European Yearbook of International Economic Law

More information about this series at http://www.springer.com/series/8165

Marc Bungenberg • Christoph Herrmann •
Markus Krajewski • Jörg Philipp Terhechte
Editors

European Yearbook of International Economic Law 2016

Springer

Editors
Marc Bungenberg
Faculty of Law
Saarland University
Saarbrücken, Germany

Christoph Herrmann
Faculty of Law
University of Passau
Passau, Germany

Markus Krajewski
Faculty of Law
University of Erlangen-Nürnberg
Erlangen, Germany

Jörg Philipp Terhechte
Competition and Regulation Institute
Leuphana University of Lüneburg
Lüneburg, Germany

ISSN 2364-8392 ISSN 2364-8406 (electronic)
European Yearbook of International Economic Law
ISBN 978-3-319-29214-4 ISBN 978-3-319-29215-1 (eBook)
DOI 10.1007/978-3-319-29215-1

Library of Congress Control Number: 2009932417

Printed on acid-free paper

This Springer imprint is published by Springer Nature
The registered company is Springer International Publishing AG Switzerland

Contents

Part II Regional Developments: Focus on Megaregionals and Plurilaterals

1. Perspectives on TPP

2. Perspectives on TTIP

3. Other Megaregionals and Plurilaterals

Part III International Economic Institutions

In Memoriam John H. Jackson (1932–2015)

Thomas Cottier

It takes generations to build a new field of law, to develop a new academic discipline, addressing and conceptualising newly emerging grounds. The inception is the most difficult phase: it requires full dedication, curiosity, vision and the courage to enter new realms. This is what characterises John H. Jackson and his work. Informed by his education in international relations at the Woodrow Wilson of Public and International Affairs and in law at the University of Michigan, he turned to explore the history, principles and rules of GATT while he was teaching contracts at the University of California in Berkeley. Other than tied to a rigid canon of established and self-repeating chairs and subjects usual in European Law Faculties, he was encouraged and able to dedicate his research to what then was an almost entirely new field of law. Albeit trade agreements range among the most important treaties in the history of international law, trade law, for strange reasons, was not part of the standard curriculum and main body of public international law, and left aside by most academics in international law. He was perhaps the first scholar to search the archives of GATT, leading to the founding treatise on the subject, *World Trade and the Law of GATT* published in 1969, 3 years after he took up work and teaching in Ann Arbor at the University of Michigan Law School.

At the time, when GATT was largely a matter for diplomats and economists, John introduced international law analysis to the field and steadily developed and promoted ideals of the rule of law and a rule-oriented system. He was very conscious of its limitations and its exposure to power politics, most of them domestic. His scholarship was considerate of all these factors. He would not advance abstract theories but remained on the ground of reality, moving step by step. Towards the end of the Uruguay Round, he inspired work on the creation of a new charter or constitution for what he called in his book *Restructuring the GATT System* (1990) '(for simplicity sake) a World Trade Organization (WTO)'. The WTO, subsequently created, has come a long way, from a mere forum of negotiations to an organisation resting on several pillars with dispute settlement today being the most prominent one. A long way indeed since John searched the archives of GATT in the 1960s. He accompanied the evolution of the GATT and WTO dispute settlement and observed the increasing role of legal analysis and thinking in the process. He realised that in a modern world of globalisation, sovereignty needs rethinking without ignoring the traditions and facts of the nation state in conceptualising *sovereignty-modern*, the term he used.

Intellectual curiosity and the need to come to grips with underlying problems would not leave John with the established disciplines of trade law, in particular goods and services. He developed a strong interest in the relationship of trade and human rights and into issues of financial regulation and monetary affairs due to the Great Recession of 2007 to 2011. He was a keen learner and listener. More than any other student, John would take notes in conferences. He would draw and share his conclusions only upon careful consideration. He most enjoyed small discussions groups rather than big audiences. In such formats new grounds were tested and discussed, leading to joint publications on emerging subjects.

John trained generations of students in the field, both in Ann Arbor and later in Washington, at Georgetown University. Many came from Europe to Ann Arbor when international trade law was yet unknown and European law was about to emerge, and he pioneered in teaching with his colleague Eric Stein at the Law Quadrangle. Later, students from Asia joined the group of the Michigan and Georgetown LL.M programmes. His teaching was based upon his textbook, regularly and carefully revised and amended. The focus was on problems, rather than solutions, and John inspired students in his calm and analytical manner behind which, however, the passion for multilateralism and its contribution to a better and more peaceful world could be felt. His teaching and educational efforts, based upon discussion of the then new Tokyo Round Agreements, prepared many for the subsequent Uruguay Round negotiations and panel work in GATT and the WTO. His teachings of the Uruguay Round results reached an increasingly wide audience of students. For a few, they were essential in preparing for future academic work in the field, inspired by John's intellectual brilliance, integrity and modesty. It is difficult to say what has been more influential, his interactive teaching or his extensive writings on the subject. Students benefited from his introductions and comments. His writings are admirably clear and precise, elegantly written and inspiring to read. But perhaps, what truly have been influential are his personality and the combination of both his teaching and writings, as they all informed each other and provided a source of inspiration.

John was interested to deal with international trade in its broader context, taking into accounts the economics but foremost the politics at work. He closely followed the work of the United States Trade Representative and worked with the office for some time; he followed the debates in the US Congress and was worried by dysfunction and isolationist trends of the American exceptionalism. He defended the status and role of public international law in an increasingly hostile environment which had left post World War II idealism and the founding fathers of the ITO and GATT behind with which he had grown and which provided the foundations of his work.

John was a close friend of Europe and European integration and the common commercial policy of the EU. He regularly visited Brussels and former students many of whom associated to the effort. He spent summers in London teaching and was a founding father of the annual WTO conference. He often would come to Geneva to talk to WTO staff and diplomats at the WTO. And he enjoyed spending a few days high above the shores of Lake Geneva with his wife Joan who would become an expert on trade on her own in accompanying John to conferences and teaching abroad.

On a long walk, John once told me that he wishes to leave once he will no longer be able to work. The moment has come, after a long and fruitful life in international law until the last summer, too early and too rapidly. The community of international trade and international economic law has lost one of its founding fathers. We mourn with his wife and companion Joan, with his family, and deplore the loss of a mentor, colleague and friend. We are most grateful to John for what he gave us and what he gave the world. In modesty, he would hardly frame it in these but true terms: a profound and inspiring contribution to world peace, to more stable and somewhat more predictable international relations on the basis of a rule-based system. His personality, teaching, works and achievements will not be forgotten. They continue to live in all of us whom he inspired through his example and his integrity. We shall keep very fond memories.

Editorial EYIEL 7 (2016)

1 Critical Perspectives on International Economic Law

In October 2015, hundreds of thousands of protesters took to the streets of Berlin to voice their concerns about the proposed free trade agreements between the EU and Canada (CETA) and the EU and the United States (TTIP). It was not the first time that international economic agreements or institutions were at the centre of public protests. International economic law has always been a politically and legally contested field. Volume 7 of the European Yearbook of International Law addresses these contestations and focuses its main section on critical perspectives of international economic law.

The editors of the yearbook invited critical scholars to voice their concerns of the main features and principles of international economic law as it stands today and outline their critical analyses of the various subfields of the discipline. In order to stimulate debate and to challenge the contestations, we asked other colleagues to comment on these critical perspectives. In most cases, especially in the most fiercely debated areas, the commentators were critical of the critics. Some chose to directly react to the claims of the main chapters, others opted for a broader defence of the system and rejected the critics' assertions more generally. Yet, others added further—sometimes also critical—perspectives and dimensions without directly challenging the claims of the first author.

The result is a unique collection of critical essays accompanied by alternative and competing views on some of the most fundamental topics of international economic law. We hope that this collection will stimulate further debate and critical research and will serve as a first source of critical essays on international economic law for newcomers and old participants of the debates alike.

1.1 Foundations

Sol Picciotto's Distinguished Essay opens our collection of critical perspectives with a personal reflection on the relationship between academic research and engagement with policy and political practices, seen through the author's own experiences of working in the field of international economic law for more than half a century. He emphasises the need to maintain academic independence and a research perspective which is based on reflexive methodology and immanent critique. Picciotto sees an increased need for engagement by critical international economic law scholars with critical political practice to challenge the current system of global economic governance.

The next two essays address the much-debated concepts of constitutionalisation of international economic law. *David Schneiderman* rejects the idea of a single, unitary global economic constitution due to the hybrid and plural setting of global economic governance. He illustrates this analysis with the current state of international investment law. In this context, he explains that the jurisprudence of investment tribunals partly resembles the output of traditional domestic constitutional jurisprudence on property rights. The emergent economic constitutional order is in tension with fundamental functions of democratic decision-making about the proper role between the state and the market.

Ernst-Ulrich Petersmann rejects this critical reading and calls for a constitutionalisation of multilevel governance of international public goods. He points out that while European legal thinking accepted the constitutionalisation of European economic law and human rights law, the discourse about global constitutionalisation remains confusing due to inadequate clarification of legal terminologies, research methods and diverse conceptions of international law and multilevel governance of public goods.

1.2 World Trade Law

The following three pairs of essays focus on issues of world trade law. *Melaku Geboye Desta* critically assesses the reality of the WTO's Agreement on Agriculture (AoA), which he sees as only the first step in a long process aimed at establishing a 'fair and market-oriented agricultural trading system'. As the Doha negotiations become less and less relevant to agriculture, the AoA remains the only framework governing agricultural trade for the indefinite future. Desta demonstrates that the treatment of agriculture as an exception to the general rules of international trade has a long pedigree, both in economic theory and regulatory practice, often used by powerful economies against developing countries. However, bilateral and regional agreements cannot be a solution in the author's view. Instead, he argues that only a multi-sectoral and multilateral forum such as the WTO allows all countries, whether they are for or against agricultural liberalisation, to make progress in this area.

Christian Häberli would not disagree. He therefore chose to describe a reform programme and shows where the development promises of the world trading system remain unfulfilled. He fears that even the completion of the Doha negotiations will fail to address specific concerns of net food-importing developing countries and resource-poor farmers. This is why additional specific commitments by developed and emerging economies are required.

From agriculture we move to trade liberalisation services. A critical academic and a politically engaged scholar at the same time, *Jane Kelsey*, challenges the dominant discourse and argues that trade in services agreements are creatures of neoliberalism. They have evolved over time as normative and disciplinary instruments and reach progressively deeper into the regulatory domain of states and limit the autonomy and authority of governments to regulate services in the national interest. A new generation free trade and investment agreements offered a way to redesign trade in services regime, align it to new technologies and corporate imperatives, and further circumscribe governments' regulatory options. Kelsey argues that new initiatives such as the plurilateral Trade in Services Agreement (TiSA) exacerbated long-standing tensions. These agreements continue to attempt to lock governments into a more extreme version of the neoliberal paradigm.

Panagiotis Delimatsis firmly defends the general approach of trade in services liberalisation. He sees the GATS as a key achievement of the Uruguay Round. However, the relevance of the GATS for the global economy has suffered from the deficiencies of the GATS legal framework. Delimatsis critically reviews the inability of the GATS to take stock of the progress made in the last 15 years of multilateral trade negotiations. He recalls that regional service-related initiatives including TTIP and TiSA threaten the very existence of the GATS. Hence, Delimatsis calls for a 'GATS 2.0' focussing on non-discrimination and good governance.

The last two essays on trade issues focus on trade-related intellectual property rights. *Carlos M. Correa* recalls that a key argument of the proponents of the TRIPS agreement was that granting intellectual property rights would boost innovation globally. He shows, however, that R&D capabilities in developing countries have not improved in the last 20 years. Pharmaceutical innovation even declined. In Correa's view the proliferation of pharmaceutical patents reflects strategies aiming at blocking generic competition. Alternative models to generate new drugs, especially those needed to address diseases prevalent in developing countries, are needed.

In the view of *Nuno Pires de Carvalho,* Correa's arguments are based on widely spread misunderstandings about the international protection of intellectual property. He claims that the TRIPS agreement should not be blamed for failing to promote invention in developing countries because that is not its aim. Instead, TRIPS aims at promoting free trade of goods and services bearing or displaying intellectual property. Also, the patent system should not be blamed for its alleged inadequacy in fostering innovation because there is no empirical evidence of whether the patent system works in one direction or the other. As a free market mechanism, the purpose of the patent system is to reduce costs.

1.3 International Investment Law and International Financial Law

The next section of our special focus addresses international investment law and international financial law, two areas which have recently been at the centre of many critical views on international economic law. The first two contributions address the relationship between investment law and development. *Muthucumaraswamy Sornarajah* who has been observing and criticising international investment law regime for decades calls it a 'fraudulent system'. He claims that when development is made the focus of the system and it is not delivered by it, the use of such a strong term is justified. While investment agreements were signed upon the promise of supporting development, investment arbitrators have brought about a system of absolute investment protection far more extensive than that contemplated by the parties to the treaties and far removed from the original goal of economic development.

In his reaction to Sornarajah's arguments, *Roberto Echandi* calls for a more balanced assessment. He agrees that the current international investment regime is not good as it is, but he claims that investment paradigms are radically shifting and development is starting to happen. However, just when developing countries are learning how to use international rule making to promote that process, many sectors in developed countries are harshly reacting against the very law they contributed to create. Echandi warns that calling a system of global governance just a manifestation of imperialism entails the risk of 'saving developing countries from development'.

Investor-state investment arbitration is subject to the fiercest criticisms in recent years. *Kate Miles* reflects upon this criticism and considers the controversies, the responses and the current debates surrounding investor-state arbitration. In particular, she reviews the discourse on the right to regulate and the arguments that investment disputes have the potential to encroach into host state regulatory space. According to Miles there is an increased acknowledgement of the problematic nature of the 'older-style' bilateral investment treaties with a more nuanced approach to investment disputes emerging. Yet, Miles remains concerned that despite these developments, public welfare regulation continues to be at risk from investor challenges and that a lack of appreciation of non-investment issues persists in arbitral decision-making.

Stephan W. Schill shares several concerns of Miles and supports reform efforts to make the system more transparent, increase possibilities of involvement for third parties, and ensure policy space. However, he argues that the present system has to be seen as a mechanism to subject international investment relations to the international rule of law, with investor-state arbitration providing a form of access to justice to foreign investors in cases where domestic courts do not sufficiently control government actions. Such a system, Schill claims, vindicates fundamental values of a just world order under law.

The latest financial crisis, especially the global crisis of 2008 and 2009, brought the international financial system once more to the centre of public and academic debates. *Celine Tan* argues that the conscription of international public finance to crisis resolution and management in recurrent sovereign debt crises highlighted the centrality of international public finance and its institutions to global economic regulation. Tan analyses the role played by international financial aid in mitigating the distributive dislocations resulting from international law's allocation of the risks and benefits of a globalised economy and examines how the use of aid finance influenced the regulatory trajectories of international economic law. She argues that the emergence of development finance as a response to the regulatory crises of the global financial system has had an adverse effect on regulatory change and sustains existing asymmetries in international economic law, thereby exacerbating its negative distributive outcomes.

A common reaction to the financial crisis was the call for better and 'more' regulation on financial market instruments to prevent future crises. However, *Christian Tietje* claims that finding adequate regulatory instruments for financial markets is not as easy as it has often been suggested and that there is a danger of overregulation with negative economic consequences. Tietje also questions Tan's understanding of the Bretton Woods system. He argues that the system was never intended to provide for any financial market regulation. Furthermore, Tietje highlights the role of soft law and similar instruments in shaping the international financial architecture.

1.4 Multinational Enterprises and Human Rights

Until very recently, multinational enterprises (MNEs) were outside the realm of international economic law, but they have become more visible in the contemporary agenda of international economic law as shown in the chapter by *Peter Muchlinski*. Preferential trade and investment agreements of the new generation address the operations of MNEs. This created worries over the loss of sovereignty by States and prompted the rise of a critical alternative position that seeks to rebalance international economic law towards a re-assertion of state regulatory power and of values other than the purely economic values. However, Muchlinski argues that this remains problematic as along as states remain wedded to the core idea of market liberalisation and corporate freedom. He shows how this conundrum can be unravelled in the context of the development of trade and investment agreements and their impact on MNE regulation.

Ibrahim Kanalan approaches the notion of regulating MNEs from a human rights perspective. He discusses the horizontal effect of human rights and proposes a new and unconventional approach to the accountability of private actors for human rights violations. He proposes a new concept for the horizontal effect of fundamental human rights borrowing elements from systems theory, especially from the work of Gunther Teubner, and demonstrates the practicability of this concept.

Human rights are a relevant normative standard not only for the regulation of MNEs, but also for international economic law more broadly. In her article, *Sarah Joseph* begins with the observation that international human rights law and international economic law seem to seek similar outcomes, namely, the protection of certain rights so as to promote human flourishing. However, compatibility between international economic law and human rights law cannot be presumed, as Joseph claims. While restrictions on, for example, protectionism can undoubtedly have positive human rights effects, there are significant areas of divergence. Joseph shows that direct conflicts between the regimes may arise with regard to the implementation of the TRIPS agreement or arbitrations under bilateral investment treaties which have posed possible threats to a state's capacity to fulfil human rights. Joseph asserts that in the end international economic law focuses on the rights of a privileged few which may clash with the human rights of others.

Lorand Bartels accepts that a state's economic policies, including the protection of intellectual property and foreign investments, and trade liberalisation, can have an impact on the enjoyment of human rights. However, even if some of these policies may be encouraged by international treaties, they do not require any specific economic policy. Bartels argues that most treaties contain exception clauses that permit states to comply with both their economic and their human rights obligations. Even if international economic law would hinder the enjoyment of human rights, Bartels' preferred solution would be to ensure that those agreements contain exceptions that can permit states to comply with their human rights obligations.

2 Regional Developments: Focus on Megaregionals and Plurilaterals

The format of EYIEL's regular section on regional developments in this volume deviates from the formats of previous issues. Instead of adopting a more or less geographical perspective, we decided to focus on the current negotiations and adoption of megaregional and plurilateral agreements. In order to capture more than one perspective, we also invited different authors to contribute short and thought-provoking insights on various aspects of these negotiations.

The first three contributors address the Trans-Pacific Partnership (TPP) which has been finalised in October 2015. *Meredith Kolsky Lewis* clarifies the political economy dynamics in the United States with respect to the TPP, focusing on the necessity of a Trade Promotion Authority (TPA) and internal political dynamics impacting support for, or opposition to, the TPP. *Henry Gao* discusses the TPP's potential implications for China arguing that the biggest challenge to China is the regulatory coherence issue. *Bryan Mercurio* broadens the perspective and highlights further potential effects of TPP on trade relations in East Asia, including the aim of the Association of Southeast Asian Nations (ASEAN) to reach deeper regional integration and Taiwan's status as an economic entity and participation in regional trade agreements.

From TPP we move to its transatlantic sister, the Transatlantic Trade and Investment Partnership (TTIP). *Jan Kleinheisterkamp* and *Lauge Poulsen* focus on investor-state dispute settlement in that agreement and argue that in order to avoid loosing support for the agreement as a whole, the parties now need to think about alternatives. Observing the developments on the other side of the Atlantic, *Simon Lester* argues that TTIP could 'smooth out' regulatory differences between the United States and the European Union and move the parties towards a single market. In his view, this requires a careful balancing of economic efficiency and national autonomy. *Charlotte Sieber-Gasser* provides us with a Swiss and hence outsider perspective on TTIP. She shows that TTIP may have considerable economic implications for Switzerland which trigger a number of legal questions concerning the democratic legitimation of the foreign policy options of Switzerland. The reflections on TPP and TTIP are complemented with observations by *Azwimpheleli Langalanga* and *Peter Draper* on the impact of these agreements on economies in sub-Saharan Africa. They ask how African countries are responding to these megaregionals and discuss various potential strategies.

Even though TPP and TTIP are the most contentious megaregional negotiations, there are other initiatives in other parts of the world which also deserve close attention. *Vincent Angwenyi* highlights the largest free trade agreement in Africa, the Tripartite Free Trade Agreement which was signed on 10 June 2015. It combines three regional economic communities in Africa: the Common Market for Eastern and Southern Africa (COMESA), the East African Community (EAC) and the Southern African Development Community (SADC). While the Tripartite FTA presents an opportunity to set in motion the establishment of a continental FTA and the eventual establishment of an African Economic Community, there are considerable challenges that need to be overcome before the Tripartite FTA can be actualised. *Emmanuel Opoku Awuku* offers a more general overview of the perspectives of developing and least-developed countries on megaregional agreements. Finally, *Billy A. Melo Araujo* provides us with an analysis of the state of play of the plurilateral negotiations on the Trade in Services Agreement (TiSA). In particular, he describes the extent to which TiSA can go beyond the current GATS framework and examines the compatibility of TiSA with WTO law.

3 Institutions and Book Reviews

This EYIEL volume is completed with our regular section on international economic institutions. *Jan Bohanes, Alejandro Sánchez* and *Alexandra Telychko* present an overview of WTO case law in the last year. *Catharine Titi* summarises recent developments in international investment law and investment arbitration case law. *Ludwig Gramlich* traces current activities of the International Monetary Fund (IMF) such as surveillance under Art. IV and various forms of financial and technical assistance. *Elisabeth Tuerk* and *Diana Rosert* outline UNCTAD's activities with regard to reforming the international investment agreement regime, in particular UNCTAD's action menu for reforming the international investment regime, as put forward in the World Investment Report 2015. *Carsten Weerth* looks at recent developments within the World Customs Organization (WCO).

Our book reviews cover *Culture and International Economic Law* (Valentina Vadi and Bruo de Witte, eds) reviewed by *Walther Michl*, *Rule of Law in International Monetary Law* (Thomas Cottier, Rosa M. Lastra and Christian Tietje, eds) reviewed by *Alexander Thiele*, *Improving the International Investment Law and Policy Regime: Options for the Future, Columbia 2013* (Karl P. Sauvant and Federico Ortino, eds) reviewed by *Julien Chaisse*, *Public Policy in International Economic Law: The ICESCR in Trade, Finance, and Investment* (Diane Desierto) reviewed by *Kholofelo Kugler* and *Investor-Staat-Schiedsverfahren nach Europäischen Unionsrecht, Zulässigkeit und Ausgestaltung in Investitionsabkommen der Europäischen Union* (Juliane Ahner) reviewed by *Till Patrik Holterhus*.

Once again, editing this yearbook would not have been possible without many helping hands and minds. We owe tremendous thanks to Rhea Hoffmann and Kholofelo Kugler of Erlangen University for their tireless efforts to turn the manuscripts into the right form and style and for dealing with numerous editorial challenges. In the last stages they were supported by Anja Nestler and Simone Schubert. Brigitte Reschke of Springer was once again our reliable 'liaison officer' in Heidelberg. To all of them: *Ein herzliches Dankeschön*!

Saarbrücken, Germany	Marc Bungenberg
Passau, Germany	Christoph Herrmann
Erlangen, Germany	Markus Krajewski
Lüneburg, Germany	Jörg Philipp Terhechte
November 2015	

List of Contributors

Vincent Angwenyi is a graduate of and a tutor at the Munich Intellectual Property Law Centre and a Doctoral Researcher at the Max-Planck Institute for Innovation and Competition.

Billy A. Melo Araujo is Lecturer in EU law at Queen's University Belfast. He graduated with a degree in law from the Catholic University of Louvain, Belgium, and an LLM in International Economic Law from the University of Warwick. After graduating, he worked as a solicitor in Brussels and later as a trainee at the WTO Appellate Body Secretariat in Geneva. He received a PhD from King's College London for a legal analysis of the regulatory disciplines included in EU free trade agreements entitled: "The Law and Policy of the EU's Deep Trade Agenda." His research interests lie in the areas of EU External Relations Law and International Economic Law.

Emmanuel Opoku Awuku is currently working for the Secretariat of the African, Caribbean and Pacific Group of States as a Legal Counsel. Dr. Awuku previously worked at the Commonwealth Secretariat, first as Senior Programme Officer at the Human Rights Unit and then later as Legal Adviser at the Legal and Constitutional Affairs Division. Before that, he worked with the United Nations and as an independent legal consultant and researcher dealing with issues ranging from foreign investment law and human rights law to trade and environmental law. Dr. Awuku has published widely in many renowned legal journals on issues relating to international trade law and sustainable development law. He is the author of International Trade and the Environment: The Impact of the WTO on Developing Countries and Environmental Protection: Ghana's timber industry and forest sector as a case study, Wolf Legal Publishers, Netherlands 2006. He holds an LL.M. and a Ph.D. degree from the University of London (Specialisation: International trade and the environment). He is a member of the Committee on International Trade Law and the Committee of International Law on Biotechnology of the International Law

Association. He is on the Editorial Advisory Board of the Commonwealth Law Bulletin. He is admitted to practice as a Solicitor of the Supreme Court of England and Wales, UK.

Lorand Bartels is a University Senior Lecturer in Law in the Faculty of Law and a Fellow of Trinity Hall at the University of Cambridge, where he teaches international law, WTO law and EU law. He holds degrees in English literature and law from the University of New South Wales and a PhD in law from the European University Institute.

Jan Bohanes has served as Senior Counsel at the Advisory Centre on WTO Law (ACWL) since 2010. He assists developing countries in WTO dispute settlement proceedings and has advised on a broad scope of WTO legal issues. Prior to joining the ACWL, Dr. Bohanes was associate attorney at the Geneva office of Sidley Austin LLP, where he advised governments and large commercial stakeholders on all issues of WTO law, including on WTO dispute settlement. Between 2002 and 2006, Dr. Bohanes worked as Legal Officer at the Appellate Body Secretariat of the World Trade Organization, assisting Appellate Body Members on appeals in the WTO dispute settlement system.

Nuno Pires de Carvalho retired from international service in the World Intellectual Property Organization (WIPO, Geneva) as Director of the Intellectual Property and Competition Policy Division. He was with the WIPO International Bureau since 1999. Before joining WIPO he was Counselor in the Intellectual Property Division of the World Trade Organization (WTO, Geneva), between 1996 and 1999.

He holds three Master of Laws degrees (LL.M.) (from the Federal University of Minas Gerais (Brazil), the Catholic University of Lisbon (Portugal), and the Washington University in St. Louis (Missouri, United States)); and two Doctorate degrees in Law (S.J.D.) (from the Federal University of Minas Gerais (Brazil) and the Washington University in St. Louis (Missouri, United States)).

He has authored several books, book chapters and articles on industrial property law, published in the United States, Europe and Brazil. His most recent book publications are: "IP and Antitrust—The Competition Policies of Intellectual Property in Eight Cases" (Wolters Kluwer, Alphen aan den Rijn, 2015), "The TRIPS Regime of Trademarks and Designs" (3rd edition, Wolters Kluwer, Alphen aan den Rijn, 2014); and "The TRIPS Regime of Patents and Test Data" (4th edition, Wolters Kluwer, Alphen aan den Rijn, 2014).

Julien Chaisse is Associate Professor at the Chinese University of Hong Kong (CUHK) and Director of the Center for Financial Regulation and Economic Development (CFRED). Dr. Chaisse is an award-winning specialist in international economic law with particular expertise in the regulation and economics of foreign investment. Apart from his academic activities, Dr. Chaisse is the World Trade Advisors' Chief Legal Counsel and Director of World Trade Advisors International

Trade Law Group. He regularly serves as a consultant to international organizations, governments, private investors and multinational law firms regarding cutting-edge issues related to international economic law.

Carlos M. Correa Special Advisor on Intellectual Property and Trade of the South Centre and Director of the Center for Interdisciplinary Studies on Industrial Property and Economics at the Law Faculty, University of Buenos Aires. He has been a visiting professor in post-graduate courses of several universities and consultant to various regional and international organizations. He has advised several governments on intellectual property, innovation policy and public health. He was a member of the UK Commission on Intellectual Property, of the Commission on Intellectual Property, Innovation and Public Health established by the World Health Assembly and of the FAO Panel of Eminent Experts on Ethics in Food and Agriculture. He is the author of several books and numerous articles.

Thomas Cottier, former Managing Director of the World Trade Institute, is an Emeritus Professor of European and international economic law at the University of Bern, Switzerland, and adjunct professor of law at the University of Ottawa, Canada.

Panagiotis Delimatsis is Professor of European and International Trade Law and Director of the Tilburg Law and Economics Center (TILEC), an interdisciplinary Center of Excellence at Tilburg University, the Netherlands. In this capacity, he leads the research cluster 'Finance, Trade and Investment' within the TILEC Research Programme 2012–2017. Previously he was a Senior Research Fellow at the World Trade Institute at the University of Bern. Panagiotis read law in Komotini, Greece; Saarbrücken and Heidelberg, Germany; and Neuchâtel, Switzerland. He is a renowned expert in the regulation of services industries. He is the author of 'International Trade in Services and Domestic Regulations—Necessity, Transparency, and Regulatory Diversity' (International Economic Law Series, Oxford University Press, 2007). Panagiotis has a keen interest in regulatory policy and regularly publishes or acts as referee for top journals and academic publishers on issues regarding public services, financial markets, energy and standardization in Europe and worldwide. Panagiotis has edited various books on these issues, the most recent of which is 'the Law, Economics and Politics of International Standardisation' (Cambridge University Press, 2016). His current research relates to standard-setting and technical barriers to trade both from an EU internal market and WTO perspective.

Melaku Geboye Desta is Principal Regional Advisor in the Capacity Development Division (CDD) of the United Nations Economic Commission for Africa (UNECA, Addis Ababa, Ethiopia) and Professor of International Economic Law at the Leicester De Montfort Law School in England (currently on leave). Prior to joining De Montfort University, Melaku was Reader in International Economic Law at the Centre for Energy, Petroleum and Mineral Law and Policy (CEPMLP), University of Dundee, in Scotland.

Peter Draper is Managing Director of Tutwa Consulting, which specialises in policy and regulatory analysis, international business expansion advisory, and corporate public affairs advisory, in Southern African and emerging markets. In South Africa he is Senior Research Fellow in the Economic Diplomacy programme at the South African Institute of International Affairs; Lecturer at Wits Business School where he has won two teaching awards; and Consultant to the India, Brazil, and South Africa think tank consortium at the Centre for Development and Enterprise. Internationally he is a member of the Board of Trustees of the Botswana Institute for Development Policy Analysis; member and vice-chair of the World Economic Forum's Global Agenda Council on the Global Trade and FDI system; member of the Board of Trustees of the International Chamber of Commerce's Research Foundation; and non-resident senior fellow of the Brussels-based European Centre for International Political Economy. Previously he worked in South Africa's national Department of Trade and Industry in various positions, including as head of economic analysis and research in the trade policy/relations division; prior to that he was an academic teaching economic history and political economy, and headed the economics department at the University of Durban-Westville.

Roberto Echandi Global Lead Investment Policy and Promotion, Trade and Competitiveness Global Practice, World Bank Group (WBG). Former Ambassador of Costa Rica to the European Union, Belgium and Luxembourg and Chief Negotiator of Costa Rica for various international investment agreements.

Henry Gao is Associate Professor of law at Singapore Management University and Dongfang Scholar Chair Professor at Shanghai Institute of Foreign Trade. With law degrees from three continents, he started his career as the first Chinese lawyer at the WTO Secretariat. Before moving to Singapore in late 2007, he taught law at University of Hong Kong, where he was also the Deputy Director of the East Asian International Economic Law and Policy Program. He has taught at the IELPO program in Barcelona and the Academy of International Trade Law in Macau, and was the Academic Coordinator to the first Asia-Pacific Regional Trade Policy Course officially sponsored by the WTO. He has advised many national governments as well as the WTO, World Bank, Asian Development Bank, APEC and ASEAN on trade issues. He sits on the Advisory Board of the WTO Chairs Program, which was established by the WTO Secretariat in 2009 to promote research and teaching on WTO issues in leading universities around the world.

Ludwig Gramlich is Professor for Public Law and Public Economic Law at Chemnitz University since 1992. He received both his doctorate in law (1978) and his Habilitation (1983) from the University of Würzburg. His main areas of research are legal issues of networks and infrastructures at national as well as international levels (in particular relating to telecommunications, energy, and banking and monetary matters).

Christian Häberli is Senior Research Fellow at the World Trade Institute of Bern University on various trade, agriculture, employment and development policy issues, adjudication of WTO disputes for tariff and non-tariff measures (SPS and TBT) affecting goods and services, regionalism and preferential trade, foreign direct investment, and human rights. Lecturer and policy advisor in Europe and in the Global South. Over 50 publications, more recently with a focus on food security from a trade and investment perspective, environmental issues and climate change implications.

Graduation in 1977 at Basel University with a Ph.D. on the subject of African Investment Law. Degrees for Development Sciences in Geneva (1975) and for Theology in Bern (2009). Professional career with the International Labour Organization (ILO) and the Swiss Government, with assignments in Madagascar, Thailand, Nepal, and Switzerland. Participation in the Uruguay and in the Doha Rounds from 1986 to 2007 as a trade negotiator for Switzerland in the GATT and the WTO. Former Chair of the Swiss—EU Joint Agriculture Committee. Assignments in the WTO include chairing the Committee on Agriculture (Regular Session) and serving in 19 stages of 5 dispute settlement cases: *EC – Bananas, EC – Biotech, Japan – Apples, China – Publications and Audiovisual Products* and *US – Country of Origin Labelling (COOL).*

Shotaro Hamamoto is professor of International Law at the Kyoto University and Professeur invite, Paris I (2009) and Sciences Po de Paris (2012). He holds an LL.B. (Kyotot) and an LL.M. (Kyoto), as well as a Docteur en droit (Paris II). He has served as Counsel and Advocate for the Japanese government in Whaling in the Atarctica case (ICJ, Australia v. Japan, New Zealand intervening, 2010–2014), Hoshinmaru (ITLOS, Japan v. Russia, 2007), and Tomimaru (ITLOS, Japan v. Russia, 2007) and as Assistant for the Spanish Government in Fisheries Jurisdiction (ICJ, Spain v. Canada, 1997–1998). He is a Japanese Representative to the UNCITRAL WG II (Arbitration/Conciliation) (2010) an to the OECD Investment Committee (2011) and has served as an Arbitrator, Japan Sports Arbitration Agency (2008). His fields of research include theory of international law, international dispute settlement, law of the sea, international investment law, international sports law, and institutional law of the European Union.

Till Patrik Holterhus, MLE. is a senior research fellow at the Institute for International Law and European Law, University of Göttingen, Germany. His main research interests are in the field of German and European constitutional law, European economic law, WTO law, international investment law and regional trade agreements.

Professor Sarah Joseph is the Director for the Castan Centre for Human Rights Law, Monash University, Melbourne. Her teaching and research interests are international human rights law and constitutional law. Particular areas of interest include economic globalisation and human rights, and the media and human rights.

She has published a number of books including Blame it on the WTO: A Human Rights Critique (OUP, 2011), Corporations and Transnational Human Rights Litigation (Hart 2004), co-authoring The International Covenant on Civil and Political Rights: Cases, Commentary and Materials (OUP, 3rd ed, 2013), Federal Constitutional Law: A Contemporary View (LBC, 4th ed, 2014), A Handbook on the Individual Complaints Procedures of the UN (OMCT, 2006) and Human Rights Translated: A Business Reference Guide (UN 2008). She has also co-edited two recent books for Edward Elgar Publishers, Research Handbook on International Human Rights Law (2010) and The World Trade Organization and Human Rights: Interdisciplinary Perspectives (2009). Sarah has also published numerous articles and presented many papers in the fields of international human rights law and constitutional law.

Ibrahim Kanalan is Research Associate at the Centre for Human Rights Erlangen-Nuremberg (CHREN) and Research Associate to the Chair for Public Law and International Public Law at University of Erlangen-Nuremberg, Germany, since April 2015. He studied law at the University of Berlin (Freie Universität Berlin) and holds a PhD in law from the University of Bremen in 2014. Between 2011 and 2014 Ibrahim Kanalan was Lecturer at the University of Berlin and from 2013 to 2014 Research Fellow at the University of Bremen. His particular areas of interest include Public International Law, International Human Rights Law, and Migration and Refugee Law.

Jane Kelsey is one of New Zealand's best-known critical commentators on issues of globalisation and neoliberalism. She has taught at the University of Auckland since 1979, specialising in law and policy and international economic regulation. She is active internationally as a researcher, analyst, adviser and commentator on globalisation, especially the Trans-Pacific Partnership Agreement, trade in services, and investment agreements. Jane's recent monographs include 'Serving Whose Interests? The Political Economy of Trade in Services Agreements' (Routledge Cavendish 2008), 'Legal Analysis of Services and Investment in the Cariforum EC EPA: Lessons for Other Developing Countries', (South Centre, 2010), and the edited 'No Ordinary Deal. Unmasking the Trans-Pacific Partnership Free Trade Agreement' (ed) (Bridget Williams Books 2010), as well as many published articles.

Jan Kleinheisterkamp is an Associate Professor of Law at the London School of Economics.

Kholofelo Kugler works as Counsel at the Advisory Centre on WTO Law (ACWL), specialising in WTO law. Prior to that she most recently worked as a Research Assistant to Professor Markus Krajewski in the area of international economic law at the University of Erlangen-Nuremberg in Erlangen, Germany, a Junior Associate at WTI Advisors in Geneva, Switzerland, and an Associate at

Bowman Gilfillan Inc. in Johannesburg, South Africa. Kholofelo is an admitted attorney in South Africa. She holds a Master of Law and Economics (MILE) degree (*summa cum laude*) from the World Trade Institute at the University of Bern, Switzerland, an LL.B degree (*cum laude*) from the University of the Witwatersrand, South Africa, together with a Bachelor's degree in Economics and International Politics from the University of South Africa. Kholofelo's areas of interest and research are in regional integration, trade in services, and investment.

Azwimpheleli Langalanga is a Research Fellow at the Mandela Institute of International Economic Law, University of the Witwatersrand. Azwimpheleli is also a Faculty Member of the African International Legal Awareness in London. In addition, he is a research associate with the Economic Diplomacy Program of the South African Institute for International Affairs, an independent liberal policy think tank. This is, in addition to being an Associate at Tutwa Consulting, where he consults on international investment law and policy. Azwimpheleli holds a Master of International Law and Economics (cum laude) from the World Trade Institute in Bern and a Master of Laws in Labor Studies from the University of KwaZulu Natal. He also has several post graduate certificates from the Mandela Institute of the University of the Witwatersrand. His research interests are in the fields of international trade and investment law and policy. He also conducts research on South African trade and industrial policy within a global economic governance framework.

Simon Lester is a trade policy analyst at the Cato Institute, and the President and founder of the trade law web site WorldTradeLaw.net. Previously, he was a Legal Affairs Officer at the Appellate Body Secretariat of the World Trade Organization.

Meredith Kolsky Lewis is Professor of Law and Vice Dean for International and Graduate Programs at the SUNY Buffalo Law School, where she also directs the Cross-Border Legal Studies Center. Professor Lewis also holds a faculty appointment at the Victoria University of Wellington Law School in New Zealand. She teaches public and private international law subjects, including International Trade Law; International Economic Law; International Business Transactions; and International Commercial Arbitration. Her research focuses on international economic law, with a particular emphasis on the WTO, free trade agreements, international dispute settlement and the Asia-Pacific region. Professor Lewis is Co-Executive Vice President and a founding member of the Society of International Economic Law. She is also co-rapporteur of the International Law Association's Committee on Sustainable Development and the Green Economy in International Trade Law and a member of the ILA Study Group on Preferential Trade Agreements.

Bryan Mercurio is Professor and Vice Chancellor's Outstanding Fellow of the Faculty of Law at the Chinese University of Hong Kong. Professor Mercurio is the author/editor of 12 books and over 75 articles/books chapters, including one of the most widely used case books on WTO law (Hart Publishing, 2012, 2nd ed, with S. Lester) and the leading collection on bilateral and regional trade agreements (Cambridge University Press, 2009, with S. Lester). He is a Visiting Professorial Fellow at the UNSW Faculty of Law and Senior Fellow at the University of Melbourne. He has served on the Founding Committee and inaugural Executive Board of the Society of International Economic Law (SIEL), Founding Member of the SIEL Intellectual Property Law Network, Founding Member and Steering Committee of the Asian International Economic Law Network and is currently a Member of the Asian WTO Research Network.

Walther Michl is Senior Research Assistant at the Chair of Public and European Law (Prof. Rudolf Streinz) at Ludwig-Maximilians-Universität (LMU) Munich (Germany). He studied law at LMU Munich and received an LL.M. in European Law from King's College London. After obtaining his Second State Exam he worked for a law firm in Munich. Since 2008 he is at the Chair of Professor Streinz.

Kate Miles (B.A., LL.B. (Auck), LL.M. (NYU), Ph.D. (Syd)) is Fellow and Lecturer in Law at Gonville and Caius College, University of Cambridge.

Peter Muchlinski is the Professor of International Commercial Law at SOAS, University of London. He is the author of Multinational Enterprises and the Law (Oxford University Press) and has published extensively on transnational business regulation and, more recently, on business and human rights and comparative corporate law. He has acted as an adviser on international investment law issues for UNCTAD and has been a contributing author and member of the editorial team for the UNCTAD Papers o Issues in International Investment Agreements.

Petersmann is emeritus Professor of International and European Law and former Head of the Law Department at the European University Institute at Florence, Italy. He was legal adviser in the German Ministry of Economic Affairs and representative of Germany in numerous European and UN institutions before becoming legal counsel in the GATT Secretariat. He worked as secretary, member or chairman of numerous GATT and WTO dispute settlement panels and as legal consultant for the EU Commission, the European Parliament, the ORCD, UNCTAD and the WTO.

Sol Picciotto (BA Oxford, JD Chicago) is emeritus professor of Lancaster University, a Senior Adviser of the Tax Justice Network, coordinator of the BEPS Monitoring Group, and a member of the Advisory Group of the International Centre for Tax and Development, where he coordinates and carries out research on taxation of transnational corporations with special reference to developing countries. He has taught at the Universities of Dar es Salaam (1964–1968), Warwick (1968–1992), and Lancaster (1992–2007); and was Scientific Director of the Oñati International Institute for the Sociology of Law (2009–2011). He is the author of International Business Taxation (1992), Regulating Global Corporate Capitalism (2011), several co-written books, and numerous chapters and articles on various aspects of international business and economic law, and on theories of state and law.

Lauge N. Skovgaard Poulsen is a Lecturer at the School of Public Policy, University College London.

Diana Rosert is Associate Legal Affairs Officer at UNCTAD's International Investment Agreements Section in the Investment and Enterprise Division. Her research interests are in international investment agreements, investor-State arbitration and, more generally, the sustainable development dimension of international investment policies. Diana has also worked as a consultant with the International Institute for Sustainable Development (IISD). She holds a Master of Arts in International Political Economy from the University of Warwick, United Kingdom.

Alejandro Sánchez has served as Counsel at the Advisory Centre on WTO Law (ACWL) since 2010. As Counsel, he has assisted developing countries in WTO dispute settlement proceedings and has advised on a broad scope of WTO legal issues. Prior to joining the ACWL, Mr. Sánchez served for 4 years as legal advisor at the Office of the General Counsel for Trade Negotiations in the Ministry of Economy of Mexico. In that capacity, he provided legal advice on a wide range of matters related to the WTO, NAFTA and other Free Trade Agreements signed by Mexico. Mr. Sánchez was also directly involved in the litigation of several WTO disputes on behalf of Mexico as well as in proceedings on trade-related matters before Mexican domestic courts.

Stephan W. Schill (Dr. iur. (Frankfurt am Main 2008); LL.M. (NYU 2006); LL.M. (Augsburg 2002)) is Professor of International and Economic Law and Governance at the University of Amsterdam, Amsterdam Center for International Law and Principal Investigator in the ERC-project on 'Transnational Private-Public Arbitration as Global Regulatory Governance: Charting and Codifying the Lex Mercatoria Publica' (LexMercPub, Grant agreement no.: 313355). He is Member of the List of Conciliators of the International Centre for Settlement of Investment Disputes and admitted to the bar as a German Rechtsanwalt and as Attorney-at-Law (New York).

David Schneiderman is Professor of Law and Political Science (courtesy) at the University of Toronto where he teaches Canadian and US constitutional law and international investment law. He has authored numerous articles and authored and edited a variety of books on constitutional law and history, socio-legal studies, and law and globalization.

Charlotte Sieber-Gasser wrote her PhD at the World Trade Institute in Bern on preferential services trade agreements between developing countries. She currently works as a Visiting Senior Research Fellow at the Graduate Institute for International and Development Studies in Geneva and as a lecturer in law at the university of Bern. She holds an MLaw degree from the universities of Fribourg and Bern in Switzerland, and an MA degree in development studies from the university of Manchester in the UK. Charlotte is a specialist in trade law and development with a particular focus on preferentialism, services trade regulation, and labour migration. Her PhD thesis will be available soon at Cambridge University Press.

Muthucumaraswamy Sornarajah, LLB (Ceylon), LLM (Yale), LLM, PhD, LLD (London) is CJ Koh Professor at the Faculty of Law of the National University of Singapore. He is Visiting Professor at the Centre for Human Rights, London School of Economics. He was the Tunku Abdul Rahman Professor of International Law at the University of Malaya at Kuala Lumpur. He was Head of the Law School of the University of Tasmania, Australia. He studied law at the University of Ceylon, the London School of Economics, King's College, London and the Yale Law School. He was Research Fellow at the Centre for International Law, Cambridge and at the Max Planck Institut fur Offentliches Auslandisches Recht at Heidelberg, Germany. He was Visiting Professor at various Universities.

Celine Tan is Associate Professor at the School of Law, University of Warwick, UK. She was previously a Lecturer in Law at the University of Birmingham and a Postgraduate Research Fellow at the University of Warwick where she completed her PhD. Her research centres on exploring aspects of international economic law and regulation with a focus on international development financing law, policy and governance.

Alexandra Telychko is a Research Assistant at the Public International Law Department of the University of Geneva Law School. She is also a Director of Fondation Vidrodgenia, a Swiss foundation promoting Ukraine's democratic development. She previously worked at the Permanent Mission of Montenegro to the WTO, at Dennis Beaver Law Office (Bakersfield, CA) and with Tudela & Associés Law Firm (Lyon, France). She studied law at the University Jean Moulin Lyon III (France). Her bachelor's degree, obtained in 2012, concentrated on French private law, while her master's degree, obtained in 2013, focused on European Union law.

Ms. Telychko also holds a master's degree in economic law from the University of Geneva Law School.

Alexander Thiele is currently substitute professor at the Ruhr-University in Bochum (Germany). After studying law he completed his Phd at the University of Göttingen in 2006, the Second State Exam followed in 2008. From 2008 to 2013 he was assistant professor in Göttingen. After finishing his habilitation in 2013 he has lectured in Göttingen, Jena and Bochum. Particular areas of interest include European and Financial Law where he has published various articles and books.

Christian Tietje, Professor of Public Law, European Law and International Economic Law, Director Institute of Economic Law and Director Transnational Economic Law Research Center (TEL), Law School, University Halle, Germany.

Catharine Titi is a Research Scientist at the French National Centre for Scientific Research (CNRS) and Member of the CREDIMI, Law Faculty of the University of Burgundy. She holds a PhD from the University of Siegen in Germany. Catharine has previously worked at the University Panthéon-Assas Paris II (CRED) and at the United Nations Conference on Trade and Development (UNCTAD).

Elisabeth Tuerk is Chief of UNCTAD's International Investment Agreements Section in the Investment and Enterprise Division. She leads the Section's work across three pillars of UNCTAD activities, encompassing research and analysis, technical assistance and capacity-building, and intergovernmental consensus-building. In her previous UNCTAD assignment, Elisabeth worked as an Economic Affairs Officer at UNCTAD's Division on International Trade and Commodities. Prior to joining UNCTAD, she worked as a staff attorney for the Trade and Investment Program of the Center for International Environmental Law (CIEL, Geneva). She holds a Magistra Degree in Law and a Magistra Degree in International Management from the Karl-Franzens University, Graz, Austria as well as a Masters Degree (MILE, Masters of International Law and Economics) from the World Trade Institute (WTI) in Bern, Switzerland. She has authored and co-authored numerous articles on trade in services, investment and development.

Carsten Weerth BSc (Glasgow) LLM (Com) MA, works for Germany's Customs Administration at the local customs authority Hauptzollamt Bremen as a customs chief inspector and has been a lecturer of Law at the Hochschule für öffentliche Verwaltung Bremen, Hochschule Bremen, Jacobs University. He is currently holding a lectureship in law at the FOM Hochschule für Oekonomie und Management—FOM University of Applied Sciences for Economics and Management.

He has published more than ten books and 100 papers on the EU Customs Union and Customs Law. He is a frequent contributor to the scientific journals AW-Prax—Zeitschrift für Außenwirtschaft in Recht und Praxis—and ZfZ—Zeitschrift für Zölle und Verbrauchsteuern—and an Editorial Board member of the Global Trade and Customs Journal (GTCJ). Dr. Weerth is contributing to three legal comments on External Trade Law (Wollfgang/Simonsen/Rogmann), Customs Law (Dorsch) and EU Law (Lenz/Borchardt) and is the founder of the Center for Customs Law and Customs Research.

Part I
Topics: Critical Perspectives on International Economic Law

1. Foundations

2. World Trade Law

3. International Investment Law and International Financial Law

4. Multinational Enterprises and Human Rights

Critical Theory and Practice in International Economic Law and the New Global Governance

Sol Picciotto

Contents

Abstract This paper discusses the relationship between academic research and engagement with policy and political practices, seen through the author's recollections of his personal experiences extending over half a century working in the field of international economic law. While stressing the importance of an interaction of theory and practice, it also emphasises the need to maintain academic independence and a research perspective, based on reflexive methodology (situating the various actors and their positions in the field) and immanent critique (close analysis of the self-understandings of practitioners in a field and detailed examination of their practices, contrasting the two). It traces the changing character of the relationship between research and political practice, and the increased need for engagement especially by critical scholars of international economic law with critical political practice. This need stems from the characteristics of global governance in the current era, dominated by corporatist public-private structures controlled by small elites, and confronting complex problems that place an increased importance on specialist expertise. This is often depoliticised as technocratic, creating a wide gap between such expert knowledge and the rhetoric of political debate.

My indebtedness to Lancaster University (UK), Tax Justice Network, and the International Centre for Tax and Development should be evident from the content of this paper.

S. Picciotto (✉)
Lancaster University, Lancaster, UK
e-mail: s.picciotto@lancs.ac.uk

M. Bungenberg et al. (eds.), *European Yearbook of International Economic Law 2016*, European Yearbook of International Economic Law 7,
DOI 10.1007/978-3-319-29215-1_1

1 The World and the Academy

It is not surprising that international economic law, and particularly the regulation of transnational corporations (TNCs), should have been such an important focus of both politics and policy-making. The world's political economy for the past century has been marked by the interacting and international processes that have transformed both national economies increasingly dominated by large TNCs, and states gradually torn apart by the contending forces of nationalism and globalisation. The study of these processes has fascinated me since my postgraduate student days. Yet I found that, while they were clearly central, their understanding posed challenges to orthodox disciplinary perspectives, as well as to the formulation of political and policy responses.

In the traditional law curriculum both international law and economic law were ill-adapted to understanding this reality, since each was separated into public and private law spheres. The international economy was considered a realm of private markets, so was dealt with only in terms of international commercial law, which largely ignored both state economic regulation and the dominant role of large corporations[1] Other disciplines were equally unsuited, as politics, economics and even sociology focused on the national state, so that 'international relations' were those of governments, and international economics dealt with flows of goods and money. Indeed, formal economics still treats TNCs in terms of 'foreign direct investment', and the study of TNCs moved to business schools, treating them predominantly from an organizational and managerial perspective. However, more independent and eclectic analyses of TNCs also emerged, from Edith Penrose to John Dunning and Grazia Ietto-Gillies, as well as some excellent work by economic sociologists.[2]

Hence, I saw that an adequate understanding of important realities required a challenge to orthodox viewpoints, in other words a critical perspective. Furthermore, such a perspective could not emerge solely from academic analysis, which seemed stuck in old orthodoxies, but from some practical engagement with the real world. Interestingly, this seemed easiest in the legal field, perhaps because the interactions of economic and political activities are centrally mediated by law. Indeed, the field of 'transnational law' was delineated as early as 1956 by a lawyer-

[1] The leading text in the UK for many years through successive editions was Schmitthoff's The Export Trade; in the US I took a course at Chicago Law School on International Business Transactions with Soia Mentschikoff, who had worked on the Uniform Commercial Code with Llewellyn, and took what was later described as a 'regulatory contracts' approach, Collins (1999); and another with Kenneth Dam, Chicago's equivalent of Philip Jessup, who later served in several US administrations before returning to teach.

[2] Notably the excellent monograph by Kristensen and Zeitlin (2005).

diplomat, Philip C. Jessup.[3] This concept quickly invaded US law schools, resulting in a proliferation of law reviews and courses in this field which helped to provide a grounding for the generations of lawyers who spread around the world, facilitating the expansion of TNCs as well as building the regulatory infrastructures of what later became known as global governance. Indeed, the initially unorthodox concepts such as transnationalism no doubt help to mould the emergence of these new forms of business and government in the past half-century.

Thus, practical engagement did not necessarily lead to a critical perspective in policy or political terms, on the contrary it tended mainly to serve politically and economically dominant, or emergent, interests. Perhaps for that reason, many in academia have been reticent or hostile towards such engagement, considering it as contaminating. This may also lead to suspicion of concepts or discourses emerging from the world of practice. Consequently, some academics prefer to stick to orthodoxies, while others develop more radical alternative frameworks aimed at escaping the grip of power, sometimes protecting themselves from it behind abstruse academic jargon. Probably the dominant tendency is to adopt a perspective of technical expertise, separating policy from politics, aiming at a "policy audience" essentially consisting of those with power, which in turn blunts the critical edge of the research agenda.[4]

It is certainly important, even essential in my view, for academic inquiry to be independent and to some extent insulated from social conflicts and power struggles. This should enable a longer-term analysis, abstracting from day-to-day professional practice or the hurly burly of politics, aiming to understand and depict the contours and ecology of the forest as a whole, and not content with knowing only the particularities of specific trees. Indeed, I have often been surprised and intrigued to find, when interviewing or simply talking with a practitioner or policy-maker, that in some ways I had a better grasp of the general policy issues in their field, although they were obviously much more immersed in and skilled at its practical detail. This detachment also means that the academic can appreciate the positions of the various participants in the debates or conflicts in a field, and can discern that each person sees and understands that field in terms which are valid from their own perspective. That appreciation in turn tends to strengthen the preference for detachment. Is it possible to retain that important detachment if one takes a position in the field?

For me it seems that some engagement is inevitable, because even academic detachment itself involves taking a position. The analyses put forward by academics of an issue or a field themselves contribute to shaping those phenomena. Certainly, a purely sociological study can avoid becoming embroiled in the

[3] Jessup was in the secretariat of the United Nations Relief and Rehabilitation Administration (UNRRA) conference in 1943, at Bretton Woods in 1944, and a technical advisor to the American delegation to the San Francisco United Nations charter conference in 1945; but his nomination by Truman as US delegate to the UN was blocked in the Senate following accusations by Senator McCarthy of 'unusual affinity for Communist causes'.

[4] Sarat and Silbey (1988).

substance of the processes, and some detachment can be created by reframing the issues using a 'reflexive' research methodology, based on analysing the positions and interests of the various actors in the field. Such an approach has been ably applied by sociologists of law inspired by Pierre Bourdieu, notably Yves Dezalay and his various collaborators and followers.[5] I have found this work very insightful, and helpful in facilitating a more dispassionate analysis, discounting preconceptions and emphasising investigation of practices and structures. Viewing the processes of construction of transnational fields, or networks of global governance, as strategies of competition between different professionals deliberately avoids taking any position about what is at stake. However, formulating such analyses in terms which claim detachment or objectivity is exactly what gives the opinions of academics power, which can be appropriated by other participants or by their own participation in a field.[6] Indeed, it may be preferable for academics to make their policy preferences explicit, rather than claim a spurious objectivity. Further, it seemed to me that analysing these processes from a pure sociological perspective was somehow missing their substance.

Involvement also has become increasingly necessary, especially in the field of international economic law. The increased necessity for more direct involvement of academics seems to me to be due to the emergence of the very phenomenon which is now central to international economic law: global governance. This form of rule rests to an unprecedented extent on knowledge, especially that of specialized professionals, including academics. This gives academics a responsibility which we cannot and in my view should not avoid.

2 Changing Interactions

Perhaps I can explain this best by reflecting on my own experience, which now spans the whole period of emergence of this phenomenon. My first job was at the new university in Dar es Salaam,[7] in a period of great political ferment, marked by post-colonial nationalism. Politics was very much in the air, and there were many urgent policy issues, but in the university our main concern was the revision of its educational approach, especially the curriculum. Our role, we thought, should to be

[5] For a good account of the methodology in the context of transnational law see Madsen (2006), pp. 33–36. I think that it can be possible to deploy the methodological techniques he discusses even while engaged in the type of participant-research I prefer. I also combine reflexive methodology with an approach of immanent critique, involving close analysis of the self-understandings of practitioners in a field and detailed examination of their practices, contrasting the two (see Conclusions for further discussion).

[6] As Madsen himself points out: "the actors often rely on academic and quasi-academic resources for legitimising their practices", Madsen (2006), p. 33.

[7] At that time a University College, part of the University of East Africa, in Tanganyika, which while I was there joined with Zanzibar to form the United Republic of Tanzania.

to ensure that both the teaching and research in this new university should be relevant to its new country, but politics and policy formation were a matter for the legislature and the government. Interestingly, the Law Faculty led the way in the process of change, in which the university became a focus of lively political and intellectual debates.

However, these stressed the 'limits of the law',[8] taking a critical view of instrumental conceptions which assumed that economic and social change could be produced by state power through legal mechanisms. In the field of international economic law this conception of economic development was expressed in the New International Economic Order Declaration of 1974 and related documents, and the hopes placed by many in nationalisations of foreign-owned assets, especially of raw materials. Although I supported strategies which aimed at reversing the legacies of colonialism and underdevelopment, my academic work took a critical view of both nationalist politics and state ownership policies, and pointed to their limitations and difficulties.[9]

Of course, in Tanzania I was an expatriate, but there were other non-Tanzanians who were closely connected with policy formulation as government advisers. Then when I returned to the UK in 1968, for me the relationship to politics was much the same. I was soon plunged into the campus movements, but their central concern was reform of universities; any wider political impact was understood to be a matter of alliances with other social forces. In the 1970s this meant working with community groups and workers' organizations, in relation to which I saw my role as providing expertise and research services. I found it very rewarding when critical theory and practice could interact, nurturing and strengthening each other, but nevertheless my academic work remained quite separate from my political engagement.

The academic and policy or political spheres have quite different dynamics and time-scales. Those engaged in the latter begin from a teleological perspective, knowing their objectives and so seeking the best means to those ends, justifications for their actions, and proof of their beliefs. The academic of course also has pre-formed views and preferences, but academic inquiry, especially if it is critical, entails adopting a sceptical stance, challenging received opinion, treating initial ideas as hypotheses to be tested. It also has a longer time horizon: a research program lasts many years, sometimes a lifetime, and even the shortest project is rarely completed in less than a year or two.[10] The policy world is of course much more fleeting, a news item disappears in hours or days at most, and while broader

[8] Shivji (1986).

[9] Faundez and Picciotto (1978).

[10] There are of course significant differences for full-time researchers and those who also have teaching and other responsibilities, but even a full-time PhD is rarely completed within the 3 years it is supposed to take. The longest I have supervised took a dozen years, but this was Yao Graham, who was drawn into direct political involvement for several years when Fl. Lt. Rawlings came to power while he was doing field work in his country, Ghana; happily, he survived a serious injury and a spell in jail to return and complete his thesis.

policy issues are not quickly resolved, proposals and campaigns usually demand papers to be written within days and to produce effects within months. Thus, from the policy perspective academic work often seems irrelevant, even utopian; so it may remain neglected outside (or even inside) academia, although it may turn out later to have been prescient and find its moment.[11]

My academic work on TNCs in the 1970s for a while came into closer conjuncture with my more political activities helping to provide research services to workplace trade union organizations. The election of a Labour government, with Tony Benn appointed as Minister for Trade and Industry (formerly the Board of Trade), sparked an attempt to introduce continental European-style co-determination, with the Industry Act of 1975. The historical strength of shop stewards in the auto industry of Coventry seemed to put them in a good position to take advantage of this, and it seemed that a more structured form of research support could help them engage with corporate strategies, especially involving internationalisation, the central challenge to the British auto industry of the time. At the same time funding for research had begun to stress relevance to policy and to users. This rightly aroused academic suspicions, and continues to do so, as disfavouring longer-term and especially critical and anti-establishment research. Nevertheless a colleague (Richard Hyman, a specialist on industrial relations) and I determined it was worth a try to submit an application for funding to the Social Science Research Council (SSRC). Somewhat to our surprise we eventually received a letter announcing that we had been successful. However, the sting in the tail was that we were required to confirm that we had the necessary 'research access', which meant a letter of approval from the company management. Needless to say, this was not forthcoming, despite the shop-floor power of our trade unionist sponsors.

In the 1980s, as my teaching and research on international economic law expanded, I planned to write a book covering the main important areas. I decided that my focus should be on TNCs, but analysed in the wider perspective of their historical development and the interaction of this process with changes in the international state system. However, I determined that it should include a chapter on international tax, a topic I had not much studied till then, but which was clearly central to both states and TNCs. As I became immersed in it, the intended chapter grew into a book.[12] As I expected, it received little attention among tax specialists, since I adopted a wider political economy and critical legal approach; at the same

[11] Among many examples I may single out Ronald Coase, whose main work was done in the left-wing intellectual context of the London School of Economics in the 1930s, but was taken up some three decades later in Chicago, resulting in the award of a Nobel Prize in 1991. Although his work probed the limits of both market-based coordination (due to 'transaction costs') and of corporate management or public planning, in the policy climate of the 1980s it sparked enormous outputs of free-market oriented work. Coase himself, however, sharply criticised the version of his views put forward especially by Richard Posner, the dominant figure in law-and-economics (his mildest comment was that it was "highly inaccurate": Coase (1993), p. 96; and see Campbell and Klaes (2005).

[12] Picciotto (1992) now enjoying a second life at http://taxjustice.blogspot.be/2013/06/international-business-taxation.html (last accessed 14 August 2015).

time, it was too technical and detailed for many of those in the policy communities; its most receptive audience was in the emerging field of international political economy, pioneered especially by Susan Strange and Robert Cox.

Once it was published I moved on, or rather back, to a wider range of issues, especially trade, which was merging with investment regulation with the establishment of the World Trade Organization (WTO) in 1995. Understanding the complexity of this phenomenon took me several years of teaching and research, mixed with other duties and a change of university. I also conducted some research into regulation of financial markets. As part of this, a colleague and I wrote a paper warning of the dangers of financial derivatives,[13] which we had difficulty getting published, and which was duly ignored by policy-makers, as were similar warnings by a few others with more influence than we had. Only finally towards the end of my academic career was I able to resume my plan to work on a more comprehensive book which was eventually completed, greatly helped by the fortuitous award of a 2-year research fellowship, as *Regulating Global Corporate Capitalism* (2011).

In the meantime, I had taken another plunge into policy arenas. In 1997 a colleague and friend, Jane Kelsey, drew my attention to the draft of the Multilateral Agreement on Investment (MAI), which had been leaked to and then publicized by activist groups. This was now the period of academic debates about 'globalisation', and of activist 'anti-globalisation' campaigns. I was critical of the academic debates, much of which seemed shallow and superficial, and I could not identify with the activists, since I regarded myself as an internationalist.

However, the text of the MAI proved fascinating, and drew me into studying its policy and political context. It created broad obligations on states for protection of property rights, derived from investment treaties, as well as the non-discrimination principles of national treatment and most-favoured-nation treatment, modelled on those in trade agreements. It applied to 'investors' and 'investments', very broadly defined to include contractual as well as property rights, but no mention of TNCs. It seemed based on a very simplistic understanding of both international political economy and of legal regulation. Interviewing some of those involved with the negotiations suggested that they were driven by short-term political considerations and ideology favouring 'free trade', with little understanding of the implications of the legal instruments they were designing. The campaigners seemed right in their opposition, but this seemed based on gut reactions. Even an academic economist, called in as a consultant by the UK Department for International Development to evaluate the campaigners' criticisms, produced what seemed to me to be a very superficial analysis, based on macro-economic assumptions about the benefits of 'open markets'. Working with researchers in some civil society organizations, especially Oxfam, we produced a volume of research-based analyses aimed at strengthening the debate.[14] I also published a more academic analysis, in which

[13] Campbell and Picciotto (2000).

[14] Picciotto and Mayne (1999).

I analysed the MAI in terms of the emergence of networks of international economic regulation.[15]

3 Academics and Global Governance

My involvement with the MAI brought home to me that my academic work in the field of international economic law was unavoidably part of the policy arena. More than that, engagement with this arena seemed a responsibility, due to the nature of the phenomena I was studying. The policy debate was dominated by neo-liberal ideologies favouring the liberalisation of markets, privatisation and deregulation. Even opponents of these ideas understood projects such as the creation of the WTO, and the proposal for the MAI, in such neo-liberal terms, and denounced them as such. Yet it seemed clear on closer examination that it was resulting in an enormous growth of regulation in many fields, from technical and health or safety standards for products to regulation of banks and other financial institutions. As Stephen Vogel pointed out, the creation of so-called free markets actually involved many more detailed and formalised rules.[16] On the other hand, what was generally described as a 'market' economy seemed to me quite different from my conception of a market, since it was dominated by corporate behemoths. Liberalisation was not a 'retreat of the state', but its transformation, into a new type of public-private corporatocracy.

I found it impossible simply to describe these phenomena in a detached way. Academics, as technical experts, had become direct participants in the creation of what was being described as global governance. International lawyers were enlisting as WTO panellists, and investment arbitrators, just as scientists were active in debates about biotechnology patenting, food safety or environmental protection. When I tried to describe the outlines of the multi-level or networked system that seemed to me to be emerging, I was denounced by some critical academics as having adopted the techno-speak of its protagonists. Yet it seemed to me impossible either to ignore or reject these processes, which like it or not were changing the world.

The world of nation-states and national economies has been dissolving, or fragmenting, restructuring around intertwined public-corporate bureaucracies.[17] This has weakened the already fragile traditional forms of democratic accountability or checks on power within states. In the political sphere, representation through class-based political parties has given way to 'audience democracy', based on the "construction of vague images prominently featuring the personality of the

[15] Picciotto (1998).

[16] Vogel (1996).

[17] I have tried to analyse this, most extensively in my book of 2011, and also by revisiting my earlier work on Marxist state theories: Picciotto (2010).

leader".[18] At the same time, policy arenas now depend much more heavily on knowledge and expertise, largely because the world and its governance have become much more complex and interconnected. The economic sphere continues to be dominated by the large corporations which had emerged in the twentieth century, but rather than growing ever bigger they have tended to become 'lean and mean', focusing on their core business, while extending their tentacles through international supply chains of subcontractors, or systems of franchising and licensing. Their cadres have become ever more expert at managing the business itself, but increasingly driven by the short-term pressures from capital markets, resulting from the disintermediation of finance and 'financialisation' of capitalism. The corporate and public policy spheres have become highly intertwined, as the competitiveness and sometimes even survival of business is highly dependent on regulatory decisions, while politicians want access to corporate funds for campaign finance, not to speak of personal enrichment. At the lower levels, regulatory officials and corporate managers also interact closely, and 'responsive regulation' has created technocratic 'epistemic communities', while also creating a seed bed for corruption.

This new world of 'governance' has spawned new organisational forms of producing, managing and deploying policy expertise. On the one hand in older professions such as law and accountancy, the large corporatist firms which had already diverged from the traditional family businesses and partnerships, have expanded their provision of policy advice and lobbying services, for both business and governments. The broadest and largest are now the Big Four (Deloitte, EY, KPMG and PwC), then the large global business consultancy and law firms (Accenture, Baker & McKenzie etc.), a number of smaller public policy advice and public relations firms, followed by an array of smaller boutique firms focusing on specific issues, such as taxation. Business or industry associations range from the Chambers of Commerce, which have a wide scope and a long history, coordinated and with a significant international presence through the International Chamber of Commerce, to more specific groupings such as the Chemicals Industry Association, which set up a global system of chemicals plant safety regulation following the Bhopal disaster.[19]

In many ways set against these was a motley range of campaigning organisations of various types. Some, especially in the fields of 'development' and the environment, are large, international, and quite well resourced—Oxfam, Friends of the Earth and others. Although their resources are mainly geared to raising funds and disbursing assistance, they have increasingly focused on campaigns around policy issues related to their concerns, which resulted in the establishment of research departments. Indeed, it was with researchers from Oxfam, the Worldwide Fund for Nature and others that I had worked on the MAI campaign. Others are targeted at more specific issues so are generally smaller, although those with a global reach can be quite large, such as Transparency International. Some trade union organisations

[18] Manin (1994); see also Manin (1997).

[19] King and Lenox (2000).

have also developed a policy role, especially the international sectoral federations. The scope of their activities has been somewhat limited, because of both their reduced resources due to declining union membership, and their reluctance to expand their concerns beyond the traditional ambit of employment conditions. Nevertheless, some of the public sector union organisations in particular have taken up wider issues, such as Education International on services liberalisation, and Public Services International on tax issues. Outside economic questions, campaigning organisations such as Amnesty have been joined by others working on broader issues of human rights and 'security', which may however include economic aspects such as corruption, money laundering and capital flight. Some position themselves less as campaigners and more like the think-tanks, which have a longer history, in many countries often linked to political parties.

Inevitably, all these organisations are dependent on, and therefore more or less beholden to, their different sources of funding. This is more direct and explicit for organisations emanating from or linked with business, which unabashedly represent the specific interests and concerns of their constituencies. Hence, although all such policy-oriented bodies have been very generally referred to as nongovernmental organizations (NGOs), those which regard themselves as working from a public interest perspective have preferred to be described as civil society organizations (CSOs). They are of course generally less well-resourced than business or professional organisations, and their need to raise funds can affect their choices of both campaigning issues and strategies. However, their staff are generally driven by ideological commitment more than career considerations, so are more likely to take independent positions, although this may result in partisanship or even fervent advocacy.

Although I have always been interested in business and economic issues, even in practical ways, my focus on understanding and analysis led me away from professional practice and to an academic career, and my concerns for emancipatory social change prompted a preference for working with CSOs. Surprisingly, this choice has not been unproblematic. It seems to be viewed by some as an abandonment of independence and of academic standards of 'objectivity', somehow undermining the integrity and reliability of my analyses and arguments. This is curious, since it seems much more acceptable for academics to have a parallel professional practice, or to work as consultants for business or professional firms. It has become increasingly normal also for such firms to finance academic research institutions especially on business and economic matters, and these institutions organise conferences and symposia with the combined participation of academics and practitioners, usually from business. These seem to me to foster shared perspectives which become received as common sense, so that the academic's commitment to critical inquiry is threatened and in many ways corrupted. These kinds of close interactions of academics with business professionals and managers seem to me much more threatening of academic integrity than work with CSOs, but they are rarely criticised.

Yet the relationship with activists is also challenging. In choosing this option it may be tempting to become a campaigner, but I have not seen this as my primary role. It seems to me more important, valuable and rewarding to prioritise critical research, since this is what is most lacking in policy arenas, yet essential for their effective functioning. Academics are in a unique and privileged position that allows them the time and independence for longer-term research from a critical perspective. Certainly, over my career, both the amount of time and the degree of independence have been reduced, with the intensification of academic work, and the shift towards private sources of funding. On the other hand, there has been some encouragement to engage in research which is relevant to policy. Although, as my experience in the 1970s with the SSRC showed, this tends to be interpreted as meaning work with business and government rather than social movements, at least it allows a space for such work. The academic's reluctance to move into this space is often due to a preference either for the easier and more financially rewarding path, or conversely to an inclination to abandon research for activism. I have preferred to maintain my focus on academic research while trying to contribute to policy debates through supporting social movement organizations.

4 International Tax Research and Activism

I was fortunate to have been able, following formal retirement from the university, to engage more fully in policy work, to a degree that would be hard or impossible for most academics with substantial teaching and other responsibilities. It is this latest experience that has brought home more directly to me the issues explored in this paper. As already mentioned, after the publication of my book on international tax in 1992, I had again broadened out my research interests, leading to my work on the WTO and the MAI, and then on financial markets. However, I remained interested in corporate taxation, especially in the ways in which international tax avoidance had led to the creation of the tax haven and 'offshore' finance system.[20] While working with Oxfam on the MAI, I suggested that this should be an area on which they do some work, and although they had too much invested in other topics to redirect their main efforts, some short-term funding did result in a report with which I helped: *Tax Havens: Releasing the Hidden Billions* (2000).

Although Oxfam did not immediately follow this up with any campaigning work on tax, other organizations did, notably War on Want. This was the period of the World Social Forums and the anti-globalisation movement, about which, as mentioned above, I had reservations. Nevertheless, the Forums provided an arena in which the international tax issue, among many others, could be debated by a combination of activists and researchers. The Tax Justice Network was launched following a discussion at the European Social Forum at Florence in 2002, mainly through the efforts of John Christensen. An economist originating from Jersey, John had worked as economic adviser there, but quit in 1998 due to his disagreement

[20] See especially Picciotto (1999).

with its government's policy of fostering the island's status as a tax haven and offshore finance centre.[21] He had contributed a chapter to the edited book in which I had also written about the offshore system,[22] and had also worked with Oxfam and helped with the report in 2000. John has been the main driving force of TJN since then, and by 2010 it had spawned a global network of tax justice groups and organisations, which in 2013 set up a new umbrella body, the Global Alliance for Tax Justice. I helped organise TJN's first conference or workshop at Essex in 2003, and seeing my role more in terms of research than activism, I was described as a Senior Adviser of TJN (with a number of others), and this remains the case. However, I travelled to Nairobi and participated in the meeting linked with the World Social Forum there which led to the foundation of TJN-Africa.

The issue of international taxation became increasingly politicised during this period, so TJN rode on the crest of a wave, which to some extent it also created. International tax evasion and avoidance had already been taken up by the G7 world leaders, and the communiqué from their meeting in Lyon in 1996 stated that "[t]ax schemes aimed at attracting financial and other geographically mobile activities can create harmful tax competition between States", and supported action on this through the Organisation for Economic Cooperation and Development (OECD), the main international tax body. This resulted in the OECD report on *Harmful Tax Competition* in 1998,[23] which was relatively timid, but was further weakened by a US volte-face in 2001, after lobbying of the new Bush administration by the far-right Centre for Freedom and Prosperity. The initiative became focused on the negotiation of bilateral treaties for exchange of information for tax matters, which was a very slow process, and was in any case limited to provision of information on request, which gave secrecy jurisdictions plenty of scope to stall.

From its formation, TJN called for a comprehensive multilateral system for automatic exchange of information, which we suggested could be based on the OECD-Council of Europe multilateral convention for administrative assistance in taxation, published in 1988 though ratified by only a handful of states by 2001. Although such a system was considered politically impossible at that time, after the renewed political pressures following the financial crisis of 2008 it became the new global standard. The multilateral convention was amended in 2010 and thrown open to all states, and in 2013 both the G8 and the newly formed G20 finally agreed to support multilateral automatic exchange of information for tax purposes. The OECD's Global Forum on Tax Transparency set about implementation, based on a Global Reporting Standard published in 2014. TJN continues to track tax transparency through a small team compiling the Financial Secrecy Index.

[21] See Warren J (2014) Tax is the Lifeblood of Democracy: An Interview with John Christensen of the Tax Justice Network. Spirit of Contradiction, http://spiritofcontradiction.eu/niebuhr/2014/08/18/interview-with-john-christensen-of-the-tax-justice-network (last accessed 13 July 2015).

[22] Hampton and Abbott (1999).

[23] OECD (1998) Harmful Tax Competition: An Emerging Global Issue, http://www.oecd.org/tax/transparency/44430243.pdf (last accessed 13 July 2015).

My main interest was international corporate taxation, which seemed to me to have further deteriorated since publication of my 1992 book. The basic tax treaty rules had been little changed since first devised under the League of Nations in 1928, and attempts to patch them up through the OECD had worsened the situation. Regulations on transfer pricing drawn up by the US in 1968, exported to other countries through the OECD, had resulted only in entrenching the 'separate entity' principle. This required adjustment of prices on transactions between entities under common control by reference to 'comparables' between independent parties, which experience showed did not exist. Based on a fundamentally faulty assumption, the approach proved ineffective in practice, as had become increasingly apparent in the 1980s, and was detailed in my 1992 book. The response of the US authorities was to develop more sophisticated methods, leading to conflicts within the OECD, and further elaborations, embodied in the OECD Transfer Pricing Guidelines of 1995. Although formally only soft law, in practice these Guidelines have come to be treated as global norms, often referred to by courts,[24] and incorporated into national law by legislation,[25] even in non-OECD countries.[26]

International tax, and especially transfer pricing, quickly emerged as an important field, and its practitioners exploited its broad principles to devise ever more elaborate corporate structures. These generally take advantage of the encouragement provided by the independent entity principle to form affiliates in convenient jurisdictions with responsibility for specific functions, with the aim of reducing

[24] In Kenya, the High Court allowed a company to use a transfer pricing method relying on the Guidelines even though those Guidelines were at that time not mentioned anywhere in Kenyan law." We live in what is now referred to as a 'global village'. We cannot overlook or sideline what has come out of the collective wisdom of tax payers and tax collectors in other countries. And especially because of the absence of any such guidelines in Kenya, we must look elsewhere". (Judge Alnashir Visram, *Unilever Kenya v KRA* 2005, 12). Similarly, a Malaysian court upheld a transfer pricing method based on the Guidelines, rejecting an adjustment made by the tax authority under local law, which it held to be invalid: *MM Sdn Berhad v Ketua Pengarah Hasil Dalam Negeri* Appeal No PKCP(R) 55/2009 (2013) MSTC ~10-046 (2013).

[25] For example as authoritative guidance for interpretation of tax treaty provisions: e.g. in the UK, the Taxation (International and Other Provisions) Act 2010 s.164 provides that treaties based on the OECD Model should be interpreted 'in accordance with' the Guidelines and with any documents published by the OECD as part of the Guidelines prior to May 1998, and any documents designated in an Order made by the Treasury after that date as comprised in the Guidelines. This is a good example of global lawmaking, in which soft and hard law become intertwined, see Picciotto (2011), pp. 20–22.

[26] The Nigerian Income Tax (Transfer Pricing) Regulations No. 1 (2012) specify that they shall be "applied in a manner consistent with" the OECD Guidelines "as supplemented and updated from time to time" (s.11); there is identical language in the Tanzania Income Tax (Transfer Pricing) Regulations 2014 s.9; the boilerplate provisions suggests a systematic process of ensuring adoption of these norms, presumably resulting from 'capacity building' through the World Bank or the OECD itself. Even where countries enact their own regulations, the Guidelines are relied on in practice, and referred to by courts, e.g. in India a Tax Tribunal even recently referred to a draft report proposing changes to the Guidelines although it had not yet been approved: Income Tax Appellate Tribunal, Mumbai, ITA No. 1565/Mum/2014, *Watson Pharma Pvt Ltd v DCIT* (9 January 2015), para. 61.

overall effective tax liability.[27] The regulations introduced in response by tax authorities still began from the independent entity assumption, so have been largely ineffective, except to create a field of complex technical rules. While some tax officials were frustrated by this, for others it provided an opportunity to invest in expertise, and many took advantage of the revolving door into private practice after a period in the public service. Private practitioners flooded into the field, offering a range of specialisations and services, and corporate tax departments grew from a handful to a hundred or more people—in the case of General Electric, which from the early 1990s built tax minimisation into its management structure, and set up its own finance affiliate, GE Capital, as many as one thousand.

In the meantime, the Oxfam report of 2000 was followed up by occasional exposés from other CSOs, often explaining the avoidance strategies of specific companies and estimating the tax losses especially for poor countries. Reports by investigative journalists followed, initially in the more liberal papers and later, especially following the fiscal crises resulting from the financial crash of 2008–2009, also in mainstream and business media channels such as Reuters and Bloomberg. Parliamentary inquiries in many countries also highlighted the issue, focusing in particular on the very low taxes paid on their non-US profits by US-based internet companies, such as Apple, Amazon, and Google. Discussion of the 'Dutch Sandwich' and the 'Double Irish' moved from specialist tax publications to mainstream media.

These political concerns generated new pressures on the OECD tax experts. An opportunity for a new direction came with the retirement in 2012 of Jeffrey Owens, who had built the OECD's Centre for Tax Policy and Administration from a handful to some 100 staff over two decades.[28] During his tenure, the OECD had continued to prioritise the role of tax treaties as preventing double taxation in order to facilitate international investment. His replacement, Pascal Saint-Amans, arrived in February 2012 with a clear agenda to redirect attention to 'double non-taxation', and he quickly launched an initially low-key project on 'base erosion and profit shifting'. The acronym BEPS soon gained high visibility after the publication in January 2013 by the OECD of a 30-month 15-point BEPS Action Plan, and its endorsement by the G20's St Petersburg Declaration of September 2013.

Work on analysing the defects of international tax rules had also taken place in parallel through TJN and other organisations. Funding from the government of

[27] For further details see Picciotto S (2013) Is the International Tax System Fit for Purpose, Especially for Developing Countries? ICTD Working Paper 13 http://www.ictd.ac/en/publications/international-tax-system-fit-purpose-especially-developing-countries (last accessed 14 August 2015); Corporate Reform Collective (2014), chs. 1 and 10.

[28] Owens J, Seminar on Liable to No Tax, 65th IFA Congress, Paris, 15 September 2011; ITR Correspondent, Jeffrey Owens Joins Ernst & Young, International Tax Review, 8 June 2012, http://www.internationaltaxreview.com/Article/3043711/Jeffrey-Owens-joins-Ernst-and-Young.html (last accessed 14 August 2015); Owens Looks Back on his Time in Office, International Tax Review, 1 February 2012, http://www.internationaltaxreview.com/IssueArticle/2967120/Archive/Owens-looks-back-on-his-time-in-office.html (last accessed 14 August 2015).

Finland enabled TJN to organize a seminar in Helsinki in June 2012, very ably planned by David Spencer, another TJN Senior Adviser. He brought together many leading specialists, including Reuven Avi-Yonah, Ilan Benshalom, Michael Durst and Michael McIntyre, and revenue officials or practitioners from several countries including Brazil, China, the Dominican Republic and India. The conclusions of the seminar were clear, that the separate entity principle created a fundamental flaw in the system, and most of those participating advocated a shift towards treating TNCs as unitary firms. I therefore followed up the event by drafting a paper arguing for 'unitary taxation' of TNCs, and discussing how a transition to such a system could be achieved, building on work especially by Michael McIntyre, Reuven Avi-Yonah and Michael Durst.[29] I also received helpful comments on the draft from others associated with TJN, except for David Spencer, who only made clear his disagreement. I was sorry that we could not find a way to debate the issue further within TJN, especially as David subsequently resigned, having failed to convince others also of his view.

This highlighted one of the problems of working with an organization like TJN, which combines research with campaigning. For me, it is important to find ways to debate different views, if they fall within the general aims of the organisation, but this can be difficult. People invest a lot in developing their understanding of issues, and hence tend to become committed to their own perspective, making it hard to be open to different ideas. The organization needs to take a stance and campaign for specific policies, and advisers who feel their views have been disregarded feel slighted. Such organisations also may attract forceful personalities with large egos, which can make it difficult to sustain open debate and team-work. Tensions can also arise over competition over access to scarce funds, and researchers dependent on grant funding may naturally feel resentful of academics in secure jobs, while academics feel conscious of the risk to their careers from identification with activism. These problems are not unique to such organisations, and academia itself is also rife with conflicts and feuds mixing clashing opinions and personal hostility. The inter-personal aspects can be dealt with to some extent by flexibility in organisational affiliation, as individuals can have different types of link with organisations, and can move between them. The more important issue is to decide the appropriate balance for each organisation between campaigning and research.

My preference is to prioritise research, not only because of my personal background and skills. A central characteristic of global governance today is both the importance of detailed or technical understanding of issues, as well as the wide gap between such understanding and the broad-brush terms in which policy debates are generally conducted.[30] That is why academics and researchers generally have a crucial part to play in helping to ensure that such debates are better informed. It is especially important, in my view, for critical views to be presented and given a fair

[29] Picciotto S (2012) Towards Unitary Taxation, http://www.taxjustice.net/cms/upload/pdf/Towards_Unitary_Taxation_1-1.pdf (last accessed 13 July 2015).

[30] Picciotto (2015).

hearing in policy arenas, which can otherwise become stuck in a stultifying consensus based on received opinions, generally supporting the dominant corporatist perspectives. This again suggests the importance of contributions from academics, who are privileged to be able to be more independent, if they wish, from big business interests.

Without any deliberate strategy, I found myself devising different ways to straddle research and campaigning. Research work emerged from my involvement as a member of the Advisory Board of the Centre for Tax and Development (ICTD), set up in 2010 and headed by Professor Mick Moore at the Institute for Development Studies at Sussex University in Brighton, with funding from the UK's Department for International Development, and Norway's Norad. He and his very able Research Directors, Odd-Helge Fjeldstad and Wilson Prichard, have pioneered research on taxation in developing countries, but were less knowledgeable about international corporate taxation, which is an important source of revenue for such countries. Finding it hard to evaluate funding applications they received in this area, they convened an informal meeting of experts in summer 2012, shortly after TJN's Helsinki seminar, and at a time when little was known about the BEPS project.

Stimulated by the discussions both in Helsinki and Brighton, I suggested that the ICTD issue a call for applications focusing especially on issues raised by a possible transition to unitary taxation of TNCs. The idea quickly snowballed as I contacted potential researchers, and we put together a program of seven (later eight) related projects, involving economists, lawyers and accountants, which after revisions eventually passed the ICTD's peer-review process for funding. It was soon shown to be very well timed, as the publication of the BEPS Action Plan laid out a high-profile agenda for international corporate tax reform. Meetings we organized to map out our research at the start (May 2013), and to review progress after some months (January 2014), attracted participants from staff of the IMF, OECD, the UN Tax Committee and the European Commission. Research outputs from all the project were published, following peer-review, within 2 years of the start of the program, which is good going for academic research.[31] We followed this up with a more targeted program for research aimed at helping developing countries to cope with the outcomes of the BEPS project, including practical ways to protect their tax base.

The launching of the BEPS Action Plan by the OECD also offered an opportunity and a challenge for policy activism, and a number of activists and researchers met in London in summer 2013 to consider how to respond to it. The BEPS project was to be run through the OECD's Committee on Fiscal Affairs (CFA), which had been the main custodian of international tax rules for over half a century, although with the addition of non-OECD G20 member states for this purpose. The tax officials representing their governments in the CFA, and those employed in the OECD Secretariat, considered themselves to be engaged in specialist technical and

[31] See http://www.ictd.ac/en/unitary-taxation-transnational-corporations-special-reference-developing-countries (last accessed 14 August 2015).

therefore 'non-political' work, while also conducting consultations aimed essentially at business representatives and tax advisers. My main concern was that it would clearly take considerable effort to track, analyse and provide comments from an independent perspective on all the proposals which would flow from the Action Plan. We also considered it important to try to widen the debate beyond the international tax specialists. These considerations led us to formulate two initiatives.

To tackle the task of analysis, we decided to create an international network of international tax specialists, academics, researchers working for CSOs, and perhaps even practitioners, which I agreed to coordinate. We chose to call it the BEPS Monitoring Group (BMG), on which we were later commended by a tax insider, who thought it made the group sound semi-official, though probably some activists considered the name too obscure. Certainly, once we had set up a rudimentary blog website, one of the first comments pointed out that we needed to explain first what BEPS meant. I drew up some basic procedural rules, which in the event worked well. Individuals would be members for their expertise, and not representing organizations; the BMG's comments and reports would be prepared by those who volunteered for each topic (a minimum of three people), and should be approved by a majority of those who had worked on drafting each paper, who would normally be identified as its authors. We had no funding,[32] so participation was necessarily limited to people already interested in tracking the issues, and with the time to do so. Starting with a handful of members, it grew to over 30, although with a much smaller core of active members.

The second suggestion, aimed at fostering a wider debate, was that we try to establish a Commission, consisting of high-profile public intellectuals from around the world. A Steering Group was set up, and some seed funding from CSOs enabled us to employ a part-time consultant, for the organisational work such as drafting funding proposals and meeting representatives of funding bodies. The Independent Commission for the Reform of International Corporate Taxation (ICRICT) met in New York in March 2015, and issued an impressive report, officially launched at the UN Conference on Finance for Development in Addis Ababa in July,[33] though we did not succeed in hitting our ambitious funding target, which would have enabled the Commission to have even higher visibility and hold several hearings around the world.

---

[32] We later received a grant of $10,000, which helped fund travel to meetings or consultations by members who had no other access to such support. I considered it legitimate to use ICTD funds for my own expenses, which became significant once the OECD consultations got underway, because the ICTD research benefited enormously from the intimate knowledge I gained, as well as contacts made, from following the process so closely. However, the BMG was not a sponsor or supporter of the ICTD, since this might be considered by some to compromise its academic independence. In wearing several hats, I in some ways resembled the tax advisers also participating in the BEPS consultations, such as Mary Bennett, who works for law firm Baker McKenzie (after spending some years as an OECD official), but has also represented various industry groups.

[33] The Report is available, together with other details of the ICRICT, www.icrict.org (last accessed 13 July 2015).

5 Conclusions

I hope that these very personal reflections have helped to map some of the tangled terrain of policy formation in global governance, as well as explaining how I have seen my role. I would like to close by briefly drawing out a few general analytical points.

The first concerns the concept of critique. For me being critical does not mean being oppositional or subjecting ideas to criticism from the outside, or from an alternative criterion of value. I apply what I understand to be a Marxian approach of immanent critique,[34] which begins from a thorough historical examination of the social practices and institutions concerned, and their associated ideologies. The critique emerges from contrasting the self-understanding of practitioners in a field with a detailed examination of their actual practices, and demonstrating the contradictions between the two. However, the aim is not to denounce hypocrisy, but to understand how and why these understandings developed, and point the way to a transformation. I should say that I did not begin with such a worked out methodological strategy or theory, but have groped my way towards it, through actual practice.

Thus, my research on the history of international business taxation revealed that from the beginning there was a tension between the reality of TNCs as they emerged as internationally-integrated businesses, and the methods developed by tax authorities to regulate them according to the bureaucratic rationality of national accounting and tax systems. I discovered a plea for a global approach to business taxation, made to the UK Royal Commission on Income Taxation in 1920:

> In a business of this nature you cannot say how much is made in one country and how much is made in another. You kill an animal and the product of that animal is sold in 50 different countries. You cannot say how much is made in England and how much is made abroad. That is why I suggest that you should pay a turnover tax on what is brought into this country...[i]t is not my object to escape payment of tax. My object is to get equality of taxation with the foreigner, and nothing else.[35]

This was from none other than William Vestey, co-founder of a family-owned global food supply business, who went on to pioneer international tax avoidance techniques, resulting in long-running disputes with the British tax authorities.

I traced the emergence and development of the rules for adjustment of accounts between related entities, and saw how they led to the development of tax avoidance techniques using intermediary entities in convenient jurisdiction, and how this in turn led the formalisation of rules on transfer pricing, which only reinforced the 'arm's length principle'. When I wrote my book, starting in the late 1980s, others were advocating a shift towards a worldwide unitary taxation system, but this was controversial, and I analysed the reasons for the divergent perspectives, without

---

[34] See e.g. Stahl T (2013) What is Immanent Critique? SSRN: http://ssrn.com/abstract=2357957 (last accessed 13 July 2015).

[35] UK Royal Commission on Income Tax 1920, Evidence, p. 452 Question 9460.

taking a position. In the more recent period of my more direct engagement with policy, I became an advocate for such an approach. It was nevertheless very important not to present such proposals as a mere alternative developed from outside the existing system, but to show how existing rules in many ways had already shifted towards it, as the only effective way of dealing with the business reality. Equally, the obstacles and objections could be explained in terms of the positions in the field of the practitioners and policy advocates expressing them.

Secondly, it seems to me that the special position of academics gives them both a responsibility and a unique opportunity. This is not only because that position gives them a degree of independence of special interests. This is certainly important, especially in relation to business and economic law and regulation, which is so dominated by corporate and pro-business views that some counter-weight is essential to ensure a genuine debate. However, academics are also subject to pressures, especially from career concerns. Research funding can also create restrictions, not only when it derives from business sources, as my experience in the 1970s with the SSRC showed me.

More importantly, an academic position offers the chance to take a long-term view, and engage in proper research. Policy fields today are teeming with pressure groups and lobbyists, often with their own policy departments, or employing consultants. However, the research which they carry out tends to be geared to the short-term agendas and timescales of campaigning and policy advocacy. Its aim is to buttress the arguments for existing policy positions, rather than to evaluate evidence, or identify and study alternative approaches. Too often policy research institutes and think tanks are also driven by short-term agendas. The impetus for the emergence of TJN and its agenda came from researchers and practitioners such as John Christensen and Richard Murphy, who did not begin as campaigners. I am sure that the same can be said for other CSOs that have helped to define important global governance issues from outside the accepted orthodoxies.

Hence, my call is not for academics to become campaigners, far from it. I consider that it is much more important that they remain rooted in a commitment to research, especially from a critical perspective. There are many specialists in designing media campaigns and crafting snappy sound-bites. There are even more professionals, lawyers, accountants, and others, making a lucrative career practising in fields such as international economic law. In my experience it is much more rewarding to aim to combine critical theory with some form of critical practice in this field.

References

Campbell D, Klaes M (2005) The principle of institutional direction: Coase's regulatory critique of intervention. Camb J Econ 29:263–88

Campbell D, Picciotto S (2000) The justification of financial futures exchanges. In: Hudson A (ed) Modern financial techniques, derivatives, and law. Kluwer Law International, The Hague, pp 121–33

Coase R (1993) Coase on Posner on Coase and concluding comment. J Inst Theoretical Econ 149 (1):96–98
Corporate Reform Collective (2014) Fighting corporate abuse. beyond predatory capitalism. Pluto Press, London
Faundez J, Picciotto S (1978) The nationalization of multinationals in peripheral economies. Macmillan, Basingstoke
Hampton M, Abbott J (eds) (1999) Offshore finance centres and tax havens. The rise of global capital. Palgrave Macmillan, London
King A, Lenox M (2000) Industry self-regulation without sanctions: the chemical industry's responsible care program. Acad Manage J 43(4):698–716
Kristensen H, Zeitlin J (2005) Local players in global games: the strategic constitution of a multinational corporation. Oxford University Press, Oxford
Madsen M (2006) Transnational fields: elements of a reflexive sociology of the internationalisation of law. Retfærd Nordisk Juridisk Tidsskrift 29(3/114):23–41, http://retfaerd.org/retfaerd-nr-114-20063/transnational-fields-elements-of-a-reflexive-sociology-of-the-internationalisation-of-law/ (last accessed 21 August 2015)
Manin B (1994) The metamorphoses of representative government. Econ Soc 23(2):133–171
Manin B (1997) The principles of representative government. Cambridge University Press, Cambridge
Picciotto S (1992) International business taxation: a study of the internationalization of business regulation. Quorum Books, Westport, http://taxjustice.blogspot.be/2013/06/international-business-taxation.html (last accessed 14 August 2015)
Picciotto S (1998) Linkages in international investment regulation: the antinomies of the draft multilateral agreement on investment, University of Pennsylvania. J Int Econ Law 19 (3):731–768
Picciotto S (1999) Offshore: the state as legal fiction. In: Hampton M, Abbott J (eds) Offshore finance centres and tax havens: the rise of global capital. Palgrave Macmillan, London, p 43–79
Picciotto S, Mayne R (eds) (1999) Regulating international business: beyond liberalization. MacMillan, Basingstoke
Picciotto S (2010) International transformations of the capitalist state. Antipode 43(1):87–107. doi:10.1111/j.1467-8330.2010.00812.x
Picciotto S (2011) Regulating global corporate capitalism. Cambridge University Press, Cambridge
Picciotto S (2015) Indeterminacy, complexity, technocracy and the reform of international corporate taxation. Soc Leg Stud 24(2):165–184. doi:10.1177/0964663915572942
Sarat A, Silbey S (1988) The pull of the policy audience. Law Policy 10:97–166
Shivji I (1986) Limits of legal radicalism: reflections on teaching law at the University of Dar es Salaam. University of Dar es Salaam, Dar es Salaam
Vogel S (1996) Freer markets, more rules. Cornell University Press, Ithaca

Global Constitutionalism and International Economic Law: The Case of International Investment Law

David Schneiderman

Contents

Abstract Are there discernable the outlines of an emergent global economic constitutional order? If the current global scene is understood as hybrid and plural, there will be no single, unitary global economic constitution in place at the present moment. There only will be partial manifestations—observable, regime-specific instances—of what might become part of such a global order. Regime specific instances can be found, for instance, in the domain of international investment law. Though there is variation among the web of 2800 bilateral investment treaties, there are sufficient commonalities that will be familiar to constitutional lawyers. It also is apparent that the body of jurisprudence produced by investment tribunals resembles, in some important ways, the output of high court decision making under national constitutional law. The paper begins by outlining two principal modes of understanding global constitutional developments, identifies some familiar constitutional tropes found in investment law, and closes with a discussion, by way of illustration, of an investor's claim, unresolved on the merits, that resembles an early nineteenth century US constitutional dispute concerning the sanctity of contracts.

D. Schneiderman (✉)
Faculty of Law, University of Toronto, 78 Queen's Park, Toronto, ON, Canada, M5S 2C5
e-mail: david.schneiderman@utoronto.ca

M. Bungenberg et al. (eds.), *European Yearbook of International Economic Law 2016*, European Yearbook of International Economic Law 7,
DOI 10.1007/978-3-319-29215-1_2

1 Introduction

Can we see the outlines of an emergent global economic constitutional order? Less ambitiously, we might ask: Does international economic law emulate, in some important ways, national constitutional law? As the international legal scene is dynamic and evolving, it is only possible to address such questions in a provisional way. I begin framing the exercise by generalizing between two principal contending views, though they are not the only available ones. The first unabashedly promotes the constitutionalisation of international economic law ('constitutionalism as project') and, the second, accepts that there is some evidence of constitutionalisation but uses it to critique this tendency ('constitutionalism as critique'). After outlining these contending views, the chapter identifies some provisional hypotheses. Generalizations are drawn primarily, but not exclusively, from work in the realm of international investment law. They lead to the conclusion that we are unlikely to observe a single unitary economic constitutional order, but a number of discrete regimes performing constitution-like functions. Following the admonition that studies of constitutionalisation should be regime specific, the third part turns to a discussion of the field of investment law. This is a legal order made up of over 3000 bilateral investment treaties (BITs) and regional free trade agreements, incorporating standards of protection that will be familiar to those working in constitutional law and, in particular, those operating in the legal systems of the global North. The fourth part takes up a recent dispute, unresolved on the merits, which resembles claims made in early nineteenth century U.S. constitutional law. The objective is to not only to highlight these constitutional linkages but, in a more critical vein, to give reason to press the pause button when it comes to deepening these constitution-like commitments.

2 Discovery, Project, and Critique[1]

There is a tendency, David Kennedy has observed, among those most enthusiastic about promoting constitutional metaphors in international law. They tend to want either to 'discover' such connections or to 'promote' constitutionalism as a 'project.'[2] In this part, I take up representative figures who work, first in the discovery mode and, second, in the project mode. Finally, I turn to the critical mode of inquiry. I consider Dunoff and Trachtman as exhibiting well the characteristics of the first 'discovery' mode. In an introduction to their edited collection, they identify three primary functions served by international constitutional law: an enabling function, a constraining function, and a supplemental or gap-filling function. If a "measure performs [any of] these functions, it is a rule of international

[1] This part draws upon Schneiderman (2010b).

[2] Kennedy (2009), p. 40.

constitutional law," they proclaim.[3] Practically speaking, enabling and constraining functions operate formalistically. They are confined to framing mechanisms that either enable the production of international law or check its production—the UN Charter, for instance, exhibits both features. The constraining version, they emphasize, is not about limiting domestic actors, such as national states, rather it is about constraining the production of international law. For this reason, a candidate for constraining constitutionalism, according to Dunoff and Trachtman, is a proposed appellate body to review the decisions of *ad hoc* international investment tribunals.[4] Supplemental constitutionalism is more interesting not only because it encompasses a wider range of practices but also because it is here that national and domestic actors become the subjects of international constitutional law. These are norms that 'arise in response to domestic constitutional deficiencies' and so fill in the gaps resulting from globalization so as 'promote domestic constitutional values at the international level.'[5] They cite, as examples, circumstances where international institutions, such as the European Court of Justice, respond to pressures 'from below' to develop international constitutional norms.

It is only a short step from discovering constitutional linkages to promoting internationalism constitutionalism as project. "If you think that constitutionalism has worked well at home, and that your own constitution may even be threatened by global pressure of one sort or another," observes Kennedy, "it can feel like a project of the utmost seriousness and urgency to interpret the world in constitutional terms."[6] This captures well the advocacy work of those who seek to repackage the institutions of economic law within a constitutional frame. I consider Ernst-Ulrich Petersmann emblematic of constitutionalism in its project mode as he has been discovering and promoting constitutional linkages for well over 30 years. For Petersmann, international economic law enlarges individual rights both at home and abroad. The end game is to generate a system of limited government that promotes economic freedom, which he associates with the spread of individual human rights.[7] In a recent iteration, he promotes a 'cosmopolitan constitutionalism' that brings norms of 'justice' to the currently fragmented international economic legal order.[8] These norms, which he associates with human rights and the rule of law, are capable of being promoted by a variety of institutions currently policing state behaviour. Petersmann is as much interested in respecting the rights of traders and investors as he is the rights of ordinary citizens to be governed by institutions that promote fairness and human dignity. For this reason, both the World Trade Organization (WTO) and investment arbitration serve as loci for the constitutionalisation of international economic adjudication.

[3] Dunoff and Trachtman (2009a, b), p. 10.

[4] Dunoff and Trachtman (2009a, b), p. 13.

[5] Dunoff and Trachtman (2009a, b), p. 14.

[6] Kennedy (2009), p. 40.

[7] Petersmann (1991), p. 406; Petersmann (1992), p. 33; Petersmann (2000), p. 22.

[8] Petersmann (2012, 2013, 2014).

Others, working in a more descriptive mode, have been more cautious about the constitutional functions served by institutions like the WTO. Deborah Z. Cass, for instance, claims that there are six elements that comprise processes of 'constitutionalisation.' These six elements or features are: a set of social practices that constrain behaviour, a belief in their foundational nature, authorized by a political community, with the requisite legitimacy, through processes of deliberative law-making, resulting in a structural realignment between the new entity and its sub-parts.[9] Testing these claims against features of the WTO, Cass concludes that that it has "some ground to make up before it deserves the label 'constitutional'"[10] Petersmann's account, moreover, elides these 'core constitutional elements' whilst being fixated on a cramped version of human rights that is focussed on individual economic rights.[11] Walker develops seven similar indices of constitutionalism, including the generation of an explicit constitutional discourse, and concludes likewise, although the European Union fares better along these indicia.[12] In a more normative vein, Howse and Nicolaïdis argue that conceiving of the WTO as constitutionalised is a counterproductive response to the WTO's legitimation problems. Rather than raising WTO dispute settlement to a 'higher law' above the fray what is needed is more politics, not less.[13] Dunoff similarly remarks that there is a self-defeating aspect to dressing up the WTO in constitutional garb, as it sparks "the contestation and politics that it seeks to pre-empt".[14]

This is precisely one of the factors animating what I label 'constitutionalism as critique.'[15] In a critical constitutional account, power and political economy are prominently brought back into the fold of international economic law. The spread of rights discourse, akin to national constitutional rights, is understood as benefiting principally powerful economic actors and their host states. Their end game is to remove barriers to trade, persons, and capital, namely, those that prove to be intolerable to economically powerful states. According to the critical constitutional account, the rules of international economic law are the product of a struggle between capital exporting and capital importing states—between the global North and South—over stamping the imprimatur of 'international law' on their preferred legal rules and institutions.[16] Dezalay and Garth chronicled such a struggle going on in the field of commercial arbitration in the 1990s. They documented a competition between Anglo-American and continental European-based legal elites over

---

[9] Cass (2005), p. 19.

[10] Cass (2005), p. 23.

[11] Cass (2005), pp. 172, 176 and Alston (2002).

[12] Walker (2002), p. 355.

[13] Howse and Nicolaïdis (2001), p. 229.

[14] Dunoff (2006), p. 675.

[15] For the purposes of this essay, I do not distinguish between notions of 'constitutional law', 'constitutionalism', and 'constitutionalization'. For a parsing of these terms, see Peters (2006).

[16] I am operating here under the influence of Pierre Bourdieu. See, for instance, Bourdieu (2000), p. 71.

the terms under which international commercial arbitration would be conducted. Their provisional conclusion was that the Anglo-American side was gaining ground.[17]

Another instance of this competition within international economic law can be found in the field of intellectual property. Susan Sell details how U.S.- and European-based conglomerates were able to successfully enlist states of the global North to advance a trade-centred conception of intellectual property that worked mostly to their own benefit. Sell describes the Trade-Related Aspects of International Property Rights (TRIPS) as "a stunning triumph of the private sector in making global IP rules and in enlisting states and international organizations to enforce them".[18] There are many aspects of the global legal order that replicate this rule making process. Powerful business interests and their host states simply are better situated to influence global rule making outcomes. Büthe and Mattli, for instance, find that U.S. firms are better situated at standard setting in financial reporting while Europeans are better at influencing product standard setting.[19] The issue is who gets access to the means by which 'international law' is made. Critical constitutionalists are attuned to these processes, desirous of bringing conceptions of power and political economy into discussions about the production of international economic law.[20]

This is not to deny that critical constitutionalists have their own projects that they wish to pursue.[21] This may or may not take shape via constitutional forms. States, even international norms, may be conscripted in these efforts. The distinguishing feature of the critical approach, in contrast to the project mode, is that global legal rules are expected to mostly get out of the way. For this reason, the question of constitutionalism is subsidiary to the question of the proper legal form with which to pursue alternative futures. For critical constitutionalists, the principal aim is one of opening up possibilities by undoing the constitution-like constraints embodied within the structures of international economic law.

3 A Constitutionalism of Bits and Pieces[22]

Kennedy admits that he has always found constitutionalism a "rather weak sociology of the way power functions." This may be a product, he admits, of U.S. legal origins, where the constitution "is a lousy description of power in American society

[17] Dezalay and Garth (1996), p. 91.

[18] Sell (2003), p. 163.

[19] Büthe and Walter (2011), p. 221.

[20] For a discussion situating this approach to post-national constitutionalism, see Anderson (2012).

[21] I am grateful to Gavin Anderson for this point. For a more general discussion of constitutionalism as critique, see Anderson (2014).

[22] With apologies to Curtin (1993).

and a quite inaccurate map of how Washington works".[23] This scepticism is likely compounded by the phenomenon of 'constitution mongering,' where American constitutionalism is promoted as a model for the rest of the world to follow. [24] It is precisely as a result of these suspicions—in the way in which constitutionalism occludes, institutionalises, and produces relations of power—that a critical constitutionalist account turns out to be a preferred heuristic with which to diagnose the current scene.

Critics, however, need to be sceptical about claims that there is a single, unitary global economic constitution in place at the present moment. There only will be partial manifestations—observable, regime-specific instances—of what might *become* global constitutional law. The particular manifestations of such an emergent, but not yet fully realized, regime are legal orders that exhibit 'constitution-like' features[25] or are 'constitutions-in-the-making'.[26] Such regimes will resemble national constitutional systems in a number of dimensions, principally in respect of rights and structures. Methodologically, this suggests that we undertake thick and detailed descriptions of these regimes rather than engage in abstract and grand theorizing about such things as global law.

The current scene, then, is hybrid and pluralistic.[27] With seemingly little consensus on questions of distributive justice in economic matters, any purported constitutional settlement will be hotly contested. So although a discourse of constitutionalism suggests an overarching legal order, this is unlikely to be presently in place. Yet it will not be the case that the regimes that govern international economic law will be disjointed or closed off from each other. Instead, there will be an elective affinity, if not evidence of deliberate coordination, amongst and between them. One can foresee, for instance, regime-specific interpretations of a principle of national treatment (or non-discrimination) that may conflict, or converge, with other of the regimes that comprise the field of international economic law.[28] In which case, we need not juxtapose constitutionalism with pluralism.[29] Instead, we should envisage 'multiple sites' where both constitutionalism and pluralism comfortably coexist.[30]

If we are looking for evidence of global constitutionalism, what sorts of constitutional features might we find? We should be on the lookout not only for a system of rights—analogous to individual rights within domestic constitutional orders—but also structural features that mimic national scenes, such as federalism, consociationalism, methods of amendment and enforcement, etc. Constitution

[23] Kennedy (2009), p. 61.

[24] Twining (1993).

[25] Schneiderman (2008), p. 4.

[26] Peters (2006), p. 582.

[27] Also Twining (2000), p. 89.

[28] See e.g. Kurtz (2009).

[29] As does Krisch (2012).

[30] Walker (2002), p. 337.

drafters of the past, Linda Colley observes, were 'assiduous and deliberate plagiarizers'.[31] The same might be going on today. We should be on the lookout, then, for attempts to elevate national norms and institutions to global legal fields. We need not go so far as to say that there is no 'genuine globalization',[32] only that a research agenda attending to a global economic constitutional order should be attentive to national constitutional origins and affiliations and, indeed, the ways in which the shape of a global economic constitution may advantage certain states and their home actors over others.[33] We also should be attentive to the phenomenon of how both rights and structures combine to discipline states in ways that dampen citizen expectations of what states can be expected to do on their behalf. For many lawyers, this merely amounts to counting cases and tallying up winners and losers. I would suggest, instead, that we attend to the subtle (and not so subtle) effects that constitution-like regimes unevenly generate for polities in the world.[34]

The discussion so far suggests that states are deeply implicated in the structuration of global constitutionalism. Teubner's view is that states largely are irrelevant to the creation of autonomous legal orders he associates with 'societal constitutionalism.'[35] To the contrary, we should be open to the prospect that states paradoxically are conceding space to the rules and institutions of transnational economic law. This suggests that global constitutionalism does not so much 'compensate' for states losing authority to transnational economic actors[36] or allow states to 'catch up' with markets,[37] rather, states are authoring the very rules and institutions that bind them well into the future.

What about the people themselves? Is there no room for democracy in either the authoring or maintenance of these constitution-like orders? To the extent that a nascent global constitutional economic order is 'demos-constraining' might not the demos be key to the legitimacy of these specific regimes?[38] Though there is much more that can be said about such questions, I would suggest a couple of different paths for thinking through this problem. First legitimacy for these orders will reside principally within the national political systems that authored them. This is how Habermas, in several essays, explains away legitimacy problems associated with the rise of the WTO. Such agreements, he writes, were 'the product of political voluntarism,' not imposed unilaterally by any one state but the consequence of

[31] Colley, L 'Written Constitutions and Writing World History' Margaret MacMillan Lecture in International Relations, University of Toronto, 4 April 2013 [unpublished].

[32] de Sousa Santos (2006).

[33] Weiss (2005).

[34] We should attend, in other words, to the complex ways in which power operates. See, for instance, the three-dimensional view of power in Lukes (2005), p. 25–29.

[35] Teubner (2012).

[36] Peters (2006).

[37] Habermas (2006), p. 83.

[38] The phrase is from Stepan (2001).

'negotiated path-dependant cumulative decisions'.[39] Relatedly, states themselves will provide many of the supports necessary to sustain the legitimacy of these transnational regimes, successfully deploying legitimating discourses associated with comparative advantage, the rule of law, and consumer freedom.[40] Ironically, such regimes may also have a disdainful view of democratic processes, though democratic consent remains a prerequisite for the establishment and ongoing maintenance of these regimes. Citizens consequently are marginalized by these mechanisms, ones that are in the service of more powerful economic forces.

For processes of constitutionalisation to be occurring, might there be a need for some self-consciousness on the part of states and citizens? Both Deborah Cass and Neil Walker, as mentioned, insist that there should be evidence of constitutional explicitness on the part of the relevant actors. On the basis of these and other criteria, they conclude that the WTO has some distance to go before being fully 'constitutionalized'.[41] This suggests that there should be some evidence of a constitutional 'big bang' which helps to kick-start the constitutionalisation process. In the context of the rise of a global economic constitution, I would propose that we consider the 1980s, in particular, the end of the Cold War—the period of global 'lift-off' for much international economic law—as having possibly generated such a constitutional moment, if not for citizens, then at least for global legal elites.[42] It is by this time that home states, channelling the preferences of their national champions and operating within the interstices of international financial institutions and international law, kicked into gear processes giving rise to regimes aiming to bring constitutional order to international economic law.

4 Investment Law's Domains

International investment law, though it has its roots in the international law for the diplomatic protection of aliens,[43] largely is a product of this post-1989 environment. By the 1990s, the rules and institutions of investment law emerged as an effectively enforceable sub-field of international law. I propose turning to a discussion of this regime, as it brings into focus elements of what a global economic constitutional order might look like. I begin by highlighting some of the regime's ideological presuppositions and then turn to its constitution-like features.

[39] Habermas (2006), p. 81.

[40] Schneiderman (2013). Thornhill's proposal that rights regimes generate de facto constituent power that can legitimate law-making authority at transnational levels is intended to elide this problem. See Thornhill (2013), p. 555. The problem is that this looks like a version of constitutionalism without a demos that can be likened to earlier practices of imperialism. On this, see Newton (2006).

[41] Cass (2005), p. 23; Walker (2002), p. 50.

[42] Dezalay (1990).

[43] Borchard (1915).

The ascendance of investment law is associated with the demise of the Soviet Union and the stark choice facing states in need of new inward capital to finance public improvements and economic development. Pushed onto the international agenda by actors within capital-exporting states, working in conjunction with coordinated pressures generated by international financial institutions, states all over the world rushed into the embrace of the investment treaty regime. It perhaps is a little too easy to line up the regime's presuppositions with the neoliberal thinking associated with Reagan, Thatcher, and the 'Washington Consensus', none of which has ever been able to settle precisely upon the appropriate limits to state functions.[44] For this reason alone, we are unlikely to find complete concordance among the various regimes that may comprise a global economic constitutional order (WTO, TRIPS, investment law). We are, instead, as likely to find conflicting trend lines (even within a single regime) as regards the proper boundaries of state regulation of markets. What we will find in common is that such regimes will be reliant upon a vigorous set of norms and institutions for their enforcement.

For this reason, it turns out that the investment law regime needs states both to establish the legal order of its rules and institutions but also to legitimate the reduction in authority that citizens and states have surrendered. Its neoliberal presuppositions are more complex then we have been led to believe, better resembling the ordoliberal version of the rule of law promoted by a loose grouping of inter-war economic and legal thinkers associated with the University of Freiburg.[45] For ordoliberals, markets were not natural and unplanned but required the active complicity of states. Rather than blindly advocating the retreat of the state in every policy realm, as do some variants of neoliberal thought, institutional solutions to the generation of market freedoms are considered necessary. Law, according to this account, has a special role to play in the structuration of free markets by laying down the rules of the game via an economic constitutional order.[46] Ordoliberals would associate this legal-institutional framework with the securing of an economic constitution. The investment rules regime, like the ordoliberal version of constitutional ordering, places economic policy front and centre—one might say, squarely within its sights.

Though there remains some variety amongst some 3000 BITs,[47] it should be uncontroversial to say that there are disciplines common to most of them and it is

[44] Neo-liberalism's curse, Peck observes, "has been that it can live neither with, nor without the state" in Peck (2008), p. 25.

[45] Both Michel Foucault, in his discussion of the origins of modern neoliberalism, and Christian Joerges, in his discussion of the European model of governance, have resuscitated an interest in the mid-war economic and legal thought of the Freiburg school. See Foucault (2008), Joerges (2005). Crouch, by contrast, denies that ordoliberalism "realistically describes today's economy" in Crouch (2011), p. 165.

[46] Compare Vanberg (1998) and Dardot and Laval (2013).

[47] Muchlinski, P (2011) Corporations and the Uses of Law: International Investment Arbitration as a 'Multilateral Legal Order.' Oñati Socio-Legal Series. 1 (4), http://ssrn.com/abstract=1832562 (last accessed 24 May 2015).

these commonalities that will be familiar to the constitutional lawyer. For one, investment treaty law disciplines are enforced by private actors, and not by states, before international investment tribunals. Tribunals are modelled upon commercial dispute resolution processes, removed from the jurisdiction of national courts, which are considered either inadequate to the task or biased in favour of one or the other of the parties. Tribunals are made up of practicing lawyers, full-time arbitrators, and academics, some of whom will self-identify as judges performing judicial functions.[48] Nevertheless, inconsistent and conflicting jurisprudence, latitudinarian interpretations, concerns about bias in investment arbitration outcomes, arbitral conflicts of interest, and doubtful benefits in terms of new inward foreign investment are generating an increasingly vocal critique of the regime and its actors.[49] A few states even have begun to check out.[50]

It is indisputable that investment treaty norms will have their analogues in typical constitutional orders of capital-exporting states. In what follows, I draw out some of these similarities. Treaties typically will include non-discrimination rights, like the standard of 'national treatment'. Broadly speaking, foreign investors cannot be treated differently from national economic actors. The distinctions relevant for the purposes of establishing discrimination have not proven to be controversial: they concern all variety of economic activities and sectors in which foreign investors participate. The question that continues to perplex in this domain, as it does in the domain of national constitutional law, is: Who is the relevant comparator for the purpose of establishing discrimination? The controversy specific to investment law has turned on the question of what the treaty language (typically, 'in like circumstances') means. Does it entail a search for sameness,[51] for competitors operating in the same market,[52] or for a much broader set of comparators loosely engaging in similar macroeconomic behaviour?[53]

So as to underscore these domestic analogues, the tribunal in the *SD Myers* case made reference to the Supreme Court of Canada's discussion of this question in the *Andrews* case.[54] There the Court eschewed a mechanical test of formal equality in favour of one of 'substantive equality' attentive to context. While it is not precisely clear what advantage the tribunal gained from this comparative constitutional law exercise, and though the Supreme Court of Canada has swung wildly in its approach

---

[48] Schneiderman (2010a), p. 383.

[49] See Sornarajah (2008); Yackee (2008).

[50] For example, Bolivia, Ecuador, South Africa and, for a time, Australia. See discussion in Schneiderman (2013).

[51] Or a 'mirror comparator' in *Methanex Corp.* v. USA, UNCITRAL, Final Award of the Tribunal on Jurisdiction and Merits, 3 August 2005, 44 ILM 1345–1464 (2005).

[52] *S.D. Myers, Inc. v. Government of Canada*, UNCITRAL, Partial Award, 13 November 2000, 40 ILM 1408 (2001).

[53] E.g. 'all exporters' in *Occidental Exploration and Production Company* v. *Ecuador*, UNCITRAL LCIA Case No UN3467, Final Award, 1 July 2004, 43 ILM 1248 (2004).

[54] *Andrews v. Law Society of British Columbia* (1989) 1 SCR 143.

to comparator groups since *Andrews*,[55] it should be apparent that investment tribunals, like high courts, are preoccupied with similar methodological questions associated with the resolution of equality rights claims.

Prohibitions against nationalisation and expropriation, or measures tantamount thereto, directly invite parallels between this new global legal order and national constitutional systems. I have argued elsewhere that it has been the desire of the United States (U.S.) and other capital-exporting states to elevate to the plane of the international this sort of 'Fourteenth Amendment psychology'[56] that is preoccupied with protecting 'vested rights'.[57] Following the ratification of the North American Free Trade Agreement (NAFTA), I predicted that Canadian constitutional lawyers would have to become familiar with the constitutional law of the fifth and fourteenth amendments to the U.S. constitution, of which Canadians have no constitutional analogue.[58] In particular, lawyers would have to attend to the categorical distinction between a compensable taking and a non-compensable exercise of police power jurisdiction.[59] This has been borne out in the recent *Chemtura* case,[60] where the investment tribunal absolved the government of Canada for instituting a phase-out of the pesticide Lindane—solely on the basis that the U.S. export market was cracking down on Lindane-treated canola—because it was in the pursuit of 'a valid exercise of ... [its] police powers.'[61] This is one of the first known instances where police power authority vindicated state policy intended to address environmental concerns.[62]

Though there remains some scholarly controversy over whether investment law standards exceed those found in U.S. constitutional law,[63] there will be no disagreement that, at a minimum, foreign investors will be entitled to standards of

---

[55] See *Withler* v. *Canada (Attorney General)* (2011) 1 SCR.

[56] Wild (1939), p. 10.

[57] Schneiderman (2008), ch. 2.

[58] Ziff (2005) and *Mariner Real Estate Ltd.* v. *Nova Scotia (Attorney General)* (1999) 68 LCR 1 (NSCA).

[59] Schneiderman (1996).

[60] *Chemtura Corporation v Canada* Award, *Ad hoc*—UNCITRAL Arbitration Rules (2 August 2010).

[61] *Chemtura Corporation v Canada* Award, *Ad hoc*—UNCITRAL Arbitration Rules (2 August 2010), p. 266.

[62] Other cases only hinted at its availability. See Lévesque (2011), p. 427, fn. 93. The *Methanex* case (*Methanex Corp.* v. USA, UNCITRAL, Final Award of the Tribunal on Jurisdiction and Merits, 3 August 2005, 44 ILM 1345–1464 (2005)) might be interpreted as having vindicated the exercise of police power jurisdiction in the state of California, but the tribunal did not use that term. Nor does the tribunal's reasoning resemble the structure of analysis associated with the exercise of police powers jurisdiction. Instead, the tribunal was focused on 'method,' namely, whether the state was intentionally targeting *Methanex*. On the tribunal's focus on method, see Paparinskis (2011), who does not, curiously, acknowledge that police powers jurisdiction plays a role in the regulatory expropriation jurisprudence.

[63] Compare Been and Beauvais (2003) and Johnston and Volkov (2013) with Parvanov and Kantor (2012).

protection equivalent to those found in U.S. regulatory takings doctrine.[64] The U.S. Congress made such national constitutional linkages explicit in 2002 when it directed that the executive branch incorporate constitutional standards into its model investment treaty.[65] The executive branch sought to achieve this synthesis by incorporating into the model treaty text the multi-factor analysis authored by the U.S. Supreme Court in *Penn Central*.[66] Curiously, the Government of Canada followed suit, incorporating almost identical language into its model investment treaty, though the doctrine remains, as mentioned, foreign law. In subsequent debates over whether to confer fast-track authority so as to finalize negotiations leading toward the Trans-Pacific Partnership (TPP) agreement, it was similarly claimed that investment disciplines mirrored obligations under U.S. law.[67] This helps to explain, so it was argued, why the U.S. had yet to lose an investment arbitration dispute as a respondent state.[68]

There is, lastly, a 'minimum standard of treatment' (MST) and 'fair and equitable treatment' standard (FET)—often treated as virtually synonymous—that have been interpreted in ways analogous to a due process clause or to clauses guaranteeing the enforceability of contracts. Consider the tribunal decision in the CMS case concerning Argentinian emergency measures taken in the midst of the 2000–2001 economic meltdown, an event that has been likened to the great depression of 1929.[69] The *CMS* tribunal held that by delinking the Argentinian peso from the U.S. dollar (and for refusing to undertake periodic adjustments of tariffs), the state had 'profoundly altered the stability and predictability' of the economic environment upon which the investor had relied.[70] The operative legal framework, together with a gas transportation licence held by CMS, amounted to a 'guarantee' that

---

[64] Parvanov and Kantor (2012), p. 779.

[65] Schneiderman (2013), pp. 81–83.

[66] *Penn Central Transportation Co. v. New York City* (1977) 438 US 104, p. 124.

[67] United States Trade Representative [USTR] (2014) The Facts on Investor-State Dispute Settlement. Tradewinds: The Official Blog of the United States Trade Representative (March), https://ustr.gov/about-us/policy-offices/press-office/blog/2014/March/Facts-Investor-State%20Dispute-Settlement-Safeguarding-Public-Interest-Protecting-Investors (last accessed 23 May 2015).

[68] Penny Pritzker, U.S. Secretary of Commerce, interviewed by Al Hunt on "Charlie Rose" (airing on PBS 11 May 2015), http://www.charlierose.com/watch/60560245 (last accessed 24 May 2015) and Miller S, Hicks G, Investor-State Dispute Settlement: A Reality Check. A Report of the CSIS Scholl Chair in International Business, January 2015, Lanham: Rowman and Littlefield/CSIS, http://csis.org/files/publication/150116_Miller_InvestorStateDispute_Web.pdf (last accessed 16 June 2015), p. 4. A better explanation for this record, discounting the unmeritorious claims, is that arbitrators are acting strategically so as to dampen blowback from the U.S. Congress. See discussion in Schneiderman (2010a).

[69] Emmott, B, A Survey of Capitalism and Democracy: Liberty's Great Advance. The Economist, 28 June 2003, p. 4.

[70] *CMS Gas Transmission Company v. The Republic of Argentina,* Award. ICSID Case No. ARB/01/08, ILM 44, 1205-63, 12 May 2005, para. 267.

bound the state far into the future.[71] As a consequence, the state was liable for both sunk costs and a sum representing future lost profits. This has been the case for most every investor dispute launched against Argentina flowing out of its economic emergency actions in this period.[72]

Again underscoring linkages between national constitutional law and investment law, the *CMS* tribunal weighed into the question of whether the state measures complied with Argentinian constitutional law. According to the account provided by Spector, Argentinian courts would not have interpreted the constitution as requiring the provision of compensation in these circumstances. The Court's long settled doctrine was to tolerate the 'most diverse invasions of private property and contractual freedom,' Spector observes.[73] Departing, however, from prior precedent in the midst of the currency crisis—for political reasons, complains Spector—the Argentinian Supreme Court in *Smith*,[74] and again in *Provincia de San Luis*,[75] declared that the emergency measures amounted to a 'flagrant violation' of constitutional property rights.[76] Shortly afterwards, the Court reverted back to its longstanding approach.[77] Spector likens this property rights interregnum to the resurrection of vested rights doctrine commonly associated with the *Lochner* era in the late-nineteenth century U.S. Well aware that it was eschewing the Court's return to the status quo ante, the CMS tribunal preferred to embrace the Court's aberrant precedent. The tribunal declared that the return to earlier doctrine 'does not overrule other decisions of the Supreme Court,' and so triumphantly declared that the content of Argentinian constitutional was entirely in accord with the norms of international investment law.[78]

5 A Bridge to the Constitutional Past?

In this final section, I want to explore the relationship between constitutional contract clauses and investment law's constitution-like disciplines (MST and FET standards, in particular) by taking up a claim made by the Detroit International

[71] *CMS Gas Transmission Company v. The Republic of Argentina,* Award. ICSID Case No. ARB/01/08, ILM 44, 1205-63, 12 May 2005, para. 161.

[72] See discussion of these disputes in Alvarez and Brink (2012) and Schneiderman (2014).

[73] Spector (2008), p. 141.

[74] *Smith, Carlos Antonio v. PE.N.*/medidas cautelares (2002) CSJN, 1/2/2002, Fallos (2002-325-28).

[75] *Provincia de San Luis v. Estado Nacional*/amparo (2003) CSJN, 5/3/2003, Fallos (2003-326-417).

[76] Spector (2008), p. 140.

[77] The Court reverted to its prior stance in *Bustos, Alberto Roque v. Estadio Nacionale*/amapro (2005) CSJN, 26/10/2004, J.A. (2005-III-189).

[78] *CMS Gas Transmission Company v. The Republic of Argentina,* Award. ICSID Case No. ARB/01/08, ILM 44, 1205-63, 12 May 2005, para. 215.

Bridge Company and its subsidiary, the Canadian Transit Company, against the Government of Canada. This dispute was never resolved. A NAFTA tribunal concluded in April 2015 that it was deprived of jurisdiction to continue hearing the claim. This was because the investor improperly pursued litigation in U.S. courts. By complaining about identical measures that gave rise to the NAFTA dispute, and without having filed an appropriate waiver, the investor had deprived the tribunal of its jurisdiction.[79] The NAFTA tribunal, therefore, never had an opportunity to evaluate the investor's claims against Canada. It may very well be that there was no merit to the claim on the facts of this case. For the purposes of my argument, we need not worry about this. Instead, my focus is on how the claim was articulated in ways that resonate in both investment and constitutional law terms.

Governments in Canada together with the State of Michigan have been working towards a new U.S. $1 billion international bridge crossing the Detroit River. This will help to alleviate congestion on the Ambassador Bridge which currently connects Detroit, Michigan to Windsor, Ontario and which accounts for about 25 % of all of the trade in goods that passes between Canada and the U.S. The Ambassador Bridge, together with its lucrative toll-collection rights, has been owned by a privately-held U.S. corporation since 1927. Michigan state residents defeated in November 2012 a state-wide ballot proposal for a constitutional amendment that would have barred the construction of the new international bridge. The family owning the Ambassador Bridge (the Morouns) reportedly spent about U.S. $31 million in support of their constitutional ballot proposal.[80]

In the year prior to the vote, the Detroit International Bridge Company (DIBC) launched a NAFTA investment dispute on behalf of its wholly-owned subsidiary, The Canadian Transit Company. The DIBC claimed that, in return for constructing and operating the bridge, they were granted "a perpetual right to maintain the bridge and collect tolls from vehicles using the bridge." Since the day the bridge opened, the DIBC "has invested hundreds of millions of dollars . . . in reliance on these rights."[81] The Canadian government, it was alleged, arbitrarily and discriminatorily planned road construction that would steer traffic away from the Ambassador Bridge toward the newly planned bridge across the Detroit River.[82] The DBIC claimed denials of national treatment, most-favoured nation treatment, and MST.

It is more than coincidental that this dispute resembles, in significant respects, the 1837 dispute between the proprietors of the Charles River Bridge and the Warren Bridge regarding an alleged exclusive right to operate a toll bridge over

[79] The investor declined to waive any claim for damages in U.S. courts while also seeking damages on similar grounds before an investment tribunal.

[80] See Ballotpedia, http://ballotpedia.org/wiki/index.php/Michigan_International_Bridge_Initiative,_Proposal_6_(2012) (last accessed 1 July 2015).

[81] *Detroit International Bride Company v Canada* (2013) Amended Notice of Arbitration, PCA Case No. 2012-25 (15 January 2013).

[82] *Detroit International Bride Company v Canada* Amended Notice of Arbitration, PCA Case No. 2012-25, 15 January 2013.

the Charles River, connecting Boston to Charlestown, for a period of 70 years. The Charles River Bridge owners claimed that the 1828 act of the Massachusetts legislature authorizing the construction of the Warren Bridge was an act impairing the obligation of contracts barred by Article I of the U.S. constitution.[83] It was predictable that, as the Warren Bridge would revert to the state after a period of 6 years and thereafter become a free public thoroughfare, the value of the Charles River Bridge would be close to nil.[84] Chief Justice Taney dismissed the suit. In so doing, Taney was forced to depart from Marshall Court precedent that held corporate charters to be sacrosanct, according to the constitution's contract clause. Earlier, Chief Justice Marshall had declared that the transfer of governing authority over privately funded, though Crown incorporated, Dartmouth College to a state-controlled body violated the constitution's contract clause. That clause, the Chief Justice declared, was intended to guard against "a power, of at least doubtful utility, the abuse of which had been extensively felt; and to restrain the legislature in future from violating the right to property."[85] Marshall's successor, Roger Brooke Taney in the Charles River Bridge case, concluded otherwise: no irrevocable rights could be inferred from the grant of a corporate charter to operate a bridge. It could "never be assumed," he wrote, that the "government intended to diminish its powers of accomplishing the end for which it was created," namely, "to promote the happiness and prosperity of the community by which it is established."[86]

Faithful to Marshall Court doctrine with which he was long affiliated, and consistent with his concurring opinion in Dartmouth College, Justice Story in dissent adjudged the reliance interest of the original bridge owners as paramount. He acknowledged that 'men may differ' on topics of this sort, but he could:[87]

> conceive of no surer plan to arrest all public improvements, founded on private capital and enterprise, than to make the outlay of that capital uncertain and questionable, both as to security and as to productiveness. No man will hazard his capital in any enterprise, in which, if there be a loss, it must be borne exclusively by himself; and if there be success, he has not the slightest security of enjoying the rewards of that success, for a single moment.

What is startling is that this is almost precisely where battle lines are drawn in many investor-state disputes. The question in many of these cases, particularly in cases of alleged expropriation or denial of MST/FET where investor expectations are considered paramount, is whether the legitimate expectations of investors can be upset in light of countervailing public interests.

The Argentinian disputes, most of which resulted in an award of damages for having upset expectations by enacting laws to combat the country's 2001 economic crisis, suggest that the structural tilt of the investment rules regime is in the

---

[83] U.S. Constitution of 1787, section 10, ¶ 1.

[84] Generally, see Kutler (1971).

[85] *Dartmouth College v. Woodward* (1819) 17 U.S. (4 Wheat.) 518, p. 628. Compare *Providence Bank v. Billings* (1830) 4 Peters 514.

[86] *Charles River Bridge v. Warren Bridge* (1837) 36 U.S. 420, p. 546.

[87] *Charles River Bridge v. Warren Bridge* (1837) 36 U.S. 420, p. 607.

direction of Justice Story's 'reaping-the-rewards' account. Changes to host state laws that upset investor expectations will attract investment treaty liability. On other occasions, countervailing public interests are weighed into the equation. On many, but not all, occasions any public interest that may have been a factor in prompting state behaviour is either belittled or concealed. This helps to explain the increasingly vocal calls for the introduction of proportionality analysis into the domains of investment law.

Until 2000, there was little in the way of balancing going on in the work of investment tribunals.[88] Tribunals were single-minded about protecting investor interests at the expense of important, countervailing public interests. Yet tribunals, it is said, are performing important judicial-like functions, failing to appreciate investor-state arbitration as a "form of governance."[89] In a handful of subsequent cases, there have been halting attempts at weighing relations between ends and means in ways that high courts in many parts of the world perform constitutional review.[90] In light of increasing legitimacy concerns, scholars now advocate the embrace of full-blown proportionality analysis within international investment law. This path appears as the most appropriate means of resolving the legitimacy problems that continue to plague the system.[91] "Intense concerns about legitimacy in the system. . .should drive a rapid adoption of proportionality analysis as a standard technique," prescribe Kingsbury and Schill.[92] It would be 'suicidal,' observes Stone Sweet, for arbitrators to proceed with "a heavy thumb pressed permanently down on the investor's side of the scale in cases with very high political stakes."[93]

The empirical evidence suggests that tribunals are beginning to hear more about proportionality from legal counsel and are exhibiting openness to applying these considerations in the context of resolving investment disputes.[94] Yet there is a

[88] Stone Sweet (2010).

[89] Kingsbury B, Schill S (2009) Investor-State Arbitration as Governance: Fair and Equitable Treatment, Proportionality and the Emerging Global Administrative Law. International Law and Justice Working Paper 2009/6, http://www.iilj.org/publications/documents/2009-6.KingsburySchill.pdf (last accessed 1 July 2015), p. 50; also Kingsbury and Schill (2010) and Schill (2012).

[90] Stone Sweet (2010), p. 68.

[91] Kingsbury B, Schill S (2009) Investor-State Arbitration as Governance: Fair and Equitable Treatment, Proportionality and the Emerging Global Administrative Law. International Law and Justice Working Paper 2009/6, http://www.iilj.org/publications/documents/2009-6.KingsburySchill.pdf (last accessed 1 July 2015), p. 52.

[92] Kingsbury B, Schill S (2009) Investor-State Arbitration as Governance: Fair and Equitable Treatment, Proportionality and the Emerging Global Administrative Law. International Law and Justice Working Paper 2009/6, http://www.iilj.org/publications/documents/2009-6.KingsburySchill.pdf (last accessed 1 July 2015), p. 40.

[93] Stone Sweet (2010), p. 75; Stone Sweet and Matthews (2008).

[94] Schneiderman (2011), pp. 491–494. In the period 1994–2010, I identified a total of 23 decisions where proportionality was mentioned expressly or impliedly in tribunal decisions. Of these, in only 13 decisions did tribunals approvingly invoke proportionality analysis in discussing the law and, of these, only eight tribunals applied some semblance of a proportionality analysis, p. 491.

significant amount of learning yet to be done. When proportionality has been applied, the record is, to put it charitably, uneven. The case of Tecmed is often singled out as having exhibited good technique,[95] yet it failed to distinguish between proportionality's place in determining whether a treaty breach is justifiable (or non-compensable)—the proper mode of inquiry—as opposed to determining whether a treaty breach had occurred.[96] These methodological problems do not bode well for the future. The rise of proportionality review in the investment law context, nevertheless, is singled out as evidence of an emerging world-wide consensus in constitutional matters.[97] It underscores the close relationship between the work of investment tribunals and constitutional and regional courts around the world.

6 Conclusion

We can conclude that the features of what we might associate with a new global constitutional order exhibit characteristics associated with older, national state, constitutional orders. At least in the case of international investment law, we are witness to a continuing preoccupation with the protection of property.[98] It is reminiscent of vested rights doctrine and Lochnerism of the nineteenth century,[99] coupled with a 'fanatic' and fundamental view of property rights that 'underwrites every expectation of profit.'[100] These are insights that 'constitutionalism as project' elides and that 'constitutionalism as critique' helps to elucidate. The revival of this older tradition is not only in tension with functions expected to be performed by

---

[95] Krommendijk and Morijn (2009), p. 444.

[96] Leonhardsen (2012), p. 124. Perrone calls this a 'double check' on whether there has been a compensable event in Perrone, N (2013) The International Investment Regime and Foreign Investors' Rights: Another View of a Popular Story. A thesis submitted to the Department of Law of the London School of Economics for the Degree of Doctor of Philosophy, London, September 2013, http://etheses.lse.ac.uk/776/1/Perrone_International_Investment_Regime.pdf (last accessed 15 June 2015), p. 240. Another problem with *Tecmed: (Tecnicas Medioambientales Tecmed SA v. United Mexican States,* ICSID Case No ARB(AF)/00/2, Final Award, 29 May 2003, 43 ILM 133 (2004)) the tribunal considered that public protests could not be reconciled with the impact on investor rights, deliberately ignoring the environmental considerations that prompted those protests. On this, see Guntrip, E (2014) International Human Rights Law, Investment Arbitration and Proportionality Analysis: Panacea or Pandora's Box? EJIL: Talk! 7 January 2014, http://www.ejiltalk.org/international-human-rights-law-investment-arbitration-and-proportionality-analysis-panacea-or-pandoras-box/ (last accessed 15 June 2015).

[97] Cohen-Eliya and Porat (2013), pp. 12–13.

[98] Lazzarato (2012), p. 7.

[99] Spector (2008), p. 140; Zumbansen (2013).

[100] Waldron (2012), p. 72.

democratic states, it reduces states to the role of 'debt collection agencies on behalf of a global oligarchy of investors.'[101]

What is also apparent is that this emergent economic constitutional order is revisiting issues of economic policy that national constitutional orders, such as the U.S., mostly resolved in favour of political authority.[102] What is on display via constitution-like rules, then, is a partial and cramped view of the proper relation between states and markets, one that remains contestable at the level of national states. The remaining question is how resilient this view will remain in the light of sub-global counter-hegemonic pressures, which are proving to be stubbornly resilient.

References

Alston P (2002) Resisting the merger and acquisition of human rights by trade law: a reply to Petersmann. Euro J Int Law 13:815–844

Alvarez J, Brink T (2012) The Argentine crisis and foreign investors: a glimpse into the heart of the investment regime. Yearb Int Invest Law Pol 2010–2011:319–362

Anderson G (2012) Beyond 'constitutionalism beyond the state'. J Law Soc 39:359–383

Anderson G (2014) Constitutionalism as critical project: the epistemological challenge to politics. In: Gill S, Cutler C (eds) New constitutionalism and world order. Cambridge University Press, Cambridge, pp 281–294

Been V, Beauvais JC (2003) The global fifth amendment? NAFTA's investment protections and the misguided quest for an international "regulatory takings" doctrine. N Y Univ Law Rev 78:30–143

Borchard E (1915) The diplomatic protection of citizens abroad or the law of international claims. The Banks Law Publishing, New York

Bourdieu P (2000) Pascalian meditations. (trans. R. Nice), Stanford University Press, Stanford, CA

Büthe T, Walter M (2011) The new global rulers: the privatization of regulation in the world economy. Princeton University Press, Princeton, NJ

Cass D (2005) The constitutionalization of the World Trade Organization: legitimacy, democracy, and community in the international trading system. Oxford University Press, Oxford

Cohen-Eliya M, Porat I (2013) Proportionality and constitutional culture. Cambridge University Press, Cambridge

Crouch C (2011) The strange non-death of neo-liberalism. Polity, Cambridge

Curtin D (1993) The constitutional structure of the union: a Europe of bits and pieces. Common Mark Law Rev 30:17–69

Dardot P, Laval C (2013) The new way of the world: on neo-liberal society. Verso, London

de Sousa SB (2002) Toward a new legal common sense: law, globalization and emancipation, 2nd edn. Routledge, New York

de Sousa SB (2006) The rise of the global left: the world social forum and beyond. Zed Books, London

Dezalay Y (1990) The big bang and the law: the internationalization and restructuration of the legal field. Theor Cult Soc 7:279–293

[101] Streeck (2011), p. 28.

[102] Underkuffler (2003).

Dezalay Y, Garth B (1996) Dealing in virtue: international commercial arbitration and the construction of a transnational legal order. University of Chicago Press, Chicago
Dunoff J (2006) Constitutional conceits: The WTO's "constitution" and the discipline of international law. Eur J Int L 17:647–675
Dunoff J, Trachtman J (2009a) A functional approach to international constitutionalization. In: Dunhoff J, Trachtman J (eds) Ruling the world? constitutionalism, international law and global governance. Cambridge University Press, Cambridge, pp 3–35
Dunoff J, Trachtman J (eds) (2009b) Ruling the world? constitutionalism, international law and global governance. Cambridge University Press, Cambridge
Foucault M (2008) The birth of biopolitics: lectures at the College de France, 1978–1979. Trans. Burchell G. Palgrave Macmillan, Houndmills
Habermas J (2006) Euroscepticism, market Europe, or a Europe of (world) citizens. In: Habermas J, Time of transitions. Trans. Cronin C, Pensky M. Polity Press, Cambridge
Howse R, Nicolaïdis K (2001) Legitimacy and global governance: why constitutionalizing the WTO is a step too far. In: Porter RB, Sauvé P, Subramanian A, Zampetti AB (eds) Efficiency, equity, legitimacy: the multilateral trading system at the millennium. Brookings Institution Press, Washington, DC, pp 227–252
Joerges C (2005) What is left of the European economic constitution? a melancholic eulogy. Eur Law Rev 30:461–489
Johnston L, Volkov O (2013) Investor-state contracts, host-state "commitments" and the myth of stability in international law. Am Rev Int Arb 24:361–415
Kennedy D (2009) The mystery of global governance. In: Dunhoff J, Trachtman J (eds) Ruling the world? constitutionalism, international law and global governance. Cambridge University Press, Cambridge, pp 37–68
Kingsbury B, Schill S (2010) Public law concepts to balance investors' rights with state regulatory actions in the public interest—the concept of proportionality. In: Schill S (ed) International Investment Law and Comparative Public Law. Oxford University Press, New York
Krisch N (2012) The case for pluralism in postnational Law. In: de Búrca G, Weiler J (eds) The worlds of European constitutionalism. Cambridge University Press, Cambridge, pp 203–261
Krommendijk J, Morijn J (2009) 'Proportional' by what measure(s)? Balancing investor interests and human rights by way of applying the proportionality principle in investor-state arbitration. In: Dupuy PM, Petersmann EU, Francioni F (eds) Human rights in international investment law and arbitration. Oxford University Press, Oxford, pp 422–451
Kurtz J (2009) The use and abuse of WTO Law in investor–state arbitration: competition and its discontents. Eur J Int Law 20:749–771
Kutler S (1971) Privilege and creative destruction: the Charles River bridge case. J.B. Lippincott Company, Philadelphia
Lazzarato M (2012) The making of indebted man: an essay on the neoliberal condition. Semiotext (e), Los Angeles
Leonhardsen EM (2012) Looking for legitimacy: exploring proportionality analysis in investment treaty arbitration. J Int Dispute Settl 3:95–136
Lévesque C (2011) Investment and water resources: limits to NAFTA. In: Segger MC, Gehring M, Newcombe A (eds) Sustainable development in world investment law. Kluwer Law International, The Netherlands, pp 409–428
Lukes S (2005) Power: a radical view, 2nd edn. Palgrave Macmillan, Basingstoke
Newton S (2006) Constitutionalism and imperialism sub specie spinozae. Law Crit 17:325–355
Paparinskis M (2011) Regulatory expropriation and sustainable development. In: Segger MC, Gehring M, Newcombe A (eds) Sustainable development in world investment Law. Kluwer Law International, The Netherlands, pp 295–328
Parvanov P, Kantor M (2012) Comparing U.S. law and recent U.S. investment agreements. Yearbook on International Investment Law & Policy 2010–2011. Oxford University Press, Oxford, pp 741–836
Peck J (2008) Remaking laissez-faire. Prog Hum Geogr 32:3–43

Peters A (2006) Compensatory constitutionalism: the function and potential of fundamental international norms and structures. Leiden J Int Law 19:579–610

Petersmann EU (1991) Constitutional functions and constitutional problems of international economic law. University Press/Westview Press, Fribourg Switzerland/Boulder

Petersmann EU (1992) National constitutions, foreign trade policy and European community law. Eur J Int Law 3:1–35

Petersmann EU (2000) The WTO constitution and human rights. J Int Econ Law 3:19–25

Petersmann EU (2012) International economic law in the 21st century: constitutional pluralism and multilevel governance of interdependent public goods. Hart, Oxford

Petersmann EU (2013) Human rights require "cosmopolitan constitutionalism" and cosmopolitan law for democratic governance of public goods. Contemp Read Law Soc Justice 5:90–119

Petersmann EU (2014) Need for a new philosophy of international economic law and adjudication. J Int Econ Law 7:639–669

Schill S (2012) Cross regime harmonization through proportionality analysis: the case of international investment law, the law of state immunity and human rights. ICSID Rev 27:87–119

Schneiderman D (1996) NAFTA's takings rule: American constitutionalism comes to Canada. Univ Toronto Law J 46:499–537

Schneiderman D (2008) Constitutionalizing economic globalization: investment rules and democracy's promise. Cambridge University Press, Cambridge

Schneiderman D (2010a) Judicial politics and international investment arbitration: seeking an explanation for conflicting outcomes. Northwestern J Int Law Bus 30:383–416

Schneiderman D (2010b) A new global constitutional order? In: Dixon R, Ginsburg T (eds) Research handbook on comparative constitutional law. Edward Elgar, Cheltenham, pp 189–207

Schneiderman D (2011) Legitimacy and reflexivity in international investment arbitration: a new self-restraint? J Int Dispute Settl 2:471–495

Schneiderman D (2013) Resisting economic globalization: critical theory and international investment law. Palgrave Macmillan, Basingstoke

Schneiderman D (2014) Compensating for democracy's "defects": the case of international investment law. In: Joerges C, Glinski C (eds) The European crisis and transformation of European governance: authoritarian managerialism versus democratic governance. Hart, Oxford, pp 47–70

Sell S (2003) Private power, public law: the globalization of intellectual property rights. Cambridge University Press, Cambridge

Sornarajah M (2008) A coming crisis: expansionary trends in investment treaty arbitration. In: Sauvant K, Cheswick-Patterson M (eds) Appeals mechanism in international investment disputes. Oxford University Press, Oxford, pp 39–77

Spector H (2008) Constitutional transplants and the mutation effect. Chicago-Kent Law Rev 83:129–145

Stepan A (2001) Arguing comparative politics. Oxford University Press, Oxford, pp 315–361

Stone Sweet A (2010) Investor-state arbitration: proportionality's new frontier. Law Ethics Hum Rights 4:47–76

Stone Sweet A, Matthews J (2008) Proportionality balancing and global constitutionalism. Columia J Transnat Law 47:72–164

Streeck W (2011) The crises of democratic capitalism. New Left Rev 71:5–29

Teubner G (2012) Constitutional fragments: societal constitutionalism and globalization. Oxford University Press, Oxford

Thornhill C (2013) A sociology of constituent power: the political code of transnational societal constitutions. Ind J Global Legal Stud 20:551–603

Twining W (1993) Constitutions, constitutionalism, and constitution-mongering. In: Stotzky I (ed) Transition to democracy in Latin America: the role of the judiciary. Westview Press, Boulder, pp 383–391

Twining W (2000) Globalisation and legal theory. Butterworths, London

Underkuffler L (2003) The idea of property: its meaning and power. Oxford University Press, Oxford

Vanberg V (1998) Freiburg school of law and economics. In: Newman P (ed) The new Palgrave dictionary of economics and the law, vol 2. Macmillan, London, pp 172–179

Waldron J (2012) The rule of law and the measure of property. Cambridge University Press, Cambridge

Walker N (2002) The idea of constitutional pluralism. Modern Law Rev 65:317–359

Weiss L (2005) Global governance, national strategies: how industrialized states make room to move under the WTO. Rev Int Polit Econ 12:723–749

Wild P Jr (1939) International law and Mexican oil. Q J Inter-Am Relat 1:5–21

Yackee J (2008) Bilateral investment treaties, credible commitment, and the rule of (international) law: do BITs promote foreign direct investment? Law Soc Rev 42:805–831

Ziff B (2005) Taking liberties: protections for private property in Canada. In: Cooke E (ed) Modern studies in property law, vol III. Hart, Oregon, pp 341–360

Zumbansen P (2013) Lochner disembedded: the anxieties of law in a global context. Ind J Global Legal Stud 20:29–69

From Fragmentation to Constitutionalisation of International Economic Law? Comments on Schneiderman's 'Constitutionalism'

Ernst-Ulrich Petersmann

Contents

Abstract This short comment on the preceding article by Prof. Schneiderman calls for the clarification of legal methodologies in research on international economic law (IEL) and on the 'constitutionalisation' of multilevel governance of international public goods (PGs). While European lawyers and courts throughout Europe accept the 'constitutionalisation' of European economic law and human rights law (HRL) as legal facts and normative challenges, legal discourse about 'constitutionalisation' of UN and WTO law and governance remains contested and often confusing due to inadequate clarification of legal terminologies, research methods and diverse conceptions of international law and multilevel governance of PGs.

E.-U. Petersmann (✉)
Law Department, European University Institute, Via Boccaccio 121, I-50133 Florence, Italy
e-mail: ulrich.petersmann@eui.eu

M. Bungenberg et al. (eds.), *European Yearbook of International Economic Law 2016*, European Yearbook of International Economic Law 7,
DOI 10.1007/978-3-319-29215-1_3

1 Legal Methodology: Constitutionalism as Discovery, Critique and Project

David Schneiderman begins his critique of 'global constitutionalism' with a chapter on 'Discovery, Project and Critique'. Having myself started my academic career as a lecturer in German constitutional law and having devoted more than 20 years of my academic teaching to European Union (EU) law, I always proceeded from the same methodological premise 'that a critical constitutionalist account turns out to be a proper heuristic with which to diagnose the current scene.'[1] Analysing IEL from such a 'discovery mode', I also concluded like Schneiderman "that we are unlikely to observe a single unitary economic constitutional order, but a number of discrete regimes performing constitution-like functions".[2] My own publications—since the 1980s—on potential 'constitutional functions' of IEL in the regulation of customs unions and common markets inside federal states (like the United States of America, Switzerland and Germany), among the 31 member states of what is today the European Economic Area (EEA), and also in multilevel governance of world trade on the basis of the law of the General Agreement on Tariffs and Trade (GATT) 1947 and the World Trade Organization (WTO) focused on the *empirical discovery* of the 'constitutional principles' underlying multilevel market regulation, their *normative interrelationships* and often *diverse justifications*.[3] Having practised IEL for more than 40 years in order to advance 'constitutional piecemeal reforms' at national and international levels of trade governance and adjudication, my answers to the rhetorical questions opening Schneiderman's contribution—'Can we see the outlines of an emergent global economic constitutional order?' 'Does international economic law emulate, in some important ways, national constitutional law?'—remain negative. The main reason why *European* law methodologies often lead to policy proposals that differ from those of *American* international lawyers (e.g. advocating 'constitutional nationalism' and hegemonic foreign policies) and *Australian* constitutional lawyers (e.g. advocating 'parliamentary sovereignty' without a human rights charter and with only limited judicial review), is due to diverse legal methodologies and value premises. '*Legal methodology*' can be defined as the 'best way' for identifying the 'sources' of IEL, the methods of legal interpretation, the 'primary rules of conduct' and 'secondary rules of recognition, change and adjudication', the relationship between 'legal positivism', 'natural law', and 'social theories of law', and the 'dual nature' of modern legal systems.[4] The etymological origins of the word methodology—*i.e.* the Greek word '*meta-hodos*', referring to 'following the road'—suggest that globalisation and its transformation of most national PGs into transnational 'aggregate PGs'—

[1] Schneiderman (2016), section 2.

[2] Schneiderman (2016), section 1.

[3] These earlier publications were summarised in Petersmann (1991).

[4] Petersmann (2012a, b).

like human rights, rule of law, democratic peace and mutually beneficial, international monetary, trading, development, environmental, communication and legal systems promoting 'sustainable development'—require new legal methodologies in order to enable citizens and peoples to increase their social welfare through global cooperation. Yet, due to their Anglo-Saxon constitutional traditions (e.g. of 'legal dualism', prioritisation of civil and political over economic and social rights) and influenced also by the continental size of their resource-rich economies, Australian, Canadian and United States (US) lawyers tend to favour utilitarian and power-oriented 'IEL methodologies' that differ from my own methodological approaches at least in the following four respects:

1.1 'Constitutionalism' as Critique of Multilevel European Governance Practices

My publications used, since the 1980s, 'constitutionalism as critique' mainly for identifying 'constitutional deficits' in national and European trade governance by using as a benchmark the constitutional recognition—in both German and European constitutional law—of citizens as holders of constituent powers ('democratic principals') and 'agents of justice' (e.g. in terms of constitutional rights and 'access to justice'), who should hold multilevel governance agents and their limited, 'constituted powers' legally, democratically and judicially more accountable for their power-oriented abuses of trade policy discretion aimed at redistributing 'economic protection rents' to powerful 'rent-seeking industries' in exchange for political support (e.g. as illustrated by illegal 'voluntary export restraints' and the EU's agricultural protectionism disregarding about 20 GATT/WTO dispute settlement findings on its illegal import restrictions on agricultural products like bananas and genetically modified products). Anglo-Saxon critics often downplay such 'constitutional criticism' of European trade politics, for instance because Australian, Canadian and US constitutional law do not protect 'individual market freedoms', multilevel constitutional regulation and multilevel judicial review of trade restrictions in similar ways as German and European constitutional law. EU citizenship, free movement rights of persons beyond state borders (e.g. due to liberalisation of services), multilevel EU parliamentarianism, recognition of transnational rights of migrants (e.g. to take up employment and receive social security benefits while residing in another common market member country) and multilevel judicial remedies are, however, no longer 'unique European experiments' in rights-based, regional common markets and integration law. Their 'enabling', 'legitimating', 'enforcement' and 'republican functions'—e.g. as decentralised means for limiting implementation deficits of free trade agreements (FTAs) and other PGs regimes—and their 'derivative nature' (i.e. being linked to state citizenship rather than to human rights) are increasingly recognised in African, Latin American and Central American integration regimes.[5] My comparative constitutional analyses of European and US common market and trade policy regulations criticised the 'judicial deference' of US courts towards authoritarian political claims "that no one has a vested right to trade with foreign nations": "When the people granted Congress the power 'to regulate Commerce with foreign Nations' (...) they thereupon relinquished at least whatever right they, as individuals, may have had to insist upon the importation of any product".[6] The common law and utilitarian traditions and power-oriented practices of Australian, Canadian and US trade policies seem to render it more difficult for Anglo-Saxon lawyers to challenge 'constitutional problems' in multilevel trade governance from the perspective of constitutional and cosmopolitan rights of citizens—including economic liberty rights and 'common market freedoms' that need to be balanced with all other (e.g. civil, political, social and cultural) constitutional rights—as recognised in EU law and European HRL.

1.2 Human Rights Law as Integral Part of Constitutional Law

The polemic misrepresentations by P. Alston of my 2001 proposals for "mainstreaming human rights into the law of worldwide organizations",[7] and its uncritical repetition by other Anglo-Saxon lawyers (like D. Cass), reflected the frequent neglect by Anglo-Saxon UN human rights advocates for clarifying the

---

[5] On the increasing recognition of transnational economic, labour, social and political citizenship rights (e.g. in the EU, the EEA, the Andean Community, MERCOSUR, the Central American Common Market, the Economic Community of West-African States, the Gulf Cooperation Council) and of regional parliamentary institutions see Closa C, Vintila D (2015) Supranational citizenship: rights in regional integration organizations. EUI Florence (unpublished conference paper).

[6] *Arjay Associates Inc. v Bush*, 891 F.2d 981, 898 (Fed. Cir. 1989). See also the US Supreme Court decision in *Buttfield v Stranahan*, 192 U.S. 470, 493, where the Court held 'that no one has a vested right to trade with foreign nations, which is so broad in character as to limit and restrict the power of Congress to determine what articles (...) may be imported into this country and the terms upon which a right to import may be exercised'. While this decision could have been construed as part of a democratic 'principal-agent relationship' to imply a limited 'right to import' subject to Congressional regulation, subsequent US Court decisions have inferred from this Supreme Court decision the absence of any individual right to trade with foreign nations (similar to a 'master-slave interpretation' of the ruler/subject relationship). For a criticism of US trade law see also Garcia (2013), criticising US attitudes of 'regulating my market at home, and deregulating markets abroad in order to facilitate exploitation of other markets internationally', as well as US power politics in NAFTA and CAFTA dispute settlement procedures (at p. 260 ff. as illustrating 'how U.S. trade policy is not always consistent with notions of justice inherent in domestic law', p. 257 and p. 324.

[7] Petersmann (2002).

complex interrelationships between multilevel constitutional law and HRL with due respect for comparative constitutional law and for the legitimate reality of 'constitutional pluralism'. This lack of interest is understandable, for instance in view of the fact that Australia, Canada and the US recognise neither the jurisdiction of regional human rights courts nor constitutional protection of economic, social and cultural human rights similar to the EU Charter of Fundamental Rights (EUCFR). The regional economic integration agreements of these Anglo-Saxon democracies—such as the North American Free Trade Agreement (NAFTA) and their very limited institutional powers (e.g. of NAFTA institutions)—does not prompt their national courts to engage in comparative constitutional research (e.g. similar to national and European courts in the EU and EEA) so as to identify constitutional principles common to all member states that constitutionally limit also multilevel economic governance (e.g. as in the EU and EEA). Alston's claims—e.g. that my arguments for constitutional protection of economic liberty rights misinterpreted UN HRL—failed to understand that my constitutional arguments were based on German and EU constitutional law and HRL rather than on Australian conceptions of UN HRL. Both constitutional law and HRL can be construed as being based on constitutional contracts among citizens, as explained by 'discourse theories' recognising mutual recognition of human rights among citizens as foundation of HRL and constitutional law.[8] UN HRL may be construed and implemented inside constitutional democracies in legitimately diverse ways in response to the democratic preferences and constitutional 'margins of appreciation' of the peoples (e.g. protecting human dignity in terms of 'maximum equal freedoms' in German constitutional law going beyond the more limited 'common law freedoms' protected in Australian constitutional law). Alston's advice—i.e. that GATT/WTO bodies, due to their lack of knowledge about UN HRL, should leave human rights discourse to UN human rights bodies—sounded like a plea for submitting GATT governance to Platonic 'philosopher kings'. Such pleas are hardly justifiable in view of the constitutional task of institutionalising 'public reason' in all areas of social cooperation and the empirical facts that UN HRL is not effectively implemented in UN governance nor in many UN member states and has not prevented the unnecessary poverty of two billion people in less developed UN members. My own constitutional approach follows the advice by J. Rawls

[8] On discourse theory, and the implicit, moral respect of discourse partners as having reasonable autonomy and dignity, as justification of human rights 'without metaphysics' see : Alexy (2004), pp. 15–24. For a comparison of Kant's moral and Rawls' contractual justifications of principles of justice, human rights and hypothetical 'social contracts', and for their criticism from communitarian perspectives, see, e.g. Sandel (2009), Chapters 5 and 6. Similar to Kant's justification of his cosmopolitan 'right of hospitality' on moral grounds, the legal interpretation of EU 'market freedoms' as 'fundamental rights' can be justified on moral and constitutional rather than only utilitarian grounds (e.g., as being constitutionally protected also by the 'general freedom of action' guaranteed in Article 2 of the German Basic Law and representing 'generalizable human interests' of all EU citizens). Also the derivation of individual investor rights and judicial remedies from international investment treaties, like the derivation of labour rights from ILO conventions, can be justified not only on utilitarian grounds, but also on human rights principles.

that—in order to enhance 'democratic capabilities' through 'public reason'—democratically agreed 'principles of justice' must be progressively transformed into democratic legislation, administration, adjudication and international agreements—also in multilevel governance of the world trading system as a global PG that remains indispensable for social welfare and poverty reduction. While human rights lawyers rightly criticise economic lawyers and WTO diplomats for their frequent disregard for HRL, most WTO diplomats justify their inattention to UN human rights advocates by the latter's neglect for 'law and economics' and for the contribution of WTO law to the lifting of hundreds of millions of poor people out of poverty (e.g. in China, India and Latin-America).

1.3 Need for an 'Overlapping Consensus' on 'Principles of Justice' Justifying IEL

As international customary law requires interpreting treaties and settling related disputes "in conformity with the principles of justice and international law", including "human rights and fundamental freedoms for all" and other "relevant rules of international law applicable in the relations between the parties" (Preamble and Article 31 Vienna Convention on the Law of Treaties (VCLT)), my publications have explored long since the principles of procedural, distributive, corrective, commutative and cosmopolitan justice and equity underlying and justifying IEL.[9] This need for clarifying 'constitutional principles of justice' is obvious for European constitutional lawyers, for instance in view of the multilevel cooperation among national and European courts of justice inside the EU as well as in the EEA on the basis on their common constitutional principles and traditions (e.g. of 'proportionality balancing' of national and EU restrictions of civil, political, economic, social and cultural rights). Due to their 'realist' rather than 'constitutional' trade policy approaches, Australian, Canadian and US trade lawyers are less inclined to insist on 'judicial administration of justice' and the relevance of constitutional liberties and human rights in multilevel trade adjudication. After having been requested to serve as member or chairman in various GATT and WTO dispute settlement panels involving Canada and the US, I was told by US trade lawyers that my later publications on HRL as relevant context for interpreting WTO rules had prompted the US Trade Representative to delete my name from the list of potential WTO panelists for the settlement of trade disputes involving the US. From the multilevel European constitutional law perspective, justifying law and governance vis-à-vis citizens requires taking more seriously the customary law requirements of treaty interpretation and adjudication "in conformity with the principles of

[9] Petersmann (1991), Chapters III, VII and VIII; Petersmann (2012a), Chapters III, VI and VIII.

justice and international law", including "human right and fundamental freedoms for all"[10] and clarification of what the Preamble to the WTO Agreement calls "the basic principles underlying this multilateral trading system". GATT/WTO rules reflect a variety of 'principles of justice' such as:

- 'procedural justice principles' as defined in the WTO Dispute Settlement Understanding (DSU) and in additional dispute settlement procedures adopted by WTO dispute settlement bodies;
- principles of distributive and corrective justice which underlie, e.g., WTO 'violation complaints' pursuant to GATT Article XXIII:1(a), the legal presumption of 'nullification or impairment' of treaty benefits in case of violations of GATT/WTO rules, and the legal obligation of GATT/WTO members to terminate illegal measures;
- 'commutative justice' principles underlying 'non-violation complaints' pursuant to GATT Article XXIII:1(b) over the nullification of the reciprocally agreed 'balance of tariff commitments', which may give rise to authorised withdrawal of concessions in order to re-establish the agreed 'reciprocal balance of concessions';
- 'equity principles' underlying 'situation complaints' pursuant to Article XXIII:1 (c) GATT in case of unforeseen 'other situations'; and
- 'cosmopolitan principles of justice' underlying the GATT/WTO legal guarantees of individual 'access to justice' in domestic courts (cf. GATT Article X) or to private arbitration.[11]

Even if UN and WTO members and their citizens are unlikely to ever agree on any comprehensive 'theory of justice' justifying IEL, the constitutional and human rights obligations of all UN and WTO member states confirm the existence of an 'overlapping consensus' on basic 'principles of justice' among governments and citizens—notwithstanding their 'reasonable disagreement' on most other dimensions of their individual and national conceptions of social and legal justice. As Australian, Canadian and US constitutional law systems differ so much from European constitutional law, it is not surprising that most Anglo-Saxon constitutional lawyers do not perceive intergovernmental power politics in UN and WTO governance as a 'constitutional problem' in spite of its lack of democratic and judicial control, its 'disfranchisement' of citizens (e.g. through FTAs without rights and remedies for citizens), and the obvious contradictions between the citizen-driven 'network conceptions' guiding the global division of labour (e.g. 'global supply chains') and the 'executive dominance' and power-oriented 'chessboard mentality' of national governments in their discretionary UN/WTO management of the world economy.

[10] Preamble and Article 31 of the VCLT.

[11] E.g. pursuant to Article 4 of the WTO Agreement on Preshipment Inspection.

1.4 Need for Multilevel 'Republican Constitutionalism' Constituting, Limiting, Regulating and Justifying Multilevel Governance of Transnational PGs

A *fourth methodological difference* relates to my use of 'constitutionalism' as a multilevel, legal methodology for constituting, limiting, regulating and justifying multilevel governance of transnational 'aggregate PGs' that must be produced for the benefit of citizens through a summation process of local, national, regional and global PGs regimes.[12] The more globalisation transforms *national PGs* into *transnational PGs*—and, thereby, *national Constitutions* into '*partial constitutions*' that can no longer protect domestic citizens and their demand for transnational PGs without international law and multilevel governance institutions—the stronger becomes the need for extending 'rights-based republican constitutionalism' to multilevel governance of transnational PGs. My publications emphasise the need for learning from the history of legal experimentation with 'republican constitutionalism' since the ancient Greek and Roman city republics 2500 years ago; these political 'trials and errors' reveal that 'mixed constitutions' at local and national levels of governance—if they combine *mono-*, *oligo-* and *democratic* structures of political governance, 'checks and balances' among multilevel legislative, executive, judicial powers and regulatory agencies, and decentralised, participatory and deliberative governance methods (like economic markets, democratic politics, constitutional rights, judicial litigation)—can protect 'aggregate PGs' more effectively 'bottom up' than alternative, authoritarian 'top down' governance systems. The universal recognition of human rights aimed at protecting individual and democratic freedoms and development of human capacities reinforces civil society claims for cosmopolitan citizenship rights and 'democratisation' in multilevel governance of regional common markets and multilevel governance of other PGs.[13]

---

[12] Petersmann (2013) Constituting, Limiting, Regulating and Justifying Multilevel Governance of Interdependent Public Goods: Methodological Problems of International Economic Law Research. EUI Law Working Papers 2013/08, http://cadmus.eui.eu/handle/1814/27559 (last accessed 8 September 2015). Pure 'PGs' (like sunshine, clean air, inalienable human rights) tend to be defined by their non-rival and non-excludable use that prevents their production in private markets. Most PGs are 'impure' in the sense that their use is either non-excludable (like common pool resources) or non-rival (like club goods, patented pharmaceutical knowledge) and impedes their supply in private markets.

[13] On the diverse legal traditions of republicanism and the disagreement on whether the core values of republicanism should be defined in terms of liberty, republican virtues of active citizenry finding self-realisation in political participation and collective supply of PGs, communitarianism, social and political equality, or deliberative democracy, see Besson and Marti (2009).

1.5 'Constitutional Advocacy' as a 'Human Rights Imperative'?

My different methodological premises prompt me to underline the 'constitutional imperative' of HRL to protect 'principles of justice' and PGs demanded by citizens against the ubiquity of abuses of public and private powers in IEL. Even though I agree with Schneiderman that 'constitutionalism as a discovery mode' reveals numerous 'constitutional linkages' in multilevel governance of international PGs, I disagree with his policy recommendation "to press the pause button when it comes to deepening these constitution-like commitments".[14] Neglect for the multilevel governance problems among the 47 member states of the Council of Europe, or for the unnecessary poverty of some two billion poor people in less-developed countries and their increasing migration to Europe, may appear to be a 'rational option' for Australian, Canadian and US citizens protected by their rich economies and constitutional democracies. My own decision to combine my academic career with now 40 years of practice in national, European, UN, GATT and WTO governance of transnational economic cooperation continues to be motivated by the 'moral imperative' to limit intergovernmental power politics by 'constitutionalism as a project mode' aimed at incremental piecemeal reforms of IEL for the benefit of citizens. Such 'struggles for justice' in intergovernmental diplomacy—e.g. by establishing an Office of Legal Affairs in the GATT Secretariat in 1982/83, establishing its jurisdictions for GATT dispute settlement proceedings, persuading trade diplomats of the need for respecting the customary rules of treaty interpretation, and participating in the elaboration of the DSU during the Uruguay Round negotiations - can be tantalising[15]; yet, one can also enjoy—like a 'happy Sisyphus' (A. Camus)—the incremental 'constitutionalisation' of 'GATT's diplomats jurisprudence' by the compulsory jurisdiction of the WTO panel and Appellate Body dispute settlement system. My positive law recommendations of interpreting German and European constitutional law guarantees of equal freedoms, non-discrimination and transnational rule of law in conformity with the GATT/WTO guarantees of equal economic freedoms, non-discrimination and transnational rule of law—as, arguably, required by the EU Treaty commitments to 'strict observance of international law'[16] and the customary rules of treaty interpretation[17]—may remain incomprehensible for 'realist' Australian, Canadian and US lawyers in view of their different constitutional law systems, power-oriented trade policy traditions, and their lack of experiences with 'multilevel European constitutionalism' as a precondition for 'democratic peace' throughout Europe. Multilevel constitutional protection of human rights in Europe (e.g. by the EU and European

---

[14] Schneiderman (2016), section 1.

[15] Petersmann (2015).

[16] Article 3 of the Treaty on European Union.

[17] Article 31:3(c) of the VCLT.

Free Trade Association courts of justice in cooperation with national courts and the European Court of Human Rights) remains a 'sisyphean task'. Yet, the current European crises (e.g. due to Russia's military annexation of parts of Ukraine, Greece's disregard for the Eurozone rules, immigration of millions of poor refugees from Africa and the Middle East) and the unnecessary poverty in less-developed countries do *not* justify—contrary to what Schneiderman suggests from his different Canadian worldview—"to press the pause button when it comes to deepening these constitution-like commitments" in economic integration law and HRL.

2 'A Constitutionalism of Bits and Pieces' Without Coherent Foundations? Need for Clarifying IEL Methodologies

In his second chapter on 'A Constitutionalism of Bits and Pieces', Schneiderman rightly rejects academic phantasies (e.g. "that there is a single, unitary global economic constitution in place" and other "grand theorizing about such things as global law") and calls for empirical analyses of the "effects that constitution-like regimes unevenly generate for polities in the world".[18] He also rightly notes that some of these regimes have "a disdainful view of democratic processes, though democratic consent remains a prerequisite for the establishment and ongoing maintenance of these regimes"; "citizens consequently are marginalized by these mechanisms, ones that are in the service of more powerful economic forces."[19] Yet, his description of 'constitution-like features' of bilateral investment treaties (BITs) since the 1980s as "aiming to bring constitutional order to international economic law' and resembling 'the ordoliberal version of the rule of law"[20] remains methodologically and normatively unconvincing for German constitutional lawyers who, like myself, studied 'law and economics' at the University of Freiburg's 'school of *ordo*-liberalism'.

2.1 Transformation of International Investment Law as 'Constitutionalism'?

In the third chapter of his contribution, Schneiderman refers to the non-discrimination, 'full protection and security', and 'fair and equitable treatment' requirements of BITs and to related investment arbitration as illustrating legal

[18] Schneiderman (2016), section 3.

[19] Schneiderman (2016), section 3.

[20] Schneiderman (2016), section 3.

problems similar to those in Canadian and US constitutional law, such as identifying the relevant comparator for the purpose of establishing discrimination, the scope of police power jurisdiction for limiting private property rights, protection of due process of law and enforceability of contracts. In his concluding fourth chapter, he also refers to the increasing use of 'proportionality analysis' in investor-state arbitration as another illustration of what he calls "investment law's constitution-like disciplines". Yet, does the international recourse to such 'constitutional principles' justify Schneiderman's conclusion of an "emergent economic constitutional order", albeit limited to international investment law and "reminiscent of vested rights doctrine and Lochnerism of the nineteenth century"?[21] My own publications have argued that—from the perspective of European constitutional law and its multilevel guarantees of judicial protection of 'inalienable' and 'indivisible' civil, political, economic, social and cultural rights of citizens—the vaguely defined 'principles of justice' exported through BITs in order to compensate for the lack of impartial and independent judiciaries in many less-developed, capital-importing countries do not adequately protect impartial and independent 'constitutional balancing' of all public and private interests involved. This is illustrated by the often one-sided domination of investor-state arbitral tribunals by commercial lawyers from big law firms that advise transnational corporations and are reluctant to interpret the 'applicable law' and 'jurisdiction' of investment tribunals as including HRL and constitutional law. In the Comprehensive Economic and Trade Agreement (CETA) between Canada and the EU as well as in the ongoing EU-US negotiations on a Transatlantic Trade and Investment Partnership (TTIP), the 'commercial arbitration paradigm' of UNCITRAL and ICSID investor-state arbitration is being limited by additional 'constitutional safeguards' protecting the sovereign duties to regulate the economy and protect constitutional rights. Yet, as illustrated by the intergovernmental exclusion of rights and effective judicial remedies of citizens in domestic courts in Article 14.16 CETA, investor-state arbitration amounts to the provision of arbitration privileges to foreign investors—especially in relations among transatlantic democracies—that circumvent constitutional commitments of governments to protect equal rights and judicial remedies for all adversely affected citizens through constitutionally constrained, permanent courts of justice.[22] Investor-state arbitration offers advantages if compared with 'diplomatic protection' and investment disputes in the International Court of Justice (ICJ). The out-sourcing of judicial protection of rule of law and of other public interests to commercial arbitrators is, however, justifiable only as a second-best substitute of 'transitional justice' as long as multilevel judicial protection of investor rights and of 'constitutional justice' remains underdeveloped in capital-importing countries, notably if the latter are ruled by despotic and corrupt governments that have often colluded with foreign investors in appropriating domestic resources to the detriment of general consumer welfare. As BITs fail to

[21] Schneiderman (2016), section 6.

[22] Petersmann (2015a).

effectively limit 'market failures' as well as 'governance failures' and 'constitutional failures' in host states and avoid references to the human rights obligations of both home and host states of investors, they do not meet the 'constitutive' and 'regulative principles' advocated by the diverse German schools of '*ordo*-liberalism' and 'economic constitutionalism' aimed at protecting a 'social market economy' based on equal constitutional rights, institutional 'checks and balances' and legislative restraints of 'market failures' through competition, environmental and social laws and remedies.[23]

2.2 *Does 'Constitutional Justice' Require a 'Cosmopolitan Methodology' of IEL?*

Is it contradictory to argue—as I have done for many years—that multilevel governance of international PGs needs to be 'constitutionalised' in order to protect human and constitutional rights more effectively, and to criticise, nonetheless, the "cosmopolitan transformations of international investment law" and "transatlantic FTAs without rights and remedies for citizens" for inadequately protecting impartial 'constitutional justice' and equal constitutional and human rights of all citizens? Schneiderman cites my publications advocating a "new philosophy of IEL" and a citizen-oriented "cosmopolitan IEL methodology" embedded into the multilevel human rights and constitutional obligations of all UN member states. Yet, his discussion of 'constitution-like commitments' in international investment law remains *descriptive* without clarifying his own legal methodology and conception of constitutionalism. In order to make the global discourse on 'constitutionalisation of IEL' more comprehensible, the underlying 'constitutional assumptions' and legal methodologies need to be clarified more precisely. Which '*legal methodology*' offers a coherent way for identifying the 'sources' of IEL, the methods of legal interpretation, the 'primary rules of conduct' and 'secondary rules of recognition, change and adjudication', the relationship between 'legal positivism', 'natural law', and 'social theories of law', and the 'dual nature' of modern legal systems?

One major methodological problem of IEL results from the fact that the different actors—like producers, investors, traders, consumers, governments, intergovernmental and non-governmental organisations—conceptualise international economic regulation from different perspectives and value premises. For instance,

- governments insisting on 'state sovereignty' and pursuing 'national interests' tend to perceive *IEL as public international law regulating the international economy* (e.g. the 1944 Bretton Woods Agreements, GATT 1947, the 1994 WTO Agreement);

[23] Petersmann (1991), p. 61 ff.

- private economic actors using their private legal and economic autonomy in the global division of labour perceive *IEL* primarily *as private international transaction, commercial and 'conflicts law'*;
- citizens, democratic institutions and courts of justice in constitutional democracies tend to perceive *IEL* from a republican perspective *as multilevel democratic regulation of 'market failures', 'governance failures' and other PGs* (e.g. national competition, trade, environmental, labour and social legislation as precondition for the proper functioning of a 'social market economy');
- EU citizens and their 28 EU member states and representative EU institutions view *European economic law as multilevel constitutional regulation* of their common market and of multilevel governance of other European PGs (like transnational rule of law, multilevel protection of human and constitutional rights of EU citizens, a common monetary union);
- UN Specialized Agencies, the WTO and ever more regional economic organisations recognise that their primary and 'secondary' treaty law is increasingly limited by '*global administrative law*' principles protecting transparency, legal accountability and rule of law in multilevel governance of international monetary stability, the world trading system, world food security, global health protection and other transnational PGs.[24]

In order to develop a coherent *theory of IEL* and clarify the legal interrelationships between such different value premises, one can use the distinction by the American legal philosopher Ronald Dworkin of 'four stages of legal theory':

- at the *semantic stage* of law, many legal terms (like 'IEL', human rights, investment and constitutional law standards of regulation like non-discrimination and 'fair and equitable treatment') remain indeterminate 'interpretive concepts' that are used by different actors with different meanings;
- at the *jurisprudential stage*, IEL requires justification in terms of 'principles of justice' (e.g. state-centered vs cosmopolitan, constitutional and global administrative law conceptions of IEL) and elaboration of a convincing theory of 'rule of law' that citizens can accept as legitimate;
- at the *doctrinal stage*, the 'truth conditions' have to be constructed of how particular fields of law-making and administration can best realise their values and justify their practices and ideals (e.g. ordo-liberal insistence on competition, environmental and social law limitations of 'market failures' as pre-conditions of a well-functioning 'social market economy');
- *judicial administration of justice* must apply, clarify and enforce the law in concrete disputes by independent and impartial rule-clarification and protection of social peace.[25]

[24] For a discussion of these competing conceptions of IEL see Petersmann (2012a), chapter 1.

[25] Dworkin (2006), p. 9 ff.

Anglo-Saxon critics of 'constitutionalisation' of IEL rarely define their use of the terms 'constitution', 'constitutionalism' and 'constitutionalisation'[26]; they also rarely question their 'constitutional nationalism' and neglect for the multilevel governance problems resulting from the transformation of most *national PGs* into *transnational 'aggregate PGs'* due to globalisation. Nor do most treatises on IEL coherently reveal and justify their respective conceptions of procedural, distributive, corrective, commutative justice and equity which, since Aristotle, continue to be recognised as diverse 'spheres of justice' in the design of dispute settlement systems (e.g., for 'violation complaints', 'non-violation complaints' and 'situation complaints' pursuant to GATT Article XXIII). Post-colonial IEL also includes 'principles of transitional justice' based on preferential treatment of less-developed countries (e.g., in Part IV of GATT, in the dispute settlement system of the WTO) as well as 'cosmopolitan principles of justice' based on the universal human rights obligations of all UN member states, including individual access to justice.[27] Yet, even though doctrinal conceptions and adjudication regarding competition law, environmental law or social law become ever more sophisticated, their overall coherence in terms of jurisprudential 'principles of justice' and transnational rule of law for the benefit of citizens in multilevel governance of international PGs is rarely questioned and justified. For instance, does Schneiderman think that the explicit exclusion of rights and remedies of citizens under CETA reflects intergovernmental power politics or 'constitutional wisdom'? Why does he argue for pressing the 'pause button' rather than for 'deepening constitution-like commitments' in view of the failures of UN and WTO governance to prevent the unnecessary poverty of two billions of poor people, climate change, and ever more conflicts (notably in Africa) and international mass migration of refugees caused by irresponsible governments? Does he agree with my normative claim that HRL requires cosmopolitan conceptions of IEL recognising 'normative individualism', citizen-driven market mechanisms and democratic consent as constitutional restraints of the 'rules of recognition' and adjudication in IEL?

2.3 *Does HRL Require 'Cosmopolitan IEL' and 'Multilevel Constitutionalism'?*

The search for the 'sources' of IEL, the best methods of legal interpretation, the 'primary rules of conduct' and 'secondary rules of recognition, change and adjudication' of IEL is usually approached from the point of view of *legal positivism* as a discovery of legal facts in the sense of authoritative law-making and effective law-enforcement. For example, Article 38 of the ICJ Statute codifies the sources of international law in terms of "international conventions", "international custom,

[26] My own definitions in Petersmann (2012a), p. 140 ff.

[27] See e.g., Francioni (2007).

as evidence of a general practice accepted as law", and "general principles of law recognized by civilized nations". The same article defines the 'rules of recognition' not only in terms of recognition by states; the references to "civilized nations" and to "judicial decisions and the teachings of the most highly qualified publicists. . .as subsidiary means for the determination of rules of law" qualify state consent in conformity with the customary rules of treaty interpretation as codified in the VCLT. For instance, the Preamble and Articles 31–33 VCLT require not only that "a treaty shall be interpreted in good faith in accordance with the ordinary meaning to be given to the terms of the treaty in their context and in the light of its object and purpose."[28] Article 31(3)(c) also clarifies that "(t)here shall be taken into account, together with the context.... (c) any relevant rules of international law applicable in the relations between the parties." As all UN member states have accepted human rights obligations as well as other 'principles of justice' under the UN Charter and under additional UN conventions, the Preamble of the VCLT emphasises

> that disputes concerning treaties, like other international disputes, should be settled by peaceful means and in conformity with the principles of justice and international law. . .,
>
> *Recalling* the determination of the peoples of the United Nations to establish conditions under which justice and respect for the obligations arising from treaties can be maintained,
>
> *Having in mind* the principles of international law embodied in the Charter of the United Nations such as the principles of the equal rights and self-determination of peoples, of the sovereign equality and independence of all States, of non-interference in the domestic affairs of States, of the prohibition of the threat of use of force and of universal respect for, and observance of, human rights and fundamental freedoms for all.

Arguably, the human rights obligations of all UN member states imply that these UN Charter principles of state sovereignty, popular sovereignty and peaceful settlement of disputes have become constitutionally constrained by the universal "recognition of the inherent dignity and of the equal and inalienable rights of all members of the human family (as) the foundation of freedom, justice and peace in the world",[29] notwithstanding the inadequate legal protection of human rights in many UN member states. The more 'principles of justice' and 'inalienable human rights' are recognised as integral parts of national and international legal systems, the more does this *'dual nature' of modern legal systems*—e.g. as legal facts and normative objectives that are inadequately realised in the non-ideal reality of national and international legal systems—also challenge traditional distinctions between *legal positivism*, *natural law theories* and *sociological conceptions of law* focusing on the 'law in action' as a 'reality check' for the 'law in the books'. The universal recognition of the 'inalienable' and 'indivisible nature' of civil, political, economic, social and cultural human rights deriving from respect for the human dignity and reasonableness of human beings has not only incorporated natural law theory into positive national and international legal systems. The

[28] Article 31, para. 1.

[29] Preamble of the Universal Declaration of Human Rights 1948.

universal recognition of a human right to democratic self-governance also reflects the concern of social theories of law that mere authoritative issuance of legal rules may not create 'positive law' unless the rules are also legitimised by democratic consent and voluntary rule-compliance by free and equal citizens.

In regional customs union and FTAs among European countries, trade rules addressed to governments have been consistently interpreted and protected by national and European courts as protecting also equal freedoms and rights of citizens rather than only reciprocal rights of governments. As stated by the EU Court of Justice,

> the fact that certain provisions of the Treaty are formally addressed to the Member States does not prevent rights from being conferred at the same time on any individual who has an interest in compliance with the obligations thus laid down.[30]

Such interpretation of liberal trade rules recognising private economic actors and citizens as legal subjects of IEL is in conformity with the citizen-oriented, rights-based nature of international commercial law (e.g. based on private contract law, property rights and autonomously agreed arbitration), international investment law (e.g. protecting investor rights and remedies though investment treaties), HRL and constitutional law (e.g. protecting basic rights of citizens as 'constituent powers' and 'democratic principals' vis-à-vis government agents with limited, delegated powers). It is also supported by the comprehensive GATT/WTO guarantees of individual access to judicial remedies, for instance in the field of GATT (Article X), the WTO Antidumping Agreement (Article 13), the WTO Agreement on Customs Valuation (Article 11), the Agreement on Preshipment Inspection (Article 4), the Agreement on Subsidies and Countervailing Measures (Article 23), the General Agreement on Trade in Services (Article VI), the Agreement on Trade-Related Intellectual Property Rights (Articles 41–50, 59) and the Agreement on Government Procurement (Article XX). Yet, as WTO institutions remain dominated by government executives interested in limiting their legal, democratic and judicial accountability vis-à-vis citizens, WTO dispute settlement bodies are reluctant to balance public and private interests (e.g. in 'fair price comparisons' in the determination of 'dumping margins' and antidumping duties) in terms of individual rights of citizens. Also in the external FTAs of the EU with third countries, including the CETA (Article 14.16), governments increasingly exclude 'direct applicability' of FTA provisions by citizens and other non-governmental, economic actors in domestic courts.[31] The increasing opposition in European civil society and in European parliaments against ratification of power-oriented—rather than citizen-oriented—CETA and TTIP provisions reflects the constitutional insight that the future development of IEL and of its underlying 'principles of justice' also depends on 'struggles for justice' by citizens defending their constitutional and human rights against abuses of public and private powers. As Schneiderman seems to support the

[30] See Case 43/75 *Defrenne v Sabena* ECR 1976, 455, par. 31; Case C-281/98, *Angonese* ECR 2000, I-4139.

[31] Semertzi (2014).

derivation of individual investor rights and judicial remedies from international investment treaties: Does his conception of 'constitutionalism' also support deriving individual trading rights and judicial remedies from FTAs, especially in relations among constitutional democracies? His "constitutionalism as discovery, project and critique" does not explain his normative premises for projecting and critiquing "constitution-like commitments" in IEL. His advice to "press the pause button" seems to imply that he perceives no urgent need for protecting domestic citizens against intergovernmental power politics (like US blockage of NAFTA Chapter 20 dispute settlement proceedings, intergovernmental NAFTA interpretations limiting Chapter 11 arbitral proceedings, CETA provisions excluding private rights and judicial remedies).

2.4 Lessons from 'Republican Constitutionalism' for Multilevel Governance of Transnational PGs?

Does Schneiderman accept a constitutional obligation of democratic governments to protect transnational PGs demanded by citizens? As the Preamble of CETA recognises "the importance of ... human rights and the rule of law for the development of international trade and economic cooperation": Should 'rule of law' in economic relations between Canada and the EU be designed as protecting constitutional rights and judicial remedies rather than excluding private rights and domestic judicial remedies pursuant to Article 14.16 CETA? Does Schneiderman agree that 'constitutionalising' multilevel governance of international PGs (like a common transatlantic market) requires exploring the lessons from past experiences with republicanism, comparative institutionalism and 'PGs theories' for limiting abuses of 'governance failures' and 'market failures'? Depending on their respective 'provision paths', some PGs can be supplied unilaterally by 'single best efforts' (e.g. a medical invention). The supply of some other PGs depends on the 'weakest links' (e.g. dyke-building, global polio eradication, nuclear non-proliferation). 'Aggregate global PGs'—like a mutually beneficial world trading system—tend to be supplied through a 'summation process' of local, national and regional PGs. They are confronted with numerous 'collective action problems' such as:

- 'prisoner dilemmas' and 'free-riding' due to attempts at avoiding the costs of producing PGs (like protection of world food security through WTO subsidy disciplines opposed by India, climate change prevention opposed by countries dependent on fossil fuels) that benefit also the 'free-riders' refusing to share the adjustment costs;
- 'jurisdiction gaps' and 'governance gaps' due to power politics (e.g. veto-powers preventing consensus-based conclusion of the WTO Doha Round negotiations, non-ratification of the International Criminal Court jurisdiction by China, Russia and the US, non-implementation of the Nuclear Non-Proliferation Treaty and its circumvention by 'failed states' like North-Korea and Pakistan);

- lack of resources, inadequate protection of property rights and 'capture' of regulatory institutions (e.g. impeding protection of biodiversity and tropical forests in many less-developed countries);
- 'constitutional gaps' and 'accountability gaps' (e.g. for protecting human rights and rule of law in UN governance) due to inadequate leadership for 'responsible sovereignty' and 'duties to protect internationally agreed common concerns'; or
- 'incentive gaps' and 'discourse failures' due to non-inclusive 'executive dominance' of intergovernmental organisations treating citizens as mere objects rather than as 'democratic principals' of all governance institutions and 'agents of justice'.

PGs theories explore techniques for limiting the collective action problems, for example:

- by limiting 'free-riding' through transformation of PGs (like the world trading system) into 'club goods' (like the WTO);
- by circumvention of veto-powers (e.g. in the WTO) by more limited 'plurilateral agreements' among 'coalitions of the willing' (e.g. FTAs pursuant to Article XXIV GATT);
- by 'differential and preferential treatment' compensating less-developed countries for 'positive externalities' (e.g. of protecting tropical forests and their greenhouse gas absorption capacities) and sharing of transitional adjustment costs (e.g. of moving from fossil fuels to 'green energy');
- by public education and subsidisation of 'public reason' (e.g. information on climate change and its harmful effects) in order to limit 'discourse failures';
- by limiting domestic 'governance failures' through multilevel commitments (e.g. through competition and environmental rules, HRL), assistance (e.g. for national health protection and tobacco control measures), stronger legal and democratic accountability mechanisms, 'countervailing rights' of adversely affected citizens, and multilevel judicial remedies; or
- by limiting the 'executive dominance' in 'disconnected UN and WTO governance' by multilevel parliamentary and judicial involvement promoting 'republican governance' and multilevel 'democratic constitutionalism'.

Only a few UN Specialized Agencies have been established through functionally limited (small c) 'treaty-constitutions' (*sic*) that explicitly link their respective multilevel governance of international PGs—for instance, in the International Labour Organization (ILO), World Health Organization (WHO), Food and Agriculture Organization (FAO) and UN Educational, Scientific and Cultural Organization (UNESCO)—to corresponding human rights, such as labour rights and human rights to protection of health, food, education, and rule of law. Yet, with the exception of the 'tri-partite' composition of the ILO institutions (by representatives of governments, employers and employees), all UN institutions tend to be dominated by intergovernmental decision-making without effective democratic participation and accountability for the frequent non-implementation of UN and WTO obligations inside many countries. Most UN and WTO government executives insist on their 'diplomatic privileges' and 'member-driven governance' and pursue self-interests in avoiding rights of citizens to hold governments accountable by invoking and enforcing UN and WTO obligations in domestic jurisdictions. Hence, multilevel UN and WTO governance of international PGs remains 'disconnected' and often ineffective: the reciprocal rights and obligations among governments in international relations are not effectively implemented inside many states due to the treatment of citizens as mere objects rather than legal subjects of international law. 'Westphalian conceptions' of IEL as reciprocal contracts among governments that government executives may freely violate in order to advance 'national interests', reflect political self-interests in preventing citizens and domestic courts to hold governments accountable for violations of international trade, investment and environmental rules.[32] Does Schneiderman's 'economic constitutionalism' argue for a stronger transnational rule of law? Can this be achieved without protecting stronger rights and remedies of citizens and without challenging Canada's 'legal dualism' in its implementation of international legal obligations inside the federation and in Canadian provinces?

3 Conclusion: Fragmentation and Integration as Dialectic Driving Forces in the 'Constitutionalisation' of IEL?

Legal, institutional and methodological 'fragmentation' and progressive 're-integration' through diverse 'constitutional' and 'judicial methods' are dialectic processes characterising national and international legal systems, as reflected in the history of federal states and in the customary law requirement of interpreting treaties and settling related disputes "in conformity with the principles of justice and international law".[33] This comment has argued that—in view of the human rights obligations and corresponding constitutional limitations of all governance institutions—legal interpretations of IEL should embrace an *inclusive 'cosmopolitan methodology'* that acknowledges the reasonable, common interests of all human beings in protecting producers, investors, workers, traders and consumers in their mutually beneficial, global division of labour as legal subjects, who are entitled to corresponding government duties to respect, protect and fulfil the human rights of citizens and their democratic demands for more effective protection of international PGs. Such a cosmopolitan methodology perceives IEL as being embedded in multilevel HRL and constitutional law. The 'constitutional functions' of international law for protecting 'aggregate PGs' inside societies can succeed only within 'constitutional checks and balances' protecting equal constitutional rights of citizens and their democratic 'public reason' in multilevel governance of

---

[32] On the exclusion by governments of 'direct applicability' of GATT/WTO rules see Petersmann (1997), p. 18 ff.

[33] Preamble and Article 31 of VCLT.

international PGs, with due respect for 'methodological pluralism'. As politics is often controlled by local and national interests, the task of doctrinal rethinking and reordering of incoherencies among local, national, transnational and international rules, principles and governance institutions also falls on civil society, legal scholars and courts of justice whenever they are confronted with injustices of UN and GATT/WTO rules and policies.

'*Comparative institutionalism*' can assist in finding out whether multilevel regulation of transnational PGs should rely on decentralised regulatory methods (like citizen-driven markets, democratic decision-making, contract law and litigation) or on more centralised regulatory agencies and intergovernmental organisations for limiting the ubiquity of 'market failures' and 'governance failures' in transnational economic relations. For example, the 15 UN Specialized Agencies rely on very diverse treaty rules, institutions and decision-making processes for the collective supply of functionally limited, yet often interdependent global PGs. Some UN Specialized Agencies justify their law and governance on *deontological grounds*, such as labour rights justifying the law and governance of the ILO and the 'enjoyment of the highest attainable standard of health (as) one of the fundamental rights of every human being' justifying the law and governance of the WHO.[34] Other organizations refer to *consequentialist* and *utilitarian justifications*, such as 'ensuring humanity's freedom from hunger' as explicit objective of the FAO, or "raising standards of living, ensuring full employment and a large and steadily growing volume of real income and effective demand".[35] The UNESCO recognises the importance of promoting 'public reason' and *'republican virtues'* through "education of humanity for justice and liberty and peace" in view of the fact that "since wars begin in the minds of men, it is in the minds of men that the defences of peace must be constructed".[36] The jurisprudence of UN tribunals increasingly reflects the structural and transformational changes of international law, for instance:

- by increasing references in ICJ jurisprudence to other international, regional and also national courts of justice "as subsidiary means for the determination of rules of law"[37] in order to conclude that state practice continues to support and accept as law (*opinio juris*), e.g., the jurisdictional immunity of states even if *jus cogens* is involved[38];
- by emphasising that the settlement of disputes among states must remain in conformity with their human rights obligations[39];

[34] cf. the Preamble of the WHO Constitution.

[35] Preamble of the GATT 1947.

[36] Preamble of the UNESCO Constitution.

[37] Article 38(1)(d) of the ICJ Statute.

[38] *Jurisdictional Immunities of the State, Germany v Italy*, 2012 ICJ, at 99.

[39] *Arctic Sunrise, Netherlands v Russia*, International Tribunal on the Law of the Sea (ITLOS), Case No. 22, Order of 22 November 2013: "The settlement of such disputes between two states

- by evolutionary interpretation and development of international environmental law in ICJ judgments like *Gabcikovo-Nagymaros*, *Pulp Mills* and *Whaling in the Antarctic*[40]; or
- by ascertaining international legal practice no longer only in terms of state consent and recognising also individuals, corporate actors and international organisations as legal subjects of ever more fields of international law, whose rights limit traditional principles of 'international law among states' (e.g. lack of reciprocity as not limiting the application of human rights treaties; recognition of *erga omnes* and *jus cogens* obligations limiting the legal relevance of state consent and enlarging the scope of rights of diplomatic protection against human rights violations; different allocation of burden of proof in case of certain human rights violations by authoritarian governments; award of damages in the 2012 ICJ judgment as reparation for the violation of the human rights of Mr. *Diallo*).[41]

The reality of 'institutional pluralism' and 'constitutional pluralism' at worldwide, regional and national levels of governance confirms that different 'PGs regimes' pursuing different policy objectives and 'principles of justice' may also require different governance institutions depending on their specific 'collective action problems'. For instance, the tripartite structures of ILO institutions are justifiable by the competing rights and interests of labour representatives (e.g. interested in high wages), employer representatives (e.g. interested in low production costs) and governments (e.g. interested in 'social peace' and avoidance of costly strikes). The compulsory WTO dispute settlement system offers a mutually beneficial PG due to its reduction of transaction costs, promotion of legal security, and progressive clarification of indeterminate legal rules and principles through impartial and independent adjudication. In contrast to the replacement of GATT 1947 by the WTO Agreement, the intergovernmental structures and 'executive dominance' in UN institutions have hardly changed over the past decades. Without stronger support from academics—also from countries outside Europe—the civil society struggles for 'civilising' and 'constitutionalising' UN and WTO governance of transnational PGs are unlikely to succeed.

---

should not infringe upon the enjoyment of individual rights and freedoms of the crew of the vessels concerned."

[40] See the overview of international environmental adjudication and of human rights courts identifying human rights provisions with environmental content in Dupuy and Vinuales (2015), p. 244 f. and p. 307 ff.

[41] For a discussion of the relevant ICJ judgments in *Congo v Uganda* (2005), *Diallo* (2010) and *Belgium v Senegal* (2012), see Andenas (2015), p. 712 ff.

References

Alexy R (2004) Menschenrechte ohne Metaphysik? Deutsche Zeitschrift für Philosophie 52 (1):15–24

Andenas M (2015) Reassertion and transformation: from fragmentation to convergence in international law. Georgetown J Int Law 46:685–734

Besson S, Marti J (eds) (2009) Legal republicanism: national and international perspectives. Oxford University Press, Oxford

Dupuy P, Vinuales J (2015) International environmental law. Cambridge University Press, Cambridge

Dworkin R (2006) Justice in robes. Harvard University Press, Cambridge

Francioni F (ed) (2007) Access to Justice as a Human Right. Oxford University Press, Oxford

Garcia F (2013) Global justice and international economic law—three takes. Cambridge University Press, Cambridge

Petersmann E (1991) Constitutional functions and constitutional problems of international economic law. International and domestic foreign trade law and policy in the United States, the European Community and Switzerland. Fribourg University Press/Boulder Publishers, Fribourg/Boulder

Petersmann E (1997) The GATT/WTO dispute settlement system: international law, international organizations and dispute settlement. Kluwer Law International, The Hague

Petersmann E (2002) Taking human dignity, poverty and empowerment of individuals more seriously: rejoinder to Alston. Eur J Int Law 13(4):845–851. doi:10.1093/ejil/13.4.845

Petersmann E (2012a) International economic law in the 21st century: constitutional pluralism and multilevel governance of interdependent public goods. Hart, Oxford

Petersmann E (2012b) Methodological pluralism and its critics in international economic law research. J Int Econ Law 15(4):921–970. doi:10.1093/jiel/jgs040

Petersmann E (2015) The establishment of a GATT Office of legal affairs and the limited public reason in the GATT/WTO dispute settlement system. In Marceau G (ed) A history of law and lawyers in the GATT/WTO. The development of the rule of law in the multilateral trading system. Cambridge University Press, Cambridge, p 182–207

Petersmann E (2015a) Transformative transatlantic free trade agreements without rights and remedies of citizens?. J Int Econ Law 18(3) (forthcoming). doi: 10.1093/jiel/jgv030

Sandel M (2009) Justice. What's the right thing to do?. Farrar, Strauss and Giraux, New York

Schneiderman D (2016) Global constitutionalism and international economic law: the case of international investment law. In: Bungenberg M, Hermann C, Krajewski M, Terhechte J (eds) European Yearbook of International Economic Law, vol 7. Springer, Heidelberg, pp 23–43

Semertzi A (2014) The preclusion of direct effect in the recently concluded EU free trade agreements. Common Mkt L Rev 51:1125–1158

Trade in Agricultural Products: Should Developing Countries Give Up on the WTO Promise for a Fair and Market-Oriented Agricultural Trading System? A Historical and Theoretical Analysis

Melaku Geboye Desta

Contents

Abstract Although the World Trade Organization (WTO) can rightly claim credit for establishing the first ever truly multilateral framework of rules for trade in agricultural products in the form of the Agreement on Agriculture (AoA), the AoA itself recognizes that it is only the first step in a long process aimed at establishing a "fair and market-oriented agricultural trading system." The Doha negotiations have been increasingly looking irrelevant to agriculture until the 10th Ministerial Conference in Nairobi in December 2015, which adopted several decisions pertaining particularly to agriculture. Despite this recent development, and considering the

The views expressed in this article are exclusively personal and do not represent the views of any institution I am affiliated with.

M.G. Desta (✉)
Capacity Development Division (CDD), United Nations Economic Commission for Africa (UNECA), Addis Ababa, Ethiopia

Leicester De Montfort Law School, De Montfort University, Leicester, UK
e-mail: Melaku.desta@dmu.ac.uk

M. Bungenberg et al. (eds.), *European Yearbook of International Economic Law 2016*, European Yearbook of International Economic Law 7,
DOI 10.1007/978-3-319-29215-1_4

manifest divergence of positions among the membership on the future of the Doha negotiations, it is clear that the present AoA, as modified by these latest Ministerial Decisions, is likely to remain the only framework governing agricultural trade for the indefinite future. Developing countries in general, and the poorest amongst them in particular, will be the primary losers of such an outcome. Reflecting on the history of agricultural trade regulation over the last two centuries, this article aims to demonstrate that the treatment of agriculture as an exception to the general rules of international trade has a long pedigree, both in economic theory and regulatory practice, often used by powerful states against the less fortunate. If multilateral negotiations fail to deliver on agriculture, developing countries cannot look to bilateral and regional agreements for solution. The article concludes that developing countries cannot afford to give up on multilateralism, for only a multi-sectoral and multilateral forum such as the WTO allows all countries, whether they are for or against agricultural liberalisation, to make progress in this area through issue linkages and cross-sectoral trade-offs.

1 Background

The World Trade Organization's (WTO) Agreement on Agriculture (AoA) declares in its preamble that the long-term objective of WTO members is "to establish a fair and market-oriented agricultural trading system."[1] The agriculture negotiations within the framework of the WTO's Doha process were part of the endeavour to bring this objective closer to reality. Regrettably, however, attainment of that objective has eluded WTO members until the 10th Ministerial in Nairobi in December 2015, where a decision to abolish export subsidies became among the most notable accomplishments in the 20-year history of the WTO itself. I believe developing countries in general, and the poorest amongst them in particular, have been the primary losers from the WTO's inability to deliver on its promises in the agricultural sector for so long. In this contribution, I will attempt to show that the General Agreement on Tariffs and Trade (GATT)/WTO treatment of agricultural trade issues, while in line with long-established traditions of exceptional protectionism in the sector, has increasingly served as a tool to deny opportunities for the poorest countries in the world to trade their way out of poverty. With the promise of Doha fading away by the day and new mega-regional agreements threatening to push the WTO further and further from the centre of global economic policy—and rule-making, the poorest developing countries are inevitably losing hope in the capacity of the multilateral trading system to respond to their enduring quest for a fair and market-oriented agricultural trading system. If this pessimistic scenario materializes, the poorest developing countries that have been complaining about a

[1] Agreement on Agriculture in Final Act Embodying the Results of the Uruguay Round of Multilateral Trade Negotiations, Marrakesh, 15 April 1994, para. 2.

trading system that did not give them the voice they deserved might soon find themselves yearning for the days when the WTO was still relevant.

2 The Agriculture Negotiations: Dynamic Markets and Slow-Moving Diplomats

Agriculture as an economic sector[2] is undergoing rapid transformation while the WTO agricultural trade negotiations have been stuck in the past. When the WTO Agreement on Agriculture was negotiated in the late 1980s and early 1990s, the world agricultural market was suffering from a structural oversupply caused by generous subsidies linked to production in rich countries, which frequently resorted to export subsidies in order to dispose excess supplies on the world market. This then became a major source of resentment in developing countries whose farmers found it increasingly difficult to sell their products on the international market; at its worst, developing countries could not even protect themselves against highly subsidised imports that displaced domestic production. As a result, the Uruguay Round negotiations on agriculture were essentially negotiations on agricultural subsidies, and the resulting AoA largely an agreement on agricultural subsidies. With the exception of Articles 4 and 5, which deal respectively with the tariffication of then existing non-tariff barriers in the sector and the agriculture-specific safeguards mechanism respectively, and Article 12 on export restrictions, all other substantive provisions of the AoA relate to agricultural domestic support and export subsidies.[3] In an innovative move by the negotiators, the AoA rules on agricultural subsidies were supplemented by country-specific commitments on trade-distortive domestic support and commitments limiting the amount of budgetary outlays supporting the exportation of particular products as well as the quantity of each product that can benefit from export subsidies. Those countries that did not schedule such commitments effectively accepted a commitment not to introduce or maintain any trade-distortive domestic support or export subsidies. On market access, the major achievement of the Uruguay Round negotiations lies in the

[2] By agriculture I mean the production of food and non-food items through farming or animal husbandry. For purposes of WTO law, Annex 1 of the Agreement on Agriculture provides a list of the covered products by reference to the Harmonized Commodity Description and Coding System, the product nomenclature developed by the World Customs Organization (WCO). See http://www.wcoomd.org/en/topics/nomenclature/instrument-and-tools/hs_nomenclature_2012/hs_nomenclature_table_2012.aspx (last accessed 6 August 2015).

[3] The AoA contains 21 articles and five annexes. Of the 21 articles, Article 1 defines the key terms; Article 2 defines the concept of agricultural products; Articles 3, 6–11, and 13 are all about agricultural subsidies. Articles 4 and 5 on market access are the only other substantive provisions in the AoA; the remaining being: Article 12 on export restrictions, Article 14 cross-referring to the SPS Agreement; Articles 15 and 16 on special and differential treatment; Articles 17 and 18 on institutions; Article 19 on dispute settlement; Article 20 on the built-in agenda to continue the reform process and Article 21 incorporating the annexes to become an integral part of the AoA and governing the AoA's relations with the rest of the multilateral agreements in the WTO system.

tariffication of innumerable non-tariff market access barriers that had been put in place especially in rich countries in order to protect their highly distorted domestic markets from foreign competition.

World agricultural markets and the issues facing national policy makers cannot look more different today. In 2008 the World Bank reported that global models were predicting the possibility of rising food prices for the first time since the world food crisis of the 1970s,[4] a forecast that was confirmed by developments since then. Over the past few years, agricultural prices stood at or close to record highs,[5] export restrictions replaced export subsidies in many countries,[6] concerns about access to supplies largely replaced traditional market access challenges,[7] agriculture became

[4] See World Bank (2007) World Development Report 2008: Agriculture for Development, http://siteresources.worldbank.org/INTWDR2008/Resources/WDR_00_book.pdf (last accessed 27 July 2015), p. 69.

[5] The Food and Agriculture Organization's (FAO) index of international food commodity prices reached its highest recorded level in February 2011. See FAO and OECD (2011) OECD—FAO Agricultural Outlook 2011–2020, http://www.oecd-ilibrary.org/agriculture-and-food/oecd-fao-agricultural-outlook-2011_agr_outlook-2011-en (last accessed 5 October 2015), p. 20.

[6] Between 2008 and 2011, a large number of countries, including Argentina, China, India, Russia, Ukraine, and Vietnam, have imposed export restrictions on agricultural products. See Demeke M, Pangrazio G, Maetz M (2009) Country Responses to the Food Security Crisis: Nature and Preliminary Implications of the Policies Pursued, http://www.fao.org/3/a-au717e.pdf (last accessed 7 August 2015) (noting that 25 countries, not all of them WTO members, had restricted or banned exports as of December 2008). See also Kim J (2010) Recent Trends in Export Restrictions. OECD Trade Policy Working Paper No. 101, TAD/TC/WP(2009)3/FINAL, http://www.oecd-ilibrary.org/docserver/download/5kmbjx63sl27.pdf?expires=1438759955&id=id&accname=guest&checksum=05CF1D2847070816D91D95CAD828F31B (last accessed 27 July 2015).

[7] Following the 2007–2008 food crisis, the FAO surveyed the policy responses of 81 developing countries; it found that 43 countries had reduced import taxes; 25 either banned exports or increased taxes on them; 45 implemented measures to provide relief or partial relief from high prices to consumers in the form of cash transfers, direct food assistance or increases in disposable income (by reducing taxes or other charges), or some combination of these measures; a significant number of countries also granted support to producers in order to offset rapidly rising input costs, such as fertilizer and animal feed for livestock producers. See FAO, IFAD, IMF, OECD, UNCTAD, WFP, World Bank, WTO, IFPRI, UN HLTF, Price Volatility in Food and Agricultural Markets: Policy Responses. 2 June 2011, http://www.oecd.org/tad/agricultural-trade/48152638.pdf (last accessed 7 August 2015), para. 37. As Javier Blas et al. noted, the 2007–2008 food crisis caused widespread unrest and open riots in more than 30 countries around the world. See Blas J, Farchy J, Weaver, C, Mundy S, Fears Grow Over Global Food Supply. Financial Times, 3 September 2010, http://www.ft.com/intl/cms/s/0/5f6f94ac-b6bc-11df-b3dd-00144feabdc0.html#axzz3oA3RFXwT (last accessed 5 October 2015).

one of the most attractive areas for foreign direct investment,[8] in short, there have been indications that a possible structural deficit has replaced structural surplus as the problem of world agricultural markets, which is increasingly looking likely to remain the case for the foreseeable future.[9] Needless to say, short-term price volatility will always remain a characteristic feature of the market for agricultural products,[10] but the key factors determining the supply-demand balance appear to be undergoing a fundamental shift. There have been significant declines in prices recently, which the FAO/OECD predict to continue for the next 10 years; it is notable, however, that even these prices are "projected to remain at a higher level than in the years preceding the 2007–2008 price spike."[11] Three major factors are usually mentioned as responsible for the high prices: (1) the drive for alternative energy sources, especially biofuels,[12] in response to climate change and energy security concerns; (2) rising demand for high-protein foods, including meat and other animal products, as a result of rising prosperity in many parts of the world, especially China and India; and (3) rising overall demand for food as a result of

---

[8] See, e.g., UNCTAD (2009) World Investment Report 2009: Transnational Corporations, Agricultural Production and Development, http://unctad.org/en/docs/wir2009_en.pdf (last accessed 5 October 2015), noting that the long-running decline in foreign direct investment flows to agriculture in developing host countries has been reversed in recent years, even suggesting a resurgence may be under way. The report also noted that "some forms of foreign participation—not least the so-called 'land grabs' by investors—are causing concern by some quarters in the development community", p. 95. UNCTAD attributes this turn mainly to three major factors: the 2008 food crisis, new investment to meet the Millennium Development Goal to halve, between 1990 and 2015, the proportion of people who suffer from hunger, and the rise of biofuel production, pp. 103–105, 110. For a recent analysis linking 'land grabs' in Cambodia with the EU's Everything but Arms (EBA) system of preferences for goods coming from LDCs, see Bradsher K, Sugar Industry Highlights Conflicts Over Trade Pacts and Land. New York Times, 30 September 2013, http://www.nytimes.com/2013/10/01/business/international/in-cambodias-cane-fields.html?_r=0 (last accessed 5 October 2015).

[9] According to the FAO and the OECD, agricultural commodity prices are expected to fall from the peaks recorded in early 2011, but they are projected to average around 20–30 % higher in real terms over the 2011–2020 period compared to the last decade. See FAO and OECD (2011) OECD—FAO Agricultural Outlook 2011–2020, http://www.oecd-ilibrary.org/agriculture-and-food/oecd-fao-agricultural-outlook-2011_agr_outlook-2011-en (last accessed 5 October 2015), p. 25.

[10] See, e.g., Meyer G, Russia's Wheat Supply Turnaround Stalks US Prices. Financial Times, 27 January 2012, p. 32 (noting that the world's wheat supply "has gone from grave to generous" within a matter of months and showing a 24 % fall in the price of wheat within a year).

[11] See OECD/FAO (2015), OECD-FAO Agricultural Outlook 2015, http://www.fao.org/3/a-i4738e.pdf (last accessed 6 August 2015), p. 15.

[12] In the US, 40 % of annual maize crop is used for ethanol production. See FAO and OECD (2011) OECD—FAO Agricultural Outlook 2011–2020, http://www.oecd-ilibrary.org/agriculture-and-food/oecd-fao-agricultural-outlook-2011_agr_outlook-2011-en (last accessed 5 October 2015). See also Trostle R (2008) Global Agricultural Supply and Demand: Factors Contributing to the Recent Increase in Food Commodity Prices, Revised. A Report from the Economic Research Service of the US Department of Agriculture (WRS-0801), http://www.ers.usda.gov/media/218027/wrs0801_1_.pdf (last accessed 7 August 2015).

demographic changes.[13] The impact of climate change on agriculture, both in its weather-related damage as well as through the impact of climate-change-mitigation measures on the sector, is also expected to be significant.[14]

Left to their own devices, these factors can cause serious humanitarian problems around the world, particularly in poor developing countries. Their solution will require a multidimensional and globally coordinated approach that involves everyone from the subsistence farmers in Africa and their governments to the largest agri-businesses and the governments of developed countries. Seen from this perspective, the current WTO negotiations focusing on the reduction of agricultural subsidies were already looking more and more out of touch with the reality on the ground. While market forces will naturally play a role, the current situation appears to require once again a fundamental re-examination of the role of the state in the agricultural sector. Such re-examination is likely to show the need for a readjustment in the objectives of WTO agricultural negotiations. This might not mean a lesser role for the multilateral trading system in international agricultural trade; it only suggests a potentially different role. As Orden et al. rightly pointed out, "[t]he relevance of the multilateral rules to guide the global agricultural trade system became apparent in an environment of high prices just as it was earlier in the

---

[13] The world population is expected to reach nine billion by 2050. In order to meet the food needs of this increased population, it is believed that annual agricultural production will have to rise by around 70 %. See Murray S, Small Farmers Have a Critical Role. Financial Times: Special Report on World Food 2011, 13 October 2011, http://www.ft.com/intl/cms/s/0/f98fbb7c-f00c-11e0-bc9d-00144feab49a.html#axzz3oA3RFXwT (last accessed 5 October 2015). See FAO, IFAD, IMF, OECD, UNCTAD, WFP, World Bank, WTO, IFPRI, UN HLTF, Price Volatility in Food and Agricultural Markets: Policy Responses. 2 June 2011, http://www.oecd.org/tad/agricultural-trade/48152638.pdf (last accessed 7 August 2015), para. 18 (forecasting the expected demand for food in 2050 to increase by between 70 % and 100 %).

[14] For more on this, see Blandford (2012), pp. 223–249. Note, however, that agriculture is not expected to suffer in all countries because of climate change. As a recent Interagency Report noted, there is "widespread agreement that agriculture, particularly in developing countries, will be for the most part negatively affected by climate change". See Interagency Report to the Mexican G20 Presidency (2012) Sustainable Agricultural Productivity Growth and Bridging the Gap for Small-Family Farms, http://www.oecd.org/tad/agricultural-policies/50544691.pdf (last accessed 7 August 2015), pp. 9–10. For a recent extensive assessment of the risks posed by climate change, including to agriculture in the UK, see UK Department for Environment, Food and Rural Affairs (Defra) (2012) The UK Climate Change Risk Assessment 2012: Evidence Report, https://www.gov.uk/government/uploads/system/uploads/attachment_data/file/69487/pb13698-climate-risk-assessment.pdf (last accessed 7 August 2015). The report found both threats and opportunities from climate change, including the following: Threats: Crop losses and other impacts on high quality agricultural land due to flooding; Higher summer soil moisture deficits, increasing demand for irrigation to maintain crop yields and quality; Increased competition for water resources in the summer and pressures to reduce abstractions; Potential for increased potency in existing, or introduction of new livestock diseases; and More intense rainfall with greater potential for soil erosion. Opportunities: Increased yields for current crops (e.g., wheat and sugar beet, potatoes) due to warmer conditions and/or CO_2 effects; Increased grass yields benefiting livestock production; New crops and tree species may be able to enter production, due to warmer conditions; Opportunities to grow a wider range of non-food crops for energy and pharmaceuticals; and Increased yields of rain-fed potatoes due to greater CO_2 and climate effects, p. 73.

decade when concern focused on the price-depressing effects of agricultural support policies."[15] However, in order for the multilateral trading system to adequately serve its objectives, it must also respond to changes on the ground.

A clear example where a WTO response is needed but still lacking is in the area of export regulation. According to *The Economist*, 33 countries imposed export restrictions on food between 2007 and 2011.[16] In today's high-price agricultural market, the traditional focus of the trading system on disciplining import restrictions will need to be supplemented with an equally effective discipline against export restrictions. Regrettably, the Doha negotiations that were hoped to bring the rules in line with the evolving needs of the market are not delivering on their promises.[17] The current version of the AoA, with the few changes introduced to it under the Bali package,[18] and more recently from the Nairobi Ministerial, is thus likely to stay with us for much longer than originally expected or intended, making it potentially less and less relevant than it is today. The next section provides an overview of the theoretical foundations and the historical evolution of the multilateral trading system and show that agricultural trade has always challenged both the theory and the practice of international trade policy from the very early days to the present time.

3 The Multilateral Trading System: A Historical Note from an Agricultural Perspective

The development of a rules-based liberal multilateral trading system has been a long and painful process.[19] The fundamental economic and philosophical tenets for free trade have been in place since at least the eighteenth century when Adam Smith used the theory of absolute advantage to explain why it would be in the interest of a country to import those goods that could be acquired more cheaply abroad than if

[15] Orden et al. (2011), p. 4.

[16] Food and Trade: The New Corn Laws. The Economist, 15 September 2012, http://www.economist.com/node/21562912 (last accessed 26 July 2015).

[17] "The Doha trade talks are dead", declared The Economist in 2012, with agriculture once again the main culprit: "The villains are powerful lobbies, notably in agriculture, such as America's cotton and sugar industries and Japan's rice farmers and fishermen." See Goodbye Doha, Hello Bali. The Economist, 8 September 2012, p. 12, Online edition: http://www.economist.com/node/21562196 (last accessed 26 July 2015).

[18] For more on this, Lamy (2008).

[19] Jeffrey Dunoff summarised what he calls "the leading economic, game theoretic and political science models that are commonly used to explain the trade regime" as follows: (1) the 'efficiency model' based on the theory of comparative advantage and gains from trade; (2) the 'collective action model' under which countries use the trading system as a way to overcome prisoner's dilemma type coordination problems, and (3) the 'embedded liberalism model' under which countries were allowed to continue to exercise their regulatory powers internally while avoiding 'mutually destructive protectionist policies' in international trade. See Dunoff (1999), pp. 733–762.

they were produced domestically. Smith argued that "if a foreign country can supply us with a commodity cheaper than we ourselves can make it, better buy it of them with some part of the produce of our own industry, employed in a way in which we have some advantage."[20] Smith's powerful argument in support of free trade was followed by an even more powerful insight that showed that two countries could both benefit from trade even where just one of them had absolute advantage (or disadvantage) in the production of all commodities. While the theory of absolute advantage "illustrated the gains when countries differed in their ability to produce different goods", the theory of comparative advantage demonstrated that two countries would still benefit from trade even where one of them is superior to the other in producing all goods, because these countries would still "specialise in the production of the good in which their opportunity cost (in terms of the implicit sacrifice of other, foregone goods, not in terms of absolute cost) was the lowest."[21]

The theory of comparative advantage demonstrated that what matters is the relative cost advantage, or disadvantage, of a country in a particular product compared to its partner. In as long as there is a difference in their relative level of productive efficiency, which is normally the case, "there is potential from trade *for all* trading partners, regardless of how countries compare absolutely."[22] Two reasons are often given as to why productive efficiency might differ across countries—differences in technology and in factor endowments. Since no two countries are the same in all respects, 'the case for specialisation through trade is a general case, applying to all countries.'[23] Specialisation in a few products allows each country to produce at a larger scale and more efficiently than would otherwise be the case—it enables them to achieve economies of scale in production.[24] As Nobel Laureate Paul Samuelson put it in his 1948 book,

> international trade is mutually profitable even when one of the two countries can produce every commodity more cheaply (in terms of all resources) than the other country. One country has an *absolute advantage* in the production of every good; the other country has an absolute disadvantage in the production of every good. But so long as there are differences in the *relative* efficiencies of producing the different goods in the two countries, one can always be sure that even the poor country has a *comparative advantage* in the production of those commodities in which it is relatively most efficient; this same poor country will have

---

[20] Smith (1776), p. 364.

[21] See Irwin (1996), p. 90. While the credit for developing the theory of comparative advantage often goes to David Ricardo and his 1817 book entitled On the Principles of Political Economy and Taxation, Irwin argues that it was Robert Torrens who "first recognized the essence of the comparative advantage argument" in a book he wrote in 1815, 2 years before Ricardo's famous book came out, p. 90.

[22] WTO (1998), p. 38 (emphasis added).

[23] WTO (1998), p. 38. For an interesting illustration with the help of examples as to how a country that is less efficient in absolute terms at producing everything can still have comparative advantage in some products and can potentially benefit from trade, see Krugman and Obstefeld (1997), p. 14.

[24] "In many industrial processes", writes Samuelson, "when you double all inputs, you may find that your output is more than doubled; this phenomenon is called 'increasing returns to scale'". Samuelson (1976), p. 28 (italics in original). See Krugman and Obstefeld (1997), pp. 13–37.

> a *comparative disadvantage* in those commodities in which it is more than averagely inefficient. Similarly, the rich, efficient country will find that it should specialize in those fields of production where its absolute advantage is comparatively greatest, planning to import those commodities in which the greatly inefficient country has the least absolute disadvantage.[25]

Stated in policy terms, the theory teaches that international trade based on the comparative advantages of countries, and not on the artificial incentives resulting from protective trade barriers (such as quotas or tariffs) or stimulants (such as export subsidies), enhances global welfare in the interest of all trading nations. In line with the laissez-faire philosophy of Adam Smith,[26] the theory of comparative advantage makes a compelling case in favour of the least possible level of government intervention on the flow of international trade.[27] This is what Professor Jeffrey Dunoff more recently called 'the efficiency model' of international trade relations.[28]

The theory has long been one of the most robust and widely-accepted propositions in economics.[29] However, only Britain had a history of fairly long and consistent adherence to free trade as government policy.[30] Outside Britain, acceptance of free-trade principles "had always been partial, half-hearted and short-lived."[31] But, as Carr pointed out, even Britain chose to be an exception because,

[25] Samuelson (1948), p. 539 (emphasis in original).

[26] In one of his often-quoted paragraphs, Adam Smith wrote the following: "As every individual ... endeavours as much as he can both to employ his capital in the support of domestic industry, and so to direct that industry that its produce may be of the greatest value; every individual necessarily labours to render the annual revenue of the society as great as he can. He generally, indeed, neither intends to promote the public interest, nor knows how much he is promoting it. By preferring the support of domestic to that of foreign industry, he intends only his own security; and by directing that industry in such a manner as its produce may be of the greatest value, he intends only his own gain, and he is in this, as in many other cases, led by an invisible hand to promote an end which was no part of his intention." Smith (1776) p. 477.

A 'full laissez faire' situation is defined by Paul Samuelson as a situation of "complete governmental noninterference with business." Samuelson (1976), p. 28 (italics in original). Carr credits Smith as the founder of the 'laissez-faire school of political economy'. Carr (1939), p. 43.

[27] In the words of Alan Sykes, "[t]he normative economic case for free trade ... in one way or another rest[s] on the premise that government intervention into international trade flows creates economic 'inefficiency' and that inefficiency is a bad thing." Sykes (1998), p. 57.

[28] See Dunoff (1999), p. 737.

[29] See WTO (1998), p. 38; Krugman and Obstefeld (1997), p. 13; and WTO (2001) Introduction to the WTO: Trading into the Future, 2nd rev. ed., https://www.wto.org/english/res_e/doload_e/tif.pdf (last accessed 26 July 2015), p. 9.

[30] According to Trentmann, Britain 'gave' free trade to the world. See Trentmann (2008), p. 2. Note also that, as Carr noted in 1939, universal free trade was "an imaginary condition which has never existed". Carr (1939), p. 7.

[31] Carr (1939), p. 46.

in those days "free trade promoted British prosperity".[32] A famous exception to this aspect of British economic history that has particular relevance to this piece, and to this day, are the 1815 Corn Laws which prohibited or restricted the importation of grains unless the price of domestic grain rose beyond certain politically-set levels.[33] The Corn Laws were repealed in 1846, but they were neither the first, nor the last, act of agricultural protectionism even in free-trading Britain. As Adam Smith showed in 1776:

> The law of England ... favours agriculture not only indirectly by the protection of commerce, but by several direct encouragements. Except in times of scarcity, the exportation of corn is not only free, but encouraged by a bounty. In times of moderate plenty, the importation of foreign corn is loaded with duties that amount to a prohibition. The importation of live cattle, except from Ireland, is prohibited at all times, and it is but of late that it was permitted from thence. Those who cultivate the land, therefore, have a monopoly against their countrymen for the two greatest and most important articles of land produce, bread and butcher's meat.[34]

Almost exactly a century after the Corn Laws were enacted, the First World War dealt a deadly blow to Britain's unilateral free trade policy, bringing it closer to the rest of the world at the time, and particularly to continental Europe and the US

[32] Carr (1979), p. 76. Until WW I, Britain avoided tariffs or other measures that discriminated against imports. Describing the situation at the beginning of the twentieth century, Trentmann wrote: "Free Trade in Britain meant that there were no tariffs at all that discriminated against imports in order to assist any branch of industry or agriculture. Customs duties were for revenue only. To prevent any protectionist effect, they were always matched by an excise tax on equivalent domestic goods. Britain stuck to Free Trade irrespective of the protectionist measures of other countries." See Trentmann (2008), p. 6. According to Professor Azar Gat, Britain used its economic and military power "to negotiate with and pressurize foreign political authorities in order to secure free trade or at least low tariff barriers for British goods. Although requesting no preference over other powers, the British were of course positioned to gain the most from the lifting of trade sanctions." See Gat (2006), p. 546.

[33] As Paul Bairoch has shown, the special treatment of agriculture in international trade policy had its roots in the desire to balance food security on the one hand and agricultural protection on the other in most European countries. In the United Kingdom, wrote Bairoch, "the political struggle between supporters of free trade and those in favour of protectionism began ... in 1815... when the gentry voted in a new Corn Law aimed at protecting local agriculture against grain imports. It should be noted that 'Corn Laws' were a quasi-permanent feature of tariff history in most European countries. They had always aimed at a precarious balance between protecting local agriculture and preventing the price of bread from rising too steeply. In England, the first national laws of this kind date back to 1436." Bairoch (1989), pp. 7–8. For more on the Corn Law, Bairoch (1989), pp. 7–13.

[34] Smith (1776) Book III Chapter IV, p. 443. One can also learn from this book that subsidies on the exportation of corn from England, called by then 'bounties', were introduced in 1688. There was an "act for ... encouraging the exportation of corn," the preamble of which states that "it hath been found by experience, that the exportation of corn and grain into foreign parts, when the price thereof is at a low rate in this kingdom, hath been a great advantage not only to the owners of land but to the trade of this kingdom in general." Smith (1776) Book I, Ch. XI, p. 215.

where the mercantilist philosophy that "imports are bad, exports good"[35] was influential.[36] The War ended in 1918, but the policy of unilateral free trade effectively disappeared for good.[37] The War also speeded up the transition of global economic and technological supremacy from Britain to the US (and to a certain extent to Japan). Unlike Britain, however, the emerging power, the US, believed in negotiated and reciprocal free trade and commercial diplomacy, rather than unilateral free trade. Indeed, the US passed its most protectionist law, the notorious Hawley-Smoot Tariff Act, in May 1930,[38] which elevated the level of customs tariffs to their highest in the history of that country.[39] Many other countries followed suit and introduced similar trade-restrictive measures, often as a response to the US move.[40] Non-tariff measures, including subsidies, quotas and quantitative restrictions proliferated, and tensions increased in the sphere of inter-state economic relations. The effect was a drastic decline in the volume of trade by as much as 60 % in the early 1930s, which "is now seen as an important reason for the depth of the depression at that time and the rise of nationalism, which ultimately led to World War II."[41] Describing the international situation which prevailed in the 1930s, Clair Wilcox wrote:

> Intensive economic nationalism marked the rest of the decade. Exports were forced; imports were curtailed. All of the weapons of commercial warfare were brought into play: currencies were depreciated, exports subsidized, tariffs raised, exchanges controlled, quotas imposed, and discrimination practiced through preferential systems and barter deals.

[35] Jackson (1977), p. 435.

[36] For a useful summary of the mercantilist trade literature, see Irwin (1996), p. 26–44.

[37] As Trentmann put it, when peace returned in 1918, "the global trade system was in tatters." See Trentmann (2008), p. 189.

[38] Krugman and Obstefeld (1997) call it "a remarkably irresponsible tariff law." See p. 237. According to Kindleberger, the origins of the Hawley-Smoot Tariff Act 'reach back to 1928 when Herbert Hoover, campaigning for the presidency, promised to do something to help farmers suffering under the weight of agricultural prices.' See Kindleberger (1989), p. 170.

[39] Paul Bairoch reported that "in 1932 the revenue raised from goods liable to import duty amounted to 59.1 % of their value." See Bairoch (1989), p. 144.

[40] Canada, Cuba, France, Mexico, Italy, Spain, Australia, and New Zealand may be mentioned as examples. See Hudec (1975), p. 5. Bacchus traced the history of the US agricultural subsidies programme to the New Deal economic programmes of the 1930s, which were introduced as "emergency measures during the depths of the Great Depression, when the nation was awash with farm surpluses and in agony over plummeting farm prices." It is interesting to note that by the late 1930s, President Franklin D. Roosevelt's administration "began to 'fear it had created a Frankenstein monster' in agricultural subsidies. 'Rural pressure groups called for larger and larger subsidies,' and, in 1939, Roosevelt lamented that 'the silly Congress gave me three hundred million dollars more than I wanted for farm subsidies.'" Bacchus J (6 July 2011) Time to Cut Farm Subsidies Now. The Hill, http://thehill.com/blogs/congress-blog/economy-a-budget/169807-time-to-cut-farm-subsidies-now (last accessed 7 August 2015).

[41] WTO (1998), p. 37.

> Each nation wanted to sell much and buy little. A vicious spiral of restrictionism produced a further deterioration in world trade.[42]

In 1934, the US passed the Reciprocal Trade Agreements Act and, by 1939, it had concluded 20 bilateral agreements that contained varying degrees of trade liberalisation, particularly in the form of tariff reductions.[43] During the same period, the League of Nations also sponsored a number of highly ambitious initiatives for multilateral trade liberalisation, but they were not successful.[44] Intensive and meaningful efforts to develop multilateral treaties of an economic nature took place mainly in the post-WWII period.[45]

4 Laying the Legal and Institutional Foundations for Freer Trade

The process to lay the groundwork for the post-War international trading arrangement was started already before the Second World War ended. A liberal and multilateral arrangement for trade was considered an essential part of the overall post-war strategy for peace. The long-accepted economic case for free trade thus found strong political support from the realisation that international peace is very much linked with, if not dependent upon, mutually-beneficial international economic relations.[46] As soon as the war was over, countries formally commenced the negotiations for the establishment of an international institution in the name of the International Trade Organization (ITO) and, on 24 March 1948, signed its Charter with a number of important objectives. The first of these objectives was to create conditions of stability and well-being which are necessary for peaceful and friendly

---

[42] Wilcox (1949), pp. 8–9.

[43] See Kindleberger (1989), pp. 193–194. Note that the use of bilateral treaties to regulate trade between states has had a long and difficult history. See, for instance, the treaty of commerce between England and Portugal, concluded in 1703 and reproduced in Adams (1776) Vol. II Book IV Chapter IV, pp. 54–55.

[44] See, e.g., Irwin et al. (2008), p. 5.

[45] For an enlightening review of European trade policy in the 100 years preceding WW I, see Bairoch (1989), pp. 1–160. For trade policy during the inter-War period, see Kindleberger (1989), pp. 160–196. See also Hudec (1975), p. 4.

[46] US President Truman is quoted to have said in 1947 that "trade and peace are inextricably linked." See WTO (1998), p. 37. According to Professor Hudec, "the postwar design for international trade policy was animated by a single-minded concern to avoid repeating the disastrous errors of the 1920s and the 1930s." Hudec (1975), p. 4.

relations among nations.[47] True to this peace-building mission, the principles of non-discrimination and transparency constituted the central pillars of the proposed system. This system embodied the lessons learnt from those devastating World Wars—the 'lessons of disaster' as Robert Hudec put it.[48] The most important lesson was that the policy of trade restriction and discrimination has been proved wrong.[49]

The ITO was designed to be one of the specialised agencies of the United Nations (UN),[50] but the Charter never entered into force due mainly to the withdrawal of support from its original 'sponsor'—the US. As a result of this failure of the ITO project, the GATT, which had initially been negotiated to serve as an interim arrangement pending the entry into force of the ITO Charter, was made operational on a 'provisional' basis.[51] The chapter of the draft ITO Charter on commercial policy was incorporated into the GATT with only little modification, opened for signature on 30 October 1947, and entered into force on 1 January 1948.

GATT was a successful international agreement administered by a structurally weak but resilient and adaptable 'institution'. It imposed a degree of discipline on

[47] Final Act of the United Nations Conference on Trade and Employment (held at Havana, Cuba from 21 November 1947 to 24 march 1948) UN doc. E/Conf. 2/78 (hereafter the Havana Charter) Article 1, first paragraph. Article 1 provides the other purposes and objectives of the ITO and may be summarized as follows: to attain higher standards of living, full employment and conditions of economic and social progress and development; to assure a large and steadily growing volume of real income and effective demand, to increase the production, consumption and exchange of goods, and thus to contribute to a balanced and expanding world economy; to foster and assist industrial and general economic development, particularly of those countries which are still in the early stages of industrial development, and to encourage the international flow of capital for productive investment; to further the enjoyment by all countries, on equal terms, of access to the markets, products and productive facilities which are needed for their economic prosperity and development; to promote on a reciprocal and mutually advantageous basis the reduction of tariffs and other barriers to trade and the elimination of discriminatory treatment in international commerce; to enable countries, by increasing the opportunities for their trade and economic development, to abstain from measures which would disrupt world commerce, reduce productive employment or retard economic progress; and to facilitate through the promotion of mutual understanding, consultation and co-operation the solution of problems relating to international trade in the fields of employment, economic development, commercial policy, business practices and commodity policy.

[48] Hudec (1975), p. 4.

[49] Hudec (1975), pp. 5–6. International trade economists still uphold the validity of this conclusion. According to Alan Winters, "[h]istory has definitely taught us one huge lesson: closed and tightly managed economies do not prosper." Winters A (1999) Trade Policy as Development Policy: Building on 50 Years' Experience. Paper prepared for the UNCTAD X High-Level Round Table on Trade and Development, Bangkok, 12 February 2000, http://unctad.org/en/Docs/ux_tdxrt1d2.en.pdf (last accessed 26 July 2015).

[50] See Article 86.1 of the Havana Charter; on specialized agencies in the UN system, see Article 57 of the UN Charter.

[51] Note that the General Agreement entered into force on the basis of a document entitled 'Protocol of Provisional Application of the General Agreement on Tariffs and Trade' according to which contracting parties undertook to apply "provisionally on and after 1 January 1948" Parts I and III of the GATT, and "Part II of that Agreement to the fullest extent not inconsistent with existing legislation." PPA (Geneva, 30 October 1947) para. 1(a) and (b) (italics added).

national trade policy based on the principles of reciprocity, predictability and non-discrimination; it served as a forum for a series of successful trade negotiations that led to a steady and broad-based reduction in market access barriers; it provided a highly flexible and reasonably effective dispute settlement mechanism, and generally it promoted the values of a largely market-based capitalist system of international economic relations. And once the Communist bloc was out of the way, which took place while the GATT Uruguay Round was entering its most critical phase, the provisional and defective GATT gave birth to the permanent, powerful and fully-formed WTO. What is remarkable for our purposes is that this legal and institutional history of free trade has been continually challenged by the agricultural sector, to which we will now turn briefly.

5 Agriculture in the Multilateral Trading System

Just as the well-known British history of unilateral free trade was punctuated by the Corn Laws of the nineteenth century, the multilaterally-based free trade agenda of the twentieth century also had to create a special exception for agriculture in different forms, an exception that is being asserted and defended just as passionately in the twenty-first century. Agricultural protectionism has always been a difficult force for governments to control. Writing about European trade policy in the early 1830s, Bairoch observed that the "main obstacle to effective free trade ... was still the substantial protection of agriculture".[52] The repeal of the British Corn Laws in 1846 represented a significant step towards free trade by the then leading European power.[53]

But when, exactly a century later, governments got together to negotiate for the multilateral liberalisation of international trade, even the UK was insistent that agricultural products should be treated differently from all other products.[54] Then UK Agriculture and Fisheries Minister Hudson was "worried about exposing British farmers to foreign competition".[55] By 1944 the UK "wanted to create a special arrangement for agricultural trade outside any main Agreement", and "abandoned the idea of bringing agriculture wholly within the general provisions of the multilateral convention on commercial policy" on the grounds that

[52] Bairoch (1989), p. 10.

[53] According to Paul Bairoch, the date 15 May 1846, when the Corn Laws were repealed, "is rightly held to mark the beginning of the free trade era in the United Kingdom." See Bairoch (1989), p. 13. Bairoch further noted that the repeal of the Corn Laws meant that import duties were abolished for livestock and nearly all meat but, "contrary to what is generally thought, grains remained liable to duties until 1869." Bairoch (1989), p. 13. See also WTO (2007) World Trade Report 2007, https://www.wto.org/english/res_e/booksp_e/anrep_e/world_trade_report07_e.pdf (last accessed 26 July 2015), p. 36.

[54] See Irwin et al. (2008), p. 43.

[55] See Irwin et al. (2008), p. 43.

"agricultural production is particularly subject to wide fluctuations", that there was a need to regulate imports, and that "no single method is adequate for the purpose of such regulation, and that either tariffs or subsidies or quotas or a combination of two or all of them might have to be used in particular cases."[56]

The UK was far from alone in this. Chief US negotiator for the ITO Charter Clair Wilcox described the paradoxical position of the United States government at the time on agriculture and a few other issues as 'the beam in our own eye'.[57] In the words of Wilcox:

> We are accustomed to speak as if the practice of economic planning is anathema in the United States. But, in a major segment of our economy this is not the case. We are no more willing than any other country to leave production in agriculture to the mercies of the market. The maintenance of farm prices at levels unrelated to those obtaining elsewhere in the world is a settled policy of our government. When supplies are ample, this means that we control production and marketing. Where we produce a surplus to sell abroad, we subsidize in order to compete. Where we produce less than we consume at home, we restrict imports so that they will not undercut the established price. The wisdom of our agricultural policy is not here in question, but the fact that it is inconsistent with our belief in private enterprise and with our efforts to restore a freer trading system should be clear.[58]

Indeed, all the 20 bilateral agreements the US had concluded less than a decade earlier had excluded agriculture. The tariff reductions under those agreements

> went side by side with US protection against agricultural imports and subsidies on agricultural exports. Protection was required under those domestic programmes which raised prices in the United States and would, without new restrictions, have attracted further supplies from abroad; and subsidies were deemed necessary to offset the price disadvantage this imposed on American producers in their traditional markets.... On the whole, the trade agreements marked the beginning of regarding liberal commercial policies as appropriate only to manufactures, and their inputs, and leaving agricultural trade largely to special arrangements.[59]

This policy of exclusion of agriculture from bilateral agreements had short-term and long-term consequences. In the short term, 1930s agricultural over-protection in industrialised countries was blamed as 'the root of the world's economic troubles'[60] at the time. A recent authoritative study on the history of GATT also concluded that agricultural interests in the US led the protectionist tide that brought about the Hawley-Smoot law and precipitated the Great Depression.[61] In the long

---

[56] Irwin et al. (2008), p. 53.

[57] Wilcox (1949), p. 35.

[58] Wilcox (1949), pp. 35–36.

[59] See Kindleberger (1989), p. 194.

[60] See League of Nations, League of Nations Official Journal, 86th Session of the Council, Fourth Meeting (24/V/1935), June 1935, p. 631. The representative described his country, Australia, as "a new, young and undeveloped country."

[61] See Irwin et al. (2008), p. 6 noting that the US "bore some responsibility" for the collapse of international trade starting in 1929: "What started out in 1929 as a legislative attempt to protect farmers from falling agricultural prices led to the enactment of higher import duties across the board in 1930. The Hawley-Smoot tariff of that year pushed already high protective tariffs much higher and triggered a similar response by other countries."

term, this US policy effectively planted the seeds of the Uruguay Round Agreement on Agriculture as well as the Doha agriculture negotiations of the twenty-first century.

The special treatment of agriculture in national and international trade policy is often approached merely as a matter of poor policy resulting from short-term calculation by politicians. Electoral politics do indeed play a significant role in agricultural policy-making, but it is also notable that historically ardent champions of free trade, including Thomas Malthus and Adam Smith, looked at agriculture differently. Malthus argued that while free trade in agricultural products would allow a steady flow of cheap imports in normal times, grain-importing countries "merited a special exception from the general rule of free trade" to ensure their very survival is not left in the hands of exporting countries.[62] According to Douglas Irwin,

> In fact, Adam Smith had also raised questions of this sort regarding the grain trade because few countries had free trade in corn. Should a large neighboring country have a crop failure, the small neighbor might restrict its exports to prevent domestic shortages. 'The very bad policy of one country may thus render it in some measure dangerous and imprudent to establish what would otherwise be the best policy in another.[63]

Finally, Hillman claims that Ricardo himself had implied in his works that "'agriculture is different' and must be treated differently."[64]

The effect of all these old and established theoretical concessions about agriculture's possible unsuitability for a free trade arrangement by some of the most influential free trade thinkers and the protectionist policy choices by the most powerful and traditionally liberal-minded countries was reflected in the content of the first drafts as well as the final versions of both the Havana Charter[65] and the General Agreement.[66] Two particularly important trade-restrictive and protective measures generally outlawed by the Havana Charter, and later the General Agreement, were explicitly, albeit conditionally, permitted for agricultural products. They concern the use of quantitative restrictions and export subsidies—the two traditional weapons used by governments to protect their producers from foreign

---

[62] See Irwin (1996), p. 95.

[63] Irwin (1996), p. 95.

[64] Hillman (1978), p. 35. According to Hillman "[o]ne may also detect in certain free-trade arguments—e.g., in Ricardo—a selective attitude in the deliberate writing off of land lords as too reactionary to make good economic agents in comparison with entrepreneurs. The implication is that 'agriculture is different' and must be treated differently." It is notable however that other theorists, such as John Stuart Mill and Friedrich List, who argued in favour of infant industry protection in the industrial sector did not recommend protection for the agricultural sector. See WTO (2007) World Trade Report 2007, https://www.wto.org/english/res_e/booksp_e/anrep_e/world_trade_report07_e.pdf (last accessed 26 July 2015), p. 36.

[65] See, inter alia, ITO Charter Articles 20 (on quantitative restrictions), and 27 and 28 (on export subsidies on primary products).

[66] As Stewart put it, GATT rules on agriculture were drafted "to be consistent with the agricultural policies of the major signatories rather than vice versa." Stewart (1993), p. 134.

competition in the domestic market and to artificially enhance the competitive standing of their producers in foreign markets, respectively.[67]

When the Havana Charter with all its agriculture exceptions was brought before the US Congress for approval, farm interests and farm organisations 'led the opposition' that precipitated the ITO's stillbirth.[68] In order to fully escape what little GATT discipline was left for agriculture, some countries, notably the US, secured 'country-specific derogations' in the form of waivers.[69] In cases where no such exemptions were available, countries maintained several trade-distorting practices "a large proportion [of which were]... maintained in blatant violation of the General Agreement."[70] An observer of the evolution of the multilateral trading system was thus quoted as saying: "GATT came into existence in the immediate aftermath of the war as a pure fruit of the industrial society, of machinery. *It largely disregarded what makes up our past—agriculture*—and what constitutes our future—services..."[71] Corbet summarised the reality well at the time when he observed: "agricultural commodities have been given a 'special status', which has put them outside the process of trade liberalization."[72]

It is notable that even after the Uruguay Round succeeded in bringing 'our past' and 'our future' together in the form, *inter alia*, of the Agreement on Agriculture and the General Agreement on Trade in Services (GATS), agriculture still casts a long shadow against services and non-agricultural products in both the diplomatic and 'judicial' activities of the WTO. To cite just one final and most recent example, agriculture's traditional role in wrecking trade liberalisation initiatives was in full display at the July 2015 negotiations for the Trans-Pacific Partnership (TPP) in Hawaii, which Jonathan Weisman captured as follows:

> In the end, a deal filled with 21st-century policies on Internet access, advanced pharmaceuticals and trade in clean energy foundered on issues that have bedeviled international

[67] See inter alia Krugman and Obstefeld (1997), p. 5. The special treatment of agriculture in the General Agreement reflected the power and influence of the US at the end of the Second World War. As Dam observed "no treaty that impinged upon the U.S. Farm program could receive the constitutionally-required senatorial approval." See Dam (1970), p. 260.

[68] Hillman (1994), p. 29. Further back in history, opposition from US agricultural interests had served as one of the main causes for US cancellation in 1865 of what is known as the 'Reciprocity Treaty' of 1854 between Canada and the US. See Trebilcock and Howse (1999), p. 38. More general concerns were also at play here. As Professor Robert Howse observed, it was 'sovereignty concerns' in the US that "foiled ... the proposed governance mechanism for trade" under the ITO Charter. See Howse (2002), pp. 96–97.

[69] The other notable case in this respect is Switzerland whose protocol of accession effectively exempted its agriculture from GATT disciplines.

[70] Jackson (1977), p. 981.

[71] Journal de Genève, quoted in GATT Focus Newsletter. No. 41, October 1986, p. 8 (italics added).

[72] See Corbet (1979), p. V.

trade for decades: access to dairy markets in Canada, sugar markets in the United States and rice markets in Japan.[73]

Indeed, the agricultural shadow can stretch far beyond trade diplomacy and sometimes reach some unexpected terrain, which was vividly witnessed in 1999 when a high-level EU-US meeting over Kosovo was hijacked by that never-ending bananas dispute at the WTO. Exasperated by the situation, US Secretary of State Madeline Albright is quoted to have said: "I never in my life thought I would spend so much time on bananas."[74] Pascal Lamy, writing about the role he played as EU trade commissioner in the early 2000s pushing for Common Agricultural Policy (CAP) reform, observed that his stance "earned [him] lasting enmity" with French President Chirac.[75]

The next question that naturally follows from here is a simple one: What makes agriculture so different and so difficult?

6 Why Is Agriculture Treated So Differently?

Different factors, including the special dependence of agriculture on the vagaries of nature, food security, culture, the environment, etc., have been invoked to justify and defend the special treatment of agricultural trade. Writing about the thinking behind the introduction of the first government policies to intervene in the agriculture sector in the US in the 1933 Agricultural Adjustment Act, Sumner and others noted that the "core observation, going back to the 1920s, was that agriculture suffered from low returns on human and other capital, low incomes for farm families, and undue variability (and especially downside shocks) on investment returns and incomes."[76] The League of Nations in 1935 underlined "the necessity to retain agricultural populations throughout the countries of Europe, not merely for economic, but for social, historic and psychological reasons."[77] A survey carried out by the 1982 GATT Working Party found that, in developing their agricultural policies, governments attached particular importance to one or more of the

[73] Weisman J, Talks for Pacific Trade Deal Stumble. The New York Times, 31 July 2015, http://www.nytimes.com/2015/08/01/business/tpp-trade-talks-us-pacific-nations.html (last accessed 5 October 2015).

[74] See Porter E, Banana Wars: Editorial Notebook. New York Times, 29 December 2009, http://www.nytimes.com/2009/12/29/opinion/29tue4.html?_r=0 (last accessed 26 July 2015).

[75] See Lamy (2013), p 74.

[76] See Sumner et al. (2010), p. 405. They further observed that: "Early supply control policies were developed together with trade barriers that insulated domestic markets from imports. Exports were important for products such as wheat, and economists recognised that programs that caused high domestic prices would reduce or eliminate commercial exports (i.e., a relatively elastic export demand). The proposals therefore included stocks management and government export dumping policies to shift production out of the domestic market", p. 406.

[77] See League of Nations (1935), p. 631.

following objectives: securing a standard of living for their agricultural population comparable with that of the population in other sectors; security of supply; maintenance of a sizeable population in certain regions; and protection of the environment.[78]

The influence of the agriculture lobby on electoral politics in many countries is also considered a significant factor.[79] Anne Krueger refers to modern-day agriculture as a 'classic example' of government capture by special interest groups.[80] In 1948 Paul Samuelson noted that "society may feel that there is some special sanctity about farm life, or something worth preserving in the way of life of the 'stout agricultural yeoman or happy peasant.'" Samuelson then added: "It is to be doubted that most people who rhapsodize in this fashion have ever lived on a farm."[81] Nearly 30 years later, Professor Samuelson observed: "[a]griculture may be the unlucky stepchild of nature, but it is often the favoured foster child of government."[82]

In the late 1990s, a new term called 'multi-functionality' was added to the trade vocabulary as a kind of shorthand expression for non-trade concerns involved in agricultural liberalisation.[83] The European Commission, one of the early proponents of the multi-functionality of agriculture, restated the three main objectives for

---

[78] GATT, Working Party on Structural Adjustment and Trade Policy: Report to the Council (L/5568, 20 October 1983), para. 30.

[79] Christina Davis argues that "high levels of agricultural protection have arisen because farm lobbies are an influential pressure group" and quotes Peter Lindert as saying: "the farm sector gets the most protection when it employs 3–4 % of the employed labor force" because "as their numbers decline, farmers become better organised and have greater incentives to seek protection, and governments can more easily subsidize the small group of remaining farmers." See Davis (2003), p. 5.

[80] See Krueger (2004), p. 488.

[81] See Samuelson (1948), p. 561.

[82] Samuelson (1976), p. 412. Southgate observed that nineteenth century export subsidies to sugar led to 'dumped exports' that reduced the London price for raw sugar "from £35 10s. in 1872 to £7 5 s. in 1902. As a result, the sugar-producing colonies and refining industries were in great difficulty, but industries based on sugar developed rapidly. ... After several abortive technical conferences, the Brussels Convention met in 1901 and by the agreement of 1903 the bounties were abolished." Southgate (1967), pp. 599–600.

[83] For a recent analysis of this concept in the context of EU agriculture policy, see Cardwell (2012), pp. 27–299. Japan's use of multi-functionality in agriculture has been described recently as a 'protectionist banner'. See Sutton M, Reconstruction and Healing Must Precede Entry into TPP [Trans-Pacific Partnership]. The Japan Times, 7 November 2011, http://www.japantimes.co.jp/print/eo20111107a1.html (last accessed 8 November 2011).

the future CAP as: viable food production, sustainable management of natural resources and climate action, and balanced territorial development.[84]

While the above concerns and policy objectives are important, it is far from settled why they should lead to the creation of a wholly unique regulatory regime for agricultural trade. In the words of some critics, these are only "arguments of convenience, concealing the primary motive of jobs, or firm, protection."[85] Instead, the fact that most developing countries stand to benefit from freer agricultural trade because of their comparative advantage in this sector has been accepted as one of the important reasons for developed countries' lack of will to liberalise agricultural trade.[86]

7 The Special Treatment of Agriculture and Developing Countries

As early as 1967, the Group of 77 developing countries lamented in their Algiers Charter that developed countries "have increased the degree of protection in many of those agricultural products in which developing countries are more efficient producers" and exhorted them to "adopt measures to discourage uneconomic production of commodities which compete with those originating in developing countries and should abolish subsidies on such competing products."[87] However, in virtually all developed countries agricultural market access barriers continued to grow, matched only by the concomitant growth of subsidies for production and export. Owing to the large subsidies provided by virtually all developed countries, the competition has long been between (tax-paying) developing country farmers and developed country treasuries. Thanks to these subsidies, the world market price of agricultural products has typically declined at the same time as the share of

[84] See European Commission, Communication From the Commission to the European Parliament, the Council, the European Economic and Social Committee and the Committee of the Regions the CAP towards 2020: Meeting the Food, Natural Resources and Territorial Challenges of the Future. COM(2010) 672 final, 18 November 2010, http://ec.europa.eu/agriculture/cap-post-2013/communication/com2010-672_en.pdf (last accessed 26 July 2015). Another EU Commission study reported that EU agriculture was responsible for about 471 million tonnes of CO_2 equivalents, which represented 9.6 % of the EU emissions of greenhouse gases in 2008. See EU Commission, Situation and Prospects for EU Agriculture and Rural Areas. December 2010, http://ec.europa.eu/agriculture/publi/situation-and-prospects/2010_en.pdf (last accessed 7 August 2015), p. 18. The same report noted that the average annual greenhouse gas emissions from agriculture have decreased at a rate of 0.7 % per year between 2000 and 2008 as a result of "improved production methods and diminishing cattle numbers", which represents a much quicker pace than GHG reductions in other sectors of the economy, p. 18.

[85] Krueger (2004), p. 491.

[86] See Matthews (2012), pp. 104–132.

[87] See First Ministerial Meeting of the Group of 77: Charter of Algiers, Algiers, 10–25 October 1967, at http://www.g77.org/doc/algier~1.htm (last accessed 7 August 2015).

regions with proven comparative disadvantage in agriculture has risen dramatically over the past four decades,[88] while the opposite has been the case particularly for the developing countries most of which had strong comparative advantage in agriculture. In the words of former GATT Director-General Peter Sutherland, developed country subsidies "led to wasteful surpluses like the 'butter mountains' and 'wine lakes' amidst poverty, and sometimes famine, in the developing world whose farmers have been shut out of the world market by industrialized countries' subsidies."[89] The EU CAP has been the prime example in this respect,[90] though by no means the only one. In 2001, the International Monetary Fund (IMF) and the World Bank in a joint paper noted that

> Although border protection, including tariff and nontariff measures, has declined substantially over the past three decades, it remains significant in both industrial and developing countries, particularly in areas such as agriculture and labor-intensive industrial products where developing countries have comparative advantage.[91]

More recently, the World Bank observed that Sub-Saharan Africa enjoys comparative advantage in agriculture, which comes from three sources: factor endowments (that "most African and agriculture-based economies are relatively rich in natural resources, but poor in skilled labor, suggesting comparative advantage for unprocessed primary products"), the difference in productivity and costs (while "indirect costs ... are higher on average in Africa than in their competitors in the developing world", the "business environment is more important for manufacturing and high-value services"); and dynamic economies of scale ("based on current and emerging comparative advantage, a diverse portfolio of processed and unprocessed primary-based exports (including services such as tourism) will remain the main

---

[88] The EU is a textbook example of this development. See, inter alia, Krugman and Obstefeld (1997), p. 199 (italics added). Recent data from the EU Commission show that the EU imported annually an average of €81 billion in 2007–2009, making the EU by far the largest importer; with a yearly average export of about €76 billion in 2007–2009, the EU is at a par with the US as one of two leading agricultural exporters. See EU Commission, Situation and Prospects for EU Agriculture and Rural Areas. December 2010, http://ec.europa.eu/agriculture/publi/situation-and-prospects/2010_en.pdf (last accessed 7 August 2015), p. 27.

[89] Sutherland P, GATT Focus Newsletter. No. 102, October 1993, p. 2.

[90] A recent appraisal by the EU Commission described the CAP as "very successful in meeting its objective of moving the EU towards self-sufficiency" but also acknowledged that "by the 1980s the EU had to contend with almost permanent surpluses of the major farm commodities, some of which were exported (with the help of subsidies), others of which had to be stored or disposed of within the EU." EU Commission, Situation and Prospects for EU Agriculture and Rural Areas. December 2010, http://ec.europa.eu/agriculture/publi/situation-and-prospects/2010_en.pdf (last accessed 7 August 2015), p. 73. The Commission also listed some of the other major problems associated with the CAP, including high budgetary cost, distortion of world markets, growing unpopularity with consumers and taxpayers, and environmental sustainability concerns.

[91] See IMF and World Bank (2001) Market Access for Developing Countries' Exports, https://www.imf.org/external/np/madc/eng/042701.pdf (last accessed 7 August 2015), p. 4.

option for generating foreign exchange in the medium term").[92] However, successive efforts by developing countries, more recently supported by a number of developed countries such as Australia and even the US, to bring agriculture into the mainstream rules of the GATT/WTO system have been largely a failure. Divisions among developing countries themselves over the subject, together with staunch and persistent resistance to agricultural liberalisation by several developed countries, including Japan, Norway, Switzerland and the EU, have ensured that agriculture would stay outside the mainstream rules to this day.

8 Attempts at Liberalising Agricultural Trade

Agriculture's place in the GATT/WTO system has been variously described in the literature—as the 'long-neglected' sector,[93] the most heavily protected and distorted sector of international trade, the sector that was "bedevilled by the twin problems of protectionism and export subsidies,"[94] the sector that was "kept out of GATT negotiations and remained riddled with tariff and non-tariff barriers",[95] and so on.

Successive attempts were made to bring agriculture into the mainstream rules of the multilateral trading system, but until the Uruguay Round they were largely a failure. Over time, agricultural trade became a subject of considerable tensions in international relations.[96] The twelfth Ministerial session of the GATT Contracting Parties in 1957 identified "agricultural protectionism, fluctuating commodity prices and the failure of export earnings to keep pace with import demand in developing countries . . . as undesirable features of the international trading environment."[97] It is enlightening to see that the 1958 Haberler Report identified market access restrictions, export subsidies, and domestic support as the three forms of national measures that protect agriculture. According to the Haberler Report, "[p]ractically all schemes of agricultural protection, however complicated in detail, can in the last resort be analysed into some combination of these three elements": (1) measures

---

[92] World Bank (2007) World Development Report 2008: Agriculture for Development, http://siteresources.worldbank.org/INTWDR2008/Resources/WDR_00_book.pdf (last accessed 27 July 2015), p. 14.

[93] See Arthur Dunkel, as quoted in GATT Focus News Letter. No. 41, October 1986, p. 8.

[94] Matsushita et al. (2003), p. 135.

[95] See Rodrik (2011), p. 72.

[96] It has been reported that "of the 82 disputes submitted to the dispute settlement process between 1980 and 1990, 60 % concerned agriculture." Steenblik R, Previous Multilateral Efforts to Discipline Subsidies to Natural Resource Based Industries. Paper Prepared for the Workshop on the Impact of Government Financial Transfers on Fisheries Management, Resource Sustainability, and International Trade, 17–19 August 1998, Manila, Philippines, http://www.oecd.org/greengrowth/fisheries/1918086.pdf (last accessed 27 July 2015), p. 11.

[97] WTO (2003), pp. 26–44, 152.

which directly discourage imports, including import duties, quantitative import restrictions, state trading enterprises (STEs), and 'voluntary restraint agreements'; (2) measures which directly encourage exports, including straightforward export subsidies, STEs, and export credit facilities; and (3) measures which directly encourage home production, including such straightforward domestic subsidies as deficiency payments and market price support.[98] A key recommendation of the Haberler report in this respect was a "gradual moderation of the degree of agricultural protection in exporting and importing countries."[99] Based on the recommendations of the Haberler Report, the 13th Session of GATT established three committees in 1958, with one of them, Committee II, given the mandate to review the agricultural policies of Contracting Parties.

The Haberler Report came out at a time when the US was beginning to consider agricultural liberalisation as potentially beneficial to its trade interests. As a result, the US was keen to follow on this recommendation in the first trade negotiation round that was launched shortly after the Haberler Report, i.e., the Dillon Round of 1960–1962. However, the six EEC member countries at the time, as part of their preparation for the launch of the European Common Agricultural Policy, refused to include agriculture in the negotiations. A recent WTO analysis reported that "differences between the EEC and the United States on this issue brought the negotiations to the brink of failure, but finally the United States decided that the further integration of the European market should take priority over certain US agricultural export interests."[100] It was only during the Kennedy Round (1964–1967) that, "for the first time, the negotiating parties agreed on the inclusion of agricultural products as a major negotiating topic."[101] However, this was only as far as countries were able to go—fundamental differences between the United States and the EEC made agreement impossible and the EEC "managed to keep its CAP largely intact".[102] The only noticeable agriculture-related achievement from the Kennedy Round was an agreement on the basic elements of a commodity agreement for grains that later became the International Grains Arrangement (IGA) replacing the International Wheat Agreement (IWA)—an agreement that was more

[98] GATT (1958), pp. 81–83.

[99] See GATT (1958), p. 102.

[100] See WTO (2007) World Trade Report 2007, https://www.wto.org/english/res_e/booksp_e/anrep_e/world_trade_report07_e.pdf (last accessed 26 July 2015), p. 183.

[101] WTO (2007) World Trade Report 2007, https://www.wto.org/english/res_e/booksp_e/anrep_e/world_trade_report07_e.pdf (last accessed 26 July 2015), p. 184. Referring to significance of the Kennedy Round, the FAO also observed: "Although the major part of the tariff reductions concerned industrial products, agriculture was included in a comprehensive manner in trade negotiations for the first time in the 20-year history of GATT." See FAO (1967), p. 42.

[102] WTO (2007) World Trade Report 2007, https://www.wto.org/english/res_e/booksp_e/anrep_e/world_trade_report07_e.pdf (last accessed 26 July 2015), p. 184.

about managing the agriculture market than about liberalising it.[103] Indeed, the very aim of the Kennedy Round of negotiations on three key agricultural products—cereals, meat and dairy products—was to establish 'general arrangements' in the nature of ICAs designed to manage markets and not to liberalise them. To this extent, the negotiations were a relative success in respect of cereals, but not in meat and dairy products.[104] However, GATT contracting parties did not give up on dairy and meat. In 1967, they established a Working Party on Dairy Products,[105] which later resulted in the *Arrangement Concerning Certain Dairy Products*.[106] The *Dairy Arrangement* set minimum export prices and entered into force on 14 May 1970[107] but its product coverage was initially limited to skimmed milk powder

[103] The IGA had two distinct components, the Wheat Trade Convention and the Food Aid Convention. The FAO called the IGA "the main achievement [of the Kennedy Round] in the agricultural field", whose main objective was managing the market for cereals by setting minimum export prices and maximum prices at which exporters will provide agreed quantities to importers. See FAO (1967), p. 42. The International Wheat Conference translated these basic objectives into reality in the form of the IGA. The 1967 Wheat Trade Convention was however a failure. As the FAO later observed, the price provisions of that Convention "were virtually ineffective from the start to prevent international wheat prices from falling below the agreed minima." FAO (1971), p. 23. The new International Wheat Agreement (IWA), and its Wheat Trade Convention (WTC), which in 1971 replaced the 1967 IGA and its WTC, contained no price-related obligations because "no agreement could be reached either on the range of prices to be established or on the definition of a reference wheat to which prices of other wheat would be related." The new WTC thus effectively became a framework agreement with mechanisms for cooperation and consultation through a new advisory subcommittee to keep the world wheat market under constant review. See FAO (1971), p. 23.

[104] The result of the Kennedy Round negotiations on these key agricultural products was summarised in a 1968 GATT Report as follows: "The negotiation of cereals resulted in agreement on basic minimum and maximum prices for wheats of major importance in international trade and the provision of food aid for developing countries to the amount of [4.5] million metric tons of grains each year initially for a period of 3 years. These agreements were subsequently incorporated in the International Grains Arrangement 1967 negotiated under the auspices of the International Wheat Council in co-operation with UNCTAD. Some bilateral arrangements were concluded on meat. In the case of dairy products very little was obtained in the negotiations." See GATT, Second United Nations Conference on Trade and Development, New Delhi, February-March 1968: Activities of GATT in the Field of Trade and Development 1964–1967 (L/2967 7 February 1968), p. 15.

[105] The Working Party was mandated to "conduct, on behalf of the CONTRACTING PARTIES, consultations under Article XXII:2 on urgent problems in international trade in dairy products with a view to arriving at mutually acceptable solutions to these problems and to report to the Council." See GATT, Working Party on Dairy Products (L/2951, 8 December 1967).

[106] See GATT, Arrangement Concerning Certain Dairy Products (L3324, 12 January 1970).

[107] See GATT, Arrangement concerning Certain Dairy Products—Entry into Force on 14 May 1970—[Addendum] (L/3324/Add.1, 20 May 1970). This Arrangement entered into force for eight contracting parties: Australia, Canada, Denmark, the EEC, Japan, New Zealand, South Africa, and the UK.

alone.[108] In April 1973, a similar arrangement—the *Protocol Relating to Milk Fat*—followed with the same minimum-export-price-setting objectives.[109] Following a New Zealand proposal in 1977 to broaden the scope of these sub-sectoral arrangements,[110] the dairy negotiations under the Tokyo Round finally produced the *International Dairy Arrangement*, which covered all dairy products and superseded the two preceding arrangements on skimmed milk powder and milk fat. Parallel efforts for the poultry sector in the 1960s produced no result,[111] but Australia's proposal for the establishment of an *International Meat Consultative Group*, modelled after the *GATT Working Party on Dairy Products*, ultimately proved successful.[112] The proposed Group was established in February 1975,[113] whose work culminated with the conclusion of the *Arrangement Regarding Bovine Meat* during the Tokyo Round. Unlike in its dairy equivalent, there are no minimum export price requirements under the latter Arrangement.[114]

At a more general level, the Tokyo Round (1973–1979) was notable for its 'explicit inclusion of agriculture' in the negotiations,[115] but the end result was almost a repeat of the Kennedy Round experience. When differences between the EEC and the US, once again over agriculture, "held up progress in almost every other area of the negotiations" and threatened the entire round with collapse, the two parties "agreed to drop most substantive questions dividing them" thus allowing the round to be concluded.[116] The ambition to develop "a new multilateral framework in the GATT for the whole agricultural sector" did not materialise; instead the Trade Negotiations Committee recommended to the GATT contracting parties to develop active co-operation in the agricultural sector within an 'appropriate consultative framework' and urged that "the definition of this framework and

[108] The GATT Secretariat was of the view that the Arrangement worked' satisfactorily'. See GATT, Safeguards for Maintenance of Access: Factual Note by the Secretariat (COM.IND/W/104, 13 April 1973), p. 4.

[109] GATT, Protocol Relating to Milk Fat (L/3855, 2 April 1973).

[110] See GATT, Multilateral Trade Negotiations Group "Agriculture" Sub-Group Dairy Products: New Zealand Statement (MTN/DP/W/25, 7 October 1977).

[111] See generally GATT, Group 3(d)—Safeguards for Maintenance of Access: Factual Note by the Secretariat (MIN/3D/2, 30 August 1974), p. 4.

[112] GATT, Australia—Proposed International Meat Consultative Group (L/4119, 26 November 1974).

[113] See GATT, Participation in the Work of the International Meat Consultative Group: Note by the Secretariat (L/4171, 9 April 1975).

[114] For more on this, see GATT, Agriculture in GATT: Note by the Secretariat (CG. 18/W/59, 15 September 1981).

[115] See FAO (1979), pp. 1–59.

[116] WTO (2007) World Trade Report 2007, https://www.wto.org/english/res_e/booksp_e/anrep_e/world_trade_report07_e.pdf (last accessed 26 July 2015), p. 186. The same report also shows that besides the two largely unsuccessful product-specific agreements (on bovine meat and dairy products), the only agricultural 'success' story to come out of the Tokyo Round related to tropical products, in which 'a majority' of developed countries acceded to the request of developing countries for the removal of all trade barriers faced by tropical products in developed countries.

its tasks be worked out as soon as possible."[117] As shown earlier, the commodity-specific arrangements in dairy and bovine meat evolved to become the *International Dairy Arrangement* and the *Arrangement Regarding Bovine Meat*, two of the many Codes produced by the Tokyo Round negotiations.[118] However, it is notable that while the results of the Kennedy and Tokyo Rounds were modest, the technical work undertaken during and between those two rounds "contributed in significant ways to the outcomes of the Uruguay Round."[119]

By the beginning of the 1980s, fear of an economic slump, even a depression, was hanging in the air, bringing with it fear of the old adage that "depressions are farm-led and farm-fed."[120] The 1982 GATT Ministerial Conference recorded the "widespread dissatisfaction with the application of GATT rules and the degree of liberalisation in relation to agricultural trade,"[121] but also recognised that there was "an urgent need to find lasting solutions" to those problems.[122] The same Ministerial Conference decided to establish a Committee on Trade in Agriculture with the mandate to carry out a two-year programme of work and to recommend strategies for greater liberalisation in agricultural trade.[123] The recommendations of the Committee clearly envisaged the two agreements that resulted from the agriculture negotiations during the Uruguay Round—the AoA and the SPS Agreement.[124] Armed with these recommendations, the 1986 Punta del Este Declaration which launched the Uruguay Round reiterated the old call and reaffirmed: "there is an

[117] GATT Multilateral Trade Negotiations: Trade Negotiations Committee, Multilateral Agricultural Framework (MTN/27, 11 April 1979).

[118] Efforts to create a similar Code for wheat were not successful, however. See FAO (1979), pp. 1–58. The negotiations for a successor to the 1971 IWA were conducted under the auspices of the United Nations Negotiating, which could not reach agreement "because of differences on a number of major issues regarding the size and distribution of reserves, prices and special assistance to developing countries."

[119] See Santana and Jackson (2012), p. 466. Santana and Jackson then refer to a 1972 GATT Secretariat Working Paper (COM.AG/W/77, 26 March 1972) as having reflected "most of the elements now contained in the UR Agreement on Agriculture."

[120] Hillman describes this fear as follows: "If substantial agricultural adjustment is not achieved soon and if agricultural protectionism is not reduced or checked there is a danger that, as on two occasions in the past the agriculture sector will be associated with a mass movement toward general economic protection, trade wars, and political breakdown." Hillman (1978), p. 35.

[121] GATT, Thirty-Eighth Session at Ministerial Level: Ministerial Declaration (L/5424, BISD 29S/9-22) adopted on 29 November 1982, p. 10.

[122] GATT, Thirty-Eighth Session at Ministerial Level: Ministerial Declaration (L/5424, BISD 29S/9-22) adopted on 29 November 1982, p. 16. See also Statement by Mr. A. Dunkel, Director-General, to the Punta del Este Ministerial Conference (MIN(86)/5) 15 September 1986.

[123] See GATT, Thirty-Eighth Session at Ministerial Level: Ministerial Declaration (L/5424) adopted on 29 November 1982, p. 9. The Committee was constituted by the Council on 26 January 1983. See GATT Council, Minutes of Meeting Held in the Centre William Rappard on 26 January 1983 (C/M/165, 14 February 1983).

[124] See GATT Committee on Trade in Agriculture, Recommendations Adopted by the Committee Meeting at Senior Policy Level on 15 November 1984 (L/5732).

urgent need to bring more discipline and predictability to world agricultural trade."[125]

The Uruguay Round negotiations showed that, just as in the previous three Rounds, agriculture held the key to the success or failure of the entire round. But unlike in the previous negotiations, several countries, including the US and the so-called Cairns Group, "insisted that there would be an agreement on agriculture or no agreement at all."[126] Developing countries also put success in agriculture as a critical precondition for the success of the Round, but they soon learnt that if they really wanted agriculture to be brought into the GATT system fully, they had to agree to the inclusion of new rules and commitments in areas that thitherto remained totally outside the trading system—services and intellectual property. Commenting particularly about how the WTO agreements on intellectual property and on services became part of the WTO covered agreements, Professor Trachtman observed that these agreement were "the product of political linkage: in the famous 'Grand Bargain', the United States, the European Union (EU), and others exchanged concessions in agriculture and textiles for concessions in intellectual property protection and services trade."[127] But the US in particular wanted both outcomes, and the 'grand bargain' for the US involved little by way of a concession in this particular respect.

And the result of all those developments was, at least from the legal perspective, encouraging. A separate AoA emerged out of it.[128] The issues of sanitary and phytosanitary measures, which formed part of the agriculture negotiations for part of the process, were later put into a separate agreement altogether.[129] The AoA stands on the three pillars of market access, export subsidies and domestic support, exactly the same three major policy areas identified by the Haberler report over three decades earlier.[130] Also for the first time, the AoA defines the term agricultural products for its purposes. It does this by reference to headings of the Harmo-

[125] GATT, Ministerial Declaration on the Uruguay Round (MIN.DEC) adopted in Punta del Este, Uruguay, on 20 September 1986, often referred to as the Punta del Este Declaration, reproduced in, GATT Focus Newsletter. No. 41, October 1986, p. 4.

[126] See United States Department of Agriculture (December 1996), p. 22.

[127] See Trachtman (2002), pp. 78–79. See also Daemmrich A (2011) The Evolving Basis for Legitimacy of the World Trade Organization: Dispute Settlement and the Rebalancing of Global Interests. Harvard Business School Working Paper 12-041, http://www.hbs.edu/faculty/Publication%20Files/12-041.pdf (last accessed 7 August 2015), p. 8 describing the Uruguay Round agreement as a new deal under which the OECD countries "would open their markets to agricultural and labor-intensive manufactured goods, including foodstuffs and clothing; in exchange, developing countries would enforce IP and open financial markets to outside investors".

[128] For more on this, see Desta (2002) and McMahon (2006).

[129] For a discussion of the SPS Agreement, see Scott (2007).

[130] See GATT (1957), pp. 81–83.

nized System to mean HS Chaps. 1–24, but excluding fish from within these Chapters and adding a number of other products from outside these Chapters.[131]

Although its practical impact remains modest in the short-run, the existence of an AoA with a detailed set of legal rules governing the sector brought some degree of certainty, predictability, and rule of law in international relations involving the agricultural sector. The AoA laid the groundwork for a rules-governed and operationally effective discipline for international trade in agricultural products. At the same time, this discipline is still in its infancy. Even today, agriculture is a class in itself. To mention only a few examples, two decades after the conclusion of the AoA, agriculture is still the area where three-digit tariff levels are most common and trade-distortive agricultural domestic support measures as well as export subsidies explicitly permitted. Thanks largely to this special treatment of agriculture in the WTO, developed countries are

> the biggest exporters of food commodities in the international markets. This is in large part due to heavy subsidies to their agriculture. In fact, the inability of developing countries to compete with the subsidized agriculture of developed countries has turned them into net importers of food produced in developed countries.[132]

9 The Doha Process

Stuart Harbinson, the former chairman of the Special Session of the WTO Committee on Agriculture, wrote of agriculture's role in the Doha negotiations in the following terms:

> It was clear from the outset that agriculture would be the main driving force for the negotiations. Agriculture lagged behind other sectors of trade in terms of both liberalization and rule-making. Indeed the main accomplishment of the Uruguay Round Agreement on Agriculture was to bring the trade within the scope of GATT/WTO disciplines for the first time. But, as a price for that, little was achieved in terms of liberalization through Uruguay Round commitments, and rule-making was basic. Further steps would have to be taken, which was one of the reasons underlying the 'built-in agenda' approach. While agriculture

[131] See Article 2 and Annex 1 of the AoA. As the Appellate Body observed more recently, "it is undisputed that the Uruguay Round tariff negotiations for agricultural products were held on the basis of the Harmonized System and that all WTO Members have followed the Harmonized System in their Schedules to the GATT 1994 with respect to agricultural products." Appellate Body Report, *European Communities—Customs Classification of Frozen Boneless Chicken Cuts*, WT/DS269/AB/R, WT/DS286/AB/R, adopted 27 September 2005, and Corr. 1, DSR 2005:XIX, p. 9157, para. 198.

[132] See UNCTAD, Recent Commodity Market Developments: Trends and Challenges: Note by the UNCTAD Secretariat. (TD/B/C.I/MEM.2/2, 23 December 2008), http://unctad.org/en/Docs/cimem2d2_en.pdf (last accessed 27 July 2015), p. 13 para. 33.

> accounted for only a small portion of international trade, it was – and is – politically sensitive in both exporting and importing countries.[133]

The drafters of the AoA knew that what they achieved was only the beginning of a reform process; meaningful agricultural liberalisation needed much more work yet to be undertaken. In recognition of this, Article 20 of the AoA contained a built-in agenda for further negotiations, which was used to start sector-specific negotiations in March 2000 following the failure of the 1999 Seattle Ministerial Conference to launch the widely anticipated comprehensive round of negotiations. When the Doha Ministerial Conference of November 2001 succeeded in launching the Doha Development Agenda (DDA), the then on-going agriculture negotiations were also brought under its umbrella.

Not surprisingly, however, the agriculture negotiations remain as complex, sensitive and divisive as ever. Writing on the Doha process, Peter Sutherland, the first Director General of the WTO, lamented:

> It has been very unfortunate that, as usual, agriculture, a diminishing and relatively tiny part of the global trade fabric, has dominated the debate and was put up front. I would have preferred to have seen a much faster process in terms of services liberalization because I think services liberalization could have developed earlier a constituency of support for the completion of the Doha Round, which would have been formidable.[134]

But, of course, agriculture is too important—and too distorted—for countries to ignore it; indeed even the WTO itself would ignore agriculture at its peril. If there is one sector that symbolises a global economic system that is skewed against the poor, agriculture is certainly it. Two decades after the agriculture breakthrough of the Uruguay Round, agricultural subsidies and other trade-distorting policies are still largely in place in nearly all Organization of Economic Cooperation and Development (OECD) countries. At the time the Uruguay Round was being negotiated, the EU CAP took about 60 % of the EU's overall budget; in 2010 the CAP still took about 41 % of it.[135] As Krueger put it, agricultural protection in rich industrial countries is 'shocking' and 'indefensible'. Krueger tells the story of subsidies in amusing and entertaining terms:

> And, if you think I exaggerate, let me tell you about the cows. The annual cost to consumers and taxpayers of 29 OECD members' support for agriculture and horticulture is so large that it could pay for each of the 56 million cows in the OECD dairy herd to enjoy a first class air ticket around the world. Each cow would also have $1450 spending money to finance

---

[133] Harbinson S (2009) The Doha Round: "Death-Defying Agenda" or "Don't Do it Again"? ECIPE Working Paper No. 10/2009, http://www.ecipe.org/app/uploads/2014/12/the-doha-round-a-death-defying-act.pdf (last accessed 27 July 2015), p. 5.

[134] See Pretzlik C, View from the Top: Peter Sutherland. Financial Times, 14 December 2007, p. 18, Online version: http://www.ft.com/intl/cms/s/0/151f7e72-a9e9-11dc-aa8b-0000779fd2ac.html#axzz3oA3RFXwT (last accessed 5 October 2015).

[135] In the 2000s 0.5 % of the EU GDP was spent on supporting EU farmers and rural areas; in 2009 that stood at 0.45 %. See EU Commission, Situation and Prospects for EU Agriculture and Rural Areas. December 2010, http://ec.europa.eu/agriculture/publi/situation-and-prospects/2010_en.pdf (last accessed 7 August 2015), p. 12.

> stopovers in the US, Europe and Asia. If the cows were willing to slum it in business class, they could have $2800 spending money instead. And they could enjoy this luxury holiday every year.[136]

Anderson and Valenzuela have shown quantitatively how subsidies on cotton could affect particularly developing countries. They argued that the removal of subsidies to cotton production and exports, and of tariffs on cotton imports,

> would boost global economic welfare by $283 million per year, and would raise the price of cotton in international markets by an average of 12.9 per cent. . . . What is striking about the welfare effects is their distribution among developing countries. . . . Especially noteworthy is the relatively large benefit bestowed on Sub-Saharan Africa, of $147 million per year. About two-fifths of that would go to the Cotton-4 and another one-fifth to other West African countries. This is driven by an estimated increase in Sub-Saharan African cotton output and value added in cotton production (net farm income) of nearly one-third, and in the real value of the region's cotton exports of more than 50 per cent. By contrast, cotton output and exports would fall by one-quarter in the United States and would halve in the EU. . .. That would raise Sub-Saharan Africa's share of global cotton exports from 12 to 17 per cent, and the share of all developing countries from 52 to 72 per cent.[137]

Anderson and Valenzuela further demonstrate that the benefits in the cotton sector come almost exclusively from reform of domestic support programmes. More importantly, these reforms would lead to a rise in farmers' incomes "a huge 30 % in Sub-Saharan Africa and around 40 % in West Africa in particular."[138]

However, a number of eminent economists also caution that the developmental benefits of agricultural liberalisation could be very limited, particularly for the poorest countries. In his influential 2005 book on *The End of Poverty* Jeffrey Sachs argued that reduction or elimination of agricultural subsidies in the OECD countries could even harm some of the poorest, mainly net-food importing, countries.[139] Likewise, Dani Rodrik warns that the developmental impact of agricultural liberalisation in the rich countries is not just 'small and highly uneven' across developing countries; it can also be detrimental particularly to those that are net food importers.[140] More recently, Rodrik added that while African cotton growers would benefit from the removal of subsidies in the US, "poor urban consumers who do not grow their food and low-income food-importing countries would be hurt by the increase in the world price of agricultural commodities as rich country subsidies are phased out."[141]

While the wisdom of these cautionary notes about the potential benefits and challenges of agricultural liberalisation to the poor are beyond doubt, it is also notable that the story of subsidies in agriculture goes beyond the economics of it. At a conference organised by Columbia University in 2006 to commemorate the tenth

---

136 Krueger (2004), p. 488.

137 See Anderson and Valenzuela (2007), p. 1290.

138 Anderson and Valenzuela (2007), p. 1292.

139 Sachs (2005), pp. 281–282.

140 Rodrik (2007), pp. 184, 222.

141 Rodrik (2011), p. 258.

anniversary of the WTO, Pascal Lamy used WTO rules on agriculture as an example to make his point that the WTO system is biased against developing countries.[142] The rules reflect that "while political decolonization took place more than 50 years ago, we have not yet completed economic decolonization."[143] Lamy underlined that a fundamental challenge for the DDA is "to correct the remaining imbalances in the trade rules in favour of developing countries and to improve the rules by providing developing countries with authentic market opportunities."[144] With hindsight, Lamy clearly foresaw the difficulties ahead when he said: "There is no way this Round can be successfully concluded if the existing agriculture bias in favor of rich countries is not properly addressed."[145] For a long time, and despite the progress at the Bali Ministerial Conference of December 2013, Doha stood at the edge of the precipice, for the same reasons Lamy identified in 2006. Writing in 2011, James Bacchus, a former member of the US Congress and a former Chairman of the WTO Appellate Body, put the responsibility for the Doha deadlock at the time on US policy on agricultural subsidies.[146] The same can be said about the relevant policies of other WTO members, particularly the EU.

Prospects for any breakthrough in the negotiations by the 10th WTO Ministerial Conference, which took place in Nairobi from 15 to 18 December 2015, were not looking promising until quite late in the process. Indeed, a look at the agriculture negotiations over the past few years would lead one to wonder whether we were not going in circles. For example, it was not reassuring to learn that, as recently as July 2015, several WTO members were heard reiterating: "the draft text reflecting the negotiations up to 2007–2008, known as the fourth revision of the draft modalities

---

[142] Lamy (2008), pp. 5–14.

[143] Lamy (2008), p. 9.

[144] Lamy (2008), p. 9.

[145] Lamy (2008), p. 10.

[146] Bacchus said: "the stubborn refusal of the United States to make additional cuts in our agricultural subsidies is by far the biggest obstacle to a global trade breakthrough." See Bacchus J, Time to Cut Farm Subsidies Now. The Hill, 6 July 2011, http://thehill.com/blogs/congress-blog/economy-a-budget/169807-time-to-cut-farm-subsidies-now (last accessed 7 August 2015). Bacchus quoted figures from the US Congressional Budget Office which showed that, in 2011, US taxpayers would pay about $16 billion in aid to farmers through various programs and argued that this was the time to cut these 'unneeded subsidies' because: the US was under enormous budgetary pressure; the money was going to some of the largest corporate farmers; the price of agricultural products on the market was high enough for the farmers to sell their produce profitably without any need for subsidies; these subsidies are making a Doha deal impossible, and thereby preventing enormous opportunities for overall economic gain for the US and the rest of the world; and that some of the US's subsidy programmes could easily be found illegal under WTO rules. In a more recent article, Paul Krugman, the Nobel Prize Winning Economist, wrote that farm subsidies in the US have become "a fraud-ridden program that mainly benefits corporations and wealthy individuals." See Krugman P, Hunger Games, U.S.A. New York Times, 14 July 2013, http://www.nytimes.com/2013/07/15/opinion/krugman-hunger-games-usa.html?_r=0 (last accessed 27 July 2015).

for agriculture or 'Rev 4', should be the basis for the agriculture discussions."[147] Developing countries have been the principal losers of that continuing drift in the Doha agriculture negotiations.[148] Against this historical background, the Nairobi Ministerial must be recognised as a significant step forward in the decades-old effort to bring fairness and market orientation to the rules governing international trade in agricultural products.

10 Conclusion

"Farm protection is like a weed," observed *The Economist;* "it grows everywhere and seems impossible to eradicate."[149] The number of unsuccessful attempts to deal with agriculture throughout the history of the GATT/WTO system provides ample evidence to support this observation. Indeed, the position of agriculture in the multilateral trading system is rich with paradoxes. While the trading system is able to boast a high degree of success in the liberalisation of trade in industrial goods whose global average tariffs have progressively fallen from above 40 % down to below 4 %, and over half of world trade is MFN duty free,[150] the level of effective protection against the flow of agricultural trade rose for most of GATT's lifetime.[151] The dramatic fall in the share of agriculture in total GDP[152] or merchandise trade[153] over time was matched by a rising share of agricultural disputes

[147] See WTO, Agriculture Negotiations: Informal Meeting, WTO members remain divided on how to advance agriculture negotiations (news item 22 July 2015) https://www.wto.org/english/news_e/news15_e/agng_22jul15_e.htm (last accessed 5 August 2015).

[148] Epps and Trebilcock observed that "While there is debate over the precise extent to which liberalization of agricultural markets will contribute to growth of the sector in developing countries, there is a strong consensus that the outcome of the Doha Round negotiations in agriculture is critical for developing countries." See Epps and Trebilcock (2009), p. 326.

[149] Food and Trade: The New Corn Laws. The Economist, 15 September 2012, http://www.economist.com/node/21562912 (last accessed 26 July 2015).

[150] See Lamy P, speech delivered on the tenth anniversary of the World Trade Institute, University of Bern, 1 October 2010, https://www.wto.org/english/news_e/sppl_e/sppl173_e.htm (last accessed 7 August 2015).

[151] For example, "agricultural support in 22 industrialised countries rose from an average of about $98 billion per year during the period 1979–1986 to an estimated $ 163 billion in 1993." United States General Accounting Office (1994), p. 133. See also Jackson (1977), p. 981.

[152] According to UNCTAD, between 2003 and 2007, agriculture accounted for as little as 3 % of global GDP. This average of course masks a wide range between different countries and groups—less than 2 % in developed countries and less than 6 % in Latin America and the Caribbean, but about one third in West and East Africa. See UNCTAD (2009) World Investment Report 2009, http://unctad.org/en/Docs/wir2009_en.pdf (last accessed 27 July 2015), p. 101.

[153] According to WTO sources, while the share of agricultural exports fell from 47 % of total merchandise exports in 1970 to just 12 in 1996, the corresponding share of manufactures rose from 38 % to 77 % over the same period. See WTO (1998), p. 34.

relative to all GATT cases.[154] While agricultural taxes are an important source of government revenue in most developing countries, agricultural subsidies are an important area of budgetary expenditure in the developed countries. Indeed, with few exceptions, the poorer the country, the higher the agricultural taxes; and the richer the country the higher the agricultural subsidies. According to the World Bank, "the poorest developing countries taxed agriculture the most, and reinvestments of tax revenues in agriculture were low and inefficient."[155] When a country's economy grows steadily and reaches a certain level, it is likely to introduce some form of farm support. The latest examples come from China and India, who are "following the ignoble path trodden by Japan, America and Europe in the 1980s: developing an agricultural industry dependent on handouts." According to *The Economist,* "[t]otal state support to Chinese farmers has more than doubled since 2004."[156] A recent *Financial Times* article observed that agricultural subsidies in middle-income Thailand have led to the formation of a 'rice mountain'.[157]

Agriculture was the 'most explosive issue'[158] during the Uruguay Round negotiations. As Clayton Yeutter, former US Secretary of Agriculture and a key player in the Uruguay Round negotiations for agriculture, put it,

> agricultural trade policy has long been enigmatic, often inexplicable, always exasperating, and frequently counter to the long-term best interests of a nation's own agriculturalists. For half a century, it has provided more distortions to the multilateral trading system than any other segment of the global economy. ... Why so many nations have worked so hard over so many years to impede agricultural trade is almost beyond comprehension![159]

The latest validation of Yeutter's observation came from the US when it recently agreed to pay Brazilian cotton farmers $147.3 million a year in return for Brazil's agreement not to apply WTO-authorised trade sanctions. As a *Financial Times* editorial put it, this in effect means that the US has now extended its "wasteful and distorting agricultural support programme" to some Brazilian farmers, "thus creating another group with a stake in preserving the inefficient status quo."[160] No

---

[154] The share of agricultural disputes in GATT for the 1950s was 23 % of all disputes, while its share for the following three decades (from 1960 to 1989) stood at 50 %. See Hudec (1993), p. 327.

[155] See World Bank (2007) World Development Report 2008: Agriculture for Development, http://siteresources.worldbank.org/INTWDR2008/Resources/WDR_00_book.pdf (last accessed 27 July 2015), p. 98.

[156] Food and Trade: The New Corn Laws. The Economist, 15 September 2012, http://www.economist.com/node/21562912 (last accessed 26 July 2015).

[157] Terazono E, Thai Farm Subsidy Creates Rice Mountain. Financial Times, 18 July 2013, p. 8, Online version: http://www.ft.com/intl/cms/s/0/644225ee-e3f5-11e2-b35b-00144feabdc0.html#axzz3oA3RFXwT (last accessed 5 October 2015). Comparing this to the impact of EU agricultural policy, Teranozo observed: "Europe has had its butter mountain and wine lake. Now the Thai government is sitting on a rice hoard large enough to supply half of global imports for a year..."

[158] Odell (2005), pp. 425–448, 437.

[159] Yeutter (1998), p. 61.

[160] See Pay to Play in Trade. Financial Times, 22 June 2010.

wonder then that agriculture has once again been to blame for Doha's long and agonising life on death's edge. Developing countries have been doomed to be the primary victims, yet again, of that lack of progress in the negotiations.

However, developing countries could not afford to give up on the multilateral trading system. The difficulties in the sector are such that the WTO remains the only forum in which any meaningful solution can be attempted. For example, the Doha negotiations promised the tantalising prospect of abolition of the anomalous and totally unfair and unjustifiable agricultural export subsidies that are a preserve of the rich few. At the Nairobi Ministerial, Doha finally delivered on this promise, but this could not even be contemplated in any other forum. At a broader level, too, only the WTO offers developing countries the opportunity to form coalitions, amongst themselves as well as with several developed countries that share the same goals, in order to extract concessions in agriculture or other sectors. Only a multi-sectoral and multilateral forum such as the WTO allows all countries, whether they are for or against agricultural liberalisation, to make progress in this area through issue linkages and cross-sectoral trade-offs. Indeed, experience in the cognate field of international investment law teaches that the regional and/or bilateral routes—the only plausible options available outside multilateralism—are fraught with danger for developing countries. Developing countries have been complaining, often rightly, about the multilateral trading system for not giving them the voice they deserve. However, the challenges set by the agricultural sector make clear that an imperfect WTO is likely to serve their interest better than no WTO at all.

References

Anderson K, Valenzuela E (2007) The World Trade Organisation's Doha cotton initiative: a tale of two issues. World Econ 30(8):1281–1304. doi:10.1111/j.1467-9701.2007.01053.x

Bairoch P (1989) European trade policy, 1815–1914. In: Mathias P, Pollard S (eds) The Cambridge economic history of Europe volume viii, the industrial economies: the development of economic and social policies. Cambridge University Press, Cambridge, pp 1–160

Blandford D (2012) Climate change policies for agriculture and WTO agreements. In: McMahon J, Desta M (eds) A research handbook on the Agreement on Agriculture. Edward Elgar, Cheltenham, pp 223–249

Cardwell M (2012) Stretching the boundaries of multifunctionality? an evolving common agricultural policy within the world trade legal order. In: McMahon J, Desta M (eds) A research handbook on the Agreement on Agriculture. Edward Elgar, Cheltenham, pp 272–299

Carr E (2001) The twenty years' crisis, 1919–1939: an introduction to the study of international relations, with new introduction by Michael Cox. Palgrave Macmillan, Basingstoke

Corbet H (1979) Preface. In: Corden W (ed) The NIEO proposals: a cool look. Trade Policy Research Centre, London

Dam K (1970) The GATT: law and international economic organization. University of Chicago Press, Chicago

Davis C (2003) Food fights over free trade. Princeton University Press, Princeton

Desta M (2002) The law of international trade in agricultural products: from GATT 1947 to the WTO Agreement on Agriculture. Kluwer, The Hague

Dunoff J (1999) The death of the trade regime. Eur J Int Law 10(7):733–762
Epps T, Trebilcock M (2009) Special and differential treatment in agricultural trade: breaking the impasse. In: Thomas C, Trachtman T (eds) developing countries in the WTO legal system. Oxford University Press, Oxford, pp 323–362. doi:10.1093/acprof:oso/9780195383614.001.0001
FAO (1967) The state of food and agriculture. Rome, FAO
FAO (1971) The state of food and agriculture. Rome, FAO
FAO (1979) The state of food and agriculture. Rome, FAO
Gat A (2006) War in human civilization. Oxford University Press, Oxford
GATT (1958) Trends in international trade: report by a panel of experts (Gottfried Haberler, Roberto de Oliveira Campos, James Meade, and Jan Tinbergen). Sales No. GATT/1958-3
Hillman J (1978) Non-tariff agricultural barriers. University of Nebraska Press, Lincoln
Hillman J (1994) The US perspective. In: Ingersent K, Rayner A, Hine R (eds) Agriculture in the Uruguay round. St. Martin's Press, New York
Howse R (2002) Symposium: the boundaries of the WTO: from politics to technocracy—and back again: the fate of the multilateral trading regime. Am J Int Law 96(1):94–117
Hudec R (1975) World trade diplomacy and the law of GATT. Praeger, Santa Barbara
Hudec R (1993) Enforcing international trade law: the evolution of the modern GATT legal system. Butterworth, Salem
Irwin D (1996) Against the tide: an intellectual history of free trade. Princeton University Press, Princeton
Irwin D, Mavroidis P, Sykes A (2008) The genesis of the GATT. Cambridge University Press, Cambridge
Jackson J (1977) Legal problems of international economic relations. West, St. Paul
Jackson J (1997) The world trading system: law and policy in international economic relations, 2nd edn. MIT Press, Cambridge
Kindleberger C (1989) Commercial policy between the wars. In: Mathias P, Pollard S (eds) The Cambridge economic history of Europe, volume viii, the industrial economies: the development of economic and social policies. Cambridge University Press, Cambridge, pp 161–296
Krueger A (2004) Wilful ignorance: the struggle to convince the free trade sceptics. World Trade Rev 3(3):483–493
Krugman P, Obstefeld M (1997) International economics: theory and practice, 4th edn. Addison-Wesley, Boston
Lamy P (2008) The WTO Doha development agenda: working for a fairer global trading system. In: Janow M, Donaldson V, Yanovich A (eds) The WTO: governance, dispute settlement & developing countries. Juris, Huntington
Lamy P (2013) The Geneva consensus: making trade work for all. Cambridge University Press, Cambridge
Matsushita M, Schoenbaum T, Mavroidis P (2003) The World Trade Organization: law, practice, and policy. Oxford University Press, Oxford
Matthews A (2012) The impact of WTO agricultural trade rules on food security and development: an examination of proposed additional flexibilities for developing countries. In: McMahon J, Desta M (eds) A research handbook on the Agreement on Agriculture. Edward Elgar, Cheltanham, pp 104–132
McMahon J (2006) The WTO Agreement on Agriculture: a commentary. Oxford University Press, Oxford
Odell J (2005) Chairing WTO negotiations. J Int Econ Law 8(2):425–448. doi:10.1093/jielaw/jgi028
Orden D, Blandford D, Josling T (eds) (2011) WTO disciplines on agricultural support: seeking a fair basis for trade. Cambridge University Press, Cambridge
Rodrik D (2007) One economics many recipes: globalization, institutions and economic growth. Princeton University Press, Princeton

Rodrik D (2011) The globalization paradox: democracy and the future of the world economy. Oxford University Press, Oxford

Sachs J (2005) The end of poverty: economic possibilities for our times. Penguin, New York

Samuelson P (1948) Economics: an introductory analysis, 1st edn. McGraw Hill, New York

Samuelson P (1976) Economics, 10th edn. McGraw-Hill, New York

Santana R, Jackson LA (2012) Identifying non-tariff barriers: evolution of multilateral instruments and evidence from the disputes (1948–2011). World Trade Rev 11(3):462–478. doi:10.1017/S1474745612000316

Scott J (2007) The WTO agreement on sanitary and phytosanitary measures: commentary. Cambridge University Press, Cambridge

Smith A (1776) An inquiry into the nature and causes of the wealth of nations. W. Strahan and T. Cadell, London

Southgate J (1967) World trade in sugar. J World Trade Law 1(6):595–631

Stewart T (1993) The Uruguay round: a negotiating history (1986–1992), vol I. Kluwer Law and Taxation Publishers, Deventer

Sumner D, Alston J, Glauber J (2010) Evolution of the economics of agricultural policy. Am J Agric Econ 92(2):403–423

Sykes A (1998) Comparative advantage and the normative economics of international trade policy. J Int Econ Law 1(1):49–82

Trachtman J (2002) Symposium: the boundaries of the WTO: institutional linkage: transcending trade and.... Am J Int Law 96(1):77–93

Trebilcock M, Howse R (1999) The regulation of international trade, 2nd edn. Routledge, London

Trentmann F (2008) Free trade nation: commerce, consumption, and civil society in modern Britain. Oxford University Press, Oxford

United States Department of Agriculture (USDA) (1996) Agricultural outlook. Economic Research Service Stock #AO-235. USDA, Washington, DC

United States General Accounting Office (1994) Report to Congress the General Agreement on Tariffs and Trade: Uruguay Round Final Act should produce overall U.S. economic gains, vol 2. (GAO/GGD-94-83b). GAO, Washington, DC

Wilcox C (1949) A charter for world trade. MacMillan, New York

WTO (1998) Annual report 1998. WTO, Geneva

WTO (2003) World trade report 2003. WTO, Geneva

Yeutter C (1998) Bringing agriculture into the multilateral trading system. In: Bhagwati J, Hirsch M (eds) The Uruguay round and beyond: essays in honour of Arthur Dunkel. Springer, Heidelberg, pp 61–78

Agricultural Trade: How Bad Is the WTO for Development?

Christian Häberli

Contents

Abstract On the face of it, many developing countries, even least developed ones, seem to be doing just fine in terms of agricultural production and trade expansion. This paper cannot answer the question whether the present multilateral rules framework strengthens or imperils resource-poor countries and farmers. Instead, it describes a 'reform programme' which is far from being completed, and it shows where the 'development promises' of the General Agreement on Tariffs and Trade (GATT) and the World Trade Organization (WTO) remain unfulfilled. Based on the experiences with the Uruguay Round, it argues that even the completion of the Doha *Development* Round is likely to fail to address some specific concerns of net food-importing developing countries (NFIDC) and resource-poor farmers. A number of additional specific commitments by developed and emerging economies are required to fulfil the promise "to establish a fair and market-oriented agricultural trading system".

Research for this paper, and editing, was funded by the Swiss National Science Foundation under a grant to the National Centre of Competence in Research on Trade Regulation, based at the World Trade Institute of the University of Berne, Switzerland.

C. Häberli (✉)
NCCR Trade Regulation, World Trade Institute (WTI), Bern, Switzerland
e-mail: christian.haeberli@wti.org

M. Bungenberg et al. (eds.), *European Yearbook of International Economic Law 2016*, European Yearbook of International Economic Law 7,
DOI 10.1007/978-3-319-29215-1_5

1 Introduction

There are many ways to look at the impact on development of what was formerly the General Agreement on Tariffs and Trade (GATT) and is now the World Trade Organization (WTO). Agriculture is certainly a good litmus test when we consider its importance for many developing countries. It was easy to pinpoint protectionism and the lack of commitments as one of the main reasons for pre-WTO agricultural stagnation, and then to praise the results of the Uruguay Round as a boost provided to the multilateral trading system. While various shortcomings in the new agricultural trade rules and the consequences of the very limited tariff and subsidy reductions have become clear, it is less easy to analyse the development impact after 1995.

On the ground, agricultural production and trade appear to have found a path towards more fairness and market-orientation at least in some countries. A multitude of trade-distorting policies and practices persist; but a new interest in farming, after decades of neglect by investors and an apparently structural decline of world market prices, may actually have come as a collateral effect of the food price crisis of 2007–2009. When the Food and Agriculture Organization of the United Nations (FAO) announced that the world's hungry had for the first time in history exceeded one billion people, everybody called for action, including in the WTO. Regrettably, there have been no rules or institutional changes since then, let alone a single tariff reduction (except for European Union (EU) banana imports) nor a lower subsidy ceiling.[1] Nonetheless, since 2012, prices have stabilised at somewhat lower levels, and production keeps increasing almost everywhere. According to the United Nations, the Millennium Development Goal of halving, between 1990 and 2015, the proportion of people who suffer from hunger "should be almost met by 2015".[2]

The rules negotiated more than 20 years ago are being criticised for their lack of development-friendliness. The same goes for today's tariff and subsidy limits. The continuation of the 'reform programme' promised in Article 20 of the Agreement on Agriculture (AoA) collapsed in 2008 with the Doha *Development* Agenda (DDA), leaving the 'haves' with spending ceilings way above those of the (mostly) developing country 'have nots'.

For this and for several other reasons the reform programme remains far from complete. From a general development point of view, the frustration in respect of broken promises is particularly understandable. The contention here is that even if 'Doha' is resuscitated and brings the WTO back on a path of trade liberalisation, the "losers" will not be able to enjoy even the low-hanging fruits unless their situation is recognised and duly taken into consideration in the final package.

[1] Häberli (2012), p. 76.

[2] UN, The Millennium Development Goals Report 2015. New York, 1 July 2015, http://www.un.org/millenniumgoals/2015_MDG_Report/pdf/MDG%202015%20rev%20%28July%201%29.pdf (last accessed 16 July 2015).

Melaku Desta discusses this key question based on a comprehensive account of the history of the multilateral trading system. He submits that the 'development promise' made right at the inception of the GATT in 1947, and consistently repeated especially for agriculture, has remained unfulfilled. The 'long-term objective' of the AoA which is "to establish a fair and market-oriented agricultural trading system"—a unique formula in any WTO agreement, and again enshrined in the DDA adopted in 2001—has eluded especially the poorest developing countries. Market dynamics, and the focus of trade diplomacy on the so-called mega-regionals, may yet exacerbate the gap between the rich trading nations and poor countries with major structural impediments. The latter not only have little food to export but now lack even some of the defense mechanisms available pre-WTO against surplus disposal. Their import bill increases with rising world market prices, but their (mostly subsistence) farmers lack the resources necessary to kick-start production and to cash in on the price bonanza.

For Desta, the 'efficiency model' role of international trade, as advocated by Malthus, Smith, Ricardo, Samuelson, Dunoff and Hudec, simply cannot work on an uneven playing field. He refers to Sumner and others, noting that the decade-long efforts to reverse the structural decline and the low returns on agricultural investment and labour could not succeed as long as rich farmers are allowed to address the 'non-trade concerns' of their governments in their 'multifunctional' role with border protection and trade-distorting subsidies. In 2008 the World Bank (International Bank for Reconstruction and Development, IBRD) observed that "Sub-Saharan Africa enjoys competitive advantage in agriculture." Yet the United Nations Conference on Trade and Development (UNCTAD) noted in the same year that developed countries are "the biggest exporters of food commodities in the international markets. This is in large part due to heavy subsidies to their agriculture. In fact, the inability of developing countries to compete with the subsidized agriculture of developed countries has turned them into net importers of food produced in developed countries."[3]

Desta argues that it is largely due to the special rules for agriculture in the WTO that the theory of competitive advantage fails to prevail: "Even today, agriculture is a class in itself." Agriculture symbolises a global economic system that is skewed against the poor. He even quotes former Director-General Pascal Lamy as seeing in the WTO a bias against developing countries: 10 years after the inception of the organisation Lamy noted that "while political decolonization took place more than 50 years ago, we have not yet completed economic decolonization."[4]

In his conclusions, Desta acknowledges the progress GATT and WTO have brought about for industrial goods whose share in merchandise trade rose from 38 % to 77 % in the period from 1970 to 1996. But the corresponding loss of world market shares for agriculture continues, mainly because of WTO-legal subsidies in rich countries, and agricultural taxes in poor countries. Hence, "[d]eveloping

[3] As quoted by Desta (2016), Section 8.

[4] As quoted by Desta (2016), Section 9.

countries are doomed to be the victims, yet again, of this lack of progress in the agriculture negotiations."[5]

This paper tries to show two things: It first concurs with Desta that under the present rules framework agriculture indeed remains 'special', even after tariffication and a (modest) reduction of border protection and factor-distorting subsidisation. It then looks at some recent policy changes and trade data possibly indicating a three-track development. On the first track, while rich countries have considerably reduced the trade-distorting subsidies to which they remain entitled, many now list 'food security' as a new objective for policies which in effect shield their farmers from competition, at the expense of their own consumers, and of more efficient farmers abroad. On the second track we note an increasing number of potentially or effectively trade-distorting practices in emerging economies, despite relatively constraining WTO limits. Some of these new support policies are notified under the so-called 'Developing Country Green Box'. However, many seem to consist in market management methods which in effect are comparable to (earlier) rich country practices. Some of them may even be damaging for developing countries without sufficient financial resources and thus adding to their problems confining them to a third track with few prospects for their poor farmers.

If this research hypothesis is correct, what would be required is a 'Doha Final Act' addressing these development issues beyond the too ambitious yet overly simplistic tariff and subsidy reduction arithmetic envisaged under the DDA. Failing such a comprehensive approach, both rich country and emerging economy policies may yet again deprive resource-poor governments and farmers of their chance to benefit from the increasing trade opportunities which demographic and economic growth provide at least in theory to all producers with comparative advantages.

Section 2 describes the present rules and their failure from a development perspective. In Sect. 3 the potential Doha negotiation results envisaged back in 2008 are shown as bringing about both partial improvements and setbacks. But more recent farm policy and trade developments demand a refocusing of the negotiations from a development perspective, different from the old non-reciprocity and preference concepts. The intra-developing country divisions marring the Ninth WTO Ministerial Conference in Bali, in November 2013 should have sounded an alarm bell for development analysts.[6] In order to avoid yet another broken promise we can draw guidance both from the meaningless 'Marrakesh NFIDC Decision' and from the implementation of some 'Developing Country Green Box' measures. The conclusions in Sect. 5 suggest a way forward taking into account the growing differences between developing countries.

[5] Desta (2016), Section 10.

[6] Häberli C (2014) After Bali: WTO Rules Applying to Public Food Reserves. FAO Commodity and Trade. Policy Research Working Paper No. 46, http://ssrn.com/abstract=2556233 (last accessed on 9 September 2015).

2 The Agricultural Reform Programme: Progress and Shortcuts

Considering that presently all agricultural tariffs are bound (i.e. can no longer be increased without compensating affected suppliers), and that all subsidies for exports and for trade-distorting domestic support are limited, the Uruguay Round has achieved a substantial part of the reform programme of agricultural trade liberalisation. However, even a cursory look into the three pillars of the AoA provides a picture of a job at best half-done, and increasingly fragile.

First, it should be remembered that complete tariff bindings were a constant demand of agricultural exporters for half a century, together with the abolition of export subsidies. Today, tariffication in agriculture has been achieved. From a systemic point of view and compared with industrialised goods, this is remarkable, even though some rather 'dirty' tariffication had to be accepted in the Uruguay Round negotiations and verifications (as well as very high ceiling bindings across the whole tariff range of some poor developing countries). Yet, after the very modest tariff reductions, many agricultural tariffs remain very high. The so-called 'tariff overhang' (i.e. the fact that the applied rates are often much lower, through regional or preferential trade agreements, or by way of unilateral measures) is no reason for contentment, because a re-increase to the bound levels is always possible, without WTO sanctions. This lack of ambitious market access commitments will neither reduce consumer prices nor improve food security by facilitating trade flows.

Secondly, it is in the domestic subsidy disparities that we find the biggest problems. All trade-distorting farm support is now limited. But the mandatory global reduction of only 20 % in the previously high spending levels of rich subsidisers leaves them with a lot of leeway to support their farmers against foreign competition. Here too, the re-instrumentation of support, and the decline in world market prices after 1995, brought about a huge 'subsidy overhang': most developed countries have shifted much of their farm support from market and price interventions to publicly-funded government programmes and measures with "no, or at most minimal, trade-distorting effects or effects on production".[7] In March 2015 the so-called Cairns Group (of agricultural exporting nations lobbying for agricultural trade liberalisation) compiled the notified domestic support data from 2001 to 2013 (Fig. 1). These data suggest that the current total aggregate measurement of support (CTAMS) of the top ten global traders of agricultural products in 2012 (sum of exports and imports) 'declined dramatically' in most developed countries, "sometimes very significantly to levels well below the legally agreed limits".[8] However,

---

[7] AoA Annex 2 ('Green Box'), paragraph 1.

[8] WTO Committee on Agriculture, Trends in Domestic Support. Communication from the Cairns Group. (Document G/AG/W/141 dated 2 March 2015), with a summary by the WTO Secretariat, https://www.wto.org/english/news_e/news15_e/agcom_04mar15_e.htm (last accessed on 8 July 2015).

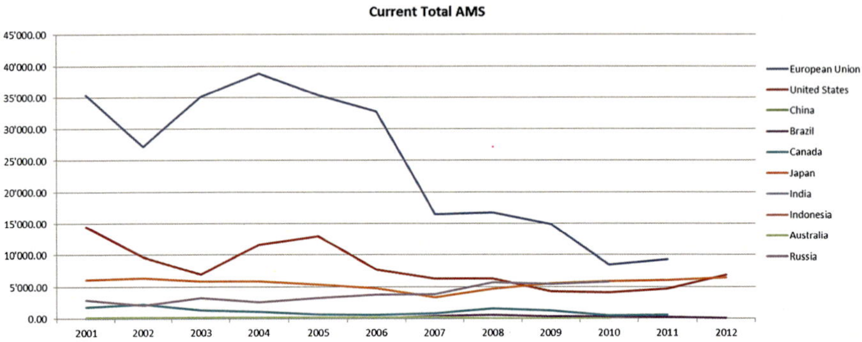

Fig. 1 Trends in Domestic Support. *Sources*: Document G/AG/W/141, and the spreadsheet in the Annex, https://www.wto.org/english/news_e/news15_e/agcom_04mar15_e.htm (last accessed on 8 July 2015)

developed countries increased Green Box expenditures, reaching on average 14.2 % of the value of production. The four developing countries covered also increased Green Box support, which rose on average to 7 % of the value of their production.

The Cairns Group paper further underlines that

> in absolute terms, the total support of all 10 increased between 2001 and 2012, growing more rapidly in the four developing countries (China, Brazil, India and Indonesia) where the starting base was much lower. When compared to the value of production, support in developed countries was stable while in developing countries the proportion increased, although at the end of the period developed countries' support was still proportionately higher, at, on average, 19.3 % of the value of production, whereas in these developing countries it was on average 12.4 %.[9]

Let us presume that this massive shift into the Green Box is not another case of 'box painting' and will indeed eliminate trade-distorting effects. We would still argue that such measures may have a negative development impact, simply because farmers benefiting from them can better displace non-subsidised imports, and because poor countries lack the financial resources for such support.[10] Indeed, those figures fail to reflect the difference between large amounts paid per farm in commercial operations, and the often much smaller amounts paid to poor farmers—let alone the incentives for agricultural foreign direct investment.[11] Worse, a re-increase of CTAMS within the bound ceilings always possible, and this is a serious handicap for poor countries.

Meanwhile, China, India and Brazil have considerably increased their CTAMS (and Japan its Blue Box expenditures, see Fig. 2). Not reflected in these figures are—as expounded further down—input and investment subsidies notified under

[9] Summary by the WTO Secretariat downloaded, https://www.wto.org/english/news_e/news15_e/agcom_04mar15_e.htm (last accessed on 8 July 2015).

[10] Häberli (2015), chapter 20.

[11] Häberli and Smith (2014).

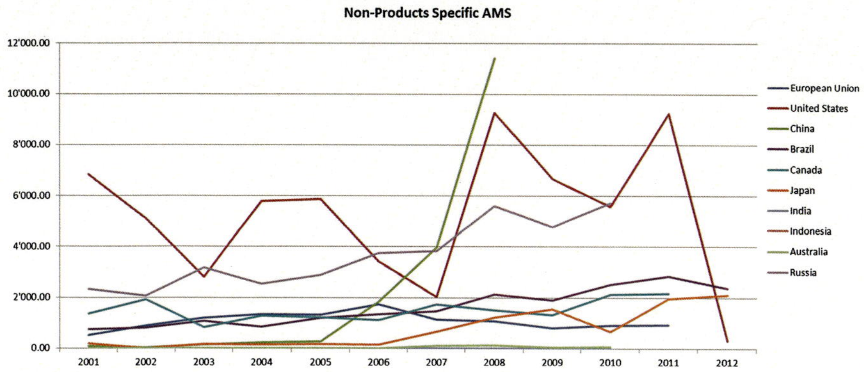

Fig. 2 Domestic support by the top ten agricultural traders (2001–12). *Sources*: Document G/AG/W/141, and the spreadsheet in the Annex, https://www.wto.org/english/news_e/news15_e/agcom_04mar15_e.htm, (last accessed 8 July 2015). Green Box and Art. 6.2 support measures are not reflected here

AoA Article 6.2. Such subsidies, whether trade-distorting or not—have at least trebled in Brazil, India and Indonesia; they have also increased as a proportion of production value.

Thirdly, export subsidies provide the best example of non-completion of the reform programme: only countries which had provided export subsidies during the base period may still maintain them, at a reduced amount, albeit not for other products. All other countries, including newly acceded ones, have no such rights. Moreover, it is in this third pillar of the AoA that we also find the largest 'overhang' between possible and applied expenditures, notwithstanding the declarations of intent made by WTO Ministers in Hong Kong (2005) and Bali (2013), to eventually abolish this form of farm support which Desta calls "anomalous and totally unfair and unjustifiable". Moreover, when considering the whole picture of *export competition* it is also the pillar with the fewest overall disciplines. This deplorable lack of export competition disciplines will only change when the decision taken at the Tenth Ministerial Conference in Nairobi, in December 2015, to abolish all export subsidies and instruments with a similar effect will have been fully implemented. This is even more significant when we analyse the Doha Round 'modalities' from a development perspective.

3 Doha: What About the Poor Countries?

On 6 December 2008 the chairperson of the Agriculture Committee in Special Session, Ambassador Crawford Falconer of New Zealand, submitted the 'Revised Draft Modalities for Agriculture', a text of 131 pages reflecting 7 years of negotiations and summarised in Box 1.[12] It shows the considerable progress achieved since 2001, as well as the outstanding issues.

[12] WTO, Committee on Agriculture in Special Session, Revised Draft Modalities for Agriculture, Document TN/AG/W/4/Rev. 4, dated 6 December 2008, https://www.wto.org/english/tratop_e/agric_e/agchairtxt_dec08_a_e.pdf (last accessed on 9 September 2015).

Box 1 The 2008 'Modalities' for the Doha Round Agricultural Negotiations

For *market access*, tariffs would be mainly reduced according to a formula, with steeper cuts on higher tariffs and ranges of cuts all in single figures. For developed countries the cuts would rise from 50 % for tariffs below 20 %, to 70 % for tariffs above 75 %, subject to a 54 % minimum average, with penalties for *peak* tariffs above 100 % (*capping*). For developing countries the cuts in each tier would be two-thirds of the equivalent tier for developed countries, subject to a maximum average of 36 %. Some products would have smaller cuts thanks to a number of flexibilities designed to take into account various concerns (1) *sensitive products* (available to all countries) with smaller cuts offset by tariff quotas allowing more access at lower tariffs (2) *special products* (for developing countries only, for specific vulnerabilities). The existing *special agricultural safeguard* (SSG) allowed for all tariffied products under AoA Article 5 to be scrapped, and replaced by a new, still hotly contested *special safeguard mechanism* (SSM) for developing countries only.

For *domestic support*, the most important result would be a general commitment limiting the *overall trade-distorting domestic support* (OTDS).[13] Reductions by way of a *tiered formula*—implying higher cuts for higher levels—would have the EU reduce its base period OTDS by 80 %, the US by 70 % and Japan by 75 %. All other countries would reduce OTDS by 55 % (developed countries with high relative levels of OTDS to make an additional effort). Implementation in 6 steps over 5 years, with a "down payment" of one-third on the first day of implementation (25 % for developing countries), and then in equal annual instalments. Developing countries with *de minimis* entitlements would make two-thirds of the cut over 3 years to 6.7 % of production, except for support mainly destined for subsistence/resource-poor farmers. A modest but systemically important innovation would be to separately list and limit domestic support by major products, in order to avoid easy support shifting and *product targeting*. NFIDC without Blue Box programmes, and recent new Members, would not have any OTDS limits, but still face Amber Box and de minimis constraints.

Export subsidies would be eliminated by 2013 (2016 for developing countries), subject to DDA completion. Three other forms of *export competition* would have new rules and limits: (1) *export credits, insurance and*

(continued)

[13] OTDS adds up Amber Box support, de minimis expenditures and Blue Box support. The so-called de minimis expenditures allow for farm support of 5 % or less in the case of developed countries and 10 % or less for developing countries, compared with the total value of the product or products supported. Blue Box support is linked to production, but subject to production limits, and therefore minimally trade-distorting.

Box 1 (continued)

guarantees by way of a new Article 10.2 of the AoA. (2) New disciplines for *food aid* would try to prevent "commercial displacement" of other Members (but not food dumping at the expense of local farmers).[14] (3) *Exporting state trading enterprises* would be subject to a slight revision of GATT Article XVII with specific rules for monopolies.

Least-developed countries (LDC) would not be obliged to make any commitments for tariff or subsidy reductions.

Cotton issues are being addressed in three types of activities: (1) since 2004 in a specific Sub-Committee of the agriculture negotiations, since the 2013 Bali Ministerial Conference (2) through discussions dedicated to the evolving trade situation, and (3) in the Consultative Framework Mechanism, chaired by the Director-General or a Deputy Director-General of the WTO. This third activity is to track developments and to exchange information on aid for cotton through its monitoring tool, the "Evolving Table on Cotton".

Export restrictions—very frequent during the 2007 to 2009 food crisis—remain a big, and still unaddressed, issue affecting especially NFIDC. The same goes for the development-sensitive issue of *differential export taxes* (a common practice in revenue-poor states). Unfortunately for countries negatively affected by such measures, these topics are not even included in the DDA.

No other comprehensive negotiating texts have emerged since 2008 and up to the time of writing this chapter. Many, namely developing country negotiators, still consider this as a basis to finalise the agricultural negotiations. In the next section the question of the development impact will be addressed on the basis of the existing rules and the changes and new disciplines foreseen in 2008 and of recent agricultural policy and trade developments.

4 Outstanding Development Issues: Food Security Governance

Looking at some of the production and trade data, one may think that despite its shortcomings, the WTO-induced reform programme has had at least some success. Agricultural production in developing countries and their world market shares have substantially increased since 1995.[15] The FAO and the Organisation for Economic

---

[14] Heri and Häberli (2011).

[15] In 2013, 8 developing countries were among the 15 leading exporters of agricultural products. (EU = 1; see Table II.14 in WTO International Trade Statistics 2014, Merchandise trade, https://www.wto.org/english/res_e/statis_e/its2014_e/its14_merch_trade_product_e.htm (last accessed

Co-operation and Development (OECD) note that crop production growth among the three groups of least-developed, other developing and developed countries is particularly strong for LDC. Brazil is poised to become the world's foremost food supplier in meeting additional global demand over the next 10 years. By 2024 real prices may have declined from their 2014 levels, but will remain above their pre-2007 levels.[16] Lastly, according to Grant and Boys and contrary to earlier research and despite the relatively modest extent of actual trade liberalisation in agriculture "participation in the GATT/WTO approximately doubles members' agricultural trade."[17]

The food crisis 2007-08 and the ensuing financial crisis also hit agricultural trade, exposing some of the weaknesses of the multilateral trading system. By employing data on specific trade-distorting domestic subsidies and on export incentives beyond a narrow class of import restrictions, Evenett and Fritz estimated the impact on LDC exports of different classes of foreign trade liberalisation and foreign trade distortions. They computed the total reduction in LDC export growth due to foreign trade distortions for each of the years from 2009 to 2013, finding

> that foreign trade distortions, principally in the form of state-provided export incentives, are responsible for cutting LDC exports by on average 5.5 % per annum. This retrograde step has occurred despite WTO rules on subsidies, calling into question the faith that should be placed in the rules-based trading system. That such trade distortions are frequently buried in the minutiae of national tax systems is a further example of murky protectionism and the tendency of governments to substitute transparent for more opaque policy instruments. [. . .] Not only are the development prospects of the LDCs at stake, so is the reputation of a rules-based trading system during the greatest 'stress test' since its creation.[18]

This last study is not limited to agriculture. But given the importance of this sector in many LDC, and the importance of trade distortions caused by agricultural policies, Desta's contention of a broken promise looks all the more solid, even though the causal link between the AoA and the extent and the impact of these positive and negative developments is debatable.

As trade lawyers we must look at the legal content of the Uruguay (and Doha) rules and commitments to see whether they are "fair and market-oriented" and

---

on 16 July 2015)) Also see Anderson K and Strutt A (2011) Asia's Changing Role in World Trade: Prospects for South-South Trade Growth to 2030, Asian Development Bank, ADB Economics Working Paper Series No. 264, http://adb.org/sites/default/files/pub/2011/Economics-WP264.pdf (last accessed on 9 September 2015); and European Commission, Directorate-General for Agriculture and Rural Development, Monitoring Agri-trade Policy, Agricultural Trade in 2013: EU Gains in Commodity Exports, June 2014, http://ec.europa.eu/agriculture/publi/map/index_en.htm (last accessed on 13 July 2015).

[16] Increase in volume and percentage, 2024 relative to 2012–2014. OECD/FAO (2015), OECD-FAO Agricultural Outlook, OECD Agriculture Statistics (database), http://dx.doi.org/10.1787/agr-outl-data-en, (last accessed on 13 July 2015). See also Table II.15 in WTO International Trade Statistics 2014, Merchandise trade, https://www.wto.org/english/res_e/statis_e/its2014_e/its14_merch_trade_product_e.htm (last accessed on 13 July 2015).

[17] Grant and Boys (2012), p. 2.

[18] Evenett and Fritz (2015).

whether "in implementing their commitments on market access, developed country Members would take fully into account the particular needs and conditions of developing country Members." A particularly pertinent question is whether they can not only promote agricultural development generally but also prevent negative impacts. It is probably impossible to agree on the normative value of such terms, and on the commitments they imply for developed countries. What seems clear is that negotiations must be guided by principles such as

> commitments under the reform programme should be made in an equitable way among all Members, having regard to non-trade concerns, including food security and the need to protect the environment; having regard to the agreement that special and differential treatment for developing countries is an integral element of the negotiations, and taking into account the possible negative effects of the implementation of the reform programme on least-developed and net food-importing developing countries.[19]

If and when a negotiation is concluded, the result will have to be either ratified on the assumption that the envisaged commitments reflect those principles—or rejected, if it does not. True, the notion of a *Single Undertaking* (requiring acceptance of all agreements and commitments) makes it difficult to oppose specific results on the grounds that they do not fulfil the development promise. Nonetheless, the consensus rule prevailing in the WTO gives even its smallest Member a tool to block a result which goes against its fundamental interest. Mindful of past broken promises, countries failing to obtain development-specific rules and measures in the WTO's longest package negotiation may want to use one last chance for real improvement in a *Doha Final Act* which will one day, perhaps, mark the end of the Development Round.

Ever since 1979 when the 'Enabling Clause'[20] opened the door for non-reciprocal trade diplomacy and concessions, the traditional way to redeem development promises has been to provide special and differential treatment (SDT) to developing countries. The WTO Secretariat has produced several information notes on the utilisation of the umpteen SDT provisions contained in all WTO agreements. They allow for non-reciprocal concessions, longer implementation periods, and smaller tariff and subsidy cuts for developing countries (with no such obligations for LDC).[21] The opinions on the general usefulness of SDT vary widely.[22] But perhaps two Uruguay Round legal texts specifically addressing agricultural development concerns allow for an assessment of their success and of

[19] AoA Preamble, Recital 6.

[20] Differential and More Favourable Treatment, Reciprocity and Fuller Participation of Developing Countries (Enabling Clause), GATT Doc L/4903, Decision of 28 November 1979, paras 1 and 2(a).

[21] WTO, Information on the Utilization of Special and Differential Treatment Provisions. The last document in this series is WT/COMTD/W/77/Rev.1/Add.4 dated 7 February 2002.

[22] For a proposal to stabilise preferential tariffs in order to increase its efficiency, see Bartels and Häberli (2010).

possible pitfalls. Both texts had unforeseen consequences: the first turned out to be a blind alley, while the second might quickly become a tool for justifying increased farm support limited only by the financial capacity of the developing country concerned.

1. The special situation of the NFIDC gave rise to a last-minute addition to the Legal Texts agreed in Marrakesh, in March 1994. Apparently aware of the limits to an automatic spread of the trade liberalisation benefits to all and sundry, the AoA negotiators anticipating 'possible negative effects of the reform programme' also adopted the Marrakesh NFIDC Decision, which foresees four possibilities for mitigating such effects: (1) food aid in grant form; (2) technical and financial assistance; (3) special conditions applying to agricultural export credit disciplines; and (4) new international financing facilities.[23] To cut a long story short, the Marrakesh Decision was never used.[24] It can hardly be said that no one claimed negative effects from trade liberalisation.[25] Rather, there was no consensus on such a correlation. Hence, when the world leaders and international financial institutions called for immediate solutions to the food crisis of 2007–2009, this so-called NFIDC Decision was not even mentioned by the WTO Director-General.[26]
2. The second text is the so-called 'Developing Country Green Box' in AoA Article 6.2. It provides that for certain government assistance programmes encouraging agricultural and rural development in developing countries, or diversification from growing illicit narcotic crops, the support provided under these programmes does not count in their CTAMS. The exact size of the window allowing for investment subsidies (for all farmers) or agricultural input subsidies (for low-income or resource-poor producers) is quite difficult to assess. Perhaps for this reason it was a long time before such programmes started to be notified (Box 2 summarises actual use).[27]

[23] Decision on Measures Concerning the Possible Negative Effects of the Reform Programme on Least-Developed and Net Food-Importing Developing Countries. Document G/AG/5/Rev. 10 dated 23 March 2012 lists 32 developing countries, and all LDC, as possible beneficiaries of the Marrakesh Decision.

[24] Document WT/COMTD/W/77/Rev. 1 dated 21 September 2001 has 57 pages of SDT measures. On the implementation of the NFIDC Decision it notes that the World Bank considered that "the impact of the Uruguay Round on food prices was small and that it did not consider it necessary to establish a special UR adjustment facility."

[25] Howse and Teitel (2009), p. 48.

[26] Häberli (2013).

[27] It may also be noted that the Committee on Agriculture, until a few years ago, had received very few "counter-notifications" under AoA Article 18.6.

Box 2 "Developing Country Green Box" (AoA Article 6.2)
More than 50 Members have notified Article 6.2 programmes. For instance, Bahrain has a subsidy specific to poultry. Brazil has a debt rescheduling and various other credit programmes. Chile offers different investment incentives. Honduras introduced a productive solidarity voucher and a technology voucher. India supports with few further specifications or delimitations its low-income and resource-poor farmers and provides other input subsidies. Namibia has a livestock marketing scheme. Nigeria has a domestic fertiliser programme. Oman has a national project for date palm development. Thailand provides soft loans for agricultural investment and farming input assistance. Uruguay has a project simply called 'Rural Uruguay'. Vietnam offers freight subsidies for the transport of commodities and production inputs to mountainous and remote regions.[28]

All of these programmes were critically examined by other WTO Members in the Committee on Agriculture. But until today their compatibility with the intricate conditions in Article 6.2 has never been formally challenged in dispute settlement.

The question relevant for this paper is whether the financial sums spent under these new farm support practices—apparently none by an LDC—can 'more than minimally' impact on production and trade by other (developing) countries, over and above the Aggregate Measurement of Support (AMS) entitlements of the countries involved. Looking at the countries that have notified such programmes it also becomes clear that the poorest developing countries have yet to support their farmers in any comparable way or extent. At this point we would note that the increasing recourse to Article 6.2, especially by large countries, is unlikely to reduce trade distortions.

5 Conclusions: Fix It While It Ain't Broke

This overview of evolving agricultural trade rules, present (non-)negotiations and unfulfilled development promises is but a summary of the development challenge narrative aptly outlined by Melaku Desta. This paper presents the development fault lines in the Uruguay Round texts with the help of the NFIDC Decision and of the growing farm support (1) by developed countries (including measures notified under the Green Box) and (2) by emerging economies (e.g. measures notified under AoA Article 6.2). A scenario emerges of a new and also rapidly growing inequality not only between developed and emerging economies but—and here lies

[28] Cf. WTO Agriculture Information Management System and the 'Transparency Toolkit', http://agims.wto.org/ (last accessed on 15 July 2015).

the 'development crux'—also in respect of the poorest WTO Members, although many of them are increasing their agricultural production and trade. The Doha Development Agenda with its export-biased and unilinear duty and subsidy reduction approach fails to provide these countries and their farmers with the tools they need when facing their better-supported competitors both at home and on regional and world markets. Still less can the classic SDT measures—nor, for that matter, the ever eroding tariff preferences—address this issue.

In conclusion, a way forward can only be suggested here by way of a to-do list for a more equitable development outcome. A Doha Final Act, if carefully drafted on the basis of new proposals by the potential losers of the ensuing competition for market shares, might be the place for providing for some sort of compensation, in a way not dissimilar to some of the 'cohesion measures' offered at each EU enlargement, or in most North–South Regional Trade Agreements. Such a package of coordinated measures should comprise the following elements, irrespective of their implementation at the multilateral and regional or sectoral levels:

1. Poor developing countries without the capacity to substantially distort trade must retain ample policy space for at least the temporary protection of fragile agricultural producers. It should be remembered that tariffs are just about the only policy tool available to many poor countries which can hardly afford to subsidise their farmers. This calls for effective and easy-to-activate safeguards (rather than tariffs which will disappear one way or the other).
2. An increase in domestic support flexibility for developing countries may be necessary given the context in which the present rules and spending ceilings were negotiated. However, new 'races of finance ministers' cannot be allowed. AoA Article 6.2 needs to be revisited; both for stricter disciplines to ensure that such measures have no detrimental effect on other (developing) countries and to strictly limit all input subsidies to poor countries unable to provide other forms of support to their resource-poor farmers.
3. As became clear at the Bali Ministerial Conference, it is imperative to prevent 'Basmati Wars'. Risk management tools such as national and regional (and 'virtual') food reserves and new production risk insurance schemes may require a special provision in the Green Box, and under the relevant export competition disciplines.
4. The absence of new disciplines in export restrictions and export competition, especially by way of food aid, are the most blatant threats to food security. These problems have yet to be addressed. As a minimum, the November 2011 G20 decision to exempt food aid supplies from export restrictions should be made mandatory. Here too, however, additional food aid disciplines are needed which not only prevent 'commercial displacement' but also protect local producers, so as to ensure that such food aid only reaches beneficiaries unable to pay for their minimum daily intake.
5. The foreseeable agricultural negotiation results are likely to benefit mainly those producers and exporters who are already competitive today. Three additional

food security-enhancing commitments should thus be undertaken which would benefit less resilient developing countries and producers.

(a) Mandatory and quantified Aid for Trade, a specific part of which should then be earmarked for food crop production in NFIDC.
(b) A formal commitment not to decrease food aid when food prices on the world market increase.
(c) Securing non-reciprocal trade preferences for countries whose food security depends on their exports.

References

Bartels L, Häberli C (2010) Binding tariff preferences for developing countries under article II GATT. J Int Econ Law 13(4):969–995. doi:10.1093/jiel/jgq051

Desta MG (2016) Trade in agricultural products: should developing countries give up on the WTO promise for a fair and market-oriented agricultural trading system? A historical and theoretical analysis. In: Bungenberg M, Hermann C, Krajewski M, Terhechte J (eds) European Yearbook of International Economic Law, vol 7. Springer, Heidelberg, pp 67–102

Evenett S, Fritz J (2015) Crisis-era trade distortions cut LDC export growth by 5.5 % per annum. In: Hoekman B (ed) The global trade slowdown: a new normal?. Centre for Economic Policy Research (CEPR). CEPR Press, London, pp 267–278. http://www.voxeu.org/sites/default/files/file/Global%20Trade%20Slowdown_nocover.pdf (last accessed 9 September 2015)

Grant J, Boys K (2012) Agricultural trade and the GATT/WTO: does membership make a difference? Am J Agric Econ 94(1):1–24. doi:10.1093/ajae/aar087

Häberli C (2012) Do WTO rules secure or impair the right to food? In: Desta MG, McMahon J (eds) Research handbook on international agricultural trade. Edward Elgar, Cheltenham, UK and Northampton, US, pp 70–103

Häberli C (2013) God, the WTO—and hunger. In: Nadakavukaren Schefer K (ed) Poverty and the international economic law system: duties to the poor. Cambridge University Press, Cambridge, pp 79–106, 10.1017/CBO9781139507097.010

Häberli C (2015) The story of community preference for food security. In: McMahon J, Cardwell M (eds) Research handbook on EU agriculture law. Edward Elgar, Cheltenham, UK and Northampton, US, pp 437–462

Häberli C, Smith F (2014) Food security and agri-foreign direct investment in weak states: finding the governance gap to avoid "land grab". Modern Law Rev 77(2):189–222. doi:10.1111/1468-2230.12062

Heri S, Häberli C (2011) Can the World Trade Organization ensure that food aid is genuine? Dev World Rev Trade Comp 1(1):1–70

Howse R, Teitel R (2009) Beyond the divide: the International Covenant on Economic, Social and Political Rights and the World Trade Organization. In: Joseph S, Kindley D, Waincymer J (eds) The World Trade Organization and human rights. interdisciplinary perspectives. Edward Elgar, Cheltenham, pp 39–68. doi:10.4337/9781781953044.00007

From GATS to TiSA: Pushing the Trade in Services Regime Beyond the Limits

Jane Kelsey

Contents

Abstract Trade in services agreements are creatures of neoliberalism. As normative and disciplinary instruments, they have evolved over time, reaching progressively deeper into the regulatory domain of nation states and imposing fetters on the autonomy and authority of governments to determine the best way to regulate

J. Kelsey (✉)
Faculty of Law, The University of Auckland, Auckland, New Zealand
e-mail: j.kelsey@auckland.ac.nz

M. Bungenberg et al. (eds.), *European Yearbook of International Economic Law 2016*, European Yearbook of International Economic Law 7,
DOI 10.1007/978-3-319-29215-1_6

services in the national interest. With the paralysis in the World Trade Organization (WTO), new generation free trade and investment agreements offered a way to redesign the General Agreement on Trade in Services (GATS), align it to new technologies and corporate imperatives, and further circumscribe governments' regulatory options. Ever-more aggressive ambitions, now being pursued through a plurilateral Trade in Services Agreement (TiSA) with a view to exporting it back into the WTO, have exacerbated the long-standing tensions that beset the GATS. As these agreements continue to push the boundaries, their attempts to lock governments into a more extreme version of the troubled neoliberal paradigm will heighten the problems of legitimacy confronting the agreements themselves and the WTO.

1 Introduction

Trade in services agreements are creatures of post-1970s neoliberalism, when services were reconceived as market phenomena and the rules that govern them redesigned to serve a globally integrating mode of capitalism. They have evolved over time, reaching progressively deeper into the regulatory domain of nation states and imposing fetters on the autonomy and authority of governments to determine the best way to regulate services in the national interest.

Harnessing services to 'trade' treaties offered a potent means of embedding neoliberalism, binding governments to maintain the model even when it was no longer the accepted orthodoxy. That time is imminent. The global financial crisis shattered the seeming omnipotence of deeply integrated and lightly regulated financial markets, while Europe's sovereign debt crisis has sharpened calls to end an agenda that rewards the rich and punishes the rest. The super-powers are not so super any more.

More broadly, high-level debates on burgeoning inequality, job insecurity, and market and regulatory failures within and between countries, rich and poor, signal a crisis of legitimacy for neoliberalism.[1] In its wake there is a renewed recognition that the state, not the market, bears the primary responsibility for addressing these failings.

Far from retreating, the champions of trade in services agreements have gone on the offensive. For both political and technical reasons, the General Agreement on Trade in Services (GATS) in the World Trade Organization (WTO) never achieved their original goals and a second attempt fell victim to the failed Doha round. Frustrated, rich services exporting states and corporate lobbies intensified their

[1] Eg. Stiglitz J, Report of the Commission of Experts of the President of the United Nations General Assembly on Reforms of the International Monetary and Financial System, United Nations, 21 September 2009; Piketty (2013) and Wolf (2014).

efforts to redesign and extend the GATS architecture, rules and technical tools through bilateral and regional deals, paradoxically making the regime more complex and fragmented. The quest to consolidate and refine those agreements into a single 'gold standard' set of global rules has led to a trio of mega-negotiations, including a plurilateral Trade in Services Agreement (TiSA). The end game for TiSA is to supplant the GATS within the WTO, a provocative move that could imperil both TiSA and the WTO.

These developments may have bypassed trade lawyers who struggle with the concept of trade in services and dismiss it as not being real trade. They are right. Traditional commodities trade, which dominated the GATT until the Uruguay round, has been swamped by the incorporation of intellectual property, foreign investment, government procurement, services, and other non-trade areas of law into the global 'trade' regime.

Trade in services agreements are really about expanding globalised markets by restricting what states can do. From their inception, they targetted domestic laws and policies behind the border. The main goals were to take down barriers to foreign direct investment and constrain the freedom of governments to regulate. In the oft-quoted words of former WTO Director-General Renato Ruggiero in 1998, the GATS reached 'into areas never before recognized as trade policy. I suspect that neither governments nor industries have yet appreciated the full scope of these guarantees or the full value of existing commitments'.[2]

Unlike other areas of international economic regulation, trade in services has very little case law.[3] And, perhaps more than in any other area, the texts are constantly changing. This chapter focuses on trade in services agreements as evolving normative and disciplinary instruments, and argues that attempts to lock governments into a troubled 'orthodoxy' through progressively deeper trade in services obligations will heighten its problems of legitimacy.

The paper explains how the original GATS was framed by the compromises of the Uruguay round. With the paralysis of the Doha round, new generation 'free trade' agreements offered a way to redesign the GATS model, align it to new technologies, and further circumscribe governments' regulatory options. While

---

[2] Ruggiero R, Towards GATS 2000—A European Strategy, address to the European Commission Conference on Trade in Services, Brussels, 2 June 1998, https://www.wto.org/english/news_e/sprr_e/bruss1_e.htm (last accessed 21 April 2015).

[3] As of April 2015 23 cases had cited the GATS in the request for consultations, but only six had been subject of a panel or Appellate Body decision and most involved some form of e-commerce: Appellate Body, *European Communities – Regime for the Importation, Sale and Distribution of Bananas – Complaint by Ecuador*, (WT/DS27/AB/R), 9 September 1997; Appellate Body, *Canada – Certain Measures Affecting the Automotive Industry,* (WT/DS139/AB/R), 31 May 2000 (also DS142); Panel, *Mexico – Measures Affecting Telecommunications Services,* (WT/DS204/R), 2 April 2004; Appellate Body, *US – Measures Affecting the Cross-Border Supply of Internet Gambling and Betting Services*, (WT/DS285/AB/R), 7 April 2005; Appellate Body, *China – Measures Affecting Trading Rights and Distribution Services for Certain Publications and Audiovisual Entertainment Products,* (WT/DS363/AB/R), 21 December 2009; Panel, *China – Certain Measures Affecting Electronic Payment Services*, (WT/DS413/R), 16 July 2012.

these agreements have successfully pushed the boundaries, they also erected new barriers to the ideal of a globally integrated services regime. The ever-more aggressive ambitions for that 'twenty-first century regime', now being pursued through TiSA, have exacerbated the long-standing tensions that beset the GATS.

2 Pressure Points

Three themes run through this narrative. The first is the development divide between: services-exporting countries and corporations whose interests have dominated the trade in services regime; newly-ascendant large developing countries who are asserting their right to influence the rules; and the majority of the global South who face being crippled by new obligations they have no control over negotiating. Those tensions have been inflamed by blatant moves by services demandeurs to bypass opposition in the WTO, negotiate TiSA on its margins under conditions of secrecy, and then dock it onto the GATS. Whether or not the old superpowers' succeed in reasserting their dominance, their actions threaten to bring three decades of geopolitical tension over services to a head.

The second theme is the quest to make and re-make a 'trade in services' regime that is coherent, workable, and reflects the commercial realities it is intended to serve. The failure to achieve that goal reflects the intrinsic flaws of the project itself. These agreements seek to abstract services from the social relations in which they are inextricably embedded. Services are and will always be social phenomena, however much the agreements try to screen out this reality. Insurance, tourism, telecommunications and the Internet, broadcasting, supermarkets and e-retailers, rubbish disposal, mining companies and construction firms, dental treatment, lawyers and accountants all involve social relations that frame people's everyday existence.

The 'trade' discourse reconceives them as monetised commodities, abstracted from their social context and functions, and transacted in transnational markets where buyers and sellers, transnational corporations and corner businesses supposedly have equal power. Specific services are then fettishised into comparable legal artefacts (described by numerical product classifications) so they can be subjected to generic rules. The commercial dimension of these services is privileged over all their other functions under the veneer of a neutral, rules-based system. The discourse is closed, with legal rules providing no entry point for those elements that are excluded, except through the limited exceptions provisions.

Constructing a legal architecture, rules and techniques that can give effect to this fiction is a complex task that has so far proved unachievable. Even were those techniques perfected, the project itself would fail. Binding and enforceable constraints that force governments to choose between their treaty obligations and domestic imperatives are not sustainable. Governments have an inescapable responsibility to regulate services as complex phenomena that perform multiple social, cultural, economic and commercial functions for their national or localised communities.

This conflict has deepened since the financial crisis, as critiques of the market paradigm have broadened beyond public services to encompass the risk-tolerant and highly liberalised approach to regulating all services. Moves to extend, rather than retract, the GATS financial services agreement and introduce a far-reaching chapter on e-commerce, revealed in leaked TiSA documents, confirm its potential to heighten the contradictions that are destabilising neoliberal globalisation and financialised capitalism.

The third theme is the state-corporate nexus under neoliberalism, an intimacy that is evident throughout the negotiating history from GATS to TiSA, and the corresponding democratic deficit that excludes legislators and citizens from the negotiating process. Once global citizens came to understand the implications of the GATS and other WTO agreements, the secrecy that protected the Uruguay round from scrutiny became untenable and the WTOs working documents and negotiating texts were exposed to greater public scrutiny. Resort to bilateral and regional FTAs allowed the demandeurs to retreat once more behind a wall of secrecy. The extraordinary confidentiality agreement that aims to shield the TiSA negotiations from public scrutiny even past its conclusion, and the disclosures in leaked documents, have revived claims of a democratic deficit and a corporate-led assault on national sovereignty. These concerns are shared by a number of WTO members who risked becoming unwilling recipients of its outcome.

3 Genesis of the GATS

The GATS was,[4] as the European Commission said, "not just something that exists between Governments. It is first and foremost an instrument for the benefit of business".[5] In the mid-1970s a handful of powerful players in the American finance industry, led by executives from AIG and American Express, recognised that the finance, transport and telecommunications sectors were key to the transformation of industrial capitalism. They had two main goals: to secure a multilateral agreement on investment, and to preempt regulation of the technologies that were beginning to revolutionise the cross-border movement of capital, data and related services.

They wanted rules that were binding and enforceable, yet generic and flexible enough to apply to the as-yet unknown. The analogy with the General Agreement

[4] This historical account draws on four sources: Aronson J (1988), Negotiating to Launch Negotiations: Getting Trade in Services onto the GATT Agenda, Pittsburgh PA: Pew Program in Case Teaching and Writing in International Affairs, Case Study No. 125–92-R; Drake and Nicolaidis (1992), pp. 37–100; Feketekuty (1988), pp. 295–322; Kelsey (2008), pp. 58–81.

[5] European Commission (2000) Opening World Markets for Services—Towards GATS 2000, p. 17 (no longer cached) quoted in Corporate Europe Observatory, GATS: Undermining Public Services Worldwide, CEO Observer, Issue 9, June 2001.

on Tariffs and Trade (GATT) was a convenient artifice. Concepts of market access, national treatment, most-favoured-nation (MFN) status, and non-tariff barriers could be adapted to justify restraints on government regulation. Influential US officials were recruited to the cause and seeded the novel idea of 'trade in services' in the OECD trade committee. By 1984 they had secured a critical mass of support. The US made inclusion of a trade in services agreement a non-negotiable component of any new GATT round.

The legal vehicle was new, but the goals were familiar and provoked determined opposition from the global South, led by India and Brazil. According to SP Shukla, India's ambassador during the formative pre-round period, the prospect that services would transcend the narrow confines of cross-border transactions and include foreign investment "had the potential of rendering [the GATT] into an effective instrument to support and promote the activities of the transnational corporations."[6] His predictions were informed by recent battles in the United Nations over the New International Economic Order and the stalemate over a code of conduct for transnational corporations.[7] By the early 1980s South governments who were being pushed into the liberalisation and privatisation of services through World Bank and International Monetary Fund's structural adjustment programmes were very protective of what is today called their 'policy space'.

Shukla observed that "no other round in the GATT was preceded by such a long gestation period and such acute labour pains. That is precisely because the developing countries saw through the game."[8] Formally, the services negotiations were conducted on a parallel track to the rest of the Uruguay round. Coverage of investment was limited to commercial presence—in effect, foreign direct investments in services sectors.[9]

4 The GATS 1994

Once the negotiations began, developing countries' resistance was worn down by a strategy of divide and rule.[10] At one level the USTR and corporate lobbies were remarkably successful, securing a novel multilateral agreement within the umbrella

[6] Shukla SP (2000) From GATT to WTO and Beyond, Working Paper 195, Helsinki: UNU World Institute for Development Economic Research (UNU/WIDER), p. 14.

[7] The UN and Transnational Corporations, UN Intellectual History Project, Ralph Bunche Institute for International Studies, The CUNY Graduate Center, Briefing Note no. 17, July 2009, http://www.unhistory.org/briefing/17TNCs.pdf (last accessed 15 October 2015).

[8] Interview with SP Shukla by Sol Picciotto, 8 December 2005, New Delhi (on file with author).

[9] The other main text dealing with foreign investment was the Agreement on Trade-Related Investment Measures.

[10] Aronson J (1988) Negotiating to Launch Negotiations: Getting Trade in Services onto the GATT Agenda, Pittsburgh PA: Pew Program in Case Teaching and Writing in International Affairs, Case Study No. 125–92-R, p. 21.

of the new WTO. As the WTO Secretariat recognised, rules and commitments that were enforceable through its new judicial system provided a bulwark against change: "bindings undertaken in the GATS have the effect of protecting liberalization policies, regardless of their underlying rationale, from slippages and reversals and, thus, improve domestic conditions for investment, trade and growth".[11] The rubric of a non-discriminatory rules-based system gave instant legitimacy to a pro-market, business-friendly model of regulating services. Concepts of national treatment, market access, MFN and transparency were transposed from the GATT with minimal scrutiny.

Despite this, Shukla considered the final GATS 1994 text was a victory. WTO members could limit their MFN obligations.[12] Developing countries were promised special and differential treatment through access to new commercial opportunities, while their own obligations would be limited, especially for least developed countries (LDCs).[13] Although no emergency safeguard mechanism had been agreed, there was a 3-year deadline on its completion.[14]

But the most significant and durable compromises involved the GATS architecture and schedules of commitments. Two experimental trade in services agreements had been negotiated during the round as potential precedents for the GATS—a services protocol to the Australia New Zealand Closer Economic Relations Trade Agreement (ANZCERTA) that came into force in 1989,[15] and the Canada US Free Trade Agreement 1989 that was expanded to include Mexico under the North American Free Trade Agreement (NAFTA), coming into force in January 1994.[16] However, the final GATS text diverged from them in important ways as noted below.

4.1 *'Trade in Services'*

The concept of 'trade in services' was novel, so it had to be defined.[17] The 'supply' of a service extended across the entire supply chain: the production, distribution, marketing, sale and delivery of a service at all levels of government, including entities exercising delegated authority.[18] The rules were applied broadly to measures "in the form of a law, regulation, rule, procedure, decision, administrative

[11] Council for Trade in Services, Recent Developments in Services Trade—Background Note by the Secretariat, S/C/W/94, 9 February 1999, p. 10 at para 23.

[12] GATS Article II.2.

[13] GATS Article IV.

[14] GATS Article X.1.

[15] The Services Protocol to the Australia New Zealand Closer Economic Relations Trade Agreement 1989.

[16] North American Free Trade Agreement 1994.

[17] See Feketekuty (1988), ch 5.

[18] GATS Article XXVIII(b).

action, or any other form",[19] which directly and indirectly affected trade in services.[20]

Specifying what constituted 'international trade' was more difficult. The ANZCERTA services protocol simply granted rights to persons of the other State and the services they supplied, including through commercial establishments in the other country. The Canada-United States Free Trade Agreement (CUSFTA) was more developed, with inter-related chapters on services and investment and a separate chapter on temporary movement of business personnel.

The GATS adopted a much more abstract definition. 'Trade' between service suppliers and consumers of different countries was disaggregated into four 'modes'[21]: from a supplier in one country to a consumer in another (mode 1); a national of one country consuming the service in the territory of the supplier (mode 2); by a service supplier of one country through a commercial presence in the territory of another (mode 3); and a natural person from one country delivering a service in another country (mode 4).

This approach was hopelessly dysfunctional for states and corporate lobbies seeking to liberate the transnational supply chains for services from government regulation. But it was essential for defensive reasons, so governments could delineate and restrict their obligations, including by different commitments for each mode of delivery, especially in sensitive services sectors.

The 'modes' also disguised a form of doublespeak. Commercial presence was code for foreign direct investment in services. The definition of mode 4 and an Annex on Temporary Movement of Natural Persons was open ended, suggesting that any form of services labour might be given rights of temporary presence; in practice, governments of preferred destinations limited its application to professionals, executives, higher skilled workers and inter-corporate transferees.

4.2 Classifying Services

Having defined what was meant by 'trade in services', the next challenge was to identify the services that would be governed by the national treatment and market access rules in each mode. The GATT Secretariat prepared a document for governments to use when preparing their schedules during the Uruguay round. Known as W/120,[22] it was based on a provisional UN Central Product Classification from

[19] GATS Article XXVIII(a).

[20] Appellate Body, *European Communities – Regime for the Importation, Sale and Distribution of Bananas – Complaint by Ecuador*, (WT/DS27/AB/R), 9 September 1997, p. 63 at para 136.

[21] GATS Article I.2.

[22] WTO, Services Sectoral Classification List, MTN.GNS/W120, 10 July 1991.

1991 (UNCPCprov).[23] Its use was not mandatory; some countries, notably the US, made up their own classification or chose not to specify one.[24]

The W/120 list of 'product classifications' assigned services to 11 sectors and more than 160 sub-sectors. These classifications reflected how commercial service suppliers perceived them, not how they were experienced by people and their communities. Midwives were a business service, shops were distribution services, cruise ships were transportation. The classifications were also limited in scope, reflecting the fact that in 1991 many services were still viewed as social phenomena, privatisations were relatively new, and the worldwide web had just been invented.

4.3 Schedules

The proposed precedents of ANZCERTA and NAFTA used a negative list to identify service sectors, areas of policy or measures that were *not* subject to the core rules. South governments insisted the GATS instead used a positive list that specified which sectors were governed by the market access and national treatment rules, and any additional commitments[25]; that would, in turn, determine whether the disciplines on domestic regulation of professional qualifications, licensing and technical standards applied to a service.[26]

The GATS schedules that were signed off in 1993 were a technical nightmare. It takes considerable technical skill to deconstruct the complex architecture of different commitments on a specific service sub-sector for market access, national treatment and any voluntary additional commitments, in each of the four modes of supply, overlaid by horizontal commitments and limitations that apply across all the listed services. Negotiators had problems drafting them and government policy makers had problems interpreting and applying them. Business complained of incoherence where governments committed only some sub-sectors in a services supply chain and that the combination of the GATS text, appendices and schedules were "not user friendly and are somewhat opaque".[27]

These complexities created the risk of unintended commitments. An analysis by the WTO secretariat in 1999 concluded that 1420 of 7040 market access

---

[23] United Nations, Provisional Central Product Classification, Statistical Papers, Series M. No 77, New York, 1991, http://unstats.un.org/UNSD/cr/registry/regcst.asp?Cl=9&Lg=1 (last accessed 21 April 2015).

[24] In *US – Gambling*, the US was held to the W/120 meaning in the absence of clear words to the contrary. Appellate Body Report, *US – Gambling*, WT/DS285/AR/R, pp. 58–59, para 176.

[25] GATS Article XX.

[26] GATS Article VI.1 and VI.5.

[27] Quoted in Feketekuty G (1999) Assessing the WTO General Agreement on Trade in Services And Improving the GATS Architecture, Institute for Trade and Commercial Diplomacy, http://www.commercialdiplomacy.org/articles_news/brookings.htm (last accessed 21 April 2015).

commitments in GATS schedules appeared to be mis-scheduled.[28] Even the powerful players incurred obligations they did not foresee. In its report on a complaint by Antigua and Barbuda against a US ban on Internet gambling, the WTO Panel made it clear that the US was bound by the commitment, even if it was an unintentional mistake.[29] The EU failed to list an MFN exception for distribution services in the case of banana imports from the African, Caribbean and Pacific (ACP) states under the Lomé agreements.[30] That was a catalyst for the EU to end its preferential arrangements with its former colonies and require six groups of ACP countries to negotiate separate regional Economic Partnership Agreement (EPA) with Europe.

Once GATS commitments were made they became impossible to rescind without consent, which in practice reflected the relative power of the interested players. Technically, a Member could withdraw a commitment after 90 days notice if there was no objection.[31] That mechanism has rarely been invoked. The EU negotiated adjustments to its own schedule and those of its newly acceded member states as a consequence of enlargement.[32]

In November 2008 the Bolivian government of Evo Morales sought to rescind a commitment made by a previous neoliberal government that allowed foreign control of hospital services, because its new constitution declared health care a human right that could not be privatised.[33] The EU consented to the change. At the last minute, the Bush administration lodged an objection requiring the Bolivian government to negotiate compensatory liberalisation in other services sectors with the US.[34] As of March 2015 Bolivia's request remained unresolved.

By contrast, the US announced in May 2007 it would amend the commitment on 'recreational services' that was the subject of the *US-Gambling* case. The US

[28] WTO, Structure of Commitments for Modes 1, 2 and 3. Background Note by the Secretariat, S/C/W/99, 3 March 1999, p. 4.

[29] Panel, *United States – Measures Affecting the Cross-border Supply of Gambling and Betting Services*, WT/DS285/R, 10 November 2004, p. 169 at para 6.138.

[30] Appellate Body, *European Communities – Regime for the Importation, Sale and Distribution of Bananas – Complaint by Ecuador*, (WT/DS27/AB/R), 9 September 1997, pp. 101–103 at paras 240–248.

[31] GATS Article XXI.

[32] See, eg. Council for Trade in Services, Communication from the European Communities and its Member States. Certification, S/C/W/273, 9 October 2006.

[33] James D, New US Trade Officials Have Opportunity to Stand Up for Health Care Rights, Centre for Economic and Policy Research, Washington DC, 10 March 2009 (on file with the author); James D, Trade in Services Agreement. How will it affect consumers?, The Real News, 3 October 2014, http://therealnews.com/t2/index.php?option=com_content&task=view&id=31&Itemid=74&jumival=10792 (last accessed 21 April 2015).

[34] Weisbrot M, The United States and Bolivia: A New Beginning?, Huffington Post, 25 May 2011, http://www.huffingtonpost.com/mark-weisbrot/the-united-states-and-bol_b_170006.html (last accessed 21 April 2015).

successfully negotiated the change with the EU in 2007.[35] In 2015, Antigua was still awaiting a resolution of the dispute it won in 2005.[36]

In sum, the GATS was an uneasy compromise. Its cumulative design features meant the text and schedules of commitments fell well short of the original ambitions. Positive lists allowed governments to make cautious and fragmented commitments, the converse of what generic trade in services rules were meant to achieve. From the perspective of most South governments, the unlevel commercial playing field, the denial of concessions in areas of their primary interest, and the power politics of the WTO made them reluctant to go any further.

5 Reforming the GATS from Within

Pressure to address the imperfections in the GATS 1994 and extend its rules and commitments began even before the deal was inked, with some early success.

The US refused to conclude some elements, insisting that negotiations continued past 1994. According to Geza Feketekuty, who had seeded the trade in services idea through the OECD, one of the principal goals was to stop restrictive regulation of telecommunications and new technologies that would enable 'new services' such as consulting, data processing and information services.[37] Negotiations on scheduled commitments on telecoms were extended until February 1997. The Annex on Telecommunications Services established rights of non-discriminatory access for foreign services providers to every member's public telecommunications networks. The Reference Paper on Basic Telecommunications that was modelled on the US domestic regulatory regime could be adopted and scheduled as an additional commitment.[38]

The US was also dissatisfied with other members' commitments to liberalise financial services, especially larger developing countries. Negotiations continued until December 1997, with a reluctant Malaysia the last to sign in the wake of the Asian Financial Crisis. An Understanding on financial services where governments voluntarily adopted stricter disciplines, was inscribed by mainly-OECD members

[35] The US agreed compensatory market access to its postal and courier, research and development, and storage and warehouse sectors. Canada, Japan and Australian also reportedly settled. However, the US said it was only binding existing liberalisation, subject to approval of Congress. ICTSD, Antigua Awarded Modest Cross-Retaliation Rights in Gambling Dispute with US, Bridges, Volume 12, no. 1, 16 January 2008, http://www.ictsd.org/bridges-news/bridges/news/antigua-awarded-modest-cross-retaliation-rights-in-gambling-dispute-with (last accessed 21 April 2015).

[36] At the Dispute Settlement Body meeting on 28 January 2013, Antigua and Barbuda requested and was granted authorisation to suspend concessions and obligations to the US in respect of intellectual property rights. https://www.wto.org/english/tratop_e/dispu_e/cases_e/ds285_e.htm (last accessed 21 April 2015).

[37] Interview with author, Washington DC, 3 May 2005 quoted in Kelsey (2008), p. 157.

[38] Under GATS Article XVIII.

in the ‘additional commitments’ column of their schedules. The resulting raft of instruments—collectively known as the WTO’s Financial Services Agreement[39]—was estimated to cover 95 % of international commerce in banking, securities, insurance, and information services as measured by revenue.[40]

Moves to conclude strong disciplines on domestic regulation of qualifications, technical standards and licensing under GATS Article VI.4 began in April 1995. Three years later the Big Five (later four) accounting firms became the beneficiaries of new disciplines that required governments to use a least trade-restrictive approach to regulating accountancy services to fulfil a ‘legitimate objective’.[41] The narrow indicative field of ‘legitimate objectives’—the protection of consumers, the quality of the service, professional competence, and the integrity of the profession—was devoid of the social and public good responsibilities traditionally expected of the accounting and auditing professions, such as protection of the tax base. However, those disciplines have still not entered into force.[42]

The momentum to extend the GATS stopped quite abruptly. There was no pressure or incentive to reach consensus on anything. The services exporting countries blocked the promise to conclude emergency safeguard mechanisms within 3 years. Ongoing talks on ‘trade-distorting subsidies’[43] and government procurement[44] went nowhere as well. A general Working Party on Domestic Regulation was established to pursue further ‘disciplines’ under Article VI.4. It made little progress[45]—in part because the US was known to oppose rules that fettered the regulatory autonomy of own sub-federal governments, which for it was a constitutional issue.

6 GATS 2000

The GATS contained an inbuilt commitment to begin negotiations for ‘a progressively higher level of liberalization’ no later than 2000 and periodically thereafter.[46] This allowed new services negotiations to begin, despite the failure to launch a ‘Millennium round’ at Seattle in 1999.

---

[39] The Financial Services Agreement comprises the GATS text, Members’ schedules of commitments and the Annex on Financial Services, supplemented by the voluntary Understanding on Commitments in Financial Services.

[40] Sauvé and Gillespie (2000), p. 430.

[41] Arnold (2005), pp. 299–330, referring to the Guidelines for Mutual Recognition Agreements or Arrangements in the Accountancy Sector, adopted May 1997; Disciplines on Domestic Regulation in the Accountancy Sector, adopted on 14 December 1998, SL/64, 17 December 1998.

[42] Newberry S, PPPs: An International Web of Relationships, Invited Forum on PPPs, University of Sydney, Sydney, 8 December 2003, p. 6.

[43] GATS Article XV.1.

[44] GATS Article XIII.2.

[45] Council for Trade in Services, Negotiations on Trade in Services. Report by the Chairman, Ambassador Fernando de Mateo, to the Trade Negotiations Committee, TN/S/36, 21 April 2011, pp. 11–12, paras 73–78.

[46] GATS Article XIX.1.

The GATS 2000 negotiations followed a largely North/South fault-line. The development promises in the GATS 1994 text proved a sham. The Council on Trade in Services was required to conduct an 'assessment of trade in services in overall terms and on a sectoral basis with reference to the objectives of the Agreement', including those on development, *before* guidelines and procedures were established.[47] Shukla saw this as an important safeguard. It was effectively bypassed; in 1998 the Secretariat prepared 15 background notes on economic potential, barriers, and current commitments in different services sectors, but no proper impact assessment was conducted.[48]

The GATS 2000 negotiations were required to show "due respect for national policy objectives and the level of development of individual members, both overall and in individual sectors". They would also "promot[e] the interests of all participants on a mutually advantageous basis and to securing an overall balance of rights and obligations", albeit within the overall obligations to liberalise.[49]

The demandeurs set out to rewrite the rules and secure new liberalisation on behalf of their transnational services firms, while Southern governments insisted on flexibility, policy space, support for development and more commitments in 'mode 4' (temporary movement of natural persons). A road map for the new negotiations was agreed in May 2000 and the negotiating guidelines and procedures were adopted in March 2001. The GATS 1994 was accepted as a basic framework: the request and offer style of negotiating commitments; the positive list approach to scheduling; the classification list used to identify sectors and sub-sectors; and members' use of inconsistent terminology.[50] But there were battles over technical 'modalities'.

Initially, South governments prevailed, using the defensive tools that Shukla and others had put in place. The guidelines for the negotiations and scheduling of sectoral commitments reiterated the need to respect the existing GATS structure and principles, and the right of members to specify commitments in sectors and modes, with 'appropriate flexibilities' for developing and least developed countries. The request-offer approach would be the main method for negotiation. Significantly, however, both Article XIX:4 and the Uruguay round negotiating guidelines said liberalisation could be advanced through bilateral, plurilateral or multilateral negotiations.[51]

---

[47] Under GATS Article XIX.3.

[48] Discussed in Kelsey (2008), p. 44.

[49] WTO, Guidelines and Procedures for the Negotiations on Trade in Services, S/L/93, 29 March 2001, p. 1.

[50] WTO, Guidelines for the Scheduling of Specific Commitments under the General Agreement on Trade in Services (GATS), S/L/92, 23 March 2001.

[51] WTO, Guidelines and Procedures for the Negotiations on Trade in Services, S/L/93, p. 2 at para 11.

7 The Doha Round

Once the Doha round was launched in late 2001, the GATS 2000 negotiations were folded into the 'single undertaking'. That created a triangular linkage between agriculture, non-agricultural market access and services. The Doha Work Programme set deadlines of 30 June 2002 for members to submit initial GATS requests and 31 March 2003 for tabling initial offers in response.[52] The round was supposed to conclude no later than 1 January 2005.

New critical alliances were formed, with some of the same players but in a quite new geopolitical context. The G-20 emerged as a force during the Cancun ministerial meeting in 2003, with India, Brazil and Malaysia playing crucial roles.[53] The subsequent ascent of the BRICS (Brazil, India, China and South Africa[54]), presented a systemic challenge to the superpowers and their dominance over the WTO for the previous decade, although each had their own offensive and defensive interests in services.

7.1 'Complementary Approaches'

The main demandeurs became impatient. The EC insisted on services concessions as a quid pro quo for market access on agriculture. A group of OECD countries (including the US, the EC, Japan, Australia, Switzerland, South Korea, Taiwan and New Zealand) floated the idea of 'complementary approaches' to advance their offensive interests.[55] Despite objections from other members, they continued meeting behind the scenes with the support of the chair of the services negotiations, facilitated by the WTO Secretariat. Their informal papers suggested a two-tier process: 'quantitative' targets would set minimum levels of commitments; 'qualitative' targets would promote 'commercially meaningful' liberalisation (rather than simply locking in the status quo), including model schedules or checklists for particular sectors or modes of supply. This approach aimed to create a critical mass of commitments in key sectors and make negotiations more efficient.

The most radical proposal was to create minimum 'benchmarks'. The EC circulated a non-paper in June 2005 suggesting every member should commit a minimum number of sectors in all modes of supply.[56] Developed countries should make new or improved commitments in 139 of the 163 services subsectors, and developing countries in at least 93, including the removal of all restrictions on

[52] WTO Ministerial Declaration, WT/MIN(01)/DEC/1, 14 November 2001, para 15.

[53] Kelsey (2008), p. 46.

[54] The Russian Federation did not become a Member until 2012.

[55] Kelsey (2008), pp. 46–47.

[56] EC non-paper, 27 October 2005. On file with author.

foreign investment in those subsectors. Consistent with the Doha Work Programme, LDCs would be encouraged, but not required, to make commitments.[57]

The idea that countries would be compelled to make GATS commitments provoked outrage. Because rich countries could count their more numerous GATS 1994 commitments, most of the new commitments would come from the South, giving the developed countries a 'round for free'.[58] Transnational corporations and foreign firms that controlled new technologies would intensify their control over international services markets and squeeze out medium and small local services providers in poorer countries. Speaking from its new position of strength within the ascendant BRICS, Brazil took the hardest line on benchmarks, warning that departure from agreed processes could derail, rather than energise, the negotiations.

A second 'complementary approach' sought to cut through the fragmentation of commitments based on subsectoral CPCs. Ideas included clusters of sub-sectors that reflected the functional operations of corporations in particular activities, model schedules for broadly defined sectors, and horizontal commitments for a particular mode of supply across all services. Groups of likeminded (services exporting) countries could design ambitious schedules on priority sectors, which they would invite others (including developing and least developed countries) to adopt, and build a critical mass of commitments to the position within the GATS.

Because the idea of benchmarks was so outrageous, and the negotiating guidelines did refer to plurilateral methodologies, there were fewer objections to the latter.

Unlike the Doha and Cancún ministerial meetings, services became a major issue at the sixth ministerial conference in Hong Kong in December 2005.[59] A draft of the ministerial declaration allowed for sector- or mode-specific plurilateral negotiations, numerical targets and indicators, and multilateral approaches that could include qualitative parameters. After an outcry from South members and NGOs the text forwarded to the conference omitted the reference to benchmarks. But Annex C on services required members to consider any plurilateral requests they received.

The final Hong Kong declaration was issued under controversial circumstances when critical members were literally silenced.[60] This manoeuvre cleared the way for pro-liberalising countries, who dubbed themselves 'friends' of different services sectors, to develop plurilateral requests. More than 20 plurilateral requests had been submitted by the next services negotiating 'cluster', with the major players

[57] Council for Trade in Services, Modalities for the Special Treatment for Least-Developed Country Members in the Negotiations on Trade in Services, adopted 3 September 2003, consistent with GATS Article IV.3.

[58] Khor (2005), p. 5.

[59] Kelsey (2008), p. 48.

[60] Kelsey (2008), p. 48.

participating in almost all. Despite these efforts, relatively few revised GATS 2000 offers had been tabled by the mid-2011. Telecommunications and financial services attracted the most offers; education, environmental or health had comparatively few.[61]

7.2 Accessions

The one area where major players did secure extensive new concessions was from the predominantly South countries seeking to join the WTO. Accession is a ruthless and largely rule-less process.[62] Any acceding country must secure the consent of existing members through bilateral and collective decisions. Any existing member effectively has a veto. A decision of the General Council in 2002 that promised restraint in market access demands from acceding LDCs,[63] reiterated in the Doha work programme,[64] was ignored.

Acceding countries were invariably required to make far more extensive GATS commitments than originating WTO members, including the most affluent. Some obligations even go beyond the agreement, for example privatisations, government procurement of services, and competition policy.[65] Often there was no commercial purpose to these demands. Their value to services exporters was as precedents for the accessions of China, Russia, Taiwan and various Arab states, with no regard for the economic, social or political consequences for small vulnerable economies or LDCs.

Similar practices later emerged for accessions to regional and mega-agreements. Canada, Mexico and Japan were required to secure bilateral and collective agreement to join the TPPA talks—and they were required to adopt the text as then agreed by the existing parties sight unseen.[66] Countries seeking to join the TiSA negotiations, or acceding to a completed agreement, could expect the same demands, irrespective of their development status.

[61] WTO Negotiations on Market Access, https://www.wto.org/english/tratop_e/serv_e/market_access_negs_e.htm (last accessed 21 April 2015).

[62] Kelsey (2005), p. 247.

[63] WTO General Council, Accession of Least-Developed Countries, Decision of 10 December 2002, WT/L/508.

[64] WTO Ministerial Declaration, WT/MIN(01)/DEC/1, 14 November 2001, para. 42.

[65] Grynberg et al. (2006).

[66] National Coalition for Commenting on TPP, Open letter to Prime Minister Abe, 13 March 2013, see translation at http://www.scoop.co.nz/stories/PO1303/S00188/terms-of-japans-entry-to-tppa-talks-bad-news-for-nz.htm (last accessed 21 April 2015).

8 The Bilateral Path

Bilateral and regional FTAs took off from the late 1990s; almost all included a chapter on services or made provision for one.[67] Supporters of multilateralism fretted about what the surge of these agreements meant for the WTO. The 10-year review of the organisation warned that the 'spaghetti bowl' of inconsistent, overlapping and partial agreements would be inefficient to negotiate and undermine multilateralism.[68] Others offered a positive spin, suggesting bilaterals could act "as laboratories for change and innovation and may provide guidance for the adoption of new trade disciplines at the multilateral level".[69]

The paralysis in the Doha round gave services demandeurs a new incentive to apply their technical work from the GATS 2000 to bilateral and regional agreements. But instead of streamlining the regime, the rules and commitments they created were complex, overlapping and sometimes contradictory.

The more powerful parties to such negotiations could tailor the legal texts in ways that proved impossible in the GATS. The US and EU led the way in what has variously been labelled competitive liberalisation or competitive imperialism.[70] Both major powers crafted GATS-plus templates to suit their services industries, whilst protecting their sensitivities and promoting their preferred regulatory models. Countries negotiating with them had to work within those parameters, although the EU was generally more flexible than the US.

These templates prescribed the acceptable rules, sectoral priorities, definitions of modes, form of commitments, regulatory disciplines, institutional arrangements and implementation periods for all their FTAs. The EU's 'Global Europe' strategy, formalised in 2006 to serve the Lisbon Agenda for Growth and Employment, sought to replicate the EU's internal model and rules for integration externally. That was replaced in 2010 by the 'Europe 2020' strategy that sought to re-assert the EU's external position in 'the rapidly changing landscape of global trade'.[71] The US operated according to the Trade Act 2003 that set out agreed terms with Congress, even after it expired, and the US model bilateral investment treaty, which was minimally modified in 2012. A 2006 study for the WTO that examined

[67] The NZ-Thailand FTA 2005 provided for subsequent negotiations of services; the Pacific Island Countries Trade Agreement (PICTA) came into force in 2006 for goods, followed by a services protocol that was opened for signature in 2012; the interim EPAs negotiated by the EU with ACP regions were for goods only.

[68] WTO, The Future of the WTO: Addressing Institutional Challenges in the New Millennium. Report by the Consultative Board to the Former Director-General Supachai Panitchpakdi, 2005, Geneva: WTO; Mattoo and Fink, Regional Agreements and Trade in Services, 2002, World Bank Policy Research Working Paper, 2852; Panagariya (1999) pp. 477–451.

[69] Crawford and Fiorentino, The Changing Landscape of Regional Trade Agreements, 2005, WTO Discussion Paper Series, No. 8, p. 16.

[70] Bhala (2007), pp. 77–105.

[71] Bendini, The European Union's Trade Policy, 5 Years After the Lisbon Treaty, Directorate General for External Policies of the European Union, 2014, p. 9.

the GATS-plus content of recent bilateral agreements identified the US FTAs as the most far-reaching.[72]

There were important differences between the two templates. The US favoured a negative list approach with two annexes, one listing all sectors exempted permanently and the second reserving specified measures at their current level of liberalisation ('standstill'). The EU maintained the positive list model. That divergence was not a problem for them (at least until they began negotiating the Transatlantic Trade and Investment Partnership and TiSA), but countries who concluded agreements with both the US and EU were left to reconcile obligations based on different structures and rules.[73] Agreements among other players had their own variations.

Occasionally, governments clawed back previous commitments on politically sensitive issues, corrected errors in their original schedules, or attached soft side-agreements or exchanges of letters to placate domestic pressures in particular areas. But the overall effect of the new architecture, scope, rules, and approaches to scheduling commitments in FTAs was to intensify the incursions into national policy and regulation. Most of these innovations had been proposed and rejected in the WTO.[74]

Almost every item on the shopping list for a GATS-plus agreement has been included in at least one bilateral FTA:

- coverage of services-related investment, government procurement, competition and e-commerce;
- relocating mode 3 (commercial presence) to the investment chapter that included protections for foreign investors on minimum standards of treatment and direct and indirect expropriation;
- annexes on new sectors, such as computer services and express delivery;
- commitments to further liberalisation;
- a negative list that imposes a standstill on existing measures and commits to rollback reservations;
- a ratchet that automatically locks in further liberalisation;
- no explicit mechanism to withdraw or amend commitments, even with compensatory adjustments;
- comprehensive model schedules and clusters of commitments;
- updated classifications for identification of services;
- multi-layered 'necessity' tests for domestic regulation of services;

[72] Roy et al., Services Liberalization in the New Generation of Preferential Trade Agreements (PTAs): How Much Further than the GATS?, 2006, WTO Staff Working, Paper Economic Research and Statistics Division, available at http://www.wto.org/english/res_e/reser_e/ersd200607_e.pdf (last accessed 21 April 2015). See also Kelsey (2008), pp. 55–57.

[73] See, for example in relation to the US and EU FTAs with South Korea: Kelsey (2011), pp. 845–868, esp. 857–868.

[74] Kelsey (2008), pp. 42–50.

- no or narrowed general exceptions for investment, including commercial presence;
- a more restrictive prudential defence for financial services;
- requirements for governments to consult foreign firms about proposed regulations;
- restrictions on means for delivering universal service obligations, such as post and telecommunications; and
- inbuilt rounds of negotiations to achieve further liberalisation.

There were also GATS-minus features that worked to dominant countries' advantage. Mode 4 was narrowed to provide special terms of entry only for élite personnel, usually professionals, managers and trainees linked to foreign investments, and skilled personnel. Another GATS-minus feature was the exclusion of public subsidies from coverage in many services chapters—this time reflecting the effectiveness of the international campaign to protect public services.

8.1 Extended Scope and Disciplines

Sectoral chapters or annexes with new or altered disciplines on regulating air transport, movement of persons, financial services and telecommunications, energy, e-commerce and government procurement became common.

Leading advocates of light-handed regulation, such as New Zealand and Australia, used FTAs to promote proposals that had stalled in the GATS. Sometimes these constraints applied across the board, even in sectors excluded from commitments to the core rules through negative list annexes or positive list schedules.[75] Where a link was retained, the wording that triggered the disciplines was often just that 'trade' in the sector had been 'liberalised'.[76] A minimalist positive list commitment of one sub-sector for any mode on either market access or national treatment, subject to strong limitations, could potentially be enough to bring the entire sector under sweeping disciplines, even though a government had clearly sought to limit the exposure of that sector.

The reach of existing rules was also deepened. The GATS required central governments to take 'reasonable steps to ensure compliance' by their state, provincial and local governments and those exercising delegated authority.[77] Many FTAs directly bound all levels of government, subject to any exceptions listed in negative

---

[75] Eg. Article 8.10 of the Free Trade Agreement between New Zealand and the Republic of Korea 2015.

[76] Eg. Article 88.1 on Computer services and Article 89.1 on Courier Services in the Economic Partnership Agreement Between the Cariforum States and the European Community and its Member States 2008.

[77] GATS Article I.3(a).

list annexes.[78] Sub-central governments were also subject to investment protections on minimum standards of treatment or direct and indirect expropriation, which the annexes of non-conforming measures did not apply to. The more extensive disciplines on domestic regulation also applied to the sub-central level, affecting such core functions as licensing (liquor outlets or rubbish dumps) and technical standards (environmental services or town planning), and to the recognition of professional qualifications by non-government bodies.

8.2 GATS-Compatibility

The WTO sets minima, not maxima, for what it calls Regional Trade Agreements (RTAs). Although the requirements for WTO-compatibility are vague, they ensure that agreements are neoliberal and contain GATS-plus elements.

The GATS Article V on RTAs is an exception to the MFN rule, which would otherwise require all WTO members to receive equally favourable treatment.[79] To qualify, parties to the RTA must undertake more extensive market access commitments and accompanying national treatment obligations than are demanded in the WTO. However, the threshold is very vague. An RTA must have (undefined) 'substantial' sectoral coverage. It must eliminate, phase out or prevent the introduction of 'substantially all discrimination' (also undefined) in those sectors. And it must be implemented immediately or within an (undefined) 'reasonable timeframe'. Barriers to non-parties cannot be raised 'overall'. This lack of precision allows the dominant player in a services negotiation to insist on its interpretation.

South governments, having been allowed to limit their exposure under the GATS, were supposed to enjoy ongoing protection when negotiating RTAs with developed countries. Unlike the GATT, the GATS requires regional trade agreements on services between rich and poor countries to recognise development asymmetries,[80] and give developing countries greater, but undefined, 'flexibility', especially in the liberalisation of market access and implementation.

This was yet another broken GATS promise. As with accessions, these flexibilities are mandatory. Yet South governments have been required to make extensive new commitments on commercial presence and cross-border supply. The EU, for example, required Cariforum countries to commit between 60 % and 70 % of services sectors in the EU-Cariforum EPA.[81] That threshold exceeded the

[78] That was a standard feature of US FTAs. Some negative list annexes grandfathered all existing local government measures without requiring them to be listed.

[79] Kelsey (2008), pp. 42–50.

[80] Under GATT Article XXIV and the Enabling Clause, development flexibilities are limited to agreements between developing countries.

[81] Kelsey J, Legal Analysis of Services and Investment in the Cariforum EC EPA: Lessons for Other Developing Countries, Research Paper 31, July 2010, South Centre, Geneva, p. ii.

controversial 'benchmarks' the EU proposed during the GATS 2000 negotiations, and required a massive increase in commitments from developing countries over their GATS 1994 schedules and GATS 2000 offers, especially compared to minimal new commitments from the EU.

The inclusion of sector specific chapters, especially on telecommunications, courier and financial services, and mobility of élite business personnel, also imposes GATS-plus regulatory constraints on South governments, as well as costly institutional, disclosure and review obligations.

Parties to RTAs are required to notify the Council on Trade in Services so it can investigate and report on compliance, and provide periodic reports on implementation. This requirement is largely academic. As of January 2015 some 143 agreements containing services had been notified.[82] Not one report had been forwarded from the Council to the WTO for review, reflecting the inability or reluctance of members to agree on an interpretation. A review to clarify and improve disciplines and procedures relating to RTAs was part of the Doha Work Programme. The General Council issued a Decision on a Transparency Mechanism for RTAs in December 2006,[83] which resulted in provisional rules for notification and review of goods and services agreements. But there was no agreement to clarify the interpretation.

8.3 GATS-Plus Commitments

A WTO study of the services content of bilaterals published in 2006 examined the mode 1 and 3 commitments of 29 WTO members in 28 bilateral agreements signed since 2000.[84] The number of commitments for all sectors, except for health, was higher than even in the GATS 2000 offers. First time and 'improved' commitments were made in key infrastructure areas, such as financial services and telecommunications, and in the traditionally sensitive areas of education and audiovisual services. Some new liberalisations involved phasing out of laws and regulations by specified dates.

The US agreements contained the broadest and deepest commitments: "the US, a key services demandeur and also signatory to many [RTAs], has gotten very significant access in various services where its industry sees particular interest,

[82] https://www.wto.org/english/tratop_e/region_e/region_e.htm (last accessed 21 April 2015).

[83] WTO General Council, Transparency Mechanism for Regional Trade Agreements. Decision of 14 December 2006, WT/L/671, 18 December 20016.

[84] Roy M et al. (2006) Services Liberalization in the New Generation of Preferential Trade Agreements (PTAs): How Much Further than the GATS?, 2006, WTO Staff Working, Paper Economic Research and Statistics Division, http://www.wto.org/english/res_e/reser_e/ersd200607_e.pdf (last accessed 21 April 2015).

e.g., financial services, express delivery, distribution, audiovisual".[85] Agreements that used negative lists—primarily those involving the US—were more likely to lock in the parties' existing levels of liberalisation. They also pre-empted new, more restrictive regulation, including of unregulated service activities such as digital technologies. Smaller, especially developing, countries tended to make the deepest commitments. Significantly, developed countries made fewer new commitments and their sensitive areas remained protected.

The Doha round was still underway during that study. The authors speculated that it was easier to convince services exporters about the gains from bilaterals than from the GATS. Governments might also be reluctant to squander their negotiating coin for bilaterals by making GATS 2000 offers. The study suggested the GATS would remain important for liberalisation between the major powers, given there were then very few North/North agreements. However, if the US got what it wanted through bilaterals, its diminishing appetite for the GATS could reduce the scope for trade offs in the broader Doha round.

8.4 Schedules

One of the strategies carried over from the GATS 2000 negotiations to achieve these outcomes was the use of clusters of commitments and model schedules, sometimes with updated classifications. Whilst those changes might have improved coherency when applied within the GATS, the lack of consistency among FTAs added to the overall incoherence. Different configurations of modes, scheduling modalities and classifications, along with positive or negative lists, created a complex matrix of schedules.

Regional agreements in which individual countries had different commitments made this worse. The Cariforum-EC EPA illustrates the problem. Neither party was required to use a specific or shared format. The EU followed its own template, with four schedules that covered: (1) commercial presences and investors[86]; (2) cross-border supply of services; (3) movement of key personnel; and (4) movement of contractual service suppliers and independent professionals. The Cariforum states had two collective schedules, configured in a different way from the EU: (1) a collation and extension of the positive list GATS schedule of each state, disaggregated by sectors and all four modes of supplying a service, which was

[85] Roy M et al, (2006) Services Liberalization in the New Generation of Preferential Trade Agreements (PTAs): How Much Further than the GATS?, WTO Staff Working, Paper Economic Research and Statistics Division, http://www.wto.org/english/res_e/reser_e/ersd200607_e.pdf (last accessed 21 April 2015), p. 54.

[86] Article 69 in the chapter on Commercial Presence refers to both commercial presences and investors and is not restricted to services. At the time, the European Commission did not have a mandate to negotiate for investor protections, but included market access and national treatment for non-services investors, which was not included in the GATS.

subject to a (seemingly redundant) standstill obligation in the headnote; and (2) a schedule for non-services investment that was effectively a negative list of five very broad categories of investment.

Further, each party scheduled its commitments using different combinations of the W/120 list, an updated version of the UN CPCs, and the International Standard Industrial Classification of All Economic Activities (ISIC), which takes a functional approach to an activity (such as mining) and does not distinguish between services and non-services. This worked for the EU because it used ISIC for scheduling both commercial presences and investors. However, Cariforum only used ISIC for its non-services investment,[87] creating overlaps and anomalies with its commitments for commercial presence (mode 3) which were based on the UN CPCs. That became even more complicated because the former was a negative list and the latter a positive list. Some Cariforum commitments had no accompanying classification at all. Not surprisingly these complex configurations produced errors and contradictions, some of which affected important social services like waste and wastewater management and hospital services.[88]

8.5 *The Multiplier Effect*

The most-favoured-nation provisions in the FTAs progressively ratcheted up countries' commitments and constraints on their regulatory autonomy in unpredictable ways.

The Cariforum-EU EPA again illustrates these complexities. If the EU gave any better treatment on commercial presence and cross-border supply of services to any other country or region, the Cariforum states would automatically receive that treatment too.[89] This entitled them to new concessions that other countries with more negotiating power could secure from the EU (although the economic asymmetries meant new entitlements would not automatically convert into concrete commercial opportunities). This obligation related only to commercial presence and cross-border supply, not to the sought-after mobility of services personnel.

Conversely, each Cariforum state was required to give the EU any better treatment on commercial presence and cross-border supply that it gave another country and/or integrated economic grouping that met the threshold for 'a major commodity trading economy'. The EU would have to consent to waive this obligation.[90] If that other country (for example, Canada) insisted that the FTA included MFN provisions that applied retrospectively, it would be entitled to the

[87] Cariforum-EC EPA, Annex IV-E.

[88] Kelsey J (2010) Legal Analysis of Services and Investment in the Cariforum EC EPA, South Center, Research paper 31, pp. 40–43.

[89] Cariforum-EC EPA, Article 70.1(a).

[90] Cariforum-EC EPA, Article 70.1(b), 70.4 and 70.5.

best treatment that Cariforum gave the EU on services and investment effectively for free.

The cross-fertilisation of commercial establishment in the EPA and investment in bilateral investment treaties (BITs) between European and Cariforum states would add further liabilities. As of December 2008, when the EPA applied provisionally, there were 34 such BITs in force.[91] While BITs often do not create strong pre-establishment rights for investors, they do grant strong investor protections that are enforceable directly through investor-state dispute settlement. A European investor could secure a right to establish a commercial presence under the EPA, and use the BIT to sue the Cariforum state for not providing 'fair and equitable treatment' or indirectly expropriating its investment by some kind of regulatory action.

According to the UNCTAD database, there were also 23 BITs in force between Cariforum states and non-EU countries. Most of these had MFN provisions that entitled the investors and investments of those states to any better treatment the Cariforum state gave to third countries, including the sectoral commitments and disciplines on regulation of commercial establishments; whether that applied in a specific BIT would depend on whether it included an exception for 'free trade areas'.

8.6 *Lessons from the FTAs*

During the 2000s these agreements supplanted the WTO as the main vehicle to advance the ambitions of the national and global services lobbies and their patron states. The negotiations also heightened the tensions identified at the start of this paper: the development divide and the inability to construct an international services regime that was both legally coherent and politically tenable, especially when they were underpinned by the asymmetries of geopolitical and corporate power.

From the perspective of the global South Yash Tandon divided these FTAs into three categories: 'integrative partnerships' where partners have compatible interests and work on the principles of solidarity and subsidiarity to benefit the weakest members; 'enforced partnerships' where one side dictates the terms and the other side either has to 'take it or leave it'; and 'structured regionalism' where the partnership is enforced and located in structures that are linked to historical relationships.[92] The first was the most benign, yet still circumscribed by neoliberal

[91] UNCTAD, Investment Policy Hub, http://investmentpolicyhub.unctad.org/IIA/IiasByCountry#iiaInnerMenu (last accessed 21 April 2015).

[92] Quoted in Shashikant and Tayob, UNCTAD Meeting Warns of Effects of Bilateral, Regional FTAs, 2007, South-North Development Monitor (SUNS), No. 6214.

requirements of WTO compatibility. But it was the second and third that dominated the era.

The plethora of treaties with variable texts and scheduling structures served an ideological purpose in re-restablishing momentum lost in the WTO and pushing the normative boundaries of the trade in services regime. But in operational terms they were technically problematic and generated interpretations that were contestable by policy makers and regulators, let alone by ad hoc state-state and increasingly investor-state dispute tribunals under the investment chapters of the FTAs.

9 TiSA

As the Doha round limped on, the most aggressive demandeurs dubbed themselves the ‘Really Good Friends of Services’. Ultimately giving up on the WTO, they decided to reconvene on its margins and pursue a ‘gold standard’ twenty-first century Trade in Services Agreement (TiSA). This plurilateral approach exemplified what one corporate lobbyist called “creating alternative ‘play-by-the-rules’ clubs of like-minded countries”.[93] Two other new mega-agreements were being negotiated in parallel: the Trans-Pacific Partnership Agreement (TPPA) and the Transatlantic Trade and Investment Partnership (TTIP). The US was a dominant player in all three. Other champions of services liberalisation, such as the EU, Japan, Australia, New Zealand, Canada, and Chile, were parties to two.

The TiSA talks began formally in March 2013.[94] As of December 2015 the participants were Australia, Canada, Chile, Chinese Taipei (Taiwan), Colombia, Costa Rica, Hong Kong China, Iceland, Israel, Japan, Liechtenstein, Mauritius, Mexico, New Zealand, Norway, Pakistan, Panama, Peru, South Korea, Switzerland, Turkey, the USA and the European Union, including its 28 member states. Singapore, Uruguay and Paraguay had withdrawn.

9.1 *A Preview of TiSA*

Suspicions about TiSA among critical publics and non-participating states were heightened as the negotiations retreated behind a wall of secrecy. The cover note to

[93] Atkinson R, Information Technology and Innovation Foundation, Hearing on The Impact of Information Technology Transfer on American Research and Development before the House Science Committee, Subcommittee on Investigations and Oversight of the US House of Representatives, 5 December 2012, http://www2.itif.org/2012-international-tech-transfer-testimony.pdf (last accessed 21 April 2015).

[94] European Commission, Trade in Services Agreement (TiSA), http://ec.europa.eu/trade/policy/in-focus/TiSA/ (last accessed 21 April 2015); Office of the Unites States Trade Representative, Trade in Services Agreement, https://ustr.gov/TiSA (last accessed 21 April 2015).

leaked TiSA documents shows the parties have agreed to ‘Declassify on: 5 years from entry into force of the TiSA agreement or, in no agreement enters into force, 5 years from the close of the negotiations’.[95] Significantly, the EU Ombudsman has spoken out against the secrecy of TTIP on the grounds that citizens have the right of input into an agreement that would have such a deep potential impact.[96] It remains to be seen if she will do the same regarding TiSA.

Secrecy begets leaks. The two most significant in 2014 were a draft TiSA financial services annex and US proposed text on e-commerce.[97] The financial services text confirmed the position taken by TiSA parties in the WTO, as they refused to address concerns about the GATS model of liberalisation and pro-market regulation, including of cross-border financial services, and the inadequacy of the prudential defence.[98]

Even if TiSA remained outside the WTO, the coverage of the financial services annex would impact on other countries. IMF researchers have described a ‘state of denial’ among affluent economies over the potential for further devastating financial crises if they maintain the current policy and regulatory regime.[99] Yet the US and EU, who bore primary responsible for the global financial crisis, are seeking to extend those rules through TiSA, TTIP and TPPA. The TiSAfication of the GATS would require developing countries that took prudent steps following the Asian Financial Crisis and similar traumas[100] to adopt those flawed rules as the new ‘best practice’ through the WTO.[101]

The e-commerce agenda is less well known, so is discussed here in some more detail. E-commerce moved slowly within the WTO. A work programme on global

---

[95] A similar provision in the TPPA applies for 4 years.

[96] Decision of the European Ombudsman closing her own-initiative inquiry OI/10/2014/RA Concerning the European Commission, 6 January 2015, http://www.ombudsman.europa.eu/cases/decision.faces/en/58668/html.bookmark (last accessed 21 April 2015).

[97] TiSA, Financial Services Annex Consolidated Text, 19 June 2014, https://wikileaks.org/TiSA-financial/ (last accessed 21 April 2015); US, Trade in Services Agreement TiSA Proposal. New Trade in Services Commitment Applicable to All Services, 25 April 2014, https://data.awp.is/filtrala/2014/12/17/19.html (last accessed 21 April 2015).

[98] For analysis of those developments and risks in the context of the financial services and investment in TPPA see: Kelsey (2010), pp. 1–43.

[99] Reinhart and Rogoff (2013), pp. 4557–4573; Reinhart CM, Rogoff KS, Financial and Sovereign Debt Crises: Some Lessons Learned and Those Forgotten. IMF Working Paper WP/13/266, December 2013.

[100] Jeasakul P, Lim CH, Lundback E, Why Was Asia Resilient? Lessons from the Past and for the Future, IMF Working Paper WP/14/38, February 2014, p. 9.

[101] The leaked annex did not disclose the proposed approach to capital account liberalization US demanded that its FTAs require full capital account liberalisation with no provision for balance of payments emergencies, despite even the IMF endorsing capital controls as a valid stabilisation mechanism. It is conceivable that other TiSA members would agree to this, but the US may insist on some tighter restrictions than are currently in GATS Articles XVI footnote 8, XI and XII.

electronic commerce was established in 1988.[102] The ministerial conference in Geneva in 2009 expressed concern that the programme was still incomplete, and promised to 'intensively reinvigorate' the work.[103]

That meant e-commerce for services was governed by the GATS 1994, which was negotiated from 1987 to 1993. The worldwide web was created only in 1989. The GATS connected with this embryonic development in four ways[104]:

(a) cross-border trade in services (mode 1) and consumption abroad (mode 2). The boundary between the two was uncertain,[105] which mattered because there were many more commitments in mode 2 than modes 1 or 3[106];
(b) services classifications (CPCs for computer services, data processing, audiovisual services). The W/120 scheduling list remains based on the 1991 UN CPCs, which does not list services like web hosting and cloud operators; it is unclear whether they would be caught by a commitment to computer services, professional services, telecommunications, or none at all. During GATS 2000 the US and EC proposed clusters of internet-enabled services—telecommunications, distribution, express delivery, computer, advertising and certain financial services—with variations that reflected their priorities and Europe's cultural sensitivities.[107] However, updating the scheduling classifications would have created new inconsistencies and potentially altered the meaning of original commitments.
(c) sectoral telecommunications commitments and the Annex on Basic Telecommunications.[108] This was the subject of a long battle between the US, which stressed the convergence of carriage and content, supported by the principle of 'technological neutrality'; and the Europeans who sought to advance their offensive interests in the telecommunications sector, while maintaining the 'cultural exception' (effectively audiovisual services) by requiring that

[102] Declaration on Global Electronic Commerce, Adopted on 20 May 1998, WT/MIN(98)/DEC/2, 25 May 1998 (98–2148).

[103] Work Programme on Electronic Commerce, 2 December 2009.

[104] See discussions in Wunsch-Vincent (2003); Wunsch-Vincent S (2005) WTO, E-commerce, and Information Technologies: From the Uruguay Round through the Doha Development Agenda: A Report for the UN ICT Task Force, Markle Foundation, http://www.iie.com/publications/papers/wunsch1104.pdf (last accessed 21 April 2015); Kelsey (2008), pp. 167–173.

[105] The Scheduling Guidelines differentiated on the basis of whether the service is delivered inside or outside the territory. MTN.GNS/W/164. The Secretariat suggested the decisive factor was whether the government's measure impinged on the supplier (mode 1) or the consumer (mode 2), Council for Trade in Services, Work Programme on Electronic Commerce, S/C/W/68, 31 March 1999, p. 3.

[106] Council for Trade in Services, Structure of Commitments for Modes 1, 2, and 3, Background Note by the Secretariat, S/C/W/99, 3 March 1999, excluding financial services commitments. p. 2, Table A1 p. 6; and Electronic Commerce. Market Access Issues—Existing GATS Commitments for Online Supply of Services, Working Party of the Trade Committee, OECD, Paris p. 6.

[107] Wunsch-Vincent (2005), p. 80.

[108] S/C/W/15/Rev. 1, 20 July 1999, discussed in OECD, 'Electronic Commerce', fn. 14.

content-based services that required telecommunications were dealt with in content-specific sectors.

(d) Under the principal of 'technological neutrality', a new means of delivering a service within a particular mode of supply is automatically covered by a commitment, even if the technology did not exist when the commitment was made.[109] The *US-Gambling* case affirmed that any means could be used to deliver a service committed in a particular mode, even if the technology that did not exist and the application was unforeseen when the commitment was made—and, by implication, if the government would have withheld the commitment or imposed limitations had it known.[110]

A joint paper on e-commerce by the US and EU in 2011 underpinned their positions in TTIP, TiSA and the TPPA. The leaked US's TiSA proposal on 'E-Commerce, technology Transfer, Cross-border Data Flows and Net Neutrality' from April 2014[111] revealed three imperatives.[112] First, it sought to protect the competitive advantage of US firms and their monopoly rights over intellectual property and technology through rules against requirements for local content, use of local facilities or technology transfer.

Second, government regulation that might impede the activities and profits of the major global services industries was restricted or prohibited, including local presence requirements, and unrestricted cross border data flows were guaranteed. Provisions on open networks and network access were subject to an ambiguous caveat for 'reasonable network management' and not harming the network.

Third, there was no effective protection for privacy, but there was a sweeping right for a government to take action it deemed necessary to protect its own security interests. Combined with the previous rules, that meant location of data in places that have minimal privacy protections and maximum rights to intercept and collect data in the name of security.

Again, this has troubling implications for democracy, and threatens to deepen the technological divide. In 2005 a World Bank report wrote approvingly:

> The GATS can be viewed as a multilateral investment agreement, granting rights to the service suppliers of other WTO members, and allowing foreign ownership and control in telecommunications, a sector of the economy often seen as having particular political and

---

[109] A mode 1 commitment meant relinquishing regulatory control over the service and its supplier to the source country and effectively accepting its consumer protection and privacy laws.

[110] Panel, *US-Gambling,* p. 202 at para 6.285.

[111] US, Trade in Services Agreement TiSA Proposal. New Trade in Services Commitment Applicable to All Services, 25 April 2014, https://data.awp.is/filtrala/2014/12/17/19.html (last accessed 21 April 2015). The US proposed seven articles: local presence; local content; local technology; movement of information; open networks, network access and use; electronic authentication and signatures; and exceptions.

[112] See Kelsey J and Kilic B, Briefing on US Proposal on E-Commerce, Technology Transfer, Cross-Border Data Flows and Net Neutrality, 17 December 2014, http://www.world-psi.org/sites/default/files/documents/research/briefing_on_TiSA_e-commerce_final.pdf (last accessed 21 April 2015).

strategic importance. For developing countries, this investment agreement often results in foreign ownership and/or the transfer of control of the incumbent carrier due to lack of domestic capital.[113]

Most South governments have reluctantly taken commitments on e-commerce in their various forms through accession or FTAs. Imposing a TiSA-version on them, even if it falls short of the US ambitions, would likely prove a step too far.

9.2 TiSAfying GATS

The USTR Ron Kirk made no secret of the ultimate goal: to establish new negotiating rules in TiSA, extend the framework to more countries, build a new international consensus on trade in services rules that 'someday could be introduced to the WTO'.[114] That would be easier said than done.

There are two options under WTO rules. The parties to TiSA could seek to add it to the Annex 4 list of plurilateral trade agreements. That would require consensus of all WTO parties. Any changes to TiSA would be governed by TiSA's rules.[115]

Alternatively, or having achieved that, any party could formally propose to the Ministerial Conference an amendment to the GATS.[116] If that was not supported by consensus after 90 days, two thirds of the members could decide to submit an amendment to the Members for approval (provided it is not to amend the MFN provisions in Article II.1). An amendment to the GATS Parts I (Scope and Definitions), II (General Obligations and Disciplines) or III (Specific Commitments) and related annexes would only take effect if accepted by two-thirds of members; it would only apply to them, and subsequently to any additional members that accepted it.[117] However, three quarters of all members could decide that an amendment that came into effect was of such a nature that any member who did not accept it within a certain time could either withdraw from the WTO or remain a member with the consent of the Ministerial Conference (presumably requiring a consensus of all the other members). Amendments to Parts IV (Progressive Liberalisation, including positive list schedules), V (Institutional Provisions) and VI (Final Provisions) would take effect for *all* members on acceptance by two thirds of them.

---

[113] Bressie et al. (2005), p. 5.

[114] US Trade Representative Ron Kirk, Remarks to the Coalition of Service Industries 2012 Global Services Summit, 19 September 2012, https://ustr.gov/about-us/policy-offices/press-office/speeches/transcripts/2012/September/ustr-kirk-remarks-csi-services-summit-2012 (last accessed 21 April 2015).

[115] Agreement Establishing the World Trade Organization, Article X.9 and X.10.

[116] Agreement Establishing the World Trade Organization, Article X.1.

[117] Agreement Establishing the World Trade Organization, Article X.5.

In 2013 the European Commission set out a three-stage strategy by which this goal might be achieved.[118] The TiSA should be built around a series of easily exportable modules. The central pillar would replicate the core GATS provisions, supplemented by a series of sectoral chapters. Parties' schedules would be supported by an 'understanding' that spelt out new scheduling rules, such as a standstill, ratchets that locked in new unilateral liberalisation, and transparency to give corporate interests more influence over the development of domestic policy and regulation.

The TiSA negotiations would begin as a plurilateral, protected from the MFN obligations to all WTO members by the GATS Article V. Other countries would be encouraged to accede to TiSA during the negotiations or afterwards, until it had reached a critical mass of parties. As WTO members, those parties would then seek to have TiSA adopted as a WTO plurilateral agreement or as an amendment to the GATS. New rules and disciplines, for example on domestic regulation, e-commerce, and ICT services, could be brought into the parties' GATS schedules in the form of reference papers inscribed in the column for 'additional commitments', as could the 'understanding on commitments'.[119] New (positive list) market access and (negative list) national treatment commitments could be added to members' schedules unilaterally.

10 A Looming Legitimation Crisis

TiSA is a brazen attempt to neutralise the resistance of many WTO Members from the global South during the GATS 2000 and Doha round and reclaim the power of rich countries to write the global rules. There are major barriers in the way of their ambitions, even assuming the US and EU can settle their own longstanding conflicts.[120]

Even if they got the numbers to force a vote in the WTO, the backlash from the most economically and politically significant non-OECD members could threaten not just the legitimacy of the GATS, but of the WTO itself. Brazil, India and South Africa warned early on against using the plurilateral strategy.[121] The US has

[118] European Commission, Negotiations for a Plurilateral Agreement on Trade in Services, Memorandum, 15 February 2013, http://europa.eu/rapid/press-release_MEMO-13-107_en.htm?locale=FR (last accessed 21 April 2015).

[119] Pursuant to GATS Article XVIII.

[120] The US sensitivities include domestic regulation disciplines and maritime transport and cabotage, while the EU maintains a cultural exception for the content of services, especially audiovisual.

[121] Stanica O, International Services Agreement. Towards a New Plurilateral Agreement, European Parliamentary Research Service, http://epthinktank.eu/2013/03/01/international-services-agreement-towards-a-new-plurilateral-trade-agreemeent/ (last accessed 21 April 2015).

blocked China's attempt to join the negotiations by setting untenable conditions.[122] South governments that resisted the worst demands of the GATS and the services wing of the Doha round, and would end up with something more severe, are unlikely just to surrender.

At the same time, TiSA has revitalised the international campaign against the GATS that made its mark during the Doha round. By 2003, the WTO secretariat felt sufficiently threatened to publish a booklet entitled *GATS – Fact and Fiction*, which simply fuelled the critique.[123] The champions of trade in services agreements failed to understand how influential this opposition has been, nationally and internationally, and are repeating their mistake with TiSA by imposing an extreme level of secrecy, which has predictably proved futile.

They seem equally unaware that intimacy between transnational corporate lobbies and their patron states is even less tolerable after the global financial crisis. New tensions have also emerged. The blending of services and investment brought the growing controversy over investor-state dispute settlement into the TiSA debate, and saw it publicly ruled out.[124] Champions of the knowledge commons and net neutrality are challenging the monopoly powers and protectionism of the big IT players through cross-border, computer and telecommunications services and e-commerce.[125]

These challenges overlap the campaigns against TTIP and the TPPA, making all three agreements into domestic political issues in the participating countries. That is especially potent in Europe, where the European Parliament had gained more say in the adoption of commercial agreements under the Lisbon Treaty. The European Parliament rejected the ratification of the Anti-Counterfeiting Trade Agreement in 2013. As of 2015, the vigorous debates on TiSA foreshadow an equally contested passage.

---

[122] China Categorically Rejects U.S. Preconditions To Participation In TiSA, Inside US Trade. World Trade Online, 22 November 2013, 31(46). The EU supported China's expression of interest (EU Backs China Joining Talks on Trade in Services Agreement (TiSA), 31 March 2014, http://eeas.europa.eu/delegations/wto/press_corner/all_news/news/2014/20143103_TiSA_press_release_en.htm (last accessed 21 April 2015).

[123] https://www.wto.org/english/tratop_e/serv_e/gats_factfiction_e.htm (last accessed 21 April 2015).

[124] Eg, a question in the European Parliament on 13 March 2015 asked the European Commission if the negotiating directives for TiSA included investor-state dispute settlement. http://www.europarl.europa.eu/sides/getDoc.do?type=WQ&reference=E-2015-004250&format=XML&language=EN (last accessed 21 April 2015).

[125] Eg, Sutton M, It Doesn't Matter who Does the Lobbying: Trade Agreements aren't the Place for Internet Regulations, Electronic Frontier Foundation, 19 December 2014, https://www.eff.org/deeplinks/2014/12/it-doesnt-matter-who-does-lobbying-trade-agreements-arent-place-internet (last accessed 21 April 2015).

Thirty years since the Uruguay round began, TiSA reflects the contradictions of embedded neoliberalism. This paper began by suggesting that the neoliberal era to which trade in services regime belongs has almost run its course, and that a transformation to an as-yet-undefined post-neoliberalism may occur over the next decade, or perhaps two.

If true, that poses a conundrum. Trade in services agreements have no place in a post-neoliberal world that seeks to reverse the development divide and to restore equality, if not primacy, to social objectives when governments exercise their responsibility to regulate services in the national interest. Yet disarming those agreements is an extraordinary political and legal challenge. Paradoxically, the TiSA project has the potential to push the trade in services regime to the brink by further delegitimising the agreements themselves and deepening the crisis in the WTO.

References

Arnold PJ (2005) Disciplining domestic regulation: The World Trade Organization and the market for professional services. Acc Organ Soc 30(4):299–330

Bhala R (2007) Competitive liberalization, competitive imperialism, and intellectual property. Liverpool Law Rev 28:77–105

Bressie K, Kende M, Williams H (2005) Telecommunications trade liberalisation and the WTO. Info J Policy Regul Strateg Telecommun Inf Med 7(2):3–24

Drake W, Nicolaidis K (1992) Ideas, interests and institutionalization: "trade in services" and the Uruguay Round. Int Organ 46(1):37–100

Feketekuty G (1988) International trade in services: an overview and blueprint for negotiations. Ballinger, Cambridge

Grynberg R, Dugal M, Razzaque MA (2006) An evaluation of the terms of accession to the World Trade Organization. A comparative assessment of services and goods commitments by the WTO members and acceding countries. Commonwealth Secretariat, London

Kelsey J (2005) World trade and small nations in the south pacific region. Kansas J Law Public Policy 14:247–306

Kelsey J (2008) Serving whose interests? the political economy of trade in services agreements. Routledge, Abingdon

Kelsey J (2010) How the trans-pacific partnership agreement could heighten financial instability and foreclose governments' regulatory space'. N Z Yearb Int Law 8:1–43

Kelsey J (2011) The conundrum of shifting orthodoxies: FTAs and Korea's currency controls. J Int Econ Law 14(4):845–868

Khor M (2005) Developing countries object to "benchmarking" services proposals. Third World Econ 363:5

Panagariya A (1999) The regionalism debate: an overview. World Econ 22(3):477–51

Piketty T (2013) Capital in the twenty-first century. Harvard University Press, Cambridge

Reinhart C, Rogoff K (2013) Banking crises: an equal opportunity menace. J Bank Financ 37:4557–4573

Sauvé P, Gillespie J (2000) Financial services and the GATS 2000 round. In: Litan R, Santomero A (eds) Brookings-Wharton papers on financial services. Brookings Institution, Washington DC, pp 423–452

Wolf M (2014) The shifts and the shocks: what we've learned-and still have to learn-from the financial crisis. Penguin Press, New York

Wunsch-Vincent S (2003) The digital trade agenda of the U.S.: parallel tracks of bilateral, regional and multilateral liberalisation. Aussenwirtschaft 58(1):7–46

Trade in Services and Regulatory Flexibility: 20 Years of GATS, 20 Years of Critique

Panagiotis Delimatsis

Contents

Abstract The General Agreement on Trade in Services (GATS) was a key achievement of the multilateral trade negotiations during the Uruguay Round. Twenty years later, the service sector is probably the most dynamic economic sector. The expansion of global value chains and of the on-demand economy will only increase the importance of services. However, the relevance of the GATS for the global economy has suffered from the deficiencies of the GATS legal framework. The purpose of the present article is not to defend the GATS. The GATS is an artefact of the 90s that struggles to remain a living instrument amidst the most severe existential crisis that has ever hit the multilateral trading system. Rather, this contribution aims at offering an account of the GATS birth defects, critically review its inability to take stock of the progress made the last 15 years of multilateral trade negotiations, discuss its development-related potential and assess its future prospects amidst regional service-related initiatives that threaten its existence, including the Transatlantic Trade and Investment Partnership (TTIP) and the Trade in

P. Delimatsis (✉)
European and International Trade Law, Tilburg Law School, Tilburg University, Tilburg, The Netherlands
e-mail: p.delimatsis@uvt.nl

M. Bungenberg et al. (eds.), *European Yearbook of International Economic Law 2016*, European Yearbook of International Economic Law 7,
DOI 10.1007/978-3-319-29215-1_7

Services Agreement (TiSA). A key conclusion of this paper is that a 'GATS 2.0' is warranted and should be focused on guaranteeing non-discrimination and ensuring good governance.

1 Introduction

The global financial crisis of 2008 has shaken the foundations of deregulatory practices of three decades of neoliberal orthodoxy in the banking sector, mostly hailed by developed countries for their adequacy.[1] There is no doubt that the financial crisis was the culmination of ill-fated regulatory choices at the domestic, regional and international level mostly made in the 80s. Such choices, which were premised on the shibboleth that 'the State cannot do it all' and the merits of technocracy, undeniably affected the course and ultimate outcome of the Uruguay Round negotiations (notably in the field of services) in the early 90s as well, wrapped in immeasurable optimism about the virtues and effects of trade liberalisation.

The financial turmoil and its negative repercussions on employment and welfare particularly for the young and poor who bore the brunt of the recession signals 'a crisis of legitimacy for neoliberalism'.[2] The critique against neoliberalism is in full swing. Post-crisis, the relative resilience of financial service industries of certain economies such as India or China to the crisis cannot go unnoticed[3] and brings about a reconsideration of several decades of conventional wisdom regarding financial regulation. The role of the 'public' versus the 'private' in finance is being reassessed, without necessarily changes in regulatory philosophy taking place.[4] The quest of a new orthodoxy seems to be more easily said than done, as in the financial sector in particular the extant interdependence among financial institutions is irreversible.

Regardless, and more fundamentally for our purposes, such discussions appear to be predominantly, if not exclusively, focused on the *regulation* of the financial sector. But do they also shake the foundations of the World Trade Organization

---

[1] Cf Avgouleas (2009), p. 24.

[2] See Kelsey's article in this volume (Kelsey 2016, section 1), quoting Stiglitz J (2009) Report of the Commission of Experts of the President of the United Nations General Assembly on Reforms of the International Monetary and Financial System, United Nations.

[3] Again, and quite ironically, this resilience may be the result of isolation from the global economy and underdevelopment of the financial system. See Huang (2010), p. 219.

[4] Take the case of the scandal-tainted Libor benchmark. In the aftermath of the Libor scandal, and despite previous pledges relating to future management of Libor by the UK Financial Services Authority (now split into the Financial Conduct Authority and the Prudential Regulation Authority), it is a *private* corporation, IntercontinentalExchange (ICE), that administers the Libor benchmark. ICE is supervised by the Financial Conduct Authority. See Intercontinental Exchange to take over running Libor benchmark. Financial Times, 17 January 2014.

(WTO) and its legitimacy in pursuing its liberalisation-centered objectives? Arguably, not. The WTO has largely achieved what it was expected to achieve, institutionally speaking: it reduced transaction costs; increased access to information (through mandatory notifications) for those who cannot buy it and thus 'popularized' otherwise highly technical information; created an independent forum for managing international commerce, solving disputes (extra-judicially or after recourse to the WTO adjudicating bodies), and enforcing sanctions.[5]

Twenty years down the road, the WTO has changed the way international law and relations function. Truth be told, the substantive law that the WTO agreements generated did not live up to the expectations of a big part of its membership in a number of areas, including in the field of services. Admittedly, the GATS has had birth defects and certain constraints *ab initio*. However, it would be erroneous to say that the creation of the WTO and the ensuing implementation of the WTO Agreements, including the GATS, did not create wealth. On the contrary, substantial growth recorded in the 4 corners of the world in the last 20 years is the result of openness mainly agreed upon in the WTO in the mid-90s, or more recently in preferential trade agreements (PTAs), which mirror the WTO trade-liberalizing logic.

Regardless of whether PTAs are friends or foes of the WTO (an issue that has come to the forefront on the occasion of the ongoing Transatlantic and Transpacific trade negotiations), the fact remains that PTAs borrow concepts, rules and principles developed in the GATT/WTO. This means that the *regulatory philosophy* of the WTO is hale and hearty. In addition, and quite crucially, practice shows that a positive relationship exists between development and trade liberalisation: the more developed a country becomes the more willing it is to open up.[6] This appears to be a diachronic axiom regarding the gains from trade. Countries are not concerned with *whether* they will liberalize but with the *timing* of such a liberalisation.

This is no less true about trade in services. Take telecommunication, transport, distribution or business services. Trade relies on adequate infrastructure and indeed such trade-enabling services sectors expanded exponentially in recent times to establish trade-supporting mechanisms and procedures. The supply of services has never before been more global. Disruptive innovation in information and communication technology (ICT) services is so significant and pervasive that regulators have difficulties following—and, even less, regulating—these activities.

The service sector is probably the most dynamic and promising economic sector; its overarching trait, that is, intangibility, allows services to cross borders much more quickly than goods. With global value chains (GVCs) becoming increasingly less regional and more global and the rapid expansion of the on-demand economy, the importance of services and their contribution to the creation of wealth is bound to grow. Statistics traditionally underestimate the value of services, but it is quite

---

[5] See Delimatsis (2013), p. 139.

[6] Again, more trade liberalization does not ipso facto guarantee more development. Social policies and pro-poor strategies for vulnerable groups are essential.

telling that the value of world exports of commercial services almost doubled between 2007 and 2013, from US$ 2.7 to US$4.6 trillion.[7]

Amidst the most severe budgetary crisis of its history, the European Union (EU) remains the largest exporter and importer of commercial services, responsible for over one fourth of global trade in services (excluding intra-EU trade). Having said that, the growth in global services trade has been unequally distributed. Still, with the exception of Africa where services trade exports declined, trade in services grew by at least 2 % in the rest of the world. Even if not all regions have benefited from trade in services, the gains from trade in services still have been more substantial and equally distributed globally when compared to merchandise trade in the last 2 years.

In addition, recent studies suggest that the rise of the South is more important and fairly broadly distributed than it was initially suggested. Indeed, the BRICS continue to have the lion's share; yet success stories of above-average economic growth that helped alleviate domestic social inequalities are to be found in the four corners of the world, from Tunisia, Rwanda and Ghana to Bangladesh, Malaysia and Vietnam. As the UN Human Development Report in 2013 put it, '[t]he rise of the South is unprecedented in its speed and scale. Never in history have the living conditions and prospects of so many people changed so dramatically and so fast'.[8] Such developments lead to the emergence of a new global middle class, with obvious societal benefits relating to equality and inclusion. As these countries grow, trade in services will grow with them.

The purpose of the present article is not to defend the GATS. The GATS is just a legal instrument, an artefact of the 90s that struggles to remain a living instrument amidst the most severe existential crisis that has ever hit the multilateral trading system. Indeed, the GATS is a victim of the current stalemate at the WTO; the current GATS negotiations started later than they were supposed to and were held hostage by the lack of progress in other fields of the WTO agenda such as agriculture or NAMA.[9] Viewed from this angle, a lot of criticism against the GATS is unjustified. Most of the global challenges nowadays regarding social cohesion, employment or the environment are not due to the rules set out in the GATS. They rather are the result of a long-lasting economic paradigm that has proven unable to cater for certain injustices.

This paper aims at offering an account of the GATS birth defects; critically review its inability to take stock of the progress made the last 15 years of multilateral trade negotiations; discuss its development-related potential; and assess its future prospects amidst regional service-related initiatives that threaten its

[7] See WTO, World Trade Report (2014), p. 24.

[8] United Nations Development Programme, Human Development Report 2013—The Rise of the South: Human Progress in a Diverse World, p. 11.

[9] See, for instance, the very important progress that was achieved and the advanced draft text produced in the negotiations relating to domestic regulation 4 years ago. Very little was done ever since due to unsatisfactory progress in other negotiating areas.

existence. Sections 2 and 3 discuss the main features of the GATS focusing on its birth defects and the critique offered by Jane Kelsey in this volume. Section 4 deals with the failed attempts to complete the GATS regulatory framework and the challenges that the current discussions at the regional level (bilateral or plurilateral) pose. Section 5 concludes. A key conclusion of this paper is that the GATS 2.0 in the aftermath of the Doha round (whenever this occurs) should focus on what the multilateral trading system has done best: guarantee non-discrimination (if needed, through recourse to an expedited dispute settlement system) and ensure good governance.

2 The GATS and Its 'Birth Defects'

2.1 Inevitable Flexibility, Constructive Ambiguity

Once regarded as non-tradable, services currently dominate economic activity in most countries around the world irrespective of their level of development. Services are a growth engine, not only in terms of economic growth but also social growth. While financial, telecommunications or transport services come to mind, other services such as health or education can also be key inputs and determinants of the stock and growth of human capital.[10] New technological means 'democratize' the supply of services globally, opening new pathways for interaction. The new collaborative consumption opportunities that are given through the internet expand the pool of potential service suppliers but also raise new questions that regulators may have hard time answering.

Taking into account the negotiating history that led to the introduction of the GATS in the WTO 'single undertaking' approach at the end of the Uruguay Round, the GATS was a milestone. It is the first multilateral agreement that establishes rules for the international supply of services. However, the GATS has also been a compromise among centrifugal forces that sought to influence the approach taken vis-à-vis trade in services. For the proponents of the GATS, mostly developed countries, this was a Pyrrhic victory. Initially, the GATS was part of a concerted attempt to consolidate at the international level previous privatization efforts made at the domestic level. Indeed, privatization of financial or telecommunication services but also healthcare or education services took place prior to the conclusion of the GATS with a view to reaping the benefits of still incomplete internal markets at the moment.[11] Competition law, at least in the EU, contributed to this trend, through the condemnation of restrictive arrangements or of abuse of dominant position and State aid rules.

[10] See Hoekman and Mattoo (2008), p. 23.

[11] Cf. Hancher and Sauter (2010).

Viewed from thin angle, then, the GATS was the result, rather than the cause, of the erosion of the public service tradition in the 1980s and transformations in previously non-marketable services that created new business opportunities for private parties and companies. It was an attempt of several trading powers but also smaller developing economies to multilateralize these transformations—and induce other WTO Members to join them in this deregulatory verve. The final deal reached at the WTO did not fully meet the aspirations of these countries. The end of the Uruguay Round found the GATS incomplete: a soft set of general obligations which should always be read in combination with a given Member's schedule; legal provisions that called for negotiations (eg, on government procurement or subsidies and domestic regulation); Members' schedules that did not reflect the actual level of openness; a future promise for progressive liberalisation, starting 5 years after the end of the Uruguay Round at the latest; and, finally, an abstract sunset review of MFN exemptions.

Whereas the substantive scope (*ratione materiae*) of the GATS is virtually unlimited, covering any possible measure affecting trade in services taken by governments, public authorities at all levels of government or by non-governmental bodies with delegated regulatory powers, the applicability of the GATS largely depends on the liberalizing decisions of each WTO Member, most notably the commitments, limitations and conditions made under market access (Article XVI GATS) or national treatment (Article XVII GATS). These commitments, limitations and conditions are inscribed in each Member's Schedule of Commitments (hereinafter 'the Schedule').

Members first decide whether they will liberalize market access and/or national treatment in a given services sector (say, professional services, which is a sub-sector of business services), and afterwards can list the types of limitations they want to maintain in this sector for each one of the four modes of supply.[12] These limitations are inscribed in a negative manner.[13] For instance, a given Member may decide, out of the entire business service sector, to fully liberalize only the supply of architectural services in a cross-border manner (that is, neither the supplier nor the consumer move, but only the service through remote means), but still maintain limitations against the establishment of foreign architects in the domestic market.

If a service sector does not form part of the Schedule of a given Member, then the GATS has a very limited influence on the regulation of this sector domestically. For instance, if a Member decides not to include health services in its Schedule, then only the MFN principle applies and some other minor (so-called 'unconditional')

[12] Cross-border supply; consumption abroad; commercial presence; and temporary movement of natural persons. There is no doubt that the GATS is an investment agreement, as over 50 % of services trade is conducted through Mode 3. See Magdeleine J and Maurer A (2008) Measuring GATS Mode 4 Trade Flows. WTO Staff Working Paper ERSD-2008-05.

[13] The so-called 'negative list' approach means in the GATS jargon that, other than the sectors and sub-sectors that are explicitly listed in a Member's Schedule of MFN exemptions, the MFN principle applies to all other sectors.

obligations, eg to publish all relevant measures of general application affecting trade in services (Article III:1 GATS) or to allow for independent review of and appropriate remedies for administrative decisions affecting trade in services (Article VI:2). The former is subject to the view of each Member as to whether a given measure affects trade in services. In any case, such obligation could be regarded as anything but burdensome, as most democracies of the world do publish their laws in the respective official journal. As to the second obligation, it is true that independent review of administrative decisions may be a controversial issue even in advanced democracies, notably in the case of self-regulatory bodies.[14]

Even the utmost principle of most-favoured-nation treatment (MFN) is not uniformly applicable; rather, each Member was given the opportunity to inscribe exemptions to the MFN. These exemptions, listed in a negative manner, are still in place although Members had agreed in the end of the Uruguay Round to review them after 10 years with a view to eliminating them.

Thus, a Member's Schedule and list of MFN exemptions determine the applicability of key GATS rules to the territory of that Member. WTO Members can tailor their obligations based on their country-specific needs and capacities. WTO Members have a wide margin of discretion as to the substantive (that is, the sectoral choice) and temporal (that is, the starting date of the pledge made) features of their liberalizing commitments.

This flexibility embedded in the GATS was the only means that would allow the acceptance of the GATS during the Uruguay Round. Variable geometry has been a trait of the global regime in services since its inception, whereby certain countries would decide to liberalize access to certain sectors, whereas other countries would leave liberalisation for a later date.

2.2 *The Outdated GATS Schedules: What Is and What Could Be*

Learning by doing has been an essential feature of the early GATS negotiations. The counterpart for services of the Harmonized System for Goods was the Central Product Classification (CPC) List of the United Nations, which found its place in the GATS in a simplified form document, the Services Sectoral Classification List (the so-called 'W/120').[15] A problematic feature of the Classification List has been its lack of adaptability to future developments. The Classification List is everything

[14] See, among many, Case C-439/99, *Commission v. Italy* [2002] ECR I-305, para. 39–40; and Joined Cases C-94/04 & C-202/04, *Cipolla* [2006] ECR I-11421.

[15] GATT, Services Sectoral Classification List MTN.GNS/W/120, 10 July 1991. The CPC 1991 that was used for the W/120 has been subsequently revised, but the W/120 remained unchanged. However, some WTO Members that acceded after the end of the Uruguay Round used subsequent versions of the CPC.

but a living instrument: First and foremost, it failed to keep up with the developments in classification made at the CPC List. Subsequent revisions of the latter have never been taken up at the GATS level. Technological advances are transforming the way services are supplied. The world nowadays is much different than 20 years ago, but the GATS has no internal mechanism that would allow updating its sectoral list. More crucially, there is no mechanism that would allow a coordinated effort to update the Schedules. Modification of Schedules is a burdensome, time-consuming process that takes place in an unorganized manner.[16]

Divided into several sectors and subsectors which are regarded as mutually exclusive,[17] the Classification List fails to cater for, simplify and thus facilitate liberalisation in certain sectors, as services related to a given activity are dispersed among various sectors and subsectors.

Take the case of health-related services whereby the relevant sector in the List 'health and social services' does not exhaust the categories of activities associate with healthcare. Whereas hospital and ambulance services form part of the health and social services sector, medical and dental services, veterinary services or those offered by midwives are listed under professional services, a sub-sector of business services.[18]

Another example of a fragmented outdated approach is energy services, which also reflects previous sectoral realities. Back in the 80s, electricity and gas were predominantly provided by state-run vertically integrated monopolistic suppliers. Such suppliers were responsible for all energy-related activities, from exploration to production to marketing.[19] These sectoral characteristics led to the conclusion that substantial trade in energy services could not yet occur and therefore preference was given to other sectors where trade was already significant. The relative insignificance of the sector at that time is also reflected in the Classification List: transport, construction, engineering, distribution and energy-related financial services are dispersed across various services sectors included in the Classification List.[20]

At the same time, the three energy-specific sectors in the Classification List can potentially be more far-reaching than one might think at first blush: services incidental to energy distribution and to mining (both classified under business services) include both downstream and upstream energy-related activities, whereas

[16] For instance, in the aftermath of the United States—Measures Affecting the Cross-Border Supply of Gambling and Betting Services (*US – Gambling*) saga, the US sought to change the entry of its schedule with respect to the cross-border supply of gambling and betting services. However, this has been impossible for more than 2 years now.

[17] Also Appellate Body Report, *US – Gambling*, para. 180.

[18] The distinction is allegedly based on whether a health-related services is associated with a given type of institutional nursing. See WTO, Council for Trade in Services, Health and Social Services, Background Note by the Secretariat, S/C/W/50, 18 September 1998, p. 20.

[19] See WTO, Council for Trade in Services, Energy Services, S/C/W/311, 12 January 2010, p. 2.

[20] See also See WTO, Council for Trade in Services (Special Session), Energy Services, Communication from the United States, S/CSS/W/24, 18 December 2000, Annex A.

pipeline transportation of fuels (classified under transport services) covers all services that relate to the actual operation of a pipeline. Thus, careless scheduling may lead to unforeseen results and requests to liberalize sub-sectors which was not initially intended.

This brings us to the importance of scheduling in services, one of the issues that has been at the epicenter of criticism against the GATS. Being a relatively short list of sectors and subsectors, the W/120 and the ensuing Schedules of commitments prepared by the WTO Members have left room for ambiguity and varying interpretations, which would not always converge with the intentions and regulatory purposes of the drafters of those Schedules. According to the 1993 Scheduling Guidelines, Members were allowed to use their own nomenclature and undertake commitments based, for instance, on a cluster approach, as long as the scope of the commitments and the classification used is sufficiently clear.[21] Nevertheless, the 'fear of the unknown' led WTO Members at the time to more often than not use the CPC classification as a basis when preparing their respective Schedules. The latter would allow "a higher degree of disaggregation and precision to be attained should it become necessary, at a later stage."[22]

Since the early years of the GATS, starting with the *EC – Bananas* dispute, it was made clear that the GATS schedules, more than anything, are the centerpieces of trade liberalisation in services. For instance, it is no coincidence that all disputes relating to services before the WTO adjudicating bodies tackled the interpretation of GATS schedules and the scope of the commitments made therein. Being an integral part of the GATS pursuant to Article XX:3 GATS, the GATS schedules, once verified, became treaty text, that is, multilateral obligations that determine the applicability and purview of the GATS. Thus, even if schedules are the results of 'a process of reciprocal demands and concessions, of "give and take"',[23] the intents and perceptions of a given Member alone regarding certain concepts will not matter.[24] As Schedules represent a treaty and a common agreement among all Members, their interpretation inevitably triggers the application of the rules of interpretation of the Vienna Convention on the Law of Treaties (Articles 31–33 VCLT). Thus, commitments made are treaty terms that must be interpreted in good faith, in accordance with the ordinary meaning of the inscribed commitments of a

[21] Also Appellate Body Report, *US – Gambling*, para. 202–203.

[22] Appellate Body Report, *US – Gambling*, para. 200.

[23] Appellate Body Report, European Communities—Customs Classification of Certain Computer Equipment, WT/DS62/AB/R, WT/DS67/AB/R, WT/DS68/AB/R, adopted 22 June 1998 (*EC – Computer Equipment*), para. 109.

[24] As the Appellate Body noted in *EC – Computer Equipment* [para. 82] when interpreting GATT Schedules, "the security and predictability of tariff concessions would be seriously undermined if the concessions in Members' Schedules were to be interpreted on the basis of the subjective views of certain exporting Members alone".

given Member taken in their context and understood in the light of the object and purpose of the GATS and the WTO, more generally.[25]

On the other hand, the manner Members draft their schedules and other members perceive similar concepts was regarded as context within the meaning of the VCLT.[26] The latter is of particular importance in the GATS whereby the reference point is the Classification List *in combination with* the CPC.[27] Thus, panels and the Appellate Body, when interpreting a GATS Schedule, will routinely have recourse to GATS Schedules of other Members to extract, if possible, the common understanding of Members regarding—and a reliable, objective meaning of—a particular concept or term. This may not always be possible, though, as certain terms used may be country-specific and unique to a particular Member. In those cases, the ordinary meaning of the term will play the most important role, and thus taking into account the unilateral origin of the commitment will be inevitable.[28]

The two landmark cases whereby the interpretation of GATS Schedules came to the fore are the gambling dispute against the US and the audiovisual services dispute against China. In *US – Gambling*, at stake was the meaning of the US entry in its GATS schedule relating to 'other recreational services (except sporting)'.[29] Interestingly, the US did not specify that, in preparing its Schedule, it used the Classification List and the CPC. The Appellate Body found that, unless Members clearly indicate that they plan to deviate from the W/120 and the CPC, they are regarded as having followed it, which would lead to the W/120 and the CPC becoming the reference points for the interpretation of a given commitment. However, this finding, as surprising as it was considered by some GATS critics in the aftermath of the *US – Gambling* dispute, should not be viewed in isolation. On the contrary, various case-specific and GATS-specific elements have played a role in the decision of the Appellate Body: first, the US contention that it generally followed the W/120 structure in its Schedule; second, the fact that the GATS Scheduling Guidelines[30] showed a clear preference for adherence to the CPC and W/120 unless an *unambiguous* indication to the contrary was given; third, a cover note in previous drafts of the US Schedule indicating that specific commitments

[25] Cf. Leroux (2007), p. 757. The Appellate Body confirmed that treaty interpretation 'is ultimately a holistic exercise that should not be mechanically subdivided into rigid components'. See Appellate Body Report, China—Measures Affecting Trading Rights and Distribution Services for Certain Publications and Audiovisual Entertainment Products, WT/DS363/AB/R, adopted 19 January 2010 (*China – Publications and Audiovisual Products*), para. 348.

[26] See, for instance, Appellate Body Report, *US – Gambling*.

[27] This can be contrasted to the GATT where only the Harmonized System of the World Customs Organization (WCO) is the relevant benchmark.

[28] See also Ortino (2006), p. 124. The Appellate Body implicitly agreed with this limitation in *US – Gambling*, para. 182.

[29] See also Krajewski (2005), p. 417.

[30] The Appellate Body considered these Guidelines to be relevant preparatory work under Art. 32 VCLT, reversing the Panel's previous finding that they constitute context within the meaning of Art. 31 VCLT.

were made according to the W/120 nomenclature; and, fourth, an explanatory text of the US International Trade Commission which included a table of concordance indicating the correspondence between the US Schedule and the CPC nomenclature.

In *China – Publications and Audiovisual Products*, China's policy relating to content review of publications and audiovisual products was at stake. The case raised several questions of systemic importance for both the GATT and the GATS, but also on the relationship between them. The GATS-related issue touched upon the electronic distribution of sound recordings and whether China had liberalized such distribution services in its Schedule or not. China suggested that the entry 'sound recording distribution services' only covers the supply of such services in physical form, while the electronic supply of such services should be regarded as coming under a new type of service sector, that is, 'network music services', which has emerged as a result of changes in digital technologies and communication networks.

The Panel appeared to sympathize with China's argument that technical feasibility and commercial reality of a services at the time a commitment was inscribed in a Member's Schedule should be taken into account in any future interpretation of that commitment.[31] This would most likely also be in line with the principle of contemporaneity, which requires that the meaning and scope of a given term be ascertained as of the time when the commitment was made. The Appellate Body underscored that "GATS Schedules...are multilateral treaties with continuing obligations that WTO Members entered into for an indefinite period of time."[32] When this is combined with sufficiently generic terms in a given Schedule (like China's) whose scope of application may change over time, then the result is that that the correct meaning of a given entry can only be the one that is ascertained at the moment of interpretation.

This evolutionary approach, based on the doctrine of 'living instrument' as first identified in *US – Shrimp*, can be quite intrusive, admittedly. However, it is also an accepted approach in general international law when it comes to international legal instruments adopted for an indefinite period of time. The Appellate Body justified its interpretive choice suggesting that any other choice would lead to similar commitments being given varying meanings, content and coverage depending on the date of their entry into force, thereby undermining the legal security, predictability and clarity of GATS specific commitments.[33] However, the opposite argument can also be made: the evolutionary approach can also undermine the abovementioned values of GATS specific commitments.

As one can infer from the above, trade in services could greatly benefit from more clarity and precision in the scheduling of GATS commitments. However, the

[31] Panel Report, *China – Publications and Audiovisual Products*, para. 7.1237.

[32] See Appellate Body Report, *China – Publications and Audiovisual Products,* para. 396.

[33] Appellate Body Report, *China – Publications and Audiovisual Products*, para. 397; also Delimatsis (2011), p. 281.

draft Schedules circulated in the Doha Round services negotiations seem to follow the same pattern as the scheduling exercise in the Uruguay Round. More crucially, it was argued that the current offers on the negotiating table still do not reflect existing levels of openness in Members' services markets.[34] Many of these offers date in any event back in 2008, so an update would certainly be necessary before any WTO round can be concluded. At the PTA level, liberalisation levels have not been far more ambitious, which, arguably, has to do with the existing uncertainties at the WTO/GATS level and the prospective finalization of the negotiating Round.

While flexible at first blush, the GATS does not seem to offer sufficient flexibility when it comes to modification of schedules and experimenting with liberalisation. The only exception to this observation is the EU, which has had the opportunity to amend the GATS by amending its Schedule of Commitments as a result of the EU's waves of enlargement after the end of the Uruguay Round.[35]

The existing mechanism of Article XXI GATS is fairly formalistic and time-consuming. Arguably, financial compensation and expedited arbitration setting the level of damages would be reliable options. By the same token, allowing Members to experiment with liberalizing commitments (for instance, in mode 4) for a pre-agreed number of years could lead to higher levels of liberalisation and also better, more responsive regulation. The idea of rolling-back liberalisation in services has been a taboo for several years; however, the lack of such a possibility may be one of the reasons for the current low level of ambition in the GATS.

3 'Sensitive' Services and Denied Liberalisation

The *pace* of liberalisation and openness to foreign competition is a matter of adequate planning. In certain sectors, liberalisation may never occur; this is the case of the core public services such as healthcare or education: services which would be undersupplied if left to private suppliers. In such cases, governments invariably intervene to pursue legitimate non-economic objectives and thereby serve the public interest. Indeed, certain services activities can be regarded as non-market services, that is, services which should not be regarded as a tradable commodity.[36] Certain financial services can also fall in this category, as openness may undermine the capacity of countries to implement, for instance, monetary policy or to ensure the viability of a statutory system of social security or public retirement plans.[37] Thus, as certain services have public good characteristics, the fear of under-provision or market failure leads the State to interfere with their

[34] Borchert et al. (2011), p. 115.

[35] See the Opinion of the Court of Justice of the European Union (CJEU) 1/2008 on the modification of the EU GATS Schedule [2009] ECR I-11129, para. 114.

[36] Cf European Commission, Green Paper on Services of General Interest, COM(2003) 270 final.

[37] GATS Financial Services Annex, paragraph 1(b).

regulation, management and supply. This was recognized in the GATS through the insertion of a rule excluding services in the exercise of governmental authority from the scope of the GATS.[38]

The threshold for such an exemption from the purview of the GATS has been regarded as quite high: such services should be neither supplied on a for-profit basis nor in competition with one or more service suppliers, the two conditions being cumulative. Regarding the first condition, intent to make a profit or obtain a financial gain would suffice. Such an intent may also be unrelated to the operational basis of the service supplier, meaning that, increasingly nowadays, public service suppliers may offer services on both a commercial and non-commercial basis.[39] As to the second condition, it seems that competition-related aspects would be crucial here, including the geographical market, end-uses, price relationships, distribution channels and equality of competitive opportunities.

When regarded together with the bottom up ("positive list") scheduling approach and the possibility of invoking the general exception provision enshrined in Article XIV GATS, the GATS appears to have all the necessary guarantees for ensuring a high level of regulatory flexibility for a sensitive core of services traditionally offered by the State. However, it would appear utopian to continue discussing the room left for regulatory autonomy at the domestic level, in particular for those WTO Members which undertook significant liberalisation commitments, for instance, in financial or telecommunication services. For those Members, the purview of the GATS is pervasive. A transfer of sovereignty takes place through international contracting and the functioning of the WTO dispute settlement system has amply demonstrated the repercussions, be it positive or negative, that such a transfer may have.

For certain WTO Members such as the EU, this transfer of sovereignty becomes clear through the internal legislative process: notably with regard to sensitive services such as cultural and audiovisual, educational, social and human healthcare, international agreements, by way of derogation, fall within the shared competence of the Union *and* its Member States (rather than the exclusive competence of the EU regarding the Common Commercial Policy) and the Council of the European Union has to decide by unanimity (rather than the qualified majority rule that characterizes the Common Commercial Policy of the EU).[40] The willingness to transfer sovereignty is then confirmed either in the pre-established negotiating mandate addressed to the EU negotiator or through the Decision that adopts the final outcome of a given WTO negotiating round.

Again, the less risk-averse (in terms of breadth of commitments) Members are offered in return the possibility to reap the benefits from liberalisation commitments made by other Members, as typically their commitments have been the result of mutually advantageous concessions made by trading partners of interest to them. If

[38] See Art. 1:3(c) GATS and para. 1(b) of the Financial Services Annex.

[39] Cf. Krajewski (2003), p. 341.

[40] Treaty on the Functioning of the European Union, Art. 207:4.

many times this group of Members consists of developed countries, this does not mean that the GATS has an inherent pro-developed-country bias. On the contrary, in view of the above-mentioned observations, the GATS, more than any other WTO agreement, appears to offer opportunities and choices to the entire membership, guaranteeing a minimum policy space for genuine regulatory intervention and the right to deny liberalisation through the safety valve of Article XIV. Even if it is true that this provision has never been invoked successfully,[41] this is a telling result not about its inefficacy but rather about the ingenuity of Members when they want to conceal protectionism in favour of the domestic industry.[42] The GATS, with all its imperfections, has an intrinsic logic and structure that condones regulatory flexibility and diversity.

Does this structure undermine the view of services as important social phenomena? From what preceded, we would rather answer this question in the negative. Even if services 'involve social relations that frame people's everyday existence',[43] this does not undermine nor supersede their nature as economic, gainful activities. The Court of Justice of the European Union (CJEU) has dealt with similar arguments in a series of cases relating to professions in services and found that any special character of a given service should be discussed under the provision relating to the protection of a non-economic objective and, if applicable, exempt a particular activity from the scope of the EU economic constitution relating to the fundamental freedoms.[44]

4 (Failed) Rule-Making in the GATS and Mega-Regionals

4.1 The Myth of Positive Integration in the GATS

The GATS, just as every WTO agreement, is an overtly incomplete contract.[45] The wording of several GATS obligations is drafted in an ambiguous manner, whereas other obligations such as those on subsidies (Article XV), safeguards (Article X), government procurement (XIII)[46] or domestic regulation (Article VI:4), which

---

[41] Delimatsis (2011), p. 281.

[42] The *US – Gambling* saga is telling in this respect: for its own domestic reasons, the US was willing to protect the horseracing industry from the otherwise general prohibition on remote gambling and betting.

[43] See Kelsey (2016), section 2.

[44] See, among others, cases such as *Reyners*, *Gebhard* and *Wouters*.

[45] On the incompleteness of the WTO agreements, see Horn H, Maggi G and Staiger R (2006) Trade Agreements as Endogenously Incomplete Contracts. NBER Working Paper No 12745.

[46] As to government procurement, the Understanding on Commitments in Financial Services, under section B.2, entails an exception to the overall absence of disciplines on government procurement by requiring that public entities respect MFN and non-discrimination when they purchase financial services.

constitute the so-called 'built-in agenda', remain to be finalized, with variable likelihood of ultimate success.

And yet, the end of the Uruguay Round was full of optimism about the future of the regulation of international trade in services. A large part of this optimism was based on the momentum relating to the regulatory work to be concluded in the aftermath of the creation of the GATS. Already agreeing among the WTO membership that rules would have to be created on subsidies, safeguards, government procurement and domestic, non-discriminatory measures was regarded as a big step forward.

Government procurement, that is, the procurement by governmental agencies of services purchased for governmental purposes and not with a view to commercial resale or with a view to use in the supply of services for commercial resale, has been initially one of the most promising areas for creative rule-making; that was in particular because similar concepts and terms were discussed under the aegis of the negotiations on trade in goods for a WTO agreement on government procurement in goods. However, the progress of the Working Group on GATS Rules, which was also discussing the issue of services subsidies and emergency safeguards, has been disappointing. Substantial divergence of views still exist among Members, with safeguards remaining the thorniest issue.

Negotiations on domestic regulation (aiming to create rules to ensure that measures relating to qualifications, licensing and technical standards do not constitute unnecessary barriers to services trade) are the biggest victim of lack of progress on the WTO negotiating table in other areas. Recognizing that this is the most important area of services regulation, Members have early on tabled various proposals with a view to influencing potential draft texts. Such drafts would establish important procedural obligations for WTO Members when preparing, drafting and adopting measures relating to qualifications, licensing or technical standards.[47] Measures aiming to regulate the conduct of both public and private bodies and facilitate market access for both legal and natural persons. Due process has been a recurring theme in the most recent draft of the rules on domestic regulation, along with extensive transparency-related obligations, calling for substantial levels of positive integration for the first time in the history of international regulation of trade in services. Some of these draft rules would go far beyond the TBT provisions on due process and transparency.

4.2 *The Termites from Above: The Mega-Regionals*

With so many open issues in the Doha development agenda and an increasing number of Members, failure at the negotiating table has become a self-fulfilling prophecy. Absent any significant development in the multilateral trade negotiating

[47] See Delimatsis (2010).

arena the last 5 years, important regional and preferential trade initiatives have emerged that may indeed undermine multilateralism and put into question the very existence and necessity of multilateral rules on services. Beyond doubt, such a fragmentation is the result of intransigent positions and lack of leadership at the multilateral level. The biggest trade powers in the world have laboriously worked on initiating and establishing bilateral or small plurilateral partnerships rather than advancing the WTO cause.

Some would argue that such initiatives are triggered by a corporate-led attempt to serve their self-interests. To be sure, a look at the negotiations for a Transatlantic Trade and Investment Partnership (TTIP) would nicely fit into this frame. Trade diversion, in certain areas at least, appears to be the fear of many when this agreement materializes. However, this would be too simplistic an observation for both developed *and* developing countries move towards the 'preferential route'. BRICS have also moved more resolutely towards stronger forms of integration. More crucially for our purposes, this can be a sign of increasing distrust and doubt as to the potential of the WTO to overcome differences, build sustainable bridges among varying views and function within an increasing diversity of Members.

In the area of services, the most interesting development by far is the Trade in Services Agreement (TiSA), currently, negotiated by 25 WTO Members (taking the EU as one). Mauritius is the last addition to the group of participants, becoming the first African country to join the discussions. TiSA negotiations cover about 70 % of world trade in services; they include major service-led economies such as the EU, US, Japan, Canada and the Republic of Korea. However, one of the most interesting developments around this initiative is the participation (or not) of China. BRICS have kept a distance from these discussions, but they will most likely think anew if and when China joins the TiSA negotiations.

TiSA is a US-led initiative and the stakes for the US are clear: almost 80 % of US exports and about 90 % of US imports through commercial presence would be covered by a forthcoming agreement in these negotiations.[48] By July 2015, 13 negotiating rounds have taken place, showing the magnitude of the endeavour but also the lack of available resources that could also focus on the GATS negotiations. The possibility for multilateralizing the negotiating process and/or the results of the negotiations was intentionally left open. For the EU at least, it has always been important that the trade block is not accused of undermining the multilateral negotiations. Thus, it is telling that the negotiating mandate of the Council addressed to the European Commission many times refers to the need to act consistently with the GATS, adopt its basic architecture, but at the same time try to address those elements that did not seem to work at the GATS level.[49]

[48] See Marchetti J and Roy M (2013) The TISA Initiative: An Overview of Market Access Issues. WTO Staff Working Paper ERSD-2013-11, p. 27.

[49] See Council of the European Union, Draft Directives for the negotiation of a plurilateral agreement on trade in services, 6891/13, ADD1, 8 March 2013.

The possibility to eventually include TiSA in the GATS framework limits the leeway for any innovation or alternative paths in the negotiations and offers. Some of the key features of TiSA include a standstill obligation (locking-in autonomous levels of liberalisation); a ratcheting clause (capturing any future removal of discriminatory measures); possibility for phase-in commitments (bind to future liberalisation); a positive list approach for market access, but a negative list approach for national treatment. This means that, contrary to the GATS, national treatment would apply horizontally subject to the reservations/exemptions that the TiSA parties would list. This is an indirect acceptance by the EU of the limits of an exclusively positive list approach that the EU has traditionally opted for.

Discussions for a TiSA have been taking place in secrecy and the quest for more transparency regularly makes headlines. The same goes for the trans-pacific negotiations within TPP and the EU-US TIP. However, transparency in trade negotiations only comes ex post, typically after the trade deal is struck. Many of the most decisive documents that determined the fate of the Uruguay Round negotiations circulated in all secrecy; some of them were room documents that remained secret for a long period of time. The WTO negotiations have also advanced through a particular category of WTO documents, the so-called JOB documents, which are only available to a restricted group of WTO and trade officials. Some of these documents are declassified months or years later.

Due to the magnitude of the current negotiations and the economies involved, curiosity about the actual proposals and drafts on the negotiating table is mounting. This bottom-up transparency may be unsatisfactory, but gives an indication as to the directions chosen by negotiators. For instance, the leaked text on domestic regulation within TiSA[50] is very similar to the most recent draft text discussed within the WPDR at the WTO. This would suggest that there is a certain level of frustration as to the unjustified deadlock that the services negotiations were led to due to uncompromising views in other areas. Thus, whereas, for a long time, the possibility to have trade-offs among various trade areas was regarded as one of the WTO's advantages, it seems now that a 'services-only' agreement may have much better chances of being finalized.

Regarding TiSA, we currently know most of the contours of the proposed agreement. What remains to be clarified is the level of openness. This is crucial because previous PTAs have delivered mediocre liberalisation results, sometimes even not going as far as the GATS. This begs the question: why abandon the negotiating table at the WTO for a second-best option? Knowing more ex ante about the liberalisation offers would allow trade experts and scholars to make sure that any negotiations outside the WTO are monitored and critically reviewed. If Members are to work with alternatives to the WTO, then they have to make a strong case for it.

---

[50] See https://wikileaks.org/tisa/domestic/TiSA%20Annex%20on%20Domestic%20Regulation.pdf (last accessed 25 July 2015).

4.3 Trade in Services and the Role of Developing Countries

Is the GATS a development-friendly trade agreement? To be sure, the central objective of the GATS is not directly development-related. The main objective of the GATS is the expansion of trade in services. In this regard, the GATS is a success story, although, arguably, trade in services has flourished many times in the shadow of GATS rules due to the discrepancy between the scheduled commitments and the actual levels of liberalisation. Trade expansion brings about economic growth, which in turn is a prerequisite for any benign government that wishes to adopt pro-development policies that address inequalities and resilient social divides. The GATS cannot impose on its Members pro-poor and pro-resilient policies that are needed to redistribute the wealth created. However, it is clear by now that without strong and bold domestic governance mechanisms, the current levels of inequality *among* and *within* States are bound to deteriorate.

Having said this, the GATS preamble has pro-development features: it reiterates the importance of the right to regulate and to use domestic regulatory preferences as to the *manner* of regulating; it calls for the increased integration of developing countries in the multilateral trading system; and espouses the importance of the principle of progressive liberalisation, commensurate with a country's needs and reciprocal moves. In addition, the GATS can promote good governance policies internally and this was the central objective of the GATS negotiations on domestic regulation (the so-called 'Article VI:4 mandate'): diminish administrative arbitrariness; increase procedural rights of service suppliers; ensure fair review of negative decisions affecting trade in services; require minimum levels of due process.

It is true that requiring non-discrimination among countries which do not start from the same point of departure may be an unfair obligation. However, national treatment in the GATS has always been a conditional obligation, subject to the discriminatory limitations of the regulating Member. The same applies to TiSA and, for all practical purposes, to all other PTAs that have a services component. More importantly, the possibility for positive discrimination in the GATS did not exist. This led several developing countries to seek the adoption of (renewable) transitional periods which would allow developing countries and LDCs to be exempted from the application of certain rules. As a result, participation and legitimacy were severely damaged, whereas the beneficial effects of such special and differential treatment provisions were doubtful at best. Thus, calls for more active advocacy by and for developing countries has become one of the most important *desiderata* of the Doha Round. The recent adoption of the LDC waiver (the Enabling Clause for Services) in the 8th WTO Ministerial Conference in Geneva in 2011 constitutes a first-rate opportunity for those most hurt by globalisation to get their share of the pie. At the same time, it is a litmus test for those that benefited the most from globalisation to share the same, growing pie. The first 3 years have been disappointing: no concrete steps were taken to operationalize the waiver. Such phenomena will only lead to increased—and justifiably so—criticism against the GATS and the willingness of the developed world to have a trading system in place from which all countries can benefit. This coincided with the launch of the TiSA negotiations, which again for some has been a signal that certain developed countries pursue self-interest strategies, which are self-defeating in the long run, as practice has shown. Viewed through this lens, it is correctly argued that TiSA may cause irreparable harm to the rationale behind the GATS and the WTO as a whole.[51] This is most likely one of the reasons why the TiSA parties have suggested that, once finalized, TiSA could simply become part of these countries' Schedules, which would then mean application of those significant commitments on an MFN basis. Free-riding by non-participants would be an issue in that case, but, on the other hand, the Uruguay Round negotiations have demonstrated that this can be overcome.

5 Conclusion

The GATS has achieved its objectives only in part. In that sense, in its 20 years of existence, WTO Members could have sought more actively to complete the agreement to see what its actual impact could be. The novelty of the service-related issues involved created substantial levels of reluctance which are reflected in the progress of the current negotiations, but also the willingness to bind existing liberalisation even at the bilateral, preferential level.

Already at the moment of its creation, the GATS was outdated and thus little relevant for services trade, as WTO Members failed to ensure the accuracy of the commitments made at the time; recall that Members failed to reach an agreement to lock-in existing openness in all services sectors. If combined with the complexity of the Schedules of commitments—a technical nightmare for some[52]—then one can easily understand that the future of the GATS was uncertain at best. Thus, the very rationale for having a multilateral instrument, that is, increased transparency, was undermined from the outset. The relatively low number of cases adjudicated before the WTO judiciary is telling. All these suggest that problems in the services sectors of the economies around the world exist not because of the GATS, but rather because the GATS' bite in many cases is not sufficiently strong. In other cases, like the recent financial crisis, the existing international financial institutions such as the Bank for International Settlements (BIS) and the banking-related 'Basel standards' as well as lax domestic regulations are to blame.

The present contribution brought forward several suggestions that could improve the GATS system: bind the status-quo; lock-in future liberalisation; create an expedited mechanism for experimenting with or reversing commitments (financial compensation would be a reliable complement of this); finalize the rule-making work on domestic regulation to ensure the appropriate review of unnecessary

[51] See Kelsey (2016), section 10.

[52] See Kelsey (2016), section 4.3.

barriers to services trade; complete rules that allow for the implementation of emergency safeguards. Arguably, these suggestions could lead to a better use of the opportunities that a multilateral instrument can create. Such changes could be encapsulated in the following observation: The GATS 2.0 in the aftermath of the Doha round (whenever this occurs) should focus on what the multilateral trading system has done best: guarantee non-discrimination (if needed, through recourse to an expedited dispute settlement system) and ensure transparency and good governance.

Notably with respect to good governance, I have argued elsewhere that an enhanced GATS system of market access could greatly benefit mobility of service suppliers, an issue that even in very integrated customs territories like the EU has been quite problematic. Due to the many times tailor-made character of service supply, many service suppliers act as individuals rather than through big commercial legal forms. Lack of mechanisms to enforce their rights may discourage them from offering their services to a broader group of clients. A complaint mechanism at the national level could thereby be created, which will receive complaints by service suppliers. Individual service suppliers would be given the right to refer directly to the multilateral rules and describe how their rights were nullified at the domestic level. The current State-to-State complaints resolution system is largely inadequate for disputes relating to services.

In a world in which economies become increasingly intertwined and service suppliers exhaust the business opportunities that technological advances create every day, we can no longer advocate for a choice between international cooperation and domestic autonomy; but rather between complementary activities of institutions at the international and domestic levels, on one side, and uncoordinated State action, on the other.[53] Regulatory flexibility will remain a State prerogative but embedded into a multilateral trustworthy system of cooperation.

References

Avgouleas E (2009) The global financial crisis, behavioural finance and financial regulation: in search of a new orthodoxy. J Corp Law Stud 9(1):23–59

Borchert I, Gootiiz B, Mattoo A (2011) Services in Doha: what's on the table? In: Martin W, Mattoo A (eds) Unfinished business? the WTO's Doha Agenda. Centre for Economic Policy Research, The World Bank Group, Washington, DC, pp 115–144

Delimatsis P (2010) Concluding the WTO services negotiations on domestic regulation—hopes and fears. World Trade Rev 9(4):643–673

Delimatsis P (2011) Protecting public morals in a digital age: revisiting the WTO rulings on US—Gambling and China—Publications and Audiovisual Products. J Int Econ Law 14(2):257–293

Delimatsis P (2013) Institutional transparency in the WTO. In: Bianchi A, Peters A (eds) Transparency in international law. Cambridge University Press, Cambridge, pp 112–141

[53] Keohane et al. (2009), p. 23.

Hancher L, Sauter W (2010) One step beyond? from Sodemare to DocMorris: the EU's freedom of establishment case law concerning healthcare. CML Rev 47(1):117–146

Hoekman B, Mattoo A (2008) Services trade and growth. In: Marchetti J, Roy M (eds) Opening markets for trade in services—countries and sectors in bilateral and WTO negotiations. Cambridge University Press, Cambridge, pp 21–58

Huang H (2010) Institutional structure of financial regulation in China: lessons from the global financial crisis. J Corp Law Stud 10(1):219–254

Kelsey J (2016) From GATS to TiSA: pushing the trade in services regime beyond the limits. In: Bungenberg M, Hermann C, Krajewski M, Terhechte J (eds) European yearbook of international economic law, vol 7. Springer, Heidelberg, pp 119–151

Keohane R, Macedo S, Moravcsik A (2009) Democracy-enhancing multilateralism. Int Organ 63:1–31

Krajewski M (2003) Public services and trade liberalisation: mapping the legal framework. J Int Econ Law 6(2):341–367

Krajewski M (2005) Playing by the rules of the game? Leg Issues Econ Integr 32(4):417–447

Leroux EH (2007) Eleven years of GATS case-law: what have we learned? J Int Econ Law 10 (4):749–793

Ortino F (2006) Treaty interpretation and the WTO Appellate Body report in US—Gambling: a critique. J Int Econ Law 9(1):117–148

The Current System of Trade and Intellectual Property Rights

Carlos M. Correa

Contents

Abstract One of the key arguments of the proponents of the Agreement on Trade-related Aspects of Intellectual Property Rights adopted as a component of the World Trade Organization was that the grant of intellectual property rights would boost innovation globally. The world map of R&D, however, does not show a general improvement of R&D capabilities in developing countries in the last 20 years. While the pharmaceutical industry was an active promoter of that Agreement, the innovation in this sector has declined. The proliferation of pharmaceutical patents reflects strategies aiming at blocking generic competition rather than a genuine increase in innovation. Alternative models to generate new drugs, especially those needed to address diseases prevalent in developing countries, are needed.

C.M. Correa (✉)
Center for Interdisciplinary Studies on Industrial Property and Economics, University of Buenos Aires, Buenos Aires, Argentina

South Centre, Geneva, Switzerland
e-mail: ceidie@derecho.uba.ar

M. Bungenberg et al. (eds.), *European Yearbook of International Economic Law 2016*, European Yearbook of International Economic Law 7,
DOI 10.1007/978-3-319-29215-1_8

1 Introduction

International intellectual property law developed since the end of the nineteenth century as an independent normative area. Three international conventions were adopted at the end of that century,[1] two of which became the very foundation on an international system on industrial property and copyright law. Thereafter, it took a long time to develop additional international rules on the subject, as it was only in 1952 that a new convention on copyright was established.[2] The internationalisation of intellectual property gained momentum in the 1960s and 1970s when various negotiations led to the conclusion of new treaties in this field.[3]

The governance of the emerging set of international conventions on intellectual property was ensured through specialized bodies established by the same conventions. The union of the governing bodies of the Paris Convention and the Berne Convention gave rise to the United International Bureaux for the Protection of Intellectual Property (BIRPI as per its French acronym), which eventually provided the grounds for the creation of the World Intellectual Property Organization (WIPO) in 1967 with the mission of encouraging creative activity and promoting "the protection of intellectual property throughout the world".[4]

The system of rules created by these international instruments operated in isolation from the multilateral trade system established by the General Agreement on Tariffs and Trade (GATT) in 1947. The creation of a linkage between the two systems was the result of an initiative of a group of US-based industries that sought to establish a framework for intellectual property protection of broad geographic coverage and capable of ensuring not only the recognition of rights, but also their effective enforcement. The role that the CEOs of large US companies played in inducing the US government to bring intellectual property as a 'trade-related' issue into the GATT is well documented.[5] It is also well known that developing countries were strongly opposed to this strategy. The government of India, for instance, argued that it would not be appropriate to establish within the framework of the

[1] Paris Convention on the Protection of Industrial Property (1883), Berne Convention for the Protection of Literary and Artistic Works (1886) and Madrid Agreement for the Repression of False or Deceptive Indications of Source on Goods was also adopted at that time (1891).

[2] Universal Copyright Convention (UCC), adopted in Geneva, Switzerland in 1952.

[3] See Rome Convention for the Protection of Performers, Producers of Phonograms and Broadcasting Organizations (1961), the International Convention for the Protection of New Varieties of Plants (UPOV) (1961), the Lisbon Agreement for the Protection of Appellations of Origin and their International Registration (1967), the Patent Cooperation Treaty (1970), the Geneva Convention for the Protection of Producers of Phonograms against Unauthorized Duplication of their Phonograms (1971), the Brussels Convention Relating to the Distribution of Programme-Carrying Signals Transmitted by Satellite (1974) and the Budapest Treaty on the International Recognition of the Deposit of Microorganisms for the Purposes of Patent Procedure (1977).

[4] Convention Establishing the World Intellectual Property Organization signed at Stockholm on July 14, 1967, Preamble, second recital.

[5] Deveraux et al. (2006).

GATT "any new rules and disciplines on intellectual property rights".[6] Brazil attempted to narrow down the scope of any negotiation to the examination of trade issues that involved, in some way, the protection of intellectual property based on GATT principles, "provided that such principles are restricted to the trade-related aspects of the matter".[7]

Indeed, the opposition of developing countries to establish a comprehensive agreement on intellectual property in the context of GATT led them to refuse the developed countries' interpretation of the ambiguous mandate approved at the GATT Ministerial Conference in Punta del Este (Uruguay) in 1986, and to avoid engaging into negotiations on the subject until 1989. The change in their position is attributable to many factors, but the primary one is likely to have been the developed countries' confessed strategy to link concessions in the areas of agriculture and textiles—the main targets for developing countries' negotiators—in the Uruguay Round to the acceptance of a new set of binding international rules on multiple aspects of intellectual property that would reflect the patterns of protection generally available in developed countries.[8]

Of course, the proponents of such rules articulated a discourse around the advantages that new disciplines on intellectual property would bring about to *all* participants in the multilateral trading system, including developing countries. Increased innovation, growing flows of foreign direct investment and technology transfer to these countries, and better prospects for economic growth were central components in this rhetoric.[9]

While a number of econometric studies have been conducted correlating intellectual property (or the 'strength' thereof) with these and other variables,[10] none of

[6] See Group of Negotiations on Goods (GATT) Negotiating Group on Trade-Related Aspects of Intellectual Property Rights, including Trade in Counterfeit Goods, Applicability of the Basic Principles of the GATT and of Relevant International Intellectual Property Agreements or Conventions—Communication from India, GATT Doc. MTN.GNG/NG11/W/39, 5 September 1989, https://www.wto.org/gatt_docs/English/SULPDF/92080040.pdf (last accessed 5 October 2015), para. 2.

[7] Group of Negotiations on Goods (GATT) Negotiating Group on Trade-Related Aspects of Intellectual Property Rights, including Trade in Counterfeit Goods, Communication from Brazil, GATT Doc. MTN.GNG/NG11/W/57, 11 December 1989, https://www.wto.org/gatt_docs/English/SULPDF/92090039.pdf (last accessed 5 October 2015), para. 11(a).

[8] Correa (2011).

[9] See e.g., Group of Negotiations on Goods (GATT) Negotiating Group on Trade-Related Aspects of Intellectual Property Rights, including Trade in Counterfeit Goods, Suggestion by the United States for Achieving the Negotiating Objective, GATT Doc. No. MTN.GNG/NG11/W/14, 20 October 1987, https://www.wto.org/gatt_docs/English/SULPDF/92030039.pdf (last accessed 5 October 2015), p. 2; Group of Negotiations on Goods (GATT) Negotiating Group on Trade-Related Aspects of Intellectual Property Rights, including Trade in Counterfeit Goods, Trade-related Aspects of Intellectual Property Rights: Submission from the European Communities, GATT Doc., No. MTN.GNG/NG11/W/49, 14 November 1989, https://www.wto.org/gatt_docs/English/SULPDF/92080171.pdf, (last accessed 5 October 2015), p. 7.

[10] See e.g., Maskus K, Yang L (2013) The Impacts of Post-TRIPS Patent Reforms on the Structure of Exports. The Research Institute of Economy, Trade and Industry, http://www.rieti.go.jp/jp/publications/dp/13e030.pdf (last accessed 2 May 2015).

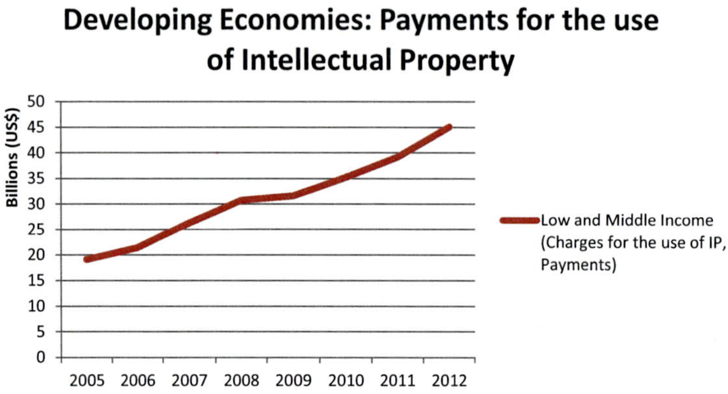

Fig. 1 Payments for the use of Intellectual Property in Developing Countries. *Source*: Kithmina V, Hewage (2014) A Delicate Truth—Remittances and Royalty Payments in Financing Development. South Centre, based on World Development Indicators, World Bank (2014)

them conclusively show that the claimed benefits have actually emerged from the implementation of high intellectual property standards. For instance, a literature review concluded, in relation to patents, that 'the sheer size and growth of the recent literature might lead one to assume that patents are an extremely important instrument of economic development and growth, which therefore attract a great deal of interest from researchers and policy makers. But this seems at odds with the weak evidence that patents serve as an incentive for innovation and the fact that relatively few firms find them an important means of securing returns to innovation'.[11] A study on the impact of the TRIPS Agreement in four developing countries concluded that

> [p]revious studies in this area have been quick to attribute the changes in these dependent variables (increased FDI, R&D, etc.) to a strengthening of the patent regime. However, based on the four country case studies, we found very little evidence for such optimism with respect to TRIPS compliance.[12]

One clear outcome of the increased levels of protection for intellectual property seems to be the enormous increase in US receipts for the use of intellectual property abroad, which doubled between 1994 and 2014. Although most payments for the use of intellectual property are done by developed countries, those by developing countries have increased dramatically. As shown in Fig. 1, they have more than doubled since 2005, the year when the TRIPS Agreement became fully enforceable (except for Least Developed Countries).

---

[11] Hall B, Helmers C, Rogers M, Sena V (2012) The Choice between Formal and Informal Intellectual Property: A Literature Review. National Bureau of Economic Research (NBER) Working Paper No. 17983, http://www.nber.org/papers/w17983.pdf (last accessed 5 October 2015), p. 35.

[12] Mani and Nelson (2013), p. 235.

Table 1 Global distribution of R&D expenditures

OECD countries 78 %
Asia (excluding Japan) 19 % (China: 11.8 %)
Latin America 2.4 % (Brazil: 1.3 %)
Near and Middle East 1.2 %
Africa 0.7 %

2 The TRIPS Agreement and Innovation

One of the key arguments underpinning the grant of intellectual property rights and, in fact, the claimed benefits of implementing the standards of the TRIPS Agreement, is the positive role that such rights would play in promoting innovation. The global map of R&D, however, does not show a general improvement of R&D capabilities in developing countries in the last 20 years, with a few exceptions, notably in the case of China. In accordance with a study[13] the distribution of global R&D was as indicated in Table 1.

Although the participation in global R&D may have improved after 2010, still, the U.S., China, Japan and Europe together account for about 78 % of the $1.6 trillion total investment in R&D.[14] R&D investment has increased in India, Brazil and China in the last 20 years, but other developing countries, especially in Africa, still perform low levels of R&D and there are no reasons to expect significant changes in the short term. The extent to which the increase in R&D investment in those three countries is related to or caused by the introduction of TRIPS-compatible rules on intellectual property is at least questionable. Significantly, none of these countries have entered into free trade or other agreements imposing TRIPS-plus standards. Hence, they would not qualify as granting 'stronger' intellectual property rights protection, one of the variables considered in some studies to assess the impact of such rights.[15] The case of China deserves special consideration and, certainly, further research. China's has sustained a high rate of R&D investment for nearly 20 years, and its total R&D investments are now more than 60 %

[13] Gaillard (2010).

[14] See Batelle (2013) 2014 Global R&D Funding Forecast, http://www.battelle.org/docs/tpp/2014_global_rd_funding_forecast.pdf (last accessed 2 May 2015), p. 4.

[15] See, e.g., Falvey R, Foster N, Memedovic O (2006) The Role of Intellectual Property Rights in Technology Transfer and Economic Growth: Theory and Evidence. United Nations Industrial Development Organization (UNIDO), Vienna http://www.unido.org/fileadmin/user_media/Publications/Pub_free/Role_of_intellectual_property_rights_in_technology_transfer_and_economic_growth.pdf (last accessed 2 May 2015); Shapiro R, Mathur A (2014) How India Can Attract More Foreign Direct Investment, Create Jobs, and Increase GDP: The Benefits of Respecting the Intellectual Property Rights of Foreign Pharmaceutical Producers. SONECON, http://www.ipdelivers.com/resources/wp-content/uploads/2014/01/Report-on-FDI-IP-and-the-Pharmaceutical-Sector-in-India-Shapiro-Mathu-.pdf (last accessed 5 May 2015).

those of the U.S. At the current rates of growth, China's total funding of R&D is expected to surpass that of the U.S. by 2022.[16] The growth of R&D budget in China explains, in fact, the largest part of the increased participation of developing countries in global R&D.

How much of the increment in R&D that has taken place in the last two decades may be attributed to intellectual property protection? It is not easy to respond to this question. However, if leading economists from the USA are right, it cannot be simply argued that innovation only or mainly occurs because such a protection is conferred. Moser, for instance, concluded a historical analysis indicating that '[o] verall, the weight of the existing historical evidence suggests that patent policies, which grant strong intellectual property rights to early generations of inventors, may discourage innovation'.[17] Bessen and Meurer noted that "...nations with patent systems were not more innovative that nations without patents systems. Similarly, nations with longer patent terms were no more innovative than nations with shorter patent terms".[18] They also found that

> patents *do* provide profits for their owners, so it makes sense for firms to get them. But taking the effect of *other* owners' patents into account, including the risk of litigation, the average public firm outside the chemical and pharmaceutical industries would be better off if patents did not exist.[19]

A survey by Lerner of patent laws in over sixty countries showed that strengthening of patent rights resulted in an increase in filings from foreign applicants, with no effect on filings by local inventors.[20] Posner has argued that "in most [industries], the cost of invention is low; or just being first confers a durable competitive advantage ... so there's no point to a patent monopoly that will last 20 years... Most industries could get along fine without patent protection".[21]

In addressing the importance of non-intellectual property incentives for innovation, Shavell and Van Ypersele noted that "there is no necessity to marry the incentive to innovate to conferral of monopoly power in innovations",[22] while

---

[16] Shapiro R, Mathur A (2014) How India Can Attract More Foreign Direct Investment, Create Jobs, and Increase GDP: The Benefits of Respecting the Intellectual Property Rights of Foreign Pharmaceutical Producers. SONECON, http://www.ipdelivers.com/resources/wp-content/uploads/2014/01/Report-on-FDI-IP-and-the-Pharmaceutical-Sector-in-India-Shapiro-Mathu-.pdf (last accessed 5 May 2015).

[17] Moser (2013), pp. 23–44.

[18] Bessen and Meurer (2008), p. 16.

[19] Bessen and Meurer (2008), p. 16.

[20] Lerner J (2002) Patent Protection and Innovation Over 150 Years, http://www.epip.eu/papers/20030424/epip/papers/cd/papers_speakers/Lerner_Paper_EPIP_210403.pdf (last accessed 5 May 2015).

[21] Posner R, Why There Are Too Many Patents in America, The Atlantic, 12 July 2012 http://www.theatlantic.com/business/archive/2012/07/why-there-are-too-many-patents-in-america/259725/ (last accessed 5 May 2015).

[22] Shavell S, van Ypersele T (1999) Rewards Versus Intellectual Property Rights. NBER Working Paper 6956, http://www.nber.org/papers/w6956 (last accessed 5 May 2015), p. 32.

Torrance and Tomlinson similarly concluded that "[a] growing body of empirical research appears to support the view that patent systems do not necessarily 'promote the Progress of ... useful Arts".[23] Other scholars have gone as far as suggesting the abolition of patents:

> [i]n general, public policy should aim to decrease patent monopolies gradually but surely, and the ultimate goal should be the abolition of patents. After six decades of further study since Machlup's testimony in 1958 has failed to find evidence that patents promote the common good, it is surely time to reassess his conclusion that it would be irresponsible to abolish the patent system.[24]

The same scholars had noted earlier that "historical evidence provides little or no support that innovative monopoly is an effective method of increasing innovation".[25] They further stated that in spite of the enormous increase in the number of patents and in the strength of their legal protection we have neither seen a dramatic acceleration in the rate of technological progress nor a major increase in the levels of R&D expenditure ... there is strong evidence, instead, that patents have many negative consequences. Both of these observations, the evidence in support of which has grown steadily over time, are consistent with theories of innovation that emphasize competition and first-mover advantage as the main drivers of innovation and directly contradict 'Schumpeterian' theories postulating that government granted monopolies are crucial in order to provide incentives for innovation.[26]

A draft report prepared for the Australian government has also been critical of the way in which the patent system operates:

> Despite the fact that patents are available for inventions in all technologies, it is arguable whether the patent system is of general benefit across the full range of technologies. Where a technology is relatively inexpensive to develop and can be quickly brought to market, innovators may be better served by simply entering the market quickly: recouping their costs through first mover advantage. Specific industries and the public may also benefit through fewer patents impeding their freedom to operate. In this respect patents are a blunt instrument, with generally the same duration and extent of rights being granted regardless of the development costs or market size of the invention.[27]

It is true that when the TRIPS Agreement was proposed and later adopted, there was much less interest in the academy on the impact of intellectual property rights, and the literature on the subject was not as abundant as it is today. However, there

---

[23] Torrance and Tomlinson (2009), p. 164.

[24] Boldrin and Levine (2013), p 20.

[25] Boldrin M, Levine D (2007) Against Intellectual Monopoly, http://levine.sscnet.ucla.edu/papers/ip.ch.8.m1004.pdf (last accessed 9 May 2015), p. 2.

[26] Boldrin M, Levine D (2012) The Case Against Patents. Federal Reserve Bank, Research Division, https://research.stlouisfed.org/wp/2012/2012-035.pdf (last accessed 2 July 2015), p. 1.

[27] Pharmaceutical Patents Review Report. 2013, http://www.ipaustralia.gov.au/pdfs/2013-05-27_PPR_Final_Report.pdf (last accessed 2 July 2015), p. 5.

were many studies[28] (including the seminal contributions of Penrose[29] and Machlup[30]) that made it clear that the effects of such rights were strongly context-dependent, that is, it is not possible to expect the same outcomes when intellectual property is applied in countries with very different levels of technological capacity and industrial profile. It was also known that developed countries pursued imitative paths of development at the early stages of their industrialization process. In 1986, for instance, an office of the US Congress had concluded that "[w]hen the United States was still a relatively young and developing country, it refused to respect international intellectual property rights on the grounds that it was freely entitled to foreign works to further its social and economic development".[31]

The inappropriateness of a 'one-size-fits-all' approach in the area of intellectual property has been highlighted in various reports[32] and in abundant academic works. Dosi and Stiglitz, for instance, have warned about the negative consequences of pretending that a system of intellectual property adapted to a developed country could work in the same way in a developing country:

> As badly designed as the American IPR regime is for the United States, it is even worse suited for developing countries. But even if the American IPR regime *were* ideal for the United States, that does not mean that it would be ideal for others. . .In particular, the IPR regimes of the advanced developed countries are likely to be inappropriate for many developing countries, and this is likely to be especially so in areas like health and agriculture. . . Indeed, one-size-fits-all, policy prescriptions are rarely a good idea in any field, but this is one area where they may work particularly badly. . .There are, for instance, large distributional consequences of different IPR regimes, and developing countries may not have the resources to easily offset those effects.[33]

Swanson and Goeschl examined the impacts of enhanced property right regimes in agriculture in countries with different levels of development. They found that

---

[28] See, e.g. Siebeck W, Evenson R, Lesser W, Primo Braga C (eds) (1990) Strengthening Protection of Intellectual Property in Developing Countries A Survey of the Literature. World Bank World Bank Discussion Papers 112, http://www-wds.worldbank.org/servlet/WDSContentServer/IW3P/IB/2000/01/06/000178830_98101903544215/Rendered/PDF/multi_page.pdf (last accessed 9 May 2015).

[29] Penrose (1951).

[30] Machlup F (1958) An Economic Review of the Patent System. Subcommittee on Patents, Trademarks and Copyrights. Committee on the Judiciary, U.S. Senate, Study no. 15, https://mises.org/sites/default/files/An%20Economic%20Review%20of%20the%20Patent%20System_Vol_3_3.pdf (last accessed 2 July 2015).

[31] U.S. Congress, Office of Technology, Assessment, Intellectual Property Rights in an Age of Electronics and Information. OTA-CIT-302 U.S. April 1986, Government Printing Office, Washington DC, http://www.princeton.edu/~ota/disk2/1986/8610/8610.PDF (last accessed 2 July 2015). Moreover, historical studies have shown that the United States emerged as the world's industrial leader by illicitly appropriating mechanical and scientific innovations from Europe and that the leaders of the republic supported the piracy of European technology in order to promote the economic strength and political independence of the new nation (Ben-Atar 2004).

[32] See e.g., Commission on Intellectual Property, Final Report. 2002, http://www.iprcommission.org/graphic/documents/final_report.htm(last accessed 9 May 2015).

[33] Dosi and Stiglitz (2014), pp. 3–4.

> there are frictions within the system of technological dissemination that inhibit the flows of beneficial information, and that enhanced property right regimes will work most prominently against the interests of those states furthest from the frontier. Whenever this is the case, enhanced IPR regimes will have the impact of skewing the distribution of benefits towards those states on or near the technological frontier. In the case of those countries furthest from the frontier, it is probable that the impact of heightened IPR is likely to be negative over any reasonable time horizon.[34]

Significantly, the already mentioned report produced for the government of Australia not only seems to reach conclusions similar to those reflected in the referred to analyses, but it also highlights the lack of proportionality between the (limited) benefits that accrue to the developed countries that impose high standards of intellectual property on small economies, and the (large) ensuing costs that the latter need to bear:

> A small country can have very little influence on the global economics of IP production by changing its own IP [intellectual property] protection policies. Given that Australia contributes less than 2 per cent of the world economy, extensions of Australian IP rights on their own are unlikely to influence a global firm's decisions as to whether or not to invest in IP…
>
> As a system stretching back many centuries, there are numerous aspects of IP regimes that remain poorly designed. Yet international IP agreements have tended to be made without regard to such matters…As a result, intellectual agreements lock us into a number of inefficiencies which have clear costs to Australia and yet which confer benefits on other countries that are either small or negligible.[35]

Similarly a report by the Australian Productivity Commission affirmed that an increase in intellectual property rights in a country which is a net importer of technology is "likely to benefit overseas rights holders disproportionately compared with domestic rights holders".[36]

In summary, while the proponents of the TRIPS Agreement operated on the premise that that minimum standards of protection would be equally beneficial for countries with diverse levels of socio-economic and technological development, the dominant view flowing from academic and other analyses seems to strongly reject that premise. As discussed in the following section, this is particularly the case of pharmaceuticals.

---

[34] Swanson and Goeschl (2014), p. 284.

[35] Pharmaceutical Patents Review Report. 2013, http://www.ipaustralia.gov.au/pdfs/2013-05-27_PPR_Final_Report.pdf (last accessed 9 May 2015), pp. 22 and 32.

[36] Productivity Commission 2012, Trade Assistance Review 2010–2011. Annual Report Series, http://www.pc.gov.au/about/governance/annual-reports/annual-report-2010-11/annual-report-2010-11.pdf (last accessed 2 July 2015), p. 100.

3 Declining Innovation in the Pharmaceutical Industry

The case of the pharmaceutical industry illustrates well the disconnection between innovation and the geographically broader and more extensive protection of intellectual property introduced by the TRIPS Agreement.

It is generally accepted that patents are not among the important means to appropriate returns to innovation in most sectors, with the notable exception of pharmaceuticals.[37] As noted by Harvard's economist Scherer, "patents are unusually important in pharmaceuticals".[38] The pharmaceutical industry played a major role in the development of the US strategy leading to the adoption of the TRIPS Agreement; this Agreement may have never existed in the absence of the effective lobbying made by that industry. The implementation of global rules ensuring the patenting of pharmaceutical products—which was denied in more than 50 countries at the beginning of the Uruguay Round[39]—and the protection of test data—for which there were no international rules before the TRIPs Agreement—was presented by that industry as an indispensable platform to sustain and increase investment in the development of new drugs.[40]

A study by Scherer published in 2004 predicted that the increase in the development of new drugs that would result from the implementation of the TRIPS rules in developing countries would be minimal, and that "global welfare is maximized by letting low-income nations free-ride on the patented inventions of first-world nations".[41] In fact, the post-TRIPS Agreement period has been characterized by a continuous decline in pharmaceutical innovation, as measured by the number of new drugs approved for marketing. Figure 2 shows that the average number of

[37] See Hall B, Helmers C, Rogers M, Sena V (2012) The Choice between Formal and Informal Intellectual Property: A Literature Review. National Bureau of Economic Research (NBER) Working Paper No. 17983, http://www.nber.org/papers/w17983.pdf (last accessed 2 July 2015), p. 15.

[38] Scherer F, A Note on Global Welfare in Pharmaceutical Patenting. Working Paper No. 03-11 Federal Reserve Bank of Philadelphia, November 2002, https://www.philadelphiafed.org/research-and-data/publications/working-papers/2003/wp03-11.pdf (last accessed 11 May 2015), p. 2

[39] See, e.g., United Nations Conference on Trade and Development, The TRIPS Agreement and Developing Countries. 1996, UN, Geneva http://unctad.org/en/Docs/ite1_en.pdf (last accessed 11 May 2015).

[40] See, e.g., Deveraux et al. (2006).

[41] Scherer F, A Note on Global Welfare in Pharmaceutical Patenting. Working Paper No. 03-11 Federal Reserve Bank of Philadelphia, November 2002, https://www.philadelphiafed.org/research-and-data/publications/working-papers/2003/wp03-11.pdf (last accessed 11 May 2015), p. 10.

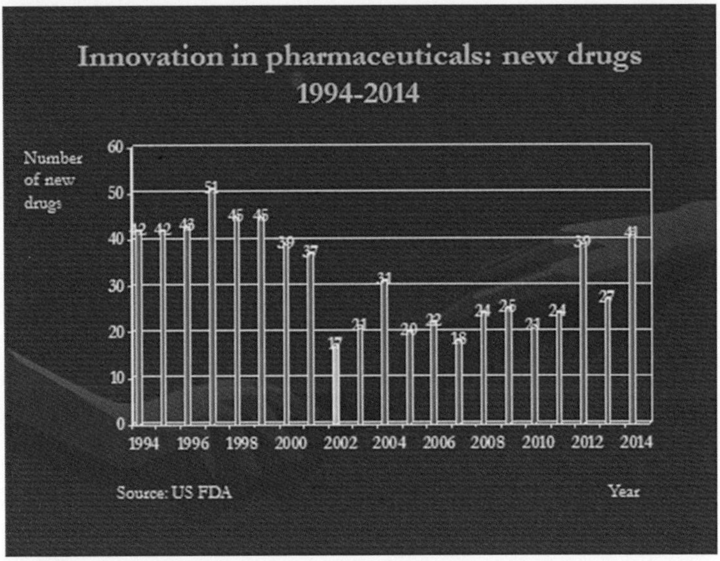

Fig. 2 Innovation in pharmaceuticals: new drugs 1994–2014

new drugs[42] developed after 2000 (when the TRIPS Agreement became enforceable in developing countries)[43] was almost half of the average in the 5 previous years.

The extension to developing countries and the strengthening of patents and test data protection for pharmaceuticals have done nothing to prevent the plummeting efficiency of the pharmaceutical industry in developing new drugs.[44] Thus, the "number of new drugs approved per billion US dollars spent on RD has halved roughly every 9 years since 1950, falling around 80-fold in inflation-adjusted terms".[45]

---

[42] The figure includes drugs that are classified as 'new molecular entities' (NMEs), which are characterized as 'new' for administrative purposes by the US Food and Drug Administration (FDA), but nonetheless contain active moieties that are closely related to active moieties in products that have previously been approved by FDA, FDA, New Drugs at FDA: CDER's New Molecular Entities and New Therapeutic Biological Products. January 2015, http://www.fda.gov/Drugs/DevelopmentApprovalProcess/DrugInnovation/ucm20025676.htm Scherer F, A Note on Global Welfare in Pharmaceutical Patenting. Working Paper No. 03-11 Federal Reserve Bank of Philadelphia, November 2002, https://www.philadelphiafed.org/research-and-data/publications/working-papers/2003/wp03-11.pdf (last accessed 11 May 2015), p. 10.

[43] See Article 65 of the TRIPS Agreement.

[44] See e.g., Hurley D, A Diabetes Drug Made the Old-fashioned Way, International New York Times, 15 November 2014, p. 12.

[45] Scannell et al. (2012), pp. 191–200. As a result of the observed decline, the authors suggest that in the field of pharmaceuticals an inverse Moore's Law (which predicated that the number of transistors in an integrated circuit would double every 2 years) applies ('Eroom's Law').

In addition, the extension of product patent and test data protection has not helped developing countries—the primary target of the whole TRIPS exercise—to address the diseases prevalent in those countries (often referred to as 'neglected diseases'), since the lack of interest—and, consequently, low investment in R&D—of the pharmaceutical industry in this area continues to be an outstanding feature of its business model. A report by the WHO Commission on Intellectual Property Innovation and Public Health (CIPIH) of April 2006 already noted that "[t]here is no evidence that the implementation of the TRIPS Agreement in developing countries will significantly boost R&D in pharmaceuticals on TYPE II and particularly Type III diseases. Insufficient market incentives are the decisive factor".[46] A more recent report confirmed that patents alone do not drive sufficient investment to counter diseases that predominantly affect poor people, because they do not offer a sufficiently profitable market; as a result, some diseases—or rather, some populations—are neglected.[47]

While in 1975–1999, only 1.1 % of new therapeutic products had been developed for neglected diseases, between January 1, 2000, and December 31, 2011 only four new chemical entities were approved for neglected diseases (three for malaria, one for diarrhoeal disease), accounting for 1 % of the 336 new chemical entities approved during the this period.[48]

Most of the new R&D addressed to find treatments for the diseases prevalent in developing countries has not been driven by the expectation of profits sustained on the legal monopoly granted by intellectual property. A number of collaborative Product Development Partnerships (PDPs) has been set up to work on such diseases with the aim of developing affordable treatments.[49] Despite their limitations and financial vulnerability,[50] PDPs have become the only mechanism that may generate new drugs for diseases mainly affecting those countries.

The effects of an expanded protection of intellectual property have been particularly tangible in the case of treatments for HIV/AIDS. Prices of HIV treatments vary greatly between middle-income countries (MICs) depending, *inter alia*, on patent landscape, while the price of drugs for third-line treatments remains a major

---

[46] World Health Organization (WHO), Public Health: Innovation and Intellectual Property Rights. Report of Commission on Intellectual Property Rights, Innovation and Public Health, April 2006, http://www.who.int/intellectualproperty/documents/thereport/CIPIH23032006.pdf (last accessed 11 May 2015). Type II diseases are incident in both developed and developing countries, but with a substantial proportion of the cases in the latter. Type III diseases are those that are overwhelmingly or exclusively incident in developing countries, such as malaria and Chagas disease.

[47] The Lancet–University of Oslo Commission on Global Governance for Health, The Political Origins of Health Inequity: Prospects for Change. 11 February 2014, http://dx.doi.org/10.1016/S0140-6736(13)62407-1 (last accessed 11 May 2015), p. 12.

[48] Pedrique et al. (2013).

[49] See, e.g., Muñoz et al. (2015).

[50] Velásquez G (2014) Public-Private Partnerships In Global Health: Putting Business Before Health? South Centre Research Paper 49 http://www.southcentre.int/wp-content/uploads/2014/02/RP49_PPPs-and-PDPs-in-Health-rev_EN.pdf (last accessed 11 May 2015).

challenge as they are likely to be patented in key countries with manufacturing capacity.[51] In accordance with the Global Commission on HIV and the Law,

> IP [intellectual property] protection is supposed to provide an incentive for innovation but experience has shown that the current laws are failing to promote innovation that serves the medical needs of the poor. The fallout from these regulations—in particular the TRIPS framework—has exposed the central role of excessive IP protections in exacerbating the lack of access to HIV treatment and other essential medicines.[52]

In addition to the low number of new drugs developed after the TRIPS Agreement entered into force, innovation in pharmaceuticals presents other shortcomings. The great majority of the new drugs are 'me-toos', that is, drugs that do not perform better than previously existing treatments, but which are generally more expensive. For example, a specialized journal noticed that "a 'new generation' of antipsychotics was systematically prescribed by doctors, yet these drugs proved to be no more effective than the prior generation and were 10 times more expensive".[53] More generally, it has been found that by the 1980s drugs were less than four times better than placebo; by the 1990s, twice as good, and by the 2000s just 36 % better than a placebo.[54]

Intellectual property is deemed to be necessary to drive private investment in drug research, which is believed to constitute the primary source of new treatments. The evidence suggests, however, that a large part of the new medicines with a genuine therapeutic impact emerge from public, not private, R&D laboratories: "...innovation depends on bold entrepreneurship. But the entity that takes the boldest risks and achieves the biggest breakthroughs is not the private sector; it is the much-maligned state."[55]

A common argument for the justification for the minimum standards imposed by the TRIPS Agreement has been that it would effectively lead to more innovation in pharmaceuticals in developing countries, especially in those with a significant scientific and technological capacity such as India. While the TRIPS Agreement did not encourage the so-called 'research-based' pharmaceutical industry to improve drug innovation, has it promoted R&D in this field in developing countries? An analysis for pharmaceutical patents in 85 countries over the 1978–1999 period found that "national patent protection did not stimulate domestic innovation

[51] See WHO (2014) Increasing Access to HIV Treatment in Middle-Income Countries: Key Data on Prices, Regulatory Status, Tariffs and the Intellectual Property Situation, http://www.who.int/phi/publications/WHO_Increasing_access_to_HIV_treatment.pdf?ua=1 (last accessed 12 May 2015).

[52] Global Commission on HIV and the Law, HIV and the Law: Risks, Rights & Health. July 2012, http://www.hivlawcommission.org/resources/report/FinalReport-Risks,Rights&Health-EN.pdf. (last accessed 12 May 2015), p. 8.

[53] Gagnon (2012), p. 192.

[54] Olfson and Marcus (2013), pp. 1116–1125.

[55] Wolf M, A Much-maligned Engine of Innovation, Financial Times, 4 August 2013, http://www.ft.com/cms/s/2/32ba9b92-efd4-11e2-a237-00144feabdc0.html (last accessed 12 May 2015) comment on the book by Mazzucato (2013).

activities, except at higher development levels, and that above a certain level of patent protection, innovation activities are actually reduced".[56]

There has been, in particular, great speculation about the boost that TRIPS rules could give to R&D on new drugs by Indian companies. The evidence so far available shows that this has not been the case. Local companies adapted in different ways to the post-TRIPS scenario, depending on their size and productive profile.[57] Some of the large local generic companies were taken over by pharmaceutical multinational companies,[58] thereby triggering the concern of the Indian government and civil society about the future of an industry that became the 'pharmacy of the developing world'.[59]

A recent study on the TRIPS Agreement's impact on the pharmaceutical industry in India concluded that TRIPS may have accelerated R&D related to improvement of existing medicines, "[b]ut in the absence of TRIPS, such activities would still have been undertaken. With larger domestic operations, Indian companies. . .would have had access to larger resources and would have been better placed to undertake such R&D".[60]

An increase in patenting by large local and foreign companies, but an insignificant patent activity by small and medium local pharmaceutical companies has also been observed.[61] While some Indian companies initiated R&D activities after the TRIPS Agreement came into effect, none of these companies has been

> engaged in the entire process of drug development because they are not ready for a start-to-finish model in NCEs [new chemical entities] research and do not have the skills and funds required for development and marketing of a drug. The model adopted by Indian companies is to develop new molecule up to a certain stage and then license it out to partners from developed countries, primarily to MNCs [multinational enterprises].[62]

Patenting by local companies focuses on "new or improved processes for products rather than products themselves. The product related applications are concerned with intermediates and formulations with maximum contribution in modified-release dosage forms".[63]

---

[56] Hall B, Helmers C, Rogers M, Sena V (2012) The Choice between Formal and Informal Intellectual Property: A Literature Review. National Bureau of Economic Research (NBER) Working Paper No. 17983, http://www.nber.org/papers/w17983.pdf (last accessed 2 July 2015), p. 15.

[57] See, e.g., Oyelaran-Oyeyinka and Gehl Sampath (2010).

[58] Ranbaxy, one of the firms taken over by a foreign (Japanese) company, was the local firm with the largest R&D budget in India. See, e.g., Srinivasan S, Gupta N, Dabade G, Phadke A, Sengupta A, Takeover of Indian Pharma Companies. Economic & Political Weekly XLV(43), 23 October 2010; Sreedhar et al. (2011), pp. 343–344.

[59] See, e.g., t'Hoen and Passarelli (2013).

[60] Mani and Nelson (2013), p. 108.

[61] Bedi et al. (2013), p. 107.

[62] Bedi et al. (2013), p. 109.

[63] Bedi et al. (2013), p. 109.

Table 2 Pharmaceutical products that overcome the objection under Sect. 3(d) of the Indian Patent Act

Indian patent no	Title of the invention	Patentee
223,589	A crystalline polymorph of an Epothilone analog of Formula I	Bristol-Meyers Squibb Co
223,767	Indolylakylamine derivatives	Wyeth
223,849	8-Azabicyclo [3.2.1] Octane-3-Methanamine derivatives compounds	Sanofi-Synthelabo
224,394	Amorphous ammonium salt of Eprosartan	Smithkline Beecham Corporation
225,283	Crystal of Diuridine Tetraphosphate or salt thereof and method for preparing the same, and method for producing said compound	Yamasa Corporation
239,408	Novel tyrosine derivatives	Orchid Research Laboratories Ltd
242,111	Crystalline Clopidogrel Besylate and process for preparation thereof	Cadila Healthcare Limited
254,576	Morpholine derivatives as Norepinephrine Reuptake inhibitors	Eli Lilly and Company Limited
254,839	Polymorphic forms of Rifaximin, processes for their production and use thereof in medicinal preparations	Alfa Wassermann S P A
254,845	Prodrugs containing novel bio-cleavable linkers	Piramal Enterprises Limited
254,845	Prodrugs containing novel bio-cleavable linkers	Piramal Enterprises Limited
255,388	Novel crystalline polymorhic form of a Camptothecin analogue	Cipla Limited

Source: Nair and Fernandes (2014), p. 13

While Sect. 3(d) of the Indian Patent Act bans, in principle, the patentability of pharmaceutical formulations and other developments relating to existing drugs, the objection to patentability may be overcome if a significant increase in efficacy is found. In fact, many patents have been granted on such 'incremental' developments in India.[64] Table 2 shows examples of such patents, obtained by both local and foreign companies. In some cases, and despite the anti-evergreening purpose of Sect. 3(d), a number of drugs received in India an extended patent protection through 'secondary' patents.[65]

The TRIPS Agreement requires a minimum protection for patents of 20 years counted from the date of filing.[66] This is an arbitrary term, as there is no evidence

[64] See in Chaudhuri S, Park C, Gopakumar K, Five Years Into the Product Patent Regime: India's Response. United Nations Development Programme (UNDP), December 2010, http://apps.who.int/medicinedocs/documents/s17761en/s17761en.pdf (last accessed 19 May 2015), p. 80.

[65] Nair and Fernandes (2014), p. 14.

[66] Article 33 of the TRIPS Agreement.

suggesting that this is the optimum duration, particularly if applied to inventions of very different nature (both major or radical as well as incremental or minor) and the development of which require completely different levels of skill and investment. G. Becker, a Nobel Prize laureate has argued in relation to the 20-year term that '[t] he current patent length of 20 years (longer for drug companies) from the date of filing for a patent can be cut in half without greatly discouraging innovation. One obvious advantage of cutting patent length in half is that the economic cost from the temporary monopoly power given to patent holders would be made much more temporary. In addition, a shorter patent length gives patent holders less of an effective head start in developing follow on patents that can greatly extend the effective length of an original patent. Even pharmaceutical and biotech companies usually do not need more than about a decade of monopoly power to encourage their very large investments in new drugs.[67]

A study on research in the area of cancer has called attention to the negative impact that the fixed term of patents may have on what type of research is conducted by the pharmaceutical industry. Eric Budish (Univ. Chicago), Benjamin N. Roi (Harvard) and Heidi Williams (MIT) found that "...under a fixed patent term, research and development (R&D) investments may be distorted away from technologies with long time lags between invention and commercialization". This means that companies focus on research for drugs that may be commercialised and generate profits as soon as possible:

> [s]ince society cares about an invention's total useful life, but private firms care only about monopoly life, a distortion emerges not just in the level of R&D..., but also in the composition of R&D: society might value invention A more highly than invention B, but private industry may choose to develop B but not A.[68]

The TRIPS Agreement, in summary, has done nothing to stop the decline in the innovation of the pharmaceutical industry in developed countries nor to induce R&D on new drugs in developing countries. Despite this, in many of these countries there has been a massive proliferation of patents in this area, based on 'evergreening' strategies, that is, the practice of filing for patents, such as on derivatives, crystal forms, formulations or new uses of existing medicines, in order to block the market entry of generic producers.

A telling example of 'evergreening' is offered by one of the patents revoked in Canada which gave rise to a complaint by the patent owner, the US company Eli Lilly, under the investment chapter of NAFTA.[69] The origin of the revoked patent

---

[67] Becker G, On Reforming the Patent System, The Becker-Posner Blog, 21 June 2013, http://www.becker-posner-blog.com/2013/07/on-reforming-the-patent-system-becker.html (last accessed 19 May 2015).

[68] Budish E, Roin B, Williams H (2014) Do Firms Underinvest in Long-term Research? Evidence from Cancer Clinical Trials, http://economics.mit.edu/files/8651 (last accessed 19 May 2015).

[69] See, e.g., Correa C (2013) Investment Agreements: A New Threat to the TRIPS Flexibilities? South Bulletin 72 http://www.southcentre.int/question/investment-agreements-a-new-threat-to-the-trips-flexibilities/ (last accessed 3 July 2015).

can be traced to a broad patent filed in 1975, drafted on the basis of a 'Markush claim',[70] which covered 15 trillion compounds "useful in the treatment of mild anxiety states and certain kinds of psychotic conditions such as schizophrenia".[71] Olanzapine was indicated as one of the 'most preferred compounds'. In 1991, Eli Lilly obtained a new patent on Olanzapine (as a 'selection' from the genus of compounds of the previous patent) and the use of Olanzapine for the treatment of schizophrenia. Between 1995 and 1998 16 separate additional patents were filed for the use of Olanzapine in the treatment of health conditions as diverse as fungal dermatitis, bipolar disorder, sexual dysfunction, insomnia, anaesthetic agent, nicotine withdrawal, tic disorder, anorexia, depression, autism and mental retardation, pain, migraines, dyskinesia, addictive substance withdrawal, and Alzheimer's disease.[72]

The proliferation of pharmaceutical patents—in many cases covering minor technical developments obvious for a person trained in the pharmaceutical field—does not reflect technological progress. As noted by Mercurio, "…there is no evidence that the increase in the volume of patents has had a positive or beneficial effect on innovation. This is problematic, and the lack of competition in certain sectors could potentially hamper innovation".[73] The already mentioned draft report produced for the Australian government also reflects this concern:

> Patents also have negative effects. They may increase prices – and so restrict supply – by more than the amount that would be required to provide the necessary incentives to innovate. This is important for pharmaceuticals because of their importance to human health. And though innovators seeking a patent must disclose considerable information about their inventions - thus providing a platform to others for further innovation - patents can also restrict follow-on innovators…

Countries that are major net exporters of intellectual property have tended to seek longer and stronger patents, not always to the global good.[74] In fact, the patenting strategies of large pharmaceutical firms often aim not only at delaying the market entry of generic producers, but also at discouraging or blocking innovation. This "fencing" strategy is based on the acquisition of a series of patents, ordered in some way, to block certain lines or directions of R&D.[75]

---

[70] A 'Markush claim' consists of the generic description of a chemical formula which includes a multiplicity of closely related compounds.

[71] Patent CA 1,075,687.

[72] See Government of Canada Counter Memorial of January 27, 2015 in *Eli Lilly and Company and Government of Canada* (Case No. UNCT/14/2).

[73] Mercurio B (2014) TRIPs, Patents and Innovation: A Necessary Reappraisal? ICTSD and World Economic Forum, www.e15initiative.org/ (last accessed 19 May 2015).

[74] Harris T, Nico D, Gruen N, 2013 Pharmaceutical Patents Review Report. Canberra, http://www.ipaustralia.gov.au/pdfs/2013-05-27_PPR_Final_Report.pdf (last accessed 3 July 2015), p. iv.

[75] Granstrand (1999), pp. 221–222.

4 Alternative Models for R&D in Pharmaceuticals

"[A] re the incentives provided by the patent system appropriate...? Sadly, the answer is a resounding 'no'."[76] This statement by Nobel Prize laureate Stiglitz encapsulates the growing scepticism in academic and other public circles about the role that intellectual property may play to effectively generate the new treatments needed in both developed and developing countries. An essential point is that innovation as such is not sufficient for a system of incentives to properly work. It must also ensure that the outcomes of the innovation process are accessible and affordable, an objective that becomes unachievable when patent owners can determine prices in exercising a monopolistic right.

High prices of pharmaceuticals, based on the exercise of patent rights,[77] severely affects developing countries where the States' purchasing capacity is low and medicines often need to be paid by the patients themselves, if they can afford them at all. But high pharmaceutical prices are also shocking patients and creating financial problems to social security systems in developed countries. For instance, 11 of the new drugs approved for cancer in 2012 cost at least US$100,000 a year in the USA,[78] where a 12-week treatment with a patented drug for hepatitis C costs US $ 84.000.[79]

The declining productivity in pharmaceutical innovation and the unaffordable costs of the patented outcomes of R&D have prompted analyses and proposals for new models of innovation in this field. Thus, a Consultative Expert Working Group on Research and Development: Financing and Coordination established by the World Health Assembly of the World Health Organization in 2010, produced a

[76] Stiglitz J (2007) Prizes, Not patents, http://www.project-syndicate.org/commentary/prizes--not-patents (last accessed 24 May 2015).

[77] High prices may also be the result of data exclusivity regimes, i.e., those that prevent generic companies to use or rely test on data for a certain period after the first approval of a drug to introduce a generic version thereof. For instance, a study found that 'of all the current forms of intellectual property protection in Jordan, the provision for data protection has the most significant effect on the price of medicines' (Abbott R, Access to Medicines and Intellectual Property in Jordan. Intellectual Property Watch, 23 July 2012, http://www.ip-watch.org/2012/07/23/access-to-medicines-and-intellectual-property-in-jordan/ (last accessed 19 May 2015). See also, for the case of Colombia, Cortés Gamba M, Rossi Buenaventura F, Vásquez Serrano M (2012) Impacto de 10 Años de Protección de Datos en Medicamentos en Colombia. IFARMA, Bogotá http://web.ifarma.org/index.php?option=com_content&view=article&id=70:serie-buscando-remedio-qimpacto-de-10-anos-de-proteccion-de-datos-en-medicamentos-en-colombiaq&catid=22:buscando-remedio (last accessed 3 July 2015).

[78] See, e.g. The New Drug War, Hard Pills to Swallow, The Economist, 1 July 2014, http://www.economist.com/news/international/21592655-drug-firms-have-new-medicines-and-patients-are-desperate-them-arguments-over (last accessed 24 May 2015).

[79] See, e.g., Armstrong D, At $84,000 Gilead Hepatitis C Drug Sets Off Payer Revolt, Bloomberg, 27 January 2014, http://www.bloomberg.com/news/articles/2014-01-27/at-84-000-gilead-hepatitis-c-drug-sets-off-payer-revolt#q (last accessed 24 May 2015).

set of recommendations[80] in view of the failure of the present incentive systems, in particular, intellectual property, to generate enough R&D in either the public or private sector in order to meet the health needs of developing countries.[81] Based on the evaluation of close to 100 proposals for mechanisms to promote better financing and coordination of research, the report concluded that an open approach to R&D should be promoted, with the results of R&D being treated as public goods not subject to the exclusive rights conferred by patents. It recommended new forms of shared financing, direct subventions, prizes and patent pools (to increase access to health products), including, in particular, a legally binding convention on R&D (see Table 3).

A starting point of these and other initiatives is that, as stressed by Dosi and Stiglitz,

> [i]ntellectual property is only one way of incentivizing innovative research; it is only one part of what might be thought of as a country's *innovation system,* the collection of institutions that promote innovation; there has been too much emphasis on IPR, to the exclusion of other ways of stimulating innovation and learning. . ..Moreover, much innovation occurs within and is supported by non-market systems.[82]

The idea that innovation may flourish better in 'open' systems rather than in those relying on the private appropriation of its results is growingly explored. It is not new, however, and it has been tested in some sectors. Mowery, Nelson and Martin, for instance, identified policies in the USA based on a knowledge base open and available to a wide range of firms and other users, which were successfully implemented in the area of semiconductors, the human genome and the development of new seeds. They concluded that '[i]n all of these areas, the support provided by public R&D programs for the broad dissemination of fundamental knowledge neither discouraged industry R&D investment nor does it appear to have discouraged privately funded innovation'.[83]

In the field of drug discovery and development, an interesting example of 'open research' is provided by the Open Source Drug Discovery, launched in 2008 by the Council of Scientific and Industrial Research of India by providing a global platform for scientific collaboration to tackle the complex problems related to discovering novel therapies for neglected tropical diseases. With more than 4500 registered users from over 130 countries, it has become 'the largest collaborative effort in drug discovery'.[84]

---

[80] WHO (2012) Research and Development to Meet Health Needs in Developing Countries: Strengthening Global Financing and Coordination. Report of the Consultative Expert Working Group on Research and Development: Financing and Coordination. http://www.who.int/phi/CEWG_Report_5_April_2012.pdf (last accessed 24 May 2015).

[81] See also Velazquez G (2012) Rethinking the R&D Model for Pharmaceutical Products: A Binding Global Convention. South Centre Policy Brief 8 http://www.southcentre.int/wp-content/uploads/2013/06/PB8_Binding-Global-Convention_EN.pdf (last accessed 3 July 2015).

[82] Dosi and Stiglitz (2014), p. 4.

[83] Mowery et al. (2010), p. 20.

[84] Open Source Drug Recovery, http://www.osdd.net/about-us (last accessed 24 May 2015).

Table 3 Suggestions for an alternative model of R&D in pharmaceuticals[a]

1. Open approach to R&D:
● Use "open knowledge" innovation, such as precompetitive research and development platforms, open source and open access schemes, prizes, particularly milestone prizes.
● Increased sharing of outputs via equitable licensing and patent pools.
2. Funding mechanisms:
● All countries should commit at least 0.01 % of GDP on government-funded R&D for product development.
● Developing countries with a potential research capacity should aim to commit 0.05–0.1 % of GDP to government-funded health research of all kinds.
● Developed countries should aim to commit 1.5–2 % of GDP to government-funded health research of all kinds.
3. Pooling resources:
● Make use of pooled funding mechanisms for increased efficiency and better coordination of financial resources.
● Portion of funds should be developed to capacity-building in developing countries through measures such as direct grants to companies.
● 20–50 % of funds raised for R&D should be channelled through a pooled mechanism.
4. Strengthening research and development capacity and technology transfer:
● Address the capacity needs of academic and public research organisations in developing countries.
● Give direct grants to companies in developing countries.
5. Coordination:
● Give WHO a central role in strengthening coordination in R&D for efficient use of resources.
● Establish a global health R&D observatory and relevant advisory mechanisms under the auspices of the WHO.
6. New binding global instrument for R&D and innovation for health:
● Kick-start formal negotiations on an international treaty/convention on global health R&D.[b]

[a]WHO (2012) Research and Development to Meet Health Needs in Developing Countries: Strengthening Global Financing and Coordination. Report of the Consultative Expert Working Group on Research and Development: Financing and Coordination. http://www.who.int/phi/CEWG_Report_5_April_2012.pdf (last accessed May 24, 2015)

[b]These negotiations have not started yet. A decision on the subject would have to be made in the WHO by 2016. See, e.g., (2013) Follow-up of the Report of the Consultative Expert Working Group on Research and Development: Financing and Coordination. Global Health Watch, http://www.ghwatch.org/node/1932 (last accessed 24 May 2015)

While this is not the place to consider this and other options (such as prizes and advanced purchasing commitments) in detail, the basic point to be made here is that the TRIPS Agreement has failed to increase innovation and generate benefits equitable distributed among all members of the WTO system. The same can be said with regard to the free trade agreements promoted by the USA and the European Union that entail a further expansion of intellectual property protection ('TRIPS-plus' standards), such as:

- extended term of patent protection (in the case of US FTAs);
- data exclusivity for pharmaceuticals and agrochemicals;
- linkage between drug registration and patent protection (in the case of US FTAs)[85];
- strengthened enforcement measures.

There is an abundant literature on the TRIPS-plus provisions in FTAs that highlights their likely negative impact in on access to medicines, including reports by UN organizations and the UN Special Rapporteur on health issues.[86] The 'Principles for Intellectual Property Provisions in Bilateral and Regional Agreements',[87] developed under the auspices of the Max Planck Institute for Innovation and Competition, have noted the imbalances inherent to the intellectual property provisions in FTAs:

> ...these deals are driven by export interests and other objectives external to the IP system rather than the common goal to achieve a mutually advantageous, balanced regulation of IP among the parties. While these agreements may pursue an overall balance of concessions, they usually do not lead to international IP rules that address the interests of all countries affected'.

5 Conclusions

The incorporation of intellectual property into trade agreements has not proven to bring about the promised benefits. The premises that have underpinned the global strengthening and expansion of intellectual property through such agreements—namely that the same standards of protection are suitable for countries with different levels of development and that innovation will be boosted—do not match the reality.

The effects of high standards of protection—as those mandated under the TRIPS Agreement and further extended under FTAs—have been critically examined in the developed countries themselves: '[i]ntellectual property is ...a social contrivance purportedly designed to increase welfare, by supposedly enhancing innovation (though... it may actually have exactly the opposite effect)'.[88] If intellectual

[85] See, e.g., Correa (2008).

[86] See, e.g. UNDP/UNAIDS (2012) The Potential Impact of Free Trade Agreements on Public Health. Issue Brief, http://www.unaids.org/sites/default/files/media_asset/JC2349_Issue_Brief_Free-Trade-Agreements_en_0.pdf (last accessed 24 May 2015); Grover A (2009) Report of the Special Rapporteur on the .Right of Everyone to the Enjoyment of the Highest Attainable Standard of Physical and Mental Health. A/HRC/11/12, http://www2.ohchr.org/english/bodies/hrcouncil/docs/11session/A.HRC.11.12_en.pdf (last accessed 24 May 2015); Manoranjan A (2013) Free Trade Agreements and Access to Medicines: Need for Regulation. SSRN: http://ssrn.com/abstract=2273275 (last accessed 24 May 2015).

[87] http://www.ip.mpg.de/fileadmin/user_upload/Principles_for_IP_provisions_in_Bilateral_and_Regional_Agreements_final1.pdf (last accessed 24 May 2015).

[88] Dosi and Stiglitz (2014), p. 3.

property does not work in developed countries as generally described by their proponents, the situation can only be worse in developing countries with weak science and technological infrastructures, scarcity of risk capital and unsophisticated production profiles. These countries are currently paying the cost of a system which primarily serves as a platform to extract rents (in the form of royalty payments and high prices) and which does little to promote local innovation and economic development.

The scenario for innovation in the pharmaceutical sector, discussed above, illustrates well that the conception underpinning the TRIPS Agreement was flawed from a global perspective. The rate of innovation has not increased, but declined, and while developing countries struggle with high prices for medicines, R&D necessary to address their particular health needs continues to be marginalized.

References

Bedi N, Bedi P, Sooch B (2013) Patenting and R&D in Indian pharmaceutical industry: post-TRIPS scenario. J Intellect Prop Rights 18:105–110

Ben-Atar D (2004) Trade secrets: intellectual piracy and the origins of American industrial power. Yale University Press, New Haven

Bessen J, Meurer M (2008) Patent failure: how judges, bureaucrats, and lawyers put innovators at risk. Princeton University Express, Princeton

Boldrin M, Levine D (2013) The case against patents. J Econ Perspect 27(1):3–22

Correa C (2008) Expanding patent rights in pharmaceuticals: the linkage between patents and drug registration. In: Netanel N (ed) The development agenda; global intellectual property and developing countries. Oxford University Press, Oxford

Correa C (2011) Globalisation and intellectual property rights: the struggle of developing countries to influence TRIPS. In: Alam S, Klein N, Overland J (eds) Globalisation and the quest for social and environmental justice: the relevance of international law in an evolving world order. Routledge, London

Deveraux C, Lawrence R, Watkins M (2006) Case studies in US trade negotiation, vol 1: making the rules. Institute for International Economics, Washington DC

Dosi G, Stiglitz J (2014) The role of intellectual property rights in the development process, with some lessons from developed countries: an introduction. In: Cimoli M, Dosi G, Maskus K, Okediji R, Reichman J (eds) Intellectual property rights legal and economic challenges for development. Oxford University Press, Oxford

Gagnon M (2012) Corporate influence over clinical research: considering the alternatives. La Revue Prescrire 32(342):311–314

Gaillard J (2010) Measuring research and development in developing countries: main characteristics and implications for the frascati manual. Sci Technol Soc 15(1):77–111. doi:10.1177/097172180901500104

Granstrand O (1999) The economics and management of intellectual property. Edward Elgar Publishing, Cheltenham

Mani S, Nelson R (2013) TRIPS compliance, national patent regimes and innovation: evidence and experience from developing countries. Edward Elgar, Cheltenham

Mazzucato M (2013) The entrepreneurial state: debunking public vs private sector myths. Anthem Press, London

Moser P (2013) Patents and innovation: evidence from economic history. J Econ Perspect 27 (1):23–44. doi:10.1257/jep.27.1.23

Mowery D, Nelson R, Martin B (2010) Technology policy and global warming: why new policy models are needed (or why putting new wine in old bottles won't work). Res Policy 39:1011–1023. doi:10.1016/j.respol.2010.05.008

Muñoz V, Vinsentin F, Foray D, Gaulé P (2015) Can medical products be developed on a non-profit basis? Exploring product development partnerships for neglected diseases. Sci Public Policy 42(3):315–338. doi:10.1093/scipol/scu049

Nair G, Fernandes A (2014) Patent policies and provisions relating to pharmaceuticals in India. J Intellect Prop Rights 19:7–17

Olfson M, Marcus S (2013) Decline in placebo-controlled trial results suggests new directions for comparative effectiveness research. Health Aff 32(6):1116–1125. doi:10.1377/hlthaff.2012.1353

Oyelaran-Oyeyinka B, Gehl Sampath P (2010) Latecomer development: innovation and knowledge for economic growth. Routledge, New York

Pedrique B, Stub-Wourgaft N, Some C, Olliavo P, Trouiller P, Ford N, Pécoul B, Bradol J (2013) The drug and vaccine landscape for neglected diseases (2000–11): a systematic assessment. Lancet Global Health 1(6):e371–e379. doi:10.1016/S2214-109X(13)70078-0

Penrose E (1951) The Economics of the international patent system. Johns Hopkins University Press, Baltimore

Scannell J, Blanckley A, Boldon H, Warrington B (2012) Diagnosing the decline in pharmaceutical R&D efficiency. Nat Rev Drug Discov 11(3):191–200. doi:10.1038/nrd3681

Sreedhar D, Janodia M, Ligade V (2011) Buyouts of Indian pharmaceutical companies by multinational pharmaceutical companies: an issue of concern. J Young Pharm 3(4):343–344

Swanson T, Goeschl T (2014) The distributive impact of intellectual property regimes: a report from the "natural experiment" of the green revolution. In: Cimoli M, Dosi G, Maskus K, Okediji R, Reichman J (eds) Intellectual property rights legal and economic challenges for development. Oxford University Press, Oxford

t'Hoen E, Passarelli C (2013) The role of intellectual property rights in treatment access: challenges and solutions. Curr Opin HIV AIDS 8(1). doi:10.1097/COH.0b013e32835b6e5a

Torrance A, Tomlinson B (2009) Patents and the regress of useful arts. Columbia Sci Technol Law Rev 10:130–168

The Current System of Intellectual Property Rights Aims to Promote Trade and Not Innovation

Nuno Pires de Carvalho

Contents

Abstract This paper challenges three widely spread misunderstandings about the international protection of intellectual property: the TRIPS Agreement should not be blamed for failing to promote invention in developing countries because that was not its aim—its aim was (and still is) to promote free trade of goods and services bearing or displaying intellectual property. In this regard, the TRIPS Agreement has actually been very successful. Besides, the patent system should not be blamed for its alleged inadequacy in fostering innovation. There is no data that show the patent system works in one direction or the other. The patent system is a proprietary tool, a free market mechanism, and its purpose is to reduce costs as regards the transactions involving inventions, as compared to the significant transaction costs stemming from trade secrets and the enormous transaction costs arising from government patronage. Therefore, it is imprudent to suggest that the patent system should be abolished in the pharmaceutical field and replaced by open innovation and prizes. These mechanisms are already available, and inventors should be left free to select those that best serve their interests.

In his paper,[1] Prof. Correa makes three points: (1) the adoption and the implementation of the Agreement on Trade-Related Aspects of Intellectual Property Rights

[1] Correa (2016) in this volume.

N.P. de Carvalho (✉)
World Intellectual Property Organization (WIPO) (retired), Geneva, Switzerland
e-mail: npirescarvalho@yahoo.com

M. Bungenberg et al. (eds.), *European Yearbook of International Economic Law 2016*, European Yearbook of International Economic Law 7,
DOI 10.1007/978-3-319-29215-1_9

(TRIPS Agreement) has failed to promote invention and innovation in developing countries, and has led to an increase in payments by developing countries for the use of intellectual property; (2) the patent system, as currently designed (primarily by the provisions of Section 5 of Part II of the TRIPS Agreement), is not adequate to promote invention, in particular the possibility it gives of appropriating technical creations without inventiveness, like incremental pharmaceutical inventions, as well as excessively long terms of protection; and (3) there are alternative methods of promoting invention in the pharmaceutical sector that would be more appropriate for developing countries, like shared financing, direct subvention, prizes, and open innovation (which is based on freely accessible and usable research and development (R&D) databases).

Prof. Correa's paper is well researched, but logically and conceptually misguided. The first problem lies in a mismatch between the title of the paper and its contents. The title implies an association between the trade system and intellectual property rights but the paper only looks at patents and at some point focuses exclusively on pharmaceutical patents. The problem with this approach is that patents are a small portion of intellectual property, and pharmaceutical patents an even smaller portion. The title would therefore be more accurate if it read 'The Current System of Trade and Pharmaceutical Patents'.

But this correction would not solve other problems in Prof. Correa's paper.

1 The Objective of the TRIPS Agreement Is Not to Promote Invention, but Free Trade

Firstly, the idea that the TRIPS Agreement has failed to promote invention and innovation is an obvious one. As a matter of course, the TRIPS Agreement does not have and never had the purpose of promoting invention. Its Article 7, which is so often cited to support this idea, actually reads: "The protection and enforcement of intellectual property rights *should contribute* to the promotion of technological innovation [...]." *Should contribute* implies programmatic language, and means that World Trade Organization (WTO) Members could effectively use intellectual property protection to promote invention but protection by itself is not enough. However, the result would be the same if the provision read *shall contribute*. This would be more peremptory language, but likewise ineffective. If the adoption of high standards of protection were enough to promote invention, those least developed countries that have anticipated the implementation of TRIPS obligations would show high rates of invention and innovation.

Moreover, there is a conceptual flaw in Article 7 of the TRIPS Agreement, which makes it largely ineffective. Only a small part of intellectual property supports the promotion of technological innovation. Several areas of intellectual property, like copyright, geographical indications, most trademarks, commercial secrets, and esthetically determined designs, just to mention a few, have nothing to do with technological invention. Article 7 was extracted from the proposal submitted in 1990 by a group of developing countries to the TRIPS negotiating group.[2] That proposal was almost exclusively concerned with patents, but in transposing it to the Agreement, the drafters failed to adapt its language, broadening its reach. The title of Prof. Correa's paper implies that same reductionist approach: it mentions intellectual property but it covers patents only. The common denominator to all areas of intellectual property is their differentiating function, as suggested by Edward Chamberlin.[3] It is the appropriation of intangible differences in products and services that permits merchants and manufacturers to lure clients. Differences may be internal (technical features, designs, processes, uses, styles, qualities, materials, and ingredients) or external (prices, location, technical assistance, courtesy treatment, origin). And it is the preference of clients for those differences that allows those manufacturers and merchants to set prices—higher or lower, depending on the operation of market forces. Inventions are just one type of difference that manufacturers introduce in products. In some cases, they are essential for the commercial success of a product. In other cases, they are not. It follows that to reduce the function of intellectual property to the promotion of invention is a reductionist misunderstanding.

The fundamental objectives of the TRIPS Agreement are defined in the first paragraph of its Preamble: To reduce distortions and impediments to international trade by means of the promotion of effective and adequate protection of intellectual property, but ensuring that measures and procedures to enforce intellectual property rights do not themselves become barriers to legitimate trade.

The purpose of the TRIPS Agreement in protecting intellectual property is not to promote invention, but rather to promote free trade of goods and services embodying or displaying intellectual property. Moreover, the purpose of the TRIPS Agreement was not even to promote higher protection of intellectual property rights (IPRs). The first paragraph of the Preamble does not say that. Instead, it refers to 'effective and adequate' protection. Where the absence or the low protection of IPRs was seen as a barrier to trade, the Agreement raised the minimum levels generally accepted by developing countries. But where the very presence of IPRs was deemed to be the barrier, the TRIPS Agreement called for a reduction in its protection—as it happened with copyright moral rights and geographical indications.

In a book I published in 2013, defending the idea that the time had come for granting patents for service inventions,[4] I inserted a section with statistical data showing the real objective of the TRIPS Agreement: promoting international trade

[2] See Group of Negotiations on Goods (GATT) Negotiating Group on Trade-Related Aspects of Intellectual Property Rights, including Trade in Counterfeit Goods MTN.GNG/NG11/W/71, of 14 May, 1990, https://www.wto.org/gatt_docs/English/SULPDF/92100147.pdf (last accessed 8 September 2015). The proposing GATT Contracting Parties were Argentina, Brazil, China, Colombia, Cuba, Egypt, India, Nigeria, Peru, Tanzania and Uruguay.

[3] Chamberlin (1946).

[4] Pires de Carvalho (2012).

in goods and services displaying or bearing IPRs. Because that section deals exactly with the same topic as covered by Prof. Correa's paper, here goes a transcript of its conclusive part:

> In conclusion, developing countries may have really believed that their proposal to include in the TRIPS Agreement the language that is now in Article 7 could be persuasive in transforming higher standards of patent protection into an operative and efficient tool for the promotion of technological creation and transfer. However, they were flatly wrong in their belief. Instead, those standards, [. . .] served the purpose set in the first paragraph of the Preamble of eliminating a barrier to trade of products that previously were not or were insufficiently protected by patents.
>
> In a nutshell, the TRIPS Agreement, like the rest of the WTO Agreement, is not about inventions or innovation—it is about trade. [. . .].[5]

2 The Current Patent System and Its Appropriateness to Promote Invention

The second point of Prof. Correa's paper is unfortunately a matter of pure speculation. Nobody can accurately make a correspondence between the standards of patent protection and the amount of invention it promotes. In this regard, the quotes from Stiglitz, Dosi, Swanson and Goeschl, despite the authors' reputation, are not helpful. Significantly, both quotes employ the terms 'likely' ("the IPR regimes of the advanced developed countries are *likely* to be inappropriate for many developing countries"[6]) and 'it is probable' ("In the case of those countries furthest from the frontier, *it is probable* that the impact of heightened IPR is *likely* to be negative over any reasonable time horizon."[7]). Those particular terms just reveal that the authors, as distinguished as they may be, were not sure of what they said. And indeed they could not be. There is simply no way of measuring the impact of property rights on the functioning of the economy. One may find here and there hints that well designed property rights—in inventions and in real estate alike—reduce transaction costs, and therefore contribute to the growth of the economy and the smooth functioning of markets. But there is no econometric tool to show unambiguously that by granting 20-year term patents increases invention by a certain percentage in a given year in a given country. After all, no entrepreneur has ever opened a supermarket just because he or she has read the Civil Code and was thrilled by the guarantees given to property rights in real estate. Nor has a CEO ever determined the opening of a research department after reading the patent statute.

Another quote in Prof. Correa's paper that appears not to be based on sound data is Becker's statement that "[t]he current patent length of 20 years (longer for drug companies) from the date of filing for a patent can be cut in half without greatly

[5] Pires de Carvalho (2012), p. 142.

[6] Correa (2016), section 2 quoting Dosi and Stiglitz (2014), pp. 3–4.

[7] Correa (2016), section 2 quoting Swanson and Goeschl (2014), p. 284.

discouraging innovation."[8] Of course, the countries that give pharmaceutical inventions a longer term of patent protection do so only by breaching their TRIPS obligations—because under Article 27.1, in combination with Article 1.1 of the TRIPS Agreement, protection that is more extensive than that required by the Agreement must comply with all its provisions, including the prohibition to discriminate against or in favour of any technological field. But that is a detail (even if an important one) that Becker would not be supposed to be aware of. This is mentioned just to underline the idea that most economists who write about the patent system do not possess more than vague ideas (mostly wrong) about how it works. Important in Becker's statement is that the reduction of the minimum patent term would not 'greatly' discourage invention. This, of course, shows that the distinguished economist believes that the reduction in patent terms would to some extent reduce the role of patents as incentives. That reduction might not be great, but it would not be nonexistent.

But this is not the point here. The point is: where is the factual basis for asserting such a thing? Has ever a country tried to reduce the term of protection from 20 years to, say, 18 years, for any given period, just for the sake of experimenting and study the impact of that reduction on invention? The answer is no. Without such an empirical background, Becker's assertion is a mere guess—which one can accept or not for its face value (which, in my opinion, is zero).

The flaw in this sort of analysis lies in a misunderstanding of the meaning of patent terms. Certain authors tend to associate the length of patent terms with the inventors' need to recoup the sunken costs of inventing and obtaining enough profits that may lure them to continue inventing. This notion, as vastly spread as it is, is flatly wrong. It is also commonly said that patents, like all IPRs, are naturally time-limited because after the patent owner having exclusively enjoyed its rights, the inventions should be generally available to be used by anyone else. Like many other general views on patent law, that view is squarely incorrect. Such a deal has never been formulated (except under very specific circumstances, like the patent granted to Brunelleschi by the city of Florence, in 1421) and historically there have been patents with indefinite duration. Today's patents, after 20 years, tend to cover technology that no one else wishes to use. The time-limited nature of patents does not result from that sort of deal. The rights conferred by patents are time-limited because their subject matter, like the subject matter of every property right, has a limited duration. Actually, all property rights are time-limited. The notion of perpetual property rights is mistaken. There are no such rights. The duration of property rights is that of their subject matter. Property rights in a flower are more fleeting than property rights in a tree. And rights in a tree are much briefer than rights in land (which, in its turn, disappears as natural phenomena, like erosion and flooding, destroy it). Technology also deteriorates by means of technical obsolescence. Unlike rights in land or other tangible goods, the rights in inventions must have a predefined duration for the reason that, being immaterial, inventions do not deteriorate physically. The duration of a patent corresponds to the average period of

[8] Correa (2016), section 3.

life that society attributes to the subject technology. This period may vary according to each specific technical field. In the steel industry, for instance, technology changes more slowly than in communications. In the pharmaceutical sector, inventions keep their technical and economic utility for much longer. However, for practical purposes, patent laws adopt an average lifespan criterion rather than create a specific duration for each industrial branch. In other words, the duration of patents corresponds the cycles of what Schumpeter named 'creative destruction'. On the one hand, patents are the engine of creative destruction, in the sense that they promote alternative inventions that tend to overcome previous inventions and make them obsolete. But, on the other hand, the average rhythm of that replacement of old technologies by new ones determines the average duration of patents. Or, rather, it should.

Some economists, like Becker, have raised, in connection with the terms of patent protection, the issue of "overprotection". Inventions with a very short technological life span are necessarily overprotected by a term of 20 years. Inventions in other sectors, like the pharmaceutical industry, may be indeed underprotected. A solution could be found by assigning a different term of protection according to the field of technology. That would raise a problem of discrimination, however, because national laws would necessarily tend to assign terms of protection according to considerations of national policy.[9] Thus, some technological fields would be more encouraged than others. That sort of discrimination would be overcome only by international arrangements, in which terms would be harmonised in accordance with the different fields of technology. To bring this absurd scenario even further, one might devise a system under which the terms of patent protection would be linked to the International Patent Classification: based on the specific classification of patent applications, patent examiners would assign the patents, when granted, the correspondent term of protection. However, the best mechanism, which would better correspond to the creative destruction rationale mentioned above, would be to assign specific and individual terms to patents, according to their duration on the market. This was the practice of proto-patents in Venice and other European countries from the fourteenth century onwards. Each patent would have its own term. However, if adopted today, this scheme would create extreme uncertainty. Actually, a system is already in place that establishes in a simple manner the necessary linkage between the patented inventions and their evolving economic and technical utility, thus reflecting the pace of creative destruction: progressive maintenance fees. As time goes by and the patented inventions lose their economic value, patent owners simply stop paying maintenance fees because they become too expensive as compared to the benefits that the patent owners can extract from the inventions, thereby letting the respective patents lapse. This shows that the market is able to provide for a situation of equilibrium between terms of patent protection and the technical utility of inventions without the need for arbitrary and artificial legal measures.

---

[9] A commentator has proposed that the term of patents should be proportionate with the economic level of the granting country. See Donoso Crespo (2013).

Prof. Correa's paper mentions other aspects of the current patent system that are generally indicated as hurdles to a smooth operation of the economy, like the relaxing of the criteria of patentability by patent offices, which leads to the granting of too many patents covering technical solutions with little inventive content. That is correct, in my view. But that is not a problem of the design of the system, but rather of its operation. The fact is that many patent offices see themselves as providers of services to inventors. In this way, the granting of patents is seen as the service and inventors are treated as customers. And the ultimate result is obtaining increased revenues for the patent offices. This happened in the middle of the nineteenth century with the United States Patent and Trademark Office, when the United States' Congress determined that it should find its own ways of funding itself.[10] The crisis of excessive and abusive patenting of trifling inventions that followed that measure is well known, and it stopped only after the United States Supreme Court requested that patents should be granted for genuine inventions only.[11]

The solution to the problem of over-patenting could eventually be introduced in the patent statutes, by making patent offices liable for patents wrongly granted—which is not the case. Moreover, patent examiners who granted 'bad' patents could also be deemed administratively liable and sanctioned for their mistakes—instead of being rewarded for the patents granted, as it is today the general practice, and which naturally encourages easing the criteria for examination.

Nevertheless, the relation between the level of patent protection and the level of inventiveness is impossible to quantify. Many countries, for example, do not care for inventing. Before the TRIPS Agreement entered into force, they were happy with free riding on inventions made in other countries. This happened in particular in sectors in which developing countries had no expertise or the means to invent, such as in the pharmaceutical sector. The national treatment principle of the Paris Convention permitted those countries to free ride on other countries' inventions provided they did not grant pharmaceutical patents to their own citizens. In the field of patents it was this sort of parasitism that the TRIPS Agreement aimed at stopping. In exchange for the reduction of subsidies and the alleviation of sanitary measures in developed countries, developing countries accepted to stop free riding on inventions made abroad with the goal of increasing exports of their commodities. To look at the TRIPS Agreement in isolation, therefore, is misguided: its impact on developing countries should be assessed in terms of the increase in exports by developing countries. As said above, the TRIPS Agreement is a free trade agreement, so its positive or negative impact should be assessed in terms of trade, not of invention.

Another aspect that makes it absolutely impossible to assess the impact of the patent system in terms of the quantity of invention is that most inventions are not

---

[10] Usselman (2002). See also Hayter (1947).

[11] *Atlantic Works v. Brady*, 107 U.S. 192 (1882). On the patent controversy in the United States, in the nineteenth century, see also Pires de Carvalho (2009), pp. 350–369.

covered by patents—in spite of the proliferation of patents in some countries in recent years. A large (but unquantifiable) part of new technology is kept secret. Because it is secret nobody knows what and how much it is. Inventors are expected to feel confident that their efforts will be rewarded by the market if an effective patent system is in force, but no one can say if that confidence is enough to persuade inventors to engage in R&D, given that many other factors interfere in the commercial success of an invention. After all, only a few patented inventions reach the market. A vast proportion of patents remain just pieces of paper, without any economic dimension.

But there is a third factor that makes it impossible to evaluate the impact of a national patent system on the quantity of invention: the size of national markets. Very competitive and inventive countries, like Switzerland and Singapore, have small markets, which would not justify the significant number of inventions made by national companies. The same can be said of large conglomerates that are legally based in large national markets, like the United States or Japan, but given their global dimension, also take the prospects of selling in other markets as a factor for inventing. This element eliminates the significance of the evaluation proposed by Prof. Correa's paper. The patent system in Brazil or in China may have a stronger impact on the drive of a company like Novartis to invent than the patent system in Switzerland.

3 Alternative Ways of Promoting Invention

The last point of Prof. Correa's paper is the possibility of resorting to alternative mechanisms of promoting pharmaceutical inventions as a way to overcome problems arising from patent exclusivity. The paper mentions open innovation (which means non-proprietary, freely available technology), public funding, and prizes.

Of course, there is an undeniable ideological motivation behind this sort of proposal. Those alternative tools of incentivising invention in the pharmaceutical sector—or in any other sector, for that matter—are already available. Inventors are free to rely on those mechanisms, when they are available. But the bottom line of such proposals is that, in the face of those alternative ways of incentivising inventions, the patent system should be banned. This is, of course, an ideologically motivated proposition.

The patent system is about private property rights. It is a tool inherent to free markets. Therefore, patents give the power to make economic decisions to consumers, who can decide to buy or not a given patented product. When it comes to pharmaceutical or agrochemical products, things may be different, as a result of government interference. But, in general, the rationale of patents corresponds to the rationale of free markets. In countries presided by the principles of free entrepreneurship and economic initiative, there is no appropriate substitute to private property. To rely exclusively on prizes and public funding to incentivise inventions is to leave in the hands of third parties—generally motivated by other interests—the decision on what and how to invent. For those who take this sort of proposition seriously, I would strongly recommend the reading of the book 'Longitude', which in vivid colours and beautiful literary style, describes the misadventures of John Smith, the genial inventor who solved the problem of determining longitude.[12] For almost all his life, he pursued the goal of receiving the prize promised to the person who found the solution. He found it—but never received the prize. Conflicting interests, corruption, and jealousy of the board members, denied him the just reward promised in a statute. To leave in the hands of national or international bureaucrats and academics, all with their own vested interests and political motivations, the possibility to decide what inventions are to be made just does not make any sense. Besides running counter the fundamentals of free-market based economies, it would raise transaction costs enormously without any guarantee of effective results. After all, there is no historical experience that countries that at some point in time have adopted a centralised mechanism of dictating the inventive activity—I am thinking of the Soviet Union and North Korea—have ever been successful in bringing effective medicines to patients. For that matter, the proponents of banning patents for pharmaceutical inventions system in favour of prizes, awards, public funding and open innovation, might also propose that private pharmaceutical companies should be prevented from inventing. But, seriously, if in countries like the United States there are a few deviations of the patent system in a background of sound free market principles—like allowing private pharmaceutical companies to appropriate the results of publicly funded research—this problem should be solved by the United States within its law and democratic political regime, but it is not a systemic problem, in the sense that it does not have to occur necessarily.

4 Conclusion

The patent system should be seen as a private mechanism of appropriation of human labour. It serves an ultimate objective that goes much beyond merely operating as an incentive to inventing: it serves the differentiation of products, which is the engine that makes free markets to function and grow by means of consumers' free choices.

Messing with the patent system can only be done at the risk of putting in peril the functioning the free markets for inventions and for inventive products. The patent system that we have was inherited from the Industrial Revolution, and it evolved as an alternative tool to technical trade secrets and government patronage given the enormous transaction costs associated with these two other tools. With all its shortcomings, the patent system has not prevented the global society from progressing technologically. Of course, the patent system has a different impact for those countries that do not invent than in those that have a strong technological

[12] Sobel (1995).

basis. But the former, in 1994, promised the latter to grant patents in accordance with certain harmonised higher standards in exchange for more opportunities to export. This was the deal in 1994. And the deal has not changed thus far.

References

Chamberlin E (1946) The theory of monopolistic competition—a re-orientation of the theory of value. Harvard University Press, Cambridge

Donoso Crespo E (2013) Correctivo a la protección mundial de las invenciones. Imprenta Visión, Quito

Dosi G, Stiglitz J (2014) The role of intellectual property rights in the development process, with some lessons from developed countries: an introduction. In: Cimoli M, Dosi G, Maskus K, Okediji R, Reichman J (eds) Intellectual property rights legal and economic challenges for development. Oxford University Press, Oxford

Hayter E (1947) The patent system and agrarian discontent, 1875–1888. Miss Val Hist Rev 34 (1):59–82

Pires de Carvalho N (2009) A Estrutura dos sistemas de patentes e de marcas—passado, presente e futuro [The structure of the patent and trademark systems—past, present, and future]. Lumen Juris, Rio de Janeiro

Pires de Carvalho N (2012) Patently outdated: patents in the post-industrial economy—the case for service patents. Wolters Kluwer, Alphen aan den Rijn

Sobel D (1995) Longitude—the true story of a lone genius who solved the greatest scientific problem of his time. Fourth Estate, London

Swanson T, Goeschl T (2014) The distributive impact of intellectual property regimes: a report from the "natural experiment" of the green revolution. In: Cimoli M, Dosi G, Maskus K, Okediji R, Reichman J (eds) Intellectual property rights legal and economic challenges for development. Oxford University Press, Oxford

Usselman S (2002) Regulating railroad innovation—business, technology, and politics in america, 1840–1920. Cambridge University Press, Cambridge

International Investment Law as Development Law: The Obsolescence of a Fraudulent System

Muthucumaraswamy Sornarajah

Contents

Abstract Fraudulent is a strong term to describe a system of investment protection that has come about over the course of the last three decades. But, when development is made the focus of the system and it is not delivered by it, the use of the strong term is justified. The investment treaties were signed upon the promise that development will result. That has not been the case. Instead, through interpretation, arbitrators have brought about a system of absolute investment protection far more extensive than that contemplated by the parties to the treaties and far removed from the original goal of economic development. The article analyses the process through which this has been brought about.

M. Sornarajah (✉)
Faculty of Law, National University of Singapore, 469G Bukit Timah Road, Singapore 259776, Singapore
e-mail: lawsorna@nus.edu.sg

M. Bungenberg et al. (eds.), *European Yearbook of International Economic Law 2016*, European Yearbook of International Economic Law 7,
DOI 10.1007/978-3-319-29215-1_10

1 Introduction

Developing countries were led into making investment treaties providing for standards of protection and compulsory arbitration at the instance of the foreign investor on the basis that such treaties were necessary to promote the flow of foreign investment necessary for economic development. The link between the system of investment protection through treaties and economic development was the assumption on which the system was built up. The link is based on an unproven hypothesis cultivated by the developed states and the financial institutions that they control, like the World Bank and the International Monetary Fund. The making of the treaties was conditional on the availability of certain facilities like loans granted by these institutions. The assumption that the investment treaties will lead to economic development is undergoing challenge. Many argue that there is no evidence to show that investors choose to invest in developing countries because these countries have investment treaties.[1] Instead, any cursory look at the picture will show that foreign investors invest not because there are investment treaties, the existence of which some investors do not even know of, but for other reasons such as a the ready availability of mineral resources, cheaper labour, large markets for manufactured goods and the need to meet competition of other investors who would move into these states if they did not.

The present is an age where there is a competition for available natural resources between states with the large industrializing countries of the developing world, China, India and Brazil, aggressively moving into states which possess natural resources, cheap labour and large markets. The canard that investment treaties are necessary for the flows of foreign investment can no longer be accepted. If investors from one state do not move in, investors, particularly state owned investors from other states like China will move in. If it is true that there is no correlation between investment flows and the signing of investment treaties, host states lose sovereignty unnecessarily by entering into investment treaties.

The only rationale for investment treaties is that, for the loss of control over foreign investment that results from conformity with the standards in the investment treaty, the *quid pro quo* is the greater flow of foreign investment. If this equation, however, does not hold, no rationale for investment treaties exists. As indicated, economic studies throw great doubts on the validity of this rationale.[2]

---

[1] There is an increasing debate amongst economists as to whether there is any link between investment treaties and flows of foreign investments. The studies are inconclusive. See Aisbett (2009), p. 395; Hallward-Driemeier M (2003) Do Bilateral Investment Treaties Attract Foreign Investment? Only a Bit and They Could Bite, World Bank Policy Research Working Paper No 3121; Yackee (2010). This is not an exhaustive list. There is a summary of these articles in Bellak C (2013), How Bilateral Investment Treaties Impact on Foreign Direct Investment, available at http://www2.gre.ac.uk/__data/assets/pdf_file/0006/822705/Christian-Bellak-How-Bilateral-Investment-Treaties-Impact-on-Foreign-Direct-Investment-A-Meta-analysis-of-Public-Policy.pdf (last accessed 3 September 2015).

[2] A good assessment can be found in Poulsen (2015).

The need for dismantling the system that has been built up for the economic development of the large law firms, arbitrators and multinational corporations and not for the economic development of the poor of the world is the focus of this study. The law that has been built up is the law of the development of greed, not the law that caters to need. It is for this reason that the system is described as a fraudulent system as it is one that is maintained on the fraudulent assumption that its continuation is to the benefit of the poor in the states in need of economic development when in fact it acts to their detriment.

This contribution, in the second part, begins with an identification of the four phases of bilateral investment treaties and the law that had been created under the treaties, on the basis of their interpretation by arbitrators. The third part examines the issues of legitimacy that have been raised as regards the system. The fourth part deals with changes to and the termination of the treaties. The final part deals with the nature of foreign investment protection that would remain if the treaty system is dismantled and the fifth part contains the conclusion.

2 The Phases of Investment Treaty Law

Investment treaties and the law that was created under them underwent four major phases. The optimist assertion that a regime had been created on foreign investment is a fallacious assertion.[3] If one was created perhaps during the second and third phases identified below, it is in shambles now. It was an ephemeral regime not worth writing about. It is necessary to set out these different phases and discuss the trends that identify them.

2.1 The First Phase (1959–1989)

Investment treaties underwent several stages of development. In the first phase, beginning with 1959, the year of the first bilateral investment treaty between Germany and Pakistan, the treaties were rather innocuous stating standards of treatment and safeguards against expropriation in loose terms and providing for arbitration as a possibility.

[3] On the existence of a regime of foreign investment, see Salacuse (2015).

2.2 The Second Phase (1990–2001)

The second phase of the treaties can be said to begin form 1990 with the award in *AAPL v Sri Lanka*[4] which announced that an appropriately worded dispute resolution provision could create a unilateral right in the foreign investor to take a state that had violated treaty standards to arbitration. It this award and its interpretation of a type of dispute settlement provision in investment treaties that is the characteristic of the second phase. Consequent on the AAPL award, the number of arbitrations brought before ICSID rose exponentially.

At the time too, the prevalent neoliberal philosophy and the dominant power of the United States and the institutions it controlled ensured that developing countries were induced into the making of a large number of investment treaties. The so called "Washington Consensus" based on the liberalization of flows of trade, assets and investments ensured that there was an adoption of international law rules that favoured the type of development strategy that was advocated by this market driven philosophy.[5] There was a massive explosion in numbers of investment treaties during this period based on the belief that they were necessary to create a framework for liberalization of flows of foreign investment.

The law on the subject was also set on a course for expansion. The term, "tantamount to an expropriation", for example, was seen as applying to measures which caused any depreciation in value of investment.[6] The second phase lasted through what Stiglitz called "the roaring nineties", the last decade of the twentieth century when neoliberalism had a near total sway. But, cracks in the acceptance of that ideology were beginning to appear towards the end of the decade. The optimistic effort at a Multilateral Agreement on Investment begun by the Organization for Economic Cooperation and Development ended in failure in 1998. Successive economic crises began in Russia and Asia. Neo-liberalism began to fray.

2.3 The Third Phase (2001–2008)

The third phase lasted till 2008. It began to a large extent with the cases associated with the Argentinian crisis, the first of which was CMS v Argentina,[7] decided in

---

[4] *Asian Agricultural Products Ltd v Republic of Sri Lanka*, ICSID Case No ARB/87/3, Award (27 June 1990).

[5] The competing notion of a "Beijing Consensus" indicates that there could not a single prescribed method of economic organization or of economic development. China's own development was achieved in the context of a heavily regulated economy within which foreign investment was fitted in.

[6] In the *Ethyl Case* (*Ethyl Corporation v Canada*) (1999) 38 ILM 708, the theory of litigation was that the statement made by the Minister that she contemplated a ban on the production of a chemical because it was thought to be carcinogenic was suggested to be tantamount to an expropriation.

[7] *CMS Gas Transmission Company v Argentina*, ICSID Case No. ARB/01/8 (17 July 2003).

2001. The Argentinian cases began a slide into chaos. The first case shows an opening up of a wide notion of fair and equitable treatment as the focus of a new law. That law, based on an expansive view, takes hold in the first few years but becomes mired in controversy. The facts of the Argentinian cases do not support claims to expropriation as physical dispossession did not take place. It was necessary to jump onto another bandwagon to keep investment arbitration and the industry that had grown up alive. Fair and equitable treatment, the amorphous phrase, was dusted up and blown up into what it was not, a treatment standard that enabled the claimant to argue that the frustration of any legitimate expectation created at the time of his entry amounted to a violation of the standard.

A mushroom of arbitral awards sought to stabilize the view but equally, another set of awards sought to restrict the meaning of the standard. Progressively, Argentina argued successfully for exceptions to liability based on necessity. The possibility of defences to liability came to be explored. Schisms began to appear in the way the treaties were interpreted. States themselves reacted to the tendency towards the expansionary law by drafting new model treaties that contained wide defences based on subjective assessments of national security and necessity as well as defences for environmental measures and labour standards.

2.4 *The Fourth Phase (2008-Today)*

The fourth phase begins with 2008. This year is chosen only because the so-called global crisis, which largely affected the rich states, began that year. Neoliberalism gets dented with this crisis. Belief in an unregulated market left to create imperfections by itself was no longer thought valid. Yet, the chances were that the vitality of neoliberalism was not ended by the crisis. It could survive through mutation into other forms. It is unlikely that the classes that prospered under neoliberalism would want to give up the system of investment arbitration that brought them so many profits, without a struggle. For our purposes, one can see that there is an effort to relieve pressure for change through suggestions for reform, such as the establishment of an appellate system (which will create more work) or the creation of an advisory centre (which will create more work for the boys).

The disputes that resulted from the withdrawal from neoliberal policies or from potential economic crises began to appear.[8] The states reacted by discovering new doctrines such as the regulatory exception to expropriation. They began to withdraw from investor-state arbitration, from the arbitral system and announce termination of treaties. South Africa, in addition to terminating treaties, announced that it would hereafter depend on its own legislation for foreign investment protection. New model treaties began to appear with limitations on arbitration through adoption of the local remedies rule and wide circumstances in which liability would be

[8] There are many anticipated litigation. On the Greek crisis, see Chaisse (2015), p. 306.

excluded. The law was in chaos. While the conservatives scurried to recover scope for the old law they had constructed, there were signs towards efforts to displace it.

3 Legitimacy of Investment Arbitration

Through the third phase, neoliberalism came to be challenged as a dominant philosophy. In the second phase, there was a veritable dance of the witchdoctors of neoliberalism, formulating theories of economic development that were based on an assumption that flows of foreign investment will ensure economic development. It was a one size fits all thesis that justified uniform and inflexible investment protection.[9]

There was a package of norms that were involved in promoting the objectives of neoliberal development. Most of these norms were to be found in the laws of the United States. What was in effect attempted was the universalization of the standards of American law on the basis that that the adoption of these norms would assure the success it had brought the United States. It required the protection of property, a feature strong in the American constitution, though over the years that notions in terms of US constitutional law had undergone a variety of meanings.[10] These different meanings were overlooked in preference of the view that full compensation must be paid if the property rights of a foreign investor are violated. Similar sanctity was extended to contracts.[11] Though domestic American constitutional law had long ago moved from the notion of sanctity of contracts, the cornerstone of investment protection was the view that contractual rights, which are the basis on which the foreign investor entered the host state, are sacrosanct.

Liberalization of movement of assets also required that there be a right of entry guaranteed to foreign investment. This right to enter and set up business has been an aim of American policy from the time its practice of Friendship, Commerce and Navigation Treaties. These treaties had political objectives. In that sense, one may attribute political motives to the United States in requiring the right of entry as the market is made subject to the entry of its powerful multinational companies which have the capacity to overwhelm the economies of states they enter. The treaties made in the second phase had uniform dispute settlement provisions making it mandatory for the state to permit foreign investors to submit disputes to arbitration usually before the International Centre for the Settlement of Investment Disputes.

---

[9] For the rejection of the one size fits all nature of neoliberal policies, see Rodrick (2012).

[10] American lawyers have suggested that property protection under investment treaties extend beyond the standard of protection in American constitutional law. Bean and Beauvais (2003), p. 30.

[11] The stabilization clause in contracts came to be protected on the ground that the umbrella clause in the treaties protects contractual commitments or that it created legitimate expectation that were protected by the fair and equitable standard.

This ensured that there was an effective compliance mechanism in cases of violations of the treaty standards.

The problem that arose in the beginning of the third phase was that the compliance mechanism became the instrumentality through which the cart and the horse of neoliberalism was driven into what was considered the regime of foreign investment treaties created by a network of treaties. Investment treaty arbitration exploded onto the scene exponentially. The case load of ICSID, a once dormant institution, increased dramatically with measures of a state affecting foreign investment being questioned as to whether they measured up to the treaty standards. There was a whipping up of investment disputes brought before arbitrators on the basis of litigation strategies that had not been contemplated before. Certainly, the states, which made the treaties, had not contemplated the possibility of such interpretations of the treaty. The law that was made by the arbitrators who accepted these strategies and expanded on them was widely at variance with the law under the treaties that a normal, linguistic interpretation of the words would indicate.[12]

Arbitrators are appointed by the parties. The arbitral institution appoints them where the parties are not in agreement. Where the arbitrators are not in agreement as to the chairman of the tribunal, the arbitral institution would appoint the chairman. The structure of arbitration and its support system, where arbitrators have a self-interest in ensuring that the course of events are such as to promote their reappointment. The new industry of investment arbitration was set off on a rampage by a group of arbitrators and large law firms set on drumming up business for themselves. The law is developed in a manner that ensures that more disputes are brought to arbitration. New methods of recourse to jurisdiction of the tribunals are fashioned.[13] New theories of substantive liability are stated.[14] This, coupled with the growth of large law firms whose business is dependent on the rapid development of this area of the law, raises the inherent possibility of continuous expansion of the law through interpretation. Studies indicate that the law came to be made by a handful of arbitrators.[15] They also indicate that there was a bias towards multinational corporations in the making of the awards.[16]

[12] For a work pointing out these extensive interpretations in the investment treaties, see Yen (2014).

[13] Examples are many. Some are given below. Eg. the notion of corporate migration where sandwich companies are made so as to enable jurisdiction (*Tokio Tokeles v Ukraine*, ICSID Case No. ARB/02/18 (29 April 2004); use of the MFN clause to expand jurisdiction (*Maffezini v Kingdom of Spain*, ICSID Case No ARB/97/7 (25 January 2000); enabling bond holder jurisdiction (*Abaclat v Argentina*, ICSID Case ARB/07/5 (4 August 2011).

[14] Some examples are given below. For further discussion of this trend of expansion, see Sornarajah (2015a).

[15] Puig (2014), p. 387; Eberhardt P, Olivet C (2012), Corporate Europe Observatory, Profiting from Injustice: How Law Firms and Arbitrators are Fuelling an Investment Arbitration Boom. http://corporateeurope.org/trade/2012/11/profiting-injustice (last accessed 24 April 2015); Waibel M, Wu Y (2012) Are Arbitrators Political?, available at http://www.wipol.uni-bonn.de/lehrveranstaltungen-1/lawecon-workshop/archive/dateien/waibelwinter11-12 (last accessed 20 April 2015).

[16] Schultz and Dupont (2014), p. 1148.

Lest it be thought that these are adverse assessments made by an inveterate opponent of the system, the opinion in agreement stated in an issue of the sedate and conservative journal, the *Economist*, in its issue of 11 October, 2014, may be reproduced:

> If you wanted to convince the public that international trade agreements are a way to let multinational companies get rich at the expense of ordinary people, this is what you would do: give foreign firms a special right to apply to a secretive tribunal of highly paid corporate lawyers for compensation whenever a government passes a law to, say, discourage smoking, protect the environment or prevent a nuclear catastrophe. Yet that is precisely what thousands of trade and investment treaties over the past half century have done, through a process known as "investor-state dispute settlement", or ISDS.

As indicated, the functioning of this system within a climate of neoliberalism further ensured that an instrumental expansion of the standards of treatment in the investment treaties was developed through the arbitration awards. The expansionism was justified largely on the basis that economic development was identified as the object of the different treaties in their preambles. This fitted in with the ICSID Convention. The Convention also stated that its objective in providing arbitration was economic development. The vision of development was neoliberal simply because ICSID, being a part of the World Bank, could not have a vision that it did not share with the World Bank, a part of the Washington Consensus. Arbitrators had a compulsion to demonstrate their fidelity to the system, the hand that feeds them so many riches.

Consequently, the stage was set for the fashioning of rules that would ensure that the principles of neoliberalism are furthered through the expansionist interpretation of the treaty standard. It is necessary to establish this proposition by indicating the instances of such expansion. Space does not permit an exhaustive analysis.[17] The expansionist tendencies may be indicated briefly in order to draw conclusions from them and to show that they had hardly anything to do with the economic development of the host states. Rather, it may be that the system that emerged was a system of legal plunder for the exorbitant sums awarded as damages and the fees involved for lawyers indicate a drain on the economies of the host states that was anything but promotive of their economic development. The damages in some cases have exceeded sums that a weak state could hardly afford. They were awarded in circumstances in which the law that was applied was based on flimsy grounds. The costs involved in arguing some cases have been crippling. A developing economy could have used the funds involved for better purposes of its development.[18]

---

[17] For a more exhaustive analysis, see Sornarajah (2015a).

[18] The Philippines Parliament was told that over 55 million dollars were spent on the *Fraport v Philippines* arbitration. The sum would have funded several development projects. *Fraport AG Frankfurt Airport Services Worldwide v The Republic of the Philippines*, ICSID Case No ARB/03/25, Award (16 August 2007). Further see Rosert D, The Stakes are High: A Review of Financial Costs of Investment Treaty Arbitration (International Institute of Sustainable Development, Paper, 2 October, 2014).

3.1 Expansionary Interpretation on Jurisdictional Issues

Expansionary techniques adopted by arbitrators include both assumption of jurisdiction and the interpretation of treaty standards. Arbitrators are reluctant to let go of the opportunity of assuming jurisdiction as this would mean loss of income. Consequently, even fraudulent schemes of manipulating the means of obtaining jurisdiction have been condoned.

An instance is the use of corporate nationality, widely relied on in the treaties to define the investor who is protected.[19] Here one sees cases, like *Tokios Tokelés v. Ukraine,*[20] holding that assets, which originally belonged to the host state, could be taken into another treaty state and brought back as protected investment. Obviously, such a view subverts the purpose of the investment treaty which is to promote economic development through the injection of fresh funds. It is downright fraudulent to say that any economic development purpose is achieved through the protection of such an investment.

Another fraudulent manipulation of the investment treaty system is the so called 'Dutch sandwich' whereby the mere insertion of a subsidiary in the corporate structure enables a large multinational corporation to exploit the better protection under an investment treaty, usually the Dutch treaty with the disputing state. This is again a fraud on the system as the subsidiary so incorporated to achieve jurisdiction is not the one which sends out the investment. Relief has been provided on the most spurious basis after the assumption of such jurisdiction, *ConocoPhillips v. Venezuela*[21] being the classic example of such an award. In that dispute, jurisdiction was assumed under a Dutch treaty on the basis of the insertion of a Dutch subsidiary in the corporate structure with no proof that any investment was channeled through that subsidiary. Again, the issue is whether any economic development is promoted, as the Dutch treaty promises, in Venezuela through such a technique of insertion of a mailbox Dutch subsidiary into the corporate structure. To assume jurisdiction on the basis of a technicality defeats the object of the treaty. The Dutch may be happy with the fact that their treaties enable post-box companies to sue under them.[22] But, it is an unhappy situation that a state should be a party to bringing about malpractices within an international system so that it may secure some minor profit. After assuming jurisdiction, the majority of the tribunal

---

[19] Sornarajah (2015b).

[20] *Tokios Tokelés v Ukraine*, ICSID Case No ARB/02/18, Decision on Jurisdiction (29 April 2004) (2005) 20 ICSID Rev 205.

[21] *ConocoPhillips Petrozuata BV, ConocoPhillips Hamaca BV and ConocoPhillips Gulf of Paria BV v Bolivarian Republic of Venezuela*, ICSID Case No ARB/07/30, Decision on Jurisdiction and Merits (3 September 2013).

[22] In a television interview, a Dutch minister agreed that these practices should be terminated. http://nos.nl/nieuwsuur/artikel/2040608-nederland-is-claimwalhalla-voor-multinationals.html?title=nederland-is-claimwalhalla-voor-multinationals (last accessed 3 September 2015).

found liability on a point hardly argued in the case, namely that there were no good faith negotiations in fixing compensation.

The case demonstrates a situation in which some arbitrators will find rather atrocious ways of ensuring that resource-rich developing countries toe the line that is drawn in order to ensure that foreign investors are given secure protection. They assume jurisdiction on flimsy grounds and then find liability on a spurious basis that had hardly been argued by the parties in the proceedings. The legitimacy of investment arbitration becomes suspect as a result. It is, as if once gunboat diplomacy had failed,[23] investment arbitrators are the insidious troops that are the hidden guardians of foreign investment dressed up in expensive civilian suits instead of military uniform.

When states react by taking remedial action through denial of benefits provisions which enable a party to determine whether or not corporate nationality of the claimant should be recognized, the provisions have been interpreted narrowly. The pro-investment bias of the tribunals is evident in the manipulation of such treaty interpretation as a means of ensuring that the claimant's ability to establish jurisdiction are not stymied.

Likewise, the whole saga relating to the use of the most-favoured-nation (MFN) clause to widen jurisdiction in a manner favourable to the claimant has yet to run its course.[24] It is evident that a tribunal should first have jurisdiction to pronounce on the effect of the MFN clause and the clause itself cannot be the basis of its jurisdiction to pronounce on the issue. It defies logic to say that a tribunal can extend its jurisdiction through the MFN clause when it does not have jurisdiction to so rule unless it can use that very clause. But logic has never mattered. In investment arbitration, it is possible to pull oneself up by one's own bootstraps. The only consideration has been to ensure that the goal of foreign investment protection is advanced, future earnings of arbitrators are made plentiful and the similar interests of large law firms is guaranteed. The altruistic aim of advancing the economic development of the poor is a fraudulent argument that supports transfer of wealth to the greedy, not the needy. Such fraudulent altruism characterized the excuses given for colonialism in the past.

The acme of aberrations occurred when two tribunals held that class actions were possible where several hundred bond holders who had bought their bonds from banks in Italy could bring claims against Argentina when payments were not

[23] Apologists admit that the area of investment protection was once the area for gunboat diplomacy but that it has been replaced by arbitration. The admission is instructive only for the reason that the rules that are applied are insidious and further the purpose of investment protection more effectively than gunboat diplomacy, which was direct, whereas the system of investment arbitration comes cloaked as 'neutral rules' applied by 'neutral' tribunals.

[24] There is a whole array of awards on the use of the MFN clause to obtain jurisdiction. They split evenly. It is not necessary to discuss the problem in detail here. There are several articles commenting on the cases. See Maupin (2011), p. 157; Douglas (2011), p. 97.

made on the bonds on the basis of the investment treaties.[25] Class actions had hitherto not been known in investment arbitration. Parties could simply not have contemplated such actions. Neither arbitration involved assets that would fall within the definition of investments in the treaties. The transactions had not taken place in Argentina. The awards demonstrate a mindset that seeks vigorously to expand the scope of investment arbitration. The dissenting awards in both cases point out these factors but the majority were oblivious to these concerns.

The litany of extensions does not stop with jurisdiction. It extends into the expansion of the substantive provisions of the treaties on the basis of which claims are brought. Space does not permit the accounting of all the instances. As before, a selective account is sufficient to indicate that economic development of host states is not the motive behind the law that is created. Rather, it is driven by motives of investor protection and the economic development of the profession of investment arbitration and the benefit of the law firms that work in the field.

3.2 *Expansionary Interpretation on Substantive Issues*

There are many examples of such expansionary interpretation. Space does not permit all of them to be detailed here.[26]

The area relates to the expansionary changes that have been made to the substantive law relating to the causes of action under the treaties. These include expropriation as well as other standards of treatment. Such expansion means that there is encroachment on the sovereignty of developing states. The most glamorous change through expansionist interpretation concerns the fair and equitable treatment standard. When I wrote the first edition of my book, the International Law on Foreign Investment in 1994, I researched the standard and found that it was without any substantive content.[27] I dealt with that standard in two pages. The international minimum standard had been around for over 100 years, and beyond the notion of denial of justice and the standards for a lawful expropriation, the standard had no definite content. I asked around from my colleagues and students as to what was meant by fair and equitable treatment at that time. They told me that they were just lawyers' terms for standards that were subjective and did not exist in any concrete sense.

Yet, this dormant standard once without concrete content has sprouted into life. Suddenly, we are told that it is the ceiling with the old international minimum standard being the floor. This is new wisdom that did not exist previously. The standard acquires new meaning which no state making the investment treaties or no

[25] *Abaclat v Argentina* (2011) UCSUD ARB/07/5 (4 August 2011; *Ambiente Ufficio v Argentina* ICSID ARB/08/0 (8 February 2013).

[26] They are detailed in the present author's recent work: Sornarajah (2015a).

[27] Sornarajah (1994), pp. 250–252.

writer in earlier times could have contemplated. Created by the magic wands of a selected group of arbitrators, this amorphous standard assumed strange meanings that very competent lawyers could not have dreamed it had. In 1999, there was an exhaustive study of the fair and equitable standard in the British Yearbook of International Law.[28] In it, Stephen Vasciannie concluded by saying that the standard had no precise content.[29] Yet, in five short years from that study, Christoph Schreuer wrote saying that the standard had now become an autonomous standard with definite content.[30] Clearly, there was law-creation that had taken place by persons who were vested with no power to create law. The legitimacy of their power to do so is greatly suspect.[31] Yet, there was no way that this arrogation of power could be challenged within the system.

The most important rule that constitutes the content of fair and equitable treatment, we are told in a series of contemporary awards in which certain arbitrators belonging to the exclusive club recurrently feature, is the rule that where a state creates legitimate expectations in a foreign investor, a failure to ensure that the expectations are met results in liability for the breach of fair and equitable treatment.[32] The quick effort to conserve this rule, developed by a group of identifiable arbitrators, as customary international law demonstrates the febricity and the imagination of the neoliberal vision.

It is interesting to know that when major international lawyers argue about the difficulties of creating norms of international law through the practice of sovereign states, it is possible for a pack of individuals to create customary international law through just a few arbitral awards. The world is being conned. The pitifulness of it is that the poor of the world are being deceived of their natural resources by the 'college' of international lawyers who are supposed to stand as a bulwark against injustice. It is a matter for sadness. But, leaving this aside, it is necessary to explore the soundness of the development of the view that violation of assurances given at the time of investments are actionable as violations of fair and equitable treatment and the protection it is said to grant to 'legitimate expectations'.

The rule is to a large extent the work of identifiable arbitrators. Sergio Puig identifies 18 arbitrators as commanding the field of investment arbitration.[33] It would be interesting to study the role of the 16 in creating or contributing to new doctrines in the field of international investment law. It is possible to trace the influence of individual arbitrators. The creation of the rule that the violation of the

---

[28] Vasciannie (1999), p. 99.

[29] Vasciannie (1999), pp. 130–147.

[30] Schreuer (2005) p. 385.

[31] The more ambitious among the arbitrators arrogate to themselves the power to create customary international law. This can be dismissed as an attempt at humour if not for the fact that serious arguments are made that the increasing number of tribunals that exist in international law now are creating constitutional norms. Theory is not far away to support humour in the service of private power.

[32] See Schill and Jacob (2015).

[33] Puig (2014), p. 416.

legitimate expectations of the foreign investor at the time of entry could amount to a violation of the fair and equitable standard could be taken of as an example. Such a content in the standard could not even have been contemplated in dreams when the treaties were originally drafted. Yet, it has become one of the most often used rules in investment arbitration now. Its course may be traced. Francisco Orrego Vicuña had written several articles suggesting the rule in international investment law largely by drawing parallels between it and the English administrative law principles on legitimate expectations.[34] He later sat on several arbitrations, the facts of which lent themselves to the application of such a principle.

The Argentinian arbitrations, arising from the economic crisis in that country, provided an ideal setting for the articulation of the rule that violations of assurances made at the point of entry by the state will be actionable as violations of the fair and equitable treatment standard.[35] The Argentinians, in a change of policy advised and supported by the neoliberal institutions of the Washington Consensus had announced full protection for all incoming investments. In the energy sectors in particular, they had announced that there would be parity between the US Dollar and the Argentine Peso and that the prices of commodities would be in accordance with an American price index. After holding out for some time after the economic crisis had set in as a result of sudden withdrawal of funds from banks, the Argentine government responded to a severe public emergency arising from widespread riots by devaluing the Peso and refusing to keep the prices fixed to the American index. This resulted in loss to several US investors who had entered Argentina through share purchases in the privatized industries. 52 different arbitrations resulted on the basis of the violation of treaty provisions.

The claims of expropriation were dismissed as the facts did not show dispossession or that the investors could not have continued to remain shareholders despite the devaluation. As expropriation became difficult to establish under the circumstances, some other avenue had to be found. The dormant fair and equitable treatment standard was given the kiss of life by the arbitrators. The easy way was to identify the rule they were formulating that the violation of assurances given at the commencement of the investment would amount to a violation of the fair and equitable treatment standard in the idea of legitimate expectations in domestic English law and farm it off as a general principle of law. So, there was investment of effort in this by a small group of arbitrators formulating the rule in exorbitant terms, which, as one writer was to point out, even the most sophisticated state could

[34] Vicuña (2003), p. 180.

[35] *CMS Gas Transmission Company v The Republic of Argentina*, ICSID Case No ARB/01/8, Award (12 May 2005), pp. 273–284; *Enron Corporation and Ponderosa Assets, LP v Argentine Republic*, ICSID Case No ARB/01/3, Award (22 May 2007), pp. 256–268; *Sempra Energy International v The Argentine Republic*, ICSID Case No ARB/02/16, Award (28 September 2007), pp. 296–304.

not meet.[36] That did not matter. All that mattered was that developing countries could hardly aspire to the standards as formulated. After all, this was law that was aimed at the vassalage of the developing countries, not at the liability of developed countries.

To justify this line of jurisprudence, the idea was that it reflected a formulation of a public law standard of governance. There was sycophantic scurrying for the discovery of the principle in the public law of some European systems, but no one has done sufficient work to show that there was indeed a notion in European public law that hampered change of public policy because legitimate expectations had been created by the state in a person. It would indeed be difficult to find such a notion in the public law of any state. Changes of policy are necessary in any constitutional system so as to meet public emergencies and changes in public circumstances. It is for that reason that in the English law-based administrative systems, there is ready interference on the basis of procedural unfairness in violating expectations but not in the ready offering of relief for the violation of any substantive rights. In fact, it is in the remotest of situations, as where a special right is granted to an individual in very special circumstances as in the *Coughlan Case*,[37] that the English courts think of providing a substantive remedy.

The extraction of the rule of legitimate expectations does not depend on a general principle of law as there are no general principles relating to this that could be exacted from European systems. Rather, it is a concocted rule that owes its existence to the whim of a small group of arbitrators who price investment protection above other values. They have made law on the basis of an error but, since only a handful of them have made the error, it is a reversible error. No arbitrator has sought to reverse the error.

Armies of young PhD students will write theses, some of them already published,[38] without questioning the legitimacy of how this principle had come to be such a major part of modern investment protection law. It is symbolic of the malaise in legal academia that no young scholar has dared to question the basis of the doctrine. The theses usually assume that the proposition regarding legitimate expectations is well-founded. How does a young scholar invest years of her life in a project to substantiate an assumption whose base is not tested out? How does a doctoral supervisor, (appropriately, 'Doktorvater' in Germany) fulfill his fiduciary function towards such a person writing on an area that is based on fraudulent assumptions? Academia has been caught up in this whirl of fraud, subverted by simple greed. It should have been seen as an uncertain basis on which to establish

[36] Zachary Douglas referred to the Tecmed standard as "the description of perfect public regulation in a perfect world, to which all states should aspire but very few (if any) will ever attain". Douglas (2009), p. 28; In *El Paso v Argentina* (p. 342) the Tribunal said that "the description of the FET standard looks like a programme of good governance that no State in the world is capable of guaranteeing at all times".

[37] *R v North and East Devon Health Authority Ex Parte Coughlan* [1999] EWCA Civ 1871 (16 July 1999).

[38] Eg. Tudor (2008); Kläger (2011); Diehl (2012); Paparinskis (2013).

what one young author called the “core standard” of investment protection. It was an ephemeral phenomenon built on error that would soon be ended.

Some tribunals have sought to question the legitimate expectations doctrine by pointing out that the legitimate expectations rule exists in domestic systems to question the discretionary decisions of subsidiary officers or organs like ministers or provincial councils but not the legislature of a state as where such a legislature changes policy to meet an economic crisis.[39] Most tribunals that have hesitated to apply the doctrine of legitimate expectations, by contrast, have sought to restrict its scope by pointing out that the specific circumstances of the case may not give rise to expectations or that such expectations in the given situation could not be considered legitimate.[40] So, those arbitrators who want to keep away from the rule do not confront it simply because it is not politic to do so, but merely avoid its use by finding that the facts show that it would be difficult to show that there could be legitimate expectations in the given situation. It is not politic for the arbitrators to dismiss it as unfounded simply because the chances of the next arbitration for such an arbitrator would become remote. The system does not promote honesty.

Thus, there are cases where it has been held that countries emerging from socialist rule were not ones in which expectations of stability could be considered legitimate.[41] Some have held that the rule is not there to provide an insurance policy against obvious risks that should have been anticipated by a prudent businessman.[42] So, there is a group of arbitrators, who are not adventurous enough to be expansionist, yet not bold enough to question the basis of a rule which cannot be maintained as it has no basis for recognition as a rule under the investment treaty. One has to explain this absence of boldness in the second group of arbitrators. They do not state the obvious fact that the first group has erred in identifying legitimate expectations rule as a part of fair and equitable treatment without showing a sufficient basis for such identification. Instead, they compound the error, by finding ways around applying the rule on legitimate expectations.

[39] *Total S.A. v. The Argentine Republic*, ICSID Case No. ARB/04/01, Decision on Liability (27 December 2010), p. 313.

[40] *Saluka Investments B.V. v. Czech Republic*, UNCITRAL, Partial Award (17 March 2006), p. 304; *Continental Casualty Company v. Argentine Republic*, ICSID Case No. ARB/03/9, Award (5 September 2008), p. 261; *Total S.A. v. The Argentine Republic*, ICSID Case No. ARB/04/01, Decision on Liability (27 December 2010), pp. 120, 121, 164.

[41] Genin v Estonia (2002) 17 ICSID Rev. 395.

[42] *Emilio Agustín Maffezini v. The Kingdom of Spain*, ICSID Case No. ARB/97/7, Award (13 November 2000), p. 29; *Waste Management Inc. v United Mexican States*, Award, ICSID Case No. ARB(AF)/00/3 (30 April 2004), pp. 160, 177.

3.3 Investment Treaties as Unequal Treaties

Investment treaties are asymmetric treaties. They benefit only multinational corporations from developed states.[43] Consequently, they are unequal treaties. Though stated as creating reciprocal obligations, this is a fallacy as developing states are hardly capable of sending substantial investments into the major developed economies of the world. There is little evidence that investment flows are enhanced as a result of the investment treaties. Investment treaties are based on lies. Developing states derive no benefit from the system of protection devised through arbitration. What is more, they stand in peril of multi-million dollar arbitral awards resulting from the violation of the treaties at times when they are least able to meet such awards. The experience of Argentina, which had to face 52 arbitrations involving claims of several billion dollars while recovering from an economic crisis,[44] illustrates this. The damages are so exorbitant that they undermine economic plans of the state. The costs of litigation are equally high. The enforcement of the awards are difficult. Argentina has not moved in the settlement of the sums awarded so far. The benefits of the system to states and to investors therefore need to be examined afresh.

3.4 Assessment of the Legitimacy of Investment Treaty Arbitration

From the point of view of states, investment treaties have been disastrous. The regulatory powers of states to deal with abusive investments are considerably curtailed as a result of these treaties. The ability of the state to deal with environmental crises, to protect the health of its people or to promote the public interest have been curtailed by investment treaties. They bring about a regulatory chill in that the threat of investment arbitration they contain results in states drawing back from measures that are necessary to deal with issues of public interest.[45] If the safety and security of the people are the highest law of a state (Salus populi suprema lex esto) states also have other competing interests that are imposed through multilateral treaties. These involve matters of global interests, such as measures necessary to deal with climate change or to protect human rights, cultural property and global health. The need for investment treaties therefore has to be re-examined.

To reiterate a point already made, investment treaties are not the reasons for the flow of foreign investments. Multinational companies have many reasons for going into developing countries. It makes sense to invest in large markets of developing

---

[43] They are technically invalid as unequal treaties. For the notion of unequal treaties, see Craven (2005), p. 335.

[44] Di Rosa (2004), p. 41.

[45] Tienhaara (2009).

countries. In imperialist days, the imperial outposts served as markets for manufactured goods of the imperial power. The same situation prevails now as it is obvious that multinational corporations need large markets found in China, India and other parts of Africa and Asia. If they do not enter these states, their competitors will. The profits the competitors make will affect the home markets as the profits will be used for innovation and expansion.

If a multinational corporation operates in the resources sectors, it will enter states that have the resources, whether or not they have treaties. For example, energy companies enter Ecuador not because it has investment treaties but because it has plenty of energy resources. If they do not enter, their competitors will. In the modern world, China, India and other states are hungry for resources and provide effective competition. Their national oil companies are as effective as any Western oil company. They do not necessarily depend on investment treaties. The largest investors in Ecuador are from Brazil and Mexico, two states with which Ecuador has no investment treaties. The largest investors in South-East Asia are the multinational companies of the United States. The United States has no investment treaties with the states of the region (except Singapore). It is pretty obvious that resource-based multinational corporations will enter states which have an abundance of resources. With heavy competition for resources, such entry simply has to be made for these corporations to survive in business. Equally, large manufacturing companies will enter lucrative markets whether they are protected by treaties or not. It is a canard to say that investment treaties promote investment flows or aid in economic development. This is only how investment treaties have been sold to developing countries.

Recent studies in this field indicate that the law had been made by a handful of aging men with a few token women in attendance. Very few of them come from the developing world. Those who come from the developing world have drunk deeply not only of the exquisite wine that is offered at the parties of arbitrators, but equally deeply of the notions of neoliberalism and the prevailing culture of investment arbitration. You cannot join the club without servilely subscribing to the holy tenets of the absolute standards of investment protection. The members of the select club are touted as 'highly qualified publicists' though there is little evidence of their deep learning, but greater evidence of their deep prejudice. They make law for the world without any legitimate power to do so. The poor of the world, in whose name this chicanery takes place, have their resources robbed and the ignominy of being recalcitrant offenders against treaty standards heaped on them. Their states stand in peril of being prey to vulture funds. Their states were induced into signing investment treaties in the belief that good would come out of such action. Instead, what has resulted is a heaping of misery in times of crises.

The hegemonic world legal order is founded on many lies. Grotius lied when he spoke of natural law basis of the international law on freedom of the seas when all the while he was seeking to justify the right of the nascent Dutch naval power to traverse the world and found colonies in Asia. Hegemonic English international lawyers lied when they argued that Australia was *terra nullius* and so could be occupied by white settlers, ignoring the nomadic aborigines who could not hold land. Hegemonic power has used the instrumentality of international law to provide justifications in altruistic terms so that it could justify its domination. Colonialism was justified through the lie that it was the white man's civilizational burden when in fact there was a massive plunder of the wealth of the colonies. International law's founding in lies is an unfortunate history that it has been unable to shake off. Investment treaty law comes in the long line of lies which have supported different principles of international law.

4 Changing Treaty Forms and Termination of Treaties

The contention that I make is that there is simply an inordinate expansion of the law well beyond the original intention of the parties through an interpretation of the provisions of the treaty by using methods of interpretation that seem unsound. The interpretation makes economic development more illusory than when the treaties were made. At the time of the making of these asymmetrical treaties, the only justification could have been that they contributed to the economic development of the host developing countries. It was an unprovable assumption but at least this mere hope provided a ground for the loss of sovereignty the treaties entailed. But, with the unwarranted expansion of the law through interpretation, the original intention of the parties has been clearly bypassed beyond the range of the surrender of sovereignty the treaties entailed. What has come about is a series of awards imposing crippling debts on developing states which they can never hope to satisfy without destroying their economies. Clearly, the time has come to ditch these treaties. The treaties cannot contribute to the economic development of the states. Instead, the type of investments that get shelter under the treaties through enormous sums awarded in their favour are ones that were clearly deleterious to the interests of the states. If one were to look at some of the cases against Ecuador, the statement would become clear. In the *Texaco-Chevron* case,[46] for example, massive desecration of tribal lands of the Amazonian people were involved, but the tribunal was bent on awarding large sums to the foreign investor almost as a prize for his environmental pollution of a pristine area of the world.

There is an obvious cause for concern that is reflected even in the attitudes of rich countries themselves. As a result of NAFTA, two rich states, the US and Canada, have been targets of investment arbitration. They have fought these cases hard. Some of them have resulted in the revival of doctrines such as the regulatory right of the state to act in the public interest or the right to license patens compulsorily, which destroy premises on which investment protection has been built. The rich states feel that their regulatory space has been constrained by investment treaties. They believe that they need to act in order to protect public

[46] PCA Case No 2009-23.

interests against foreign investors and cannot be deterred by reasons of investment protection from acting in the public interest.

When poor countries engaged in regulatory expropriations and were condemned to pay heavy compensation, no one raised an eyebrow in concern. One wonders whether the archetypal Mexican expropriation in pursuance of land-reform following the Zapatist Revolution in Mexico, from 1910 to 1940, in the context of which much expropriation law is discussed, were not regulatory expropriations as the state was seeking to free land from the exploitative domination of monopoly capital and redistribute it to the landless who cultivated it. Many post-colonial expropriations were similarly regulatory in that they sought to redirect the economy into the hands of the local people and divest it from the hands of nationals of the imperial powers. The premises on which investment protection law was based were purposefully tilted against the developing state, which simply did not have the power to object. Now that the targets of arbitration suits are developed countries, we see the emergence of the regulatory expropriation exception to provide for the situation, despite the fact that no meaningful distinction can be made between regulatory expropriation and non-regulatory expropriation in the case of measures taken by the modern state.

The picture is now changing dramatically. Developed states like the United States and Canada are fast becoming the largest recipients of foreign investment. They are becoming restrictive of flows of foreign investment, using national security exceptions to keep foreign investment out. They have been subjected to several arbitrations and can anticipate very many more. This picture is repeated as far as European states are concerned. German views have been considerably altered as a result of the *Vattenfall* arbitration. The boots which kicked the developing countries with fervour are now on other feet. The attitudes are consequently changing. The US Model and the Canadian Model investment treaties, released in 2004 are replete with defences against liability.[47] They provide for environmental safeguards, labour standards and, most of all, contain provisions stating that measures taken to protect the health, welfare and safety of the public should not be considered as violations of the investment treaty. They contain subjective statements of the national security defence. The new Model treaties shift the focus of investment treaties from investment protection and seek to balance them against other interests, such as the environment, labour standards and other public interests.

So are born the balanced treaties. The balanced treaties have now become established practice with the new American and Canadian treaties being based on their respective model treaties. The call for balance also has resulted in other

[47] Article 12 (environment protection), Article 13 (labour standards), Article 18 (essential security interests), Article 19 (disclosure of information), Article 20 (prudential measures for financial services), Article 21 (taxation measures), Annexure B (Letter on Expropriation: exemption of regulatory measures). See US Model BIT of 2004 and Article 10 (general exceptions), Article 11 (health, safety and environmental measures), Article 16 (taxation measures), Article 17 (prudential measures).

so-called balanced treaties, instances being the ASEAN Investment Treaty (2009),[48] the SADC Model Treaty[49] and the Commonwealth Guide for Developing Country[50] These treaties strike the balances within them differently. Stephan Schill optimistically suggested that investment treaties multilateralize investment law.[51] It is like talking of the BITs Revolution on the basis that the investment treaties create customary international law. Both are figments of imagination. The internal structures of investment treaties are carefully negotiated striking different compromises and they can neither create custom nor multilateralize the law.

Of course, much is going to depend on how the neoliberal arbitrators are going to read these developments. Their usual approach has been to read whatever inroads states make on investment protection as narrowly as possible. It could well be that such an approach would be attempted with the so-called balanced treaties. But, this would provoke states into rasher reactions. It could also be that the newer, balanced treaties would become a larger playing field for lawyers. The balanced treaties, with a plethora of defences and with the rule on regulatory expropriations are essentially unworkable because they contain considerable subjectivity, the need to provide a margin of appreciation to the state exercising its discretionary power and the uncertainty involved in the wide formulation of regulatory space.

The reaction of arbitrators has been the discovery of the proportionality rule, picked out of the air without any basis in treaty language.[52] There is no demonstration as to how this is made applicable to the situation of investment disputes. As in other instances, a rule of domestic law, of uncertain origin and not demonstrably a general principle, is plucked out of thin air as if through a magical process and made relevant to control the new threat to investment protection and to investment arbitration.[53] The proportionality test reserves some power in the arbitrator to determine whether the measure taken was proportionate to the end achieved by the state. The domestic courts give a large margin of appreciation to the state in these matters. Arbitrators are hardly qualified to perform such an exercise as they are by no means acquainted with the internal situation of the state within its political

---

[48] ASEAN Comprehensive Investment Agreement (26 February 2009).

[49] South African Development Community Model Bilateral Investment Treaty (2012).

[50] VanDuzer JA, Simons P, Mayeda G (2012) Integrating Sustainable Development into International Investment Agreements: A Guide for Developing Countries, available at https://www.iisd.org/pdf/2012/6th_annual_forum_commonwealth_guide.pdf (last accessed 3 September 2015) (also published as a book by the Commonwealth Secretariat in 2013).

[51] Schill (2009).

[52] See further also *LG&E Energy Corp, LG&E Capital Corp, LG&E International Inc v Argentine Republic*, ICSID Case No ARB/02/1, Decision on Liability (3 October 2006), p. 194; *Total SA v The Argentine Republic*, ICSID Case No ARB/04/1, Decision on Liability (27 December 2010), pp. 123 and 197; *El Paso Energy International Company v The Argentine Republic*, ICSID Case No ARB/03/15, Award (31 October 2011), pp. 241–243 and 373. *Occidental Petroleum Corporation v Ecuador* ICSID Case No ARB/06/11, (5 October, 2012) pp. 402–404.

[53] One recent text (Bücheler (2015, p. 35) states that the proportionality test is borrowed from German law. It is difficult to demonstrate how other states were aware of this law and made treaties subjecting the principles in it to a German doctrine.

and social context, have arrogated unto themselves the power of performing such a function. They will only alienate states further from investment arbitration and bring more contempt for investment arbitrators as self-serving mercenaries who do not want to give up on the system that produces good earnings for them.

5 What of the Future?

What then are the answers for the problems that attend investment treaty arbitration? We see that many states of Latin America have terminated treaties and have withdrawn from the ICSID Convention. The trend will continue with the return of Latin American states to the Calvo doctrine. The Australians attempted to give up investor-state arbitration in their treaties as well. Their experience with the *Philipp Morris* arbitration may well see them have an entrenched view on this. It could well be that other states will also dispense with investor-state arbitration and there is growing evidence as to this taking place. Many treaties are approaching termination. The chances are that the treaties will not be extended beyond their period of validity. In this way, the treaties will lapse, though of course, the rights of existing investors would continue for the period specified. Eventually, one can see the system of investment treaty arbitration going into desuetude. But, in its last years, it will like all wild beasts, thrash about for life, giving rise to unimaginable crudities.

To me, the episode of investment treaty arbitration, which began with *AAPL v. Sri Lanka* in 1990,[54] brought out the worst tendencies in international law and in international lawyers. The neoliberal age sought to use international law instrumentally in order to advance the precepts of its own market driven agenda. It sought to construct a law that conduced to liberal flows of foreign investment. The ethos for it was created by international financial institutions—the International Monetary Fund and the World Bank—which saw in instruments like BITs the means of purveying the tenets of neoliberalism. They encouraged these treaties. Often, through conditionalities imposed on loans and other financial assistance, they required developing states to make these investment treaties holding out the economic advice that the treaties would promote flows of foreign investment and result in economic development. These premises were acted upon by arbitrators who enhanced the scope of the law that was contained in the treaties. All this has been explained above.

But, what is unconscionable was the active participation of international lawyers in maintaining this system built on unprovable assumptions and aimed at only the poorer states of the world despite the fact that the system had turned against the interests of the humanity that inhabited these states. If the international law

---

[54] *Asian Agricultural Products Ltd v Republic of Sri Lanka*, ICSID Case No ARB/87/3, Award (27 June 1990).

profession did so because its members profited personally from the maintenance of this system, it is indeed an indictment of the international lawyers of this particular age that they knowingly subverted the system of international law in order to serve their selfish interests. One may say that this was not a phenomenon of this age alone but previous ages as well, but one can speak with the authority of observation only of the age in which one has lived and worked.

The ending of the system of investment arbitration will not be calamitous. It may result in arbitrators and lawyers being out of work but given the earnings they have made, it is no discomfort to them. Foreign investors have not gained from the system as many awards were not paid up. Recovering them will only add to costs and may be illusory as funds for attachment would have been transferred into account that are covered by immunity. Foreign courts have been reluctant to proceed against sovereign property. Systems of protection are still left open. It is possible to create effective protection through contract. The system of diplomatic protection still remains. State to state arbitration also is an alternative as is the International Court of Justice. The domestic courts are open. In developed countries, domestic courts are the system of protection. In the past, the absence of an effective judiciary was the reason for the externalization of protection. In most countries, that reasoning does not hold. South Africa, for example, ensures that its domestic legislation and courts are the means through which remedies are sought. It is necessary to explore more equitable means of relief than investor-state arbitration.

This was an age in which international law served the interests of greed. The sooner that situation is ended, the better for the credibility of international law. As Mahatma Gandhi once put it, the world has sufficient to meet man's need but never enough to meet man's greed.[55] It is time that international law is redirected to serve man's need rather than his greed. I talk of man's greed for it is man who lusts for power, sex and wealth. A woman is guided, it is said, by considerations of motherly love, care for the hungry child and the easing of suffering. At a time when few women have now emerged into arbitration, let us hope that they may show a change towards a need-based law that is yet not visible despite their entry. Let not history show that their kind also acted with the same chicanery and pursued greed rather than the need of mankind.

References

Aisbett E (2009) Bilateral investment treaties and foreign direct investment: correlation versus causation. In: Sauvant K, Sachs L (eds) The effect of treaties on foreign direct investments. Oxford University Press, Oxford, p 395

Bean V, Beauvais J (2003) Global fifth amendment? New York Univ Law Rev 78:30

Bücheler G (2015) Proportionality in investor-state arbitration. Oxford University Press, Oxford

[55] Nayyar (1956), p. 522.

Chaisse J (2015) Greek debt restructuring, Abaclat v Argentina and investment treaty commitments. In: Lim CL, Mercurio B (eds) International economic law after the global crisis. Cambridge University Press, Cambridge, pp 306–328

Craven M (2005) What happened to unequal treaties? the continuities of informal empire. Nordic J Int Law 74:335

Di Rosa P (2004) The recent wave of arbitrations against Argentina under bilateral investment treaties: background and principal legal issues. University of Miami Inter-Am L Rev 36(1):41-?

Diehl A (2012) The core standard of international investment protection. Kluwer, Alphen aan den Rijn

Douglas Z (2009) International law of investment claims. Cambridge University Press, Cambridge

Douglas Z (2011) The MFN clause in investment treaty arbitration: treaty interpretation off the rails. J Int Dispute Settlement 2:97

Kläger R (2011) Fair and equitable treatment in international investment law. Cambridge University Press, Cambridge

Maupin J (2011) MFN based jurisdiction in investor-state arbitration: is there any hope of a consistent approach? J Int Econ Law 14:157

Nayyar P (1956) Mahatma Gandhi: the last phase, vol 2. Navajivan Publishing House, Ahmedabad

Paparinskis M (2013) International minimum standard and the fair and equitable treatment. Oxford University Press, Oxford

Poulsen L (2015) Bounded rationality and economic diplomacy: the politics of investment treaties in developing countries. Cambridge University Press, Cambridge (forthcoming)

Puig S (2014) Social capital in the arbitration market. Eur J Int Law 25:387–425

Rodrick D (2012) The globalization paradox. W. W. Norton & Company, New York

Salacuse J (2015) The law of investment treaties. Oxford University Press, Oxford

Schill S (2009) The multilateralization of international investment law. Cambridge University Press, Cambridge

Schill S, Jacob M (2015) Fair and equitable treatment, content, practice, method. In: Bungenberg M, Griebel J, Hobe S, Reinisch A (eds) International investment law. Nomos, Baden-Baden

Schreuer C (2005) Fair and equitable treatment in arbitral practice. J World Invest Trade 6:357–385

Schultz T, Dupont C (2014) Investment arbitration: promoting the rule of law or empowering foreign investors? A quantitative empirical study. Eur J Int Law 1148

Sornarajah M (1994) The international law on foreign investment, 1st edn. Cambridge University Press, Cambridge

Sornarajah M (2015a) Resistance and change in the international law on foreign investment. Cambridge University Press, Cambridge

Sornarajah M (2015b) Good faith, corporate nationality, and denial of benefits. In: Mitchell A, Sornarajah M, Voon T (eds) Good faith in international economic law. Oxford University Press, Oxford

Tienhaara K (2009) The expropriation of environmental governance: protecting foreign investors at the expense of public policy. Cambridge University Press, Cambridge

Tudor I (2008) The fair and equitable standard in international foreign investment law. Oxford University Press, Oxford

Vasciannie S (1999) The fair and equitable treatment standard in international investment law and practice. Br Yearb Int Law 70(1):99–164

Vicuña FO (2003) Regulatory authority and legitimate expectations: balancing the rights of the state and the individual under international law in a global society. Int Law Forum 5:180

Yackee J (2010) Do bilateral investment treaties promote foreign direct investments?. Vanderbilt J Int Law 50:397

Yen TH (2014) The interpretation of investment treaties. Brill, Nijhoff, Leiden

Be Careful with What You Wish: Saving Developing Countries from Development and the Risk of Overlooking the Importance of a Multilateral Rule-Based System on Investment in the Twenty-First Century

Roberto Echandi

Contents

Abstract This essay aims to stress the key role of international investment law for development in times of globalisation. It does not argue that the current international investment regime is good as it is, nor that it does not require adjustments. Instead, it is argued here that regardless of how power shaped international investment law during the nineteenth and twentieth centuries, currently investment

---

All opinions and potential errors expressed in this note do not represent the views of the World Bank Group and are full responsibility of the author.

R. Echandi (✉)
Investment Policy and Promotion, Trade and Competitiveness Global Practice, World Bank Group, Washington, DC 20433, USA
e-mail: rechandi@ifc.org

M. Bungenberg et al. (eds.), *European Yearbook of International Economic Law 2016*, European Yearbook of International Economic Law 7,
DOI 10.1007/978-3-319-29215-1_11

paradigms are radically shifting and development is starting to happen. For the first time in history foreign direct investment (FDI) is in fact enabling developing countries to become major exporters of goods and services of increasing value added. An economic multipolar world is emerging and not only inward but also outward FDI from developing countries have a lot to do in this process. Just when developing countries are finally learning to insert themselves into a globalised economy, and just when they are learning how to use international rule-making to promote that process, many sectors in developed countries—not used to any external regime limiting their historical discretion in national decision-making—are harshly reacting against the very law they contributed to create. Within this radically new context, to argue that a system of global governance is just a manifestation of imperialism entails the risk of saving developing countries from development.

1 Introduction

Over the past three decades, investment has become one of the most dynamic areas of international economic law. Such a trend stems not only from the negotiation of a patchy but extensive network of International Investment Agreements (IIAs) around the globe[1]—rising from less than 200 in the late 1980s to more than 3000 in 2015—but also from the increasing application of these agreements in order to address conflicts surging between foreign investors and States hosting the investment.

Provisions relating to investor-State dispute settlement have been included in IIAs since the late 1960s. However, active use of these provisions to institute arbitral proceedings was rare until the early 2000s. For instance, from 1987 to mid-1998, only 14 BIT-related cases were brought before the investor-State arbitration proceedings of the International Centre for Settlement of Investment Dispute (ICSID), and only two awards and two other settlements were issued over this period.[2] The period since the late 1990s has witnessed growing judicial activism.

[1] The term 'International Investment Agreement' (IIA) is used in this note as a term to refer to those international agreements negotiated among States to regulate their conduct with respect to cross-border investments, and thus comprises Bilateral Investment Treaties (BITs), Preferential Trade Agreements (PTAs) with investment chapters and the investment-related provisions of the Agreements of the World Trade Organization (WTO) with the caveat that the latter does not provide for investor-State dispute settlement procedures.

[2] All cases can be found on the ICSID webpage at www.worldbank.org/icsid/cases/cases.htm, or at http://ita.law.uvic.ca/chronological_list.htm (last accessed 29 October 2015).

The cumulative number of known treaty-based cases had risen to more than 600 by 2014.[3]

Increasing recourse to investor-State arbitration has fueled the development of a growing volume of jurisprudence which is still evolving and has been subjected to extensive analytical scrutiny within the legal and academic communities. An interesting dynamic has emerged between such evolving case law and investment treaty-making, as governments pay closer attention to the legal impacts of the wording of particular clauses included in their IIAs. Arbitral awards have demonstrably led the governments of numerous countries to revise their IIA templates based on the interpretations arising from international arbitral decisions.[4]

These new developments in international investment law are generating debate among investment stakeholders. Clearly, given the relative youth of the IIAs, the increase in litigation has evidenced the need to adjust both the wording of texts and features of the investor-State dispute settlement (ISDS) clauses. However, while certain sectors consider such increase in litigation—and derived normative evolution in IIAs—to a great extent as a natural trend of normative evolution towards the development of a rule-oriented international investment regime, others argue that the problem lies in the very nature and features of international investment law.

It is within this context, that Prof. Sornarajah's article "International Investment Law as Development Law: The Obsolescence of a Fraudulent System" as well as this commentary are being written. These two essays are just the tip of the iceberg of a deep and complex discussion about the role of international investment law and development that often lumps together numerous issues of different nature. Today, the discussion about international investment law covers a wide range of issues. Moreover, the debate on IIAs means different issues for different sectors.

To illustrate this point, let's take the discussion on one of the features of international investment law: ISDS. While for some, the problem with ISDS is the need to improve certain specific features of investor-State arbitration procedures, for instance, whether they are transparent enough, and contain appropriate safeguards to prevent frivolous claims or conflict of interest between legal counsel and arbitrators, or mechanisms to control too much activism by arbitrators, for others ISDS is about the more fundamental issue as to whether arbitration in itself is the appropriate vehicle to address legal disputes between investors and governments. For others the problem is even more basic, that is, whether investors—domestic or foreign—should have a private right of action to challenge measures of governments in an international venue—be it arbitration or any other type of adjudication.

Other sectors' criticism against international investment law goes even beyond ISDS. Their objections relate to the very existence of international investment law

[3] Source: UNCTAD (2015) Investor-State dispute Settlement: Review of Developments in 2014, IIA Issues Note No. 2, 2015, Geneva, United Nations.

[4] This point has been developed in detail in UNCTAD (2007) Investor-State Dispute Settlement and Impact on Investment Rulemaking, New York and Geneva.

as a vehicle to establish standards of protection within the logic of a market-oriented economy coupled with effective enforcement mechanisms. Last but not least—and not attempting to be exhaustive in the list of issues generating controversy today—for others the problem is with the very existence of an international legal framework that by definition will foster certain values and policies and that will inevitably erode sovereignty of States to unilaterally determine how to better pursue their interests—whatever they may be.

This mixing of different level of issues about international investment law, IIAs, and ISDS tends to exacerbate confusion rather than elucidation about the role of international investment law and development. Thus, from the outset, let me clarify what this essay is and it is not about.

This essay purports to focus the attention on the importance of international investment law for development in times of globalization. This note does not argue that the current international investment regime is good as it is, nor that it does not require adjustments. Further, this commentary to Prof. Sornarajah's article does not challenge his opinion that asymmetries in real power between developed and developing countries have historically played a role in the evolution of international law. This essay does not either challenge the view that "[h]egemonic power has used the instrumentality of international law to provide justifications in altruistic terms so that it could justify its domination."[5] However, the central argument of this essay is that regardless of how power shaped international law in the nineteenth century and the early stages of the twentieth century, the development of a globalized economy over the last six decades is challenging traditional views and paradigms about sovereignty and development, and thus about the role of international investment law should play in that context.

This note argues that international investment law—including the private right of action of investors to enforce investment protection guarantees either through arbitration or an international court system—has not been fraudulent and is far from becoming obsolete. Rather, international investment law is evolving and it is becoming increasingly relevant for development. Moreover, it is argued here that as developed countries are now discovering the existence of international norms and disciplines on investment as they become applicable for all countries alike, developing countries have a particular interest now in keeping international investment law not only alive, but also strong if they want to defend their interests in the economy of the twenty-first century.

Today we are living in a world where development has taken significant steps over the last four decades. Over the past 40 years, life expectancy in developing countries has increased by 20 years—about as much as was achieved in all of human history prior to the middle of the twentieth century. Over the past 30 years, adult illiteracy in the developing world was nearly halved to 25 % from 47 %. Over the past 20 years, the absolute number of people living on less than one dollar a day has for the first time begun to fall, even as the world's population has grown by 1.6

[5] Sornarajah (2016), section 3.4.

billion people. Thanks in particular to poverty reduction efforts in China and India, the proportion of people living on less than one dollar a day by 2015 is projected to decrease to just over 12 % from more than 28 %, bringing half a billion people out of poverty. Over the last decade, economic growth in the developing world has outpaced that in the developed countries.[6]

Evidence is showing how thanks precisely to the opening of trade and investment flows, the world has witnessed how hundreds of millions of people in the developing world have been taken out of poverty, new emerging economies have transformed their exports from commodities to sophisticated manufactures and services, and are using international economic law to safeguard their interests in an increasingly interdependent world where closer interaction is likely to generate conflict.

From China to Mexico, from Turkey to Ethiopia or Morocco, to geographically smaller countries such as Singapore, Chile, Ireland or Costa Rica, today, evidence shows that the issue is no longer whether developing countries should integrate to an international economy characterized by constantly evolving global value chains entangling international production of goods and services. Instead, the issue is *how to facilitate* developing economies to use investment as a vehicle to insert themselves in this process and thus attract, retain and link international investment with their domestic economies and thus generate more and better paid jobs for their citizens.

Thus the challenge today is how to incorporate in this virtuous cycle of development the bottom billion of people who still, precisely for not being yet dynamically integrated into the international flows of production, investment, technology and know-how, are still trapped in poverty. They are becoming the victims of an increasing gap between the richer and poorer countries.[7]

Indeed, the paradox today is that poverty reduction is not leading to a smaller gap between richer and poorer countries. Given the key role that technical knowledge plays in determining the higher value added of goods and services, today it is not only necessary to increase productivity of existing production and exports. In order to grow, countries have to qualitatively change the composition of their exports towards higher value added goods and services. In other words, "it is not the same to produce potato chips than microchips". Thus, the role of investment in development has increased from being just a source of capital to become the key vehicle to transfer that technical knowledge and change the composition of countries' exports. The challenge then, is to get more investment not less, and international investment law has a key role to play in this process.

Within this context, this essay respectfully disagrees with many of the key fundamental arguments expressed by Prof. Sornarajah's article and that are often tabled to argue for the dismantlement—rather than reform—of the international

---

[6] Source: World Bank. Data available at: https://www.worldbank.org/progress/reducing_poverty.html (last accessed 29 October 2015).

[7] Collier (2007).

investment law regime. For reasons of time and space, this essay will address three assertions that seem particularly concerning as they are based on many implicit assumptions that are not only conceptually flawed but factually incorrect.

The first assertion that merits comment is a commonly argued one in the current debate about IIAs, that is that the existing web of IIAs are the historical result of some sort of conspiracy by developed countries and international financial institutions which induced developing countries to adopt these agreements with very little understanding by the latter about their content and implications. In this regard, Prof. Sornarajah writes: "... states were induced into signing investment treaties in the belief that good would come out of such action. Instead, what has resulted is a heaping of misery in times of crisis."[8]

Second, there is the argument that IIAs have failed to deliver development. In this regard, Prof. Sornarajah asserts:

> The link between the system of investment protection through treaties and economic development was the assumption on which the system was built up. The link is based on an unproven hypothesis cultivated by the developed states and the financial institutions that they control, like the World Bank and the International Monetary Fund.[9]

Third and as a result, Prof. Sornarajah also argues that an additional problem with the existing investment protection regime is that it unduly limits developing countries' sovereignty and policy space to pursue policies that are necessary to ensure development: "If it is true that there is no correlation between investment flows and the signing of investment treaties, host states lose sovereignty unnecessarily by entering into investment treaties."[10] And he adds: "It is untrue that development takes place on the basis of investment treaties. States without investment treaties like Brazil have made spectacular economic progress... It would appear that investment treaties only bring trouble. They impose a regulatory chill through the threat of arbitration by an investor, and make states forge action in the public interest." [11]

At this point it is important to stress that this essay does not argue that everything is fine with the current legal status quo of international investment law. What this note argues is that in addition to other issues which countries are currently resolving through new generation IIAs—clarifying substantive provisions and modernizing investor-State dispute settlement procedures and even considering the establishment of an international investor-State court—there are three structural problems with the existing international investment law regime as it stands today that require deeper attention by stakeholders and that unfortunately are being overlooked by the current debate.

First, the current regime is patchy, conformed by a confusing web of similar and yet differently worded BITs and more recently Preferential Trade Agreements

[8] Sornarajah (2016), section 3.4.

[9] Sornarajah (2016), section 1.

[10] Sornarajah (2016), section 1.

[11] Sornarajah (2016), section 3.4.

(PTAs).[12] Such fragmentation and diversity inherently promotes incoherence in both rule-making and jurisprudential development. Despite the evolution of "new generation" IIAS that address most of the criticism that stakeholders have made to the original European model BITs,[13] a myriad of old fashioned, imprecisely worded agreements still remain in place. Second, the current investment regime is disconnected with the multilateral trading system, and thus, the multiple layers of interaction between trade and investment is often overlooked in a world where international production no longer differentiates between these two.[14] And third, the implementation dimension of international investment law is currently envisaged by stakeholders as limited exclusively to dispute resolution, rather than systematically promoting to use of international investment law as a tool to manage relationships among investment stakeholders in a non-litigious way.[15]

In addition to this introduction this essay contains four additional sections. Section 2 focuses on the discussion of Prof. Sornarajah's key arguments stated above. Section 3 presents some reflections of the author with respect to key existing challenges of the international investment regime as it stands now. Last but not least, Sect. 4 includes some concluding remarks. In full disclosure to the reader, most of the views expressed in this essay draw from the experience of the author as a former trade and investment negotiator of a developing country for almost two decades, both in dealing not only with legal issues when negotiating but also applying IIAs, but also with the domestic and international political economy of negotiations of those agreements.[16]

---

[12] This point has been developed in detail in UNCTAD (2006) International Investment Arrangements: Trends and Emerging Issues, Geneva, United Nations.

[13] Echandi (2010).

[14] Echandi and Sauve (2013).

[15] This point is further developed in Echandi (2011) Investor-State Dispute Prevention Mechanisms: Why are they so important for developing countries and for the healthy evolution of the international investment regime? in UNCTAD (2011) Investor-State Disputes: Prevention and Alternatives to Arbitration II, Proceedings of the Washington and Lee University and UNCTAD Joint Symposium on International Investment and Alternative Dispute Resolution, held on 29 March 2010 in Lexington, Virginia, USA (New York and Geneva: United Nations).

[16] Clearly, the insights included in this note are coloured by the experience of my own country and region. I come from Costa Rica, a very small nation in Central America which has been quite successful in attracting foreign direct investment (FDI) and using it to foster a qualitative transformation of its economy. A little more than 20 years ago, the overwhelming majority of Costa Rican exports were concentrated on a few agricultural products, basically bananas and coffee. Today, Costa Rica exports more than five thousand products among which microchips, high-tech medical devices and exports of services rank at the top of the export supply. Clearly, international trade and investment have been critical in enabling Costa Rica to migrate from being a commodity exporter into a provider of higher value added goods and services. For more detailed information, see: Ferreira, G. (2009), From Coffee Beans to Microchips: Export Diversification and Economic Growth in Costa Rica, Louisiana State University, mimeo, http://ageconsearch.umn.edu (last accessed 29 October 2015).

2 Setting the Record Straight: Reflections on Common Criticisms to the International Investment Regime

2.1 IIAs Are the Result of a "Grand Bargain" Imposed by Developed Countries and International Financial Institutions on Developing Countries

In the field of international investment policy, the motivations of developed countries to promote the negotiation of IIAs are well-known and documented. Historically, these countries have been visualized as capital exporting economies seeking protection to their investors' assets when invested abroad. Instead, the motivations leading developing countries to limit their sovereignty and undertake international obligations through IIAs are less obvious, and have been subject to more debate. Academic and experts from the developed world have commented on this matter, attempting to interpret legal views and socio-economic events in developing countries.

The accounts attempting to explain why developing countries subscribe IIAs are varied, and have ranged from extremely simplistic and somewhat patronizing views of developing countries to more sophisticated analyses. However, a common idea underlying the explanations of many scholars when trying to explain developing countries' acceptance of IIAs is that developing countries believed in these treaties' "grand bargain": the expectation to receive greater capital inflows in exchange for a commitment to protect foreign investment. Although this is a rational proposition, to explain developing countries' intentions to enter into IIAs exclusively on the basis of this "grand bargain" has three fundamental problems.

First, it presupposes that there is causal link between investment protection and an increase in investment inflows. As will be explained in section B below, it is an uncontested fact that the amount of investment flowing into a host country depends on a series of variables. Second, framing the rationale of IIAs exclusively on the existence of such a "grand bargain" leads to a wrong benchmark against which to assess the utility IIAs. Indeed, according to this logic, if investment protection through IIAs does not translate into increased investment inflows, then the "grand bargain" would be frustrated, suggesting therefore an unfair result against developing countries if they continue to keep their part of the deal. Furthermore, and more important, this view also presupposes that for developing countries, the exclusive rationale of IIAs is to foster investment inflows. As will be explained below, that is not the exclusive function these international instruments perform in developing countries.

Last but not least, the third problem with framing developing countries' intentions to enter into IIAs exclusively in terms of this "grand bargain" logic is that it turns out to be somewhat inaccurate from an historical perspective. Indeed, this view assumes that developing countries opted to undertake the obligation to protect foreign investment as a result of IIAs. This perspective presupposes a sequential

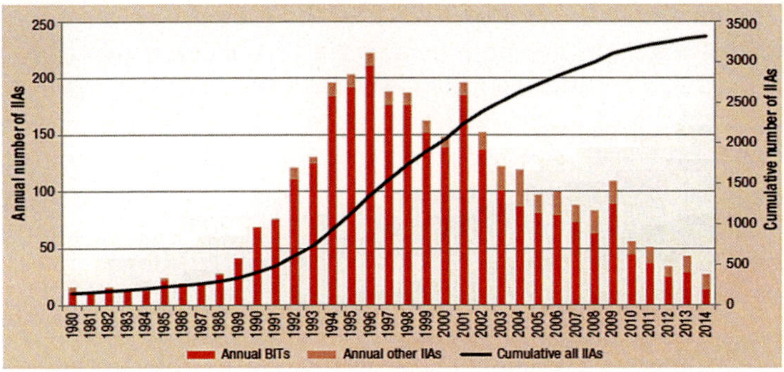

Fig. 1 Number of IIAs negotiated per year 1980–2014. *Source*: UNCTAD, IIA database. *Note*: Preliminary data for 2014

process under which developing countries had to adjust their domestic legislation as a result of IIAs. In fact, in the case of most developing countries the sequence was the other way around. That is, negotiation of IIAs took place only after profound economic and legal transformations resulting from the debt crisis and the fall of the Iron Curtain had already started and not vice versa. Thus, as historical accounts demonstrate, IIAs were just a by-product—and not a factor—of market-oriented domestic reforms in developing countries and economies in transition.

The widespread negotiation of IIAs is really a phenomenon of the 1990s. Although the first BIT was negotiated in 1959, it is very revealing that during the 1960s and until the 1980s, negotiation activity of BITs was very limited. Between the first BIT negotiated in 1959 between Germany and Pakistan, and up to 1979 there were less than 200 BITs negotiated, representing an average of less than 10 BITs negotiated every year. During the 1980s, negotiation activity almost doubled, elevating the average number of BITs negotiated every year to 19. However, it was not until the 1990s when the "IIA negotiation boom" took place. As Fig. 1 illustrates, during that decade, the average number of BITs negotiated every year was more than 8 times higher than during the 1980s, reaching 144 BITs negotiated every year. During the first decade of the twenty-first century, that annual average decreased significantly.

Figure 1 clearly illustrates how the increase in IIA negotiation activity—in particular BITs—became a trend during the 1990s, gradually decreasing during the last decade. Which factors can explain this trend? If BITs were "imposed" on developing countries, how can it be explained that at the moment European powers were advocating BITs in the 1960s most developing countries in fact rejected BIT negotiations and instead advocated the establishment of a New International Economic Order (NIEO) at the United Nations?

The determination of the States' intention when entering into IIAs is an exercise that has to be undertaken with caution. Specific motivations leading governments to subscribe IIAs are multiple and varied, and any attempt to provide a single explanation may be misleading. However, evidence shows that, regardless of such specificities, IIAs are a by-product of the profound economic and political reforms that most developing countries and economies in transition undertook during the 1980s and 1990s. History evidences a sequence by which most developing countries first undertook structural adjustment programs, reformed their domestic legal orders and then subsequently undertook legal obligations through IIAs, rather than the other way around.

The dramatic impact of the debt crisis of the 1980s, had forced most Latin American countries to question the old import-substitution industrialization policies implemented for more than three decades. The winds of the "Washington consensus" were blowing hard, and given the evident failure of policies implemented over the previous three decades, most developing countries undertook very painful structural adjustment reforms. Such reforms entailed elements such as to embrace fiscal discipline, to reorient public expenditures, to engage in tax reform, to liberalize the capital accounts and interest rates, to privatize government owned-enterprises, to liberalize tariffs and non-tariff barriers, to promote deregulation and to promote effective protection to property rights and contractual relations.

Market-oriented policies reformulated the different variations of the State-led inward looking economic model that prevailed in most Latin American countries since the 1940s. Widespread privatization of multiple State enterprises was promoted not only to balance huge fiscal deficits, but also as the result of the shift in the conception of the role of the State in the economy. The State would no longer be conceived as an entrepreneur, but rather as a regulator of private economic activity. Further, the orientation of the economic development model, until then geared towards promoting the development of domestic markets, shifted towards promoting integration of the national productive sector into the international economy.

In the midst of the debt crisis, among the top objectives of policy makers in most developing countries and economies in transition was to find effective means to increase and diversify exports. Such goal was critical not only to stabilize the economies in the short term, but also to foster growth in the long term. Further, most governments aspired not only to export more, but rather, to increase the value-added to their exports. Thus, it quickly became evident for policy makers that for such purpose, attracting greater inflows of FDI would be critical.

Governments understood the potential advantages of FDI to achieve key objectives such as capital, transfer of technology, access to international distribution networks and generation of jobs. Furthermore, if productive investment was going to be lured, most governments of developing countries understood that the deep reforms would have to transform the chaotic state of their economies, into an environment competitive enough where international business could thrive and generate backward linkages with the domestic productive sector.

Within this context, at least in the case of Latin American countries, the process of domestic reform started well before the negotiation of IIAs. While reforms started in the 1980s, negotiations of IIAs took place one decade later, in the 1990s. The shift towards market-oriented policies in the 1980s was also reflected on reforms to domestic legislation affecting foreign investment. The wave of reform of national regulatory frameworks affecting foreign investment during the 1980s is well documented.[17] Thus, the negotiation wave of IIAs took place only once governments had already started the process of market-oriented reforms that lead to modify their domestic laws and regulations applicable to foreign investment. In other words, it was the process of domestic reforms triggered by structural adjustment programs, what enabled government officials to undertake international commitments in IIAs, and not the other way around.

The fact that the content of IIAs did not entail additional reforms to national laws and regulations beyond those already carried out in the context of structural adjustment programs, explains why negotiations of IIAs during the 1990s were not controversial in the national parliaments of most developing countries. Indeed, if authorities had already paid the political price of unilaterally undertaking the harsh structural adjustment programs that entailed a major overhaul of national economic legislation, it is easy to understand why to negotiate international agreements that could give developing countries something in return—even in theory—was a very rational course of action to follow.

Furthermore, the debt crisis made any chance to finance development through public barrowing or official aid illusory, leaving private foreign investment as practically the only source of funding to foster development and expansion of economic activity in developing countries. The thirst for FDI was extraordinary, and having unilaterally adopted practically all the standards of protection included in IIAs, the next challenge for governments was then to make those reforms known and credible to foreign investors—thus the key role of IIAs as signaling devices, a point which is further developed below.

An important additional aspect often overlooked by investment literature when explaining the negotiation boom of IIAs is that, at least in the case of Latin America and most economies in transition, the winds of liberalism were not limited to economic policy. By the 1990s, Latin America had already experienced a wave of democratization and the fall of most of the military dictatorships that had ruled for decades most of the countries of the region. Democratization was also in vogue in Eastern Europe and other parts of the developing world. Within this context, the promotion of guarantees protecting individuals against the potential abuse of the

[17] By 1991, when the wave of negotiation of IIAs was just starting, UNCTAD's World Investment Report was already commenting the significant reforms undertaken at the domestic level by developing countries during the 1980s. "The trend towards reducing restrictions on the activities of transnational corporations in host developing countries is one of the more important policy developments of the past decade. A sample of more than 300 instances of changes in policies and regulations affecting foreign direct investment by transnational corporations covering 46 countries (20 developed market economy countries and 26 developing countries, including five newly industrializing countries) over 11 years (1977–1987) illustrates the scope and direction of the changes. More than two thirds of the changes in the sample were in the direction of reducing restrictions on the activities of transnational corporations. In the case of the newly industrializing countries, more than three fourths of the changes were in the direction of reducing restrictions on transnational corporations." (UNCTAD (1991) World Investment Report 1991, Geneva: United Nations Conference on Trade and Development, p. 28.)

power of the State—the typical underlying logic of standards of protection included in IIAs, such as the standards of fair and equitable treatment, due process of law and transparency—were also coherent with the new democratic and administrative reforms taking place in most developing countries and economies in transition—a process which to a great extent, has not yet been concluded in many of these countries.

2.2 Developing Countries Did Not Understand the Implications Nor Impacts of IIAs

So far we have explained how during the 1990s there was an economic and political context that facilitated the negotiation of IIAs by developing countries and economies in transition. However, the fact that negotiating these international agreements practically did not entail any additional reform to the domestic legal order—and thus, no associated political cost—does not yet explain what were the benefits or positive incentives that governments might have expected from subscribing IIAs.

The specific motivations leading a government to subscribe a particular IIA varied government from government, and negotiation from negotiation. Each negotiation had its own particular history, and it would be pretentious to come up with a single set of explanations for each of the thousands of negotiations of IIAs that took place after the 1990s. Thus, rather than focusing on identifying the specific intentions of each State from a developing country when entering each IIA, this section explains in more detail why, given the economic and political context previously described, IIAs were visualized by many developing countries as instruments worth negotiating actively.

In addition to the low political cost associated with their negotiation, IIAs were instruments that perfectly fitted within the new development strategy pursued by most developing countries and economies in transition. With the debt crisis and the implementation of structural adjustment programs, the ruling elites—at least in most Latin American countries—had incorporated within the government several cadres of sophisticated young technocrats, most of them trained in the best universities of the U.S. and Europe. These teams of technocrats were in charge of the major economic policy decisions during the 1990s, and most of them clearly visualized IIAs as instrumental to achieve, both at the international and domestic level, various objectives which were critical for the success of the new outward-oriented development strategy. In this regard, IIAs were expected to fulfill various functions, both at the international and domestic level.[18]

[18] This point is further developed in Echandi (2011).

2.2.1 The Functions of IIAs in the International Front

In the external front, IIAs were expected to pursue at least two critical objectives. First, IIAs were expected to serve as signaling device to foreign investors inducing greater levels of confidence with respect to the welcoming environment and the effective level of protection their investments would receive in host countries. The second key function that many governing elites understood that IIAs could play would be to de-politicize international investment conflicts.

2.2.1.1 Signaling

Developing economies with big emerging domestic markets, such as Brazil, Russia, India, China or South Africa (BRICS) enjoy an advantage that many other governments from smaller developing countries envy: they are constantly visible in the international economic setting. For better or for worse, international investors in the major economic hubs of the world—as well as the specialized mass media—constantly monitor and tend to be quite familiar with everyday economic and political developments in the BRICS economies. That is not the situation of most other developing countries. In fact, one of the main challenges for most of the smaller developing countries—which constitute the numerical majority of nations in the world—is to become visible in the radar screen of international investors. Some countries even struggle to be acknowledged of their existence.

In a world where wealth increasingly depends on how a particular country inserts itself into the international economy, to be invisible for foreign investors is a matter to be taken quite seriously by governments. Further, by lacking important emerging domestic markets to lure foreign investors, smaller economies tend to depend more on natural resource-seeking FDI or efficiency-seeking FDI. The latter is the kind of FDI that most developing countries are interested to attract due to its potential benefits in terms of the increase, diversification, and transformation of their export supply and generation of jobs. However, this is the kind of FDI for which there is more international competition, and given its export-orientation, efficiency-seeking FDI is also quite sensitive to the level of market access—in terms of tariff and non-tariff barriers—that exports originating in the host country may enjoy in major export market destinations.

Within this context, it becomes evident that for smaller developing economies, to undertake the challenge to foster a more welcoming domestic environment to investment in the 1980s was only half of the story. It was also necessary for these countries to demonstrate that the new regulatory framework was effective, and that in fact it was going to be implemented.

Further, smaller countries had also to overcome the burden of convincing private investors why they should locate their business in their economies rather than somewhere else. That is why, many developing countries started to negotiate Preferential Trade Agreements (PTAs) incorporating investment chapters. Through these agreements, host governments could ensure foreign investors—who were also exporters—that by locating their investments in their countries, their production would in fact enjoy free access in the export markets they were interested to target.

Furthermore, having many IIAs would demonstrate the existence of a uniform investment policy in the host country, and would also increase the opportunities to promote the host country as attractive investment destination. Thus, it is true that Presidents and Ministers seized every chance they had to maximize the publicity of the signature of an IIAs, but this was not because ruling elites did not understand the contents or implications of these instruments, but rather because they thought such agreements mirrored their national investment policies, and that was precisely the message that politicians were eager to convey to the international investment community in order to attract FDI.

Another variable explaining the multiplicity of IIAs negotiated by many developing countries relates to the fact that, in most cases, ruling elites perceived that attracting productive investment into the country was good no matter its national origin or the dimension of the investment transaction. Further, as a new development model was been implemented, most policies tended to be forward-looking, thus governments were more interested in promoting future FDI inflows rather than regulating existing ones. Within this logic, the non-existence of FDI inflows with a particular country at the time of negotiation did not prevent political authorities to sign IIAs.

2.2.1.2 IIAs as Devices to Depoliticize International Investment-Related Conflicts

An important number of current critics of international investment law seem to have forgotten that international investment disputes are as old as international economic activity. There have been investor-State disputes for centuries. What has changed are the means to settle them. An important role governments that many developing countries have expected IIAs to perform is to depoliticize international investment-related conflicts. History is plagued with examples of political conflicts resulting from investment-related interests. Throughout the nineteenth and early twentieth century, diplomatic protection was a common way to deal with investment-related disputes. In many instances, the abuse of diplomatic protection led to "gun-boat" diplomacy and other power-oriented manifestations against developing countries.[19] The inclusion of investor-State dispute resolution mechanisms in IIAs was then intended to provide investors with avenues to enable them to directly enforce their rights, in exchange for a legal obligation to both investors and their home States to refrain from exerting any diplomatic protection against the host country during arbitration proceedings.

---

[19] This point is further developed in Cable (1981).

This additional "grand-bargain" implicit in the negotiation of IIAs was consistent with a fundamental policy objective that most ruling elites of developing countries in the 1980s and 1990s clearly understood, and that it was critical within the new economic model fostering the international insertion of their countries. Governments understood that in an increasingly interdependent world, developing countries should strongly advocate for the development of rule-oriented—and not power-oriented—international economic institutions. Governments clearly understood that globalization meant that the world would be increasingly prone to frequent international tensions. Within that context, developing countries—especially the smaller ones—would have very limited economic, political and/or military power to defend their interests. Consequently, one of the few instruments that smaller economies would have at their disposal to promote their agenda in an interdependent economic setting would be, despite all its limitations, international law.

Developing countries then started to promote greater participation in international rule-making, not only through IIAs, but also acceding to institutions like the General Agreement of Tariffs and Trade (GATT) and later the World Trade Organization (WTO). Indeed, it is not a coincidence that during the end of the 1980s and the 1990s, there was a wave of accessions of developing countries and economies in transition to the WTO. Within this context, the interest of developing countries was not only to attempting to participate as much as possible in international rule-making, but also to ensure that international economic conflicts, such as in trade and investment, were solved not according to unilateral power-oriented diplomacy, but rather through bilateral or multilateral rule-oriented dispute resolution.

From the 1990s on, the promotion of the legalization of international trade and investment relations has then become an important systemic objective for many developing countries. Promotion of rule-oriented dispute resolution has been envisaged not only as a means to attempt to compensate asymmetries of power, but also to depoliticize potential economic conflicts among developing countries themselves.

South-South investment flows have significantly increased over the last two decades. Although trade patterns among developing countries have tended to be shaped by leading emerging "local" multinationals, during this period small and medium enterprises have also fuelled regional integration. It is often easier for firms of developing countries to do business in geographically adjacent markets, where they are amidst more familiar and similar business practices and market conditions. However, in the developing world, it is frequent that bilateral political agendas of neighbouring countries are loaded with extremely sensitive political issues. Territorial border disputes, immigration, smuggling, and other types of irregular activities taking place in the borders are just some of the thorny issues that typically comprise bilateral agendas. In these scenarios, it is easy to envisage that any dispute arising between the host State and an investor from a neighbouring country would easily become politicized. Thus, the role of IIAs as instrument to depoliticize investment disputes also becomes critical in the context of promoting a stable environment to foster South-South regional integration.

2.2.2 The Functions of IIAs in the Domestic Front

In addition to the signaling and depoliticizing effects that IIAs could play in the external front, since the 1990s government technocrats in many developing countries also visualized these agreements as instrumental to achieve some important objectives at the domestic level. In particular, there were two objectives that were going to be critical for the success of the outward-oriented development strategy starting to be implemented at the time. One of those goals would be to attempt to ensure long-term continuity in the implementation of the new market-oriented economic policies. A second aim of IIAs would be to contribute to modernize the public administration, and make it become more efficient, transparent, accountable and respectful of the rights of individuals.

2.2.2.1 Lock-in Domestic Reforms

One of the features that for a long time has characterized most developing economies is their political and economic volatility. Until the 1980s, coups d' Etat orchestrated by various military factions were typical in many Latin American, Asian and African nations. Describing in detail the causes of this economic and political volatility would go beyond the scope of this essay. The relevant point to stress here is that numerous developing countries have traditionally been highly vulnerable to the influence of powerful economic and/or political interest groups.

In the developing world, the strength of the legal and political institutions has tended to vary significantly country to country. In countries with weak institutions, policy coherence and consistency over an extended period of time have traditionally been trumped by short-term policy reversals that are imposed by strong vested interest groups which temporarily capture government action until the another power group repeats the cycle. It is evident that erratic and inconsistent implementation of economic policy one sure way to perpetuates underdevelopment.

The shift in the economic development strategy undertaken in the 1980s and 1990s in many developing countries and economies in transition was radical. Such transformation was only possible because the impact of the economic crisis was harsh enough to provide the new democratically-elected governments with enough political leeway to undertake the necessary measures to stabilize their national economies. However, that does mean that all political forces had homogenous views regarding economic policy. Even within the same political party, there were factions promoting reform and other factions resisting it. The policy shift not only entailed a different mindset and vision of development, but also a generational change. Popular humor used to characterize this clash of perspectives as the fight between "modernists" and "dinosaurs", the latter resisting to accept the end of an era.

Within this context, it should not surprise why ruling elites suspected that those groups that used to benefit from the old inward-looking and State-led import-substitution model would sooner or later attempt to reverse the process of reform. That is why, reformist groups opted to use various international instruments to "lock-in" the political and economic transformations undertaken during the period.

The use of international economic agreements—including IIAs—to "lock-in" the processes of market-oriented reforms undertaken by many developing countries and economies in transition during the 1980s and 1990s is a trend that has been widely acknowledged by literature.[20] An additional point to be made here is that experience shows that the use of international legal instruments to "lock-in" process of domestic economic reform has its limitations. Clearly, from a political perspective, sound economic policies should generate their own critical mass of support from society, which should back them as a consequence of the benefits derived from their implementation.[21] However, the opportunity cost of policy reversals may also depend on the kind of legal instruments used to lock-in the process of reform.

For instance, today it would simply be unthinkable to expect the countries of Eastern Europe that acceded into the European Union, to return to their former State-planned economic model. Something similar could be said for Mexico and its integration to the U.S. economy institutionalized by NAFTA. Also in Latin America, the experiences of Chile, Colombia, Peru and most Central American countries are some examples where the new development strategy tended to deliver positive results. However, the case of the countries members of the "Alianza Bolivariana de las Americas" (ALBA), i.e. Venezuela, Bolivia and Ecuador are examples where sharp policy reversals have taken place, and where governments have attempted to get rid of the obligations imposed by IIAs, so far, with limited success.

2.2.2.2 Pressure for the Modernization of the Domestic Administrative Legal System

Just as structural adjustment programs had forced the private sector to learn how to survive in an open and competitive domestic environment, ruling elites believed that in a politically liberal and modern market-oriented economy, the public administration would also have to become more efficient, transparent, accountable and respectful of the rights of individuals. Today it is easy to forget that for many

[20] For instance, see Schneiderman (2007).

[21] However, as the current situation in some Latin American countries evidences, the problem is that political and economic liberalism are not enough *per se* to generate sustainable development in many countries that for centuries have had quasi-feudal social structures. Effective policies leading to greater social investment and poverty alleviation are also required. When governments fail to provide these services, it is easy for societies to fall prey of authoritarian populist leaders promising the masses what they want to hear.

decades, the public administration in many developing countries and economies in transition was just part of a bureaucratic machinery of an authoritarian regime—either under a right-wing military dictatorship or under a communist system of government.

Despite their huge differences, right or left wing authoritarian regimes had something in common: values such as efficiency, transparency and accountability to citizens were just alien ideas to a public administration used to be the "supreme law of the land" and accustomed to exert almost unlimited power over individuals who did not have any other choice than to quietly accept government *dicta*—no matter how arbitrary they were. However, during the 1980s and 1990s, both national citizens—who would no longer tolerate authoritarian rule—as well as foreigners—who were accustomed to enjoy the individual guarantees respected in their home countries—expected a different pattern of administrative behavior. Indeed, in modern market-oriented economies, despite having key regulatory powers, the State is conceived as serving the citizenry rather than the other way around.

Just as in the international level, ruling elites of many developing countries understood the importance of promoting the rule of law to govern inter-State relations, in the domestic level they also recognized the critical need to develop strong law-abiding institutions to make the new liberal and market-oriented development strategy succeed. The role of institutions in fostering development in modern societies has been widely acknowledged by literature. However, as experience shows, shifting the culture of the public administration from an authoritarian to liberal mindset would prove to be one of the most difficult challenges for developing countries and economies in transition. In fact, one could argue that up to today, such endeavor remains an unfinished task in many countries.

Within this context, one may ask how IIAs were seen as instrumental to strengthen the rule of law and to modernize the public administration in developing countries. In this regard, IIAs were perceived to be instrumental in three different ways.

First, in many developing countries international agreements not only have equal or higher hierarchy than domestic laws and regulations, but also have direct effect, enabling any natural or legal entity to invoke international obligations in any domestic legal tribunal. The principle of equality between nationals and foreigners, which is incorporated in many Constitutional orders, prevents discrimination against foreigners, but also against nationals. Thus, in some developing countries, citizens have invoked IIAs in conjunction with the Constitutional right of non-discrimination between nationals and foreigners in order to make domestic courts enforce the rights that nationals get as a result of IIAs against actions of the administration.[22]

Second, investor-State dispute settlement mechanisms constitute effective enforcement mechanisms of norms and disciplines included in IIAs. As those

[22] This is the case of Costa Rica, where the Constitutional system has actively incorporated international law within the domestic legal order. See, Echandi (1997).

norms and disciplines also tended to be incorporated in domestic legislation, IIAs would indirectly become enforcement mechanisms to foster the same patterns of administrative behaviour mandated by national laws. Ruling elites in many developing countries understood that no matter how modern domestic legislation may be, the new legal framework would remain death letter if it did not translated in a concrete shift in patterns of behaviour by the administration. In this sense, IIAs generate a "spill over" effect that benefits national citizens and residents as the host country gradually develops better administrative practices to comply with international obligations.

Third, another way—albeit more recently discovered—through which IIAs can contribute to make the public administration in developing countries more transparent and accountable is by including specific obligations in this respect. Some IIAs include explicit and specific commitments fostering the transparency and due process of law of the public administration in the host country, not only exclusively with respect to foreign investors, but with respect to all residents in general.[23] In fact, one of the recent developments in investment rule-making over the last decade is a trend towards a more frequent inclusion in IIAs of explicit obligations concerning access to administrative proceedings, including the right of an impartial review and appeal from administrative decisions.[24]

---

[23] A clear example of this trend is article 19 of the 2004 Canadian Model BIT (Canadian Foreign Investment Promotion and Protection Agreements, at: Agreement Between Canada and [...] for the Promotion and Protection of Investments, http://www.italaw.com/documents/Canadian2004-FIPA-model-en.pdf (last accessed 29 October 2015), which states:

"1. Each Party shall, to the extent possible, ensure that its laws, regulations, procedures, and administrative rulings of general application respecting any matter covered by this Agreement are promptly published or otherwise made available in such as manner as to enable **interested persons** and the other Party to become acquainted by them.

2. To the extent possible, each Party shall: (a) publish in advance any such measure that it proposes to adopt; and (b) provide **interested persons** and the other Party a reasonable opportunity to comment on such proposed measures.

3. Upon request by a Party, information shall be exchanged on the measures of the other Party that may have an impact on covered investments." (emphasis added).

[24] For example Article 18.5 of the DR-CAFTA (The Dominican Republic-Central America-United States Free Trade Agreement, United States, Costa Rica, El Salvador, Guatemala, Honduras, and Nicaragua, 28 May 2004) which states:

"1. Each Party shall establish or maintain judicial, quasi-judicial, or administrative tribunals or procedures for the purpose of the prompt review and, where warranted, correction of final administrative actions regarding matters covered by this Agreement. Such tribunals shall be impartial and independent of the office or authority entrusted with administrative enforcement and shall not have any substantial interest in the outcome of the matter.

2. Each Party shall ensure that, in any such tribunals or procedures, the parties to the proceeding are provided with the right to:

(a) a reasonable opportunity to support or defend their respective positions; and

(b) a decision based on the evidence and submissions of record or, where required by domestic law, the record compiled by the administrative authority.

3. Each Party shall ensure, subject to appeal or further review as provided in its domestic law, that such decisions shall be implemented by, and shall govern the practice of, the office or authority with respect to the administrative action at issue."

The three mechanisms described above unveil an important feature of IIAs: the "bi-dimensional" regulatory nature of international economic law. Indeed, with the legalization of international investment relations, a rule-oriented international governance system is emerging. Such legal framework regulates not only horizontal relations among States, but also vertical relations between States' authorities and individuals. This is a major shift. Traditionally public international law used to deal exclusively with horizontal relations between States, attempting to co-ordinate sovereignty and territorial jurisdiction, rather than regulating vertical relations between authorities and individuals. As pointed out by Cottier:

> Policing states was not an original task of international law . . . [t]he advent of human rights protection, but also protection of market access, non-discrimination and investment in international economic law, have introduced elements of vertical relations to the extent that states, in their horizontal relations, increasingly addressed issues concerning vertical relations of States and foreign individuals, both humans and corporations.[25]

IIAs have two regulatory dimensions. First, as a result of the norms and disciplines undertaken between States, each Contracting Party expects a certain pattern of behavior by the other Contracting Parties in their horizontal inter-State relationship. Second, IIAs also bind the States among themselves to honor certain patterns of behavior with respect to individuals. It is in this second dimension, where IIAs acquire their major relevance as instruments generating pressure for the modernization of public administration. It is in this vertical dimension where IIAs are contributing to the generation of what some scholars have called the emergence of a Global Administrative Law.[26]

2.3 *IIAs Do Not Generate Investments Nor Development*

According to some critics of international investment law, since IIAs were to automatically generate investments and development, and in their view none of such outcomes have taken place, IIAs then have no reason to exist and should therefore been dismantled. The problem with this argument is that it is simplistic, misleading and factually inaccurate.

The argument is simplistic and misleading because it presupposes that just by signing an international agreement providing investment protection clauses—regardless as to whether in fact such agreements reflected regulatory conduct in practice by signatory States—international investment flows will pour into

---

[25] Cottier T, et al. (2012) The principle of proportionality in International Law, Working Paper No 2012/38 Swiss National Centre of Competence in Research, http://www.wti.org/fileadmin/user_upload/nccr-trade.ch/wp3/publications (last accessed 29 October 2015).

[26] See for instance Kingsbury B, Schill, SW (2009) Investor-State as Governance: Fair and Equitable Treatment, Proportionality and the Emergence of a Global Administrative Law, New York University School of Law, Public Law and Legal Theory Research Paper Series, Working Paper No. 09–46, http://ssrn.com/abstract=1466980 (last accessed 29 October 2015).

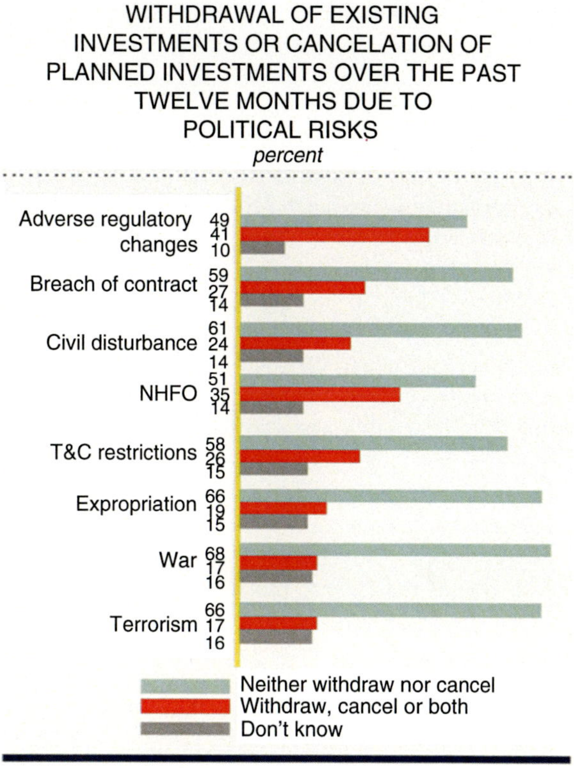

Fig. 2 Withdrawal of existing investments or cancelation of planned investments over the past 12 months due to political risks. *Source*: MIGA EIU Political Risk Survey 2013

signatory countries and as a result, development will automatically follow. It would be great if such assumption was true. All developing countries would need to do in order to develop would be then to sign a treaty!

As clearly such a position would not be serious, let's assume that the argument is more sophisticated. Let's assume that what it is really meant is that there is no evidence showing at least some causal link between an improvement in the level in investors' confidence the signature of IIAs are supposed to generate and actual investment inflows into the host countries. In this regard, recent surveys undertaken by the Multilateral Investment Guarantee Agency (MIGA) show a very revealing trend.

Surveys show that among the key constraints for increasing investment in many developing countries are investors' perception of high political risk, in particular risks derived from governments' sovereign conduct. In particular, as shown in Fig. 2 data shows that over the last 4 years in developing countries one out of four investors has either refrained from expanding their investments or even withdrawn their business due to government conduct related to breach of contracts, expropriation, transfer of payments and adverse regulatory changes.[27] Thus, there seems to be clear evidence between certain government conduct and the lack of investment retention in developing countries and economies in transition.

Without questioning the undeniable need for States to have policy space to regulate in the public interest, these trends suggest that many governments still have a long way to go in exercising their regulatory powers according to principles of transparency, predictability and due process of law.

Within this context, the surveys referred to above evidence that investment protection guarantees granted by IIAs, in particular the prospect of obtaining effective redress if they are not respected, operate as risk management tools for investors. From this point of view, IIAs may contribute to increase investors' confidence to undertake investments in environments they perceive as risky, in particular in countries where they may not be able to easily predict government conduct. In fact, this is exactly the function that capital exporting countries assigned to BITs when they started to promote them in the 1960s. During that period, economic nationalism was rife, developing countries were asserting their sovereignty over their natural resources and nationalizations were not uncommon in many countries. Governments promoted BITs, together with political risk insurance instruments, precisely to protect their investors against political risks.[28]

Retaking the issue of the impact of IIAs on attraction—and not retention—of investment flows, abundant evidence has accumulated in recent years. Sauvant and Sachs (2009) compiled a list of studies investigating the effectiveness of IIAs in attracting investment and found very different conclusions. One trend seems evident, however. While evidence is mixed in the case of bilateral investment treaties, evidence clearly suggest and impact on investment and trade flows in the case of Preferential Trade Agreements (PTAs) with investment provisions. In fact, the impact of PTAs on investment and trade is becoming so recognized, that now, in the context of the negotiation of the so called "mega regional agreements" such as the Trans Pacific Partnership Agreement (TPP) or the Transatlantic Trade and Investment Partnership Agreement (TTIP) between the EU and the United States, the concern is what will be the impact of those treaties to countries not participating in the negotiations in terms of trade and investment diversion.

Coming back to the discussion on the impact of IIAs on investment flows is that there are many types of agreements and many variables determining FDI flows. Differences in the type and strength of investment provisions, problems in disentangling effects relative to other liberalization reforms, and data quality and availability for larger samples are some of the challenges that many studies have faced. Most new evidence tries to address one or more of these concerns, and suggests that IIAs can be important mechanisms in attracting investors in certain contexts.

Table 1 summarizes these studies. However, it is important to stress that any of the studies cited have to be read with care and within context. One cannot

---

[27] See World Investment and Political Risk Reports 2013–2009, Multilateral Investment Guarantee Agency (MIGA) Word Bank Group, http://www.miga.org/resources/index.cfm?stid=1866 (last accessed 29 October 2015).

[28] For more on the historical origins of BITs see, *inter alia*: Alvarez (2011); Vandevelde (2010).

Table 1 Effects of bilateral investment agreements, and preferential trade agreements on foreign direct investment and other variables

Country	Study	Investor protection measure studied	Effect
Cross-country	Berger and others (2013)	Ratification of bilateral investment agreements and preferential trade agreements with all source countries (83 developing host countries and 28 source countries)	In the short term, a host country could increase its share of FDI flows from all source countries by 17 % through bilateral agreements and by 23 % through preferential trade agreements. The long-term effect increases to 37 % for bilateral agreements and to 50 % for preferential trade agreements. The long-term impact of switching from preferential trade agreements without national treatment provisions to agreements with them (with all source countries) is about 29 %
Cross-country	Busse et al. (2010)	Ratification of bilateral investment agreements (83 developing host countries and 28 source countries)	A nearly 25 % increase in host country share of FDI flows from all source countries. The long-term effect is about 31 %
Cross-country	Büthe and Milner (2014)	Ratification of a preferential trade agreement; moving from a preferential trade agreement without an investment clause to one with a strict investment clause; moving from an agreement without any dispute settlement mechanism to one with such a mechanism (122 developing and transition economies)	It increases FDI by an equivalent of 0.274 % of GDP. No effect for signed preferential trade agreements; increases FDI by an equivalent of 0.316 % of GDP; increases FDI by an equivalent of 0.252 % of GDP, respectively. All results reported over 5-year period
Cross-country	Colen, Persyn, and Guariso (2014)[a]	Ratification of a bilateral investment agreements (13 countries in the former Soviet Union and Central and Eastern Europe)	It increases the stock of FDI by 1–2 %. Investments are highest for utilities and real estate and, to a lesser extent, banking and mining. No effect was found for manufacturing and services
Cross-country	Egger and Merlo (2012)	Ratification of a bilateral investment agreement (Germany and 86 host countries)	A 12.6 % increase in the number of affiliates, a 45 % increase in FDI flows, a 25 % increase in employment, and a 49 % increase in assets. The FDI generated by signing and ratifying a bilateral agreement averages about €5 million per firm and €130 million per host country

(continued)

Table 1 (continued)

Country	Study	Investor protection measure studied	Effect
Cross-country	Haftel (2010)	Ratification of a bilateral investment agreement relative to its signing (U.S. and 120 host countries)	FDI to host country increases from 0.07 to 0.24 % of GDP. There are no effects for signed bilateral agreements
Cross-country	Lesher and Miroudot (2006)[b]	Ratification of a preferential trade agreement with substantive investment provisions (177 countries)	It is associated with a 57.1 % increase in FDI flows and a 20.8 % increase in exports
Cross-country	Paniagua and Myburgh (forthcoming)[c]	Ratification of New York international convention on the recognition and enforcement of foreign arbitral awards	It increases host country greenfield FDI flows by an average of 40 %
Cross-country	Yackee (2009)	Signing of bilateral investment agreements between the top 18 FDI source countries and the rest of the world	There was no effect on FDI flows

[a]Colen L, Persyn D, Guariso A (2014) What Type of FDI Is Attracted By Bilateral Treaties?, Discussion Paper 346/2014. LICOS Centre for Institutions and Economic Performance. Leuven
[b]Lesher M, Miroudot S (2006) Analysis of the Economic Impact of Investment Provisions in Regional Trade Agreements, OECD Trade Policy Papers 36, OECD Publishing
[c]Paniagua J, Myburgh A (forthcoming) Does International Commercial Arbitration Promote Foreign Direct Investment?, Catholic University of Valencia, Faculty of Economics and Business, Spain, and World Bank Group, Washington, DC

presuppose that all IIAs are the same—in fact BITs and Preferential Trade Agreements with investment provisions are not the same despite both categories including investment protection clauses. Further, one cannot assume that investment is an homogenous phenomenon and, as such, its determinants and socio-economic effects on development are also the same. There are various types of FDI, each with different impacts, and determinants, and thus, the role of IIAs in influencing investors' locational decisions are different too. For instance, investment in mining does not raise the same economic, social and environmental challenges that other types of investments may raise, such investments in manufacturing plants, or hotels, or call centers may generate. With such diversify of types of FDI, it is also too simplistic to expect that the role of IIAs in influencing investors' locational decisions in different countries with different market sizes, natural resource endowments and level of international competitiveness will be comparable.

The most important clarification on the role of IIAs and development is to put the role of those agreements in their proper context. It is not realistic to expect that just by signing a particular type of agreement, countries will automatically develop. The question as to why are some countries rich and others poor is one that has been attempted to be answered in many different historical periods by numerous academics, politicians, social scientists and economists. However, clearly none has argued that such endeavour can be automatically resolved by just negotiating an investment agreement.

Today we face a very interesting paradox. On the one hand, according to World Bank Statistics, the number of people in the world living on extreme poverty—that is, on less than $1.25 per day—has decreased dramatically in the past three decades. While in 1981 on average half of the citizens in the developing world used to live in extreme poverty, in 2010 that figure had decreased to 21 %—despite a 59 % increase in the developing world population. It is precisely through increasing flows of trade and investment that these results have been achieved. The rescue of hundreds of millions of people from poverty in countries like China and India and most of the developing world is not the result of lack of investment but on the contrary. This fact shows that it is more investment what is needed, not less.

On the other hand, the gap between the richest and poorest countries in the world is increasing. Indeed, in 1776, when Adam Smith wrote "The Wealth of Nations", the richest country in the world was approximately four times wealthier than the poorest country. The richest country in the world is now more than 400 times richer than the poorest country. What separates them? Knowledge, diversification and the composition of exports are part of the answer, all areas in which foreign investment has an important role to play.

History shows that at the end of the day, countries grow because they produce new and better goods and services, or find better ways to produce those goods and services, and retain more of the value added from their exports. Throughout this process, the key is how to connect the domestic economy with the international private sector. Foreign investment is a necessary and important vehicle to promote this connection—although not sufficient.

International investment is a necessary—although not sufficient—driver for economic growth and diversification. Shifting a country's work force from lower into higher value added jobs will depend on fostering a wider range of opportunities for private economic activity, and on the ability of local companies to integrate into global production value chains. Foreign investment is the pathway to those global value chains, allowing developing countries the opportunity to engage with and benefit from the world economy. Foreign investors can create jobs, bring capital and new technologies, and create knowledge spillovers. But these benefits are not automatic. Some countries attract large quantities of foreign investment and never move up the value chain. In order to maximize the development impacts of foreign investment, a suitable investment policy framework is needed.

When defining a modern investment vision for development in the era of globalization, there are three fundamental propositions that policy makers should keep in mind. First investment policy and development is not about choosing to privilege foreign investment over domestic or vice-versa. It is about connecting both of them.

Second, investments are more than just transactions, they entail multi-staged relationships among different stakeholders. For instance, in the case of FDI, there are foreign investors, governments and domestic investors and civil society. Such relationships have multiple dimensions, but one way to visualize them is to follow a sequential approach, by which, in the case of FDI, the main objective of maximizing its potential benefits entail previous stages, covering the stage by which foreign investors are attracted to invest into the host country, the stage when such investment is materialized and it is established, then the stage when the investment starts to be managed, operated and once retained hopefully begins to expand, leading to linkages and thereby "rooting" the FDI with the domestic economy.

Third, and most important it is to recognize that investments, and in particular foreign direct investment (FDI) are not homogenous phenomena. Different types of investment have different effects on socio-economic development and thus require different policies. On the basis of the investors' motivations to locate their investments, a frequently used typology of FDI is based on John Dunning's distinction between natural resource-seeking, market-seeking, efficiency-seeking and strategic asset-seeking FDI.[29]

While the amount and quality of natural resources explain why some countries attract more natural resource-seeking FDI than others—regardless of whether they have IIAs or not—, the size and rate of growth of the domestic market is the key determinant for market-seeking FDI. In fact, market-oriented economies with large domestic markets like the United States, the European Union, Japan and even developing countries like Brazil tend to attract significant amounts of market-seeking FDI. This fact explains why until less than one decade, most FDI inflows used to take place among developed countries. Fortunately this has changed. More than half of the FDI in the world today flow to developing countries and economies in transition.

As the main driver of market-seeking FDI is to have access to have access to bigger domestic markets to supply more goods and services, the role of IIAs vary a lot depending on the size of the domestic market of the host country and on the possibility to do business there. This may explain why Brazil is attracting significant FDI inflows with no IIAs and yet countries like China, a key leader in negotiating BITs, has become the main recipient and exporter of FDI in the developing world. In the case of China, in the early 1990s the need of a communist regime to ensure foreign investors that private property was going to be protected despite not being a market economy definitively explains the key signaling role that BITs played in that context. Who could argue that in the case of China such message did not have an effect in attracting FDI? However, and more important, is the fact that contrary to Brazil where efficiency seeking FDI has been limited, in China that has become the main type of FDI inserting the country in international markets.

Efficiency-seeking FDI is among all, probably the type of investment that has greater potential to transform developing countries' exports from commodities to

[29] These three key ideas are the main conceptual pillars for the new investment policy framework designed by the investment policy and promotion team of the Trade and Competitiveness Global Practice of the World Bank. For a full explanation on such framework please visit Investment Policy and Promotion site at: https://www.wbginvestmentclimate.org/advisory-services/international-trade/investment-policy/ (last accessed 29 October 2015).

higher value added goods and services. Efficiency-seeking FDI is export oriented by definition, and as such it requires certainty in the long term on the possibility to effectively export to key export markets. Further, in this type of investment, the investor becomes an exporter, and thus, the host country not only has to ensure predictability on conditions to do business in the host country, but also on market access conditions abroad, where the investors' exports will be directed. In a world where international production is happening more and more, Preferential Trade Agreements are in fact investment agreements, attempting to influence investors' decisions to locate efficiency-seeking FDI in countries that enable them to compete and have access to international markets. This reality explains the increasing proliferation of Preferential Trade Agreements containing investment provisions while the rate of increase in the negotiations of BITs has been in decline.

Last but not least, Dunning's typology also mentions strategic-asset-seeking FDI, which is the type of FDI that is motivated by investors' interest in acquiring strategic assets in specific firms. The relevance of this type of investment for the discussion on IIAs, is that in the twenty-first century, developing countries are no longer just recipients of FDI, but also generate FDI outflows. According to UNCTAD's 2015 World Investment Report, 39 % of all outward FDI flowing into the international markets is generated by developing countries and economies in transition. This phenomenon is illustrated by the case of the acquisition by the Indian Conglomerate TATA of the British firms Land Rover and Jaguar. In that operation, TATA's acquisition entailed not only enterprises, but the intangible strategic assets owned by those firms, such as brands, know how, distribution networks, human capital etc, The TATA example is just one among many illustrations one could cite today. In fact, in areas such as production of cement and bread, the leading firms in the world today are from Mexico.

These types of outward investments are also becoming instrumental for developing countries in joining international value chains and productive networks. In a world where South-South and South-North flows of investment are growing, we are also witnessing an increase in investment protectionism in developed countries. The political resistance to allow Dubai ports to acquire interests in a port in the United States is just one example of a trend that has been started to be documented by data.[30] Within this context is fair to ask, why the certainty and predictability that European investors were looking for in promoting BITs in the 1960s, and the predictability regarding the protection and the right of establishment that the United States and Canada sought to promote in the late 1980s and 1990s could not be values that investors from developing countries may seek to protect through IIAs in the twenty-first century? In other words, why should not developing countries seek protection to their investments abroad?

In sum, these factual data evidences two key points. First, it is not rational to expect that just by signing IIAs development will automatically happen. IIAs are

[30] In this regard, please see UNCTAD's 2015 World Investment Report data on the direction on regulatory changes on investment regimes in host countries.

just one part of a policy mix that has to be designed and implemented taking into consideration many factors. What is clear is that without IIAs, in particular PTAs, as evidence suggests, it would be extremely difficult, if not impossible, to countries to attract efficiency-seeking investment, which is the main vehicle for export diversification and enabling factor for developing countries to join global value chains. Second, it is not true that most developing countries are not in the path of development, on the contrary as data shows poverty has decreased precisely due to the increase in flows of trade and investment into developing economies. These trends evidence that more than ever before, it is in the interest of developing countries to promote the development and respect of rules fostering predictability and certainty in investment flows.

2.4 IIAs Are Bad for Development Because They Unnecessarily Erode the Sovereignty of the State and the Policy Space Governments Need to Pursue Public Policy Objectives

Another criticism against international investment law is that rules and disciplines included in IIAs unduly limit the possibilities for development as a result of preventing governments from adopting and implementing the policies required to foster economic growth and shared prosperity. There many fundamental problems with this argument. First, it presumes, in a political naïve way, that governments—both in developed and developing countries—have adequate domestic mechanisms to shield themselves from powerful interest groups. According to this line of thought, national governments' public policies always tend to promote the general interest of their respective societies, and never are vulnerable to short-term opportunistic political behaviour. Moreover, this argument also presupposes that in the case of developing countries, domestic legal systems are adequate enough to ensure optimal accountability of governments vis-à-vis their residents. Consequently, according to this view, IIAs hurt developing countries because they erode the "regulatory space" public authorities would otherwise have to pursue the common good of their citizens.

That is precisely the second problem with the argument challenging international investment law on grounds of sovereignty. Even assuming that IIAs do erode the policy space, the argument presupposes a clash between the obligations of IIAs and the discretion that host governments should have when exerting their regulatory powers and sound policy making. Such reasoning can lead to absurd results. To illustrate this point, that argument would lead to the conclusion that in order to undertake modern policy making, countries may, *inter alia*: First, unilaterally change the domestic legislation prevailing at the time of the establishment of foreign investors, or moreover: allow de facto discrimination on the basis of nationality against foreign investors. Second, countries should not take into account the principles of proportionality, due process, transparency, protection of legitimate expectations, and predictability in when regulating. Third, governments should be free to take private property without existing a legitimate public interest, disregarding due process, and without fair market value compensation.

Clearly, as governments themselves have explicitly stated in the texts of their new generation of IIAs, nothing in these agreements preclude public authorities from adopting transparent and nondiscriminatory regulatory measures to protect legitimate public welfare objectives, such as public health, safety, and the environment. The arguments against this assertion are often based on particular claims submitted by investors that may be interpreted as going against this principle. However, what should matter is not what investors claim—just as in national courts, any person can submit any baseless claim—what matters is what the adjudication system has found. In this regard, there is no evidence that arbitration tribunals have ruled against a State for legitimately exercising is regulatory powers. In fact, empirical evidence shows that arbitration tribunals tend to dismiss the majority of the claims submitted against States, rather than the other way around.

Perhaps the most important criticism to any argument advocating for the elimination international investment law in the name of development is that it ignores the multiple roles that a strong rule-oriented international investment regime may play in the best interest of developing countries.

In the current international economic context, a rule-oriented international investment regime can be instrumental to developing countries in various contexts—whether economic, political or legal. This plays out in three ways.

First, to some extent, ISDS limits the State-to-State politicization of investment disputes. Contrary to pure trade disputes where the private sector must enlist the aid of its home State to espouse a claim through a unified and multi-lateral dispute settlement process, investors do not require any assistance from their home State to submit a claim to investment treaty arbitration. Further, numerous IIAs provide that an investor's home State can be prevented from getting involved in the conflict via diplomatic protection while an investor-State arbitration is pending.

Second, ISDS provides the means to solve investor-State differences not in accordance to the parties' relative power but rather on the basis of agreed legal principles, rules and disciplines. As State relationships become increasingly intertwined and complex, where tensions arise, developing countries—especially the smaller ones—have limited economic, political and/or military power to defend their interests. Consequently, international law—despite all its limitations—is one of the few instruments that smaller economies have at their disposal to promote their agendas. Thus, it is in the best interest of developing countries to foster the development and effective implementation of the rule of law in international affairs, including investment relations.

Third, ISDS has gained importance for developing countries as their local investors and business grow and also begin to seek investment opportunities abroad to develop their businesses at home. This is not insignificant, as UNCTAD's 2015 World Investment Report suggests FDI from the developing world accounts increased from for 25 % of worldwide FDI outflows in 2009 to 39 % in 2014. A rule-oriented international investment regime helps developing countries provide their investors with the same level of protection that investors from developed countries enjoy when doing business abroad.

3 The Need for a Multilateral Rule-Based System on Investment for the Twenty-First Century: Some Initial Reflections

As stated in the previous sections, FDI continues to play a crucial role in development, connecting low- and middle-income countries to the global economy through multinational companies' value chains and providing opportunities for upgrading the capabilities of their local businesses. In 2014, more than 55 % of the world's $1.23 trillion FDI inflows went to developing countries, and this share continues to increase. Furthermore, the role of developing countries as a source of FDI is also growing—last year, more than a third of global FDI originated in low- and middle-income countries. Despite the increasing weight of FDI in economic growth and in the diversification of exports in developing countries, the international investment regime continues to have three key structural shortcomings. First, it lacks a multilateral umbrella and instead is based on a patchy web of different types of IIAs with similar yet different norms and disciplines, leading among other problems to an inherently incoherent jurisprudential development. Second, the current discussion on ISDS is deviating the attention from a key role that international investment law should play in a world increasingly interconnected by international production patterns. That is, rather than exclusively solving legal disputes between investors and States, international investment law should become an instrument to facilitate retention of investment in developing countries by giving stakeholders the opportunity to manage conflicts before they escalate into legal disputes. Third, despite the increasing incorporation of investment provisions clauses to Preferential Trade Agreements, the international investment regime remains significantly disconnected from the multilateral trading system.

3.1 The Need to Address Fragmentation

In the absence of a comprehensive multilateral framework for investment akin to what exists for cross-border trade, FDI flows are regulated by a combination of the countries' domestic legislation, bilateral treaties, and, increasingly, investment-related provisions in regional trade and investment agreements. There is an existing patchy framework of international investment rules and disciplines sparsely located in more than 3000 bilateral investment treaties, almost 300 PTAs and relevant agreements of the WTO. The negotiation of mega-regional agreements and the negotiation of the US-China bilateral investment treaty (BIT) and China-EU BIT may represent some steps towards greater coherence to the regime, but clearly not full convergence as many countries are not parties of these negotiations.

As stated before, while the core elements of this regime of intertwined and interrelated international instruments have existed for more for many decades, investment rule making has in the recent years been evolving on multiple fronts.[31] First, there has been some clarification that investment protection guarantees are not intended to erode government's regulatory capacity in pursuit of legitimate public policy objectives. Second, countries have also agreed to provide greater precision on the rules that govern resolution of investor-state grievances and disputes. Third, there is increased attention paid to responsible investment—with a particular focus on environmental and social issues—and with a broader objective of equitable growth and sustainable development. Fourth, there has been recognition of the increase multiplicity of the types and forms of foreign investment, including non-equity modes, state-owned or state-affiliated enterprises and funds, and institutional investors.

Despite these international initiatives, the complexity, fragmentation, and the evolving nature of the investment regimes worldwide requires a more coordinated and coherent approach to domestic, bilateral, regional and trans-regional investment rule-making and implementation. There is an evident need to promote greater coherence of the international investment regime in order to effectively harness international investment relations for sustainable development.

Despite the emerging consensus on the need to promote greater coherence, the key question is what would be the concrete policy steps governments may adopt in the near or medium term. Depending on the level of ambition of different countries a range of different options could be considered to achieve such objective. Paradoxically, the negotiation of a multilateral agreement with binding and enforceable disciplines would be clearly be the most ambitious and yet less plausible option given the current debate on the international investment regime. The failed negotiations sponsored by the OECD on the Multilateral Agreement on Investment (MAI) and the failed attempt to incorporate investment in the final agenda of the WTO Doha Negotiation Round may still be too recent in the collective memory of investment stakeholders.

There are however, other initiatives that could be explored to foster greater coherence within the international investment regime. Other possible alternatives to consider would entail building on work by the international organizations such as UNCTAD, OECD, the WBG, the WTO and others, articulating a basic framework organizing existing norms, to develop a set of guidelines or even just a set of principles to inform domestic investment rule-making, ensuring that these rules work for the benefit of both home and host countries. Various concrete initiatives could be undertaken to prepare the discussion of such an endeavour. One possible step could be to build on the new generation of IIAs and identify the legal level

[31] This point is developed in Echandi (2010).

playing field of international rules and disciplines resulting from the interaction of the noodle bowl of bilateral investment treaties in conjunction with the numerous PTAs and the WTO applicable disciplines on investment.

3.2 The Need to Use International Investment Law to Enhance Investor-State Relations Rather Than Focus Only on Investment Disputes

From a systemic perspective, there is a more important negative consequence of investor-State litigation besides economic and political cost which should not be overlooked. Increased litigation undermines the development of long-term harmonious relationships between foreign investors and host States. In a sense such outcome is in fact contrary to one of the key objectives that international investment agreements (IIAs) should promote, that is, to contribute towards the creation of an investment climate favouring the growth of investment inflows. International investment law, should entail much more than investor-State disputes, it should be an instrument for governance. In a globalized world where patterns of international production are leading every day to a higher level of interaction among foreign and local investors, governments and civil society, there is an evident need for an international investment regime promoting the maximization of the positive impact of foreign investments in host countries as well as the mitigation of any potential negative effect.

In particular, among other functions, international investment law should be used to respond to the real social need of finding effective ways to enable investors and host States to address their problems—the number of which may naturally arise from their increasing interaction—in an efficient manner, without necessarily incurring in the costs associated with litigation. How to better adjust those problem-solving techniques to the particular context of investor-State disputes is an ongoing important discussion in many academic and policy circles. However, a key point already recognized by experts is that, regardless of which particular ADR technique may be explored, given the complex political economy of investor-State disputes, the best chance to resolve a dispute between a foreign investor and a host government is likely before the investment conflict escalates into a legal dispute under an international investment agreement. This raises the question as to how can this objective be achieved.[32]

States are complex organizations. Further, given their broad scope of application, norms and disciplines of IIAs may touch upon a plethora of policy matters that are handled by multiple governmental agencies. Such agencies do not have the

[32] This point is further developed in Echandi R (2014) Investor-State Conflict Management: A preliminary sketch, Transnational Dispute Management Vol. 1 Issue 1, January 2014, www.transnational-dispute-management.com (last accessed 29 October 2015).

same policy priorities. Further, no all agencies may be even aware of the existence of IIAs, or may have among their top priorities to act in compliance with such treaties or domestic investment protection laws. Within this context, it may be relevant to note that a majority of the investor-State disputes submitted to international arbitration have involved measures adopted by sub-national or sector-specific regulatory agencies.

In order for alternatives to investor-State arbitration to have a better chance to succeed in the future, it is necessary to provide governments with a minimum institutional infrastructure that can enable them to identify, track and manage conflicts arising between investors and public agencies as early as possible. Governments need to be able to react in a coordinated manner with respect to a conflict with an investor at a very early stage, well before the aggrieved investor submits a legal claim for compensation under an IIA.

To enable States to promptly assess conflicts, and determine the better course of action to address such conflict, is precisely the key role that investor-State conflict management mechanisms purport to perform. Currently, such institutional infrastructure does not exist in many countries. Investor-State conflict management mechanisms (CMMs) can be defined as those institutional or contractual mechanisms that are meant to enable host States and investors to effectively address their grievances at a very early stage, preventing their conflicts from escalating into full-blown legal disputes. CMMs may enable the use of various preventive ADR techniques—such as mediation, conciliation or early neutral evaluation—as problem solving techniques to properly manage a conflict.

Avoiding the economic and political costs entailed by investor-State arbitration is one of the most attractive potential advantages of developing conflict management mechanisms, both for investors and governments. An early management of the conflict will likely prevent any measure from inflicting significant damage to any of the parties involved in the conflict, erasing thus any potential claim for compensation. Further, a conflict can be resolved through solutions that may not entail the use of any public resources at all. For instance, an agency may simply implement a measure addressing the issue that motivated the conflict in the first place.

From the outset, it is important to clarify that CMMs cannot—nor should they—guarantee that all investment-related conflicts will be prevented from escalating into investor-State disputes. Conflict management mechanisms presuppose the use of interest-based techniques—such as early neutral evaluation or preventive mediation—rather than adjudication. Interest-based techniques may not be adequate to deal with certain kinds of conflicts. For instance, where the parties need to clarify the interpretation of a legal obligation, or where the host State may be interested in setting a public policy precedent for the future, adjudication may turn out to be necessary.

The main objective of CMMs is also not to avoid investor-State litigation at all cost. Rather, their rationale is to enable the parties the possibility to select the best problem solving technique to manage their conflicts—being direct negotiation, mediation, early neutral evaluation or any other including arbitration when it is the best option. Providing the parties with such possibility may not only reduce transaction costs, but also, more important, may lead to a more stable and harmonious environment where investors and host States can focus their attention in maximizing the benefits of investments for all stakeholders involved.

CMMs may be particularly useful to deal with investment-related conflicts stemming from the application of inconsistent policies or lack of coordination among different government agencies—inconsistencies which could entail the liability of the host State under an IIA. In this respect, CMMs may be a vehicle to enable international investment law in general, and IIAs in particular, to play a more constructive role in strengthening the rule of law in host countries. CMMs may promote such outcome by allowing a Lead Agency to use international and domestic investment law as a tool to persuade other public agencies generating a conflict with the investor, to consider whether their actions are in fact in conformity with the applicable investment frameworks, well before the conflict had escalated into a dispute. Further, by opening new additional channels to address conflicts, CMMs may also prevent frivolous claims by investors who may see in investor-State arbitration the only available outlet to attract the attention of the host State to address a particular problem.

Establishing the necessary institutional infrastructure to enable governments to properly operate CMMs is a domestic endeavour. However, the CMM agenda also has an international dimension. The success of the Investor-State CMMs is to a great extent based on the notion of enabling both States and investors to negotiate on the shadow of the law. From this point of view, this approach is based on the idea that the prospects of facing international responsibility for an unlawful act—and the associated pecuniary consequences for the budget of the agency incurring in the violation of an obligation—would act as a deterrent for an agency to adopt a measure inconsistent with domestic and international law. Clearly, for such assumption to operate in practice, two conditions would in fact be necessary.

First, countries require technical assistance in setting up their institutional or contractual CMMs. Second, to foster negotiations on the shadow of the law, there is a need to continuing promoting greater clarity regarding the contents of international investment law. Both of these approaches could be promoted through international cooperation. The World Bank Group has recently started to develop a program specifically directed to assist developing countries in setting up CMMs. It is a new initiative being piloted in some developing countries which could be further expanded.

Further, State-to-State cooperation could also promote initiatives to foster greater clarification of key elements of international investment law. Negotiation of interpretative declarations and or inclusion of specific clauses in IIAs providing for clarification of the scope and content of substantive provisions of these agreements are also other specific steps which could be undertaken in this direction. For instance, certain IIAs, establish joint administrative commissions comprising government authorities of the Contracting Parties with the capacity to enact jointly agreed interpretative notes clarifying particular provisions of the IIAs. Further, States could also agree on other initiatives geared at promoting, to the extent possible, greater coherence in the interpretation of IIAs, such as establishing a mechanism of preliminary rulings, or alternatively, mechanisms of appellate review. Another approach would be to promote the inclusion in the texts of IIAs of more effective incentives inducing both investors and governments to undertake real, serious and good faith attempts to effectively explore interest-based conflict management processes before any notice of intent for arbitration can be submitted by the foreign investor.

In the current inter-dependent world, the search for alternatives to investor-State dispute resolution entails much more than procedural and institutional solutions and discussions. In fact it raises a profound philosophical question: which should be the parameters of governance orienting the evolution of the international investment regime? The differentiation between power-based, rights-based and interest-based dispute resolution used in the context of conflict theory results quite useful when translated to the context of the historical evolution of international investment relations and international investment law in particular. From a trend where investor-State investment disputes used to be predominantly resolved through diplomatic protection—an approach that in practice led to power-based dispute resolution—with the proliferation of IIAs and the increase in investor-State arbitration the trend has shifted towards rights-based dispute resolution.

International investment relations have become increasingly "rule-oriented" In general, that should be considered a positive development for both international and domestic investment governance. However, the legalization of international investment relations is also exerting strong pressures over host countries' administrations, leading various political actors to resist to those pressures, and to challenge the legitimacy of the current international investment regime. Within this context, it is not surprising that a significant share of the literature on international investment law has recently focused on how the international investment regime—and investor-State dispute settlement procedures in particular—should be revisited and adjusted to properly respond to the realities of the twenty-first century.

No one could argue that the current international investor-State arbitration mechanisms in IIAs do not need to be improved—there are, however, significant disagreements as to what kind of improvements to make and how they should be implemented. Nevertheless, and regardless of this discussion, the main point of this note is that any serious attempt to modernize the international investment regime should bear in mind that, to properly perform its function, the regime can no longer afford to leave all problems arising between investors and host States to be exclusively addressed through investor-State arbitration.

It is time to conceive the application of international investment law as going beyond litigation. After evolving from power-based to rule-based dispute settlement, it is time for the international investment regime to evolve once again, now in the direction of incorporating within its structure interest-based conflict management mechanisms.

3.3 The Need to Better Integrate Trade and Investment

With the dramatic growth of international trade in services and the increasing fragmentation of production on a global scale, governments in developed and developing countries alike have become acutely aware of the central role that foreign investment plays in positioning their national economies in an interdependent world market and in fueling the well-being of citizens.

Over the last decade, IIA negotiations have addressed an expanded range of issues. A growing number of IIAs include more sophisticated investment protection provisions as well as liberalization commitments. Compared to BITs, PTAs show far more variation in their scope, approach and content. Moreover, recent PTAs tend to encompass a broader range of issues that in the most comprehensive agreements may include not only investment protection and liberalization, but also trade in goods and services, intellectual property rights, competition policy, government procurement, temporary entry for business persons, transparency, as well as protection of the environment and of labor rights.

Moreover, despite the ever deeper interaction between international investment and trade, investment law has tended to evolve separately from the regulatory regime governing international trade. The failed attempt at crafting a Multilateral Agreement on Investment (MAI) in the 1990s was very much reflective of these two "solitudes". Experts from both fields all too rarely interact with one another. This has fuelled an artificial and unduly segmented vision of these two fundamental pillars of international economic law and policy. Indeed, despite their particular features and complexities, international trade and investment are no longer two competing but rather complementary ways to serve and integrate international markets. There is, accordingly, a genuine need to assess and study both subject areas through a more integrated lens and to strive to identify and exploit the natural synergies between them and extend them to other rising fields of international economic law, such as competition law and policy, to which they are inextricably linked.

The inclusion of investment chapters into PTAs is clearly representing a step in integrating trade and investment law as part of the governance system of an global economy characterized by international production patterns in which the investor has become a trader—both importer and exporter—and vice versa. Some experts have expressed concern over the integration of these two areas of law—arguing that while investment is rooted in the law on protection trade is rooted on the law on transactions. However, regardless of any legal and theoretical discussion, the features of investment flows are showing how old paradigms are quickly being challenged by economic and technological realities. In less than two decades, trade in services—which in the not so far past used to be denominated as "non-tradeable"—has become a rising component in trade and investment flows. In sum, the greater the share of international production becomes government by megaregional agreements covering trade and investment among other subjects, the clearer the need to have a multilateral system governing not only trade but also other areas of economic law, including investment.

4 Conclusion

A significant part of the international investment regime—in particular the traditional model BIT originally negotiated by European Member States—was designed in an historical context where FDI used to flow from North to South, and when it used to be concentrated on natural resource-seeking FDI and to a lesser extent on market-seeking FDI. Over the last three decades, investment flows have changed significantly not only in terms of its determinants, but also in the direction that is flowing, the sectoral composition of investment, the modalities of investment as well as the subjects who have become international investors. Investment and trade have become two sides of the same coin of international production.

Yet, despite these key transformations, the current patchy international investment regime is generating significant controversy among investment stakeholders due to the increase in investor-State litigation, which is not only distracting the attention of the need to update international investment law in the direction towards a modern—yet strong- rule-oriented governance system, but also in the direction to learn non-litigious means to use law to as a basis of rule-based negotiation among stakeholders to address problems and prevent them from escalating into legal disputes.

The controversy on the multiple issues related to international investment law should not deter stakeholders from discerning a huge opportunity for legal systemic advancement in this field. For this first time ever, because of IIAs, governments in many developing countries have become accountable in situations where basic guarantees such as due process, transparency, proportionality, and discrimination are compromised. The problem is not the existence of international investment law, the challenge to be overcome is to use it to upgrade the domestic legislation and level the playing field with domestic investors too. The solution is not to dismantle the law, but rather to continuing developing it so it can permeate and benefit investors regardless of nationality and whether they are natural people or companies.

On the other hand, for the first time ever, industrial countries are also becoming accountable to international rules and disciplines being enforced beyond their own legal borders. This may be generating discomfort in many sectors of developed countries, who perceive that national sovereignty is being eroded.

Paradoxically, in the majority of developing countries with societies more used to adjust to international pressures, the use of international law as a tool to protect their own investors and conditions for their exports—including those of international investors from their territories—is becoming more familiar. Many developing countries are understanding that in an increasingly interactive world the issue is not whether conflict is avoidable, but rather whether conflicts will be solved according to political or military might, or according to pre-agreed legal principles.

In an interdependent world, where nation States must learn to cooperate in order to deal with issues affecting the common good, what is obsolete is to safeguard the notion of absolute State sovereignty as a dogma. International law—which by the way enjoys the same original political legitimacy as domestic law as it is also approved by national parliaments to become legally binding and enforceable—will become increasingly necessary. In every corner of the world, the most common demand of citizens to their governments is to implement policies conducive to generate more and better paid jobs. Today, such outcome is increasingly dependent on how each country inserts itself into the international value chains of production of goods and services. As international investment is the key vehicle to join such production networks, the question is not whether investment law is necessary or not, but rather how to modernize it to ensure that developing countries can have adequate means to pursue their interests. Thus, let's be careful that in that endeavour, developing countries do not end suffering from dismantling a legal system in the absence of which, we go back to the era of raw-power oriented dispute settlement.

References

Alvarez J (2011) International law regime governing international investment. Hague Academy of International Law, The Hague

Berger A, Busse M, Nunnenkamp P, Roy M (2013) Do trade and investment agreements lead to more FDI? Accounting for key provisions inside the black box. Int Econ Econ Policy 10 (2):247–75

Busse M, Koniger J, Nunnenkamp P (2010) FDI promotion through bilateral investment treaties: more than a BIT? Rev World Econ 146(1):147–77

Büthe T, Milner HV (2014) Foreign direct investment and institutional diversity in trade agreements: credibility, commitment, and economic flows in the developing world, 1971–2007. World Polit 66(1):88–122

Cable J (1981) Gunboat diplomacy 1919–1979: political applications of limited naval force. Macmillan, London

Collier P (2007) The bottom billion: why the poorest countries are failing and what can be done about. Oxford University Press, New York

Echandi R (1997) The Uruguay round agreements: constitutional and legal aspects of their implementation in Costa Rica. In: Jackson JH, Sykes A (eds) Implementing the Uruguay round. Oxford University Press, Oxford

Echandi R (2010) Bilateral investment treaties and investment provisions in regional trade agreements: recent developments in investment rulemaking. In: Yannaca-Small K (ed) Arbitration under international investment agreements: A guide to key issues. Oxford University Press, Oxford

Echandi R (2011) What do developing countries expect from the international investment regime?. In: Alvarez J, Sauvant K et al (eds) The evolving international investment regime: expectations, realities, options. Oxford University Press, Oxford

Echandi R, Sauve P (2013) Prospects in international investment law and policy: world trade forum. Cambridge University Press, Cambridge

Egger P, Merlo V (2012) BITs bite: an anatomy of the impact of bilateral investment treaties on multinational firms. Scand J Econ 114(4):1240–66

Haftel YZ (2010) Ratification counts: U.S. investment treaties and FDI flows into developing countries. Rev Int Polit Econ 17(2):348–77

Sauvant KP, Sachs LE (2009) The effect of treaties on foreign direct investment: bilateral investment treaties, double taxation treaties, and investment flows. Oxford University Press, Oxford

Schneiderman D (2007) Constitutionalizing economic globalization. Cambridge University Press, Cambridge

Sornarajah M (2016) International investment law as development law: the obsolescence of a fraudulent system. In: Bungenberg M, Hermann C, Krajewski M, Terchechte JP (eds) European yearbook of international economic law, vol 7. Springer, Heidelberg, pp 209–232

Vandevelde K (2010) Bilateral investment treaties, history, policy, and interpretation. Oxford University Press, Oxford

Yackee J (2009) Do BITs really work? Revisiting the empirical link between investment treaties and foreign direct investment. In: Sauvant KP, Sachs LE (eds) The effect of treaties on foreign direct investment: bilateral investment treaties, double taxation treaties, and investment flows. Oxford University Press, Oxford

Investor-State Dispute Settlement: Conflict, Convergence, and Future Directions

Kate Miles

Contents

Abstract This article reflects upon the criticisms directed towards investor-state arbitration over the last decade. It considers the controversies, the responses and the current debates surrounding investor-state arbitration. In particular, it reviews the discourse on the right to regulate and the arguments that investment disputes can impact on matters of public interest and have the potential to encroach into host state regulatory space. It also considers concerns expressed at the structural, institutional, and procedural frameworks for investor-state arbitration. In examining both the procedural and substantive responses to such criticisms, the argument is put forward that, increasingly, there is an acknowledgement of the problematic nature of the 'older-style' bilateral investment treaties, that attempts are being made to address this through new emphases in treaty-drafting, and that a more nuanced approach to investment disputes may be emerging. Concerns remain, however, that even despite these developments, public welfare regulation continues to be at risk from investor challenges and that a lack of appreciation of non-investment issues persists in arbitral decision-making. For this reason, the article ultimately adopts an ambivalent view of the future impact of the changes currently occurring within the field.

K. Miles (✉)
Gonville and Caius College, University of Cambridge, Cambridge CB3 9DZ, UK
e-mail: klm66@cam.ac.uk

M. Bungenberg et al. (eds.), *European Yearbook of International Economic Law 2016*, European Yearbook of International Economic Law 7,
DOI 10.1007/978-3-319-29215-1_12

1 Introduction

Investor-state arbitration has been the subject of intense scrutiny for well over a decade now, with controversy surrounding both the substance of international investment agreements and procedural aspects of the dispute settlement system. In particular, the concerns have focused on the potential for investment disputes to impact upon matters of public interest and to encroach upon host state regulatory space.[1] Stemming from a series of high-profile investment claims,[2] criticism has also been directed towards the rather opaque system of investor-state arbitration, in which proceedings are conducted under confidential conditions.[3] Questions have also been raised regarding the systemic independence of arbitrators as they are permitted to act as counsel in proceedings, whilst sitting as arbitrators in other matters.[4] And there is no appeals mechanism to ensure consistency in arbitral decision-making.[5] In essence, the arguments are that, with its substantive focus on investment protection and procedure modelled on commercial dispute resolution, investor-state arbitration is ill-equipped to address adequately the wider issues implicated by investment disputes.[6]

Since the late 1990s, the debates have, at times, become polarised and, until a few years ago, criticism of investor-state arbitration was periodically dismissed within certain investment law circles as having little validity.[7] However, there has recently been an increasing acknowledgement that the 'older style' bilateral

---

[1] See, for example, the discussion in Soloway (2000); see also Tienhaara (2009).

[2] See, for example, *Methanex Corporation v United States of America*, (2005) 44 *International Legal Materials* 1345; *S.D. Myers, Inc v Canada*, Partial Award (Decision on the Merits), November 2000; *Ethyl Corporation v Canada*, Jurisdiction Phase, (1999) 38 *International Legal Materials* 708; *Metalclad Corporation v The United States of Mexico*, Award, 25 August 2000, (2001) 40 *International Legal Materials* 35; *CMS Gas Transmission Co v Argentine Republic* (2005) 44 *International Legal Materials* 1205; *Philip Morris Asia Limited v The Commonwealth of Australia*, In the Matter of Arbitration under the Arbitration Rules of the United Nations Commission on International Trade Law 2010, Notice of Arbitration, (21 November 2011).

[3] Tienhaara (2006).

[4] Van Harten (2007), pp. 172–173.

[5] See, for example, the *Lauder Cases*: In the Matter of a UNCITRAL Arbitration between Ronald S. Lauder and the Czech Republic, Final Award, 3 September 2001; *CME Czech Republic B.V. (the Netherlands)* v. *Czech Republic* (UNCITRAL, Partial Award of 13 September 2001; Final Award of 14 March 2003); see also the discussion in Yannaca-Small (2008), pp. 1009–1010; see also Joubin-Bret (2008).

[6] Sornarajah (2003); see the discussion on the views of members of the investment sector "that an arbitrator is not the guardian of public policy, that his duties are towards the parties only, and that he must confine himself to the determination of disputes involving private interests" in Mayer (2001), pp. 246–247.

[7] See, for example, the characterisation of critics of investor-state arbitration in Weiler (2005); see also the view set out in Baker (2006); see also Wälde and Kolo (2001).

investment treaties (BITs) are, indeed, problematic and possess the potential to encroach upon legitimate host state policy-making and regulatory development.[8] Appreciation of this aspect increased amongst developed states as a result of the Canadian and American experience under the North American Free Trade Agreement (NAFTA)[9] and recent cases brought against Germany[10] and Australia.[11] Furthermore, the context in which new international investment agreements are being negotiated has also changed. Indeed, a large number of states are both capital exporters and importers and it is now commonplace to see such agreements concluded between two developed states and also as between two developing states.[12]

For these reasons, key areas of contention have shifted to the exploration of potential responses to such acknowledged shortcomings. For example, the issues include whether substantive reform of standard treaty protections is desirable, whether further procedural reform is necessary or whether the reform measures recently adopted are sufficient to remedy procedural deficiencies in the system, or whether abandonment of the investor-state dispute settlement system (ISDS) altogether is the best option for certain states.

Such reform attempts have manifested in the so-called 'new generation BITs', importing World Trade Organization (WTO)-style exceptions provisions into the body of the treaties.[13] There have been numerous examples of drafting reform in the

---

[8] See, for example, European Commission Statement, Improving ISDS to Prevent Abuse—Statement by EU Trade Commissioner Karel De Gucht on the Launch of a Public Consultation on Investment Protection in TTIP, 27 March 2014, http://europa.eu/rapid/press-release_STATEMENT-14-85_en.htm (last accessed 4 April 2015).

[9] Adopted 17 December 1992, (1992) 32 ILM 612 (entered into force 1 January 1994). Notable examples include *Methanex Corporation v United States of America*, (2005) 44 *International Legal Materials* 1345; *Dow AgroSciences LLC v Government of Canada*, Notice of Arbitration, 31 March 2009 http://www.naftaclaims.com/disputes/canada/dow/dow-01.pdf (last accessed 7 August 2015).

[10] *Vattenfall AB et al v Federal Republic of Germany*, Request for Arbitration, 30 March 2009, ICSID No. ARB/09/6, http://www.italaw.com/documents/VattenfallRequestforArbitration.pdf (last accessed 6 June 2015); *Vattenfall AB et al v Federal Republic of Germany*, ICSID No. ARB/12/12.

[11] *Philip Morris Asia Ltd v The Commonwealth of Australia*, In the Matter of Arbitration under the Arbitration Rules of the United Nations Commission on International Trade Law 2010, Notice of Arbitration, 21 November 2011, http://www.ag.gov.au/tobaccoplainpackaging (last accessed 6 June 2015).

[12] UNCTAD (2005) South-South Investment Agreements Proliferating. IIA Monitor No. 1 UNCTAD/WEB/ITE/IIT/2006/1, http://unctad.org/en/Docs/webiteiit20061_en.pdf (last accessed 10 June 2015).

[13] See, for example, Art. 9 of Agreement Between Canada and the Czech Republic for the Promotion and Protection of Investments, (adopted 6 May 2009, entered into force 22 January 2012), http://www.treaty-accord.gc.ca/text-texte.aspx?id=105128&lang=eng (last accessed 4 April 2015).

inclusion of references to 'sustainable development' within more recent bilateral investment treaties.[14] There have been suggestions within the European Commission of significant departures from traditional approaches for the Trans-Atlantic Trade and Investment Partnership (TTIP),[15] including a permanent investment court, an appeals mechanism, and express requirements for the preservation of host state regulatory space.[16] There have also been substantial moves to improve transparency embodied in procedural reforms of the major sets of arbitration rules such as those of the International Centre for the Settlement of Investment Disputes (ICSID)[17] and the United Nations Commission on International Trade Law (UNCITRAL).[18]

The concrete nature of these reform measures suggests that the criticisms of earlier days in the ISDS controversy did, in fact, make in-roads into what was, for quite some time, a particularly hard-line mainstream position within the investment arbitration community. Indeed, over the last few years, there has been a discernible shift in the tone of scholarly commentary in which an appreciation of the adverse impacts of investor-state arbitration sits alongside accounts of its benefits. Suggesting the need for more balanced international investment agreements so as to take account of non-investment public interest issues is no longer considered radical as it once was even just 5–10 years ago. Bastions of extreme views, of course, remain in which critics continue to be dismissed and characterised as ill-informed activists with questionable agendas, including even critics who are scholars and experts in the field.[19] However, given the significant cultural change in temperature and that a softened, more nuanced discussion is now the norm, unquestioning pro-ISDS advocacy increasingly appears out of touch. Mainstream

[14] See, for example, Agreement between Canada and the Federal Republic of Nigeria for the Promotion and Protection of Investments (signed 6 May 2014), http://www.international.gc.ca/trade-agreements-accords-commerciaux/agr-acc/fipa-apie/nigeria.aspx?lang=eng (last accessed 12 June 2015); see also Agreement between Canada and the Republic of Peru for the Promotion and Protection of Investments (signed 14 November 2006, entered into force 20 June 2007), http://www.treaty-accord.gc.ca/text-texte.aspx?id=105078&lang=eng (last accessed 12 June 2015).

[15] Trans-Atlantic Trade and Investment Partnership, currently being negotiated by the European Union and the United States of America, see the European Commission website for its negotiating texts, http://ec.europa.eu/trade/policy/in-focus/ttip/documents-and-events/index_en.htm#eu-position (last accessed 5 July 2015).

[16] European Commission Speech, Discussion on Investment in TTIP at the Meeting of the International Trade Committee of the European Parliament, Cecilia Maelström, Commissioner for Trade, 18 March 2015, http://europa.eu/rapid/press-release_SPEECH-15-4624_en.htm (last accessed 8 May 2015).

[17] ICSID, Rules of Procedure for Arbitration Proceedings (2006) https://icsid.worldbank.org/ICSID/StaticFiles/basicdoc/CRR_English-final.pdf (last accessed 15 June 2015).

[18] UNCITRAL Arbitration Rules (as revised in 2010) https://www.uncitral.org/pdf/english/texts/arbitration/arb-rules-revised/arb-rules-revised-2010-e.pdf (last accessed 10 July 2015).

[19] The closed list-serve OGEMID (Oil-Gas-Energy-Mining-Infrastructure Dispute Management), which operates on a Chatham House Rules basis, is one such forum, http://www.transnational-dispute-management.com/ogemid/ (last accessed 16 April 2015).

intellectual discourse tends now to engage with theoretical framings of international investment law,[20] continued analysis of the interactions between investment law and non-investment issues,[21] explorations into various institutional and procedural reform options and models,[22] and ways in which international investment law structures can stimulate more environmentally and socially responsible approaches to foreign investment.[23]

Criticisms remain. Some I share; others I do not. In particular, despite the climate of reform and the inclusion of WTO-type exceptions within, for example, more recent Canadian international investment agreements,[24] there has not yet been a widespread recalibration of the substantive protections contained in international investment agreements. The majority of BITs currently in force are those of the old model and, for that reason, it is likely that we will still see a number of *Philip Morris* and *Vattenfall*–style claims for some time yet.[25] Once the older generation-style BITs are no longer in force, however, disputes of this ilk are less likely to appear if carefully drafted safeguards are introduced.

Even then, the risk of public welfare-related claims emerging in some form or another is, of course, not eliminated. In this regard, it is worth noting that the way in which treaty protections have been used since the late 1990s was certainly not anticipated at the time of signing the majority of bilateral investment treaties.[26] In some respects, therefore, there now needs to be 'an eyes wide open' approach to the negotiating and concluding of new international investment agreements—if there are investment agreements in place, it is inevitable that there will be investor claims that encroach in some form on government policy space. The inclusion of carve-out clauses and exceptions provisions can reduce the frequency with which states face investor claims of this nature, but the substantive law remains relatively untouched and the interpretation and application of investment treaties can, at times, take unexpected turns. And this tendency alludes to the central role of arbitrators in the development of the law in this field.

---

[20] See, for example, Schill (2015); see also, for example, Douglas et al. (2014).

[21] See, for example, Baetens (2013).

[22] See, for example, Kalicki and Joubin-Bret (2015).

[23] See, for example, Dupuy and Viñuales (2013).

[24] See, for example, Agreement between Canada and the Federal Republic of Nigeria for the Promotion and Protection of Investments (signed 6 May 2014), http://www.international.gc.ca/trade-agreements-accords-commerciaux/agr-acc/fipa-apie/nigeria.aspx?lang=eng (last accessed 12 June 2015).

[25] *Philip Morris Asia Ltd v The Commonwealth of Australia*, In the Matter of Arbitration under the Arbitration Rules of the United Nations Commission on International Trade Law 2010, Notice of Arbitration, 21 November 2011, http://www.ag.gov.au/tobaccoplainpackaging (last accessed 6 June 2015); *Vattenfall AB et al v Federal Republic of Germany*, Request for Arbitration, 30 March 2009, ICSID No. ARB/09/6, http://www.italaw.com/documents/VattenfallRequestforArbitration.pdf (last accessed 6 May 2015); *Vattenfall AB et al v Federal Republic of Germany*, ICSID No. ARB/12/12.

[26] Sands (2005), pp. 121, 141.

Key criticisms of ISDS have pointed to structural and procedural features of the appointment of arbitrators, but they have also extended to more amorphous aspects such as 'cultural approaches', an apparent reluctance to address adequately non-investment issues within awards, and a lack of appreciation of the distinct character of ISDS from that of international commercial arbitration.[27] These critiques do not question the integrity of individual arbitrators; rather, the concern is that there are systemic factors at play, operating on arbitrators at a subconscious level and feeding into the conduct of hearings, decision-making processes, and drafting of awards. These more subtle concerns, in my view, have also been influential in the increasingly widespread sense of disquiet at the use to which investment treaties have been put and that it is not solely the way in which investment treaties have been drafted, but the interpretations that have been given to their provisions that are problematic.

At a deeper conceptual level, I also continue to have concerns. An aversion to appreciating the modern legacy of the field's historical origins in imperialism is, in my view, unhelpful. There is a reluctance to acknowledge that power dynamics operate within this field and that, whilst they do, indeed, have different actors and different interests are at play, at its heart, such dynamics are grounded in the history of the development of the law. Leading proponents of the importance of historical perspectives within international law include those scholars identifying with the group Third World Approaches to International Law (TWAIL).[28] This mode of critique questions core assumptions of international law and explores the ways in which ostensibly neutral doctrines have been applied throughout history so as to construct and support conventional narratives of international law and obfuscate the disempowering of non-Western peoples. In my view, these patterns also find form in international investment law. I have explored the far-reaching nature of those patterns elsewhere, examining in depth their history back to the seventeenth century.[29] In this article, however, I am limiting my discussion to contemporary controversies, cases, and criticisms, and, in this vein, I have particular concerns at recent attempts to frame investor-state arbitration as a mode of global administrative law, an instrument of good governance, and a purveyor of the rule of law. I also continue to be concerned at the direction of arbitral interpretation, not only at the outcomes in isolated cases, but also at the way in which it is influencing the development of the law.

With all this in mind, Part 1 of this article sets out many of the criticisms that have been directed at both investor-state arbitration and the substantive rules of international investment law. It considers both the scholarly discourse that has surrounded investment arbitration and the protest actions of public pressure groups. Part 2 explores the response to the criticism. This includes both the dismissing of

[27] Sornarajah (2003), pp. 13–17; Van Harten (2007), p. 159.

[28] See, for example, Anghie (2004); see also Pahuja (2011); see Mickelson (1998); see also Gathii (2008).

[29] Miles (2013).

those criticisms as well as the measured re-thinking of approaches to foreign investment protection and the attempts to re-design its treaties and dispute settlement mechanisms. I conclude, however, with an assessment as to why concerns remain. In particular, I consider the implications of the recent *Clayton & Bilcon* Award[30]; not only for state decision-making, but also in a wider sense for the direction in which reform measures have been travelling. In essence, I take the view that there is a seductive quality to the reasoning in this Award, so that when the issue is framed in a certain way, it appears reasonable; however, when encapsulated from a contrary position, the more troubling aspects become apparent. In other words, it is likely that concerns expressed at the Award, and, indeed, those articulated in the Dissenting Opinion of Professor Donald McRae,[31] will be answered by arguing at cross purposes through a re-framing of the issues, rather than an addressing of the concerns themselves. This tends to suggest that despite the incremental procedural reforms and shifting attitudes within the field, arbitrators' decisions are likely to continue to impact upon non-investment issues for some time yet.

2 Criticism of Investor-State Arbitration

Much of the criticism directed towards investor-state arbitration over the last decade or so has emerged out of the potential loss of state control over health and environmental regulation. The core intent behind the BITs and free trade agreements containing investment protection provisions signed throughout the 1960s to late 1990s had been to promote foreign investment flows into developing states and to protect the investments made within the signatory states from arbitrary seizure or discriminatory treatment. The new dispute settlement mechanism contained within many of these treaties, through which the investor could directly seek recourse at the international level, had the advantage of no longer needing to engage the investor's state and rely on its political decision as to whether or not to pursue the claim on behalf of its national. As it transpired, however, this advantage would also be its disadvantage, as there would now be no external filter operating on the decision-making processes—in other words, the decision to pursue the claim would rest entirely with the investor. And it is the way in which investors have ultimately sought to use international investment agreements that has been particularly problematic and at the root of so much of the controversy surrounding investor-state arbitration.

---

[30] In the Matter of an Arbitration under Chap. 11 of the North American Free Trade Agreement and the UNCITRAL Rules of 1976 between *William Ralph Clayton et al v Government of Canada*, Award, 10 March 2015.

[31] In the Matter of an Arbitration under Chap. 11 of the North American Free Trade Agreement and the UNCITRAL Rules of 1976 between *William Ralph Clayton et al v Government of Canada*, Dissenting Opinion of Professor Donald McCrae, 10 March 2015.

Popular discontent took the form of widespread protests at the negotiations of the Multilateral Agreement on Investment (MAI) in the late 1990s.[32] There was certainly a more generalised anti-globalisation element to the demonstrations, but core concerns surrounded the potential impact of the MAI on host state regulatory space and the effective prioritising of the interests of foreign investors over domestic needs.[33] Similar sentiments are currently manifesting in public opposition to TTIP and TPP. Although concerns from public interest groups have figured throughout the intervening period, particularly at the extent of the substantive protections contained within BITs and the operation of investor-state arbitration, wider public engagement with the controversial issues surrounding ISDS subsided somewhat following the shelving of the MAI.

The opposition to TTIP has reportedly taken some officials by surprise,[34] apparently unanticipated because, as there are already more than 3000 international investment agreements in place, it was thought that this agreement would be relatively uncontroversial. However, much like the MAI in the 1990s, the spectre of a particularly significant treaty has again galvanised large sections of public opinion, operating almost as a lightning rod for a variety of globalisation-type complaints.[35] Given the size of the trading blocs involved, the scale of the treaty certainly sets it apart from the several thousand BITs that are already in existence. And it is this sense of scale that also generates an idea or image of the treaty and what it represents in a way that individual BITs do not. It is this, perhaps, that has captured the imagination of the public.

There are, of course, concrete concerns behind the public protests. And, although some activist material is wildly inaccurate and incendiary, there have recently been several high-profile cases against developed states that illustrate the adverse consequences of being a party to international investment agreements. In this regard, it

---

[32] See the text of the draft Multilateral Agreement on Investment (MAI) at OECD Negotiating Group on the Multilateral Agreement on Investment, Draft Consolidated Text, 22 April 1998 http://www1.oecd.org/daf/mai/pdf/ng/ng987r1e.pdf (last accessed 27 April 2015).

[33] McDonald (1998); Tieleman K (2000) The Failure of the Multilateral Agreement on Investment and the Absence of a Global Public Policy Network: A Case Study for the UN Vision Project on Global Public Policy Networks. http://old.gppi.net/fileadmin/gppi/Tieleman_MAI_GPP_Network.pdf (last accessed 27 April 2015); see also the activist commentary at Nova S and Sforza-Roderick M (undated) "Worse than NAFTA": A Commentary on the Multilateral Agreement on Investment. Preamble Center for Public Policy, www.globalpolicy.org/socecon/bwi-wto/mai2.htm (last accessed 27 April 2015); for a further example of NGO commentary, see Joint NGO Statement on the Multilateral Agreement on Investment, NGO/OECD Consultation on the MAI, 27 October 1997, http://bocs.hu/igaz-a-1.htm (last accessed 27 April 2015).

[34] Barkin N, Thousands in Germany Protest against Europe-US Trade Deal, Reuters, 18 April 2015 http://www.reuters.com/article/2015/04/18/us-trade-protests-germany-idUSKBN0N90LO20150418 (last accessed 20 April 2015).

[35] Barkin N, Thousands in Germany Protest against Europe-US Trade Deal, Reuters, 18 April 2015 http://www.reuters.com/article/2015/04/18/us-trade-protests-germany-idUSKBN0N90LO20150418 (last accessed 20 April 2015), for example, one demonstrator interviewed in Barkin's article is protesting against increased importation of genetically-modified food rather than ISDS *per se*.

is the two Vattenfall claims brought against Germany and the Philip Morris arbitration brought against Australia that have, in particular, crystallised for the public the objections to the inclusion of ISDS within TTIP. The concerns expressed at these cases, in fact, reflect criticisms that have been directed towards both the substantive protections guaranteed in international investment agreements and the procedural frameworks of ISDS for some time. Accordingly, those core criticisms are examined in the next sections of this article.

2.1 Substantive Protections

International investment agreements provide a series of standard protections to the investing nationals of state parties to the treaties and, although the specific terminology varies from treaty to treaty, the key protections are essentially the same. They tend to consist of prohibitions on uncompensated expropriation and guarantees of fair and equitable treatment, national treatment, most-favoured-nation treatment, and full protection and security.[36] On the face of it, the provisions themselves appear relatively innocuous. Aimed at ensuring that foreign investors are not subjected to arbitrary and discriminatory seizures of their investments, there is no serious question as to the need for some form of foreign investment protection within international law. However, it is the way in which these provisions have been used, the interpretations that have been given to these rather vague terms, and their application to public welfare regulation and decision-making that have generated so much controversy.

In the late 1990s and into the 2000s, international investment agreements began to be invoked to challenge public welfare regulation and governmental decision-making that impacted in a negative way on foreign-owned investments.[37] Scholarly criticism emerged almost immediately highlighting the very different way in which investor protection measures were being used in these cases from their traditional purpose as a ‘shield’ against arbitrary state action.[38] Commentators were quick to point out that this amounted to using the instrument as a ‘sword’, attacking legitimate public welfare regulation and encroaching into domestic host state policy space. And that this was inappropriate; that the policy decisions of governments on the health and environment of their citizens should not be determined by investment

[36] McLachlan et al. (2007), p. 207.

[37] See, for example, *Ethyl Corporation v Canada*, Jurisdiction Phase, (1999) 38 *International Legal Materials* 708; *Pope & Talbot v Canada*, Award on the Merits of Phase II, 10 April 2001; *S. D. Myers Inc* v. *Canada* (UNCITRAL, First Partial Award of 13 November 2000); *Compania del Desarrollo de Santa Elena S.A.* v. *The Republic of Costa Rica*, (2000) 39 *International Legal Materials* 1317; *Metalclad Corporation* v. *United Mexican States*, ICSID Case No. ARB(AF)/97/1, Award of 30 August 2000; *Methanex Corporation* v. *United States of America*, (2005) 44 *International Legal Materials* 1345.

[38] Soloway (2000), pp. 123–125; Been and Beauvais (2003), pp. 33–37; Sands (2002).

rules alone; and that governments should not be forced to look over their shoulders, factoring into their public welfare decision-making the threat of investor-state arbitration.[39]

The retort often made was that illegitimate, protectionist motives were behind policy decisions made in these early cases in the guise of public welfare regulation.[40] My view has always been that while there are undoubtedly examples of capricious state decision-making from which foreign investors rightly need compensation, it is unacceptable to include legitimate public welfare regulation within the scope of investment protection. The risk that legitimate measures taken to protect the health and environment of citizens could impact on commercial activities is a standard business risk. However, there have been investment awards that state otherwise, notably the award in *Azurix*, in which the tribunal stated: "For the Tribunal, the issue is not so much whether the measure concerned is legitimate and serves a public purpose, but whether it is a measure that, being legitimate and serving a public purpose, should give rise to a compensation claim."[41]

These sentiments were also behind well-known statements made by the tribunal in the *Santa Elena* award[42]:

> While an expropriation or taking for environmental reasons may be classified as a taking for a public purpose, and thus may be legitimate, the fact that the Property was taken for this reason does not affect either the nature or the measure of the compensation to be paid for the taking. That is, the purpose of protecting the environment for which the Property was taken does not alter the legal character of the taking for which adequate compensation must be paid. The international source of the obligation to protect the environment makes no difference.
>
> Expropriatory environmental measures – no matter how laudable and beneficial to society as a whole – are, in this respect, similar to any other expropriatory measures that a state may take in order to implement its policies: where property is expropriated, even for environmental purposes, whether domestic or international, the state's obligation to pay compensation remains.

The argument that environmental or health-related regulation can be used for protectionist purposes does not answer the criticism that investment law encompasses those measures that are not. There have, of course, been decisions that reflect such a viewpoint, the leading case being *Methanex*, in which the tribunal stated[43]:

---

[39] Soloway (2000); Sands (2002); Mann H, von Moltke K (1999) NAFTA's Chap. 11 and the Environment: Addressing the Impacts of the Investor-State Process on the Environment. International Institute for Sustainable Development (IISD) www.iisd.org/pdf/nafta.pdf (last accessed 27 April 2015); Peterson (2005); Tienhaara (2011).

[40] See, for example, Weiler (2005).

[41] *Azurix Corp.* v. *Republic of Argentina*, ICSID Case No. ARB/01/12, Award of July 14, 2006, para. 310.

[42] *Compania del Desarrollo de Santa Elena, S.A.*, v. *The Republic of Costa Rica*, (2000) 39 *International Legal Materials* 1317, 1329.

[43] *Methanex Corporation v United States of America* (2005) 44 International Legal Materials 1345, 1456.

> As a matter of general international law, a non-discriminatory regulation for a public purpose, which is enacted in accordance with due process and which affects, inter alia, a foreign investor or investment is not deemed expropriatory and compensatory unless specific commitments had been given to the then putative foreign investor contemplating investment that the government would refrain from such regulation.

This line of reasoning was a positive development, but it also drew attention to a core structural issue within investor-state arbitration—there is no appeals mechanism or system of precedent by which subsequent cases would be obliged to follow the *Methanex* approach. It is open to arbitrators to take a contrary view. In fact, it was the *Azurix* case that illustrated this problematic aspect of the decentralised structure of investor-state arbitration. The case was decided after *Methanex*, but followed the more expansive approach to legitimate public welfare regulation of a decision taken prior to *Methanex*,[44] *Tecnicas Medioambientales Tecmed, SA v United Mexican States* (*Tecmed*).[45] In so doing, it ensured that environmental and health-related measures remained exposed to challenges from foreign investors. And this concern that legitimate policy decisions are being targeted has been borne out by the *Vattenfall*[46] and *Philip Morris*[47] claims.

2.1.1 Vattenfall I and II

The *Vattenfall* disputes are a two-step story of a Swedish company's use of ISDS against Germany—the first stage constituting arbitration triggered by environmental conditions attached to emissions and water use permits for the operation of a coal-fired power plant; the second set of arbitral proceedings by a planned nuclear energy phase-out. In the 2009 proceedings filed with ICSID, the complaint arose out of the planned construction and operation by Vattenfall of a new coal-fired power plant on the River Elbe in Germany. The local authority issued a licence but with requirements on water quality, emissions restrictions and water use constraints that allegedly rendered the project unviable. Vattenfall filed a Request for

[44] *Methanex Corporation v United States of America* (2005) 44 International Legal Materials 1345, 1456.

[45] *Tecnicas Medioambientales Tecmed, SA v United Mexican States* (2004) 43 *International Legal Materials* 133.

[46] *Vattenfall AB et al V Federal Republic of Germany*, Request for Arbitration, 30 March 2009, ICSID No. ARB/09/6 http://www.italaw.com/documents/VattenfallRequestforArbitration.pdf (last accessed 30 May 2015); *Vattenfall AB et al v Federal Republic of Germany*, ICSID No. ARB/12/12.

[47] *Philip Morris Asia Limited v The Commonwealth of Australia*, In the Matter of Arbitration under the Arbitration Rules of the United Nations Commission on International Trade Law 2010, Notice of Arbitration, (21 November 2011), available at http://www.ag.gov.au/tobaccoplainpackaging (last accessed 30 May 2015).

Arbitration with ICSID seeking €1.4 billion in damages. Ultimately, the matter was settled with Germany agreeing to slacken the environmental standards and issue a significantly less exacting permit.[48]

Vattenfall II was prompted by Germany's policy review of its nuclear energy programme following the 2011 Fukushima disaster in Japan, which resulted in a governmental decision to phase-out the use of nuclear energy by 2022.[49] This shift in environmental policy was inherently directed towards the nuclear industry and would inevitably have substantial financial implications for those industry actors in the field. Vattenfall and several other owners of nuclear facilities within Germany took exception to the new regulation, asserting that this was not a permitted measure under the Energy Charter Treaty.[50] A Notice of Arbitration was filed by Vattenfall on 31 May 2012 and the matter is currently progressing through a series of procedural hearings.[51] The company is said to be suing for compensation in the realm of €4.7 billion. However, as the documents have not been made public, which is troubling given the public interest issues at stake, it is not possible to verify this or the exact bases for the complaint under the Energy Charter Treaty. The assumption is that the complaint will involve allegations of uncompensated expropriation and a breach of the fair and equitable treatment standard. Despite the opaque nature of the conduct of this particular arbitral claim, what is clear is that it is a direct attack on the legitimate domestic environmental policy-making of the host state. And, irrespective of the outcome, the very fact that claims such as this can be filed against host states under international investment agreements is a cause for concern.

2.1.2 Philip Morris

Actions taken by Philip Morris against the increasingly restrictive tobacco measures implemented by several states illustrate exactly the potential problems of international investment agreements and their dispute settlement systems. In Uruguay's case, the restrictions take the form of conditions on marketing, prohibitions on the descriptions 'mild' and 'light', and requirements of graphic public

---

[48] See the discussion in Bernasconi-Osterwalder N and Hoffman R (2013) The German Nuclear Phase-Out Put to the Test in International Investment Arbitration: Background to the New Dispute *Vattenfall v Germany II*. IISD https://www.tni.org/files/download/vattenfall-icsid-case_oct2013.pdf (last accessed 6 June 20015).

[49] The Thirteenth Amendment to the Atomic Energy Act (13. AtGÄndG v. 31.07.2011, BGBl I S. 1704 (No. 43)).

[50] Energy Charter Treaty, Annex I, Final Act of the European Energy Charter Conference, 17 December 1994, 34 ILM 373.

[51] *Vattenfall AB et al v Federal Republic of Germany*, ICSID No. ARB/12/12.

health warnings on the packaging of cigarettes.[52] Philip Morris alleges that this constitutes an uncompensated expropriation of the company's intellectual property, a breach of the fair and equitable treatment standard, and unreasonable impairment of the use of its investment in violation of the Switzerland–Uruguay BIT.[53]

Philip Morris Asia Ltd is also pursuing a claim against Australia under the Hong Kong–Australia BIT.[54] The new Australian measures require tobacco products to be packaged in plain material devoid of all logos or branding images.[55] The allegations are that this prevents the full use of Philip Morris' intellectual property and, accordingly, expropriates its investment, violates the fair and equitable treatment standard, and fails to provide full protection and security to its investments as required under the treaty. A further argument relates to the suitability of the particular measures taken. In this regard, Philip Morris argues that the plain packaging requirements do not assist with the purported public health purpose of the regulation, but will, instead, feed the black market trade in illegal cigarettes.[56] The proceedings are on-going. However, as other countries are considering the introduction of 'plain packaging' tobacco legislation, the outcome of this investor-state dispute will be significant.[57]

---

[52] Peterson L, Uruguay: Philip Morris Files First-Known Investment Treaty Claim Against Tobacco Regulations, Investment Arbitration Reporter, 3 March 2010 https://www.iareporter.com/articles/philip-morris-files-first-known-investment-treaty-claim-against-tobacco-regulations/ (last accessed 7 August 2015).

[53] *Philip Morris Brand Sàrl (Switzerland), Philip Morris Products S.A. (Switzerland) and Abal Hermanos S.A. (Uruguay) v. Oriental Republic of Uruguay*, (ICSID Case No. ARB/10/7); Accord entre la Confédération Suisse et la République Orientale de l'Uruguay Concernant la Promotion et la Protection Réciproques des Investissements (entered into 7 October 1988), http://investmentpolicyhub.unctad.org/Download/TreatyFile/2327 (last accessed 7 August 2015); see also the discussion in International Centre for Trade and Sustainable Development, Tobacco Company Files Claim Against Uruguay Over Labelling Laws, Bridges Weekly Trade News Digest, 10 March 2010, http://www.ictsd.org/bridges-news/bridges/news/tobacco-company-files-claim-against-uruguay-over-labelling-laws (last accessed 15 June 2015).

[54] Agreement between the Government of Hong Kong and the Government of Australia for the Promotion and the Protection of Investments, 1748 UNTS 385 (signed 15 September 1993, entered into force 15 October 1993); *Philip Morris Asia Limited v The Commonwealth of Australia*, In the Matter of Arbitration under the Arbitration Rules of the United Nations Commission on International Trade Law 2010, Notice of Arbitration, 21 November 2011, https://www.ag.gov.au/Internationalrelations/InternationalLaw/Documents/Philip%20Morris%20Asia%20Limited%20Notice%20of%20Arbitration%2021%20November%202011.pdf (last accessed 07 August 2015).

[55] *Tobacco Plain Packaging Act* (2011), Cth Act No. 148 of 2011.

[56] *Philip Morris Asia Limited v The Commonwealth of Australia*, Notice of Arbitration, 21 November 2011.

[57] The United Kingdom, New Zealand, Ireland, France, Canada, Finland, Norway and Turkey have introduced initiatives, enacted legislation, or are considering proposals to introduce more restrictive tobacco regulations, ASH, Standardised Tobacco Packaging, (March 2015), http://ash.org.uk/files/documents/ASH_877.pdf (last accessed 24 May 2015); see also Saez C, 'France Spearheads Push for Plain Packaging of Tobacco Products', Intellectual Property Watch, 23 July 2015, http://www.ip-watch.org/2015/07/23/france-spearheads-push-for-plain-packaging-of-tobacco-products/ (last accessed 24 August 2015).

There is no serious contention that the regulation in these instances was not enacted for legitimate health purposes. In light of this, the particularly aggressive approach adopted by Philip Morris has attracted the attention of the public more generally, causing consternation at the encroachment into host state domestic policy space. Rather unreasonably, the public disquiet at this case is often characterised within sectors of the investment legal community as an ill-informed over-reaction and that this claim has become the 'poster-boy case for anti-ISDS lobbyists'.[58] The dismissive way in which legitimate public concerns are framed is unfortunate. It would seem that even raising concerns is, at times, equated with being uninformed. In fact, far from being the 'one-off', outlier claims pro-ISDS advocates assert,[59] the *Philip Morris* cases are precisely the type of challenge that is permitted under a substantial number of existing international investment agreements.

Whether a particular claim is ultimately successful is, of course, another issue. And certainly there are commentators strongly suggesting that these tobacco claims will not succeed on the merits.[60] Interestingly, this has also been put forward as a reason to discredit those who cite the *Philip Morris* cases when expressing concern at ISDS. The argument is that to condemn ISDS at this point is to pre-judge the outcome of the *Philip Morris* arbitrations and that the cases may well result in decisions favourable to the states involved.[61] However, this *ad hoc* approach to answering a systemic question does not address a fundamental issue—whether investor-state arbitration is a process governments should have to endure in order to implement legitimate public welfare measures at all, a process that can last years and can require vast legal resources to defend.

The inappropriate encroachment into domestic policy and regulatory space that is clear in the *Vattenfall* and *Philip Morris* cases has, however, made an impact on the way in which ISDS is viewed more generally. And that awareness has generated new explorations into retaining ISDS but in a form designed to prevent such cases arising in the future. In particular, this is one debate that is currently occurring in the TTIP negotiations. This and other responses to the criticisms of ISDS are considered below in Part II of this article. First, however, further issues relating to the structural and procedural frameworks of ISDS will be addressed.

[58] Sentiments such as this are regularly expressed on the email list-serve OGEMID, which operates on a Chatham House Rule basis so that statements cannot be attributed to individuals.

[59] Statements expressed on E-mail list-serve OGEMID.

[60] See, for example, Voon and Mitchell (2011).

[61] Statements expressed on E-mail list-serve OGEMID.

2.2 Procedural, Institutional and Cultural Concerns

Criticism over the last 15 years has also been directed at aspects of ISDS that go beyond the substantive provisions contained within international investment agreements. It has extended to the procedural and institutional structures of investor-state arbitration, focusing on the lack of transparency, restrictions on public participation, arbitral practice, its commercial emphasis, and the lack of an appeals mechanism. The sum of these individual issues has pointed to fundamental systemic problems within ISDS, leading commentators to question the legitimacy of investor-state arbitration altogether.[62]

In some respects, the issues arise out of the institutional borrowing from international commercial arbitration, which, while appropriate in a private, commercial setting, is inappropriate for matters involving actions against states. Furthermore, counsel and arbitrators often work in both arbitral fields, which has contributed to the blurring of the cultures. In particular, it is the confidentiality that is such an important feature of international commercial arbitral proceedings that has been so controversial in its translation into investor-state arbitration.[63] Critics have long pointed to the difference in nature of the disputes in these two separate forms of international arbitration, emphasising the public interest that is inherently at play in investment claims. For example[64]:

(a) Investment disputes often involve public service sectors;
(b) Government public welfare regulation may be in dispute;
(c) Defence costs and funding compensation awards will be drawn from public budgets; and
(d) The threat of arbitration may have a 'chilling' effect on government policy, decision-making or regulation.

For these reasons, it is important that the proceedings and resolution of investment disputes are not confidential; these reasons serve to explain why the international commercial arbitration model is so inappropriate for ISDS.[65] The transparency concerns arising out of the public interest element of ISDS have

---

[62] Van Harten (2007); Tienhaara (2006); Brower et al. (2003).

[63] Van Harten (2007); see also Editorial, The Secret Trade Courts, The New York Times, 27 September 2004 http://www.nytimes.com/2004/09/27/opinion/27mon3.html?_r=0 (last accessed 5 July 2015); DePalma A, Nafta's Powerful Little Secret; Obscure Tribunals Settle Disputes, but Go Too Far, Critics Say, The New York Times, 11 March 2001 http://www.nytimes.com/2001/03/11/business/nafta-s-powerful-little-secret-obscure-tribunals-settle-disputes-but-go-too-far.html (last accessed 5 July 2015).

[64] See Tienhaara (2007); see also the discussion in Miles (2010); IISD (2007) Revising the UNCITRAL Arbitration Rules to Address Investor-State Arbitrations. http://www.iisd.org/pdf/2007/investment_revising_uncitral_arbitration.pdf (last accessed 8 June 2015).

[65] Tienhaara (2007); IISD (2007) Revising the UNCITRAL Arbitration Rules to Address Investor-State Arbitrations. http://www.iisd.org/pdf/2007/investment_revising_uncitral_arbitration.pdf (last accessed 8 June 2015); see also the discussion in De Brebandere (2014), pp. 149–152.

essentially been two-fold, centring, on the one hand, on access to documents; and, on the other, on access to the oral hearings. As the default position for many years in ISDS has been that of little or no public access to even basic documents and pleadings and of closed hearings, transparency became a particularly controversial issue. This debate also flowed into the separate but linked issue of public participation and whether *amicus curiae* briefs and participation in oral hearings should be permitted. Resistance stemmed from the concern that such exposure and involvement could compromise confidential information, delay or lengthen proceedings, increase costs, or waste time with irrelevant material.[66]

At a certain level, there has increasingly been a greater appreciation that procedural structures, frameworks, and the specific rules themselves impact not only on the practical aspects of the conduct of hearings, but can, in fact, also shape the cultural setting for the hearing and the way in which substantive issues are considered by tribunals. Steps have recently been taken to increase transparency and public participation in ISDS through different mechanisms, largely in response to criticisms of the system. This can be seen in the express inclusion of measures in more recent investment treaties[67]; through the creative use of rules by arbitral tribunals,[68] and in the revision of procedural rules as seen with ICSID in 2006,[69] so that provision can be made for open hearings, access to documents, and the submission of amicus briefs. And, undoubtedly, the most significant moves in this direction have been the recent adoption of the UNCITRAL procedural rules on transparency in 2013[70] and the UN Convention on Transparency in Treaty-Based Investor-State Arbitration in 2014.[71]

In terms of public participation, there have, of course, been a number of controversial issues. Certainly, the extent of public access in individual cases has been one; and, indeed, whether public participation makes any difference to outcomes has been another. But with procedural issues such as transparency and public participation, the point is perhaps not so much whether in any particular case, the

---

[66] Rubins (2006); see also Bastin (2012).

[67] See, for example, Agreement between Canada and the Federal Republic of Nigeria for the Promotion and Protection of Investments (signed 6 May 2014), http://www.international.gc.ca/trade-agreements-accords-commerciaux/agr-acc/fipa-apie/nigeria.aspx?lang=eng (last accessed 12 June 2015); see also the discussion in Newcombe (2007).

[68] See, for example, the creative interpretation of Article 15(1) of the UNCITRAL Rules in *Methanex Corporation v United States of America* (2005) 44 International Legal Materials 1345 to permit the submission of *amicus curiae* briefs.

[69] ICSID, Rules of Procedure for Arbitration Proceedings (2006) https://icsid.worldbank.org/ICSID/StaticFiles/basicdoc/CRR_English-final.pdf (last accessed 15 June 2015).

[70] UNCITRAL, Rules on Transparency in Treaty-based Investor-State Arbitration (adopted 16 December 2013, entered into force 1 April 2014) https://www.uncitral.org/pdf/english/texts/arbitration/arb-rules-revised/arb-rules-revised-2010-e.pdf (last accessed 15 June 2015).

[71] United Nations Convention on Transparency in Treaty-based Investor-State Arbitration (adopted 10 December 2014, opened for signature 17 March 2015), http://www.uncitral.org/pdf/english/texts/arbitration/transparency-convention/Transparency-Convention-e.pdf (last accessed 15 June 2015).

actual submissions from an *amicus* brief were influential in the outcome of the dispute. The significance is more generalised than that—it is more that with a culture of openness, where there are procedures for open hearings and receiving *amicus* briefs, then the system as a whole benefits, certainly in terms of questions of legitimacy. And the legitimacy of ISDS has not been served well by a number of other features of investor-state arbitration.

One such controversial feature is the lack of an appeals mechanism. ISDS has a decentralised, flat structure under which the disputes are determined by non-permanent tribunals assembled to hear solely the immediate claim. As a system, it follows the model developed for international commercial arbitration, which, as it not only prioritises confidentiality, but also finality of result and speed of resolution, does not have any facility for appeals. Whilst appropriate for international commercial arbitration, there are other factors at play in ISDS. In particular, the public interest involved in investor-state disputes means that ensuring consistency of approach and the capacity to correct errors of law are imperatives—and these are not given the same significance within the international commercial arbitration model. Inconsistency in investment awards has become increasingly problematic where decisions on the same issues conflict, even to the extent of contrary outcomes on essentially the same set of facts.[72] For critics, this has added to the legitimacy deficit within the current investor-state dispute resolution system and driven calls for the establishing of an appeals mechanism.[73]

In response to the controversy, ICSID turned its attention to the need for an appeals facility, acknowledging the potential for inconsistent awards as a systemic problem.[74] After initially exploring the issue with gusto, the review slowed somewhat as several states took a negative view of the proposal.[75] The arguments against an appeals mechanism are varied. However, recurring grounds have included that there are no fundamental problems with ISDS to justify such a significant structural change, that there are no realistic options currently 'on the table' for consideration,

[72] See, for example, the *Lauder Cases: In the Matter of a UNCITRAL Arbitration between Ronald S. Lauder v the Czech Republic*, Final Award, 3 September 2001; *CME Czech Republic B.V. (the Netherlands)* v. *Czech Republic* (UNCITRAL, Partial Award of 13 September 2001; Final Award of 14 March 2003); see also the discussion in Yannaca-Small (2008), pp. 1009–1010; see also Joubin-Bret (2008).

[73] For views supportive of an appellate facility, see, for example, the discussion in Van Harten (2007), pp. 153–75, 180; see also Brower (2003); Gal-Or (2008); Gantz (2006).

[74] ICSID (2004) Possible Improvements of the Framework for ICSID Arbitration. Discussion Paper https://icsid.worldbank.org/apps/ICSIDWEB/resources/Documents/Possible%20Improvements%20of%20the%20Framework%20of%20ICSID%20Arbitration.pdf (last accessed 7 August 2015).

[75] Tams C (2006) An Appealing Option? The Debate about an ICSID Appellate Structure. 57 Essays in Transnational Economic Law, Institut für Wirtschaftsrecht, http://www.wirtschaftsrecht.uni-halle.de/sites/default/files/altbestand/Heft57.pdf (last accessed 7 August 2015), p. 6; Investment Treaty News, ICSID Member-Governments OK Watered-Down Changes to Arbitration Process, (29 March 2006), www.iisd.org/pdf/2006/itn_mar29_2006.pdf (last accessed 17 May 2015); see the discussion in Walsh (2006), pp. 444–445.

and that an appeals facility goes against the *raison d'être* of international arbitration as a relatively quick and less expensive alternative to domestic litigation.[76] And despite the conclusion of treaties that anticipated the future creation of an appeals facility for investor-state disputes,[77] there was little progress on this point.

Recently, however, the debate on an appellate mechanism has experienced a resurgence in the controversy surrounding TTIP with proposals not only for an appeals facility being discussed, but also those for a permanent investment court to hear both disputes at first instance and on appeal.[78] In particular, the European Union (EU) paper asserts that a restructured investment dispute settlement system with an appellate body would not only assist with attaining consistency in awards and predictability in the law, but also with enhancing the legitimacy of the system. And it is not limiting its proposals to the TTIP context, but envisages a wider, permanent, multilateral, two-tier adjudication system, stating[79]:

> [The proposals] suggest steps that can be taken to transform the system towards one which functions more like traditional courts systems, by making their appointment to serve as arbitrators permanent, to move towards assimilating their qualifications to those of national judges, and to introduce an appeal system.
>
> The sections below suggest that in parallel the EU should work towards the establishment of an international investment court and appellate mechanism with tenured judges with the vocation to replace the bilateral mechanism which would be established. This would be a more operational solution in the sense of applying to multiple agreements with multiple partners but it will require a level of international consensus that will need to be built. It is suggested to pursue this in parallel with establishing bilateral appeal mechanisms. These changes are intended to be the stepping stones towards a permanent multilateral system for investment disputes.

As can be seen from the TTIP EU proposal, the legitimacy issues are not limited to the need for an appellate mechanism, but also involve the lack of independence of arbitrators; not at an individual level, but as a systemic issue. In particular,

---

[76] See the discussion in Tams C (2006) An Appealing Option? The Debate about an ICSID Appellate Structure. 57 Essays in Transnational Economic Law, Institut für Wirtschaftsrecht, http://www.wirtschaftsrecht.uni-halle.de/sites/default/files/altbestand/Heft57.pdf (last accessed 7 August 2015), p. 34; see also the discussion on the origins of commercial arbitration as an alternative to litigation in Van Harten (2007), pp. 59–61; see the critiques in Legum (2008); see also Paulsson (2008); see also the discussion in Sammartano (2003), pp. 388–391.

[77] See for example Treaty Between the United States of America and the Oriental Republic of Uruguay Concerning the Encouragement and Reciprocal Protection of Investment (2005) Art. 28.10, http://investmentpolicyhub.unctad.org/Download/TreatyFile/2380 (last accessed 7 August 2015).

[78] EU (2015) Investment in TTIP and Beyond—the Path for Reform: Enhancing the Right to Regulate and Moving from Current ad hoc Arbitration towards an Investment Court. Concept Paper http://trade.ec.europa.eu/doclib/docs/2015/may/tradoc_153408.PDF (last accessed 8 June 2015).

[79] EU (2015) Investment in TTIP and Beyond—the Path for Reform: Enhancing the Right to Regulate and Moving from Current ad hoc Arbitration towards an Investment Court. Concept Paper, p. 4 http://trade.ec.europa.eu/doclib/docs/2015/may/tradoc_153408.PDF (last accessed 8 June 2015).

concerns have been expressed at what has been termed 'the revolving door' of appointments, whereby arbitrators in one dispute are not only permitted to act as counsel in other investment disputes, but where 'counsel selecting an arbitrator who, next time around when the arbitrator is counsel, selects the previous counsel as arbitrator.[80] Potentially, the decisions arbitrators make can impact upon the law applicable to later cases on which they also work as counsel.[81] Critics have pointed to the conflict of interest that arises in such circumstances and the rule of law principles this implicates.[82] I consider that such systemic issues also raise significant questions about the idea that investor-state arbitration promotes the rule of law.[83] Proponents of this view come at the issue from the perspective of monitoring host state conduct and encouraging domestic compliance with rule of law principles, but, in so doing, and in the rush to embrace the term 'global administrative law', perhaps, overlook the less admirable and rather more problematic rule of law implications of the way in which ISDS itself operates in practice.

There are, in fact, also further troubling issues relating to the appointment process for arbitrators. There is no central governing framework, there is no security of tenure, and the parties, or the arbitral facility, select the arbitrators. It essentially operates as a market place for obtaining appointments and one that values not only business acumen, but also the level of authority that will likely be generated within the internal dynamics of the arbitral tribunal.[84] In this regard, Puig

---

[80] Van Harten, (2007), pp. 172–173; Buergenthal (2006), p. 498; Cosbey A et al. (2004) Investment and Sustainable Development: A Guide to the Use and Potential of International Investment Agreements International. IISD http://www.iisd.org/pdf/2004/investment_invest_and_sd.pdf (last accessed 8 May 2015).

[81] Buergenthal (2006), p. 498; Van Harten (2007), pp. 172–173; Cosbey A et al. (2004) Investment and Sustainable Development: A Guide to the Use and Potential of International Investment Agreements International. IISD, p. 6 http://www.iisd.org/pdf/2004/investment_invest_and_sd.pdf (last accessed 8 May 2015); see also the comments of Philippe Sands in Sulaimain U, London Barrister Opposes Arbitrators Acting as Counsel, Global Arbitration Review, 7 October 2009 http://globalarbitrationreview.com/news/article/18979/london-barrister-opposes-arbitrators-acting-counsel/ (last accessed 8 May 2015).

[82] Cosbey A et al. (2004) Investment and Sustainable Development: A Guide to the Use and Potential of International Investment Agreements International. IISD http://www.iisd.org/pdf/2004/investment_invest_and_sd.pdf (last accessed 8 May 2015); Buergenthal (2006), p. 498; Van Harten, (2007), pp. 172–173; Philippe Sands in Sulaimain U, London Barrister Opposes Arbitrators Acting as Counsel, Global Arbitration Review, 7 October 2009 http://globalarbitrationreview.com/news/article/18979/london-barrister-opposes-arbitrators-acting-counsel/ (last accessed 8 May 2015); Miles (2013), p. 377.

[83] See, for example, Schill S (2006) Fair and Equitable Treatment under Investment Treaties as an Embodiment of the Rule of Law. IILJ Working Paper 2006/6 (Global Administrative Law Series) http://iilj.org/publications/documents/2006-6-GAL-Schill-web.pdf (last accessed 25 August 2014); Kingsbury B and Schill S (2009) Investor-State Arbitration as Governance: Fair and Equitable Treatment, Proportionality and the Emerging Global Administrative Law. IILJ Working Paper 2009/6 (Global Administrative Law Series) http://www.iilj.org/publications/documents/2009-6.KingsburySchill.pdf (last accessed 25 August 2014); Kalderimis (2011); Kotuby (2011), p. 164; Postiga (2013).

[84] Sornarajah (2003), p. 17; Dezalay and Garth (1996), pp. 8–9, 70; Puig (2014).

describes an awareness and valuing within the market of individual arbitrators' 'symbolic capital' and 'insider status'.[85] It is, therefore, an inherently conservative model that does not reward bold decision-making and is less inclined to welcome interpretations incorporating principles from other fields that will significantly shift prevailing approaches.[86]

There has also long been criticism of the lack of diversity amongst arbitrators in investor-state arbitration.[87] As Puig discusses, the statistics reveal that, even now, appointments still go overwhelming to men, from a small number of developed states, and that experience in business transactions and commercial agreements is significant in obtaining arbitral appointments.[88] This is not to say that arbitrators are not drawn from a pool of academics and judges as well as commercial private practice, nor that they do not, at a conscious level, operate in an independent and impartial manner. Nor is it to say that host states do not ever prevail in the claims they face—of course, many do. But, rather, the suggestion is that the market for appointments functions in subtle ways so as to encourage emulating the established model of 'successful' arbitrators and commercial expertise is an important component of that community.[89] The concern is that these influences filter down into the interpretative approaches and decision-making processes adopted by arbitrators.[90] As essentially an epistemic community or issue network, the arbitrators in the investment sector are central to knowledge-creation within, and the development of, international investment law.[91] If the cultural base and social norms of the group operate subconsciously so as to prioritise commercial values and conservative decision-making, this will inevitably produce a particular kind of arbitral law-making. And this, in turn, suggests that progressive readings of treaties and innovation to give weight to non-commercial considerations may well be stifled through the operation of subconscious constraints before they are even conscious propositions.[92] In his discussion on the pervasive influence of a small number of elite arbitrators at the centre of the investment arbitral network, Puig argues that[93]:

> Once arbitrators become central, they are likely to remain central – indeed become even more central. This could have (and probably already has had) an impact on doctrine since

[85] Puig (2014), p. 421.

[86] Miles (2013), p. 342–345.

[87] See, for example, Shalakany (2000).

[88] Puig (2014), pp. 402, 404–405. Puig uses recent data from ICSID appointments showing that 93% of appointments went to men and, of the women appointed, three-quarters of those appointments were held by two women, Professors Brigitte Stern and Gabrielle Kaufman-Kohler, statistically pushing the overall figure to 95 %.

[89] Puig (2014); Miles (2013), pp. 342–345; Dezalay and Garth (1996), pp. 8–9, 16, 29; Borgen, (2007), pp. 724–728.

[90] Van Harten (2007), pp. 111, 125, 172–173; Dezalay and Garth (1996), pp. 8–9, 16, 29; Borgen (2007), pp. 724–728; see also the discussion in Trinh (2014), pp. 25–31.

[91] Miles (2013), pp. 342–345.

[92] Miles (2013), pp. 342–345.

[93] Puig (2014), pp. 422.

> central arbitrators will be appointed to a large number of tribunals, connect and engage with more arbitrators, and hence will influence international investment law to a greater extent. Thus, legal knowledge advanced and preferred by power-brokers, and with that their political preferences, will probably become more dominant.

In this way, the dynamics of the arbitral process operate so as to ensure that prevailing doctrines remain dominant and criticisms go unanswered.

There has, of course, been some engagement with aspects of public international law in several awards.[94] In certain instances, it resulted in an erroneous use of rules of customary international law.[95] But, more commonly, while there were references to non-investment treaties or other international instruments, there has been very little actual application of their rules.[96] Interpretative mechanisms to use principles from other fields of international law and bring about a more contextualised interpretation of international investment agreements already exist—the key one of which is Article 31(3)(c) of the Vienna Convention on the Law of Treaties. And yet, it is not readily utilised for the resolution of investment disputes.[97] Indeed, scholars have commented on the reluctance of arbitral tribunals to contextualise investor rights or interpret them against a background of non-investment obligations.[98] There is, however, an exception: One isolated way in which non-investment principles have been used within investment awards is in the context of human rights. Not so as to justify host state action or to support local communities affected by investor activities, but, rather, so as to incorporate rights to private property and to the peaceful enjoyment of possessions, framing investors' claims as human rights violations.[99] This form of selectivity in the methodology of interpretation within investor-state arbitration fuels concerns that the system prioritises commercial

---

[94] See, for example, *Marvin Roy Feldman Karpa v United Mexican States* (2001) 40 *International Legal Materials* 615; *Pope & Talbot Inc* v. *Canada* (Award on Damages) (2002) 41 *International Legal Materials* 1347; *MTD Equity Sdn. Bhd. & MTD Chile S.A.* (Decision on Annulment of 2007); *Compañía del Desarrollo de Santa Elena S.A. v. The Republic of Costa Rica,* (2000) 39 *International Legal Materials* 1317; *CMS Gas Transmission Company* (2005) 44 *International Legal Materials* 1205; *LG&E Energy Corp* ICSID Case No. ARB/03/26, Award, 25 July 2007; *CMS Gas Transmission Company* ICSID Case No. ARB/01/8, Decision on Annulment (2007).

[95] See, for example, the treatment of necessity under customary international law in *CMS Gas Transmission Co v Argentine Republic* (2005) 44 *International Legal Materials* 1205.

[96] *Compania del Desarrollo de Santa Elena S.A.* v. *The Republic of Costa Rica*, (2000) 39 *International Legal Materials* 1317; *S.D. Myers, Inc v Canada*, Partial Award (Decision on the Merits), November 2000.

[97] See the discussion in Miles (2013), pp. 307–308, 319–320; Hirsch (2008); see the discussion on a public law approach involving the use of Article 31(3)(c) in Schill (2010), pp. 23–27.

[98] Reinisch (2008), pp. 201–202; McLachlan (2008), p. 376.

[99] See, for example, *In the Matter of a UNCITRAL Arbitration between Ronald S Lauder v the Czech Republic*, Final Award, 3 September 2001; *Tecnicas Medioambientales Tecmed, SA v United Mexican States* (2004) 43 *International Legal Materials* 133; *In the Matter of a NAFTA Arbitration under UNCITRAL Arbitration Rules between International Thunderbird Gaming Corp* v. *United Mexican States*, Award, Separate Opinion, 26 January 2006, http://www.iisd.org/pdf/2006/itn_award.pdf (last accessed 10 August 2015).

interests at the expense of others and that this has negative implications for host states, which need to balance multiple interests.[100]

This approach has contributed to a further key criticism of ISDS—that, as a system, it deals with non-investment issues in an inadequate fashion. This criticism induces different responses, one of which is that such engagement is not provided for within the treaties and it is, therefore, inappropriate even to consider non-investment issues within investment claims. This position overlooks the reality that investment arbitration rarely involves solely questions of investment law, but, in fact, often engages with extraneous issues, matters of policy, and law. It is more likely, in my view, that there are at play the cultural factors discussed above. There has certainly been a reluctance to incorporate principles from other fields of international law in interpreting investment treaties and my sense is that this stems largely from the viewpoint of arbitrators that it is inappropriate to do so.

In line with this approach, I recently heard a senior scholar and arbitrator within the field assert at length during a conference presentation that it was entirely inappropriate to consider environmental matters within an ISDS context and that the drive to do so was generated by the ineffectual nature of international environmental dispute settlement bodies and therefore a desire to 'piggy-back' onto the success of ISDS. Not only did such a statement seem inherently inaccurate, but it also represented a misunderstanding of the nature of environmental disputes and the way in which they tend to be resolved through either one of a two-path structure: that of adjudication under the auspices of courts and tribunals such as the International Court of Justice or the International Tribunal for the Law of the Sea; or through the more consultative non-compliance procedures established within specific treaty regimes.[101] Specialised environmental issues *per se* and of the kind that would be seen in environmental dispute settlement mechanisms are unlikely to appear in investment arbitration. Although I may be venturing into anecdote, those statements were representative of views I have repeatedly heard for years at such events. The more usual expression of opinions along the lines of this arbitrator is to suggest that a consideration of principles from international human rights law, environmental law or labour standards would constitute an inappropriate straying into areas of social, environmental or economic policy.[102] Again, in my view, this represents a fundamental misunderstanding of the intertwining of investment with non-investment issues. These aspects are often multi-layered in investment disputes, the outcomes of which will impact not only on investment matters, but also on public welfare measures designed to protect the environment and health of a host state's citizens. And, as other critics have argued, I also share the view that the deliberate decision not to engage with the interaction and operation of these principles and explore creative interpretations of BITs is, in itself, a political decision.[103]

[100] Miles (2013), p. 330.

[101] See Sands and Peel (2012); see also Stephens (2009).

[102] Sornarajah (2003), pp. 13–17; Muchlinski (2008), p. 683.

[103] Muchlinski (2008), pp. 683–684.

3 Responses and Shifting Viewpoints

There has, indeed, been movement in response to criticisms directed towards investor-state arbitration. The core issue is whether this is the beginning of a ground-swell to continue to reform ISDS at a fundamental level; or whether this is it. Concrete responses to date have included those of the NAFTA parties, following their experiences as respondent states, drafting more 'state-friendly' Model BITs, and this in turn resulting in the emergence of the 'new generation' BITs.[104] The response to criticisms has included significant procedural shifts in ensuring greater transparency.[105] There have been calls for carve-outs to ensure host state regulatory space.[106] States have pulled out of the ICSID Convention.[107] Other states have reviewed their policies towards ISDS, Australia having a particularly pendulum-like relationship with investor-state arbitration as it swings between including and excluding ISDS provisions.[108]

Overall, there is a sense that even if the substantive law on investment protection has not yet changed dramatically, the wider environment in which it is operating has—whilst the importance of foreign investment protection is appreciated, tolerance for investment rules that operate so as to trump other interests has waned. It is clear that further reforms are still required. In particular, modifying substantive investment rules is needed so as to respond adequately to the demand for more balanced treaties and interpretations of investor protection provisions that are more responsive to host state public welfare priorities. The question is whether influential components of the investment legal community are responding appropriately to this shift yet. And, in my view, the decision of *Clayton & Bilcon v Canada* suggests that there is still some way to go in this regard.

[104] United States State Department, Treaty between the Government of the United States of America and the Government of [Country] Concerning the Encouragement and Reciprocal Protection of Investments (2012) www.ustr.gov/sites/default/files/BIT%20text%20for%20ACIEP%20Meeting.pdf (last accessed 29 April 2015); Canada, Model Foreign Investment Protection Agreement (2004) http://www.italaw.com/documents/Canadian2004-FIPA-model-en.pdf (last accessed 10.08.2015); see the discussion in Newcombe (2007), p. 9; Miles (2013), pp. 231–236.

[105] See the 2006 reforms of ICSID Arbitration Rules; see also the 2013 UNCITRAL Rules on Transparency.

[106] See, for example, European Commission Statement, Improving ISDS to Prevent Abuse - Statement by EU Trade Commissioner Karel De Gucht on the Launch of a Public Consultation on Investment Protection in TTIP, 27 March 2014, http://europa.eu/rapid/press-release_STATEMENT-14-85_en.htm (last accessed 04.04.2015).

[107] For example, Bolivia, which gave notification of its withdrawal from ICSID on 2 May 2007.

[108] See the discussion in Kurtz and Nottage (2015).

3.1 *Substantive Responses and the Right to Regulate*

The pressure to reform the substantive rules on investment protection generated in the mid–2000s several small steps towards a more balanced approach. This shift produced the so-called 'new generation BITs', in which references to sustainable development, protection of the environment, labour rights, and the health and safety of the public appeared.[109] The new emphasis tended to manifest in reoriented preambles that included the promotion of sustainable development as an objective of the treaty, the tightening of provisions on expropriation, and the introduction by Canada of a 'General Exceptions' provision modelled on that of the WTO.[110] These changes were welcome and signalled a shift in attitude, but did not significantly alter the substantive protections provided under investment treaties, particularly as, even under the Canadian exceptions clause, state measures still had to meet stringent requirements as to their application.[111] It also became clear that the state's right to regulate had remained at risk of challenge under investment treaties and, as such, pressure for further reform intensified.

Arbitrator interpretations of the treaty guarantee fair and equitable treatment have been particularly problematic in the context of governmental regulation and administrative decision-making. Expansive readings have meant that the vague treaty term is now understood to include the 'legitimate expectations' of the investor and to require a 'stable legal and business environment'. The *Tecmed* award elaborated on what this meant[112]:

> The foreign investor expects the host State to act in a consistent manner, free from ambiguity and totally transparently in its relations with the foreign investor, so that it may know beforehand any and all rules and regulations that will govern its investments, as

[109] See the discussion in Newcombe (2007), p. 399; see also Miles (2013), pp. 231–236; UNCTAD (2015) Recent Trends in IIAs and ISDS. IIA Issues Note, p. 3 http://unctad.org/en/PublicationsLibrary/webdiaepcb2015d1_en.pdf (last accessed 6 June 2015); see, for example, Agreement between Canada and the Federal Republic of Nigeria for the Promotion and Protection of Investments (signed 6 May 2014), available at http://www.international.gc.ca/trade-agreements-accords-commerciaux/agr-acc/fipa-apie/nigeria.aspx?lang=eng (last accessed 12 June 2015).

[110] See, for example, Agreement between Canada and the Federal Republic of Nigeria for the Promotion and Protection of Investments (signed 6 May 2014) http://www.international.gc.ca/trade-agreements-accords-commerciaux/agr-acc/fipa-apie/nigeria.aspx?lang=eng (last accessed 12 June 2015); see also Agreement between Canada and the Republic of Peru for the Promotion and Protection of Investments (signed 14 November 2006, entered into force 20 June 2007) http://www.treaty-accord.gc.ca/text-texte.aspx?id=105078&lang=eng (accessed 12 June 2015).

[111] Newcombe (2007), p. 401.

[112] *Tecnicas Medioambientales Tecmed, SA v United Mexican States* (2004) 43 *International Legal Materials* 133, 173. This approach has been adopted in a number of subsequent awards, such as, *MTD Equity Sdn Bhd & anor v Republic of Chile* (Award) (2005) 44 *International Legal Materials* 91, 105–106; *CMS Gas Transmission Co v Argentine Republic* (2005) 44 *International Legal Materials* 1205, 1235; *Azurix Corp. v Argentine Republic* (Award) (2006) ICSID Case No. ARB/01/12, para. 360–361, 372, 392, 408.

well as the goals of the relevant policies and administrative practices or directives, to be able to plan its investment and comply with such regulations.

Although such an approach does not mean that regulation can never change, it does have the potential to constrain governmental options in designing new public policy or seeking to implement good faith shifts in direction on public welfare issues. Certainly, the *Vattenfall II* and *Philip Morris* cases drew attention to this potential. And, reflecting the increased awareness of, and disquiet at, the use of BITs as a 'sword' rather than a 'shield', states negotiating new investment agreements have been responding to expansive arbitral interpretations of treaty standards. For example, the drafters of the EU–Canada Comprehensive Economic and Trade Agreement attempted to restrict the application of fair and equitable treatment to a specific set of circumstances.[113] The concerns, however, have remained. EU representatives recently acknowledged the potential for inappropriate encroachment into public welfare regulation and policy-making in investor-state arbitration and are seeking to ensure that TTIP ring-fences the right to regulate in the public interest from investor challenge. In this regard, the Commission stated[114]:

> To be perfectly clear, I fully agree with the many critics who claim that ISDS up until now has resulted in some very worrying examples of litigation against the state – to give you the most cited example: the case of a tobacco company against Australia challenging Australian law which obliges tobacco companies to sell their products with plain packaging.
>
> But this case is still pending and we should not prejudge the outcome or jump to conclusions on what the final outcome will be.
>
> What really does matter is that irrespective of the outcome in this case, we can already today improve the ISDS system. What we are working on already for some years will help to prevent frivolous legal actions in the future.
>
> We need to ensure the right of the state to legislate in the public interest is fully preserved.

In the course of the TTIP debate, France has also expressed its reservations at the way in which ISDS has developed and put forward its proposals for what it calls a 'new approach for solving disputes in the twenty-first century'.[115] Whatever the outcome of the TTIP deliberations, there has been a considerable shift in the negotiating environment. The response from states to a significant component of the substantive criticisms of ISDS has been to seek to draft more state-friendly treaties and it is likely that such attempts will continue. And, conceptually, then, the

---

[113] EU–Canada Comprehensive Economic and Trade Agreement, Consolidated CETA Text, 26 September 2014 http://trade.ec.europa.eu/doclib/docs/2014/September/tradoc_152806.pdf (last accessed 8 June 2015).

[114] European Commission Statement, Improving ISDS to Prevent Abuse—Statement by EU Trade Commissioner Karel De Gucht on the Launch of a Public Consultation on Investment Protection in TTIP, 27 March 2014, http://europa.eu/rapid/press-release_STATEMENT-14-85_en.htm (last accessed 4 April 2015).

[115] Hiault R, Tribunaux d'arbitrage entre entreprises et Etats: ce que défend la France, Les Echos, 2 June 2015, http://www.lesechos.fr/journal20150602/lec1_monde/021103436220-tribunaux-darbitrage-ce-que-defend-la-france-1124446.php# (last accessed 2 June 2015).

next move is to explore balancing investor rights with responsibilities. More recent BITs have tended to include provisions expressly stating that investors are obliged to comply with national laws of the host state. Tentative moves into more controversial manifestations of investor obligations have been made and it will be interesting to see the way in which this aspect develops over the next 15 years.[116]

3.2 Procedural Responses

One of the most remarkable transformations over the last decade has been the attitude towards procedural reform. Meaningful steps began to be taken with the 2006 ICSID reforms and continued with the UNCITRAL review through to the 2014 conclusion of the UN Convention on Transparency, to the point that transparency and public participation have been described as "the new normal".[117]

It was particularly significant when, in 2006, ICSID implemented a series of reforms that included new rules relating to non-disputing party access to the proceedings and the acceptance of *amicus curiae* briefs.[118] ICSID Rule 37(2) allows arbitral tribunals to receive *amicus* briefs even without the consent of the parties. The tribunal is still required to consult with the parties, but it can override their wishes. This signalled a move away from the almost absolute party autonomy of the international commercial arbitration model and a recognition of the public interest element in investor disputes. The reforms to the ICSID Rules on access to the oral hearings, however, did not go far enough as ICSID Rule 32(2) only allows non-disputing party access if the parties agree. If one party objects, therefore, the non-disputing party will be excluded from the oral hearings.[119]

Alongside the reforms to the ICSID Rules, there have also been attempts to address transparency issues in more recent bilateral investment treaties. The vast majority of current BITs do not contain transparency measures. However, following on from the inclusion of non-party participation and transparency specifications in the United States' and Canadian Model BITs,[120] 'new generation BITs' have

---

[116] See, for example, the suggestions in UNCTAD (2012) Investment Policy Framework for Sustainable Development, http://unctad.org/en/PublicationsLibrary/diaepcb2012d5_en.pdf (last accessed 24 June 2015), p. 58.

[117] Calamita (2014), p. 645.

[118] The amended ICSID Rules https://icsid.worldbank.org/ICSID/StaticFiles/basicdoc/CRR_English-final.pdf (last accessed 10.08.2015); see also the discussion in Tienhaara (2007); see Newcombe (2007), p. 388; see also McLachlan, Shore and Weiniger (2007), pp. 57–60.

[119] ICSID Rule 32(2); Newcombe (2007), p. 391; see also Tienhaara (2007).

[120] United States State Department, Treaty between the Government of the United States of America and the Government of [Country] Concerning the Encouragement and Reciprocal Protection of Investments (2012) Arts 28 and 29 www.ustr.gov/ (last accessed 29 April 2015); Canada, Model Foreign Investment Protection Agreement (2004) Arts 34, 35, 38 and 39, http://www.italaw.com/documents/Canadian2004-FIPA-model-en.pdf (last accessed 10 August 2015).

adopted a more transparent approach to the conduct of hearings.[121] These have included provisions requiring the public disclosure of pleadings, submissions, orders, and awards, and requiring that hearings must be open to the public subject to the need to protect confidential information.[122]

It was against this background of moves to modernise investor-state proceedings that attention also turned to the UNCITRAL Rules. Having been designed as a set of procedural rules to govern the conduct of international commercial arbitral proceedings, the presumption was one of confidentiality and closed hearings. A review to update the 1976 UNCITRAL Rules was undertaken from 2006, producing the revised Rules of 2010, the additional 2013 UNCITRAL Rules on Transparency in Treaty-Based Investor-State Arbitration, and, ultimately leading to the 2014 Convention on Transparency. Of primary concern in these developments was both transparency and public participation issues, such as, notification of the initiation of arbitral proceedings, publication of statements of claim and defences, access to other pleadings, capacity to accept non-disputing party and *amicus* submissions, open hearings, and publication of awards. The 2010 revisions did not address transparency or public participation concerns, leaving the presumption in place that hearings are closed unless the parties agree otherwise and that even awards are only to be made public with the consent of both parties.[123] However, recognising the distinct nature of investor-state arbitration, the Working Group was charged with drafting a set of UNCITRAL transparency rules applicable solely to treaty-based investor-state arbitration. Given the place from which transparency within the UNCITRAL Rules was starting, the document that emerged from this process was nothing short of transformative.

The 2013 Transparency Rules require the public dissemination of the notice of arbitration, the statements of claim and defence, submissions, non-disputing and third party submissions, transcripts of hearings, and orders, decisions and awards of the arbitral tribunal.[124] Hearings are also to be public.[125] There are conditions and

[121] Newcombe (2007); see also Shan (2007), pp. 652, 656; Treaty between the United States of America and the Oriental Republic of Uruguay Concerning the Encouragement and Reciprocal Protection of Investment (2005) Arts 28 and 29 http://investmentpolicyhub.unctad.org/Download/TreatyFile/2380 (last accessed 7 August 2015); see also Agreement between Canada and the Republic of Peru for the Promotion and Protection of Investments (2006) Arts 34, 35, 38 and 39 http://www.treaty-accord.gc.ca/text-texte.aspx?id=105078&lang=eng (last accessed 12 June 2015).

[122] United States State Department, Treaty between the Government of the United States of America and the Government of [Country] Concerning the Encouragement and Reciprocal Protection of Investments (2012), Arts 28 and 29 www.ustr.gov/ (last accessed 29 April 2015); Canada, Model Foreign Investment Protection Agreement (2004), Arts 38 and 39, http://www.italaw.com/documents/Canadian2004-FIPA-model-en.pdf (last accessed 10 August 2015).

[123] UNCITRAL Arbitration Rules (as revised in 2010), Arts. 28 and 34.

[124] UNCITRAL, Rules on Transparency in Treaty-based Investor-State Arbitration (adopted 16 December 2013, entered into force 1 April 2014), Art. 3.

[125] UNCITRAL, Rules on Transparency in Treaty-based Investor-State Arbitration (adopted 16 December 2013, entered into force 1 April 2014), Art. 6.

exceptions attached to these transparency measures for both documents and hearings, namely non-disclosure for protection of confidential material, the protection of the integrity of the arbitral process, and in respect of essential security interests.[126] These new requirements apply to disputes arising out of treaties concluded on or after 1 April 2014 when investor-state arbitration is initiated under the UNCITRAL Arbitration Rules, unless the parties agree otherwise. They only apply to disputes arising out of treaties concluded prior to 1 April 2014 when the Parties to the relevant treaty, or the disputing parties, agree to their application. And therein lay the problem—the new approach to transparency would not automatically apply to most of the disputes that would arise in the immediate future. Recognition of this issue led to the conclusion of the UN Convention on Transparency, the purpose of which is to extend the application of the 2013 UNCITRAL Rules of Transparency to the vast number of already existing investment treaties.[127] To date there are 11 signatories to the Convention.[128] And although it may take some time before the full transparency measures are consistently applied in investor-state arbitration, the steps taken over the last decade have not only changed the procedural landscape dramatically, but have shifted the expectations and culture of confidentiality surrounding investment disputes. Which is why it is somewhat surprising to see current high-profile investor-state arbitral proceedings under a black-out of information.

Both Germany and Sweden are signatories to the Convention and are publicly supportive of transparency and public participation measures within investor-state arbitration. And yet, the proceedings in *Vattenfall II* are being conducted under blanket confidentiality. No documents are available, no official information has been released as to the specific allegations, the basis for the claim, the sums involved, nor the defences, and there is certainly no opportunity for *amicus* submissions or public scrutiny through open hearings.[129] On issues of such importance, and in the current climate embracing transparency in investor-state arbitration, it is disappointing to see a veil of confidentiality settle across this dispute, keeping it from public view. It would be a shame if this approach were to be adopted generally in the future whenever particularly contentious matters of public interest are involved in a dispute.

---

[126] UNCITRAL, Rules on Transparency in Treaty-based Investor-State Arbitration (adopted 16 December 2013, entered into force 1 April 2014), Art. 7.

[127] United Nations Convention on Transparency in Treaty-based Investor-State Arbitration (2014).

[128] United Nations Convention on Transparency in Treaty-based Investor-State Arbitration (2014).

[129] Peterson L, Germany's Openness to ISDS Transparency and the Vattenfall Arbitration, Investment Arbitration Reporter, 2 June 2015, http://www.iareporter.com/articles/germanys-openness-to-isds-transparency-and-the-vattenfall-arbitration/ (last accessed 8 June 2015).

4 Remaining Concerns

At the outset of this article, I referred to the concerns that I still have at the substance and structure of investor-state arbitration. In particular, I mentioned the lack of appreciation of the deeper history of the field and its implications for contemporary controversies, as well as the recent attempts to frame ISDS as a component of global administrative law and a mechanism to promote the rule of law so as to bolster its legitimacy. The issues are nuanced and complex. I have recently written in depth on these aspects elsewhere,[130] so I will concentrate my comments here on one key issue—arbitral interpretation.

For all the progress made in shifting attitudes towards non-investment issues within investor-state arbitration, I am concerned that a decision such as that in the recent *Clayton & Bilcon* Award could be issued in 2015. In its dismissive treatment of the Canadian Joint Review Panel's considered and detailed analysis of the investor's sub-standard Environmental Impact Statement, the Award embodies an approach that is reminiscent of the earliest investor-state disputes involving environmental matters. There is very little regard given to the sustainability principles guiding the state bodies responsible for the decision-making at issue in this dispute and what appears to be a significant, and, in the circumstances, inappropriate, deference to the investor's stated expectations.

This case against Canada involved a proposal to develop a quarry and marine terminal at Whites Point, an ecologically sensitive area within Nova Scotia. The regulatory frameworks in place in Nova Scotia and federal Canada include requirements for environmental assessment and approval for projects such as that proposed by Bilcon. They also both have official policies of 'sustainable development', so as to encourage and promote economic development while conserving and promoting environmental quality.[131] Bilcon approached the local authorities with the proposal, whom provided encouragement. In the course of applying for the relevant approvals, the proposal was referred to a Joint Review Panel for consideration, a body established by both federal and provincial authorities, and which entailed a process requiring public hearings and the issuing of an independent report. Bilcon submitted an Environmental Impact Statement addressing the physical, biological and social impacts of the project.[132] The Joint Review Panel concluded that the assessment provided by Bilon was inadequate and recommended to the Nova Scotia and federal governments that the project be rejected.

Bilcon challenged the decision of the Joint Review Panel, not as might be expected through the Canadian court system of judicial review or appeals, but by filing a claim under NAFTA, alleging that the decision constituted a violation of

---

[130] Miles (2013); see also Miles (2014).

[131] *In the Matter of an Arbitration under Chapter 11 of the North American Free Trade Agreement and the UNCITRAL Rules of 1976 between William Ralph Clayton et al v Government of Canada*, Award, 10 March 2015, para. 10.

[132] *William Ralph Clayton et al v Government of Canada*, para. 18.

Articles 1102 and 1103 on non-discrimination and Article 1105 guaranteeing fair and equitable treatment. The basis of the complaint was two-fold: On the one hand, it rested on the argument that its legitimate expectations, created by the regulatory environment and the initial encouragement from the authorities, had been breached; and, on the other, Bilcon argued that NAFTA's protections had also been violated because the Panel's reliance on 'community core values' was a fundamentally novel term unknown to environmental assessment and that Bilcon had not been made aware that its proposal would be assessed against this criteria.

The arbitral award released earlier this year containing the decision of the majority found in favour of Bilcon, accepting the company's main arguments. I referred at the start of this article to the 'seductive' reasoning of the majority because the logic is particularly persuasive when framed in a certain way. For this, Howse, a consultant to the investor's legal team, provides an example, stating[133]:

> The panel did not dispose of the investor's proposal on the basis of an environmental analysis but rather on the motive that it was against "community values", a concept not part of the relevant legal and regulatory framework; as the majority award held, the investor had no advance notice about the employment of this extralegal analytic or any opportunity to confront it.
>
> ...Since, as I mentioned, I was involved in this dispute on behalf of Bilcon, I have to leave it to other followers of this blog to debate whether, under a treaty like NAFTA, a decision fatal to the investment that is on grounds other than those provided by law, and without prior notice of those grounds, is a matter of sufficient seriousness to be of international concern.

Described in such terms, it is impossible not to agree with Howse's view and the majority decision. But that was not quite what happened. Rather, the Joint Review Panel had a mandate "to identify, evaluate and report on the potential environmental effects of the Project on the physical, biological and human environments." In an area that has been described as a "small scale scenic, rural fishing community and economy on the ecologically sensitive and unique Bay of Fundy with its endangered right whales",[134] the Panel assessed "terrestrial effects", "marine effects", "human environment effects" and "cumulative effects". In its analysis of the human environment effects, the Panel considered that Bilcon had failed to address adequately a raft of matters, including Aboriginal peoples' resource use, community history and heritage resources, community character and attitudes, and community health and wellness. An 'umbrella' term, "community core values", was used by the Panel to group all these aspects together. It was not a "novel" or "extra-legal" term

---

[133] Howse R, The Bilcon Decision: The Environment, Local Politics and the Rule of Law, International Economic Law and Policy Blog, 20 March 2015, http://worldtradelaw.typepad.com/ielpblog/2015/03/the-bilcon-decision-the-environment-local-politics-and-the-rule-of-law.html (last accessed 11 August 2015).

[134] Eaton J, Digby Neck Quarry Bilcon Case: Tribunal Decision and Dissent, Sierra Club Canada, 11 May 2015, http://www.sierraclub.ca/sites/sierraclub.ca/files/JANET201505.pdf (last accessed 4 June 2015).

of which Bilcon had no notice. It was a convenient overarching framework under which all the aspects of the category "human environment effects" could be grouped. McRae sets this out in his dissent, stating[135]:

> Rather than being unaware of what was required of a human environment effects analysis, what the Panel was to call "community core values", the Claimant simply did not or was unable to satisfy the Panel that the project could operate consistently with those core values. The Panel was entitled to make that assessment; it was clearly within its mandate to do so.

In the Award, it is recorded that Bilcon was aware of the local and state policies promoting sustainable development and it included sections in its environmental impact statement on the social impacts of the project.[136] It was not unaware of the need for community impact to be addressed—it just did not deal with this aspect in a satisfactory way. What the Panel did not do, however, was set out expressly the links between the relevant regulation, local, federal and international, and the sustainability principles on which its decision was based.[137] And that omission allowed the ambiguity to arise and grounds for the challenge to be constructed. In discussing this aspect, VanderZwaag and May welcome the practical application of sustainability principles encapsulated in domestic and international environmental law and point to specific Canadian statutes and international instruments, such as the Canadian *Environmental Assessment Act*, the Nova Scotia *Environment Act*, and the Akwé: Kon Voluntary Guidelines,[138] the essence of which, if not explicit references, were reflected in the Joint Review Panel's Report. VanderZwaag and May make the comment that[139]:

> The Nova Scotia Environmental Assessment Regulations have defined an 'environmental effect' as including, 'any effect on socio-economic conditions, on environmental health, physical and cultural heritage or on any structure, site or thing including those of historical, archaeological, paleontological or architectural significance'. This wording provides a firm

[135] *In the Matter of an Arbitration under Chapter 11 of the North American Free Trade Agreement and the UNCITRAL Rules of 1976 between William Ralph Clayton et al v Government of Canada*, Dissenting Opinion of Professor Donald McRae, 10 March 2015, para. 26.

[136] *In the Matter of an Arbitration under Chapter 11 of the North American Free Trade Agreement and the UNCITRAL Rules of 1976 between William Ralph Clayton et al v Government of Canada*, Award, 10 March 2015, para 10.

[137] VanderZwaag D and May J (2008) Quarrels over a Proposed Quarry in Nova Scotia: Successful Application of Sustainability Principles in Environmental Impact Assessment but not a Perfect Ending. In Bosselmann K, Engel R and Taylor P (eds), Governance for Sustainability: Issues, Challenges, Successes. IUCN Environmental Policy and Law Paper No. 70, http://cmsdata.iucn.org/downloads/eplp_70_governance_for_sustainability.pdf (last accessed 11 August 2015), p. 111.

[138] Secretariat of the Convention on Biological Diversity (2004) Akwé: Kon Voluntary Guidelines for the Conduct of Cultural, Environmental and Social Impact Assessments Regarding Developments Proposed to Take Place on, or which are Likely to Impact on, Sacred Sites and on Lands and Waters Traditionally Occupied or Used by Indigenous and Local Communities, https://www.cbd.int/doc/publications/akwe-brochure-en.pdf (last accessed 10 July 20015).

[139] VanderZwaag and May (2008).

basis in law to justify the inclusion of social, economic, and community-based concerns within the assessment of the Whites Point Quarry proposal.

Other Canadian environmental law experts have echoed these sentiments. Doelle, in particular, having been called as an independent expert in the *Clayton & Bilcon* case, expressed his concern at the misunderstanding of the relevant environmental law amongst members of the arbitral tribunal other than McRae. After the decision was released, he wrote[140]:

> I have found a NAFTA Tribunal that lacked, with the exception of the dissenting member, even a basic understanding of the legal context within which the decisions it was asked to rule on were made. It also lacked any real appreciation for the factual context within which the decisions being challenged were made.

Doelle explained that under the Nova Scotian environmental assessment process, all the socio-economic effects are considered as environmental law. For this reason, the arbitral tribunal's decision that the Joint Review Panel went outside its mandate in applying a test of 'core community values' represents a misunderstanding of what the Panel was asked to do, that is, being to examine "not just biophysical effects and socio-economic effects that flow from biophysical effects," but all the socio-economic effects.[141] In other words, the Panel's process, methodologies, analysis, and outcomes were all exactly within its brief. Doelle emphasises that[142]:

> The report is clear in applying appropriate and well-established methodologies to its analysis of the socio-economic effects of the project. As pointed out by the dissent, the concept of "core community values" only appears toward the end of the report, making it clear that it is a way of summing up the Whites Point Panel's conclusions rather than a methodology for evaluating the project.

It is somewhat surprising to see in 2015 an approach from an investor-state arbitral tribunal that is not more embracing of the non-investment issues involved in the dispute. Those working with domestic or international environmental law will be familiar with the broad scope generally given to such concepts as 'sustainable development' and 'environmental effects' and that an expansive view of what is to be encompassed within environmental impact assessments is well-understood within environmental legal circles.[143] This is, perhaps, where greater engagement as between investment law and other fields would be beneficial. However, it also highlights that the 'ways of seeing' of the various experts can be so different and are

[140] Doelle M, Clayton White Points NAFTA Challenge Troubling, Marine and Environmental Law News, 25 March 2015 https://blogs.dal.ca/melaw/2015/03/25/clayton-whites-point-nafta-challenge-troubling/ (last accessed 27 April 2015).

[141] Doelle M, Clayton White Points NAFTA Challenge Troubling, Marine and Environmental Law News, 25 March 2015 https://blogs.dal.ca/melaw/2015/03/25/clayton-whites-point-nafta-challenge-troubling/ (last accessed 27 April 2015).

[142] Doelle M, Clayton White Points NAFTA Challenge Troubling, Marine and Environmental Law News, 25 March 2015 https://blogs.dal.ca/melaw/2015/03/25/clayton-whites-point-nafta-challenge-troubling/ (last accessed 27 April 2015).

[143] VanderZwaag and May (2008).

dependent on the perspective from which one already comes. The discourse following the issuing of the *Bilcon* decision certainly revealed the very different ways in which the dispute and outcome have been framed and, in so doing, also illustrated the deep divisions between a section of investment lawyers and environmental lawyers. And, in these concluding remarks, I am not entirely convinced that those barriers can be overcome immediately in the current climate of arbitral decision-making. There has, indeed, been a significant shift in the last few years in the cultural approach to non-investment issues, transparency, and host state regulatory space in treaty-making and in much of the discourse. However, it seems it will take more time for this shift to filter down into arbitral decision-making on anything like a consistent basis.

References

Anghie A (2004) Imperialism, sovereignty and the making of international law. Cambridge University Press, Cambridge

Baetens F (ed) (2013) Investment law within international law: integrationist perspectives. Cambridge University Press, Cambridge

Baker M (2006) Denial of justice in local courts. In: Ortino F, Sheppard A, Warner H (eds) Investment treaty law: current issues, vol I. British Institute of International and Comparative Law, London, p 187

Bastin L (2012) The amicus curiae in investor-state arbitration. Camb J Int Comp Law 1 (3):208–234. doi:10.7574/cjicl.01.03.57

Been V, Beauvais J (2003) The global fifth amendment? NAFTA's investment protections and the misguided quest for an international "regulatory takings" doctrine. N Y Univ Law Rev 78 (30):31–143

Borgen C (2007) Transnational tribunals and the transmission of norms: the hegemony of process. George Wash Int Law Rev 39:685–764

Brower C II (2003) Structure, legitimacy, and NAFTA's investment chapter. Vanderbilt J Transnat Law 36:37–94

Brower C, Brower C II, Sharpe J (2003) The coming crisis in the global adjudication system. Arbitr Int 19(4):415–440. doi:10.1093/arbitration/19.4.415

Buergenthal T (2006) The proliferation of disputes, dispute settlement procedures and respect for the rule of law. Arbitr Int 22(4):495–500. doi:10.1093/arbitration/22.4.495

Calamita N (2014) Dispute settlement transparency in Europe's evolving investment treaty policy. J World Invest Trade 15(3–4):645–678. doi:10.1163/22119000-01504014

De Brebandere E (2014) Investment treaty arbitration as public international law: procedural aspects and implications. Cambridge University Press, Cambridge

Dezalay Y, Garth B (1996) Dealing in virtue: international commercial arbitration and the construction of a transnational legal order. University of Chicago Press, Chicago

Douglas Z, Pauwelyn J, Viñuales J (2014) The foundations of international investment law: bringing theory into practice. Oxford University Press, Oxford

Dupuy P, Viñuales J (eds) (2013) Harnessing foreign investment to promote environmental protection: incentives and safeguards. Cambridge University Press, Cambridge

Gal-Or N (2008) The concept of appeal in international dispute settlement. Eur J Int Law 19 (1):43–65. doi:10.1093/ejil/chm054

Gantz D (2006) An appellate mechanism for review of arbitral decisions in investor-state disputes: prospects and challenges. Vanderbilt J Transnat Law 39:39–76

Gathii J (2008) Third world approaches to international economic governance. In: Falk R, Rajagopal B, Stevens J (eds) International law and the third world: reshaping justice. Routledge-Cavendish, Abingdon, pp 255–268
Hirsch M (2008) Interactions between investment and non-investment obligations in international investment law. In: Muchlinski P, Ortino F, Schreuer C (eds) The Oxford handbook of international investment law. Oxford University Press, Oxford, pp 154–181. doi:10.1093/oxfordhb/9780199231386.001.0001
Joubin-Bret A (2008) The growing diversity and inconsistency in the IIA system. In: Sauvant KP (ed) Appeals mechanism in international investment disputes. Oxford University Press, Oxford, p 137
Kalderimis D (2011) Investment treaty arbitration as global administrative law: what this might mean in practice. In: Brown C, Miles K (eds) Evolution in investment treaty law and arbitration. Cambridge University Press, Cambridge, pp 145–160. doi:10.1017/CBO9781139043809
Kalicki J, Joubin-Bret A (eds) (2015) Reshaping the investor-state dispute settlement system: journeys for the 21st century. Brill, Leiden. doi:10.1163/9789004291102
Kotuby C (2011) 'Other international obligations' as the applicable law in investment arbitration. Int Arbitr Law Rev 14(5):162–172
Kurtz J, Nottage L (2015) Investment treaty arbitration 'down under': policy and politics in Australia. ICSID Rev 30(2):465–480. doi:10.1093/icsidreview/siv001
Legum B (2008) Options to establish an appellate mechanism for investment disputes. In: Sauvant P (ed) Appeals mechanism in international investment disputes. Oxford University Press, Oxford, pp 231–240
Mayer P (2001) Reflections on the international arbitrator's duty to apply the law: the 2000 Freshfields lecture. Arbitr Int 17(3):235–248. doi:10.1023/A:1011248016716
McDonald J (1998) The multilateral agreement on investment: heyday or MAI-day for ecologically sustainable development? Melb Univ Law Rev 22(3):617–656
McLachlan C (2008) Investment treaties and general international law. Int Comp Law Q 57 (2):361–401. doi:10.1017/S0020589308000225
McLachlan C, Shore L, Weiniger M (2007) International investment arbitration: substantive principles. Oxford University Press, Oxford
Mickelson K (1998) Rhetoric and rage: third world voices in international legal discourse. Wisconsin Int Law J 16(2):353–419
Miles K (2010) Reconceptualising international investment law: bringing the public interest into private business. In: Kolsky Lewis M, Frankel S (eds) International economic law and national autonomy. Cambridge University Press, Cambridge, pp 295–319. doi:10.1017/CBO9780511760471
Miles K (2013) The origins of international investment law: empire, environment and the safeguarding of capital. Cambridge University Press, Cambridge
Miles K (2014) International investment law and universality: histories of shape-shifting. Camb J Int Comp Law 3:986–1010. doi:10.7574/cjicl.03.04.247
Muchlinski P (2008) Corporate social responsibility. In: Muchlinski P, Ortino F, Schreuer C (eds) The Oxford handbook of international investment law. Oxford University Press, Oxford, pp 637–687. doi:10.1093/oxfordhb/9780199231386.001.0001
Newcombe A (2007) Sustainable development and investment treaty law. J World Invest Trade 8 (3):357–407
Pahuja S (2011) Decolonising international law: development, economic growth and the politics of universality. Cambridge University Press, Cambridge
Paulsson J (2008) Avoiding unintended consequences. In: Sauvant P (ed) Appeals mechanism in international investment disputes. Oxford University Press, Oxford, pp 241–265
Peterson LE (2005) All roads lead out of Rome: divergent paths of dispute settlement in bilateral investment treaties. In: Zarsky L (ed) International investment for sustainable development: balancing rights and rewards. Earthscan, London, pp 123–150

Postiga A (2013) The emergence of global administrative law as a means of transnational regulation of foreign direct investment. Braz J Int Law Spec Issue Int Econ Law 10(1):171–193
Puig S (2014) Social capital in the arbitration market. Eur J Int Law 25(2):387–424. doi:10.1093/ejil/chu045
Reinisch A (2008) 'Investment and …'—broader picture of investment law. In: Reinisch A, Knahr C (eds) International investment law in context. Eleven International Publishing, The Netherlands, pp 201–207
Rubins N (2006) Opening the investment arbitration process: at what cost; for what benefit?. Transnat Dis Manag 3
Sammartano M (2003) The fall of a taboo: review of the merits of an award by an appellate arbitration panel and a proposal for an international appellate court. J Int Arbitr 20(4):387–392
Sands P (2002) Searching for balance: concluding remarks; colloquium on regulatory expropriations in international law. N Y Univ Environ Law J 11:198
Sands P (2005) Lawless world: America and the making and breaking of global rules. Penguin, London
Sands P, Peel J (2012) Principles of international environmental law. Cambridge University Press, Cambridge
Schill S (2010) International investment law and comparative public law—an introduction. In: Schill S (ed) International investment law and comparative public law. Oxford University Press, Oxford, pp 3–37
Schill S (2015) The overlooked role of arbitration in international adjudicatory theory. ESIL Reflect 4(2): European Society of International Law, http://www.esil-sedi.eu/node/934 (last accessed at 09.05.2015)
Shalakany A (2000) Arbitration and the third world: bias under the sceptre of neo-liberalism. Harv Int Law J 41:419
Shan W (2007) From "north–south divide" to "private–public debate": revival of the Calvo doctrine and the changing landscape in international investment law. Northwest J Int Law Bus 27(3):631–664
Soloway J (2000) Environmental regulation as expropriation: the case of NAFTA's chapter 11. Can Bus Law J 33:92–127
Sornarajah M (2003) The clash of globalizations and the international law on foreign investment: the Simon Reisman lecture in international trade policy. Can Foreign Policy 10(2):1–20. doi:10.1080/11926422.2003.9673321
Stephens T (2009) International courts and environmental protection. Cambridge University Press, Cambridge
Tienhaara K (2006) What you don't know can hurt you: investor-state disputes and the protection of the environment in developing countries. Glob Environ Pol 6(4):73–100
Tienhaara K (2007) Third party participation in investment-environment disputes: recent developments. Rev Eur Community Int Environ Law 16(2):230–242
Tienhaara K (2009) The expropriation of environmental governance: protecting foreign investors at the expense of public policy. Cambridge University Press, Cambridge
Tienhaara K (2011) Regulatory chill and the threat of arbitration: a view from political science. In: Brown C, Miles K (eds) Evolution in investment treaty law and arbitration. Cambridge University Press, Cambridge, pp 606–628. doi:10.1017/CBO9781139043809
Trinh H (2014) The interpretation of investment treaties. Martinus Nijhoff, Leiden. doi: 10.1163/9789004274549
Van Harten G (2007) Investment treaty arbitration and public law. Oxford University Press, Oxford
Voon T, Mitchell A (2011) Time to quit? assessing international investment claims against plain tobacco packaging in Australia. J Int Econ Law 14(3):515–552. doi:10.1093/jiel/jgr030
Wälde T, Kolo A (2001) Environmental regulation, investment protection and 'Regulatory Taking' in international law. Int Comp Law Q 50(4):811–848. doi:10.1093/iclq/50.4.811

Walsh T (2006) Substantive review of ICSID awards: is the desire for accuracy sufficient to compromise finality? Berkeley J Int Law 24(2):444–462

Weiler T (2005) Good faith and regulatory transparency: the story of Metalclad v. Mexico. In: Weiler T (ed) International investment law and arbitration: leading cases from the ICSID, NAFTA, bilateral treaties and customary international law. Cameron May, London, pp 701–745

Yannaca-Small K (2008) Parallel proceedings. In: Muchlinski P, Ortino F, Schreuer C (eds) The Oxford handbook of international investment law. Oxford University Press, Oxford, pp 1008–1048. doi:10.1093/oxfordhb/9780199231386.001.0001

In Defense of International Investment Law

Stephan W. Schill

Contents

Abstract The present article responds to the critical perspective Kate Miles offers on international investment law in her article "Investor-State Dispute Settlement: Conflict, Convergence, and Future Directions", published in this Yearbook. While sharing several concerns Miles identifies, and supporting present reform efforts to make the system more transparent, increase possibilities of involvement for third parties, and ensure policy space, this article presents a generally positive perspective on the foundations of international investment law. It argues that the present system has to be seen as a mechanism to subject international investment relations to the international rule of law, with investor-state arbitration providing a form of access to justice to foreign investors in cases where domestic courts are not sufficiently well-placed to effectively control government action and enforce investment treaty obligations. The system, in other words, vindicates fundamental values of a just world order under law. Furthermore, the article argues that Miles paints a misleading picture of the power arbitrators exercise in the interpretation and application of investment treaties. Rather than developing the system to the detriment of public interests, arbitrators are subject to numerous mechanisms of state control; moreover, they regularly apply interpretative techniques that are

S.W. Schill (✉)
Faculty of Law, University of Amsterdam, Amsterdam, The Netherlands
e-mail: s.w.b.schill@uva.nl

M. Bungenberg et al. (eds.), *European Yearbook of International Economic Law 2016*, European Yearbook of International Economic Law 7,
DOI 10.1007/978-3-319-29215-1_13

respectful of public interests. Finally, the article discusses the cases Kate Miles presents as pathologies of the system and argues that they are not encroachments on governments' policy space, but involve legitimate disputes that are appropriate for resolution in an international forum.

1 Introduction

Not even a decade ago, international investment law and investor-state dispute settlement (ISDS) were considered to be "exotic and highly specialized knowledges."[1] It was the ambit of a relatively small group of *conoscenti* who, with the exception of the handful of academics in public international law involved, had their principal background in the practice of international commercial arbitration in large transnational law firms in Paris, London, Stockholm, New York, or Washington DC. By now, investment law has moved mainstream. It has boomed in academia (scholarship and teaching) and international dispute resolution,[2] and has become a subject of general public debate, chiefly in connection with the negotiation of mega-regionals, such as the Trans-Pacific Partnership (TPP) and the Transatlantic Trade and Investment Partnership (TTIP).[3]

From a democratic perspective, this is a positive development given that international investment agreements (IIAs) do not only deal with technical issues,[4] but are relevant for society at large. It is cases, such as Vattenfall challenging

[1] Koskenniemi M (2006) Fragmentation of International Law: Difficulties Arising from the Diversification and Expansion of International Law. Report of the Study Group of the International Law Commission, International Law Commission, UN Doc A/CN.4/L.682, http://legal.un.org/ilc/documentation/english/a_cn4_l682.pdf (last accessed 28 September 2015), para. 8.

[2] For the mainstreaming of investment law in academia and dispute resolution see Schill (2011b); Schill and Tvede (2015).

[3] This is most emblematically reflected in the online public consultation on investment on investment protection and investor-to-state dispute settlement (ISDS) in the Transatlantic Trade and Investment Partnership Agreement (TTIP) the European Commission conducted from 27 March to 13 July 2014, which elicited close to 150,000 replies, many of which were however submitted collectively through online platforms of opponents of ISDS that contained pre-defined answers. See Report of the European Commission, Commission Staff Working Document, SWD (2015) 3 final, 13 January 2015, http://trade.ec.europa.eu/doclib/docs/2015/January/tradoc_153044.pdf (last accessed 28 July 2015).

[4] This is how IIAs were often regarded by governments negotiating and parliaments ratifying the treaties. In fact, under-politicisation of the content and effect of investment treaties is a recurring theme in the study conducted by Poulsen L (2011) Sacrificing Sovereignty by Chance: Investment Treaties, Developing Countries, and Bounded Rationality. PhD Thesis, London School of Economics, http://etheses.lse.ac.uk/141/1/Poulsen_Sacrificing_sovereignty_by_chance.pdf (last accessed 29 September 2015).

Germany's nuclear power phase-out under the Energy Charter Treaty,[5] Philip Morris challenging plain-packaging of cigarettes in Australia under the Hong Kong-Australia bilateral investment treaty (BIT),[6] or Lone Pine Resources tackling a ban on fracking in Quebec under the North American Free Trade Agreement (NAFTA),[7] that show how investment law can touch on general public interests and affect core aspects of domestic law and policy-making. Consequently, IIAs should be developed in transparent and democratic procedures, strike a fair balance between investment and non-investment concerns, leave states sufficient policy space to pursue public policies, and ensure that the resolution of investment disputes conforms to accepted standards of the rule of law. At the same time, it must be recognised that the protection of investors is not only a private, but equally a public interest.[8]

The burgeoning public debate notwithstanding, the long-lasting niche-existence of the field and little public knowledge about the principal actors in investment dispute settlement has created an aura of obscurity and suspicion. It is therefore hardly surprising that criticism of IIAs and ISDS is vocal and seemingly dominant in the public discourse. Critics are found in political parties from across the democratic spectrum, non-governmental organisations, civil society networks, and academia. Relying on the backlash in state practice, including the retreat of some countries from the existing system and the wide-spread recalibration of investment disciplines,[9] they have characterised investment law as facing a deep "legitimacy crisis".[10] Only more recently have supporters of international investment law undertaken more extensive steps in trying to rebalance the public debate and reclaiming argumentative grounds in defense of the system.[11]

As Kate Miles' article shows, there are plenty critical points, including the lack of transparency, problems with the independence of arbitrators, the existence of inconsistent and incoherent decision-making, and the concern whether IIAs leave states sufficient policy space for regulating in the public interest. Miles correctly summarises these concerns and pulls them together as arising from the tension

[5] *Vattenfall AB and others v. Federal Republic of Germany*, ICSID Case No. ARB/12/12 (registered 31 May 2012).

[6] *Philip Morris Asia Limited (Hong Kong) v. The Commonwealth of Australia*, UNCITRAL, Notice of Arbitration (21 November 2011).

[7] *Lone Pine Resources Inc. v. The Government of Canada*, UNCITRAL, Notice of Arbitration (6 September 2013).

[8] Thus, states protect and promote foreign investment in order to further their own policy goals, including the transfer of technology, the creation of employment, economic growth, and other development interests through instruments under domestic and international law. For an overview see UNCTAD (2012) World Investment Report 2012: Towards a New Generation of Investment Policies, http://unctad.org/en/PublicationsLibrary/wir2012_embargoed_en.pdf, (last accessed 15 October 2015), p. 97 ff.

[9] See Waibel et al. (2010).

[10] Brower and Schill (2009), p. 473 (with further references).

[11] See, for example, Brower and Blanchard (2014); Brower et al. (2013), p. 3; Schwebel (2015).

between a private law-inspired dispute settlement mechanism and its public interest implications.[12] At the same time, Miles also acknowledges that many concerns are already being addressed on an incremental basis.[13] Thus, modern, 'recalibrated' IIAs take pains to clarify treaty standards and introduce appropriate exceptions in order to ensure policy space to protect public interests; arbitration rules are being reformed in order to ensure transparent proceedings and allow participation of affected third parties; and a number of reform initiatives, at the regional and multilateral level, are under way that aim at building a system that better meets the requirements for fair and democratic dispute settlement under the rule of law. Moreover, there may even be renewed interest in a more institutionalised investment dispute settlement system, with the possible creation of an appeals mechanism or even a permanent investment court, as recently suggested by the European Commission.[14] Overall, these are welcome developments as the lack of transparency and the dismissive attitude of large parts of the arbitration community towards critical voices have understandably raised doubt as to whether arbitration is a suitable mechanism to settle what are, in essence, public and not private law disputes.[15]

The current reform efforts notwithstanding, Kate Miles remains critical of international investment law and ISDS. She castigates the hegemonic nature and pedigree of investment law in imperialism and in the post-imperialist contractions of decolonisation and goes on record as a critic of "recent attempts to frame investor-state arbitration as a mode of global administrative law, an instrument of good governance, and a purveyor of the rule of law."[16] Unfortunately, she does not elaborate in depth on any of these intriguing points. What she concentrates on instead as being the core of her continued criticism are two issues. First, there is the

[12] Miles (2016), section 1. In my own explanation of the criticism, I go a step further and read it as stemming from a clash between domestic constitutional values—democracy, the rule of law, and human or fundamental rights—and the basic institutional structures of ISDS. This framing helps not only to see better why investment law is facing such strong headwind, but also allows to draw parallels to the legitimacy debates, and possible solutions to it, that surround other forms of global governance rather than debates about the legitimacy of international commercial arbitration. See Schill (2011a, 2015a).

[13] Miles (2016), sections 3, 3.1 and 3.2. For further analysis of the changes IIAs and ISDS are undergoing see the contributions in Hindelang and Krajewski (2016).

[14] See European Commission, Press Release: Commission Proposes new Investment Court System for TTIP and Other EU Trade and Investment Negotiations, 16 September 2015, http://europa.eu/rapid/press-release_IP-15-5651_en.htm (last accessed 15 October 2015). For a succinct overview over the most recent reform debates and options more generally see UNCTAD (2015) World Investment Report 2015: Reforming International Investment Governance, http://unctad.org/en/PublicationsLibrary/wir2015_en.pdf (last accessed 28 September 2015), p. 119 ff. See further, inter alia, the contributions in Kalicki and Joubin-Bret (2015).

[15] On the public nature of investment law see Schill (2010), p. 10 ff.

[16] Miles (2016), section 1.

option for investors, even under reformed IIAs, to bring "public welfare-related claims" that "encroach in some form on government policy space."[17] This concerns the justification of investor access to ISDS regardless of the results of individual disputes. Second, Miles casts doubts on whether arbitration, due to the socialisation and composition of the arbitration bar, is well-placed to resolve investment disputes and to further develop investment law in a manner consonant with the public interest.[18]

While I agree with Miles' identification of the legitimacy concerns investment law is facing as a system of global governance,[19] I differ with her on a number of points. First, and most importantly, investment law, and particularly individual access to ISDS, fulfils an important function in subjecting international investment relations to the rule of law, to the benefit of investors, states, and their populations (Part II). Second, my assessment of the power the 'arbitration community' has in the present system is fundamentally different. Rather than being able to shape investment law at will, arbitrators are subject to various mechanisms of state control; this ensures that arbitral jurisprudence can develop, and in fact develops, in ways that are intended by states (Part III). In addition, rather than having given short thrift to non-economic public interests, arbitrators regularly make use of interpretative techniques that are sovereignty-friendly and respectful of public interests (Part IV). Finally, I disagree with Miles that the cases she portrays as particularly problematic (*Vattenfall, Philip Morris,* and *Bilcon*), are pathologies of the system. Rather than representing illegitimate encroachments on policy space, I consider them as involving legitimate disputes about the relationship between private rights and governmental powers in a global economy that are appropriate for being resolved in an international forum (Part V). All of this leads me to a generally positive assessment of the basic structures of IIAs and ISDS that should be defended against criticism, but that nonetheless can benefit from further reform for which the criticism can serve as a catalyst (Part VI).

2 International Investment Law and Investor-State Dispute Settlement and the Rule of Law

In her account of international investment law and ISDS, Kate Miles remains silent on the consequences of the criticism she formulates. She deconstructs and points to biases and blind spots, but leaves us without a hint on how a better world of investor-state relations and investment dispute settlement would look like. Would she suggest to get rid of the current system? To reform it, and, if so, along which path? Should we return to state-to-state dispute settlement? Or domestic courts? It is

[17] Miles (2016), section 1.

[18] Miles (2016), section 1.

[19] See Schill (2011a, 2015a).

unfortunate that she leaves these questions unanswered, as evaluating alternatives to the present system is important for a considered assessment of the pros and cons of the status quo. Doing so explains why IIAs and ISDS have developed in the first place and why the system carries structural benefits that are worth preserving. These benefits relate to the function of IIAs and ISDS to subject international investment relations to the rule of law.

Under a rule of law focus, individual access to ISDS should not be seen as an encroachment on government policy space, as Miles suggests, but as a form of judicial review that enables investors to have the legality of government action under international law controlled by independent and impartial institutions. As such, ISDS responds to the fundamental rule of law postulate found in international human rights law and many domestic constitutions[20] that government action must be reviewable as to its legality by independent and impartial adjudicatory institutions. In this perspective, ISDS is a form of granting access to justice,[21] which helps to ensure compliance of states with principles contained in IIAs. These principles, in turn, are not overly onerous. They either parallel restrictions governments regularly face under their own constitutional laws or are necessary for integrating national economies into a global economic space. They include the obligation not to discriminate against foreign investors in comparison to nationals or third-party nationals, not to treat them unfairly and inequitably, not to expropriate them without compensation, and to protect them against other government interference that is contrary to the rule of law. In addition, IIAs require free transfer of capital in respect of the investment and, more recently, also provide, albeit subject to a considerable number of exceptions, for market access and investment liberalisation.

What a rule of law perspective considers as a matter of accountability under legal standards can also be looked at in economic terms.[22] From this perspective, the availability of access to ISDS transforms IIAs from political declarations into readily enforceable promises. ISDS, in other words, makes government promises to foreign investors in IIAs credible.[23] This reduces the political risk of foreign investment, lowers the risk premium connected to it, and makes foreign investment projects more cost-efficient to the benefit of investors, host states, and, as products

[20] See, for example, *Golder v. United Kingdom*, Judgment (21 February 1975), ECHR Series A No. 18, paras. 28–36 (interpreting Article 6(1) of the European Convention on Human Rights to grant a right to access to justice); Basic Law of the Federal Republic of Germany, Article 19(4); Constitution of the Italian Republic, Article 24; Spanish Constitution, Section 24(1); Political Constitution of the Republic of Chile, Article 20. On access to justice under international law see also the contributions in Francioni (2007).

[21] Cf. *Lithgow and Others v. United Kingdom*, ECtHR (Application No 9006/80, Series A102), Decision (8 July 1986), para. 201 (where the European Court of Human Rights held that Member States could comply with their obligation under Article 6(1) ECHR to provide access to justice by submitting disputes to an arbitral tribunal provided that the principles of fair trial and due process are guaranteed).

[22] The following discussion draws on Schill (2015c), pp. 628–633.

[23] Cf. Schwartz and Scott (2003), pp. 556–562.

and services offered become cheaper, their populations.[24] Certainly, the credibility of commitments of the host state is not only a matter of the availability of dispute settlement mechanisms. Reputation, community pressure, the moral obligation to keep promises, or host states' self-interest to be seen as reliable, may also contribute to states living up to promises made in IIAs.[25] Yet, such mechanisms sometimes work imperfectly because states can benefit by reneging on promises made after an investor has made its investment, for example, by imposing additional obligations or even expropriating the investment without compensation.[26] For host states to make credible commitments, a mechanism to uphold their original promises, such as independent third-party dispute settlement in courts or arbitration, is necessary.[27]

Mechanisms to settle disputes between foreign investors and host states that fulfil the rule of law requirement of access to justice can be set up at the domestic and/or the international level. However, host state courts are often not well-positioned to enforce governments' promises vis-à-vis foreign investors. Often these courts are not, or are not perceived to be, sufficiently neutral in resolving disputes with their own governments. Sometimes, independent courts that administer justice efficiently are missing altogether. Sometimes, corruption and lengthy court proceedings may frustrate efforts to hold host states accountable in domestic courts.[28] While such problems are often encountered in the domestic courts of developing and transitioning countries, well-developed legal systems are not exempt from similar concerns.[29] In respect of Germany, to take my home

---

[24] See Jandhyala and Weiner (2014) (showing that IIAs reduce the premium for political risk that would make foreign investment projects more costly). It is less clear, however, whether investment treaties on the whole are able to attract additional foreign investment. There is an increasing amount of studies on this topic, with diverging results. Contrast only Tobin and Rose-Ackerman (2009) (finding a positive correlation between investment agreements and investment flows) with Aisbett (2009) (negating a correlation between investment agreements and investment flows). In more recent and refined studies, however, evidence is becoming more robust that there is a positive correlation between investment agreements and the inflow of foreign investment. See, for example, Berger et al. (2012); Büthe and Milner (2014) (with further references).

[25] Particularly on reputation as a mechanism to induce States' compliance with their obligations under international law see Guzman (2008), pp. 71–117.

[26] The underlying change in the incentive structure after one party has started performing or placed an asset under the control of the other party is also described as a hold-up problem. See Williamson (1985), p. 52 ff. See also Guzman (1998), p. 658 ff.; for a game-theoretic reconstruction see Cooter and Ulen (2004), p. 195 ff.

[27] Cf. Elkins et al. (2006), pp. 823–824.

[28] On corruption in the judiciary see Buscaglia and Dakolias (1999); Dakolias and Thachuk (2000). For the length of some court proceedings in the Member States of the Council of Europe see European Commission for the Efficiency of Justice, Length of Court Proceedings in the Member States of the Council of Europe Based on the Case Law of the of the European Court of Human Rights, December 2006, http://siteresources.worldbank.org/INTLAWJUSTINST/Resources/CEPEJCourtDelayEnglishUPDATED.doc (last accessed 17 October 2013).

[29] For a commonly cited example of a court in a developed legal system engaging in biased and discriminatory conduct vis-à-vis a foreign investor see *Loewen Group, Inc. and Raymond L. Loewen v. United States of America*, ICSID Case No. ARB(AF)/98/3, Award (26 June 2003).

jurisdiction as an example, the European Court of Human Rights (ECtHR) has handed down various judgments deciding that the length of court proceedings was contrary to the 'reasonable time'-requirement in Article 6(1) of the European Convention on Human Rights (ECHR).[30] The Court even determined that overly long court proceedings and the inexistence of a domestic remedy at the time constituted a "systemic problem" in the German legal system.[31]

Yet, domestic courts may not only in fact fail to provide efficient access to justice. Sometimes, there are legal barriers, such as access restrictions for foreigners. In Germany, to stay with my example, domestic law contains significant restrictions for foreigners concerning access to justice. While access to general courts is unrestricted, Germany's Basic Law (i.e., the German Constitution) excludes foreign juridical persons from the enjoyment of fundamental rights and hence excludes their access to the German Constitutional Court.[32] In other countries, certain government measures may be completely exempt from domestic judicial review, such as those that constitute 'political questions' under the jurisprudence of the US Supreme Court, including in matters touching upon foreign economic policy.[33] In again other countries, such as Australia, obligations arising under international law, including those granted in an IIA, may not be enforceable in domestic courts due to their inapplicability within the domestic legal order.[34] In all of these cases, not providing for access to an international forum would effectively frustrate the enforcement of standards granted in IIAs against non-compliant governments and therefore fall short of the rule of law requirement to access to justice.

Another option for the enforcement of IIA disciplines, and granting access to justice, would be international courts and tribunals. In existing international courts, however, investors face limitations as regards standing. Instead of being able to pursue claims independently, only their respective home state is able to espouse a

[30] See, amongst others, *Sürmeli v. Germany*, ECtHR (Application No 75529/01), Decision (8 June 2006), para. 134; *Kressin v. Germany*, ECtHR (Application No 21061/06), Decision (22 December 2009), para. 26; *Spaeth v. Germany*, ECtHR (Application No 854/07), Decision (29 September 2011), para. 42.

[31] *Rumpf v. Germany*, ECtHR (Application No 46344/06), Decision (2 September 2010), paras. 64 ff.

[32] Under Article 19(3) of the German Basic Law, foreign corporations cannot rely on fundamental rights granted in the Constitution. There is an exception, however, for juridical persons from other Member States of the European Union (EU) who can invoke their rights of non-discrimination under EU law to claim equal treatment with German juridical persons, and hence access to the Constitutional Court. See BVerfGE 129, 78, 97 f. (German Constitutional Court, 19 July 2011).

[33] For an overview over the jurisprudence of the US Supreme Court and lower federal courts in the US see Cole J (2014) The Political Question Doctrine: Justiciability and the Separation of Powers, Congressional Research Service Report No. R43834, https://www.fas.org/sgp/crs/misc/R43834.pdf (last accessed 28 July 2015), pp. 10–12, 15–19.

[34] See French (2015), pp. 159–161.

claim through diplomatic protection.[35] Apart from the potential to cause rifts in inter-state relations, this has a number of significant drawbacks for efficient access to justice: First, the exercise of diplomatic protection is at the discretion of home states—they can, but do not have to, take up their national's claim; second, home states exercise exclusive control over the rights of their nationals on the international level[36] and can settle, waive or modify them;[37] third, the entitlement to receive compensation for the violation of international law is not vested in the alien, but in the home state—home state can, but does not have to pass on the compensation to those who have actually suffered harm;[38] and, finally, diplomatic protection is subject to the exhaustion of local remedies.[39] While the latter requirement affords host states an opportunity to review and remedy their conduct, it brings the shortcomings of domestic courts back into the picture. Existing international courts dealing with investment disputes at an inter-state level are therefore hardly a viable option for the effective enforcement of IIA standards and for granting access to justice to affected investors. Conversely, a return to inter-state enforcement of IIAs may also bring power-relations between states that are reminiscent of gunboat diplomacy, and therefore contravene the idea of the rule of law, back into international investment relations.[40]

Contractual solutions for dispute resolution, including alternative means for settling disputes, such as conciliation or mediation, that some suggest as an alternative,[41] also have considerable drawbacks in respect of access to justice under the concept of the rule of law. Above all, they are only available to investors with sufficient negotiating power. While large-scale investment contracts have always contained arbitration, choice of law, stabilisation, or internationalisation clauses, small- or medium-sized investors, who play an important part in foreign investment relations, often lack the necessary bargaining power to negotiate such protections. Moreover, contractual solutions are unavailable to investors that make their investments based on a country's general investment legislation. For them, reaching agreement with the host state on non-domestic dispute settlement will be difficult once a dispute has arisen. In such cases, treaty-based arbitration clauses are

[35] See *The Mavrommatis Palestine Concessions (Greece v. Britain)*, Judgment (30 August 1924), PCIJ Series A, No. 2 (1924), 12. See generally on diplomatic protection Amerasinghe (2008).

[36] See *Barcelona Traction, Light and Power Company, Limited (Belgium v. Spain)*, Judgment (5 February 1970), ICJ Reports 1970, 42, para. 70.

[37] In practice, this has led to the settlement of international claims concerning the violation of the rights of foreigners by lump-sum agreements. See Lillich and Weston (1975); Weston et al. (1999).

[38] Borchard (1915), pp. 356–359, 383–388; Hagelberg (2006), p. 51. Home states are therefore under no obligation to pass the compensation on to those investors that have actually suffered the harm.

[39] See Amerasinghe (2005); Cancado Trindade (1983).

[40] See Johnson and Gimblett (2012).

[41] Public Statement on the International Investment Regime, 31 August 2010, http://www.osgoode.yorku.ca/public-statement-international-investment-regime-31-August-2010/ (last accessed 28 July 2015), para. 10; see also Yackee (2008).

the only fall-back option to hold host states efficiently accountable and therefore fulfilling rule of law ideals for investor-state relations.

In sum, ISDS compensates for a number of limitations that may exist for foreign investors under domestic law, other instruments of international law, and contracts as regards access to justice as a requirement of the concept of the rule of law. In many cases, domestic courts in developing and developed countries will not be able, for the reasons discussed above, to ensure the comprehensive and neutral enforcement of IIA disciplines.[42] Existing international courts would not be sufficient either. As a consequence, proposals to limit access to ISDS by foreign investors should be analysed critically and assessed in light of the question of whether alternatives are able to serve not only the interests of host states in preserving policy space, but also the interest in holding states accountable for compliance with obligations contained in IIAs under the concept of the rule of law.

Certainly, a newly created international court in which investors have direct access to enforce IIA disciplines would be an alternative, but such a court, while recently discussed in various quarters[43] does not yet exist, and it is highly uncertain whether it will ever come into existence. For the moment, investor-state arbitration is therefore the only viable option to grant access to justice to foreign investors and to allow enforcement of IIA disciplines in a neutral forum. This notwithstanding, ISDS is not immune from criticism. On the contrary, viewing it as an instrument furthering the rule of law requires that investor-state arbitration itself, and those serving as arbitrators, have to be faithful to the requirements of the rule of law. However, unlike critics, I have faith that arbitrators are able to live up to high rule of law standards and fulfil the expectations commonly vested in adjudicatory institutions that administer justice and control the exercise of public authority. This requires that arbitrators orient their decision-making towards administering justice in accordance with the idea of the rule of law and with sufficient respect for competing public interests. That they can, and in many cases already do so, is what the next section will address.

[42] Certainly, the situation of investors behaving opportunistically and attempting to renege on their original promises also exists. However, the host state as a sovereign actor does not depend on dispute settlement mechanisms to make investors comply with his or her obligations, but can typically react to such conduct by unilaterally imposing sanctions. The states' ability to impose and enforce decisions unilaterally is also the deeper justification for having a unilateral right of recourse for foreign investors. It is a corollary and no more than a modest limitation on host state sovereignty.

[43] See the European Commission's proposal for a permanent TTIP Tribunal, European Commission, Press Release: Commission Proposes New Investment Court System for TTIP and Other EU Trade and Investment Negotiations, 16 September 2015, http://europa.eu/rapid/press-release_IP-15-5651_en.htm (last accessed 15 October 2015). See further UNCTAD (2015) World Investment Report 2015: Reforming International Investment Governance, http://unctad.org/en/PublicationsLibrary/wir2015_en.pdf (last accessed 28 September 2015), p. 152.

3 Mechanisms of State Control of Arbitration

Kate Miles' criticism of the international investment regime not only stems from its institutional structure involving a right of action of foreign investors against government conduct at the international level; it is closely connected to her assessment of the sociological consequences choosing arbitration to settle investor-state disputes has on how public interests are dealt with. In her view, the sociological composition of the arbitration bar is responsible for interpretations of IIA standards, conduct of hearings, and drafting of awards that show an "apparent reluctance to address adequately non-investment issues within awards and a lack of appreciation of the distinct character of ISDS from that of international commercial arbitration."[44] It is the cultural context that arbitration brings with it in the resolution of investor-state disputes that Miles views as a fundamental problem for the protection of public interests in the international investment regime. Echoing other critical voices in the field, she suggests that ISDS is subject to capture by a small group of particularly influential arbitrators that have preponderant influence on how the law is applied and further developed.[45]

The point I take issue with here is not that many of those who regularly sit as arbitrator have a commercial arbitration mind-set. I have criticised this myself and advocated that more attention should be paid to both public international and comparative public law in order to make the international investment regime more legitimate, produce better and fairer results, provide more convincingly reasoned decisions, and ensure regard for competing non-investment concerns and public policies.[46] I also do not cast into doubt that the investment arbitration community has developed its own epistemic, or interpretive culture,[47] and that that community's core of repeatedly appointed arbitrators is particularly influential in further developing international investment law.[48] What I take issue with in Kate

[44] Miles (2016), section 1.

[45] See the discussion of the community of investment arbitrators in Miles (2016), section 2.2. For other particularly critical views of how a small group of arbitrators allegedly captured the investment field see Eberhardt P, Olivert C (2012) Profiting from Injustice: How Law Firms, Arbitrators and Financiers Are Fuelling an Investment Arbitration Boom, Corporate Europe Observatory and the Transnational Institute, http://www.tni.org/profitingfrominjustice.pdf (last accessed 29 July 2015), pp. 35–55; Sornarajah (2015), pp. 27–28.

[46] See Schill (2010).

[47] On the influence of epistemic communities on interpretation see Karton (2013); see further Waibel (2015).

[48] The structure of the community of investment arbitrators and their influence on how investment disputes are decided is the subject of a number of recent empirical sociological studies. See Franck et al. (2015); Pauwelyn J (2015) WTO Panelists Are from Mars, ICSID Arbitrators Are from Venus—Why? And Does It Matter?, http://dx.doi.org/10.2139/ssrn.2549050 (last accessed 29 July 2015); Puig (2014). Earlier studies include Kapeliuk (2010); Fontoura Costa (2011); Waibel M, Wu Y (2011) Are Arbitrators Political? Working Paper, http://www.wipol.uni-bonn.de/lehrveranstaltungen-1/lawecon-workshop/archive/dateien/waibelwinter11-12 (last accessed 29 September 2015).

Miles' account is the suggestion that a certain commercial mind-set of arbitrators is a given and cannot be changed, that states have little possibilities for changing it, and that in consequence arbitrators, rather than states dominate the system. What Miles disregards, in my view, are the control mechanisms states have at their disposal to ensure that arbitrators stay within their mandate and develop the law in line with states' expectations.

First, it is important to see that investment treaty arbitrators are not self-entitled, neither individually nor as a group, nor is the legal basis upon which the resolution of investor-state disputes rests removed from state control. On the contrary, arbitrators derive their power to adjudicate and decide individual disputes from the choice of the parties to IIAs. It is states that chose to provide for the possibility to settle investment disputes by means of arbitration between foreign investors and host states; it is states that provided for the choice of arbitrators by investors and states as disputing parties. Furthermore, in their appointment decisions disputing parties are not limited to certain individuals or members of a specific group, but are free to choose anybody as arbitrator who meets the necessary standards of independence and impartiality. Thus, the decisions arbitral tribunals produce, the way they interpret IIA standards, and the attention they give to non-investment concerns, is not an unavoidable consequence of a specific *esprit des corps* of the arbitration community, but results from the choices of contracting parties to IIAs. It is states who tailor the contours of investment dispute settlement, not arbitrators. For example, arbitral rules can be tailored, as is actually the case with the most-used rules in investor-state disputes, namely the rules applicable pursuant to the Convention on the Settlement of Investment Disputes Between States and Nationals of Other States (ICSID Convention),[49] to ensure that the majority of arbitrators on individual tribunals can trace their appointments either directly to the respondent state's consent, or are indirectly legitimised through the consent given by the contracting states of the ICSID Convention to the appointing authority, which is the Chairman of ICSID's Administrative Council, and to the individuals nominated by states as members of ICSID's List of Arbitrators.[50] Similarly, it is states, not

[49] Convention on the Settlement of Investment Disputes Between States and Nationals of Other States (adopted 18 March 1965, entered into force 14 October 1966) 575 UNTS 159.

[50] Pursuant to Article 37(2) ICSID Convention the respondent state has to agree to a sole arbitrator deciding the dispute (lit a) or, in addition to appointing one arbitrator at will, agree to the president of the Tribunal (lit b). Failing such agreement, the Chairman of the Administrative Council shall appoint the presiding arbitrator after consulting both parties (Article 38 ICSID Convention). In making appointment choices, the Chairman is limited to individuals that Member States have nominated to be included in the List of Arbitrators (see Article 40(1) ICSID Convention). Other arbitration rules frequently applied in investment treaty arbitrations, such as the United Nations Conference on International Trade Law (UNCITRAL) Arbitration Rules (the revised version of 2010, and the latest version of 2013 incorporating the UNCITRAL Rules on Transparency for Treaty-Based Investor-State Arbitration are available at http://www.uncitral.org/uncitral/en/uncitral_texts/arbitration/2010Arbitration_rules.html (last accessed 29 July 2015) or the Rules Governing the Additional Facility for the Administration of Proceedings by the Secretariat of the International Centre for Investment Disputes (ICSID Additional Facility Rules) (latest version

arbitrators, who crafted the applicable law under IIAs. States, in other words, are the actors responsible for creating international investment law and ISDS and controlling its further development.

Second, it is crucial to note that the power of arbitral tribunals is limited to an individual case. This one-off nature of arbitration increases the influence of states over the dispute settlement process as compared to a permanent international court, concomitantly reducing the power of arbitrators. Although arbitral tribunals, through the use of precedent, contribute to the further development of international investment law, there is no institutional rationale for them to do so that is comparable to that of a permanent international court, which would strive for interpretive hegemony. Santiago Montt designates the underlying logic of the investment arbitration system as a "BIT lottery",[51] arguing that states had no interest in creating a permanent investment court because that would have increased the risk of such a court going in the wrong direction in interpreting vague IIA standards. Instead, states deliberately risked incoherence by opting for arbitration in order to reduce systemic effects of individual decisions. If, for example, the decision in *Bilcon v. Canada*, as Miles argues,[52] is incorrect, it is less likely to perpetuate itself in a system of one-off arbitration as compared to a system that is subject to the jurisdiction of a permanent international court or appellate body.

Furthermore, the state's influence in the appointment of arbitral tribunals arguably brings arbitrators closer to domestic democratic processes than judges in permanent international courts who are appointed for a term of several years, are empowered to hear an indeterminate number of cases, and are subject to complex inter-governmental bargains about positions in international organisations.[53] Likewise, the ratio of party-appointed ad hoc judges to permanent members is smaller (for example, 1–15 or 16 in the International Court of Justice) than in a three-member tribunal where one out of three members has been directly appointed by the state and the presiding arbitrator may also have its consent. This is a democratic advantage of international arbitration over permanent international courts that is often disregarded.

Third, the appointment system in investor-state arbitration also ensures on the long-term that arbitrators have an interest in settling investment disputes and further developing investment law in ways that are consistent with the expectations of states parties to IIAs. Unlike critics who argue that arbitrators as a group, independently of whether they are usually investor- or state-appointed, have an interest in

---

effective as of 10 April 2006) reprinted in ICSID Additional Facility Rules, Document ICSID/11, April 2006, https://icsid.worldbank.org/apps/ICSIDWEB/icsiddocs/Documents/AFR_English-final.pdf (last accessed 30 July 2015) are slightly more complicated, but they can be applied so as to ensure that states face a majority on the arbitral tribunal that they are comfortable with or that is legitimised through appointment by a truly neutral appointment authority in a process in which the state party participates.

[51] Montt (2009), p. 157.

[52] Miles (2016), section 4.

[53] For this argument see Schill (2015b), p. 4.

rendering investor-friendly decisions because only investors can bring future claims that may result in reappointments,[54] I see the reappointment system as functioning in the reverse fashion. Assuming (with critics) that all arbitrators have an interest in being reappointed, and therefore assuming that they have an incentive to align their decision-making and interpretative methods, including the extent of policy space they grant, with the interests of those actors that keep the system running, it is states, and not investors, that are relevant for ensuring the long-term viability of international investment law. It is states, and not investors, that can make, and in fact have made, use of their treaty-making powers, their powers to terminate investment treaties, and their powers of interpretation, to bring change to the system. What is more, they could, if they choose to do so, even bring down the system altogether. It is therefore states, not investors, upon whom the long-term viability of the system depends.

Given that states have crafted ISDS as a mechanism for the neutral resolution of investment disputes, arbitrators not only have an incentive to be independent and impartial, but also to adapt their decision-making to changing expectations, including the increasing respect for what states parties to IIAs consider as part of their public interests. What these interests are can be brought to the attention of arbitral tribunals through the submission of respondent states and of the non-disputing state party.[55] The reappointment process for arbitrators can therefore function as a mechanism by means of which states can implement changes among the group of decision-makers and their prevalent thinking. Accordingly, what some perceive as a fundamental flaw in system-design, namely dispute settlement by one-off arbitral tribunals, could be viewed as a gateway for change and adaptation to outside criticism, rather than a threat to the legitimacy of ISDS. In the end, it is the parties themselves, in particular states, who are not only responsible for the jurisprudence arbitral tribunals produce and the sociological composition of the core group of investment arbitrators that are particularly influential in further developing investment law, but are also in a position to use their appointment powers to change the sociological composition of those who serve as arbitrators, as well as their treaty-making powers to adapt the legal bases for resolving investor-state disputes.

Finally, ISDS does not take place in a void, but is embedded in a functioning system of separation of powers between arbitrators as adjudicators and contracting states as legislators. States are not at the mercy of arbitral interpretations of IIA standards, but retain influence over the way tribunals further develop international investment law. Apart from their powers to terminate, modify, and amend IIAs,

---

[54] For this argument see Van Harten (2007), p. 167 ff.; Van Harten (2010).

[55] Some IIAs provide expressly for the possibility of non-disputing party submissions; see eg Article 10.20.2 of the Dominican Republic–Central America–United States Free Trade Agreement (CAFTA-DR), https://ustr.gov/trade-agreements/free-trade-agreements/cafta-dr-dominican-republic-central-america-fta/final-text (last accessed 15 October 2015). Yet, even in the absence of such an explicit provision, tribunals are generally able to suggest such submissions, and in practice have done so (see eg *Aguas del Tunari, S.A. v. Republic of Bolivia*, ICSID Case No. ARB/02/3, Decision on Respondent's Objections to Jurisdiction (21 October 2005), paras. 45–49).

they can influence arbitral jurisprudence, and correct arbitral interpretations they disagree with, through joint interpretations, which are binding on tribunals pursuant to Art. 31(3)(c) of the Vienna Convention on the Law of Treaties.[56] Such interpretations have at times occurred in the investment treaty context and been generally respected by arbitral tribunals. Binding interpretations by the Free Trade Commission (FTC) under NAFTA, a treaty organ mandated inter alia for this purpose, are probably the prime example for how arbitral tribunals can be embedded into a functioning separation of powers framework.[57] Another example of a joint interpretation[58] are the diplomatic notes Argentina and Panama exchanged after the jurisdictional decision in *Siemens v. Argentina*[59] in order to clarify that the most-favoured-nation clause in their BIT would not apply to more favourable access conditions granted under the host state's third-country BITs along the lines first set out in *Maffezini v. Spain.*[60]

All in all, through the appointment and reappointment of arbitrators, the parties to individual disputes, and amongst them predominantly states, exercise control over arbitral tribunals and are able to influence the future direction of arbitral jurisprudence. Similarly, states' powers to terminate and renegotiate IIAs, as well as to issue joint interpretations allow states to limit the systemic effects of arbitral decisions they disagree with. All of this shows that states retain power to ensure a fair balance between investment and non-investment concerns within the existing system and are not at the mercy of arbitral discretion. Instead, states in investment treaty arbitration receive what they have bargained for and are able to continuously monitor and to react to imbalances of that bargain.

[56] See further on the impact of states' interpretations of IIAs, Roberts (2010).

[57] The FTC has issued an Interpretive Note through which the interpretation of fair and equitable treatment under NAFTA was tied to customary international law and that infused transparency into the decision-making of arbitral tribunals. See NAFTA Free Trade Commission, Notes of Interpretation of Certain Chapter 11 Provisions, 31 July 2001, http://www.sice.oas.org/tpd/nafta/Commission/CH11understanding_e.asp (last accessed 30 July 2015). Arbitral tribunals have, with some initial quarrels as to whether interpretations should affect ongoing proceedings, accepted and followed that interpretation. Most recently see *Clayton and others and Bilcon of Delaware, Inc. v. Government of Canada*, UNCITRAL (NAFTA), Award on Jurisdiction and Liability (17 March 2015), paras. 432–433.

[58] This incident is reported in *National Grid plc v. The Argentine Republic,* UNCITRAL, Decision on Jurisdiction (20 June 2006), para. 85.

[59] See *Siemens AG v. The Argentine Republic,* ICSID Case No. ARB/02/8, Decision on Jurisdiction (3 August 2004), paras. 82-110.

[60] *Emilio Agustín Maffezini v. The Kingdom of Spain*, ICSID Case No. ARB/97/7, Decision of the Tribunal on Objections to Jurisdiction (25 January 2000), paras. 38-64.

4 Arbitral Tribunals and Their View of Public Interests

Turning away from the institutional relations between states and arbitral tribunals, it is also difficult to see how a commercial mind-set prevails in the practice of investment treaty arbitration and operates to the detriment of public interests. Not only does Miles not mention actual examples of cases that she considers have incorrectly cut short non-investment concerns or reduced host states' regulatory power to protect them; she also gives short thrift to the long string of cases in which arbitral tribunals expressly have recourse to what I call public law thinking and public law rationales in order to interpret IIA standards in ways that are respectful of non-investment concerns, thus granting states considerable leeway to pursue what they consider to be in their public interests. The existence of these cases casts doubt on the argument that the commercial-mindedness of the arbitral community has undue impact on the interpretation of IIAs to the detriment of public interests.

One example of an argumentative technique that has its root in public law thinking which arbitral tribunals frequently use in order to take account of non-investment concerns in the interpretation of investment treaty standards, thereby safeguarding host states' policy space, is recourse to proportionality balancing.[61] Already early on, the Tribunal in *Tecmed v. Mexico* was strongly influenced by the jurisprudence of the ECtHR on the First Optional Protocol to the ECHR when adopting the Court's proportionality test in order to determine when state measures turn from a regulation not requiring compensation into a compensatory indirect expropriation.[62] The Tribunal's point of departure was that "[t]he principle that the State's exercise of its sovereign powers within the framework of its police power may cause economic damage to those subject to its powers as administrator without entitling them to any compensation whatsoever is undisputable."[63] Only measures that interfered with foreign investment to achieve a public purpose in a disproportionate manner would require compensation.[64] Alternatively, discriminatory action or the existence of specific commitments

---

[61] For more in-depth discussion of the principle of proportionality in investment treaty arbitration see Bücheler (2015); Kingsbury and Schill (2010); Stone Sweet (2010); Leonhardsen (2012); Henckels (2012).

[62] See *Tecnicas Medioambientales Tecmed S.A. v. United Mexican States*, ICSID Case No. ARB (AF)/00/2, Award (29 May 2003), paras. 113-122.

[63] *Tecnicas Medioambientales Tecmed S.A. v. United Mexican States*, ICSID Case No. ARB (AF)/00/2, Award (29 May 2003), para. 119.

[64] *Tecnicas Medioambientales Tecmed S.A. v. United Mexican States*, ICSID Case No. ARB (AF)/00/2, Award (29 May 2003), para. 122 (stating that one needed to "consider, in order to determine if [the interferences] are to be characterised as expropriatory, whether such actions or measures are proportional to the public interest presumably protected thereby and to the protection legally granted to investments, taking into account that the significance of such impact has a key role upon deciding the proportionality").

given to the foreign investor that the government would refrain from such regulation could also trigger compensation.[65] Applied in this way, proportionality reasoning helps to achieve a balance between the interest of the affected investor and the public interest that is to be protected by the host state's measure in question.

Yet, proportionality analysis is not limited to the expropriation context. It is increasingly also used by arbitral tribunals when applying the concept of fair and equitable treatment. For example, far from constituting an absolute and fixed threshold that government conduct cannot pass without incurring liability, the Tribunal in *Saluka v. Czech Republic* considered that "[t]he determination of a breach of [fair and equitable treatment] ... requires a weighing of the Claimant's legitimate and reasonable expectations on the one hand and the Respondent's legitimate regulatory interests on the other."[66] Under this reasoning, fair and equitable treatment does not prohibit changes to the regulatory framework in place; it only requires that host states give due consideration to the position of investors and weigh the importance of the continuation of a specific regulatory framework against the benefits and need for change. All in all, as this interpretation shows, fair and equitable treatment does not immunise investors from regulatory changes unless host states have made specific promises to the contrary.[67]

Most recently, the Tribunal in *Occidental v. Ecuador* applied the principle of proportionality to determine the legality of a revocation of an operating license by the host state and expressly placed it into a comparative public law context:

> The application of the principle of proportionality may be observed in a variety of international law settings, including cases in which the proportionality of countermeasures taken in trade disputes is challenged before a WTO Panel under the General Agreement on Tariffs and Trade ("GATT").

---

[65] See *Methanex Corporation v. United States of America,* UNCITRAL (NAFTA), Final Award of the Tribunal on Jurisdiction and Merits (3 August 2005) Part IV, ch D, para. 7 ("In the Tribunal's view, Methanex is correct that an intentionally discriminatory regulation against a foreign investor fulfils a key requirement for establishing expropriation. But as a matter of general international law, a non-discriminatory regulation for a public purpose, which is enacted in accordance with due process and, which affects, inter alios, a foreign investor or investment is not deemed expropriatory and compensable unless specific commitments had been given by the regulating government to the then putative foreign investor contemplating investment that the government would refrain from such regulation.").

[66] *Saluka Investments B.V. v. Czech Republic*, UNCITRAL, Partial Award (17 March 2006), para. 306.

[67] For another example that fair and equitable treatment does not suppress the host state's power to legislate in the public interest see *Parkerings-Compagniet AS v. Republic of Lithuania,* ICSID Case No. ARB/05/8, Award (11 September 2007), para. 332 (stating that "[i]t is each State's undeniable right and privilege to exercise its sovereign legislative power. A State has the right to enact, modify or cancel a law at its own discretion. Save for the existence of an agreement, in the form of a *stabilisation* clause or otherwise, there is nothing objectionable about the amendment brought to the regulatory framework existing at the time an investor made its investment. As a matter of fact, any businessman or investor knows that laws will evolve over time. What is prohibited however is for a State to act unfairly, unreasonably or inequitably in the exercise of its legislative power.").

> On the application of proportionality generally in the context of administrative action, the most developed body of jurisprudence is in Europe. It is very well-established law in a number of European countries that there is a principle of proportionality which requires that administrative measures must not be any more drastic than is necessary for achieving the desired end. The principle has been adopted and applied countless times by the European Court of Justice in Luxembourg, and by the European Court of Human Rights in Strasbourg.
>
> Against that background, the Tribunal observes that there is a growing body of arbitral law, particularly in the context of ICSID arbitrations, which holds that the principle of proportionality is applicable to potential breaches of bilateral investment treaty obligations.[68]

These decisions are not exceptions. Rather there is a more general trend to use proportionality balancing as a method to bring public interest considerations into the interpretation of IIA standards.[69] While proportionality analysis itself raises concerns as to its legal basis and the power it confers on arbitral tribunals, what is important for present purposes is that in practice arbitral tribunals by no means one-sidedly decide disputes in favour of foreign investors, nor disregard competing non-investment concerns.

Moreover, as an argumentative technique proportionality reasoning is typical for public law thinking; its use therefore illustrates a clear break with commercial law thinking that has long prevailed in investment arbitration. Through this and similar public law argumentation, tribunals ensure policy space for host states to determine and implement what they determine to be in their public interest. In addition, proportionality analysis also serves as a tool to coordinate and reconcile IIA disciplines with obligations under other international treaties, whether for the protection of the environment, human rights, or rights of indigenous people.[70]

In addition to recourse to proportionality reasoning, tribunals also secure that states have sufficient policy space to pursue public interests through various

---

[68] *Occidental Petroleum Corporation and Occidental Exploration and Production Company v. The Republic of Ecuador*, ICSID Case No. ARB/06/11, Award (5 October 2012), paras. 402–404.

[69] See *MTD Equity SDN BHD and MTD Chile S.A. v. Republic of Chile*, Award (25 May 2004), para. 109; *Azurix Corp. v. The Argentine Republic*, ICSID Case No. ARB/01/12, Award (14 July 2006), para. 311; *Fireman's Fund Insurance Company v. The United Mexican States*, ICSID Case No. ARB(AF)/02/01, Award (17 July 2006), para. 176(j); *LG&E Energy Corp, LG&E Capital Corp, LG&E International Inc. v. Argentine Republic*, ICSID Case No. ARB/02/1, Decision on Liability (3 October 2006), para. 194; *BG Group Plc. v. Republic of Argentina*, UNCITRAL, Final Award (24 December 2007), para. 298; *National Grid P.L.C. v. Argentine Republic*, UNCITRAL, Award (3 November 2008), para. 175; *Joseph C. Lemire v. Ukraine*, ICSID Case No. ARB/06/18, Decision on Jurisdiction and Liability (14 January 2010), para. 285; *Total S.A. v. The Argentine Republic*, ICSID Case No. ARB/04/1, Decision on Liability (27 December 2010), paras. 123 and 197; *El Paso Energy International Company v. The Argentine Republic*, ICSID Case No. ARB/03/15, Award (31 October 2011), paras. 241–243 and 373; *Deutsche Bank AG v. Democratic Socialist Republic of Sri Lanka*, ICSID Case No. ARB/09/2, Award (31 October 2012), para. 522; cf. also *Antoine Goetz & Consorts et S.A. Affinage des Metaux v. Republique du Burundi*, ICSID Case No. ARB/01/2, Sentence (21 June 2012), para. 258.

[70] See van Aaken (2009), pp. 502–506; Schill (2012a).

doctrines of deference, that is, restrictions in the depth of review of government conduct.[71] The Tribunal in *S.D. Myers v. Canada* perhaps most clearly caught the different dimensions of deference when it stated that investment treaty tribunals:

> d[o] not have an open-ended mandate to second-guess government decision-making. Governments have to make many potentially controversial choices. In doing so, they may appear to have made mistakes, to have misjudged the facts, proceeded on the basis of a misguided economic or sociological theory, placed too much emphasis on some social values over others and adopted solutions that are ultimately ineffective or counterproductive. The ordinary remedy, if there were one, for errors in modern governments is through internal political and legal processes, including elections.[72]

Likewise, the Tribunal in *Tecmed v. Mexico* observed that, in determining whether a regulatory act constituted an indirect expropriation,

> the analysis starts at the due deference owing to the State when defining the issues that affect its public policy or the interests of society as a whole, as well as the actions that will be implemented to protect such values, such situation does not prevent the Arbitral Tribunal, without thereby questioning such due deference, from examining ... whether such measures are reasonable with respect to their goals, the deprivation of economic rights and the legitimate expectations of who suffered such deprivation.[73]

While there is not yet a uniform line of reasoning, nor a uniform standard of deference applied by arbitral tribunals, tailoring the standard of review is a widespread technique arbitral tribunals use to ensure that states dispose of sufficient room for manoeuvre in implementing public policies to protect non-investment concerns. What is more, just as proportionality reasoning, recourse to deference and similar concepts indicating a reduced standard of review reflects public law and public international law thinking, thus constituting a clear break with commercial law-inspired techniques of interpretation and dispute resolution.[74]

Finally, there is a notable move in investment treaty arbitration more generally to interpret IIA standards against the benchmark of comparative public law. While this development is only starting to take hold of investment treaty arbitration more broadly, it shows that the hitherto prevailing commercial law spirit is subsiding. For example, the Tribunal in *Total v. Argentina* observed in relation to the fair and equitable treatment standard:

> In determining the scope of a right or obligation, Tribunals have often looked as a benchmark to international or comparative standards. Indeed, as is often the case for general standards applicable in any legal system (such as "due process"), a comparative analysis of what is considered generally fair or unfair conduct by domestic public

[71] For more in depth discussion see Schill (2012b); Burke-White and von Staden (2010a, b); Henckels (2012). For a different reading of arbitral decisions as not showing sufficient restraint see Van Harten (2013).

[72] *SD Myers, Inc v. Canada*, UNCITRAL (NAFTA), Partial Award, 13 November 2000), para. 261.

[73] *Tecnicas Medioambientales Tecmed S.A. v. United Mexican States*, ICSID Case No. ARB (AF)/00/2, Award (29 May 2003), para. 122.

[74] For an in-depth discussion of the conceptual foundations of deference in public and public international law see Schill (2012b), pp. 585–594.

> authorities in respect of private firms and investors in domestic law may also be relevant to identify the legal standards under BITs. Such an approach is justified because, factually, the situations and conduct to be evaluated under a BIT occur within the legal system and social, economic and business environment of the host State.[75]

Similarly, the Tribunal in *Toto v. Lebanon* stated that "[t]he fair and equitable treatment standard of international law does not depend on the perception of the frustrated investor, but should use public international law and comparative domestic public law as a benchmark."[76] And finally, the Tribunal in *Gold Reserve v. Venezuela* gave an extensive overview over the parallels that existed between the concept of legitimate expectations in IIAs and parallel doctrines of domestic public law:

> With particular regard to the legal sources of one of the standards for respect of the fair and equitable treatment principle, *i.e.* the protection of 'legitimate expectations', these sources are to be found in the comparative analysis of many domestic legal systems. ... Based on converging considerations of good faith and legal security, the concept of legitimate expectations is found in different legal traditions according to which some expectations may be reasonably or legitimately created for a private person by the constant behavior and/or promises of its legal partner, in particular when this partner is the public administration on which this private person is dependent. In particular, in German law, protection of legitimate expectations is connected with the principle of *Vertraensschutz* [sic] (protection of trust) a notion which deeply influenced the development of European Union Law, pointing to precise and specific assurances given by the administration. The same notion finds equivalents in other European countries such as France in the concept of *confiance lé gitime*. The substantive (as opposed to procedural) protection of legitimate expectations is now also to be found in English law, although it was not recognized until the last decade. This protection is also found in Latin American countries, including in Argentina ... and exists equally in Venezuelan administrative law....[77]

As these decisions show, Miles' critique conveys a one-sided picture of the sociological and legal implications the choice for arbitration entails in ISDS. Her view suggests that power in the existing system resides in the hands of arbitrators, either individually or as a group. Yet, the community of investment arbitrators is far from the 'old boys club' Miles depicts, which controls the fate of individual disputes and the future of the entire field to the detriment of public interests. For once, states have it in their hands to diversify the group of investment arbitrators by appointing people with a different mind-set and different characteristics—and indeed, a diversification in terms of gender, age, nationality, professional background and pedigree of investment arbitrators is already taking place in recent years. At the same time, investment tribunals are themselves increasingly breaking with the mind-set of international commercial arbitration by making use of argumentative techniques known from (national and international) public law, such as

---

[75] *Total S.A. v. The Argentine Republic*, ICSID Case No. ARB/04/1, Decision on Liability (27 December 2010), para. 111 (internal citations omitted).

[76] *Toto Costruzioni Generali S.p.A. v. Republic of Lebanon*, ICSID Case No. ARB/07/12, Award (7 July 2012), para. 166.

[77] *Gold Reserve Inc. v. Bolivarian Republic of Venezuela*, ICSID Case No. ARB(AF)/09/1, Award (22 September 2014), para. 576 (internal citations omitted).

proportionality balancing, doctrines of deference, and comparative public law reasoning. These developments illustrate that arbitrators, already in the existing system, dispose of the tools to interpret IIA disciplines in a way that respects the policy space states need to regulate in the public interest. What remains in Miles' account of ISDS are then no more than half a handful of 'problematic' cases that I will turn to next.

5 Vattenfall, Philip Morris, Bilcon: Pathologies of the System?

When considering the effect of IIAs on regulatory powers of states, decisions by arbitral tribunals have always been the focal point of criticism—and rightly so as a dispute settlement system should not only be assessed in respect of its structural features, including who has access, who decides, under which procedures, and at what cost, but also in terms of its outcomes. Over time, however, there has been a curious shift in how investor-state cases have been used to criticize ISDS' impact on regulatory space. When the first ISDS cases were handed down in the late 1990s and early 2000s, critics castigated the outcome of certain decisions as paying insufficient respect to public interests and unduly restricting a government's policy space, for example to protect the environment.[78] Yet, soon such arguments became difficult to sustain because few, if any, cases were convincing examples of undue restrictions of government policy space to protect public interests.[79] Consequently, criticism shifted to the potential 'regulatory chill' that interpretations of IIA

[78] Reactions to *Metalclad Corporation v. The United Mexican States*, ICSID Case No. ARB(AF)/97/1 (NAFTA), Award (30 August 2000), were such an example, as the case was criticised for expanding the concept of indirect expropriation in IIAs so as to encompass a particularly broad version of regulatory taking that required compensation for any general measure that aimed at the protection of the environment and was harmful to the profits of foreign investors. What often went unnoticed, however, was that the case concerned not a 'regulatory taking' at all, but involved the frustration of an assurance that the central Mexican government had given to the investor in question that all permits to operate the envisioned waste landfill had been granted and that construction could start.

[79] On the contrary, a host of decisions recognised, not much differently from the restrictions domestic constitutional standards imposed, that general regulation was usually exempt from compensation, unless there was discrimination, unnecessary and disproportionate negative impact, or specific assurances to refrain from the measure in question. See *Methanex Corporation v. United States of America,* UNCITRAL (NAFTA), Final Award of the Tribunal on Jurisdiction and Merits (3 August 2005). See also *Saluka Investments BV v. Czech Republic*, UNCITRAL, Partial Award (17 March 2006), para. 255 ("It is now established in international law that States are not liable to pay compensation to a foreign investor when, in the normal exercise of their regulatory powers, they adopt in a non-discriminatory manner bona fide regulations that are aimed at the general welfare.").

standards by arbitral tribunals, and governments' fear for incurring liability for breach of IIAs, could cause.[80] However, since actual examples showing such a chill by arbitral interpretations are equally rare, the regulatory chill-argument was largely devoid of legal bite and hence equally weak.[81]

With little problematic outcomes to point to, critics have now resorted, as does Kate Miles in her discussion of *Vattenfall*, *Philip Morris*, and *Bilcon*, to taking the very fact that certain claims are even brought as an "inappropriate encroachment into domestic policy and regulatory space".[82] Viewing claims as a problem for a dispute settlement system says much about the critic's view of the concept of the rule of law and the idea of access to justice—it propagates that the better alternative to government control through adjudicatory mechanisms is no effective government control at all. I have refuted the value of such an argument already in Part 2 above. Yet, even when taking a closer look at *Vattenfall*, *Philip Morris*, and *Bilcon*, we see that Miles' assessment of these cases as pathologies of the system is little convincing. Instead, a more detailed assessment of these cases shows that they have ended up in ISDS for entirely legitimate reasons. In both, *Vattenfall* and *Philip Morris*, legitimate controversies existed as to whether the government's concrete conduct, not the underlying policies themselves, which nobody doubted were legitimate, were in line with the applicable investment disciplines. The same holds true with respect to the *Bilcon* case. Not the legitimacy of a government policy to protect the environment was at stake here, but the concrete implementation of that policy and its compliance with NAFTA's investment chapter.

First, let me turn to the two *Vattenfall* cases.[83] These cases are entirely separate from each other and not part of a "two-step story".[84] *Vattenfall I* concerned the legality of environmental conditions attached to an operating license issued by the

---

[80] See, for example, Tienhaara (2011).

[81] See, for example, the conclusion of a study for the Minister for Foreign Trade and Development Cooperation, Ministry of Foreign Affairs, The Netherlands by Tietje C, Baetens F (2014) The Impact of Investor-State-Dispute Settlement (ISDS) in the Transatlantic Trade and Investment Partnership, Ref. MINBUZA-2014.78850, http://www.rijksoverheid.nl/bestanden/documenten-en-publicaties/rapporten/2014/06/24/the-impact-of-investor-state-dispute-settlement-isds-in-the-ttip/the-impact-of-investor-state-dispute-settlement-isds-in-the-ttip.pdf (last accessed 31 July 2015), p. 9 ("We recognize that regulatory chill is difficult to prove or disprove, but a close examination of case law from NAFTA and CAFTA does not support this theory. Most investment claims do not challenge the government's ability to legislate or regulate as such, but are administrative in character, challenging a government's treatment of an individual investor in the context of a particular license, permit, or promise extended by government officials. So far under NAFTA, direct challenges to the government's legislative or regulatory rights have never succeeded."); see further at pp. 39–48.

[82] Miles (2016), section 2.1.

[83] These are *Vattenfall AB, Vattenfall Europe AG, Vattenfall Europe Generation AG v. Federal Republic of Germany*, ICSID Case No. ARB/09/6, Award (11 March 2011) (*Vattenfall I*) and *Vattenfall AB and others v. Federal Republic of Germany*, ICSID Case No. ARB/12/12 (registered 31 May 2012) (*Vattenfall II*).

[84] Miles (2016), section 2.1.1.

City of Hamburg under existing environmental laws for a coal-fired power plant. *Vattenfall II* concerned a legislative change to the federal law governing nuclear power plants. While *Vattenfall I* thus involved a question tied to administrative law; *Vattenfall II* involved restrictions of the legislator and hence a constitutional matter. There was no other connection between these two cases except for the fact that the same energy company operated the plants in question and that the basis for the claims were the investment provisions in the Energy Charter Treaty. More importantly, however, both *Vattenfall* cases are not presented in full by Kate Miles, but in a selective fashion that has the effect of suggesting conclusions that both cases simply do not support, namely that Vattenfall was and is using ISDS to circumvent uncontested and flawless public interest regulation. Rather, a full reading of the facts of both cases shows that legitimate disputes about the appropriateness of the government measures under international law are at issue and that these disputes are apt for an international adjudicatory system, such as investor-state arbitration, to decide.

Turning to *Vattenfall I*, this is not a case where a settlement of the parties of the ICSID proceedings resulted in the City of Hamburg (not Germany) "agreeing to slacken the environmental standards and issue a significantly less exacting permit."[85] What Miles does not mention is that Vattenfall had challenged the environmental conditions in Hamburg's administrative courts and that it was in these domestic court proceedings that a settlement was reached, as permitted under German administrative law, regarding certain conditions of a water permit that was necessary for the operation of the plant. The settlement of the ICSID proceedings, which is publicly available,[86] only procedurally implemented the parties' earlier settlement in domestic courts and has no independent regulatory content. It is of course possible that the ICSID proceedings exercised pressure on the City to settle the domestic court case, but such an argument has not been put forward.

In addition, Miles also does not tell us the full background of *Vattenfall I*. Importantly, this was not a case where an investor used ISDS to reach an exemption from environmental standards required under domestic law. Instead, the case was concerned with a situation in which the ministry in charge changed policy after local election, even though the investor had already been promised by the Hamburg City Government, then under the sole control of the Christian Democrats, that an operating license with certain environmental parameters was going to be issued and on that basis had been granted permission to start the construction of the power plant. However, before all final licenses were issued, the Green Party joined the City Government after the elections alongside the Christian Democrats, took over the ministry in charge and issued a license that the investor claimed made the operation of the plant economically unviable because it imposed environmental conditions that were harsher than originally promised. The full background of

[85] Miles (2016), section 2.1.1.

[86] *Vattenfall AB, Vattenfall Europe AG, Vattenfall Europe Generation AG v. Federal Republic of Germany*, ICSID Case No. ARB/09/6, Award (11 March 2011)

Vattenfall I should make clear that this is not a straightforward situation of a government agreeing to slacken environmental regulations facing an ISDS claim. On the contrary, it concerns a legitimate dispute about whether a government that indicates that it would exercise administrative discretion in issuing a license in a certain way and thereby induces a specific investment, can simply renege on that promise without standing in for the damage caused. The modus of implementation of environmental policies was thus the true problem, not the environmental policy as such.

Likewise, *Vattenfall II* is not so much about the legitimacy of phasing out nuclear power *per se*, but about the procedure of doing so. Above all, the case cannot be limited to the law phasing out nuclear power that was ultimately passed, but needs to be seen against the background of consecutive governments engaging in roller coaster ride-type politics in respect of nuclear energy.[87] Thus, after nuclear power was first made into one of the corner stones of Germany's strategy to secure an autarkic energy supply, the coalition government between the Social Democrats and the Green Party under Chancellor Schröder decided in 2002, in agreement with the energy industry, a long-term plan to phase-out nuclear power by 2032. In October 2010, however, the newly elected federal government under Chancellor Merkel consisting of a coalition between Christian Democrats and the Liberal Party, essentially undid the earlier phase-out of nuclear power, again in consultation with the nuclear industry. This deal, however, came at a price, so that the government would also benefit from the additional income. In return for the extension of operating capacity for nuclear plants, power producers were required to invest in their plants and pay a new tax on nuclear fuel that would benefit the public purse.

Only a few months later, in March 2011, the Fukushima incident happened, and because of impending elections in Germany's South-Western State of Baden-Württemberg, which Chancellor Merkel's Christian Democrats risked losing inter alia due to having undone the original nuclear phase-out, an immediate moratorium on producing nuclear power was declared by executive order on the basis of existing legislation. In August of the same year the permanent phase-out was then decided by federal law. The end date of that second phase-out was 2022—10 years earlier than the phase-out decided under the Schröder government in 2002; at the same time, the tax on nuclear however was not repealed. This additional background gives *Vattenfall II* a very different flavour and moves it far from an "illegitimate encroachment on regulatory space". It is the back-and-forth of law and policy-making in an area requiring significant investments and long-term planning that is brought to ISDS here, not the phase-out of nuclear power as such.

That legal action against the nuclear power phase-out itself is not an encroachment of regulatory space can also be seen from the domestic court cases that are pending in the matter. The highest German administrative court, the Bundesverwaltungsgericht, has already held that the temporary moratorium declared

[87] For a short discussion of the factual background with further references see Wikipedia, Atomausstieg, https://de.wikipedia.org/wiki/Atomausstieg (last accessed 31 July 2015).

immediately following the Fukushima incident was contrary to the governing statutory law, thus requiring the government to pay damages to affected power producers.[88] Other aspects of the nuclear power phase-out are still pending in domestic courts, such as the question whether maintaining the nuclear fuel tax was legal, even though the rest of the 'phase-out deal' was undone.[89] Similarly, Vattenfall and some of its German competitors have brought constitutional challenges against the nuclear power phase-out in the German Constitutional Court.[90] If the ICSID proceedings in *Vattenfall II* encroach on regulatory space, the same would hold true of the domestic proceedings in the matter.

Certainly, one may argue that domestic proceedings control government conduct sufficiently. Yet, Vattenfall faces additional hurdles that ISDS remedies help to smoothen. Thus, none of the domestic proceedings is likely going to address the legality of the measures under the Energy Charter Treaty. Moreover, with Vattenfall being in essence a foreign state-owned company, it is unclear whether the company can invoke fundamental rights under the German Constitution. And finally, the case illustrates the possible lack of neutrality, from the perspective of foreign investors, of domestic courts. After all, one could ask how the German Constitutional Court can deliver a strictly neutral and apolitical decision when each judge on the court is likely to have a political view on the issue at stake. After all, apart from German reunification, nuclear power has been perhaps the most political of all topics in Germany in the past decades. For all of these reasons, it is entirely legitimate that the dispute between Vattenfall and the German government about the legality of the measures at stake under the Energy Charter Treaty is pending in an international, and not only in a national forum. What is highly problematic, however, is the confidentiality with which the *Vattenfall II* case is handled. So far, little is known about the case itself and the parties' arguments except for minor details that were leaked from unknown sources. This aspect, in my view, is the true problem with *Vattenfall II*, because it is contrary to the principles of openness and transparency that govern dispute settlement between private and public actors in democratic societies, not the fact as such that the case is brought.

[88] See German Federal Administrative Court (Bundesverwaltungsgericht—BVerwG), Decision of 20 December 2013 (7 B 18/13) [2014] Deutsches Verwaltungsblatt 303. See also the pointed analysis of the moratorium by Rebentisch (2011). On the liability of the state under domestic law see Schmitt and Wohlrab (2015).

[89] See German Federal Constitutional Court (Bundesverfassungsgericht), 2 BvL 6/13 (pending) following an order for reference by the Hamburg Fiscal Court, Decision of 29 January 2013 (4 K 270/11). The Federal Fiscal Court (Bundesfinanzhof—BFH) declined the application of interim measures until the Bundesverfassungsgericht renders its judgment, thereby annulling prior decisions by the FG Hamburg and the FG Munich that granted repayment claims put forward by power plant operators, see BFH, Decision of 9 March 2012 (VII B 171/11) and Decision of 25 November 2014 (VII B 65/14).

[90] See constitutional complaints submitted by E.ON Kraftwerke GmbH (1 BvR 2821/11), RWE Power AG (1 BvR 321/12), Kernkraftwerk Krümmel GmbH & Co OHG and Vattenfall Europe Nuclear Energy (1 BvR 1456/12) (all pending).

Second, turning to *Philip Morris*, in my view this is also not a good example of an illegitimate claim *per se* that reflects badly on the entire investment treaty system. Independently of the low likelihood many observers attribute to Philip Morris' chances of winning,[91] and independently of how the implementation of plain packaging in Australia should be decided, the very fact that this dispute is brought in ISDS is not part of an illegitimate encroachment of Australia's policy space, but responds, entirely legitimately, to a shortcoming the Australian legal system has with the domestic enforcement of international treaties, including IIAs. After all, under Australian law, IIAs are not enforceable within the domestic legal order and before Australia's courts. As Australia's Chief Justice recently stated: "[t]he capacity of international treaties to confer rights on non-state actors has long been accepted. But such rights are not enforceable under the domestic law of dualist states, unless those states are constitutionally empowered to give effect to them and have done so."[92] Australia, being a dualist state, faces exactly this limitation with respect to IIA disciplines: they cannot be invoked in domestic courts. Where then, other than in an international forum, should an investor bring claims for non-compliance with the Australia-Hong Kong BIT? Under the circumstances at hand, ISDS is the only available forum in which access to justice to review Australia's conduct under the BIT in question is granted.

Finally, turning to *Bilcon*, I cannot see how this case "embodies an approach that is reminiscent of the earliest investor-state disputes involving environmental matters", as Kate Miles argues.[93] To start with, *Bilcon* is a pending dispute, which makes it a bad example to argue a general point about the dangers of arbitral discretion. The Tribunal has only ruled on liability, but left damages open. It is therefore too early to assess the impact of the decision and the consequences of the breach of NAFTA that the Tribunal found. Possibly, the damages attached to the breach found by the Tribunal will remain very low, given that the project at issue was not a going concern. Furthermore, there are remedies in case the decision was wrong before the Canadian courts that exercise supervisory jurisdiction at the seat of the arbitration, which have been used by the respondent.[94] Only upon completion of that process will one be able to assess whether the current ISDS system does not dispose of the necessary powers of self-correction, if they were needed. *Bilcon* may be correctly or incorrectly decided, it may be good or bad from an environmentalist's perspective, but I do not think it is a good example to illustrate the dangers of arbitral interpretations.

---

[91] See, for example, Voon and Mitchell (2011). Meanwhile, Philip Morris' claim has reportedly been dismissed, albeit on jurisdictional grounds. See 'Australia Prevails in Arbitration with Philip Morris over Tobacco Plain Packaging Dispute' IAReporter (17 December 2015), http://tinyurl.com/jd7qwlf (last accessed 27 February 2016).

[92] See French (2015), p. 159.

[93] Miles (2016), section 4.

[94] *Attorney General of Canada v. William Ralph Clayton and others*, Notice of Application (16 June 2015), Court File No. T-1000-15, http://italaw.com (last accessed 31 July 2015).

Certainly, it is problematic if an arbitral tribunal steps entirely into the shoes of a domestic administrative court in reviewing the measures in question, and engages in an exercise of second-guessing the application of national law by a national institution. Yet, this is not what the majority in *Bilcon* did. It set out the deferential and well-accepted NAFTA standard of fair and equitable treatment, as developed by the tribunal in *Waste Management v. Mexico*[95] as the basis of its holding, emphasising "that there is a high threshold for the conduct of a host state to rise to the level of a NAFTA Article 1105 breach."[96] Already this statement should counter the argument about *Bilcon* rolling back the deferential character of arbitral review under NAFTA. The majority in *Bilcon* did also not review the measure in question under the standards of Canadian law, saying that the treatment of the foreign investor was simply illegal under that law. The majority went further than that and held that the way the environmental assessment was conducted in the case at hand was arbitrary and contrary to how Canadian companies were treated in comparable circumstances.[97] The Tribunal therefore applied a lenient standard and held that the administrative process carried out in the case at hand fell blatantly short of the international minimum standard.

A finding of arbitrariness, which requires a high threshold, should not be taken as an illustration of unpredictable arbitral discretion, but rather throws a critical light on the administrative process in the case in Canada. Keeping in mind that we are here in an international, transborder, not a purely inner-Canadian context, is important because what may seem arbitrary for lawyers from outside Canada, such as the Tribunal's President, a German, and the investor's nominee, an American, may be just perfectly fine for a Canadian, such as the dissenter, and vice versa. Importantly, the transborder context has to be taken into account when considering whether certain government conduct withstands scrutiny under basic notions of fairness and the rule of law not only within a domestic legal and cultural context, but also under the eyes of lawyers that have been socialised elsewhere and that may take issue with conduct found perfectly agreeable in the host state. After all, differing legal culture is one of the obstacles that international law tries to overcome by providing legal standards that are independent of national law and compliance with which is determined by independent and neutral legal institutions.

---

[95] *Clayton and others and Bilcon of Delaware, Inc. v. Government of Canada*, UNCITRAL (NAFTA), Award on Jurisdiction and Liability (17 March 2015), paras. 427-446.

[96] *Clayton and others and Bilcon of Delaware, Inc. v. Government of Canada*, UNCITRAL (NAFTA), Award on Jurisdiction and Liability (17 March 2015), para. 444.

[97] *Clayton and others and Bilcon of Delaware, Inc. v. Government of Canada*, UNCITRAL (NAFTA), Award on Jurisdiction and Liability (17 March 2015), para. 591 (concluding that "that the conduct of the joint review was arbitrary. The JRP [i.e. Joint Review Panel] effectively created, without legal authority or fair notice to Bilcon, a new standard of assessment rather than fully carrying out the mandate defined by the applicable law, including the requirement under the *CEAA* [i.e. the applicable legal framework] to carry out a thorough 'likely significant adverse effects after mitigation' analysis.").

That conduct that is legal under domestic law, suddenly becomes illegal under international law is the most normal of consequences the acceptance of, and submission to, international law by states can have. This holds true in international law generally, and international investment law in particular. Likewise, falling short of international standards in individual cases, and losing an arbitration here or there, should be appreciated as a normal consequence of engaging in international adjudicatory institutions. Rather than casting the adjudicatory institutions dealing with such disputes into doubt, losing a case should inspire states to aim at further perfecting the way they exercise public authority in transborder relations. What one should rather wonder about is why only cases against developed countries, such as Germany, Canada, and Australia, are depicted as pathologies of international investment law and ISDS? Developed countries are in no way exempt from the need of occasional and well-balanced control by international courts tribunals that smoothen the unavoidable edges of less-than-ideal law- and policy-making, which, at times, affects foreigners more than nationals.

6 Conclusion: Pathways for Future Reform

The current international investment regime is certainly not perfect—no system of adjudication is. It suffers from a number of shortcomings, which Kate Miles has rightly mentioned. I agree that a fundamental problem with ISDS is the unfortunate blending between a model for the resolution of private (commercial) disputes with public law issues. I agree that these disputes should not be conducted behind closed doors, but should be fully transparent, that public participation should be ensured to reflect the fundamental democratic principle that those affected by a decision should be heard and involved in their making. I also agree that legitimate public welfare regulation should not be prevented or even chilled by international investment protection, but that host states need policy space to regulate in the public interest. At the same time, I consider it important that foreign investors—in fact any investor, independent of nationality—benefit from sufficient protection against arbitrary, discriminatory or otherwise illegitimate government conduct and have recourse to a neutral and efficient forum to settle disputes with governments. This is called for not only in the interest of investors, but is—as a postulate of the rule of law—itself in the public interest.

What we are looking for in the end, is a balance between protecting investors against illegitimate government interference, while ensuring sufficient policy space to pursue legitimate regulation in the public interest. Yet, what is legitimate in the eyes of one side (whether investors, states, third parties, or outside observers), may not be so in the eyes of the other. It is for this reason that somebody neutral and independent needs to decide on where the boundaries of legitimate government and investor conduct lie, and do so not on the basis of political preference, but based on legal principle. Arbitration is an appropriate instrument to achieve such ends and is capable, in both principle and fact, to distinguish illegitimate opportunistic government behaviour from legitimate regulation in the public interest. What is more, looking at past performance of investment treaty arbitration, there is little concern about systemic pro-investor and anti-public interest biases. On the contrary, arbitrators have fared well in resolving the often complex investor-state disputes without disregarding competing non-investment concerns. This does not mean that arbitration is necessarily the best possible alternative, but it is at present the only workable one we have to enforce IIA disciplines effectively and neutrally.

As I have argued above in discussing and refuting the criticism of IIAs and ISDS, my own assessment of the present system is much more positive than the one depicted by Kate Miles. This notwithstanding, the criticism investment treaty arbitration has been and continues to be subject to is an important source of dynamism and change without which the investment regime would be much worse off than at present. The criticism of the investment regime and particularly ISDS is to be credited for making governments, the general public, as well as specialists, aware of potential biases and shortcomings. It has functioned as a wake-up call for governments to watch arbitral decision-making and to assess whether the system stays within its intended mandate. The criticism has also contributed to governments starting to remedy certain shortcomings through the introduction of more transparency and third-party participation, clarifications to IIA standards, and tighter control mechanisms vis-à-vis arbitral decision-making. And the criticism has led to an improvement in how arbitrators conduct arbitral proceedings, reason awards and decisions, deal with competing public interests, and how the arbitration community is starting to self-regulate in order to ensure the benefits of the system.

Finally, the criticism continues to fuel much of the current debates about the reform of the investment treaty regime, in particular the debates about renewed efforts at multilateralism, the thinking about international investment law as part of policies of sustainable development, and possibly the creation of new and more permanent institutions for ISDS, such as an appellate mechanism or a permanent investment court.[98] Thus, instead of continuing to argue that the existing international investment regime is fundamentally flawed, it is these reform efforts that critics should direct their attention to and actively engage with in order to tweak the system to better live up to the ideals of democracy, the protection of human rights, and the rule of law they aspire to. After all, it is not the basic structure of the system, in particular recourse to an international forum in order to review government action as to their compliance with certain basic rule of law principles enshrined in international treaties, which are rotten. It is rather some excrescent rank growth that needs trimming. Critics of the investment regime could do a lot on this end by

[98] See European Commission, Press Release: Commission Proposes New Investment Court System for TTIP and Other EU Trade and Investment Negotiations, 16 September 2015, http://europa.eu/rapid/press-release_IP-15-5651_en.htm (last accessed 15 October 2015). For a succinct overview over the most recent reform debates and options more generally see UNCTAD (2015) World Investment Report 2015: Reforming International Investment Governance, http://unctad.org/en/PublicationsLibrary/wir2015_en.pdf (last accessed 28 September 2015), p. 119 ff. See further, inter alia, the contributions in Kalicki and Joubin-Bret (2015).

turning from deconstruction to constructive engagement and help build a better system of international investment law.

Acknowledgments The author acknowledges support in preparing this article under a European Research Council Starting Grant on 'Transnational Private-Public Abitration as Global Regulatory Governance: Charting and Codifying the Lex Mercatoria Publica' (LexMercPub, Grant agreement no.: 313355).

References

Aisbett E (2009) Bilateral investment treaties and foreign direct investment: correlation and causation. In: Sauvant K, Sachs L (eds) The effect of treaties on foreign direct investment: bilateral investment treaties, double taxation treaties, and investment flows. Oxford University Press, Oxford, pp 395–435. doi:10.1093/acprof:oso/9780195388534.003.0015

Amerasinghe C (2005) Local remedies in international law, 2nd edn. Cambridge University Press, Cambridge

Amerasinghe C (2008) Diplomatic protection. Oxford University Press, Oxford. doi:10.1093/acprof:oso/9780199212385.001.0001

Berger A, Busse M, Nunnenkamp P, Roy M (2012) Do trade and investment agreements lead to more FDI? accounting for key provisions inside the black box. Int Econ & Econ Policy 10 (2):247–275. doi:10.1007/s10368-012-0207-6

Borchard E (1915) The diplomatic protection of citizens abroad. Banks Law Publishing Company, New York

Brower C, Blanchard S (2014) What's in a meme? The truth about investor-state arbitration: why it need not, and must not, be repossessed by states. Columbia J Transl Law 52(3):689–777

Brower C, Schill S (2009) Is arbitration a threat or a boon to the legitimacy of international investment law? Chicago J Int Law 9(2):471–498

Brower C, Pulos M, Rosenberg C (2013) So is there anything really wrong with international arbitration as we know it? In: Rovine A (ed) Contemporary issues in international arbitration and mediation: the Fordham Papers. Brill Nijhoff, Leiden, pp 1–13. doi:10.1163/9789004260207_002

Bücheler G (2015) Proportionality in investor-state arbitration. Oxford University Press, Oxford

Burke-White W, von Staden A (2010a) The need for public law standards of review in investor-state arbitrations. In: Schill S (ed) International investment law and comparative public law. Oxford University Press, Oxford, pp 689–720. doi:10.1093/acprof:oso/9780199589104.003.0022

Burke-White W, von Staden A (2010b) Private litigation in a public law sphere: the standard of review in investor-state arbitrations. Yale J Int Law 35:283–346

Buscaglia E, Dakolias M (1999) An analysis of the causes of corruption in the judiciary. Law Policy Int Bus 30:95–116

Büthe T, Milner H (2014) Foreign direct investment and institutional diversity in trade agreements: credibility, commitment, and economic flows in the developing world, 1971-2007. World Pol 66(1):88–122. doi:10.1017/S0043887113000336

Cancado Trindade A (1983) The application of the rule of exhaustion of local remedies in international law. Cambridge University Press, Cambridge

Cooter R, Ulen T (2004) Law and economics, 4th edn. Addison Wesley, Boston

Dakolias M, Thachuk K (2000) The problem of eradicating corruption from the judiciary: attacking corruption in the judiciary: a critical process in judicial reform. Wis Int Law J 18:353–406

Elkins Z, Guzman A, Simmons B (2006) Competing for capital: the diffusion of bilateral investment treaties, 1960-2000. Int Organ 60(4):811–846. doi:10.1017/S0020818306060279

Fontoura Costa J (2011) Comparing WTO panelists and ICSID arbitrators: the creation of international legal fields. Oñati Socio-Legal Series 1(4), http://opo.iisj.net/index.php/osls/article/view/63/207

Francioni F (ed) (2007) Access to justice as a human right. Oxford University Press, Oxford

Franck S, Freda T, Lavin K, Lehmann T, van Aaken A (2015) The diversity challenge: exploring the "invisible college" of international arbitration. Columbia J Transl Law 53:429–506

French R (2015) ISDS: litigating the judiciary. Public Law Rev 26(3):155–165

Guzman A (1998) Why LDCs sign treaties that hurt them: explaining the popularity of bilateral investment treaties. Virginia J Int Law 38:639–688

Guzman A (2008) How international law works: a rational choice theory. Oxford University Press, Oxford

Hagelberg J (2006) Die völkerrechtliche Verfügungsbefugnis des Staates über Rechtsansprüche von Privatpersonen. Nomos, Baden-Baden. doi:10.5771/9783845225081

Henckels C (2012) Indirect expropriation and the right to regulate: revisiting proportionality analysis and the standard of review in investor-state arbitration. J Int Econ Law 15 (2):223–255. doi:10.1093/jiel/jgs012

Hindelang S, Krajewski M (eds) (2016) Shifting paradigms in international investment law: more balanced, less isolated, increasingly diversified. Oxford University Press, Oxford

Jandhyala S, Weiner R (2014) *Institutions sans frontières*: international agreements and foreign investment. J Int Bus Stud 45(6):649–669. doi:10.1057/jibs.2013.70

Johnson OT, Gimblett J (2012) From gunboats to BITs: the evolution of modern international investment law. In: Sauvant K (ed) Yearbook on international investment law and policy 2010–2011. Oxford University Press, New York, pp 649–692

Kalicki J, Joubin-Bret A (eds) (2015) Reshaping the investor-state dispute settlement system: journeys for the 21st century. Brill Nijhoff, Leiden. doi:10.1163/9789004291102

Kapeliuk D (2010) The repeat appointment factor: exploring decision patterns of elite investment arbitrators. Cornell Law Rev 96:47–90

Karton J (2013) The culture of international arbitration and the evolution of contract law. Oxford University Press, Oxford

Kingsbury B, Schill S (2010) Public law concepts to balance investors' rights with state regulatory actions in the public interest—the concept of proportionality. In: Schill S (ed) International investment law and comparative public law. Oxford University Press, Oxford, pp 75–104. doi:10.1093/acprof:oso/9780199589104.003.0003

Leonhardsen E (2012) Looking for legitimacy: exploring proportionality analysis in investment treaty arbitration. J Int Disp Settlement 3(1):95–136. doi:10.1093/jnlids/idr014

Lillich R, Weston B (1975) International claims: their settlement by lump-sum agreements. University Press of Virginia, Charlottesville

Miles K (2016) Investor-state dispute settlement: conflict, convergence, and future directions. In: Bungenberg M, Hermann C, Krajewski M, Terchechte JP (eds) European yearbook of international economic Law, vol 7. Springer, Heidelberg, pp 273–308

Montt S (2009) State liability in investment treaty arbitration. Hart Publishing, Oxford

Puig S (2014) Social capital in the arbitration market. Eur J Int Law 25(2):387–424. doi:10.1093/ejil/chu045

Rebentisch M (2011) "Kraftwerks-Moratorium" versus Rechtsstaat. Neue Zeitschrift für Verwaltungsrecht 30:533–535

Roberts A (2010) Power and persuasion in investment treaty interpretation: the dual role of states. Am J Int Law 104(2):179–225

Schill S (2010) International investment law and comparative public law: an introduction. In: Schill S (ed) International investment law and comparative public law. Oxford University Press, Oxford, pp 3–37. doi:10.1093/acprof:oso/9780199589104.003.0001

Schill S (2011a) Enhancing international investment law's legitimacy: conceptual and methodological foundations of a new public law approach. Virginia J Int Law 52(1):57–102

Schill S (2011b) W(h)ither fragmentation? On the literature and sociology of international investment law. Eur J Int Law 22(3):875–908. doi:10.1093/ejil/chr062
Schill S (2012a) Cross-regime harmonization through proportionality analysis: the case of international investment law, the law of state immunity, and human rights. ICSID Rev-Foreign Investment Law J 27(1):87–119. doi:10.1093/icsidreview/sis002
Schill S (2012a) Deference in investment treaty arbitration: re-conceptualizing the standard of review. J Int Disp Settlement 3(3):577–607. doi:10.1093/jnlids/ids010
Schill S (2015a) Developing a framework for the legitimacy of international arbitration. In: van den Berg A (ed) Legitimacy: myths, realities, challenges. ICCA Congress Series, vol. 18, Miami 2014, Wolters Kluwer, Alphen aan den Rijn, pp 789–827
Schill S (2015b) The overlooked role of arbitration in international adjudicatory theory. ESIL Reflection 4(2)
Schill S (2015c) The sixth path: reforming investment law from within. In: Kalicki J, Joubin-Bret A (eds.) Reshaping the investor-state dispute settlement system: journeys for the 21st century. Brill Nijhoff, Leiden, pp 621–652
Schill S, Tvede K (2015) Mainstreaming investment treaty jurisprudence: the contribution of investment treaty tribunals to the consolidation and development of general international law. Law Pract Int Courts Trib 14(1):94–129. doi:10.1163/15718034-12341287
Schmitt T, Wohlrab S (2015) Haftung des Bundes in der Auftragsverwaltung am Beispiel des so genannten "Moratoriums" für Kernkraftwerke. Neue Zeitschrift für Verwaltungsrecht 34 (14):932–937
Schwartz A, Scott R (2003) Contract theory and the limits of contract law. Yale Law J 113:541–619
Schwebel S (2015) In defense of bilateral investment treaties. In: van den Berg A (ed) Legitimacy: myths, realities, challenges. ICCA Congress Series, vol. 18, Miami 2014, Wolters Kluwer, Alphen aan den Rijn, pp 1–11
Sornarajah M (2015) Resistance and change in the international law on foreign investment. Cambridge University Press, Cambridge, doi:10.1017/CBO9781316156339
Stone Sweet A (2010) Investor–state arbitration: proportionality's new frontier. Law Ethics Hum Rights 4(1):48–76. doi:10.2202/1938-2545.1044
Tienhaara K (2011) Regulatory chill and the threat of arbitration: a view from political science. In: Brown C, Miles K (eds) Evolution in investment treaty law and arbitration. Cambridge University Press, Cambridge, pp 606–657
Tobin J, Rose-Ackerman S (2009) When BITs have some bite. In: Rogers C, Alford R (eds) The future of investment arbitration. Oxford University Press, New York, pp 131–144
van Aaken A (2009) Defragmentation of public international law through interpretation: a methodological proposal. Indiana J Glob Leg Stud 16(2):483–512
Van Harten G (2007) Investment treaty arbitration and public law. Oxford University Press, New York. doi:10.1093/acprof:oso/9780199552146.001.0001
Van Harten G (2010) Investment treaty arbitration, procedural fairness, and the rule of law. In: Schill S (ed) International investment law and comparative public law. Oxford University Press, Oxford, pp 627–657. doi:10.1093/acprof:oso/9780199589104.003.0020
Van Harten G (2013) Sovereign choices and sovereign constraints: judicial restraint in investment treaty arbitration. Oxford University Press, Oxford. doi:10.1093/acprof:oso/9780199678648.001.0001
Voon T, Mitchell A (2011) Time to quit? assessing international investment claims against plain tobacco packaging in Australia. J Int Econ Law 14(3):515–552. doi:10.1093/jiel/jgr030
Waibel M, Kaushal A, Chung KH, Balchin C (eds) (2010) The backlash against investment arbitration. Kluwer Law International, Alphen aan den Rijn
Weston B, Bederman D, Lillich R (1999) International claims: their settlement by lump-sum agreements 1975–1995. Brill Nijhoff, Leiden
Williamson O (1985) The economic institutions of capitalism: firms, markets, and relational contracting. The Free Press, New York

Yackee J (2008) Do we really need BITs? Asian J WTO Int Health Law Policy 3(1):121–146
Waibel M (2015) Interpretive communities in international law. In: Bianchi A, Peat D, Windsor M (eds) Interpretation in international law. Oxford University Press, New York, pp 147–164. doi:10.1093/acprof:oso/9780198725749.003.0007

Shifting Sands: Interrogating the Problematic Relationship Between International Public Finance and International Financial Regulation

Celine Tan

Contents

Abstract International public finance and international financial institutions have regained prominence in wake of the global financial crisis. The conscription of international public finance to crisis resolution and management in recurrent sovereign debt crises has highlighted the centrality of international public finance and its institutions to global economic regulation. In particular, the financial crisis has underscored the fundamental role of international public finance in managing the negative externalities caused by failures of international economic law and governance.

This paper interrogates the problematic relationship between international public finance and international economic law, in particular their shared responsibility for the distribution of international economic resources. It investigates the role played by international financial aid in mitigating the distributive dislocations resulting from international law's allocation of the risks and benefits of a globalized

C. Tan (✉)
School of Law, University of Warwick, Coventry, UK
e-mail: Celine.Tan@warwick.ac.uk

M. Bungenberg et al. (eds.), *European Yearbook of International Economic Law 2016*, European Yearbook of International Economic Law 7,
DOI 10.1007/978-3-319-29215-1_14

economy and examines how utilisation of aid finance in this manner has influenced the regulatory trajectories of international economic law.

Drawing on the example of sovereign debt relief and international financial regulation, this paper argues that the deployment of development finance as responses to the regulatory crises of the global financial system have had adverse effects on regulatory change, especially on efforts to reorient international financial law towards a more progressive social and economic agenda. It demonstrates how current practices of financial aid not only fail to address the systemic failings of the international financial system, they serve to sustain, if not entrench, existing asymmetries in international economic law, thereby exacerbating its negative distributive outcomes.

1 Introduction

International public finance and international financial institutions (IFIs) have regained prominence in wake of the global financial crisis. The conscription of international public finance to crisis resolution and management in the series of sovereign debt crises since 2008 has once again highlighted the centrality of international public finance and international financial institutions to global economic regulation. In particular, the financial crisis has underscored the fundamental role of international public finance in managing the negative externalities caused by failures in international economic law and governance. Resources from the public purse have been mobilised, both at national and international levels, to both contain the social and economic fallout from the regulatory shortcomings that have contributed to the crisis and to compensate for the absence of effective regulatory responses to its aftermath.

This paper interrogates the problematic relationship between international public finance and international economic law in the context of their shared responsibility for the distribution of international economic resources. The paper demonstrates how changes in the nature, scope and rationale of international financial regulation in the postwar period have resulted in the increasing deployment of official sector financing as a default response to regulatory challenges in the international financial system and considers the impact of these developments on international financial law and governance. It argues that these changes in the relationship between finance and regulation exemplify the conceptual shift in the normative foundations of the international financial architecture from a financial system governed by international law and inter-state coordination towards one primarily disciplined by market mechanisms.

The paper further argues that the practice of using financial transfers to compensate for the asymmetries of international economic law and regulation stymies legal and regulatory reform and serves to sustain, if not entrench, systemic market and regulatory failings and exacerbate the negative distributive outcomes of the international financial architecture. This disembeds the policies and practices of international public finance from the conduct of international economic relations and inserts recipient and financier states into relationships of power, with implications on their engagements with each other and with the global economy.

The remainder of this paper is organised as follows: the next section reviews the historical and contemporary relationship between international public finance and international economic law, namely international financial law, and examines the shifting rationales for international public finance in the context of changes in the global financial system in the postwar period. The following section investigates the function of public finance in the current international financial architecture, particularly its role in responding to the regulatory deficits and compensating for distributive dislocations of international financial law. The penultimate section of the paper then maps the concerns that arise from deploying international public finance as a mechanism for compensating for market and regulatory failures in a globalised economy and the challenges these pose for the reform of the international financial architecture.

2 Revisiting the Foundations

2.1 The Postwar Economic Compact

The growth and evolution of international economic law is intimately linked with the development of international public finance and its policies and institutions. Officially mobilised finance was a principal feature in the design of the postwar economic order and a fundamental complement to the regulatory architecture for trade and monetary affairs established, first, by the Bretton Woods agreement in 1944 and, latterly, by the formation of the General Agreement on Tariffs and Trade (GATT) in 1947, the precursor to the World Trade Organisation (WTO). Where the International Monetary Fund (IMF) and the GATT sought to provide the disciplinary framework for the conduct of international financial flows and trade in goods and services, multilateral financing formed the basis of support for financial stabilisation and reconstruction and economic development from the IMF and the International Bank for Reconstruction and Development (IBRD) (now part of the World Bank Group) respectively.[1]

At the core of the design of the postwar economic architecture was the political recognition that legal and policy cooperation was necessary to provide a stable base for an increasingly interdependent global economy. Collective global legal, regulatory and financial action were rationalised on the grounds that markets did not serve as efficient nor equitable mechanisms for the distribution of economic

[1] See Akyüz (2006), pp. 486–491; Arner and Buckley (2011), pp. 2–15.

resources nor could they be relied upon to ensure that international trade and financial flows led to politically or socially acceptable outcomes.[2]

This framework of international economic governance depended on complementarity between international economic law and the deployment of international public finance. Internationally binding rules and regulatory institutions were required to supervise national economies and prevent negative externalities generated by uncoordinated and self-interested national policies while multilateral financial assistance was necessary to provide for global public goods,[3] including support for international financial stability, and on humanitarian and distributive justice grounds. Embodied in the postwar political compromise termed by Ruggie as 'embedded liberalism'[4] the postwar framework of financial regulation was focused on establishing effective international regulatory mechanisms but at the same time, recognising that nation states had primary responsibility and autonomy to regulate financial flows in and out of national borders.

The IMF was placed centre of this regulatory architecture with the mandate to promote international monetary cooperation and international monetary stability, primarily through securing 'multilateral discipline in exchange rate policies' and the provision of short-term 'liquidity in for current account financing'.[5] The former responsibility saw the IMF endowed with the authority—under Article IV of its original IMF Agreement—to supervise member states' exchange rates so that they operated within a narrow range of multilaterally negotiated par values backed by the US dollar and underpinned by gold, and to impose sanctions[6] on members that failed to comply.[7] The Fund's mandate to promote international trade also resulted in obligations on member states to maintain current account convertibility under Article VIII, Sect. 2(a) but members retained their right to exercise controls over international capital flows under Article VI, Sect. 3.[8] The latter provision,

[2] Akyüz (2010), p. 40; Akyüz (2006), p. 487; Picciotto (2011), pp. 64–65.

[3] A global public good is defined as a service or policy whose production and consumption are in the public domain and whose benefits extend beyond national borders and across socio-economic groups (Kaul et al. 2003, p. 3).

[4] Ruggie (1982), p. 393.

[5] Akyüz Y, Reforming the IMF: Back to the Drawing Board, TWN Global Economy Series 7, p. 7; see also Article I of the IMF Articles of Agreement, hereinafter, the 'IMF Agreement'.

[6] This included the withholding of access to IMF resources, suspension or even withdrawal from the organisation.

[7] Akyüz Y, Reforming the IMF: Back to the Drawing Board, TWN Global Economy Series 7, p. 7; Alexander et al. (2006), p. 84; Chowla P, Sennholtz B, Griffiths J, At Issue: Dollars, Devaluations and Depressions: How the International Monetary System Creates Crisis, 23 September 2009, London: Bretton Woods Project, http://www.brettonwoodsproject.org/art-565403 (last accessed 21 April 2015), p. 1.

[8] Article VIII, Sect. 2(a) stipulates that subject to certain exceptions, 'no member shall, without the approval of the Fund, impose restrictions on the making of payments and transfers for current international transactions' while Article VI, Sect. 3 provides that members 'may exercise such controls as are necessary to regulate international capital movements' as long as such controls' do not restrict payments for current transactions' or 'unduly delay transfers of funds in settlement of commitments'.

according to the IMF's General Counsel, reflected 'the view—prevailing when the Fund was established—that speculative capital movements had contributed to the instability of the pre-war system'.[9]

Regulatory powers aside, the IMF was also entrusted with financial powers, the objective of which was to enable member states experiencing short-term balance-of-payments imbalances to draw upon a common pool of resources[10] to support stabilisation efforts in times of financial crisis.[11] The purpose for providing such liquidity was to prevent member states from undertaking domestic adjustment measures during a crisis that may have deflationary and destabilising consequences for the international economy (Article I(v) of the IMF Agreement[12]). The language of credit (for example, repayment and interest) was deliberately avoided in the IMF Agreement out of some deference to the founding rationale of the Fund as a credit union and the IMF's constitutional obligation under the aforementioned Article I (v).[13] Instead, drawing upon the IMF's resources has traditionally been construed as a right of members to access collective funds towards which it has contributed although since 1952, the IMF has introduced conditionalities for drawings above a member's reserve tranche (equivalent to 25 % of a member's quota subscriptions at the IMF).[14]

The historical relationship between international economic law and international public finance was therefore ostensibly built upon a shared responsibility for managing and mitigating the destabilising effects of global market failures. In discharging this responsibility, international economic law, including international financial law, and international institutions of public finance have played critical roles in the distribution of international economic resources and in the allocation of the risks and benefits of international economic activity. Over the years, the

[9] Hagan (2010), p. 966.

[10] These resources are traditionally drawn primarily from subscriptions to the IMF from member countries in the form of quota payments—each member is allocated a quota based broadly on its relative weight in the global economy which determines not only the aforementioned subscriptions but also their entitlement to borrow from the IMF and their voting rights (IMF, Where the IMF Gets Its Money, A Factsheet, 3 October 2014, http://www.imf.org/external/np/exr/facts/finfac.htm (last accessed 21 April 2015); IMF, IMF Quotas, A Factsheet, 3 October 2014, http://www.imf.org/external/np/exr/facts/quotas.htm) (last accessed 21 April 2015) . Over the years, the IMF has supplemented its resources through gold sales and arrangements to borrow from member states under multilateral and bilateral arrangements (see Sect. 3.1).

[11] Alexander et al. (2006), pp. 20–21; Akyüz (2006), pp. 489–491.

[12] Article I (v) of the IMF Agreement provides that one of the purposes of the IMF is '[t]o give confidence to members by making the general resources of the Fund temporarily available to them under adequate safeguards, thus providing them with opportunity to correct maladjustments in their balance of payments without resorting to measures destructive of national or international prosperity'.

[13] Akyüz Y, Reforming the IMF: Back to the Drawing Board, TWN Global Economy Series 7, p. 9 f.; Tan (2013), p. 103; Tan (2010a), pp. 169–171.

[14] Akyüz Y, Reforming the IMF: Back to the Drawing Board, TWN Global Economy Series 7, p. 9 f.; Tan (2013), p. 103; Tan (2010a), pp. 169–171; see discussion in Sect. 3.2.

regulatory and financial framework established by international monetary and trade law and the international financial institutions (IFIs) have been pivotal in assigning rights and access to transnational economic resources and establishing rules for cross-border trade, investment and financial flows as well as determining entitlements to and obligations for official financial support. Accordingly, international economic law and the policies and practice of international public finance have had a significant impact in shaping distributive outcomes in the global economy by influencing not only access to economic resources but also how these resources and the risks and benefits of global processes of production and consumption are shared among different actors and communities around the world.

2.2 *The Post-Bretton Woods Financial Architecture*

The current international financial architecture bears little resemblance to the framework conceived at Bretton Woods and contemporary legal and political arrangements for global financial cooperation operate in a vastly changed geopolitical and economic environment. First, the process of decolonisation saw the rapid entry of previously peripheral countries into the global economic system, necessitating the reorganisation of international economic law and governance to accommodate new postcolonial international relations, including the maintenance of political influence and access by former imperial countries to resources and markets in the newly independent states. A fundamental aspect of this reorganisation has been the conscription of international economic law and IFIs in the process of managing the entry and participation of postcolonial states in the global economy through the restructuring of state engagement with external economic actors and of the institutions of the domestic political economy.[15] This process was extended in the post-Cold War era to accommodate the accession of former Eastern bloc countries into the global economic order.[16]

Second, there have been major transformations in the constitution of international financial markets and the structures of financial intermediation in the postwar period. The progressive liberalisation of capital movements since the 1960s and the collapse of the fixed exchange rate system in the 1970s, along with advances in technology, created the conditions for the rapid globalization of financial markets in the 1980s and 1990s. This, along with the development of complex financial

[15] This included the reorientation of postcolonial economies to facilitate the entry of foreign capital, ostensibly for industrial, infrastructural and agricultural development, and the restructuring of economic sectors towards a market-led, export-oriented model of economic organisation. See Anghie (2005), pp. 3–4; Pahuja (2005), p. 465; Tan (2013), pp. 26–29.

[16] Like postcolonial states, many of the former communist states lacked the institutional and regulatory framework to deal with entry into a globalized market and were particularly vulnerable to economic shocks, particularly the impact of rising oil and other commodity prices and 'currency volatility arising from the privatization of foreign exchange risk' Alexander et al. (2006), p. 92.

instruments, the growth in the scope and scale of financial institutions, changes in corporate funding and the activities of multinational companies, and technological links between different financial systems have led to a worldwide increase in the volume of financial assets and financial trading and the speed and sophistication of cross-border financial transactions.[17]

The cumulative effect of these geopolitical, economic and legal changes in the postwar period has been a gradual shift in the purpose, organisation and application of international financial law and international public finance. This has notably restructured the relationship between international financial law and international public finance. Crucially, the primary concern of international economic law in recent decades has been with the facilitation of greater market integration through the elimination of national barriers to cross-border trade, investment and finance.[18] Accordingly, the regulatory framework for international finance has been chiefly preoccupied with the liberalisation of financial sectors and less focused on regulating systemic risks arising from such liberalisation. For example, despite the aforementioned constitutional right of IMF member states to exercise capital controls, the IMF has long been a primary advocate of capital account liberalisation, utilising its surveillance powers and financing conditionalities to pursue liberalisation of capital regimes within member states, although this stance has been considerably muted following recent regional and global financial crises.[19]

These changes have resulted in a fundamental reorganisation of the international financial architecture in the post-Bretton Woods era, including a progressive decentralisation of international financial governance and the outsourcing of regulatory authority to quasi or non-state actors, such as central banks and private industry bodies, and the movement away from a central, supranational structure for financial governance towards a 'fragmented regulatory domain'.[20] Although the current regulatory system remains centred on the IMF, the constitution and operational premise of today's international financial governance differ considerably from the framework established by the postwar planners.

Most significantly, the role of the IMF has changed substantially since its establishment, especially since the collapse of the par value system in 1971 (see

[17] Picciotto (2011), pp. 260–265; also Alexander et al. (2006), pp. 22–32; Brummer (2011), pp. 265–266; Weber and Arner (2007), p. 403.

[18] Akyüz (2010), pp. 39–40; Faundez (2010), pp. 17–18.

[19] Attempts in the 1990s to amend these provisions to allow for the IMF to pursue capital liberalisation in member states were thwarted by the onset of the Asian financial crisis and there has been a rethinking of the IMF's stance since the inception of the current global financial crisis, including an acknowledgment by Fund staff that such controls may be necessary under certain circumstances (Chowla P, Rethinking the IMF's Capital Account Mandate, Briefing Paper, 28 September 2010, London: Bretton Woods Project, http://www.brettonwoodsproject.org/art-566692#_edn4 (last accessed 21 April 2015); Ostry JD et al., Capital Inflows: The Role of Controls, IMF Stuff Position Note, 19 February 2010, at: https://www.imf.org/external/pubs/ft/spn/2010/spn1004.pdf (last accessed 21 April 2015).

[20] Brummer (2012), pp. 63–65.

Article IV (2) of the amended Agreement). Members today have to inform the Fund of any changes in its exchange arrangements but need not do so prior to the change nor seek the institution permission to do so.[21] This legislative amendment, coupled with the aforementioned ideological shift towards capital liberalisation, has meant that while it remains an important institution for delivering multilateral financing, the IMF no longer plays a central role in the regulation of international financial flows.

The IMF's primary regulatory task in the global economy post-1979 has been to provide bilateral and multilateral surveillance of the global economy through a combination of mandatory evaluations of individual member states (including exchange rate policies) and reviews of global and regional economic trends under Articles IV, Sect. 3(a) & (b) of the IMF Agreement.[22] Since the Asian financial crisis, the IMF, together with the World Bank, have also been involved in the implementation and monitoring of international financial standards, such as through its Financial Sector Assessment Programmes (FSAPs). These assessments, incorporating evaluations of a member's adoption and implementation of standards in identified policy areas, inform both the IMF's surveillance work and the Bank's country assistance strategies.[23]

However, both the IMF's work on standards and codes and its surveillance role remain mainly advisory as the institution does not have the constitutional authority to impose sanctions on member states that fail to comply with its policy recommendations although it can, and have, translated such recommendations into conditionalities for financing or criteria for determining access to contingent financing (see Sect. 3.1). The latter practice has resulted in an asymmetry in the way that IMF surveillance activities operate in reality, with one set of members—those that draw on IMF resources—subjected to the institutions' supervision while another set of members—those not dependent on IMF financing—remaining outside the control of the IFI.[24]

Instead of the IMF, a patchwork of regulatory networks and political coordination structures has emerged over the years to deal with the challenges of global financial integration. These increasingly involve normative arrangements and institutions facilitated directly between regulatory communities rather than through formal diplomatic channels and international organisations. In other words, constituent parts of states—especially specialised regulatory agencies—are networking with their counterparts abroad to develop financial regulatory standards outside usual international legal or diplomatic arenas. Much of contemporary international

[21] Brummer (2012), pp. 63–65.

[22] See also IMF, IMF Surveillance, A Factsheet, 3 October 2014, http://www.imf.org/external/np/exr/facts/surv.htm (last accessed 21 April 2015).

[23] IMF, The Financial Sector Assessment Program (FSAP), A Factsheet, 30 September 2014, http://www.imf.org/external/np/exr/facts/fsap.htm (last accessed 21 April 2015).

[24] Akyüz Y, Reforming the IMF: Back to the Drawing Board, TWN Global Economy Series 7, pp. 48–49; Bradlow DD, The Governance of the IMF: The Need for Comprehensive Reform, Paper prepared for the G 24 technical committee, Singapore, September 2006, p. 15.

financial regulation has also been delegated to private or quasi-public regulatory agencies and a great deal of supervision of financial actors, markets and transactions is conducted through self-regulation by private market participants.[25] Consequently, aside from some limited areas—notably the legislative framework of the European Monetary Union (EMU)—the bulk of the regulatory framework developed outside the Bretton Woods architecture consists of non-binding legal norms and non-judicial supervisory structures.

The current international financial system is therefore regulated through a loose assemblage of legal, quasi-legal and non-legal mechanisms that include international organisations, notably the IMF; what Pan terms 'state-to-state contact groups', such as the Group of Seven/Eight (G7/8) and Group of 20 countries; transgovernmental regulatory networks, such as the Basel Committee on Banking Supervision (Basel Committee) and the Financial Stability Board (FSB) (formerly the Financial Stability Forum or FSF); bilateral and regional networks, such as the EMU; and a host of private standard-setting agencies and industry associations, including the International Accounting Standards Board (IASB) and the International Swaps and Derivative Association (ISDA).[26] Most of international financial regulation is conducted, via these multiple channels, through the development and implementation of non-binding international financial standards, such as codes, guidelines, recommendations, principles or best practices, which may or may not be adopted as national legislation by states, but which do not constitute obligatory international law per se.[27]

This piecemeal approach to international financial regulation and the proliferation of multiple sites of regulation have led to significant problems of coordination, fragmentation of law and the increasing incoherence in international financial rulemaking. The reliance on 'soft law' developed through the decentralised, highly technocratic regulatory networks and political coordination mechanisms has resulted in a haphazard development of international financial norms and regulatory structures and the uneven implementation of these rules, not only between countries, especially developed and developing countries, but also between different economic sectors.[28] Systematic oversight of international financial markets, cross-border financial flows and domestic economic policies has been difficult given the lack of what Picciotto terms 'functional cooperation'[29] between these discrete regulatory networks and compounded by deeply embedded power relations within

---

[25] Bruner (2008), p. 1; Picciotto (2011), pp. 13–15 and 269–271; Stephan PB, Privatising International Law, University of Virginia School of Law John M Olin Law and Economics Research Paper Series No 2011-02, March 2011.

[26] Pan (2010), pp. 247–248.

[27] Alexander et al. (2006); Giovanoli (2009), p. 84; Weber and Arner (2007), pp. 410–411.

[28] Alexander et al. (2006), p. 134.

[29] Picciotto (2011), p. 270.

these networks that have led to the pursuit of regulatory agendas of interest to dominant state and non-state actors within those regimes.[30]

The fragmented nature of contemporary international financial governance is further exemplified by the absence of a central mechanism for the management and resolution of financial crises. While the IMF retains its mandate as the only 'permanent institution' providing 'the machinery for consultation and collaboration on international monetary problems' (Article 1(i) of the IMF Agreement), the Fund has not effectively facilitated coordination or supervision of national policy and regulatory responses to financial crises, leaving open the potential for negative spillovers of domestic adjustment efforts, including distorted stimulus packages that favour domestic stakeholders and 'beggar thy-neighbour' policies, such as competitive currency devaluations and trade restraints, that precipitated the establishment of the Bretton Woods institutions.[31]

Further, despite recurrent episodes of sovereign debt crises, there remains no formal, legal framework for orderly sovereign debt workouts, with debt restructurings contingent upon *ex-post*, voluntary and *ad-hoc* negotiations, often initiated and directed by the G-groups, notably the G7/8 and/or the G20, in concert with the IMF. The lack of clear, transparent and predictable rules for evaluating creditor claims on sovereign states can and have resulted in protracted discussions between a debtor state and its creditors. This not only postpones the resolution of a crisis and generates greater uncertainty in financial markets, as witnessed during the Eurozone crisis, but can also lead to asymmetries in the treatment of debtors and creditors and in the burden of adjustment between different stakeholders by privileging creditors, and certain classes of creditors, over other stakeholders, and discounting domestic social and economic welfare claims on government revenue in the process (see Sect. 4).

3 Credit and Containment

3.1 Responding to Regulatory Deficits

The progressive reorientation of international financial regulation away from its original objectives of mitigating and managing global market failures has meant that the responsibility for moderating the excesses of unfettered markets and compensating for the negative externalities resulting from market failures have

[30] Raustiala's study of transgovernmental networks, for example, demonstrates that 'power plays a critical role' in the export of 'regulatory ideas, rules and practices' from economically dominant states to weaker states, with 'economically weak jurisdictions' frequently embracing 'as substantial part of the regulatory models of the dominant powers' Raustiala (2002), pp. 51, 59–60.

[31] See United Nations, Report of the Commission of Experts of the President of the United Nations General Assembly on Reforms of the International Monetary and Financial System, 21 September 2009, para 29–34; also Sect. 4.2.

fallen primarily on the institutions and mechanisms of international public finance. In particular, limited global collective action on regulatory coordination in the financial sphere has meant that international public finance, mobilised and disbursed mainly through the IMF but also other international and regional financial institutions, has assumed a pivotal role in the mitigation and management of financial crises resulting from both market and regulatory failures. At the same time, the shift in the regulatory environment for international finance has resulted in regulatory failures that have generated their own distributional asymmetries which have necessitated the interventions of international public finance.

Indeed, a key feature of financial crises in recent decades has been the often large-scale accompanying loans or rescue packages, usually disbursed by the IMF to affected countries and often in conjunction with financing from other IFIs, such as the World Bank and, more recently, European stabilisation funds, as well as bilateral contributions from other IMF members.[32] Officially mobilised resources were central to the resolution of the 1980s debt crisis under the Baker and Brady Plans and again, to the response of the international community to the Latin American and Asian financial crises of the late 1990s.[33] They are also a fundamental element in the delivery of debt relief to low-income countries under multilaterally and bilaterally negotiated schemes (see Sect. 3.2).

Since the onset of the global financial crisis in 2008, the IMF has disbursed a record of almost US$400 billion to 38 member states to support crisis interventions.[34] There has also been a substantial increase in IMF resources, supported by the G20, that include the doubling of quota resources[35] and expanding its borrowing capacity.[36] This increase in the availability of Fund resources has been matched by a corresponding doubling of members' standard access limits to Fund resources—from 100 % of quota annually and 300 % cumulatively to 200 and 600 % respectively[37]—and accompanied by a major overhaul of the IMF's lending facilities with the introduction of new financing instruments, enhancing the flexibility of existing arrangements and streamlining lending procedures to enable speedier access to Fund resources.[38]

---

[32] See Akyüz Y, Why the IMF and the International Monetary System Need More than Cosmetic Reform, South Centre Research Paper 32, November 2010, http://www.southcentre.int/research-paper-32-November-2010/#more-1364 (last accessed 16 October 2015), p. 27.

[33] Arner and Buckley (2011), chapters 2 and 3; Salamanca (2010).

[34] Independent Evaluation Office (IEO) of the IMF, IMF Response to the Financial and Economic Crisis, Evaluation Report, 2014, p. 18.

[35] These quota reforms form part of a wider reform of IMF governance reforms (see discussion in Sect. 4.1).

[36] Independent Evaluation Office (IEO) of the IMF, IMF Response to the Financial and Economic Crisis, Evaluation Report, 2014, p. 18.

[37] See IMF, IMF Standby Arrangement: A Factsheet, 10 April 2015, https://www.imf.org/external/np/exr/facts/sba.htm (last accessed 21 April 2015).

[38] Independent Evaluation Office (IEO) of the IMF, IMF Response to the Financial and Economic Crisis, Evaluation Report, 2014, pp. 19–20.

Outside the IMF, a permanent lending facility, the European Stability Mechanism (ESM) was established in 2012 with a paid-in capital of €80 billion to provide financial assistance to troubled Eurozone member states.[39] From July 2013, this replaced the temporary mechanisms which have been set up since 2009 to deal with the Eurozone crisis, including the Greek loan facility and the European Financial Stability Facility (EFSF).[40] Financial support will take the form of loans to eligible states and, in exceptional cases, the purchase of bonds issued by the beneficiary country.[41]

This historical record of official funds pledged to international and regional financial institutions to support crisis-stricken countries exemplify how international regulatory failures have been increasingly compensated by international public finance. In particular, the inadequate regulation of international financial activity discussed in the previous section, including the failure to adequately monitor international financial flows and systemic financial institutions, has meant that official resources have increasingly served to underwrite the risks of international financial activity and manage financial contagion. The IMF, in particular, views its lending facilities as forming a core part of its responsibility for crisis resolution in the contemporary international financial system, developed in pursuant to its mandate under Article I(v) of its Agreement (see Sect. 2.2). The availability of large-scale public financing is seen as key to maintaining international financial stability by ‘reducing the likelihood of a run by private creditors that would trigger or exacerbate a crisis’ and/or, in the event of a crisis, by providing a cushion for national adjustment efforts that is not disruptive to the international system as a whole.[42]

Towards this end, two significant policy shifts at the IMF have contributed significantly to the expansion in the use of official sector finance in the management and resolution of financial crises. First, the introduction of the IMF’s lending into arrears (LIA) policy during the 1980s debt crisis—codified in an Executive Board decision in 1989—has enabled the Fund to extend financing to member states that have fallen into arrears with their private creditors—initially commercial banks and latterly extended to bondholders—under specific circumstances. Prior to this change, financial support from the Fund required ‘the elimination of existing arrears and the non-accumulation of new arrears during the program period’[43] and while

[39] European Central Bank (ECB), The European Stability Mechanism, ECB Monthly Bulletin, July 2011, pp. 74–77.

[40] European Central Bank (ECB), The European Stability Mechanism, ECB Monthly Bulletin, July 2011, pp. 74–77.

[41] European Central Bank (ECB), The European Stability Mechanism, ECB Monthly Bulletin, July 2011, pp. 74–77.

[42] IMF, Review of Fund Facilities: Analytical Basis for Fund Lending and Reform Options, 6 February 2009, para 5–11.

[43] IMF, Fund Policy on Lending into Arrears to Private Creditors: Further Consideration of the Good Faith Criterion, 30 July 2002, para 7.

this remains the general rule, the LIA now allows the IMF lend to countries in arrears provided that certain conditions are met.

Current rules permit the Fund to lend in arrears where 'prompt Fund support is considered essential for the successful implementation of the member's adjustment programme' and where 'the member is pursuing appropriate policies and is making a good faith effort to reach a collaborative agreement with its creditors'.[44] The latter requirement conditions IMF rescue packages to indebted states on such countries entering into debt rescheduling negotiations with their private creditors but allows the IMF to continue extending financial support to the debtor state if such negotiations stagnate due to creditor demands that are 'inconsistent' with the 'financing parameters' established under the IMF programme.[45]

In December 2015, the IMF extended its policy of tolerating arrears to official creditors, now allowing it to lend to countries which have outstanding arrears to bilateral sovereign creditors under certain circumstances.[46] Previously, a country in arrears to official creditors would not have been allowed to access IMF financing except where a Paris Club restructuring agreement was in place or where consent of the creditors owed arrears have been obtained.[47] The reformed policy on non-toleration of arrears to official creditors now enables the Fund to lend into arears owed to official bilateral creditors where certain criteria are satisfied. These conditions include the necessity of 'prompt financial support' from the IMF and the pursuit of 'appropriate policies' by the requesting member state; the assessment by the Fund that 'the debtor is making good faith efforts and that the absence of a debt restructuring is due to the unwillingness of the creditor to reach an agreement consistent with the parameters of the Fund-supported program' and that 'the decision to lend into arrears would not have an undue negative effect on the Fund's ability to mobilize official financing packages in future cases'.[48]

Second, in recent decades, the IMF has become increasingly reliant on supplementary financing to increase its lending capacity beyond its own resources drawn primarily from members' quota contributions and, to some extent, its investment

---

[44] Simpson L, The Role of the IMF in Debt Restructurings: Lending into Arrears, Moral Hazard and Sustainability Concerns, UNCTAD, G 24 Discussion Paper Series No 40, May 2006, https://www.imf.org/external/pubs/ft/privcred/073002.pdf (last accessed 16 October 2015), p. 10; also IMF, Fund Policy on Lending into Arrears to Private Creditors: Further Consideration of the Good Faith Criterion, 30 July 2002, https://www.imf.org/external/pubs/ft/privcred/073002.pdf (last accessed 16 October 2015), para 14.

[45] IMF, Fund Policy on Lending into Arrears to Private Creditors: Further Consideration of the Good Faith Criterion, 30 July 2002, https://www.imf.org/external/pubs/ft/privcred/073002.pdf (last accessed 16 October 2015), para 51.

[46] IMF, IMF Executive Board Discusses Reforming the Fund's Policy on Non-Toleration of Arrears to Official Creditors, Press Release No 15/555, 10 December 2015, https://www.imf.org/external/np/sec/pr/2015/pr15555.htm (last accessed 29 April 2016).

[47] IMF, Reforming the Fund's Policy on Non-Toleration of Arrears to Official Creditors, IMF Policy Paper, December 2015, para 11.

[48] IMF, Reforming the Fund's Policy on Non-Toleration of Arrears to Official Creditors, IMF Policy Paper, December 2015, para 18.

income and proceeds from gold sales. In particular, the IMF maintains two standing multilateral borrowing arrangements—the General Arrangements to Borrow (GAB) and the New Arrangements to Borrow (NAB)—that can be activated in the event of a predicted shortfall in usable Fund resources available to countries, notably during a major financial crisis.[49] The NAB was expanded in 2011 to incorporate new participants, mainly emerging markets such as Brazil, China and India, and increase credit capacity to about US$520 billion from US$47 billion although this was rolled back to around US$253 billion following quota increases implemented as part of the 2010 agreement to double quotas.[50] Since 2009, the IMF has also entered into a series of bilateral loan agreements with individual countries to significantly bolster resources and as of September 2014, 34 agreements are in effect, providing credit of up to US$395 billion.[51] These arrangements have bolstered the IMF's capacity to extend finance to its member states but have, in turn, rendered the institution susceptible to the influence of these supplementary financiers.[52]

The evolving role of the IMF and the expansion of its crisis lending portfolio in the post-Bretton Woods era highlight the growing dissonance between international economic law and international public finance. In fact, the proliferation and expansion of the IMF's financing portfolio have coincided with the decline of the Fund as an international supervisory institution. As Akyüz notes: '[t]he more the IMF has failed in crisis prevention, the more it has become involved in crisis management and lending.'[53] These developments represent an important shift in the rationale for international public finance whereby official sector financing is increasingly deployed to supplement market discipline of the debtor state rather than to constrain market failures.

Most notably, the limited regulatory role of IFIs, especially the IMF, coupled with the traditional reluctance to impose capital controls and the absence of a legal mandate to organise debt standstills has meant that official sector financing is increasingly pursued as mechanism for insuring against a disorderly default by indebted states and bolstering market confidence to prevent exit of finance, maintain liquidity within countries facing crisis and catalyse new financing. In particular, the provision of crisis financing today is targeted less at preventing destabilising national adjustments and stimulating economic activity in crisis-stricken states but to preserve countries' market 'creditworthiness', notably by keeping them current

[49] IMF, IMF Standing Borrowing Arrangements, 6 April 2016, http://www.imf.org/external/np/exr/facts/gabnab.htm (last accessed 29 April 2016).

[50] IMF, IMF Standing Borrowing Arrangements, 6 April 2016, http://www.imf.org/external/np/exr/facts/gabnab.htm (last accessed 29 April 2016).

[51] IMF, Where the IMF Gets its Money, 6 April 2016, http://www.imf.org/external/np/exr/facts/finfac.htm (last accessed 29 April 2016).

[52] Gould (2003) and further discussion in Sect. 4.3.

[53] See Akyüz Y, Why the IMF and the International Monetary System Need More than Cosmetic Reform, South Centre Research Paper 32, November 2010, http://www.southcentre.int/research-paper-32-November-2010/#more-1364 (last accessed 16 October 2015), p. 30.

on debt payments to creditors, to prevent credit outflows and maintain access to international capital markets.[54]

Responses to the global financial crisis have thus emphasised the creation of so-called 'firewalls', large buffers of contingent financing made available to eligible countries through IFIs, to serve as precautionary instruments to stabilise financial markets. The introduction of 'precautionary credit lines' at the IMF—the Flexible Credit Line (FCL) and the Precautionary and Liquidity Line (PLL) (replacing the Precautionary Credit Line)—signals the extension of the scope of public finance from a tool for crisis resolution to one of crisis prevention. Under these new instruments, countries are pre-approved for exceptional access to loans—with no hard cap under the FCL and up to 500 of quota under the PLL—from the Fund and drawings are subjected to limited or no conditionality in the case of the PLL and FCL respectively.[55] By extending upfront financial support to pre-qualifying countries without the stigma of traditional conditionality, these instruments have been designed to bring more countries under the supervision of the IMF, thereby ostensibly increasing IMF oversight over more of its member states, particularly, large emerging countries, and, by extension, expanding its supervision over the financial system as a whole.[56]

It has also been argued that the availability of contingent financial support will incentivise the implementation of 'stronger crisis prevention policies' in member states in order to pre-empt future crises while reducing countries' need for self-insurance through stocks of large reserves and overcoming problems associated with global imbalances.[57] At the same time, it is expected that the upfront access to large buffers of financial support will serve as a mechanism of insurance by maintaining investor confidence in financial markets, preventing capital outflows and mobilising additional financing during periods of financial stress by signalling the IFIs' approval and underwriting of qualifying countries' economic policies.[58] In

[54] See Akyüz (2006), pp. 498–499; Rieffel (2003), pp. 49–50.

[55] IMF, The IMF's Flexible Credit Line (FCL), A Factsheet, 22 March 2016, http://www.imf.org/external/np/exr/facts/fcl.htm (last accessed 29 April 2016); IMF, The IMF's Precautionary Credit Line (PLL) A Factsheet, 30 March 2016, http://www.imf.org/external/np/exr/facts/pll.htm (last accessed 29 April 2016).

[56] IMF, Review of Fund Facilities: Analytical Basis for Fund Lending and Reform Options, 6 February 2009, para 8; IMF, The Fund's Mandate: The Future Financing Role: Reform Proposals, 29 June 2010, para 13).

[57] See Akyüz Y, Why the IMF and the International Monetary System Need More than Cosmetic Reform, South Centre Research Paper 32, November 2010, http://www.southcentre.int/research-paper-32-November-2010/#more-1364 (last accessed 16 October 2015), p. 32; IMF, The Fund's Mandate: The Future Financing Role—Reform Proposals, 29 June 2010, p. 2; IMF, Review of Fund Facilities: Analytical Basis for Fund Lending and Reform Options, 6 February 2009, para 1–16.

[58] IMF, The Fund's Mandate: The Future Financing Role—Reform Proposals, 29 June 2010, p. 2; IMF, Review of Fund Facilities: Analytical Basis for Fund Lending and Reform Options, 6 February 2009, para 1–16; also European Central Bank (ECB), The European Stability Mechanism, ECB Monthly Bulletin, July 2011, pp. 73–74.

this manner, the IMF, and to a lesser extent, other IFIs such as the ECB, are attempting, through their roles as a lenders of last resort, to both influence the regulatory, fiscal and monetary environment of its members to prevent financial contagion as well as manage the behaviour of financial actors during a financial crisis.

3.2 Debt and Discipline

A critical component in the utility of financial aid as a regulatory instrument in the international financial system is the application of conditionality which governs the use of such resources. Conditionality—generally used to refer to the terms of the economic programme accompanying the use of financial resources disbursed by IFIs[59]—is today a fundamental element in international financial regulation. Most notably, its use is now central to IMF financing, whether made through its General Resources Account (GRA) pursuant to Article I(v) of the IMF Agreement or via the IMF's concessional financing facilities established through trust funds pursuant to Article V(2)(b).[60] The use of conditionality is also seen as an important component of the viability of the aforementioned newly established precautionary credit lines at the IMF and crucial to the implementation of the ESM.

Policy conditionality reinforces the market-based disciplinary framework of the contemporary international financial architecture by providing a mechanism through which countries can demonstrate their adherence to market norms. For the IMF, conditioning its financial support provides recipient countries with 'a policy commitment device' that demonstrates to an external audience, namely financial markets and investors, that authorities 'will implement policies necessary to address the member's [balance of payments] difficulties'.[61] Here, the IMF plays a crucial role as a 'reputational intermediary', helping member states establish or, in many cases, reestablish financial and economic credibility through their demonstration of adherence to or commitment to 'market-friendly policies' that minimises the risk of policy reversal by domestic law and policymakers.[62]

---

[59] Tan (2010b), p. 114.

[60] This provision, which was inserted as part of the IMF's Second Amendment to its Articles of Agreement, stipulates that 'If requested, the Fund may decide to perform financial and technical services, including the administration of resources contributed by members that are consistent with the purposes of the Fund'. The Fund's concessional lending framework has undergone a number of revisions since it was first introduced in 1979, the latest overhaul taking place in 2009 and establishing three facilities—the Extended Credit Facility (ECF), the Rapid Credit Facility (RCF) and the Standby Credit Facility (SCF)—with different terms for access under the umbrella of the Poverty Reduction and Growth Trust (PGRT) for which the Fund serves as trustee (IMF, A New Architecture of Facilities for Low-Income Countries, 26 June 2009, pp. 3–4).

[61] IMF, Review of Fund Facilities: Analytical Basis for Fund Lending and Reform Options, 6 February 2009, para 8, 11.

[62] Broome (2010), pp. 41–42; Broome (2008), pp. 130–132.

Conditionality thus enables the financing institution, notably the IMF, to signal confidence in a country's economic policies and institutional environment through *ex-ante* assurances to extend liquidity based on prior commitments by the country or to rehabilitate the financial standing of crisis-stricken countries within the international financial markets through an *ex-post* programme of supervised economic adjustment. In the former arrangement, conditionality usually takes the form of prior actions or pre-qualification criteria, such as under the FCL and PLL, while in the latter, conditionality will be implemented through programme reviews of the borrower's compliance with policy actions linked to phased disbursements of financial support. The linking of financial disbursements to a plan of economic action by the borrowing state provides a disciplinary instrument through which the 'policy credibility' of a state in financial or prolonged structural economic crisis can be constructed or rehabilitated in order to either stem capital outflows or incentivise new lending into the country.[63] While not legally binding per se, the reputational effect of these programmes mean that conditionalities can generate expectations governing the use of official resources that have as much normative force as binding legal obligations.[64]

Accordingly, the rationale for conditionality has gradually evolved from its original purpose of safeguarding common resources to serving as an instrument for enforcing fiscal and monetary discipline in member states. This expansion of the role and content of conditionality reflects the underlying premise of the post-Bretton Woods regulatory environment in which threats to the international financial system have largely been perceived as stemming from errant domestic policies of countries in crisis rather than from inherent systemic problems of the international financial system or spillovers from policies of other, notably economically influential, member states.[65] Without explicit authority to enforce exchange rate policies or effectively manage transnational capital flows and limited enforcement powers in respect of its surveillance function, control over domestic policies of crisis-stricken countries via the instrument of conditionality and the implementation of an adjustment programme has emerged as the IMF's default means of safeguarding international financial stability.[66] Conditionality also enables the IMF and, to a lesser extent, the World Bank, to perform a quasi-regulatory function by 'locking-in' policy recommendations made via other channels, such as the IMF's Article IV surveillance and FSAP reports (see Sect. 2.2).

The importance of conditionality as a default regulatory instrument is reinforced by the aforementioned signalling and catalytic role of IMF financing. Compliance with the terms of an IMF adjustment programme is often a precondition for access to financing from other multilateral and bilateral lenders as well as a pre-requisite for most debt rescheduling and debt relief arrangements, including under the newly

---

[63] Broome (2010), pp. 41–42; Broome (2008), pp. 130–132.

[64] Broome (2010), pp. 41–42; Broome (2008), pp. 130–132.

[65] Tan (2010b), pp. 188–193.

[66] Tan (2010b), pp. 188–193.

established ESM. This has placed the IMF at the helm of sovereign debt management, providing financial support as well as mobilising supplementary financing from other financiers, coordinating countries' relations with their private and sovereign creditors, and establishing and monitoring the terms and conditions for debt renegotiations.[67] As Gould observes, '[t]he IMF, through its conditionality, facilitates cooperation between creditors and borrowers, by vouching for a borrower's reputation and enabling it to more credibly commit to a particular course of action'.[68]

In the absence of an international sovereign insolvency process with pre-determined rules for orderly debt restructuring, the brokerage function of IMF financing is particularly important for countries facing acute financial crises. The Fund's LIA policy, coupled with its ability to supervise the economic policies of borrowing member states, has enabled the institution to exert significant influence over the behaviour of both parties to a sovereign debt agreement during the restructuring period. As a result, the IMF plays a critical role in providing the platform for organising the aforementioned 'rescue packages' for stricken member states and for coordinating debt renegotiations. It was a key player in the organisation of financial support packages to Greece, Spain and other Eurozone countries and remains a pivotal actor under regional initiatives, such as the ESM and multilateral currency swap arrangement under the East Asian Chiang Mai initiative[69] where loans (or drawings above 30 % of a member's quota in the latter) are conditional on an IMF adjustment programme.

The IMF also plays a prominent role in sovereign debt relief operations for low-income countries. Not only is an IMF programme a precondition for debt restructuring under the auspices of the Paris Club, the first port of call for countries seeking rescheduling of debt owed to sovereign creditors—which make up the bulk of creditors for low-income countries—but the Fund is also responsible for assessments of countries' debt sustainability which determines eligibility for various debt rescheduling and debt relief schemes.[70] The Fund is also currently trustee to and administrator of two debt relief schemes – the enhanced Heavily Indebted Poor Countries (HIPC) initiative, successor to the original HIPC initiative and the

[67] Tan (2010a), pp. 48–49; also Woods (2006), pp. 164–165.

[68] Gould (2003), p. 559.

[69] The Chiang Mai initiative (CMI) was originally a series of bilateral currency swaps arrangements established in the aftermath of the Asian financial crisis. In 2010, the CMI was transformed into a multilateral arrangement, the Chiang Mai Initiative Multilateralization (CMIM), involving the finance ministries and central banks of the countries of the Association of Southeast Asian Nations (ASEAN) plus China, Japan and South Korea (ASEAN + 3) and the Hong Kong Monetary Authority, aimed at providing currency swaps under pooled reserves governed by a single contractual agreement (see Bangko Sentral ng Pilipinas (BSP), Chiang Mai Initiative Multilateralization, March 2012, Philippines Central Bank FAQs, http://www.bsp.gov.ph/downloads/Publications/FAQs/CMIM.pdf (last accessed 21 April 2015).

[70] Tan (2010a), p. 49; also Villanov and Martin, The Paris Club, Debt Relief International (DRI) Publication 3, 2001, p. 2.

Catastrophe Containment and Relief (CCR) Trust—which aim to reduce the debt burdens of eligible countries through reductions in their debt service or debt stock owed to official lenders subsidised by IMF and other bilateral and multilateral donors.[71] Support from the IMF has been crucial to the success of these schemes, particularly in mobilising bilateral and multilateral contributions to the trust funds that meet the cost of debt relief as clearance of debt stock and/or suspension of debt servicing here is operationalised not through conventional debt write-downs by creditors but are offset instead by official donor resources, usually of aid budgets.[72]

4 Financial Aid as Financial Regulation

4.1 Masking Regulatory Failures

The progressive expansion in the use of official financial resources to compensate for the regulatory deficits of the international financial architecture over the postwar period is problematic on a number of levels and can, and have, serve to entrench, if not exacerbate, existing regulatory failures and stymie reforms to the international financial architecture. Firstly, the deployment of official sector resources as an instrument for financial crisis containment, resolution and, increasingly, prevention, does not address the underlying regulatory deficits of the current international financial architecture discussed in Sect. 2.2 above. While adequate financial resources have been necessary to provide effective counter-cyclical liquidity and create a buffer to destructive adjustment policies in the event of crisis, there remains an imperative for effective international regulation over cross-border financial flows and supervision of major financial actors, including domestic policies of systematically important countries and the activities of major global financial institutions.

Commitment of financial resources, however substantial, has been and continues to be insufficient to overcome the underlying volatility in financial markets resulting from these regulatory failures, as demonstrated by the mounting frequency of financial crises and the increasing speed of financial contagion in the post-Bretton Woods era. The decline of the IMF as an international supervisory organisation has not been matched by a corresponding development of similarly constituted inter-state mechanisms for global financial governance. In particular, the focus of international financial regulation since the Asian financial crisis has been on the development of international financial standards via a range of political

---

[71] IMF, Debt Relief Under the Heavily Indebted Poor Countries (HIPC) Initiative, A Factsheet, 8 April 2016, http://www.imf.org/external/np/exr/facts/hipc.htm (last accessed 29 April 2016); IMF, The Catastrophe Containment and Relief Trust, 18 March 2016, http://www.imf.org/external/np/exr/facts/ccr.htm (last accessed 29 April 2016).

[72] Cosio-Pascal (2010), pp. 250–251 and section 4.2.

and technocratic agencies and networks and implemented through domestic law, regulatory and institutional reform, leveraged by a combination of market forces—using 'market discipline and market access channels to provide incentives for the adoption of sound supervisory systems'[73]—and the operational activities of the IFIs—such as surveillance activities, technical assistance or loan conditionalities—without the corresponding development of a clear central coordinating or supervisory structure and limited legal enforceability (see Sect. 2.2).

The contemporary regulatory landscape for international financial activity therefore continues to be hampered by a lack of coordination among regulatory agencies and suffused with entrenched power dynamics that impede efforts at regulatory reform. As Alexander et al. observes: 'A major weakness in the existing international regime is that IFI standard setting is dominated by a few rich or large countries that exercise regulatory control over the major financial institutions'.[74] Although the decision-making platform has been broadened in the years following the Asian financial crisis—notably with the formation of the G20 in 1999 and its elevation of status in 2008[75] and the corresponding establishment of the FSF, also in 1999, and subsequent expansion into the FSB in 2009—involving a greater number of countries, especially emerging economies, in the process of global financial governance, these changes have been incremental at best.

Governance arrangements within these groups and networks have not been formalised and non-G8 countries remain, by and large, marginalised from regulatory discussions that are undertaken both within transgovernmental networks as well as within the IFIs. Importantly, despite its high profile, the G20 continues to function primarily as a political agenda-setting forum without a formal constitution or legal powers and with negotiations remaining heavily dominated by interests of the G8 industrialised countries.[76] While the G20 has served as a high-level

[73] Weber and Arner (2007), p. 411.

[74] Alexander et al. (2006), p. 171.

[75] The G20 was created initially as a forum for 'finance ministers and central bank governors from systematically important industrialized and developing countries to discuss issues relating to the global economy' but was elevated to an inter-governmental forum with the convening of annual summits of heads of states and governments from 2008. See: Carrasco (2010), pp. 199–200; also Gnarth K, Schmucker C (2011) The Role of the Emerging Countries in the G20: Agenda-Setter, Veto Player or Spectator?, Bruges Regional Integration and Global Governance Papers 2/2011, www.cris.unu.edu/fileadmin/.../BRIGG_2011-2.pdf (last accessed 16 October 2015). The group is comprised of Argentina, Australia, Brazil, Canada, China, France, Germany, India, Indonesia, Italy, Japan, Mexico, Russia, Saudi Arabia, South Africa, South Korea, Turkey, the United Kingdom, the United States and the European Union. Representatives from international organisations, including the IMF, OECD and the World Bank, also attend the meetings (see Gnarth K, Schmucker C (2011) The Role of the Emerging Countries in the G20: Agenda-Setter, Veto Player or Spectator?, Bruges Regional Integration and Global Governance Papers 2/2011), www.cris.unu.edu/fileadmin/.../BRIGG_2011-2.pdf (last accessed 16 October 2015).

[76] See Gnarth K, Schmucker C (2011) The Role of the Emerging Countries in the G20: Agenda-Setter, Veto Player or Spectator?, Bruges Regional Integration and Global Governance Papers 2/2011, www.cris.unu.edu/fileadmin/.../BRIGG_2011-2.pdf (last accessed 16 October 2015).

mechanism for cooperative dialogue and inter-state policy coordination, the implementation (and technicalities) of decisions taken at this forum fall on existing networks and institutions, notably the IMF where governance power asymmetries remain deeply rooted despite some changes to voting shares and the constitution of the Executive Board agreed in 2010 and scheduled for implementation in 2012.[77]

At the same time, without the regulatory mandate to undertake more comprehensive surveillance over systematically important countries and to enforce policy prescriptions outside the mechanism of conditionality, the role of the Fund in ensuring international financial stability remains limited and reliant primarily on its financing function discussed in Sect. 3. Using finance as a default mechanism for financial governance masks the regulatory deficits that contribute to financial instability as well as creating further asymmetries in international financial regulation, with one set of members subjected to international financial supervision via *ex-ante* or *ex-post* conditionalities (see Sects. 2.2 and 3.2) while members not in need of financing falling outside the supervisory jurisdiction of the institution. As a United Nations (UN) commission[78] notes, 'much of the effort to coordinate international economic policy has focused on putting constraints on countries whose behaviour is not systematically significant, while doing little about countries whose policies can have systematically significant consequences'.[79]

Similarly, without effective international coordination of national responses to financial crises, the policy reforms necessitated by economic restructuring programmes accompanying IMF financing may exacerbate inequalities in the

[77] In December 2010, the IMF's Board of Governors approved a package of governance reforms that will double quotas and realign shares to shift 6 % of quota shares to emerging market and developing countries at a small expense (around 1.35 %) to industrialised, mostly European countries, the outcome being that the ten largest shareholders of the Fund now include Brazil, Russia, India and China (the BRICs) (IMF, IMF Approves Far-Reaching Governance Reforms, IMF Survey Online, 5 November 2010, http://www.imf.org/external/pubs/ft/survey/so/2010/NEW110510B.htm (last accessed 21 April 2015)). The reforms also include a restructuring in the Executive Board composition to decrease by two seats held by European countries and to move towards an all-elected Executive Board as opposed to the current mix of appointed representatives for the top five shareholders and elected representatives for the rest (IMF, IMF Approves Far-Reaching Governance Reforms, IMF Survey Online, 5 November 2010, http://www.imf.org/external/pubs/ft/survey/so/2010/NEW110510B.htm (last accessed 21 April 2015)). The reforms have yet to be implemented due to the lack of ratification by the US of necessary agreements (Independent Evaluation Office (IEO) of the IMF, IMF Response to the Financial and Economic Crisis, Evaluation Report, 2014, p. 19).

[78] The Commission of Experts on Reform of the International Financial and Monetary System was convened by the President of the 63rd Session of the United Nations General Assembly Miguel d'Escoto Brokmann under the leadership of economist Joseph Stiglitz in November 2008 to assist member states 'in their deliberations on the world financial and economic crisis' (United Nations, Report of the Commission of Experts of the President of the United Nations General Assembly on Reforms of the International Monetary and Financial System, 21 September 2009, para 7).

[79] United Nations, Report of the Commission of Experts of the President of the United Nations General Assembly on Reforms of the International Monetary and Financial System, 21 September 2009, para 29.

burden of adjustment between developed and developing countries while failing to tackle the externalities arising from an uncoordinated global approach to crisis intervention and resolution. The aforementioned UN commission has argued that this regulatory vacuum can worsen crisis conditions and aggravate existing asymmetries in global trade and financial markets, especially where protectionist trade measures and competitive currency devaluations impact upon multilateral trade and where fiscal stimulus packages in industrialised countries are distorted 'so that more benefits accrue domestically'.[80] On the latter point, the commission experts noted that government 'bailouts, guarantees and asymmetric expansionary fiscal policies' within industrialised countries can distort financial market incentives by redirecting capital away from developing and least developed countries as financial actors focus lending and investment activities within home countries for politically expedient and economic reasons.[81]

4.2 Cartelisation of Debt Management

The absence of a framework for the coordination of international responses to financial and economic crises is compounded by the lack of a formal legal regime for sovereign insolvency. As previously discussed, current approaches to crisis resolution, including for the restructuring of sovereign official and private sector debt, remain premised on informal, *ad-hoc* and *ex-post* negotiations.[82] The restructuring of sovereign debt, in particular, is heavily dependent on the political mediation of dominant industrialised states and the IMF and, importantly, contingent on the availability of officially mobilised finance attached to the discipline of an IMF stabilisation programme discussed in Sect. 3. This system, described by Herman et al. as 'embodying informal and imperfect coordination of the debtor and its creditors' is fundamentally political, often involving high-level inter-state diplomacy and the participation of IFIs and other multilateral agencies in addition to negotiations with private commercial creditors.[83]

While various mechanisms have been established in the postwar period to deal with the problem of sovereign insolvency—from the creation of the Paris Club in 1956 to renegotiate debt owed to official creditors to the formation of the bank advisory committees (BACs) or London Clubs and the accompanying Baker and Brady Plans in the 1980s to restructure commercial bank loans of developing

[80] United Nations, Report of the Commission of Experts of the President of the United Nations General Assembly on Reforms of the International Monetary and Financial System, 21 September 2009, para 30–31.

[81] United Nations, Report of the Commission of Experts of the President of the United Nations General Assembly on Reforms of the International Monetary and Financial System, 21 September 2009, para 32–34.

[82] Herman et al. (2010a), pp. 4–5; Rieffel (2003), pp. 1–7.

[83] Herman et al. (2010a), p. 4.

countries to the introduction of 'market-based' approaches, such as collective action clauses (CACs) and codes of conduct, to deal with the 'collective action' problems of restructuring sovereign bond contracts in the late 1990s and early 2000s—these piecemeal initiatives have been developed in response to specific sovereign debt crises and/or aimed at resolving discrete aspects of sovereign indebtedness. They have not provided a formal overarching *ex-ante* framework for the orderly resolution of sovereign debt distress similar to those available to individuals, corporations or municipalities (in the case of the US) under domestic bankruptcy regimes.[84]

The centrality of international public finance to the resolution of sovereign debt crises in the absence of a formal process of debt arbitration has meant that debt restructuring continues to be managed by a small cartel of states, private creditors and international financial institutions, notably the IMF, leading to significant asymmetries in the treatment of debtor states. As Herman et al. argue, current 'debt workout regimes treat sovereign borrowers differently, depending on the degree of political power of debtor governments and their willingness to use it', placing 'smaller less strong, or less 'strategically' important countries at a disadvantage'.[85] Differential treatment has been accorded to both middle-income and low-income indebted countries seeking debt relief over the past decade, with politically expedient countries, such as Russia and Argentina, accorded more favourable restructuring terms (including the restructuring of defaulted debt in the case of Argentina) than less influential states.[86] Both Iraq and Nigeria also secured unprecedented packages of debt relief from its Paris Club creditors outside usual Paris Club rescheduling terms in 2004 and 2005 respectively[87] due to their strategic importance and economic weight relative to their regional neighbours.

The lack of predictability resulting from the absence of a formal framework for debt renegotiation with pre-established and binding rules of conduct and terms of engagement for debtors and creditors that can shape the expectations of market and public actors in the event of a financial crisis generates not only significant instability in financial markets but also contributes to rising political tensions, both within the crisis-stricken state and in the international economy. The closed-door nature of sovereign debt negotiations coupled with the executive nature of sovereign debt contracts—where legislative consent is rarely required for renegotiations—marginalises stakeholders outside the immediate cartel of creditors, IFIs and related transnational commercial actors from the process. Further, the absence of a mechanism to trigger automatic, temporary standstills on debt repayments in a sovereign debt crisis has meant that debt rescheduling negotiations are often

[84] See Bolton and Skeel (2010); Herman et al. (2010a, b).

[85] Herman et al. (2010b), p. 489.

[86] Herman et al. (2010b), p. 489.

[87] Paris Club, Paris Club Agrees on a Comprehensive Treatment of Nigeria's Debt, 20 October 2005, Press Release; Paris Club, The Paris Club and the Republic of Iraq Agree on Debt Relief, 21 November 2004, Press Release.

conducted under the shadow of an imminent sovereign default with its attendant impact on the indebted states' access to capital from public and private sources. Consequently, debt is often renegotiated under severely exigent economic circumstances, leading to high restructuring costs, both financially as well as in social welfare and human development terms.

At the same time, the changing profile of sovereign debt—from official and bank lending to bond financing—and the widespread practice of debt securitisation has meant that sovereign debt, particularly of high- and middle-income countries, is dispersed among increasingly heterogeneous creditors, creating significant coordination problems in the event of a debt crisis.[88] These difficulties, involving reconciling the interests of parties with diverse and inconsistent priorities, can in turn generate additional problems, including what is known as a rush to exit (to sell the debt) or a rush to the courthouse (to litigate to recoup the debt) or cause creditor holdouts where individual creditors refuse to agree on a settlement, either as a strategy to later free ride on a restructuring agreement or to recover debt through litigation.[89] The problem of holdout creditors has been compounded by the securitisation of debt and the reselling of sovereign debt on the secondary market which has increased the practice of commercial litigation by so-called 'vulture funds' or investment companies that speculate on and purchase distressed debt of countries at a discount with hope of collecting the full amount in litigation at a future date.

Although the introduction of the aforementioned CACs has mitigated some collective action problems in sovereign debt restructuring, they have not fully resolved the holdout problem as the case *NML Capital Ltd v Republic of Argentina*[90] in the US has demonstrated. As the IMF itself has argued, the decision by the New York courts to prohibit Argentina from making payments to creditors holding restructured bonds without paying holdout creditors in full 'enhances the leverage of holdouts' and 'increased the risk that holdouts will multiply'.[91] Recent experi-

[88] Bolton and Skeel (2010) pp. 449–485.

[89] Gelpern and Gulati (2010), p. 350.

[90] In June 2014, the US Supreme Court declined Argentina's appeal of a New York federal court decision that Argentina had violated the parri passu clause in defaulted bonds by making payments to bondholders who participated in unilateral exchanges of Argentinean debt in 2005 and 2010 without also paying the holdout creditors and prohibited Argentina from 'making future payments on restructured bonds unless it paid the defaulted bondholders' in full (IMF, Strengthening the Contractual Framework to Address Collective Action Problems in Sovereign Debt Restructuring, October 2014, Box 1). Argentina finally settled with the holdout creditors in early 2016, putting an end to its 15-year legal battle with the holdout creditors but setting a worrying precedent for other similar debt negotiations by raising 'the likelihood that a variety of 'creative' holdout strategies will be developed, reducing overall efficiency and increasing the long-term transaction costs of credit' (Mario Blejer, Argentina's Deal with the Holdouts is A Mixed Blessing, *Financial Times*, 31 March 2016).

[91] IMF, Strengthening the Contractual Framework to Address Collective Action Problems in Sovereign Debt Restructuring, October 2014, para 14.

ence with Greek bond restructurings have also highlighted the potential for holdout creditors to obtain so-called 'blocking positions' to prevent the operation of CACs within particular bond series, rendering the restructuring process much more difficult.[92] Further, despite the existence of CACs, debt restructuring negotiations remain lengthy and contingent upon political leverage and the involvement of official sector financing to underwrite significant portions of debt write-downs.[93]

The politicisation of debt negotiations is further compounded by Fund's increasing dependence on supplementary financing for the success of its financial packages. The IMF's own Independent Evaluation Office (IEO) highlights that 'the IMF remains reliant on borrowing for 70 % of its credit capacity and access to more than half of the IMF's credit capacity is controlled by a super-majority of creditors'.[94] As observed by Gould, supplementary finance 'is often crucial for the short-run success of individual Fund programs because the Fund only provides a fraction of the amount of money necessary for a borrowing country to balance its payments and implement the Fund designed program successfully'.[95] The contingency of the IMF's credibility as a catalytic lender on the willingness of these external financiers to extend resources means that these financiers are often 'both able and willing to influence' the design of borrowers' programmes, notably the terms and conditions under which IMF programmes are extended.[96]

This highly political characteristic of sovereign debt management inserts states into relationships of power with dominant economic states, private creditors and other international financial actors, notably credit ratings agencies whose rankings determine the capacity of governments to borrow on international capital markets. Without *ex-ante*, predictable rules and pre-established processes for sovereign insolvency, official financial support packages remain the only viable solution for countries seeking to stabilise domestic markets and for the international community seeking to contain financial contagion. However, the introduction of conditionality and the progressive changes to the lending regime in the postwar period (see Sect. 3.2) has meant that there is no longer automaticity in access to financial resources and eligibility for such resources, including volume and scope of support from the IFIs and other international actors, are determined on an ad-hoc, case by case basis by these institutions controlled by G7/8 countries. Studies by political economists, such as Copelovitch (2010), Gould (2003) and Woods (2006), have shown that the size and terms of IMF lending will vary depending on the political and economic circumstances of the countries requesting financing, including, *inter*

---

[92] IMF, Strengthening the Contractual Framework to Address Collective Action Problems in Sovereign Debt Restructuring, October 2014, para 25.

[93] Bolton and Skeel (2010), pp. 449–485; Stiglitz (2010), pp. 35–69.

[94] Independent Evaluation Office (IEO) of the IMF, IMF Response to the Financial and Economic Crisis, Evaluation Report, p. 19.

[95] Gould (2003), pp. 555–556.

[96] Gould (2003), pp. 552–555.

alia, the exposure of G7/8 commercial banks in the countries concerned and the composition of private external debt held by the countries.[97]

Accordingly, countries in need of financial support are reliant on assessments of their debt sustainability and projections of economic recovery drawn up primarily by IMF staff and approved by a largely political process of consensus among major economic powers. Considerations of how much to lend and under what conditions are often determined by geo-strategic, political and/or economic interests of external actors, with policy prescriptions accompanying loan packages 'based neither on clear evidence nor on pure expert analysis or predictions' but instead 'reflect bureaucrats trying to square political pressures and institutional constraints'.[98] In the case of official lending, the result of using official development aid (ODA) to write-off portions of sovereign debt has meant that the debt workout processes under the Paris Club and other official debt relief schemes 'have essentially been merged into the foreign aid regimes of their donors' with 'the financial relationships of these debtors [effectively] governed by donor-recipient partnerships',[99] with all their attendant connotations of power and strategic influence.

Consequently, the lack of a rules-based process for determining access to financial support from the IFIs further disembeds the practice of sovereign debt restructuring from the general conduct of international economic activity by conditioning post-crisis decisions of states and their creditors on an external process over which the original parties to a debt contract have no real control. This means that resolution of fundamental contractual issues concerning the rescheduling of obligations is contingent upon decisions made by third parties via a discretionary, inherently political process with indeterminate outcomes. This not only enhances international financial fragility but also complicates relations between debtor and creditor states in other spheres of the economy.

4.3 Aiding Asymmetries

The use of public resources to mitigate the dislocations of the international financial system both reinforces existing and creates further asymmetries in the regulation of international finance and the distribution of international economic resources. In compensating for the deficits in international financial governance, the policies and practices of international public finance can and have exacerbated the global inequalities in income and wealth, generating a disproportionate exposure to consequences of regulatory failure on some segments of the international economy than on others. Specifically, the deployment of public resources, particularly where there are no corresponding policy or regulatory measures to alleviate prevailing nor prevent future distributional impacts, can have adverse consequences on economic

[97] Copelovitch (2010), pp. 63–67.

[98] Woods (2006), p. 4; see also Copelovitch (2010); Gould (2003), p. 551 et al.

[99] Herman et al. (2010b), p. 490.

development, poverty and social welfare, both domestically and internationally, when resources are diverted from one community of actors to another through direct financial transfers or indirect budgetary decisions.[100]

Utilising public resources to keep countries current on debt obligations to official and private creditors give rise to what economists term a 'moral hazard' on the part of both sovereign debtors and its creditors. This, in turn, can create asymmetries in the allocation of financial risk. Legal scholars, economists and political scientists have long argued that the possibility of financial bailouts from IFIs during a financial crisis changes the behaviour of financial actors and financial markets by enabling excessive risk-taking in sovereign debt markets due to inefficiently priced sovereign risk.[101] While the prospect of official financial intervention can encourage imprudent borrowing and lax economic policies by sovereign debtors, it has been argued that such bailouts, without corresponding mechanisms for private sector involvement in sovereign debt restructuring, create a much more serious risk of creditor moral hazard.

Crucially, while debtor states assume the financial obligations of financing from the IFIs and sustain the political and economic ramifications of an accompanying adjustment programme, official bailouts relieves private creditors from the consequences of excessive risk-taking and lack of due diligence in financial decision-making. Further, the assumption of the role of domestic lender of last resort by governments, particularly since the Latin American and Asian financial crises, has meant that governments have increasingly assumed the liabilities of insolvent financial institutions, either through the process of nationalisation or recapitalisation, effectively converting private debt into public liabilities that need to be funded from public resources. This means that private risk is increasingly underwritten by public resources, leading to unequal burden sharing between creditors and debtors and between private commercial actors and other stakeholders.

Consequently, financial bailouts, of domestic institutions and/or sovereign states, can be costly and lead to 'a massive redistribution of wealth from ordinary taxpayers to those bailed out'.[102] This asymmetry has meant that the burden of adjustment to a financial or sovereign debt crisis has been borne primarily by the citizens of debtor states. For example, Herman et al. argue that without a structured process of sovereign debt resolution that prioritises the equitable treatment of debt obligations, primacy has been given to debt servicing over and above a state's other contingent liabilities, such as obligations for 'pensions and unemployment insurance' that warrant as much representation within a debt renegotiation process as

---

[100] Akyüz (2010), pp. 1–5; United Nations, Report of the Commission of Experts of the President of the United Nations General Assembly on Reforms of the International Monetary and Financial System, 21 September 2009, para 19.

[101] Alexander et al. (2006), p. 96; Bolton and Skeel (2010), pp. 450–456.

[102] United Nations, Report of the Commission of Experts of the President of the United Nations General Assembly on Reforms of the International Monetary and Financial System, 21 September 2009, para 60.

creditor claims.[103] Large scale financial support from IFIs also exacerbate the north-south income divide in a globalized economy where debt service benefits transnational commercial investors and external creditors, leading to greater credit outflows while correspondingly disadvantaging domestic stakeholders who pay for debt servicing through increased taxation and fiscal contraction, exacerbated by the fiscal and monetary austerity imposed by financing conditionalities.

Global distributional asymmetries are further aggravated by the policies and practices of international public finance, particularly in the allocation of resources to countries in need of financial support. First, the use of official sector financing to subsidise commercial or official creditors diverts resources from other domestic or international priorities, including the mitigation of social and economic dislocations of crisis, economic recovery and the attainment of international development objectives such as the Millennium Development Goals (MDGs). The use of official development aid under the HIPC and associated schemes to alleviate the debt of low-income countries, for example, has reduced the amount of ODA available to support other international development or poverty reduction initiatives.[104] Moreover, under the terms of the now completed Multilateral Debt Relief Initiative (MDRI), countries with eligible debt cancelled under the initiative saw the amount of their foregone debt service to the International Development Association (IDA) in any given year being deducted from its annual financing allocation from the institution.[105]

Second, the access policies and practice of conditionality at IFIs have resulted in differential and often, discretionary, treatment of countries in terms of eligibility for and terms of financing. Concerns, for example, have been expressed over the two-tiered system of the precautionary lines introduced by the IMF in 2009 which allows for upfront access to an uncapped amount of resources for a select group of pre-approved countries (see Sect. 3.1) while subjecting other members to strict access policies and conditions of lending. Akyüz, for example, argues that these new instruments can 'lead to a further fragmentation of IMF membership by creating different categories in terms of their eligibility of access' to resources and privileging 'a small number of more prosperous emerging economies while the discretionary nature of the loans and levels of access 'open[s] the door for political influence'.[106] At the same time, the expansion of the IMF's lending portfolio and

---

[103] Herman et al. (2010b), p. 492.

[104] Tan C (2013) Life, debt, and human rights: contextualizing the international regime for sovereign debt relief. In: Nadakavukaren Schefer K (ed) Poverty and the international economic legal system poverty and the international economic legal system: duties to the world's poor. Cambridge University Press, Cambridge, pp 307–324.

[105] International Development Association (IDA), Report from the Executive Directors of the International Development Association to the Board of Governors, 15 February 2011 (modified 18 February 2011), Annex 2, para 16.

[106] Akyüz Y, Why the IMF and the International Monetary System Need More than Cosmetic Reform, South Centre Research Paper 32, November 2010, http://www.southcentre.int/research-paper-32-November-2010/#more-1364 (last accessed 16 October 2015), pp. 32–33.

the record injection of official sector resources into the international financial system without efforts to design and implement a mandatory system for involving private sector creditors in crisis resolution 'could not only overstretch [...] resources, but also endanger [the] financial integrity' of the IMF and other official institutions engaged in delivering financial aid.[107]

Finally and importantly, the use of international public finance in mitigating regulatory failures recast the negative consequences of regulatory asymmetries as domestic problems rather than systemic failings that require a radical revision of the rules of international finance. Financial support from IFIs to countries facing balance of payments difficulties continue to problematise the state in receipt of such resources, with accompanying economic adjustment programmes focused on restructuring domestic economic policies and institutions. While there is international recognition of the international sources of financial crises, the conscription of official financing as the primary regulatory and compensatory mechanism without corresponding regulatory measure to address the aforementioned external drivers of crisis places the burden of adjustment on domestic constituencies. It is national governments that must bear responsibility for restoring fiscal and monetary stability within the macroeconomic parameters determined by the IFIs and domestic stakeholders who assume the costs of doing so. This stymies reform by mitigating the effects of such crises on other international financial actors, notably private creditors, and forecloses wider reform of an asymmetrical financial system.

5 Conclusion

The postwar period has seen major shifts in the operation and constitution of international financial markets and the size, scale and composition of international financial flows, particularly since the breakdown of the Bretton Woods system. This new order of international finance has generated a much greater risk of financial instability and potential for financial contagion than any other time in history. The enhanced fragility of a heavily interconnected global financial system has left national regulatory regimes ill-equipped to deal with the 'extraterritorial nature of systemic risk that arises from the cross-border trade of financial services and associated payments, cross-border portfolio capital flows and the increasing scope of activities of multifunctional financial institutions and conglomerates'.[108] At the same time, the 'sophisticated technological linkages between financial systems' and 'the extensive global reach of many major financial institutions'[109] has meant that

[107] Akyüz Y, Why the IMF and the International Monetary System Need More than Cosmetic Reform, South Centre Research Paper 32, November 2010, http://www.southcentre.int/research-paper-32-November-2010/#more-1364 (last accessed 16 October 2015), p. 37.

[108] Alexander et al. (2006), p. 32.

[109] Alexander et al. (2006), p. 32.

the speed at which the negative repercussions of national regulatory and policy failures, such as inadequate supervision of domestic financial institutions, is transmitted has been increased dramatically in recent decades.

This messy and incongruent regulatory landscape has been a contributor to global financial instability. The current framework has not been able to establish effective mechanisms for the prevention of financial crises nor has it been able to generate effective and coordinated responses to such crises when they have occurred as demonstrated by past and current experiences with global and regional crises. In particular, the absence of a central coordinating structure of international financial governance has meant that there has been a 'haphazard development' of international financial norms and regulatory structures and an 'uneven application' of these rules to developed and developed countries[110] as well as lack of effective mechanisms for effective and equitable interventions in times of crises.

Importantly, these developments have led to a growing disjuncture between the rationale for and scope of international financial law and regulation and international public finance, with important implications for international financial governance. Accompanying the regulatory shift away from centralised governance and classical liberal international law as the normative framework for the global financial system has been the diminishing importance of law and other non-legal regulatory norms as mechanisms for global collective action in the financial sphere. Instead, law and regulation have increasingly operated as instruments to facilitate liberalisation of international financial markets rather than mechanisms to correct market failures and ensure equitable outcomes of international economic transactions.

As a result of these changing regulatory trajectories, international public finance has been progressively conscripted to manage and mitigate the negative externalities caused by both market and regulatory failures. This has heightened the gap between the policies and practices of international public finance and the development of international financial law and regulation. In particular, the increasing use of official sector resources as a default regulatory instrument for the prevention, mitigation and resolution of financial crises has meant that the evolution of mechanisms of international finance public finance has been pursued separately to regulatory reform and have served to compensate for regulatory failings rather than complement regulatory measures to maintain international financial stability. This disembeds the governance and disbursement of international public finance from the conduct of international financial affairs and has exacerbated the regulatory failings of the international financial system. At the same time, this paper has also demonstrated that despite the centrality of official financing to the mitigation and management of sovereign debt crises, the current architecture of international public finance does not provide a sustainable nor equitable framework for effective mobilisation, disbursement or utilisation of public resources to maintain or restore international financial stability.

[110] Alexander et al. (2006), p. 134.

This, in turn, has generated significant asymmetries in the way in which risks and benefits of a globalized financial system are allocated between financial actors and between states and communities in different parts of the world. While some lightly regulated financial actors, including systematically important financial institutions, reap the benefits of the mispricing of risk of global financial transactions, other stakeholders in the international financial system shoulder the burden of adjustment when the consequences of excessive risk-taking is manifested in financial and economic crises. Here, developing countries and emerging economies, and especially low-income developing countries, and the communities within them, are especially affected by contractions in the global economy resulting from these regulatory failures and distributional asymmetries due to fewer economic and institutional resources for crisis mitigation and management, inherent economic fragilities and greater susceptibility to external shocks.[111]

Consequently, the current regulatory framework for international financial governance lacks not just the political legitimacy but also the legal authority to prevent, intervene in or resolve financial crises effectively or equitably. Reform of the international financial architecture must therefore focus not only on establishing effective and equitable mechanisms for the regulation of international financial markets but also on rehabilitating the complementary link between international financial law and regulation and international public finance, particularly in reinscribing their shared responsibility for the mitigation and management of global market failures. As Akyüz notes, capital market failures need not always necessitate multilateral financing where other 'forms of collective action', notably legal and other regulatory interventions, 'may be able to address such failures'.[112] Utilising official sector financing as a means of overcoming market and regulatory deficits will only fuel further instability the international financial system.

References

Akyüz Y (2006) Rectifying capital market imperfections: the continuing rationales for multilateral lending. In: Kaul I, Conçeiçào P (eds) The new public finance: responding to global challenges. Edward Elgar, Aldershot, pp 486–491

Akyüz Y (2010) Multilateral disciplines and the question of policy space. In: Faundez J, Tan C (eds) International economic law, globalization and developing countries. Edward Elgar, Aldershot

Alexander K, Dhumale R, Eatwell J (2006) Global governance of financial systems: the international regulation of systemic risk. Oxford University Press, Oxford

Anghie A (2005) Imperialism, sovereignty and the making of international law. Cambridge University Press, Cambridge

[111] United Nations, Report of the Commission of Experts of the President of the United Nations General Assembly on Reforms of the International Monetary and Financial System, 21 September 2009.

[112] Akyüz (2006), p. 489.

Arner D, Buckley R (2011) From crisis to crisis: the global financial system and regulatory failure. Kluwer, Alphen aan den Rijn
Bolton P, Skeel DA (2010) How to rethink sovereign bankruptcy: a new role for the IMF? In: Herman B, Ocampo JA, Spiegel S (eds) Overcoming developing country debt crisis. Oxford University Press, Oxford, pp 449–485
Broome A (2008) The importance of being earnest: the IMF as a reputational intermediary. New Polit Econ 13(2):125–151
Broome A (2010) The International Monetary Fund, crisis management and the credit crunch. Aust J Int Aff 64(1):37–54
Brummer C (2011) How financial law works (and how it doesn't). Georgetown Law J 99:257–327
Brummer C (2012) Soft law and the global financial system: rulemaking in the 21st century. Cambridge University Press, Cambridge
Bruner C (2008) States, markets and gatekeepers: public-private regulatory regimes in an era of economic globalization. Mich J Int Law 30(1):125–176
Carrasco E (2010) An opening for voice in the global economic order: the global financial crisis and emerging economies. Oreg Rev Int Law 12(2):179–211
Copelovitch M (2010) The international monetary fund in the global economy: banks, bonds and bailouts. Cambridge University Press, Cambridge
Cosio-Pascal E (2010) Paris club: intergovernmental relations in debt restructuring. In: Herman B, Ocampo JA, Spiegel S (eds) Overcoming developing country debt crisis. Oxford University Press, Oxford, pp 231–276
Faundez J (2010) International economic law and development: before and after neo-liberalism. In: Faundez J, Tan C (eds) International economic law, globalization and developing countries. Edward Elgar, Aldershot, pp 10–33
Gelpern A, Gulati M (2010) How CACs became boilerplate: governments in market-based change. In: Herman B, Ocampo JA, Spiegel S (eds) Overcoming developing country debt crisis. Oxford University Press, Oxford, pp 347–388
Giovanoli M (2009) The reform of the international financial architecture after the global crisis. J Int Law Polit 42(1):81–123
Gould ER (2003) Money talks: supplementary financiers and the international monetary fund conditionality. Int Organ 57(3):551–586
Hagan S (2010) Enhancing the IMF's regulatory authority. J Int Econ Law 13(3):955–968
Herman B, Ocampo JA, Spiegel S (2010a) Introduction: the case for a new international reform effort. In: Herman B, Ocampo JA, Spiegel S (eds) Overcoming developing country debt crisis. Oxford University Press, Oxford, pp 1–31
Herman B, Ocampo JA, Spiegel S (2010b) Conclusion: towards a comprehensive sovereign bankruptcy regime. In: Herman B, Ocampo JA, Spiegel S (eds) Overcoming developing country debt crisis. Oxford University Press, Oxford, pp 489–496
Kaul I, Conceiçao P, Le Gouven K, Mendoza RU (2003) Why do global public goods matter today? In: Kaul I, Conceiçao P, Le Gouven K, Mendoza RU (eds) Providing global public goods: managing globalization. Oxford University Press, Oxford, pp 1–16
Pahuja S (2005) The postcoloniality of international law. Harv Int Law J 46(2):459–469
Pan EJ (2010) Challenge of international cooperation and institutional design in financial supervision: beyond transgovernmental networks. Chic J Int Law 11(1):243–284
Picciotto S (2011) Regulating global corporate capitalism. Cambridge University Press, Cambridge
Raustiala K (2002) The architecture of international cooperation: transgovernmental networks and the future of international law. Va J Int Law 43(1):1–92
Rieffel L (2003) Restructuring sovereign debt: the case for ad hoc machinery. Brookings Institution Press, Washington, DC
Ruggie J (1982) International regimes, transactions and change: embedded liberalism in the postwar economic order. Int Organ 36(2):379–415

Salamanca LJG (2010) The 1980s crisis in syndicated bank lending to sovereigns and the sequence of mechanisms to fix it. In: Herman B, Ocampo JA, Spiegel S (eds) Overcoming developing country debt crisis. Oxford University Press, Oxford, pp 111–139

Stiglitz J (2010) Sovereign debt: notes on theoretical frameworks and policy analyses. In: Herman B, Ocampo JA, Spiegel S (eds) Overcoming developing country debt crisis. Oxford University Press, Oxford, pp 35–69

Tan C (2010a) Regulation and resource dependency: the legal and political aspects of structural adjustment programmes. In: Bradlow D, Hunter D (eds) International financial institutions and international law. Kluwer Law, Alphen aan den Rijn, pp 167–198

Tan C (2010b) The new disciplinary framework: conditionality, new aid architecture and global economic governance. In: Faundez J, Tan C (eds) International economic law, globalization and developing countries. Edward Elgar, Aldershot, pp 112–137

Tan C (2013) Life, debt, and human rights: contextualizing the international regime for sovereign debt relief. In: Nadakavukaren Schefer K (ed) Poverty and the international economic legal system poverty and the international economic legal system: duties to the world's poor. Cambridge University Press, Cambridge, pp 307–324

Weber R, Arner D (2007) Toward a new design for international financial regulation. Univ Pa J Int Econ Law 29(2):391–453

Woods N (2006) The globalizers: the IMF, the World Bank and their borrowers. Cornell University Press, Ithaca and London

Problematic Relationships: Why International Economic Law Is Sometimes More Complicated Than It Appears

Christian Tietje

Contents

Abstract The international financial crisis of 2008 has gained a lot of attention from scholars from different disciplines. For many participants in the debate, the crisis was nothing else than an expression of a lack of effective international financial market regulations. Thus, to have better and "more" regulation on financial market instruments was seen as the key to preventing future crises. However, taking stock after about 7 years since the breakdown of Lehman Brothers makes clear that, first, finding adequate regulatory instruments for financial markets is certainly not as easy as it has often been suggested, and second, that there is a severe danger of overregulation with negative economic consequences. Celine Tan is not much interested in the intensive debate on possibilities, limitations and concepts on international financial market regulation. Instead, she simply asserts that there is a lack of "effective and equitable mechanisms for the regulation of international financial markets". This assertion is supplemented by a description of public institutions such as the International Monetary Fund (IMF) providing financial resources to States that suffer from financial crises. Based on these two observations, it is clear for the author that "international public finance has been progressively conscripted to manage and mitigate the negative externalities caused by both market and regulatory failures".

C. Tietje (✉)
Martin-Luther-University, Halle-Wittenberg, Germany
e-mail: christian.tietje@jura.uni-halle.de

M. Bungenberg et al. (eds.), *European Yearbook of International Economic Law 2016*, European Yearbook of International Economic Law 7,
DOI 10.1007/978-3-319-29215-1_15

1 Introduction

The international financial crisis of 2008 has gained a lot of attention from scholars from different disciplines. For many participants in the debate, the crisis was nothing else than an expression of a lack of effective international financial market regulations. Thus, to have better and "more" regulation on financial market instruments was seen as the key to preventing future crises. However, taking stock after about 7 years since the breakdown of Lehman Brothers makes clear that, first, finding adequate regulatory instruments for financial markets is certainly not as easy as it has often been suggested, and second, that there is a severe danger of overregulation with negative economic consequences.[1]

Celine Tan is not much interested in the intensive debate on possibilities, limitations and concepts on international financial market regulation. Instead, she simply asserts that there is a lack of "effective and equitable mechanisms for the regulation of international financial markets".[2] This assertion is supplemented by a description of public institutions such as the International Monetary Fund (IMF) providing financial resources to States that suffer from financial crises. Based on these two observations, it is clear for the author that "international public finance has been progressively conscripted to manage and mitigate the negative externalities caused by both market and regulatory failures".

I have doubts whether the author can make a convincing point. This is due to the following main issues, which will be addressed in the following parts of this comment: First, the author misunderstands the historical conception and idea of the so-called Bretton Woods system—this system was never intended to provide for any financial market regulation. Second, as already indicated, the author does not take into account the inherent problems of international financial market regulation. Third, the author underestimates the role of soft law and similar instruments in shaping the international financial architecture. Fourth, there is no proof for any causal relationship between an alleged lack of international financial regulation and an increase in international public finance.

2 Public Finance and Financial Market Regulation in Historical Perspective

Public finance and political influence on the receiving state by third states and/or private creditors is not at all a new phenomenon.[3] Indeed, international financial markets have not been developed as primarily private financial markets. Instead, cross-border financial transactions in history largely fulfilled the purpose of

[1] For details on the systemic problems of regulating global financial markets see Lehmann and Tietje (2010); for a topical overview on the entire debate see Cottier et al. (2014).

[2] Tan (2016), section 5.

[3] This and the next sections of this comment are largely based on Tietje (2011, 2014).

financing state budgets.[4] At the peak of this earlier development, at the end of the nineteenth century, there were hardly any restrictions on capital movement. Thus, substantial international capital flows to emerging markets took place in the form of bonds. Because of this, the time before World War I has been termed the 'golden age for emerging market bonds and international capital flows to emerging markets'.[5]

The difference between before World War I and today is the number of creditors involved in international capital transactions. Before World War I, there was no real globalised financial market. After World War I, the international financial centre moved from London to New York. Furthermore, at the end of the 1920s, about 800,000 US citizens held foreign bonds. At that time, bonds were the most important international financial market instrument. States were almost exclusively the recipients of international financial transactions, thus an international financial market with private parties on both sides of the transaction, i.e. a real international private financial market, did not exist.[6] However, the interdependence of bonds, sovereign debts, and private capital markets was already becoming apparent.

The establishment of the Bretton Woods system in 1944 was the first truly multilateral attempt to establish an international monetary system. The Bretton Woods System was created on the basis of the prevailing factual setting of the international financial markets. The most important influencers were the head of the US delegation, Harry Dexter White, and British economist John Maynard Keynes. Although White and Keynes sometimes disagreed,[7] the traumatic experience of the world economic crisis of 1929 and what is known today as 'Keynesianism' united them. Moreover, both agreed that fixed but adjustable exchange rates are necessary in order to enable free international trade in goods and services. This must be supplemented by general (Keynes) or at least possible (White) capital controls, they argued.[8] Indeed, the discussion about financial markets at Bretton Woods involved only capital controls. With regard to further aspects of financial markets, everybody at that time accepted what *Keynes* wrote in 1933: '[. . .] above all, let finance be [. . .] national'.[9]

---

[4] Held et al. (1999), p. 191 et seq.

[5] Mauro P et al. (2000) Emerging Market Spreads: Then versus Now. IMF Working Paper WT/00/190, p. 3, http://info.tuwien.ac.at/ccefm/workshop/imf_wp00190.pdf (last accessed 25 August 2015); Szodruch (2008), p. 73.

[6] For details see Szodruch (2008), p. 73 et seq.

[7] See Boughton JM (2002) Why White, not Keynes? Inventing the Postwar International Monetary System. IMF Working Paper, WP/02/52; Lastra (2006), p. 345, 351 et seq.

[8] Boughton JM (2002) Why White, not Keynes? Inventing the Postwar International Monetary System. IMF Working Paper, WP/02/52, p. 11; for details on the opinion of John Maynard Keynes concerning capital controls see, e.g., Cohen (2006), p. 45 ff. comprehensively Moschella (2010), p. 5.

[9] Keynes (1933), p. 769.

In spite of some common beliefs, some fundamental differences concerning the appropriate approach towards the international monetary systems remained, and in the end White's position prevailed. This is true not only regarding the regulation of bilateral monetary relations between the US and the United Kingdom (Keynes), but also in establishing a multinational and integrated system for monetary, investment and trade issues.[10] However, the IMF was kept small and was prevented from being a lender of last resort as a consequence of this approach.[11]

As a result of the Bretton Woods conference in July 1944, the International Bank for Reconstruction and Development (IBRD) (also called World Bank) and the International Monetary Fund (IMF) were established. The original idea of the World Bank was just to function as a bank and to give money via credits or guarantees to those regions of the world severely affected by World War II.[12] In this regard, the World Bank was originally seen as representing the investment pillar of the international economic system of which trade and finance were the other two pillars.[13] However, since the US started its own financial support programme in 1948, the European Recovery Program,[14] the World Bank actually never got a chance to fulfil its original mandate. Thus, the Bank quickly changed its focus and became a development institution.[15]

The original mandate of the IMF, as the second Bretton Woods institution, was restricted to stable currency systems in direct connection to liberalised trade in goods and services.[16] Of course, this mandate was dependent on the establishment of a third Bretton Woods institution responsible for liberalised international trade in goods and services. The establishment of an International Trade Organization (ITO), as designed by the Havana Charter of 1948, would have completed the architecture of the international economic system. Since the Havana Charter never

---

[10] Boughton JM (2002) Why White, not Keynes? Inventing the Postwar International Monetary System. IMF Working Paper, WP/02/52, p. 13 ff.

[11] Boughton JM (2002) Why White, not Keynes? Inventing the Postwar International Monetary System. IMF Working Paper, WP/02/52, p. 16 ff.

[12] For details see, e.g., Schlemmer-Schulte (2015), para 85 et seq.; Lowenfeld (2008), p. 93 et seq.

[13] Arner DW and Buckley RP (2010) Redesigning the architecture of the global financial system https://www.law.unimelb.edu.au/files/dmfile/download13c41.pdf (last accessed 24 September 2015), p. 6; Lastra (2006), p. 345, 354 et seq.

[14] For details see de De Zayas A (2009) Marshall Plan (European Recovery Program). http://opil.ouplaw.com/view/10.1093/law:epil/9780199231690/law-9780199231690-e654?prd=EPIL (last accessed 25 August 2015).

[15] Schlemmer-Schulte (2015), para 81.

[16] See Article 1 Articles of Agreement of the International Monetary Fund, 27 December 1945, UNTS 2, 40 (IMF Agreement): 'The purposes of the International Monetary Fund are: [. . .] (2) To facilitate the expansion and balanced growth of international trade, and to contribute thereby to the promotion and maintenance of high levels of employment and real income and to the development of the productive resources of all members as primary objectives of economic policy. (3) To promote exchange stability, to maintain orderly exchange arrangements among members, and to avoid competitive exchange depreciation'.

entered into force and the ITO was never established,[17] the IMF was thus never able to fulfil its original mandate in a comprehensive way, even though it worked quite successfully after its establishment. This was largely due to the rather simple structure and thus also due to the limited rule of law in the original Bretton Woods system of fixed exchange rates. The IMF essentially had the task of negotiating the initial exchange rates of a country and had the power to grant permission to countries to devalue their currencies in specific situations. This was supplemented with the possibility for the IMF to lend money to countries facing balance of payment problems. In turn, Member States of the IMF were obliged to maintain the value of their currency and to purchase or sell the currency by use of reserve in case of a deviation from the fixed value.[18] Regarding international financial markets, however, it is important to note that the legal order of the IMF only provided for the possibility of control of capital transfers. Based on Article VI (Sect. 3) IMF Agreement,[19] the entire issue of financial markets was therefore left to the sovereign discretion of States, which is in alignment with the above-mentioned quote by Keynes to 'let finance be [...] national'.[20] The idea of nationalising finance was based on the firm belief that the international financial and economic crisis of 1929 was due to speculative financial transactions, and that capital controls could therefore have prevented it.[21] As a logical consequence of this prevailing opinion at the time, states envisaged the dissolution of the Bank for International Settlements (BIS) while establishing the Bretton Woods System.[22] As this never happened, the deficiencies of the system became obvious.[23] Moreover, this historical conception and development makes it clear why international law did not play much of a role in international monetary affairs after World War II. This was exactly what was planned by States and the way they designed it. Because of the design (architecture) of the original Bretton Woods System, it was clear that public finance would be the only international tool to influence domestic financial and monetary structures. Bretton Woods was thus not intended to establish a comprehensive international economic or financial order in terms of an integration of trade, finance, investment and currency based on the rule of law. Furthermore, a

---

[17] See, e.g., Lowenfeld (2008), p. 23 et seq.

[18] See, e.g., Lowenfeld AF (2011) Monetary Law International. http://opil.ouplaw.com/view/10.1093/law:epil/9780199231690/law-9780199231690-e1537?rskey=lUyMEE&result=1&prd=EPIL (last accessed 25 August 2015).

[19] 'Members may exercise such controls as are necessary to regulate international capital movements [...]'.

[20] Keynes (1933), p. 769.

[21] For details on this opinion namely of Keynes see Boughton JM (2002) Why White, not Keynes? Inventing the Postwar International Monetary System. IMF Working Paper, WP/02/52, p. 10; Moschella (2010), p. 5.

[22] Lastra (2006), p. 345, 354 et seq.

[23] Arner DW and Buckley RP (2010) Redesigning the architecture of the global financial system https://www.law.unimelb.edu.au/files/dmfile/download13c41.pdf (last accessed 24 September 2015), p. 5 ff.

genuine lender of last resort was not established. With the exception of capital control, financial market stability was not addressed, and with the exception of balance of payment questions, the entire issue of sovereign debt was left open. International public finance was thus the only regulatory instrument of the Bretton Woods system.

New challenges occurred at the end of the 1960s due to the introduction of 'Eurobonds'. Eurobonds are bonds issued in a currency other than that of the country of issuance, which are usually placed on different domestic financial markets simultaneously by big banks or banking consortiums. Some consider Eurobonds to be a 'genuinely de-territorialised form of finance'.[24] Eurobonds had the effect that the international financial market, which was almost totally controlled and restricted by states until the 1960s, opened up to the private sector. However, at that time, the important private actors in the financial market were exclusively large banks and banking consortiums.

In addition to the factual changes in the international financial market, important structural developments occurred in the 1970s: the shift from fixed to flexible exchange rates after the United States removed the link between the US Dollar and the gold standard on 15 August 1971; the reaction of Member States of the IMF to this by a substantial revision of Article VI IMF Agreement and thus an extension of the IMF mandate in 1976 in order to give the IMF the mandate to supervise the international currency system with regard to macroeconomic considerations.[25] This development goes hand in hand with the introduction of conditionality as an essential policy tool of the IMF, which marked the beginning of the IMF's slow transformation into a development institution.[26]

The shift in the mandate of the IMF at the beginning of the 1970s goes hand in hand with a fundamental change in the global structure of sovereign debts. Most developing countries financed their state budgets after World War II with the help of credits they received from developed countries and the Bretton Woods institutions. Private capital played hardly any role and only became relevant with the introduction of Eurobonds. However, the energy crisis at the beginning of the 1970s led to massive profits being made by the oil-exporting countries. These countries placed their currency reserves—known as Petro Dollars—on the Euro-Dollar markets, i.e. in accounts held with branches of US Banks in the United Kingdom, namely in London. The banks themselves used these savings to invest in, i.a., Latin American States.[27]

[24] Szodruch (2008), p. 52, with further references on Eurobonds in general; Lastra (2006), p. 371, 396 et seq.

[25] See, e.g., Arner DW and Buckley RP (2010) Redesigning the architecture of the global financial system https://www.law.unimelb.edu.au/files/dmfile/download13c41.pdf (last accessed 24 September 2015), p. 10.

[26] Schlemmer-Schulte (2015), para 50 et seq.

[27] Szodruch (2008), p. 52, 89 et seq.

The Bretton Woods system was more or less unaffected by these developments. Instead, a structure parallel to Bretton Woods, and largely based on soft law dealing with the emerging challenges described above, developed. These developments occurred under the auspices of the BIS in Basel, Switzerland. As a result of the insolvency of the German Herstatt Bank, the US Franklin National Bank, and the Israel-British Bank in London, the governors of the central bank of the G-10 countries founded the Standing Committee on Banking Regulations and Supervisory Practices, which was renamed the Basel Committee on Banking Supervision in 1990.[28] The insolvencies of these banks however were only the immediate cause of the establishment of the Basel committee. The real genesis lies in the introduction of new actors and an increase in the volume of international financial markets, i.e. in the emerging globalisation of financial markets in the 1970s. Essentially, the establishment of the Basel committee was a reaction to the lack of international standards for the globalised financial market at that time.[29] However, it is obvious that the task of the Basel committee was and is limited to rather microeconomic issues. Exchange rate stability, sovereign debts and other challenges to the international economic system are not of primary interest for the Basel system.

The developments in the 1970s concerning administrative and political cooperation and coordination finally led, in the 1990s, to the establishment of what was called the New International Financial Architecture I (NIFA I).[30] The immediate background for the NIFA I was the financial crisis in Mexico in 1994 ('Tequila crisis'), the Asian crisis in 1997, and the Brazilian and Russian crises in 1998–1999. The G-7 finance ministers reacted to these crises in May 1998 with a report entitled 'Strengthening the Architecture of the Global Financial System'. With this report, a new dimension of international cooperation based on the rule of law concerning the global financial markets began. This system was successful at least until September 11, 2001. Following the terrorist attacks, the focus shifted away from international financial market stability.

As we know today, this was a fatal development, because some of the real causes of the financial crisis in 2007 and 2009 emerged during that time. Even though it is hard to single out any one cause of the financial crisis in 2007 and 2009, the low interest rates policy of the Federal Reserve played a role. This policy was only possible because of the surplus of financial resources in the US market due to China's policy of investing its foreign currency reserves in the US.[31] The foreign currency reserves of China are, to some extent, a result of the export performance of the country after its accession to the WTO on December, 11 2001.

---

[28] For details see Rost (2009), p. 319.

[29] Norton (2010), p. 266.

[30] Very comprehensively on this Norton (2010), p. 272 et seq.

[31] On the causes of the crisis see, e.g., Hellwig (2010), p. 365 ff.; Ohler (2010), p. 6 et seq.; comprehensively Obstfeld M, Rogoff K (2009) Global Imbalances and the Financial Crisis: Products of Common Causes, http://www.frbsf.org/economics/conferences/aepc/2009/09_Obstfeld.pdf (last accessed 25 August 2015); Lastra and Wood (2010), p. 531.

As Celine Tan rightly points out, the topic of state insolvency has been left out from any legal regulation in the international monetary system.[32] However, the real problem of this is not that much the stepping in of international public finance in case of state insolvency or some spectacular bankruptcies of states in the last few years, but the phenomenon of 'private sector involvement', i.e. the historically unprecedented interdependence of private international financial markets, currency stability and sovereign debts.[33] Private sector involvement has its roots in developments that occurred at the end of the 1980s. It became obvious around 1989 that something had to be done to break the everlasting cycle of financing state budgets by credits provided by a limited number of international banks, leading to sovereign default of that state some years later, necessitating financial aid from international organisations such as the IMF and debt restructuring based on new international credits by large banks, further sovereign default a number of years later and so on. To get out of this everlasting cycle, a radical restructuring of sovereign debt was necessary. Such a new system was proposed with the Brady Plan. According to the principles developed by US Treasury Secretary Nicholas F. Brady in March 1989, large credits to emerging economies are restructured to bonds which are put on the international financial markets in order to finance the original credit. With this, the structure and indeed the number of creditors dramatically changes. In the past, only a limited number of international banks had served as creditors; now, theoretically, an unlimited number of bondholders in different jurisdictions have this ability. Due to private sector involvement in state budget finance, today sovereign defaults necessarily entail crises in the financial and also the currency markets. However, with the exception of certain attempts to harmonise the law of collective action clauses,[34] the international political and legal community hardly reacted to this radical new structure of state debts or its inherent interdependence with private international financial and public currency markets. Celine Tan points this out in her contribution.

3 Domestic Embeddedness of Financial Market Instruments

In order to understand the inherent limits of any attempt to develop international harmonized rules on financial market regulation, the domestic embeddedness of financial market instruments must be realised. Financial market products are inherently linked to a specific domestic legal order; they are indeed the progeny of domestic jurisdiction. For instance, an investor buying shares in a Luxembourg investment fund is trusting not only the issuer, but also Luxemburg's well-known

[32] Tan (2016), section 3.2.

[33] Comprehensively Szodruch (2008).

[34] For details see Koch (2004), p. 665; Schill (2008), p. 65.

quality of legislation and administrative practices in the area of finance. This is a unique feature of financial market products. Unlike physical products and most services, financial market products always feature a particular jurisdiction. Thus, they are products that are deeply rooted in one specific domestic legal order, on the one hand, and increasingly traded on global markets on the other. They are offered not only on their domestic market, but also worldwide, and in this sense they are 'international' or better—'transnational'. Therefore, one may speak of transnational financial products and markets by highlighting the above-described double character of products and markets as being both domestic and international.[35]

This unique feature of financial market products has consequences for any attempt at international regulation because there are inherent limitations due to the domestic embeddedness, which may also be characterised in terms of regulatory competition.[36] Because of the domestic embeddedness of financial market products, in most instances regulation and supervision in this area are aimed not only at financial market stability, but are also influenced by many other considerations, including consumer protection, protection of creditors, and the fiscal interests of the government.[37] These regulatory aims are not necessarily connected to the character of financial market products as (global) public goods; they can be based on purely political considerations.

Further, one must realise that there is no one-size-fits-all optimal monetary policy for all countries worldwide. Already the theoretical concept of optimal monetary policy is unclear and in dispute. Moreover, the effects of monetary policy of central banks leading to inflation or deflation depend to a certain and maybe even large extent on specific micro- and macroeconomic circumstances in a given country or economic region.[38] Furthermore, there is increasing demand for a more integrated and comprehensive policy by central banks concerning monetary issues. The Committee on International Economic Policy and Reform made this point convincingly in its September 2011 report 'Rethinking Central Banking':

> Central banks should make clear that monetary policy is only one part of the policy response and cannot be effective unless other policies – fiscal and structural policies, financial sector regulation – work in tandem.[39]

The inherent complexity and the lack of a single globally applicable optimal monetary policy create serious obstacles for international coordination and

---

[35] Lehmann and Tietje (2010), p. 6668 et seq.; see also Weber (2010), p. 683.

[36] Lehmann and Tietje (2010), p. 663 seq.; similar Weber (2010), p. 684: "International regulation and supervision is not' naturally superior' to regional or national rules and supervisory practices or vice versa"; for details see also Trachtman (2010), p. 719.

[37] Garicano and Lastra (2010), p. 599.

[38] For a comprehensive discussion on this see Posner EA, Sykes AO (2012) International Law and the Limits of Macroeconomic Cooperation. Institute for Law and Economics Working Paper No. 609, p. 41 et seq., http://ssrn.com/abstract=2120890 (last accessed 7 September 2015).

[39] Committee on International Economic Policy and Reform, Rethinking Central Banking, September 2011, iii.

cooperation in monetary affairs. As Eric A. Posner and Alan O. Sykes wrote, '[a]bout the most one can expect is occasional ad hoc cooperation among the subset of central banks confronting an immediate short-term problem'.[40]

In sum, there are limitations on comprehensive international harmonisation, coordination and cooperation concerning financial market regulation and supervision and monetary affairs. Thus, the international financial and monetary order will always be characterised by a certain element of decentralisation. The rule of law in international financial and monetary affairs thus also has inherent limits. This is the challenge and not some alleged relationship between financial market and public finance.

4 The Role of Soft Law

It is true, as highlighted and criticized by Celine Tan, that the current international financial system is dominated by soft institutions and soft law.[41] However, the significance of soft law in the global financial and monetary system is not necessarily a negative phenomenon. Chris Brummer has discussed this and further aspects in his book, *Soft law and the Global Financial System*.[42] This is not to say that soft law may be adequate for any regulatory challenges in the international financial system. However, it is necessary to look into the large literature on soft law and, directly linked to this, what is today called global administrative law (GAL), in order to be able to weigh and balance the pros and cons of soft law and soft institutions in the international financial systems as an important part of GAL.[43] Indeed, most phenomena of the international financial/monetary system are typical for GAL and have been intensively and comprehensively discussed in the GAL literature.

[40] Posner EA, Sykes AO (2012) International Law and the Limits of Macroeconomic Cooperation. Institute for Law and Economics Working Paper No. 609, p. 44, http://ssrn.com/abstract=2120890 (last accessed 7 September 2015).

[41] Tan (2016), section 2.2.

[42] Brummer (2012).

[43] On Global Administrative Law see, e.g., Kingsbury et al. (2005), p. 15; Cassese S et al. (2008) Global Administrative Law—Cases, Materials, Issues. 2nd ed., http://www.iilj.org/GAL/documents/GALCasebook2008.pdf (last accessed 7 September 2015); for a comprehensive overview on Global Administrative Law see: Bibliographical Resources, http://www.iilj.org/GAL/documents/GALBibliographyMDeBellisJune2006.pdf (last accessed 7 September 2015).

5 The Relationship Between International Financial Regulation and International Public Finance

Finally, it seems necessary to conduct more research on the empirical assumptions Celine Tan makes in her paper. Tan basically assumes that a financial crisis leads to an intensive increase in foreign public finance of a respective country and, by means of conditionality, thus also an increase in foreign (or international) policy influence. However, empirical studies seem to come to a totally different conclusion. In an IMF Working Paper, Jochen R. Andritzky argues as follows:

> During the last decades, investors from abroad have increased their presence in government bond markets. The financial crisis broke this trend. Domestic financial institutions allocated a larger share of government securities in their portfolios, as Japan has done since its crisis in the 1990s. Increases in the share held by institutional investors or non-residents by 10 percentage points are associated with a reduction in yields by about 25 or 40 basis points, respectively.[44]

The quote indicates that, overall, a financial crisis within a state might not lead to more public finance from sources outside the respective country, but rather to more finance of the state budget by domestic investors, namely domestic commercial banks and central banks. This is not the place to make an in depth assessment of this. However, it is necessary to conduct more economic research before making the assumption that there is a causal relationship between international public finance and a financial crisis.

6 Conclusions

It has become obvious that the international financial system was designed without any attempt for international regulation of financial markets. Thus, the developments since the 1970s that led to the NIFA I and to today's system, which occurred largely outside but closely connected to the Bretton Woods system, were not a "fundamental reorganisation of the international financial architecture",[45] as claimed by Celine Tan. Instead, developments such as the Basel Banking Committee, the Financial Stability Forum/Board, international standardisation, etc., occurred in order to close those gaps that were left open by Bretton Woods. Moreover, international public finance, originally by the World Bank, later by the IMF, and of course also by states was always part of the system. This has not changed. At least there is no empirical evidence for any significant increase in public finance by third states or international institutions in causal connection to

[44] Andritzky JR (2012) Government Bonds and Their Investors: What Are the Facts and Do They Matter? IMF Working Paper (WP/12/158).

[45] Tan (2016), section 2.2.

financial crises. Thus, overall, Celine Tan is telling a story that is known and has been told several times already. This is the story about the pro and cons of conditionality and the systemic problems of the international financial system.

References

Brummer C (2012) Soft law and the global financial system—rule making in the 21st century. Cambridge University Press, Cambridge

Cohen BJ (2006) Monetary governance and capital mobility in historical perspective. In: Grote R, Marauhn T (eds) The regulation of international financial markets—perspective for reform. Cambridge University Press, Cambridge, pp 27–53

Cottier T, Lastra RM, Tietje C, Satragno L (eds) (2014) The rule of law in monetary affairs. Cambridge University Press, Cambridge

Garicano L, Lastra RM (2010) Towards a new architecture for financial stability: seven principles. J Int Econ Law 13(3):597–621

Held D, McGrew AG, Goldblatt D, Perraton J (1999) Global transformations. Stanford University Press, Stanford

Hellwig M (2010) Finanzkrise und reformbedarf. In: Hellwig M, Höfling W, Zimmer D (eds) Finanzmarktregulierung: Welche Regelungen empfehlen sich für den deutschen und europäischen Finanzsektor? Gutachten E/F/G zum 68. Deutschen Juristentag. Verlag C.H. Beck, München, pp E5—E 57

Keynes JM (1933) National self-sufficiency. Yale Rev 22(4):755–769

Kingsbury B, Krisch N, Stewart RB (2005) The emergence of global administrative law. Law Contemp Probl 68:15–61

Koch EB (2004) Collective action clauses—the way forward. Georgetown J Int Law 35 (4):665–692

Lastra RM (2006) Legal foundations of international monetary stability. Oxford University Press, Oxford

Lastra RM, Wood G (2010) The crisis of 2007–09: nature, causes, and reactions. J Int Econ Law 13 (3):531–550

Lehmann M, Tietje C (2010) The role and prospects of international law in financial regulation and supervision. J Int Econ Law 13(3):663–682

Lowenfeld AF (2008) International economic law, 2nd edn. Oxford University Press, Oxford

Moschella M (2010) Governing risk—the IMF and global financial crises. Palgrave Macmillan, Basingstoke

Norton JJ (2010) NIFA-II or “Bretton-Woods-II”? The G-20 (Leaders) Summit process on managing global financial markets and the world economy—Quo Vadis? J Bankng Regul 11 (4):261–301

Ohler C (2010) International regulation and supervision of financial markets after the crisis. Eur Yearb Int Econ Law 1:3–29

Rost B (2009) Basel committee on banking supervision. In: Tietje C, Brouder A (eds) Handbook of transnational economic governance regimes. Martinus Nijhoff, Leiden, pp 319–328

Schill S (2008) Der völkerrechtliche Staatsnotstand in der Entscheidung des BVerfG zu Argentinischen Staatsanleihen—Anachronismus oder Avantgarde? Zeitschrift für ausländisches öffentliches Recht und Völkerrecht 68:45–67

Schlemmer-Schulte S (2015) Internationales Währungs—und Finanzrecht. In: Tietje C (ed) Internationales Wirtschaftsrecht, 2nd edn. De Gruyter, Berlin, pp 434–508

Szodruch A (2008) Staateninsolvenz und private Gläubiger—Rechtsprobleme des Private Sector Involvement bei staatlichen Finanzkrisen im 21. Jahrhundert. Berlin, Berliner Wissenschafts-Verlag

Tan C (2016) Shifting sands: interrogating the problematic relationship between international public finance and international financial regulation. In: Bungenberg M, Hermann C, Krajewski M, Terchechte JP (eds) European yearbook of international economic Law, vol 7. Springer, Heidelberg, pp 343–375

Tietje C (2011) The international financial architecture as a legal order. Ger Yearb Int Law 54:11–45

Tietje C (2014) The role of law in monetary affairs: taking stock. In: Cottier T, Lastra RM, Tietje C, Satragno L (eds) The rule of law in monetary affairs. Cambridge University Press, Cambridge, pp 11–44

Trachtman JP (2010) The international law of financial crisis: spillovers, subsidiarity, fragmentation and cooperation. J Int Econ Law 13(3):719–742

Weber RH (2010) Multilayered governance in international financial regulation and supervision. J Int Econ Law 13(3):683–704

Regulating Multinational Enterprises

Peter Muchlinski

Contents

Abstract Multinational Enterprises (MNEs) were, until relatively recently, deemed to be outside the purview of International Economic Law (IEL). More recently this has changed. MNEs are visible and much of the contemporary agenda of IEL concerns the facilitation of their operations, specifically, through the increasing integration of trade and investment issues in new generation Preferential Trade and Investment Agreements (PTIAs). These developments have created growing worries over the loss of sovereignty by States and have prompted the rise of a critical alternative position that seeks to rebalance IEL towards a re-assertion of State regulatory power and of values other than the purely economic values. Here Non-Governmental Organisations (NGOs), or Civil Society Groups (CSGs), play a significant role seeking to curb what they perceive as unaccountable excesses of corporate power supported by the retreat of the State from regulatory control. This trend does not obviate the need to address issues of distributive justice, social solidarity and sustainable development that challenge any purely facilitative calculation about corporate freedoms. It requires action to rebalance both domestic and international rules concerning the operations of MNEs and to reign in corporate excesses. The problem is how to do this if the State remains wedded to the core idea

P. Muchlinski (✉)
School of Law, SOAS, University of London, London, UK
e-mail: pm29@soas.ac.uk

M. Bungenberg et al. (eds.), *European Yearbook of International Economic Law 2016*, European Yearbook of International Economic Law 7,
DOI 10.1007/978-3-319-29215-1_16

of market liberalisation and corporate freedom. This paper will seek to unravel this conundrum in the context of the development of PTIAs and their impact on MNE regulation.

1 Introduction

Multinational Enterprises (MNEs) were, until relatively recently, deemed to be outside the purview of International Economic Law (IEL). As private non-State actors, their legal existence was purely a matter of, and for, domestic law. The result was that MNEs were invisible to international law. Accordingly, IEL saw its focus as being the regulation of State conduct, particularly in the trade field. Investment by non-State actors, so far as it was addressed at all, was limited to the legal consequences of State nationalisations, as an aspect of the law relating to diplomatic protection.[1]

More recently this has changed. MNEs are visible and much of the contemporary agenda of IEL concerns the facilitation of their operations.[2] Specifically, the operations of transnational business are viewed through the lens of trade and investment liberalisation.[3] The rise of investor protection through international investment law is perhaps the strongest indicator of this trend. It is furthered by the increasing integration of trade and investment issues in new generation Preferential Trade and Investment Agreements (PTIAs). This has prompted negotiations for new inter-regional agreements such as the proposed Transatlantic Trade and Investment Partnership (TTIP) and Trans Pacific Partnership (TPP) and has created a number of regional arrangements following a similar policy model.[4]

These developments have created growing worries over the loss of sovereignty by States and have prompted the rise of a critical alternative position. This seeks to rebalance IEL towards a re-assertion of State regulatory power and of values other than the purely economic value of financial maximisation that is displayed by the neo-liberal mantra of privatisation, deregulation and liberalisation. Here Non-Governmental Organisations (NGOs), or Civil Society Groups (CSGs), play

[1] For a fuller discussion see Muchlinski (2012a).

[2] For a general discussion of the nature of contemporary international economic law see further the collection of articles in JIEL (2014). It is striking that this collection does not include a paper specifically dedicated to international investment law or MNE regulation, though aspects of these issues are discussed in the contributions. For a socio-legal perspective see further Perry-Kessaris (2013).

[3] For a wider discussion of market promoting legal measures, covering both international and domestic developments, see Muchlinski (2011b).

[4] See further Joubin-Bret (2013), p. 289 and UNCTAD (2014) World Investment Report 2014 http://unctad.org/en/PublicationsLibrary/wir2014_en.pdf (last accessed 22 July 2015), pp. 118–124.

a significant role seeking to curb what they perceive as unaccountable excesses of corporate power supported by the retreat of the State from regulatory control. Indeed the State, and the existing political processes through which it operates, are seen as part of the neo-liberal project and not to be trusted to regulate in the public interest.

There is no doubt that, in recent decades, governments have accepted their use of legislative and executive power to facilitate corporate freedom as part of the wider move towards a truly liberal global economy that offers the widest possible geographical space for global markets to flourish.[5] This has resulted in some specific characteristics for MNE regulation under domestic laws. First, the free movement of corporations across the global economy is required so that firms can make the best use of their specific competitive advantages in combination with the location specific advantages of host countries.[6] This requires easy incorporation through company law and a reduction of restrictions on foreign investment, a continuing trend in domestic laws, despite some notable counter-examples.[7] Such domestic laws are reinforced by market liberalisation rules in international economic instruments.[8]

Secondly, investment risk needs to be reduced by way of protective laws, which ensure that investors' competitive advantages are not undermined by host countries' regulations and that the economic value of investments is upheld. Here the protection of intellectual property rights is significant, a matter already given international protection under the WTO TRIPs Agreement.[9] Also important is the creation of structures conducive to the growth of large corporations, something which was achieved historically with the acceptance of corporate group structures under domestic corporate laws in the late nineteenth century,[10] and which today is reflected in the reduction of foreign ownership restrictions and the abovementioned reduction of restrictive foreign investment screening laws. A further factor is the creation of favourable production costs through incentives such as tax breaks and other aids, including the use of export processing zones and similar policy enclaves, subject to limits ensuring that public money is not wastefully employed in such support.[11] Connected to this is the control of labour costs through labour laws that

---

[5] For a full discussion see Muchlinski (2013a), pp. 286–304.

[6] Muchlinski (2011a), p. 671.

[7] See UNCTAD (2014) World Investment Report 2014 http://unctad.org/en/PublicationsLibrary/wir2014_en.pdf (last accessed 17 August 2015), pp. 106–114; UNCTAD (2015) World Investment Report 2015. http://unctad.org/en/PublicationsLibrary/wir2015_en.pdf (last accessed 17 August 2015), pp. 102–104.

[8] Muchlinski (2011a), p. 672.

[9] Muchlinski (2011a), pp. 672–673 and see too Muchlinski (2007), pp. 33–34.

[10] Muchlinski (2007), p. 35. The role of competition law in this process is harder to determine, Muchlinski (2007), p. 35.

[11] Muchlinski (2007), pp. 219–237.

ensure that such costs are placed at an economically efficient level so as to increase the enterprise's return on investment. Thus the trend is towards the limitation of worker rights to the extent possible without compromising basic labour standards as contained in ILO Conventions.[12]

The abovementioned trend in domestic laws does not obviate the need to address issues of distributive justice, social solidarity and sustainable development that challenge any purely facilitative calculation about corporate freedoms. It requires action to rebalance both domestic and international rules concerning the operations of MNEs and to reign in corporate excesses. The problem is how to do this if the State remains wedded to the core idea of market liberalisation and corporate freedom.

This paper will seek to unravel this conundrum in the context of the development of PTIAs and their impact on MNE regulation. Perhaps these instruments do more than anything else to show how the initial separation between trade and investment issues in IEL has been superseded by a more integrated approach.[13] This comes at a time when the nature and content of International Investment Agreements (IIAs) is being questioned and recalibrated to allow for a better balance between investor rights and State interests in regulatory space based on the need to further sustainable development goals.[14] Thus the focus of the first section on PTIAs is justified not only as an illustration of the current trends in IEL towards facilitative regulation of trade and investment but also as a magnet for contemporary critical currents that inform the development of IEL. These currents are examined in more detail in the second section. In turn this raises the question of whether PTIAs contain the kernel of a new approach to MNE regulation, a matter to be discussed in the final part of the paper.

---

[12] Muchlinski (2011a), p. 674. Of course this does not preclude violations of basic labour standards in certain cases: see further Muchlinski (2007), ch. 12.

[13] On the conceptual separation of trade from investment issues see further Muchlinski (2012b), pp. 56–60. See too Hofmann et al. (2013), p. 9.

[14] Hofmann et al. (2013), p. 10. See further UNCTAD (2012) Investment Policy Framework for Sustainable Development. UN Pub. UNCTAD/DIAE/PCB/2012/5, http://unctad.org/en/PublicationsLibrary/diaepcb2012d5_en.pdf (last accessed 20 July 2015); UNCTAD (2015) Investment Policy Framework for Sustainable Development UNCTAD/WEB/DIAE/PCB/2015/3, http://investmentpolicyhub.unctad.org/Upload/Documents/INVESTMENT%20POLICY%20FRAMEWORK%202015%20WEB_VERSION.pdf (last accessed 13 August 2015); VanDuzer A, Simons P, Mayeda G (2012) Integrating Sustainable Development into International Investment Agreements: A Guide for Developing Countries, http://www.iisd.org/pdf/2012/6th_annual_forum_commonwealth_guide.pdf (last accessed 20 July 2015), also published as VanDuzer et al. (2013). See too OECD Informal Ministerial Meeting on Responsible Business Conduct Investment Treaty Law, Sustainable Development and Responsible Business Conduct: A Fact Finding Survey http://www.oecd.org/investment/2014RBCMinisterial-TreatyRBC.pdf (last accessed 20 July 2015).

2 Market-Oriented Liberalisation Through PTIAs

PTIAs have become increasingly important in recent years especially as attempts to push forward the coverage of the WTO Agreements under the Doha Round have stalled.[15] According to UNCTAD data, by the end of 2013, a total of 334 IIAs other than Bilateral Investment Treaties (BITs) were concluded. Fourteen of these were concluded in 2013.[16] These are divided by UNCTAD into three groups. The largest, consisting of seven agreements, are those with BIT equivalent provisions, including substantive standards of investment protection and investor-State dispute settlement (ISDS).[17] Two agreements have limited investment provisions, with national treatment regarding commercial presence or free movement of capital relating to direct investments,[18] while the third group consists of five agreements with investment co-operation provisions and/or a future negotiations mandate.[19] In addition, in early 2014, Chile, Colombia, Mexico and Peru signed a comprehensive protocol that includes an investment chapter.[20] Also negotiations for new "other IIAs" are continuing including the EU, with more than 20 agreements in progress, Canada with 12 FTA negotiations, the Republic of Korea with 10, Japan and Singapore with 9 each and Australia and the US with 8 each.[21]

A further important development identified by UNCTAD involves the negotiation of what it terms "Megaregional Agreements". These are defined as: "broad economic agreements among a group of countries that together have significant

[15] See Johnston and Trebilcock (2013), p. 243.

[16] UNCTAD (2014) World Investment Report 2014 http://unctad.org/en/PublicationsLibrary/wir2014_en.pdf (last accessed 17 August 2015), p. 114. See too Bungenberg (2013), Berger (2013), Tevini (2013) and Joubin-Bret (2013) that analyse the legal impact of PTIA provisions and on regional development. According to the UNCTAD (2015) World Investment Report 2015. http://unctad.org/en/PublicationsLibrary/wir2015_en.pdf (last accessed 17 August 2015), p. 106, by the end of 2014, 31 new IIAs were concluded, of which 18 are BITs and 13 are "other IIAs" bringing the overall total to 3271 (2926 BITs and 345 "other IIAs") by year-end with the annual number of BITs continuing to decline.

[17] UNCTAD (2014) World Investment Report 2014 http://unctad.org/en/PublicationsLibrary/wir2014_en.pdf (last accessed 17 August 2015), p. 115. These include the Canada-Honduras Free Trade Agreement (FTA), The China-Iceland FTA Columbia's FTAs with Costa Rica, Israel, The Republic of Korea and Panama, and New Zealand's FTA with Taiwan.

[18] China-Switzerland FTA and EFTA-Costa Rica-Panama FTA: UNCTAD (2014) World Investment Report 2014 http://unctad.org/en/PublicationsLibrary/wir2014_en.pdf (last accessed 17 August 2015), p. 115.

[19] Chile-Thailand FTA, EFTA-Bosnia and Herzegovina FTA, US trade and investment framework agreements signed with the Caribbean Community (CARICOM), Myanmar and Libya: UNCTAD (2014) World Investment Report 2014 http://unctad.org/en/PublicationsLibrary/wir2014_en.pdf (last accessed 17 August 2015). p. 115.

[20] UNCTAD (2014) World Investment Report 2014 http://unctad.org/en/PublicationsLibrary/wir2014_en.pdf (last accessed 17 August 2015).

[21] UNCTAD (2014) World Investment Report 2014 http://unctad.org/en/PublicationsLibrary/wir2014_en.pdf (last accessed 17 August 2015).

economic weight and in which investment is only one of several subjects addressed."[22]

They include the proposed TTIP and TTP Agreements.[23] In particular these agreements raise prominent public issues relating to the potential for economic benefits and their likely impact on the regulatory space of participating countries and sustainable development.[24] This can be seen from their proposed contents and coverage, which appear to extend the scope of investor protection and substantive areas of liberalisation in ways conducive to the more unimpeded operation of MNEs in the global economy.

Of especial significance in this regard are a number of questions that pertain to the scope of the investment protection offered. First, the trend in existing PTIAs is towards the extension of investor protection to the pre-establishment stage of the investment, allowing for a restriction of State discretion in the regulation of entry and establishment for foreign investors. For example in the consolidated text of the Canada-EU Trade Agreement (CETA) it is made clear that the Contracting Parties shall not apply market access restrictions or performance requirements, other than those that are exempted, and that non-discrimination protection shall apply to the pre-entry stage.[25] The exemptions to free market access are listed in Article X.4 (1) as follows:

> Measures concerning zoning and planning regulations affecting the development or use of land, or other analogous measures.
>
> Measures requiring the separation of the ownership of infrastructure from the ownership of the goods or services provided through that infrastructure to ensure fair competition, for example in the fields of energy, transportation and telecommunications.
>
> Measures restricting the concentration of ownership to ensure fair competition.
>
> Measures seeking to ensure the conservation and protection of natural resources and the environment, including limitations on the availability, number and scope of concessions granted, and the imposition of moratoria or bans.
>
> Measures limiting the number of authorizations granted because of technical or physical constraints, for example telecommunications spectrum and frequencies.

---

[22] UNCTAD (2014) World Investment Report 2014 http://unctad.org/en/PublicationsLibrary/wir2014_en.pdf (last accessed 17 August 2015), pp. 118–124 on which this account draws.

[23] UNCTAD (2014) World Investment Report 2014 http://unctad.org/en/PublicationsLibrary/wir2014_en.pdf (last accessed 17 August 2015), pp. 118–119. UNCTAD asserts that some 88 countries are currently involved in negotiations for mega-regional agreements. See ibid Table III.5 for a selected list of the most important negotiations. The largest is the Regional Comprehensive Economic Partnership (RCEP) involving the ASEAN countries, Australia, China, Japan, India, the Republic of Korea and New Zealand, covering for close to half the global population. The TTIP is the biggest in economic terms covering 45 % of global GDP and in terms of global inward investment the TTP is the biggest.

[24] UNCTAD (2014) World Investment Report 2014 http://unctad.org/en/PublicationsLibrary/wir2014_en.pdf (last accessed 17 August 2015), p. 118. See too UNCTAD (2015) World Investment Report 2015. http://unctad.org/en/PublicationsLibrary/wir2015_en.pdf (last accessed 17 August 2015), pp. 106–108.

[25] CETA Consolidated text as of 26 September 2014, Articles X.4–X.7.

> Measures requiring that a certain percentage of the shareholders, owners, partners, or directors of an enterprise be qualified or practice a certain profession such as lawyers or accountants.

Thus while the general approach is to restrict the State's right to regulate market access certain core regulatory powers are preserved, including land planning, environmental protection and fair competition. Nonetheless this represents a major shift from first generation European BITs, which covered only post-entry treatment and left entry and establishment issues, including market access and performance requirements, to exclusive domestic legal control.[26] These new agreements in effect limit the power of the State to regulate at the point of entry where State power in relation to foreign investors is at its strongest.

Secondly, PTIAs include elements outside the investment chapter, which have significant impacts on the State's right to regulate. In particular, the inclusion of intellectual property protection and services liberalisation commitments significantly increase the capacity of such agreements to protect corporate interests and rights in these areas.

In relation to intellectual property, PTIAs tend to echo the WTO TRIPs Agreement in offering protection and, indeed in some cases, greater protection than under TRIPs through, for example, increased periods of protection beyond what is required by TRIPs.[27] This has led to concerns about the scope of protection and whether this will undermine legitimate interests in the conservation of natural and cultural resources and the appropriation of such resources by private owners through intellectual property rights affecting developing countries which rely on such resources for their welfare.[28] In addition, the protection of pharmaceutical patents led to a major debate in the early 2000's about the power of private pharmaceutical firms to control access to essential drugs through their assertion of such rights, leading to the adoption of the Doha Declaration on the TRIPS Agreement and Public Health.[29] This recognises the Members' rights to use the

---

[26] As regards performance requirements this follows the NAFTA approach and is also a novel development in European practice.

[27] UNCTAD (2014) World Investment Report 2014 http://unctad.org/en/PublicationsLibrary/wir2014_en.pdf (last accessed 17 August 2015), p. 120. See, for an example of TRIPs related protection, CETA Chap. 22 Article 2, which states that the intellectual property rules in CETA complement the rights and obligations of the Contracting Parties in the TRIPs Agreement. On "TRIPs plus" protection see further Xiong (2012).

[28] See Roffe (2010), p. 307.

[29] WT/MIN(01)/DEC/2 20 November 2001 http://www.wto.org/english/thewto_e/minist_e/min01_e/mindecl_trips_e.pdf (last accessed 20 July 2015) as amended by Implementation of paragraph 6 of the Doha Declaration on the TRIPS Agreement and public health Decision of the General Council of 30 August 2003 GENERAL COUNCIL WT/L/540 and Corr.1 1 September 2003 http://www.wto.org/english/tratop_e/trips_e/implem_para6_e.htm (last accessed 20 July 2015) and Amendment of the TRIPS Agreement GENERAL COUNCIL WT/L/641 8 December 2005 Decision of 6 December 2005 at http://www.wto.org/english/tratop_e/trips_e/wtl641_e.htm (last accessed 20 July 2015) amending Art.31(f) of the TRIPs Agreement by way of Article 31[bis] which excludes the operation of Art.31(f) for exporting Members who supply pharmaceuticals to eligible non-producing Members.

provisions of the TRIPS Agreement to further public health and that the Agreement should be interpreted in a manner that is permissive of such policies.[30]

As regards services, a major regulatory effect of PTIAs has been to provide stronger protection for services-based investment by following the WTO GATS Agreement in allowing for direct investments in services provision, through "commercial presence" to be protected by the non-discrimination provisions of the services chapter.[31] This has led to concerns that services liberalisation will be used as a means of privatising health and education services. In relation to health services, the debates surrounding the TTIP have identified two problem areas: "that TTIP will require publicly run health services to be opened up to competition from private sector healthcare providers; and that a 'ratchet clause' and negative listing in TTIP would preclude the possibility of privatised public services being returned to state operation".[32]

The main concern about health services, put by trade unions and NGOs in particular, is that health is not suitable for traditional market competition and as such should be fully or partially excluded from the trade in services provisions within TTIP.[33] Similar concerns have been expressed about education services, especially in the light of increased private sector involvement in educational provision both at school and college level.[34]

EU negotiators have made a clear commitment that there will be an exemption for public services from TTIP.[35] However, the CETA contains a rather general exclusion in Chap. 11 Article X.01(2) which states, "This Chapter does not apply to

---

[30] The Doha Declaration is specifically mentioned in CETA in Chap. 22 Article 3.

[31] UNCTAD (2014) World Investment Report 2014 http://unctad.org/en/PublicationsLibrary/wir2014_en.pdf (last accessed 17 August 2015), p. 120.

[32] Khan U, Pallot R, Taylor D, Kanavos P (2015) The Transatlantic Trade and Investment Partnership: International Trade Law, Health Systems and Public Health. London School of Economics and Political Science, http://www.epha.org/IMG/pdf/LSE_study-TTIP_International_Trade_Law_Health_Systems_and_Public_Health_website.pdf (last accessed 20 July 2015), p. 9 and see pp. 41–42.

[33] See for example Hilary J (2015) What is TTIP? War on Want, http://www.waronwant.org/campaigns/trade-justice/more/inform/18078-what-is-ttip (last accessed 20 July 2015).

[34] See for example the UK Universities and College Union (2014) The Transatlantic Trade and Investment Partnership: What it is and why we Should be Worried http://www.ucu.org.uk/media/pdf/6/n/ucu_translantictradebriefing_jan14.pdf (last accessed 21 July 2015); European Trade Union Committee for Education (2015) Will Education Services be Covered by the TTIP? http://www.csee-etuce.org/en/actions/campaigns/exclude-education-from-ttip/262-what-is-the-ttip#Will education services be covered by the TTIP? (last accessed 21 July 2015).

[35] Khan U, Pallot R, Taylor D, Kanavos P (2015) The Transatlantic Trade and Investment Partnership: International Trade Law, Health Systems and Public Health. London School of Economics and Political Science, http://www.epha.org/IMG/pdf/LSE_study-TTIP_International_Trade_Law_Health_Systems_and_Public_Health_website.pdf (last accessed 20 July 2015), p. 9. See too EU (2015) About TTIP—Basics, Benefits, Concerns http://ec.europa.eu/trade/policy/in-focus/ttip/about-ttip/questions-and-answers/index_en.htm (last accessed 21 July 2015), EU (2015) Protecting Public Services in TTIP and Other EU Trade Agreements at http://trade.ec.europa.eu/doclib/press/index.cfm?id=1115&title=Protecting-public-services-in-TTIP-and-other-EU-trade-agreements (last accessed 21 July 2015).

measures affecting: (a) services supplied in the exercise of governmental authority…"[36] In addition, by Chap. 11 Article X.06 the Contracting Parties can opt out of liberalisation of any services sector by way of a negative list of excepted sectors.[37] Thus while it is true that Contracting Parties can opt out of liberalisation once they have committed to this there is no further opportunity to opt out and national treatment must apply to the private service provider.

A third area of contention concerns investor protection and the possible introduction of Investor State Dispute Settlement (ISDS). Again this has been a major issue in negotiations for the TTIP. The fear exists that inclusion of ISDS will undermine the capacity of domestic courts and tribunals to act as fora for the settlement of investor-State disputes, giving foreign investors a privilege not enjoyed by their domestic competitors, and also that this process leads to the privatisation of important disputes with a public interest dimension, preventing proper transparency and accountability.[38]

Indeed UNCTAD expresses concern over investor-state arbitration in its comprehensive *Investment Policy Framework for Sustainable Development* (IPFSD).[39] It says that ISDS can create unjustified liabilities and high procedural costs. Together, these put a significant burden on defending host countries and exacerbate concerns over the balance between investor protection and the preservation of national policy space for development, especially in the case of less developed host countries.[40] In addition, ISDS claims have been used by investor claimants in hitherto unanticipated ways to challenge measures adopted in the public interest (such as measures to promote social equity, foster environmental protection or protect public health) showing that, "the borderline between protection from political risk and undue interference with legitimate domestic policies is becoming increasingly blurred."[41] Accordingly, UNCTAD asserts that this problem needs a

[36] CETA.

[37] CETA.

[38] See further for example Osgoode Hall Law School Public Statement on the International Investment Regime 31 August 2010 http://www.osgoode.yorku.ca/public_statement (last accessed 21 July 2015).

[39] UNCTAD (2012) Investment Policy Framework for Sustainable Development. UN Pub. UNCTAD/DIAE/PCB/2012/5, http://unctad.org/en/PublicationsLibrary/diaepcb2012d5_en.pdf (last accessed 20 July 2015), UNCTAD (2015) Investment Policy Framework for Sustainable Development UNCTAD/WEB/DIAE/PCB/2015/3, http://investmentpolicyhub.unctad.org/Upload/Documents/INVESTMENT%20POLICY%20FRAMEWORK%202015%20WEB_VERSION.pdf (last accessed 13 August 2015) and UNCTAD (2015) World Investment Report 2015. http://unctad.org/en/PublicationsLibrary/wir2015_en.pdf (last accessed 17 August 2015), Ch.IV.

[40] UNCTAD (2012) Investment Policy Framework for Sustainable Development. UN Pub. UNCTAD/DIAE/PCB/2012/5, http://unctad.org/en/PublicationsLibrary/diaepcb2012d5_en.pdf (last accessed 20 July 2015), pp. 39–40.

[41] UNCTAD (2012) Investment Policy Framework for Sustainable Development. UN Pub. UNCTAD/DIAE/PCB/2012/5, http://unctad.org/en/PublicationsLibrary/diaepcb2012d5_en.pdf (last accessed 20 July 2015), p. 40.

solution involving treaty design that looks at options both in ISDS provisions and in the scope and application of substantive clauses.[42]

In a similar vein, the Commonwealth Secretariat has published an extensive study authored by three leading Canadian legal scholars entitled *Integrating Sustainable Development into International Investment Agreements: A Guide for Developing Countries* (the Guide).[43] As with the UNCTAD IPFSD, the Guide lays the problem with current IIAs at the feet of the outcomes of ISDS claims.[44] The proposed solution is again to rebalance new IIAs taking into account such concerns.[45]

Both organisations seek to place sustainable development at the heart of the IIA reform project. They do not reject ISDS outright. Rather ISDS is seen to have a role but one that needs to address the shortcomings identified above so that it fits in with the wider sustainable development agenda.[46] Equally, substantive provisions may need reformulation so as better to meet the goals of sustainable development. These issues are discussed further in Sect. 3 below.

The preceding issues all add up to a picture of increased accommodation for the interests of private undertakings in the global economy, resulting in a model of regulation that places business facilitation at its heart. IEL plays a key role in this process through the international economic agreement, which limits State discretion and power in the unilateral use of command and control methods of business regulation. This has the important effect of creating an international legal obligation to observe certain methods of regulation that transcends periodic governmental change, and so ensures the succession of these regulatory methods regardless of changes in domestic political conditions. This creates an apparently stable legal framework within which business can operate freely in the knowledge that certain types of regulatory practices and policies will not be pursued by States except on pain of a breach of international obligations, which, in the case of investor rights,

[42] UNCTAD (2012) Investment Policy Framework for Sustainable Development. UN Pub. UNCTAD/DIAE/PCB/2012/5, http://unctad.org/en/PublicationsLibrary/diaepcb2012d5_en.pdf (last accessed 20 July 2015), p. 40.

[43] VanDuzer A, Simons P, Mayeda G (2012) Integrating Sustainable Development into International Investment Agreements: A Guide for Developing Countries, http://www.iisd.org/pdf/2012/6th_annual_forum_commonwealth_guide.pdf (last accessed 20 July 2015).

[44] VanDuzer A, Simons P, Mayeda G (2012) Integrating Sustainable Development into International Investment Agreements: A Guide for Developing Countries, http://www.iisd.org/pdf/2012/6th_annual_forum_commonwealth_guide.pdf (last accessed 20 July 2015, p. 7.

[45] VanDuzer A, Simons P, Mayeda G (2012) Integrating Sustainable Development into International Investment Agreements: A Guide for Developing Countries, http://www.iisd.org/pdf/2012/6th_annual_forum_commonwealth_guide.pdf (last accessed 20 July 2015).

[46] UNCTAD (2012) Investment Policy Framework for Sustainable Development. UN Pub. UNCTAD/DIAE/PCB/2012/5, http://unctad.org/en/PublicationsLibrary/diaepcb2012d5_en.pdf (last accessed 20 July 2015), p. 43; VanDuzer A, Simons P, Mayeda G (2012) Integrating Sustainable Development into International Investment Agreements: A Guide for Developing Countries, http://www.iisd.org/pdf/2012/6th_annual_forum_commonwealth_guide.pdf (last accessed 20 July 2015), Section 4.5 'Dispute Settlement'.

can result in costly arbitral claims. That this may be an apparent, rather than a real, stability comes from the reaction to this arrangement from within local political communities, which offer a developing critique of market-liberalisation and which challenge the facilitative model of business regulation contained in PTIAs.

3 The Contemporary Critique of Market-Liberalisation and MNE Regulation[47]

The debate on the proper relationship between state and corporate power is not new. It involves the question of how to treat collective action in an organised society.[48] The MNE as a transnational institution creates, in particular, the problem of extraterritoriality, whereby, in order to regulate effectively, the national regulator may need to apply their national laws and legal claims to entities and events arising outside the regulator's home jurisdiction, thereby infringing the sovereignty of the target jurisdiction. Historically, that has led to conflicts of jurisdiction in a wide range of areas including competition, tax, securities and financial services.[49] Conflicts are liable to flare at any time where the regulating jurisdiction perceives that activity in a target jurisdiction is infringing its regulatory policy goals and there is no direct territorial nexus between the activities and the regulating jurisdiction.[50]

Such concerns generated the "sovereignty at bay" debate in the 1970s, named after the title of Raymond Vernon's famous book of 1971.[51] Some versions of this approach foresaw the end of the nation-state. In the words of Charles Kindleberger, writing in 1969, "the nation-state is just about through as an economic unit."[52] The

[47] This section draws upon material in Muchlinski (2013b), pp. 292–296. My thanks to Natasha Fleming of OUP for permission to use this material.

[48] This question is as pertinent in an acephalous society as it is in the modern centralised sovereign state. On which see further Smith (1974).

[49] On which see further Muchlinski (2007) ch. 4 and Zerk J (2010) Extraterritorial Jurisdiction: Lessons for the Business and Human Rights Sphere from Six Regulatory Areas. A Report for the Harvard Corporate Social Responsibility Initiative to Help Inform the Mandate of the UNSG's Special Representative on Business and Human Rights, Working Paper No. 59, http://www.hks.harvard.edu/m-rcbg/CSRI/publications/workingpaper_59_zerk.pdf (last accessed 21 July 2015).

[50] A distinction is made between pure extraterritoriality, where the targeted actor has no direct or indirect presence or assets in the regulating jurisdiction, and the territorial exercise of jurisdiction with overseas impacts, where the targeted actor is present in the regulating jurisdiction, or has assets there, and the actor and/or the assets are involved in foreign conduct unlawful under the regulating state's law: see further Zerk J (2010) Extraterritorial Jurisdiction: Lessons for the Business and Human Rights Sphere from Six Regulatory Areas. A Report for the Harvard Corporate Social Responsibility Initiative to Help Inform the Mandate of the UNSG's Special Representative on Business and Human Rights, Working Paper No. 59, http://www.hks.harvard.edu/m-rcbg/CSRI/publications/workingpaper_59_zerk.pdf (last accessed 21 July 2015).

[51] Vernon (1971). For a useful analysis see Korbin (2010), p. 183.

[52] Kindleberger (1969), p. 207; Ball (1968).

constitutional implications of the rise of MNEs gave rise to the view that they had to be controlled if state sovereignty was not to be lost to an unaccountable coalition of the executive branch of government and the management of MNEs.[53]

Vernon's own work was less alarmist. His main concern was to deal with the issue of extraterritorial regulation. Accordingly, he recommended greater international co-operation over taxation issues and in resolving the problem of overlapping regulatory jurisdictions between the States in which the MNE operated through regulatory co-operation on the basis of bilateral treaties that further the principle of comity between the signatories.[54] In a sense the rise of PTIAs exemplifies this approach, in that basic issues of economic and social organisation entail regulatory responses that can no longer remain at the level of the nation-state and necessitate at least a minimal agreement between States as to policy. Whether PTIAs, in their current form, achieve what is actually required at the policy level remains the key question and not the preservation of exclusive single State control, which appears increasingly illusory.

Vernon and others also considered the possible establishment of some supranational body to which MNEs could be accountable.[55] The most tangible result in policy terms was the establishment in the UN of the Commission on Transnational Corporations (TNCs are the UN terminological equivalent of MNEs[56]) and the Centre on Transnational Corporations (UNCTC).[57] These bodies were tasked with negotiation of a new binding Code of Conduct for TNCs and to offer legal and policy advice to developing countries in their dealings with MNEs. The proposed Code of Conduct floundered by the early 1990s when neo-liberal ideas gained ground seeing it as an unwarranted interference with corporate freedom and the need for investment in host countries. The UN TNC bodies were downgraded and restructured as a research branch of the United Nations Conference on Trade and Development (UNCTAD) without any negotiating mandate.[58]

A further solution to the problem of limited territorial sovereignty is to create a new level of regulatory space at the supranational level. In effect this is one of the

[53] See for example Miller (1973). By contrast, Seymour Rubin vocally denied that MNEs challenged the nation-state. Rather they appeared to be rather well controlled by it. However Rubin also accepted the need for at least an international forum in which the operations of MNEs could be discussed. See Rubin (1974).

[54] See for example European Communities-United States Agreement on the Application of Their Competition Laws: 30 ILM 1487 (1991) as supplemented by the 1998 European Communities-United States Agreement on the Application of Positive Comity Principles in the Enforcement of Their Competition Laws Agreement of 4 June 1998, 37 ILM 1070 (1998).

[55] Korbin (2010), p. 271; Rubin (1974) and see too Goldberg and Kindleberger (1970).

[56] On which see Muchlinski (2007), p. 6.

[57] See further UN Secretary General's Group of Eminent Persons Report on The Role of MNEs on Development and International Relations 1974 UN Doc. E/5500/Add 1 (Part I) 24 May 1974: 13 ILM 800 (1974).

[58] See Muchlinski (2000a), p. 97. See further Sagafi-Nejad (2008), chps 5 and 6.

aims of the EU—its larger territorial reach allows for a reduction of the mismatch.[59] This has had significant impacts on corporate regulation particularly in the fields of competition law and the development of harmonised principles of corporate law including the establishment of supranational corporate entities such as the European Economic Interest Grouping (EEIG) and the *Societas Europea* (SE).[60] On the other hand such thinking is coming under increased scrutiny from Eurosceptic perspectives, which fear that transfers of sovereignty of this kind reduce the ability of the nation-state to regulate effectively or to act in the interests of its corporate actors.[61]

Since the 1990s a number of developments have highlighted a renewal of concern over private corporate power, especially the power of MNEs as the prime movers of globalisation. For example, in 1998, Amnesty International went beyond its traditional concern over the civil and political rights of individuals and published its *Human Rights Guidelines for Companies*.[62] This was one aspect of a wider movement among NGOs to add to their agendas the effects of MNEs on human rights, labour rights and sustainable development,[63] spurred on, in part, by their opposition to negotiations on a Multilateral Agreement on Investment (MAI). The MAI failed when France pulled out on the ground that the provisions on the protection of foreign investors, and their right to challenge national policy decisions before international arbitral tribunals, represented too great an inroad into national sovereignty over economic policy.[64]

By the late 1990s, a second wave of academic and popular literature emerged, critical of the power of MNEs, which is still developing. Like "sovereignty at bay" the "new corporate accountability" literature also expresses alarm at the impact of the global business practices of MNEs on the sovereignty of states. It goes further by considering the impact of transnational corporate power on the popular democracy that is rooted within the boundaries of Western states. Alarming titles have appeared such as "When Corporations Rule the World" "The Silent Takeover: Global Capitalism and the Death of Democracy" and "Post-Democracy".[65]

---

[59] See Muchlinski (2007), p. 118.

[60] See generally Muchlinski (2007), ch 10 and pp. 72–75.

[61] As argued by David Cameron when he vetoed the Euro zone pact in December 2011 on the grounds that he was defending City of London financial interests against excessive regulation: Traynor I, Watt N, Gow D, Wintour P, David Cameron Blocks EU Treaty with Veto, Casting Britain a Drift in Europe. The Guardian, 9 December 2011, http://www.guardian.co.uk/world/2011/dec/09/david-cameron-blocks-eu-treaty (last accessed 21 July 2015).

[62] Amnesty International UK Business Group (1998).

[63] On which see further Yaziji and Doh (2009).

[64] On the MAI see further MAI Negotiating Text (as of 24 April 1998), http://unctad.org/sections/dite/iia/docs/Compendium/en/96%20volume%204.pdf (last accessed 22 July 2015). For background see: OECD (1996); Muchlinski (2000b); Fatouros (1995); Engering (1996); Picciotto and Mayne (1999); Picciotto (1998); Canner (1998); UNCTAD Lessons from the MAI Series on issues in international investment agreements (New York and Geneva, United Nations, 1999), http://unctad.org/en/Docs/psiteiitm22.en.pdf (accessed 20 July 2015); Henderson (1999); Clarke and Barlow (1997).

[65] See Korten (2001); Hertz (2002); Crouch (2004).

This literature foretells the possible end of popular democracy in the West as a result of the hollowing out of popular power by the ever closer association of corporations and politicians, of all major persuasions, who accept that the furtherance of corporate interests is the main objective of contemporary governance, to the exclusion of alternative aims, and to the benefit of an increasingly unaccountable elite of the super-rich.[66] A lot of weight is placed on the ability of major firms to lobby the political process, especially in the US, thereby threatening the balance of democratic pluralism.[67] This is seen as being reinforced by the power of MNEs to set agendas of consumption through mass marketing and branding creating the illusion that a good life can be achieved through individualistic consumerism.[68]

The critique of PTIAs is also rooted in such concepts. As noted above, the major fear is that these agreements will further the process of hollowing out State power to the detriment of local accountability and participation in meaningful political processes. Equally the unbridled liberalisation of trade and investment, accompanied by a reduction of State regulatory rights could lead to the erosion of basic human rights protection. According to Alfred de Zayas, the UN Special Rapporteur on the promotion of a democratic and equitable international order, there should be a moratorium on the negotiations over the TTIP on the grounds that, "we don't want a dystopian future in which corporations and governments call the shots. We don't want an international order akin to post-democracy or post-law."[69] In particular, and despite the proposed safeguards for the right to regulate in the proposed agreement, he feels that the adoption of ISDS would constitute a threat to basic human rights.[70]

It is the view of the present author that such critiques, while containing some important warnings, are exaggerated and unduly pessimistic. This is said in the belief—that some will no doubt dismiss as naïve—that the global political system is not necessarily deaf to popular concerns and basic civilised values, such as those embodied in human rights, environmental and other social standards championed in international instruments and domestic laws alike. Equally, there is no going back to the mass regulatory State exemplified by the State capitalism of the old Soviet Bloc or the corporatism of the early post-World War II West (notwithstanding the continued existence of centralised State capitalist economies such as China, a political and economic work in progress whose outcome is "too early to say"). Furthermore, it is increasingly clear that libertarian types of deregulation and

---

[66] For an expression of this view see Monbiot G, Our Economic Ruin Means Freedom for the Super-rich. The Guardian, 31 July 2012, p. 26.

[67] See Korten (2001), ch. 10; Crouch (2011), pp. 124–134; Palast (2003).

[68] See further Korten (2001), ch. 11 'Marketing the World' and see further Klein (2000).

[69] Quoted in Inman P, Halt to Trade Talks Urged Amid Fears Over Secret Courts. The Guardian, 5 May 2015, p. 22.

[70] Inman P, Halt to Trade Talks Urged Amid Fears Over Secret Courts. The Guardian, 5 May 2015, p. 22.

laissez-faire are not an option as a viable method of fostering capitalism. This depends too much on the view that actors will self-deny when confronted with opportunities for improper self-enrichment at massive social and economic cost. This much must be plain after the global banking crisis of 2007–2009. Thus, the challenge for the contemporary regulation of MNEs lies in acknowledging these elements and seeking ways of creating viable regulatory agendas. In this process the content of PTIAs may indeed offer much scope for creative adaptation which preserves the benefits of market capitalism while creating clear boundaries, based on consensus building, to market behaviour that leads to unacceptable social, environmental or economic outcomes. This in itself is a radical, difficult, agenda. Its parameters will form the final part of this paper.

4 Building a New Regulatory Agenda and the Rebalancing of International Economic Law

This section is divided into two parts: the first will elaborate further on the theoretical and institutional underpinnings underlying the creation of a more inclusive, socially and environmentally relevant IEL, while the second will apply this reasoning to the development of PTIAs that now characterise the normative content of IEL as regards State regulatory space in an increasingly inter-connected global economy and society.

4.1 Theoretical and Institutional Underpinnings

The development of a recalibrated regime of MNE regulation requires some discussion of theory and institutional context. Guidance can be found from liberal theories of development, as espoused by Amartya Sen, and social democratic theories of modified sovereignty, as posited by Neil McCormick. This discussion must be rooted in an integrated model of international political economy in which trade and investment are properly treated as aspects of the same process—the transnational supply of goods and services—and not as self-contained disciplines. This latter issue is, in a sense, already answered by the coverage of PTIAs, which do not rigidly differentiate between trade and investment, and so need not be discussed any further here (though numerous technical legal issues arise out of this historical divide.)[71]

Turning first to the contribution of Sen, a distinction can be made between two attitudes to development:

[71] For more detailed discussion of this issue see further de Brabandere (2013); Binder (2013); Jacob (2013); Baetens (2013); Braun (2013); Albites-Bedoya (2013).

> One view sees development as a 'fierce' process, with much 'blood sweat and tears' – a world in which wisdom demands toughness. In particular, it demands calculated neglect of various concerns that are seen as 'soft-headed' [including] social safety nets that protect the very poor, providing social services for the population at large, departing from rugged institutional guidelines in response to identified hardship and favouring – 'much too early' – political and civil rights and the 'luxury' of democracy...This hard-knocks attitude contrasts with an alternative outlook that sees development as essentially a 'friendly' process. Depending on the particular version of this attitude, the congeniality of the process is seen as exemplified by such things as mutually beneficial exchanges (of which Adam Smith spoke eloquently), or by the working of social safety nets, or of political liberties, or of social development – or some combination or other of these supportive activities.[72]

Sen is persuaded by the latter approach, from which he builds his thesis that development can only occur as a process of expanding 'the real freedoms that people enjoy'.[73] Such freedoms include the provision of elementary capabilities for life but also run to political freedoms, access to economic facilities, social opportunities such as access to education or health care, transparency guarantees allowing for freedom to deal with one another in conditions of disclosure and lucidity, and protective security based on essential welfare support against abject misery.[74]

This approach is echoed in the new UN Sustainable Development Goals (SDGs), which are used by UNCTAD to frame its IPFSD. The SGDs are outlined in Chapter IV of the UNCTAD *World Investment Report 2014*.[75] They are seen as the next step from the Millennium Development Goals offering a concerted effort to shift the global economy, both developed and developing, onto a more sustainable trajectory of long-term growth and development.[76] The main focus areas are the economic infrastructure for power, transport, telecoms, water and sanitation in developing countries, food security, the social infrastructure of health and education, environmental sustainability involving climate change adaptation and mitigation, the conservation and safeguarding of ecosystems and sustainable agriculture.[77] In addition, investment to assist marginalized groups, such as isolated communities or the excluded poor, and gender and equality issues are considered.[78]

The role of the private sector is seen as key to investment in these areas, given the significance of such investment in global capital flows, and its ability to reduce

---

[72] Sen (1999), p. 35.

[73] Sen (1999), p. 36.

[74] Sen (1999), pp. 38–40.

[75] UNCTAD (2014) World Investment Report 2014 http://unctad.org/en/PublicationsLibrary/wir2014_en.pdf (last accessed 17 August 2015), Ch. IV 'Investing in SDGs: An Action Plan for Promoting Private Sector Contributions'. The following paragraphs are taken from Muchlinski (2016).

[76] UNCTAD (2014) World Investment Report 2014 http://unctad.org/en/PublicationsLibrary/wir2014_en.pdf (last accessed 17 August 2015), p. 136.

[77] UNCTAD (2014) World Investment Report 2014 http://unctad.org/en/PublicationsLibrary/wir2014_en.pdf (last accessed 17 August 2015), pp. 140–143.

[78] UNCTAD (2014) World Investment Report 2014 http://unctad.org/en/PublicationsLibrary/wir2014_en.pdf (last accessed 17 August 2015), pp. 144–145.

pressure on public funding.[79] On the other hand the essential role of the public sector is stressed. This appears in two key ways. First, the use of Public Private Partnerships (PPPs) may need to be widened, but with caution over the well-known financial risks run by the public partner which need to be adequately addressed in the applicable contractual arrangements.[80] Secondly, effective regulation will be required to avoid negative private sector impacts. This is particularly relevant in relation to maintenance of standards and capabilities, effective competition and consumer protection, including affordability to the poorest, especially in basic needs sectors such as water and sanitation.[81] This requires guiding principles for investment in SDGs to offer clear direction and to ensure that the needs of all stakeholders are met.[82]

These development-oriented ideas can be placed in a wider social and political context, relevant to the actual needs of contemporary political conditions by reference to McCormick's theory of modified sovereignty.[83] McCormick's theory of sovereignty offers an 'optimistic' view (as opposed to a 'pessimistic' view that sees the contest between state and corporate power as a zero sum game with one winner) which allows for an accommodation between the possible dilution of traditional state sovereignty, in the face of the twin challenges of internal devolution and economic globalisation, through a pluralistic concept of sovereignty that can be shared at a number of levels from the local, the regional, the national to the supranational. The key question is how to allocate the various exercises of sovereignty to their most appropriate level. This is achieved through the idea of subsidiarity, a concept that allows for considerable market freedom for corporate actors but which is delimited by communal concerns based on a social democratic ideal of equality.[84]

---

[79] UNCTAD (2014) World Investment Report 2014 http://unctad.org/en/PublicationsLibrary/wir2014_en.pdf (last accessed 17 August 2015), p. 146.

[80] UNCTAD (2014) World Investment Report 2014 http://unctad.org/en/PublicationsLibrary/wir2014_en.pdf (last accessed 17 August 2015), pp. 167–168.

[81] UNCTAD (2014) World Investment Report 2014 http://unctad.org/en/PublicationsLibrary/wir2014_en.pdf (last accessed 17 August 2015), p. 150. These sectors have attracted attention over the relationship between investor rights and responsibilities and the right to regulate in investment awards. Notably in *Biwater Gauff (Tanzania) Ltd. v. United Republic of Tanzania* (Procedural Order No. 5), ICSID Case No. ARB/05/22, 2 February 2007, para. 52, the tribunal accepted, at the procedural stage, that human rights considerations might be raised by the dispute, in that it concerned the operation of a privatised water company and that this involved significant public interests in relation to the right to water and to health. At the award stage, in *Biwater Gauff (Tanzania) Ltd. v. United Republic of Tanzania* (Award), ICSID Case No. ARB/05/22, 24 July 2008, para. 358, the tribunal noted that the public interest issues surrounding the right to water in this case were admissible though the tribunal did not explore the United Republic of Tanzania's human rights law obligations in further detail holding, rather, that the claimants had not made out their case on the facts.

[82] UNCTAD (2014) World Investment Report 2014 http://unctad.org/en/PublicationsLibrary/wir2014_en.pdf (last accessed 17 August 2015), pp. 151–152.

[83] The following analysis was first posited in Muchlinski (2013b). Here it is linked expressly to the liberal approach to sustainable development.

[84] See McCormick (1999), pp. 150–153.

Here CSGs, including various social and environmental NGOs, can play an important role, first, by offering an alternative narrative concerning the relationship between corporate freedom and the right to regulate and, secondly, by operating as an institutional alternative to the market-State, which seeks to further corporate freedom.[85] CSGs/NGOs may be expected to advocate a model of corporate regulation that takes into account non-economic values of the kind argued for in Sen's conception of development, and which are given institutional force through the SDGs.

This approach does not see the corporation as an insuperable obstacle to progress, which must be reigned in completely, through some unlikely revival of the mid-twentieth century Corporatist State. Rather it rests on the process of 'experimental governance'.[86] This approach highlights the complex web of institutions and actors that seek to manage the global economic system in the absence of global government. It involves the internal management systems of MNEs and inter-firm supply chains, the various normative standards developed by inter-governmental organisations, states and sub-state entities with legislative and regulatory powers, and the activities of CSGs/NGOs. This approach is also termed 'civil regulation'.[87] This has come about as a result of a perceived 'regulatory gap' between traditional legal regulation by the territorial state and the increasingly transnational character of business activities and the resulting 'polycentric governance' of the globalising world in which traditional State and inter-governmental governance structures are operating in tandem with civil regulation by CSGs and self-regulation by corporate actors.[88]

Applied to the development of IEL, the abovementioned theoretical and institutional developments would require new international norms that counterbalance corporate freedoms with corporate and State responsibilities to operate in line with sustainable development norms. In turn McCormick's views on subsidiarity can guide policy-makers as to the best level of regulation that would serve to achieve these goals most effectively, and on the appropriate role of local stakeholders in the policy-making and dispute resolution process. Thus IEL needs to remain aware of the close interactions between local, regional, inter-regional, plurilateral and multilateral sites of regulation that, together, from a regulatory net within which globalised economic operations occur. In this environment the role of PTIAs as possible vehicles for the enactment of such policies becomes evident, as they provide a ready-made vehicle for IEL reform.

---

[85] See further Crouch (2004, 2011). On the relationship between CSGs/NGOs and corporations see further Yaziji and Doh (2009).

[86] See further Zeitlin (2011); Kristensen and Zeitlin (2005) esp.chs.11 and 12.

[87] See further Bendell and Murphy (2002), p. 24; Zadek (2007), ch. 5.

[88] See Ruggie J (2015) Life in the Global Public Domain: Response to Commentaries on the UN Guiding Principles and the Proposed Treaty on Business and Human Rights. SRRN http://ssrn.com/abstract=2554726 or http://dx.doi.org/10.2139/ssrn.2554726 (last accessed 22 July 2015).

4.2 Reconciling Corporate Freedom and the Right to Regulate in PTIAs

The starting point should be a clearer idea of which issues need international rules to control State powers, and which do not. That is at the heart of subsidiarity. Perhaps the greatest problem with current generation IIAs is that they assume the inadequacy of host country regulatory and dispute settlement bodies and procedures. This may have been an understandable reaction by market-oriented States to the rise of newly independent post-colonial developing countries, many of which were governed by charismatic nationalist leaders who could play off the West and the East during the Cold War, to the possible detriment of Western investors. However, in 2015, can such a world-view prevail, and, moreover, find a place in agreements such as the TTIP and TTP, which are to be concluded by countries with largely reliable legal and political systems that broadly support private commercial rights?

To assume that relatively advanced societies cannot be trusted to administer foreign trade and investment without some form of delocalised regulatory net seems to show a lack of respect for local political and social communities, which is at odds with true liberal sentiment. The result is, as noted above, that while current PTIAs make some concessions towards local regulatory rights, and temper some of the more glaring procedural shortcomings of ISDS, more could still be done. In particular, PTIAs could do more to accept subsidiarity as a core goal that is consistent with the goals of market liberalisation and the preservation of legitimate corporate freedoms. This assertion can be discussed further under three headings: the State right to regulate, increasing accountability and transparency, and reform of dispute settlement procedures.

4.2.1 The State Right to Regulate

The first principle of all international economic agreements should be, in accordance with international law, that the State is sovereign and has the right to regulate within its territory. Any modification to this is an exception to the general principle and has to be so treated.[89] This is the embodiment of the principle of subsidiarity as well. Thus in the EU legal order, according to Article 5(3) of the Treaty on European Union

> Under the principle of subsidiarity, in areas which do not fall within its exclusive competence, the Union shall act only if and in so far as the objectives of the proposed action cannot be sufficiently achieved by the Member States, either at central level or at regional and local level, but can rather, by reason of the scale or effects of the proposed action, be better achieved at Union level.[90]

---

[89] See Muchlinski (2007), pp. 177–178 and Muchlinski (2011a), pp. 676–677.

[90] Article 5(3) Treaty on European Union OJ [2010].

This principle would be useful in guiding PTIA negotiators in constructing provisions dealing with the limits of State powers. In each case where the commercial right of a corporate actor is in issue, the question should be when must the order of the PTIA take over from the State as the principal regulator? The usual answer in IIAs has been whenever there is a breach of the protective investor rights contained in the agreement.

However, as pointed out by UNCTAD, the formulation of these protections leaves much to the discretion of the interpreter when deciding when this line has been crossed. Accordingly, UNCTAD recommends new formulations of rights, which draw clearer lines as to when the intervention of the treaty is proper. Here the IPFSD provides a set of principles specifically focused on designing sound SDG friendly investment policies. This requires co-ordination between national and international investment policies and commitments in IIAs. In particular, such treaties must not unduly undermine the regulatory space required for sustainable development policies.[91] Indeed, they must be designed to be proactive in mobilising and channelling investment into SDGs.[92]

Thus, for example, the fair and equitable treatment standard can be limited to gross violations of the international minimum standard of treatment, or be based on an exhaustive list of unacceptable types of maladministration such as not to deny justice in judicial or administrative proceedings, treat investors in an arbitrary manner, flagrantly violate due process, engage in manifestly abusive treatment involving continuous, unjustified coercion or harassment and infringing investors legitimate expectations based on investment-inducing representations or measures.[93] Another example is to provide a clear definition of regulatory takings so as to preclude any interpretation that colours a legitimate exercise of regulatory power as such.[94]

In addition to reformulating investor rights in a more SDG friendly way, future agreements could also reserve rights to regulate by excluding certain sectors or

[91] UNCTAD (2014) World Investment Report 2014 http://unctad.org/en/PublicationsLibrary/wir2014_en.pdf (last accessed 17 August 2015), p. 152; UNCTAD (2015) World Investment Report 2015. http://unctad.org/en/PublicationsLibrary/wir2015_en.pdf (last accessed 17 August 2015), p. 135.

[92] UNCTAD (2014) World Investment Report 2014 http://unctad.org/en/PublicationsLibrary/wir2014_en.pdf (last accessed 17 August 2015), p. 181.

[93] UNCTAD (2012) Investment Policy Framework for Sustainable Development. UN Pub. UNCTAD/DIAE/PCB/2012/5, http://unctad.org/en/PublicationsLibrary/diaepcb2012d5_en.pdf (last accessed 20 July 2015), p. 51; UNCTAD (2015) World Investment Report 2015. http://unctad.org/en/PublicationsLibrary/wir2015_en.pdf (last accessed 17 August 2015), p. 137 and see further UNCTAD (2012) Fair and Equitable Treatment: A Sequel. http://unctad.org/en/Docs/unctaddiaeia2011d5_en.pdf (last accessed 20 July 2015).

[94] See UNCTAD (2012) Expropriation: A Sequel, http://unctad.org/en/Docs/unctaddiaeia2011d7_en.pdf (last accessed 20 July 2015), p. 12; and the US Model Bilateral Investment Treaty 2012 Annex B paragraph 4 http://www.ustr.gov/sites/defalt/files/BIT%20text%20for%20ACIEP%20Meeting.pdf (last accessed 22 July 2015).

activities from treaty coverage altogether. For example, under the MFN clause, some more recent treaties have restricted its operation to exclude procedural matters.[95] This option is offered in the UNCTAD and Commonwealth Secretariat model clauses.[96] In addition, other exclusions can be included to heighten the development friendliness of the MFN clause by way of carve-outs for selected policies and measures, such as subsidies, specific sectors or industries and issues of a social character such as minorities, rural populations and marginalized or indigenous peoples.[97] Similarly, the national treatment clause can allow for derogations by way of reservations for specific sectors or specific measures from national treatment.[98] In addition, PTIAs could use a GATS style 'opt-in' or 'positive list' approach to sectoral liberalisation, whereby contracting State parties do not commit to national treatment in general, and then provide a "negative list" of excluded sectors, but, rather, only list those sectors that they are ready to open up and any restrictions on national treatment that apply to the sector in question.[99] Furthermore, the scope and definition clause can include a list of excluded types of investments which ensure that purely contractual claims and other controversial types of claims (for example claims based on portfolio investments, sovereign debt instruments or intellectual property rights not covered by domestic laws) are excluded.[100]

---

[95] UNCTAD Most-Favoured-Nation Treatment: A Sequel, http://unctad.org/en/Docs/diaeia20101_en.pdf (last accessed 20 July 2015), pp. 84–87.

[96] UNCTAD (2012) Investment Policy Framework for Sustainable Development. UN Pub. UNCTAD/DIAE/PCB/2012/5, http://unctad.org/en/PublicationsLibrary/diaepcb2012d5_en.pdf (last accessed 20 July 2015), p. 51; UNCTAD (2015) World Investment Report 2015. http://unctad.org/en/PublicationsLibrary/wir2015_en.pdf (last accessed 17 August 2015), p. 136; VanDuzer (2012), pp. 136 and 138.

[97] UNCTAD (2012) Investment Policy Framework for Sustainable Development. UN Pub. UNCTAD/DIAE/PCB/2012/5, http://unctad.org/en/PublicationsLibrary/diaepcb2012d5_en.pdf (last accessed 20 July 2015), p. 5; UNCTAD (2015) World Investment Report 2015. http://unctad.org/en/PublicationsLibrary/wir2015_en.pdf (last accessed 17 August 2015), p. 137.

[98] UNCTAD (2012) Investment Policy Framework for Sustainable Development. UN Pub. UNCTAD/DIAE/PCB/2012/5, http://unctad.org/en/PublicationsLibrary/diaepcb2012d5_en.pdf (last accessed 20 July 2015), p. 50; VanDuzer A, Simons P, Mayeda G (2012) Integrating Sustainable Development into International Investment Agreements: A Guide for Developing Countries, http://www.iisd.org/pdf/2012/6th_annual_forum_commonwealth_guide.pdf (last accessed 20 July 2015), p. 125.

[99] On 'negative' and 'positive' lists in IIAs see further Muchlinski (2007), p. 254.

[100] UNCTAD (2012) Investment Policy Framework for Sustainable Development. UN Pub. UNCTAD/DIAE/PCB/2012/5, http://unctad.org/en/PublicationsLibrary/diaepcb2012d5_en.pdf (last accessed 20 July 2015), p. 49; UNCTAD (2015) World Investment Report 2015. http://unctad.org/en/PublicationsLibrary/wir2015_en.pdf (last accessed 17 August 2015), p. 143; VanDuzer A, Simons P, Mayeda G (2012) Integrating Sustainable Development into International Investment Agreements: A Guide for Developing Countries, http://www.iisd.org/pdf/2012/6th_annual_forum_commonwealth_guide.pdf (last accessed 20 July 2015), p. 91. As a separate issue, the umbrella clause may also need to be modified, or omitted, so as to exclude contractual claims arising out of the investment contract from being turned into treaty violations subject to ISDS: see

4.2.2 Increasing Accountability and Transparency

To date transparency has been discussed in IIAs as an aspect of State accountability. According to UNCTAD, existing transparency provisions concentrate on State duties to disclose, "adequate information to foreign investors to enable informed investment decisions and to enhance the predictability and stability of the on-going investment relationship between the host State and the investor."[101]

However it has two further aspects relevant to a new form of PTIA: accountability of investors to stakeholders and accountability through stakeholder participation in PTIA procedures and dispute settlement (discussed in the next sub-section).[102]

This reflects the need for what McCormick has termed 'communal subsidiarity', that is, "the need to have a rich and varied range of institutions within which self-realisation can be fostered and developed."[103] The aim is to create a mixed state/civil society approach to the pursuit of non-market goals, which opens the door to a civil society sector that supplements the state. Translated into PTIAs this would require a widening of the notion of transparency and accountability into new institutional formats, and obligations on commercial actors, which have hitherto been absent. It seeks to temper pure market-liberalism with an accommodation for individual self-realisation which, according to McCormick, requires not only extensive political and economic liberty for individuals, but also

> depends on a substantial degree of support for individuals so that each may have social and economic backing with which coming to maturity as a potentially self-realising individual is possible. It also gives reason to oppose acceptance of legally conferred economic liberties so extensive that differences of wealth between different persons can reach an extent that makes impossible any serious adherence to an ideal of equality of self-respect among different persons. Equality of this sort is essential to their participation as equals in the same political community. . .[104]

Obviously PTIA provisions alone could not achieve this, and any reforms in these agreements must be seen as part of a wider multi-level approach to regulation. However, given their potential as vehicles for constraining the capacity of States to act domestically as guardians of wider stakeholder interests, by favouring the pursuit of specific corporate liberties, such developments appear to be entirely consistent with emerging transnational notions of social justice as embodied in the SDGs.

UNCTAD (2014) World Investment Report 2014 http://unctad.org/en/PublicationsLibrary/wir2014_en.pdf (last accessed 17 August 2015), p. 54.

[101] UNCTAD Transparency: A Sequel, http://unctad.org/en/PublicationsLibrary/unctaddiaeia2011d6_en.pdf (last accessed 21 May 2015), p. 5.

[102] UNCTAD Transparency: A Sequel, http://unctad.org/en/PublicationsLibrary/unctaddiaeia2011d6_en.pdf (last accessed 21 May 2015), pp. 7–12.

[103] McCormick (1999), p. 152.

[104] McCormick (1999), pp. 176–177.

Accordingly, within their sphere of operation PTIAs should strive to include provisions on investor disclosure as part of the recognition of corporate responsibility standards in IEL instruments.[105] More broadly corporate responsibilities could also form part of future agreements, echoing existing standards found in domestic laws and regulations. To date any references to corporate responsibility in IIAs have been purely hortatory or couched in terms of State obligations not to lower regulatory standards in relation to labour and environment.[106] However, more developed clauses could be included. Indeed, in relation to environmental protection, some progress has already been made with specific protections of regulatory rights contained in international environmental agreements.[107]

Further options include Section 7 of the UNCTAD model, which provides a clause on investor obligations and responsibilities.[108] This can contain a general obligation to obey host state laws with a concomitant denial of rights under the treaty if an investment is made in violation of host country law.[109] In addition, following the adoption by the UN Human Rights Council of Guiding Principles for Business and Human Rights, a provision could be developed encouraging (or, in the alternative, requiring) an investor to follow the corporate human rights due diligence process contained in the Guiding Principles relating to economic development social and

[105] For detailed discussion see UNCTAD Transparency: A Sequel, http://unctad.org/en/PublicationsLibrary/unctaddiaeia2011d6_en.pdf (last accessed 21 May 2015), pp. 30–36.

[106] See further UNCTAD (2012) Investment Policy Framework for Sustainable Development. UN Pub. UNCTAD/DIAE/PCB/2012/5, http://unctad.org/en/PublicationsLibrary/diaepcb2012d5_en.pdf (last accessed 20 July 2015), p. 59. UNCTAD proposes that such clauses could be expanded to include health and human rights.

[107] See Potestà (2013).

[108] UNCTAD (2012) Investment Policy Framework for Sustainable Development. UN Pub. UNCTAD/DIAE/PCB/2012/5, http://unctad.org/en/PublicationsLibrary/diaepcb2012d5_en.pdf (last accessed 20 July 2015), p. 58; UNCTAD (2015) Investment Policy Framework for Sustainable Development UNCTAD/WEB/DIAE/PCB/2015/3, http://investmentpolicyhub.unctad.org/Upload/Documents/INVESTMENT%20POLICY%20FRAMEWORK%202015%20WEB_VERSION.pdf (last accessed 13 August 2015), p. 106.

[109] UNCTAD (2012) Investment Policy Framework for Sustainable Development. UN Pub. UNCTAD/DIAE/PCB/2012/5, http://unctad.org/en/PublicationsLibrary/diaepcb2012d5_en.pdf (last accessed 20 July 2015), p. 58; UNCTAD (2015) Investment Policy Framework for Sustainable Development UNCTAD/WEB/DIAE/PCB/2015/3, http://investmentpolicyhub.unctad.org/Upload/Documents/INVESTMENT%20POLICY%20FRAMEWORK%202015%20WEB_VERSION.pdf (last accessed 13 August 2015), p. 106. See too VanDuzer A, Simons P, Mayeda G (2012) Integrating Sustainable Development into International Investment Agreements: A Guide for Developing Countries, http://www.iisd.org/pdf/2012/6th_annual_forum_commonwealth_guide.pdf (last accessed 20 July 2015), pp. 287–290.

environmental risks.[110] Furthermore, investors may be encouraged (or required) to observe applicable corporate social responsibility standards.[111]

Turning to stakeholder participation in institutional structures, UNCTAD proposes a co-operative institutional structure under which the parties can discuss the interpretation of the IIA, so as to facilitate consistency in awards, and to provide a forum for co-operation in the furtherance of the sustainable development goals of the agreement.[112] This builds upon the idea of a Joint Committee set up by the parties to administer the treaty, an institutional innovation that was contained in the Norwegian Model BIT of 2007.[113] It would follow that, in order to further wider stakeholder interests, some form of stakeholder participation could be provided for on such a committee. It would amount to an extension of the principle of co-determination to the transnational sphere and go some way to reducing the suspicion of pro-corporate bias that accompanies the current critique of transnational economic agreements.

4.2.3 Reform of ISDS[114]

The UNCTAD IPFSD focuses on three key issues here: conditions of access to investment arbitration, ISDS institutions and procedures and remedies and

[110] See UN Human Rights Council Seventeenth Session 21 March 2011: Guiding Principles on Business and Human Rights Implementing the United Nations "Protect, Respect and Remedy" Framework, http://www.ohchr.org/documents/issues/business/A.HRC.17.31.pdf Guiding Principle 17 (last accessed 22 July 2015), adopted by Resolution 17/4 of the Human Rights Council 16 June 2011 UN Doc A/HRC/RES/17/4 6 July 2011 http://www.business-humanrights.org/media/documents/un-human-rights-council-resolution-re-human-rights-transnational-corps-eng-6-jul-2011.pdf (last accessed 22 July 2015). See further Muchlinski (2012a); Business and Human Rights Initiative (2010) How to Do Business with Respect for Human Rights. https://commdev.org/userfiles/files/2651_file_how_to_business_with_respect_for_human_rights_gcn_netherlands_june2010.pdf (last accessed 21 May 2015); Abrahams D, Wyss Y (2010) International Finance Corporation Guide to Human Rights Impact Assessment and Management (HRIAM) http://www.ifc.org/wps/wcm/connect/8ecd35004c0cb230884bc9ec6f601fe4/IFC_HIRAM_Full_linked.pdf?MOD=AJPERES (last accessed 23 July 2015). See too OECD Guidelines for Multinational Enterprises (2011 revision) Chapter VI "Human Rights", http://www.oecd.org/dataoecd/43/29/48004323.pdf (last accessed 22 July 2015).

[111] UNCTAD (2012) Investment Policy Framework for Sustainable Development. UN Pub. UNCTAD/DIAE/PCB/2012/5, http://unctad.org/en/PublicationsLibrary/diaepcb2012d5_en.pdf (last accessed 20 July 2015), p. 58; UNCTAD (2015) Investment Policy Framework for Sustainable Development UNCTAD/WEB/DIAE/PCB/2015/3, http://investmentpolicyhub.unctad.org/Upload/Documents/INVESTMENT%20POLICY%20FRAMEWORK%202015%20WEB_VERSION.pdf (last accessed 13 August 2015), p. 107.

[112] UNCTAD (2012) Investment Policy Framework for Sustainable Development. UN Pub. UNCTAD/DIAE/PCB/2012/5, http://unctad.org/en/PublicationsLibrary/diaepcb2012d5_en.pdf (last accessed 20 July 2015), p. 6.

[113] See Norway Model BIT 2007, Article 23.

[114] This section draws upon Muchlinski (2016).

compensation.[115] As to conditions of access, these can be restricted so as to avoid the costs of investor-state arbitration to the host country, mentioned above. In some cases this may lead to the exclusion of ISDS altogether, or to its availability only for a limited list of claims, and/or the exclusion of certain types of claims, such as those arising out of measures to protect health or human rights, which are key to sustainable development.

In addition the availability of ISDS could be conditional on the prior exhaustion of domestic remedies in the host country,[116] and/or be made subject to a 'fork-in-the-road' provision by which the investor agrees not to bring, or a 'no U-turn' provision, by which the investor undertakes to discontinue, proceedings in the same case before another forum. Furthermore, strict limitation periods could be added to prevent 'old' cases from being brought. UNCTAD is keen to stress that the use of alternative dispute resolution mechanisms should be encouraged, especially as resort to investor-state arbitration often results in the breakdown of the relationship between the investor and the host country.[117] Both the UNCTAD and Commonwealth Secretariat models suggest the availability of counterclaims arising out of investors' non-compliance with domestic laws or a breach of investors' obligations under the treaty.[118]

On the issue of institutions and procedures, of the many reforms proposed to make ISDS more legitimate and consistent the most important are: the adoption of an appellate mechanism; accessibility to proceedings, including public documentation and hearings and *amicus curiae* participation; a means of disposing of

---

[115] UNCTAD (2012) Investment Policy Framework for Sustainable Development. UN Pub. UNCTAD/DIAE/PCB/2012/5, http://unctad.org/en/PublicationsLibrary/diaepcb2012d5_en.pdf (last accessed 20 July 2015), pp. 56–57 on which this paragraph draws. See too UNCTAD (2015) Investment Policy Framework for Sustainable Development UNCTAD/WEB/DIAE/PCB/2015/3, http://investmentpolicyhub.unctad.org/Upload/Documents/INVESTMENT%20POLICY%20FRAMEWORK%202015%20WEB_VERSION.pdf (last accessed 13 August 2015), pp. 103–106.

[116] See too VanDuzer A, Simons P, Mayeda G (2012) Integrating Sustainable Development into International Investment Agreements: A Guide for Developing Countries, http://www.iisd.org/pdf/2012/6th_annual_forum_commonwealth_guide.pdf (last accessed 20 July 2015), p. 413.

[117] UNCTAD (2012) Investment Policy Framework for Sustainable Development. UN Pub. UNCTAD/DIAE/PCB/2012/5, http://unctad.org/en/PublicationsLibrary/diaepcb2012d5_en.pdf (last accessed 20 July 2015), pp. 43 and 56; UNCTAD (2015) Investment Policy Framework for Sustainable Development UNCTAD/WEB/DIAE/PCB/2015/3, http://investmentpolicyhub.unctad.org/Upload/Documents/INVESTMENT%20POLICY%20FRAMEWORK%202015%20WEB_VERSION.pdf (last accessed 13 August 2015), p. 105.

[118] UNCTAD (2012) Investment Policy Framework for Sustainable Development. UN Pub. UNCTAD/DIAE/PCB/2012/5, http://unctad.org/en/PublicationsLibrary/diaepcb2012d5_en.pdf (last accessed 20 July 2015), p. 57; UNCTAD (2015) Investment Policy Framework for Sustainable Development UNCTAD/WEB/DIAE/PCB/2015/3, http://investmentpolicyhub.unctad.org/Upload/Documents/INVESTMENT%20POLICY%20FRAMEWORK%202015%20WEB_VERSION.pdf (last accessed 13 August 2015), p. 103; and VanDuzer A, Simons P, Mayeda G (2012) Integrating Sustainable Development into International Investment Agreements: A Guide for Developing Countries, http://www.iisd.org/pdf/2012/6th_annual_forum_commonwealth_guide.pdf (last accessed 20 July 2015), pp. 468–469.

frivolous claims, consolidation of multiple claims arising from the same facts and a joint interpretation mechanism for the Contracting Parties to control tribunal interpretations of IIA clauses.

Finally, as regards remedies and compensation, at present most IIAs do not specify any rules on this issue. This may allow a tribunal to require, for example, the modification or annulment of laws or regulations thus unduly intruding into host country sovereignty.[119] To avoid such consequences the dispute settlement clause can limit available remedies to monetary compensation and restitution of property, or compensation only. Guidance as to the measure of compensation may also be provided, as it already is for expropriation. Thus the clause could specify that compensation will be equitable and take into account all relevant circumstances, including the host country's level of development, and exclude certain types of damages by agreement of the parties such as moral damages and lost profits past a certain date.[120]

The above list of reforms goes some way to making ISDS more palatable as a system of dispute settlement. However, they do not require a fundamental re-think of whether such a system is at all needed in the current legal and political environment of foreign investment. As the present author has argued elsewhere, the existing system of ISDS is largely an unforeseen historical accident, developed as an act of legal entrepreneurship by specialist lawyers.[121] It was never seen as a general substitute for domestic legal dispute settlement, but as a stopgap in cases of extreme maladministration carried out by governments in weak governance zones. As noted above, the availability of ISDS in IIAs was also very much involved with the decolonisation process and was rooted in the mistrust placed in early post-colonial governments' ability to offer impartial justice to foreign investors, and their habitual disregard for the procedures of ad hoc international arbitration.[122]

Indeed, there is still a good case to be made that, in relation to weak governance situations, some kind of delocalised system of dispute settlement is desirable as a means of reducing investment risk. However that is not true of many of the countries that are now considering adding ISDS to the range of remedies offered by mega-regional agreements. It is difficult, for example, to describe the legal systems of the US, EU and the more advanced economies of the Asia-Pacific region

[119] UNCTAD (2012) Investment Policy Framework for Sustainable Development. UN Pub. UNCTAD/DIAE/PCB/2012/5, http://unctad.org/en/PublicationsLibrary/diaepcb2012d5_en.pdf (last accessed 20 July 2015), p. 57.

[120] UNCTAD (2012) Investment Policy Framework for Sustainable Development. UN Pub. UNCTAD/DIAE/PCB/2012/5, http://unctad.org/en/PublicationsLibrary/diaepcb2012d5_en.pdf (last accessed 20 July 2015); UNCTAD (2015) Investment Policy Framework for Sustainable Development UNCTAD/WEB/DIAE/PCB/2015/3, http://investmentpolicyhub.unctad.org/Upload/Documents/INVESTMENT%20POLICY%20FRAMEWORK%202015%20WEB_VERSION.pdf (last accessed 13 August 2015), p. 106; VanDuzer A, Simons P, Mayeda G (2012) Integrating Sustainable Development into International Investment Agreements: A Guide for Developing Countries, http://www.iisd.org/pdf/2012/6th_annual_forum_commonwealth_guide.pdf (last accessed 20 July 2015), pp. 467–468.

[121] See Muchlinski (2013a) and Muchlinski (2011b).

[122] See Muchlinski (2007), p. 709.

as lacking adequate domestic remedies to satisfy the claims of foreign investors. Rather what is being proposed is preferential treatment of foreign investors by offering additional remedies over and above domestic remedies as a matter of routine. This may be inconsistent with long established norms of domestic law, which have worked out procedural safeguards for due process and access to justice.[123] The possibility of unconstitutionality is also present, particularly under US law.[124]

In addition, the economic advantages of ISDS appear to be rather small while the political risks are high. For example, according to an LSE Enterprise study on the costs and benefits of a EU-US treaty undertaken for the UK Department of Business Innovation and Skills,

> investment treaty arbitration has become politically controversial in Canada because of the frequency and character of investor challenges to Canadian government policies, and the Canadian government has had to invest considerable resources in an investment-treaty defence capacity as a result of its more than 30 NAFTA claims. While few of these cases were lost on the merits, Canada has faced incentives to settle cases either by paying compensation or, in some reported cases, by changing government policies.[125]

The study concludes that, were the UK to become a party to an EU-US treaty containing ISDS, little would change in the pattern of US investment into the UK while the political risks and costs of defending claims would increase, in line with the abovementioned Canadian experience of NAFTA.[126]

Given these findings in the context of developed countries, the costs created by ISDS would no doubt represent far greater challenges for less developed countries. That said such countries are also more likely to suffer from weak governance and inadequate systems of justice. Here the solution may well be to have reformed ISDS. However, this should be accompanied by other policies designed to improve the quality of local governance and justice. In this regard home country obligations of technical assistance may have to be introduced to help alleviate such local

[123] See further Johnson L, Sachs L, Sachs J (2015) Investor-State Dispute Settlement, Public Interest and US Domestic Law. Columbia Center on Sustainable Development Policy Paper http://ccsi.columbia.edu/files/2015/05/Investor-State-Dispute-Settlement-Public-Interest-and-U.S.-Domestic-Law-FINAL-May-19-8.pdf (last accessed 22 July 2015).

[124] Johnson L, Sachs L, Sachs J (2015) Investor-State Dispute Settlement, Public Interest and US Domestic Law. Columbia Center on Sustainable Development Policy Paper, http://ccsi.columbia.edu/files/2015/05/Investor-State-Dispute-Settlement-Public-Interest-and-U.S.-Domestic-Law-FINAL-May-19-8.pdf (last accessed 22 July 2015).

[125] Skovgaard Poulsen L, Bonnitcha J, Yackee J (2013) Costs and Benefits of an EU-USA Investment Protection Treaty, https://www.gov.uk/government/uploads/system/uploads/attachment_data/file/260380/bis-13-1284-costs-and-benefits-of-an-eu-usa-investment-protection-treaty.pdf (last accessed 22 July 2015).

[126] Skovgaard Poulsen L, Bonnitcha J, Yackee J (2013) Costs and Benefits of an EU-USA Investment Protection Treaty, https://www.gov.uk/government/uploads/system/uploads/attachment_data/file/260380/bis-13-1284-costs-and-benefits-of-an-eu-usa-investment-protection-treaty.pdf (last accessed 22 July 2015), pp. 44–45.

problems. Equally increased use of alternative dispute resolution systems and home-host State co-operation could also avoid the costs and burdens of ISDS.[127]

5 Concluding Remarks

This paper suggests that PTIAs can be drawn up in a manner that ensures a fair balance between market liberalisation, corporate rights and responsibilities and the State's right to regulate. This may be essential if the legitimacy of such agreements, and of transnational economic regulation more generally, is to be maintained. The criticisms made of this emerging normative regime are, as noted, important, though they can be exaggerated into an apocalyptic dystopian image of a future controlled by unaccountable mega-corporations, bent on human exploitation, leading to massive inequality, a trope found in numerous contemporary films[128] and books.[129] It is clear that while such dangers exist, real life can—and should—take a different turn. There is still much mileage possible from a liberal idea of sustainable development, and a social democratic ideal of fair and balanced distribution of resources, which can shape the content of essentially pro-market transnational legal instruments, which, in turn, impact on the domestic right to regulate.

However, we do not live in a world in which corporatism and State control is central to life. That created its own terrors and tropes.[130] Our world is more polycentric and varied and this should inform how we develop the new balance in international economic agreements and in MNE regulation. This requires the imaginative leap towards a world in which corporate actors are counter-balanced by communities and, indeed, controlled by them. In this the State plays a facilitative role as well. It requires a mix of formal legal regulation, civil regulation and self-regulation. It can use the idea of subsidiarity as a method for determining what should, and should not, be taken to the supranational level of normative regulation. PTIAs offer a vehicle for such experimental governance to develop, if the political will is there. For now it may not be, and the neo-liberal obsession with corporate freedom appears to remain prevalent.

The dangers of this approach are evident. We need the imagination to go beyond the idea that corporate freedom equates with personal freedom and any control over that freedom undermines freedom of the individual. It's just not true, as McCormick

[127] UNCTAD (2012) Investment Policy Framework for Sustainable Development. UN Pub. UNCTAD/DIAE/PCB/2012/5, http://unctad.org/en/PublicationsLibrary/diaepcb2012d5_en.pdf (last accessed 20 July 2015), pp. 56–63; UNCTAD (2015) Investment Policy Framework for Sustainable Development UNCTAD/WEB/DIAE/PCB/2015/3, http://investmentpolicyhub.unctad.org/Upload/Documents/INVESTMENT%20POLICY%20FRAMEWORK%202015%20WEB_VERSION.pdf (last accessed 13 August 2015), p. 110.

[128] A good recent example being Elysium (Dir: Neill Blomkamp, Tristar Pictures 2013).

[129] See for example Collins (2008) film version (Dir: Gary Ross, Color Force, 2012).

[130] See classically Orwell (1949) and Animal Farm (London, Secker and Warburg, 1945).

shows. Thus it is open to us to do more and to develop IEL as part of a wider system of balancing individual freedoms and corporate powers, and using corporate capacity for good and useful work to the full while controlling the risk of malevolent corporate action.

References

Albites-Bedoya J (2013) Internal consistency of PTIAs: overlapping trade and investment obligations and dispute resolution mechanisms. In: Hofmann R, Schill S, Tams C (eds) Preferential trade and investment agreements: from recalibration to reintegration. Nomos, Baden-Baden, pp 157–166

Amnesty International UK Business Group (1998) Human rights guidelines for companies. Amnesty International, London

Baetens F (2013) Preferential trade and investment agreements and the trade/investment divide. In: Hofmann R, Schill S, Tams C (eds) Preferential trade and investment agreements: from recalibration to reintegration. Nomos, Baden-Baden, pp 91–128

Ball G (1968) COSMOCORP: the importance of being stateless. Atl Commun Q 6(2):163–170

Berger A (2013) Investment rules in Chinese PTIAs—A partial "NAFTA-ization". In: Hofmann R, Schill S, Tams C (eds) Preferential trade and investment agreements: from recalibration to reintegration. Nomos, Baden-Baden, pp 297–333

Bendell J, Murphy D (2002) Towards civil regulation: NGOs and the politics of corporate environmentalism. In: Utting P (ed) The greening of business in developing countries: rhetoric, reality and prospects. Zed Books, London

Binder C (2013) An international law approach to interactions between preferential trade and investment agreements and the BIT world. In: Hofmann R, Schill S, Tams C (eds) Preferential trade and investment agreements: from recalibration to reintegration. Nomos, Baden-Baden, pp 71–80

Braun T (2013) Investment chapters in future European preferential trade and investment agreements: two universes or an integrated model? In: Hofmann R, Schill S, Tams C (eds) Preferential trade and investment agreements: from recalibration to reintegration. Nomos, Baden-Baden, pp 129–156

Bungenberg M (2013) Preferential trade agreements and regionalism. In: Hofmann R, Schill S, Tams C (eds) Preferential trade and investment agreements: from recalibration to reintegration. Nomos, Baden-Baden, pp 269–287

Canner S (1998) The multilateral agreement on investment. Cornell Int Law J 31:657–681

Clarke T, Barlow M (1997) MAI: the multilateral agreement on investment and the threat to Canadian sovereignty. Stoddart, Toronto

Collins S (2008) The hunger games. Scholastic Press, New York

Crouch C (2004) Post-democracy. Polity Press, Cambridge

Crouch C (2011) The strange non-death of neo-liberalism. Polity Press, Cambridge

de Brabandere E (2013) Co-existence, complementarity or conflict? interaction between preferential trade and investment agreements and bilateral investment treaties. In: Hofmann R, Schill S, Tams C (eds) Preferential trade and investment agreements: from recalibration to reintegration. Nomos, Baden-Baden, pp 37–69

Engering F (1996) The multilateral investment agreement. Transl Corp 5(3):147–161

Fatouros A (1995) Towards an international agreement on foreign direct investment? ICSID Rev-FILJ 10:181–207

Goldberg P, Kindleberger C (1970) Toward a GATT for investment: a proposal for supervision of the international corporation. Law Policy Int Bus 2:295–325

Henderson D (1999) The MAI affair: a story and its lessons. RIIA, London

Hertz N (2002) The silent takeover: global capitalism and the death of democracy. Arrow, London
Hofmann R, Schill S, Tams C (2013) Preferential trade and investment agreements: from recalibration to reintegration. In: Hofmann R, Schill S, Tams C (eds) Preferential trade and investment agreements: from recalibration to reintegration. Nomos, Baden-Baden, pp 9–23
Jacob M (2013) Technique and contents of international investment treaties: can the form affect the substance? In: Hofmann R, Schill S, Tams C (eds) Preferential trade and investment agreements: from recalibration to reintegration. Nomos, Baden-Baden, pp 81–89
Johnston A, Trebilcock M (2013) The proliferation of preferential trade agreements: the beginning of the end of the multilateral trading system? In: Hofmann R, Schill S, Tams C (eds) Preferential trade and investment agreements: from recalibration to reintegration. Nomos, Baden-Baden, pp 243–267
Joubin-Bret A (2013) Preferential trade and investment agreements and regionalism: a stepping stone towards a multilateral set of investment rules or another type of noodles in the spaghetti bowl? In: Hofmann R, Schill S, Tams C (eds) Preferential trade and investment agreements: from recalibration to reintegration. Nomos, Baden-Baden, pp 289–295
Journal of International Economic Law (JIEL) (2014) Symposium in Honor of John H. Jackson. J Int Invest Law 17:3
Kindleberger C (1969) American business abroad. Yale University Press, New Haven
Klein N (2000) No logo. Harper Collins, London
Korbin S (2010) Sovereignty@bay: globalisation, multinational enterprise and the international political system. In: Rugman A (ed) The Oxford handbook of international business, 2nd paperback edn. Oxford University Press, Oxford
Korten D (2001) When corporations rule the world, 2nd edn. Kumarian Press/Conn & Berrett-Koehler Publishes, West Hartford/San Francisco
Kristensen P, Zeitlin J (2005) Local players in global games: the strategic constitution of the multinational corporation. Oxford University Press, Oxford
McCormick N (1999) Questioning sovereignty: law state and practical reason. Oxford University Press, Oxford
Miller A (1973) The multinational corporation and the nation-state. J World Trade Law 7 (3):267–292
Muchlinski P (2000a) Attempts to extend the accountability of transnational corporations: the role of UNCTAD. In: Kamminga M, Zia-Zariffi S (eds) Liability of multinational corporations under international law. Kluwer Law International, The Hague, pp 97–118
Muchlinski P (2000b) The rise and fall of the multilateral agreement on investment: where now? Int Law 34:1033–1054
Muchlinski P (2007) Multinational enterprises and the law, 2nd edn. Oxford University Press, Oxford
Muchlinski P (2011a) The changing face of transnational business governance: private corporate law liability and accountability of transnational groups in a post-financial crisis world. Indiana J Glob Leg Stud 18(2):665–705
Muchlinski P (2011b) Corporations and the uses of law: international investment arbitration as a "multilateral legal order". Oñati Socio-Legal Series 1(4): https://doaj.org/toc/2079-5971/1/4. Last accessed 22 July 2015
Muchlinski P (2012) Implementing the new UN corporate human rights framework: implications for corporate law, governance and regulation. Bus Ethics Q 22(1):145–177. doi: http://dx.doi.org/10.5840/beq20122218
Muchlinski P (2012b) Multinational enterprises and international economic law: contesting regulatory agendas over the last twenty years. Yearb Jap Assoc Int Econ Law 21:53
Muchlinski P (2013a) The role of preferential trade and investment agreements in international investment law: from unforeseen historical developments to an uncertain future. In: Hofmann R, Schill S, Tams C (eds) Preferential trade and investment agreements: from recalibration to reintegration. Nomos, Baden-Baden, pp 211–227

Muchlinski P (2013b) Sovereignty and private corporate power: the case of multinational enterprises. In: Rawlings R, Leyland P, Young A (eds) Sovereignty and the law: domestic, European, and international perspectives. Oxford University Press, Oxford, pp 286–304

Muchlinski P (2016) Negotiating new generation international investment agreements: new sustainable development oriented initiatives. In: Krajewski M (ed) Shifting paradigms in international investment law. Oxford University Press, Oxford

OECD (1996) Towards multilateral investment rules. OECD, Paris

Orwell G (1949) 1984. Secker and Warburg, London

Palast G (2003) The best democracy money can buy. Constable and Robinson, London

Perry-Kessaris A (ed) (2013) Socio-legal approaches to international economic law: text, context, subtext. Routledge, London

Picciotto S (1998) Linkages in international investment regulation: the antinomies of the draft multilateral agreement on investment. Univ Pa J Int Econ Law 19(3):731–768

Picciotto S, Mayne R (eds) (1999) Regulating international business: beyond liberalisation. Macmillan/Oxfam, London

Potestà M (2013) From mutual supportiveness to mutual enforcement? the contribution of US preferential trade and investment agreements to the effectiveness of environmental norms. In: Hofmann R, Schill S, Tams C (eds) Preferential trade and investment agreements: from recalibration to reintegration. Nomos, Baden-Baden, pp 167–185

Roffe P (2010) Intellectual property, development concerns and developing countries. In: Faundez J, Tan C (eds) International economic law, globalization and developing countries. Edward Elgar, Cheltenham, pp 307–330

Rubin S (1974) The multinational enterprise at bay. Am J Int Law 68(3):475–488. doi:10.2307/2200516

Sagafi-Nejad T (2008) The UN and transnational corporations: from code of conduct to global compact. Indiana University Press, Bloomington and Indianapolis

Sen A (1999) Development as freedom. Oxford University Press, Oxford

Smith M (1974) Corporations and society. Duckworth, London

Tevini A (2013) Regional investment protection and liberalization within the Association of Southeast Asian Nations. In: Hofmann R, Schill S, Tams C (eds) Preferential trade and investment agreements: from recalibration to reintegration. Nomos, Baden-Baden, pp 335–353

VanDuzer J, Simons P, Mayeda G (2013) Integrating sustainable development into international investment agreements: a guide for developing country negotiators. Commonwealth Secretariat, London

Vernon R (1971) Sovereignty at bay: the multinational spread of US enterprises. Penguin, Harmondsworth

Xiong P (2012) Patents in TRIPS-plus provisions and the approaches to interpretation of free trade agreements and TRIPS: do they affect public health? J World Trade 46(1):155–186

Yaziji M, Doh J (2009) NGOs and corporations: conflict and collaboration. Cambridge University Press, Cambridge

Zadek S (2007) The civil corporation, Revth edn. Earthscan, London

Zeitlin J (2011) Pragmatic transnationalism: governance across borders in the global economy. Soc Econ Rev 9:187. doi:10.1093/ser/mwq027

Horizontal Effect of Human Rights in the Era of Transnational Constellations: On the Accountability of Private Actors for Human Rights Violations

Ibrahim Kanalan

Contents

Abstract This article discusses the horizontal effect of human rights and proposes a new and unconventional approach to the accountability of private actors for human rights violations. It argues that current theoretical and doctrinal approaches are not able to provide adequately for the protection of human rights, as these approaches are underpinned by state-centric perspectives of law and classical theoretical concepts of human rights. The article aims to highlight the gap in accountability that exists within international and national law as well as the weaknesses of the existing theoretical and doctrinal approaches. It proposes a new concept for the horizontal effect of fundamental human rights borrowing

I would like especially to thank Chris Thornhill and Andreas Fischer-Lescano for their critical comments.

I. Kanalan (✉)
Centre for Human Rights Erlangen-Nuremberg, Friedrich-Alexander-Universität Erlangen-Nürnberg, Schillerstraße 1, 91054 Erlangen, Germany
e-mail: Ibrahim.kanalan@fau.de

M. Bungenberg et al. (eds.), *European Yearbook of International Economic Law 2016*, European Yearbook of International Economic Law 7,
DOI 10.1007/978-3-319-29215-1_17

elements from systems-theory, especially from the work of Gunther Teubner. Finally, this article demonstrates the practicability of this concept.

1 Introduction

In July 2008, over a 100 civil society organisations, Non-Governmental Organisations (NGOs) and other social actors filed a 'lawsuit' at the Permanent Peoples' Tribunal (PPT) against a number of diverse, transnational agrochemical corporations, including the German companies Bayer and BASF, Swiss corporation Syngenta, and the US corporations Monsanto, DuPont, and the Dow Chemical Company. The lawsuit claimed that these corporations have caused, "massive death, terrible harm to health, plunder of the environment and destruction of ecological balance and biodiversity".[1] The corporations were accused of having violated fundamental human rights, such as the right to health, life, food, and the right to a safe and healthy environment. In another case in February 2007, the human rights NGO Global Witness filed a complaint with the so-called Organisation of Economic Co-operation and Development (OECD) National Contact Point of the United Kingdom (the UK NCP) against the UK transnational corporation Afrimex UK Ltd. The complaint alleged that Afrimex had paid taxes to rebel forces in the Democratic Republic of Congo and had violated human rights through the company's failure to implement and adhere to sufficient due diligence measures in its supply chain. This led to the sourcing of minerals from mines that use child labour and forced labour, and that operate under unacceptable health and safety conditions.[2] Lastly, in August 2008, a group of Nigerian citizens claimed before the US national courts that the transnational corporations Royal Dutch Petroleum Co. and Shell Petroleum Development Company of Nigeria had violated diverse human rights of indigenous communities in Nigeria.[3]

Despite their taking place in different locations and at different times, and on diverse platforms, the central issue behind these complaints is the allegation of human rights violations committed by private entities, namely, transnational corporations. However, the accountability of private actors, especially the accountability of transnational corporations (TNCs), for human rights violations is one of

[1] Permanent Peoples' Tribunal, Session on Agrochemical Transnational Corporations, Bangalore, December 2011, http://agricorporateaccountability.net/sites/default/files/tpp_bangalore3dec2011.pdf (last accessed 28 September 2015).

[2] Statement of United Kingdom National Contact Point, *Global Witness* v *Afrimex (UK) Ltd*, 28 August 2008 http://oecdwatch.org/cases/advanced-search/cases/advanced-search/keywords/casesearchview?b_start:int=60&search=en_Human%20rights&type=Keyword (accessed 16 March 2015).

[3] See, for instance, the US Supreme Court, *Kiobel et al* v *Royal Dutch Petroleum Co. et al*, (No. 10-1491), 17 April 2013; United States Court of Appeals, *Kiobel* v *Royal Dutch Petroleum*, 621 F 3d 111, 2nd Cir 17 September 2010.

the most hotly disputed issues at present, not only in the academic world, but also in international, regional and national politics.[4] The question as to whether TNCs should be bound by specific human rights obligations, and, if so, through which means and to what extent they should be held accountable, is today more controversial than ever. This question is one of the major challenges of the twenty-first century.[5] Consequently, a number of approaches and concepts have been developed in the last decades which aspire to solve this very question. These generally proceed from the realities of economic globalisation and therefore stress the enormous power that private actors hold in order to justify the accountability of private actors for human rights violations.[6]

The emergence of the enormous power and the ascending role of private actors in general, and the power of TNCs in particular, render their influence on the diverse platforms and processes indisputable. It is, for instance, generally recognised that TNCs are among the strongest economic entities, with some boasting turnovers higher than the Gross Domestic Product (GDP) of many nation states.[7] And that TNCs can significantly affect law and policy-making processes on both international and national levels.[8] Similarly indisputable is the human rights record of these private actors. In the last decades, TNCs have often found themselves under increased public scrutiny, due to their involvement in human rights violations and their interference in domestic affairs.[9] They violate human rights in different ways. These violations encompass areas such as inhumane working conditions, substantial impacts on the rights to life, health, and food, as well as cases of massive environmental destruction and damage.[10]

---

[4] See, for example, for an overview, Scherer and Palazzo (2011), p. 903ff.

[5] The Panel of Eminent Persons, Protecting Dignity: Agenda for Human Rights, Report 2008, www.UDHR60.ch (last accessed 16 March 2015).

[6] Interim Report of the Special Representative of the Secretary-General on the Issue of Human Rights and Transnational Corporations and Other Business Enterprises, UN Doc. E/CN.4/2006/97, 22 February 2006; Ratner (2001), p. 443; Monshipouri et al (2003), p. 965. Briefly, for the concepts from the 1970s onwards, see Nolan (2005), pp. 582–583.

[7] See, for example, www.forbes.com/global2000/list (last accessed 16 March 2015); www.globaltrends.com/knowledge-center/features/shapers-and-influencers/190-corporate-clout-2013-time-for-responsible-capitalism (last accessed 16 March 2015); Nolan (2005), pp. 582–583; Joseph (2004), p. 1ff.

[8] Interim Report of the Special Representative of the Secretary-General on the Issue of Human Rights and Transnational Corporations and Other Business Enterprises, UN Doc. E/CN.4/2006/97, 22 February 2006, para. 9ff; Westaway (2012), p. 63.

[9] Interim Report of the Special Representative of the Secretary-General on the Issue of Human Rights and Transnational Corporations and Other Business Enterprises, UN Doc. E/CN.4/2006/97, 22 February 2006, para. 15; Teubner (2006), pp. 327, 328; Monshipouri et al (2003), p. 973ff; Joseph (2004), p. 2ff., with diverse examples; European Coalition for Corporate Justice, With Power come Responsibility, May 2008, http://www.corporatejustice.org/IMG/pdf/ECC_001-08.pdf (last accessed 5 October 2015).

[10] For instance, the involvement of transnational corporation Shell was not only in the violation of human rights, but also in the massive destruction of the environment; see, for example, the United Nations Environment Programme, Environment Assessment of Ogoniland, 2011.

The provisions concerning the accountability of private actors for human rights violations are asymmetrical to the ascending role and power of private actors, and their involvement in human rights violations.[11] This matter is therefore high on the agenda not only of scholars and politicians, but also of social movements and NGOs.[12]

This paper aims to address this topic from a different perspective and proposes an unconventional approach for the horizontal effect of human rights. First, I will argue that the existing concepts with regard to the responsibility of private actors for human rights violations are insufficient to hold private actors—and TNCs in particular—accountable, and to protect human rights sufficiently. I further claim that, in order to hold private actors accountable for human rights violations, and thus to bind them to fundamental human rights standards, it is necessary to go beyond classical human rights concepts. It is essential for a new approach to detach itself from the traditional understanding of human rights and to consider the origins of human rights as a starting point in order to justify the validity of human rights in a 'private sphere'. In doing so, we must first derive the justification for the normative validity of human rights for private actors from the normative power of the human rights provisions itself. Secondly, the abstract idea of human rights has to be transferred to private actors by taking their specific constellations in multifarious societies as well as in transnational constellations into consideration. According to this premise, this paper will attempt to demonstrate the manner in which the state-centric concept can be overcome and to justify a new theory for the comprehensive binding of private actors to human rights standards.

After sketching the concept of horizontality of human rights (Sect. 2), I briefly address the accountability of private actors for human rights violations *de lege lata* (Sect. 3). On the one hand, I examine the accountability of such actors under state law and non-state law, that is, according to 'voluntary' initiatives such as codes of conducts and corporate social responsibility (CSR) measures. On the other, I analyse theoretical and doctrinal approaches concerning the horizontal validity of human rights. In the second part of this article (Sect. 4), I propose a new theory of horizontal effect (the direct effect of human rights) that endeavours to go beyond classical concepts of horizontal effect. Firstly, I address the origins of the human rights concept in order to explain the general reason for the normative justification of human rights beyond the relationship between the state and individuals. Subsequently, I further justify the direct effect of human rights for private actors by arguing that the necessity for making human-rights standards binding on private actors arises from the differentiation of society in various functional systems. Finally, I seek to demonstrate the practicability of my approach. In this section, I borrow elements from systems-theory, especially from the work of Gunther

[11] Monshipouri et al. (2003), p. 983ff.

[12] Report of the Special Representative of the Secretary-General on the Issue of Human Rights and Transnational Corporations and other Business Enterprises, UN Doc. A/HRC/8/5, 7 April 2008.

Teubner, in order to develop the concept of horizontal effect of fundamental human rights.

2 The Concept of Horizontality of Human Rights

The question of the horizontality of human rights entails a number of disputes and problems.[13] These include, among others, a lack of clarity concerning the terminology, definition and the exact content of the concept itself. Even though the concept of horizontal effect of human rights is utilised almost in an inflationary manner, there is hardly any consensus concerning the precise meaning and content of this concept.[14] In this paper, I articulate the concept of the horizontal effect of human rights with regard to whether human rights norms apply *directly* in relations between private actors. In other words, whether human-rights provisions serve as a cause of action in private litigations.[15]

3 Can Private Actors Be Held Accountable for Human Rights Violations?

3.1 State Law

It is no doubt possible to make human rights standards binding on private actors within the framework of legal order of the state. This can be performed by means of international conventions, international customary law or national laws, among others. Leaving aside the question of whether private actors can be the subjects of international law, the international community is able to bind private actors through explicit regulation by an international treaty.[16] Hence, there are occasionally treaties that regulate the binding of private actors to human rights standards, for instance, the provisions under the Charter of the International Military Tribunal (Nuremberg), the Statute of International Criminal Tribunal Rwanda (ICTR) or the Rome Statute of International Criminal Court.[17] However, these existing provisions are generally related to the criminal liability of individuals; they are not provisions concerning the general accountability of private actors under human rights law. Furthermore, the international community has been either unable or unwilling to

---

[13] See, for an introduction and a brief summary, for instance, Uitz (2005), p. 1.

[14] See, for example, Beyleveld and Pattinson (2002), p. 623; Young (2007), p. 35.

[15] See, for example Garlicki (2005), p. 129; Gardbaum (2003), p. 393ff., 404; Tushnet (2003), pp. 87–88; Hunt (1998), pp. 428–429.

[16] See Ratner (2001), pp. 538–539.

[17] See Clapham (1993), pp. 95–96; Ratner (2001), p. 467.

adopt such a treaty. Also, customary international law does not recognise the accountability of private actors for human rights violations.[18]

Another option for the creation of legally-binding regulations exists within domestic law.[19] States are able to create legal obligations for private actors to prevent human rights violations and to hold them accountable in the event of a violation. And indeed, a small number of states have already utilised this option for holding private actors to account. Perhaps the most prominent example is the United States' (US) Alien Tort Claims Act (ATCA).[20] Since the decision of the Supreme Court of the US in April 2013, however, the relevance of this approach for future cases is unclear. The Supreme Court tends to marginalise the scope of this litigation and rejected the universal jurisdiction of US courts in general.[21] In addition to the US, provisions exist in other countries, such as the UK, and have been discussed in Canada.[22] However, domestic provisions are, for a number of reasons, inadequate to provide sufficient protection of human rights.[23] On the one hand, these kinds of regulations are practiced exclusively in a small number of countries. On the other, the home states of TNCs are often not interested in producing comprehensive binding regulations; due to the asymmetrical power and economic relations, host states are also often either not interested or not able to regulate the human rights violations of private actors.[24] Furthermore, this option poses difficulties and uncertainties concerning the legal procedural criteria and the political relevance of these cases can significantly influence the judicial process.[25]

---

[18] See Business and Human Rights: Mapping International Standards of Responsibility and Accountability for Corporate Acts, UN Doc. A/HRC/4/035, 9 February 2007, para. 34.

[19] Detailed analysis with sufficient examples can be found by Joseph (2004), p. 1ff. See, also, Ratner (2001), pp. 533–536.

[20] Steinhardt and D'Amato (1999); Wouters J, De Smet L and Ryngaert C (2003) Tort Claims Against Multinational Companies for Foreign Human Rights Violations Committed Abroad: Lessons from the Alien Tort Claims Act? Institute for International Law K. U. Leuven, Working Paper No 46, www.law.kuleuven.be/iir/nl/onderzoek/wp/WP46e.pdf (last accessed 16 March 2015); Weschka (2006), p. 625.

[21] US Supreme Court, *Kiobel et al.* v *Royal Dutch Petroleum Co. et al.*, (No. 10-1491), 17 April 2013, (569 U.S. (2013)).

[22] Weschka (2006), p. 625; De Schutter O (2004) The Accountability of Multinationals for Human Rights Violations in European Law. CHRGJ Working Paper No 1, http://chrgj.org/wp-content/uploads/2012/07/s04deschutter.pdf (last accessed 5 October 2015).

[23] See De Jonge (2011), p. 91ff, 117; Joseph (2004), p. 153ff.

[24] Report of the Special Representative of the Secretary-General on the Issue of Human Rights and Transnational Corporations and other Business Enterprises, UN Doc. A/HRC/8/5, 7 April 2008, para. 14ff; Land and Power—The Growing Scandal Surrounding the New Wave of Investments in Land, Oxfam Briefing Paper, September 2011, p. 23ff.

[25] Joseph (2004), p. 21ff, 83ff, 113ff.

3.2 Non-State Law

3.2.1 Codes of Conduct

The fact that neither international law nor domestic law has been able to provide an adequate solution has led to the emergence of new considerations and concepts. Over the past decades, public and private codes of conduct (the self-regulation of private actors) have become prominent.[26] The most well-known instruments are, among others, the Guidelines of the OECD regarding the duties of multinational corporations (Guidelines for Multinational Enterprises)[27] and the Tripartite Declaration of the International Labour Organization (ILO) concerning multinational enterprises and social policy[28] and the Global Compact initiative of the United Nations (UN).

All these instruments have a common objective, in that they operate on a voluntary basis and contain general recommendations for states and business enterprises. They utilise a vague language with regard to the obligations of corporations. Analysing them within the framework of state law and utilising the language and concepts of domestic legal practices, these instruments have hardly any legally-binding nature. The OECD Guidelines, for instance, are state recommendations to business enterprises without legally-binding character.[29] The Guidelines did not even contain any assertive reference to human rights and international law until their update in 2011. Following this update, there is now a reference to the protection of human rights according to the UN 'Protect, Respect and Remedy' Framework Concept developed by John Ruggie.[30] Another weakness of the Guidelines are their insufficient and non-coercive monitoring system.[31] The Declaration

[26] Interim Report of the Special Representative of the Secretary-General on the Issue of Human Rights and Transnational Corporations and Other Business Enterprises, UN Doc. E/CN.4/2006/97, 22 February 2006; Business and Human Rights: Mapping International Standards of Responsibility and Accountability for Corporate Acts, UN Doc. A/HRC/4/035, 9 February 2007; Clapham (2006), p. 195ff; De Schutter (2006), p.1; De Jonge (2011), p. 21ff; McLeay (2006), p. 219.

[27] OECD, Guidelines for Multinational Enterprises—2011 updated version, OECD Publishing; Clapham (2006), p. 201ff; Weschka (2006), p. 647ff; Karl (1999), p. 89.

[28] It has been adopted at the 204th Session (1977) and amended lastly at its 295th Session (2006), www.ilo.org/wcmsp5/groups/public/---ed_emp/---emp_ent/---multi/documents/publication/wcms_094386.pdf (last accessed 16 March 2015). See, for example, Clapham (2006), p. 211ff.

[29] OECD, Guidelines for Multinational Enterprises—2011 updated version, OECD Publishing, p. 17, Concepts and Principles, para. 1.

[30] OECD, Guidelines for Multinational Enterprises—2011 updated version, OECD Publishing, Chapter IV, Commentary on Human Rights, para. 36–46.

[31] The Guidelines grant "National Contact Points" but the object and tasks of these points are very general, OECD, Guidelines for Multinational Enterprises—2011 updated version, OECD Publishing, Part II, Implementation Procedure; Amnesty International, The 2010-11 Update of the OECD Guidelines for Multinational Enterprises has come to an end: the OECD must now turn into effective implementation, 23 May 2011, http://www.amnesty.org/en/documents/IOR30/001/2011/en/ (last accessed 5 October 2015).

of the ILO faces similar difficulties. The principles are comprehensively recommended to governments, multinational business enterprises and employers' and workers' organisations. In contrast to the OECD Guidelines, the Declaration's mandate is restricted to human rights violations in the fields of "employment, training, conditions of work and life and industrial relations".[32] Comparable to the Guidelines of the OECD, the main weakness of the Declaration are its non-binding nature according to state law, its formulation of merely vague duties and the lack of an effective implementation and monitoring mechanism, which, in turn, is due to the absence of independent enforcement mechanisms.[33] In conclusion, attempts to bind private actors in accordance with codes of conduct initiatives are welcome, since they are not of irrelevance and may be potentially helpful to supplement other mechanisms of accountability.[34] Nevertheless, as outlined above, voluntary means are generally not able to provide sufficient protection of human rights and thus fail to close the existing accountability gap. Simply by virtue of their 'voluntary' character, vague obligations and ineffective implementation and monitoring mechanisms, these initiatives are neither intended nor suitable to provide acceptable solutions for the accountability of private actors, and are even less appropriate to replace legally-binding instruments.[35] In particular, when considering the state-centric concept of law, this approach cannot serve as an alternative solution. Subsequently, it is not surprising, that experiences do, in practice, demonstrate that these mechanisms are hardly appropriate to operate against human rights violations by corporate actors.[36]

The UN Norms which were drafted in 2003 by the Sub-Commission of the Human Rights Committee of the Economic and Social Council[37] tended to go beyond the weaknesses of codes of conducts and corporate social responsibility initiatives and were an exception to previous guidelines. Contrary to most existing 'voluntary' initiatives, the Norms were designed as legally-binding provisions.[38]

[32] ILO Declaration, www.ilo.org/wcmsp5/groups/public/---ed_emp/---emp_ent/---multi/documents/publication/wcms_094386.pdf (last accessed 5 October 2015), para. 4, 7.

[33] Nolan (2005), p. 587; Kinley and Tadiki (2004), p. 950; Weschka (2006), pp. 646–647.

[34] Indeed, circumstances exist in which codes of conduct contribute to the prevention of human rights violations. See for instance, Land and Power—The Growing Scandal Surrounding the New Wave of Investments in Land, Oxfam Briefing Paper, September 2011, p. 33ff, with a few positive examples. See, also, Teubner (2011a), pp. 619–620.

[35] Kinley and Tadiki (2004), p. 950; Narula (2006), pp. 752–753.

[36] See, for example, The London School of Economics and Political Science, The Reality of Rights, 2009, http://www.lse.ac.uk/businessAndConsultancy/LSEEnterprise/pdf/reality_of_rights.pdf (last accessed 5 October 2015), p. 36f; Action Aid International, Power Hungry, 2005, http://www.actionaid.org.uk/sites/default/files/doc_lib/13_1_power_hungry.pdf (last accessed 5 October 2015), pp. 47–48.

[37] Economic and Social Council, Sub-Commission on the Promotion and Protection of Human Rights, "Norms on the responsibilities of transnational corporations and other business enterprises with regard to human rights" (UN-Norms) UN Doc. E/CN.4/Sub.2/2003/12/Rev.2, 26 August 2003. See, also, Weissbrodt and Kruger (2003), p. 901; Backer (2006), p. 287; Nolan (2005).

[38] Weissbrodt and Kruger (2003), p. 903, 913; Backer (2006), p. 333ff, 343.

They did not merely impose a negative obligation to respect human rights (the obligation to respect) but the provisions were also intended to impose positive obligations on private actors, namely, the "obligation to promote, secure the fulfillment of, respect, ensure respect of and protect human rights".[39] However, the Human Rights Committee rejected the draft of the Sub-Commission and emphasised that the draft was not of a legally-binding nature.[40]

3.2.2 Corporate Social Responsibility

Ultimately, the approach of business actors to regulate their accountability for human rights violations by themselves might be discussed as an alternative to close the accountability gap. Within the concept of CSR, business actors are expected to commit themselves to regulating their human rights responsibilities in order to prevent human rights violations.[41] This concept includes the voluntary, self-binding provisions of business actors to take 'social responsibility' for human rights violations.[42]

However, this approach has also ultimately failed, due to the non-legally binding character of such measures, and the lack of effective implementation and enforcement mechanisms,[43] along with the concomitant lack of commitment from corporate actors to enforce these responsibilities.[44] These measures are not without importance and may, in some respects, be regarded as an achievement. In specific circumstances, these instruments can be of a legally-binding character and become the object of judicial assessment, in so far as they set standards as part of private contracts or statements of intent or commitment, which are relevant to consumer

[39] Economic and Social Council, Sub-Commission on the Promotion and Protection of Human Rights, "Norms on the responsibilities of transnational corporations and other business enterprises with regard to human rights" (UN-Norms) UN Doc. E/CN.4/Sub.2/2003/12/Rev.2, 26 August 2003, at para. 1.

[40] Commission on Human Rights, Decision of 20 April 2004 in Commission on Human Rights, Report on the Sixtieth Session, UN Doc. E/2004/23—E/CN.4/2004/127, para. 525–527.

[41] Business and Human Rights: Mapping International Standards of Responsibility and Accountability for Corporate Acts, UN Doc. A/HRC/4/035, 9 February 2007, para. 63ff; European Commission, A Renewed EU Strategy 2011-14 for Corporate Social Responsibility, COM (2011) 681, 25 October 2011, p. 4ff; European Commission, Green Paper, COM (2001) 366, 18 July 2001, para. 20ff.

[42] See European Commission, Green Paper, COM (2001) 366, 18 July 2001, para. 8f; for a comprehensive concept, see European Commission, A Renewed EU Strategy 2011-14 for Corporate Social Responsibility, COM (2011) 681, 25 October 2011, p. 6f.

[43] European Commission, Green Paper, COM (2001) 366, 18 July 2001, para. 55f; Action Aid International, Power Hungry, 2005, http://www.actionaid.org.uk/sites/default/files/doc_lib/13_1_power_hungry.pdf (last accessed 5 October 2015), p. 41f; Narula (2006), p. 754.

[44] Land and Power—The Growing Scandal Surrounding the New Wave of Investments in Land, Oxfam Briefing Paper, September 2011, p. 35f.

protection law and competition law. However, despite these measures, the impact of these instruments remains rather minor.[45]

3.3 New Concepts – Old Patterns: Operating in the Shadow of the State-Centric Concept

Having outlined that currently neither state law nor non-state law (soft law) is able to produce an adequate solution to this problem within the existing state-centric legal order, I will now focus on a selection of theoretical and doctrinal approaches and new developments which aim to create a foundation for binding human rights standards for private actors. The following analysis will demonstrate that these proposals operate in the shadow of traditional concepts of international law and human rights law, and, accordingly, are not able to provide solutions to the challenges of human rights in the era of transnational constellations, since these traditional concepts are themselves ill-equipped to provide solutions to new problems.

According to the traditional concept of international law, two criteria are essential for any actor to be directly bound by human rights standards. Firstly, the actor must be recognised as a subject of international law (international legal personality)—that is, that subject quality is only present when an actor has rights and obligations under a system[46]; and secondly, there must be human rights provisions that impose an obligation on these actors.[47] Consequently, almost all approaches are focused on these criteria and serve only to entrench their existence further. The first of these concepts—which I refer to as the formalistic-positivist concept—approaches the foundation of directly binding law via the prevailing international law principles, and thus argues that private actors (TNCs) should be recognised as the subjects of international law due to the fact that these actors possess a number of rights which are also enforceable.[48] The advocates of this approach argue that the normative recognition of TNCs as *rights-holders* is already indisputably existent, but dispute the human rights obligations of private actors, that is, the assignation of TNCs as *duty-bearers*. Accordingly, the notion of the human rights obligations of private actors is partially rejected in accordance with the argument that neither human rights treaties nor customary international law provide for such an obligation. In contrast, many others have demanded recognition of these duties, although there remains much dispute over the precise details and legal foundations that such

[45] Ruggie (2007), p. 835f; Narula (2006), p. 755.

[46] Reinisch (2005), p. 70; Alston (2005), p. 20, with other references.

[47] See, for example, for an overview, Clapham (1993), p. 94ff.

[48] Clapham (1993), pP. 94–124; Ratner (2001), p. 467ff; Kinley and Tadiki (2004), p. 944ff; Jägers (1999), p. 264ff.

duties should have.[49] The second approach (legal-sociological or functional concept) focuses on the factual, economical and political power of TNCs, and argues that, even in the absence of any assertive declaration of the international human rights duties of private actors, the latter should be considered to be the subjects of international law.[50] Due to their economic power and social function, private actors should be recognised not only as the subjects of international law, but also as rights-holders and duty-bearers as well.[51] Similar to the previous approach, the details regarding the precise foundations and the duties themselves are contested and vary widely.[52]

Lastly, the proposal of the former UN Special Representative, John Ruggie, provides a valuable basis for analysis. Ruggie's work was based upon a consensus that is rooted in the societal expectations of business actors. After rejecting the draft of the Sub-Commission concerning the responsibility of business enterprises, the UN Human Rights Committee created a new mandate for this matter. Initially, under this mandate Ruggie formulated the 'Protect, Respect and Remedy' Framework,[53] and later elaborated this concept through the Guiding Principles,[54] which provide recommendations for the implementation of the Framework. The 'Protect, Respect and Remedy' Framework articulates the human rights obligations of corporate actors in three core principles: "the State's duty to protect against human rights abuses by third parties, including businesses; the corporate responsibility to respect human rights; and the need for more effective access to remedies."[55] The concept of the Framework includes a broad range of obligations, and does not operate exclusively within the realm of the obligations of private actors. However, my focus will be precisely on the obligations of private actors, since the other principles concerning the duties of the states are—at least for this inquiry—of less relevance. The duty to respect basically compels TNCs not to violate human rights and to respect the exercise of human rights.[56] Although the obligation to

[49] Ratner (2001), p. 494ff; Kinley and Tadiki (2004), p. 960ff; Clapham (1993), p. 94ff, 134ff.

[50] See, for example, Kamminga and Zia-Zarifi (2000), p. 5ff; Dahm et al. (2002), p. 245ff, 257.

[51] Bilchitz (2010), pp. 208–211.

[52] See, for comprehensive duties beyond the duty to respect human rights, for instance, Bilchitz (2010), pp. 207–211.

[53] Report of the Special Representative of the Secretary-General on the Issue of Human Rights and Transnational Corporations and other Business Enterprises, UN Doc. A/HRC/8/5, 7 April 2008.

[54] Report of the Special Representative of the Secretary-General on the Issue of Human Rights and Transnational Corporations and other Business Enterprises, UN Doc. A/HRC/17/31, 21 March 2011.

[55] Report of the Special Representative of the Secretary-General on the Issue of Human Rights and Transnational Corporations and other Business Enterprises, UN Doc. A/HRC/8/5, 7 April 2008, para. 9. For a detailed analysis, see Deva (2012), p. 101; Simons (2012), p. 5; Bilchitz (2010).

[56] Report of the Special Representative of the Secretary-General on the Issue of Human Rights and Transnational Corporations and other Business Enterprises, UN Doc. A/HRC/8/5, 7 April 2008, para. 23f, 51ff; Report of the Special Representative of the Secretary-General on the Issue of Human Rights and Transnational Corporations and other Business Enterprises, UN Doc. A/HRC/17/31, 21 March 2011, Annex para. 11ff.

respect is mainly conceived as a 'negative obligation', it does not only refer to the obligation to omit violations, but also contains positive components, so that, in the event of private actors exercising certain public functions or undertaking additional commitments voluntarily,[57] the private actors could be obliged to take positive measures to avoid human rights violations.[58] As far as the normative foundation for the recognition of private actors as the 'subjects' of international law and the imposition of obligations on private actors is concerned, Ruggie suggests that business corporations already possess particular rights and duties in accordance with international law and are already recognised as 'participants' at the international level, with the capacity to bear both rights and duties under international law.[59] With regard to imposing obligations, he justifies this by means of societal expectations. He states that society has at least the 'basic expectation' that a business should respect human rights—also referred to as a 'company's social license to operate'.[60]

Summarising these approaches the question no longer appears to be whether private actors—in particular TNCs—can be recognised as subjects of international law, but, rather, the manner in which the 'subject' criteria and the foundation of the obligation for private actors, its content and extent, can be normatively justified and determined.[61] Analysing the core arguments of these proposals concerning the imposition of human rights obligations on private actors, the main arguments that emerge are, firstly, that private actors often perform public functions, and, secondly, that enormous power is imputed to the private actors, especially TNCs.[62] It has been

---

[57] Report of the Special Representative of the Secretary-General on the Issue of Human Rights and Transnational Corporations and other Business Enterprises, UN Doc. A/HRC/8/5, 7 April 2008, para. 24; Report of the Special Representative of the Secretary-General on the Issue of Human Rights and Transnational Corporations and Other Business Enterprises, UN Doc. A/HRC/11/13, 22 April 2009, para. 61ff.

[58] Report of the Special Representative of the Secretary-General on the Issue of Human Rights and Transnational Corporations and other Business Enterprises, UN Doc. A/HRC/17/31, 21 March 2011, Annex para. 13; Report of the Special Representative of the Secretary-General on the Issue of Human Rights and Transnational Corporations and other Business Enterprises, UN Doc. A/HRC/8/5, 7 April 2008, para. 55; Report of the Special Representative of the Secretary-General on the Issue of Human Rights and Transnational Corporations and Other Business Enterprises, UN Doc. A/HRC/11/13, 22 April 2009, para. 59. See, also, Bilchitz (2010), p. 204ff.

[59] Business and Human Rights: Mapping International Standards of Responsibility and Accountability for Corporate Acts, UN Doc. A/HRC/4/035, 9 February 2007, para. 20; Ruggie (2007), p. 824.

[60] Report of the Special Representative of the Secretary-General on the Issue of Human Rights and Transnational Corporations and other Business Enterprises, UN Doc. A/HRC/17/31, 21 March 2011, para. 6; Report of the Special Representative of the Secretary-General on the Issue of Human Rights and Transnational Corporations and other Business Enterprises, UN Doc. A/HRC/8/5, 7 April 2008, para. 9, 54.

[61] Ruggie (2007), p. 824ff; Kinley and Tadiki (2004); Ratner (2001); Muchlinski (2007); Alston (2005), p. 3ff; Weissbrodt and Kruger (2003); Jägers (1999); Clapham (1993), p. 89ff.

[62] Monshipouri et al (2003), p. 966 with further references; Scherer and Palazzo (2011), p. 901ff; Ratner (2001), p. 461 ff. Knox (2008), p. 39 with further references; Nolan (2005), p. 581ff.

concisely observed that, "[w]ith power should come responsibility [. . .]".[63] Despite the positive observation that most analyses go partially beyond the classical concept and recognise the possibility that actors other than states can also be bound by human rights, it is also notable that these analyses are generally based upon traditional understandings of human rights and international law.[64] Even though these approaches do constitute important steps forward,[65] they nevertheless still have shortcomings since they are loyal to the traditional concept of international law and to the liberal construction of human rights, and operate in the shadow of these concepts.

Commencing with the criteria for the subjects of international law within Ruggie's Framework, Ruggie tends to go beyond the classic understanding and, instead, pleads for recognition of business corporations as subjects of international law by stating that business corporations are at least 'participants' of international law.[66] This approach, which was initially proposed and promoted by Rosalyn Higgins,[67] goes beyond the classic concept and corresponds more to the realities of international law than to the traditional concept of the 'subjects' of international law. Questioning the normative base of the Ruggie's concept and the determination of the content of the obligations, his concept lacks innovation and persuasiveness. As far as the normative foundation is concerned, Ruggie analyses international law and comes to the conclusion that international law does not impose direct legal obligations on corporations.[68] He argues that the normative base for imposing obligations on corporations originates in the expectations of the society[69] and

Critical to this approach, see Report of the Special Representative of the Secretary-General on the Issue of Human Rights and Transnational Corporations and Other Business Enterprises, UN Doc. A/HRC/11/13, 22 April 2009, para. 65 with other references.

[63] Weissbrodt and Kruger (2003), p. 901. See, also, European Coalition for Corporate Justice, With Power come Responsibility, May 2008, http://www.corporatejustice.org/IMG/pdf/ECC_001-08.pdf (last accessed 5 October 2015); Nolan (2005); Kinley and Tadiki (2004), p. 1021.

[64] See, for instance, Ratner (2001), p. 449ff.

[65] Despite the critique concerning the concept of Ruggie, a large number of states has stressed that the question of accountability of business will not end with the proposal of Ruggie; rather, this concept should be elaborated further; HRC, Council holds dialogue with Experts on summary executions, independence of judges and lawyers, transnational corporations, Information Release, 30 May 2011, www.ohchr.org/en/NewsEvents/Pages/DisplayNews.aspx?NewsID=11082&LangID=E (last accessed 16 March 2015).

[66] Business and Human Rights: Mapping International Standards of Responsibility and Accountability for Corporate Acts, UN Doc. A/HRC/4/035, 9 February 2007, para. 20; Ruggie (2007), p. 824.

[67] Higgins (1994), p. 48f.

[68] Business and Human Rights: Mapping International Standards of Responsibility and Accountability for Corporate Acts, UN Doc. A/HRC/4/035, 9 February 2007, para. 35–44.

[69] See Report of the Special Representative of the Secretary-General on the Issue of Human Rights and Transnational Corporations and other Business Enterprises, UN Doc. A/HRC/8/5, 7 April 2008, para. 24; Report of the Special Representative of the Secretary-General on the Issue of Human Rights and Transnational Corporations and Other Business Enterprises, UN Doc. A/HRC/11/13, 22 April 2009, para. 61ff.

claims that the obligation to respect is the "the baseline norm for all companies in all situations" which have acquired "near-universal recognition".[70] He bases his concept upon voluntary obligation to respect the expectation of the society, and, in the end, also refers to moral obligations.[71] But if the normative base is exclusively understood as being voluntary and moral, it is not comprehensible why this approach should ultimately be more promising than the diverse initiatives and standards that exist already and are similarly based upon voluntarism or morality.[72] Furthermore, the reason for the reduction of the extent of the obligation is neither plausible nor undisputable. Limiting the obligations of corporations solely to *respect* human rights and not to operate with the obligation to *protect* and *fulfil*, would mean deviating from the 'respect-protect-fulfil' concept without any convincing reasons.[73] In conclusion, his concept lacks persuasive normative foundations, on the one hand, while, on the other, its explanation for the content and extent of his concept is weak and remains faithful to an existing concept of human rights as primarily negative rights (the obligation to respect).[74] It is ultimately unsuitable to protect human rights comprehensively or to justify the accountability of private actors sufficiently. In fact, this approach—except the proposal concerning the legal personality of transnational corporations—does not really move beyond the existing initiatives and standards, apart from those that already recognised the obligations of private actors.

Other concepts that focus on the power to argue for binding human rights standards struggle with fundamental difficulties and are the object of much

[70] Report of the Special Representative of the Secretary-General on the Issue of Human Rights and Transnational Corporations and Other Business Enterprises, UN Doc. A/HRC/11/13, 22 April 2009, para. 46–48; Report of the Special Representative of the Secretary-General on the Issue of Human Rights and Transnational Corporations and other Business Enterprises, UN Doc. A/HRC/8/5, 7 April 2008, para. 54–55.

[71] Vandenhole W (2012) Emerging Normative Frameworks on Transnational Human Rights Obligations. EUI Working Papers (RSCAS 2012/17), p. 12ff; Simons (2012), p. 37.

[72] Simons (2012), p. 38 with further references. From view of NGO's: UN Human Rights Council: Weak Stance on Business Standards. Human Rights Watch, 16 June 2011, www.hrw.org/news/2011/06/16/un-human-rights-council-weak-stance-business-standards (last accessed 16 March 2015); Resolution of Human Rights Council on Business and Human Rights fails victims of transnationals. FIAN, 17 June 2011, www.fian.org/en/news/article/detail/resolution_of_human_rights_council_on_business_and_human_rights_fails_victims_of_transnationals/ (last accessed 16 March 2015).

[73] At international level, progressive approaches exist which operate in accordance with the 'respect, protect, fulfil' concept and argue that the expectation of society includes positive obligations, that is, the obligation to promote the protection and fulfilment of human rights; see Special Rapporteur on the Right of Everyone to the Enjoyment of the Highest Attainable Standard of Health—Mission to GlaxoSmithKline, UN Doc. A/HRC/11/12/Add.2, 5 May 2009, para. 16ff, 35ff. See, critically, also Bilchitz (2010), pp. 204–208. In fact, Ruggie does not intend to propose a new concept with binding obligations, but, instead, draws existing weak obligations through a pragmatic approach and abandons important human rights principles; see, especially, Bilchitz (2010).

[74] See, also, Deva (2012), p. 104.

criticism. Firstly, instead of focusing on the explanation of the normative validity of human rights beyond the state and the individual, the focus is primarily based upon the demonstration of the international legal personality of private actors (especially business corporations). In the end, these approaches remain loyal to conventional concepts without questioning either the role of international law or the concepts themselves regarding the existence of accountability gap. Both aspects are, in fact, of significant relevance.[75] Secondly, as previously mentioned, these approaches are referred for grounding the international legal personality of private actors and imposing obligations on them, primarily because of the power which business corporations possess. However, this is an enormously problematical approach, firstly, because the power phenomena is truly not a new one,[76] and, secondly, because it is decisive, the discussion regarding human rights cannot exclusively be conceived in terms of power phenomena, and, accordingly, the solution cannot be restricted to such concepts. In addition, operating with the traditional concept of human rights and international law, and primarily conceiving the political system as the relevant actor that endangers human rights, while merely recognising other actors as the subjects of international law, produces the side effect that everything is interpreted from a state-centric perspective and leads to the attempt to transfer the specifics of the relationship between the state and the individual to other relationships.[77] The risk of human rights violations is no longer exclusively produced by the political system and its most organised and differentiated agent, the state; instead, a host of other autonomous systems, with expansionist tendencies (expansive self-dynamics) and the potential to endanger human rights, are able to violate human rights as well.[78] Provided that the possession of power is crucial for recognising the international legal personality, why should the imposition of binding human rights obligations—and thus the accountability for human rights violations—be restricted to business corporations?[79] What about other powerful systems and their actors, for instance, in sports (Fédération Internationale de Football Association (FIFA), Union of European Football Associations (UEFA) or the International Olympic Committee (IOC)), religion (religious organisations or associations), academia (universities, schools), the media and NGOs?[80] Focusing on

[75] See, for example, McLean (2004), p. 363; Simons (2012). In general, for a critical analysis of international law, see Marks (2003); Anghie (2005); Koskenniemi (2002).

[76] Hale (1935), p. 149, had already in 1935 emphasised the aspect of power phenomena of private actors and asserts that there is no difference to that of the power of states, quoted, in Clapham (1993), pp. 126–127. In addition, it will be demonstrated below that business corporations have always been in possession of power.

[77] In line with this primarily 'formalistic-positivist' approach, for instance, see Kinley and Tadiki (2004), p. 945ff, 960ff. In general, concerning (human) rights as a construction positivising, producing and shaping political power, see Thornhill (2010) and Thornhill (2008).

[78] Teubner (2006), p. 342; Verschraegen (2006), p. 112; Knox (2008), p. 19. On this point, see the following section.

[79] Critical, also, is Ratner (2001), pp. 541–542; Knox (2008), p. 39.

[80] See, also, Teubner (2006), p. 342.

power also leads to another false assumption, namely, that human rights can be restricted to the communicative media of politics. But this is an error: the communicative media of politics is just one of a large number of other communicative media.[81]

The most important point is the fact that the possession of power does not imply a normative foundation for the validity of human rights between private persons. The validity of obligations has to be derived from human rights provisions themselves, and not from the fact that particular actors are in possession of power. In a similar manner, focusing on the undertaking of public functions does not operate to establish a normative foundation. It is doubtful that the imposition of such obligations on private actors can be explicated by the function that they perform. Here, as well, the normative validity can exclusively be rooted in the idea of human rights itself and not in the function or action which the duty-bearer is performing.

4 Going Beyond Classical Concepts

4.1 Proposal for a New Theory of Horizontal Effect of Human Rights

Gunther Teubner has argued that the actual problem of binding private actors by human rights standards appears to lie in the totalising conceptualisation of human rights as a construction between the state and the individual and the attempt to transfer this concept to the relation between individuals and new actors.[82] However, this traditional concept is unable, by means of its legal doctrine, to operate satisfactorily as a response to global human rights problems in the era of transnational constellations.[83] This is primarily due to the fact that the conception of national and international law is not uniform. Furthermore, the constellations of functionally-differentiated societies in the age of transnationalism differ from the era in which the traditional concepts of law emerged. Thus, even despite a gradual modification, the transference of a theory-construction to new relationships between individuals and other actors does not offer an adequate solution.[84] What is needed is a separation from the state-centric concept, and a return to the origin and general idea of human rights as the starting-point to introduce a new concept.

[81] Teubner (2011b), p. 208f; Verschraegen (2006), p. 121; Teubner (2012), p. 206ff.

[82] Teubner (2006), p. 330f. See, also, Teubner (2003), p. 5ff.

[83] For a critique of the traditional concept as a solution against human rights violations from another perspective, see, also, Narula (2006).

[84] For his initial critique concerning a global constitution, see Teubner (2003), p. 3.

4.1.1 Generalising the Idea of Human Rights: Addressing the Roots of Human Rights

The origin and idea of human rights is one of the most contested and disputed issues within rights discourse.[85] It would exceed the intentions and limitations of this paper to reopen this discussion, so, in the following, I seek only to elaborate the main points as a background to my discussion.

Beyond most disputes in this area, a historical examination shows the formation of human rights as a result of societal struggles that are related to the expectations of society. It should, however, not be ignored that the formation of rights in general was more probably determined by functional reasons than by normative ones.[86] In its normative conception, human rights are the outcome of diverse struggles, protests and resistance against injustice generally, and particularly against the absence of freedom, equality, independence, as well as against imperialism, colonialism, oppression and humiliation, to name but a few.[87] Put briefly, human rights in their modern formation are responses to structural experiences of injustice.[88] In consequence, and contrary to what liberal theory suggests, they do not operate solely as negative rights against the interference of the state—that is, the obligation to respect. Rather, they must be conceived comprehensively serving as positive rights that enable the inclusion of individuals in diverse functional systems—that is, the obligation to protect and fulfil.[89] Due to the interdependence of the structural experiences of injustice and societal expectations, as well as the formation and shape of human rights, this positivisation of demands—with its initial focus on 'negative rights' and subsequent focus on 'positive rights'—is primarily due to political-sociological circumstances. This operates in a dialectical manner according to the needs and interests of society.[90] The fact that the endangerment of rights was originally essentially caused by the state is due to the political system with the state in its centre—which was the most differentiated system of society.[91] On the other hand this is a very narrow narrative of human rights from liberal European perspective. From the perspective of Third World there has hardly been a

[85] See, for instance, Baxi (2008); Beitz (2009); Kennedy (2002); Shestack (1998); Mutua (1996); Nickel (2008); Donnelly (1984); Freeman (1994); Perry (1997).

[86] Thornhill (2011a), p. 181ff.

[87] See, for example, the preamble of the Universal Declaration of Human Rights. See also Barreto (2013), p. 140.

[88] Brugger (1989), p. 537; Barreto (2013), p.140.

[89] Teubner (2012), p. 207f; Teubner (2011b), p. 200ff; Verschraegen (2006); Luhmann (2009), p. 136ff. Thornhill has elaborated the inclusionary function of (human) rights especial for the political system, Thornhill (2011b), p. 381, 390ff. See, also, Thornhill (2010), Thornhill (2008). This accomplishment of human rights is, however, not exclusively normatively conditioned, but functional as well. See Thornhill (2011b).

[90] In general, regarding human rights, see Marshall (1950). See, also, Thornhill (2008).

[91] Teubner (2006) p. 336ff; Graber and Teubner (1998), p. 61, 64f, 68f.

solid distinction between the state and private actors. States and corporations were together the actors of colonisation and oppression.[92]

However, the idea of human rights is comprehensive, and is not limited to the endangerment caused by its operating exclusively in one system. Quite apart from the source of the endangerment, the normative idea behind the purpose of human rights was the prevention and elimination of injustice in all forms which pose a threat to the most important interests of individuals, such as integrity, life, freedom, and equality. This is the reason why human rights do not operate as 'pre-legal absolute' rights, but, rather, as 'pre-political' and 'pre-legal' 'latent rights' that arise out of, and are shaped by, conflicts both in and between diverse systems, for politics, morals, religion, law, economy, science, etc.[93] Accordingly, the normative basis of human rights[94] is its universal demand for justice: justice both within each different functional system, and between the systems and their environment. Therefore, all theories have to consider this premise as a starting-point and have to prevent all the conditions and circumstances that threaten or endanger human beings in their basic interests and fundamental rights. It is not the source of the danger that is critical, but the existence of the danger itself. Therefore, the prevention of endangerment must be considered as a central point, provided that all actors are addressed and can possess the potential to threaten and endanger human rights. The connectivity point for any actor to be bound by human rights law has to be the potential and the real possibility of the actors endangering or threatening human rights.[95] Contrary to the power-centric approach, the question of whether or not an actor should be bound does not depend on his or her possession of power,[96] since the possession of power does not provide a normative foundation with which to bind them. Instead, the normative power of human rights to prevent violations of integrity, life, freedom, interests, and needs, and the potential of actors to violate human rights are the central determinants. The reason for binding them is the normative power of human rights itself.

4.1.2 Foundation of Human Rights Obligations for Private Actors

With the assertion in mind, that the general reason for having binding human-rights law for any actor arises from the normative idea of preventing the violation of the

---

[92] McLean (2004); Barreto (2013).

[93] Teubner (2006), p. 336.

[94] As Thornhill accurately states, the base of (human) rights is not exclusively normative, but functional instead, as rights provide the means for political system to articulate the reserves of power; Thornhill (2011a).

[95] Ratner (2011), pp. 524–525, 540. Ratner also tends to consider the potential of TNCs to violate human rights as being decisive.

[96] See, also, Teubner (2011b), p. 199ff.

interests and rights of human beings I now analyse why private actors should be bound by human rights law.

In the eighteenth century, when the positivisation of human rights commenced, the state was powerful and was the most important actor that could cause a major danger to human rights. However, the evolution of human rights has undergone significant alterations. The differentiation and fragmentation of society has produced new functional social systems and thus new (autonomous) actors.[97] Having previously been under the dominance of political power (the state), diverse functional systems began to emerge as autonomous independent systems, still under the shadow of the political system.[98] In accordance with this evolution, business corporations also developed into 'global players' in the twentieth century. Accordingly, the systems-theory approach is based upon this diagnosis and constitutes new terrain in the discourse surrounding corporate human rights obligations.[99]

Niklas Luhmann diagnosed that the maximisation of the intrinsic rationality of diverse functional systems, which is caused by functional differentiation, involves an enormous potential of endangerment for human beings, nature and society.[100] Accordingly, Andreas Fischer-Lescano and Gunther Teubner observe that it is insufficient to indicate exclusively the political conflicts and thus the political-legal conflict solutions for the problems of the 'global society'. They argue that problems would not be generated primarily as 'interests- and power-conflicts', but that the fragmented 'operative closed functional systems' of the global society would be generated instead, and that in their expansionist tendencies the main problem of the global society would be generated.[101] Subsequently, Teubner claims, "it is the fragmentation of society that is today central to the human rights question".[102] Following Teubner, I argue that human rights do not involve solely the relation between the political system and individuals, but rather—and contrary to the traditional understanding—the diverse relations of individuals to all other functional systems.[103] In accordance with this, a large number of expansionist systems with their sub-systems, organisations and institutions, as well as diverse interactions, constitute a large number of communications and, at the same time, entail an enormous potential of danger to human rights.

> There is not just a single boundary concerning political communication and the individual, guarded by human rights. Instead, the same problems arise in numerous social institutions, each forming their own boundaries with their human environments: not only politics/

[97] In detail, see Fischer-Lescano and Teubner (2006).

[98] Teubner (2012), p. 179ff.

[99] Teubner (2011b); Teubner (2012), p. 189ff; Teubner (2006). For the first approach, see, also, Graber and Teubner (1998).

[100] Luhmann (1997), p. 630f, 1088ff. See, also, Fischer-Lescano and Teubner (2006), p. 25ff.

[101] Fischer-Lescano and Teubner (2006) p. 28ff; Fischer-Lescano and Teubner (2007), p. 37, 41ff.

[102] Teubner (2006), p. 339.

[103] Teubner (2011b), p. 211ff; Teubner (2006), p. 336ff.

individual, but also economy/individual, law/individual, science/individual, medicine/individual.[104]

The traditional concept was based upon the principle that the state was able to produce a solution so long as the political system was able to be identified with society and was perceived as essential actor. The failure of this concept occurs as a result of the fragmentation of society, causing multiplication of the boundary zones of the autonomous communication matrices to individuals.[105] The consequence of these events is that endangerment does not exclusively arise from the communications of the political system, and thus does not concern the relationship between the state and the individual, but instead concerns the relation among individuals and all the systems with all their diverse sub-systems.[106] Accordingly, the new 'equation' with regard to the function of human rights is: *functional system X* vs. *the individual*. The endangerment and thus the violation do not result from a single process, with a single source or actor (political system and state), but instead result from a large number of anonymous and autonomous globalised communication processes of diverse functional systems.[107] Thus, and due to its multiplicative systems, this new constellation with its diverse institutions, actors and communications requires new solutions, 'new types of guarantees', which "limit the destructive potential of communication".[108] What is necessary is a concept that is sensitive and responsive to modifications of this kind and considers this diagnosis as its starting-point.

The *ecological concept of fundamental rights* observes precisely this diversification and attempts to offer an adequate solution.[109] According to this concept, the problem of human rights should not be understood as tradition assumes—as a balance between society as a whole and its parts—instead as a problem of the relations of the expansive social systems to their social, human, and natural ecologies.[110] Simultaneously, human rights are consequently conceptualised as a "response to problems that transcend society" and "demand an ecological sensitivity of communication".[111] The consequence of such a perception is primarily that the problem of human rights is transformed to the question of the transcendence of system boundaries. On the one hand, human rights have the function of constraining communications,[112] that is, the entire or sole question revolves around the safeguarding of 'boundary relations' between social systems and their environment.[113] On the other hand, the function of human rights does not exclusively exist

[104] Teubner (2006), p. 339.

[105] Teubner (2006), p. 338 ff. Teubner (2011b), pp. 209–212.

[106] Teubner (2012), p. 213; Teubner (2011b), p. 211.

[107] Teubner (2012), p. 215f; Teubner (2006), pp. 339–341.

[108] Teubner (2006), p. 339.

[109] Teubner (2006), p. 333ff; Teubner (2012), p. 189ff; Teubner (2011b), p. 199ff.

[110] Teubner (2006), p. 330ff.

[111] Teubner (2006), p 333.

[112] Teubner (2006), p 334; Graber and Teubner (1998), p. 68ff.

[113] Similar to the function of the constitution; Teubner (2003), p. 10ff.

in its negative dimension as prevention of exclusion, but also exists in its positive dimension as enabling inclusion (rights to access).[114] Even if this function is gradually neglected,[115] human rights still serve as a means to acquire access to diverse societal systems, their institutions and goods in order to enable *de facto* the exercise of human rights. Ultimately, under these circumstances, the question no longer concerns access to the political system (the relationship of the individual with the state) but instead concerns all functional systems (the relationship of the individual with the functional system X).[116] As a consequence, human rights have to be conceived as a concept that includes all societal institutions and actors which are able to communicate and thus possess the potential to violate human rights. Conceived as such, the problem of human rights always occurs consequentially in relation to communicative processes, in so far as, whenever a communication is performed, boundaries are transcended and rights are violated.[117]

The matter concerns the re-formulation of human rights from conflicts between individuals within society to conflicts between society and its ecologies, or rather a transformation "from the paradigm of interpersonal conflicts between individual bearers of fundamental rights to that of ecological conflicts between anonymous communicative processes, on the one hand, and concrete people, on the other".[118] Translated into the language of law, one might define the issue as that of individual lawsuits against private actors, for example against TNCs, private associations, religious or sports institutions, hospitals, universities, schools, NGOs, which concern, on the one hand, structural violence and exclusion from systems, institutions and actors, and, on the other, the claim to access to the diverse systems, institutions and goods.[119]

The question which then arises is: What does this concretely entail in order for private actors to be bound by human rights law? Considering the true assertion of the emergence of the power of private actors, especially of TNCs, the thesis of fragmentation, and the potential of these actors to violate human rights within the new concept of human rights, one can draw the conclusion concerning the accountability of private actors. The necessity of having binding human-rights obligations for private actors arises from the differentiation of the societal systems. Since the political system is not the only differentiated system, its exclusive consideration is insufficient to meet the challenge of constellations in the age of functionally-differentiated societies. Accordingly, the traditional concept of human rights, which was designed for relations between political systems and individuals (and within the jurisdiction of nation states), is not able to produce an appropriate and

---

[114] Teubner (2011b), p. 202ff; Teubner (2012), p. 202ff; Luhmann (2009), p. 41f; See also Verschraegen (2006).

[115] See also Teubner (2011b), p. 202; Teubner (2012), p. 207ff.

[116] Teubner (2011b), p. 204–205; Teubner (2012), p. 208ff; Verschraegen (2006), p. 107ff, 120ff.

[117] Teubner (2006), p. 333ff.

[118] Teubner (2006), p. 342; See also Teubner (2011b), p. 210ff.

[119] Teubner (2006), pp. 343–344; Teubner (2011b), p. 212ff.

persuasive solution, either. Thus, according to the new concept of human rights private actors, as the actors of diverse functional systems, are bound by human rights due to the fact that they participate as the *subjects of law*[120] in communicative processes, which are of relevance for human rights. Being able to participate in communicative processes entails the potential to violate human rights and cause endangerment. Thus, whether these actors possess enormous power is not crucial—even though power as a communicative medium of politics is important for other functional systems[121]—but what is central is their participation in communications, and thus the possibility of violating human rights. Focusing on the point of participation in communicative processes enables this concept to be responsive for the binding of various actors without considering their power or even their performance in a public or private sphere. The only thing of importance is the fact that they participate in communications. This liberation from the power relations at the core of this thesis is supported by the different initiatives of the UN, which do not restrict the circle of duty-bearers exclusively to powerful TNCs, but instead extend it to corporations in general, as long as the latter are involved in human rights violations, without focusing on the question of how powerful they are.[122]

Due to this formation—that is, the shifting of focus from the question of power to the question of participation in communications and the violations of human rights—we are able to ask the question as to why TNCs alone should be bound by human rights law, when other actors are able to violate human rights as well. In addition, the shift and concentration on functional fragmentation make this concept adaptable to further developments, since it is responsive to future developments. The comprehensiveness of this concept enables to use it in general for questions of the validity of human rights, for instance, with regard to extraterritorial application—which the current concept is hardly able to solve convincingly and sufficiently.[123] The emancipation from the state-centric approach, the separation of human rights from the political system, and the focus on their connectivity in the communicative processes of diverse functional systems means that functional systems other than political systems are also able to be bound by human rights. Furthermore, because of the factual abolition of the boundaries between the diverse functional systems, such as economics, the media or science, the spatial range of validity (*ratio loci*) can, in fact, be universalised. As a result, not only private actors but also the political system can be held accountable for human rights violations

---

[120] See to this concept Teubner (2003), p. 4f; Fischer-Lescano (2002), p. 349.

[121] Teubner (2012), p 175ff.

[122] The extension of the circle of duty-bearer to all corporations was initially formulated by the UN Norms of the Economic and Social Council, Sub-Commission on the Promotion and Protection of Human Rights, "Norms on the responsibilities of transnational corporations and other business enterprises with regard to human rights", UN Doc. E/CN.4/Sub.2/2003/12/Rev.2, 26 August 2003 and later Report of the Special Representative of the Secretary-General on the Issue of Human Rights and Transnational Corporations and other Business Enterprises, UN Doc. A/HRC/8/5, 7 April 2008, para. 24.

[123] See also critically Teubner (2011b), pp. 192–194.

beyond its jurisdiction where it operates and communicates beyond its boundaries.[124]

Another complex issue is the content and extent of the obligations of the new actors, that is, the re-specification of human rights in diverse functional systems. It is important to avoid the categorical error of other approaches and not to attempt to modify and to transfer the state human rights and obligations to the particularities of other functional systems. Instead, it is proposed that the details should be determined according to the specifics of concrete systems and regimes (regime-specific determination)[125]; in other words, re-formulating the concept of human rights for the relationship between individuals and other societal institutions.[126] According to this premise, it is natural that not all human rights are able to be applied in all functional systems or impose obligations on all actors. For instance, the right to asylum or the right to a fair trial has hardly any relation to corporations, NGOs or private organisations. As a consequence, these actors are less likely to threaten or violate these rights.[127] Whether the right or obligation is threatened or violated by a concrete actor due to the fact that there is interference with a right, or the access to a right is denied, should be the decisive factor. The content and extent of the obligations can be precisely determined in accordance with the following principles: firstly, it is of the utmost importance to conceptualise human rights as provisions concerning the obligations to respect, protect, and fulfil; subsequently, one must determine the details of the specific system, without considering only the preventive function of human rights (obligation to respect).[128] Contrary to a reductionist approach, human rights can impose comprehensive obligations on private actors as well. As the UN Norms stated, human rights encompass the obligation "to promote, secure the fulfillment of, respect, ensure respect of and protect human rights recognized in international as well as national law".[129]

Advocating for comprehensive obligations for business corporations—especially the obligation to protect and fulfil—is likely to be disputed. Nevertheless, such a comprehensive approach can be justified, firstly, because of the important role that business corporations play in the realisation of human rights, and, secondly, due to their function, which does not differ significantly from the function of the state. Business corporations are important institutions of society. They interfere with and take over the functions of other social systems, impact on political

[124] Kanalan (2014), p. 495.

[125] Similarly Teubner (2012), p 195ff, 204ff.

[126] Teubner (2011b), p. 195ff.

[127] Similar, but with other arguments, Ratner (2001), p. 492ff, 511ff.

[128] Accurately Teubner (2012), p. 203.

[129] Economic and Social Council, Sub-Commission on the Promotion and Protection of Human Rights, "Norms on the responsibilities of transnational corporations and other business enterprises with regard to human rights", (UN-Norms), UN Doc. E/CN.4/Sub.2/2003/12/Rev.2, 26 August 2003, para. 1 and the preamble.

processes, and perform functions of the state.[130] Whether through granting the right to food, health, labour or non-discrimination, the realisation of human rights is strongly impacted by the conduct of private actors. As such, violations of human rights are no longer exclusively committed by states but also by private actors.[131] With this in mind, it is necessary to broaden the responsibility for the realisation of fundamental human rights to diverse actors and not solely restrict it to states, since a diverse range of actors commit violations and, consequently, the achievement of human rights depends upon the contributions of these diverse actors.[132]

In addition, the law grants business corporations a large number of privileges, rights and freedoms.[133] These actors differ from the state essentially due to the fact that they are legal entities under private law, and, consequently, have no monopoly on power, and they are not law-making authorities. In contrast to this, however, corporations are, due to their economic capacity, often more powerful than a number of states, and, by means of this power, are able to impact upon and shape a number of legal processes. Furthermore, corporations are assisted by international and domestic law, tax advantages, subsidies, infrastructure, and protection by the state, which grants them extensive freedoms; without having any of the power or privileges of the state, they may be considered as being of comparable importance and have comparable impact. It is worth mentioning that corporations are also as dangerous as states.[134] Privileges and rights should be equitable to responsibilities and obligations. Due to the particular role of business corporations,[135] and the privileges they enjoy, it is justifiable to impose particular obligations on them,[136] according to the premise of 'no rights without obligations'.[137] If corporations benefit the most from globalisation, the global abolition of boundaries and trade

[130] See for example Peters (2006), p. 100.

[131] See for instance The impact of business corporations on the rights to food; Narula (2010), p. 403, 407ff; Land and Power—The Growing Scandal Surrounding the New Wave of Investments in Land, Oxfam Briefing Paper, September 2011, p. 23ff; Murphy (2006) Concentrated market power and agricultural trade. ECOFAIR Trade Dialog and Heinrich Böll Stiftung (eds).

[132] See for instance, in context of the right to health, Hunt (1998), para. 16.

[133] Bilchitz (2010), p. 207ff; Narula (2010), p. 403, 407ff.

[134] See for the power, impact and privileges of the corporations, for example Interim Report of the Special Representative of the Secretary-General on the Issue of Human Rights and Transnational Corporations and Other Business Enterprises. UN Doc. E/CN.4/2006/97, 22 February 2006, para. 7ff.

[135] See also Westaway (2012), p. 63.

[136] See, for other arguments and approaches Lichtenberg (2009), p. 76; ECHR, *Van der Mussele* v *Belgium*, Application No 8919/80 (= Series A Nr. 70) (27 October 1983), para. 29, noticed the privileges and equipment of private actors with special authorization. However, due to the state-centric concept and procedural necessity—that the court can only examine states obligation to protect—it has recognized the accountability of private actors mediated that is with means of imputation of the violation of privates to the state; See also Ziemele I (2009), Human rights violations by private persons and entities: The case-law of International Human Rights Courts and Monitoring Bodies. EUI Working Paper, AEL (22 August 2009), p. 25.

[137] Similarly Beitz and Goodin (2009), p. 17.

restrictions, and if corporations acquire the most national and international protection, then it is justified and consistent to globalise or transnationalise solidarity and thus extend such responsibilities to all members of the global society.[138] John Ruggie also recognised the particular role of business corporations, stating that the scope of their obligations is defined by societal expectations (the social licence to operate).[139] However, he inconsistently limited social expectations in general to the obligation to respect.[140] Contrary to Ruggie's approach, the obligations must be comprehensive—especially with regard to fundamental rights (basic rights)[141]—due to the fact that business corporations possess the capacity and the ability to contribute to the realisation of these rights, for instance, by granting access to important goods and services.[142] Thus, the obligations of TNCs must include, in addition to the obligation to respect, the obligations to protect and to fulfil without prioritising any of these obligations.[143] For the obligations to protect and fulfil, it is necessary to take into consideration the actual capability, ability, and competency of business corporations to perform in accordance with these obligations (the potential of realisation).[144] Consequently, business corporations are obliged—besides their obligation to respect the exercise of human rights and according to their capacity and competence—to endeavour, by all means at their disposal, to protect against human rights violations by other actors (the obligation to protect), as well as to prevent violations of human rights by means of granting access to the exercise of such rights (obligation to fulfil), for example, by granting access to fundamental goods and interests, such as the right to food or health.[145]

To sum up, as Gunther Teubner states, beyond the obligation to respect, the principle of inclusion has to be generalised in such a manner that "access to the communicative media in all function systems is not only permitted, but is actually guaranteed by means of fundamental rights".[146] Thus, this also applies to business

---

[138] In detail, regarding global responsibility, see Crawford (2009), p. 131.

[139] For instance Report of the Special Representative of the Secretary-General on the Issue of Human Rights and Transnational Corporations and other Business Enterprises, UN Doc. A/HRC/8/5 (7 April 2008), para. 54. See, for this argument also Hunt (1998), para. 35ff.

[140] Ruggie, however, relativizes his concept and broadens the obligation in certain circumstances to an obligation to protect, that is, to perform actively to prevent human-rights violations; see, for instance Report of the Special Representative of the Secretary-General on the Issue of Human Rights and Transnational Corporations and other Business Enterprises, UN Doc. A/HRC/8/5, 7 April 2008, para. 24.

[141] Appealing in general for restrictions of human-rights violations to the 'crass' matter of society threatening mental and physical integrity; Teubner (2006), p. 335. Similarly, already prior to Teubner, Luhmann (1993), p. 578ff.

[142] Bilchitz (2010), p. 209, 216.

[143] Similarly Bilchitz (2010), p. 210ff.

[144] Similarly, Hunt (1998), para. 37ff. In general, for capacity and potential as criteria to determine obligations, see Shue (1988) p. 687; Shue (1996), p. 164f; Beitz and Goodin (2009), p. 14ff.

[145] Hunt has, according to these principles, elaborated the obligation of business corporations to contribute to the fulfilment of the right to health; see Hunt (1998), para. 16ff.

[146] Teubner (2011b), p. 204 (footnote omitted).

corporations, since “the functional differentiation of the societal system, the regulation of the relationship of inclusion and exclusion is transferred to function systems”.[147]

4.2 *The Practicability-Test*

With this result in mind, the following question arises: Can this concept indeed operate for the question of human rights in the ‘private sphere’? The response depends on the practicability of this concept. Can human rights advocates, law practitioners, and dogmatists face the challenge to apply this concept to real life cases or are we left with the current conception of international law and human rights conventions, the consequences of which were described by the Permanent Peoples’ Tribunal in the following damning terms:

> The directions in which the world is developing leave no doubt as to the fact that, if alternatives are not found to these trends, we are heading towards a world in which the power of a few hundred human beings (political, economic and military leaders), of Kafkaesque remoteness and inaccessibility, in many cases totally unknown, will leave the majority of people no option but to be slaves, to be eliminated or excluded.[148]

A detailed analysis demonstrates that the application of this concept in practice is not a hopeless project. I will illustrate this through addressing both state law and non-state law (the so-called *new lex mercatoria*).

4.2.1 State Law

The first indication for the effect of human rights beyond the relation of the individual to the state presents the Universal Declaration of Human Rights (UDHR). The UDHR states in its preamble that human rights are a response against tyranny and oppression, and stresses simultaneously that “every individual and organ of society” has the duty to contribute to the realisation of human rights.[149] Certainly, this statement alone cannot offer sufficient evidence to justify the binding of private actors by state law. However, the statement does not exclude other actors from being bound by human rights standards and provides grounds for such an argument as well.[150] This is especially true for binding provisions in

---

[147] Luhmann (2000), p. 427; quoted in Teubner (2011b), p. 205.

[148] Permanent Peoples’ Tribunal, The European Union and transnational corporations in Latin America. Madrid, 14–17 May 2010, Transnational Institute (December 2010), p. 6.

[149] See preamble and Article 29 UDHR; See also preamble of the International Covenant on Economic, Social and Cultural Rights and International Covenant on Civil and Political Rights.

[150] Beyleveld and Pattinson (2002), p. 632; The provisions at national level do not operate for an objection and, furthermore, some constitutions assertively include provisions which recognise the accountability of private actors as well; see Oliver and Fedtke (2007), p. 3, 9ff.

universal and regional human rights documents since they also indicate duties for private actors.[151] Accordingly, a thorough analysis of the European Convention of Human Rights (ECHR), for instance, Articles 17 and 10 (2) ECHR, present us with assistance for the possibility of binding human rights obligations for private actors.[152] More significant still are the new human rights conventions which indisputably illustrate the fact that human rights do not only impose obligations on states, but also on other actors. The African Charter, for example,[153] explicitly states that human rights obligations are imposed on actors other than the state.[154] In the case of Inter-American Human Rights System the horizontal effect is recognized by the jurisprudence of the Court. The Inter-American Court of Human Rights (I-ACtHR) has ruled that the principle of non-discrimination has horizontal effect, and thus binds private actors as well[155]; in effect, this means that private employers must consider this principle and are not allowed to discriminate against individuals.

Furthermore, at the domestic level as well the binding of actors other than states by human rights law is well recognised.[156] England provides an interesting example concerning the question of horizontal effect, as its common law does not recognise a right of privacy, which the European Convention on Human Rights (Article 8) explicitly requires. Even the question of binding private actors is controversial,[157] an analysis of jurisprudence can nonetheless serve to ground legal arguments. In jurisprudence, this issue has been inconsistently addressed, in particular due to the fact that there is a lack of clarity as to what horizontal effect actually entails. Thus, initially, courts have implicitly tended to find that Article 8 ECHR cannot provide a cause of action, thereby ruling out horizontal effect.[158] However, later in a case concerning the question if the press has to respect the right of privacy of a child and thus can be prohobited to publish for example the name, address and pictures of the child, the UK Supreme Court stated that the rights of the Convention can be applied in litigation between private parties, that is, that Convention rights can provide a

---

[151] Clapham (1993), pp. 94–124.

[152] In detail, Beyleveld and Pattinson (2002), p. 629ff.

[153] Articles 27–29 African Charter on Human and Peoples' Rights, OAU Doc. CAB/LEG/67/3 rev. 5, 21 I.L.M. 58 (1982).

[154] See also Ziemele I (2009), Human rights violations by private persons and entities: The case-law of International Human Rights Courts and Monitoring Bodies. EUI Working Paper, AEL, 22 August 2009.

[155] I-ACtHR, Juridical Condition and rights of undocumented migrants—advisory opinion OC-18/03 (17 September 2003), p. 146ff.

[156] For instance Oliver and Fedtke (2007).

[157] For instance Hunt (1998), pp. 428–429; Beyleveld and Pattinson, (2002), p. 623; Young (2007), p. 35.

[158] For instance UK Supreme Court, *Wainwright v Home Office*, [2003] UKHL 53; UK Supreme Court, *Campbell v MGN Ltd*, (n24) UKHL [2004] 22, pp. 17–18, 132.

cause of action with all the consequential rights and obligations that arise from it.[159] In a similar manner, the Constitutional Court of India has recognised that private actors are bound by human rights provisions, stating that the normative obligations of human rights bind private persons and corporations as well. Referring among others to the Universal Declaration of Human Rights, International Convention on Political, Social and Cultural Rights and the Constitutional Provisions, the Court imposed positive obligations on private persons in order to facilitate the exercise of human rights.[160] The Court stated:

> It would thus be clear that in an appropriate case, the Court would give appropriate directions to the employer, be it the State or its undertaking or-private employer to make the right to life meaningful; to prevent pollution of work place; protection of the environment; protection of the health of the workman or to preserve free and unpolluted water for the safety and health of the people. The authorities or even private persons or industry are bound by the directions issued by this Court under Article 32 and Article 142 of the Constitution.

Similarly, the courts in Nigeria and Uganda have ruled that human rights provisions have horizontal effect and can provide a cause of action.[161] The Federal High Court of Nigeria has in a litigation between an individual and the Shell Petroleum Nigeria and others applied the human rights provisions as enshrined in the Constitution of Nigeria and declared that the action of the corporations is a gross violation of the Applicant's fundamental right to life and dignity of human persons.[162]

4.2.2 Non-State Law (New Lex Mercatoria)

4.2.2.1 Codes of Conduct

As mentioned above, governments, diverse international organisations, NGOs and transnational corporations have all developed a large number of regulations over the last decades which endeavour to regulate 'voluntarily' the human rights obligations of corporations. The scope and content of these regulations, their binding effect as well as their efficacy does, as discussed above, vary widely. Since its update in 2011, the Guidelines of the OECD seem to be indisputably the most

---

[159] *Re S*, UK Supreme Court, [2004] UKHL 47, p. 23ff; See also Court of Appeal (Civil Division) *Murray v Big Pictures (UK) Ltd*, [2008] EWCA Civ 446 (07 May 2008); Young (2007), p. 42ff.

[160] Indian Constitutional Court, *Consumer Education and Research Centre v Union of India*, 1995 AIR 922, 1995 SCC (3) 42, 27 January 1995, p. 22ff.

[161] See for example Federal High Court of Nigeria, *Gbemre v Shell Petroleum Development Company Nigeria Limited and others*, AHRLR 151 (NgHC 2005) (14 November 2005); High Court of Uganda, *Kasha Jacqueline* et al. *v Rolling Stone Ltd*, Case No 163 of 2010 (30 December 2010).

[162] Gbemre v Shell Petroleum Development Company Nigeria Limited and others, Federal High Court of Nigeria, (2005) AHRLR 151 (NgHC 2005) (14 November 2005), Declaration No 2.

elaborated regulations with a unique implementation mechanism—namely, the National Contact Points (NCPs)—for challenging human rights violations committed by transnational corporations.

According to its initiators, the Guidelines 'express the shared values of the governments' which 'provide principles and standards of good practice consistent with applicable laws and internationally recognized standards'.[163] Corporations are obliged to respect internationally-recognised human rights (Section II (General Policies), A.2.) and are encouraged to support human rights facilitation (Section II (General Policies), B. 1-2). Furthermore, the Guidelines specify the human rights obligations of private entities (Section IV. Human Rights). Accordingly, the enterprises should respect human rights, avoid infringing the human rights of others, and avoid causing or contributing to adverse human rights impacts. Furthermore, they have the positive obligation to 'seek ways to prevent or mitigate adverse human rights impacts', by carrying out human rights 'due diligence', and providing for or co-operating in the remediation of adverse human rights impacts. In line with these principles, the NCPs assess the compliance of corporations with the Guidelines. According to the OECD Watch, there have been more than 200 cases to date, in which different human rights organisations had approached the NCPs alleging violations of the Guidelines by corporations and thus violations of human rights law.[164] In some cases, the NCPs have confirmed the obligations that human rights law imposes on private corporations mediated through the Guidelines. Thereby, the question of whether the conduct of transnational corporations is in compliance with the Guidelines provide a medium for the examination of human rights violations through enterprises. Within the framework of assessing the violation of the Guidelines, the NCPs also examine violations of human rights.

Accordingly, NCPs have addressed compliance with the Guidelines by assessing the compliance of transnational corporations with their human rights obligations. For instance, in the case of *Global Witness* vs. *Afrimex Ltd*, the UK NCP scrutinised diverse allegations against the British corporation and declared the violation of a large number of human rights, including a violation of its obligation to respect and its positive obligation to contribute to the protection of human rights. The NCP initially stated:

> SOCOMI [business partner of Afrimex] paid taxes and mineral licences to RCD-Goma and these payments contributed to the continuation of the conflict. Therefore the NCP concluded that Afrimex failed to meet the following requirements of the OECD Guidelines for Multinational Enterprises: II.I 'Respect the human rights of those affected by their activities consistent with the host government's international obligations and commitments.' and II.2 'Contribute to economic, social and environmental progress with a view of achieving sustainable development.'[165]

[163] OECD, Guidelines for Multinational Enterprises—2011 updated version, OECD Publishing, Concepts and Principles I.1.

[164] See for example the documentation of OECD Watch, http://oecdwatch.org/cases (last accessed 16 March 2015).

[165] Statement of United Kingdom National Contact Point, *Global Witness* v *Afrimex (UK) Ltd*, para. 59.

Furthermore, the NCP affirmed:

> The NCP has found insufficient evidence that Afrimex encouraged business partners or suppliers [. . .] to apply principles of corporate conduct compatible with the Guidelines. [. . . The] NCP has concluded that Afrimex failed to meet the following requirements of the OECD Guidelines for Multinational Enterprises: II.I 'Respect the human rights [. . .]'. II.10 Encourage, where practicable, business partners, including suppliers and subcontractors, to apply principles of corporate conduct compatible with the Guidelines.[166]

Lastly, the NCP declared that the corporation had not encouraged the avoidance of violations of children's rights and labour rights.

Another case in which the UK NCP has confirmed the effect of human rights on corporations and declared that human rights violations were committed by private corporations is that of *Survival International* vs. *Vedanta*, a British transnational corporation. The UK NCP has stated that Vedanta had the obligation to respect the rights of an indigenous community of Donria Kondh in the Niyamgiri Hills in India. Since the corporation failed to comply with its obligation to respect human rights and failed to take positive measures to avoid infringements of human rights (*the obligation to protect*), it violated human rights and therefore was not in compliance with the Guidelines.[167] The relevance of human rights law for transnational corporations has also been articulated by NCPs in other OECD countries. Concerning the question of applicable law, the Swedish NCP has stated that:

> Applicable public international law includes the UN Universal Declaration on Human Rights, the International Convention on the Elimination of All Forms of Racial Discrimination (CERD) and the International Covenant on Civil and Political Rights (ICCPR).[168]

The claim that codes of conducts are based upon voluntarism, and that they do not have a legally-binding character beyond the regimes that created them, is not valid. This can be refuted by two arguments. Firstly, the 'voluntary' regulations are the result of intense external pressure, generated by civil society and other societal actors.[169] Secondly, after they are created, these codes detach themselves from their creators and operate as norms, without source or authority respectively. At the end of the creation process, they can be attributed neither to traditional sources of international law nor to a particular author.[170] For this reason, it has been accurately stated that the obligations of corporations exist '*independently of what governments*

[166] Statement of United Kingdom National Contact Point, *Global Witness v Afrimex (UK) Ltd*, para. 61.

[167] Statement of United Kingdom National Contact Point, *Survival International* v *Vedanta Resources plc* (25 September 2009).

[168] Statement of National Contact Point Sweden, *Jijnjevaerie Sami Village* v *Statkraft AS* (14 February 2013).

[169] Teubner (2005), p. 109.

[170] See, for example, Zumbansen (2012), p. 305, 329f; Peters et al. (2009) p. 544, 575f; Tietje (2003), p. 27, especially p. 38f;

and/or private stakeholders do'.[171] It is no longer the structure which is decisive, but the process, instead.[172] This theoretical assumption can be empirically demonstrated within jurisprudence and practice. In this sense, the South African Human Rights Commission (SAHRC) has, in a case alleging the human rights violations of local inhabitants through the mining activities of the corporation Anglo Platinum, referred to non-state law and considered this in its review.[173] The Commission considered, in addition to state law—*inter alia* international law and constitutional law—different codes of conduct, in assessing the human rights violations of the mining company.[174] The Commission took into consideration, among other documents, the Performance Standards[175] of the International Finance Corporation (IFC). The Commission did not consider these codes of conduct as necessarily mediated through state law—for example, competition or consumer protection law—but rather as being directly effective without referring to state law.

The analysis of the statements of the NCPs, as well as of the jurisprudence of state *fora*, demonstrates that binding human rights law for private actors is recognised. This is, in other words, a confirmation of the validity of the horizontal effect of human rights in the 'private sphere'.

4.2.2.2 Private Dispute Arbitrations

Another example for demonstrating the practicability of the distinguished concept of the horizontal effect of human rights for private actors is the practice of private dispute arbitrations. Private dispute arbitrations increasingly apply human rights norms directly for disputes in which private actors are involved. This can be observed, for example, in the practice of the World Intellectual Property Organization (WIPO), and the Internet Corporation for Assigned Names and Numbers (ICANN), which is delegated to resolve disputes concerning domain names for the Internet. ICANN is a private legal person according to the private law of the federal state of California in the US. The nature of the law of this regime is, in fact, private, and it resolves disputes between private actors who do not have a direct relationship

---

[171] OECD, Report by the Chair of the 2011 Meeting of the National Contact Points, p. 2, emphasis added. See also Business and Human Rights: Mapping International Standards of Responsibility and Accountability for Corporate Acts, UN Doc. A/HRC/4/035, 9 February 2007, para. 61.

[172] Teubner (1996), p. 255, 270f.

[173] South African Human Rights Commission (SAHRC) (2008), Mining-related observations and recommendations: Anglo Platinum, affected communities and other stakeholders, in and around the PPL Mine, Limpopo, November 2008.

[174] South African Human Rights Commission (SAHRC) (2008), Mining-related observations and recommendations: Anglo Platinum, affected communities and other stakeholders, in and around the PPL Mine, Limpopo, November 2008, p. 27, 51f, 75ff.

[175] See for example International Finance Corporation (2012), Sustainability Framework—Policy and Performance Standards on Environmental and Social Sustainability Access to Information Policy, January 2012.

with one another. However, being a private legal order beyond the legal order of states, the WIPO has, in the past, referred to human rights norms of diverse legal regimes and apply human rights norms in arbitrating disputes.[176] Accordingly, WIPO has declared in its seminal ruling in the year 2000 that even the right to free speech is not listed in the Uniform Dispute Resolution Policy (UDRP)—the policy which codifies the applicable law: 'The Internet is above all a framework for global communication, and the right to free speech should be one of the foundations of Internet law.'[177] The court directly applied the norm of free speech in its codified form in the First Amendment of the US Constitution and declared that a private corporation, Bridgestone Firestone Inc., was bound by this norm. Later, the court went beyond this, referring to the norm in the US Constitution and referring to the provisions of diverse legal orders regarding the right to free speech.[178] In one case from 2007, the court stated that:

> [. . . R]espect for the principle of freedom of speech is not confined to the United States, just as recognition that it cannot be absolute is not unknown within the United States. The principle of freedom of expression is enshrined, for example, in article 10 of the European Convention on Human Rights and article 19 of the Universal Declaration of Human Rights.[179]

Even WIPO relativised this statement and stated that the primary basis for determining the application of the UDRP policy has to be the terms of the policy itself. Simultaneously however, it emphasised that "these provisions may in places import or refer to principles or rules of national law, and they have to be interpreted in the context of established principles and rules of national and international law".[180] In fact, the court has applied the norms of diverse legal orders in private legal disputes between private actors, which is an acknowledgement of the validity of human rights for private actors.

Another example of the relevance for human rights in private disputes is the practice of the International Centre for the Settlement of Investment Disputes (ICSID). ICSID is in charge of disputes regarding investments between states and private actors. The state parties and the private parties are in equal relation, as private actors. That means that international public law and human rights law are not, *per se*, applicable law. The parties can according to the Convention on the

---

[176] In detail, see for example, Renner (2010), p. 187ff.

[177] WIPO Arbitration and Mediation Center, *Bridgestone Firestone, Inc., Bridgestone/Firestone Research, Inc., and Bridgestone Corporation v. Jack Myers*, Case No D2000-0190, 5.

[178] See, for example, WIPO Arbitration and Mediation Center, *Equality Charter School, Inc. v. Mona Davids / A Happy DreamHost Customer*, Case No. D2011-1226; WIPO Arbitration and Mediation Center, *Nippon Paper Industries Co., Ltd. v. Harriett Swift*, Case No. D2011-0832; WIPO Arbitration and Mediation Center, *Fundación Calvin Ayre Foundation v. Erik Deutsch*, Case No. D2007-1947.

[179] WIPO Arbitration and Mediation Center, *Fundación Calvin Ayre Foundation v. Erik Deutsch*, Case No. D2007-1947, para. 6.12.

[180] WIPO Arbitration and Mediation Center, *Fundación Calvin Ayre Foundation v. Erik Deutsch*, Case No. D2007-1947, para. 6.12.

Settlement of Investment Disputes Between States and Nationals of Other States determine the applicable law (Article 42). However, in the past, even where the parties did not agree on human rights law as applicable law, ICSID tribunals have considered human rights law in their decisions. By means of *amicus curiae* briefs, the court has also referred to human rights norms and considered them in the process of reconciliation. In the case of *Suez/Vivendi* v *Argentina*, the tribunal stated, referring to a prior decision in 2005, that:

> Even if its [the courts] decision is limited to ruling on a monetary claim, to make such a ruling the Tribunal will have to assess the international responsibility of Argentina. In this respect, it will have to consider matters involving the provision of 'basic public services to millions of people'. To do so, it may have to resolve 'complex public and international law questions, including human rights considerations'.[181]

Also, in other cases, it can be observed that the court takes human rights into consideration in its decisions.[182] In fact, in ICSID cases, the statements are not as clear as in the case of the disputes heard by ICANN. That is, the court does not declare the direct human rights obligations of private actors, but it does, however, consider human rights in its decisions.

Lastly, the recognition and application of the human rights responsibilities of private actors and, thus, the horizontal validity of human rights can be observed in the practice of Law of the Civil Society, in other words, the Customary Transnational Law[183] of civil society. The diverse tribunals of civil society, for example, Permanent Peoples' Tribunal (PPT), have applied human rights norms directly against private corporations and emphasised the obligations of private actors under human rights law. The PPT in particular has discussed, in the last decades, the human rights violations of private actors, including those committed by transnational corporations.[184] Recently, the violations of human rights by transnational corporations were discussed by the tribunals *Agrochemical Transnational Corporations* (2011), *Neoliberal Policies and European Transnationals in Latin America and the Caribbean* (2008), *The Role of Transnational Corporations in Colombia* (2006–2008) and *Global Corporations and Human Wrongs* (2000). These tribunals

[181] ICSID, *Suez, Sociedad General de Aguas de Barcelona, S.A. and Vivendi Universal, S.A.* v *Argentina*, Case No ARB/03/19, Order in Response to a Petition by Five Non-Governmental Organisations for Permission to make an *Amicus Curiae* Submission (12 February 2007), para. 18.

[182] See for example ICSID, *Biwater Gauff (Tanzania) Ltd.* v *United Republic of Tanzania*, Case No ARB/05/22, Procedural Order No 5 (02 February 2007), para. 46ff; ICSID, *Azurix Corp.* v *The Argentine Republic*, Case No ARB/01/12 (23 June 2006), para. 254ff; See, in general, also Marrella (2010) p. 335. However, the court has recently rejected an *amicus curiae* brief, where violations of human rights and violations of duty of states to respect human rights were stressed. See ICSID, *Bernhard von Pezold* et al. v *Republic of Zimbabwe*, Case No ARB/10/15, *Border Timbers Limited* et al. v *Republic of Zimbabwe*, Case No ARB/10/25, Procedural Order No. 2 (26 June 2012), para. 58.

[183] For Customary Transnational Law in general, see for example Müller (2008), p. 19.

[184] For an overview, see Permanent Peoples' Tribunal, Session on Neo-liberal Policies and European Transnationals in Latin America and the Caribbean, Lima, 6 May 2008, www.tni.org/sites/www.tni.org/archives/reports/altreg/pptlima.pdf (last accessed 16 March 2015).

reviewed the human rights violations of private entities, referred to human rights law, and substantiated the validity of human rights provisions for private actors.[185]

In its decision in 2008, the PPT referred to the "protection of the principles and rules of international public law, the Universal Declaration of Human Rights, the international Human Rights Conventions and Covenants and the Universal Declaration of the Rights of Peoples",[186] and identified diverse human rights violations by European transnational corporations. The tribunal stated:

> To [. . .] denounce in the international arena those multinational corporations with private and state capital originating in Europe, for serious, clear and persistent violations of the international principles, laws, conventions and covenants that protect the civil, political, economic, social, cultural and environmental rights of the communities, nationalities, families and individuals of the peoples of Latin America and the Caribbean diverse human rights violations of transnational corporations.[187]

5 Conclusion

The analysis in this paper has shown that the current state of international and national law is not able to provide for the general accountability of private actors for human rights violations. There is a serious accountability gap within both international and national law. Besides the interests of powerful states and non-state actors, the main obstacle to making human rights obligations for business corporations binding is the state-centric understanding of law and human rights. This is also the weakness of the current theoretical and doctrinal concepts concerning the horizontal effect of human rights.

Therefore, this paper has proposed a new concept of horizontal effect. The main pillars of this concept are the normative power of human rights and the consideration of the functional differentiation of society. In this concept, systems theory provides an outstanding tool with which to explain why transnational corporations must be made accountable for human rights violations, and how the validity of human rights for relations beyond the state and individuals should be established. This concept is not merely confined to the accountability of corporations, but also applies to the accountability of all private actors.

The most challenging question is, however, the practicability of this concept. Is it realistic to impose human rights law on private actors? The Sub-section of the last part of this article has demonstrated that human rights do, indeed, have a binding

[185] Permanent Peoples' Tribunal, 2011; Permanent Peoples' Tribunal, 2008; Permanent Peoples' Tribunal, Session on Global Corporations and Human Wrongs, Coventry (UK) 22–25 March 2000, Findings and Recommended Action. Law, Social Justice & Global Development Journal 2001, http://www2.warwick.ac.uk/fac/soc/law/elj/lgd/2001_1/ppt (accessed 16 March 2015). See, also, Permanent Peoples' Tribunal, 2010.

[186] Permanent Peoples' Tribunal, 2008, p. 12.

[187] Permanent Peoples' Tribunal, 2008, p. 12.

effect on private actors as well. The horizontal effect has been illustrated in particular through the jurisprudence of diverse *fora*, not only within the regimes of state law, but also within the regimes beyond state law.

References

Alston P (2005) The "not-a-cat" syndrome: can the international human rights regime accommodate non-state actors. In: Alston P (ed) Non-state actors and human rights. Oxford University Press, Oxford, pp 3–36

Anghie A (2005) Imperialism, sovereignty and making of international law. Cambridge University Press, Cambridge

Backer LC (2006) Multinational corporations, transnational law: the United Nations norms on the responsibilities of transnational corporations as a harbinger of corporate social responsibility in international law. Columbia Hum Rights Law Rev 37:287–389

Barreto JM (2013) Imperialism and decolonization as scenarios of human rights history. In: Barreto JM (ed) Human rights from a third world perspective. Cambridge Scholars Publishing, Cambridge, pp 140–171

Baxi U (2008) The future of human rights. Oxford University Press, Oxford

Beitz CR (2009) The idea of human rights. Oxford University Press, Oxford

Beitz CR, Goodin RE (2009) Basic rights and beyond. In: Beitz CR, Goodin RE (eds) Global basic rights. Oxford University Press, Oxford, pp 1–24

Beyleveld D, Pattinson SD (2002) Horizontal applicability and horizontal effect. Law Q Rev 118:623–646

Bilchitz D (2010) The Ruggie Framework: an adequate rubric for corporate human rights obligations? Sur - Int J Hum Rights 7(12):198–228

Brugger W (1989) Menschenrechte im modernen Staat. Archiv des öffentlichen Rechts 114:537–588

Clapham A (1993) Human rights in the private sphere. Clarendon, Oxford

Clapham A (2006) Human rights obligations of non-state actors. Oxford University Press, Oxford

Crawford N (2009) No borders, no bystanders: developing individual and institutional capacities for global moral responsibility. In: Beitz CR, Goodin RE (eds) Global basic rights. Oxford University Press, Oxford, pp 131–156

Dahm G, Delbrück J, Wolfrum R (2002) Völkerrecht, vol I/2. De Gruyter, Berlin

De Jonge A (2011) Transnational corporations and international law. Edward Elgar, Cheltenham/ Northampton

De Schutter O (2006) The challenge of imposing human rights norms an corporate actors. In: De Schutter O (ed) Transnational corporations and human rights. Hart, Oxford, pp 1–40

Deva S (2012) Guiding principles on business and human rights: implications for companies. Eur Company Law 9(2):101–109

Donnelly J (1984) Cultural relativism and universal human rights. Hum Rights Q 6:400–419

Fischer-Lescano A (2002) Globalverfassung: Verfassung der Weltgesellschaft. Archiv für Rechts- und Sozialphilosophie 88(3):349–378

Fischer-Lescano A, Teubner G (2006) Regime-Kollisionen. Suhrkamp Verlag, Frankfurt am Main

Fischer-Lescano A, Teubner G (2007) Fragmentierung des Weltrechts. In: Albert M, Stichweh R (eds) Weltstaat und Weltstaatlichkeit. Verlag für Sozialwissenschaft, Wiesbaden

Freeman M (1994) The philosophical foundations of human rights. Hum Rights Q 16(3):491–514

Gardbaum S (2003) The "horizontal effect" of constitutional rights. Michigan Law Rev 102:388–459

Garlicki L (2005) Relations between private actors and the European convention on human rights. In: Sajó A, Uitz R (eds) The constitution in private relations. Eleven International Publishing, Utrecht, pp 129–143
Graber CB, Teubner G (1998) Art and money: constitutional rights in the private sphere. Oxf J Leg Stud 18:61–73
Hale RL (1935) Force and the state: a comparison of political and economic compulsion. Columbia Law Review 35(2):149–201
Higgins R (1994) Problems and process: international law and how we use it. Oxford University Press, Oxford
Hunt M (1998) The "horizontal effect" of the human rights act. Public Law 423–443
Jägers N (1999) The legal status of the multinational corporation under international law. In: Addo MK (ed) Human rights standards and the responsibility of transnational corporations. Kluwer Law International, The Hague, pp 259–270
Joseph S (2004) Corporations and transnational human rights litigation. Hart, Oxford
Kamminga MT, Zia-Zarifi S (2000) Liability of multinational corporations under international law: an introduction. In: Kamminga MT, Zia-Zarifi S (eds) Liability of multinational corporations under international law. Kluwer Law International, The Hague, pp 1–13
Kanalan I (2014) Extraterritoriale Staatenpflichten jenseits der Hoheitsgewalt: Ein neues Konzept für umfassende extraterritorial Staatenpflichten. Archiv des Völkerrechts 52(4):495–521. doi:10.1628/000389214X14271941530745
Karl J (1999) The OECD guidelines for multinational enterprises. In: Addo MK (ed) Human rights standards and the responsibility of transnational corporations. Kluwer Law International, The Hague, pp 89–106
Kennedy D (2002) The international human rights movement: part of the problem? Harv Hum Rights J 15:101–125
Kinley D, Tadiki J (2004) From talk to walk: the emergence of human rights responsibilities for corporations at international law. Va J Int Law 44(4):931–1023
Knox JH (2008) Horizontal human rights law. Am J Int Law 102:1–47
Koskenniemi M (2002) The gentle civilizer of nations. Cambridge University Press, Cambridge
Lichtenberg J (2009) Are there any basic rights. In: Beitz CR, Goodin RE (eds) Global basic rights. Oxford University Press, Oxford, pp 71–91
Luhmann N (1993) Das Recht der Gesellschaft. Suhrkamp Verlag, Frankfurt am Main
Luhmann N (1997) Gesellschaft der Gesellschaft, vol 2. Suhrkamp Verlag, Frankfurt am Main
Luhmann N (2000) Die Politik der Gesellschaft. Suhrkamp Verlag, Frankfurt am Main
Luhmann N (2009) Grundrechte als Institution, 5th edn. Duncker & Humblot, Berlin
Marks S (2003) Empire's law. Indiana J Glob Leg Stud 10(1):449–466
Marrella F (2010) On the changing structure of international investment law: the human right to water and ICSID arbitration. Int Commun Law Rev 12:335–359
Marshall TH (1950) Citizenship and social class. Cambridge University Press, Cambridge
McLean J (2004) The transnational corporation in history: lessons for today? Indiana Law J 79 (2):363–377
McLeay F (2006) Corporate codes of conduct and the human rights accountability of transnational corporations: a small piece of a larger puzzle. In: De Schutter O (ed) Transnational corporations and human rights. Hart, Oxford, pp 219–240
Monshipouri M, Welch CE, Kennedy ET (2003) Multinational corporations and the ethics of global responsibility. Hum Rights Q 25(4):965–989
Muchlinski PT (2007) Multinational enterprises and the law, 2nd edn. Oxford University Press, Oxford
Müller T (2008) Customary transnational law: attacking the last resort of state sovereignty. Indiana J Glob Leg Stud 15(1):19–47
Mutua MW (1996) The ideology of human rights. Va J Int Law 36:589–657
Narula S (2006) The right to food: holding global actors accountable under international law. Columbia J Transnational Law 44:691–800

Narula S (2010) Reclaiming the right to food as a normative response to the global food crisis. Yale Hum Rights Dev Law J 13(2):403–420

Nickel J (2008) Rethinking indivisibility: towards a theory of supporting relations between human rights. Hum Rights Q 30:984–1001

Nolan J (2005) With power comes responsibility: human rights and corporate responsibilities. Univ NSW Law J 28(3):581–613

Oliver D, Fedtke J (2007) Human rights and private sphere. In: Oliver D, Fedtke J (eds) Human rights and the private sphere. Routledge, London

Perry MJ (1997) Are human rights universal? The relativist challenge and related matters. Hum Rights Q 19:461–509

Peters A (2006) Privatisierung, Globalisierung und die Resistenz des Verfassungsstaates. Archiv für Rechts- und Sozialphilosophie Beiheft 105:100–159

Peters A, Förster T, Köchlin L (2009) Towards non-state actors as effective, legitimate, and accountable standard setters. In: Köchlin T, Förster T, Zinkernagel GF, Peters A (eds) Non-state actors as standard setters. Cambridge University Press, Cambridge, pp 492–563

Ratner SR (2001) Corporations and human rights: a theory of legal responsibility. Yale Law J 111:443–545

Reinisch A (2005) The changing international legal framework for dealing with non-state actors. In: Alston P (ed) Non-state actors and human rights. Oxford University Press, Oxford, pp 37–89

Renner M (2010) Zwingendes Transnationales Recht. Nomos Verlag, Baden-Baden

Ruggie JG (2007) Business and human rights: the evolving international agenda. Am J Int Law 101:819–840

Scherer AG, Palazzo G (2011) The new political role of business in a globalized world: a review of a new perspective on CSR and its implications for the firm, governance, and democracy. J Manag Stud 48(4):899–931

Shestack JJ (1998) The philosophic foundation of human rights. Hum Rights Q 20(2):201–234

Shue H (1988) Mediating duties. Ethics 98(4):687–704

Shue H (1996) Basic rights, 2nd edn. Princeton University Press, Princeton

Simons PC (2012) International law's invisible hand and the future of corporate accountability for violations of human rights. J Hum Rights Environ 3:5–43

Steinhardt RG, D'Amato AA (eds) (1999) The Alien Tort Claims Act: an analytical anthology. Transnational, New York

Teubner G (1996) Globale Bukowina. Zur Emergenz eines transnationalen Rechtspluralismus. Rechtshistorisches J 15:255–290

Teubner G (2003) Globale Zivilverfassung: Alternativen zu staatszentrierten Verfassungstheorie. Zeitschrift für ausländisches öffentliches Recht und Völkerrecht 63:1–28

Teubner G (2005) Codes of conduct multinationaler Unternehmen: Unternehmensverfassung jenseits von Corporate Governance und gesetzlicher Mitbestimmung. In: Höland A et al (eds) Arbeitnehmermitwirkung in einer sich globalisierenden Arbeitswelt. Berliner Wissenschafts-Verlag, Berlin, pp 109–117

Teubner G (2006) The anonymous matrix: human rights violations by "private" transnational actors. Mod Law Review 69:327–346

Teubner G (2011a) Self constitutionalizing TNCs? on the linkage of "private" and "public" corporate codes of conduct. Indiana J Glob Leg Stud 18(2):617–638

Teubner G (2011b) Transnational fundamental rights: horizontal effect? Rechtsfilosofie & Rechtstheorie 40:191–215

Teubner G (2012) Verfassungsfragmente. Suhrkamp Verlag, Frankfurt am Main

Thornhill C (2008) Towards a historical sociology of constitutional legitimacy. Theory Soc 37:161–197

Thornhill C (2010) Re-conceiving rights revolutions: the persistence of a sociological deficit in theories of rights. Zeitschrift für Rechtssoziologie 31(2):177–207

Thornhill C (2011a) A sociology of constitutions. Cambridge University Press, Cambridge

Thornhill C (2011b) The future of the state. In: Kjaer P, Teuber G, Febbrajo A (eds) The financial crisis in constitutional perspective: the dark side of functional differentiation. Hart, Oxford, pp 357–393

Tietje C (2003) Recht ohne Rechtsquellen? Zeitschrift für Rechtssoziologie 24(1):27–42

Tushnet M (2003) The issue of state action/horizontal effect in comparative constitutional law. Int J Constitut Law 1(1):79–98

Uitz R (2005) Yet another revival of horizontal effect of constitutional rights: why? and why now? In: Sajó A, Uitz R (eds) The constitution in private relations. Eleven International Publishing, Utrecht, pp 1–20

Verschraegen G (2006) Systems theory and the paradox of human rights. In: King M, Thornhill C (eds) Luhmann on law and politics. Hart, Oxford, pp 101–126

Weissbrodt D, Kruger M (2003) Norms on the responsibilities of transnational corporations and other business enterprises with regard to human rights. Am J Int Law 97:901–922

Weschka M (2006) Human rights and multinational enterprises. Zeitschrift für ausländisches öffentliches Recht und Völkerrecht 66:625–661

Westaway J (2012) Globalization, transnational corporations and human rights – a new paradigm. Int Law Res 1(1):63–72

Young AL (2007) Horizontally and the Human Rights Act 1998. In: Ziegler K (ed) Human rights and private law. Hart, Oxford, pp 35–51

Zumbansen P (2012) Defining the space of transnational law. Transnational Law Contemp Prob 21 (2):305–336

Human Rights and International Economic Law

Sarah Joseph

Contents

Abstract Ostensibly, international human rights law and international economic law (incorporating international trade law and international investment law) seek to achieve similar outcomes, namely the protection of certain rights so as to promote human flourishing. However, compatibility between international economic law and human rights law cannot be presumed. While restrictions on, for example, protectionism can undoubtedly have positive human rights effects, there are significant areas of divergence. For example, international trade law is widely acknowledged as being biased against poorer countries, and swift trade liberalisation may in fact undermine a State's ability to implement its obligations regarding economic social and cultural rights. Direct conflicts between the regimes may arise with regard to the implementation of the agreement on Trade Related Aspects of Intellectual Property Rights (TRIPS). A number of arbitrations under bilateral

S. Joseph (✉)
Faculty of Law, Monash University, Melbourne, VIC 3800, Australia
e-mail: sarah.joseph@monash.edu

M. Bungenberg et al. (eds.), *European Yearbook of International Economic Law 2016*, European Yearbook of International Economic Law 7,
DOI 10.1007/978-3-319-29215-1_18

investment treaties have posed possible threats to a State's capacity to fulfil human rights. Finally, a chilling impact on human rights implementation may arise from the loss of policy space which flows from international economic law. Ultimately, international economic law focuses on the rights of a privileged few, namely foreign traders and investors, which may lead to the inevitable prioritisation of their rights when they clash with or otherwise detract from the human rights of others. Such a prioritisation is unfortunate if it adds to the capacity for powerful entities to override the interests of the powerless and marginalised.

1 Introduction

International human rights law emerged around the same time as modern international economic law, out of the ruins of the Second World War.[1] The Bretton Woods conference focused on building the architecture of global economic cooperation and security, while the newly formed United Nations (UN) recognised that human rights were a matter of legitimate international focus and regulation in the wake of the shocking crimes of World War II. The original General Agreement on Tariffs and Trade (GATT) was adopted in 1947, while the Universal Declaration of Human Rights (UDHR) was adopted in 1948.

Most globally recognised human rights are listed in the International Bill of Rights, comprising the UDHR and the two treaties which enshrine its norms, the International Covenant on Civil and Political Rights 1966 (ICCPR) and the International Covenant on Economic Social and Cultural Rights 1966 (ICESCR). These rights are complemented by seven other core UN human rights treaties, which focus on particular types of human rights victims (eg children, migrant workers, people with disabilities) or particular types of human rights abuses (eg discrimination on the basis of race or sex, torture, disappearances). Human rights are also protected under regional treaties, as well as customary international law.

For ease of analysis, the International Bill of Rights, particularly the two Covenants, will be the focus of 'human rights' for the purposes of this paper. Below I address the extent to which international economic law is compatible with those human rights. The commentary will largely focus on international trade law, as represented by World Trade Organization (WTO) law, with the final part of the paper focusing on potential conflicts between human rights law and international investment law.

[1] Much of the following commentary is adapted from Joseph (2011) and Joseph (2013), pp. 841–870.

2 International Human Rights Law: Some Basics

The ICCPR protects civil and political rights.[2] It has 168 States parties as at June 2015. Civil and political rights can be categorised as encompassing rights of (1) physical and spiritual integrity and autonomy; (2) rights of fair treatment; and (3) rights to participate meaningfully in the political process.[3] Category 1 includes the rights to life and freedom from torture and other ill treatment, freedom of movement and the right to privacy. Spiritual autonomy is ensured by rights such as the freedoms of expression, religion, belief and thought. Category 2 encompasses fairness in a narrow procedural sense, such as the right to a fair trial, and in a broader sense, such as a general right of equal protection of the law and freedom from non-discrimination. Category 3 obviously encompasses the right to vote and to stand for election, and also includes rights which are essential for a healthy political process, such as the freedoms of assembly and association. The three categories overlap considerably. The ICCPR has a strong obligation provision in Article 2(1), whereby States parties are required to immediately guarantee all of the rights therein to all within jurisdiction.

The ICESCR protects economic social and cultural (ESC) rights, and has 164 States parties as at June 2015. Economic rights are rights related to labour and employment, contained in Articles 6–8 of the ICESCR,[4] as well as the accrued benefits of labourers and social safety nets for those who cannot work in Article 9 (the right to social security). Social rights are those needed to function adequately in society such as the right to family life (Article 10), the right to an adequate standard of living (Article 11), the right to health (Article 12) and the right to education (Articles 13 and 14). Article 15 covers cultural rights, including the right to participate in the cultural life of society and to benefit from scientific progress. The distinction between the three categories is not watertight, and indeed is often ignored.[5] The ICESCR has a weaker obligation provision than the ICCPR: its Article 2(1) requires the progressive implementation of the rights therein, and is qualified by the resources available to a State.

States have duties to respect, protect, and fulfil all human rights. The duty to *respect* is a duty to refrain from activities that harm human rights. The duty to *protect* is the duty to take reasonable measures to protect people from harm to their human rights by other entities, such as individuals or corporations. States are required to regulate private entities in order to ensure, as far as is reasonably possible, that they do not harm the human rights of others. For example, the regulation of health and safety standards helps to ensure that workers' rights are not infringed by their employers. The duty to *fulfil* includes the duty to take the

---

[2] The following commentary is adapted from Joseph (2010), pp. 89–90.

[3] See also Davidson (2004), p. 2.

[4] Articles 6–8 cover, respectively, the rights to work, to just and favourable conditions of work, and to join trade unions.

[5] Alston and Goodman (2013), p. 286.

measures necessary to ensure that individuals enjoy their human rights. Examples of implementation of this obligation would be the provision of subsidies to ensure access by the poor to essential goods and services such as water, health care and education.

It has been argued in a number of philosophical and political circles that ESC rights are not 'real' human rights,[6] or that they lack sufficient content to be useful in an international economic context.[7] Such an argument ignores the fact that three quarters of the world's nations have committed to international legal obligations under the ICESCR, and that such rights are enforceable in numerous domestic courts.[8] The adoption of an Optional Protocol to the ICESCR in 2008, which allows for individual complaints of ICESCR violations at the international level, puts to bed the contention that such rights are non-justiciable.[9] Such arguments are essentially ideological, or reflect a lack of understanding of international human rights law.[10]

The Achilles heel of the international human rights system lies in its enforcement, or lack thereof. No global body, apart from the UN Security Council and the International Court of Justice, is empowered to make legally binding decisions on human rights.[11] The Security Council and ICJ rarely deal with human rights matters, though the number of human rights cases before the ICJ has increased in recent years. Enforcement against recalcitrant States takes place largely by the process of naming and shaming. While shame can prompt behavioural change by a State, it is clearly a weak enforcement measure compared to the economic consequences that ensue from non-compliance with the rulings of dispute resolution bodies in the WTO,[12] or from ignoring the decision of an investment tribunal. The record of compliance with the rulings of UN human rights bodies pales in comparison to the record of compliance by WTO members with the WTO dispute settlement bodies.

The discrepancy in the strength of the enforcement regimes means that a *de facto* hierarchy can develop, with trade and investment rules prevailing over human rights rules, due to the stronger enforcement system under the WTO and bilateral investment treaties (BITs) compared to the global human rights system.[13] The disproportionate strength of the trade and investment regimes compared to the

[6] Harrison (2007), p. 26 (noting but not agreeing with the argument). See, eg, Human Rights Survey, The Economist (5 December 1998), p. 9, suggesting that economic social and cultural rights are issues that "should be left to politics and the market".

[7] See, eg., Marceau (2002), pp. 786–789; Alvarez (2001), p. 10.

[8] See Langford (2008), pp. 3–4.

[9] The Optional Protocol came into force on 5 May 2013, after its tenth ratification. At the time of writing, it had 19 States parties.

[10] Howse and Teitel (2009), p. 40.

[11] Regional human rights courts are stronger, as they are empowered to make legally binding decisions.

[12] See Alston (2012), p. 833; Vázquez (2003), p. 803–804.

[13] Salomon (2007), p. 155.

human rights regime can lead to prioritisation of the former norms if they conflict with human rights norms, or regulatory chill as States may fail to adopt measures to protect human rights because they fear that such measures might breach trade and investment law.[14]

3 International Trade Law and ESC Rights

3.1 Congruence

Freer trade across borders is said to increase net wealth in the world. The economic advantages of liberalised trade regimes are supported by David Ricardo's nineteenth century theory of comparative advantage. Ultimately, the theory holds that global free trade will generate greater global wealth, a goal that is congruent with human rights law, given that it should increase the capacity of States to protect ESC rights.

Free trade can facilitate people's access to important products and services which facilitate their enjoyment of ESC rights. For example, in 2002 Oxfam International noted that some African countries imposed a very high tariff on mosquito nets, surely a measure that cost lives by increasing the exposure of the poor to malaria, in probable breach of the right to health.[15]

There is little doubt that trade obstacles can harm overall welfare and also specific human rights. For example, the World Bank reported that US and European cotton subsidies depressed world cotton prices by 71 % in 2001-2 with devastating effects for the incomes of cotton growers in Africa and central Asia,[16] and therefore their rights to work and to a livelihood.[17] The potential generation of human rights harms by protectionist measures indicates that, in principle, some

[14] The issue of the actual hierarchy in law between the two sets of norms is beyond the scope of this paper. See Joseph (2011), pp. 46–50.

[15] Oxfam International (2002) Rigged Rules and Double Standards, p. 62.

[16] World Bank (2006) World Development Report 2006, p. 212.

[17] See, eg, WTO, Poverty reduction: sectoral initiative in favour of cotton, WTO Committee on Agriculture, WTO doc. TN/AG/Gen.4 (16 May 2003). For an update, see Lazzeri T, Western Cotton Subsidies Endanger African Farmers, Africa Europe Faith and Justice Network, http://www.aefjn.org/index.php/352/articles/western-cotton-subsidies-endanger-african-farmers.html (last accessed 16 March 2015). There are strong arguments that a State, such as the US, owes human rights obligations to people in other countries, such as cotton growers in Africa, in certain circumstances. See Maastricht Principles on Extraterritorial Obligations in the area of Economic, Social and Cultural Rights, a set of principles adopted by international experts in 2010, http://www.etoconsortium.org/nc/en/library/maastricht-principles/?tx_drblob_pi1%5BdownloadUid%5D=23 (last accessed 26 March 2015).

limitation on the regulatory power of the State to restrict free trade is welcome from a human rights point of view.[18]

3.2 Bias Against the Poor

WTO rules favour the interests of developed States over poorer developing States, a systemic bias conceded by the immediate past WTO Director General Pascal Lamy in 2006.[19] Cambridge University economist Ha-Joon Chang agrees, stating that WTO trading rules "favour free trade in areas where the rich countries are stronger but not where they are weak".[20]

Such a state of affairs is hardly surprising if one considers the economic and political power equations in existence at the time the WTO treaties were negotiated and concluded in the 1980s and early 1990s. Imbalances of power have continued during negotiations for further liberalisation in the Doha round. Certainly, emerging economies such as China, India and Brazil, have asserted themselves in current negotiations, which is one reason why they have stalled. Meanwhile, the current biased rules prevail.

With current rules tilted against poorer States, the WTO is not achieving optimal outcomes in alleviating poverty, and therefore in promoting the capacity of States to fulfil ESC rights. At worst, unbalanced WTO rules hamper development and exacerbate poverty in the poorest states, thereby prejudicing the realization of ESC rights. In this respect, the economists Joseph Stiglitz and Andrew Charlton reported in 2005 that, by some estimates, 48 of the least developed countries had suffered economic losses of close to US $600 million per year since they began implementing WTO agreements.[21]

The bias in WTO rules against developing nations is demonstrated by the WTO's Agreement on Agriculture (AoA). Many developing States have a comparative advantage in agricultural products, but the AoA allows significant protectionism to their detriment. For example, the AoA does not combat 'tariff escalation', that is the escalation of tariffs imposed on processed agricultural goods compared to raw goods. Such tariff schemes, commonly imposed by developed States, stunt the growth of more sophisticated and lucrative agricultural industries in source countries.[22] Other egregious examples of agricultural protectionism include Europe's

[18] Joseph (2011), p. 119.

[19] Lamy P, It's Time for a new "Geneva Consensus" on making trade work for development, Emile Noel Lecture New York University Law School, New York, 30 October 2006, https://www.wto.org/english/news_e/sppl_e/sppl45_e.htm (last accessed 15 March 2015).

[20] Chang (2008), p. 13.

[21] Stiglitz and Charlton (2005), p. 47.

[22] See Oxfam International (2002) Rigged Rules and Double Standards, pp. 102–103.

sugar markets[23] and US cotton markets (as mentioned above). It is unsurprising that some of the most prominent demands of developing States in the current round of WTO negotiations are for further agricultural liberalisation.

3.3 Does Free Trade Alleviate Poverty?

A more fundamental issue is whether trade liberalisation generally assists States in alleviating poverty and promoting and protecting ESC rights.[24] Over time, the strategy may well be beneficial, but swift liberalisation as pushed in bilateral and regional treaties, and in the Doha round, may not be favourable for ESC rights. For example, the loss of tariff revenue creates a significant hole in the budgets of developing States which is difficult to replace, because tariffs are relatively simple to administer compared to internal taxes.[25]

Premature trade liberalisation may trap a developing State in primary production and low cost unskilled manufacturing, where it has a current comparative advantage, but which is disadvantageous in the long term. Ha-Joon Chang argues that liberalisation is "absolutely right" for States that are willing to accept their "current levels of technology as given", but it is not appropriate where States wish to "acquire more advanced technologies" and develop their economies.[26] A gradual sequenced approach to liberalisation in developing States, incorporating the development of appropriate institutional capacities and dynamic niche industries, is preferable to the reduced policy space entailed in rapid and potentially premature liberalisation.[27] Therefore, it is possible that liberalised trade can hinder the capacity of States to abide by their obligations to progressively guarantee ESC rights.

3.3.1 The Rights of the Losers from Free Trade

Fundamentally, WTO rules compel States to liberalize their trade regimes. Trade liberalization undoubtedly creates winners and losers, with the latter being those in uncompetitive industries. Those "losers" do not inevitably find new jobs, especially in the developing world where there is already an oversupply of labour,[28] and therefore suffer detrimental social consequences and loss of enjoyment of ESC

[23] Vandenhole (2007), p. 73.

[24] Joseph (2011), pp. 164–169.

[25] The International Monetary Fund has estimated that, between 1980 and 2005, less than 30 % of lost tariff revenue was recovered by developing States through other means: Baunsgaard and Keen, Trade Revenue and (or?) Trade Liberalisation, IMF Working Paper No. 05/112 (2005).

[26] Chang (2008), p. 47.

[27] See Rodrik (2007), p. 1.

[28] Stiglitz and Charlton (2005), p. 6, 26 and 194.

rights. WTO rules do not demand that States take measures to compensate the losers, nor do they require States to ensure that the gains from free trade are equitably distributed. Those matters are left to the discretion of Member States. Therefore, the WTO mandates that States adopt policies that harm certain people, yet it does nothing to ensure recompense for those harmed. In contrast, the treatment of losers from trade liberalization is crucial from a human rights point of view. This does not mean that there can be no losers. Rather, it means that appropriate measures must be taken to alleviate the detrimental human impact of free trade reforms. Unfortunately, developing States often lack the capacity to do so.

Why are obligations regarding the dismantling of free trade obstacles felt to be worthy of explicit internationalisation within the free trade agenda, while measures regarding redistribution and other social welfare issues associated with trade, such as labour protections and fair distribution of the gains of trade, are omitted? As noted by Andrew Lang, 'what we currently think of as "trade issues" and "trade values" are not predetermined but are in part a matter of choice'.[29] The exclusion of the 'welfare' side of the 'embedded liberal' free trade bargain from the WTO[30] is a political choice, rather than an incontestable given.

The problem is exacerbated by the adoption of prevailing WTO rules in an era where neo-liberal economic theories have predominated. Neo-liberalism has also influenced the contemporaneous policies of other key international economic bodies such as the International Monetary Fund and the World Bank,[31] and the philosophy underlies international investment law. Neoliberalism upholds the invisible hand of the market as the appropriate guiding force for economies with minimal state intervention. Given that redistribution and compensation for "the losers from trade" normally requires State intervention, neoliberalism does not ideologically support such measures.

Neoliberal thinking dictates that the market should be cordoned off from politics and be left to its own devices. "[D]emocracy is acceptable to neo-liberals only in so far as it does not contradict the free market".[32] However, such a demarcation of economics and politics *is* a political position: state abstention has consequences just like state intervention.[33] If the market is left unregulated by public power, market forces may be distorted by imbalances of private power. The "market" does not form a neutral baseline. Rather, non-intervention "assumes that the existing distribution of wealth and entitlements is legitimate".[34] As colourfully stated by Frank

[29] Lang (2007), p. 545.

[30] Ruggie (1982), pp. 393–398, famously suggested the pre-WTO GATT regime was based on a premise of 'embedded liberalism', whereby GATT members agreed to reduce protectionist measures, whilst simultaneously promulgating domestic welfare policies to provide safety nets for the losers from liberalised trade.

[31] See, eg., Gathii (2001), pp. 152–153; Stiglitz (2010), p. 220.

[32] Chang (2008), pp. 176.

[33] Gathii (2001), pp. 168–169.

[34] Gathii (2001), pp. 167–168.

Garcia, the "efficiency model" promoted by the WTO and most economists needs to be "flushed ... out of its assumed neutrality and into the mud pit of normative brawling, where it belongs".[35]

3.3.2 Case Study: The Right to Food

The right to food is recognised in Article 11 of the ICESCR. Article 11(1) generally guarantees the right to an adequate standard of living for a person and his/her family, including "adequate food". In General Comment 12, the Committee on Economic Social and Cultural Rights confirmed that the right to food entails, for all, "physical and economic access at all times to adequate food or means for its procurement".[36]

Major concerns exist about the impact of liberalised trade on the enjoyment of the right to food. Trade literature emphasises that free markets will divert to those who sell for less, but markets also divert to those willing to pay more.[37] For example, more of the finite amounts of arable land are being used to cultivate and feed livestock for meat to satisfy the more expensive tastes of a growing middle class in Asia instead of growing staple foods for the poor and the hungry.[38] Similarly, biofuel production has diverted many crops which traditionally feed the poor[39] into products which are used by the rich to drive their cars.[40]

International agricultural markets suffer from a number of flaws that can exacerbate hunger and prejudice enjoyment of the right to food, given that 50 % of the world's hungry are in fact small agricultural producers.[41] Agricultural commodities markets have generally delivered poor and erratic returns to producers over the last 3 decades.[42] A number of factors cause these markets to defy the orthodox

[35] Garcia (2003), pp. 17.

[36] Committee on Economic, Social and Cultural Rights, General Comment 12: The right to adequate food (Art. 11), UN doc. E/C.12/1999/5 (12 May 1999), para 6.

[37] De Schutter O (2009) International Trade in Agriculture and the Right to Food, Dialogue on Globalization Occasional Paper No. 46, pp. 10–11.

[38] Murphy, Concentrated Market Power and Agricultural Trade, Ecofair Trade Dialogue Discussion Paper No. 1 (English Version), August 2006, p. 27.

[39] Human Rights Council, Report of the Special Rapporteur on the right to food, De Schutter, Building resilience: a human rights framework for world food and nutrition security, UN doc. A/HRC/9/23 (8 September 2008), para 28.

[40] Commission on Human Rights, Report of the Special Rapporteur on the right to food, Ziegler, UN doc. E/CN.4/2005/47 (24 January 2005), para 23; Annex 2, para 10.

[41] UN Millennium Project, Halving Hunger: It can be done, summary of the report of the task force on hunger, The Earth Institute, Columbia University, 2005, pp. 4–6, available at: http://www.unmillenniumproject.org/documents/HTF-SumVers_FINAL.pdf (last accessed 16 March 2015).

[42] UNGA, Report of the Special Rapporteur on the Right to Food, De Schutter, UN doc. A/63/278 (21 October 2008), para 18.

economic theories regarding supply and demand.[43] It is difficult to tailor supply to demand due to the vagaries of climatic conditions, and the fact that land cannot be easily moved 'in and out of production'[44] to suit market conditions. Low prices mean that many farmers cannot make a decent living. Price hikes are too unpredictable for those farmers to take advantage of, and they also suffer as consumers with sudden rises in food prices.

Global agricultural trade is dominated by large-scale single-crop farms owned by multinational agribusiness companies.[45] Indeed, many commodities markets are dominated by only a few agribusiness multinationals.[46] To some extent, the growth of global supply chains benefits smaller farmers by connecting them to global markets.[47] However, cartelisation within these supply chains has created severe power imbalances between producers and buyers, allowing the latter to exercise effective monopsony power to drive down prices paid to producers.[48] Yet measures to combat private monopolies are 'conspicuously absent' from the WTO.[49]

The dominant agribusiness corporations are 'more likely to be concerned with profitable trade than with local-level food security'.[50] Export orientation in agriculture has prompted switches from subsistence products to non-food cash crops, such as coffee, cocoa and tobacco.[51] The diversion of resources from food can weaken local food security and transform a country into a net food importing country, with all of the vulnerabilities associated with that status.

The above problems conspire to leave vast numbers of small farmers extremely vulnerable in the world economy. Economists might advise many of them to move into more efficient industry sectors. But modern mechanised agribusiness cannot employ them all and their skills are not easily adaptable to non-agricultural or urban industries. Furthermore, the ability of the many poor rural women to simply "move" to new areas and jobs is seriously hindered by cultural barriers. Further, extensive reduction in smallholders will only exacerbate some of the problems regarding the

---

[43] Human Rights Council, Report of the Special Rapporteur on the right to food, De Schutter: Mission to the World Trade Organization, UN doc. A/HRC/10/5/Add.2 (25 June 2008), para 21; Wolf (2005), p. 206.

[44] Murphy (2005), p. 3.

[45] Breining-Kaufman (2005), p. 368.

[46] World Bank (2008) World Development Report 2008: Agriculture for Development, pp. 135–136.

[47] De Schutter O (2009), International Trade in Agriculture and the Right to Food, Dialogue on Globalization Occasional Paper No. 46, p. 30.

[48] United Nations Development Programme (UNDP) (2005) Human Development Report 2005: International Cooperation at a Crossroads: Aid, Trade and Security in an Unequal World, pp. 142–143.

[49] United Nations Development Programme (2005) Human Development Report 2005: International Cooperation at a Crossroads: Aid, Trade and Security in an Unequal World, p. 139.

[50] Dommen (2002), p. 34.

[51] United Nations Human Settlements Programme (2006) Global Report on Human Settlements 2006: The Challenge of Slums, p. 41.

lack of competition in markets and overemphasis on cash crops. Finally, the assertion that smallholders should give up their land and independence arguably treats them as economic units rather than as human beings with human rights.

Agricultural activities are commercial activities, but they are also truly multifunctional, serving purposes beyond the production of commodities. They promote human welfare, traditional cultural practices, and the provision of environmental and ecological services.[52] While the AoA acknowledges 'non-trade' concerns in some of its provisions, such as food security and environmental protection, overall it "clearly fits into a programme of trade liberalization in agricultural products".[53] In contrast, many experts, including from economic fields, argue that new agricultural management systems must be devised so as to serve these multifunctional purposes.[54]

4 Trade Law and Civil and Political Rights

Free trade and investment can facilitate the introduction of products and services that boost civil and political rights. For example, the use of social media, involving access to the internet and social media sites (services), mobile phones, and computers (products) in the Arab Spring facilitated the overthrow of long-standing dictatorships in Tunisia and Egypt in early 2011.[55] Having said that, the souring of that revolution in Egypt gives us pause to wonder whether it was premature, with technology perhaps driving the revolution forward before its proponents were properly organised for the aftermath.[56] These days social media is proving to be an effective recruitment tool for the barbaric Islamic State group. Technology is of course neither 'good' nor 'bad'—it depends on the context in which it is used. After all, surveillance technology, to assist in the identification and suppression of dissidents, can also be traded across borders.[57]

[52] International Assessment of Agricultural Knowledge (2009) Science and Technology for Development, Agriculture at the Crossroads, 2009, Executive Summary, p. 6; World Bank (2008) World Development Report 2008: Agriculture for Development, p. 2.

[53] Human Rights Council, Report of the Special Rapporteur on the right to food, De Schutter: Mission to the World Trade Organization, UN doc. A/HRC/10/5/Add.2 (25 June 2008), para 14.

[54] International Assessment of Agricultural Knowledge (2009), Science and Technology for Development, Agriculture at the Crossroads, p. 50.

[55] See Dubai School of Government (2011) Civil Movements: The Impact of Facebook and Twitter Arab Social Media Report vol. 1, no. 2; Howard PN, Duffy A, Freelon D, Hussain MM, Mari W, Mazaid M (2011) Opening Closed Regimes: What Was the Role of Social Media during the Arab Spring?, Working Paper 2011.1, http://pitpi.org/wp-content/uploads/2013/02/2011_Howard-Duffy-Freelon-Hussain-Mari-Mazaid_pITPI.pdf (last accessed 7 March 2015).

[56] Morozov (2011), p. 196.

[57] Joseph (2012a), p. 168.

Could trade rules directly assist in the protection and fulfilment of civil and political rights? In this regard it is intriguing to speculate on whether China's infamous internet censorship rules breach its WTO obligations. China censors internet access via the "Great Firewall", which blocks or slows foreign internet sites. The level of censorship imposed by China breaches the human right to freedom of expression.[58] The firewall apparently "degrades the performance of websites based outside the country",[59] so an argument may be made that it impairs foreign competition via the internet in China's huge market. Indeed, Google rapidly lost market share in China after moving its operations outside the firewall, temporarily, early in 2010.[60]

WTO law could therefore prove to be an ally of those who seek greater internet freedom in China. We will not find out unless a State instigates a relevant complaint. The key issue, however, in any resultant dispute would not be human rights, but the scope of China's WTO obligations and the extent of impairment to foreign trade.[61]

More generally, Pascal Lamy has stated that global trade rules are "a rampart against totalitarianism".[62] Indeed, it is commonly argued that economic openness promotes political openness in the following ways. Economic openness promotes economic growth, which helps to create new economic elites, who can challenge the authority of dictatorial government power, creating further space for civil society. It leads to the creation of a middle class, which is more educated and which eventually demands greater political and social freedom.[63]

These theories are backed up by evidence: democracy and civil and political freedoms tend to flourish more in richer developed States, which generally have more liberal trade and investment regimes, than in poorer developing countries, which generally have more restrictive regimes.[64]

---

[58] Freedom of expression is recognised in Article 19 of the UDHR and Article 19 of the ICCPR. While China is not a party to any treaty that guarantees freedom of expression, it is arguable that the right is protected under customary international law. In any case, greater enjoyment of freedom of expression in China would boost the enjoyment of an internationally recognized right in that country, regardless of China's strict human rights obligations.

[59] Scheer, Obama should back Google with more than rhetoric: the US should challenge China's "firewall" before the WTO, The Huffington Post, 25 May 2011, http://www.huffingtonpost.com/peter-scheer/obama-should-back-up-goog_b_425724.html (last accessed 15 March 2015).

[60] See, eg, Google losing market share in China, The Boston Globe, 23 April 2010.

[61] See, generally, Wu T, The World Trade Law of Censorship and Internet Filtering, 3 May 2006, http://papers.ssrn.com/sol3/papers.cfm?abstract_id=882459 (last accessed 15 March 2015), p 10.

[62] Lamy P, Towards Shared Responsibility and Greater Coherence: Human Rights, Trade and Macroeconomic Policy, Speech at the Colloquium on Human Rights in the Global Economy, Co-organized by the International Council on Human Rights and Realizing Rights, Geneva, 13 January 2010, http://www.wto.org/english/news_e/sppl_e/sppl146_e.htm (last accessed 15 March 2015).

[63] See Garcia (1999), p. 59; Bhagwati (2002), pp. 43–44.

[64] See Griswold D, Trading Tyranny for Freedom: How Open Markets till the soil for Democracy, Cato Institute, 6 January 2004, http://www.cato.org/publications/trade-policy-analysis/trading-tyranny-freedom-how-open-markets-till-soil-democracy (last accessed 16 March 2015).

However, the above arguments are contestable. Singapore has long had an open economy, yet has only slowly increased its observance of civil and political freedoms. Similarly, economic reforms in China have not been matched by significant improvements in civil and political rights.[65] And, as noted above, some developing States have experienced poor economic performance rather than growth in eliminating trade barriers.

Furthermore, the spread of marketisation across the world has accompanied greater global inequality.[66] Trade and investment policies do not mandate any form of domestic wealth distribution. The benefits of economic growth might flow only to a small elite. When gaps between elites and the poor grow, there is a more pronounced divergence in their interests, leading to the possible generation of rules and institutions which favour the latter over the former.[67] Greater inequality may therefore lead to greater marginalisation and intolerance of the poor.

Harvard Professor Amy Chua has questioned the assumption that the twin trajectories of free trade and democracy in the developed world will recur in the developing world. First, she notes that the development of democracy and free trade regimes in industrialised States was slow; universal suffrage and economic liberalisation evolved over centuries.

In contrast, comparable economic transitions in developing States have been remarkably swift, and have not allowed time for the development of economic safety nets, or the development of aspirational pro-market ideologies amongst a population.[68] In such circumstances, the impoverished majority may be very hostile to the inequalities created by free markets, at least until a substantial middle class emerges, so democratisation and marketisation may pull in different directions for a time. In order to stave off internal hostility in such situations, States must ensure that domestic inequality is contained and that appropriate redistributive measures are in place,[69] again indicating that the process should be managed and properly sequenced.

5 Chilling Impact

A systemic issue which arises with regard to the interaction of human rights law and trade law is the extent to which the latter rules may have a 'chilling effect' on the will of States to implement their human rights obligations. In respect to the right to health, for example, a State may wish to ban or prevent the importation of toxic products which harm consumer health.

---

[65] Gervais (2009), p. 393.

[66] See statistics cited in Joseph (2011), pp. 166–167.

[67] Pogge (2008).

[68] See generally Chua (2000), p. 287.

[69] Wolf (2005), p. 29.

WTO obligations have a very broad scope. Free trade rules have traditionally targeted protectionism, that is measures that discriminate in favour of local products against foreign products. Other WTO obligations suggest a more broad-based "freedom to trade" divorced from notions of discrimination, which imposes greater restrictions on the regulatory capacities of a State.[70] This shrinkage of policy space could limit the ability of a State to regulate in respect to essential services and utilities, thereby failing to meet such core human rights obligations as the provision of safe drinking water and sanitation.[71]

WTO agreements do contain exceptions which might facilitate reconciliation with human rights law in the case of conflict. In particular, Article XX of the GATT and the similar Article XIV of the General Agreement on Trade in Services allow a State to adopt measures necessary to protect morals and public health. For example, the recent *Seals* dispute confirmed that measures to protect 'public morals' (under Article XX(a) of the GATT) can include measures to promote animal welfare so as to satisfy the moral tastes of the local population.[72] One could extrapolate that certain human rights measures, such as a ban on the products built by child labourers, could be enacted in a similar manner.

However, the exceptions to WTO regimes have been interpreted with very high degrees of scrutiny, to the point that a State may still hesitate to rely on them in regulating imports to support human rights. Indeed, social measures have rarely survived WTO challenges intact (though there have not been many cases). Even the *Seals* legislation has to be amended in order to be fully WTO compliant.

6 Possible Direct Conflicts: TRIPS and Human Rights Law

Direct conflicts between a State's obligations under international human rights law and WTO law may most obviously arise under the Agreement on Trade Related Aspects of Intellectual Property Rights (TRIPS). Under TRIPS, WTO Members are required to protect intellectual property (IP) rights, such as copyright, patents and trademarks. The Least Developed Countries do not have to fully comply with TRIPS until 2021.

IP rights are justified by the rewards they deliver to creators, innovators, inventors and authors, and the consequent incentives they deliver to research and development. TRIPS mandates the erection of barriers to trade in the form of

[70] Driesen (2001), p. 279.

[71] See Lang (2001), p. 801.

[72] Appellate Body Report, European Communities—Measures Prohibiting the Importation and Marketing of Seal Products, WT/DS400/AB/R and WT/DS401/AB/R, 22 May 2014; See Howse R, Langille J, Sykes K, Sealing the Deal: the WTO's Appellate Body Report in EC-Seal Products. ASIL Insights, 4 June 2014, http://www.asil.org/insights/volume/18/issue/12/sealing-deal-wto%E2%80%99s-appellate-body-report-ec-%E2%80%93-seal-products (last accessed 15 March 2015).

temporary monopoly rights, so its inclusion within the WTO is anomalous. Indeed, the inclusion of TRIPS within the WTO exposes neoliberals to charges of hypocrisy, as TRIPS mandates considerable State intervention in the economy in one particular area, which happens to generate huge benefits for corporate interests.

However, IP protection is said to indirectly boost trade because foreign investment and technology transfer is promoted when investors are confident that their valuable IP rights will be respected in the host State.[73] IP protection should also promote local innovation within a State by protecting investments in research and development from pirates and copycats.[74]

Are IP rights human rights? Article 15(1)(c) of the ICESCR recognizes the right of everyone "to benefit from the protection of the moral and material interests resulting from any scientific, literary or artistic production of which he is the author". The UN Committee on Economic Social and Cultural Rights has distinguished Article 15(1)(c) rights from IP rights. The right in Article 15(1)(c) protects "the personal link between authors and their creations and between peoples, communities, or other groups and their collective cultural heritage, as well as their material interests which are necessary to enable authors to enjoy an adequate standard of living". In contrast, IP rights "primarily protect business and corporate interests and investments".[75] In that respect, the Committee underlined that Article 15(1)(c) rights vest only in human beings, rather than corporations.[76] Furthermore, the Committee anticipates that a variety of regimes, including but not limited to IP-like regimes, could suffice to satisfy Article 15(1)(c).[77] This is quite different to the 'one size fits all' regime in TRIPS.

The most prominent human rights concern regarding TRIPS has been its alleged negative impact on access to medicines for poor people, because compulsory patent protection for pharmaceutical products raises prices beyond their reach. In his 2009 Report to the UN Human Rights Council, the Special Rapporteur on the Right to Health, Anand Grover, wrote extensively on this issue. Grover's report implies that TRIPS obligations do not conflict with the right of access to medicines, though he still found that TRIPS has "had an adverse impact on prices and availability of

[73] See Singham (2001), pp. 375–385.

[74] However, it has been argued that this rationale for TRIPS effectively put "the policy cart before the empirical horse", Gervais (2009), p. 370.

[75] Committee on Economic, Social and Cultural Rights, General Comment No. 17: The right of everyone to benefit from the protection of the moral and material interests resulting from any scientific, literary or artistic production of which he or she is the author (Art. 15, para. 1(c)), UN doc. E/C.12/GC/17, 12 January 2006, para 2.

[76] Committee on Economic, Social and Cultural Rights, General Comment No. 17: The right of everyone to benefit from the protection of the moral and material interests resulting from any scientific, literary or artistic production of which he or she is the author (Art. 15, para. 1(c)), UN doc. E/C.12/GC/17, 12 January 2006, para 7.

[77] Committee on Economic, Social and Cultural Rights, General Comment No. 17: The right of everyone to benefit from the protection of the moral and material interests resulting from any scientific, literary or artistic production of which he or she is the author (Art. 15, para. 1(c)), UN doc. E/C.12/GC/17, 12 January 2006, paras 2, 16 and 47.

medicines".[78] He urged developing States to utilise all available TRIPS flexibilities, as needed, in order to ensure access to medicines domestically. Their common failure to do so, which is often prompted by economic and diplomatic pressure from richer States, international financial institutions, and corporations, amounted in Grover's view to a violation of the right to health in Article 12 of the ICESCR.

A burgeoning debate now relates to the compatibility between global copyright regimes and human rights law. For example, copyright laws obstruct access to educational materials by raising their price.[79] Obstacles to basic education are counterproductive to a State's aspirations for economic, institutional and social development.

In late 2014, the UN Special Rapporteur on Cultural Rights, Farida Shaheed, issued a report on copyright and the right to science and culture in Article 15 of the ICESCR.[80] While the report is largely designed to help ensure the injection of human rights concerns into ongoing discussions of global copyright regimes, it also draws attention to possible ways in which modern copyright regimes might undermine human rights. She suggests that overly strong copyright regimes can unduly limit "cultural freedom and participation" (para 27), and punitive approaches to the punishment of digital piracy (eg denial of Internet access) can breach "the right to freedom of expression and the right to science and culture" (para 51). Rather, copyright regimes should "ensure a vibrant public domain of shared cultural heritage, from which all creators are free to draw" (para 50). She also notes how copyright regimes have failed to protect and respond to "the unique concerns of Indigenous peoples" (para 56).

The TRIPS regime provides weaker IP protection, and therefore allows for more policy space, than the 'TRIPS-plus' regimes which are commonly adopted within regional or bilateral trade treaties. If a State bound by TRIPS plus commitments is a Member of the WTO, it may have to guarantee equivalent rights to traders from all other States in the WTO, due to the Most Favoured Nation principle.[81]

7 Investment Law and Human Rights

Bilateral investment treaties ('BITs') emerged in the post-war decolonisation period as a means of protecting foreign investors, largely from developed States, from expropriation by developing States.[82] By the 1980s and 1990s, BITs

[78] Human Rights Council, Report of the Special Rapporteur on the right of everyone to the enjoyment of the highest attainable standard of physical and mental health, Anand Grover, UN doc. A/HRC/11/12 (31 March 2009), para 94.

[79] See, generally, Chon (2007), p. 803; 3D, The Philippines: Impact of copyright rules on access to education, June 2009, http://www.crin.org/docs/3DCRC_PhilippinesJun09.pdf (last accessed 15 March 2015).

[80] UN doc. A/HRC/28/57, 24 December 2014.

[81] Abbott and Reichmann (2007), pp. 963–964.

[82] A good history of BITs is found in Vandevelde (1998), p. 621.

proliferated, including between developing States, as they came to be seen as a norm in governing international investment.[83] However, since the turn of the century, there has been a downturn in the number of new investment treaties.

BITs are said to promote foreign investment in a country,[84] which provides jobs, tax revenue, the transfer of technology and skills, foreign currency reserves, local business for subcontractors and local competition to the benefit of consumers. Increases in wealth provide further resources which should improve the capacity of States to progressively implement their ESC rights obligations. Furthermore, foreign investors may influence States positively by demanding adherence to the rule of law, as arbitrary decision-making intolerably threatens their investments.[85]

BITs act as 'bills of rights' for a State's investors when they operate in the territory of the other party. Examples of substantive rights in BITs include guarantees against direct and indirect expropriation, non-discrimination in comparison with local investors, and fair and equitable treatment. The web of investment treaties in existence does not follow a particular model, and therefore contains materially different substantive obligations.[86]

These substantive rights are often supplemented by significant procedural rights. Numerous BITs allow investors to bring their claims against governments directly to international arbitral tribunals, bypassing local judicial systems. These provisions reflect the post-war lack of trust in post-colonial judicial systems, which may still be warranted in the many States where the judiciary lacks real independence.

Arbitral tribunals are typically made up of three arbitrators with commercial expertise. Awards can entail the payment of considerable compensation and other ameliorating measures to an investor, often in the hundreds of millions of dollars.[87] States are legally obliged to abide by arbitral awards. Failure to comply will likely attract economic and political pressure from the bilateral party to the BIT, and will jeopardise a State's reputation with regard to foreign investors generally. Therefore, as with trade regimes, enforcement under some investment treaties is strong as significant economic consequences can flow from breach.

Rights under BITs are very broad and vague, and are often claimed by investors to protect them from regulatory changes which diminish likely future profits. This is problematic as many such regulatory changes are supportive of the fulfilment of human rights, such as environmental or health regulations, and price caps or cross-subsidies to facilitate the availability of essential utilities for the poor. Furthermore,

---

[83] See Jandhyala et al. (2011), p. 1047.

[84] However, the common assumption that BITs encourage foreign investment in a State may be challengeable: see Hallward-Driemeyer M (2003) Do Bilateral Investment Treaties Attract FDI? Only a bit. . .and they could bite, World Bank Policy Research Paper No. 3121.

[85] See, eg, World Bank (2002), World Development Report 2002: Building Institutions for Markets, http://www.worldbank.org/wdr/2001/fulltext/fulltext2002.htm (last accessed 20 September 2010).

[86] Karamanian (2012), p. 243.

[87] Kriebaum (2009), p. 244.

many BITs do not explicitly allow exceptions to permit regulations in areas of public interest.

This "chilling" problem is exacerbated by unpredictability within the investment arbitration regime. There is no overarching appellate system in the world of international investment arbitration.[88] This circumstance is problematic as decisions, for example on the meaning of "expropriation" or on the existence and scope of public interest regulation exceptions, are inconsistent.[89] Furthermore, the arbitral system suffers from a lack of transparency: proceedings are often held in secret.[90] As the pool of arbitrators is quite small, the potential for conflicts of interest arises as a person may be involved in one case as counsel, and in another as an arbitrator over similar legal issues.[91]

7.1 Investment Cases

Conflicts between a State's obligations under international human rights law and international investment law can arise when a claim by a foreign investor against a government prejudices the human rights of third parties.

For example, in *Glamis Gold v United States*, a Canadian company claimed that Californian mining regulations, which diminished the value of its mining investment, breached the US obligations to Canadian investors under the North American Free Trade Agreement. Those same regulations were argued to preserve the human rights of third parties, such as their minority rights under Article 27 of the ICCPR, to which the US is a party. The Quechuan Indian nation filed an amicus brief against the Glamis claim.[92] In the result, the arbitral tribunal found that it did not have to make any ruling on the human rights issues, as Glamis's claim failed for other reasons.[93]

In *Foresti et al v South Africa*, Italian mining companies challenged the South African Black Economic Empowerment Laws, which had been adopted to redress historic economic disadvantage for non-whites. The mining companies argued that the empowerment laws rendered their mining rights less valuable and amounted to expropriation as well as breaches of requirements of 'fair and equitable

---

[88] Arbitral awards may be reviewed on narrow grounds by courts in proceedings regarding enforcement of the award. See Fry (2007), pp. 118–119.

[89] Fry (2007), pp. 83–84.

[90] Fry (2007), pp. 115–117.

[91] Goldhaber (2013), pp. 407–408.

[92] See Application for Leave to File a Non-party Submission and Submission of the Quechan Indian Nation, http://www.state.gov/documents/organization/52531.pdf (last accessed 15 March 2015) p. 8. Amicus briefs may be submitted to tribunals though the tribunals do not have to accept them, or take them into consideration in making decisions.

[93] See Tribunal Award http://www.state.gov/documents/organization/125798.pdf (last accessed 15 May 2015) p. 22.

treatment'.[94] *Aguas del Tunari v Bolivia* concerned a claim by a consortium regarding the cancellation of a contract to run water utilities in the Bolivian city of Cochabamba. Critics claimed that access to water had been limited by the consortium's high prices, which led to civil unrest. The cancellation arguably enhanced the right of access to water in Cochabamba.[95]

Foresti and *Aguas del Tunari* were discontinued after significant civil society outrage. Perhaps the perceived bark of investment law is worse than its actual bite. However, the doctrine of precedent does not operate within international investment law, and similar-sounding obligations under different BITs may be relevantly different. Furthermore, the costs involved for a State in defending arbitral challenges are considerable. South Africa's aborted defence in the *Foresti* proceedings cost €5 million of which the claimants only paid €400,000.[96] Therefore, the chilling impact of investment law upon a State's willingness to implement its human rights obligations remains apparent.

7.2 *Chevron-Ecuador*

A new possible threat posed by investment arbitration to human rights norms emerged in a dispute between Chevron and Ecuador. The case concerns long-running litigation regarding legal responsibility for grave environmental harm caused to homelands of the Lago Agrio Indigenous peoples by oilspills and dumped waste. Having won a $19 billion judgment in an Ecuadorian court, the plaintiffs face the possibility of that judgment being effectively overruled by an arbitral panel.

The facts of this dispute are contested and very complex.[97] The following is a short summary. From 1967 to 1990, Texaco was involved in oil exploration in the Lago Agrio oilfields in the Ecuadorian Amazon as part of a consortium. Terrible environmental practices prevailed, and probably continued after Texaco's exit in 1990. Litigation against Texaco in respect of grave environmental damage commenced in the US in 1993 by groups of Indigenous plaintiffs from the Lago Agrio. In 2002, US courts declined jurisdiction over the matter, deeming Ecuador to be the more appropriate forum, in line with Texaco's constant arguments. Litigation against Chevron, which had merged with Texaco in 2001, commenced in Ecuador in 2003. In 2011, Judge Zambrano ruled in favour of the plaintiffs, awarding them

[94] Award and decision to discontinue, http://icsid.worldbank.org/ICSID/FrontServlet?requestType=CasesRH&actionVal=showDoc&docId=DC1651_En&caseId=C90 (last accessed 15 March 2015).

[95] See Bechtel Bows to Bolivia, Multinational Monitor 27, January-February 2006, 1, p. 4.

[96] Peterson L, South Africa Mining Arbitration ends with a Whimper, as terms of Discontinuance are set out in the award, Investment Arbitrator Reporter, 5 August 2010, http://www.iareporter.com/articles/20100818_6 (last accessed 15 March 2015).

[97] See, eg, Joseph (2012b), pp. 70–91.

$US 19 billion, which was confirmed on appeal. Chevron does not have significant assets in Ecuador, so the plaintiffs are seeking enforcement of the judgment in other jurisdictions.

In 2009, Chevron commenced action against Ecuador in the Permanent Court of Arbitration (PCA), claiming various breaches of a BIT between the US and Ecuador, to prevent the judgment from being handed down. It claims that the proceedings were tainted by fraud by the court as well as the plaintiffs' legal team. Since Zambrano's judgment was issued in February 2011, it now seeks an order for Ecuador to do all it can to prevent execution or enforcement of the judgment, or to indemnify Chevron for any damage caused by such enforcement. The PCA has issued several interim orders to Ecuador, seeking to prevent enforcement of the judgment.[98] In late 2013, it also handed down its decision on one aspect of the merits of the case, which favoured Chevron.[99] The merits phase is expected to conclude in 2015.

Chevron is essentially attempting to thwart, via the route of investment arbitration, a judgment obtained in Ecuador by the Lago Agrio plaintiffs who are not party to, and are excluded from, the investment arbitration proceedings. That judgment was obtained after 16 years of litigation in two countries. Amici briefs submitted on behalf of the Lago Agrio plaintiffs were summarily rejected by the tribunal, even though their interests are undoubtedly at stake in the arbitration.

Chevron's complaints before the PCA focus on alleged corruption within the Ecuadorian legal system. Ironically, the adequacy of that legal system had been asserted vigorously by the predecessor company, Texaco, in order to remove the litigation from US courts against the wishes of the plaintiffs. Also ironically, the arbitral panel is judging the adequacy of Ecuadorian due process whilst failing to satisfy standard due process requirements itself: for example its proceedings are held in secret and no appeal will be available.[100]

This author is not in a position to know if Chevron's claims of fraud are true. Yet the company does not seem to have clean hands. Chevron was quite happy with the Ecuadorian legal system, as Texaco had been, prior to the ascent of the populist government of Rafael Correa in 2007. The legal system was probably no less corrupt beforehand, but prior to Correa it favoured Texaco and later Chevron.[101] While the Ecuadorian litigation was ongoing, Chevron lobbied the US government to punish Ecuador with trade sanctions, and Wikileaks cables reveal that it also sought to influence the Ecuadorian government in its favour in 2008.[102]

---

[98] See, eg, PCA Case No. 2009-23, *Chevron and Texaco v. Ecuador*, Fourth Interim Award on Interim Measures, 7 February 2013.

[99] PCA Case No 2009-23, *Chevron and Texaco v Ecuador*, First Partial Award on Track 1, 17 September 2013. This decision focused on the interpretation of remediation agreements concluded between Texaco and Ecuador in 1995 and 1998.

[100] Goldhaber (2013), pp. 406–410.

[101] Joseph (2012b), p. 87.

[102] Joseph (2012b), p. 85.

The plaintiffs' attempts to seek a remedy in the US failed, leaving them with no option but to seek a remedy in Ecuador. It may be that, as the plaintiffs had argued in the US, a fair hearing on such a complex matter with political and economic repercussions was simply not possible in Ecuador's underdeveloped legal system. Perhaps, as argued by Chevron, that unfairness fell upon it in Zambrano's judgment. But Chevron, unlike the plaintiffs, now has the option of seeking justice before an arbitral panel.

What could the plaintiffs have done if they had felt similarly aggrieved by the Zambrano judgment? As it happens, the Lago Agrio plaintiffs filed a petition with the Inter American Commission on Human Rights in 2011, seeking interim relief against Ecuador to prevent it from complying with the PCA's interim awards.[103] That petition has been discontinued. The fact of the petition confirms that the IACHR provides the plaintiffs with an international avenue of relief, a rival to the PCA route available to Chevron. A clearer potential manifestation of conflict between different areas of international law may be hard to find. There was, and even remains, the possibility of two international forums, the PCA and the IACHR, ordering Ecuador to take two diametrically courses of action. In such a contest, as noted above, Ecuador's ultimate course may be influenced by the relative strengths of the relevant enforcement regimes.

So far, the PCA's insertion into the drama has been unsuccessful. Ecuador is not complying with its interim orders, which may be why the IACHR petition was discontinued. Furthermore, a US court has declined to enforce the PCA's interim orders.[104] The current Ecuadorian government seems unlikely to comply with any final merits decision in favour of Chevron. Indeed, in presuming to effectively overrule Ecuadorian courts on the Chevron matter, the arbitral tribunal may have acted without prudence and beyond what States are actually prepared to put up with from secret three-person commercial tribunals.[105]

Meanwhile, the litigation continues outside the PCA. A US court has refused to enforce the Ecuadorian judgment (for reasons unrelated to the PCA),[106] but the plaintiffs are seeking enforcement in other jurisdictions, including Canada, Brazil and Argentina. The ongoing saga demonstrates how hard it is to hold a multinational corporation to account for harm caused in a developing State. Victims in such situations may be deprived of any practical right to a remedy. While the prolonged drama rolls on, the Lago Agrio oilfields remain polluted, with devastating impacts on the local environment, culture and health.

[103] Low L, The Chevron-Ecuador Dispute: A Paradigm of Complexity, American Society of International Law Proceedings, 28–31 March 2012, p. 419, 421.

[104] *Chevron v. Naranjo*, 667F. 3d 232 (2nd Cirt, 2012).

[105] See generally, Goldhaber (2013), pp. 373–416.

[106] *Chevron v. Donziger*, US District Court, Southern District of New York (4 March 2014), http://www.theamazonpost.com/wp-content/uploads/Chevron-Ecuador-Opinion-3.4.14.pdf (last accessed 16 March 2015).

8 Conclusion

There are certainly synergies between the relevant economic law regimes and economic social and cultural rights, as well as civil and political rights. Certainly, all three systems are concerned with the promotion of human agency and human flourishing.

However, one must not be complacent in presuming the compatibility of the international economic legal regimes with human rights law. Those regimes essentially promote the rights of a privileged few, namely foreign traders and investors,[107] which may lead to the inevitable prioritisation of their rights when they clash with or otherwise detract from the human rights of others. Such a prioritisation is unfortunate if it adds to the already great capacity for powerful entities to override the interests of the powerless and marginalised.

Acknowledgement Thanks to Adam Fletcher for assisting in preparing the footnotes and format of this paper.

References

Abbott FM, Reichmann JH (2007) The Doha round's public health legacy: strategies for the production and diffusion of patented medicines under the amended TRIPS provisions. J Int Econ Law 10(4):921–987

Alston P (2012) Resisting the merger and acquisition of human rights by trade law: a reply to Petersmann. Eur J Int Law 13(4):815–844

Alston P, Goodman R (2013) International human rights. Oxford University Press, Oxford

Alvarez JE (1997) Critical theory and the North American free trade agreement's chapter eleven. Univ Miami Inter-Am Law Rev 28(2):303–312

Alvarez JE (2001) How not to link: institutional conundrums on an expanded trade regime. Widener Law Symp J 7(1):1–19

Bhagwati JN (2002) Free trade today. Princeton University Press, Princeton

Breining-Kaufman C (2005) The right to food and trade in agriculture. In: Cottier T, Pauwelyn J, Bürgi E (eds) Human rights and international trade. Oxford University Press, Oxford, pp 341–381

Chang HJ (2008) Bad samaritans: the myth of free trade and the secret history of capitalism. Bloomsbury, London

Chon M (2007) Intellectual property from below: copyright and capability for education. UC Davis L Rev 40:803–854

Chua A (2000) The paradox of free market democracy: rethinking development policy. Harv Int Law J 41(2):287–380

Davidson S (2004) Introduction. In: Conte A, Davidson S, Burchill R (eds) Defining civil and political rights: the jurisprudence of the United Nations Human Rights Committee. Ashgate, Farnham, pp 1–16

Driesen DM (2001) What is free trade? the real issue lurking behind the trade and environment debate. Va J Int Law 41(2):279–368

[107] See, eg., Alvarez (1997), pp. 307–309.

Dommen C (2002) Raising human rights concerns in the world trade organization: actors, processes and possible strategies. Human Rights Q 24(1):1–50
Fry JD (2007) International human rights law in investment arbitration: evidence of international law's unity. Duke J Int Comp Law 18(1):77–150
Garcia FJ (1999) The global market and human rights: trading away the human rights principle. Brooklyn J Int Law 25(7):51–98
Garcia FJ (2003) Trade, inequality, and justice: toward a liberal theory of just trade. Transnational, Ardsley
Gathii JT (2001) Re-characterizing the social in the constitutionalization of the WTO: a preliminary analysis. Widener Law Symp J 7:137–173
Gervais D (2009) TRIPS 3.0: policy calibration and innovation displacement. In: Thomas C, Trachtmann JP (eds) Developing countries in the WTO legal system. Oxford University Press, Oxford, pp 363–394
Goldhaber MD (2013) The rise of arbitral power over domestic courts. Stanford J Complex Litig 1 (2):373–416
Harrison J (2007) The human rights impact of the World Trade Organisation. Hart, Portland
Howse R, Teitel R (2009) Beyond the divide: the covenant on economic, social and cultural rights and the world trade organization. In: Joseph S, Kinley D, Waincymer J (eds) The world trade organization and human rights: interdisciplinary perspectives. Edward Elgar, Cheltenham, pp 39–69
Jandhyala S, Henisz WJ, Mansfield ED (2011) Three waves of BITs: the global diffusion of foreign investment policy. J Confl Resolut 55(6):1047–1073
Joseph S (2010) Civil and political rights. In: Baderin MA, Ssenyonjo M (eds) International human rights law: six decades after the UDHR. Ashgate, Farnham, pp 89–106
Joseph S (2011) Blame it on the WTO: a human rights critique. Oxford University Press, Oxford
Joseph S (2012a) Social media, political change, and human rights. Boston Coll Int Comp Law Rev 35(1):145–188
Joseph S (2012b) Protracted lawfare: the tale of Chevron Texaco in the Amazon. J Human Rights Environ 3(1):70–91
Joseph S (2013) Trade law and investment law. In: Shelton D (ed) The oxford handbook of international human rights law. Oxford University Press, Oxford, pp 841–870
Karamanian SL (2012) Human rights dimensions of investment law. In: de Wet E, Widmar J (eds) Hierarchy in international law: the place of human rights. Oxford University Press, Oxford, pp 236–271
Kriebaum U (2009) Is the European Court of Human Rights an alternative to investor-state arbitration? In: Dupuy M, Francioni F, Petersmann EU (eds) Human rights in international investment law and arbitration. Oxford University Press, Oxford, pp 219–245
Lang ATF (2001) The GATS and regulatory autonomy: a case study of social regulation of the water industry. J Int Econ Law 7(4):801–838
Lang ATF (2007) Reflecting on 'linkage': cognitive and institutional change in the international trading system. Modern Law Rev 79(4):523–549
Langford M (2008) The justiciability of social rights: from practice to theory. In: Langford M (ed) Social economic rights jurisprudence: emerging trends in international and comparative law. Cambridge University Press, Cambridge, pp 3–45
Marceau G (2002) WTO dispute settlement and human rights. Eur J Int Law 13(4):753–814
Morozov E (2011) The net delusion. Allen Lane, London
Murphy S (2005) WTO agreement on agriculture: suitable model for a global food system? Foreign Policy Focus 7(8):3–7
Pogge T (2008) Growth and inequality: understanding recent trends and political choices. Dissent 55(1):66–75. doi:10.1353/dss.2008.0024
Rodrik D (2007) How to save globalisation from its cheerleaders. Journal Int Trade Dipl 1(2):1–33
Ruggie JG (1982) International regimes, transactions and change: embedded liberalism in the postwar economic order. Int Organ 36(2):379–415

Salomon ME (2007) Global responsibility for human rights. Oxford University Press, Oxford
Singham SA (2001) Competition policy and the stimulation of innovation: TRIPS and the interface between competition and patent protection in the pharmaceutical industry. Brooklyn J Int Law 26(2):363–416
Stiglitz JE, Charlton A (2005) Fair trade for all. Oxford University Press, Oxford
Stiglitz JE (2010) Freefall: free markets and the sinking of the global economy. Norton, New York
Vandenhole W (2007) Third state obligations under the ICESR: a case study of EU sugar policy. Nordic J Int Law 76(1):73–100
Vandevelde K (1998) The political economy of a bilateral investment treaty. Am J Int Law 92 (4):621–641
Vázquez CM (2003) Trade sanctions and human rights – past, present and future. J Int Econ Law 6 (4):797–839
Wolf M (2005) Why globalisation works. Yale University Press, New Haven

International Economic Law and Human Rights: Friends, Enemies or Frenemies?

Lorand Bartels

Abstract A state's economic policies, including the protection of intellectual property and foreign investments, and trade liberalisation, can have an impact on the enjoyment of human rights. Some of these policies may also be encouraged by international treaties. But it does not follow that any given economic policy is required by those treaties. Determining whether this is the case requires a close analysis of the treaties at issue. In fact, most treaties typically contain exceptions clauses that permit states to comply with both their economic and their human rights obligations. In sum, while Sarah Joseph is right that, in principle, international economic law could hinder the enjoyment of human rights, it is more difficult to identify cases in which this is mandated. But even if this were the case, the logical solution is not to add human rights obligations to international economic agreements. It would be sufficient to ensure that those agreements contain exceptions that can permit—without mandating—states to comply with, and further, their existing human rights obligations.

Sarah Joseph's article addresses an important question: what is the relationship between international economic law—concerning, principally, trade, intellectual property and investment—and obligations to respect, protect and fulfil human rights. While broadly agreeing with her conclusions, this comment highlights some aspects of this question that merit more detailed consideration.

Trade, intellectual property and investment rules all have the long term objective of promoting human welfare, both for individual countries and globally. Trade rules do this by restricting protectionism, which is an inefficient way to allocate resources; intellectual property rules do this by encouraging (or purporting to encourage) innovation; and investment rules do this by creating (or purporting to create) a favourable climate for attracting foreign capital made. As Sarah Joseph notes, the more economically successful a country, the more resources it will have to implement its human rights obligations, and beyond this the better able it will be

L. Bartels (✉)
University of Cambridge, Cambridge CB2 1TJ, UK
e-mail: lab53@cam.ac.uk

M. Bungenberg et al. (eds.), *European Yearbook of International Economic Law 2016*, European Yearbook of International Economic Law 7,
DOI 10.1007/978-3-319-29215-1_19

to improve life for its residents.[1] These long term objectives are perfectly consistent with human rights obligations, and, to the extent that the implementation of these obligations requires public resources, also support these obligations.

The relationship between international economic law obligations and human rights obligations become more complex as one looks at the way that these long term objectives are achieved.[2] Partly this is because the philosophical bases of international economic law (which is essentially utilitarian) and human rights (which is essentially deontological) are distinct. The difference manifests itself chiefly in that what is important for international economic law is the aggregate welfare of the group, whereas what is important for human rights law is the welfare of the individual.[3]

This said, there is a measure of congruence between international economic law and human rights law. Reducing protectionism in an importing country often improves the economic situation of those working in export industries, including those in developing countries. Likewise, there can be a congruence between the rights of intellectual property rights holders and investors can overlap with their human rights,[4] and, as Sarah Joseph notes, enhanced access to goods and services, the results of both trade and investment, can also sometimes facilitate the enjoyment of human rights.[5]

But international economic law rules can, in principle, interfere with people's enjoyment of human rights. This is most obviously the case with intellectual property obligations, which have the effect of raising the price of products and services incorporating intellectual property, as well as restricting freedom of expression. Where these products and services are required in order for human rights to be enjoyed, such as for example medicines or information, these effects can, in theory, be problematic[6]; on the other hand, it is also important to acknowledge that these obligations are typically subject to relevant exceptions.[7] The situation is also rather straightforward in relation to investment obligations. The problem arises when state regulation to comply with, or further, human rights obligations reduces the value of an investment. In some circumstances, this can result in the state becoming liable to pay compensation to the investor. The sums involved can be significant. On 9 April 2015, for example, Argentina was ordered to pay $US 405 million to a French water company after terminating a water contract

[1] Joseph (2016), section 7.

[2] See, further, Bartels (2009).

[3] Bartels (2009), p. 581 and references there cited, especially Garcia (2003), pp. 14–19. Even in cases of 'group rights' it is usually individuals that are the rights holders. See, further, Smit Duijzentkunst BL, The Concept of Rights in International Law (unpublished PhD manuscript on file with author, 2015), section 3.1.

[4] On investor rights as human rights, see Savarese (2014), p. 95 n 13 noting the result in *Mike Campbell (Pvt) Ltd v Zimbabwe*, SADCT No 2/2007, 28 November 2008.

[5] See Joseph (2016), section 3.1.

[6] Eg Hestermeyer and Broude (2014), p. 295.

[7] Mercurio (2013).

that, Argentina claimed, was necessary to be able to provide water at lower prices to its population.[8] Ultimately, the loss of income (real or threatened) can undermine a state's ability or willingness to regulate as it would prefer.

In the case of intellectual property and investment obligations, conflicts with human rights obligations are far from remote. But governments are also becoming alert to these problems. An example is the World Trade Organization (WTO) decision on essential medicines, although its effectiveness remains to be seen,[9] in particular following the impounding of generic drugs in transit by the Netherlands.[10] In relation to investment law, some recent model bilateral investment treaties, and recent treaties, are becoming more effective at protecting regulatory autonomy, both by giving more detail to the underlying obligations and by including exceptions clauses for legitimate regulation.[11]

So even though intellectual property rules and investment rules could potentially impair a country's ability to meet its human rights obligations, it also deserves to be recognized that where new rules are being drafted the game is beginning to change.

The relationship between trade rules (not including rules on intellectual property rules and investment in services) and human rights obligations is perhaps the most complex.[12] This is because trade policies—both protectionist and liberalizing—redistribute resources within societies in complicated ways. One must therefore be careful in generalising about the negative effects of trade liberalisation, because one person's loss can often be another's gain, and it is not always straightforward which of these is to be preferred. This makes it very difficult to generalise about an issue as complicated as agricultural liberalisation. Removing export subsidies on food is likely to raise world prices, thereby helping farmers from poor countries, but this could also be to the detriment of consumers in poor countries; even in the same countries;[13] vice versa, if rich countries 'dump' subsidised food in poor countries, this may be to the detriment of local production,[14] but this is only because these products find a ready market there, often the urban poor. It is also important not to

---

[8] See, eg, *Suez, Sociedad General de Aguas de Barcelona, SA and Vivendi Universal, SA v Argentina*, ICSID Case No ARB/03/19, Decision on Liability of 30 July 2010, para 240, where the tribunal stated that "[u]nder the circumstances of this case, Argentina's human rights obligations and its investment treaty obligations are not inconsistent, contradictory, or mutually exclusive. Thus . . . Argentina could have respected both types of obligations." and Final Award, 9 April 2015, para 117.

[9] Hestermeyer (2007).

[10] WTO, *European Union and a Member State—Seizure of Generic Drugs in Transit—Request for Consultations by India*, WT/DS408/1, 19 May 2010; European Union and a Member State—Seizure of Generic Drugs in Transit—Request for Consultations by Brazil, WT/DS409/1, 12 May 2010. For discussion, see Mercurio (2012), p. 389.

[11] Arts 8.9 and 28.3 of the Canada-EU Comprehensive Trade and Economic Agreement (not yet signed), (last accessed 20 March 2016).

[12] Kinley (2009), ch 2.

[13] Smith (2012), pp. 52–53.

[14] It is not clear that this practice is actually damaging. See Matthews (2012), pp. 120–121.

mistake an 'unbalanced' trade agreement for a cause of hardship. The WTO Agreement on Agriculture may permit rich countries to protect agriculture to the detriment of poor countries, including by means of 'tariff escalation', but that does not mean that it causes them any damage. The true counterfactual for causation purposes is a world without this agreement, and it cannot be doubted that in such a world poor countries would be even worse off. Trade liberalisation is not a zero sum game so much as an ultimatum game.

But even so, it is still possible that the result of one or other of these redistributionist policies can impede the enjoyment of human rights. The question then is whether this is the result of trade liberalisation, seen as a policy choice, or whether it is the ineluctable result of the multilateral and regional and bilateral trade obligations concerning trade liberalisation. In fact, it is very rare that states' trade obligations will actually ever hinder their ability to comply with their human rights obligations (leaving aside obligations that are more properly considered investment issues, as discussed above). First, trade liberalisation obligations are always negotiated, and it is typical for so-called 'sensitive' products to be excluded from the final deal, or to be included but in a way that gives a country a great deal of regulatory flexibility. For example, agricultural tariffs in poor countries are typically bound at a rate much higher than is applied. To take some examples of applied versus bound rates in percentages of the value of imported agricultural products: Angola: 10%/ 53 %; Bangladesh: 17 %/192 %; Benin: 15 %/62 %; Botswana: 9 %/38 %.[15] This means that these countries could increase their tariffs fourfold without violating their WTO obligations. The fact that they do not cannot be attributed to these countries' trade obligations, but rather to other factors.

There are also many safety valves built into the system. Some are in the form of a type of *rebus sic stantibus* clause, permitting WTO members to impose temporary 'safeguard measures' on imports causing 'serious injury' to domestic producers. Moreover, trade restrictive and discriminatory regulations are always permitted if this is necessary for a wide range of public policy reasons, including 'public morals', which doubtless include human rights.[16] Even the 'necessity' test is essentially a rule directed at good administration, and the fact that many measures have so far failed to meet this test, or a similar test under the chapeau of the general exceptions, is essentially an indication that states have shown themselves to be poor regulators (and in some cases outright protectionist). It is not a sign that there is anything inherently wrong with the rules themselves.[17] The main exception is that

[15] WTO/ICT/UNCTAD, World Tariff Profiles 2014, Geneva 2014, p. 12, https://www.wto.org/english/res_e/booksp_e/tariff_profiles14_e.pdf (last accessed 20 March 2016).

[16] Earlier more cautious approaches to the scope of the 'public morals' exception seem unwarranted. In *EC—Seal Products*, WT/DS400/AB/R, adopted 18 June 2014, the Appellate Body had no difficulty finding that EU 'public morals' include concern for the protection of seals, largely because, as the panel had found, there was a reference to animals as 'sentient beings' in one of the EU primary treaties. A fortiori, it would be inconceivable that the protection of human rights, in virtually all cases referenced in national constitutions, would not be considered to be valid 'public morals' of the respective country.

[17] Bartels (2015).

discriminatory non-agricultural subsidies lack an exceptions clause, but there is often very little policy justification for discriminatory subsidies in any case.

So one should not exaggerate the degree to which trade obligations operate as any sort of constraint on countries seeking to meet their human rights obligations. It is significant that, in relation to food, Olivier de Schutter, former UN Rapporteur on the Right to Food has also recognized this. He has said that:

> It should be emphasised that neither the failure of many developing countries to invest sufficiently in agriculture nor the damage caused to their agricultural sector by the lowering of import tariffs on agricultural products can be attributed to the WTO rules. The main responsibility for this situation lies with the international financial institutions, particularly with the structural adjustment programmes imposed on states in the 1980s as a condition for their access to loans.[18]

One might add that, in practice, it is virtually impossible to imagine the poorest WTO members being forced to defend such measures in WTO dispute settlement proceedings. No least developed country has ever had a WTO case filed against it; indeed, the same is true of all African countries apart from South Africa and Egypt, and in these cases the bulk of the complainants were other developing countries.[19] This is less likely to be because these countries religiously adhere to the rules, than because their markets are too small to make it worthwhile bringing a case, and in any case it would be disastrous public relations for a large country to take on one of these in the WTO. In short, for the poorest countries trade obligations rules are not in reality much of a constraint on what is usually called ‘policy space’.

But if the rules do not prevent countries from protecting their populations against the direct effects of trade liberalisation, there can still be problems arising at the macro level of budgetary resources. If lost tariff revenue is not replaced, if the implementation of an agreement comes with direct costs, if a country lacks the ability to manage structural adjustment, or if preferences are eroded,[20] it is possible

[18] De Schutter (2011), p. 154. See also Häberli (2013).

[19] Aside from the US, the complainants in these cases were Brazil, Turkey, India, Indonesia, Pakistan, and Thailand. See WTO, Disputes by country/territory, https://www.wto.org/english/tratop_e/dispu_e/dispu_by_country_e.htm (last accessed 20 March 2016).

[20] Sarah Joseph (Joseph (2016)), section 3.2) refers to Stiglitz and Charlton (2005), p. 47, who state that “by some estimates, 48 of the least developed countries had suffered economic losses of close to US$600 million per year since they began implementing WTO agreements.” As this has become something of a meme in this area, it is appropriate to note that Stiglitz and Charlton are misquoting their source. This source was the United Nations Development Program (UNDP) (1997) Human Development Report, http://hdr.undp.org/sites/default/files/reports/258/hdr_1997_en_complete_nostats.pdf, p. 82 forecasting in 1997—ie 2 years after the WTO agreements were signed—that “[t]he least developed countries stand to lose up to $600 million a year, and Sub-Saharan Africa $1.2 billion.” It was not clear from that report why this would be the case, but it appears likely that the basis for this claim is a different UNDP study, using identical language, which said that “the least developed countries stand to lose up to US$600 million per year in generalized system of preferences (GSP) advantages.” UNDP, High-level Meeting on the Integrated Initiatives for Least Developed Countries’ Trade Development, Trade Liberalisation and Sustainable Human Development, Doc LDC/HL/7, 9 October 1997, 27–28 October 1997, p. 3. Aside from the figures being mere forecasts, the result would be from rich countries, not poor countries, ‘implementing WTO

that a poor country may be unable to protect its people in line with its human rights obligations. What is then to be done?

There are two ways to look at this. First, each of these scenarios, except the last, depends upon the consent of the country experiencing losses, and these countries should, and typically do, negotiate for assistance as part of their promise to liberalise. It is after all these countries that are responsible for making sure that they do not put themselves in a position where they are unable to comply with their international human rights obligations. Second, to the extent that rich (and other) states engage in conduct that has direct effects on human rights in poor countries, the question arises whether these countries might potentially be responsible under human rights law. Suffice to say, the matter is not nearly as clear at the international level as the Maastricht Principles to which Sarah Joseph refers would have one believe.[21]

In reality, whether one sees this in terms of obligation, or as voluntary, much is being done to ameliorate the costs of trade liberalisation. Over $30 billion is disbursed annually in the context of the WTO's Aid for Trade initiative.[22] And sometimes commitments are made conditional on capacity, which must *de facto* then be funded where such capacity does not exist. One sees this in the recent Trade Facilitation Agreement, which states that "[w]here a developing or least developed country Member continues to lack the necessary capacity, implementation of the provision(s) concerned will not be required until implementation capacity has been acquired" and that "[a]ssistance and support for capacity building should be provided to help developing and least developed country Members implement the provisions of this agreement, in accordance with their nature and scope."[23]

This state of affairs also seems to render it unnecessary to require that trade rules themselves *mandate* "recompense for those harmed", as Sarah Joseph suggests. But there is another reason that this goes too far: that mandate already exists in the form of human rights obligations. What is required from trade regimes is that they do not *prevent* states from complying with their human rights obligations. And, for the reasons mentioned, they do not.

In summary, I agree with Sarah Joseph's appraisal of the potential difficulties that intellectual property and investment obligations cause for compliance with human rights obligations, with the proviso that these obligations are increasingly becoming subject to relevant exceptions. Likewise, while trade liberalisation itself can theoretically lead to human rights violations, this is not the same as saying that trade liberalisation *obligations* lead to such violations. These obligations are also

---

agreements'. This aside, it turns out that the figures were probably accurate: Hoekman et al. (2009), pp. 18–19.

[21] Cf Bartels (2014), p. 1071 ff.

[22] See Table A.1 in WTO, Aid for Trade at a Glance, 2013.

[23] Article 13.2 of the WTO Trade Facilitation Agreement, WT/L/931, 15 July 2014. For discussion, see Bartels, Sequencing the Implementation of Obligations in WTO Negotiations, Commonwealth Trade Hot Topics No 116, Commonwealth Secretariat, December 2014.

subject to numerous flexibilities, both formal and informal, that permit states to comply with their human rights obligations. If there are human rights violations, these are more likely to be attributable either to domestic policy choices, or perhaps the loan conditionality policies of the World Bank and the IMF. At most, one can identify certain direct budgetary costs associated with trade liberalisation, both voluntary and required by trade rules, but these costs are (at least to some extent) met by development aid, and in theory, at least, also by the gains from liberalisation.

So while one might be able identify situations in which states' economic policies have interfered—or may interfere—with the enjoyment of human rights, it is more difficult to attribute these effects to those states' international legal obligations, given the available exceptions. These effects tend rather to be the result of optional domestic policy choices instead.

Acknowledgement I am grateful to friends and colleagues for their valuable suggestions.

References

Bartels L (2009) Trade and human rights. In: Bethlehem D, McRae D, Neufeld R, Van Damme I (eds) The Oxford handbook of international trade law. Oxford University Press, Oxford, pp 571–591

Bartels L (2014) The EU's human rights obligations in relation to policies with extraterritorial effects. Eur J Int Law 25(4):1071–1091

Bartels L (2015) The chapeau of the general exceptions in the WTO GATT and GATS agreements: a reconstruction. American Journal of International Law 109(1):95–115

De Schutter O (2011) International trade in agriculture and the right to food. In: De Schutter O, Cordes K (eds) Accounting for hunger: the right to food in the era of globalisation. Hart Publishing, Oxford/Portland, pp 137–192

Garcia F (2003) Trade, inequality, and justice. Transnational, Ardsley

Häberli C (2013) God, the WTO – and hunger. In: Nadakavukaren Schefer K (ed) Poverty and the international economic legal system. Cambridge University Press, Cambridge, pp 79–106

Hestermeyer H (2007) Canadian-made drugs for Rwanda: the first application of the WTO waiver on patents and medicines. Am Soc Int Law: Insights 11(28)

Hestermeyer H, Broude T (2014) The first condition of progress? Freedom of speech and the limits of international law. Va J Int Law 54(2):295–321

Hoekman B, Martin W, Braga CAP (eds) (2009) Trade preference erosion: measurement and response. World Bank Publications/Palgrave-MacMillan, Washington

Joseph S (2016) Human Rights and International Economic Law. In: Bungenberg M, Hermann C, Krajewski M, Terchechte JP (eds) European yearbook of international economic Law, vol. 7. Springer, Heidelberg, pp 461–481

Kinley D (2009) Civilising globalisation. Cambridge University Press, Cambridge

Matthews A (2012) The impact of WTO agricultural trade rules on food security and development: an examination of proposed additional flexibilities for developing countries. In: MacMahon JA, Desta MD (eds) Research handbook on the WTO agriculture agreement. Edward Elgar, Cheltenham, pp 104–132

Mercurio B (2012) 'Seizing' pharmaceuticals in transit: analysing the WTO dispute that wasn't. Int Comp Law Q 61(2):389–426

Mercurio B (2013) TRIPS and access to essential medicines. In: Van Calster G, Prévost D (eds) Research handbook on environment, health and the WTO. Edward Elgar, Cheltenham, pp 233–269

Savarese E (2014) The coherence of EU law: the promotion of investments vs the protection of human rights. Ital Yearb Int Law 23(1):91–112

Smith F (2012) Food security and international agricultural trade regulation: old problems, new perspective. In: MacMahon JA, Desta MD (eds) Research handbook on the WTO agriculture agreement. Edward Elgar, Cheltenham, pp 31–49

Stiglitz JE, Charlton A (2005) Fair trade for all. Oxford University Press, Oxford

United Nations Development Program (UNDP) (1997) Human development report. Oxford University Press, Oxford

Part II
Regional Developments: Focus on Megaregionals and Plurilaterals

The United States' Path to Concluding the Trans-Pacific Partnership: Will TPA + TAA = TPP?

Meredith Kolsky Lewis

Contents

Abstract The political economy of international trade decision-making within the United States is ever-changing and complex. The recent debates over the merits of the Trans-Pacific Partnership (TPP,) and the associated efforts of the Obama Administration to obtain Trade Promotion Authority (TPA), highlight these complexities. This short article is an attempt to clarify the political economy dynamics in the United States with respect to the TPP. It first explains what Trade Promotion Authority (TPA) is and why President Obama needed to have TPA as a precursor to concluding the TPP negotiations. Second, it discusses some of the internal political dynamics impacting support for, or opposition to, the TPP, as well as the Administration's previous failures to obtain TPA for the TPP negotiations. Third, the piece addresses Trade Adjustment Assistance (TAA) and its interplay with TPA. The article concludes with an assessment of the ramifications for the TPP of the House and Senate having passed both the TPA and TAA bills.

M.K. Lewis (✉)
SUNY Buffalo Law School, 719 O'Brian Hall, Buffalo, NY 14260, USA
e-mail: mlewis5@buffalo.edu

M. Bungenberg et al. (eds.), *European Yearbook of International Economic Law 2016*, European Yearbook of International Economic Law 7,
DOI 10.1007/978-3-319-29215-1_20

1 Introduction

The United States is unquestionably the lead demandeur in the ongoing Trans-Pacific Partnership (TPP) negotiations. It may therefore be difficult to understand how and why internal politics in the United States have threatened to derail the Agreement. The political economy of trade within the United States is ever-changing, and the complexities have been in full force in the debates over the merits of the TPP and the associated efforts of the Obama Administration to obtain Trade Promotion Authority (TPA). This short article is an effort to clarify the dynamics unfolding in the United States with respect to the TPP. It will first explain what Trade Promotion Authority (TPA) is and why President Obama needed to have TPA to conclude the TPP negotiations. Second, it will discuss some of the internal political dynamics impacting support for, or opposition to, the TPP, as well as the Administration's previous failures to obtain TPA for the TPP negotiations. Third, the piece will address Trade Adjustment Assistance (TAA) and its interplay with TPA. The piece will conclude with an assessment of the ramifications for the TPP of the House and Senate having passed both the TPA and TAA bills.

2 Trade Promotion Authority: Why it Matters

The United States Constitution gives Congress the power to "regulate commerce with foreign nations..." and to "collect...duties..."[1] while the President has wide-ranging authority over the nation's foreign affairs, including the power "by and with the advice and consent of the Senate, to make treaties...".[2] Historically, this division of competences with respect to international trade resulted in Congress establishing tariffs, and the President negotiating friendship, commerce and navigation treaties that did not include commitments to lower or remove tariffs.[3] To the extent the Executive negotiates trade agreements that have a more direct impact on commerce, such as by lowering tariffs, such agreements require Congress to pass implementing legislation in order for them to become effective. In the ordinary course, members of Congress can edit any proposed legislation by crossing out provisions or by adding new text. Congress's ability to alter the content of proposed legislation creates a practical difficulty with respect to the ability of the President to conclude trade agreements. When other countries negotiate trade agreements with the United States, they will not be willing to make their "best and final" offers unless they feel they are receiving the same from the U.S. However, if Congress can re-write whatever deal the President has concluded, then the U.S.'s negotiating

[1] U.S. Constitution, art. I, § 8.

[2] U.S. Constitution, art. II, § 2, cl. 2.

[3] Fergusson IF (2012) Trade Promotion Authority (TPA) and the Role of Congress in Trade Policy. Congressional Research Service, p. 2.

partners cannot have any certainty that the terms to which they have agreed will not be altered by Congress. In recognition of the difficulties this dynamic creates, over time Congress has, on a limited basis, delegated some of its Commerce powers to the President.

In 1934, Congress passed the Reciprocal Trade Agreement Act[4] which gave the President the authority to negotiate tariff reductions, within certain parameters, with other countries. Congress first granted Trade Promotion Authority (TPA), or as it was then called, Fast-Track Authority, to the Executive in the Trade Act of 1974.[5] TPA gives the President the ability to present trade agreements to Congress for its consideration on an up-or-down vote basis, without the possibility of filibuster or of altering the text of the proposed agreement. Congress can, and generally does, condition this delegation of its powers. In particular, Congress has always granted TPA for a limited time period, and generally conditions the authority on the President pursuing certain objectives in any negotiations conducted.

While Congress has granted TPA to presidents on a regular basis since the 1970s, the authority is not without controversy and some Congresses are less inclined to grant it than others. TPA was last granted to President Bush in the Trade Act of 2002, and that authority expired on 1 July 2007.[6] Thus President Obama had not had TPA for the entirety of his time in office, prior to Congress granting the power in late June 2015. The lack of TPA does not and did not prevent the President from beginning trade negotiations. While it is useful to have from the beginning, TPA becomes increasingly important as negotiations reach their final phase, when negotiators are making their "best and final" offers. In the early years of the TPP negotiations, the Administration did not seem to feel any urgency to seek, or for Congress to grant, TPA. Some have criticized the President for not requesting TPA sooner. However, by mid-2013, the TPP negotiations had progressed sufficiently that the Executive felt the agreement could be concluded within a number of months. Having reached the "end game", the other TPP participants expect President Obama to have TPA before they will be willing to engage in the final, most difficult negotiations to conclude the agreement.

---

[4] Pub. L. 73-316, H.R. 8687, enacted 29 March 1934; 19 U.S.C. §§ 1351-1354.

[5] Pub. L. 93-618, H.R. 10710, enacted 3 January 1975; 19 U.S.C. 2101.

[6] Pub. L. 107-210, H.R. 3009, enacted 6 August 2002; 19 U.S.C. §§ 3803-3805. The expiration of TPA only applied to trade agreements that had not been signed as of 1 July 2007. Accordingly, although the United States' free trade agreements with Colombia, Korea and Panama were not brought before Congress until 2011, all had been signed before the expiration of TPA in 2007 and thus were submitted to Congress pursuant to the previous grant of TPA authority. Prior to the 2002 Trade Act, the President had been without TPA since 1994.

3 Political Economy Dynamics Complicate the Process

3.1 Friends in Strange Places

The factions within the U.S. that have favored or opposed trade agreements have varied over time. At present, it is largely the Republicans who are in favor of negotiating additional free trade agreements and Democrats in opposition. Within the major parties however, there are factions that disagree with their colleagues. Thus there is a group of pro-trade Democrats, and also a cohort of anti-trade Republicans. Over the past decade or more, the two parties have each pushed for controversial content in trade agreements. Democrats have emphasized the need for environmental and labor protections in trade agreements, and also want assurances that human rights will be protected. Republicans are less concerned about these issues, and instead have pushed for heightened intellectual property protections, which are often viewed as favorable to big business, in particular pharmaceutical companies.

The TPP plays into traditional party preferences in that pro-union Democrats are almost uniformly opposed, and business-oriented Republicans tend to be in favor. However, the TPP introduces new complexities because the Agreement will cover previously uncharted territory. As but a few examples, it has entailed negotiations on liberalizing trade in agricultural products and textiles to a level never before agreed to by the U.S.; the intellectual property negotiations may have significant implications for access to medicine; and having Japan as a negotiating partner for the first time creates new opportunities but is also seen by many as a threat. Furthermore, some in Congress see geopolitical strategic benefits to being a part of a major Asia-Pacific trade agreement, whereas foreign policy is less of a concern for others. As a result of these dynamics and the sheer complexity of assessing a deal involving 11 other countries, Representatives across the political spectrum will have to assess this trade agreement like none that has come before it.

3.2 You Can Ask, but Ye May Not Receive

The Obama Administration has expressed interest in TPA off and on since it decided to continue the TPP negotiations that had been begun under the Bush Administration.[7] However, it did not demonstrate any urgency to obtain TPA in the

[7] See, e.g., Kirk Says Administration Will Seek Fast Track Authority, Predicts Approval. Inside U.S. Trade, 18 December 2009.

early stages of the negotiations.[8] And in 2012, it was the Republican Congressional leadership pushing the President to seek TPA rather than the other way around.[9] The Administration indicated it wanted TPA, yet did not request it. This was likely due to the highly politicized environment that exists in Presidential election years. With President Obama seeking to be reelected in November 2012 and needing as much party support as possible, his Administration was unlikely to make any moves that could upset fellow Democrats.

Once safely reelected, President Obama finally requested TPA in a July 2013 speech, but no action was taken by Congress. Congressional leaders introduced TPA legislation in January 2014, but that bill did not progress to a vote.[10] Obama again requested TPA in his 2014 State of the Union Address, but his own party quickly poured cold water on the idea, with then-Senate Majority leader Harry Reid indicating he did not support fast-track authority and that Obama should not push this issue.[11] Mid-term elections held in the U.S. in November 2014 changed the balance of power, with Republicans gaining control over the Senate and maintaining their leadership of the House. The Administration hoped to be granted TPA in early 2015, but miscalculated Congress's willingness to give it this authority. Although the Republican majority largely supports the TPP, it was not going to give the President something he wanted without the Administration expending any effort. Even when the Republican leadership became more willing, even eager, to give President Obama TPA, differences of opinion within Congressional leaders regarding what a TPA bill should contain led to repeated delays in introducing legislation.[12]

Why such difficulty in getting a bill to be considered? Part of the challenge arises from the fact that the President's main allies on trade are from the opposing party—the Republicans. While the Republicans currently control both the House and the Senate, they are not keen to give President Obama—a Democrat—something he wants without getting something in exchange. At the same time, many Democrats in both the House and Senate are not favorably inclined towards trade agreements in

[8] At that time, the Administration was also focusing on completing FTAs with Korea, Panama and Colombia, which had been signed by President Bush but to which Congress required additional changes, which necessitated further negotiations. However, because those FTAs were signed before the expiry of the previous grant of TPA, it was only the TPP that was being negotiated without TPA.

[9] See Boehner Calls on President to Pursue New, Broad Fast-Track Authority. Inside U.S. Trade, 23 March 2012.

[10] See United States Senate Committee on Finance (2014) Baucus, Hatch, Camp Unveil Bill to Bring Home Job-Creating Trade Agreements, http://www.finance.senate.gov/newsroom/chairman/release/?id=7cd1c188-87f1-4a0b-8856-3fc139121ca9 (last accessed 11 August 2015).

[11] Colman Z, Democrats Give Obama Cold Shoulder on Trade Promotion Authority. The Washington Diplomat, 27 February 2014, http://www.washdiplomat.com/index.php?option=com_content&view=article&id=10091:democrats-give-obama-cold-shoulder-on-trade-promotion-authority&catid=1515&Itemid=428 (last accessed 11 August 2015).

[12] See, e.g., Hatch Says Congress Won't Consider TPA Before April; Hints No Bill Prior. Inside U.S. Trade, 6 March 2015.

general or the TPP in particular and therefore were not prepared to support TPA, much less expend political capital to assist the President on this matter. In order to obtain support from unenthusiastic Democrats, the majority Republicans had to negotiate over the substance of what a TPA bill would contain.

While the relevant House and Senate leaders reached agreement in April 2015 on the key elements that would need to be included in TPA legislation,[13] it still took a period of weeks to get the legislation drafted and proffered for debate and a vote. Within the ebb and flow of Congressional activity, there are periods that are inherently more or less favorable to try to pass legislation. As a starting point, Congress recesses at a number of predictable junctures throughout the year. While Congress occasionally delays a scheduled recess, it prefers not to do so. Thus legislators try to have important pieces of legislation considered in advance of certain Congressional breaks, particularly the more lengthy summer and Christmas recesses.

With summer approaching, supporters of the TPP and other trade agreements under negotiation grew increasingly anxious to get a TPA bill passed. If TPA were not passed imminently, the current window for completing the negotiations would close. Why so time sensitive? The United States will hold Presidential elections in November 2016. All of the House of Representatives seats and one-third of the U.S. Senate seats will also be up for election at the same time. The cycle of intense campaigning for these positions begins approximately a year in advance of the elections. As a practical matter, Congress is generally unwilling to consider controversial legislation during the calendar year in which elections are held. Counting backwards then, for the TPP to have a chance of being approved by Congress while President Obama is still in office, the agreement would ideally be presented to Congress for its up-or-down vote before the December 2015 recess. Under the terms of the TPA bills, any trade agreement must be made available to the public for at least 60 days before the President can formally sign the agreement. Thereafter, Congress works with the White House for a period of months to undertake "legal scrubbing"—the process by which lawyers review the entirety of the agreement to ensure that the same wording is used to convey like concepts across chapters and to identify and address any inaccuracies, confusing text, or other difficulties. Given that the TPP will comprise 29 chapters, this process will be lengthy. Finally, the President will formally submit the TPP to Congress, which will have 90 days within which to debate, and then to hold its up-or-down vote on the agreement.[14] Trade ministers from other TPP partners have been deeply concerned about this timing, and had signaled that if TPA were not attained prior to the summer Congressional recess, there would be no hope of concluding the Agreement prior to 2018.[15]

[13] See Wiseman J, Deal Reached on Fast-Track Authority for Obama on Trade Accord. The New York Times, 16 April 2015, http://www.nytimes.com/2015/04/17/business/obama-trade-legislation-fast-track-authority-trans-pacific-partnership.html (last accessed 11 August 2015).

[14] See, e.g., Barfield C (2015) Tipping Our TPP Hand. American Enterprise Institute, https://www.aei.org/publication/tipping-our-tpp-hand/ (last accessed 11 August 2015).

[15] See Robb Says Only One Week Left to Finish TPP, if TPA Passes. Inside U.S. Trade, 19 June 2015.

In addition to all of the activity that has to take place *after* the TPP negotiations are concluded, there are still substantive issues to be resolved in the TPP negotiations. Thus there will need to be further meetings amongst the parties to reach agreement on the issues that remain. In order for there to be any possibility of concluding the TPP during Obama's presidency; therefore, the Administration needed to be granted TPA as early as possible in 2015, and ideally well before Congress's summer recess.

4 Trade Adjustment Assistance

Because of the opposition to the TPP (and therefore to the granting of TPA) amongst many Democrats, the President and pro-TPP Congressional leaders decided to bundle together the consideration of TPA with something the Democrats would be more sympathetic to—namely a bill to renew Trade Adjustment Assistance (TAA), which provides worker retraining and other assistance to those workers adversely impacted by trade agreements. Absent a vote to renew, the current TAA bill was set to expire on September 30, 2015. While TPA tends to have significant Republican support but weak Democrat support, TAA is just the reverse. Thus the thinking was that if TPA and TAA were combined, both Republicans and Democrats would get something they wanted. President Obama also stated that he would not sign a bill granting him TPA unless it were to be accompanied by a TAA bill. Accordingly, a plan was devised whereby the Senate and House would each consider TPA and TAA bills, with the bills then being presented as a package to the President. On 22 May 2015, the Senate duly voted in favor of a combined TPA and TAA bill.[16] The House considered TPA and TAA separately a few weeks later. However, because the Senate had addressed TPA and TAA as a single bill, neither TPA nor TAA could progress to the President unless the House passed both the TAA and TPA bills.

In a significant blow to the White House, the House of Representatives voted convincingly *against* TAA, by a vote of 126–302. This was followed by a vote narrowly in favor of TPA.[17] Because both bills had to be passed in order for the House/Senate package to go to the President, the TAA vote effectively rendered the TPA vote meaningless, and cast into doubt the likelihood that President Obama would ever receive TPA or conclude the TPP.

Why did the House vote against TAA? Even though Democrats overwhelmingly favor TAA, and many Republicans were willing to vote in favor, if only to enable

---

[16] See Senate Approves TPA-TAA Bill with Two Changes, After Two-Week Fight Fizzles. Inside U.S. Trade, 29 May 2015.

[17] See In a Surprise Move, House Votes Down TAA, Sets Back Fast Track. Inside U.S. Trade, 19 June 2015.

the ultimate signing of a TPA bill, a significant contingent of Democrats decided as a tactical matter to vote against TAA.

Their strategy was not to kill TAA, but rather to sacrifice TAA in order to kill TPA. They knew that both bills had to pass in order for TPA to become a reality, and they also knew that the TPA bill would likely pass even without support from many Democrats. Accordingly, the only way to stop TPA was to vote against TAA, and in this regard, the anti-TPA contingent was successful. But this success was only temporary, because the pro-TPA forces regrouped and developed a new strategy.

The new strategy, again devised by Republican House and Senate leadership together with the White House, was to decouple TPA and TAA. The thought was that since there had been enough votes to support TPA, TPA could be accomplished if presented as a stand-alone bill. While the President wanted a TAA bill, this would also likely be accomplished, as the anti-TPA/pro-TAA forces would now have nothing to gain by voting against TAA. Before, a vote against TAA was effectively a vote against TPA. But by de-linking the bills, a vote against TAA would have no bearing on TPA and there would no longer be any incentive to vote against a bill that one actually supported. Furthermore, the Republican leadership issued assurances that it would immediately introduce a TAA bill following an approved TPA bill. The House voted on the stand-alone TPA bill on June 19, 2015, and passed it by a narrow margin, 218 votes in favor, 208 votes opposed.[18] The TPA bill then headed to the Senate.

The strategy had its risks within the Senate. In order to reconsider TPA and TAA in this new format, the Senate had to agree procedurally to hold the new votes. Such a decision requires a three-fifths majority of the Senate, or 60 votes to end debate on a bill. This process, called cloture, is required to overcome a filibuster by opposing Senators.[19] Therefore, if fewer than 60 Senators voted in favor of reconsidering TPA and TAA as delinked bills, then the new bills would have been filibustered and could not have been presented for a vote.[20] The ability to attain 60 votes was in question because a cohort of Democratic senators who had voted for the linked TPA/TAA bills were concerned that TPA would be approved and the Republican-led Senate would then decline to proffer a TAA bill.

However, the Senate leadership succeeded in assuring the Democrats that they would put forth a TAA bill, and on 24 June 2015, the Senate voted by the barest possible margin, 60 in favor, 37 opposed (3 senators were not present to vote), for cloture, which allowed the stand-alone TPA bill to come to a vote. With this procedural hurdle overcome, there was little drama over the Senate vote on the

---

[18] See House Approves Standalone TPA Bill as Part of Obama-GOP Plan. Inside U.S. Trade, 19 June 2015.

[19] For a discussion of filibusters and cloture, see United States Senate, "Filibuster and Cloture" http://www.senate.gov/artandhistory/history/common/briefing/Filibuster_Cloture.htm (last accessed 11 August 2015).

[20] See http://www.senate.gov/artandhistory/history/common/briefing/Filibuster_Cloture.htm (last accessed 11 August 2015).

actual TPA bill, because that type of vote only requires a bare majority of senators' support to pass. With a three-fifths majority already having voted to hold a vote on the stand-alone bill, it was widely expected that the actual vote would easily eclipse the required bare majority. And indeed, the vote on the stand-alone TPA bill was 60 senators in favor, 38 opposed.

The Senate next turned to the issue of TAA. In order to improve the prospects for TAA to pass, Congressional leaders agreed that TAA should be bundled together with other trade measures that had already attained an overwhelming level of support in previous votes, including a renewal of the African Growth and Opportunity Act (AGOA) and a renewal of the Generalized System of Preferences program. On a voice vote, the Senate agreed to pass this package of measures.

The Senate vote sent the TAA bundle of legislation to the House for its consideration. Finally, on 25 June, the House voted 286-138 in favor of the TAA and accompanying legislation, which meant that TPA and TAA had been passed by both the House and Senate.[21] The bills then progressed to the President, who duly signed both sets of legislation along with the companion bills into law on Monday, 29 June 2015.[22]

The TPA legislation authorizes the President to enter into trade agreements, consistent with a lengthy list of enumerated objectives, for a period of 3 years (until 1 July 2018), with a possibility of renewal for an additional 3 years.[23] The President is required to notify Congress in advance of initiating trade negotiations, but the legislation specifically excepts from this requirement several ongoing negotiations: the TPP; the Trans-Atlantic Trade and Investment Partnership (TTIP) with the European Union; the Doha Round of WTO negotiations; the Trade in Services negotiations; and negotiations for a WTO environmental goods agreement.[24] The legislation requires the President to follow consultations procedures to be established by the Congress. The Administration will also have to be mindful of the negotiating objectives outlined in the legislation as well as other conditions. These parameters were the result of negotiations within Congress and therefore include subject matter that the Administration would have preferred to be excluded, and which could cause some headaches for the TPP negotiations. These provisions include a negotiating objective relating to foreign currency manipulation[25] and an

---

[21] See Congress Approves TAA-Preferences Bill with Backing of House Dems. Inside U.S. Trade, 26 June 2015.

[22] The grant of Trade Promotion Authority appears in Title I of H.R. 2146, and can be cited as the Bipartisan Congressional Trade Priorities and Accountability Act of 2015. See https://www.congress.gov/bill/114th-congress/house-bill/2146/text?q={%22search%22%3A[%22\%22hr2146\%22%22]} (last accessed 11 August 2015). For a summary of all of the trade-related legislation signed into law on 29 June, see On Trade: Here's What the President Signed into Law. The White House Blog, 29 June 2015, https://www.whitehouse.gov/blog/2015/06/29/trade-here-s-what-president-signed-law (last accessed 11 August 2015).

[23] H.R. 2146, Sec. 103(a)(1)(A).

[24] H.R. 2146, Sec. 107(a)(1)-(5).

[25] H.R. 2146, Sec. 102(b)(12).

exclusion from TPA of agreements entered into with countries that do not comply with the United States' Trafficking Victims Protection Act of 2000 (22 U.S.C. 7106 et. seq.).[26]

5 With TPA and TAA Passed, Is the TPP in the Bag?

Now that President Obama has TPA, the TPP parties will enter into the end game of negotiations. Given the timeline outlined above, the parties feel urgency to conclude the negotiations in one final round, and for that round to be held as soon as possible. Otherwise, there will be no real prospect of getting Congress to consider such a contentious bill until after the 2016 elections. The parties are therefore highly motivated to wrap up the negotiations. New Zealand Trade Minister Tim Groser says now that TPA is assured, the goal is to conclude negotiations within the month: "Now that Congress has spoken, it is show time… the scenario that I and my negotiators are working to is that we have to get the basic political deal done by the end of July, including finalising all the chapter texts, leaving only legal rectification by experts to be done thereafter."[27]

Notwithstanding the motivation of the negotiators, the issues that remain to be resolved are the ones which are the most politically sensitive and those over which there is the greatest difference in negotiating positions. Accordingly, reaching final agreement on an expedited schedule may prove quite difficult, and it is always possible that a deal could unravel at the very end. Examples of major issues still requiring resolution include agreement between the U.S. and Japan on a number of issues, including market access for rice and auto parts; Canada's protection of its dairy and poultry industries; market access for New Zealand dairy products; and the degree to which intellectual property protections will be heightened—and with what degree of impact on access to medicines.[28] These are significant, substantive issues that may not be susceptible to resolution in a very compressed time period.

Furthermore, if the TPP is concluded, there will be a faction within Congress that will be vociferous in its opposition to passing the trade pact into law. Because the

[26] H.R. 2146, Sec. 106(b)(6). This provision in particular may cause issues with respect to Malaysia's inclusion in the TPP. See Weisman J, Congressional Panels Approve Fast Track for Trade Deal, with Conditions. The New York Times, 23 April 2015, http://www.nytimes.com/2015/04/24/business/international/congressional-panels-approve-fast-track-for-trade-deal-with-conditions.html?_r=0 (last accessed 11 August 2015).

[27] McBeth P, TPP Negotiations Set to Accelerate, Groser Says. Scoop Business, 30 June 2015, http://www.scoop.co.nz/stories/BU1506/S01068/tpp-negotiations-set-to-accelerate-groser-says.htm (last accessed 11 August 2015).

[28] See TPA Passage Shifts Focus to TPP, But Some Skeptical of Quick Conclusion. Inside U.S. Trade, 26 June 2015.

entire text of the Agreement will be made public for a significant period of time before Congress votes, there will be a period of sustained negative commentary by a variety of constituencies who oppose the Agreement. Thus, while those members of Congress who voted in favor of TPA likely viewed their vote as effectively a vote in favor of the TPP, with only a ten-vote margin in favor of TPA in the House, the TPP's ultimate acceptance is not assured. And the closer to the 2016 elections this debate takes place, the more contentious it will be. For these reasons, while attaining TPA was a necessary precursor to concluding the TPP, it alone is not sufficient to guarantee the ultimate conclusion of the Agreement, nor its acceptance by the U.S. Congress.

TPP, Regulatory Coherence and China's Free Trade Strategy from A to Z

Henry Gao

Contents

Abstract This article starts with an overview of the negotiation on regulatory coherence in the Trans-Pacific Partnership (TPP), and then discusses its potential implications for China. The article argues that, the biggest challenge to China is not the trade diversion caused by the market access commitments in the TPP, but the regulatory coherence issues. The article then discusses the various initiatives China has taken at the domestic, bilateral, regional and global levels in response to the TPP negotiation, and concludes with a critical assessment of the pros and cons of each initiative.

H. Gao (✉)
School of Law, Singapore Management University, 60 Stamford Rd, 178900 Singapore, Singapore

Shanghai Institute of Foreign Trade, Shanghai, China
e-mail: gaohenry@gmail.com

M. Bungenberg et al. (eds.), *European Yearbook of International Economic Law 2016*, European Yearbook of International Economic Law 7,
DOI 10.1007/978-3-319-29215-1_21

1 Introduction

While purporting to be a 'Trans-Pacific' trade agreement, the Trans-Pacific Partnership (TPP)[1] curiously doesn't include China, which is one of the most important players in the Pacific. When the TPP negotiations were first launched in 2010, China deemed it as a scheme to contain China and deliberately ignored the agreement.[2] When the negotiations gained more and more momentum in 2012, China started to take a more realistic approach by paying close attention to the negotiations and indicated that it would be willing to consider TPP as one of the possible routes to achieve regional trade integration in Asia Pacific. More recently, China even indicated its willingness to join the negotiations by noting that the US has failed to invite China to join the TPP, to which the US replied that China should be able to meet the high standards before it may be considered as a potential applicant.

Putting diplomatic speeches aside, the reality remains that China's accession to the TPP in the near future is almost impossible. On the other hand, with the recent grant of the Trade Promotion Authority to President Obama, we will most likely see the conclusion of the TPP by the end of 2015, if not before. Once concluded, the TPP will have far-reaching implications not only for its members, but also for other countries in the region as well, especially China, which is a key link in the regional supply chains in Asia Pacific.

Many commentators, especially economists, predicated that the TPP will divert trade away from China to its competitors in the trade group, such as Vietnam and Mexico. With an ambitious agenda for market access negotiations, coupled with carefully-crafted rules of origin such as the "yarn-forwarding rule" which aim to prevent non-members from taking advantage of the tariff concessions, the TPP will certainly create obstacles for Chinese exports to key markets such as the US. However, it is still possible for China to bypass these obstacles through creative use of certain exceptions such as the "short-supply list" and relocating its factories to TPP members. In contrast, it would be much harder for China to deal with the challenges brought by the efforts by TPP members to harmonize the regulatory regimes on a variety of issues across the region, as there are no easy ways to circumvent the regulatory barriers.

This article will start with an overview of the negotiations on regulatory coherence issues in the TPP, then discuss the implications for China, followed by a critical review of China's attempts to deal with the challenge.

---

[1] This article was completed in July 2015 and all information are up to date until July 2015. For an overview of the TPP, see United States Trade Representative (USTR), Overview of the Trans Pacific Partnership, https://ustr.gov/tpp/overview-of-the-TPP (last accessed 5 August 2015).

[2] For a detailed analysis on China's changing attitudes towards the TPP, see Gao (2014), pp. 77–98.

2 Regulatory Coherence in the TPP

From the very beginning, the leading protagonist of the TPP, the US, has made clear that the TPP is not just about market access, but more importantly about making rules for the twenty-first century. In the Outlines of the TPP agreement agreed in Honolulu, Hawaii on November 12, 2011, the TPP members listed regulatory coherence as one of the key cross-cutting issues in the agreement and called for commitments that "will promote trade between the countries by making trade among them more seamless and efficient".[3]

As noted by Bollyky, regulatory coherence is not a new concept and has evolved through three tracks, i.e., the regulatory reform movement at the domestic level, the promotion of good regulatory practices at the WTO, and bilateral and regional efforts on regulatory cooperation and convergence.[4] According to him, a twenty-first century approach to regulatory coherence should focus on inter-governmental cooperation and include the following elements: an integrated approach that takes into consideration of both trade liberalization and other legitimate regulatory objectives; a joint institute to formulate common technical regulations and standards; and a flexible scope that may be expanded to address future emergent regulatory concerns and trade barriers.[5] However, due to resistances from domestic constituencies, Bollyky predicted that the TPP chapter would focus on inter-governmental regulatory reform rather than intra-governmental regulatory coherence.[6]

Bollysky's prediction is largely confirmed by the October 2011 leaked draft on the regulatory coherence chapter, which mainly focuses on the establishment of coordination mechanisms and implementation of best practices at the domestic level.[7] However, the recently adopted Bipartisan Congressional Trade Priorities and Accountability Act of 2015 seems to take a different approach by mandating US negotiators to seek to "promote regulatory compatibility through harmonization, equivalence, or mutual recognition of different regulations and standards and to encourage the use of international and interoperable standards".[8] Indeed, the inclusion of more inter-governmental cooperation is not impossible given the long history of regulatory cooperation among some TPP members, such as the Trans-Tasman Mutual Recognition Arrangement between Australia and New Zealand.[9]

No matter which approach is taken, it seems certain that the regulatory regimes of the TPP members will be subject to heavy influence from the US, as we can see from the detailed languages in the Bipartisan Congressional Trade Priorities and

---

[3] USTR, Outlines of TPP, https://ustr.gov/tpp/outlines-of-TPP (last accessed 5 August 2015).

[4] Bollyky (2012), pp. 174–178.

[5] Bollyky (2012), pp. 178–181.

[6] Bollyky (2012), pp. 181–182.

[7] http://www.citizenstrade.org/ctc/wp-content/uploads/2011/10/TransPacificRegulatoryCoherence.pdf (last accessed 5 August 2015).

[8] H.R. 2146.

[9] See Bollyky (2012), pp. 176–177.

Accountability Act on various regulatory issues ranging from e-commerce to labour and environment provisions.

3 Implications for China

While regulatory coherence can help reduce trade costs for firms from TPP members, it will most likely have a negative impact on non-TPP member countries. This is because compliance with diverse regulatory requirements is increasingly costly for firms, and can easily offset savings gained from other factors of input such as labor and raw materials. Thus, once the TPP comes into being, Chinese firms will become the most direct victims, as their customers will discover that it is much cheaper to source their imports from TPP members with fewer regulatory barriers. Some Chinese firms may try to meet the technical standards prevailing in TPP countries by sending their products for testing in these countries, but this will add to their production costs. Moreover, they might even be denied the opportunity due to systemic problems in the regulatory regimes (such as those on labor and environment) in the home country and these are beyond their controls.

In addition to the negative impacts on individual Chinese firms, the TPP regulatory coherence package will also foil China's efforts to develop domestic standards through promotion of indigenous innovation programs. For the last two decades, China has been trying to develop its own technical standards on issues ranging from mobile 3G network (TD-SCDMA), Wi-Fi (WAPI), to DVD format (EVD). As the TPP harmonizes the technical standards in these areas, most foreign firms and even many domestic Chinese firms will find it makes more sense for them to comply with the standards in the TPP rather than those in China.

Last but not least, the TPP will makes it more difficult for China to influence rule-making at the global level. While the current membership of the TPP is limited to only 12 countries,[10] most of these countries are key players in the WTO. Moreover, given the ambition of the US in launching the TPP negotiations, it is very likely to further expand to include other key economies. With the support of these countries, it would be much easier for the US to push its agenda on various regulatory issues into the WTO. Conversely, China would find it more and more difficult to resist the demands from the US and its allies.

[10] The current members include the US, Australia, Brunei Darussalam, Canada, Chile, Japan, Malaysia, Mexico, New Zealand, Peru, Singapore, and Vietnam.

4 China's Responses

When the TPP negotiations were first launched, China wasn't sure what to make of it and simply chose to ignore it. As the negotiations gained more and more momentum, China started to take it seriously and even indicated its willingness to seek accession. As stated by the Mexican Economy Secretary Bruno Ferrari when Mexico applied to join the TPP in late 2011, "the most important part is to participate in designing the rules of the TPP, not just enter into the TPP".[11] By entering the TPP negotiations, China could play some role in designing the new rules. However, the US probably will not want China's participation before the conclusion of the negotiations as it would make it more difficult for the US to control the direction of the negotiations. Moreover, even if China manages to get in, it has to face procedural hurdles in the accession process. While there are no explicit rules on accession, the experience of other countries which have joined the TPP negotiations half-way suggested that the following are the likely steps for new applicants:[12]

First, in terms of the process, the applicant has to consult with current TPP members on a bilateral basis, in addition to meeting in parallel with TPP members as a group.[13] Second, in terms of the substance, the country has to demonstrate that it can "live up to the high standards of the TPP agreement"[14] by addressing issues of concern for all TPP members, and must be willing to make concessions in specific areas of interests.[15] For example, when Japan applied, it was asked to provide better access for U.S. agricultural exports such as beef, market access for autos, pharmaceuticals and medical devices, as well as insurance services.[16] Also, the new member has to accept everything that has been agreed by existing members in the new negotiations and may not re-open any concluded issue for discussion.[17] Third, to admit a new member, the existing members have to reach a consensus decision.

---

[11] Inside US Trade, Mexico Expects TPP Countries To Consider New Entrants At March Round, 23 December 2011.

[12] Inside US Trade, TPP Countries Say Canada Not Ready to Join Talks, Press Vietnam to Decide, 22 October 2011.

[13] Inside US Trade, TPP Countries Say Canada Not Ready to Join Talks, Press Vietnam to Decide, 22 October 2011; See also Inside US Trade, Brady Says New TPP Entrants Must Address Bilateral Trade Issues, 16 December 2011; Inside US Trade, Marantis Sees New Entrants On 'Separate Track' From TPP Negotiations, 16 December 2011.

[14] Inside US Trade, USTR Intensifies Focus On TPP In Face Of Potential New Entrants. 9 December 2011.

[15] Inside US Trade, Canadian Minister Says Canada Ready To Meet, Exceed TPP Standards, 23 December 2011.

[16] Inside US Trade, Brady Says New TPP Entrants Must Address Bilateral Trade Issues, 16 December 2011.

[17] Inside US Trade, Congress, Administration to Consult on Possible Japan TPP Participation, 18 November, 2011; Inside US Trade, USTR Intensifies Focus On TPP In Face Of Potential New Entrants. 9 December 2011.

Of course, for obvious reasons, the view of the US is the most important.[18] Fourth, before being admitted as a full member, an applicant may start out as an "associate member". As such, the applicant may observe three rounds of negotiations without having to assume all the responsibilities of the full members. However, it must commit to full participation by the time of the fourth round.

Given the complicated accession process, again China could be subject to high demands from the existing members, especially the US. Thus, this is not an attractive option to China.

As China could not participate in the rule-making efforts in the TPP, it is left with only one choice, i.e., making its own rules. This is indeed what China has been doing for the past two years, and it involves initiatives at three levels.

First, at the domestic level, China has been introducing various reform measures. Some of these were launched by the Central Government as part of the nation-wide reform plan. Others were first tested in the so-called Free Trade Zones (FTZ). First piloted in the Pudong area in Shanghai in September 2013, the China (Shanghai) Pilot FTZ (SPFTZ) aims to become China's testing ground for new regulatory regimes on trade and investment. Initially covering only 28 km^2, the SPFTZ quickly introduced many new regulatory reforms in a host of areas:[19]

1. Investment regulation: these include the use of negative-listing rather than the traditional positive listing approach to regulate foreign investment; replacing the old approval system with a new registration system for foreign investments in areas which are not subject to the negative list; a "single window" registration system for the establishment of new firms; and further liberalization of the investment in the services sector;
2. Customs regulation: these include full liberalization of imports into the SPFTZ; the establishment of a "single window" system for international trade; and differentiated regulatory framework based on the customs risks of individual goods;
3. Financial regulation: these include several regulatory innovations to further promote the internalization of the Renminbi; further improvement of the financial services market; and introducing new ways to deal with financial risks through prudential regulations.
4. Shift of government function: In this area, the SPFTZ tries to switch from the old ex ante regulatory system to a system that reduces entry barriers and regulate through post facto monitoring of market players. The measures include national security review, anti-monopoly review, establishment of a social credit system, publication of firms' annual reports, sharing of information among regulatory

[18] Inside US Trade, Groser Says U.S. Holds Biggest Sway In Decision On New TPP Entrants, 23 December 2011.

[19] Shizhengfu Xinwen Fabuhui Tongbao Zimao Shiyanqu Yunxing Yinian Yilai de Qingkuang (Municipal Government Held Press Conference to Report on the Progress made during the first Year of the SPFTZ), Official website of the SPFTZ, 11 October 2014, http://www.china-shftz.gov.cn/NewsDetail.aspx?NID=afa679c5-7495-4436-959a-cd2b1957eb19&MenuType=3&CID=b90374c0-e6e6-4cfe-9cfe-1a365ad8fd77 (last accessed 5 August 2015).

authorities and coordination of enforcement measures, and encouraging non-governmental actors to help monitor markets.

Once these reform measures were proven successful in the SPFTZ, they were then selected by the Central Government for adoption across the country. To provide more room for regulatory innovation, in early 2015, the Central Government added three more pilot FTZs in Tianjin, Guangdong and Fujian, and further expanded the area of the SPFTZ to 120 km^2.

Second, at the bilateral and regional level, China has been experimenting with various new regulatory approaches. For example, in its Bilateral Investment Treaty negotiation with the US, China agreed to, for the first time, the use of negative listing approach and the grant of pre-establishment rights to foreign investors.[20] In its latest FTA signed with Australia, China also agreed to cooperate with Australia on a variety of regulatory issues ranging from Technical Barriers to Trade,[21] Financial Services[22] and Electronic Commerce.[23] There are also talks of including regulatory issues in the negotiations on other regional initiatives by China, such as the Regional Comprehensive Economic Partnership Agreement[24] and the 'One Belt One Road' initiative.[25]

Third, at the global level, China has also been trying very hard to participate in rule-making initiatives in various fora. For example, in the WTO, China actively supported the negotiation on the Trade Facilitation Agreement. Beyond the WTO, China has also been actively seeking participation in other regulatory initiatives such as the Trade in Services Agreement (TiSA), but unfortunately hasn't made much progress due to strong resistance from the US.

---

[20] Jingji Cankao (Economic Information), Di 11 Lun Zhongmei Touzi Xieding Tanpan Juxing, Huo She Fumian Qingdan Neirong (China and US to hold the 11th Round of Negotiations on the Bilateral Investment Treaty, May Discuss Issues on Negative Listing), 15 January 2014, http://jjckb.xinhuanet.com/2014-01/15/content_487189.htm (last accessed 5 August 2015).

[21] Ch. 6 of the China Australia Free Trade Agreement.

[22] Annex 8-B of the China Australia Free Trade Agreement.

[23] Ch. 12 of the China Australia Free Trade Agreement.

[24] According to the NZ Ministry of Foreign Affairs and Trade, the RCEP negotiations are supposed to cover issues such as competition policy, investment, intellectual property rights, and even labor and environmental issues. See Regional Comprehensive Economic Partnership (RCEP), http://www.mfat.govt.nz/Trade-and-Economic-Relations/2-Trade-Relationships-and-Agreements/RCEP/#negs (last accessed 5 August 2015).

[25] The One Road and One Belt Initiative refers to the Silk Road Economic Belt and 21st-Century Maritime Silk Road, which seeks to enhance the economic link between China and countries in Central and Western Asia, and Southeast Asia, South Asia and Africa, respectively. See Xinhua, Vision and Actions on Jointly Building Silk Road Economic Belt and 21st-Century Maritime Silk Road, Issued by the National Development and Reform Commission, Ministry of Foreign Affairs, and Ministry of Commerce of the People's Republic of China, with State Council authorization, March 2015, http://news.xinhuanet.com/english/bilingual/2015-03/28/c_134105922.htm (last accessed 5 August 2015).

5 Conclusion

To summarize, even though China has been excluded from the TPP negotiations, the progress in the TPP, especially that on regulatory coherence, has pushed China to re-think its strategy on trade liberalization and regulatory reform. As China realized that it would run the risk of being marginalized without regulatory reform, it has been experimenting with reform initiatives at various levels. So far, most progress has been made at the domestic level, where various regulatory reform measures were introduced in China's new generation of FTZs. This is unsurprising, as China would have most autonomy for the domestic reforms. However, the limitation to this approach is that such reform measures are mainly introduced by local governments, while the reforms on many deeper regulatory issues needs the sanction of the central government and even external pressure from foreign governments. That is also why China has also been actively engaged in negotiations on regulatory coherence issues at the bilateral, regional and multilateral levels as well. These initiatives can help China to catch up with the best practices of regulatory reform at the international level, but as these negotiations typically involve trade-offs between different sectors and regulatory coherence issues are often used as bargaining chips, how much impact they can have on China's regulatory reform is still an open question. Nonetheless, by leading China to the negotiating table, these initiatives have at least taken an important step towards the right direction.

Acknowledgement This article benefits from the generous support provided by the SMU Internal Research Grant (Project Fund No. C234/MSS13L010).

References

Bollyky TJ (2012) Regulatory coherence in the TPP talks. In: Lim CL, Elms D, Low P (eds) The Trans-Pacific Partnership: a quest for a 21st century trade agreement. Cambridge University Press, Cambridge

Gao H (2014) Selected issues in TPP negotiations and implications for China. In: Hu J, Vanhullebusch M (eds) Regional cooperation and free trade agreements in Asia. Brill Academic Publishers, Leiden

The Flow-On Effect: How the TPP Will Re-Shape Trade Relations in East Asia

Bryan Mercurio

Contents

Abstract Much ink has already been spilt on the Trans-Pacific Partnership (TPP), including some quality legal and geo-political analysis and high level economic enquiry but also far too many premature predictions of textual language or economic impact. This brief article does not attempt to predict or analyse the legal text, which at the time of writing had not been finalised, but rather highlights four potential flow-on effects a finalised and in-force TPP will have on trade relations in East Asia: (1) China's response; (2) the impact on the ongoing negotiations of the Association of Southeast Asian Nations (ASEAN) aimed at deeper regional integration; (3) unilateral trade liberalization and good governance initiatives by aspiring entrants to the TPP; and (4) Taiwan's status as an economic entity and participation in regional trade agreements. To this author, the flow-on effects will have a considerable impact on and go some way in re-shaping trade relations between and among East Asian nation states.

B. Mercurio (✉)
Faculty of Law, The Chinese University of Hong Kong, 6/F Lee Shau Kee Building, Shatin, NT, Hong Kong
e-mail: b.mercurio@cuhk.edu.hk

M. Bungenberg et al. (eds.), *European Yearbook of International Economic Law 2016*, European Yearbook of International Economic Law 7,
DOI 10.1007/978-3-319-29215-1_22

1 Introduction

Much ink has already been spilt on the Trans-Pacific Partnership (TPP), including some quality legal and geo-political analysis and high level economic enquiry but also far too many premature predictions of textual language or economic impact. This brief article does not attempt to predict or analyse the legal text, which at the time of writing had not been finalised, but rather highlights four potential flow-on effects a finalised and in-force TPP will have on trade relations in East Asia: (1) China's response; (2) the impact on the ongoing negotiations of the Association of Southeast Asian Nations (ASEAN) aimed at deeper regional integration; (3) unilateral trade liberalization and good governance initiatives by aspiring entrants to the TPP; and (4) Taiwan's status as an economic entity and participation in regional trade agreements. To this author, the flow-on effects will have a considerable impact on and go some way in re-shaping trade relations between and among East Asian nation states.

2 Four Effects of the TPP on Trade Relations in East Asia

2.1 China Will Respond

The successful conclusion of the TPP will certainly have a flow-on effect on and set off a chain of events in East Asia. Perhaps the most discussed in the literature to date is the effect on and response of China.[1] While China's initial fiery rhetoric towards the TPP has been replaced by cautious acceptance of the agreement it remains weary of the economic and political weight and signalling effect of the TPP. The question is not *if* China will react to the TPP but rather *how* it will react. This author posits that China will react by expending energy and capital in order to keep (or acquire) a sphere of

[1] See, ie, Armstrong S, China's participation in the Trans-Pacific Partnership. East Asian Forum, 11 December 2011, http://www.eastasiaforum.org/2011/12/11/china-participation-in-the-trans-pacific-partnership/ (last accessed 7 August 2015); Li C and Whalley J (2012) China and the TPP: A Numerical Simulation Assessment of the Effects Involved. NBER Working Paper No. 18090; Bergsten F and Schott JJ (2012) China and the Trans-Pacific Partnership. APEC Currents, http://www.apec.org.au/docs/currentsrmit/2012-1/index.html#3 (last accessed 7 August 2015); Yuan WJ (2012) The Trans-Pacific Partnership and China's Corresponding Strategies. Center for Strategic and International Studies Freeman Briefing Report, http://csis.org/files/publication/120620_Freeman_Brief.pdf (last accessed 7 August 2015); Solís M (2013) The Containment Fallacy: China and the TPP. Brookings Upfront, http://www.brookings.edu/blogs/up-front/posts/2013/05/24-china-transpacific-partnership-solis (last accessed 7 August 2015); Petri et al (2014).

influence over the 'near-abroad' and inhibit a shift in the balance of power in favour of the United States (US).[2]

Such a reaction would be a repeat of history. China's initial response to Japan's entry into the TPP negotiations was to greatly accelerate its efforts for an 'ASEAN+6'-style agreement (later named the Regional Comprehensive Economic Partnership (RCEP))[3] and kick-start trade negotiations with Japan-Korea (dubbed the 'CJK')[4] and, separately, Korea (which has recently been concluded).[5] If the past is any indication of future behaviour, one could expect at least part of China's reaction to the conclusion of the TPP to include a redoubling of negotiating efforts to advance the somewhat stalled RCEP,[6] and possibly a reset of the frozen CJK negotiations (assuming political tensions, territorial disputes and nationalism allow for civil negotiations between China and Japan).[7] China may also seek to advance talks with the US and EU on a bilateral investment treaty (BIT) and even to export its preferred model-BIT to other nations.[8] In addition, and as significantly, China will likely attempt to exert influence in other economic-related ways, such as through its leadership in the Asian Infrastructure Investment Bank (AIIB), promotion of its

[2] On the potential for the TPP to increase US influence in the region, see Salidjanova N, Koch-Weser I and Klanderman J (2015) China's Economic Ties with ASEAN: A Country-by Country Analysis. U. S.-China Economic and Security Review Commission Staff Research Report, p. 4 ("Although TPP has many purposes, most of which are exclusively economic, it could also have an indirect bearing on the balance of power in the Asia region, in terms of solidifying U.S. partnerships in the face of China's growing influence.").

[3] Ermert M, Big trading blocs moving at breakneck pace to raise free trade standards. IP Watch, 22 May 2013.

[4] Ermert M, Big trading blocs moving at breakneck pace to raise free trade standards. IP Watch, 22 May 2013 (quoting Nakagawa as stating "Japan's move to join the TPP must have made them change their mind").

[5] http://news.xinhuanet.com/english/china/2014-11/10/c_133778436.htm (last accessed 7 August 2015). The agreement is not yet in force.

[6] The RCEP is not expected to offer substantial market access opportunities for goods or services or to be a cutting edge '21st century' agreement in addressing behind the border or other trade-related issues. For projected economic analysis of both the TPP and RCEP, see Petri PA (2012) Economics of TPP and RCEP Negotiations Draft Document, http://www.pecc.org/resources/doc_view/1942-economics-of-the-tpp-and-rcep-negotiations (last accessed 7 August 2015).

[7] On China-Japan relations, see Nagy (2013), p. 49.

[8] In regards to the BIT with the US, it has been reported that the framework agreement is completed but much remains to be done with regard to the 'negative lists', or reservations. China has not previously negotiated a trade or investment treaty using the negative list approach. See China "uncomfortable with" U.S. negative list for investment treaty talks: Lou. Xinhua English News, 20 April 2015, http://news.xinhuanet.com/english/2015-04/21/c_134167561.htm (last accessed 7 August 2015). For background information on investment treaties in Asia, see Chaisse (2015).

proposed Free Trade Area of the Asia-Pacific (FTAAP)[9] and increasing its growing presence in Africa, Central/South America and the Middle East.[10]

The one response we should not expect from China is an express desire to accede to the TPP. While China would no doubt like to counter the US move to solidify its position as the dominant economic force in the region, China simply is not ready, able or willing to implement the high standards likely to come out of the TPP negotiations. This is not to suggest that China is not progressing—on the contrary, China's recent agreements with Australia and Korea focused not only on traditional staples such as tariff rates and rules of origin, but also included advancements on earlier Chinese FTAs in areas such as information technology and services—but merely recognizes that China will be unwilling to agree to meaningful market access liberalization through deep reductions in tariff and non-tariff barriers on industrial and agricultural products or a substantial opening of its services market as well as disciplines on such matters of labour, environment, competition and state-owned enterprises (SOEs). Disciplines on such issues would strike at the core of China's industrial policy. Thus, even though China has since-2013 expressed some interest in potentially joining the TPP at a later date, it has also recognised that the agreement's tougher standards may not be appropriate for China's level of economic development and liberalization ambitions.[11] For this reason, China's cautious interest in the TPP takes the form of ambiguous statements such as the one made by Ministry of Commerce spokesman Shen Danyang that China 'will analyze the pros and cons as well as the possibility of joining the TPP, based on careful research and according to principles of equality and mutual benefit'.[12]

---

[9] See Solís M, China flexes its muscles at APEC with the revival of FTAAP. East Asian Forum, 23 November 2014, http://www.eastasiaforum.org/2014/11/23/china-flexes-its-muscles-at-apec-with-the-revival-of-ftaap/ (last accessed 7 August 2015); Salidjanova N, Koch-Weser I, Klanderman J (2015) China's Economic Ties with ASEAN: A Country-by Country Analysis. U.S.-China Economic and Security Review Commission Staff Research Report, p. 9 (arguing that the FTAAP "could detract from U.S. efforts to complete TPP, as most key economies in the region would be involved in both negotiations").

[10] See Rousseau R, The New Geography of Chinese Influence. Diplomatic Courier, 29 May 2014, http://www.diplomaticourier.com/news/regions/brics/2212-the-new-geography-of-chinese-influence (last accessed 7 August 2015).

[11] It should be noted, however, that China's level of economic development exceeds that of some current parties to the TPP, most notably Vietnam.

[12] Yao K, China to study possibility of joining U.S.-led trade talks. Reuters, 30 May 2013, http://www.reuters.com/article/2013/05/30/us-trade-asiapacific-china-idUSBRE94T0X420130530 (last accessed 7 August 2015). See also Lei H (2013) Foreign Ministry Spokesperson Hong Lei's Regular Press Conference on May 31, 2013. Chinese Ministry of Foreign Affairs, http://www.fmprc.gov.cn/eng/xwfw/s2510/t1046318.shtml (last accessed 7 August 2015); Ding Q and Boris J, 'Positive' Sign on Free Trade Pact. China Watch (Washington Post), 5 July 2013, http://chinawatch.washingtonpost.com/2013/07/positive_sign_on_free_trade_pact/ (last accessed 7 August 2015). But see Lim CL (2015) China and the Trans-Pacific Partnership. Social Science Japan 52, p. 15 (arguing China has signalled its intent to enter into an agreement with high standards).

Regardless of China's stated interest, the TPP is in the short-to-medium term a non-starter for China due to its model of economic growth, which remains led by the state and fed in part by lax understanding and enforcement of intellectual property rights.[13] Moreover, as China is currently attempting to deal with several internal difficulties—including deceleration of domestic economic growth, serious environmental issues and a plethora of problems associated with an ageing population—the time does not seem ripe for China to accede to a trade framework which would limit its toolkit in order to manage economic development. Moreover, if China were ready to undertake such initiatives or even to negotiate an agreement which promotes meaningful economic liberalization it does not need the TPP to do so, it could simply use the RCEP as the platform. The fact that the RCEP negotiations do not seem to be proceeding with the expectation of much ambition—and could even be called conspicuously unambitious—is telling in this regard.

China will react to the conclusion of the TPP with a flurry of trade-related activities, but it will not seek immediate accession to the TPP as the expected standards and disciplines of that agreement extend far beyond China's comfort zone. Instead, China will pursue alternative arrangements and seek to enhance its geo-political influence in other ways as a counterweight to the US 'pivot' to Asia.[14] In the longer term, China could perhaps come to accept greater disciplines as the price for expanded market access and/or economic influence and seek entry into the TPP—but that day is far into the future.

2.2 *ASEAN Will Face Difficult Questions*

The completion of the TPP will also likely also bring about wider, albeit less discussed, consequences on East Asia. Some of the most significant flow-on effects of a completed TPP will occur in ASEAN, as well as in the member states of ASEAN.

Four of the ten ASEAN member states are part of the TPP—Brunei, Malaysia, Singapore and Vietnam—and it is inevitable that the obligations undertaken and (expected) deeper set of rules in that agreement will have an effect on intra-ASEAN negotiations in the lead-up to the ASEAN Economic Community (AEC).[15] The ASEAN has always been beset by difficulties and discord when it comes to trade

---

[13] See Mercurio (2012), p. 23.

[14] Obama B, Remarks by President Obama to the Australian Parliament. Canberra, 17 November 2011; Donilon T, 'The United States and the Asia-Pacific in 2013' Remarks made to The Asia Society. New York, 11 March 2013, https://www.whitehouse.gov/the-press-office/2013/03/11/remarks-tom-donilon-national-security-advisor-president-united-states-an (last accessed 7 August 2015).

[15] For information on the AEC, see http://www.asean.org/communities/asean-economic-community (last accessed 7 August 2015). It should be noted that the ASEAN Comprehensive Investment Agreement, which provides for a harmonized set of principles in relation to intra-ASEAN foreign investment, entered into force in 2012. See http://www.asean.org/images/2012/Economic/AIA/Agreement/ASEAN%20Comprehensive%20Investment%20Agreement%20%28ACIA%29%202012.pdf (last accessed 7 August 2015).

and investment liberalization, but the fact that four of ASEAN's Member States will be parties to the most comprehensive FTA (covering both trade and investment disciplines) to date will only widen the schism between the 'can do' and 'can't do' countries. The potential effect of the TPP on ASEAN cannot therefore be overstated.

The ASEAN member states also demonstrate a marked variance in their negotiating skill and alacrity. While Singapore is well-suited to and experienced in negotiating meaningful trade agreements,[16] Brunei, Malaysia and Vietnam have proven in the past to be reticent or even hostile to ambitious trade agreements. Of note in this regard are Malaysia's unsuccessful negotiations with the US (which broke down after eight rounds in 2008 but never officially ceased)[17] and the EU (which broke down in 2012 after seven rounds but never officially ceased)[18] and Vietnam's resolute defence of its status as a transitional economy and recently acceded Member of the WTO.[19]

With these four ASEAN member states agreeing to what is expected to be deep reductions in tariffs and non-tariff barriers, significant liberalization commitments in goods and services as well as obligations relating to trade-related measures such as labour, environment, competition and the disciplining of SOEs, it is beyond doubt that the TPP will effect negotiations within ASEAN. One area which is both worthy of mention and highly illustrative is trade in services—commitments made in the TPP are expected to be via a 'negative list' approach, meaning every sector and subsector of services are subject to the agreement and will be liberalized subject to restrictions for existing and other measures and carve-outs listed in the annexes.[20] This format is well-known and used by most OECD nations, but unlike the GATS approach of a 'positive list' approach in which only the sectors and subsectors listed are subject to any liberalization commitment.[21] It is also likely that investment, or 'commercial presence' as it is referred to in the GATS, will be carved out of the services chapter of the TPP and instead be the sole domain of the investment chapter. Again, such an approach is common among FTAs involving an

[16] Singapore has negotiated 20 FTAs with a diverse range of developed and developing countries, including the US, Japan, Korea and China. See http://www.fta.gov.sg/sg_fta.asp (last accessed 11 August 2015).

[17] See https://ustr.gov/trade-agreements/other-agreements/malaysia-fta (last accessed 11 August 2015).

[18] See http://ec.europa.eu/trade/policy/countries-and-regions/countries/malaysia/ (last accessed 11 August 2015).

[19] Information on Vietnam and the WTO can be found at https://www.wto.org/english/thewto_e/countries_e/vietnam_e.htm (last accessed 11 August 2015).

[20] See http://dfat.gov.au/trade/agreements/tpp/news/Documents/Trans-Pacific-Partnership-Trade-Ministers-Report-to-Leaders.pdf (last accessed 11 August 2015) stating: "On services and investment, we are negotiating access to each other's services and investment markets on a 'negative list' basis, which assumes access unless countries take an exception.".

[21] On the GATS approach, see https://www.wto.org/english/Tratop_e/serv_e/guide1_e.htm (last accessed 11 August 2015). The EU has traditionally been one notable exception and maintained a preference for the positive list or hybrid-approach to scheduling, however its recent FTA with Canada does adopt a negative list approach.

OECD country. Although there is no inherent reason why a negative list approach to scheduling should be more trade liberalizing than a positive list approach,[22] in practice this has been the case almost without exception.[23]

Singapore is the only one of the four ASEAN Member States with experience in negotiating a negative list (although Brunei has compiled a 'transparency list' in its FTA with Japan[24]). In the past, Malaysia has been firmly opposed to a negative list, Vietnam has questioned its own ability to negotiate in this manner and Brunei has not signalled any intent to shift its scheduling approach. But now, all four countries will have experience with negotiating in such a manner and, perhaps more importantly, will have completed all of the necessary groundwork to enable competent negotiations using a negative list approach.[25] There is no reason for them to oppose a negative list in the ASEAN Trade in Services Agreement (ATISA), the services component of the AEC scheduled to replace the ASEAN Framework Agreement on Services (AFAS) in 2016. On the contrary, it would make more sense for these countries to at the very least offer the level concessions made to TPP partners to their ASEAN partner countries as part of the ATISA negotiations—for the remaining ASEAN member states will of course already be aware of the concessions made by the four ASEAN countries in the TPP. It would also be easier for these members to take stock of their own commitments and value the offers of negotiating partners using the negative list approach given the experience of the TPP negotiations. Such an approach may face opposition, but the negative approach to scheduling commitments will result in enhanced liberalization and deeper integration of ASEAN—which is of course one of the key objectives of the AEC.[26]

A flow-on effect of the TPP could therefore be a shift in negotiating strategies among the several member states of ASEAN, who may now have incentive to push a more aggressive and liberalized trade agenda internally at the ASEAN. As a result, the ASEAN could become a more liberalized and integrated trade area and in the process change the course and outcomes of the AEC (for the better). This would, of course, also likely result in a shift in ASEAN's negotiating positions in its external trade relations. ASEAN FTAs to date can all be characterised as rather

[22] See Adlung R, Mamdouh H (2013) How to Design Trade Agreements in Services: Top Down or Bottom-Up? WTO Staff Working Paper ERSD-2013-08.

[23] See, eg, Roy M (2011) Services Commitments in Preferential Trade Agreements: An Expanded Dataset. WTO Staff Working Paper, ERSD-11-18; Hufbauer and Stephenson (2007), p. 605; Roy et al (2007), p. 155.

[24] This approach provides for the preparation and publication of a non-binding list of existing measures not conforming to the market access and national treatment obligations. The list is identical in form to the reservations made in a negative list approach.

[25] As Annex I of a negative list approach applies to *existing* measures, it is necessary for countries to undergo a substantial amount of coordination and, preferably, a regulatory audit prior to negotiations. For more detailed information on preparing for services negotiations, see Sauvé P and Lacey S (2013) A handbook for negotiating preferential trade agreements: services liberalization, prepared for the United Nations Economic and Social Commission for Asia Pacific (UNESCAP) and Asia-Pacific Research and Training Network on Trade (ARTNeT). United Nations Publication, Thailand.

[26] See AEC Blueprint, signed November 2007, http://www.asean.org/archive/5187-10.pdf (last accessed 11 August 2015).

weak and lacking ambition—and all indications are that this remains the case in the RCEP negotiations—but it would seem likely that a rejuvenated ASEAN would also be ready to shift its external negotiating positions and seek deeper and more meaningful trade relations with partner countries.

The completion of the TPP could therefore have a significant effect on the negotiation of ASEAN's internal trade agreements as well as its negotiations with external partners. In the alternative, the schism dividing ASEAN member states could deepen. Member states may look elsewhere for economic growth, further marginalizing and ASEAN as a regional trading group. As importantly, the ASEAN could become viewed (from both the inside and outside) as merely a group that codifies the least common denominator in its trade agreements. A divided ASEAN would also have repercussions on non-trade related issues, such as the resolution of territorial disputes and its leadership role within the regional framework. In short, ASEAN would be further divided, destabilized and weakened as an economic and potentially political organization. The direction which ASEAN will take is unknown at this time, but that the successful conclusion of the TPP will bring ASEAN to a 'fork in the road' is not in doubt.

2.3 *Unilateral Behavioural Change*

The TPP is expected to deliver benefits and include obligations on a number of 'behind the border' issues, some of which could extend well beyond existing FTAs negotiated by countries in Asia. Each of these areas would require domestic reform, with some necessitating far-reaching changes in partner countries. The most notable of these behind the border issues include services, investment, product standards (including but not limited to health and safety), competition, intellectual property, labour, environment, e-commerce, SOEs and government procurement.[27]

To date, Korea and Taiwan have clearly stated their aims of acceding to the TPP,[28] while Thailand, the Philippines, Indonesia, and others have expressed an interest in entering the TPP at some point in the future.[29] Should these countries

[27] See Mercurio (2014), p. 1558, 1559–1562.

[28] See Fifield A, South Korea asks to join Pacific trade deal: Washington says not so fast. The Washington Post, 15 April 2015, http://www.washingtonpost.com/world/asia_pacific/south-korea-asks-to-join-pacific-trade-deal-washington-says-not-so-fast/2015/04/15/85d7396a-e39e-11e4-ae0f-f8c46aa8c3a4_story.html (last accessed 11 August 2015); Lee J, Taiwan must join TPP and RECP in 2014: President Ma. The China Post, 10 January 2014, http://www.chinapost.com.tw/taiwan/national/national-news/2014/01/10/398005/Taiwan-must.htm (last accessed 11 August 2015).

[29] On the nature of the TPP as an open agreement, see the comments of then-acting US Trade Representative Demetrios Marantis in March 2013: "at a certain point, economies that are interested are going to either be part of TPP as we are finalizing it, but the idea is that if economies aren't ready right now, that they'll be able to join once it's done and essentially accede to the TPP... The whole point of the agreement is to serve as a platform for regional integration in Asia".

succeed in joining the TPP, it seems natural that other Asian countries and ASEAN member states would likewise seek entry to the TPP.

Before any of these countries enter the TPP, however, they would need to show a commitment to the high standards and significant obligations of the agreement. Most of the legwork would need to be completed prior to negotiating entry, which in effect would in some cases precipitate deep structural changes in domestic setting in order to simply formally join accession negotiations.[30] In this regard, the possibility of accession to the TPP will have positive effects on trade, liberalization, and good governance in the region as more countries view accession as a realistic possibility and begin planning for negotiations and ultimate entry into the pact.

2.4 *The Taiwan Question*

As mentioned above, Taiwan has on several occasions stated its aspiration to be included as a member of the TPP.[31] Apart from staking its claim as a separate customs territory capable of negotiating trade agreements and opening new market access opportunities, Taiwan's membership in the TPP would inevitably raise further questions; namely, would accession to the TPP open up an avenue for negotiations with ASEAN and potentially even the RCEP?

Taiwan currently has negotiated FTAs with a handful of countries, including New Zealand and Singapore. Both of these agreements, however, were subsequent to these countries reaching an FTA with China and likely with its tacit approval. Membership in the TPP would not only significantly expand the size and economic weight of Taiwan's FTA partner countries but perhaps more importantly mean that Taiwan will have a pact with countries who have not negotiated an FTA with China, most prominently the US, Canada and Japan. While these nations are likely not going to be frightened any Chinese threat of retaliation, such threats will likely

---

Bracken L, Japan's TPP Negotiating Team to Be Formed Outside Cabinet, Isolated From Protectionists. BNA International Trade Daily, 21 March 2013.

[30] See, eg, Palmer D and Behsudi A (2014) Taiwan's man in D.C. pushes TPP membership. Politico Pro, http://www.politico.com/story/2014/08/taiwans-man-in-dc-pushes-tpp-membership-110111_Page2.html (last accessed 11 August 2015) discussing difficulties with Taiwan's entry to the TPP, including systemic and specific trade issues.

[31] See Fifield A, South Korea asks to join Pacific trade deal: Washington says not so fast. The Washington Post, 15 April 2015, http://www.washingtonpost.com/world/asia_pacific/south-korea-asks-to-join-pacific-trade-deal-washington-says-not-so-fast/2015/04/15/85d7396a-e39e-11e4-ae0f-f8c46aa8c3a4_story.html (last accessed 11 August 2015); Lee J, Taiwan must join TPP and RECP in 2014: President Ma. The China Post, 10 January 2014, http://www.chinapost.com.tw/taiwan/national/national-news/2014/01/10/398005/Taiwan-must.htm (last accessed 11 August 2015); Palmer D and Behsudi A (2014) Taiwan's man in D.C. pushes TPP membership. Politico Pro, http://www.politico.com/story/2014/08/taiwans-man-in-dc-pushes-tpp-membership-110111_Page2.html (last accessed 11 August 2015). See also Mercurio (2014), p. 1563.

affect the willingness of others such as Malaysia, Peru and Vietnam to proceed without China's endorsement.

Taiwan has made no secret of its desire to be a part of regional trade agreements yet most countries are hesitant to embrace the island for fear of upsetting China. This response is economically rather than ideologically driven as China is an important trading partner for every country in Asia and the expected reprisal from China could be significant. It is likewise not difficult to understand why Taiwan craves an FTA with ASEAN and membership in the RCEP; while cementing its status as an independent economic entity may play a role, it would seem economics are far more important. Taiwan is currently well-integrated into the supply chains of Asia for several products but risks exclusion should its competitors receive preferential treatment. A pact with ASEAN would go some way in protecting its market and the joining the RCEP (theoretically open to jurisdictions which have an FTA with ASEAN)[32] would not only further insulate markets but also open the door to several other key markets (including Korea and India).

That being said, Taiwan's place in the TPP and any future ASEAN-Taiwan FTA is far from certain. China has consistently pressured countries to spurn negotiations with Taiwan (unless and until they negotiate with China) and its recent rejection of Taiwan's application for entry as a founding member of the AIIB[33] indicates the stance is unlikely to shift in the near future.

3 Conclusion

Upon coming into force, the TPP will have a significant effect not only on members but also upon countries external to the agreement. This brief article limited analysis to four possible flow-on effects of the TPP on East Asia, but in so doing demonstrated the potential tectonic shift in trade policy and relations which could occur as a direct result of the TPP.

First, China will react, and its reaction will in itself have flow-on effects. In the short term, it will in all likelihood accelerate its own bilateral and regional trade and investment negotiations and seek alternative paths to exert regional influence in an attempt to counter the weight of the TPP. In the long term, China may even seek to join the TPP which could necessitate massive internal changes almost on the scale of those needed for its entry into the WTO in 2001.

---

[32] The RCEP is based on ASEAN centrality and limited to countries which have a FTA with ASEAN. On ASEAN centrality, see Fukunaga (2015), p. 103.

[33] Blanchard B and Gold M, Taiwan rejected as founding member of Beijing-led multilateral bank. Reuters, 13 April 2015, http://uk.reuters.com/article/2015/04/13/asia-aiib-taiwan-idUKL4N0XA20L20150413 (last accessed 11 August 2015).

Second, with four ASEAN member states in the TPP it seems likely that these countries will attempt to bring some of the rules, obligations and architecture of the TPP to ASEAN in some form. The fact that ASEAN is committed to deepening its internal relationship and is transitioning to an AEC only increases the likelihood of the TPP's influence on ASEAN's trade liberalization efforts. The effect could be tremendously positive and lead to a stronger and more dynamic ASEAN, but it could also have the opposite effect and lead to an attenuation of ASEAN's role in regional integration as a whole while at the same time creating conditions which further weaken its existing structure.

Third, countries desiring to seek membership in the TPP will have to conform to the rules and standards prior to admission. With so many interested observers in Asia, the finalisation of the TPP will bring about a host of positive changes in the domestic regulatory framework and trade policies of aspiring TPP entrants.

Fourth, if and when Taiwan is admitted as a member of the TPP the question of Taiwan's negotiation of an FTA with ASEAN and ultimately the RCEP would become unavoidable. While such questions have to date been carefully avoided, this will no longer be possible and the answer will impact not only trade relations but broader political issues in the region.

Acknowledgement Thanks to Stephen Nagy, Julien Chaisse, Bryan Druzin and CL Lim for commenting on draft versions of this article. All opinions and errors remain my own.

References

Chaisse J (2015) The shifting tectonics of international investment law - structure and dynamics of rules and arbitration on foreign investment in the Asia-Pacific region. George Washington Int Law Rev 47(3):187–216

Hufbauer G, Stephenson S (2007) Services trade: past liberalization and future challenges. J Int Econ Law 10(3):605–630

Fukunaga Y (2015) ASEAN's leadership in the Regional Comprehensive Economic Partnership. Asia Pac Policy Stud 2(1):103–115

Mercurio B (2012) China and the enforcement of intellectual property rights. China Perspect 1:23–28

Mercurio B (2014) The trans-pacific partnership: becoming a game changer. World Econ 37 (11):1558–1574

Nagy SR (2013) Territorial disputes, trade and diplomacy: examining the repercussions of the Sino-Japanese territorial dispute on bilateral trade. China Perspect 4:46–57

Petri PA, Plummer MG, Zhai F (2014) The TPP, China and the FTAAP: the case for convergence. In: Guoqiang T, Petri PA (eds) New directions in Asia-Pacific economic integration. East-West Center, Honolulu, pp 78–89

Roy M, Marchetti J, Lim H (2007) Services liberalization in the new generation of preferential trade agreements (PTAs): how much further than the GATS? World Trade Rev 6(2):155–192

Investment Protection in TTIP: Three Feasible Proposals

Jan Kleinheisterkamp and Lauge N. Skovgaard Poulsen

Contents

Abstract Investor-state dispute settlement (ISDS) through international arbitration has become a major stumbling block in negotiations of the Transatlantic Trade and Investment Partnership (TTIP).

Despite a number of efforts to fix shortcomings of the existing system especially by the European Commission, many stakeholders still are unconvinced that these incremental adaptations are sufficient to safeguard policy space in Europe. Right or wrong, there is little political appetite to include similar provisions into TTIP. At the time of writing, Washington also showed little appetite for a transatlantic or even multilateral investment court.

In order to avoid losing support for the agreement as a whole, the parties now need to think about alternatives. This brief article proposes three solutions, which could be politically acceptable while at the same time offering meaningful investment

We are grateful to David Gaukrodger for comments on a previous version.

J. Kleinheisterkamp (✉)
Law Department, London School of Economics, Houghton Street, London WC2A 2AE, UK
e-mail: J.Kleinheisterkamp@lse.ac.uk

L.N. Skovgaard Poulsen
School of Public Policy, University College London, London WC1H 9QU, UK
e-mail: l.poulsen@ucl.ac.uk

M. Bungenberg et al. (eds.), *European Yearbook of International Economic Law 2016*, European Yearbook of International Economic Law 7,
DOI 10.1007/978-3-319-29215-1_23

protections. Our proposals are intended as a concise but constructive input to the increasingly divisive political debates, which are detracting attention from the broader economic and geopolitical benefits of a transatlantic trade agreement.

1 Introduction

Investor-state dispute settlement (ISDS) through international arbitration has become a major stumbling block in negotiations of the Transatlantic Trade and Investment Partnership (TTIP). While trade and regulatory cooperation are at the heart of TTIP, the comparatively minor element of ISDS is dominating the current political landscape.[1]

In agreements with Canada (CETA) and Singapore, the European Commission has included several modifications to the 'traditional' investment provisions found in the bilateral investment treaties of European capital exporting countries, so as to address some of the perceived shortcomings of the traditional ISDS system. Among those, the push for greater transparency is especially laudable, as is the latest insertion of the Investment Court System in the "legal scrubbing" of the CETA text. Yet, many stakeholders remain unconvinced that these adaptations of ISDS are sufficient to justify its inclusion into TTIP.

In order to avoid losing support for the agreement as a whole, the parties need to think about alternatives. This brief article proposes three solutions, which could be politically acceptable while at the same time offering meaningful investment protections. We do not offer a full-fledged cost-benefit analysis compared to CETA, nor do we engage in a comprehensive technical legal discussion. Rather, our proposals are intended as a concise but constructive input to the increasingly divisive political debates, which are detracting attention from the broader economic and geopolitical benefits of a transatlantic trade agreement.

2 The (Political) Problem

The European Parliament stated in 2013 that future EU investment agreement should only include ISDS (be it in form of arbitration or a court system) "[i]n the cases where it is justifiable" and has affirmed its skepticism as to whether it is in fact

[1] See Poulsen, Bonnitcha, and Yackee (2015).

necessary and justifiable in TTIP.[2] Indeed, there are important policy questions that beg for answers. Since only a small minority of American investors are genuinely concerned with expropriation risks in few EU member states, why should they not just be asked to purchase political risk insurance? Why should taxpayers have to pay for protections that multinationals to a large extent can pay for themselves through the private market?[3]

These concerns are significant. Even if dismissing the loudest criticism against ISDS as unpersuasive, the intensive and growing opposition could derail the most comprehensive preferential trade agreement in history. TTIP is expected to require approval in the European Parliament as well as national parliaments, so policy-makers and especially politicians need strong justifications for not simply excluding investment protection from the agreement.

Given the current political controversy, it would arguably be wise to avoid investment protection in TTIP—at least for the moment. This would allow stakeholders and negotiators to focus their attention on the elements of the agreement expected to offer the largest gains, such as in the area of trade.[4] Moreover, it would allow European policy-makers to pause and rethink both the substantive and procedural rights in investment treaties "bottom up". Much work needs to be done to assure the consistency between investment law, on the one hand, and EU law and national laws of the member states, on the other hand.[5] Recent discussions in Europe also provide an opportunity to revisit some of the basic design elements of investment treaties.[6] This pausing, however, does not seem to be viable owing to the political pressures to finalize TTIP.

At the same time, the public debate shows that just sticking to the adaptations made in CETA seems equally politically inviable, unless the new rhetoric of the

---

[2] European Parliament (Plenary), text adopted on 23 May 2013 in Procedure 2012/0163(COD), P7_TAPROV(2013)0219, http://www.europarl.europa.eu/sides/getDoc.do?pubRef=-//EP//TEXT+TA+P7-TA-2013-0219+0+DOC+XML+V0//EN (amendment 3) (last accessed 11 August 2015); European Parliament Resolution of 8 July 2015 containing the European Parliament's recommendations to the European Commission on the negotiations for the Transatlantic Trade and Investment Partnership (TTIP) (2014/2228(INI)), http://www.europarl.europa.eu/sides/getDoc.do?pubRef=-//EP//TEXT+TA+P8-TA-2015-0252+0+DOC+XML+V0//EN&language=EN (para (2)(xv)) (last accessed 11 August 2015).

[3] Political risk insurance covers many of the risks protected by investment treaties, such as uncompensated expropriation and contract breach. See generally; Poulsen (2010). On the use of insurance to mitigate against political risks, see generally West (1999).

[4] See Ikenson (2014).

[5] See Kleinheisterkamp (2014a); Kleinheisterkamp (2015).

[6] Several design elements could be reconsidered: On the consolidation of investment disputes through the possibility of treaty claims against investors see Laborde (2010) and Bjorklund (2013). For concerns with using arbitration to resolve investment treaty disputes see Van Harten (2007); Lester (2013).

For the different use of remedies in investment treaty law compared with most advanced legal systems see Gaukrodger and Gordon (2012). For the inconsistency of investment law with corporate law in the most advanced legal systems see Gaukrodger (2013); see generally Waibel (2013).

Investment Court System manages to divert the criticism. Even then, the US would still have to agree to give up arbitration as the adjucation mechanism for investment disputes - which presently seems unlikely. The challenge is then to find a way of redrafting investment provisions in TTIP that address the political concerns over ISDS while still providing meaningful protection to European and US investors. In this brief we propose three pragmatic options that would achieve that goal. They differ from the European Commission's stated plans in important respects.

Table 1 below summarizes the proposals.

3 Proposal on Substantive Investor Rights

In response to the criticisms made against ISDS, the Commission has added 'patches' to old investment treaty models developed before the rise of investment treaty arbitration, trying to deflect criticism against the later by recasting ISDS in a court system, which only adresses part of the procedural issues. Many stakeholders still fear, however, that, in substance, European regulatory standards may be lowered through ISDS, and some of the Commission's efforts may even backfire by increasing the scope for creative lawyering and expansive interpretations. An example is the fair and equitable treatment clause in CETA.[7]

This concern could be addressed by an express general clarification in TTIP and other investment treaties that foreign investors should get the same high levels of protection as domestic investors receive in domestic law, *but not higher levels of protection*. In the EU, the benchmark would be EU law and the general principles common to the laws of the member states.[8] In the case of claims against the US, a relevant starting point would often be the rich US case law on the takings doctrine, which offers significant guidance for the balancing private and public rights.[9]

Such a clarification would set a fundamental principle for the interpretation of all substantive investment provisions in TTIP. It would force arbitral tribunals to engage with the rich national public law traditions on both sides of the Atlantic, rather than ignore them, and cap the scope of the substantive treaty rights accord-

For UNCTAD's work on sustainability concerns in the existing international investment regime, see http://unctad.org/en/PublicationsLibrary/diaepcb2012d5_en.pdf (last accessed 21 August 2015).

[7] See e.g. Bernasconi-Osterwalder and Mann (2013). A more useful formulation is offered in; Bonnitcha (2014), pp. 343–344.

[8] See, e.g., the decision of the Court of Justice of the EU in the *FIAMM* and *Fedon* case, Joined Cases C-120 & 121/06 P, [2008] ECR I-6513. The need to refer to the general principles common to the laws of the member states for determining state liability under EU law is explicitly enshrined in Article 340(2) TFEU.

[9] See e.g., Shenkman (2002). For a comparison of US domestic law and international investment law on contract breach, see; Johnson and Volkov (2013).

Table 1 Three feasible proposals for investment protection in TTIP

	Substantive protections	Dispute resolution	
	No greater rights	*Option I: The Australia-US model*	*Option II: The ISDS patches model*
Defining features	– Operative provision clarifying that the investment provisions afford foreign investors the same high levels of protection as domestic law grants domestic investors, but not higher levels of protection.	– Default reliance on domestic law and courts. – State-to-state dispute settlement based on substantive investment protection provisions as benchmark. – Institutionalized consultations about domestic investment regimes.	– Local courts first decide on the illegality of public acts. – Comprehensive state 'filter' of private claims. – Binding state interpretations. – Independent appeals mechanism.
Advantages	– As a principle of interpretation, it would prevent international tribunals from re-striking the balance between public and private interests obtained in US and EU domestic legal regimes. – Corresponds with fundamental principle expressly stated by both the EU and the US.	– Continues tradition of excluding ISDS in agreements among developed countries. – On-going consultations add to TTIP as a "living agreement". – US-Australia agreement provides a precedent.	– Avoids the 'side-lining' of domestic courts. – States retain control. – State interpretations adds to TTIP as a "living agreement". – Greater consistency and predictably. – Precedents exist in comparative legal regimes.

ingly so as not to compromise the long established balance struck between private and public interests.[10]

Our proposal is fully in line with the investment policy aims defined by both the European Parliament and the US Congress. The US Government informed Congress in 2013 that, as already laid down in the 2002 Trade Act, it would seek to secure in TTIP:

> for U.S. investors in the EU important rights comparable to those that would be available under U.S. legal principles and practice, *while ensuring that EU investors in the United States are not accorded greater substantive rights with respect to investment protections than U.S. investors in the United States.*[11]

Equally, the EU Regulation 912/2014 of 23 July 2014 framing financial responsibility for ISDS expressly states that:

> Union agreements should afford foreign investors the same high level of protection as Union law and the general principles common to the laws of the Member States grant to investors from within the Union, *but not a higher level of protection.* Union agreements should ensure that the Union's legislative powers and right to regulate are respected and safeguarded.

And in its Resolution of 8 July 2015, the European Parliament equally recommended the Commission regarding TTIP:

> to ensure that foreign investors are treated in a non-discriminatory fashion *while benefiting from no greater rights than domestic investors.*[12]

These declarations are expressions of a democratic political understanding about the intended reach of future investment agreements and for TTIP in particular. Backing this by an operative "no greater rights" provision in TTIP would be an important step for a reformed European investment treaty policy.

4 Two Options for Dispute Resolution

Giving all American investors the opportunity to bypass European courts is a highly controversial policy. This is the case whether ISDS is resolved through international arbitration or in a Transatlantic Investment Court. While EU member states have signed bilateral investment treaties with developing countries for decades, a

---

[10] Montt (2009). See also Schill (2012).

[11] Letter by US Trade Representative Marantis to the Speaker of the House of Representatives of 20 March 2013, http://www.ustr.gov/sites/default/files/03202013%20TTIP%20Notification%20Letter.PDF (last accessed 21 August 2015).

[12] See European Parliament Resolution of 8 July 2015 containing the European Parliament's recommendations to the European Commission on the negotiations for the Transatlantic Trade and Investment Partnership (TTIP) (2014/2228(INI)), http://www.europarl.europa.eu/sides/getDoc.do?pubRef=-//EP//TEXT+TA+P8-TA-2015-0252+0+DOC+XML+V0//EN&language=EN (last accessed 21 August 2015).

similar treaty arrangement with the United States will significantly increase the chances of claims given the amount of US investment in Europe.[13]

To accommodate this concern we propose two dispute resolution models for the investment protection chapter, which are both politically feasible.

4.1 *Option 1: The Australia-US Model*

Private recourse to treaty-based investment arbitration originated as an alternative to domestic legal systems that were not considered trustworthy. Until recently, Western governments only negotiated investment treaties with transition or developing countries.[14] Treaty-based arbitration was considered unnecessary between countries with well-developed legal systems.

In line with this tradition our first proposal is based on the 2005 Australia-United States Free Trade Agreement, AUSFTA, which excludes ISDS.[15] One of the main advantages of this model is that it requires little, if any, institutional innovation as a precedent has already been provided in the Australia-US agreement. This would allow negotiators to quickly settle the investment protection chapter and instead focus on the more important elements of TTIP.

4.1.1 An Investment Treaty Tailored for Countries with Highly Developed Legal Systems

AUSFTA includes a long chapter on investment protection with traditional investment treaty protections against uncompensated expropriation, discrimination, unfair and inequitable treatment, capital transfer restrictions, etc. But since both Australia and the United States have high levels of investment protection in their domestic legal regimes as well as reliable court systems, they agreed to exclude ISDS from the agreement and not make the substantive treaty provisions directly applicable in their respective courts.

---

[13] See Poulsen L, Bonnitcha J and Yackee J (2015) Transatlantic Investment Treaty Protection, http://www.ceps.eu/system/files/SR102_ISDS.pdf (last accessed 11 August 2015).

[14] An exception to this rule is the North American Free-Trade Agreement (NAFTA), but both the US and Canadian governments did not expect its investment chapter to apply to their own regulatory acts but primarily to Mexico. Another partial exception is the Energy Charter Treaty (ECT), but here again the investment protection chapter was primarily intended as a shield against political risks in the least developed parties (Eastern Europe and Russia). Note also that ECT was concluded as a mixed agreement including the European Union and its member states, yet without any possible intention to modify the existing rules for the internal EU energy market as amongst the then member states, which would have required a modification of the EU Treaties.

[15] Text can be found at: www.ustr.gov/trade-agreements/free-trade-agreements/australian-fta (last accessed 21 August 2015).

Both states are free to consent to arbitration with individual investors on an ad-hoc basis (for instance in contracts), but the default option is to resolve investment disputes in domestic courts based on domestic law. If a home state is concerned about the treatment of its investors in the other country, however, it can file an inter-state claim both for purposes of clarification and compensation of its investors.[16]

This model departs from traditional investment treaties, but as noted by the United States Trade Representative:

> [a]mong other things, Australia has an open economic environment and a legal system similar to that of the United States, U.S. investors have confidence in the fairness and integrity of Australia's legal system, and the United States has a long history of close commercial relations with Australia that has flourished largely without disputes of the type addressed by international investment provisions.[17]

This description also corresponds with most European states and transatlantic investment flows have flourished for decades without treaty-based recourse to investment arbitration. The AUSFTA model therefore fits with TTIP as well.

4.1.2 A "Living" Investment Chapter in TTIP

Another important feature of the AUSFTA Model is that the two governments commit to meet regularly to discuss the implementation of the investment protection provisions as well as other issues pertaining to the operation of their respective investment regimes. Here, the substantive provisions of the treaty—such as fair and equitable treatment—can be used to highlight perceived deficiencies in domestic regulation of foreign investment.

Extending this part of AUSFTA for the purposes of TTIP would correspond with the aim of making TTIP a "living agreement" through a continuous process of making domestic trade and investment regimes ever more compatible. On-going monitoring and consultations about domestic regulatory regimes has been highly effective for the OECD, for instance, and seems a more appropriate model to push forward transatlantic integration than litigation.

[16] For example, if a European investor in the United States were denied access to justice, as in the *Loewen* case, this would be undermine the common understanding about the equivalence of the court systems and the European Commission could take up this issue and even bring a state-to-state arbitration against the United States, both for a declaration of the violation of the substantive investment provisions and for damages of the European investor. On the often overlooked promises of state-to-state dispute settlement in international investment law, see; Roberts (2014).

[17] Text can be found at: https://ustr.gov/archive/assets/Document_Library/Reports_Publications/2005/2005_TPA_Report/asset_upload_file120_7517.pdf (last accessed 21 August 2015).

4.2 *Option 2: The ISDS 'Patches' Model*

Our second option for dispute resolution is similar to the AUSFTA Model by including traditional investment treaty protections but differs by keeping a limited recourse to ISDS. To ensure ISDS is only used in exceptional cases, the proposal includes four 'patches' to traditional ISDS provisions.[18]

4.2.1 Local Courts First Decide on Illegality of Public Acts

Local courts in Europe and the United States should have the chance to correct errors of local administration or legislation before international tribunals get involved. The first 'patch' is therefore a requirement that foreign investors seek to resolve their disputes with host states through domestic courts. This will ensure that international adjudication is the last legal resort in an investment dispute (rather than the first).[19] It will also enhance legal certainty by fostering dialogue between national courts and national regulators that consolidates national administrative law and practice.

A local litigation requirement can be structured in different ways. One option would be to insist on exhaustion of local remedies. This is similar to the obligation in the European Convention of Human Rights, for instance, including for expropriation disputes. If, however, Washington finds an exhaustion requirement unacceptable due to judicial systems in some EU member states, another option would be a local litigation requirement of a minimum of 5 years, which is a reasonable time for proceedings of such complexity.[20]

4.2.2 Comprehensive State 'Filter' of Private Claims

Our second patch is that home and host states should be allowed to block individual claims, if they *both* agree the dispute should be settled by domestic judges rather than international tribunals. A similar option is included in NAFTA for investment

[18] They would work both in a traditional investment arbitration system as well as a standing investment court, which has recently been proposed by Germany and the European Commission.

[19] For a discussion, see Kuijper, Pernice, Hindelang, Schwarz and Reuling (2014).

[20] In the light of the US Supreme Court decision in *BG Group v Argentina*, it would be necessary to clearly formulate the local litigation requirement of 5 years as a genuine condition precedent for the EU's consent to arbitration under the investment agreement. In this case, the US Supreme Court defined the local litigation requirement in the US-Argentina BIT as a mere question of admissibility. This would therefore fall within the exclusive jurisdiction of the arbitral tribunal as a procedural question and thus outside the scope of judicial review of the tribunal's jurisdiction, thus potentially allowing arbitrators to dispense with local litigation requirements. For another adjustment of the local litigation requirement, see discussion in Kuijper, Pernice, Hindelang, Schwarz and Reuling (2014).

disputes regarding tax questions with the justification that it can block particularly controversial investor disputes from proceeding. In CETA, as well, there is a similar filter mechanism for investment disputes in financial services.

Extending such filter mechanisms to all areas covered by the investment provisions addresses fundamental concerns about safeguarding public policies. Taxation and financial stability are important issues, but so are environmental protection, health concerns, consumer protection and other public interest matters. The Hong Kong government would likely have agreed to block Phillip Morris' (now failed) claim against Australia, for instance, if a filter mechanism had existed in the relevant treaty.

4.2.3 Binding State Interpretations

Third, *joint* and prospective interpretations of TTIP's investment provisions issued by the parties should be binding upon arbitration tribunals. Such interpretive powers are delegated to NAFTA's Free Trade Commission (FTC) and similar provisions are included in CETA. TTIP needs more precise language than CETA to make clear that these joint interpretations are strictly binding, as a few tribunals have disregarded FTC interpretations.[21]

This, too, would allow states greater control over the arbitral process by steering the development of the law created by them.[22] It would also correspond to the logic of making TTIP a 'living agreement', as the investment protection chapter could form the basis for a constructive dialogue between the EU and the US on the content of investment treaty standards going forward.

4.2.4 Independent Appeals Mechanism

One of the key concerns with investment arbitration raised in recent decades has been the lack of coherence, and occasional contradiction, in the decisions by tribunals. This makes it harder for states and investors to assess their rights and liabilities under an investment treaty. With respect to claims pursued under TTIP such uncertainty could be diminished if investors and states are given an opportunity to appeal through an independent appellate body similar to the one included in the WTO. The latest version of CETA now includes such an appellate instance in its Article 8.28. Both the US Government and the European Commission have

[21] On the legality and practice of state interpretation of investment treaty obligations, see; Roberts (2010).

[22] This proposal is supported even by strong defenders of investment arbitration; see e.g. commissioned report to the Dutch government by Tietje C and Baetens F (2014) The Impact of Investor-State-Dispute Settlement (ISDS) in the Transatlantic Trade and Investment Partnership.

suggested an appellate body solution, but have failed to implement it so far for TTIP.[23]

5 Responding to Potential Concerns

5.1 *Concern 1: Not All European and American Courts Are Trustworthy*

5.1.1 Domestic Courts and the AUSFTA Model

Concerns have been raised that some European and American courts are untrustworthy. Under the AUSFTA Model, countries like Romania and Bulgaria would still be free to offer broad and binding consent to investment arbitration in their domestic laws or in contracts backed up by the ICSID and New York Conventions. Even without such measures, most critics would probably find it unpersuasive that American investors should be allowed to avoid all European courts, including those of the majority of countries with excellent rule of law records, because of concerns with the legal system in a few member states in Eastern Europe. Also, it is worth recalling that individual American (and European) investors are always free to purchase political risk insurance, which covers many of the same risks as an investment treaty.

Similarly, few would seriously argue that anecdotal evidence from American judicial proceedings, for instance in Mississippi, albeit worrisome individually, are sufficient to make the case that American courts are systemically biased against foreigners.[24] Commissioner De Gucht noted that the basic justification for ISDS is when investors are faced with host states that do "not have a properly-functioning judicial system, where one can have doubts about the rule of law."[25] The United States clearly does not fit that description.

5.1.2 Domestic Courts and the ISDS Patches Model

One concern against local litigation requirements is that it would allow international tribunals to overrule highest national court decisions. This argument is unpersuasive. Moreover, the Commission's solution to include fork-in-the-road provisions that force investors to choose exclusively between national courts and international adjudication is potentially damaging. First of all, it is a common

[23] See contributions in; Sauvant (2008).

[24] See in more detail Kleinheisterkamp (2014b).

[25] http://www.europarl.europa.eu/sides/getDoc.do?pubRef=-//EP//TEXT+CRE+20130522+ITEM-019+DOC+XML+V0//EN (last accessed 21 August 2015).

principle in Europe that domestic court decisions can be scrutinized by supra-national courts, such as the European Court of Justice and the European Court of Human Rights. So given all the other areas of sovereign activity that the Commission is comfortable to entrust to international tribunals under TTIP and other investment agreements, it is not clear why domestic court decisions should not be. Moreover, domestic courts primarily will decide (first) on whether domestic law provides for a remedy; investors who question the solutions found by domestic courts can (then) request international tribunals to determine whether there is a violation of the protection standards under *international* law. Secondly, under most BITs, as well as under EU law and the ECHR, national court decisions themselves can qualify as state measures that may be considered to violate treaty obligations. Third, fork-in-the road provisions *force* investors to avoid domestic courts if they want to be able to use international adjudication to resolve disputes. This is again in direct contradiction to established legal principles in Europe, for instance in the ECHR, where supra-national courts are the last resort.

5.2 *Concern 2: Precedential Value for Agreements with Developing Countries*

5.2.1 Precedence and the AUSFTA Model

One concern with the AUSFTA Model is that it might set an unfavourable precedent and prevent policy-makers from pursuing 'traditional' ISDS provisions in future negotiations with countries, where there is a lack of trust in domestic legal systems. Yet, even if we assume that ISDS is a valid governance instrument in those cases, which is beyond the scope of this brief to address, we would caution against taking this precedent-setting argument too far. China, for instance, is a staunch proponent of ISDS and recently agreed to include ISDS in its agreement with Australia, even though there was no ISDS provision in the US-Australia. India is currently revisiting its investment treaty policy and has never been shy of blocking agreements that it considers to unduly infringe on India's sovereign rights. Brazil has never ratified an investment treaty with ISDS and has no plans of doing so. Ultimately, the 'TTIP as precedence' argument may only hold for much smaller states, like Myanmar, and most would probably find this is an insufficient reason to have ISDS cover investor-state relations in most of the Western world.

5.2.2 Precedence and the ISDS Patches Model

The main concern regarding precedence for the ISDS Patches Model regards the local litigation requirement. While this is an entirely reasonable requirement in Europe and the United States, it is less attractive in countries with less developed court systems. Again, we find the precedent-setting argument unpersuasive.

Developed countries already negotiate different (or no) investment treaties among themselves. We are unpersuaded that a country like China, for instance, would find it controversial that countries with very high rule of law standards negotiate different agreements among themselves compared to treaties with other countries.[26]

Moreover, it is worth recalling that a positive case can be made for a local litigation requirement also in treaties with developing countries. This would incentivise foreign investors to lobby for more efficient and independent domestic courts, allow the necessary dialogue between administration and courts, and reduce the risk of ISDS 'substituting' for local court reforms. It is beyond this brief to assess this argument in detail, but it is often forgotten in current policy debates about the long-term implications of investment treaties.[27]

5.3 *Concern 3: Excessive Involvement of Home States/ International Tribunals*

5.3.1 Home States and the AUSFTA Model

Proponents of ISDS occasionally argue that state-to-state dispute resolution 'politicize' investment disputes by having investors rely on home states to file a claim.[28] They therefore advocate ISDS on the ground it is "apolitical". This argument is often taken too far however. All investment disputes can be regarded as inherently political—whether resolved through investment arbitration, domestic courts, or inter-state discussions or adjudication. Moreover, there is no credible evidence that home state involvement does in fact decrease as a result of arbitration.[29]

Secondly, it is inherently difficult to see why TTIP should place companies that are 'investors' rather than 'exporters' on a different legal footing when running into disputes with host governments. If it is acceptable to rely on state-to-state adjudication for disputes involving 'behind-the-border' trade regulations, why would it be unacceptable when disputes involve investment regulations?

More generally, transatlantic diplomatic ties have remained strong for decades without an investment treaty in place: there is no evidence that they have been affected by somehow politicized transatlantic disputes. The existing differences in the context of the WTO confirm this view. Also, if a specific investment dispute were threatening to compromise broader political relations—which is exceedingly

[26] In the specific case of China note also that Beijing already require investors to go through a domestic administrative review procedure before taking claims to arbitration. See; Gallagher and Shan (2009), ch. 8.

[27] See Ginsburg (2005).

[28] See, e.g., Baetens F (2015).

[29] For a critical discussion, see Paparinskis (2010). For recent empirical evidence, see Jandhyala, Gertz and Poulsen (2015).

unlikely—the AUSFTA Model does not prevent the parties from consenting to arbitration with investors on an ad-hoc basis.

5.3.2 Investment Tribunals and the ISDS Patches Model

While the AUSFTA Model may be poorly received by proponents of investment arbitration, critics of ISDS could argue our Patches Model does not go far enough in curtailing the power of ISDS.

This brief article, however, merely addresses the situation in which policymakers decide to keep ISDS in TTIP. In that case, the combination of (1) an express 'no greater rights' clause, (2) a meaningful local litigation requirement, (3) a generalized state filters mechanism, (4) binding state interpretations, and (5) an appellate body, will not only lower the number of potential ISDS claims to those actually carrying merit. It will also increase the incentives for investment tribunals to show greater judicial constraint compared to some of the more adventurous decisions made in the past. While this approach will not eliminate the use of ISDS from the system, it will be brought closer in line with the public law standards developed in the EU over the last 5 decades.

References

Bernasconi-Osterwalder N, Mann H (2013) A response to the European Commission's December 2013 document 'investment provisions in the EU-Canada free trade agreement (CETA)'. IISD Report, International Institute for Sustainable Development, February 2014

Bonnitcha J (2014) Substantive protection under investment treaties. Cambridge University Press, Cambridge

Bjorklund A (2013) The emerging civilization of investment arbitration. Penn State Law Rev 113 (4):1269–1300

Gallagher N, Shan W (2009) Chinese investment treaties: policies and practise. Oxford University Press, Oxford

Gaukrodger D (2013) Investment treaties as corporate law: shareholder claims and issues of consistency. A preliminary framework for policy analysis. OECD Working Papers on International Investment No. 2013/3, www.oecd.org/investment/working-papers.htm. Accessed 21 August 2015

Gaukrodger D, Gordon K (2012) Investor-state dispute settlement: a scoping paper for the investment policy community. OECD Working Papers on International Investment 2012/03, http://dx.doi.org/10.1787/5k46b1r85j6f-en. Accessed 21 August 2015

Ginsburg T (2005) International substitutes for domestic institutions: bilateral investment treaties and governance. Int Rev Law Econ 25(1):107–123

Ikenson D (2014) A compromise to advance the trade agenda: purge negotiations of investor-state dispute settlement. CATO Institute Free Trade Bulletin No. 57, 4 March 2014

Jandhyala S, Gertz G, Poulsen L (2015) Legalization and diplomacy: depoliticization of investment disputes through arbitration? American power in the investment regime

Johnson L, Volkov O (2013) Investor-state contracts, host-state "commitments" and the myth of stability in international law. Am Rev Int Arbitr 24(3):361–415

Kleinheisterkamp J (2014a) Financial responsibility in the European international investment policy. Int Comp Law Q 63(2):449–476

Kleinheisterkamp J (2014b) Is there a need for investor-state arbitration in the transatlantic trade and investment partnership (TTIP)? http://ssrn.com/abstract=2410188. Accessed 21 August 2015

Kleinheisterkamp J (2015) Investment treaty law and fears for sovereignty: transnational challenges and solutions. Modern Law Review 78(5):793–825

Kuijper P, Pernice I, Hindelang S, Schwarz M, Reuling M (2014) Investor-state dispute settlement (ISDS) provisions in the EU's international investment agreements, volume 2—studies, report for Directorate-General for External Policies of the European Union, http://www.jura.fuberlin.de/fachbereich/einrichtungen/oeffentliches-recht/lehrende/hindelangs/Studie-fuer-Europaeisches-Parlament/Hindelang.pdf?1411545510. Accessed 21 August 2015

Laborde G (2010) The case for host state claims in investment arbitration. J Int Disp Settlement 1 (1):1–26

Lester S (2013) Liberalization or litigation? Time to rethink the international investment regime. CATO Policy Analysis No. 730, 8 July 2013

Montt S (2009) State liability in investment treaty arbitration: global constitutional and administrative law in the BIT generation. Hart Publishing, Portland

Paparinskis M (2010) Limits of depolitization in contemporary investor-state arbitration. Select Proc Eur Soc Int Law 3:271–282

Poulsen L, Bonnitcha J, Yackee J (2015) Transatlantic investment treaty protection. In: Hamilton D, Pelkmans J (eds) Rule-makers or rule-takers: exploring the transatlantic trade and investment partnership. Rowman and Littlefield, London

Poulsen L (2010) The importance of BITs for foreign direct investment and political risk insurance: revisiting the evidence. In: Sauvant K (ed) Yearbook on international investment law & policy 2009/2010. Oxford University Press, Oxford

Roberts A (2010) Power and persuasion in investment treaty interpretation: the dual role of states. Am J Int Law 104:179–225

Roberts A (2014) State-to-state investment treaty arbitration: a hybrid theory of interdependent rights and shared interpretive authority. Har J Int Law 55(1):1–70

Sauvant K (ed) (2008) Appeals mechanisms in international investment law. Oxford University Press, Oxford

Schill S (2012) Deference in investment treaty arbitration: re-conceptualizing the standard of review. J Int Disp Settlement 3(3):577–607

Shenkman E (2002) Could principles of fifth amendment takings jurisprudence be helpful in analysing regulatory expropriation claims under international law? NYU Environ Law J 11:174–197

Waibel M (2013) Sovereign defaults before international courts and tribunals. Cambridge University Press, Cambridge

West G (1999) Political risk investment insurance: a renaissance. J Project Finance 5(2):27–36

Van Harten G (2007) Investment treaty arbitration and public law. Oxford University Press, Oxford

Six Degrees of Integration: How Closely Will the TTIP Integrate the Transatlantic Market?

Simon Lester

Contents

Abstract There are real differences in the varying conceptions of free trade. The TTIP brings these differences to the fore and makes addressing them unavoidable. The TTIP could push the boundaries of economic integration in a number ways, most prominently by trying to 'smooth out' regulatory differences between the United States and the European Union, and in the process moving us towards a single market. There are various ways this can be done—mutual recognition and harmonization are two of the main ones—but all involve reducing the variances between the regulation of different national markets. International economic governance involves a careful balancing of economic efficiency and national autonomy, and which conception of free trade to use has a real impact. If the proper balance is not achieved, groups from a wide range of political ideologies could be upset. The challenge for TTIP negotiators is to find that right balance.

S. Lester (✉)
Cato Institute, 1000 Massachusetts Ave, NW, Washington, DC 20001, USA

WorldTradeLaw.net, Falls Church, VA, USA
e-mail: slester@cato.org

M. Bungenberg et al. (eds.), *European Yearbook of International Economic Law 2016*, European Yearbook of International Economic Law 7,
DOI 10.1007/978-3-319-29215-1_24

1 Introduction

There has been a long struggle in trade policy to define the terms of the debate. What exactly is the 'free trade' we are pursuing? Perhaps the ambiguity has been intentional, to some extent, in order to obscure fundamental disagreements. But this approach may have taken us as far as it can. As we continue to push forward, we must eventually confront our choices: There are real differences in the varying conceptions of free trade. The TTIP brings these differences to the fore and makes addressing them unavoidable.

In the TTIP, people have emphasized that the negotiators are addressing regulatory trade barriers, arguing that tariffs on U.S.-EU trade are already low.[1] But the generalizations about how TTIP will handle regulation conceal important distinctions. Addressing regulation could just mean prohibiting *protectionist* regulation; or it could mean imposing various constraints on *non-protectionist* regulations that interfere with trade in some way. There are significant differences between these approaches in terms of the degree of integration that is pursued.

The TTIP could push the boundaries of economic integration in a number ways, most prominently by trying to "smooth out" regulatory differences between the United States and the European Union,[2] and in the process moving us towards a single market. There are various ways this can be done—mutual recognition and harmonization are two of the main ones—but all involve reducing the variances between the regulation of different national markets. Separate markets become more integrated as regulatory divergence is eliminated.

Broadly speaking, there is a continuum of integration, from narrow tariff lowering all the way to a fully integrated single market. The implications of these different conceptions are much more important than proponents of trade agreements, who sometimes blur the distinctions, let on. International economic governance involves a careful balancing of *economic efficiency* and *national autonomy*, and which conception of free trade to use has a real impact. If the proper balance is

[1] This argument is something of an exaggeration, as many tariffs – some fairly high – remain. Lester S, US-EU Trade Talks: Don't Forget about the Tariffs, 22 July 2013, http://www.cato.org/blog/us-eu-trade-talks-dont-forget-about-tariffs (last accessed 4 August 2015).

[2] Remarks by the President at Meeting with the President's Export Council, 12 March 2013: "As I announced at the State of the Union address, we're also going to be launching an effort to lock in a EU-U.S. trade deal as well. And already, Europe is our largest trading partner—the EU as a whole—and we think that we can expand that even further. And some of this has to do with us being able to break down some existing barriers across the Atlantic to U.S. products and services, but some of it also has to do with smoothing out differences in regulatory approaches, just trade frictions that arise that are unnecessary that carries over from earlier periods.", http://www.whitehouse.gov/the-press-office/2013/03/12/remarks-president-meeting-presidents-export-council (last accessed 4 August 2015).

not achieved, groups from a wide range of political ideologies could be upset.[3] The challenge for TTIP negotiators is to find that right balance.

2 Degrees of Integration

In many discussions of trade and economic integration, the options are glossed over. Supporters of international trade agreements are for "free trade"; opponents are against it. But just what is free trade, and what are the possibilities for integration more generally? It is worth exploring these at the outset.

The classic explanation from the economics literature of the forms of integration was set forth by Bela Belassa in *The Theory of Economic Integration*, as follows:

> Economic integration, as defined here, can take several forms that represent varying degrees of integration. These are a free-trade area, a customs union, a common market, an economic union, and complete economic integration. In a free trade-area, tariffs (and quantitative restrictions) between the participating countries are abolished, but each country retains its own tariffs against nonmembers. Establishing a customs union involves, besides the suppression of discrimination in the field of commodity movements within the union, the equalization of tariffs in trade with nonmember countries. A higher form of economic integration is attained in a common market, where not only trade restrictions but also restrictions on factor movements are abolished. An economic union, as distinct from a common market, combines the suppression of restrictions on commodity and factor policies, in order to remove discrimination that was due to disparities in these policies. Finally, total economic integration presupposes the unification of monetary, fiscal, social, and countercyclical policies and requires the setting up of a supra-national authority whose decisions are binding for the member states.[4]

The problem with this approach is that, while it was appropriate for the era when it was developed, it falls short in describing some of the most important issues of today. In 1961, when Belassa was developing his theory, debates over whether customs unions or free trade areas were more desirable took center stage. European integration was in its early period, and its efforts to integrate were well-known. By

[3] For example, those skeptical of regulation worry that the TTIP will harmonize regulations upwards, whereas those who support more active regulation worry about 'regulatory chill' from the TTIP. For the former, see. Bromund TR, TTIP: Small Upside, Big Downside, Heritage Foundation, 19 May 2015, http://www.heritage.org/research/commentary/2015/5/ttip-small-upside-big-downside (last accessed 4 August 2015); for the latter, see Siles-Brügge G and Butler N, Beyond the Headlines on TTIP: Beware the Fine Print, Manchester Policy Blog, 1 June 2015, http://blog.policy.manchester.ac.uk/posts/2015/06/beyond-the-headlines-on-ttip-beware-the-fine-print/ (last accessed 4 August 2015).

[4] Balassa (1961). Along the same lines, Economist Steven Suranovic defines the following types of arrangements for coordinating trade, fiscal, and/or monetary policies: preferential trade agreements, free trade areas, customs unions, common markets, economic unions, and monetary unions. See 'Economic Integration: Overview' in Suranovic (1998), http://internationalecon.com/Trade/Tch110/T110-2.php (last accessed 4 August 2015).

contrast, the impact of trade governance on regulatory autonomy, and the subtle distinctions in how domestic regulation might affect trade, were not a major concern at that time. Belassa's "common market" category is the relevant one here, but it glosses over this issue too quickly.

Today, by contrast, the customs union versus free trade area debate has been all but forgotten. Now, the way trade rules affect the ability to regulate is one of the most important issues being discussed. As a result, we need a modified theory of economic integration that can help take into account the distinctions in how trade rules affect domestic regulation. To that end, I offer a slightly different take on the conventional categories, to tease out some important distinctions a little more clearly.

With the experience of the last few decades of economic integration, in particular the problems of "policy space" and "regulatory autonomy," a more precise classification system can be developed, using the following categories:

- **Border Barriers:** Only border measures such as tariffs and quotas, the traditional means of protectionism, are eliminated/reduced.
- **Customs Union:** An integration arrangement can go beyond internal trade liberalization, and set up a mechanism to coordinate external trade policy, for example through a common external tariff.
- **Anti-Discrimination:** In addition to tariffs and quotas, which are inherently discriminatory, internal laws, regulations and other measures that are protectionist in nature are also prohibited.[5]
- **Single Market:** Regulations which are not protectionist can also interfere with trade, for example, duplicative product testing requirements. Mechanisms such as mutual recognition and harmonization can deal with this problem.
- **Economic and Monetary Union:** Governments can coordinate their fiscal and monetary policies.
- **Political Union:** Political structures can be merged, creating a new sovereign entity.

The key addition here is to distinguish two forms of "deep" integration that cover domestic regulations: Anti-discrimination and a single market. Both go beyond the border, involving international oversight of domestic regulations. But an anti-discrimination approach narrowly targets discriminatory regulations, whereas a single market approach tries to address any measures that affect trade even where they do not discriminate against foreign goods or services, such as differences in regulations across countries.

In the TTIP, the main focus is on lowering border barriers and moving towards a single market. Anti-discrimination/protectionism for regulations is already enforced by the WTO, but additional rules may be included in the TTIP in particular

[5] There is an extensive jurisprudence in the GATT/WTO for identifying when measures are protectionist.

sectors. In the following sections, I define protectionism and single market more clearly.

3 Protectionism

Protectionism is a commonly used term in trade policy debates. Most people probably have a general sense of it, but it is worth looking at specific definitions.

Encyclopædia Britannica defines it as: "Policy of protecting domestic industries against foreign competition by means of tariffs, subsidies, import quotas, or other restrictions or handicaps placed on the imports of foreign competitors."[6] Black's Law Dictionary says, "[t]he protection of domestic businesses and industries against foreign competition by imposing high tariffs and restricting imports."[7] Specialized trade dictionaries say, "[t]he deliberate use or encouragement of restrictions on imports to enable relatively inefficient domestic producers to compete successfully with foreign producers,"[8] and "[e]conomic policies which prevent the exposure of domestic producers to the rigours of the international market, often under the guise of some other policy objective."[9] And the Financial Times explains it as: "The use of tariff and non-tariff restrictions on imports to protect domestic producers from foreign competition."[10]

All of these definitions have a particular theme in common: Treating foreign producers worse than domestic producers, usually by design. Note that some definitions talk of a particular "policy," or the "deliberate use" of the measures, or disguising such measures as legitimate policies.

At the GATT/WTO, the elimination of protectionist laws and regulations is a core goal. In this regard, in an early WTO dispute, the Appellate Body explained that "[t]he broad and fundamental purpose of [GATT] Article III is to avoid protectionism in the application of internal tax and regulatory measures."[11] In recent years, the case law under GATT Articles III and XX, TBT Agreement Article 2.1, SPS Agreement Articles 2.3 and 5.5, GATS Articles XVII and XIV, and TRIPS Agreement Article 3 has grown, setting out an extensive body of jurisprudence to guide the inquiry into when governments are acting in a protectionist manner.

---

[6] Encyclopædia Britannica. Encyclopædia Britannica Online. Encyclopædia Britannica Inc., 2015, 12 February 2015, http://www.britannica.com/EBchecked/topic/479643/protectionism (last accessed 4 August 2015).

[7] Garner and Campbell (2014), p. 1418.

[8] Hinkelman and Putzi (2006), p. 137.

[9] Goode (2007), p. 349.

[10] Financial Times Lexicon. 'protectionism' 12 February 2015, http://markets.ft.com/research/Lexicon/Term?term=protectionism (last accessed 4 August 2015).

[11] Appellate Body Report, *Japan – Taxes on Alcoholic Beverages*, WT/DS8/AB/R, WT/DS10/AB/R, WT/DS11/AB/R, adopted 1 November 1996, p. 16.

4 Single Market

Somewhat less familiar than protectionism is the idea of a single market. Economic integration into a single market has historically played an extremely important role in the development of today's advanced economies. Canada, Germany and the United States are prominent examples.

Prior to about a century ago, the state's role in the domestic economy was far less than it is today. As a result, integration focused mainly on removing border tariffs, in the case of free trade areas, or coordinating them externally, in the case of a customs union. By contrast, concerns about internal laws and regulations that discriminated against foreign trade, or otherwise interfered with it, were less important.

Thus, U.S. and Canadian economic integration efforts did not go into too much detail about how these countries would achieve their domestic integration. Internal tariffs were not permitted, of course, but beyond that vague principles seemed sufficient. In this regard, the Canadian constitution provides that: "All Articles of the Growth, Produce, or Manufacture of any one of the Provinces shall, from and after the Union, be admitted free into each of the other Provinces."[12] In the U.S., the Commerce Clause gives Congress the power "to regulate commerce with foreign nations, and among the several states, and with the Indian tribes," which led to the notion of a "dormant" or "negative" commerce clause that prevented states from interfering with trade.[13]

For the German Zollverein, the focus of economic integration was on the development of a customs union. German states could be unified by eliminating tariffs between them, and setting a common external tariff. A few regulations did get in the way, of course,[14] but it was not considered necessary to formulate a detailed set of rules to address this.

The European Union is the most recent example of an effort towards a single market, and there are lots of lessons to be learned from this. This integration effort

---

[12] Section 121 of the Constitution Act, 1867. It has been suggested that this provision can already guarantee free trade. James D, Infernal trade barriers: Canada's constitution already guarantees free-trade between the provinces, Financial Post, 22 July 2014, http://business.financialpost.com/fp-comment/infernal-trade-barriers-canadas-constitution-already-guarantees-free-trade-between-the-provinces (last accessed 4 August 2015). In practice, however, that has not been the case. See, e.g., Choudhry (2002), http://scholarship.law.berkeley.edu/facpubs/2240 (last accessed 4 August 2015).

[13] Legal Information Institute, Commerce Clause, "The 'dormant' Commerce Clause refers to the prohibition, implied in the Commerce Clause, against states passing legislation that discriminates against or excessively burdens interstate commerce.", https://www.law.cornell.edu/wex/commerce_clause (last accessed 4 August 2015).

[14] "The Zollverein [...] harmonized weights and measurements as well as standardized the acceptance of multiple currencies in use throughout its territory." Ploeckl F, The Zollverein and The Formation of A Customs Union, Discussion Papers in Economic and Social History, Number 84, 2010,http://www.nuff.ox.ac.uk/economics/history/Paper84/ploeckl84.pdf (last accessed 4 August 2015); see also, Henderson (1968), p. 317.

was carried out in modern times, with an extensive regulatory state to get in the way. As a result, the lessons here are probably the most relevant for new initiatives of this sort to be carried out in trade agreements. Attempts at mutual recognition and harmonization in today's trade negotiations can draw on the rich experience of the EU.

Of course, even today's national single markets are not perfect. Canada and the U.S. still have many issues with internal trade barriers. In Canada, a mid-1990s attempt at enhancing domestic economic integration, called the Agreement on Internal Trade, made some progress, and there is a mechanism in place for addressing internal trade disputes related to regulations.[15] However, the AIT is seen as insufficient to address the problem, and new initiatives are under way today.[16] Thus, despite outward appearances of being a fully integrated economic entity, apparently Canada still thinks it has more work to do.

And in the United States, litigation under the dormant commerce clause highlights the continued trade frictions that state regulation may give rise to. A recent case involves a California law requiring that eggs sold in that state be produced by hens whose cages give them sufficient room to move around. This regulation has an adverse effect on out-of-state egg producers who use smaller cages, and in this way affects trade. Egg producers from other states have challenged the California law in federal court.[17]

In the past, general principles were thought sufficient to achieve economic integration, but now we have learned that more precision is often necessary, as a formal economic union may be undermined by local regulations. The growth of the

[15] One recent case dealt with regulations in Quebec that prevent the use of the word 'butter' on dairy product substitutes. Report of Article 1706.1 Appeal Panel Regarding the Dispute between Saskatchewan and Québec Concerning Dairy Blends, Dairy Analogues and Dairy Alternatives, 26 January 2015. http://www.ait-aci.ca/en/dispute/AIT%20Final%20appeal%20decision%20jan%2026.pdf (last accessed 4 August 2015).

[16] See Geddes J, Taylor-Vaisey N, Home is where the trade barriers are, Maclean's, 29 October 2013 ("Back in 1994, the federal, provincial and territorial governments signed what's called the Agreement on Internal Trade, a sort of free trade pact for Canada's domestic economy. But the AIT hasn't eliminated a wide range of obstacles. Corporations face separate, unharmonized registration requirements in different provinces. Professionals confront different standards from province to province when it comes to recognizing their qualifications. Consumers in most provinces still can't order wine from another's vineyards. Refiners have to mix special batches of ethanol-enhanced gasoline to meet varying provincial rules.") http://www.macleans.ca/politics/home-is-where-the-barriers-are-weve-got-free-trade-with-europe-fantastic-now-how-about-all-those-trade-restrictions-between-the-provinces-2/ (last accessed 4 August 2015); Lester (2014), p. 61, http://object.cato.org/sites/cato.org/files/articles/lester-internationaleconomy-fall-2014.pdf (last accessed 4 August 2015). See also, CBC News, James Moore pitches changes to interprovincial trade, 20 August 2014, http://www.cbc.ca/news/politics/james-moore-pitches-changes-to-interprovincial-trade-1.2741641 (last accessed 4 August 2015); McKenna B, Canada's internal trade barriers must fall, The Globe and Mail, 14 June 2015.

[17] See Flynn D, Egg-Producing States File Appeal Over California's Proposition 2, Food Safety News, 8 March 2015, http://www.foodsafetynews.com/2015/03/six-egg-producing-states-file-appeal-over-californias-proposition-2/#.VVOobflViko (last accessed 4 August 2015).

regulatory state means there are many more product and service regulations that have the potential to affect trade. The tariffs might all have disappeared, but efforts to sell in other markets face a thicket of costly and burdensome regulations that must be cut through. Domestic markets such as Canada continue to search for answers here, but efforts are also underway at the international level.

5 The TTIP: Towards a Single Market?

With all of the integration possibilities in mind, where does the TTIP fall on the continuum of integration? First, the TTIP does not ignore border barriers. While people have suggested that tariffs between the U.S. and EU are already low, they do still exist, and occasionally are fairly high.[18] Thus, the TTIP will certainly play an important role in removing lingering protectionist border barriers.

As for discriminatory regulations, for trade in goods, there is no need to go beyond the existing WTO non-discrimination obligations, such as in GATT Article III or TBT Agreement Article 2.1. Any concerns with protectionist measures can be handled at the WTO. However, for trade in services and for government procurement, there is no blanket obligation to liberalize at the WTO, but rather commitments for particular sectors or government agencies. Here, additional TTIP commitments that go further than WTO commitments could provide for additional liberalization.

The biggest issue for the TTIP is non-discriminatory regulatory trade barriers. To some extent, addressing such issues would bring the U.S.-EU economic area closer to a single market. For example, increased reliance on international standards would harmonize regulations to some degree. So far, however, the two parties appear to see a different set of regulatory issues, and are pushing different solutions to the problems they associate with regulation.

For the U.S., one of the biggest issues is the transparency of the EU regulatory process. As its primary demand, the U.S. would like to see the EU add a "notice and comment" period to its process, as is used in the U.S., through which the EU would publish draft regulations, get comments from stakeholders, and respond to these comments as it formulates the final regulation. Currently, the EU does get input from stakeholders, but earlier in the process, and it does not publish a draft.[19] This

[18] Lester S, US-EU Trade Talks: Don't Forget about the Tariffs, 22 July 2013, http://www.cato.org/blog/us-eu-trade-talks-dont-forget-about-tariffs (last accessed 4 August 2015).

[19] U.S. Trade Representative Michael Froman went to Brussels to give a speech on these issues. Remarks by U.S. Trade Representative Michael Froman on the United States, the European Union, and the Transatlantic Trade and Investment Partnership, 30 September 2013, https://ustr.gov/about-us/policy-offices/press-office/speeches/transcripts/2013/september/froman-us-eu-ttip (last accessed 4 August 2015); See also, Inside U.S. Trade, Froman Calls On EU Regulators To Be More Like Their U.S. Counterparts, 04 October 2013 ("Froman implicitly criticized the European Commission's system of issuing preliminary general papers based in advance of issuing proposed

"meta-" issue does not directly integrate the U.S. and EU markets, but it does harmonize their processes, making it easier for U.S. companies to navigate the EU process.

In response, EU officials have pushed back against what they perceive as U.S. interference with the EU process.[20] Instead of these internal process issues, the EU has focused on more cooperation between U.S. and EU regulators, including the establishment of a regulatory cooperation body that would allow agencies from the U.S. and EU to coordinate their regulatory actions and exchange information.[21] This could reduce duplicative efforts, and help to reduce the burden of disparate regulations in the two markets. Several sectors have been identified as likely candidates for such cooperation, including chemicals, cosmetics and vehicles.[22] However, some U.S. agencies are resisting these efforts, calling into question the potential for success here.[23]

In addition, although the WTO already has rules on SPS and TBT measures, there are proposals in the TTIP to go further on these issues. However, it is not clear

---

rules, and seeking comments on those papers rather than the detailed rules themselves. The commission typically does not have a separate comment period once the actual regulation is promulgated. U.S. federal agencies, by contrast, issue proposed rules and then take comments before issuing a final version.").

[20] Then EU Trade Commission Karol de Gucht said the following in a speech soon after Ambassador Froman's remarks: "Neither side will be successful if it seeks to impose its system on the other.", Transatlantic Trade and Investment Partnership (TTIP)—Solving the Regulatory Puzzle, 10 October 2013, http://trade.ec.europa.eu/doclib/docs/2013/october/tradoc_151822.pdf (last accessed 4 August 2015). See also, Inside U.S. Trade, EU Official Pushes Back Against USTR Criticism Of Brussels Rulemaking, 04 October 2013.

[21] Inside U.S. Trade, EU Official Pushes Back Against USTR Criticism Of Brussels Rulemaking, 04 October 2013.

[22] See, e.g., European Commission, Ensuring transparency in EU-US trade talks: EU publishes negotiating positions in five more areas, 14 May 2014 ("The papers released today include proposals for enhancing the compatibility of each other's existing rules and regulations, or working more closely together in setting them in future, in five sectors:

1. Chemicals
2. Cosmetics
3. Pharmaceutical products
4. Motor vehicles
5. Textiles and clothing

In each sector, the papers focus on ways we can:

- end the unnecessary duplication of product testing or plant inspections
- recognise each other's existing regulations, or bring them more closely together
- align our respective procedures for approving or registering new products.")

[23] Inside U.S. Trade, FDA Seeks To Sever EU Regulatory Cooperation Efforts From TTIP Talks, 18 July 2014. There are also concerns about the impact on regulation by U.S. states: "Sharon Treat, a former state representative in Maine, said she believes the EU proposal would have a chilling effect on states' ability to regulate. She expressed doubt that underfunded, overstretched state agencies would have the ability to respond to the European Commission's request for information on how a particular regulation is crafted." Inside U.S. Trade, TTIP Negotiators Create Joint Text On Regulatory Cooperation, Discuss TBT, 30 April 2015.

how exactly such TTIP obligations would add to the already extensive WTO rules in these areas, and why such additions are needed.

What these proposals would do is move the TTIP very tentatively towards a single market. But they would not go far. There would not be a generalized effort to ensure mutual recognition across all products and services. There would, however, be small steps that go beyond what already occurs at the WTO and delicately explores the possibility of more mutual recognition.

At this point, the chances of success for the TTIP on regulatory issues are unclear. The U.S. and EU seem to have different perspectives on what the most important issues are. It is still possible that progress will be made, but it will probably require some difficult compromises from both sides. If they can do so, however, it will be a small step towards a slightly more integrated, but not yet "single," transatlantic market.

6 Economic Efficiency versus National Autonomy in International Economic Governance

The description in the previous sections puts the issues in narrow, practical terms, in the context of specific initiatives in international trade agreements or domestic law. More broadly, the principles involved here are economic efficiency and national autonomy, and the core challenge of economic integration agreements like the TTIP is achieving a balance between them. With border barriers and protectionist domestic regulations, the balance is easy. Reducing protectionism adds a lot to efficiency, but does not have much impact on autonomy. A government can regulate however it wants as long as it is not being protectionist. By contrast, as you move towards a single market, efficiency is improved further, but the effect on autonomy grows considerably. A single market constrains national regulation in a wide range of ways, with varying degrees of interference.

The establishment of a single market is widely seen as adding substantially to economic welfare. The larger size of the market creates additional opportunities for internal trade, allowing comparative advantage and specialization to expand. It also lets companies operate on a larger scale, reducing average costs. And it reduces the burden of regulation, as companies need only comply with one set of regulations, rather than many.

At the same time, a single market undermines local autonomy over policy. If the people of a jurisdiction have preferences in a particular policy area, they would like to be able to express them. If they are subject to rules from above, in the form of an international agreement, they may not be able to do so.

Thus, while a single market improves economic welfare, it reduces political autonomy. That is the inherent trade-off.

To take some examples, in the EU, as is well-known, there is great sensitivity about allowing hormone-treated meat or genetically modified food to be sold.

Dispute settlement rulings that EU restrictions violate WTO obligations have not been able to change this. It is difficult to imagine the TTIP making any more progress in these areas.

Going in the other direction, the U.S. is quite sensitive about its financial services regulations,[24] as well as a variety of more obscure regulatory issues such as headlights on cars.[25]

Thus, there are clearly limits to how far a single transatlantic market can be pushed. It is possible that it can really only be advanced in areas where there are no concerns at all about autonomy.

Moreover, to be successful, it should do so in ways that are less binding and more hortatory. Litigation over alleged trade barriers, where they are not protectionist, is probably counter-productive, leading to intense concerns about autonomy and sovereignty. Thus, instead of binding rules, the regulators simply need to agree to recognize each other's work.

By way of example, automobile safety standards might be a good place to start. Automobiles tested for safety in one jurisdiction should be able to be marketed in the other. An agreement on mutual recognition for automobiles made in the U.S. and EU would have substantial economic benefits.[26]

7 The Influence of Industry

One of the difficulties with addressing sensitive regulatory issues in trade negotiations is that industry is more interested in "market access" than with developing principles that can properly balance the various competing concerns. Companies mainly care about whether they can sell their products in foreign markets; what principles are used to bring down "barriers" is of little consequence to them.

To take an example, a recent news report on the TTIP carried the following headline: "EU dropped pesticide laws due to US pressure over TTIP, documents reveal." The article further stated that, "US trade officials pushed EU to shelve action on endocrine-disrupting chemicals linked to cancer and male infertility to

[24] Trindle J and Fairless T, U.S. Wants Financial Services Off Table in EU Trade Talks, Wall Street Journal, 15 July 2013, http://www.wsj.com/articles/SB10001424127887323394504578607841246434144 (last accessed 4 August 2015).

[25] "[S]ome non-American carmakers have developed sophisticated car headlights that adjust automatically in response to surroundings. While these headlights are available in Europe and other places, they have not been approved for sale in the United States." Lester S, Transatlantic Regulatory Trade Barriers, Huffington Post, www.huffingtonpost.com/simon-lester/transatlantic-regulatory-trade-barriers_b_3580900.html (last accessed 4 August 2015).

[26] One estimate is that harmonization of auto regulations would increase US-EU auto trade by at least 20 %, resulting in national income gains for both partners together of over $20 billion per year in the long run. Freund C and Oliver S, Gains from Harmonizing US and EU Auto Regulations under the Transatlantic Trade and Investment Partnership, Peterson Institute for Economics Policy Brief, June 2015, http://www.piie.com/publications/pb/pb15-10.pdf, p. 17.

facilitate TTIP free trade deal."[27] As is often the case with news reporting, there is some exaggeration. The influence of lobbying by U.S. companies was almost certainly not the driving factor in the EU decision, although it may have been one factor taken into account.

But perception can become reality. When companies lobby against regulations in this way, citing trade concerns and ongoing trade negotiations, it provides ammunition to critics to argue that trade agreements interfere with regulatory autonomy. In this instance, the U.S. industry stated the following in a public letter: "The potential adoption of a regulatory approach in the EU that would likely result in significant impact on U.S. commerce and international trade is of serious concern to ACC, CLA, and all of our member companies. In addition, the adoption of an approach in the EU that differs so substantially from EPA's EDSP program would likely put in place precisely the kind of regulatory barriers that a potential US-EU Free Trade Agreement would be designed to address."[28]

Industry demands of this sort can impede the development of workable principles as part of trade agreements. In the case of endocrine disruptors, the industry appears to want to prevent the adoption of a "trade barrier"—in the form of a domestic regulation under consideration—that it might face. (Such arguments are sometimes reflected in official government reports on trade barriers.[29]) But no one is suggesting that this regulation is protectionist, so here we are in the sensitive realm of the "single market." What might help is if demands for regulation to be stopped were replaced by cooperation between agencies in different countries, to see if there is the possibility for mutual recognition or harmonization. In this regard, the language used is important. One person's "trade barrier" is another person's "health regulation," and differences in regulation should not always be handled in the same way as protectionist regulations, with binding rules and litigation.

[27] Nelson A, EU dropped pesticide laws due to US pressure over TTIP, documents reveal, The Guardian, 22 May 2015, http://www.theguardian.com/environment/2015/may/22/eu-dropped-pesticide-laws-due-to-us-pressure-over-ttip-documents-reveal (last accessed 4 August 2015).

[28] Letter from Walls M, Vice President of Regulatory & Technical Affairs at the American Chemistry Council, and Glenn B, Vice President of Science and Regulatory Affairs at CropLife America, to Jim Jones, Acting Assistant Administrator at the Office of Chemical Safety and Pollution Prevention, "RE: Consideration of Endocrine Disruptors in the EU." 3 December 2012, http://www.americanchemistry.com/Policy/Chemical-Safety/Endocrine-Disruption/ACC-CropLife-America-Letter.pdf (last accessed 25 February 2016).

[29] Office of the United States Trade Representative, Proposal for Categorization of Compounds as Endocrine Disruptors from 2014 Report on Technical Barriers to Trade, April 2014, pp. 68–70, https://ustr.gov/sites/default/files/2014%20TBT%20Report.pdf (last accessed 4 August 2015).

8 Conclusion

Economic integration through trade agreements is on safest ground when it focuses on protectionism. Steps towards a single market have to be taken very carefully, with a recognition of the sensitivities that exist. Economic efficiency is important, but undermining national autonomy could put the whole negotiation in peril. It may be possible to achieve a few small degrees of integration through the TTIP, but we should not overestimate the prospects or push harder than is realistic.

References

Balassa B (1961) The theory of economic integration. Richard D Irwin, Homewood

Choudhry S (2002) The agreement on internal trade, economic mobility, and the charter. Asper Rev Int Bus Trade L 2:261–272

Garner BA, Campbell H (2014) Black's law dictionary, Tenth edn. Thomson Reuters, St. Paul

Goode W (2007) Dictionary of trade policy terms, 5th edn. Cambridge University Press, Cambridge

Henderson WO (1968) The Zollverein. Frank Cass & Co. Ltd., London

Hinkelman EG, Putzi S (2006) Dictionary of international trade, 7th edn. World Trade, Petaluma

Lester S (2014) A call for integration. Int Econ 2014:61–63

Suranovic SM (1998) International trade theory and policy. Flat World Knowledge, Irvington

TTIP and Swiss Democracy

Charlotte Sieber-Gasser

Contents

Abstract Free Trade Agreements (FTAs) are increasingly concerned with regulatory convergence, rather than with trade liberalization through elimination of tariffs. This appears to result more often in so-called dynamic trade agreements, which still evolve after adoption. Further economic integration in democracies, however, depends on the support of the constituency. This chapter takes a closer look at the democratic legitimation of global economic integration in a case study on Switzerland. It states that the current principles and institutions of democracy in Switzerland are unlikely to fully accommodate the new regulatory challenges of dynamic FTAs.

C. Sieber-Gasser (✉)
Graduate Institute for International and Development Studies, Geneva, Switzerland

NCCR Trade Regulation, World Trade Institute, Hallerstrasse 6, 3012 Bern, Switzerland
e-mail: charlotte.sieber@wti.org

M. Bungenberg et al. (eds.), *European Yearbook of International Economic Law 2016*, European Yearbook of International Economic Law 7,
DOI 10.1007/978-3-319-29215-1_25

1 The Implications of TTIP for Switzerland

A substantial trade agreement between the European Union (EU) and the United States of America (US) develops considerable economic implications for Switzerland, a recent study of the World Trade Institute in Bern found.[1] While Switzerland currently holds a complex regulatory framework for its trade and political relations with the EU (the so-called Bilateral Treaties),[2] the attempt to negotiate a Free Trade Agreement (FTA) with the US failed already in the stage of exploratory talks.[3] Thus, Swiss trade relations with the US rely today on the regulatory framework of WTO regulation, meaning that market access is limited to the global minimum standard.

The economic implications suggest that Switzerland has to react if the negotiations over the TTIP were successfully concluded. This, however, triggers a number of legal questions concerning the democratic legitimation of the foreign trade policy options of Switzerland.

This chapter elaborates first the economic implications of TTIP for Switzerland, therewith substantiating the need for adequate trade policy measures. It then turns to the regulatory framework of Swiss foreign trade policy and highlights the legal questions, which arise in the potential case of a Swiss reaction to the TTIP. The chapter concludes by outlining potential avenues for trade policy measures in reaction to the TTIP and their respective legal implications. Simon Lester discusses more generally the sensitive balance between autonomy of the constituency and regulatory convergence in the global market. In line with his argumentation, this contribution is specifically highlighting the legal challenge of multilateral regulatory convergence for democracy in the case of Switzerland.

1.1 Potential Trade Diversion for Switzerland

The potential trade distorting impact of TTIP on third countries is linked with the regulatory framework for FTAs in WTO law. Preferences granted in trade in goods[4] and in trade in services[5] are excluded from Most-Favoured Nation (MFN) treatment

---

[1] Cottier T, Egger P, Francois J, Manchin M, Shingal A and Sieber-Gasser C (2014) Potential Impacts of a EU-US Free Trade Agreement on the Swiss Economy and External Economic Relations, Rechtsgutachten erstattet Staatssekretariat für Wirtschaft SECO, http://www.wti.org (last accessed 17 August 2015).

[2] For an overview, see: Die Bilateralen Abkommen Schweiz—Europäische Union. Directorate for European Affairs, August 2014, Swiss Confederation, Bern.

[3] See e.g. Swiss-U.S. Trade and Investment Cooperation Forum, Fact Sheet and Agreement. SECO, March 2010, Swiss Confederation, Bern, p. 1.

[4] Art. XXIV of the General Agreement on Tariffs and Trade (GATT).

[5] Art. V of the General Agreement on Trade in Services (GATS).

in trade regulation, if the FTA results in substantial coverage of all trade between the EU and the US. This implies a high incentive for the EU and the US to conclude a substantial trade agreement granting a considerable increase in market access. It furthermore means that preferences granted in TTIP will be discriminatory for third countries.

The current mandate for the negotiations over the TTIP goes, however, considerably beyond market access commitments in trade in goods and services. It lists regulatory convergence and a substantial decrease in non-tariff barriers to trade as one of the primary goals of the negotiations.[6] Such commitments are not necessarily excluded from MFN treatment, since most of the non-tariff barriers (NTBs) to trade relate to technical barriers and phytosanitary and sanitary measures. Minimum standards in both areas of regulation are established in the WTO agreements[7] and do not provide for an MFN exemption for FTAs. WTO members are obliged to enter into negotiations over mutual recognition of standards, but they are not required to automatically accept equivalency of NTBs. Thus, should the TTIP establish certain commitments in regulatory convergence, such commitments would be of discriminatory nature similarly to the commitments in trade in goods and in services.

Given that global average tariffs on goods are already low for most products, the implications of the discriminatory preferences granted in TTIP in trade in goods will be limited to the number of products which are still burdened with substantial tariffs. In the case of Switzerland, tariffs are a direct concern in the US market, since Switzerland already enjoys preferential market access to the EU market. They are, however, indirectly a concern in the EU market as well, since today's preferences *vis-à-vis* US products are likely to be eliminated by the TTIP. In consequence, producers from the EU and the US will be able to sell their products at a cheaper price on the TTIP markets due to the elimination of tariffs alone, therewith increasing price-pressure on Swiss products.[8] Derived from the current numbers of exported goods to both the EU and the US market and the applied tariffs, the Swiss

[6] See Directives for the negotiation on the Transatlantic Trade and Investment Partnership between the European Union and the United States of America, Declassification, ST 11103/13, DCL 1, October 9 2014, Brussels, http://data.consilium.europa.eu/doc/document/ST-11103-2013-DCL-1/en/pdf (last accessed 31 August 2015), p. 12, para. 25: "The Agreement will aim at removing unnecessary obstacles to trade and investment, including existing NTBs, through effective and efficient mechanisms, by reaching an ambitious level of regulatory compatibility for goods and services, including through mutual recognition, harmonisation and through enhanced cooperation between regulators."

[7] The Agreement on Technical Barriers to Trade (TBT) and the Agreement on Sanitary and Phytosanitary Measures (SPS).

[8] Cottier et al. (2014), Potential Impacts of a EU-US Free Trade Agreement on the Swiss Economy and External Economic Relations, Rechtsgutachten erstattet Staatssekretariat für Wirtschaft SECO, http://www.wti.org (last accessed 17 August 2015), pp. 46–49.

industries for precision machinery and for optical lenses, as well as the Swiss motor vehicle industry will be affected substantially by TTIP.[9]

The potential scope of trade diverting implications of TTIP for Switzerland relating to regulatory convergence and rules of origin can be estimated only roughly because of the scarcity of information available on TTIP. Economic estimates show, however, that depending on the availability of mutual recognition and the character of the rules of origin, regulatory convergence in TTIP could both imply substantial losses for the Swiss economy, and substantial gains.[10] The commitments and character of TTIP in this respect are particularly important for the Swiss pharmaceutical industry because of their dependence from exports to both the TTIP markets and from mutual recognition of production standards and certification.[11] But they are equally relevant for the Swiss industries producing and exporting interim products and components to the TTIP markets.[12] Discriminatory regulatory convergence and strict rules of origin both have the potential to *de facto* impede exports of interim products and components to the TTIP markets by substantially increasing NTBs *vis-à-vis* Swiss producers.

Overall it is cautiously estimated that the Swiss economy faces a decrease of GDP of roughly 0.4 percent in the case that TTIP is limited to discriminatory liberalization in trade in goods and services.[13] However, while the general estimates of potential losses might be substantial but not detrimental *per se*, losses are unevenly distributed among sectors: individual industries in Switzerland could be facing serious economic challenges if TTIP was implemented without intervention by the Swiss government.

1.2 Potential Spill-Over Effects for Switzerland

Third countries like Switzerland have, on the other hand, also much to gain economically from TTIP: If TTIP achieves regulatory convergence, third countries

[9] Francois J and Sieber-Gasser C (2014) Zum Freihandelsabkommen EU-USA: Auswirkungen auf die Schweiz. SwissTnet, inSide online, http://www.swisst.net/cms/inside/index.php?option=com_content&task=view&id=4032&Itemid=939 (last accessed 31 August 2015).

[10] Cottier et al. (2014), Potential Impacts of a EU-US Free Trade Agreement on the Swiss Economy and External Economic Relations, Rechtsgutachten erstattet Staatssekretariat für Wirtschaft SECO, http://www.wti.org (last accessed 17 August 2015), p. 38.

[11] Cottier et al. (2014), Potential Impacts of a EU-US Free Trade Agreement on the Swiss Economy and External Economic Relations, Rechtsgutachten erstattet Staatssekretariat für Wirtschaft SECO, http://www.wti.org (last accessed 17 August 2015), p. 47.

[12] Francois and Sieber-Gasser (2014). Zum Freihandelsabkommen EU-USA: Auswirkungen auf die Schweiz. SwissTnet, inSide online, http://www.swisst.net/cms/inside/index.php?option=com_content&task=view&id=4032&Itemid=939 (last accessed 31 August 2015).

[13] Cottier et al. (2014), Potential Impacts of a EU-US Free Trade Agreement on the Swiss Economy and External Economic Relations, Rechtsgutachten erstattet Staatssekretariat für Wirtschaft SECO, http://www.wti.org (last accessed 17 August 2015), p. 38.

could adjust their production methods accordingly and—if mutual recognition is granted—export to both markets on just one standard. Furthermore, if other third countries follow suit, the TTIP-standards could potentially establish market access beyond the TTIP-markets. Since NTBs account today for a substantial share in barriers to trade, according to economists, gains from regulatory convergence and elimination of NTBs are substantial.[14]

In the case of Switzerland, the potential gains from TTIP are at the largest for the industries, which depend most heavily on mutual recognition as they operate in sectors with high levels of NTBs. Examples of such industries are the precision machinery, the motor vehicle, and the pharmaceutical industries.[15]

The potential scope of regulatory convergence could be estimated from the recently concluded negotiations over the *Comprehensive Economic and Trade Agreement (CETA)* between the EU and Canada. CETA is the result of a similarly ambitious negotiation mandate of both partners, which explicitly targeted regulatory convergence. According to the consolidated draft of CETA, the EU and Canada did not achieve substantially new levels of regulatory commitments. However, based on the institutional framework of CETA, regulatory convergence will continue to be negotiated and pursued between the EU and Canada and ought to result in higher levels of convergence in the coming years. Thus, it is rather unlikely that TTIP will immediately achieve regulatory convergence beyond what was achieved under CETA.

Nevertheless, the two regulatory areas of CETA, which resulted in some commitments in regulatory convergence, are among others the standards in the motor vehicle industry[16] and the standards for pharmaceutical products.[17] Similar regulatory convergence in TTIP would, much the same as CETA, imply considerable gains for the concerned industries in Switzerland through spill-over effects as a consequence of a unification of standards in the two main export markets of Switzerland.

---

[14] See Egger P, Francois J, Manchin M, Nelson D (2014) Non-Tariff Barriers, Integration, and the Trans-Atlantic Economy, paper prepared for the October Economic Policy Panel, Rome, p. 29.

[15] Cottier et al. (2014), Potential Impacts of a EU-US Free Trade Agreement on the Swiss Economy and External Economic Relations, Rechtsgutachten erstattet Staatssekretariat für Wirtschaft SECO, http://www.wti.org (last accessed 17 August 2015), p. 48: e.g. exports of precision instruments and watches are burdened by 22.25 percent (EU) and 24.65 percent (US) of actionable NTBs, in addition to tariffs.

[16] Consolidated CETA Text, Cooperation in the Field of Motor Vehicle Regulations, Annex, pp. 91–98.

[17] Consolidated CETA Text, Protocol on the Good Manufacturing Practices for Pharmaceutical Products, pp. 427–441.

1.3 Imperative for a Swiss Intervention

The economic analysis shows that contingent on the final scope of the agreement; a TTIP affects individual industries in Switzerland substantially. For industries exporting to the EU and the US, the TTIP both creates an opportunity for economic gains as a consequence of lower levels of NTBs, and a disadvantage as a consequence of discriminatory tariffs. In that, the industries most likely to gain substantially from the TTIP are at the same time the industries most exposed to trade distortion as a consequence of TTIP.

The characteristics of industries in Switzerland most likely affected—both positive and negative—can be summarised as follows:

- high tariffs both to the EU and to the US: TTIP will result in price-pressure both in the US and in the EU market
- interim products and components: strict rules of origin could be problematic for exports to the TTIP-markets, on the other hand, unification of standards could increase market access in TTIP-markets and reduce NTBs to exports
- sensitive products: mutual recognition of standards in TTIP could be both an opportunity to increase market access in TTIP-markets and reduce NTBs, as well as it could impede exports to TTIP-markets if equivalency of standards was not established
- EU and/or US market as the main destination of export: TTIP will increase competition *vis-à-vis* Swiss exports in both TTIP-markets compared to *status quo*

Since the EU market is the most important and the US market is the second most important market for Swiss exports worldwide,[18] the Swiss economy currently is relatively vulnerable to an increase in competition in the TTIP-markets. The industries particularly exposed are at the same time key industries for the Swiss export economy[19]: Chemical and pharmaceutical industries are the top industries in Switzerland in terms of revenues[20]; but also the industries of precision machinery, optical lenses, and components for motor vehicles are large industries and gener-

[18] See Iseli C (2015) Boomende Exporte in die USA, Press Release, February 12 2015, Swiss Confederation, Bern.

[19] Cottier et al. (2014), Potential Impacts of a EU-US Free Trade Agreement on the Swiss Economy and External Economic Relations, Rechtsgutachten erstattet Staatssekretariat für Wirtschaft SECO, http://www.wti.org (last accessed 17 August 2015), p. 47; Brändle Schlegel N, Christen A, Feubli P, Rutschi B, Stokanic V (2014) Success Factors for Swiss SMEs: Prospects and Challenges for Exports, Swiss Issues Industries, June 2014, Credit Suisse Group AG, Flawil, p. 15.

[20] Generis AG (2012) Handbook for investors: business location in Switzerland, April 2012 edition. Osec, Schaffhausen, p. 17.

ating a high number of jobs. Therefore—and independent from the final scope of the agreement—successful negotiations over the TTIP will force Swiss politics to intervene in order to protect its industries from discrimination in the TTIP-markets, and in order to take advantage of the potential for spill-over effects where it applies.

The type of Swiss trade policy reaction to TTIP largely depends on the outcome of the TTIP negotiations. International economic law offers an array of possible avenues, some of which have already been discussed publicly in Switzerland. One option is docking on-to TTIP once the negotiations have been concluded.[21] While the US sent positive signals towards welcoming the EFTA states into the TTIP framework,[22] little is known about the EU's position on this matter. Another option would be to aim for mutual recognition agreements, if substantial regulatory harmonisation or convergence was achieved in TTIP. This could be combined with bilateral agreements echoing single chapters of the TTIP, e.g. in public procurement, investment protection, or intellectual property protection. Bilateral agreements limited to mutual recognition and specific sectorial regulation, however, would not fully compensate for trade diversion as a consequence of discriminatory tariffs. Switzerland (or EFTA) could also try to negotiate a separate, individual FTA with the US, if pressure from TTIP provides the necessary incentive to overcome the obstacles of the last attempt. It would, however, have to be taken into account that a separate FTA is likely to be negotiated and implemented after the TTIP, leaving the Swiss economy exposed in the meantime. It has also been raised—in conjunction with the current challenges in the bilateral relations with the EU—whether the accession to the European Economic Area (EEA) could compensate for trade diversion as a consequence of TTIP.[23] Finally, while EU membership would eliminate trade diversion from TTIP and secure economic integration in the EU, it is unlikely that the TTIP could exert sufficient economic pressure on Switzerland to change public attitudes towards EU membership. However, all of these options have in common that they are based on a new, more or less substantial economic integration treaty.

[21] Schneider-Schneiter E (2015) Transatlantische Handels- und Investitionspartnerschaft. Interessenwahrung der Schweiz, Interpellation, 15.3638, 18 June 2015; Vonplon D, Freihandelsabkommen: Furcht vor dem Alleingang. Handelszeitung, 7 April 2015.

[22] E.g. Eisenring C, Schweiz und USA im Dialog: Die Angst vor dem handelspolitischen Abseits. Neue Zürcher Zeitung, 12 June 2014.

[23] See e.g. Schmid S, Blochers Gegner haben ein Ziel, aber noch keine Strategie. Aargauer Zeitung, 12 May 2015; also, Report on EEA-Switzerland: Obstacles with regard to the full implementation of the internal market, Motion for a European Parliament Resolution, A8-0244/2015, 24 July 2015, p. 6: it is suggested that the "conclusion of TTIP must not lead to new trade barriers being set up between the EU and the EEA EFTA states".

2 Regulatory Framework of Swiss Integration in the Global Market

Switzerland is a semi-direct democracy; a representative democracy with elements of a direct democracy. Swiss citizens have relatively broad referendum rights on the communal, the cantonal and the federal level, as well as they have the right to submit initiatives on revisions to the cantonal or the federal constitution.

Foreign trade relations are generally the authority of the Swiss federal government with subsidiary competencies of the cantons.[24] For the ratification of international treaties different procedures apply depending on the type and content of the treaty: Mandatory referendum applies in particular to international treaties concerning the accession to supranational organisations and organisations concerned with collective security.[25] If eight cantons or 50,000 voters ask for a popular vote within 100 days after the notification, an international treaty is furthermore submitted to a popular vote under the optional referendum. This applies in particular to treaties concerned with the accession to an international organisation, and to treaties, which establish important binding legal rules or require the implementation in federal law.[26]

These general provisions and procedures result in a number of legal questions concerning the negotiating process, the ratifications process and the democratic legitimation of FTAs in general and a potential intervention related to TTIP in particular.

2.1 *Foreign Trade Policy and Democracy in the Swiss Constitution*

A potential reaction to TTIP would generally consist of negotiations and subsequently of the adoption of an agreement. Thus, in terms of democratic legitimation, the two phases of the negotiation and of the ratification of a trade agreement have to be distinguished. Based on the Swiss federal constitution, procedures of foreign trade policy are specified in federal acts. They establish generally a requirement of the federal government to consult with the commissions on foreign relations of the federal assembly, and to inform the federal assembly regularly on foreign policy. However, the relevant provisions are of a rather general nature and do not specifically apply to trade negotiations alone. Furthermore, they require subsequent

[24] Art. 54-6, and Art. 101 of the Swiss federal constitution (BV, SR 101).

[25] Art. 140:1(b) of the Swiss federal constitution (BV, SR 101). Majority of both the cantons and the total votes is required.

[26] Art. 141:1(d)2-3 of the Swiss federal constitution (BV, SR 101). Majority of the total votes is required.

interpretation, which has led to a number of standard practices in foreign trade policy.

Neither the constitution nor the relevant federal acts establish rules on exploratory trade talks. It is therefore suggested that they fall entirely within the authority of the federal government. In "important" negotiations, the federal government is required to consult the negotiating mandate with the commissions on foreign policy of the federal assembly.[27] The final competence to launch trade negotiations lies with the federal government.[28] Furthermore, beyond the obligation to inform regularly on "important" issues of foreign policy, the federal government is not specifically required to share information or to consult with the commissions of the federal assembly on a regular basis during negotiations.[29] In consequence, the obligation to consult and to inform on trade negotiations depends on the assessment whether an aspect of foreign trade policy is "important" or not. While the federal assembly generally has supervising authority over foreign relations, the corresponding rights are primarily established in the ratification process.[30] In practice, the federal government thus enjoys considerable discretionary power in foreign trade policy with the exception of the ratification of a trade agreement.

Based on the Swiss federal constitution, the ratification of a trade agreement could fall within the scope of the optional referendum, since it establishes important legislative provisions and may require the amendment of federal law. However, simultaneously with the introduction of a broader scope of the optional referendum in 2003,[31] the federal government introduced the so-called «common practice of standard agreements». The federal government argued that FTAs are essentially of the same kind and normally require none to very little amendment of federal law. Accordingly, it was therefore not necessary to burden the legislative process with an optional referendum.[32] The federal assembly accepted this line of argumentation so far and until today, only one FTA of Switzerland was submitted under the optional referendum.[33]

[27] Art. 152:3 of the Federal Act on the Federal Assembly (ParlG, SR 171.10).

[28] Art. 184 of the Swiss federal constitution (BV, SR 101).

[29] Art. 152:3 of the Federal Act on the Federal Assembly (ParlG, SR 171.10).

[30] Art. 166 of the Swiss federal constitution (BV, SR 101).

[31] The partial revision of the Swiss federal constitution on strengthening direct democratic rights was accepted by the Swiss people on February 9 2003 in a popular vote. The partial revision was suggested by the Swiss federal government. See Volksabstimmung vom 9. Februar 2003: Erläuterungen des Bundesrates, Bundeskanzlei, Bern, Swiss Federal Administration, pp. 6–7.

[32] Doppelbesteuerungsabkommen mit Israel, Swiss Federal Government, BBl 2003 6475; Freihandelsabkommen mit Chile. Swiss Federal Government, BBl 2003 7136.

[33] See chronology of Swiss referenda, Swiss federal administration, available at: https://www.admin.ch/ch/d/pore/rf/ref_2_2_3_1.html# (last accessed 18 August 2015). The only exception to the rule is the FTA with Hong Kong in 2012. The Swiss federal government suggested the submission under the optional referendum because of the novelty of the legal embedding of the agreement on labour standards in the FTA. The referendum was not seized, however.

Table 1 Partner countries of the 30 FTAs of Switzerland, along with the year of their entry into force

EFTA FTAs	
Turkey (1992)	Israel (1993)
Palestine (1999)	Morocco (1999)
Mexico (2001)	EFTA revision (2001)
Macedonia (2002)	Jordan (2002)
Singapore (2003)	Chile (2004)
Tunisia (2006)	South Korea (2006)
Lebanon (2007)	Egypt (2008)
Southern African Customs Union (2008)	Canada (2009)
Albania (2010)	Serbia (2010)
Colombia (2011)	Peru (2011)
Hong Kong (2012)	Ukraine (2012)
Montenegro (2012)	Gulf Cooperation Council (2014)
Central America (2014)	Bosnia-Herzegovina (2015)
Individual Swiss FTAs	
European Economic Community (1973)	Faroe Islands (1995)
Japan (2009)	China (2014)

Source: State Secretariat for Economic Affairs (SECO) and Sieber-Gasser C (2015) Democratic legitimation of trade policy tomorrow: TTIP, democracy and market in the Swiss Constitution, Jusletter, 9 November 2015

2.2 Democratic Legitimation of Swiss Free Trade Agreements Today

With the exception of several treaties between Switzerland and the EU,[34] foreign trade relations of Switzerland were until today ratified by the federal assembly alone. Accession to the WTO was submitted under the optional referendum in 1995, but the referendum did not materialize since the requirements for a popular vote in terms of signatures and time were not met.[35] There are currently 30 FTAs in force between Switzerland and countries around the world. In addition, Switzerland is highly integrated in the European market through a number of bilateral integration treaties both with the EU and the member states of the European Free Trade Association (EFTA). Generally speaking, Switzerland is well integrated in the global market—among others through FTAs.

[34] Generally, Swiss-EU relations have resulted in a number of popular votes, be it as a referendum or as an initiative. In the past 25 years, the Swiss voting population decided at least eleven times on Swiss-EU relations. See Sieber-Gasser C (2015) Democratic legitimation of trade policy tomorrow: TTIP, democracy and market in the Swiss Constitution, Jusletter, 9 November 2015.

[35] Kübler D, Surber M, Christmann A, Bernhard L (2012) Mehr Direkte Demokratie in der Aussenpolitik? Studien ZDA No. 2, Zentrum für Demokratie, Aarau, p. 10.

Most of the 30 FTAs of Switzerland were negotiated within the EFTA framework, simultaneously with the other EFTA member states. Four out of the 30 Swiss FTAs are individual FTAs between Switzerland alone and a partner country. Table 1 lists the partner countries of the 30 FTAs of Switzerland, along with the year of their entry into force.

Within the EFTA framework, Switzerland is currently negotiating FTAs with Algeria, Georgia, India, Indonesia, Malaysia, the Philippines, Thailand, and Vietnam. Negotiations over an FTA with Russia, Belarus and Kazakhstan are on hold.[36]

Table 1 shows that the majority of the Swiss FTAs currently in force were concluded after the partial revision of the Swiss federal constitution in 2003, which enlarged the scope of the optional referendum in Art. 141:1. A closer look at the actual treaty texts reveals that there are differences with respect to the scope and structure of the agreements. The most substantial trade agreements in Table 1 are the revisions to the EFTA agreement, and the agreements with Singapore, Colombia, Peru, China and Central America.[37] Generally, a tendency to a broadening scope and increasing depth of Swiss FTAs over time can be observed. This tendency is in line with the general global evolution of preferentialism, which increasingly tends to include new areas of trade regulation and go beyond WTO minimum standards.[38]

It has been raised whether the common practice of standard agreements is compatible with the requirements of Art. 141:1(d)3 of the Swiss federal constitution. There are several reasons for this concern: (1) Swiss FTAs differ in terms of scope and depth of the commitments, *ergo*, they are individual treaties, and not one general template treaty extended to different partners; (2) Economic and political implications differ between partners of an FTA; and (3) Economic and political implications differ between times of concluding and ratifying an FTA.[39] Art. 141:1 (d)3 of the Swiss federal constitution requires submission under the optional referendum if important binding legal rule is established through an FTA, or if amendments to federal law are required by the FTA. Thus, FTAs, which cover new regulation, compared to previous FTAs (like a chapter on trade and environment,

[36] EFTA, list of on-going negotiations, available at: http://www.efta.int/free-trade/ongoing-negotiations-talks (August 31 2015).

[37] Sieber-Gasser C (2015) Democratic legitimation of trade policy tomorrow: TTIP, democracy and market in the Swiss Constitution, Jusletter, 9 November 2015.

[38] Sieber-Gasser C (2015) Democratic legitimation of trade policy tomorrow: TTIP, democracy and market in the Swiss Constitution, Jusletter, 9 November 2015. See also Mavroidis PC (2013) Gone with the wind? the diminishing relevance of the WTO to preferential trade agreements. In: Kleimann D (ed) EU preferential trade agreements: commerce, foreign policy and development aspects. European University Institute, Florence, pp 19–24.

[39] For details, see Diggelmann O (2014) Muss das Freihandelsabkommen der Schweiz mit der Volksrepublik China dem fakultativen Staatsvertragsreferendum unterstellt werden? Rechtsgutachten, http://www.ivr.uzh.ch/institutsmitglieder/diggelmann/gutachten/GA_FHA_China.pdf (last accessed 14 August 2015), pp. 52–58.

which was introduced for the first time in the FTA with Hong Kong), or FTAs, which are likely to develop a more substantial impact on the Swiss economy than previous FTAs (like the FTA with China), fulfil the requirements of "important legislative provisions" of Art. 141:1(d)3 of the Swiss federal constitution and should—from a strictly legal perspective—be submitted under the optional referendum.

2.3 CETA, TTIP, EU Bilateral Relations: Constitutional Challenges Ahead

Table 1 furthermore shows that Switzerland has no FTA with the US today, and a closer look on the FTA with Canada reveals that it is substantially less broad and deep than CETA. In the case of CETA, the EFTA member states might want to consider renegotiations of their FTA in order to achieve similar or identical treatment on the Canadian market as the EU. CETA includes regulatory convergence in the motor vehicle and pharmaceutical industries, and chapters on labour standards, temporary movement of persons, cooperation on science, technology, research and innovation, to name only a few, which go beyond what was previously covered by Swiss FTAs. In addition, CETA establishes a complex institutional framework aiming at continuously deepening mutual market integration over time.[40]

Thus, the consolidated draft of CETA suggests that the agreement introduces a number of innovations with regard to the institutional framework and the scope of an FTA. Consequently substantial renegotiations of the FTA with Canada as a reaction to CETA are likely to cover at least some of the innovative aspects of CETA as well. This means that renegotiations—if successful—result in an FTA, which covers new aspects of trade compared to previous FTAs of Switzerland, and potentially even covers so-called dynamic institutions. Normally, both would suggest that such an agreement be submitted under the optional referendum based on Art. 141:1(d)3 of the Swiss federal constitution.

Given the ambitious mandate for the negotiations over TTIP and the declared goal of moving toward regulatory convergence and institutionalised subsequent rounds of further liberalization,[41] TTIP would in general raise similar issues, as CETA. One scenario for a Swiss reaction to TTIP would be to dock-on to TTIP.

[40] Consolidated CETA Text, available: http://trade.ec.europa.eu/doclib/docs/2014/september/tradoc_152806.pdf.

[41] Directives for the negotiation on the Transatlantic Trade and Investment Partnership between the European Union and the United States of America, Declassification, ST 11103/13, DCL 1, October 9 2014, Brussels, http://data.consilium.europa.eu/doc/document/ST-11103-2013-DCL-1/en/pdf (last accessed 31 August 2015).

This implies that Switzerland would assume the institutional framework of TTIP. Depending on the level of legislative authority delegated to the TTIP institutions and contingent on the interpretation of the term "international organisation" in Art. 141 of the Swiss federal constitution, docking-on to TTIP is more closely linked to joining an international organisation (Art. 141:1(d)2) than to the ratification of a treaty establishing important legislative provisions (Art. 141:1(d)3). This is in particular the case, when the term "international organisation" is defined as "an agreement of states to engage in regular consultation under set conditions and to establish machinery for the implementation of their joint decisions".[42] If TTIP would be considered to establish "international organisation"-like institutions, the common practice of standard agreements would no longer apply, since optional referendum would be based on Art.141:1(d)2 instead of Art. 141:1(d)3 of the Swiss federal constitution.

Given the expected economic impact on Switzerland and innovative character of CETA and TTIP, the decision on the negotiation mandate should normally fulfil the requirements of "important" as in Art. 152:3 of the Federal Act on the Federal Assembly, and therewith suggest the obligation of the federal government to consult with the commissions on foreign policy of the federal assembly.

If TTIP covers the delegation of legislative power to the institutions of TTIP, a similar legal question arises, as is currently the case in EU-Swiss relations[43]: What is the legal consequence, if Switzerland ratifies an international commitment (accession to TTIP), which subsequently results in the amendment of federal law (e.g. through subsequent rounds of negotiations within the TTIP institutions), and the amendment is rejected in a referendum?[44]

To date, the Swiss federal constitution does not provide a clear answer to this potential future scenario: According to Art. 5:4 of the Swiss federal constitution, the confederation and the cantons "shall respect international law" (in this case, the commitments under TTIP), while Art. 34:1 establishes that "political rights are guaranteed". Switzerland would, therefore, be forced to limit the political rights of its citizens (e.g. to referenda on federal acts which are unrelated to TTIP, similar to the current common practice of standard agreements), or to violate its commitments in international law (e.g. non-compliance with commitments under the TTIP). The latter could trigger dispute settlement proceedings according to the relevant

[42] Claude IL (1964) Swords into plowshares: the problems and progress of international organisation, 3rd edn. Random House, New York, p. 8.

[43] Switzerland is currently debating over an institutional framework agreement, which would allow that the static Bilateral Treaties with the EU could dynamically adapt to the evolution of relevant EU law. The debate is highly controversial, specifically also because of concerns over the remaining scope of democratic rights of Swiss citizens. See also Institutional Issues. Directorate for European Affairs, May 2015, Swiss Confederation, Bern.

[44] Optional referendum not only applies to international treaties, but also to federal acts: Art. 141:1 (a) of the Swiss federal constitution (BV, SR 101).

agreement, or—if non-compliance was considered a "material breach"—to the termination of the treaty by the other parties.[45]

This implies that new regulatory innovations in FTAs will require regulatory innovations in the institutional design of the Swiss semi-direct democracy. The current debate over the institutional framework agreement of the Swiss-EU relations is therefore likely not concerned with an isolated challenge for the Swiss constitution, but touches upon a broader challenge of combining the economic imperative to integration in the global market with safeguarding domestic democratic rights.[46] If negotiations between the EU and Switzerland continue to stall, the reaction of Switzerland to TTIP could as well have an impact on the future scope of the institutional framework agreement between Switzerland and its immediate neighbour (and *vice versa*).

3 Conclusions

Economic estimations strongly suggest that Switzerland reacts to TTIP, should TTIP be successfully concluded. An intervention in the interest of the most exposed industries in Switzerland might be necessary independent from the final scope of TTIP. Given the expected economic impact of TTIP on Switzerland, the negotiating mandate for the reaction to TTIP would have to be consulted with the commissions of the federal assembly, since it would meet the requirements of "important negotiations". Furthermore, should the outcome of a reaction of Switzerland to TTIP result in an FTA with the US or in docking-on to TTIP, such an agreement should normally cover new regulation and therefore have to be submitted under the optional referendum. This would imply a change in the common principle of standard agreements, which was applied to FTAs until today and exempted FTAs from the optional referendum.

Finally, should TTIP delegate legislative authority to its institutions and result in a so-called dynamic agreement, Switzerland would face similar legal challenges in its reaction to TTIP as it currently faces with regard to the institutional framework agreement with the EU. It is suggested that the balance between domestic democratic rights and political and economic interests in integration in the global market be clarified—either in the Swiss constitution or in federal law. Taking into consideration the evolution of international trade regulation along with a rapidly increasing integration of the global market, clarifying the right balance will enable Switzerland to react more quickly to future developments in the regional and the global market.

---

[45] See Art. 60 of the Vienna Convention on the Law of Treaties (VCLT).

[46] See also Sieber-Gasser C (2015) Democratic legitimation of trade policy tomorrow: TTIP, democracy and market in the Swiss Constitution, Jusletter, 9 November 2015.

Locating African Countries within Mega-Regionals

Azwimpheleli Langalanga and Peter Draper

Contents

Abstract Mega-Regional trade negotiations, specifically the Transatlantic Trade and Investment Partnership (TTIP) and the Trans-Pacific Partnership (TPP), have the potential to transform global trade relations, if successfully concluded. They would forge new market access conditions and trading rules amongst the major developed economies in sub-Saharan African space, our core focus. This would redound in the World Trade Organization, to shape global trade rules for the future. If they fail then the decline of western, especially U.S. but also EU, trade leadership will be hastened, benefiting China in particular but also, over time, the BRICs economies. That would give smaller developing countries greater leverage in

A. Langalanga (✉)
South African Institute of International Affairs, 1 Jan Smuts Avenue, Johannesburg, South Africa
e-mail: Azwimpheleli.langalanga@tutwaconsulting.com

P. Draper
Tutwa Consulting, Pretoria, South Africa
e-mail: peter.draper@tutwaconsulting.com

M. Bungenberg et al. (eds.), *European Yearbook of International Economic Law 2016*, European Yearbook of International Economic Law 7,
DOI 10.1007/978-3-319-29215-1_26

pursuing their trade relations but with relatively uncertain consequences in a new, multipolar trading system. In this light, our interest is in how African countries are responding to the Mega-Regionals. Are they consciously forming strategic responses in anticipation of potentially being shut out of potential new trade and investment circuits? If so, what is the nature and direction of those responses? If not, why not? And what may the consequences for their trade relations be?

1 Introduction

The initiation of negotiations to conclude "Mega-Regional agreements" by the major trading powers is significant. Two of these preferential trade agreements (PTAs) stand out for their sheer size and ambition: the Transatlantic Trade and Investment Partnership (TTIP) between the United States (U.S.) and the European Union (EU), and the Trans-Pacific Partnership (TPP) between the U.S. and a number of American and Asian states; 12 countries altogether. In addition to encompassing a significant proportion of global trade, these agreements aim to promote deep integration between members, focusing not only on substantial and near-complete tariff liberalisation, but also to significantly reduce non-tariff barriers and provide harmonized, consistent rules for a range of issues.

These Mega-Regionals have the potential to reshape the global trading system. If successful, they will establish new global trade governance norms and regulations. Developing countries not participating in the formulation of these rules would be confronted by a changed regulatory landscape, one not necessarily in their interests or within their capacities to implement. These countries are rightly concerned that such agreements will substantially harm their trade preferences and prevent them from fully participating in global value chains and regional growth. Should the TTIP and TPP negotiations fail, then Western leadership of the international trading system would diminish, substantially, in favor of China and, to a lesser extent, other rapidly emerging powers. This would have a different set of implications for outsider developing countries.

This paper focuses on how the African countries could be affected by these developments. Given the vast geographical space under consideration, the analysis is necessarily high level, strategic rather than detailed, and selective in focusing on particular countries and groupings.

Sect. 2 briefly outlines the 'low politics' of what is on the negotiating agenda. It is important to appreciate the breadth and depth of this agenda, as different countries will react very differently to it, depending on the broad orientation of domestic political economy. Those reactions lie on a spectrum: from those which seek to fully embrace and leverage economic globalisation and the multinational corporations (MNCs) that drive it through their global value chains (GVCs), to those that seek to constrain economic globalisation and those MNCs in favor of domestic corporations. This is analogous to the old 'free trade' versus 'protection' debate, with the modern difference being that the latter is far more nuanced than is commonly appreciated, revolving increasingly around the pros and cons of 'smart' or 'deliberative' industrial policy, state capitalism, or both. The section concludes with a brief elucidation of the implications of the negotiating agenda for sub-Saharan African economies.

2 The Negotiating Agenda

Here, we briefly outline the contours of the core negotiating issues in both TTIP and TPP: market access, rules, new and cross-cutting issues.

2.1 Market Access

Patrick Messerlin suggests that if TTIP is completed then the more concentrated a country's industrial and agricultural exports to pre-TTIP U.S. and EU markets, the more severe the impact of those agreements on that country's exports will be; additionally, the more that country is exposed to the envisaged trade rules and regulations, the more adverse the impact on their trading arrangements will be.[1] Countries with preferential market access will suffer the risk of preference erosion arising from tariff reductions in the Mega-Regionals and there is always the risk of unilateral withdrawal of preferences, such as through generalised systems of preferences (GSP). Countries that have free trade agreements (FTAs) with the U.S. and EU might face increased competition within those markets from third party Mega-Regional participants, especially if their export basket competes with that of the other Mega-Regional participants also looking to enter the U.S. or EU market, a dynamic that currently applies only to TPP because of the high number of third parties involved.[2] Countries that trade on a most favored nation (MFN) basis will only be significantly impacted if they are highly dependent on the EU and U.S. markets and face the risk of trade diversion from new competitors.[3]

Rules of origin (RoO) regimes govern access to trade preferences, and are ostensibly adopted to prevent trade deflection or transshipment from outside the

[1] Messerlin P (2014) The Transatlantic Trade and Investment Partnership and the Developing Countries, Final Draft, Policy Brief, SciencesPo, Groupe d'Economic Mondiale, pp. 14–22.

[2] Rosales O, Herreros S (2014) Mega-regional Trade Negotiations: What is at Risk for Latin America?, Working Paper, Inter-American Dialogue, http://archive.thedialogue.org/page.cfm?pageID=32&pubID=3488 (last accessed 13 October 2015), pp. 4–5.

[3] Rosales O, Herreros S (2014) Mega-regional Trade Negotiations: What is at Risk for Latin America?, Working Paper, Inter-American Dialogue, http://archive.thedialogue.org/page.cfm?pageID=32&pubID=3488 (last accessed 13 October 2015).

PTA area. They play a critical role in determing where actual production will be geographically located within a PTA. The EU and the U.S. have such divergent approaches to RoO that one of the possible outcomes of TTIP could be the relaxation of current regimes and enhanced market liberalisation. However, considering the highly restrictive U.S. RoO regime for clothing, textiles, and footwear—a key sector for many developing countries—this possibility is highly uncertain.[4]

With regard to trade in services, it is likely that the cumulative effect of TPP, TTIP, and the Trade in Services Agreement (TiSA) negotiations involving mainly OECD[5] countries will be enhanced services trade liberalisation internationally.[6] This could lead to diversion of those services tradable across borders, but more significantly to investment diversion since investment is the most significant mode whereby services are provided internationally. The link between services provision and the operation of GVCs is well-established, so those countries outside the Mega-Regionals wishing to integrate into GVCs could face a double blow—diversion of their goods and services exports and of investment away from their markets.

Government procurement markets are an under-appreciated arena for market access in trade agreements. It is highly probable that the final text on government procurement in both TPP and TTIP will mirror the WTO's 2011 revised government procurement agreement (GPA)[7] since the domestic lobby in the U.S. prevents their government from negotiating provisions more onerous than the GPA in order to preserve their benefits from the 'buy local' campaigns and 'buy American' federal funding provisions.[8]

2.2 Rules

Many observers of the Mega-Regionals think that their real significance is not in the traditional market access agendas for goods and services, but rather in the potential

[4] Messerlin P (2014) The Transatlantic Trade and Investment Partnership and the Developing Countries, Final Draft, Policy Brief, SciencesPo, Groupe d'Economic Mondiale (last accessed 18 October 2015.

[5] Organisation for Economic Cooperation and Development.

[6] Messerlin P (2014) The Transatlantic Trade and Investment Partnership and the Developing Countries, Final Draft, Policy Brief, SciencesPo, Groupe d'Economic Mondiale.; Draper P, Lacey S, Ramkolowan Y (2014) Mega-regional Trade Agreements: Implications for the African, Caribbean, and Pacific Countries, ECIPE Occassional Paper No. 2/2014, ECIPE, pp. 18–16 (last accessed 18 October 2015).

[7] Draper P, Lacey S, Ramkolowan Y (2014) Mega-regional Trade Agreements: Implications for the African, Caribbean, and Pacific Countries, ECIPE Occasional Paper No. 2/2014, ECIPE, pp. 12–13 (last accessed 18 October 2015).

[8] Akhtar SI, Jones VC (2014) Proposed Transatlantic Trade and Investment Partnership (T-TIP): In Brief, CRS Report R43158, Congressional Research Report, March 2015, p. 10 (last accessed 17 October 2015).

to harmonize regulatory standards.[9] The issue of regulatory coherence is meant to promote regulatory consistency between the EU and U.S. and is one of the foundations of the TTIP negotiations.[10] Both parties have divergent approaches to regulation, encompassing many issues. For example, the U.S. approach to genetically modified foods is relaxed whereas the EU is very cautious.[11] TTIP would likely establish best practice provisions on standards, but it remains to be seen how demanding or effective they will be. Greater regulatory convergence between the EU and the U.S. could possibly lower transaction costs for third parties trading with both of them owing to the uniform requirements, but such standards may not necessarily be easy to comply with and therefore could constitute trade barriers.[12]

On intellectual property rights (IPRs) issues, positions remain divergent within both TPP and the TTIP. In TTIP, differences revolve around approaches to protection of IPRs such as geographical indications.[13] In TPP, disagreements are more about the depth and scope of protection, with the U.S. seeking protection well beyond the WTO's trade-related aspects of intellectual property rights (TRIPS) agreement provisions.[14] Given the widely varying knowledge conditions prevailing in different countries across the world, and the ethical issues pertaining to particular IPR issues such as access to medicines, the U.S. IPR agenda has been controversial. Speculation, however, is that both TPP and TTIP will provide for differentiated

---

[9] Draper P, Lacey S, Ramkolowan Y (2014) Mega-regional Trade Agreements: Implications for the African, Caribbean, and Pacific Countries, ECIPE Occasional Paper No. 2/2014, ECIPE, pp. 15–16 (last accessed 18 October 2015).

[10] In the TPP, by contrast, given the profound negotiating asymmetries all countries with the partial exception of Japan, will converge towards US regulatory standards since that is a core requirement of the US approach to negotiating PTAs.

[11] Akhtar SI, Jones VC (2014) Proposed Transatlantic Trade and Investment Partnership (T-TIP): In Brief, CRS Report R43158, Congressional Research Report, page 10 (last accessed 16 October 2015).

[12] Akhtar SI, Jones VC (2014) Proposed Transatlantic Trade and Investment Partnership (T-TIP): In Brief, CRS Report R43158, Congressional Research Report. Much depends on the conformity assessment procedures, and how they are implemented vis a vis third parties. Conformity assessment is akin to a RoO; an exporter needs to apply to have his/her good approved, in other words that it conforms to the standard. The U.S. and EU, for example, could automatically extend this recognition to suppliers within the TTIP jurisdiction, but not to outsiders. If a third party supplier meets the criteria for one market, the issue is whether they would have to be tested in the other market or whether approval would also automatically be extended.

[13] Geographical indications refer to names for goods that derive from a recognizable place, such as Champagne. Since the EU countries colonised much of the world, including the U.S., the EU lays claim to many such names. The U.S. contests this because not doing so would mean having to change many names, a very costly exercise.

[14] Fergusson IF, McMinimi MA, Williams BR (2013) The Trans-Pacific Partnership (TPP) Negotiations and Issues for Congress, CRS Report R42694, Congressional Research Report, pp. 42–45 (last accessed 17 October 2015).

provisions for developed and developing countries with regard to IPRs insofar as they set global rules and standards of the future.[15]

In TTIP, there are substantive differences between the EU and the U.S. over some aspects of investment protection, particularly investor-state arbitration, which is central to U.S. investment agreements.[16] The same is true of the U.S. and some TPP negotiating partners. European views on this issue are mixed; in TPP negotiations, Australia has major reservations. The U.S. is also pushing for controversial provisions such as the automatic right of establishment of foreign goods and services providers in the markets of PTA partners: non-discriminatory treatment of U.S. investors and their investments; minimum guarantees of fair and equitable treatment; disciplines on expropriation; prohibitions on capital controls; exemptions for scheduled non-conforming measures; and a ban on imposing performance requirements on such as minimum export thresholds and local content requirements.[17]

Competition policy is being pursued in TPP by the U.S., partly as an additional means of dealing with state-owned enterprises (SOEs) in developing countries and levelling the playing field for U.S. companies by doing away with the financing, regulation, and transparency issues that allegedly confer an unfair competitive advantage on SOEs.[18] Speculation is that competition policy negotiations will create centralised competition oversight authorities such as those in the EU, West African Economic and Monetary Union, and COMESA,[19] but the possibility of a substantive agreement on competition seems far-fetched, especially as OECD efforts in the area have come to nought.[20] Hence, negotiations on the regulation of SOEs, both in the OECD and in the TPP, seek to do away with any competitive advantage conferred on SOEs by governments.

2.3 Broad Implications for Sub-Saharan Africa

From the preceding brief analysis, several broad implications are apparent:

---

[15] Fergusson IF, McMinimi MA, Williams BR (2013) The Trans-Pacific Partnership (TPP) Negotiations and Issues for Congress, CRS Report R42694, Congressional Research Report.

[16] First enshrined in the North American Free Trade Agreement, investor-state dispute settlement allows for investors to sue states directly via neutral arbitration panels.

[17] Draper P, Lacey S, Ramkolowan Y (2014) Mega-regional Trade Agreements: Implications for the African, Caribbean, and Pacific Countries, ECIPE Occassional Paper No. 2/2014, ECIPE.

[18] Draper P, Lacey S, Ramkolowan Y (2014) Mega-regional Trade Agreements: Implications for the African, Caribbean, and Pacific Countries, ECIPE Occassional Paper No. 2/2014, ECIPE.

[19] Draper P, Lacey S, Ramkolowan Y (2014) Mega-regional Trade Agreements: Implications for the African, Caribbean, and Pacific Countries, ECIPE Occassional Paper No. 2/2014, ECIPE.

[20] Messerlin P (2014) The Transatlantic Trade and Investment Partnership and the Developing Countries, Final Draft, Policy Brief, SciencesPo, Groupe d'Economic Mondiale.

1. With respect to goods exports, there is potential for trade deflection and consequently reduced earnings. Concerning RoO, TPP partners such as Vietnam are lobbying for their relaxation, particularly the 'yarn-forward'[21] rule implemented by the U.S. for clothing and textile imports. Should those RoO be relaxed, then some countries will experience preference erosion. These include some African countries, particularly those whose exports benefit from the African Growth and Opportunities Act (AGOA). Furthermore, those threatened with graduation from GSP[22] access to MFN[23] in both the U.S. and EU markets could experience a double hit, especially if they do not have a PTA with either.[24]
2. African countries would be under great pressure to further liberalise their services trade. Africa, in particular, could benefit from a greater liberalisation of access to network services markets[25] through foreign direct investment (FDI).[26]
3. New and enhanced regulatory standards and disciplines will most likely apply to U.S. and EU trade relations with third parties going forward.[27] This could be positive or negative, depending on how exports from outside the qualifying PTA zone are treated by regulators. It is impossible to predict in the aggregate how this will play out; it will do so on an individual product level.
4. Competition and investment policy have implications for development in Africa. There are trends in some countries toward nationalisation and expropriation of property that could deny these countries investment opportunities. Issues such as the legal framework for investment; secure contractual and property rights for investors; investor rights and obligations; and investor protection and FDI restrictions become central to establishing an attractive investment climate. It will also be of particular interest to Africa to see just how much 'policy space' TPP carves out for developing countries.

---

[21] "This rule is intended to ensure that clothing made in a TPP member country, using fabrics or fibres originating in a non-member country, does not benefit from tariff reduction." Rosales O, Herreros S (2014) Mega-regional Trade Negotiations: What is at Risk for Latin America?, Working Paper, Inter-American Dialogue, http://archive.thedialogue.org/page.cfm?pageID=32&pubID=3488 (last accessed 13 October 2015).

[22] The GSP is an exemption from the WTO MFN principle and provides for preferential market access to qualifying developing countries as qualified by the grantor.

[23] The MFN principle provides for WTO members to treat all imported goods from other WTO members equally, without favouring one above the other.

[24] Countries to be affected by graduation from GSP are mainly those in Sub Saharan Africa. These are countries that are beneficiaries to the US's AGOA arrangement and the EU's Eeverything But Arms GSP.

[25] Refers to markets in communications, energy, finance and transport; ie services that cut across the entire economy and as such could be considered 'networked'.

[26] Draper et al. (2012), pp. 15–33 (last accessed 18 October 2015).

[27] Draper P, Ismail S (2014) The Potential Impact of Mega-regionals on Sub-Saharan Africa and LDCs in the Region, WEF Global Agenda Council on Trade & Foreign Direct Investment, Mega-regional Trade Agreements Game-Changers or Costly Distractions for the World Trading System?, World Economic Forum, July 2014, p. 30 (last accessed 16 October 2015).

5. The importance of SOEs to some developing country economies needs to be underscored here. However, an agreement on SOEs that limits their competitive advantage could provide the right kind of incentives to improve corporate governance and ensure competitive efficiency in public entities.
6. It is highly probable that a successful conclusion of these negotiations will set off a process of competitive liberalisation in other PTA negotiation processes, particularly involving TPP and TTIP members. Countries integrating into TTIP and TPP disciplines will establish a superior investment climate through the WTO-plus trade policies and, in order to attract investment and gain access to the EU and U.S. markets, African countries might have to re-evaluate their approach to such disciplines.[28] This will have implications for African countries in a range of areas where they do not currently subscribe to rules set predominantly by developed countries. For example, many countries do not participate in the WTO's GPA, but will have to revisit this consequent on TTIP and TPP implementation. It is, however, in the interest of Africa, as developing continent, to clarify government procurement policy in developed countries through the TPP and TTIP as this was one of the main instruments of protection used by developed countries during the economic crisis of 2008–2009.

Overall, those countries wishing to integrate into GVCs by aligning their trade policies to the sources of MNC investment should not be unduly troubled by these and other implications. The key issue will be the political willingness to adopt the sometimes painful reform packages required, and state capacities to implement them. This is arguably a substantially greater challenge in the sub-Saharan African context. Those countries that evince a different approach to integration into the global economy, namely a 'smart industrial policy' one, will react quite differently since the agenda involves major intrusion into domestic policy space. Others may resist the agenda on purely ideological grounds, such as opposition to western incursions or perceived diktat.

3 Implications for Atlantic Africa

3.1 Patterns of African Regional and Global Integration

Historically, economic integration in Africa was shaped by the ideology of pan-Africanism, the realities of regional state formation imposed by de-colonisation processes[29]; and the economic realities of being subsistence economies with trade

[28] Draper P, Ismail S (2014) The Potential Impact of Mega-regionals on Sub-Saharan Africa and LDCs in the Region, WEF Global Agenda Council on Trade & Foreign Direct Investment, Mega-regional Trade Agreements Game-Changers or Costly Distractions for the World Trading System?, World Economic Forum, July 2014. P. 30 (last accessed 17 October 2015).

[29] French decolonisation was quite different to British, the two constituting the dominant paradigms, and both to Portuguese decolonisation.

dominated by commodity exports. These broad characteristics also apply to some extent to Latin America and Asian countries, notwithstanding important contextual differences. Consequently, it is no surprise to find that the internal structure of regional economic arrangements in Africa mirrors Latin American and Caribean weaknesses in terms of 'hardware' and 'software' deficits. Arrangements remain weak and characterized by little internal trade.[30] Thus, notwithstanding the fact that Africa has, for the past decade or so, been going through a period of unprecedented economic growth and is expected to keep growing rapidly in the coming years, the continent remains among the least globalised regions in the world and most disconnected from GVCs, while also being the least integrated internally.

African integration attempts have taken three directions: integration with neighbors and other countries because of economic linkages, history, and security; continental efforts driven by the African Union (AU); and global integration, unilaterally, and through the WTO. Regional integration, was initially shaped by import substitution thinking, the dominant economic paradigm pursued in the 1960s and 1970s as post-colonial states sought to build industrial bases. That experience gave way to the debt crisis of the 1980s and 1990s, and adoption (many would say imposition) of structural adjustment policies embodied in the Washington Consensus. Similarly to much of the developing world, the impact of structural reforms is still widely debated, and this has implications for trade strategy going forward.

In the current context, the primary driver of continental economic integration is the African Economic Community, established through the Abuja Treaty, and expected to be achieved through a progressive, linear integration process. Eight regional economic communities (RECs) were identified as pillars: the Inter-Governmental Authority on Development (IGAD); Arab Maghreb Union (AMU); Community of Sahel-Saharan States (CENSAD); Economic Community of West African States (ECOWAS); Economic Community of Central African States (ECCAS); Southern African Development Community (SADC); Common Market for Eastern and Southern Africa (COMESA); and the East African Community (EAC). The Tripartite Free Trade Area (TFTA) is also being negotiated between COMESA, EAC and SADC, and is considered Africa's own version of a Mega-Regional trade negotiation. The TFTA is supposed to set the foundation for wider continental integration after it was launched in Johannesburg, South Africa in June, 2015. This launch was done not withstanding the fact that the real negotiations are far from complete.

These RECs are at different levels of theoretical economic integration, from PTAs to customs unions to common markets. The major challenge is the mainstreaming of regional integration nationally, or, rather, the failure thereof.[31]

---

[30] OECD/AfDB/UNDP (2014) African Economic Outlook 2014: Global Value Chains and Africa's Industrialisation, OECD Publishing, pp. 73–88 (last accessed 15 October 2015).

[31] Economic Commission for Africa (ECA) (2010) Assessing Regional Integration in Africa IV: Enhancing Intra-African Trade, Addis Ababa, http://www.uneca.org/publications/assessing-regional-integration-africa-iv (last accessed 13 October 2015), pp. 20–24 (last accessed 17 October 2015).

Given the chronic institutional weaknesses of most sub-Saharan states, there are also questions about the most appropriate institutional form RECs should take; in essence, it is difficult to see how new, institutionally challenged states could adopt a European-style integration process.[32] This underscores the point about enduring pre-colonial relationships particularly in Francophone Africa where monetary and currency policies, for example, are set in Paris under the CFA scheme.[33]

Integration with the global economy is defined by the Doha Round negotiations at the WTO, access to AGOA, and the Economic Partnership Agreements (EPAs) concluded and still being negotiated with the EU and which are intended to replace both GSP and the Everything but Arms (EBA) scheme extended to least developed countries (LDCs). The engagement between Africa and emerging economies, such as the BRICS group, which lack the formalised structures of the EU and U.S., should also be added to this mix.[34]

3.2 *Implications of Mega-Regionals for Africa*

The reaction to the Mega-Regional negotiations has been largely muted in African capitals and continental institutions. The focus is largely on infrastructure development, industrialisation, and improving intra-regional trade. A perusal of AU documents reveals a pre-occupation with Doha Round negotiation issues while emphasising the primacy of multilateralism. South Africa is one exception; the government has been particularly vocal about condemning the emergence of the Mega-Regionals as an attempt to circumvent the Doha Round and craft trade rules outside of the WTO by the global trading majors. There is no apparent public debate on the implications of these Mega-Regionals for countries and their global trading relations, which may indicate that countries view these Mega-Regional negotiations as just another regional trade agreement process not necessarily of relevance to Africa. It is also useful to point out that while Mega-Regionals may have been

[32] Draper P (2010) Rethinking the (European) Foundations of Sub-Saharan African Regional Economic Integration: a Political Economy Essay, Working Paper No. 293, OECD Development Centre, OECD, pp. 17–24 (last accessed 16 October 2015).

[33] The French Treasury backs two African currencies: the West African CFA Franc, and the Central African CFA Franc, which are exchangeable although they cannot be used in the respective zones. They are used in 14 countries, 12 former French colonies, plus Guinea Bissaau (a former Portuguese colony) and Equatorial Guinea (formerly a Spanish colony). The term CFA means *Communauté financière d'Afrique* in West Africa, and *Coopération financière en Afrique centrale* in Central Africa. See Heiko Korner, 'The Franc Zone of West and Central Africa: A Satellite System of European Monetary Union'. Interneconomics, July/August 2002 (last accessed 18 October 2015).

[34] UNDP (2011) Regional Integration And Human Development: A Pathway For Africa, http://www.undp.org/content/undp/en/home/librarypage/poverty-reduction/trade_content/regional_integrationandhumandevelopmentapathwayforafrica.html pp. 31–43(last accessed 13 October 2015).

influenced by such developments as the Doha impasse, slowdown in global trade, and a change in production patterns, among other things, the motivations for African regional integration have always been different. There is also the aspect of existing preferential trading arrangements with both the United States and the EU (AGOA, EBA, GSP) that are possibly being taken for granted as fortresses against potential negative impacts of the Mega-Regionals. AGOA covers about a third of U.S. tariff lines and utilisation of AGOA preferences has not been impressive outside of the energy sector, whereas the EU's GSP provides preferential market access for roughly 65 % of all tariff lines for qualifying developing countries. Of more relevance to African LDCs is the EBA scheme, which provides for duty-free access, subject to a quota for sensitive (to the EU) commodities, across all products except arms and armaments.

The impact of Mega-Regionals is most likely to be felt in the market access arena. Even then, this depends on: the extent to which an African country utilizes the corresponding preferential access scheme; the country's export structure; and whether any Mega-Regional country exports the same products to the market in question. On the positive side of the ledger, the fact that trade complementarities in Africa's trade with the EU and U.S. are high might lead to enhanced market access, but with the potential disadvantage of locking in African economies as commodity exporters.[35] This could affect African countries' ability to upgrade in GVCs.[36] On the other hand, diversification of export baskets would expose African economies to competition from Asian countries with more competitive products, some of which are negotiating TPP, meaning they could acquire preferential market access into the same U.S. market that Africa will be competing for.[37] Finally, the fact that TTIP, TPP, and the Regional Comprehensive Economic Partnership (RCEP) in Asia, centered on China, incorporate the major GVC hubs of the world could also disincentivise MNCs from investing in sub-Saharan Africa outside of the resource sector or for efficiency-seeking purposes.[38]

The impact on African trade is also subject to other factors. Africa's impressive growth patterns have increased its attractiveness and have seen different external partners tussle for increased engagement in trade and investment. The U.S. and EU

---

[35] Draper P, Lacey S, Ramkolowan Y (2014) Mega-regional Trade Agreements: Implications for the African, Caribbean, and Pacific Countries, ECIPE Occassional Paper No. 2/2014, ECIPE.

[36] Draper P, Ismail S (2014) The Potential Impact of Mega-regionals on Sub-Saharan Africa and LDCs in the Region, WEF Global Agenda Council on Trade & Foreign Direct Investment, Mega-regional Trade Agreements Game-Changers or Costly Distractions for the World Trading System?, World Economic Forum, July 2014.

[37] Draper P, Lacey S & Ramkolovan Y (2014) Mega-regional Trade Agreements and South Africa's Trade Strategy: Implications for the Tripartite Free Trade Area Negotiations,, South African Institute of International Affairs, Occasional Paper 206, November 2014, pp. 7–10 (last accessed 16 October 2015).

[38] Draper P, Ismail S (2014) The Potential Impact of Mega-regionals on Sub-Saharan Africa and LDCs in the Region, WEF Global Agenda Council on Trade & Foreign Direct Investment, Mega-regional Trade Agreements Game-Changers or Costly Distractions for the World Trading System?, World Economic Forum, July 2014.

are essentially competing for enhanced economic influence on the continent within the context of shifts in Africa's trade and investment patterns towards emerging economies such as China, India, and Brazil. Discussing AGOA possibilities post-2015, Mevel et al posit that an integrated Africa, with concluded EPA agreements and an extended AGOA would deflect any potential trade diversion if TTIP is implemented, especially with increased intra-African trade.[39]

Given that the EU remains Africa's biggest trading partner, TTIP has the greatest implications as far as impact on current market access is concerned. Since there are 33 LDCs in Africa, out of a total of 54 countries, the future of EBA is particularly important. No major changes seem to be in the cards, so the most serious challenge for individual African states is the possibility of being graduated from the scheme upon achieving a consistently higher development status. Since the continent as a whole is growing rapidly, this possibility is likely to assert itself in coming years. In this light, the EPAs are particularly important since they offer current and future non-LDCs the security of a PTA with the EU. However, EPAs generally do not cover much beyond market access for goods, so the regulatory agenda associated with TTIP would still have to be engaged in such cases.

Concerning AGOA, the process of renewing it beyond the scheme's October 2015 expiration is underway. There appears to be consensus on both sides of the political aisle in the U.S. Congress that the scheme should be renewed, but also revamped. At this stage, it is not clear what directions the revamping would evolve in; and Congress' failure to renew GSP does not augur well for negotiating or passing a new version. Therefore, those African states, like Lesotho, which depend on AGOA market access would be well advised not to place long-term reliance on the scheme. In addition, it is quite possible that the revamping process could culminate in some kind of graduation procedure, or a glide path towards ultimate termination. If this were to be the case, then African states would need to consider entering into PTAs with the United States in order to maintain and deepen market access.

China is reportedly moving towards formalising its trade and investment arrangements with Africa and this will add another dimension to the current EPA and AGOA discussions.[40] China will continue to constitute a growing market for traditional African exports, principally commodities. But sustained development is ultimately linked to economic diversification, which requires adding value to exports and upgrading in value chains. China could well be a part of this story,

[39] Mevel S et al (2013) The African Growth and Opportunity Act: An Empirical Analysis of the Possibilities Post-2015, Africa Growth Initiative at Brookings, United Nations Economic Commission for Africa, http://www.brookings.edu/research/reports/2013/07/african-growth-and-opportunity-act pp. 25–31 (last accessed 13 October 2015).

[40] Mevel S et al (2013) The African Growth and Opportunity Act: An Empirical Analysis of the Possibilities Post-2015, Africa Growth Initiative at Brookings, United Nations Economic Commission for Africa, http://www.brookings.edu/research/reports/2013/07/african-growth-and-opportunity-act (last accessed 13 October 2015).

particularly by relocating medium-sized manufacturing firms to the continent,[41] but the markets for such products will almost certainly be primarily in the developed countries, especially the U.S. and EU.

It is more difficult to discern how these trends will play out at country levels, let alone regional levels in sub Saharan Africa—that would require a detailed study. Nonetheless, it is apparent that three of the major economic powers in that broad arc—South Africa, Angola, and Nigeria—are pursuing increasingly inward-looking trade strategies. In Southern Africa, Namibia is increasingly mimicking its South African neighbour, a strategy which draws on and resonates with developments in some of their landlocked SADC neighbours, notably Zimbabwe and Zambia. Ghana stands out as a country which seemingly intents to pursue a more outward-looking trade strategy, and Morocco is the only African country to conclude a PTA with the United States while also participating in the Euromed agreements with the EU along with its North African counterparts in the AMU. For the rest, it is not clear that trade strategy—whether of a more liberal or inward-looking posture—features high on the policy radar screen. At the continental level, 'smart industrial policy' is being actively pushed and gaining traction in various regional policy networks.[42] These ideological currents draw from and feed growing resource nationalism, which leads to a particular take on the GVC 'narrative'. And since investment inflows into the continent are gathering pace, this trend releases pressure to reform from African states that are skeptical of trade and investment policy liberalisation. By contrast, in non-Atlantic Africa, and particularly in East Africa, a countertrend towards trade and investment liberalisation is discernible, notably in Kenya and Rwanda. Furthermore, the African Development Bank is advocating a view more consonant with the GVC agenda.[43] This also feeds into the continental conversation on trade.

Overall, we do not discern a clear continental divide among the African economies akin to the sharp three-way split in Latin America. The question is whether sharper divisions will emerge should the Mega-Regionals successfully conclude.

[41] Davies et al. (2014).

[42] United Nations Economic Commission for Africa (2013) Making the Most of Africa's Commodities: Industrializing for Growth, Jobs and Economic Transformation, Economic Report on Africa 2013, pp. 20–24 (last accessed 17 October 2015).

[43] OECD/AfDB/UNDP (2014) African Economic Outlook 2014: Global Value Chains and Africa's Industrialisation, OECD Publishing.

4 Implications for Their Trade Strategies

For sub-Saharan Africa, much depends on how two issues play out. First, will TPP and TTIP conclude? And second, how much does it matter if a country is left out of their regulatory scope? First, we set out three potential outcome scenarios.[44]

4.1 Mega-Regional Negotiations Scenarios

4.1.1 Full Success

Under a scenario of 'full success', one could expect a free trade zone spanning the Asia-Pacific region and covering 40 % of global GDP, with tariffs completely eliminated and barriers to investment completely removed; and another free trade zone covering the transatlantic space, of similar scope and magnitude. But this scenario is also commonly referred to as 'utopia', since some tariffs and some barriers to investment will inevitably remain on the most politically sensitive items, and both TPP and TTIP are only likely to go part way in tackling the now much more important issue of behind-the-border trade barriers in the form of domestic regulation. The protectionist intent lurking behind many such regulations is best unmasked in the context of dispute settlement, and for this the WTO is likely to remain the forum of choice for most, if not all, parties to TPP and TTIP.

Nonetheless, if one hews to the full success scenario, then 'competitive liberalisation' will subsequently roll across the planet and wrap all up in its path. Already, we see that China is closely watching the TPP process, and calibrating its own domestic economic reform program to mirror potential negotiating outcomes to the extent possible. Similar, albeit more embryonic discussions, are taking place in other significant developing countries such as India, Brazil, and South Africa. If China moves to join TPP, as it has in the case of the TISA negotiations, then the pressure on outsider countries will rise enormously.

4.1.2 Partial Success

The more likely scenario of the three is 'partial success', since trade agreements always involve trade-offs and compromises, and both Mega-Regionals are almost certain to fall somewhat short of the lofty and ambitious goals aspired to in their founding declarations. This is simply a manifestation of the age-old maxim that trade agreements involve a set of second- or even third-best policy choices. Be that

[44] This section is sourced from Draper P, Lacey S, Ramkolowan Y (2014) Mega-regional Trade Agreements: Implications for the African, Caribbean, and Pacific Countries, ECIPE Occassional Paper No. 2/2014, ECIPE.

as it may, even if TPP manages to consolidate existing liberalisation efforts undertaken by all the parties to it, and to provide domestic political cover for implementing reforms to some of the most intractable domestic economic problems in member countries (Japanese rice subsidies come to mind), this will still represent considerable progress. Similarly, TTIP is likely to be relatively comprehensive on the tariff front but also to involve numerous regulatory compromises. Nonetheless, this scenario would be a significant outcome from the standpoint of promoting global trade liberalisation and regulatory convergence. If the latter operates primarily through a mutual recognition agreement (MRA) modality, through which outsiders' access to both markets is enhanced, then the result could be positive for outsiders and the global trade system.

If the partial success scenario unfolds, then outsider countries will have more wriggle room, more time to adjust their trade strategies, and more policy space to pursue. However, this scenario is likely to be accompanied by ongoing stasis in the WTO, since the major developed countries that have traditionally exercised leadership over the global trading system would not have been able to decisively seize the initiative. The pressure on outsider countries to forge reciprocal trade arrangements with the major developed countries would increase somewhat, but probably not much further than where it currently stands. Much depends on the shape of the partial success outcome.

4.1.3 Failure

Given the advanced stage of TPP talks, and the enormous amount of political capital that has already been spent by leaders in such countries as the U.S., Japan, and Germany, it is unlikely that either negotiation will be allowed to fail. Instead, negotiators will do what GATT negotiators did after 6 years of negotiations in the Tokyo Round, which is to draw a line in the sand and call failure a success.[45] Here, one envisages a much more modest agreement that fails to provide a single tariff schedule for goods among all parties to TPP, significant exclusions in TTIP, and with both limited to a set of largely hortatory declarations on achieving future progress in areas where the talks have proven difficult (e.g. IPR, environment, labor).

The domestic political economy constraints in a number of countries are formidable, in particular the U.S., which is at the center of both negotiations: the Republican-dominated House of Representatives is seemingly determined to deny President Obama any kind of positive outcomes whatsoever; the Obama Administration's commitment to trade and investment liberalisation is at most lukewarm and predicated solely on the objective of increasing U.S. exports; and Obama faces

[45] We say this given the failure of GATT negotiators in the Tokyo Round to bring agricultural trade more fully under GATT disciplines, or to end the proliferation in vertical export restraints by concluding a safeguards agreement, both of which had to wait until the Uruguay Round.

opposition from much of his political supporters in the Democratic Party. The U.S. electorate has lost much of its appetite for these kinds of deals, particularly with the dominant political narrative regarding NAFTA still being that it ultimately moved many U.S. jobs offshore. One could argue that for the U.S. the electoral math for a sweeping trade deal like this one just isn't there, something we are seeing in the difficulties the Obama Administration is now having in merely obtaining trade promotion authority (TPA). Without TPA, both the TPP's and TTIP's ultimate scope and effects will be constrained. This is a scenario we might realistically be facing.

If the negotiations fail, then the immediate pressure will be off outsider countries. However, there could well be a backlash from the U.S. and the EU, since this scenario would hasten potential Chinese leadership of the global trading system. In the interregnum, positioning among the major powers would likely be intense, and pressure on outside countries to yield reciprocity in their trade relations with these powers would therefore likely escalate substantially beyond current levels. Furthermore, this scenario would likely mean that the WTO would be stuck in the doldrums with no leadership from any quarter as the major powers jostle to shore up regional alliances. In the medium term, outsider countries would need to adjust to a multipolar trading system. This may present some opportunities to play the major powers off against each other in order to bolster domestic economic priorities, although that can be a risky game to play. However, since the China card would be very much in play, outsider countries would need to ask serious questions about Chinese trade diplomacy, its underlying interests, and associated strategies for pursuing those interests. At the very least, China is likely to pursue a more hardheaded approach to securing them, which, if properly harnessed could be very beneficial to outsider countries.[46]

4.2 Does Negotiating Success Matter to Excluded Countries?

Crucially, this depends very heavily on how one defines success. Some parties, particularly certain civil society groups, may define success as a collapse in the talks and thus the failure of TPP and TTIP to culminate in the envisaged PTA. Our view is that success would be a PTA based on the solid consensus of all of the parties to the talks, with major trade liberalising effects for goods, services, and investments, as well as measurable progress in reforming some of the most intractable political economy choke-holds that a limited number of commodities have exercised on the world trade system for many decades. This is necessarily a globally systemic view, and not one rooted in the particular interests of any country or group of countries, whether insiders or outsiders. Ultimately, we believe these two negotiations do offer the prospect of positively deepening global economic

[46] Davies et al. (2014).

integration, even as we remain alive to the challenges that they pose to poorer countries less capable of matching up to the more rigorous standards they imply. Furthermore, the thread that runs through all three scenarios is that the pressure on outside countries to adhere to rigorous behind-the-border regulatory norms and to liberalise trade policies is very unlikely to disappear. It may fluctuate depending on the scenario, but to stick one's head in the sand and hope it will never return does not seem to us to be a viable strategy.

4.3 Broad Implications for Sub-Saharan Africa

Clearly, the countries in sub-Saharan Africa that are already inclined to pursue integration into GVCs by way of regulatory upgrading and trade and investment policy liberalisation will be better placed to manage the transitions heading their way. Those that adopt a more skeptical posture will play for time, meaning they will likely continue with their domestic status quo while beefing up regulatory capacities and mitigating liberalisation to the maximum extent that current policy space affords. Those that reject free trade altogether, are unlikely to be moved to change their view if TPP and TTIP pass, even if they suffer from trade diversion. Of course, nothing is predetermined, and domestic political economies, interacting with powerful external headwinds, will continue to play decisive roles in each individual state.

Based on current trends, though, a reasonably clear pattern is discernible in sub-Saharan Africa of the geographical equation. For example, in the recent fracas over concluding the protocol for accession of the WTO's Trade Facilitation Agreement agreed to in Bali in December 2013, South Africa played an active role in attempting to block adoption of the protocol. It is not inconceivable that other African trade-skeptic nations, notably Angola and Nigeria, could increasingly align their strategies along these lines. A countertrend—embryonic alliances amongst more liberal-minded states—is not currently evident.

5 Concluding Remarks

From the aforegoing, it is clear that much is at stake, from the grubby details of trade negotiating minutiae, to the strategic implications of being left outside Mega-Regional trade agreements as a new global trading system is potentially constructed. The sub-Saharan African region is in the early stages of redefining its trade and investment relations with the EU, in particular; a process that has been fraught, to say the least. The U.S. is in the early stages of reacting to the EU's evolving network of EPAs in Africa, through adjusting the AGOA framework. It has also witnessed the political fallout from the EPA saga and no doubt does not wish to unnecessarily jeopardise its position in one of the last economic growth frontiers in the world. But both, the EU and U.S., feel compelled to respond to China's embrace of the African continent, a fact which gives substantial leverage to Africans. For their part African elites seem not to have engaged fully with the rapidly changing strategic trade and investment landscape, but the new realities will increasingly intrude onto African countries' agendas. As they do, each country will have to assess the extent to which it wishes to embrace the new playing field, particularly with respect to domestic regulation. At this stage it is not clear what regional, or sub-regional, patterns of response in terms of the free trade—industrial policy spectrum, will emerge. But it would be surprising if they did not.

References

Draper P, Dube M, Nene M (2012) The Doha Development Agenda and the WTO can deliver on Africa's development priorities. In: Wilkinson R, Scott J (eds) Trade, poverty and development: getting beyond the WTO's Doha Deadlock. Routledge, London

Davies M, Draper P, Edinger H (2014) Changing China, changing Africa: future contours of an emerging relationship. Asian Econ Policy Rev 9(2):180–197

The Tripartite Free Trade Area: A Step Closer to the African Economic Community?

Vincent Angwenyi

Contents

Abstract On the 10th of June 2015 the heads of state of three Regional Economic Communities in Africa, the Common Market for Eastern and Southern Africa (COMESA), the East African Community (EAC) and the Southern African Development Community (SADC), signed a declaration launching the biggest Free Trade Area (FTA) in Africa as well as opening a Tripartite FTA Agreement (The Agreement) for signature. The Tripartite FTA has the potential to open up a market comprising more than half the population of Africa with a Gross Domestic Product (GDP) of USD 1.3 Trillion as at 2014 which was roughly 58 % of Africa's GDP.

Regional integration has largely been embraced in Africa as a means to realise economic development and sustainable growth. The formalisation by the Member States of the EAC, COMESA and SADC of the Agreement is therefore highly laudable. However, though the Tripartite FTA presents an opportunity to set in motion the establishment of a Continental FTA and the eventual establishment of

---

V. Angwenyi (✉)
Max-Planck-Institute for Innovation and Competition, Riesstrasse 82, 80993 Munich, Germany
e-mail: angwenyi@gmail.com

M. Bungenberg et al. (eds.), *European Yearbook of International Economic Law 2016*, European Yearbook of International Economic Law 7,
DOI 10.1007/978-3-319-29215-1_27

an African Economic Community, the reality is that there are considerable challenges that need to be overcome before the Tripartite FTA can be actualised.

1 Introduction

The need for integration in Africa has been expressed over the years through the crafting of various objectives and the creation of a number of legal instruments and institutions to meet these objectives. Though the ultimate intention has always been for a socially, politically and economically integrated Africa, the focal objectives have evolved over time in response to various circumstances and changes within Africa and globally.

The quest for integration can be said to have begun in the early twentieth century with the espousing of the Pan Africanist ideals that advocated for *inter alia* the civil and political rights for Africans as well as encouraging the venturing by Africans into educational, commercial and industrial enterprise as a means of alleviating the poor condition of Africans globally.[1] The initial objectives were largely political, seeking to ensure that Africans were granted a level playing field in terms of having their own voice and seeking their own ideals.

The efforts of the Pan African movement are credited with the conclusion in 1963 of the Organization of African Unity (OAU) Charter establishing the OAU, which is the predecessor of the current African Union (AU).[2] At its inception the central objective of the OAU was to ensure that after the liberation of most African States the right to self-determination was protected.[3] With increasing globalisation, economic development was acknowledged as a core aspect of self-determination and resulted in the increased focus on economic integration as a catalyst for uniting Africa.[4]

One of the core intentions of the OAU had always been to foster economic cooperation among the Member States.[5] This intention was subsequently expressed over the years that followed through the signing of various declarations and conclusion of treaties that aimed at fostering economic cooperation and development among the Member States.

---

[1] Sherwood (2012), pp. 106–126.

[2] AU in a Nutshell http://au.int/en/about/nutshell (last accessed 11.08.15).

[3] Charter of the Organization of African Unity (OAU Charter) 479 U.N.T.S. 39. The preamble reflects this intention.

[4] See, e.g., Declaration on African Cooperation, Development, and Economic Independence, I.L. M 12(4): 996–1013. The preamble for instance expressed the concern over the widening gap in economic development between Africa and the developed world.

[5] OAU Charter, Article 1 and 2.

The most concrete step towards the economic integration of Africa under the ambit of the OAU was the signing of the Treaty Establishing the African Economic Community (AEC Treaty) in 1991.[6] The AEC Treaty provides for a six stage plan towards the eventual achievement of an African Economic Community (AEC).[7]

One of these stages was set in motion on the 10th of June 2015 when the heads of state of three regional economic communities (RECs), the Common Market for Eastern and Southern Africa (COMESA), the East African Community (EAC) and the Southern African Development Community (SADC), signed a declaration launching the biggest free trade area in Africa as well as opening a Tripartite Free Trade Area (FTA) Agreement for signature. This was followed a week later by the launching of negotiations within the AU for the establishment of a Continental FTA.[8]

While the conclusion of the Agreement is certainly a bold step towards the creation of the AEC, questions still remain as to the effectiveness of the RECs in achieving their objectives. The Agreement as it presently is also presents its own challenges. This article seeks to shed some light on the Tripartite FTA by first putting into perspective the EAC, COMESA and SADC. The important milestones that led to the conclusion of the Agreement are also highlighted. The core provisions of the Agreement and the challenges facing the actualisation of the Tripartite FTA are discussed.

2 The Regional Economic Communities Perspective

2.1 Introduction

Regional integration has been largely accepted in Africa as a way to achieve economic development and sustainable growth. The AU for instance recognises eight RECs, which together cover more or less the whole of Africa. Many RECs in Africa are however lagging behind in the implementation of their objectives. The price volatility on the global market and its effect on the relatively nascent natural-resource based economies in Africa highlights the need for the RECs to expedite their integration efforts in order to bolster and increase regional economic activity. The conclusion by the Member States of the EAC, COMESA and SADC of the

[6] Treaty establishing the African Economic Community (AEC Treaty), 30 I.L.M. 1241 (1991).

[7] AEC Treaty, Article 6(2). In respect of the third stage the AEC Treaty provides that "At the level of each regional economic community and within a period not exceeding ten (10) years, establishment of a Free Trade Area through the observance of the time-table for the gradual removal of Tariff Barriers and Non-Tariff Barriers to intra-community trade and the establishment of a Customs Union by means of adopting a common external tariff."

[8] The African Union Assembly launches the Continental Free Trade Area (CFTA) negotiations, 17 June 2015, http://summits.au.int/en/25thsummit/events/african-union-assembly-launches-continental-free-trade-area-cfta-negotiations (last accessed 14 September 2015).

Agreement is in this regard highly laudable. One, however, has to take a step back and consider how effective the three RECs are in meeting their own objectives.

The core objective of the three RECs is naturally to achieve social, political and economic integration but the level of integration sought varies. Whereas on the one hand SADC and COMESA intend to eventually achieve a Monetary Union with a single currency, the EAC has the far more ambitious objective of establishing a Political Federation. The three RECs however have common objectives which if harmonised could facilitate the tapping of the great potential within the Tripartite FTA.

2.2 COMESA

COMESA is the largest of the three RECs with a membership of 19 Northern, Eastern and Southern African states.[9] The origin of COMESA goes back to the 1982 Treaty Establishing the Preferential Trade Area for Eastern and Southern African States (PTA Treaty), which was concluded under the ambit of the OAU.[10] The PTA Treaty sought the enhancement of co-operation and development among the Member States in the fields of trade, customs, agriculture, industry, natural resources, transport, monetary affairs and communications.[11] Member States were required to inter alia bring down and eventually eliminate customs duties on imports from within the PTA and establish common rules of origin (RoO) for products eligible for preferential treatment. The ultimate objective of the PTA was the establishment of an economic community for the Eastern and Southern African states.[12]

The transition of the PTA into a Common Market was set in motion with the ratification of the COMESA Treaty on 8 December 1994. The main objectives of COMESA as set out in the COMESA Treaty are geared towards sustainable growth and development within the Member States and jointly among the Member States. This objective is to be met through the creation of an economically liberalised environment that promotes domestic, cross-border and foreign investment, adoption of common policies and programs and the adoption of common positions with regards to the international agenda.[13] The ultimate aim is the implementation of specific measures that will result in the realisation of the AEC.

---

[9] COMESA Member States are Burundi, The Comoros, Egypt, The Democratic Republic of Congo, Djibouti, Eritrea, Ethiopia, Kenya, Libya, Madagascar, Malawi, Mauritius, Rwanda, Seychelles, Sudan, Swaziland, Uganda, Zambia and Zimbabwe.

[10] Treaty Establishing the Preferential Trade Area for Eastern and Southern African States (PTA Treaty), 21 ILM 479 (1981), Article 29; See also Treaty Establishing a Common Market for Eastern and Southern Africa (COMESA Treaty), 33 I.L.M. 1067 (1994), preamble.

[11] PTA Treaty, Article 3.

[12] PTA Treaty, Article 3.

[13] COMESA Treaty, Article 3.

The COMESA Treaty sets out undertakings in various economic fields which the Member States are required to meet, some of which were subject to fixed timelines. As regards cooperation in respect of trade liberalisation and development for instance, the COMESA Treaty set a timeline of 10 years from its entry into force for the creation of a Customs Union. Within this period, customs duties and similar charges on imports from the Member Countries were to be eliminated. It also entailed the removal of Non-Tariff Barriers (NTBs) and the establishment of a Common External Tariff (CET) for goods coming from third countries.[14] This in turn necessitated the adoption within this period of various requirements such as RoO, rules on dumping, restrictions on subsidies and rules on competition.[15] The COMESA Treaty also requires the Member States to cooperate in monetary and financial matters with the highly ambitious eventual goal of establishing a Monetary Union characterised by a common currency that would facilitate easier cross-border trade.[16]

Another fundamental undertaking was geared towards addressing the persistent problem of poor infrastructure. The Member States undertook to establish coordinated and complementary transport and communications policies as well as to expand and improve the current facilities and create new ones.[17] Industrial development, which is intrinsically linked to functional infrastructure, is also acknowledged as a critical development area. The Member States are required to adopt an industrial strategy that takes into account aspects such as specialisation and complementarity of industries while having regard to various comparative advantages.[18] The support of small and medium enterprises, food and agricultural industries, the promotion of industrial Research and Development (R&D), increased private sector participation and the improvement of the investment climate in the Common Market are among the many factors identified as necessary in enhancing industrial development.[19]

Various other critical development areas targeted for achievement by the Member States are: cooperation in the development of energy; efficient and sustainable use of natural resources; protection and preservation of the environment; promotion of scientific and technological progress; cooperation in agriculture and rural development and the progressive adoption of measures to facilitate the free movement of persons, labour and services.

The disparity in terms of economic development between some of the Member States is recognised as a critical integration challenge. The Member States therefore agreed to take measures to address this disparity through cooperating in capacity

[14] COMESA Treaty, Article 45.

[15] COMESA Treaty Article 46–62.

[16] COMESA Treaty, Article 4(4).

[17] COMESA Treaty, Article 84–98.

[18] COMESA Treaty, Article 99.

[19] COMESA Treaty, Article 100.

building for these regions in areas such as infrastructure, industrial development and agriculture.[20]

The COMESA FTA was launched in 2000. To date however not all the Member States are party to the FTA.[21] The Democratic Republic of Congo, Ethiopia, Uganda, and Eritrea have expressed their commitment to join and are at various stages of preparing accession instruments.

The Customs Union was launched in 2009, which was already beyond the agreed-upon 10-year timeline.[22] A three-band CET was set at 0 % for imports of raw materials and capital goods, 10 % for imports of intermediate products and 25 % for imports of finished products. The 0 % on raw materials is due to the fact that they are important for production and the cost therefore affects competitiveness of the end products. The 25 % on finished products is explained as a measure to protect domestic products from the stiff competition of foreign products.[23]

COMESA has adopted various instruments and measures meant to give full effect to the Customs Union but timelines remain largely unmet and the implementation is still low. Member States expressed various concerns including: local industries and revenues being affected by the imported goods; loss of decision-making capacity on various policy areas; some countries facing serious economic and industrial problems hence requiring time for their own economies to recover; insufficient capacity, information and coordination. One concern expressed that touches on the issue of overlaps is the fact that the EAC, a number of whose members are also members of COMESA, already has a customs union.[24]

The COMESA Secretariat pointed out that the real reasons for the non-implementation include: National policies that are incompatible with the customs union; some countries having existing free trade agreements with third countries that include duty free provisions hence making it difficult to subsequently introduce a CET; some domestic industry stakeholders feeling threatened by competition from imports, and a general lack of prioritisation of regional integration requirements as well as institutional, technical and financial constraints in some Member States.[25]

The inadequacy of existing infrastructure in the COMESA region has been noted as one of the key hindrances to the region's economic progress. Various infrastructure projects that have been identified as key in meeting the COMESA Treaty

[20] COMESA Treaty, Article 144.

[21] COMESA, Final Communiqué of The Eighteenth Summit Of The Comesa Authority Of Heads Of State And Government (COMESA 18th Summit), 31 March 2015, http://www.comesa.int/summit2015/wp-content/uploads/2015/03/150331_Final-communique_March-2015_new.pdf.pdf (last accessed 14 September 2015).

[22] Ngwenya S et al. (2013) Key Issues in Regional Integration 2, p. 131 http://www.comesa.int/attachments/article/1223/Key%20Issues%20on%20Regional%20Intergration.pdf (last accessed 14 September 2015).

[23] Ngwenya et al. (2013), p. 79.

[24] Ngwenya et al. (2013), pp. 134–135.

[25] Ngwenya et al. (2013), p. 135.

objectives have been initiated. They broadly cover transport, energy, and Information and Communications Technology (ICT).[26] The approach to the development of roads and railways envisions the construction of inter-regional corridors.[27] A Djibouti Corridor Authority has for instance been set-up to oversee the implementation of the Djibouti Corridor which links Djibouti, South Sudan, Sudan and Ethiopia.[28] As regards energy, the regional Association of Energy Regulators for Eastern and Southern Africa (RAERESA) was set up in 2009 to streamline cooperation efforts towards sustainable energy development. The current projects are targeted at hydro-electric, geothermal and wind energy, including various proposed regional interconnection projects.[29] The COMESA Infrastructure Fund was set up to raise capital to aid the funding of these proposed projects and is reported to currently have a capitalisation of around USD 22 million.[30] There are however no concrete timelines for the finalisation of the various projects.

Regarding ICT, an association of ICT regulators in the COMESA region (ARICEA) was formed in 2003. One of its objectives is to coordinate cross-border ICT regulatory issues.[31] To this end an ICT Policy and Model Bill was approved as well as various regulatory guidelines touching on for instance interconnection, satellite and wire services, licensing, cyber security being concluded.[32] The status of the expansion and modernisation of actual regional ICT infrastructure is however uncertain. Various ICT projects had been conceptualised under the ambit of a regional telecommunications project (COMTEL Project) seeking to for example increase fibre-optic linkages but the funding remains a major hindrance to their

[26] See e.g., COMESA, COMESA Region Key Economic Infrastructure Projects (COMESA Infrastructure Report), 9 April 2013, http://www.comesa.int/attachments/article/842/COMESA%20REGION%20KEY%20ECONOMIC%20INFRASTRUCTURE%20PROJECTS_19%20AUG.pdf (last accessed 14 September 2015).

[27] COMESA Infrastructure Report, para 4.1.

[28] Djibouti Corridor Authority to be Established, http://www.comesa.int/index.php?option=com_content&view=article&id=1590:djibouti-corridor-authority-to-be-established&catid=5:latest-news&Itemid=41 (last accessed 14 September 2015).

[29] COMESA Infrastructure Report, para 3.2 and 4.2; See also Mushakavanhu T (2015), Kenya is building Africa's biggest wind energy farm to generate a fifth of its power, Quartz Africa, 3 July 2015, http://qz.com/444936/kenya-is-building-africas-biggest-wind-energy-farm-to-generate-a-fifth-of-its-power/ (last accessed 14 September 2015).

[30] COMESA Infrastructure Report, para 5; See also Osemo w (2015), COMESA Infrastructure kitty hits $22 million, 21 March 2015, http://www.comesa.int/summit2015/comesa-infrastructure-kitty-hits-22-million/ (last accessed 14 September 2015).

[31] Info available on the ARICEA website, http://aricea.comesa.int/index.php?option=com_content&view=article&id=3&Itemid=12 (last accessed 14 September 2015).

[32] COMESA, Report of the 8th Annual General Meeting of Regulators of Information and Communication for Eastern and Southern Africa (ARICEA), 18 October 2012, http://aricea.comesa.int/attachments/article/18/8th%20ARICEA%20AGM%20final%20report%20with%20annexes%20(2).pdf (last accessed 14 September 2015).

implementation.[33] ARICEA also reports facing challenges in attracting private sector participation in its programs.[34]

All these factors point to a significant NTB concern, not to mention a number of lingering tariff issues. These challenges aside, reports point to a slow but somewhat steady achievement of some integration objectives. The operationalisation of the Regional Payment and Settlement System (REPSS) for instance will go a long way in cutting down financial and transaction costs in the region once all the Member States commit to participate in it.[35] As regards actual trade, reports indicate that intra-COMESA trade increased from USD 19.2 billion in 2013 to USD 22 billion in 2014, with a likelihood of seeing further increases once all Member States participate in the FTA.[36]

2.3 EAC

The EAC Member States are Kenya, Uganda, Tanzania, Rwanda, and Burundi. With the exception of Tanzania, all the other Member States are also part of COMESA. The EAC was established with the entering into force of the Treaty for the Establishment of the East African Community (EAC Treaty) in the year 2000.[37] The main objective of the EAC is the development of policies and programmes to foster cooperation among the Member States in political, economic, social and cultural fields, research and technology, defence, security and legal and judicial affairs.[38]

The EAC has a four-stage integration plan; the establishment of a Customs Union, a Common Market, a Monetary Union and eventually a Political Federation.[39] The first three stages are similar to COMESA and SADC objectives. The objective of a Political Federation however makes the EAC the most ambitious

---

[33] COMESA Infrastructure Report, para 6.3. Very little information exists about the COMTEL Project with some previous reports indicating that most Member States chose to pursue their own ICT development objectives.

[34] ARICEA Report, p. 4.

[35] See COMESA's Regional Payment and Settlement System (REPSS) Goes Live, http://www.comesa.int/index.php?option=com_content&view=article&id=395:comesas-regional-payment-and-settlement-system-repss-goes-live&catid=5:latest-news&Itemid=41 (last accessed 14 September 2015).

[36] COMESA 18th Summit (2015), p. 8.

[37] History of the EAC, http://www.eac.int/index.php?option=com_content&view=article&id=44&Itemid=54 (last accessed 14 September 2015); The EAC had however previously been in place with a customs union between Kenya, Uganda and the then Tanganyika (now Tanzania) in the 1920 as well an earlier EAC which was dissolved in 1977. Subsequent efforts to reintegrate the three states led to the reestablishment of the EAC.

[38] EAC Treaty, Article 5(1).

[39] EAC Treaty, Article 5(2).

REC in Africa. The EAC Treaty neither defines what the Political Federation entails nor elaborates further on specific steps for its achievement. A committee set up in 2004 to oversee the fast-tracking of the East African Federation specified that it would entail the drafting of a Federal Constitution, creation of the office of a Federal President and the eventual establishment of a Federal Government.[40] It is therefore presumed that the individual Member States would evolve into the constituent states. Two institutions that have been in place since 2001 and that are regarded as building blocks of the political federation are the East African Court of Justice and the East African Legislative Assembly. The committee's recommendation was for an integration approach that allows for the overlapping of the four stages so that parallel activities can take place to enable an expedited establishment of the Political Federation.[41] The proposed timelines for the political federation have however proven to have been too ambitious.

In terms of economic integration however, the EAC is lauded as having made the most significant strides among the eight RECs in Africa.[42] Of the three Tripartite FTA RECs, the EAC Customs Union was the first to be established. It should however be noted that unlike SADC and COMESA that included a FTA as a transition phase to a Customs Union, the first stage for the EAC was the establishment of a Customs Union. Its establishment was therefore pivotal to the setting into motion of the integration objectives. The Customs Union Protocol was concluded in 2004 with the aim of inter alia eliminating tariffs on imports from the Member States, elimination of NTBs and the establishment of a CET for third countries. Rwanda and Burundi joined the customs union in 2008.[43] All internal tariffs are to date reported to have been eliminated.[44]

A three-band CET similar to the COMESA CET was also established, broadly set at 0 % for meritorious goods, raw materials and capital goods, 10 % for intermediate goods and 25 % for consumer goods with a few products classified as sensitive goods going above the 25 % rate.[45] The CET rates are already fully

---

[40] EAC Secretariat, Report of the Committee on Fast Tracking East African Federation (EAC Committee Report), 29 November 2004, http://federation.eac.int/index.php?option=com_content&view=article&id=191&Itemid=138 (last accessed 14 September 2015).

[41] EAC Committee Report, para. 5.3.

[42] AfDB (2014) African Development Report 2014: Regional Integration for Inclusive Growth, http://www.afdb.org/fileadmin/uploads/afdb/Documents/Publications/ADR14_ENGLISH_web.pdf, p. 11 (last accessed 14 September 2015).

[43] Info available at http://www.eac.int/customs/index.php?option=com_content&view=article&id=123&Itemid=78 (last accessed 14 September 2015).

[44] Info available at http://www.eac.int/customs/index.php?option=com_content&view=article&id=137&Itemid=169 (last accessed 14 September 2015). The elimination had however been gradual in respect of various goods from Kenya to Uganda and Tanzania to enable their producers to adjust to the increased competition from the Kenyan imports. See Mugisa E. et al. (2009), An Evaluation of the Implementation and Impact of the East African Community Customs Union, p. 13, http://www.customs.eac.int/index.php?option=com_docman&task=doc_download&gid=84&Itemid=106 (last accessed 14 September 2015).

[45] Mugisa et al. (2009), p. 8.

operational with the most recent amendments on various qualifying goods having come into effect at the beginning of July 2015.[46] The Member States have in addition established a Single Customs Territory (SCT) which commenced at the beginning of 2014 and is in the process of implementation.[47] The main import of the SCT is to allow the assessment and collection of tax revenues at the first point of entry of imports thus facilitating the faster movement of the goods within the territory.[48]

A report published by the EAC Secretariat in December 2014 revealed that a number of NTBs have been resolved.[49] A time-bound program has additionally been put in place for the elimination of various remaining unresolved NTBs. Some of the NTBs identified for elimination include: government sanctioned or tolerated practices such as export subsidies and government monopolies; restrictive customs and administrative entry procedures such as arbitrary customs classifications and surcharges; technical barriers such as non-harmonised standards and charges such as special duties and administrative fees. There are also concerns raised over issues such as arbitrariness, discrimination and costly procedures.[50] The main arguments made to justify these NTBs centre around safeguards on health, security, safety and revenue loss and the protection of local industries and consumers.[51]

The EAC Common Market Protocol entered into force in July 2010 and broadly provides for the freedom of movement of labour, goods, services and capital.[52] The protocol is regarded as being quite ambitious and its implementation wanting.[53]

---

[46] EAC (2015), Gazette Vol. AT 1 – No. 9, http://www.eac.int/customs/index.php?option=com_docman&task=cat_view&gid=66&Itemid=123 (last accessed 14 September 2015); Ernst & Young (2015) East Africa Budget 2015/2016; Economic and Tax Focus (Ernst & Young Report), http://www.ey.com/Publication/vwLUAssets/EY-east-africa-budget-2015-2016-economic-and-tax-focus/$FILE/EY-east-africa-budget-2015-2016-economic-and-tax-focus.pdf (last accessed 14 September 2015).

[47] EALA (2014), Report of On-Spot Assessment on the EAC Single Customs Territory (EALA Report), http://eala.org/key-documents/reports/doc_details/539-on-spot-assessment-on-the-eac-single-customs-territory-eac-sct.html (last accessed 14 September 2015).

[48] EALA Report (2014), p. 1; EAC Secretariat (2015), Annual Progress Report of the Council to the Summit of EAC Heads of State for the period December 2013 to November 2014, http://www.eac.int/index.php?option=com_content&view=article&id=1807:annual-progress-report-of-the-council-to-the-16th-ordinary-heads-of-state-summit-for-the-period-december-2013-november-2014-&catid=146:press-releases&Itemid=194 (last accessed 14 September 2015).

[49] EAC Secretariat, Status of Elimination of Non-Tariff Barriers in the East African Community Vol. 8 (NTB Report), December 2014, http://www.eac.int/trade/index.php?option=com_docman&Itemid=132.

[50] NTB Report (2014), p. 25.

[51] NTB Report (l2014), p. 20.

[52] EAC Common Market: Overview, http://www.eac.int/commonmarket/index.php?option=com_content&view=article&id=80&Itemid=117 (last accessed 14 September 2015).

[53] World Bank/EAC Secretariat (2014) East African Common Market Scorecard 2014: Tracking EAC compliance in the movement of Capital, Services and Goods (EAC Common Market Scorecard), https://www.wbginvestmentclimate.org/publications/upload/East-African-Common-Market-Scorecard-2014.pdf (last accessed 14 September 2015).

The Member States are reported as all having restrictions that affect inward investments originating from within the EAC, with new restrictions on capital movement being introduced contrary to the requirements under the Protocol.[54] It is also noted that key laws, principally sectoral, within the Member States have several measures that restrict the movement of services. Most of these measures favour the local service providers over service providers from the other Member States contrary to the national treatment principle. The other measures favour service providers from outside the EAC.[55]

In respect of the Monetary Union, a Committee consisting of the Central Bank Governors of the Member States reported that some progress had already been made in the harmonisation of banking regulations, payment systems and monetary and exchange rate policy.[56] Other priority areas identified by the Committee include harmonisation of ICT aspects, integration of the payment systems and harmonisation of reporting standards of which work is reported to be in progress.[57] The Monetary Union Protocol was signed in 2013 and has thus far been ratified by all the five Member States.[58] The next steps include the creation of a Monetary Institute and a Statistics Bureau as well as one tasked with surveillance, compliance and enforcement.[59]

The EAC is reported to be the most economically uniform REC, with economic disparities in terms of fiscal policy, inflation, reserves and revenue to expenditure recording significant reductions since 2000.[60] The EAC is also projected to experience real growth of 6.2 % in 2015, with Tanzania expected to register the highest growth at 7 %.[61] The value of intra-EAC trade has also seen significant improvement with the period between 2008 and 2013 indicating a 84 % increase from USD 3,148.7 million in 2008 to USD 5805.6 million in 2013.[62]

---

[54] EAC Common Market Scorecard (2014), p. 3. Kenya's laws reportedly make it easier to move capital while Tanzania's and Burundi's are the most restrictive.

[55] EAC Common Market Scorecard (2014), pp. 3–4.

[56] UNECA (2012), Towards a Common Currency in the East African Community(EAC) Issues, Challenges and Prospects (UNECA Report), http://www.uneca.og/sites/default/files/PublicationFiles/towards_a_common_currency_in_the_eac-2012.pdf (last accessed 14 September 2015).

[57] UNECA Report (2012), p. 9–10, 47–48.

[58] Ligami C., Uganda Ratifies the Monetary Union, The East African, 7 February 2015, http://www.theeastafrican.co.ke/news/Uganda-ratifies-the-monetary-union/-/2558/2616360/-/g05itfz/-/index.html (last accessed 14 September 2015).

[59] EAC Annual Progress Report (2015) p.2; Ligami C. (2015).

[60] Mo Ibrahim Foundation (2014) Regional Integration: Uniting to Compete (Mo Ibrahim Foundation Report), http://static.moibrahimfoundation.org/downloads/publications/2014/2014-facts-&-figures-regional-integration-uniting-to-compete.pdf (last accessed 14 September 2015).

[61] Ernst and Young Report (2015), p. 3.

[62] EAC Secretariat (2014) East African Community Trade Report 2013, http://www.eac.int/trade/index.php?option=com_docman&task=cat_view&gid=49&Itemid=49 (last accessed 14 September 2015).

2.4 SADC

The SADC Treaty[63] was signed in August of 1992 and currently brings together 15 Member States.[64] Eight of the Member States are also part of COMESA and one the EAC. The main Treaty objectives are similar to those of the EAC and COMESA, seeking to achieve economic development, peace and security, and growth, alleviate poverty and enhance the standard and quality of life.[65] A number of Protocols have to date been concluded to give effect to the SADC Treaty objectives including those on trade, trade in services, energy, finance and investment and movement of persons. The SADC integration plan is similar to that of COMESA, involving a transition from a FTA, a Customs Union, a Common Market and finally to a Monetary Union with the eventual adoption of a single currency.

A Regional Indicative Strategic Development Plan was prepared and signed by the Member States to provide a roadmap for the achievement of the various SADC objectives.[66] The timeframes that the Member States set were for the FTA to be formed by 2008, the Customs Union by 2010, the Common Market by 2015, the Monetary Union by 2016 and the Single Currency by 2018.[67]

One of the core aims of the Protocol on Trade which entered into force in 2001 was for the establishment of the FTA.[68] 13 of the 15 Member States are currently party to the FTA with the Democratic Republic of Congo and Angola reportedly set to join.[69] The minimum conditions for the establishment of the FTA were achieved in 2008 when 85 % of intra-SADC trade was at zero duty following a tariff phase-down initiative that commenced in 2001. Maximum trade liberalisation was reportedly being achieved in 2012 following the phasing-down of tariffs on sensitive products.[70] There are however various derogations subsequent to 2012 that indicate that maximum liberalisation is in reality yet to be achieved. Mozambique, Malawi,

---

[63] Treaty of the Southern African Development Community, 32 ILM 116.

[64] The Member States are: Angola, Botswana, DR Congo, Lesotho, Madagascar, Malawi, Mauritius, Mozambique, Namibia, Seychelles, South Africa, Swaziland, Tanzania, Zambia and Zimbabwe.

[65] SADC Treaty, Article 5; see also http://www.sadc.int/about-sadc/overview/sadc-objectiv/ (last accessed 14 September 2015).

[66] SADC (2001), Regional Indicative Strategic Development Plan (RISDP), http://www.sadc.int/files/5713/5292/8372/Regional_Indicative_Strategic_Development_Plan.pdf (last accessed 14 September 2015). A revised RISDP has been finalised in 2015 to take into account the reallocation of the existing resources towards the achievement of the most important objectives within the 2015-2020 period. It however does not deviate from the scope and purpose of the original RISDP (see 35th SADC Summit Report, p. 18).

[67] See http://www.sadc.int/about-sadc/integration-milestones/ (last accessed 14 September 2015).

[68] Protocol on Trade in the SADC Region (1996), Article 2 http://www.sadc.int/files/4613/5292/8370/Protocol_on_Trade1996.pdf.

[69] Seychelles acceded to the FTA in May 2015, See http://www.seychellestradeportal.gov.sc/trade-agreements (last accessed 14 September 2015).

[70] See http://www.sadc.int/about-sadc/integration-milestones/free-trade-area/.

Zimbabwe, and Tanzania for instance require more time to achieve various tariff commitments. The SADC Secretariat indeed highlights that the main action points include the outstanding tariff phase-down commitments, NTBs, problems relating to the RoO, customs and trade facilitation issues as well as liberalisation of trade in services as required under the Protocol on Trade in Services.[71]

The transition from the FTA to the Customs Union did not proceed according to the agreed timeframe and is proving to be quite a challenge for the Member States. This in turn means delayed implementation of the Common Market and the Monetary Union.[72] The biggest challenge identified in this regard is the establishment of the CET which requires the convergence of the various Member State tariff policies. It is notable however that five of the Member States (Botswana, Lesotho, Namibia, South Africa and Swaziland) are already part of a Southern African Customs Union (SACU), an institution separate from and predating the SADC,[73] thus providing additional harmonisation and integration challenges.

One positive step towards the achievement of monetary integration was the launching of the SADC Integrated Regional Electronic Settlement System (SIRESS) which to date includes 11 Member States. The SIRESS has had a positive impact in ensuring secure and harmonised settlement of cross-border payments.[74]

SADC however indicates some positive figures in terms of intra-regional trade. SADC's intra-regional trade records the most development amongst the RECs in Africa, accounting for 44 % of Africa's intra-regional trade as of 2011.[75] Looking at the international picture however, intra-regional trade still has a long way to go. The highest percentage of SADC trade is still with the Asia Pacific Economic Cooperation (APEC) and the European Union (EU).[76]

2.5 *The Overlaps Challenge*

As already noted, one of the core challenges faced by the three RECs is the fact that most of the participating countries belong to more than one REC. This has resulted in instances of functional overlaps and duplication of integration efforts. One

---

[71] SADC Secretariat, 35th Summit of SADC Heads of State and Government (35th SADC Summit Report), 18 August 2015, http://www.sadc.int/news-events/news/35th-sadc-summit-brochure/ last accessed 14 September 2015); Services are recognised as generating 57 % of the regions GDP. The priority sectors for the liberalisation of trade in services are communication, construction, energy, finance, tourism and transport.

[72] See http://www.sadc.int/about-sadc/integration-milestones/customs-union/ (last accessed 14 September 2015).

[73] See http://www.sacu.int/main.php?id=471 (last accessed 14 September 2015).

[74] 35th SADC Summit Report, p. 56.

[75] Mo Ibrahim Foundation Report (2014), p. 19.

[76] See http://www.sadc.int/about-sadc/overview/sadc-facts-figures/ (last accessed 14 September 2015).

particular aspect of the overlaps concern that touches on the Tripartite FTA is the fact that COMESA, EAC and SACU already have Customs Unions in place, with the SADC Customs Union still in the pipeline. Member States belonging to both EAC and COMESA for instance already have the challenge of having to apply two conflicting CETs.

Belonging to more than one FTA may be beneficial in terms of integrating into the Tripartite FTA owing to the fact that measures to remove tariffs and NTBs would already be in place. However, belonging to a Customs Union entails the adoption of a CET which is incompatible with the Tripartite FTA because it would mean putting up a tariff barrier in respect of goods coming from FTA states that are not part of the Customs Union and are thus regarded as third countries.

The concern over various issues arising from the membership overlaps is one of the key issues that led to the formation of the EAC-COMESA-SADC Tripartite (The Tripartite).

3 The EAC-COMESA-SADC Tripartite

3.1 Background

The Tripartite was established in 2005 in order to look into ways in which the three RECs could coordinate and harmonise their efforts towards regional integration, especially in the areas of trade, customs, free movement of people and infrastructure development.[77]

The first Tripartite Summit was held in October 2008 bringing together the Heads of State and Government of COMESA, EAC and SADC. The main objective was to chart out how the three RECs can move towards deeper cooperation in their efforts towards trade and economic liberalisation, including joint programmes targeting free movement of persons and infrastructure development.[78] Indeed, as already noted before, the key challenge highlighted at the first Summit was that of overlapping memberships of countries that are already part of a Customs Union and that are negotiating terms for joining an alternative Customs Union or those that are negotiating terms of two separate Customs Unions.[79] The Tripartite was therefore recognised as the best avenue to address this concern.

The need for a road map for establishing the Tripartite FTA was also highlighted progress made towards inter alia harmonising RoO, establishment of one-stop

[77] See COMESA-EAC-SADC Tripartite, http://www.eac.int/index.php?option=com_content&view=article&id=1496&Itemid=201 (last accessed 14 September 2015).

[78] First COMESA-EAC-SADC Tripartite Summit Report (1st Tripartite Summit Report), 20 October 2008, para 9, http://www.eac.int/index.php?option=com_docman&task=doc_download&gid=478&Itemid=163 (last accessed 14 September 2015).

[79] 1st Tripartite Summit Report(2008), para 4.

border posts, and the elimination of NTBs on the Tripartite level was also noted.[80] One of the early achievements of the Tripartite has been the successful implementation of a web-based scheme for reporting, tracking and elimination of NTBs that has enabled stakeholders to efficiently report NTBs and monitor the progress in their resolution.[81]

One of the core recommendations in the first Summit was for the establishment of the Tripartite FTA within a 5 year period as well as for the adoption of a roadmap for its achievement. It was also recommended that a Memorandum of Understanding between the three RECs be concluded, setting out the broad cooperation objectives as well as the legal and institutional framework for the Tripartite process and a coordination mechanism.[82] The Memorandum of Understanding between the three RECs came into force much later in January 2011.

The draft agreement including its annexes was conveyed to the Member States of the three RECs for review and proposals in December 2009.[83] The revised version was made available in 2010 for purposes of deliberation at the second Summit.[84]

The second Summit was held in June 2011. A three-pillar development approach was adopted at this Summit: market integration, infrastructure development, and industrial development. Three key milestones towards the Tripartite FTA were also achieved at this Summit; a declaration launching the negotiations for the establishment of the COMESA-EAC-SADC Tripartite FTA was signed and the roadmap for the establishment of the Tripartite FTA and the Tripartite FTA negotiating principles, processes, and institutional framework were adopted.[85]

The negotiations as set out in the negotiating principles are to be conducted in two phases. Phase one negotiations being in respect of trade in goods aspects i.e. tariff liberalisation, RoO, dispute resolution, customs procedures and simplification of customs documentation, transit procedures, NTBs, trade remedies, technical barriers to trade and sanitary and phytosanitary measures. It was also agreed that negotiations on movement of business persons were also to be part of the phase one negotiations but as a parallel and separate track. Phase two negotiations are in respect of trade in services, cooperation in trade and development, competition policy, intellectual property (IP) rights and cross border investment. The

---

[80] 1st Tripartite Summit Report (2008), para 23.

[81] See http://www.tradebarriers.org/about (last accessed 14 September 2015).

[82] 1st tripartite Summit Report, para. 44 and 104.

[83] Mallya A (2011) COMESA-EAC-SADC Tripartite Framework: State of Play, http://www.eac.int/index.php?view=article&catid=145%3Atripartite&id=581%3Acomesa-eac-sadc-tripartite-framework-state-of-play-&format=pdf&option=com_content&Itemid=1, pp. 3–5.

[84] Draft agreement establishing the COMESA, EAC and SADC Tripartite Free Trade Area (2010), http://www.tralac.org/wp-content/blogs.dir/12/files/2011/uploads/Draft_Tripartite_FTA_Agreement_Revised_Dec_2010.pdf (last accessed 14 September 2015).

[85] Communiqué of the Second COMESA-EAC-SADC Tripartite Summit, 13 June 2011, p.1. http://www.eac.int/news/index.php?option=com_docman&task=doc_view&gid=195&Itemid=77 (last accessed 14 September 2015).

Agreement was to be finalised once the phase one negotiations were concluded.[86] According to the roadmap, the phase two negotiations would be part of a built-in agenda once the Agreement was finalised.

The Tripartite FTA was finally launched on the 10th of June, 2015 at the third Tripartite Summit in Cairo.[87] The Agreement was opened for signing and a post-signature implementation plan was adopted. It was also directed that the outstanding issues from the phase one negotiations be completed and that negotiations on the phase two be commenced.

3.2 The Tripartite FTA Agreement

The Agreement formalises the commitment to establish the FTA and gives a legal basis and framework for the participating countries to implement the objectives of the Tripartite. The intention as reflected in the preamble to the Agreement is for the Tripartite FTA to evolve into a single Customs Union.[88]

The Agreement is divided into 12 parts. The first part addresses the interpretation of terms in the Agreement as well as the establishment, objectives and principles of the Tripartite FTA. The specific objectives are stated to be the progressive elimination of tariff and non-tariff barriers, the liberation of trade in services, cooperation on customs and trade-related areas, implementation of trade facilitation measures as well as putting in place the institutional framework for implementing and administering the Tripartite FTA.[89]

The principles governing the Agreement include variable geometry, flexibility and special and differential treatment, transparency, building on the *acquis*, single undertaking with regard to the various phases of the Agreement, Most Favoured Nation Treatment(MFN), National Treatment, reciprocity, substantial liberalisation, and consensus-based decision making.[90]

[86] See Guidelines for Negotiating the Tripartite Free Trade Area among the Member/Partner States of COMESA, EAC and SADC, 12 June 2011, para 2, http://www.tralac.org/images/docs/5284/tfta-negotiating-principles-12062011.pdf (last accessed 18.9.15); See also Roadmap for Establishing the Tripartite FTA, http://www.trademarksa.org/sites/default/files/publications/Roadmap%20for%20TFTA%20Negotiation%20-%2012.06.2011.pdf (last accessed 14 September 2015).

[87] Communiqué of the Third COMESA-EAC-SADC Tripartite Summit 10 June 2015, http://www.sadc.int/files/5914/3401/0196/Communiqu_of_the_3rd_COMESA_EAC_SADC_Tripartite_Summit.pdf (last accessed 14 September 2015).

[88] Agreement Establishing a Tripartite Free Trade Area among The Common Market For Eastern And Southern Africa, The East African Community And The Southern African Development Community (The Tripartite Agreement), preamble, http://www.eac.int/legal/index.php?option=com_docman&task=doc_download&gid=205&Itemid=154.

[89] The Tripartite Agreement, Article 5.

[90] The Tripartite Agreement, Article 6.

The core international trade principles of MFN and National Treatment make up part two of the Agreement, which deals with non-discrimination. Participating countries may conclude preferential trade agreements with third countries provided that reciprocity is accorded to other participating countries. One aspect however that could affect the unity of the Tripartite FTA is the fact that the Agreement allows participating countries to enter into preferential agreements among themselves. Although such agreements are required to be on MFN basis and in accordance with the objectives of the Agreement, sanctioning such multiplicity within the FTA may ultimately complicate the integration into a single FTA which is an overarching objective of the Agreement.[91] It is not clear from the Agreement what nature of preferential agreements among the participating countries is contemplated. Unless some exceptional circumstances are provided for, it ultimately makes no sense from the perspective of the Tripartite FTA territory for participating countries to conclude among themselves preferential agreements consisting only of aspects that are within the scope of the Agreement. Such agreements would not be 'preferential' in respect of the excluded participating countries because of reciprocity and non-discrimination. One can however picture a situation where derogations are made in the Agreement in accordance with the special and differential treatment principle. This could be for instance to facilitate preferential agreements aimed at assisting the weaker countries to integrate better into the Tripartite FTA.

The principles of Variable Geometry and flexibility, special and differential treatment are specifically geared towards addressing the different levels of development among the participating countries.[92] The Agreement defines variable geometry as 'the principle of flexibility which allows for progression in cooperation amongst members in a larger integration scheme in a variety of areas and at different speeds'.[93] This is however having due regard to the principle of building on the *acquis*, by which the progress already achieved among the three RECs is meant to be built upon and consolidated.[94]

Some commentators have expressed the concern that the principle of *acquis* would result in an effort for additional and separate trade arrangements.[95] The

[91] The Tripartite Agreement, Part II.

[92] The Tripartite Agreement Article 6; The differences in economic development among the participating countries is also highlighted in the preamble to the Agreement.

[93] The Tripartite Agreement, Article 1.

[94] The Agreement does not define the term *acquis*. The term had however been explained in context earlier on in the negotiating principles for the Tripartite FTA. Building on the acquis of the existing REC FTAs in terms of consolidating tariff liberalisation in each REC FTA was one of the overarching principles guiding the negotiations. *See* Guidelines for Negotiating the Tripartite Free Trade Area among the Member/Partner States of COMESA, EAC and SADC (2011), http://www.tralac.org/images/docs/5284/tfta-negotiating-principles-12062011.pdf (last accessed 15 September 2015).

[95] Erasmus (2013) The Agreement preceding the Agreement: how the negotiating principles decided the Tripartite FTA game plan. In Hartzenberg T et al. (eds) Cape to Cairo: Exploring the Tripartite FTA agenda, tralac, Stellenbosch, pp. 9–11, http://www.tralac.org/publications/article/5548-cape-to-cairo-exploring-the-tripartite-fta-agenda.html (last accessed 15 September 2015).

reasoning is that if the Agreement allows the RECs to maintain preferential terms between their Member States, then participating countries that are not party to such arrangements would have to negotiate their own terms on the basis of the Agreement.[96] This would therefore be contrary to the idea of an all-inclusive system as envisioned in the creation of the Tripartite, in addition to exacerbating rather than resolving the overlaps challenge.

From a different perspective however, it was expressed in the Tripartite Trade Negotiations Forum that Member States that belong to an already existing FTA would not need to renegotiate tariff terms between them. They would simply have to consolidate their liberalisation levels to the agreed-upon Tripartite FTA standard, with the eventual result being that all participating countries will be harmonised to the Tripartite FTA standard.[97] Such an application of the principle of building on the *acquis* suggests that the intention is to make it easier to converge towards the Tripartite FTA. Additionally, article 30(7) of the Agreement provides, 'In the event of inconsistency or a conflict between this Agreement and the treaties and instruments of COMESA, EAC and SADC, this Agreement shall prevail to the extent of the inconsistency or conflict.' It may therefore be argued that the overriding objectives of the Agreement, inter alia the creation of a single FTA, take precedence and the principle of *acquis* would be applicable to the extent that it does not interfere with this objective. One may additionally question the validity of any preferential agreements in light of the reciprocity and non-discrimination principles.

The scope of the Agreement covers trade in goods and services as well as other trade-related matters i.e. competition policy, cross-border investment, trade and development, and IP rights.[98] The core areas of harmonisation and cooperation are set out in a more or less general manner with the intention being that the member countries will conclude protocols and annexes to the Agreement to give full effect to its provisions.

Liberalisation of trade in goods is addressed in part three of the Agreement. Finalisation of the trade in goods aspects as noted in the roadmap was the main undertaking on which the conclusion of the Agreement was to be based. Trade in goods is in fact the backbone of the Agreement. It is however noted in the Agreement that there are outstanding aspects of the phase one negotiation in respect of elimination of customs duties, trade remedies and RoO that the participating countries undertake to conclude as part of a built-in agenda.[99] The failure to come to an agreement on the core trade in goods aspects of the FTA especially on

---

[96] Zamfir L (2015) The Tripartite Free Trade Area project Integration in southern and eastern Africa, http://www.europarl.europa.eu/RegData/etudes/BRIE/2015/551308/EPRS_BRI(2015)551308_EN.pdf (last accessed 15 September 2015).

[97] Launch of African Tripartite FTA now set for June, Bridges Africa, 16 March 2015, http://www.ictsd.org/bridges-news/bridges-africa/news/launch-of-african-tripartite-fta-now-set-for-june (last accessed 21.9.15).

[98] The Tripartite Agreement, Article 3.

[99] The Tripartite Agreement, Article 44.

elimination of customs duties and RoO prior to the adoption of the Agreement has led to its workability as a comprehensive instrument being questioned.[100]

Participating countries are required to desist from imposing new import duties or charges having equivalent effect except as stipulated in the Agreement.[101] This however only applies to goods that are subject to trade liberalisation. The criteria and conditions for goods that shall be eligible for preferential treatment have however not been finalised owing to outstanding issues on RoO. Based on the report of the Technical Working Group (TWG) on RoO, some of the outstanding aspects are rather fundamental to comprehensive RoO.[102] The RoO have indeed been one of the significant harmonisation challenges, especially since SADC RoO markedly differ from those of COMESA and EAC.[103]

The report indicates that there was lack of agreement between SACU Member States and the other Member States as to what criteria of origin should be adopted, specifically in the case of materials that do not originate from the Tripartite FTA. The SACU Member States had expressed preference for the use of agreed common rules for the launch of a Partial Tripartite FTA, opting to leave out any determination based on value addition on non-originating materials. The other Member States preferred the use of agreed common rules as well as 35 % value-added on the ex-factory cost as interim RoO of the Tripartite FTA.[104]

The Agreement further provides that duties are to be eliminated progressively in accordance with schedules on elimination of import duties, the negotiation of which is not complete.[105] The goal that has been set is for 100 % tariff liberalisation under the Tripartite FTA. The benchmark for countries that are yet to fully liberalise their tariffs within their RECs or those in existing REC FTAs is at 60–85 % upon entry into force of the Agreement. The Tripartite FTA negotiations are however built on consensus based decision making. Various countries have submitted their tariff offers but not all tariff offers are ready meaning negotiations are set to continue.[106] This essentially means that the Agreement as it currently is provides no definitive guidance as to how the participating countries should go about liberalising the trade

[100] Erasmus (2015) The Tripartite Free Trade Agreement: Results of Phase One of the Negotiations, Stellenbosch, tralac, pp. 8–9 http://www.tralac.org/publications/article/7803-the-tripartite-free-trade-agreement-results-of-phase-one-of-the-negotiations.html.

[101] The Tripartite Agreement, Article 9(1) and (2).

[102] Report of the 9th Meeting of the Technical Working Group on Rules of Origin (RoO Report), 16–19 February 2015, http://www.comesa.int/index.php?option=com_content&view=article&id=1440 (last accessed 19.9.15).

[103] Erasmus G (2015), p. 19.

[104] RoO Report, para 12–17. The value addition criterion is in respect of (raw) materials that do not originate from within the FTA. The proposal therefore advocates for an added value that is not less than 35 % of the ex-factory cost of the finished product in the case of non-originating materials. Common rules here refers to rules that are the same across the three RICs and for which it was agreed no further negotiations would need to be undertaken.

[105] The Tripartite Agreement, Article 9(3).

[106] Bridges Africa (2015); See also Erasmus G (2015), p. 17.

in goods. The section dealing with the liberalisation of trade in goods, which is a core aspect of the Agreement, is in effect not operable.

The participating countries should also eliminate and refrain from imposing NTBs as well as quantitative restrictions on trade on other participating countries. The Agreement however details exceptional circumstances in which quantitative restrictions can be applied.[107]

Part four of the Agreement is in respect of customs cooperation and trade facilitation. Participating countries undertake to cooperate in terms of customs and mutual administrative assistance in the implementation of the Agreement. They should also put in place measures to facilitate trade through standardisation of trade and customs documentation and information is also prioritised.[108]

Trade remedies, which are provided for in part five of the Agreement, are also subject to ongoing negotiations.[109] Interim measures were however adopted to facilitate the conclusion of the Agreement. Anti-dumping, countervailing and safeguard measures may be applied on the basis of the existing provisions of the RECs for Member States belonging to the same REC or on the basis of World Trade Organization (WTO) rules in respect of inter-REC issues.[110] The Agreement incorporates a built-in agenda by which guidelines on the implementation of the trade remedies are expected to be concluded. The core provisions on anti-dumping, countervailing and safeguard measures as well as preferential standards are however suspended pending the finalisation of the annex on trade remedies.[111]

The Agreement points to a heavy reliance on WTO rules on trade remedies which are regarded as difficult to implement, more so for many African countries. The inclusion of WTO rules rather than a *sui generis* trade remedies regime was at the insistence of Egypt and South Africa, which already have active domestic trade remedies regimes.[112] This is also reflected in their proposals in the course of the trade remedies negotiations. South Africa, Egypt, and Malawi for instance proposed the retention of a part incorporating the global safeguard measures under Article XIX of the General Agreement on Tariffs and Trade (GATT) 1994 as well as the WTO Agreement on Safeguards.[113] The EAC however proposed that this part be

---

[107] The Tripartite Agreement, Article 11. The exceptions are those contained in Article XI.2 of GATT 1994, the WTO Agreement on Safeguards, Articles 17 and 18 of the Agreement which deal with anti-dumping, countervailing and safeguard measures and annex II of the Agreement which deals with trade remedies. The annex on trade remedies is however one of the areas in which outstanding issues still exist.

[108] The Tripartite Agreement, part IV.

[109] The Tripartite Agreement, Article 44.

[110] The Tripartite Agreement, Article 16 (1).

[111] The Tripartite Agreement, Article 16 (2) and (3).

[112] Erasmus G (2015), p. 20; See also Illy O., Trade remedies in Africa: experiences, challenges and prospects, Bridges Africa, 8 April 2015, http://www.ictsd.org/bridges-news/bridges-africa/news/trade-remedies-in-africa-experiences-challenges-and-prospects (last accessed 22.9.15).

[113] Annex on Trade Remedies, p. 2, http://www.comesa.int/attachments/article/1441/Annex%202%20on%20Trade%20Remedies%20English0001_S.pdf (last accessed 22.9.15).

deleted. Egypt in addition expressed the desire for a system that would allow an affected country to proceed with an appropriate countervailing measure without prejudice to the fact that consultations with the allegedly subsidising country may be proceeding.[114]

The rights and obligations under the WTO agreements on technical barriers to trade (TBT) and sanitary and phytosanitary measures (SPS) are reaffirmed in part six of the Agreement. The provisions do not point to any outstanding aspects in this regard. The participating countries are also permitted to establish special economic zones to speed up development. Where the circumstances require it, participating countries are allowed to adopt measures geared towards the protection of infant industries. An infant industry is defined as 'a new industry of national strategic importance that has not been in existence for more than 5 years, and that is experiencing high start-up costs and difficulties competing with like imports.'[115] The only outstanding aspect in this part of the Agreement is in respect of guidelines which are to be developed in respect of measures to alleviate severe balance of payment and external financial difficulties.

Part seven of the Agreement provides generally for cooperation in financial areas, trade policies and negotiations, research and statistics. The institutions charged with the implementation of the Tripartite FTA, including a dispute settlement body responsible for the administration of the dispute settlement are set out in part eight and nine of the Agreement.

The various general and security exceptions are contained in part 10 of the Agreement. Parts 11 and 12 cover financial provisions and the general and final provisions respectively. Amendments for instance require a consensus. Defaulting countries may be subjected to sanctions as determined by the Tripartite Summit on recommendation of the Tripartite Council of Ministers. A participating country may withdraw from the Agreement subject to it discharging its existing obligations under the Agreement.

A 2-year timeline from the entry into force of the Agreement has been put in place for the conclusion of a protocol on trade in services as well as on competition policy, cross-border investment, trade and development, and IP rights, which constitute phase two of the negotiation agenda.[116] The current Agreement therefore neither provides for IP rights aspects nor investment measures. Going by the negotiations during the drafting of the Agreement, it is expected that the protocol on IP rights will draw upon some of the WTO's Agreement on Trade-Related Aspects of Intellectual Property Rights (TRIPs) flexibilities. The annex on IP rights in the draft Agreement for instance had a provision encouraging participating

[114] Annex on Trade Remedies, p. 1 and 2.

[115] The Tripartite Agreement, Article 24.

[116] The Tripartite Agreement, Article 45.

countries to fully exploit the flexibilities contained in the Doha Declaration on TRIPs and public health to facilitate access to medicines.[117]

Another exclusion from the Agreement is in respect of the movement of business persons in spite of the fact that it was originally included as part of the phase one negotiation. As indicated before the plan was for negotiations on the movement of business persons to be part of phase one but as a parallel and separate track. It was eventually agreed that movement of business persons should not be included in the Agreement.[118] A separate agreement is now being negotiated under the aegis of the Tripartite Technical Committee on the movement of business persons.[119] Some of the provisions being considered include short-term and long-term temporary movement, identification of a business person, entry, stay, exit as well as a multi-entry multi-visa concept.[120]

The concept of a built-in agenda from the WTO perspective is in respect of continuing review or further negotiation of specific aspects in already binding agreements.[121] Its use in the Agreement is however different from this. The built-in agenda was initially targeted for phase two negotiations. It was envisioned that they would commence after the trade in goods negotiations had been concluded and the Agreement finalised. The current built-in agenda is now in respect of outstanding phase one aspects as well as the phase two negotiations. As already noted the outstanding phase one aspects include core trade in goods issues which bring to question whether the Agreement in its current state is indeed binding.[122]

Going further one questions how this concept of a built-in agenda can be reconciled with the principle of a single undertaking as used in the Agreement. The principle of single undertaking is not defined in the Agreement. According to the WTO, a single undertaking would mean that virtually every item of the negotiation is part of a whole and indivisible package and cannot be agreed separately. "Nothing is agreed until everything is agreed".[123] There is however a derogation from this principle under the Doha Ministerial Declaration. Article 47 of the Ministerial Declaration provides that "agreements that are reached at an early stage may be implemented on a provisional or a definitive basis". There is no such

---

[117] Annex on Intellectual Property Rights, Article 7, http://www.tralac.org/images/Resources/Tripartite_FTA/TFTA%20Annex%2009%20IPR%20Revised%20Dec%202010.pdf (last accessed 23.9.15).

[118] Report of 3rd TTC-MBP, Tripartite Agreement on Movement of Business Persons, November 2014 (MBP Report), https://tis.sadc.int/files/8614/1640/5306/Draft_Tripartite_Agreement_on_Business_Persons.pdf (last accessed 24.9.15).

[119] MBP Report; See also E-COMESA Newsletter, 12 November 2014, http://www.comesa.int/attachments/article/1379/e-comesa_newsletter_435.pdf (last accessed 24.9.15).

[120] MBP Report.

[121] Built-in Agenda: Work set out in existing agreements, https://www.wto.org/english/thewto_e/minist_e/min99_e/english/about_e/04agen_e.htm (last accessed 24.9.15).

[122] See also Erasmus (2015), p.14.

[123] See How the negotiations are organised, https://www.wto.org/english/tratop_e/dda_e/work_organi_e.htm (last accessed 24.9.15).

derogation under the Agreement. The principle of single undertaking as it was used in the negotiating framework had been specifically focused on trade in goods. The Agreement however provides that it is with regard to the various phases of the Agreement. If we go by the WTO definition of single undertaking one may very well argue that there is no agreement. Even if we assume that the derogation applies there is no conclusive trade in goods agreement that can be said to have been reached at an early stage.

The overall feeling one gets is that the Agreement was rushed in order to have it ready within an already extended timeline.

The entry into force of the Agreement requires 14 ratifications. Participation by accession is also provided for.[124] So far 16 countries have signed the Agreement[125] and are presumably in the process of ratification. It is however questionable whether any of the current signatories will ratify the Agreement before the outstanding phase one aspects have been finalised. The entry into force of the Agreement is therefore expected to take some time.

One big concern here is that the three RECs will continue to pursue their own individual integration agenda hence further complicating the harmonisation and integration into a single FTA. The need for renegotiation of customs aspects by the countries that are already in Customs Unions is expected to further delay the entry into force of the Agreement. This is the case for South Africa for instance, which, though being one of the most important economies in the region, has yet to sign the Agreement.[126]

The anticipation had been that the Agreement would be a game changer in view of some of the challenges faced by the three RECs. However, a lot of work still needs to be done before it can be considered to be a game changer. What is critical is for all the 26 countries to participate in the FTA. Insufficient participation would mean an additional REC hence defeating the whole purpose of the Tripartite FTA. Given the difficulties the three RECs have experienced in liberalising their markets a lot of political goodwill and commitment is needed in order to make the Tripartite FTA a reality in the foreseeable future.

4 Conclusion

The Tripartite FTA promises a market comprising 632 million people (57 % of Africa's population) with a total Gross Domestic Product (GDP) of USD 1.3 trillion as at 2014 which was roughly 58 % of Africa's GDP.[127] Africa's GDP figures for

[124] The Tripartite Agreement, Article 40 & 41.

[125] Erasmus (2015), p. 8.

[126] Erasmus (2015), pp. 8–9.

[127] 3rd Summit Communiqué, p. 1.

the past few years have generally displayed a positive trend, with real GDP growth averaging 5 % a year since the turn of the century.[128]

Trade figures likewise reflect progressive improvement. The value of exports outside of Africa has experienced encouraging growth; from a figure of USD 148 billion in 2000 to USD 657 billion in 2012, with the 2014 figure of USD 552 billion indicating some decline from the 2012 figures.[129]

Europe still remains Africa's largest trading partner. This in itself presents a challenge to regional integration owing to the fact that the EU negotiates for Economic Partnership Agreements (EPAs) on terns that in some cases may conflict with integration objectives. Some critics go as far as to label it a '*divide and conquer*' approach.[130] China has however surpassed the USA as Africa's single largest trading partner, indicating the increased competition for the African market.[131] Intra-Africa trade as well continues to post encouraging figures, with the SADC region responsible for the bulk of intra-African trade.[132]

The overall picture however shows that a lot more still needs to be done. Africa's share of global trade still remains quite low, with an export value of about 3 % as at 2014.[133] There is still a high dependence on commodities and natural resources showing very little improvement in terms of economic diversification.[134] This is in part as a result of a lack of the necessary infrastructure, technological development and technical expertise needed to enable the proper exploitation of the resources.[135]

If the objective of social, political and economic integration and development in Africa is to be achieved a lot more work needs to be done. The Tripartite FTA presents an opportunity to set in motion the establishment of the Continental FTA and the eventual establishment of an African Economic Community. However, as

[128] AFDB (2014) Tracking Africa's Progress in Figures, p. 20. http://www.afdb.org/en/knowledge/publications/tracking-africa%E2%80%99s-progress-in-figures/ (last accessed 15 September 2015); See also AfDB et al. (2015) Africa Economic Outlook 2015: Regional Development and Spatial Inclusion, p. 9 http://www.africaneconomicoutlook.org/fileadmin/uploads/aeo/2015/PDF_Chapters/Overview_AEO2015_EN-web.pdf (last accessed 15 September 2015).

[129] AfDB (2014), p. 42; see also AfDB et al. (2015), p. 6; The trade data can also be found on the International Trade Centre (ITC) website http://www.trademap.org/Country_SelProduct_TS.aspx.

[130] McDonald S et al. (2013), Why Economic Partnership Agreements undermine Africa's Regional Integration, https://www.wilsoncenter.org/publication/why-economic-partnership-agreements-undermine-africas-regional-integration.

[131] AfDB (2014), p. 42; see also AfDB et al. (2015) p. 6.

[132] AfDB (2014), p 43; see also Busuulwa B, Intra-African trade rises as market access between blocs improves, The East African, 29 August 2015, http://www.theeastafrican.co.ke/business/Intra-African-trade-up-as-market-access-between-blocs-improves–/–/2560/2850908/-/14qd2iy/-/index.html.

[133] Figure courtesy of the ITC data.

[134] AfDB (2014), p 42.

[135] UNECA, Economic Report on Africa 2008: Africa and the Monterrey Consensus: Tracking Performance and Progress, 133 (ECA 2008), http://www.uneca.org/publications/economic-report-africa-2008 (last accessed 15 September 2015); UNCTAD, Economic Development in Africa Report 2009: Strengthening Regional Economic Integration for Africa's Development, 15 (United Nations Publication 2009), http://unctad.org/en/Docs/aldcafrica2009_en.pdf.

discussed in the previous chapters, there are considerable challenges that need to be overcome before the Tripartite FTA can be actualised.

References

Erasmus G (2013) The Agreement preceding the agreement: how the negotiating principles decided the Tripartite FTA game plan, Chapter 2. In: Hartzenberg T et al (eds) Cape to Cairo: Exploring the Tripartite FTA agenda, tralac, Stellenbosch, http://www.tralac.org/publications/article/5548-cape-to-cairo-exploring-the-tripartite-fta-agenda.html

Sherwood M (2012) Pan-African Conferences, 1900–1953: what did 'Pan-Africanism' mean? JPan African Stud 4(10):106–126, http://www.jpanafrican.com/docs/vol4no10/4.10Pan-African.pdf

Developing and Least-Developed Countries and Mega-Regional Trade and Investment Agreements

Emmanuel Opoku Awuku

Contents

Abstract Regional trade agreements (RTAs) have become a very prominent feature of the multilateral trading system. These arrangements have operated as legally permitted exceptions to the General Agreement on Tariffs and Trade (GATT) since it was established in 1947. The GATT rules, which have been subsumed under the WTO rules, recognise that tariffs and other barriers to trade can be reduced on a preferential basis by countries under regional arrangements. This is based on the cardinal principle of Article XXIV of GATT, which permits a departure from the Most Favoured Nations (MFN) obligation of non-discrimination within free trade areas, customs unions or interim arrangements that lead to the formation of free trade areas or customs unions. Mega-Regional trade and investment agreements merit attention because of their sheer size and their potential implication for trade and investments. These agreements are broad economic

---

The views expressed in this article are those of the author and do not necessarily represent the views of the ACP Secretariat. The fact of the author's employment with the ACP Secretariat does not imply any endorsement of his views by the Secretariat.

E. Opoku Awuku (✉)
Caribbean and Pacific Group of States, 55 Sint Pauluslaan, Vossem, Tervuren, Belgium
e-mail: eawuku@gmail.com

M. Bungenberg et al. (eds.), *European Yearbook of International Economic Law 2016*, European Yearbook of International Economic Law 7,
DOI 10.1007/978-3-319-29215-1_28

agreements among groups of countries that together have economic weight in negotiations and also at the world stage.

1 Introduction

Regional trade agreements (RTAs) have become a very prominent feature of the multilateral trading system. These arrangements have operated as legally permitted exceptions to the General Agreement on Tariffs and Trade (GATT) since it was established in 1947. The GATT rules, which have been subsumed under the WTO rules, recognise that tariffs and other barriers to trade can be reduced on a preferential basis by countries under regional arrangements. This is based on the cardinal principle of Article XXIV of GATT, which permits a departure from the Most Favoured Nations (MFN) obligation of non-discrimination within free trade areas, customs unions or interim arrangements that lead to the formation of free trade areas or customs unions. Megaregional trade and investment agreements merit attention because of their sheer size and their potential implication for trade and investments. These agreements are broad economic agreements among groups of countries that together have economic weight in negotiations and also at the world stage.

This paper will look at Mega-Regional trade and investment agreements from the perspective of developed and developing countries. I will move on to look at how developing and developed countries perceive the on-going negotiations on Mega-Regional trade agreements. Within the context of developing countries, this paper will look at the PACER Plus and the Tripartite free trade agreement. I will conclude by looking at policy challenges arising from Mega-Regional trade agreements for both developed and developing countries.

2 Overview of Mega-Regional Trade and Investment Agreements

Megaregional trade and investment agreements are seen by developed countries as essentially geopolitical tools in response to the rise of global trading powers such as Brazil, Russia, China and South Africa (BRICS), who are emerging as newly industrialized countries. They are distinguished by their large, fast growing economies and their significant influence on regional and global affairs, all five being members of the G20. The stalemate at the World Trade Agreement (WTO) negotiations over the last decade, i.e. the Singapore issues[1] and the Doha Development Round, is also seen as one of the causes for the proliferation of bilateral and regional trade agreements and more recently Mega-Regional trade and investment agreements.[2] The following are some of the on-going negotiations on Mega-Regional trade and investment agreements:

1. the Canada—EU Comprehensive Economic Trade Agreement (CETA);
2. the EU—United States Transatlantic Trade and Investment Partnership Agreement (TTIP);
3. the Trans-Pacific Partnership Agreement (TPP) between 12 countries: Australia, Brunei Darussalam, Canada, Chile, Japan, Malaysia, Mexico, New Zealand, Peru, Singapore, United States of America and Viet Nam. Within this partnership agreement the strongest economies are the United States of America and Japan, the rest are countries with less economic weight.
4. The Regional Comprehensive Economic Partnership (RCEP) is a FTA negotiation that has been developed among 16 countries: 10 members of ASEAN (Brunei, Cambodia, Indonesia, Laos, Malaysia, Myanmar, Philippines, Singapore and Viet Nam) and the six countries with which ASEAN has existing Free Trade Agreements (FTAs)—Australia, China, Japan, India, the Republic of Korea and New Zealand. RCEP negotiations were launched by leaders of the 16 participating countries in the margins of the East Asia Summit on 20 November 2012. Leaders announced that RCEP would be "a modern, comprehensive, high-quality and mutually beneficial economic partnership agreement establishing an open trade and investment environment in the region to facilitate the expansion of regional trade and investment and contribute to global economic growth and development". The formal negotiations began in May 2013. The negotiations cover trade in goods, trade in services, investments, economic and technical cooperation, intellectual property rights, competition, rules of origin, dispute settlementand institutional issues.[3]

   Almost all these countries are in one way or another involved in other free trade agreements with either developed or developing countries.
5. The Pacific Agreement on Closer Economic Relations (PACER) Plus between the 15 Pacific Island Forum countries[4] (PICs) including Australia and New Zealand. The PACER Plus negotiations aim to deepen trade and economic

[1] December 1996, WTO Ministerial Conference in Singapore on the agenda were: Trade and Investment, Trade and Competition policy, transparency in government procurement, and trade facilitation.

[2] Ramdoo I (2014) New Mega-Trade Deals: What Implications for Africa? Briefing Note. 73, - European Centre for Development Policy Management.

[3] New Zealand Ministry of Foreign Affairs & Trade, Regional Comprehensive Economic Partnership, http://www.mfat.govt.nz/Trade-and-Economic-Relations/2-Trade-Relationships-and-Agreements/RCEP (last accessed 17 September 2015).

[4] Pacific Island Forum Countries: Australia, Cook Islands, Federated States of Micronesia, Kiribati, Nauru, New Zealand, Niue, Palau, Papua New Guinea, the Marshall Islands, Samoa, Solomon Islands, Tonga, Tuvalu and Vanuatu.

cooperation between Australia, New Zealand and Forum Island Countries (FICs). The PACER Plus arrangements are intended to provide a comprehensive framework between these parties for trade and economic cooperation to foster improved economic growth, investment and employment in the Pacific Region.
6. the Tripartite Free Trade Agreement (TFTA), which comprises three regional blocks that have come together to form a Mega-Regional trade and investment agreement: the Southern African Development Community (SADC),[5] the East African Community (EAC)[6] and the Common Market for Eastern and Southern Africa (COMESA).[7]

3 Developing Countries' Perspectives on Mega-Regional Trade and Investment Agreements

3.1 PACER Plus

PACER Plus is envisaged to be a regional FTA covering many issues, which removes barriers to trade and improves market access between the participating parties. The Pacific Island Countries (PICs) already have a FTA among themselves (PICTA), which means that the main gain for these nations will be primarily due to higher levels of trade with New Zealand and Australia. The main intent of this agreement is to facilitate economic growth through increased regional trade and economic integration. At their meeting in August 2009, the leaders of the Pacific Islands Forum agreed to prioritize the implementation of the Pacific Plan—the master strategy for strengthening regional cooperation and integration in the Pacific—by, inter alia, fostering greater international and intra-regional trade opportunities by proceeding with the implementation of key regional trade agreements and, in particular, working to allow for the freer movement of goods and services, and strengthening the ability of the private sector to participate competitively in an integrated economy through the necessary enabling environments and support mechanisms.[8]

It could be argued that liberalizing markets will make both exports and imports between the member countries easier and less costly, and encourage private sector

[5] SADC: Angola, Botswana, the Democratic Republic of the Congo, Lesotho, Madagascar, Malawi, Mauritius, Mozambique, Namibia, Seychelles, South Africa, Swaziland, the United Republic of Tanzania, Zambia, and Zimbabwe.

[6] EAC: Burundi, Kenya, Rwanda, Uganda, the United Republic of Tanzanian.

[7] COMESA: Burundi, the Comoros, the Democratic Republic of the Congo, Djibouti, Egypt, Eritrea, Ethiopia, Kenya, Libya, Madagascar, Malawi, Mauritius, Rwanda, Seychelles, Sudan, Swaziland, Uganda, Zambia and Zimbabwe.

[8] Pacific Island Forum Secretariat, Third Non-State Dialogue on Pacific Agreements on Closer Economic Relations (PACER) Plus, Deepening Engagement on PACER Plus, Stamford Plaza, Auckland, New Zealand, 29/November 2013, PIFS (13)NSAP.02.

growth. This would be significant as New Zealand and Australia account for almost half of all PICs imports. PERCER Plus is expected to increase export capacity, lead to higher standards of living through cheaper imports, reduce the price of productive inputs and potentially create more jobs in the export sector. New Zealand and Australia already provide duty free and quota free access for PICs. Thus, new concessions and agreements between the parties will likely cover customs procedures, rules of origin, dispute settlement, TBT (technical barriers to trade) and SPS (sanitary and phytosanitary, i.e. food safety and animal and plant health standards) issues, development assistance, labour mobility and removal of tariffs and quotas on the part of PICs. As all regional agreements the PACER Plus agreement would have to comply with international legal frameworks (particularly the World Trade Organization framework).

In accordance with GATT Article XXIV, there must be significant liberalization of "substantially all" trade between partner countries within a "reasonable" period of time (roughly 10 years), which imposes limits on the scope and flexibility of negotiations. It is important to note that Australia and New Zealand are involved in RCEP and TPP negotiations and it could be argued that any future preferential tariff access granted to Pacific Island Countries by Australia and New Zealand is likely to be eroded to some extent by access granted to TPP and RCEP developing country members such as a Vietnam, which may compete directly with Pacific Island Countries in specific product categories. Australia and New Zealand have recognized that PACER Plus should not be defined by commercial interests alone and therefore trade capacity building is a priority. Civil society in the Pacific region is concerned with urgent issues such as mobility of labour, intellectual property rights, access to medicines, food security and climatic change issues and they argue that these issues should be addressed.[9]

3.2 *Tripartite Free Trade Agreement*

Within the context of the African continent, the promotion of inter-regional trade has long been on the agenda of the African policy makers. African countries have seen developed countries advancing Mega-Regional trade liberalisation and investment negotiations outside the confines of the WTO Agreement. They see powerful economies coming together and lowering or eliminating tariffs between their respective exports and becoming more competitive vis a vis those from third countries such as African and other developing countries. In addition, regional integration arrangements have proliferated all over, often creating a confusing mixture of overlapping, sometimes incompatible preferential trade regimes.

[9] AFTINET, PACER Plus: Development of Free Trade in the Pacific Island Forum. See www.aftinet.org.au (last accessed 17 September 2015).

The TFTA was established to bring together three of Africa's major regional economic communities to trade among themselves and attract investments. TFTA is based on three main pillars—market integration, infrastructure development and industrial development—reflecting the fact that there are multiple obstacles to trade in the region, and that it requires effort to increase and diversify industrial production and improve transport infrastructure.

The general objectives mentioned in the Tripartite Free Trade Agreement (TFTA) are: (a) promoting rapid socio-economic development in the region; (b) creating a large single market with free movement of goods and services to promote intra-regional trade; and (c) enhancing the regional and continental integration processes, thus building a strong Tripartite Free Trade Area for the benefit of the people of the region.[10]

The specific objectives point to:(1) the elimination of all tariffs and non-tariff barriers to trade in goods and services;(2) promoting intra-regional trade; (3) cooperating on customs matters;(4) implementing trade facilitation measures; (5) establishing and promoting cooperation in all trade related areas among Tripartite member/partner states; and (6) establishing and maintaining an institutional framework for the implementation of TFTA.[11]

The TFTA Agreement stipulates that the agreement shall be built on the principle of "variable geometry", allowing groups of countries to progress at different speeds in their integration effort in various areas. This principle is complementary to the principle of the acquis, whereby what has already been concluded at the regional economic committees level will remain valid. The principle includes a provision regarding flexibility, and special and differential treatment for all products and creating transparency, which means that the different levels of economic will be taken into account.

The principles also include the Most Favoured Nations (MFN) treatment and national treatment, which means that member countries will accord to all other member countries any preferential trade conditions awarded to each other or to third parties. Products originating in other member countries will be treated no less favourably than national products. The agreement shall be governed by the principle of a "single undertaking", which means that the agreement will include all aspects of trade related issues including trade in services, intellectual property rights, competition policy, and trade and development.

TFTA is expected to bring broad benefits such as improving the business environment, attracting more foreign direct investment, enhancing the economic

---

[10] Agreement Establishing A Tripartite Free Trade Area Among The Common Market for Eastern and Southern Africa, The East African Community and the Southern African Development Community, http://www.eac.int/legal/index.php?option=com_docman&task=doc_download&gid=205&Itemid=154 (last accessed 24 September 2015).

[11] Agreement Establishing A Tripartite Free Trade Area Among The Common Market for Eastern and Southern Africa, The East African Community and the Southern African Development Community, http://www.eac.int/legal/index.php?option=com_docman&task=doc_download&gid=205&Itemid=154 (last accessed 24 September 2015).

continental free trade area, building the capacity of micro, small and medium scale enterprises, facilitating the movement of business persons, strengthening the infrastructure, and promoting competitiveness in the regions and the African continent.

Some analysts call TFTA a "big deal" and a potential game changer for the African trading system and thus for more than half a billion citizens of its member states. It is seen as a launch pad for the establishment of an even more ambitious Continental Free Trade Area to cover all of Africa.[12]

It is envisaged that when the negotiation is concluded and all outstanding issues are resolved (such as tariff liberalisation schedules, trade exemptions, trade remedies, rules of origin, and the dispute settlement mechanism), the actual implementation of the TFTA could still be a difficult, risky and lengthy process. It will require significant consultations with all relevant stakeholders and real political will from regional and national policy makers to make it operational. In addition, the TFTA would have to be ratified by member states before it can come into force in accordance with international law. It will also have to be applicable to GATT/ WTO rules, especially Article XXIV(8) of WTO/GATT.

It is envisaged that the Enabling Clause[13] will be chosen as the notification route because it is believed that it will make matters easier regarding WTO compliance. Nevertheless, substantially all trade between the parties will have to be liberalised.[14]

The African Union Action Plan for boosting intra-African trade[15] identified a number of problems affecting intra African trade. Firstly, most African countries do not trade much with each other and this means that they are not able to fully harness the synergies and complementarities of their economies and take full advantage of their economies of scale and other benefits, such as income and employment generation.

[12] Andriamananjara S, Understanding the Importance of the Tripartite Free Trade Area. Brookings, Africa Focus, 17 June 2015.

[13] It worth saying that prior to the Enabling Clause of 1979, developing countries have justified the formation of regional trade agreements among them on the basis of Part IV of GATT. In Part IV of GATT, the developing countries members including the ACP Group supported the provision of Article XXXVII:4 which provides for less-developed contracting parties "to take appropriate action in the implementation of PART IV for the benefit of trade of other less-developed contracting parties, in so far as such action is consistent with their individual present and future development, financial and trade needs taking into account past development as well as the trade interests of the less-developed contracting parties as whole". This Article gave developing countries the legal grounds to form preferential trade agreements among themselves, such as the Global System of Trade Preferences (GSTP) outside the GATT framework. However, under the rules of the Decision of 28th November 1978 (L4903) (Enabling Clause) this subject to notification to the Committee on Trade and Development (CTD), The Council on Trade in Goods and the Council on Trade in Services.

[14] Erasmus and Hartzenberg (2013), p. 347.

[15] African Union (2012) Action Plan for Boosting, Intra-African Trade, Addis Ababa, Ethiopia, http://www.au.int/en/sites/default/files/Action%20Plan%20for%20boosting%20intra-African%20trade%20F-English.pdf (last accessed 24 September 2015).

Secondly, there are a number of constraints affecting intra-African trade, such as restrictive customs procedures and regulations; administrative and technical barriers to trade; complex, inefficient and costly transit systems; numerous roadblocks along corridors of individual borders; differences in rules of origin; and problems associated with trade documentation at border posts.

Thirdly, Africa lacks productive capacity, faces inadequacies of trade related to infrastructure, and lacks trade information and trade financing.[16] These problems, as enumerated in the African Plan of Action also apply to the TFTA area. Although the TFTA is seen as a major boost for African free trade, it has many hurdles to overcome and needs to address the problems stated in the African action plan. Many developing and least-developed countries are subject to preferential trade regimes with the EU and USA such as quota free, duty free access on their export products, which gives rise to concerns as to how Mega-Regional trade and investment regimes will impact on developing and least-developed countries which are also in the process of forging a Mega-Regional trade deal.

4 Developed Countries' Perspectives on Mega-Regional Trade and Investment Agreements

Within the context of CETA, TPP, TTIP most countries involved in these agreements developed economies, which are already interdependent in their trading relations. Once the agreements are concluded, these are likely to have major impact on global trade and investment rule making and investment patterns.

They are negotiating mega deals with deeper integration covering substantive issues such as standards for trade and investment; market access to goods, services and procurement; data protection; competition policy; non-tariff barriers (NTB); regulatory cooperation; intellectual property rights; trade in services; financial services; government procurement; social responsibility; and investor state dispute settlement. These are issues which will require regulations, higher standards, norms, licensing practices, domestic taxes, government procurement, rules on investment, rules on state trading enterprises. These are issues developing countries sees as mega in nature outside the WTO framework.

A study commissioned by the European Parliament on the benefits of entering into TTIP has estimated that full tariff liberalisation and a one-quarter reduction in the costs arising from non-tariff barriers would bring between EUR 49.5 billion and EUR 119 billion per year for the EU and between EUR 49.5 billion and EUR

[16] African Union (2012) Action Plan for Boosting, Intra-African Trade, Addis Ababa, Ethiopia, http://www.au.int/en/sites/default/files/Action%20Plan%20for%20boosting%20intra-African%20trade%20F-English.pdf (last accessed 24 September 2015).

95 billion per year for the USA.[17] Despite the enormous benefits to the EU and the USA, some members of the civil society within the EU have raised concerns with regard to the transparency of the negotiations, the issue of the investor-state dispute settlement and other issues with regard to regulations and standards. There is also an argument from some African thinkers that the rise of Mega-Regional free trade areas signals the weariness of countries regarding the negotiating impasse within the WTO. This line of thinking presumes that countries seek to advance trade liberalisation outside the confines of the WTO and its single undertaking in order to create new rules and standards outside the WTO or to create a trade fortress to exclude those countries that are not part of the negotiations.[18] These agreements go deeper than what is provided in the WTO agreements, and include for example licensing practices, domestic taxes, government procurement, rules on investment, rules on state-trading enterprises; human rights, environment, labour rights, data protection, trade facilitation, competition policy and consumer protection. These issues could be classified as WTO extra standards. Other studies provides that[19]:

1. If TTIP is concluded, developing countries could benefit from the simplification and cost savings of having a single set of standards to fulfil when exporting to a much larger market;
2. For this to be possible, however, the EU and the USA need to include a clause in TTIP extending the principle of mutual recognition or equivalence to third parties;
3. While developing countries could be negatively affected if the TTIP results in higher regulatory standards, this is unlikely to happen;
4. If TTIP lead to lower standards, developing countries might find it easier to export (again, provided that mutual recognition is extended).[20]

5 Preferential Treatment

On the issue of preferential treatment, GATT Part IV on Trade and Development provides the basis for the GATT/WTO members to provide special advantageous treatment for developing and least developed country members. These include

[17] Manrique Gil M, Lerch M and Bierbrauer E (2015) The TTIP's potential impact on developing countries: A review of existing literature and selected issues. Directorate – General for External Polices, Policy Department, European Parliament, DGEXPO/B/PolDep/Note/2015_84.

[18] Richter (2014), p. 50.

[19] Agreement Establishing A Tripartite Free Trade Area Among The Common Market for Eastern and Southern Africa, The East African Community and the Southern African Development Community, http://www.eac.int/legal/index.php?option=com_docman&task=doc_download&gid=205&Itemid=154 (last accessed 24 September 2015).

[20] Manrique Gil M, Lerch M and Bierbrauer E (2015) The TTIP's potential impact on developing countries: A review of existing literature and selected issues. Directorate – General for External Polices, Policy Department, European Parliament, DG EXPO/B/PolDep/Note/2015_84.

favourable market access conditions (Article XXXVI (4) of the GATT/WTO Agreement), especially for processed and manufacture exports (Article XXXVI (5)), in the hope of increasing trade of developing countries and encouraging diversification of their export capacity. The special treatment could be provided by way of a standstill, reduction and elimination of customs duties and other charges affecting products of current or potential export interest of developing countries (Article XXVII).

On the basis of GATT/WTO rules, it is expected that TPP, TTIP and other Mega-Regional trade and investment agreements relax their rules to some degree in line with tariff preference commitments under Part IV of GATT to support developing and least-developed countries. The EU's Everything But Arms(EBA) preferential system provides for duty free access to 49 countries across Africa, Asia, the Pacific and the Caribbean. This scheme is also available from the USA to support African trade and development through the African Growth and Opportunity Act (AGOA). Eligible African countries are offered duty-free access on a range of goods to the USA market, including clothing and apparel, wine and some agricultural products. Although it is envisaged that this Act will expire on 30 September 2015, it is hoped that the USA will renew it.

The EU Generalised System of Preferences (GSP) provides for preferential (reduced duty) access to roughly 65 % of all tariff lines for developing country beneficiaries. The same tariff lines are zero-rated for GSP+ countries that meet the criteria set out by the EU, while least-developed countries receive full duty-free access across all products except arms and armaments through the Everything But Arms (EBA) scheme.

The EU began negotiations on seven EPAs with seven regional blocks of the ACP in order to achieve wider and deeper trade agreements. To date, only the Caribbean region has signed the EPA with the EU, providing the Caribbean Community (CARICOM) with duty free access to the EU.

The EU has amended Council Regulation No. 1528/2007 (known as the Market Access Regulation) so that duty-free, quota-free access to the EU market would be reserved to those EPA countries that have taken the necessary steps towards signing and ratifying the EPAs.[21] As of 1st of October 2014, the ACP countries that have not signed and ratified the EPAs will only benefit from the GSP, GSP+ or EBA regimes of doing business with the European Union.

According to the European Commission's recent trade policy report, the new GSP focuses preferences on countries-most-in-need and addresses the issue of preference erosion. The GSP concentrates the benefits on fewer eligible countries. Countries classified as high or upper middle income for the most recent 3 years by the World Bank or countries having equivalent or better preferential access under

[21] Council Regulation (EC) No. 1528/2007 applying to the arrangements for product originating in certain States which are part of the African, Caribbean, and Pacific (ACP) Group of States provided for in agreements establishing, or leading to the establishment of, Economic Partnership Agreements.

other arrangements would be removed from the list of beneficiary countries. Hence, the number of GSP beneficiaries decreased from 178 under the previous GSP to the current 92, and is expected to decrease further. However, some of the removed countries will be covered by other preferential arrangements.

The true extent to which preferential access for ACP countries could be eroded by the Mega-Regional agreements depends on a number of factors. This includes the extent to which use is actually made of the preferential access provided. ACP countries may also have a substantially different export structure to those new members within Mega-Regional agreements. In such a situation, the level of preference erosion becomes irrelevant since exporting countries are not competing across the same product lines and categories.

The countries participating in the Tripartite arrangement fall into three regional groups for the purpose of concluding EPAs with the EU, but the overlap of these three groups with the three Regional Economic Communities (RECs) is only partial, as EPAs cannot take account of the multiple membership of the RECs. These groups are: the SADC EPA Groups (including some of the SADC countries), the EAC and the ESA EPA Group (Eastern and Southern Africa). The negotiations with the SADC EPA Group and EAC were concluded in 2014 and arrangements awaiting to be signed and ratified. The EU already has bilateral free trade agreement with South Africa called Trade, Development and Cooperation Agreement.[22] The creation of the TFTA and finally of a Continental Free Trade Agreement will enable African countries to enjoy better market access to the EU and the USA.

6 Conclusion

All studies so far concur that removal of non-tariff barriers to trade, particularly through regulatory harmonisation, will have a particular impact on developing countries who are not part to these agreements. Megaregional trade and investment agreements may affect countries that are not involved in the negotiations. There is a potential risk of marginalisation of third parties, which could further turn them from "rule makers" into "rule takers". Third parties may have the option of acceding to Mega-Regional trade and investments agreements. This could, however, reinforce their role as "rule takers" and expose them to the conditionalities that sometimes emanate from accession procedures. This could be problematic, given that many countries that are not participating in Mega-Regional trade and investment agreements are least-developed and developing countries. However, it is very difficult to measure their impact. Therefore, it would be recommendable that a future study be conducted on the implementation of Mega-Regional trade and investment

[22] The Tripartite Free Trade Area Project Integration in Southern and Eastern Africa. Briefing, March 2015, European Parliamentary Research Services.

agreements and their effect on developing and least-developed countries who are non- participants of the negotiations.

The EU has a legal obligation through Article 208 of the Lisbon Treaty to take account of the objectives of the development cooperation in the policies that it implements which are likely to affect developing countries,[23] including the African, Caribbean and Pacific Group of States (ACP States).

In an effort to better integrate into the global trading system and improve their trade performance, most least-developed and developing countries, especially the ACP states, have over the last decade been involved in two major sets of negotiations: the WTO Doha Round and the EPA negotiations with the EU, with the hope and expectation that their outcomes would be development-oriented and address their interest and concerns in the global trade and investment agenda. Unfortunately, most of these negotiations are in some form of a stalemate. This has increased the need for Africa to explore other alternative means of enhancing its trade performance and using trade and investment as a key instrument for the promotion of sustainable economic growth and development.

The issue of trade facilitation constraints needs to be urgently addressed, such as the complex customs and administrative procedures and regulations, inefficient and costly transit systems, numerous informal roadblocks along trade corridors, differences in rules of origin, trade documentation.

Developing countries and their regional economic communities would need to enter into dialogue with the EU and the USA and other emerging industrial countries who are also negotiating Mega-Regional trade and investment agreements, to put forward their concerns on key issues such as preferential tariff treatment, mutual recognition of non-tariff barriers and trade and investment issues.

References

Erasmus G, Hartzenberg T (2013) The tripartite free trade area: what will it be, and how will it come about? In: Herrmann C, Krajewski M, Terhechte JP (eds) European yearbook of international economic law, vol 5. Springer, Heidelberg, pp 345–353

Richter S (2014) Reaching a consensus? Afr Investor 12(2):48–50

[23] Consolidated Treaties Charter of Fundamental Rights. European Union, March 2010, Luxembourg.

The Trade in Services Agreement (TiSA): Assessing the State of Play and Potential Pitfalls

Billy A. Melo Araujo

Contents

Abstract This article aims to provide an overview of the state of play regarding the Trade in Services Agreement (TiSA). It pinpoints some of the potentially novel aspects and limitations of the agreement and addresses some of the more problematic legal questions that surround its negotiation, particularly the issue of its potential multilateralisation and incorporation within the WTO framework. Section 2 provides a brief description of the history and rationale behind the negotiation of the TiSA. Sections 3 and 4 describe the current GATS framework in relation to liberalization commitments and non-discriminatory regulatory principles, and the extent to which TiSA can go beyond this. Section 5 examines the compatibility of the TiSA with WTO law by focusing on the issue of whether the TiSA can comply with conditions set out under Article V GATS for the establishment of a preferential trade agreements (PTAs) covering services. Finally, Sect. 6 addressees the manner and the conditions under which the TiSA may be multilateralised in the future.

The usual disclaimer applies.

B.A. Melo Araujo (✉)
School of Law, Queen's University Belfast, 28 University Square, Belfast BT7 1NN, Ireland
e-mail: B.Melo-Araujo@qub.ac.uk

M. Bungenberg et al. (eds.), *European Yearbook of International Economic Law 2016*, European Yearbook of International Economic Law 7,
DOI 10.1007/978-3-319-29215-1_29

1 Introduction

The idea of a plurilateral trade in services agreement (TiSA) was first mooted by the US and Australia in 2011 in response to the lack of progress in negotiations at the level of the World Trade Organization (WTO). The objective was to gather like-minded WTO Members (so-called "Really Good Friends" or "RGFs"[1]) keen to push forward negotiations on trade in services in order to develop a trade agreement outside the auspices of the General Agreement on Services (GATS), with the aim of addressing its deficiencies.[2] This plurilateral agreement would not only further existing market access commitments but also address new services areas hitherto untouched by the GATS, lock-in domestic liberalisation policies and establish additional regulatory disciplines. Four years on, the group of RGFs has increased from 16 to 25 members and whilst negotiations remain very much alive they also remain very much a work in progress.

This article aims to provide an overview of the state of play regarding TiSA. It pinpoints some of the potentially novel aspects and limitations of the agreement and addresses some of the more problematic legal questions that surround its negotiation, particularly the issue of its potential multilateralisation and incorporation within the WTO framework. Section 2 provides a brief description of the history and rationale behind the negotiation of the TiSA. Sections 3 and 4 describe the current GATS framework in relation to liberalization commitments and non-discriminatory regulatory principles, and the extent to which TiSA can go beyond this. Section 5 examines the compatibility of the TiSA with WTO law by focusing in particular on the issue of whether the TiSA can comply with conditions set out under Article V GATS for the establishment of a preferential trade agreements (PTAs) covering services. Finally, Sect. 6 addressees the manner and the conditions under which the TiSA may be multilateralised in the future.

[1] The coalition of Really Good Friends currently includes the following members: Australia, Canada, Chile, Chinese Taipei, Colombia, European Union, Hong Kong, Iceland, Israel, Japan, South Korea, Liechtenstein, Mauritius, Mexico, New Zealand, Norway, Pakistan, Panama, Peru, Switzerland, Turkey, the US and Uruguay, Costa Rica, Israel, Panama, Peru and Turkey.

[2] Sauve, "Dr. Jekyll or Mr. Hyde? Reflections on the Trade in Services Agreement (TISA)", Directorate-General for External Policies Workshop the plurilateral agreement on services, 1 July 2013, http://www.europarl.europa.eu/RegData/etudes/workshop/join/2013/433722/EXPO-INTA_AT(2013)433722_EN.pdf (last accessed 7 October 2015), p. 14.

2 TiSA: A Means to Circumvent the GATS Stalemate

Whilst the conclusion of GATS in 1994 represented a major breakthrough for the international trading system, some have long argued that it is no longer fit for purpose in its current format.[3] Firstly, because the liberalisation commitments included in the agreement remain modest. Most commitments do not reflect actual domestic policies meaning that WTO Members have the flexibility to backtrack on the regulatory status quo.[4] In addition, WTO Members have proved reluctant to address some key service sectors. For example, the EU has been consistent in its resolve to protect the audiovisual sector.[5] Similarly, developed countries have consistently blocked negotiations for the further liberalisation of Mode 4 services (temporary movement of natural persons), an area where developing countries have an important comparative advantage, because of the potential repercussions on migration policy.[6] Secondly, GATS suffers from serious architectural deficiencies that stunt attempts to further liberalise trade in services. The positive list approach to scheduling is not conducive to the opening of services markets.[7] The modal approach in the GATS has compartmentalised negotiations and in doing so rendered negotiations in sensitive areas such as Mode 4 service supply more difficult.[8] Thirdly, the GATS does little to address the most important barriers to trade in services: regulatory barriers.[9]

Attempts to address such limitations at the multilateral level have not been successful, largely because there is no appetite for such negotiations from developing countries. Services were not seen a priority area in the context of the Doha Round which was focused on areas such as agriculture and non-agricultural market access. The fact that developed countries remained unwilling to seriously consider liberalising mode 4 services only served to further discourage developing countries from embracing negotiations in trade in services.[10]

---

[3] See European Parliament, Working Document on Recommendations to the European Commission on the negotiations for the Trade in Services Agreement (TiSA), Committee on International Trade, DT/1071748EN.Doc, 4 September 2015.

[4] Hoekman B, Mattoo A, Liberalizing Trade in Services: Lessons from Regional and WTO Negotiations, 13 December 2012, http://globalgovernanceprogramme.eui.eu/wp-content/uploads/2012/11/Hoekman-Mattoo-Services-Cooperation_International_Negotiation_final.pdf (last accessed 7 October 2015), p. 4.

[5] Marchetti and Roy (2008), p. 63.

[6] OECD (2004) Trade and Migration Building Bridges for Global Labour Mobility, p. 135.

[7] Latrille P, Lee J, Services Rules in Regional Trade Agreements: How Diverse and How Creative as Compared to the GATS Multilateral Rules, WTO Working Paper Economic Research and Statistics Division, 31 December 2012, https://www.wto.org/english/res_e/reser_e/ersd201219_e.pdf (last accessed 7 October 2015), p. 7.

[8] Trachtman (2003), pp. 57–82.

[9] Feketekuty (2000), pp. 225–240.

[10] Panizzon M, Trade and Labor Migration—GATS Mode 4, Friedrich Ebert Stiftung, Working Paper No. 47, January 2010, http://library.fes.de/pdf-files/iez/global/06955.pdf (last accessed 7 October 2015), pp. 20–24.

The TiSA is the manifestation of the increasing frustration felt by developed country WTO Members about the lack of progress at WTO level. As Vivianne Reding—the rappoerteur for the European Parliament's Committee on International Trade—recently put it, the objective of the TiSA is to "advance the stalled WTO talks with countries that are willing to make further progress on trade in services" and "break new grounds in market access commitments and to enhance international rules in several fields such as financial, digital and transport services".[11] However, the RGFs are not content to simply secure enhanced liberalisation and regulatory disciplines amongst themselves. The TiSA has multilateral aspirations in that its proponents are hoping that it will come to represent a "stepping stone towards renewed impetus at WTO level, not an alternative to the multilateral governance".[12] To achieve this, the agreement is supposedly being crafted in a GATS-compatible manner, to secure further integration at the multilateral level. Therefore, the objective of the TiSA participants is to move the discussion to an environment that is less hostile and more conducive to negotiations on trade in services in the hope that the result of such negotiations can then be multilateralised.

3 Opening Services Markets Through TiSA

Whilst non-discrimination and market access requirements are key to both the General Agreement on Tariffs and Trade (GATT) and the GATS legal frameworks, the two agreements diverge in a number of aspects. Firstly, in recognition of the various ways in which services can be delivered, Article I:2 GATS distinguishes four modes of services supply: (1) services that are supplied from the territory of one WTO Member to another WTO Member (cross-border trade); (2) services that are supplied from the territory of one WTO Member to the consumer of another WTO Member (consumption abroad); (3) services that are supplied by a supplier from one WTO Member in the territory of another WTO Member (commercial presence); and (4) services that are supplied by a supplier from one WTO member through the presence of natural persons placed in the territory of another WTO Member. The scope of GATS is therefore wider than that of GATT, as it not only covers measures affecting services but also the suppliers of such services.

---

[11] Sauve, "Dr. Jekyll or Mr. Hyde? Reflections on the Trade in Services Agreement (TISA)", Directorate-General for External Policies Workshop the plurilateral agreement on services, 1 July 2013, http://www.europarl.europa.eu/RegData/etudes/workshop/join/2013/433722/EXPO-INTA_AT(2013)433722_EN.pdf (last accessed 7 October 2015), p. 26.

[12] Sauve, "Dr. Jekyll or Mr. Hyde? Reflections on the Trade in Services Agreement (TISA)", Directorate-General for External Policies Workshop the plurilateral agreement on services, 1 July 2013, http://www.europarl.europa.eu/RegData/etudes/workshop/join/2013/433722/EXPO-INTA_AT(2013)433722_EN.pdf (last accessed 7 October 2015), p. 26.

The GATS applies to all services sectors, barring certain exceptions and limitations (such as the Annex on Air Transport Services).

Secondly, the manner in which liberalisation commitments operate differs significantly from GATT. Under GATS, the provisions on most-favoured-nation (MFN), national treatment and prohibition of quantitative restrictions can be subject to important restrictions. The MFN obligation applies to all WTO Members and to all service sectors, barring for measures that are listed in the MFN exemption list.[13] This is what is typically referred to as a negative approach to scheduling commitments, insofar as all services are assumed to be subject to MFN commitments, except those specifically listed in the GATS schedules. The positive list approach to scheduling adopted with regard to market access obligations (Article XVI GATS) is even more restrictive in that WTO Members are only bound by such obligations in relation to the services sectors and modes of supply scheduled in commitments. Moreover, even after a market opening commitment is made, a WTO Member can circumscribe such commitment by listing limitations, qualifications or conditions in its schedules. In this respect, GATS is said to follow a 'hybrid' approach to the scheduling of commitments, in contrast to that followed by other trade agreements such as NAFTA, where all services sectors are assumed to be covered by the liberalisation commitments unless a country has scheduled a limitation to the contrary.

The conclusion of GATS did not yield significant gains in terms of liberalising global trade in services as most market opening commitments made at the time merely locked in already existing policies of WTO Members. And, whilst most WTO Members have subsequently pursued the unilateral liberalisation of domestic services markets, these policy reforms have not been inscribed under their GATS schedules, the upshot being that the commitments scheduled under GATS often do not correspond with the applied level of liberalisation.[14] More tangible progress has been made outside the realm of the GATS through preferential trade agreements (PTAs), which tend to include GATS plus commitments across all services sectors, even those where only modest commitments have been made at the WTO level.[15] However, the success of PTAs in securing GATS plus commitments should not be overstated. Firstly, despite the breadth of commitments typically undertaken in these agreements, sensitive services sectors for developed countries, such as health services, audiovisuals (for the EU) and maritime transport and professional services (for the US), remain off limits.[16] Secondly, although PTAs typically contain GATS plus commitments, few represent an improvement in the liberalisation policies of

[13] Article II.2 GATS.

[14] See the Summary and Overview in Marchetti and Roy (2009), p. 5.

[15] See the Introduction and Overview in Sauve and Shingal (2014), p. 3.

[16] Marchetti J, Roy M (2013) "The TISA Initiative: An Overview of Market Access Issues", WTO Working Paper Economic Research and Statistics Division, 27 November 2013, https://www.wto.org/english/res_e/reser_e/ersd201311_e.pdf (last accessed 7 October 2015), p. 5.

the parties.[17] Typically, only developing countries tend to carry out domestic regulatory reforms as a result of the conclusion of a PTA—a reflection of the fact that most PTAs are signed between developed and developing countries and are the result of negotiations characterised by high degrees of asymmetry. Thirdly, the temporary movement of persons—especially those engaged in low-skilled labour—remains an area where liberalisation commitments are few and far between.[18]

The TiSA is seen as an opportunity to address the limitations of both GATS and existing PTAs. The EU has stated that the TiSA should be "comprehensive in scope with no exclusion of services sectors or modes of supply at the outset"[19] and "reflect the reality on the ground, i.e. the actual level of existing liberalisation, and provide for new or improved market access".[20] The market opening offers should go beyond commitments made in the context of the GATS and existing PTAs, and at the very least correspond to the level of policies applied domestically. In addition, the TiSA participants could also consider departing from the GATS architecture and adopt legal mechanisms that encourage further liberalisation. This could be achieved by moving away from the GATS hybrid approach to listing liberalisation commitments towards a negative-list approach to scheduling where all sectors are assumed to be subject to commitments unless it is specifically excluded by a party. Similarly, it has been suggested that the TISA participants should consider including a standstill provision which requires parties to lock in their applied regulatory policies and a "ratchet" provision which obliges parties to lock in any future elimination of discriminatory measures.[21] Together, these obligations would engender a pro-liberalisation dynamic whereby any liberalisation of a measure automatically becomes a binding commitment under the TiSA.

With respect to the architecture of the agreement, there appears to be a consensus amongst parties that the TiSA should follow as closely as possible the template set by GATS notably because this would facilitate any future multilateralisation of the agreement. As a result, there are no significant deviations from the GATS. The EU has released a proposal for the core text of the TiSA (EU Core Text)[22] that

[17] Hoekman B, Mattoo A, Liberalizing Trade in Services: Lessons from Regional and WTO Negotiations, 13 December 2012, http://globalgovernanceprogramme.eui.eu/wp-content/uploads/2012/11/Hoekman-Mattoo-Services-Cooperation_International_Negotiation_final.pdf (last accessed 7 October 2015), p. 12.

[18] Panizzon (2010); Hoekman B, Mattoo A (2013) Liberalizing trade in services: lessons from regional and WTO negotiations. International Negotiation 18.1, p 135.

[19] European Commission, Negotiations for a Plurilateral Agreement on Trade in services, 5 February 2013 http://europa.eu/rapid/press-release_MEMO-13-107_en.htm (last accessed 7 October 2015).

[20] European Commission, Negotiations for a Plurilateral Agreement on Trade in services, 5 February 2013 http://europa.eu/rapid/press-release_MEMO-13-107_en.htm (last accessed 7 October 2015).

[21] Sauve (2014), p. 9.

[22] European Commission Plurilateral Services Agreement, EU Proposal March 2013. Available at: http://trade.ec.europa.eu/doclib/docs/2014/july/tradoc_152687.pdf.

replicates almost verbatim the entire text of the GATS, including the modal approach,[23] the approach to scheduling of commitments[24] and the provisions on general exceptions allowing members to derogate from the agreement to pursue public interest objectives under certain circumstances.[25] However, there are some noteworthy differences between the TiSA and GATS. With respect to the scheduling of commitments, whilst the TiSA participants have maintained a positive list approach to scheduling market concessions, there is an agreement to "adopt a negative list approach for" national treatment commitments.[26] This means that all service sectors are subject to the national treatment obligation unless a reservation or limitation is made in the relevant schedule.[27] Moreover, the TiSA participants appear to be following through on the idea of including standstill and ratchet clauses in the agreement with regard to national treatment commitments. In accordance with Article II.1 of the EU Core Text for the TiSA, the conditions, limitations and qualifications to which the national treatment obligation is subject are "limited to measures in force in the territory of the Party at the time the Schedule of Specific Commitments enters into force".[28] This standstill commitment would effectively guarantee that TiSA members will maintain policies that are no less restrictive than those applicable at the time of the entry into force of the agreement. Furthermore, Article II.2 of the same text provides that if any Party "amends a measure relating to the conditions, limitations and qualifications"[29] relating to national treatment commitments "in a way that reduces or eliminates the inconsistency of that measure, such amendment shall be binding on the party pursuant to this agreement".[30] This would require TiSA members to reflect and incorporate within the TiSA any liberalisation measures, which would go beyond existing national treatment commitment inscribed in the agreement.

As regards the market opening offers that have been made public, these fall someway short of the lofty ambitions proclaimed by the proponents of the agreement. Detailed offers from countries such as Norway and Switzerland are riddled with the type of sectoral exceptions and exemptions commonly found in the

[23] Article I-1 EU Core Text.

[24] Article I-3 EU Core Text.

[25] Article I-9 EU Core Text.

[26] European Commission, How to read a Trade in Services Agreement Schedule, November 2013. http://trade.ec.europa.eu/doclib/press/index.cfm?id=1133 (last accessed 7 October 2015); See also Godsoe (2014), p. 4.

[27] European Commission, How to read a Trade in Services Agreement Schedule, November 2013. http://trade.ec.europa.eu/doclib/press/index.cfm?id=1133 (last accessed 7 October 2015); See also Godsoe (2014), p. 4.

[28] Article II-1.2 EU Core Text.

[29] Article II-1.4 EU Core Text.

[30] Article II-1.4 EU Core Text.

GATS.[31] Elsewhere, a review of the initial offers tabled by TiSA participants has shown that many of the aforementioned sensitive sectors remain off the table.[32] The EU, for example, has voiced its commitment to protect audio-visual services, public health and education, social services and water distribution services[33] whilst the US has maintained its reluctance to make any commitments with respect to Mode 4 and maritime transport.[34] Indeed, there are reports of a growing rift within the TiSA between, on the one hand, advanced industrialized nations such as the US and EU Member States that wish to push through further liberalisation in areas such as financial services, telecommunications, postal and courier sources and electronic commerce and, on the other hand, poorer countries such as Mexico, Pakistan and Turkey that are demandeurs of liberalisation in areas such as Mode 4, maritime services and road transport services.[35] In short, many of the issues that undermined negotiations at multilateral level are currently holding back the talks on the TiSA.

4 Regulatory Disciplines

Behind-the-border measures in the form of non-discriminatory regulations are significant obstacles to international trade in services. This is due in part to the difficulty of applying border measures such as tariffs and quotas to intangible products and also because most services are not delivered through cross-border trade but rather by the establishment of a commercial presence abroad.[36] Such regulatory barriers can take various forms. Some regulations, such as licensing and qualification requirements represent up-front costs top market entry.[37] In certain cases the obstacle may not relate to the regulation itself but rather to the manner in which it is applied (or not applied) by the host country. A lack of regulatory transparency, administrative delays and arbitrary application of the law can undermine attempts of foreign service providers to access a market. And finally, mere regulatory differences between countries can significantly heighten the costs for

[31] Bosworth M (2014) The Proposed Non-MFN Trade in Services Agreement: Bad for Unilateralism, the WTO and the Multilateral Trading System, NCCR Trade Working Paper No. 2014/05, p. 20.

[32] Bosworth M (2014) The Proposed Non-MFN Trade in Services Agreement: Bad for Unilateralism, the WTO and the Multilateral Trading System, NCCR Trade Working Paper No. 2014/05, p. 20.

[33] Messerlin P (2015) The Transatlantic Trade and Investment Partnership: The Services Dimension. CEPS Special Report (No. 106/May 2015), p. 10.

[34] Sauve (2014), p. 10.

[35] Kanth R (2015), Sharp "asymmetries" in levels of ambition emerge in TiSA talks, 16 April 2015, http://www.twn.my/title2/wto.info/2015/ti150404.htm (last accessed 8 October 2015).

[36] Jackson (1988).

[37] Kox H, Nordas H (2011) Services Trade and Domestic Regulation. OECD Trade Policy Working Papers (No. 49).

services suppliers wishing to do business broad.[38] However, the attempts to discipline domestic regulation in the GATS are rather modest. Article III and Article VI GATS include a number of transparency and procedural obligations, such as the obligation to promptly publish all measures of general application pertaining to services but by far the most potentially intrusive provision in the GATS is Article VI:4 GATS which establishes a mandate to negotiate cross-sectoral substantive standards, with the intention of ensuring that measures relating to qualification requirements and procedures, technical standards and licensing requirements do not constitute unnecessary barriers to trade in services. More specifically, Article VI:4 (b) invites WTO Members to negotiate disciplines requiring that a specific set of non-discriminatory rules (qualification requirements and procedures, technical standards and licensing requirements) are not more burdensome than necessary to ensure the quality of the service. Such a necessity requirement could, controversially, pave the way for judicial assessments regarding the appropriateness of a domestic measure in order to secure a given public policy objective.[39] However, although the WTO established a Working Party on Domestic Regulations in 1996 to negotiate these horizontal disciplines as long ago as 1996, WTO members are yet to come to an agreement as to how far Article VI:4 GATS should go in terms of disciplining domestic regulation.[40]

Beyond these horizontal disciplines, the WTO has also established sector-specific rules that apply on a plurilateral basis. This is the case in the Understanding on Commitments in Financial Services[41] which imposes optional enhanced national treatment and market access commitments to WTO Members, and the GATS Annex on Financial Services, which includes a carve-out allowing WTO Members to derogate from GATS in order to adopt prudential measures such as those ensuring the protection of depositors and the maintenance of financial stability. There is also the Reference Paper on Telecommunications Services,[42] which is unique in the GATS legal framework in that it provides a number of pro-competitive disciplines and regulatory principles in the area of telecommunication services that must be incorporated into the domestic regulatory framework of WTO Members who have made commitments in the area. A peculiarity of these sector-specific agreements is that although they are plurilateral—in that they are only binding on those WTO Members that subscribe to them—the benefits of commitments relating to them are extended to all WTO Members on a MFN basis.

[38] Sykes (1999), pp. 53–57; Kox H, Lejour A (2007) Regulatory heterogeneity as an obstacle for international services trade. CPB Discussion Paper (No 49).

[39] Marchetti and Mavroidis (2004), pp. 511–562.

[40] WTO (2011) Working Party on Domestic Regulation, Disciplines on Domestic Regulation pursuant to GATS. Chairman's Progress Report Article VI:4, S/WPDR/W/45, 14 April 2011.

[41] Understanding on Commitments in Financial Services (1994), Uruguay Round Final Act, GATT Trade Negotiations Committee Document MTN/FA II-AIB, General Agreement on Trade in Services, 15 April 1994.

[42] WTO (1996) Negotiating Group on Basic Telecommunications (NGBT). Reference Paper (vol. 3) 36 I.L.M 367, 24 April 1996.

Much like the GATS, the record of PTAs in addressing non-discriminatory regulatory barriers is mixed. PTAs have not added much as far as Article VI GATS disciplines on domestic regulation are concerned. Generally speaking, the provision is either absent from many PTAs or only present in a watered down version.[43] For example, PTAs concluded by the US typically transform article VI:4 GATS into a best endeavors obligation whilst recent EU PTAs omit any reference to the 'necessity test' mandated in Article VI:4(b) GATS.[44] Moreover, both EU and US PTAs tend to include provisions that require parties to incorporate the results of any negotiations at GATS level into the agreement.[45] Therefore, both the EU and the US refrain from using their PTAs as an opportunity to develop new disciplines on domestic regulations and are satisfied by simply deferring to ongoing negotiations that are taking place under the auspices of the GATS Council for Trade in Services. In the context of the TiSA negotiations, the EU's negotiating mandate specified that it wished to develop regulatory disciplines concerning transparency and domestic regulation.[46] The EU Core Text for TiSA also shows that it plans to include of a separate chapter dealing specifically with domestic regulation in the agreement. However, no clarification has been provided thus far as to the exact content of this chapter and whether it is intended to build on Article VI GATS and the work of the Working Party on Domestic Regulations.

PTAs have been more successful in enhancing regulatory transparency and cooperation between countries. The new generation of deep and comprehensive PTAs that are increasingly being signed by developed countries generally includes provisions that go beyond GATS by requiring parties to publish measures of general application in advance of their entry into force and sometimes to adopt prior comments procedures that allow interested parties to comment on proposed legislation.[47] There are provisions requiring parties to notify other parties of any proposed or actual measure that may affect the operation or substantially affect the interests of the other party.[48] Finally, there is an emerging tendency for developed country PTAs to include ambitious regulatory cooperation mechanisms.[49] This is

[43] Krajewski (2006), pp. 175–202.

[44] Melo Araujo (2014), p. 402.

[45] Melo Araujo (2014), pp. 402–403.

[46] Council of the European Union (2015), Draft Directives for the negotiation of a plurilateral agreement on trade in services, 10 March 2015. http://trade.ec.europa.eu/doclib/press/index.cfm?id=1273 (last accessed 8 October 2015).

[47] WTO (2011) Working Party on Domestic Regulation, Disciplines on Domestic Regulation pursuant to GATS. Chairman's Progress Report Article VI:4, S/WPDR/W/45, 14 April 2011, p. 405.

[48] WTO (2011) Working Party on Domestic Regulation, Disciplines on Domestic Regulation pursuant to GATS. Chairman's Progress Report Article VI:4, S/WPDR/W/45, 14 April 2011.

[49] WTO (2011) Working Party on Domestic Regulation, Disciplines on Domestic Regulation pursuant to GATS. Chairman's Progress Report Article VI:4, S/WPDR/W/45, 14 April 2011, pp. 412–413.

the case of EU-Canada Comprehensive Economic Trade Agreement (CETA)[50] and the EU-US Transatlantic Trade and Investment Partnership (TTIP, currently under negotiation)[51] where the parties have envisaged enhanced transparency rules and the establishment of institutional mechanisms promoting regulatory dialogue.[52] This includes, for example, requirements to notify proposed regulations, to implement prior comments procedures and to facilitate exchange of data[53] as well as the creation of an institutional body entrusted with the task of assessing the feasibility of implementing regulatory harmonisation, compatibility and mutual recognition arrangements.[54] In accordance with the EU Core Text, the TiSA will include a separate chapter including horizontal disciplines on regulatory transparency, although no indication is provided as to what these rules may look like. Similarly, there has so far been no suggestion that TiSA participants intend to develop an institutional mechanism for regulatory cooperation of the time envisaged in the CETA and the TTIP.

Another area where PTAs have gone further than GATS is in including regulatory disciplines that apply to specific services sector. The EU and US have tended to replicate the content of the GATS instruments such as the Reference Paper on Telecommunication Services, the Financial Services Understanding and the Financial Services Annex in their respective PTAs. In other words, these PTAs are being used to expand the reach of plurilateral WTO rules. In addition, the EU has also sought to apply the regulatory disciplines included in the Reference Paper on Telecommunication Services to other service sectors. A notable example of this is the EU-CARIFORUM Economic Partnership Agreement (EPA)[55] which provides competition law requirements that must be imposed in the tourism sector, namely prohibitions of any "abuse of dominant position through imposition of unfair prices, exclusivity clauses, refuse to deal, tied sales, quantitative restrictions or vertical integration".[56] Such provisions are a unique feature in the PTA landscape and were introduced at the specific request of CARIFORUM States keen on ensuring that the larger EU service suppliers were not able to engage in unfair

---

[50] The negotiations for the EU-Singapore PTA and the CETA have been concluded but the agreements are yet to be ratified. See European Union, Overview of PTA and Other Trade Negotiations. http://trade.ec.europa.eu/doclib/html/118238.html (last accessed 8 October 2015).

[51] European Commission (2015) Revised EU proposal on Regulatory Cooperation in Transatlantic Trade and Investment Partnership (TTIP), 6 May 2015,http://trade.ec.europa.eu/doclib/docs/2015/may/tradoc_153432.1.1%20Explanatory%20note%20-%20revised%20Regulatory%20cooperation%20EU%20legal%20text.pdf (last accessed 8 October 2015).

[52] European Commission (2013) EU–US Transatlantic Trade and Investment Partnership, Trade Cross-Cutting Disciplines and Institutional Provisions, Initial EU Position Paper 2013.

[53] Lester and Barbee (2013), pp. 847–867.

[54] European Commission (2013) EU–US Transatlantic Trade and Investment Partnership, Trade Cross-Cutting Disciplines and Institutional Provisions, Initial EU Position Paper 2013.

[55] EU-CARIFORUM Economic Partnership Agreement, signed 15 October 2008, OJ L289/1/3, 30 October 2008.

[56] Article 127 (1), EU-CARIFORUM EPA.

practices, which would undermine the ability of CARIFORUM firms to participate in the market. The expansion of the pro-competitive regulatory disciplines included in the Reference Paper on Telecommunications Services to other services sectors also appears to represent a key aim of the TiSA. Various participants have stated that the agreement will include a number of sector specific chapters covering issues such as licencing and qualification procedures, independence of regulators, fair market access authorisation processes, competition-related provisions, and non-discriminatory access to networks.[57] In doing so, the TiSA would be building on what is currently being done at PTA level by applying regulatory disciplines that are incorporated in WTO plurilateral instruments to other services sectors (especially network industries).[58] This appears to be confirmed by the EU's proposal for an annex on financial services which follows the template set in its PTAs by copy-pasting large swathes of the Financial Services Understanding with a few deviations and additions in certain areas (e.g., requirements on new financial services, transparency, etc).[59]

5 Compatibility of TiSA with WTO Law

Having come to terms with the unlikelihood of pursuing successful multilateral negotiations in the area of trade in services, the proponents of the TiSA have been keen to emphasize that any plurilateral agreement in this area should be compatible with WTO law. There are a number of options available to the TiSA participants to ensure such compatibility. The first and most straightforward option would have been to collectively enhance their GATS commitments.[60] The advantage of this mechanism rests in its simplicity and, more importantly, the fact that commitments would apply automatically on a MFN basis to all WTO Members. However, from the perspective of TISA participants, any option that would allow the rest of the WTO membership to free ride on the liberalisation efforts of the TiSA participants was always a non-starter.[61] The TiSA participants would have also envisaged the possibility of following the examples of the Information Technology Agreement

[57] See e.g. European Commission (2015) Negotiations for a Plurilateral Agreement on Trade in services, 15 February 2013; Canada Department of Foreign Affairs (2013) Trade and Development Canada, Consultations on a Plurilateral International Services Agreement, Canada Gazette Notice 16 March 2013.

[58] Sauvé P (2013) A Plurilateral Agenda for Services? Assessing the case for a Trade in Services Agreement (NCCR Trade regulation, Working Paper (No 2013/29, May 2013).

[59] European Commission (2014) The EU publishes TiSA position papers, 22 July 2014, http://trade.ec.europa.eu/doclib/press/index.cfm?id=1133 (last accessed 8 October 2015).

[60] Adlung (2015), p. 2.

[61] Questions for the Record for Committee on Ways and Means Full Committee Hearing on President Obama's Trade Policy Agenda with U.S. Trade Representative Michael Froman, 3 April 2014. www.waysandmeans.house.gov/UploadedFiles/QFR_040314TR.pdf (last accessed 8 October 2015).

(ITA). This plurilateral instrument does away with the problematic issue of free riding in that although it applies on an MFN basis, only enter into force once a "critical mass" of WTO Members acceded to the agreement. This avenue was presumably not pursued as it could significantly delay the entry into force of the agreement.

The second option consists of pursuing, in accordance with Article X:9 of the WTO Agreement, the negotiation of a separate plurilateral trade agreement whose benefits would not be applied multilaterally but rather only to the participants to the agreements. Examples of such agreements include the WTO Government Procurement Agreement as well as the Agreement on Trade in Civil Aircraft, both of which are discriminatory agreements. Such an agreement would remove the issue of free riding whilst leaving the door open for WTO Members to accede and allowing the members of the plurilateral agreement to benefit from the WTO's dispute settlement mechanism. However, WTO Members wishing to follow this path face a considerable obstacle in the shape of Article X:9 of the WTO agreement which requires a consensus decision approving non-MFN plurilateral agreement. In other words, every single WTO Member has the power to veto the creation of a discriminatory plurilateral agreement within the WTO framework. In light of the known objections to the negotiation of the TISA by certain emerging economies this consensus requirement effectively ruled out the prospect of negotiating the TISA under the auspices of the WTO.

This being so, the TISA participants had little option but to plump for the third option—the negotiation of a PTA in accordance with Article V of GATS. According to this provision, WTO Members may be party to or enter into an agreement liberalizing trade in services, provided that such an agreement: (a) has substantial sectoral coverage, and (b) provides for the absence or elimination of substantially all discrimination. As things currently stand it could be argued that the TiSA may fail to comply with both of these cumulative conditions. Firstly, with respect to the "substantial sectoral coverage" condition, footnote to Article V:1 (a) GATS states that the "condition is understood in terms of numbers of sectors, volume of trade affected and modules of supply" and that "agreements should not provide for the a priori exclusion of any mode of supply". The requirement not to *a priori* exclude any mode of supply from a PTA reveals a desire to ensure that PTAs follow the GATS architecture but falls short of an outright prohibition on PTAs that deviate from GATS. Secondly, the reference to the "number of sectors" and "volume of trade affected" indicates that both quantitative and qualitative criteria must be taken into account when determining the extent to which a PTA has "substantial sectoral coverage". Here, again, very little guidance is given at GATS level as to what such quantitative or qualitative criteria might look like. In the context of Article XXIV GATT, the corresponding provision in the area of goods, which requires PTAs to eliminate restrictions to substantially all trade, a number of quantitative and qualitative criteria have been put forward by scholars and WTO Members alike to determine what constitutes 'substantially all trade'. The quantitative approach consists of setting the exact figure of percentage of trade that could be subject to internal restrictions. For example, in 1957, it was suggested by the European Economic Community that a "free trade area should be considered as having been achieved for substantially all the trade when the volume of liberalised trade reached 80 per cent of total trade".[62] More recently, Australia had suggested that internal restrictions should be eliminated on up to 95 % of all six-digit tariff lines listed in the Harmonized Commodity description and Coding System.[63] Other WTO Members have suggested complementing the quantitative criteria[64] with a qualitative approach imposing the abolition of trade restrictions on all major sectors of economic activities. There has been however, no agreement to date between WTO Members on the interpretation of the term "substantially". There is also very little guidance from the WTO adjudicatory bodies on this matter. For example, in *Turkey—Textiles* the Appellate Body noted that "substantially all the trade is something considerably more than merely some of the trade".[65] Moreover, the Appellate Body agreed with the Panel's finding that the assessment of this concept requires an analysis of both quantitative and qualitative criteria, but stopped short of setting out the criteria that should be taken into account for this purpose.[66]

As already discussed, at this stage, it would seem that the TiSA participants are unlikely to commit to the liberalisation of sensitive areas such as audiovisual and maritime transport services as well as Mode 4 services supply. Whilst the limited guidance provided by the GATS and the case law means that TiSA participants may have enough room for maneuver to exclude certain sectors or modes of supply in the TiSA, such exclusions would certainly open the door for the possibility of a successful legal challenge before the WTO.

Secondly, the requirement to ensure the absence or elimination of all discrimination means that at the very least, PTAs should secure liberalisation commitments that are GATS plus in nature.[67] However, as flagged by Adlung there is a very real danger that GATS minus features will be included in the TiSA.[68] Although the TISA negotiators have been keen to talk up their desire to offer liberalisation commitments that go significantly beyond GATS, PTA practice suggests that these WTO Members are by no means averse to incorporating language that reduce

[62] Report of the Sub-group Committee on the European Economic Community, L/778, adopted on 29 November 1957, 6S/70, para 30.

[63] Negotiating Group on Rules, Submission on Regional Trade Agreements by Australia, TN/RL/W/173/Rev1, 3 March 2005.

[64] Lockhart N, Mitchell AD (2005) Regional trade agreements under GATT 1994: an exception and its limits. In: Lockhart N, Mitchell AD (eds) Challenges and prospects for the WTO. Cameron May Ltd., p. 28.

[65] Appellate Body Report, Turkey—Restrictions on Imports of Textile and Clothing Products, para. 48.

[66] Appellate Body Report, Turkey—Restrictions on Imports of Textile and Clothing Products, para. 49.

[67] R. Adlung, The Trade in Services Agreement (TISA) and Its Compatibility with GATS: An Assessment Based on Current Evidence, World Trade Review 2015, pp. 19–22.

[68] R. Adlung, The Trade in Services Agreement (TISA) and Its Compatibility with GATS: An Assessment Based on Current Evidence, World Trade Review 2015, pp. 19–22.

the obligations and levels of commitments included in GATS. Examples of such practice include the reluctance of PTA parties to reproduce Article VI GATS on domestic regulation, the increased scope of the public utilities exemption in EU PTAs and the reduced level of Mode 4 commitments in US PTAs.[69] What is more, GATS minus features are currently being envisaged in relation to the TISA. For example, the EU intends to include language in the TISA that would limit commitments relating to health and social services to privately funded services.[70] Such language is not found in the EU's GATS schedules. Similarly, the EU's initial offer for the TiSA contains a horizontal exemption for subsidies[71] that exempts subsidies from national treatment. Finally, the EU's initial TiSA offer on financial services shows that it intends to deviate from GATS with regard to the treatment of 'new financial services'. The Understanding on Financial Services provides that WTO Members must "permit financial service suppliers of any other Member established in its territory to offer in its territory any new financial service".[72] This means that a home state is required to allow the supply of a new financial service provided in the territory of another WTO Member even if such services are not provided in the territory of the former.[73] However, EU's proposal reduces the scope of this obligation by adding that the host state is free to determine the juridical form through which the service may be provided and require an authorisation for the provision of the service.[74]

6 Multilateralising TiSA

The EU has issued a proposal for the architecture of the TISA which is intended to ensure that the agreement is conducive to multilateralisation.[75] The EU's plan is to subdivide the TiSA into two components: firstly, a central pillar which would replicate the entire text of GATS and, secondly, a series of chapters that would

[69] Stephenson S, Robert M (2011) Innovations of Regionalism in Services in the Americas. Swiss National Centre of Competence in Research (2011) NCCR Working Paper 2011/34 (June), www.nccr-trade.org (last accessed 8 October 2015), p. 8.

[70] European Commission (2013), EU Initial Offer—TiSA, November 2013.

[71] European Commission (2013), EU Initial Offer—TiSA, November 2013.

[72] Understanding on Commitments in Financial Services (1994), Uruguay Round Final Act, GATT Trade Negotiations Committee Document MTN/FA II-AIB, General Agreement on Trade in Services, (15 April 1994), p. 7.

[73] Tietje C, Finke J, Dietrich D (2010) Liberalization and Rules on Regulation in the Field of Financial Services in Bilateral Trade and Regional Integration Agreements, GTZ scientific study.

[74] European Commission, Proposal for a TiSA Annex on Financial Services, Article 13. http://trade.ec.europa.eu/doclib/docs/2014/july/tradoc_152688.pdf (last accessed 8 October 2015).

[75] European Commission (2012) A modular approach to the architecture of a plurilateral agreement on services September 2012, http://trade.ec.europa.eu/doclib/docs/2014/july/tradoc_152686.pdf (last accessed 8 October 2015).

complement existing GATS rules by providing additional rules and disciplines. The advantage of having two wholly separate components as part of this approach is that it would facilitate any future multilateralisation of the agreement. If the TiSA membership were to reach a critical mass, the outcome of the negotiations relating to the central pillar—that is, the specific commitments on national treatment and market access—would be easily transposable into the GATS framework. The commitments undertaken under the central pillar would therefore be multilateralised and apply on an MFN basis to all WTO members. With respect to the sector specific chapters, WTO Members could negotiate on an individual basis the incorporation of sector specific chapters within the WTO framework either repackaging such chapters as annexes to GATS or turning them into 'understandings' or 'reference papers' in accordance with Article XVIII GATS.

The architecture of the TiSA is therefore being conceived with the prospect of multilateralisation in mind. However, before the agreement can be brought within the WTO framework, its membership must reach a critical mass. The critical mass approach is one that was followed in the context of plurilateral trade instruments such as the Information Technology Agreement and the Reference Paper on Telecommunication Services whose benefits were extended to the entire WTO membership on a non-discriminatory basis once a significant proportion of WTO Members (a critical mass) had signed on the agreement.[76] In order to avoid free riding, the participants of agreements such as the ITA decided to hold back entry into force until the membership of the agreement amounted to 80–90 % of global trade in IT products.[77] However, as we have seen, in the context of the TiSA, the participants intend to pursue a different option. Rather than postponing entry into force of the agreement, the application of the MFN principle will be temporarily pushed back until a critical mass is reached.[78] How the TiSA intends to achieve and assess whether a critical mass has been reached and how the multilateralisation will occur are factors that are yet to be divulged by the TiSA participants. The EU has revealed that the parties intend to include an accession clause in the agreement that will be open to all WTO Members but has not specified what conditions will have to be met by countries wishing to accede.[79] The threshold for a critical mass has also not been identified, with concerns having been raised about whether the 90 % minimum threshold adopted with respect to previous agreements[80] would work in the context of trade in services.[81] TiSA participants currently account for

[76] Hoekman and Mavroidis (2015), pp. 101–116.

[77] Peng (2013), p. 627.

[78] European Commission, Memo, Negotiations for a Plurilateral Agreement on Trade in services, 15 February 2013, http://europa.eu/rapid/press-release_MEMO-13-107_en.htm (last accessed 21.10.2015), p. 4.

[79] European Commission (2013) The Trade in Services Agreement, http://trade.ec.europa.eu/doclib/docs/2013/June/tradoc_151374.pdf (last accessed 8 October 2015).

[80] Jones (2015), p. 105.

[81] Bosworth M (2014) The Proposed Non-MFN Trade in Services Agreement: Bad for Unilateralism, the WTO and the Multilateral Trading System, NCCR Trade Working Paper No. 2014/05, p. 27.

approximately 70 % the global trade in services[82]—some way short of the 90 % mark. However, as noted by Bosworth, a minimum 90 % threshold may not be fit for purpose in the context of the TiSA to the extent that the global share of trade in services is typically assessed by taking into account cross-border trade only, rather than other modes of supply such as commercial presence. The argument is that the TiSA participants should set the critical mass threshold at a lower level.[83]

That being said, the identity of the TiSA participants may ultimately prove to be just as relevant as the share of trade in services that these countries represent. Currently, the countries negotiating TiSA are, by and large, developed and industrialised nations (mostly OECD members) whilst most emerging economies and developing countries remain on the outside looking in. In other words, those countries appear to have maintained their position adopted in the context of the WTO—that is, not to engage in any negotiations relating to trade in services. The participation of emerging economies, in particular, may prove to be the most important factor in the eventual multilateralisation of the TiSA. Firstly, it is unlikely that the TiSA participants would allow larger emerging economies such as China, India and Brazil to free ride on the benefits of TiSA without making corresponding liberalisation commitments. Secondly, the participation of large emerging economies would effectively confirm the status of the TiSA as a truly global trade agreement and the prospect of seeing their firms being discriminated against in accessing the largest markets in the world may cause reluctant WTO Members to reconsider their positions.

However, on this issue, it is worth noting that despite the fact that China made clear its desire to join the TiSA negotiations back in 2013,[84] TiSA participants such as the US have held back on bringing China into the fray. Such reticence seems to be borne out of concerns, based on the difficult experience of the negotiation of the ITA, that China's conservative stance with respect participation in negotiations on services liberalisation negotiations could undermine the progress of TiSA negotiations.[85] It may also reflect the fact that some of the major proponents of the TiSA are quite happy to keep the TiSA primarily as an OECD-led club during negotiations. This would allow them to negotiate an agreement that reflects their interests and provide WTO Members wishing to accede the agreement in the future with a

---

[82] See European Parliament, Working Document on Recommendations to the European Commission on the negotiations for the Trade in Services Agreement (TiSA), Committee on International Trade, DT/1071748EN.Doc, 4 September 2015.

[83] Bosworth M (2014) The Proposed Non-MFN Trade in Services Agreement: Bad for Unilateralism, the WTO and the Multilateral Trading System, NCCR Trade Working Paper No. 2014/05, p. 27.

[84] Bridges Weekly, Services Talks Advance as TISA Members Prepare to Exchange Offers (26 September 2013) http://www.ictsd.org/bridges-news/bridges/news/services-talks-advance-as-tisa-members-prepare-to-exchange-offers (last accessed 8 October 2015).

[85] Bosworth M (2014) The Proposed Non-MFN Trade in Services Agreement: Bad for Unilateralism, the WTO and the Multilateral Trading System, NCCR Trade Working Paper No. 2014/05, p. 16; Raman (2014), p. 125.

simple choice to either opt-in or opt-out. It is an approach that comes with risks because whilst it may be true that smaller developing nations will have little choice but to accept the terms of an eventual agreement, this may not hold true for larger economies who would happily remain outside the scope of the TiSA if its terms are deemed unfavourable.[86] The upshot is that by excluding certain countries from current negotiations, the TiSA participants may ultimately undermine the agreement's chances of being multilateralised and ensure that the regulatory system for international trade in services remains fragmented in the long term.

In light of the above, it may be worth assessing how WTO Members not currently participating in TiSA negotiations may be tempted to join the agreement in the future. In order to attract those developing countries that rejected GATS reform proposals during the Doha round, the negotiators of the TiSA will have to devise an agreement that will give these countries a reason to accede the TiSA. Based on current evidence, the TiSA is unlikely to possess such attributes. Firstly, the priorities of the TiSA naturally reflect the offensive interests of its proponents. The emphasis has been placed on the expansion of market access for sectors such as financial services and telecommunication services that are of interests to developed countries, whilst areas that would address the demands of developing country WTO Members, notably Mode 4 liberalisation, are left relatively untouched. Secondly, so far, the TiSA participants have failed to mention the possibility of including legal mechanisms that would allow some form of differentiation in favour of developing countries. One of the problematic issues surrounding the liberalisation of trade in services at multilateral level stems from the assumption that the rationale for liberalisation in trade in goods—that is, that free trade is welfare inducing as it allows countries to better exploit their comparative advantages—holds for other sectors of economic activity. Yet, it is wrong to apply such reasoning to services markets which are heterogeneous and where trade liberalisation does not necessarily lead to welfare gains.[87] In fact, there is ample evidence to suggest that increased competition in services market can in certain cases reduce welfare.[88] The liberalisation and introduction of competition in the financial services market, for example, can be detrimental in developing countries, as in most cases the domestic industry is weak.[89] Liberalisation may tempt depositors to switch their custom to foreign financial institutions and increased competition could lead domestic banks to take more risks, potentially leading to a collapse of the national banking system.[90] Providing for an asymmetrical liberalisation feature that would allow for transitional periods during which the developing countries can progressively liberalise and economic sectors where commitments have been made would be welcome and may address some of the lingering concerns developing countries have with regard to the TiSA.

---

[86] Hoekman and Mavroidis (2015), p. 108.

[87] Whalley (2004), pp. 1223, 1231.

[88] Hay (2007), pp. 25, 39.

[89] Stiglitz (2000), pp. 443–445.

[90] Stiglitz (2000), p. 444.

On a related note, given the emphasis of the agreement on regulatory barriers, the TiSA could also allow differentiation with respect to the implementation of the regulatory disciplines included in those agreements. These pro-competitive regulatory disciplines, whilst broad, have the potential to significantly undermine regulatory autonomy. For example, as pointed out by Krajewski, the requirement that interconnection rates be "cost-oriented" may undermine the ability of governments to apply additional charges to fund universal services obligations.[91] Likewise, the obligation to maintain independent regulators can be problematic in countries whose constitutions require parliamentary accountability of administrative bodies.[92] In addition, the domestic reforms that are entailed could prove very time-consuming and costly for developing countries—something that may act as disincentive for prospective WTO Members considering whether or not to join TISA. In order to ensure an element of differentiation with respect to regulatory disciplines, the TiSA participants may wish to draw inspiration from the Reference Paper on Telecommunication Services whose impact is lessened by the fact that it provides a significant degree of flexibility for WTO Members. Indeed, WTO Members have the option to select which specific regulatory principles they wish to be bound by or even modify the Reference Paper in their commitments so as to reflect their particular interests and needs.[93]

Another factor that has played a key role in undermining efforts towards further multilateral liberalisation of trade in services is the fear harboured by governments that the opening of domestic markets could prove detrimental to the national economy, if not accompanied by the adoption of appropriate regulatory reforms to ensure that countries are able to reap the rewards of liberalisation whilst also ensuring that equity concerns are addressed.[94] In this context, domestic regulatory reform improving the contestability of markets and addressing equity concerns is a pre-requisite for the opening of services markets. The TiSA should therefore ensure that regulatory reforms conducted by developing countries as a result of compliance with the agreement are facilitated and supported by the membership. This could be achieved by establishing legal and institutional framework that sets the platform for regulatory cooperation through dialogue, the dissemination of information and technical assistance and capacity building. Cooperation between regulatory authorities should also be complemented by aid programs to assist countries in conducting regulatory reform and improve institutional capabilities.[95]

---

[91] Krajewski (2006), p. 176.

[92] Krajewski (2006), p. 171.

[93] Cowhey and Klimenko (2002), p. 275.

[94] Hoekman B and Mattoo A (2011) Services Trade Liberalization and Regulatory Reform: Re-invigorating International Cooperation, World Bank, Policy Research Working Paper 5517, p. 10.

[95] Hoekman B, Messerlin PA (1999) Liberalising Trade in Services: Reciprocal Negotiations and Regulatory Reform. World Bank and CEPR, 5 July 1999; Hoekman, et al (2007), p. 367; Hoekman B and Mattoo A (2011) Services Trade Liberalization and Regulatory Reform: Re-invigorating International Cooperation, World Bank, Policy Research Working Paper 5517, p. 10.

7 Conclusion

Given the lack of transparency that characterises trade negotiations, discussing a trade agreement in the making is, at best, an exercise in hopeful speculation. In this respect, the TiSA is certainly no exception. However, based on the little information that is available at this stage, it is not unreasonable to suggest that TiSA's proponents do not necessarily view the agreement as an opportunity to develop particularly innovative mechanisms for the liberalisation of trade in services, nor as a vehicle to address some of the unresolved issues that have blighted the progress of negotiations at the WTO level. Instead, the reality of the TiSA negotiations is far more mundane and the objectives pursued fundamentally utilitarian: the enhancement of market opening commitments in areas where developed countries have offensive interests, the liberalisation of new services areas and the enshrinement of broad regulatory principles on transparency and competition. The end product of the ongoing negotiations will most likely consist in the plurilateralisation of the PTAs concluded by the likes of the EU and the US in the past 2 decades. There is, of course, value in this approach. A trade agreement comprising a wide coalition of WTO members, whilst not ideal, may be preferable to the trade diversion and fragmentation resulting from the proliferation bilateral and regional PTAs. Furthermore, the inclusion of sector specific disciplines promoting competition and transparency of the type found in EU and US PTAs are GATS plus features that may prove to be beneficial for developing nations so long as these are complemented by appropriate support in the form of technical assistance, capacity building and regulatory cooperation.

Nevertheless, contrary the rhetoric coming from its proponents, the future multilateralisation of the TiSA should not be taken for granted. Indeed, despite the change of venue—from a multilateral to a plurilateral setting—the same problems that undermined trade in services negotiations at WTO level remain in the context of the TiSA. The major large emerging economies, the ringleaders of the opposition to GATS reforms, remain uninvolved in the negotiations. Certain TiSA participants have recoiled at the prospect of China joining the talks for fear that its demands might prove to be unpalatable for some and derail the process.[96] Meanwhile, other BRICS states such as Brazil and India have not waivered in their skepticism towards the TiSA.[97] It is also very telling that, even within the exclusive group of RGF, there are reports of disagreements mirroring those that existed at WTO level—with developed countries unwilling to open their markets in areas that are of interest to developing countries. This is where the strategy of plurilateralising EU and US PTAs may ultimately fall short. If the TiSA is viewed purely as a means to avoid cumbersome resistance from developing countries at the WTO level and

[96] Hufbauer G, Jung E, Miner S, Moran T, Schott J (2015) From Drift to Deals: Advancing the WTO Agenda. Peterson Institute for International Economics Report, June 2015, p. 31.

[97] Hufbauer G, Jung E, Miner S, Moran T, Schott J (2015) From Drift to Deals: Advancing the WTO Agenda. Peterson Institute for International Economics Report, June 2015, p. 31.

push through the disciplines put forward by a select group of advanced industrialised nations, it is very possible that instead of being seen as the event that reinvigorated WTO negotiations on services, the TiSA's major achievement will be to cement the already existing rift within the WTO membership.

References

Adlung R (2015) The Trade in Services Agreement (TISA) and its compatibility with GATS: an assessment based on current evidence. World Trade Rev 2015:1–25. doi:10.1017/S1474745615000294

Cowhey P, Klimenko M (2002) Telecommunications reform in developing countries after the WTO agreement on basic telecommunications services. J Int Dev 12(2):265–281

Feketekuty G (2000) Regulatory reform and trade liberalization in services. In: Sauve P, Stern R (eds) GATS 2000 – new directions in services trade liberalization. The Brookings institution press, Washington, pp 225–240

Godsoe H (2014) The depth of the trade in services agreement. Int Law Manag Rev 10(1):1–27

Hay C (2007) Keynote article: what doesn't kill you can only make you stronger: the Doha development round, the services directive and the EU's conception of competitiveness. J Common Mark Stud 45:25–43

Hoekman B, Mavroidis P (2015) Embracing diversity: plurilateral agreements and the trading system. World Trade Rev 14(1):101–116

Hoekman B, Mattoo A, Sapir A (2007) The political economy of services trade liberalization: a case for international cooperation? Oxford Rev Econ Policy 23(3):367–391

Jackson J (1988) International competition in services: a constitutional framework (AEI Studies). AEI Press, Washington

Jones K (2015) Reconstructing the world trade organization for the 21st century. Oxford University Press, Oxford

Krajewski M (2006) Services liberalization in trade agreements. In: Bartels L, Ortino F (eds) Regional trade agreements and the WTO. Oxford University Press, Oxford, pp 175–201

Lester S, Barbee I (2013) The challenge of cooperation: regulatory trade barriers in the transatlantic trade and investment partnership. J Int Econ Law 16(4):847–867

Marchetti J, Roy M (2009) Summary and overview. In: Marchetti J, Roy M (eds) Opening markets for trade in services: countries and sectors in bilateral and WTO negotiations. Cambridge University Press, Cambridge, pp 1–5

Marchetti J, Roy M (2008) Services liberalization in the WTO and in the PTAs. In: Marchetti J, Roy M (eds) Opening markets for trade in services: countries and sectors in bilateral and WTO negotiations. Cambridge University Press, Cambridge, pp 61–113

Marchetti J, Mavroidis P (2004) What are the main challenges for the GATS framework? Don't talk about revolution. Eur Bus Organ Law Rev 5(3):511–562

Melo Araujo B (2014) Regulating services trade agreements - a comparative analysis of regulatory disciplines included in EU and US free trade agreements. Trade Law Dev 6(2):393–416

Panizzon M (2010) International law of economic migration - a ménage à trois? GATS Mode 4, EPAs and Bilateral Migration Agreements. J World Trade 44(6):1207–1252

Peng S (2013) Is the Trade in Services Agreement (TiSA) a stepping stone for the next version of GATS? Hong Kong Law J 43(2):611–632

Raman H (2014) Implication of TISA on trade of services. J Polit Gov 3(4):121–128

Sauve P, Shingal A (2014) Introduction and overview. In: Sauve P, Shingal A (eds) The preferential liberalization of trade in services: comparative regionalism. Edward Elgar, Cheltenham, pp 1–5

Sauve P (2014) Towards a plurilateral Trade in Services Agreement (TISA): challenges and prospects. journal of international commerce. Econ Policy 5(1):1–16

Stiglitz JE (2000) Two principles for the next round or, how to bring developing countries in from the cold. World Econ 23(4):437–454

Sykes A (1999) The (limited) role of regulatory harmonization in international goods and services market. J Int Econ Law 2(1):49–70

Trachtman J (2003) Lessons for the GATS from existing WTO rules on domestic regulation. In: Mattoo A, Sauve P (eds) Domestic regulation and service trade liberalization. World Bank/ Oxford University Press, Oxford, pp 57–82

Whalley J (2004) Assessing the benefits to developing countries of liberalisation in services trade. World Econ 27(8):1223–1253

Part III
International Economic Institutions

Overview of WTO Jurisprudence in 2014

Jan Bohanes, Alejandro Sánchez, and Alexandra Telychko

Contents

J. Bohanes (✉) • A. Sánchez • A. Telychko
Advisory Centre on WTO Law, Avenue Giuseppe Motta 31-33, 1211 Geneva 30, Switzerland
e-mail: Jan.Bohanes@acwl.ch; Alejandro.Sanchez@acwl.ch; alexandra.telychko@me.com

M. Bungenberg et al. (eds.), *European Yearbook of International Economic Law 2016*, European Yearbook of International Economic Law 7,
DOI 10.1007/978-3-319-29215-1_30

Abstract This article presents an overview of the reports (judgments) of panels and the Appellate Body of the World Trade Organization (WTO) circulated in 2014. For each report, we present the key findings on the most salient issues as well as, where appropriate, observations on the systemic significance on a given finding. 2014 was a very busy year for the WTO dispute settlement system. 11 panel reports were circulated, and except for one of these 11 disputes, all of them were appealed to the Appellate Body. The Appellate Body issued five reports in 2014, four of which related to a panel report issued in 2014. One appeal related to a panel report was issued the previous year, in 2013, namely, the EU – Seals dispute. The disputes covered a broad range of issues, including anti-dumping and countervailing duties; import restrictions; sanitary and phytosanitary measures; publication requirements; and import restrictions on agricultural products.

1 WTO Jurisprudence in 2014 at a Quick Glance

2014 was a very busy year for the WTO dispute settlement system. In 2014, eleven panel reports were circulated, namely *China – Anti-Dumping and Countervailing Duties on Certain Automobiles from the United States* (DS440); *US – Countervailing and Anti-Dumping Measures (China)* (DS449); *US – Country of Origin Labelling (COOL) (21.5)* (DS384, 386); *India – Measures Concerning the Importation of Certain Agricultural Products* (DS430); *US – Anti-dumping Measures on Certain Shrimp from Viet Nam* (DS429); *US – Countervailing Measures on Certain Products from China* (DS437); *US – Countervailing Measures on Certain Hot-rolled Carbon Steel Flat Products from India* (DS436); *China – Measures Relating to the Exportation of Rare Earths, Tungsten and Molybdenum* (DS431, 432, 433); *US – Countervailing and Anti-dumping Measures on Certain Products from China* (DS449); *Argentina – Measures Affecting the Importation of Goods* (DS438, 444, 445); and *Peru – Additional Duty on Imports of Certain Agricultural Products* (DS457).

Of these 11 panel reports circulated in 2014, all but one—namely, *China – Anti-Dumping and Countervailing Duties on Certain Automobiles from the United States* (DS440)—were appealed and in four of those instances, the Appellate Body Report was also issued in 2014.[1] Together with one Appellate Body Report relating to a panel report issued in 2013 (*EC – Seals*), this brings the total number of Appellate Body Reports issued in 2014 to five.

The Agreements interpreted and applied in this disputes are primarily the *Agreement on Subsidies and Countervailing Measures ("SCM Agreement")*, the General Agreement on Tariff and Trade 1994 (the "GATT 1994"), the *Agreement on Technical Barriers to Trade* (*"TBT Agreement"*), the *Agreement on Implementation of Article VI of the General Agreement on Tariffs and Trade 1994 (the "Anti-dumping Agreement")* and the *Agreement on Agriculture.*

As in previous years, the 2014 case law has its fair share of trade remedies, that is, anti-dumping and countervailing duties. Even the dispute in *US – Countervailing and Anti-Dumping Measures (China)* (DS449), which focussed primarily on Articles X:1 and X:2 of the GATT 1994, ultimately concerned the application of trade remedy measures in the US domestic system, namely, the politically contentious issues of applying countervailing duties to non-market economies (NMEs).

On the non-trade remedy side, some remarkable case law has come out of the *Argentina – Measures Affecting the Importation of Goods* dispute, especially certain findings on unwritten measures; as well as *China – Measures Relating to the Exportation of Rare Earths, Tungsten and Molybdenum*, concerning the status of precedent as well as the relationship between China's Protocol of Accession and the WTO Agreement and the GATT 1994. The dispute *Peru – Additional Duty on Imports of Certain Agricultural Products* (DS457) featured extensive arguments by both parties about the legal import of a free-trade agreement (FTA) for the interpretation and application of WTO law; however, the panel largely sidestepped the issues, since the FTA was not yet in force.

2 US – Cool (21.5)—Panel Report

2.1 *Facts of the Case*

These proceedings are the continuation of the original *US – COOL* dispute initiated by Canada and Mexico concerning the US country of origin labelling requirements ("COOL measure").[2] In 2012, the Appellate Body declared this measure

[1] *US – Countervailing and Anti-Dumping Measures (China)* (DS449); *US – Countervailing and Anti-dumping Measures on Certain Products from China* (DS449); *US – Countervailing Measures on Certain Products from China* (DS437); and *China – Measures Relating to the Exportation of Rare Earths, Tungsten and Molybdenum* (DS431, 432, 433).

[2] *US – Country of Origin Labelling (COOL) (21.5)* (DS384,386).

WTO-inconsistent. Subsequently, Canada and Mexico alleged that the United States failed to properly comply with the Appellate Body's findings and, thus, initiated compliance proceedings pursuant to Article 21.5 of the Dispute Settlement Understanding ("DSU").

In terms of substance, the amended COOL measure was largely similar to the original COOL measure. The original measure required retailers to affix a label on certain commodities to indicate their country origin, which was determined according to the country where the animal was born, raised and slaughtered. Four different labels were established for this purpose (A, B, C and D). Label B, for example, referred to multiple countries of origin, and read "Product of country X, product of the US". The amended COOL measures retained this general structure, but rather than requiring that labels simply list the different countries involved in the production, it required an indication of the specific production steps that took place in each country.[3]

2.2 Salient Legal Findings

The Panel found that the amended COOL measure was inconsistent with the national treatment obligation of Article 2.1 of the TBT Agreement. Like in the original case, however, the Panel rejected the complainant's claims under Article 2.2 of the TBT Agreement that the COOL measures are more trade restrictive than necessary.

2.2.1 The Amended Cool Measure is Inconsistent with Article 2.1 of the TBT Agreement

Article 2.1 of the TBT Agreement stipulates: "Members shall ensure that in respect of technical regulations, products imported from the territory of any Member shall be accorded treatment no less favourable than that accorded to like products of national origin". This provision, thus, incorporates a national treatment and most-favoured-nation obligation into the context of technical regulations.

Canada and Mexico argued that, just like the original COOL measure, the amended COOL measure was inconsistent with Article 2.1 of the TBT Agreement since it provides treatment less favourable to imported livestock than that accorded to domestic livestock.

The Panel agreed with the complainants. At the outset, the Panel recalled that, according to the Appellate Body's guidance in *US – Clove Cigarettes*, the "less favourable treatment" clause in Article 2.1 involves analysing, first, whether the

[3] For example, under the amended COOL measure, Label B read "Born and raised in Mexico, Raised and Slaughtered in the United States".

technical regulation modifies the conditions of competition to the detriment of imported products vis-à-vis like domestic products, and, second, whether any such detrimental impact does stem exclusively from legitimate regulatory distinctions.[4] Under this standard, even if a technical regulation is discriminatory, it may still be in conformity with Article 2.1 of the TBT Agreement if it truly pursues a legitimate objective.

Concerning the existence of detrimental impact, the Panel found that, compared to the original COOL measure, the amended COOL measure exacerbates the source of the less favourable treatment, that is, the need for segregating meat and livestock. Because the amended COOL measure requires that labels indicate the exact country where each individual production steps took place (i.e. where the cattle was born, raised and slaughtered) upstream producers need to keep even more precise production records. The Panel thus concluded that "the amended COOL measure increases the practical necessity for private actors to choose domestic over imported livestock, and has an increased negative effect on the competitive conditions of imported livestock in the US market".[5] In light of these considerations, the Panel found that the amended COOL measure entails increased detrimental impact on imported livestock.

The second part of the analysis of "less favourable treatment" under Article 2.1 involved examining whether the detrimental impact stems exclusively from legitimate regulatory distinctions. The Panel noted a "disconnect" between the informational requirements imposed on upstream producers and the information effectively communicated to consumers. It stated that "although the amended COOL measure increases the information communicated to consumers through mandatory retail labels, it necessarily increases the associated upstream informational (recordkeeping) requirements in order to do so."[6] The Panel therefore concluded that "under the particular circumstances of this case, the detrimental impact caused by the amended COOL measure does not stem exclusively from legitimate regulatory distinctions".[7]

The Panel's ultimate conclusion was that the amended COOL measure was inconsistent with Article 2.1 of the TBT Agreement.

It is worth noting that this Panel followed the standard for Article 2.1 of the TBT Agreement set out in 2012 by the Appellate Body in *US – Clove Cigarettes*. To recall, the Appellate Body in that dispute was faced with the issue of whether Article 2.1 of the TBT Agreement gives parties policy space to pursue legitimate objectives even though the TBT Agreement lacks any "general exceptions" clause akin to Article XX of the GATT 1994. The Appellate Body found that a measure that causes a detrimental impact on imported products would not violate Article 2.1 if that detrimental impact stems exclusively from a legitimate regulatory

[4] Panel Report, *US – COOL (21.5)*, paras. 7.60–7.62.

[5] Panel Report, *US – COOL (21.5)*, para. 7.167.

[6] Panel Report, *US – COOL (21.5)*, para. 7.266.

[7] Panel Report, *US – COOL (21.5)*, para. 7.283 (emphasis added).

distinction. The Appellate Body's approach does not flow from the text of any provision of the TBT Agreement, but rather from its object, context and purpose. The Panel in the 21.5 proceedings in *US – COOL* followed this approach by first examining whether a detrimental impact exists, and then whether such impact stems exclusively from a legitimate regulatory distinction.

The Panel's application of the Appellate Body's legal standard, however, reveals that the second part of the analysis—whether the detrimental impact stems exclusively from a legitimate regulatory distinction—remains ambiguously broad. This element basically seeks to elucidate whether the reason behind the discrimination is legitimate or illegitimate. The Panel's finding that the measure's detrimental impact does not stem exclusively from a legitimate regulatory distinction was largely based on the "disconnect" between the burdensome informational requirements and the minor increase of information communicated to consumers. While this "disconnect" demonstrates the imbalance between the measure's restrictiveness and the low contribution to its objective, it is unclear why this meant that the discrimination does not stem from legitimate reasons. In order to give clarity and predictability to WTO Members on the content of the obligation under Article 2.1, it is important for the Appellate Body to clarify the precise contours of this second element of the interpretative analysis that it has developed under Article 2.1.

2.2.2 The Complainants Did Not Make a Prima Facie Case of Inconsistency with Article 2.2 of the TBT Agreement

The complainants also claimed that the amended COOL measure violates Article 2.2 of the TBT Agreement because it is more trade-restrictive than necessary to fulfill a legitimate objective.

In the original proceedings, the complainants' claim under Article 2.2 was rejected by the Appellate Body. These compliance proceedings gave the complainants a second opportunity to obtain a finding of inconsistency with Article 2.2 of the TBT Agreement with respect to the COOL measure, albeit in its amended form.

Article 2.2 is another provision of the TBT Agreement that, until a few years ago, had never been interpreted by the Appellate Body. In 2012, in the context of the dispute *US – Tuna II (Mexico)*, the Appellate Body had the first opportunity to clarify the meaning of the core obligation of Article 2.2: "technical regulations shall not be more trade-restrictive than necessary to fulfill a legitimate objective, taking account of the risks that non-fulfillment would create". As clarified by the Appellate Body, an analysis under Article 2.2 should consider (i) the measure's trade restrictiveness; (ii) the contribution made by the measure towards the country's objective; and (iii) the risks that would arise if the measure does not fulfill the country's objective.[8] On the basis of these three criteria, a Panel may conclude, for example, that the challenged measure is more trade-restrictive than necessary because it is

[8] Appellate Body Report, *US – Tuna II (Mexico)*, paras. 311–323.

highly trade-restrictive, makes a low contribution to the government's policy objective, and the non-fulfillment of the objective would not give rise to serious consequences. This is called a "relational analysis". Panels may complement this analysis with a "comparative analysis", which examines the measure's necessity in light of available alternative measures that the regulating country could have adopted.

It should be noted that, to date, no claim under Article 2.2 has been successful. As the present dispute demonstrates, the above legal standard requires certain factual findings that, in certain cases, a panel may hesitate to make.

The Panel began by conducting the aforementioned "relational analysis", recalling first that the amended COOL measure pursues the same objective as the original COOL measure, i.e. to provide consumer information on origin. While it found that the measure makes some contribution to this objective, and is trade restrictive, the Panel encountered problems with examining the measure's risks of non-fulfilment. The Panel indicated that, based on the evidence submitted, it was unable to ascertain the gravity of not fulfilling the amended COOL measure's objective. For this reason, the Panel noted that it was unable to "draw [] definitive conclusions on the complainants' Article 2.2 claims".[9] The Panel, thus, proceeded to conduct the comparative analysis under Article 2.2. To recall, this analysis entails examining alternative measures that the regulating Member could have adopted instead of the incriminated measure.

The Panel's comparative analysis consisted of examining the four alternative measures submitted by Canada and Mexico. These alternative measures all consisted of modifications to the COOL measure, such as converting certain of its mandatory elements into voluntary options for producers, and imposing a "trace-back" system which involves documenting the precise location of each production step, even if the entire production took place within the United States.

The Panel rejected all four alternative measures. In essence, the Panel found that the complainants: (i) failed to demonstrate and to explain how such measures would make an equivalent contribution to the United States objective; (ii) failed adequately to identify the content of the alternatives; and (ii) failed to explain how the alternative measures would be implemented in the United States. The complainants, therefore, were unable to demonstrate that the amended COOL measure is more trade-restrictive than necessary because, as they alleged, the US had at its disposal other less trade-restrictive means to achieve its objective of consumer information.

The Panel's overall conclusion was that the complainants did not make a *prima facie* case that the amended COOL measure violates Article 2.2 of the TBT Agreement.

The Panel's findings leave a strange aftertaste. The Panel seems to have imposed on the complainants too strict a standard concerning the identification and explanation of the alternative measures. This is particularly the case of the third and fourth alternative measures where the Panel considered that the complainants had failed to adequately identify the alternative measures and explain how they could be

---

[9] Appellate Body Report, *US – Tuna II (Mexico)*, para. 7.424.

implemented in the United States. This begs the question of what degree of precision complainants should adopt when identifying alternative measures under Article 2.2. In 2011, the panel in *US – Clove Cigarettes* faulted Indonesia for not adequately identifying the alternative measures since "Indonesia simply list [ed] numerous different measures, mostly in bullet point form".[10] It is clear that mere enumeration in bullet point form does not permit a Panel to properly examine the alternative measures. That would appear to be a fair interpretation and application of the law consistent with due process.

In the instant dispute, however, Canada and Mexico explained in detail the substance of their alternative measures. The Panel found that their level of detail was insufficient. The implications of this finding are somewhat worrying. The comparative analysis is a conceptual tool that allows panels to make an overall determination as to whether the challenged technical regulation is more trade restrictive than necessary. Complaining parties are obliged to indicate with reasonable precision the content of their proposed alternative measure. However, they are not required to present a detailed blueprint of how the alternative measure would in fact be implemented by the responding party. This would be an excessive burden on complaining parties that would make even harder to obtain a finding of inconsistency under Article 2.2 of the TBT Agreement. It may be noted that in five disputes, including Article 21.5 proceedings, no complainant has been successful with a claim under Article 2.2. Actual and potential complainants will soon start wondering whether it is at all possible to win a claim under Article 2.2.

3 EC – Seal Products: Appellate Body Report

3.1 Facts of the Case

The Appellate Body heard appeals from the complaining parties (Canada and Norway) and for the respondent (the EU) concerning the Panel's report in this dispute.

Canada and Norway challenged certain EU measures that affect the sale of seal products (the "EU Seal Regime"). The seal products at issue include those processed or unprocessed, deriving or obtained from seals, including meat, oil, blubber, organs, raw fur skins and tanned fur skins, as well as articles (such as clothing and accessories, and omega-3 capsules) made from fur skins and oil.

Under the EU Seal Regime, the placing of seal products on the EU market is prohibited unless the seal products: (i) result from hunts traditionally conducted by Inuit and other indigenous communities ("IC exception"); (ii) are brought in by travellers for their personal use ("Travellers exception"); or (iii) are by-products of

[10] Panel Report, *US – Clove Cigarettes*, para. 7.422.

hunting conducted for the sole purpose of sustainable management of marine resources ("MRM exception").

The Panel found that the EU Seal Regime contravenes the national treatment and the most-favoured-nation ("MFN") obligations under Article 2.1 of the TBT Agreement, but rejected the claim under Article 2.2 that the measure is more trade restrictive than necessary. For the same reasons, the Panel found violations of the national treatment and MFN obligations under GATT Articles I:1 and III:4, respectively. As an affirmative defence, the EU unsuccessfully invoked the general exception under Article XX(a), which permits measures necessary to protect public morals.

A detailed summary of the findings of the panel in *EC – Seals* can be found in last year's edition of the Yearbook.[11]

3.2 *Salient Legal Findings*

The Appellate Body found that the Panel erred in concluding that the EU Seal Regime is a technical regulation under Annex 1.1 of the TBT Agreement, and thus declared moot and of no legal effect all of the Panel's findings under the TBT Agreement. The Appellate Body upheld the Panel's findings of violation under Articles I:1 and III:4 of the GATT 1994, but found that the EU Seal Regime is not justified under Article XX(a) of the GATT 1994.

3.2.1 The Measure at Issue Is Not a Technical Regulation Within the Meaning of Annex 1.1 of the TBT Agreement

A threshold issue in any claim under the TBT Agreement is the determination of whether the challenged measure falls within the definition of one of the three types of measures covered by the TBT Agreement: "technical regulation", "standard", or "conformity assessment procedures". Annex 1.1 of the TBT Agreement defines "technical regulation" as follows:

> Document which lays down product characteristics or their related processes and production methods, including the applicable administrative provisions, with which compliance is mandatory. It may also include or deal exclusively with terminology, symbols, packaging, marking or labelling requirements as they apply to a product, process or production method.

The Appellate Body has clarified that a measure qualifies as a "technical regulation" if it satisfies three criteria: (i) it applies to an identifiable product or

[11] Bohanes and Salcedo (2015), pp. 354–363.

group of products; (ii) it lays down product characteristics; and (iii) compliance with the product characteristics is mandatory.[12]

In the instant dispute, the controversy was whether the EU seal regime satisfied the second of the above elements, that is, whether it lays down product characteristics. The particular structure of the EU seal regime made it difficult to ascertain this point. It established rules for the importation of seal products in three ways: (i) it prohibited the marketing of products consisting exclusively of seal; (ii) it prohibited the marketing of seal-containing products; and (iii) it set out the conditions under the three exceptions to sell seal products in the EU market (the travellers exception, the IC exception, and the MRM exception). The Panel acknowledged that the EU's measure contained both permissive and prohibitive elements. Relying on the Appellate Body's guidance in *EC – Asbestos*, the Panel concluded that the EU seal regime was a technical regulation because it "lays down a product characteristic in the negative form by requiring that all products not contain seal".[13]

The EU requested the Appellate Body to reverse the Panel's decision that the measure satisfies the definition of "technical regulation" contained in Annex 1.1 of the TBT Agreement. According to the EU, the Panel erred in not considering the various aspects of the measure at issue.

The Appellate Body agreed with the EU. It noted that while the EU Seal Regime comprised permissive and prohibitive elements, the Panel's conclusion that the measure constitutes a technical regulation rests on an assessment of only one prohibitive element, i.e. the prohibition on the marketing of seal-containing products. The Appellate Body observed that such prohibition is not the "main feature of the measure",[14] but rather "is but one of the components of the EU Seal Regime and has to be analysed together with other components of the measure before reaching a conclusion under Annex 1.1".[15] The Appellate Body concluded that the main feature of the EU Seal Regime is the establishment of conditions for placing seal products on the EU market "based on criteria relating to the identity of the hunter or the type or purpose of the hunt from which the product is derived".[16] The Appellate Body thus concluded that the measure as a whole does not lay down product characteristics.

Following common practice in WTO appellate proceedings, the complaining parties requested in advance that, if the Appellate Body were to reverse the Panel's findings that the EU Seal Regime lays down product characteristics, the Appellate Body complete the legal analysis under Annex I.1 of the TBT Agreement. However, as happens not infrequently, the Appellate Body was unable to complete the

---

[12] Appellate Body Report, EC – Asbestos, paras. 66–70; See also Appellate Body Report, *EC – Sardines*, para. 176; Appellate Body Report, *US – Tuna II (Mexico)*, para 183.

[13] Appellate Body Report, *EC – Seal Products*, para. 5.25 (quoting the Panel Report, *EC – Seal Products*, para. 7.106).

[14] Appellate Body Report, *EC – Seal Products*, para. 5.58.

[15] Appellate Body Report, *EC – Seal Products*, para. 5.39.

[16] Appellate Body Report, *EC – Seal Products*, para. 5.58.

legal analysis because it considered that the Panel had not sufficiently explored certain relevant factual issues.

Having concluded that the EU Seal Regime falls outside the scope of the TBT Agreement, the Appellate Body declared moot and of no legal effect the Panel's findings under Articles 2.1 and 2.2 of the TBT Agreement, as well as those under 5.1.2 and 5.2.1, which refer to procedures applied by the EU to assess the conformity of the EU Seal Regime, and which only apply to the extent that the underlying measure constitutes a technical regulation.

The Appellate Body's finding that the EU Seal Regime is not a technical regulation thus meant the end of the complainant's claims under the TBT Agreement. This finding came as a surprise to many. In previous rulings, the Appellate Body had signaled its willingness to interpret broadly the concept of "technical regulation". For example, in *US – Tuna II (Mexico)*, it found that a dolphin-safe label was "mandatory" (and thus a "technical regulation") even though producers were not required to obtain it as a condition for selling their tuna in the US market. In contrast, the finding that the EU Seal Regime was not a technical regulation was based on a narrow application of the concept "[d]ocument which lays down product characteristics". This finding may be an attempt by the Appellate Body to limit the application of the TBT Agreement to a small category of measures.

As discussed in next section, however, the finding that the EU Seal Regime is not a technical regulation did not affect the claims under Articles I:1 and III:4 of the GATT 1994.

3.2.2 The Appellate Body Upheld the Panel's Findings That the EU Seal Regime is Inconsistent with Articles I:1 and III:4 of the GATT 1994

The EU appealed the Panel's findings of violation under Articles I:1 and III:4 of the GATT 1994. The EU faulted the Panel for not applying the legal standard of Article 2.1 of the TBT Agreement to the analyses under Articles I:1 and III:4 of the GATT. As noted previously, the Appellate Body stated in *US – Clove Cigarettes* that while Article 2.1 of the TBT Agreement generally prescribes that technical regulations shall not cause a detrimental impact on imports, this type of treatment shall not constitute a violation of Article 2.1 when it stems exclusively from a legitimate regulatory distinction. In the EU's view, the Panel should have applied this legal standard in the context of Articles I:1 and III:4 of the GATT 1994 when analyzing the EU Seal Regime, such that the obligations contained in these provisions would not be contravened if the discriminatory treatment stems exclusively from a legitimate regulatory distinction.

The Appellate Body rejected the EU's appeal. The Appellate Body first recalled that, as found by the Panel, the legal standards under Articles I:1 and III:4 of the GATT 1994 are different from that of Article 2.1 of the TBT Agreement. The non-discriminatory obligations in Articles I:1 and III:4 are balanced against Members' right to regulate under the general exceptions of Article XX of the GATT

1994.[17] The TBT Agreement, however, lacks a clause of general exceptions similar to GATT Article XX, which explains the additional element in the legal standard of Article 2.1, that is, the consideration of whether the discriminatory treatment stems from a legitimate regulatory distinction.[18]

The Appellate Body similarly rejected the EU's argument that the legal standard of GATT Article III:4 requires an additional inquiry into whether the detrimental impact on competitive opportunities stems exclusively from a legitimate regulatory distinction. The Appellate Body disagreed with the EU that a previous Appellate Body finding in *EC – Asbestos* on the issue of "like products" supports its contention.[19]

In conclusion, the EU Seal Regime was found to be inconsistent with Articles I:1 and III:4 of the GATT 1994. The Appellate Body next examined whether this inconsistency could be justified under the general exception of Article XX(a) of the GATT 1994.

3.2.3 The Appellate Body Upheld the Panel's Findings That the EU Seal Regime is not Justified Under Article XX(a) of the GATT 1994

Before the Panel, the EU's defense under Article XX(a) of the GATT 1994 had been unsuccessful. While the Panel agreed that its measure met the requirements of subparagraph (a) of Article XX as a measure necessary to protect public morals, it found that the measure did not satisfy the conditions of the chapeau as the measure was applied in a manner that constitutes arbitrary or unjustifiable discrimination. Since the measure did not satisfy the requirements of the chapeau, the Panel's ultimate conclusion was that the inconsistencies with Articles I:1 and III:4 could not be justified under Article XX(a) of the GATT 1994.

Both the complainants and the EU appealed the Panel's substantive findings under Article XX.

With respect to the chapeau of Article XX, the Appellate Body agreed with the complainants that the Panel's legal standard was erroneous. In assessing whether the EU Seal Regime gives rise to arbitrary or unjustifiable discrimination under the chapeau of GATT Article XX, the Panel improperly applied the same legal test it applied under Article 2.1 of the TBT Agreement. The Appellate Body acknowledged that while there are important parallels between the legal standards of Article 2.1 of the TBT Agreement and the chapeau of GATT Article XX, there are also significant differences between the two provisions.[20] The Appellate Body thus found that, instead of applying the same legal test to both provisions, the Panel

[17] Appellate Body Report, *EC – Seal Products,* para. 5.77.

[18] Appellate Body Report, *EC – Seal Products,* para. 5.77.

[19] Appellate Body Report, *EC – Seal Products,* paras. 5.108–5.110.

[20] Appellate Body Report, *EC – Seal Products,* paras. 5.310–5.311.

should have conducted an independent analysis of the consistency of the EU Seal Regime with the specific terms and requirements of the chapeau.

Having reversed the Panel's finding, the Appellate Body then proceeded to complete the legal analysis under the chapeau of GATT Article XX, which involves an examination of whether the IC and MRM exceptions are "applied in a manner which would constitute a means of arbitrary or unjustifiable discrimination between countries where the same conditions prevail, or a disguised restriction on international trade". The Appellate Body observed that while the EU maintains a different regulatory treatment for IC hunts and commercial hunts, the EU failed to demonstrate how this discrimination can be reconciled with, or is related to, the policy objective of addressing EU public moral concerns regarding seal welfare. For example, the EU did not explain why the protection of economic and social interests of Inuit communities prevents the EU from protecting the welfare of seals in the context of hunts conducted by those communities. The Appellate Body found that the EU failed to demonstrate that the EU Seal Regime is designed and applied in a manner that meets the requirements of the chapeau of Article XX of the GATT 1994.

In summary, although for different reasons, the Appellate Body arrived at the same final conclusion as the Panel, that is, that the EU Seal Regime does not meet the requirements of the chapeau, and thus cannot be justified under Article XX(a) of the GATT 1994.

4 US – Carbon Steel (India): Panel Report

4.1 Facts of the Case

This dispute concerns countervailing duties imposed by the United States in 2001 on imports of certain hot-rolled carbon steel flat products from India. India challenged the original investigation of 2001, the subsequent administrative reviews of 2002, 2004, 2006, 2007 and 2008, as well as the sunset reviews of 2007 and 2013. In addition, India challenged "as such" certain provisions of the United States Tariff Act of 1930.

Article VI of the GATT 1994 and the Agreement on Subsidies and Countervailing Measures ("SCM Agreement") allow WTO Members to impose countervailing duties on imports when the country of importation has determined, through an investigation, that (i) those goods are produced by entities receiving governmental subsidies from the exporting country; and (ii) that the industry in the country of importation is suffering injury as a result of the subsidized imports.

The United States investigating authority, the US Department of Commerce ("USDOC"), found that certain Indian exporters of carbon steel received subsidies from India's National Mineral Development Corporation ("NMDC"). The alleged subsidy consisted of the provision of iron ore at less than adequate remuneration by the NMDC to certain Indian companies, namely Essar, ISPAT, JSW and Tata. The USDOC found that this subsidy was provided under the "Captive Mining of Iron Ore Programme" and the "Captive Mining of Coal Programme".

4.2 Salient Legal Findings

The Panel found that the USDOC's determination that the NMDC is a "public body" is not inconsistent with Article 1.1(a)(1) of the SCM Agreement. The Panel concluded that the USDOC's determination that the grant of mining rights constitutes a provision of goods did was not inconsistent with Article 1.1(a)(1)(iii) of the SCM Agreement. The Panel also found that the United States' practice of cross-cumulation (considering together the volume of subsidized imports and imports found to be dumped in another investigation) is "as such" and "as applied" inconsistent with Articles 15.1–15.5 of the SCM Agreement.

4.2.1 The Panel Rejected India's Claim That the USDOC's Determination That the NMDC is a "Public Body" was Inconsistent with Article 1.1(a)(1) of the SCM Agreement

India claimed that, by finding that the NMDC was a "public body", the United States acted inconsistently with Article 1.1(a)(1) of the SCM Agreement.

Article 1.1 of the SCM Agreement stipulates that a "subsidy" exists if "there is a financial contribution by a government <u>or any public body</u> within the territory of a Member".[21]

Past WTO disputes concerning the SCM Agreement show that, in certain cases, it is difficult to determine whether an entity qualifies as a "public body". In particular, this difficulty arises when a financial contribution is not granted by a governmental agency, but by an entity whose links to the government are unclear. In *US – Anti-Dumping and Countervailing Duties (China)*, the Appellate Body rejected the Panel's interpretation of "public body" as meaning an entity that is *owned* by the government. Instead, the Appellate Body clarified that a critical criterion in identifying a "public body" is whether the entity is *vested with governmental authority*, that is, whether it has the authority to perform governmental functions.[22]

In the present dispute, India claimed that the USDOC's determination that the NMDC is a public body was based solely on the fact that the Government of India holds 98 % of shares in this entity. According to India, this is at odds with the

[21] According to Article 1.1, the other element of the concept of "subsidy" is that the financial contribution confers a benefit to the recipient.

[22] Appellate Body Report, *US – Anti-Dumping and Countervailing Duties (China)*, para. 317.

Appellate Body's reasoning that the fact that a government is the majority shareholder does not mean that the government exercises meaningful control over that entity's conduct.

The Panel rejected India's claim. It noted that, according to evidence in the record, the NMDC is under meaningful control of the Indian Government. For example, the Indian Government was involved in the selection of directors of the NMDC, which, in the Panel's view, is "extremely relevant"[23] as "government involvement in the appointment of an entity's directors suggests that the relationship between the government and that entity is closer than it would be if the government simply hold a shareholding in that entity".[24]

The Panel concluded that government shareholding, when combined with other factors, may well be indicative of the government's meaningful control. The Panel thus found that the "USDOC's determination, when viewed in light of the above-mentioned record evidence, effectively amounted to a determination that the NMDC was under the 'meaningful control' of the [Government of India]".[25] For these reasons, the Panel rejected India's claim that the USDOC's determination that the NMDC is a public body is inconsistent with Article 1.1(a)(1) of the SCM Agreement.

4.2.2 The Panel Rejected India's Claim That the USDOC Acted Inconsistently with Article 1.1(a)(1)(iii) of the SCM Agreement by Determining That the Grant of Mining Rights Constitutes a "Provision of Goods" and, Thus, a Financial Contribution

The USDOC determined that the Government of India provided financial contributions to steel producers by providing them with iron ore and coal through the grant of captive mining rights, that is, rights allowing steel producers to mine iron ore and coal for their own use.

India alleged that, because of the uncertainty inherent in mining activities and the need of significant intervention through private work, the mining licence does not lead to a guaranteed transfer of marketable minerals. This, in India's view, means that there is no reasonable proximate relationship between the mining rights and the actual iron ore and coal extracted.

The Panel rejected India's argument. By granting the right to mine, the Government of India essentially made those minerals available to, and put them at the disposal of, the beneficiaries. On this basis, the Panel concluded that the grant of mining rights is "reasonably proximate" to the use or enjoyment of the minerals such that it constitutes a provision of goods within the meaning of Article 1.1(a)(1)(iii) of the SCM Agreement. Additionally, the Appellate Body distinguished the

---

[23] Panel Report, *US – Carbon Steel (India)*, para. 7.84.

[24] Panel Report, *US – Carbon Steel (India)*, para. 7.85.

[25] Panel Report, *US – Carbon Steel (India)*, para. 7.89.

facts of this case from its findings in *US – Softwood Lumber IV* where it accepted that, in certain cases, extraction rights may not be a provision of goods given the uncertainty as to what and how much the beneficiary may find. Whereas in *US – Softwood Lumber IV* the Appellate Body referred to “the right to explore and, if anything is found, extract the goods”, this case involves the grant of mining rights to extract minerals from *known* sites.

For these reasons, the Panel rejected India’s claim that the USDOC’s determination was inconsistent with Article 1.1(a)(1)(iii) of the SCM Agreement.

4.2.3 The Panel Found That United States Acted Inconsistently with Article 15.3 of the SCM Agreement by Applying Cross-Cumulation in Injury Determinations

India argued that Section 1677(7)(G) of the U.S. Code was inconsistent with Article 15.3 of the SCM Agreement “as such” (i.e. the law itself) and “as applied” in the original countervailing duty investigation (i.e. anti-subsidy investigation) on Indian carbon steel. India explained that, pursuant to this provision of US law, the US investigating authority in charge of assessing the existence of injury to the domestic industry is required to conduct a cumulative assessment of the effects of all “unfairly traded imports”, which includes considering the effects of subsidized imports as well as the effects of imports subject to a different type of investigation, namely an anti-dumping investigation.

Article 15.3 of the SCM Agreement stipulates that “[w]here imports of a product from more than one country are simultaneously subject to countervailing duty investigations, the investigating authorities may cumulatively assess the effect of such imports [. . .]”.

Article 15.3 allows authorities to cumulate the effects of subsidized imports from all countries simultaneously investigated. For example, if an authority initiates simultaneous anti-subsidy investigations on imports from countries A, B and C, the authority may take into account the cumulated effects of imports from all three sources when assessing whether the domestic industry suffers injury. The cumulative assessment of subsidized imports from various sources logically increases the possibility that injury is found to exist. In this context, the issue before the Panel was whether Article 15.3 permits “cross-cumulation”, that is, the cumulative assessment of the effects of imports subject to a countervailing investigation with the effects of imports of the same product subject *only* to an anti-dumping investigation.

The Panel upheld India’s claim that Article 15.3 does not allow cross-subsidization. The Panel noted that, according to the text of Article 15.3, cumulation is permitted when products from different countries are “simultaneously subject to countervailing duty investigations”. The Panel observed that “[i]mports which are only the subject of a parallel, simultaneous anti-dumping duty investigation plainly do not satisfy this requirement as a matter of fact".[26]

The Panel rejected the United States' argument that, while Article 15.3 only addresses cumulation in the context of simultaneous countervailing duty investigations, it leaves open the possibility to conduct cross-cumulation of other imports subject to other types of investigation. The Panel considered that it was "unable to reconcile the United States' position with the text of Article 15.3 in the overall context of Article 15 of the SCM Agreement".[27]

The Panel thus found that Section 1677(7)(G) of the U.S. Code is inconsistent with Article 15.3 of the SCM Agreement "as such" and "as applied" in the original investigation at issue.[28]

5 US – Carbon Steel (India): Appellate Body Report

5.1 *Facts of the Case*

As discussed above, India challenged the countervailing duties imposed by the United States on Indian imports of hot-rolled carbon steel products, which resulted from the anti-subsidy investigation conducted by the United States Department of Commerce (USDOC). The Panel sided with India on various claims, but rejected other important claims, such as India's challenge against the USDOC's determination that the NMDC is a "public body", and that the grant of mining rights qualifies as a "provision of goods". India appealed these and other findings by the Panel.

5.2 *Salient Legal Findings*

The Appellate Body reversed the Panel's conclusion that the USDOC's determination of "public body" was inconsistent with Article 1.1(a)(1) of the SCM Agreement. In contrast, the Appellate Body upheld the Panel's finding that the USDOC did not act inconsistently with Article 1.1(a)(1)(iii) of the SCM Agreement by determining that the grant of mining rights qualifies as a provision of goods. Finally, the Appellate Body partially upheld the Panel's conclusion that the practice of "cross-cumulation" is inconsistent "as such" and "as applied" with Article 15.3 of the SCM Agreement.

[26] Panel Report, *US – Carbon Steel (India)*, para. 7.341.

[27] Panel Report, *US – Carbon Steel (India)*, para. 7.343.

[28] Panel Report, *US – Carbon Steel (India)*, para. 7.356.

5.2.1 The Appellate Body Reversed the Panel's Finding That the USDOC's Determination on the Issue of "Public Body" Was Not Inconsistent with Article 1.1(a)(1) of the SCM Agreement

India challenged the Panel's finding that the USDOC did not act inconsistently with Article 1.1(a)(1) of the SCM Agreement by concluding that India's NMDC was a "public body". According to India, the Panel erred in interpreting the term "public body" as an entity that is "meaningfully controlled" by a government. India argued that, for an entity to be a "public body", it must be vested with governmental authority, which India interprets as having the power to regulate, control, or supervise individuals or otherwise restrain their conduct.[29]

The Appellate Body rejected India's interpretation. It stated that, although certain entities that constitute "public bodies" may possess the power to regulate, it did "not see why an entity would necessarily have to possess this characteristic in order to be found to be vested with governmental authority or exercising a governmental function and therefore to constitute a public body".[30] Nevertheless, for the different reasons, the Appellate Body agreed with India that the Panel erred in concluding that the USDOC's determination of "public body" was not inconsistent with Article 1.1(a)(1) of the SCM Agreement. The Appellate Body indicated that the evidence examined by the panel could more properly be characterized as "formal indicia of control". This evidence involved the Government's ownership interest in NMDC, the Government's power to appoint and nominate directors, and the reference to the organization's website indicating "administrative control" by the Indian Government. The Appellate Body found that this amounts to a failure by the Panel to "evaluate whether the USDOC had properly considered the relationship between the NMDC and the [Government of India] within the Indian legal order, or the extent to which the [Government of India] in fact 'exercised' meaningful control over the NMDC as an entity and over its *conduct*".[31]

After reversing the Panel's finding, the Appellate Body completed the legal analysis on this issue. It recalled its earlier observations that the USDOC did not properly evaluate the relationship between the NMDC and the Indian Government, and that the USDOC merely examined formal indicia of control, such as the Government's ownership interest in the organization and its power to appoint and nominate directors. Hence, the Appellate Body concluded that the "USDOC did not provide a reasoned and adequate explanation of the basis for its finding that the NMDC is a public body within the meaning of Article 1.1(a)(1) of the SCM Agreement".[32]

---

[29] Appellate Body Report, *US – Carbon Steel (India)*, para. 4.11.

[30] Appellate Body Report, *US – Carbon Steel (India)*, para. 4.17.

[31] Appellate Body Report, *US – Carbon Steel (India)*, para. 4.43 (original emphasis).

[32] Appellate Body Report, *US – Carbon Steel (India)*, para. 4.54.

5.2.2 The Appellate Body Upheld the Panel's Rejection of India's Claim Regarding the USDOC's Determination on "Provision of Goods" as a Final Contribution Under Article 1.1(a)(1)(iii) of the SCM Agreement

Before the Panel, India claimed that the USDOC acted inconsistently with Article 1.1(a)(1) of the SCM Agreement by determining that the grant of mining rights constitutes a financial contribution. India argued that no reasonable proximate relationship exists between the mining rights and the iron ore and coal actually extracted. The Panel rejected India's claim, finding that the grant of mining rights allows firms to extract minerals from known sites, such that there is a reasonably proximate relationship between the grant of mining rights and the extraction of minerals.

India appealed the Panel's ruling. India reiterated its arguments made before the Panel, namely that while the GOI did grant mining rights to Indian firms, the complexity and uncertainties associated with the extraction process undermined any reasonably proximate relationship between those mining rights and the final goods extracted. According to India, the circumstances of this case are different from those in *US – Softwood Lumber IV*, in which the Appellate Body examined "the connection between a right to harvest standing timber, and the standing timber itself".[33] India's point was that in *US – Softwood Lumber IV* the grant of stumpage rights implied a quasi-automatic access to timber because the extraction process was fairly simple, i.e. cutting standing trees. India argued that the connection between the grant of mining rights and the extracted iron ore and coal is severed by a series of significant actions performed by the beneficiary at its own risk and cost.

The Appellate Body disagreed with India's interpretation of the findings in *US – Softwood Lumber IV*. As explained by the Appellate Body, in *US – Softwood Lumber IV* the right over felled trees was an inevitable consequence of the harvesting rights, which meant that making timber available was the *raison d'être* of the stumpage rights. Applying this reasoning to the present case, the Appellate Body found that "rights over extracted iron ore and coal follow as a natural and inevitable consequence of the steel companies' exercise of their mining rights, which suggests that making available iron ore and coal is the *raison d'être* of the mining rights."[34] In the Appellate Body's view, this supports the conclusion that the grant of mining rights is reasonably proximate to the use or enjoyment of the minerals by the beneficiaries of those rights.

The Appellate Body, thus, upheld the Panel's rejection of India's claim that the USDOC's contravened Article 1.1(a)(1)(iii) of the SCM Agreement by determining that the granting of mining rights amounted to a provision of goods.

---

[33] Appellate Body Report, *US – Carbon Steel (India)*, para. 4.74.

[34] Appellate Body Report, *US – Carbon Steel (India)*, para. 4.74.

5.2.3 On the Issue of "Cross-Cumulation", the Appellate Body Partially Upheld the Panel's Finding that Section 1677(7)(G) of the U.S. Code is Inconsistent with Article 15.3 of the SCM Agreement

The Panel had found that the Section 1677(7)(G) of the U.S. Code is inconsistent with Article 15.3 of the SCM Agreement "as such" and "as applied" in the original countervailing duty investigation. At the heart of the Panel's finding was its interpretation that Article 15.3 does not permit "cross-cumulation" in injury determinations, that is, cumulation of the effects of imports subject to countervailing duty investigations with those of imports subject only to anti-dumping investigation. On the basis of this interpretation, the Panel also found violations of Articles 15.1, 15.2, 15.4, and 15.5 of the SCM Agreement.

Importantly, the Panel not only found "as applied" violations (i.e. with respect to the specific original investigation at issue), but also that Section 1677(7)(G) of the U.S. Code was "as such" inconsistent with the SCM Agreement as those provisions allowed the U.S. investigating authority to conduct "cross-cumulation" in "certain situations".

The United States appealed the Panel's findings on two separate grounds.

First, the United States argued that the Panel incorrectly interpreted Article 15.3 as prohibiting cross-cumulation. For this purpose, the United States basically repeated its original argumentation previously made before the Panel.

Focusing on the phrase "simultaneously subject to countervailing duty investigations" in Article 15.3, the Appellate Body observed that "[t]he text is clear in stipulating that being subject to countervailing duty investigations is a prerequisite for the cumulative assessment".[35] The Appellate Body rejected the United States' argument that Article 15.3 does not prohibit cross-cumulation because this provision is silent on that issue. The Appellate Body found that "Article 15 is not silent on the question of cumulation of the effects of subsidized imports with the effects of non-subsidized imports".[36]

The United States argued that the interpretation of Article 15.3 of the SCM Agreement should reflect the Appellate Body's findings in *EC – Tube or Pipe Fittings* that cumulation under Article 3.3 of the Anti-Dumping Agreement is permitted given the need to consider the injurious effects from imports originating from several countries that affect the domestic industry. Furthermore, the United States referred to the Appellate Body's findings in *US – Oil Country Tubular Goods* where Article 11.3 of the Anti-Dumping Agreement was interpreted as permitting cumulation in sunset reviews even though it is not expressly authorized in the Anti-Dumping Agreement. The Appellate Body rejected these arguments. It considered that its findings in *EC – Tube or Pipe Fittings* and *US – Oil Country Tubular Goods* are inapposite because they addressed regular cumulation (i.e. cumulation of effects of imports all subject to anti-dumping investigation), as opposed to cross-

[35] Appellate Body Report, *US – Carbon Steel (India)*, para. 4.579.

[36] Appellate Body Report, *US – Carbon Steel (India)*, para. 4.589.

cumulation (i.e. cumulation of the effects of dumped imports with those of subsidized, non-dumped imports). The Appellate Body thus saw "no basis in the text of Article 15.3 of the SCM Agreement for cumulatively assessing the effects of subsidized imports with those of non-subsidized imports".[37]

On the basis of the above, the Appellate Body found that the Panel did not err in concluding that Articles 15.1–15.5 do not authorize cross-cumulation.

The Appellate Body then addressed the United States' argument that the Panel acted contrary to Article 11 of the DSU because, by finding that Section 1677(7)(G) of the U.S. Code requires in certain situations the practice of cross-cumulation, the Panel failed to make an objective assessment of the matter before it. The United States' complaint therefore goes to the manner in which the Panel assessed the municipal law at issue. The Appellate Body agreed with the United States. It said that the "Panel neither analysed the text of Section 1677(7)(G) nor considered any relevant practice" and that the Panel failed to provide "reasons based on the text of the measure as to why it required the USITC to cumulate the effects of subsidized imports with the effects of dumped, non-subsidized imports".[38] Accordingly, the Appellate Body found that the Panel failed to comply with its duty under DSU Article 11 to conduct an objective assessment of the matter before it, and therefore reversed the Panel's findings that Section 1677(7)(G) is "as such" inconsistent with Articles 15.1–15.5 of the SCM Agreement.

After reversing the Panel's findings, the Appellate Body examined whether it was in a position to complete the legal analysis, that is, whether it could resolve for itself the legal issue originally before the Panel. The Appellate Body proceeded to examine whether any of the different subparagraphs of Section 1677(7)(G) indeed require the United States' investigating authority to cumulate the effects of subsidized imports with those of dumped, non-subsidized imports.

With respect to Sections 1677(7)(G)(i) and (ii), the Appellate Body concluded that it is unclear whether these provisions require cross-cumulation. It noted that "[i]n the absence of an analysis by the Panel to this effect, and given the paucity of evidence regarding the application of the measure at issue on the Panel record, we are unable to complete the legal analysis with regard to the measure in these respects".[39] However, with respect to Section 1677(7)(G)(iii), the Appellate Body found that its wording makes clear that cross-cumulation is required in certain situations, namely when petitions to initiate countervailing duty investigations or anti-dumping duty investigations are filed on the same day and either investigation is initiated by the investigating authority. Consequently, the Appellate Body found that Section 1677(7)(G)(iii) of the U.S. Code is inconsistent "as such" with Articles 15.1–15.5 of the SCM Agreement.

[37] Appellate Body Report, *US – Carbon Steel (India)*, para. 4.593.

[38] Appellate Body Report, *US – Carbon Steel (India)*, para. 4.611.

[39] Appellate Body Report, *US – Carbon Steel (India)*, para. 4.628.

6 Argentina: Import Measures—Panel Report

6.1 Facts of the Case

In this dispute, the EU, Japan, and the United States challenged alleged Argentine import restrictions covering a broad range of sectors, including foodstuffs, automobiles, motorcycles, mining equipment, electronic and office products, agricultural machinery, medicines, publications, and clothing. The complaint referred to two main measures:

First, an unwritten measure, described by the complainants as a "combination of actions" under the label of "Restrictive Trade-Related Requirements" (which the Panel referred to as "TRRs"). The complainants argued that the various "actions" taken by the Argentine government created a requirement on importers to agree to certain conditions to import into Argentina. These conditions included five distinct elements, namely, commitments: (i) to export a certain value of goods from Argentina; (ii) to limit the volume and value of imports; (iii) not to repatriate funds from Argentina to another country; (iv) to undertake investments in Argentina; and (v) to use local content in domestic production. The panel referred to each one of these five sets of actions as "trade-related requirements" (TRRs); the panel also referred to the combined single measure, consisting of these five actions taken together, as the "trade-related requirements measure" (TRRs measure).

The second measure was the Advance Sworn Import Declaration (DJAI). The DJAI was in essence an import license that a prospective importer had to fill out and submit, and that number of Argentine government agencies could review and comment on. A comment could prevent the completion of the DJAI procedure, and the importer had to submit additional information. Only upon satisfactory completion of the review process would an importer be entitled to import the goods covered by the DJAI.

6.2 Salient Legal Findings

The dispute revolved to a significant extent around evidentiary issues and the definition of a "measure" for purposes of WTO law.

6.2.1 Findings of Violation Under Article XI of the GATT 1994

Drawing on a broad range of evidence, the panel found that Argentina had imposed the five different unwritten sets of TRRs alleged by the complainants.[40] The panel also found that these five individual sets of measures together constituted a single overarching measure because they contributed "in different combinations and degrees -- as part of a single measure -- towards the realization of common policy objectives that guide Argentina's 'managed trade' policy, i.e. substituting imports and reducing or eliminating trade deficits".[41]

The panel then found that this single TRR measure constituted an "other measure" within the meaning of Article XI that had a limiting effect on imports into Argentina. This was because the various components of the measure either had a direct limiting effect (the balancing, import limiting, and local content requirement) or were linked to the right to import (the investment and non-repatriation requirement). The panel also highlighted the "uncertainty generated by the unwritten and discretionary nature of the requirements" and the additional costs resulting from activities unrelated to an operator's business activity.[42] The panel also reflected previous case law that, in order to prove a violation of Article XI, it was not necessary to establish actual trade effects based on data of trade flows.[43]

In addition, Japan requested the panel to make findings about the TRR measure "as such", which in WTO parlance refers to a measure independently of any case-specific application. "As such" challenges are routine in WTO dispute settlement; however, in this case, the "as such" challenge faced the hurdle that the alleged overarching measure—just like its five individual components—was an unwritten measure. The panel applied the criteria that the Appellate Body had previously defined for "as such" challenges of unwritten measures—namely, that the alleged rule or norm be attributable to the responding Member; its precise content; and that it has "general and prospective application".[44] The panel found that these criteria were satisfied in the present case.

Particularly interestingly, on the criterion of *general* application, the panel emphasized that the TRR measure affects a wide range of sectors and could affect any sector and was part of a broader policy implemented by the Argentine government, rather than isolated measures taken with respect to individual importers. With

[40] Appellate Body Report, *US – Carbon Steel (India)*, Panel Report, paras. 6.166–6.177 (for the requirement to balance imports with exports); Appellate Body Report, *US – Carbon Steel (India)*, paras. 6.178–6.195 (for the requirement to limit the volume and value of imports); Appellate Body Report, *US – Carbon Steel (India)*, paras. 6.196–6.207 (for the local content requirement); Appellate Body Report, *US – Carbon Steel (India)*, paras. 6.208–6.212 (investment requirement); Appellate Body Report, *US – Carbon Steel (India)*, paras. 6.213–6.216 (for the requirement not to repatriate profits from Argentina).

[41] Panel Report, *US – Carbon Steel (India)*, para. 6.228.

[42] Panel report, *US – Carbon Steel (India)*, paras. 6.249–6.263.

[43] Panel report, *US – Carbon Steel (India)*, para. 6.264.

[44] Panel report, *US – Carbon Steel (India)*, para. 6.322–6.342.

respect to *prospective* application, the panel focussed on what it considered the "deliberate policy" character of the measure, its year-long application and the resulting likelihood that it would continue to be applied in the future.[45]

With respect to the DJAI—which was a written measure—the complainants relied on Article XI, whereas Argentina argued that the DJAI was an import formality covered exclusively by Article VIII. The panel found that DJAI procedure was not a mere formality, but rather related to the right to import; and that, in any event, even if Article VIII were triggered, this would not exclude the applicability of Article XI, because these two provisions are not mutually exclusive.[46] On substance under Article XI, the panel found that the DJAI was a necessary condition to import into Argentina and the process of obtaining a DJAI in "exit" status was not automatic. Moreover—as in the case of the TRR measure—the panel found that uncertainty existed concerning the application of the measure, which uncertainty itself affected import opportunities; and that the operation of the measure also imposed a burden on importers unrelated to their business activity.[47] The panel also rejected Argentina's argument that, in order to violate Article XI, the measure had to restrict imports by reference to quantity or in a way that was "quantifiable". Rather, the panel found that Article XI:1 protects Members' expectations as to the competitive relationship between their products and those of other Members in respect of importation itself.[48]

Article III:4 The panel also found that the local content requirement—one of the five individual sets of TRRs—violated Article III:4 of the GATT 1994, because it resulted in less favourable treatment of imported products when compared to domestic products. In this rather straight-forward finding, the panel confirmed previous case law that origin-based distinctions between products created a presumption that products are "like"; that the requirement affected the level of imports purchased; and that the Argentine measured created an incentive to use domestic products over imported products."[49]

6.2.2 Examination and Evidence of an Unwritten Measure

One of the key challenges for the complainants in this case was the unwritten character of the TRRs and the TRR measure. The complainants could not point to a single written document that would set out the import-restrictive measures. Instead, they relied on a range of evidence from which the existence of these requirements

[45] Panel report, *US – Carbon Steel (India)*, paras. 6.329–6.342.

[46] Panel report, *US – Carbon Steel (India)*, paras. 6.433–6.445.

[47] Panel report, *US – Carbon Steel (India)*, paras. 6.471–6.473.

[48] Panel report, *US – Carbon Steel (India)*, paras. 6.476–6.478.

[49] Panel report, *US – Carbon Steel (India)*, paras. 6.273–6.294.

could be deduced. Argentina objected to some of this evidence. The panel therefore made certain interesting statements on the probative value of that evidence.

By way of example, with respect to *articles from newspapers and magazines*, Argentina argued that the articles in question had been published in media traditionally critical of the government and, in any event, were tainted by the "bias" of the reporters. The panel rejected this criticism, finding that previous panels had relied on newspaper articles and that it was within a panel's right to assess the objectivity and accuracy of a newspaper article on a case-by-case basis. If a party considered that a particular article contained incorrect information, the panel stated, that party could rebut that evidence.[50]

With regard to statements by Argentine officials—statements that strongly suggested the will of the Argentine government to restrict imports and provide relief to domestic industries—Argentina argued that it could not be simply presumed that such statements would necessarily translate into specific measures. However, the panel found that, even if such statements should be considered with "caution", "[c]onsistent public statements made on the record by a public official cannot be devoid of importance, especially when they relate to a topic in which that official has the authority to design or implement policies."[51] Interestingly, the panel also relied on a statement by the International Court of Justice in *Military and Paramilitary Activities In and Against Nicaragua*, to the effect that statements made by public officials "are of particular probative value when they acknowledge facts or conduct unfavorable to the State represented by the person who made them".[52]

6.2.3 Proposed Procedures for Considering Sensitive Evidence

Of additional interest in this case was a particular procedure proposed by the panel, but ultimately not accepted by the parties. The panel had intended to create a mechanism to incentivize the parties to submit particularly sensitive evidence. The panel understood from the complainants' arguments that the Argentine government's import-restriction policy was reflected, among other things, in agreements between the Argentine Government and importers/economic operators, or in letters addressed by importers/economic operators to the Argentine Government. These agreements and letters described the specific commitments stipulated by the government. However, numerous economic operators were reluctant to authorize the complaining governments to present this evidence, because they feared retaliatory action by the Argentine government.

The panel therefore proposed a set of special procedures, under which an independent expert (a Geneva-based notary public) would assess the evidence

[50] Panel report, *US – Carbon Steel (India)*, paras. 6.69–6.72.

[51] Panel report, *US – Carbon Steel (India)*, paras. 6.78–6.79.

[52] Panel report, *US – Carbon Steel (India)*, paras. 6.80.

and respond to the panel's questions, subject to particular conditions.[53] However, due to systemic concerns, the parties did not agree to the adoption of such procedures. The panel also requested Argentina to provide these documents, given that they were all in the government's possession. Faced with Argentina's reluctance to do so, the panel ultimately concluded that the substance of the complainants' allegation—including on the basis of other evidence—had been demonstrated. The panel did not explicitly draw "adverse inferences"; nevertheless, it chastised Argentina for refusing to submit the evidence on the grounds that it was not relevant, reminding all parties that "[t]here is nothing in the DSU that supports the proposition that, faced with a panel's request for specific information, a Member can decide whether that information is relevant for the settlement of a dispute or whether the other party has already made a *prima facie* case that would justify the panel's request." It also stated that, under Article 13.1, Members are "under a duty and an obligation 'to respond promptly and fully' to requests made by panels for information".[54]

6.2.4 Observations

This panel report is interesting not only because it throws a light on long-standing formal and informal import restrictions imposed by the Argentine government, policies that have for a long time been a source of professed frustration for certain other WTO Members. Once the panel found that the alleged import restrictions existed and constituted a WTO-law-relevant "measure", the resulting findings were unsurprising. However, getting to a finding that unwritten measures existed represented a challenge for the complainants, because at least with respect to the TRRs, the Argentine government had deliberately not reduced these measures in written form.

The panel report is also remarkable for its treatment of unwritten measures as well as the flexibility of a WTO dispute settlement panel to accommodate evidentiary challenges faced by complainants against trade-restrictive measures that the defendant government has made a deliberate effort not to enshrine in written measures. The panel was visibly sympathetic to the complainants' situation, even explicitly acknowledging that the complainants had a "plausible motive" for not submitting certain evidence that was in their possession or in the possession of their economic operators.[55]

[53] Panel report, *US – Carbon Steel (India)*, paras. 1.27–1.28. Such as, for instance, that the final assessment of the facts would remain the sole prerogative of the panel and that the parties would always be in a position to comment on the expert's statements.

[54] Panel report, *US – Carbon Steel (India)*, para. 6.59.

[55] Panel report, *US – Carbon Steel (India)*, para. 6.63.

7 Peru: Additional Duty on Imports of Certain Agricultural Products—Panel Report

7.1 *Facts of the Case*

In this dispute, Guatemala challenged the Peruvian "price range system" (PRS), which applied to four sets of agricultural products, including sugar, an important export commodity for Guatemala. Under the PRS, the Peruvian government would impose a fluctuating "additional variable duty" whose amount depended on the precise numerical relationship between a so-called reference price and the PRS. This additional duty was imposed on top of any otherwise applicable ordinary duty (which, however, for most of the covered products was zero).

The PRS consisted of a "price range floor" and a "price range ceiling", both of which were based on 5-year world market price data for a given commodity and were updated every 6 months. The reference price, for its part, was the average world market price for the previous 2 weeks (fortnight) for a given commodity; it was updated every fortnight. If the reference price was below the price range floor, the additional variable duty equaled the difference between these two values. If the reference price was between the price range floor and the price range ceiling, no additional duty was imposed. Finally, if the reference price was above the price range ceiling, the differential was subtracted from the otherwise applicable normal duty, by way of a "duty rebate". However, the rebate could not be higher than the normal duty; in any event, because most of the covered products attracted a zero tariff, the system almost never resulted in a rebate.

In essence, and by its explicit design, the PRS was a price stabilizing mechanism for imports. When current world market prices were low, in relation to a 5-year average, the value of imports would be artificially elevated to at least the price range floor. When current world market prices were within the pre-defined price band—as desired by the Peruvian government—no additional duty was generated and only the ordinary customs duty (zero for most products) would apply. When the current world market price exceeded the ceiling of the price band, the system would generate a rebate from any applicable ordinary customs duty. While the additional variable duty protected producers, the rebate from any applicable customs duty reflected a concern (although much weaker a concern) for consumers.

The PRS bore a conspicuous resemblance to the so-called price band system previously operated by Chile and challenged by Argentina during the 2000s.

7.2 *Key Findings of the Panel*

Guatemala challenged the additional duties under Articles 4.2 of the Agreement on Agriculture, as a variable import levy, a minimum import price or a measure "similar" to these two. Guatemala also challenged the measure as an impermissible "other duty and charged" that Peru had not recorded in its schedule of commitments. Guatemala also brought a range of claims under Article X:1 and X:3(a) of the GATT 1994, against the perceived failure by Peru to publish certain elements of the PRS as well as certain perceived discrepancies between the wording of the measure and its actual application by the Peruvian government.

The Panel first had to deal with a procedural objection by Peru. The background to this objection was a negotiated and signed free-trade agreement (FTA) between Guatemala and Peru. That agreement had been signed, but was not yet in force because Peru had decided not to ratify it; pursuant to public statements by Peruvian officials, the decision not to ratify was in direct retaliation against Guatemala's WTO challenge of the PRS. The text of the FTA stipulated that Peru was permitted to maintain the PRS; however, it also stated that both parties confirmed their WTO rights and obligations and that, to the extent of any conflict between the two, the FTA would prevail.

Peru pointed to these FTA provisions and argued that Guatemala had acted against the good faith requirement under Article 3.10 of the DSU; had failed to exercise judgment as to whether the initiation of the dispute would be fruitful (Article 3.7 of the DSU); and was frustrating the object and purpose of the FTA, under Article 18 of the Vienna Convention on the Law of Treaties (Vienna Convention). Peru argued that, for all these reasons, Guatemala was barred from bringing the dispute to the WTO. The panel rejected these objections, relying essentially on the fact that the FTA was not in force. With respect to Article 18 of the Vienna Convention, the panel stated that it was not convinced that "the violation by a Member of the obligation contained in Article 18 of the Vienna Convention with respect to a treaty that does not form part of the WTO covered agreements can constitute evidence of lack of the good faith required by Articles 3.7 and 3.10 of the DSU"; in any event, the panel found that it could not determine that the object and purpose of the FTA had been violated, because the FTA was not within its terms of reference.[56]

On substance, the panel found that the additional duty resulting from the PRS was a variable import levy, because it was "inherently variable"—namely, because it varied according to a formula built into the Peruvian legislature which ensures constant and automatic variation, without any intervening discretionary act of the Peruvian executive. The panel also found that the measure was characterized by a lack of transparency and predictability, and isolated the Peruvian market from international price fluctuations. The panel also rejected Peru's argument that domestic price trends were correlated with international price trends. The panel thus found a violation of Article 4.2 of the Agreement on Agriculture. As a consequential finding, the panel found that the additional duty was an "other duty and charge" within the meaning of Article II:1(b) of the GATT 1994 and violated this provision, because it had been not recorded in Peru's schedule of concessions.

[56] Panel Report, *Peru – Additional Duty on Imports of Certain Agricultural Products* (DS457), para. 7.92.

In contrast, the panel ruled that the additional duty was neither a minimum import price nor a measure similar to a minimum import price. Guatemala had argued that the price range floor price (or an alternative, implicit threshold) constituted such a minimum import price and that the additional duty would elevate the transaction price of shipments to at least that threshold. The panel's contrary view on both counts (minimum import price or a similar measure) revolved around the fact that the PRS did not ensure that a minimum import price would be reached in each and every case; the panel in essence relied on the fact that the reference price was different from the transaction value of a given shipment, and that Peru had demonstrated the existence of transactions whose transaction value plus any additional duty was below the PRS floor applicable at the time of shipment.

Finally, the panel exercised judicial economy on Guatemala's claims under Articles X:1 and X:3(a), on grounds that ruling on these claims would not meaningfully add to the resolution of the dispute.

7.3 *Observations*

The panel's finding of a violation under Article 4.2 of the Agreement on Agriculture and Article II:1(b) of the GATT 1994 was hardly surprising. The measure was very obviously "inherently variable" within the meaning of the Appellate Body's previous case-law, given its multiple mathematical formulae, its automaticity and constant updating in the light of evolving world-market prices. Of interest were the panel's modulation of the Appellate Body's criteria of "lack of transparency" and "lack of predictability", which are not treaty language. The panel was clearly trying to reconcile the Appellate Body's somewhat opaque precedent, treaty text as well as the common meaning of these concepts.

In contrast, the panel's ruling on "minimum import price" or a "measure similar to a minimum import price" betrayed a surprisingly narrow scope for that term. The measure was quite obviously geared towards ensuring that imports would not enter the Peruvian market below the long term average world market price. Although the panel did not explicitly state so, the linchpin of its analysis was that the additional duty imposed by the PRS did not correspond to the difference between the PRS floor price and the transaction value of a given shipment, but rather to the difference between the floor price and the reference price. However, the reference price was at least intended to function as a proxy for transaction values, a point that the panel did not explicitly analyse. Moreover, the panel's finding could mean that, by relatively simple manipulation of the design of a measure, WTO Members could escape a finding of violation under the "minimum import price" component of Article 4.2. However, they would still be condemned under the "variable import levy component".

The dispute also attracted attention because it touched on the relationship between FTA and WTO law. However, the panel ultimately failed to make any findings of material import on this issue. The panel dodged the issue by relying heavily on the fact that the FTA was not yet in force.

8 China: Rare Earths—Panel Report

8.1 Introduction and Facts

This dispute featured a challenge by the EU, Japan and the United States concerning Chinese export restrictions on certain rare earths and other elements. China uses export duties and export quotas to limit the exportation of 15 sets of rare earths (including many sub-variations) as well as certain other minerals, going by the not universally familiar names such as Praseodymium, lanthanum, tungsten and molybdenum. These elements occur either naturally in the soil or are produced after some basic processing. The commercial and policy stakes of this dispute were high. Rare earths are important elements for producing many products that are essential for modern life—cell phones, computer hard drives, loudspeakers, green technologies such as wind turbines or hybrid cars, cameras and telescope lenses. Contrary to what their names suggest, rare earths are generally abundant, but are hazardous to extract.

Over the years, China had become the dominant global supplier of these materials. China's export restrictions on rare earths (as well as on other raw materials, which had been subject to a previous similar dispute) have been used by China as an aspect of its industrial policy, namely, to reserve a significant portion for the Chinese domestic industry. They have also become a political tool and were perceived as a potential strategic economic threat by the complainants.

The Chinese export restrictions took the form of export duties and export quotas. As will be seen below, legally speaking, the crux of the dispute had been decided in the previous dispute, which went by the name of *China – Raw Materials*.[57] Nevertheless, China requested the panel to review the previous analysis.

8.2 Salient Legal Findings

In essence, the complainants challenged three sets of measures: export duties, export quotas, as well as the administration and allocation of the export quotas.

[57] China—Measures Related to the Exportation of Various Raw Materials (DS394).

8.2.1 The WTO Consistency of China's Export Duties

The complainants challenged a range of export duties imposed by China on the products at issue. Export duties—although not export quotas—are normally legal under WTO law. Nevertheless, China's Protocol of Accession contains a prohibition on export duties, unless these duties are imposed on products enumerated in an Annex to the Protocol. This is a so-called "WTO-plus" obligation, imposed on China during its long accessions process between 1988 and 2001. Frequently, countries or customs areas acceding to the WTO after 1995—that is, countries or customs areas that are not original WTO Members—have had to assume obligations that go beyond the obligations of original WTO Members. This concerns not only the extent and depth of tariff concessions, but also tightened substantive rules. In the case of China (as well as other countries, e.g. Viet Nam), these WTO-plus obligations include the prohibition of export duties. As noted above, under "standard" GATT/WTO obligations, Members are unconstrained with respect to export duties, even though relevant proposals have been made as part of the Doha Round.

China did not dispute the obvious, namely, that it was applying export duties inconsistently with Article 11.3 of its Protocol of Accession. However, China invoked Article XX of the GATT 1994 to justify this breach, arguing that the export duties at issue were intended to serve as a complement to Chinese environmental policy concerning the extraction and production of rare earths and the other minerals at issue.

An obvious problem in this regard for China was that both a panel and the Appellate Body in *China – Raw Materials* had ruled Article XX of the GATT 1994 inapplicable to China's Protocol of Accession. The basic idea behind that ruling was that, although the Protocol of Accession is part of the WTO's legal architecture, defenses under Article XX of the GATT are available only to justify violations of the GATT 1994 itself, and not also violations of other WTO legal agreements or documents. The only exception to that rule is where that other WTO legal agreement or document specifically and expressly refers to Article XX.

The panel's dilemma was to what extent it could do as requested by China—namely, to engage in a re-assessment of a legal issue previously decided by the Appellate Body in the light of what China alleged were new arguments. The Appellate Body had previously ruled that, absent "cogent reasons", panels are expected to follow the legal interpretations developed by the Appellate Body. The panel ultimately decided to engage with China's arguments, justifying this decision by referring to certain "particular circumstances", including: that it would examine these arguments to determine whether they constituted the "cogent reasons" mentioned by the Appellate Body; that doing so would assist the Appellate Body and the DSB with respect to a complex legal question; that no other party objected to the panel doing so; and that the parties to the dispute were not identical to the parties in *China – Raw Materials*.

Ultimately, the panel rejected China's arguments and reached the same decision as the Appellate Body had reached previously. It ruled that the silence in Article

11.3 of China's Protocol of Accession with respect to Article XX of the GATT (or the GATT more broadly) had to be given meaning; that the fact that the Protocol of Accession had been made an integral part of the WTO Agreement and that Article XII of the WTO Agreement provided that an accession "shall apply to the [WTO] Agreement and the Multilateral Trade Agreements annexed thereto" the did not mean that the GATT 1994 was applicable to the obligations in the Protocol or that individual provisions of the Protocol were made part of the Multilateral Agreements annexed to the WTO Agreement. The panel therefore declined to see the "systemic relationship" between the Protocol and the GATT as a cogent reason to depart from the Appellate Body's previous reasoning.

The panel also rejected the argument that the words "nothing in this Agreement" in Article XX could be read to encompass the Protocol. Similarly, the panel disagreed that non-availability of Article XX would deprive China of the ability to regulate trade on the grounds of non-trade concerns; the panel ruled that the non-availability concerned only one type of trade instruments, namely export duties (as opposed to export quotas).

8.2.2 Separate Opinion by One of the Panelists on the Availability of Article XX

Remarkably, one of the panelists issued a dissenting ("separate") opinion on this issue, siding with China. The central point in this panelist's reasoning revolves around the relationship between Article 11.3 and Article XX; the "WTO-plus" nature of Article 11.3; the alleged close relationship between Articles II and XI of the GATT 1994; the fact that in Russia's case, a prohibition on export duties was stipulated in Russia's schedule, rather than in the Protocol; and the object and purpose of the WTO Agreement.

Wherever one stands on the applicability of Article XX and on the Appellate Body's caselaw, it is safe to say that the separate opinion lags far behind the majority's view in terms of detail and thoroughness of the legal argument; at times, the separate opinion has an almost political character. For this reason alone, arguably, it is not particularly convincing.

8.2.3 The Justification of Export Duties and Export Quotas Under Article XX

A very large part of the panel's reasoning concerns Article XX and whether this provision could justify the Chinese export duties and export quotas. With respect to export duties, the panel engaged in this analysis on an arguendo basis, given that it had already found Article XX not applicable. With respect to the export quotas, the panel was required to address China's reliance on Article XX.

With respect to export duties, China invoked Article XX(b). The panel accepted that mining and production of rare earths, tungsten and molybdenum caused harm to the environment and to human, animal and plant life or health. However, the panel was not convinced that the export duties were designed so as to protect the environment or public life or health; found that the duties were not apt to make a material contribution to these goals; and also found that China had not explained why it could not, as an alternative to export duties, increase volume restrictions and pollution controls and the so-called resource or pollution taxes, which are taxes imposed on mining operations. The panel also found that China had not substantiated its arguments under the chapeau of Article XX.

With respect to export quotas—found to be illegal under Article XI of the GATT 1994 and other certain paragraphs of China's Working Party Report—the panel's analysis of Article XX was significantly longer. Here, China invoked Article XX (g). The panel examined this justification separately for rare earths, tungsten and molybdenum, respectively.

The key elements in the panel's rejection of China's arguments for all three minerals were certain asymmetrical, not "even-handed" features of China's regime. In essence, China was not restricting domestic consumption in the same manner as exports/foreign consumption. In essence, once the materials at issue had been produced, China did not apply consumption limitations to the domestic industry, but did limit foreign consumption/export by means of export quotas. The panel did not accept the defence that the quota had not been filled in the most recent period. The panel also considered that the export limitations had the "perverse" effect of increasing domestic supply and lowering prices, thereby encouraging domestic consumption, rather than limiting it (moreover, unused quota amounts were reallocated to the domestic industry). Moreover, the panel failed to see a connection between the manner in which export quotas were set and the ways in which China alleged domestic consumption was regulated. In a nutshell, the panel viewed the export restriction as China's way of ensuring a secure supply of the materials at hand for the domestic industry, as part of China's industrial policy, rather than as an element in China's environmental policy. The panel also faulted China for not explaining why it was unable to implement alternatives, such as higher production volume restrictions or higher pollution controls.

8.3 Observations on Salient Aspects of the Panel Report

The panel's finding can be described as remarkable for the following aspects.

With respect to the treatment of Appellate Body precedent, the panel very carefully walked a balancing act between adherence to the Appellate Body's previous decisions, on the one hand, and the claim by China that it deserved a fresh look at the core legal issue, on the other hand. All in all, the panel explained lucidly why it decided not simply to follow Appellate Body precedent without further analysis; but at the same time produced a systemically healthy outcome that respects the quasi-precedent status that Appellate Body decisions enjoy.

In its Article XX(g) and chapeau analysis, the panel found that the search for alternatives to WTO-inconsistent behaviour could be analysed under the chapeau. This thought has never previously been explicitly articulated and serves to underscore that the consideration of alternatives is—rightly—less driven by particular treaty terms (such as "necessary" under Article XX(b), but more by the inherent logic of weighing and balancing trade and non-trade concerns.

Finally, continuing with the analysis of "alternatives", the panel found that doing more of an already existing category of regulation (e.g. stricter pollution controls or stricter maximum mining volumes) can serve as an alternative measure. This is important, because defendant governments increasingly argue in WTO dispute settlement that the incriminated measure is part of a "comprehensive suite of measures"; doing so is sometimes driven by the wish to fight off suggestions of alternative measures on the grounds that the proposed alternatives are already being implemented. If the argument were accepted that doing more of something is not alternative, it would make it significantly more difficult to ever identify alternative measures to WTO-inconsistent behaviour. This would make challenges to regulatory protectionism much easier under, for instance, Article III and XI of the GATT 1994, Article 2.1 of the TBT Agreement or Article 5.6 of the SPS Agreement.

9 China: Rare Earths—Appellate Body Report

9.1 The Appellate Body's Ruling in a Nutshell

The Appellate Body's review of the panel findings in the China—Rare Earths dispute focussed on the relationship between the WTO Agreement (Marrakesh Agreement) and Paragraph 1.2 of China's Accession Protocol, as well as on Article XX(g).

Although the Appellate Body quibbled with certain aspects of the panel ruling, it upheld the essential core of the panel's determination. China was unable to convince the Appellate Body that its measures could be justified as environmental measures.

9.2 Salient Legal Findings

9.2.1 The Relationship Between Article XII of the WTO Agreement and Paragraph 1.2 of China's Accession Protocol

China appealed the panel's finding that Article XII of the WTO Agreement—which provides that an accession "shall apply to the [WTO] Agreement and the Multilateral Trade Agreements annexed thereto"—did not imply that the Accession Protocol was made part of each Multilateral Trade Agreement, such that an Article XX defense would be available to violations of obligations enshrined in the Accession Protocol. The panel had concluded that, by virtue of paragraph 1.2 of the Accession Protocol, the Protocol had to be treated as an "integral" part of the WTO Agreement, but not also as an integral part of each Multilateral Trade Agreement.

The thrust of the Appellate Body's detailed engagement with China's argument was that Article XII reinforces the concept of "single undertaking", whereby all WTO Members are subject to all covered agreements. However, Article XII does not create a substantive relationship between China's Accession Protocol and provisions of the covered agreements. Nor did paragraph 1.2 of the Accession Protocol contain relevant guidance on this point; instead, it simply confirmed Article XII of the WTO Agreement. The Appellate Body acknowledged that the term "WTO Agreement" in the Accession Protocol can also be understood as building a "bridge" between the Protocol and all the covered agreements. However, that "bridge" was of a general nature and had to be specified with respect to individual provision of the Protocol.

The Appellate Body pointed out that the same applied to the relationship between the covered agreements, as well as between the covered agreements and the WTO Agreement, which had to be assessed on a case-by-case basis. For instance, Article 3 of the TRIMs Agreement explicitly referred to GATT exceptions; in contrast, the Appellate Body recalled that it had declined that Article XX could be available to justify a breach of the TBT Agreement. The answer always depended on the specific wording of the relevant provision and on the closeness of the link established in the provision. Thus, China's general argument of an "intrinsic relationship" between the Protocol and the WTO Agreement was not sufficient.

9.2.2 Article XX(g) and Measures Relating to Conservation

China also appealed the panel's conclusion that its export quotas do not "relate to" conservation under Article XX(g); and that these export quotas are not "made effective in conjunction with" domestic restrictions under Article XX(g).

With respect to the interpretation of Article XX(g), the Appellate Body confirmed that the panel had not erred by focussing on the "design and structure" of the export quotas, in determining whether they "relate to" conservation. It also found that the panel did not err when it found that this analysis did not require an evaluation of actual effects of the concerned measures, although "predictable effects of a measure may be relevant for the analysis". The Appellate Body also rejected a number of arguments of China as mischaracterizing the panel's findings.

The Appellate Body also addressed the panel's use of the concept of "even-handedness". It found it unclear whether the panel had considered even-handedness to be a separate requirement or whether it considered that this concept was embodied in paragraph (g). The Appellate Body clarified that even-handedness was not a separate concept or element in the Article XX(g) test and found an error by the panel to the extent that the panel considered this criterion as a separate analytical element. As a separate point, the Appellate Body also clarified that

Article XX(g) required that, if there were limitations on international trade in the name of conservation, then domestic restrictions also had to exist that would impose limitations on domestic production or consumption; and such restrictions had to be "real", rather than merely "on the books". At the same time, it was not necessary for a successful invocation of Article XX(g) that the burden on domestic and foreign consumers be "evenly distributed".

With respect to the application of Article XX(g), the Appellate Body rejected China's appeal for more or less the same reasons as it had articulated with respect to the interpretation of Article XX(g). The Appellate Body also rejected a number of arguments by China as to the panel's treatment of evidence, under Article 11 of the DSU.

9.2.3 Simultaneous Timing of Appeals

Beyond the substance of this dispute, an interesting issue arose with regard to the timing of the appeal. The US appeal in this dispute was filed simultaneously with the appeal by China of the panel report in the US—Countervailing and Anti-dumping Measures (China) dispute. The Appellate Body assigns appeal numbers on a sequential basis, depending on the day of filing of the appeal. The random selection of the Appellate Body division is then linked to these appeal numbers. Hence, the simultaneous appeals created a problem as to how to assign appeal numbers to these two appeals. The Appellate Body resolved this problem by a random draw in the presence of the parties. It also expressed regret about this situation, exhorting parties to "coordinate, communicate and cooperate amongst themselves, as well as with the Appellate Body and the Appellate Body Secretariat, in the planning, filing and conduct of their appeals".

9.3 Observations on Salient Aspects of the Appellate Body Report

One noteworthy point is the Appellate Body's reaffirmation of its caselaw concerning Article XX and its applicability to legal texts other than the GATT 1994. The Appellate Body has emphasized that the relationship between the Protocol of Accession and Article XX cannot be determined in the abstract, but rather must be clarified on a case-by-case basis, in the light of the precise wording of a given provision. This approach has the usual virtues and drawbacks of a "case-by-case" approach—on the minus side, little predictability; on the plus side, greater flexibility for the adjudicating body.

The Appellate Body also helpfully clarified the concept of "even-handedness" under Article XX(g). For one, it emphasized that it is not a treaty term and not a separate criterion under Article XX(g), but rather a short-hand for the "made effective in conjunction with"-criterion, which obviously *is* treaty language. Secondly, the Appellate Body clarified that the "made effective in conjunction with" standard does not require precise equality in the "burden" on the domestic and on the export/import side, but does require—in the present case—that there be some equivalent limitations on domestic consumption. These limitations were missing on the domestic side in this dispute, making China's defense a very challenging task.

10 US: Countervailing and Anti-Dumping Measures (China)—Panel Report

10.1 Factual Background

The factual background to this dispute reaches back to the early 1980s. At that time, the United States Department of Commerce (USDOC) decided not to apply countervailing duties (CVDs) to non-market economies (NMEs). The basic idea behind this decision was that NMEs were so distorted due to the pervasive influence of the government on the national economy that it made little sense to determine to what extent pricing decisions by exporters were distorted through subsidies.

This practice of not imposing CVDs on exports from NMEs lasted until 2006/2007. Presumably under pressure from domestic interest groups, USDOC decided to apply CVDs to NMEs. It argued that its previous practice flowed from the discretion vested in it under the applicable legislation; in other words, the non-application practice was not mandatory, but rather discretionary, and thus could be changed.

This decision by USDOC was challenged before the US judiciary. In 2011, in the so-called GPX V case, the Court of Appeals for the Federal Circuit (CAFC) determined that the USDOC's decision to apply CVDs was in violation of US statutes. In reaction to this decision, the United States Congress promulgated a new law that requires USDOC to apply CVDs to NMEs and provides the conditions for doing so.

An interesting additional wrinkle to this legislation is that the requirement to apply CVDs to NME exports was retroactive—concerning investigations initiated on or after November 2006; however, the new statute took effect only in 2012. At the same time, an important concomitant aspect was not applied on a retrospective basis. This concomitant aspect concerned so-called "double remedies" that can arise when anti-dumping duties and CVDs are applied to the same exports from NMEs. These double remedies arise because, when an investigating authority calculates a dumping margin for exporters in NMEs, it uses a surrogate normal value that is typically derived from a proxy country (e.g. using Indonesia as a surrogate country for China, to account for the perception that prices in that industry in China are distorted through governmental intervention). By using this proxy country, one eliminates the effects of any subsidy that may have existed in the country of origin (in our example, China). If the investigating authority were now to apply both anti-dumping duties and CVDs in the full amount, it would (at least partially) double-count the effect of the subsidy, creating "double remedies", which is prohibited under WTO law. The panel phrased this problem in the following manner: "[T]o the extent that a subsidy leads to a reduction in the export price of a product, that subject will necessarily be captured in the dumping margin if that dumping margin, and the resulting antidumping duty, are calculated using a nonmarket economy methodology that calculates normal value based on surrogate values from a third country."

In recognition of this risk of double remedies, the new US statute provided the necessary tools for avoiding double remedies. However, the relevant provisions—concerning the avoidance of double remedies—were applicable only prospectively, counting from the time of promulgation of the statute. Hence, for the period between 2006 and 2012, USDOC was required to impose CVDs on NME exports, but did not have the legal tools to avoid the imposition of double remedies.

10.2 Salient Legal Findings

10.2.1 Prompt Publication of Trade Regulations: GATT Article X:1

China claimed that the United States violated Article X:1 of the GATT 1994 because the measure at issue applied over 5 years retrospectively. As is known, Article X:1 of the GATT 1994 requires Members to publish their laws, regulations, judicial decisions and international agreements related to trade matters. The overarching objective of Article X is greater transparency of national legislation, for the benefit of both exporting countries as well as of private commercial operators. Article X:1 does not specify how publication should occur, but it requires that publication occur "promptly".

China argued that, by applying to events going back to 2006, the measure had been "made effective" with respect to that year and thus had not been published "promptly". The panel disagreed, finding that the term "made effective" referred to the legal effect of the measure at the time of its promulgation, rather than referring to the temporal scope of the measure's application. The upshot of this finding is that Article X:1 does not discipline at all a Member's decision to backdate a measure and apply it retroactively. Rather, this task seems to fall on the shoulders of Article X:2.

10.2.2 No Enforcement Before Publication Pursuant to Article X:2

Article X:2 provides that trade laws and regulations that effect "an advance in a rate of duty or other charge on imports under an established and uniform practice", or a "new" or "more burdensome" requirement may not be enforced before the measure has been officially published. Thus, unlike under Article X:1, Article X:2 appears to specifically prohibit retroactive application of certain measures.

The panel agreed that the measure had been "enforced" prior to its official publication. The panel found that the term "enforced" also referred to the temporal scope of application of a measure, in the sense of a set of past events and circumstances—that occurred prior to the enactment of the measure—to which the measure was being applied retroactively.

Nonetheless, the majority of the panel found that the measure fell outside the scope of Article X:2, because it neither effected an "advance" in a rate of duty or other charge on imports under an established or uniform practice, nor imposed a "new" or "more burdensome" requirement or restriction on imports. The key question here was which aspect of domestic law should serve as the benchmark for determining whether an "advance" or a "new" or "more burdensome" requirement had been imposed. For instance, should the benchmark be the law as it stood before 2006, that is, the non-application of CVDs to NMEs? Or rather the USDOC's practice of applying CVDs, since 2006, even though it had been subsequently declared illegal by US courts?

The panel majority chose the USDOC practice between 2006 and 2012 as the benchmark—that is, the practice of applying CVDs to NMEs. This choice was in part driven by the words "under an established and uniform practice" in Article X:2. The panel majority did not consider that the practice was unlawful under US law, because no US court had, at the time when the new law was introduced, formally ordered USDOC to revise its practice. The panel majority then found that no "advance" in a duty had been "effected", because the new rates of countervailing duties, whatever rates were those appropriate in the light of the applicable U.S. CVD provisions, just like the rates previously applicable under USDOC's established and uniform practice after 2006. For the same reasons, the panel majority found that the measure at issue did not create a "new" or "more burdensome" requirement. Therefore, the panel majority concluded that the US did not act inconsistently with Article X:2 of the GATT 1994.

However, one panelist dissented from this part of the panel majority finding and reached the opposite conclusion. The dissenter used as the relevant benchmark not the post-2006 USDOC practice, but rather the applicable legal provisions before and after the legislative change. The dissenter found that, prior to the enactment of the measure, US CVD law did not apply to imports from NMEs; subsequent to the enactment, CVD law did apply to such imports. Absent the new measure, USDOC would have had to revoke all pending CVD orders. The dissenter also rejected the US argument that the measure at issue merely "clarified" the previously applicable law; it also found that—even accepting this "clarification" argument—the new state of the law required USDOC to apply CVDs to NME imports, whereas before there was discretion to do so. The dissenter ended on the interesting note of accusing the majority of eviscerating Article X:2; it stated that, under the majority's approach, a Member could circumvent Article X:2 by applying a higher rate or a more burdensome requirement some time before publishing the relevant measure; the new measure would then be compared to that pre-publication more burdensome practice, and a violation of Article X:2 would never be found.

10.2.3 Claim Under Article X:3(b)

China's third claim concerned the requirement in Article X:3(b) that tribunals "be independent of the agencies entrusted with administrative enforcement and their decisions shall be implemented by, and shall govern the practice of, such agencies unless an appeal is lodged." China contented that, if legislation such as the measure at issue were permissible, it would not be meaningful to seek judicial review of what an interested party considers to be unlawful agency conduct. This, according to China, would be because an independent tribunal's favourable finding could always be superseded by the enactment of a new law that renders the agency's actions lawful "after the fact".

The panel rejected this argument and ruled that Article X:3(b) does not prohibit a WTO member from taking legislative action such as the measure at issue, that is, supersede a judicial determination that is pending when the legislation comes into force. The key argument of the panel was that the measure at issue did not narrowly target pending court cases but amended the law in a more general manner.

10.2.4 Claim Concerning "Double Remedies"

As described above, the new 2011 "GPX" legislation required USDOC to apply retroactively CVDs to NME exports in investigations initiated as early as 2006. However, the requirement to avoid double remedies was applicable only as of 2012. Due to this time "gap", China argued that the United States had failed to investigate and avoid double remedies in 26 countervailing duty (CVD) investigations and administrative reviews initiated over the period 2008–2012.

The panel found no "cogent reason" to depart from a previous Appellate Body finding that Article 19.3 requires an investigating authority to investigate and to avoid double remedies when concurrently imposing CVDs and anti-dumping duties. The notion of "double remedies" was described in the factual background section of this summary. The Appellate Body finding made previously in DS379 has two aspects, namely, "(i) the imposition of double remedies arising from the concurrent imposition of CVDs and anti-dumping duties calculated under an NME methodology is inconsistent with the obligation in Article 19.3 to levy CVDs' in the appropriate amounts; and (ii) the burden is on an investigating authority imposing such concurrent duties to 'investigate' whether it is offsetting the same subsidies twice."[58] The United States requested the panel to review and depart from this Appellate Body finding, including by invoking specificities of the United States

[58] Appellate Body Report, *US – Anti-Dumping and Countervailing Duties*, para. 606.

trade remedy system; however, the panel declined to do so, as it saw no "cogent reasons" for departing from this Appellate Body precedent.

The panel then considered the 26 investigations at issue and found that the United States had failed to investigate whether double remedies could arise.

10.2.5 Examples of "Cogent Reasons" to Depart from Prior Appellate Body Case Law

In confronting the issue of double remedies, the panel noted that the Appellate Body had previously addressed this issue in the *US – Anti-Dumping and Countervailing Duties*.[59] The panel then considered to what extent it was bound by this Appellate Body decision and referred to the Appellate Body's statement that, absent "cogent reasons", panels were expected to follow previous Appellate Body decisions on the same issue. The panel noted that the Appellate Body had not defined the concept of "cogent reasons" and provided examples of what it considered to be such cogent reasons, namely: (i) a multilateral interpretation of a provision of the covered agreements under Article IX:2 of the WTO Agreement that departs from a prior Appellate Body interpretation; (ii) a demonstration that a prior Appellate Body interpretation proved to be "unworkable in a particular set of circumstances falling within the scope of the relevant obligation at issue"; (iii) a demonstration that the Appellate Body's prior interpretation leads to a conflict with another provision of a covered agreement that was not raised before the Appellate Body; or (iv) a demonstration that the Appellate Body's interpretation was based on a "factually incorrect premise."[60] In this dispute, the panel found that none of these scenarios existed.

10.3 Observations on Salient Aspects of the Panel Report

Our observation on this panel report is set out in the description of the Appellate Body report in the same dispute, as set out below.

[59] WT/DS379/AB/R.

[60] Panel Report, *US – Countervailing and Anti-Dumping Measures*, para. 7.317.

11 US: Countervailing and Anti-Dumping Measures (China)—Appellate Body Report

11.1 Salient legal Findings

Aside from certain procedural findings—on the sufficiency of China's panel request and the admissibility of certain evidence—the Appellate Body report in this dispute is entirely focused on the interpretation and application of Article X:2 of the GATT 1994.

It may be recalled that the panel majority found that no "advance" in a rate of duty or a "new" or "more burdensome" requirement existed, because the majority compared the new measure with the USDOC's post-2006 practice of applying CVDs to NMEs. In contrast, the dissenter compared the relevant US statute as it stood prior to and subsequent to the measure at issue. China appealed against the majority's finding.

The Appellate Body reversed the majority's finding. It characterized the function of Article X:2 as "ensuring transparency and protecting traders' expectations as to the publication and enforcement of certain measures is relevant to the interpretation of the obligations contained in this provision." For this reason, these traders' expectations about the applicable measure were the "proper baseline" for Article X:2.

The Appellate Body specified that the baseline of the comparison under Article X:2 to determine whether a measure "effects an advance in a rate of duty" should be made between the new measure and the prior published measure that it replaced or modified. The Appellate Body rejected the use of USDOC practice as such a benchmark, in part by correcting the panel majority's reliance on the phrase "under an established and uniform practice" in Article X:2. Rather, it found, the analysis should start with the language of the previous measure and its meaning should be ascertained on the basis of objective criteria. In that context, the practice of the administering agency—here, the USDOC post-2006 practice—could be relevant. However, the Appellate Body disagreed with the panel majority's approach of ascribing decisive importance to the USDOC practice, subject only to the requirement that the practice was lawful. The Appellate Body therefore reversed the panel majority's finding.

The Appellate Body then attempted to "complete the analysis" and come to its conclusion on the consistency of the US measure with Article X:2 based on the corrected legal standard. The key issue was the precise meaning of the relevant US statute prior to the enactment of the measure at issue in 2012. The Appellate Body considered that to determine this precise meaning required a comprehensive examination of legislation, judicial decisions, and expert legal opinions pertaining to CVD law in the United States. Needless to say, the legislation, decisions, and opinions relating to US CVD law that the Appellate Body had at its disposal were amenable to different interpretations. The Appellate Body also considered that USDOC's inconsistent application of CVD law to NMEs complicated the analysis.[61] Because many of the criteria for examining the meaning of US domestic law were factual in nature, and because the Appellate Body cannot establish new facts, the Appellate Body concluded that it was unable to complete the analysis. Hence, the Appellate Body was unable to resolve the question of the legality of the US measure.

11.2 Observations on Salient Aspects of the Appellate Body Report

Although this dispute was ultimately unsatisfactory from China's perspective, because the Appellate Body could not complete the legal analysis and find a violation of Article X:2, the Appellate Body's finding is nevertheless important. As the panel dissenter correctly pointed out, the panel majority's view carries in it the risk of a circular comparison, where a new measure retrospectively "blesses" a particular practice by an administering agency. Put differently, where an administering agency begins—contrary to previous practice, under the same statutory language—to apply a different practice; and that practice is subsequently cast into statutory language that differs from the previous statutory language; the panel majority's approach would deny a violation of Article X:2. The Appellate Body's approach of focussing on the statutory language as the key criterion—all the while examining administrative practice (as well as judicial decisions) as a manifestation of the meaning of domestic law—appears more principled and correct.

12 China: Anti-Dumping and Countervailing Duties on Certain Automobiles from the United States

12.1 Facts of the Case

The dispute concerned the anti-dumping ("ADDs") and countervailing duties ("CVDs") imposed by China in December 2011 on certain automobiles imported from the Unites States, as set out in Notices 20 and 84 of the Chinese Ministry of Commerce ("MOFCOM").[62] MOFCOM had identified six main respondent companies, among which were General Motors LLC, Ford Motor Company, Mercedes-Benz USA and Chrysler Group LLC.

---

[61] Appellate Body Report, *US – Countervailing and Anti-Dumping Measures*, para. 4.165.

[62] MOFCOM, *Announcement No. 20* and Appendix, "Final Determination of the People's Republic of China concerning the Anti-dumping and Countervailing Investigation on Imports of Certain Automobiles Originating in the United States" (5 May 2011); MOFCOM, *Announcement No. 84* (14 December 2011).

The duties concerned specifically certain automobiles from the US with an engine capacity of 2.5 litres or bigger. ADDs ranged from to 21.5 %, while CDDs ranged from 6.2 to 30 %.

China's ADDs and CVDs were challenged by the United States in July 2012. The US raised a series of allegations under the *Anti-dumping agreement ("ADA"), Agreement on Subsidies and Countervailing Measures ("ASCM")* and the GATT 1994.

While the WTO dispute was pending, China announced that it would discontinue the duties it had imposed on the vehicles at issue. This, however, did not prevent the Panel from making a ruling, notably on the ground that China "has not brought any official documentation that would support this contention". The DSB issued a report in May 2014. In the absence of an appeal by either party, the DSB adopted the Panel Report in June 2014.

12.2 Salient Legal Findings

The Panel found a series of Chinese duties on imports of US-made cars and SUVs to be inconsistent with the *ADA* and the *SCM Agreement*, notably because of procedural and substantive violations. As is well-known, these two agreements prevent WTO Members from imposing AD or CVD measures unless its relevant authorities conduct an investigation that determines the existence of dumping or subsidization respectively as well as consequential injury to the domestic industry.

The United States argued that China had not followed the appropriate procedures when examining potential subsidies and dumping and applying these particular duties, determined by MOFCOM. According to the US' complaint, the investigations were based on insufficient evidence; entailed a faulty definition of the domestic industry; withheld relevant data and calculations; failed to objectively examine the evidence; and made unsupported findings of injury to the domestic industry.

12.2.1 Confidential Data and Non-Confidential Summaries

Anti-dumping and anti-subsidy proceedings involve considerable amounts of confidential and sensitive business information because they require exporting companies to submit to the importing Member authorities information concerning price and cost of the products in a detailed manner. In order to build a strong case, interested parties ideally need access to the confidential information submitted by the opposing side. At the same time, they will be reluctant to provide their own confidential information to their opponents. Thus, equal access to information should be given to the parties.

Article 6.5 of the *ADA* and Article 12 of the *SCM Agreement* contain a principle that information, which is by nature confidential, should be treated as such by the authorities and should not be disclosed without the authorization by the party submitting it. However, the authorities require interested parties providing such confidential information to present meaningful non-confidential summaries thereof. The summary should allow a reasonable understanding of the information withheld in order for the opposing party to respond and defend its interests.

The United States challenged the adequacy of 12 non-confidential summaries submitted in the petition. The Panel found some of them to be consistent with Articles 6.5.1 of the *ADA* and Article 12.4.1 of the *SCM Agreement*, since they permitted a reasonable understanding of the redacted confidential information. However, the Panel also found that MOFCOM failed to require the submission of adequate non-confidential summaries of confidential information concerning certain other injury factors in the petitions for both ADDs and CVDs. These findings of violation are part of a longer series of disputes against China in which findings were made against MOFCOM with respect to non-confidential summaries of confidential information.[63] It remains to be seen to what extent these findings will lead to adjustment in MOFCOM practice that may in the future give rise to fewer challenges.

12.2.2 Determination of the "Residual Rate"

The panel faced a series of claims by the United States about how China determined what the panel called the "residual rate". This is the rate applied to exporters who were not known to the investigating authority and were therefore not included in the investigation. The panel distinguished this rate from the "limited examination" rate, which is the rate applied to exporters that are known to the investigating authority, but not included in a sample pursuant to Article 6.10 of the Anti-dumping Agreement. The panel deliberately declined to use the term "all others rate", which is popular among trade remedy lawyers but, according to the panel, obfuscates the difference between the "limited examination" rate and the "residual rate".

It may be noted that it is not clear—either from the text of the Anti-dumping Agreement or from the case law—whether investigating authorities may indeed apply to unknown exporters a rate that is different (or higher, as investigating authorities typically do) from the "limited examination" rate. This point was described in detail in the analogous article in the last edition of the Yearbook.[64] This panel assumed that it was permissible. It would, of course, be useful for the Appellate Body to clarify this important point.

The panel found that China violated Article 6.8 and Annex II, because the notice of initiation did not sufficiently inform exporters about the precise information required of them (volumes and prices) and therefore did not satisfy the "facts

[63] Panel Report, *China – GOES,* para. 7.223–7.225. Panel Report, *China – Broiler Products,* para. 7.65. Panel Report, *China – X-Ray Equipment,* para. 7.364.

[64] Bohanes and Salcedo (2015), pp. 346–349.

available" requirements. In other words, there was a mismatch between the information requested in the notice of initiation, and the facts available used. However, the panel rejected the United States' claim that China had not properly disclosed the essential facts relevant to this residual rate; and that it had not provided sufficient public notice.

Interestingly, the panel found that, the SCM Agreement does not contain the equivalent of Articles 6.10 and 9.4 of the Anti-Dumping Agreement, and that it was therefore also not clear whether the notion of a "residual rate" applied to countervailing duties. However, the panel assumed that this was the case, for reasons of logic. The panel also assumed that, although the SCM Agreement does not contain an Annex II of the Anti-dumping Agreement, nevertheless the same requirement apply under the SCM Agreement for purposes of determining the legality of the recourse to facts available. The findings under the SCM Agreement mirrored the analogous claims under the Anti-dumping Agreement.

12.2.3 Definition of the Domestic Industry

An interesting finding was made in the context of defining the domestic industry. During an investigation, the investigating authority must determine the domestic industry for purposes of the injury determination. This requires examination of which domestically produced products are like the exported products. Article 4.1 of the Anti-dumping Agreement establishes two methods for the determination of the domestic industry: either the domestic industry is constituted of the domestic producers of the like product, or it corresponds to a group of producers whose collective output constitutes a major proportion of the domestic production of the like product.

The Appellate Body had indicated that given the context in which the term "a major proportion" is situated, it should be properly understood as a "relatively high proportion of the total domestic production", so as to ensure that the domestic industry defined on this basis is capable of providing ample data that ensure an accurate injury analysis.[65]

The Appellate Body had also noted that while an investigating authority is provided with a certain flexibility to define the domestic industry in the light of what is reasonable and practically possible, the determination should be made in an unbiased manner. Particularly, an investigating authority "must not act as to give rise to a material risk of distortion in defining the domestic industry, for example, by excluding a whole category of producers of the like product."[66]

In *EC – Fasteners*, the European Commission contacted and received information from a large number of domestic producers and from that number it excluded those who did not indicate a willingness to be part of the sample. The Commission

[65] Appellate Body Report, *EC – Fasteners*, para. 412–413.

[66] Appellate Body Report, *EC – Fasteners*, para. 414.

further concluded that this smaller group still qualified as a "major proportion" since it represented more that 25 % of total domestic production. The Appellate Body had found that the Commission acted inconsistently with the requirement of objectivity by defining the domestic industry as only those producers willing to be included in a sample for the injury determination, because this introduced the possibility of bias towards an affirmative finding of injury.[67]

Unlike in the *EC – Fasteners*, the panel did not find a similar inconsistency in the fact that MOFCOM had excluded certain producers from the scope of the domestic industry.[68] Specifically, the United States relied on the *EC – Fasteners*, claiming that China had defined the industry in a biased fashion by including within the domestic industry only those producers that had been "registered", based on their willingness to provide data for the injury investigation.

The panel rejected this claim, stating that the mere use of a registration requirement by MOFCOM did not introduce a material risk of distortion. Furthermore, the Panel found that, unlike in *EC – Fasteners*, MOFCOM had not defined the domestic industry on the basis of willingness to be included in a sample, and that the US had not shown that the process used by MOFCOM to define the domestic industry was biased towards a category of domestic producers. Indeed, MOFCOM communicated its notices, forms and questionnaires in an open manner, allowing any interested party to participate in the investigations. The choice of some of the producers not to participate in the investigation could not be attributed to the investigating authority or the registration process, since these producers were equally aware of the need to register in order to participate.

Moreover, MOFCOM did not define the domestic industry on the basis of willingness to be included in a sample, since there was no sampling in the investigations at issue, and thus no question of excluding some of the producers unwilling to be included in a subset of the domestic industry.

This finding highlights the difficult balance to be found between administrative efficiency and an investigating authority's need to be pragmatic in its investigation, on the one hand; and the need for objectivity, on the other hand. Limiting the injury determination to producers that are willing to participate in the investigation creates, as the United States argued, a serious risk of distortion and bias. As difficult as this issue may be in practice, it is not clear whether this panel finding adequately balances the competing concerns and whether it is not tilted too much in favour of administrative expedience and too lenient on an investigating authority.

---

[67] Appellate Body Report, *EC – Fasteners,* paras. 422 and 427.

[68] Panel Report, *China – Broiler Products,* para. 7.428.

13 India: Agricultural Products—Panel Report

13.1 Facts of the Case

The dispute concerned an import prohibition series of measures imposed by India on certain agricultural products from countries reporting Notifiable Avian Influenza ("NAI") to the World Organization for Animal Health ("OIE"). The WTO uses the OIE as the reference organization for standards relating to animal health and infectious diseases of animals. The Terrestrial Animal Health Code ("OIE Code") is the principle reference for WTO members for purposes of the *Sanitary and Phytosanitary Measures Agreement ("SPS Agreement")*. Chapter 10.4 of the OIE Code deals specifically with avian flu, requiring members to notify the OIE of any cases of domestic highly pathogenic notifiable avian flu ("HPNAI") in birds and the occurrence of certain types of low pathogenicity notifiable avian flu ("LPNAI") in poultry.

The measures at issue were: the Indian Livestock Importation Act 1898 ("Livestock Act"); a number of orders issued by India's Department of Animal Husbandry, Dairying, and Fisheries pursuant to the Livestock Act, most recently Statutory Order ("S.O.") 1663 (E); as well as any amendments, related measures, or implementing measures.

India's import ban on US poultry and other farm goods was challenged by the United States in 2012, raising a series of allegations under the *SPS Agreement* and the GATT 1994.

The DSB issued a report in October 2014. In January 2015, India notified the DSB of its decision to appeal to the Appellate Body certain issues of law and legal interpretation in the panel report. The Appellate Body report in this dispute was issued in June 2015, and is therefore not covered by this article.

13.2 Salient Legal Findings

The Panel found that India had violated WTO law on a number of counts. The following five sections highlight the most salient legal findings from a systemic perspective.

13.2.1 Presumption of Consistency Under Article 3.2

SPS measures vary across countries due to the differences in national regulations, interests of domestic stakeholders, consumers' preferences etc. The resulting diversity of SPS measures has a negative impact on trade, as exporters must ensure to comply with different standards in order to gain market access. The *SPS Agreement* intends to address this issue by promoting harmonization of SPS measures, by providing an obligation and an incentive for WTO Members to use international standards for their domestic legislation. Members are required to "base" their domestic legislation on international standards, unless certain exceptions apply.

Harmonization around international standards is encouraged in the *SPS Agreement* by means of a presumption of consistency of measures conforming to international standards with the GATT 1994 and the *SPS Agreement.* Indeed, pursuant to Article 3.2, when a Member's legislation "conforms" to an international standard—rather than merely being "based on" that standard—that legislation enjoys a presumption of consistency with the SPS Agreement.[69]

The concept of "conformity" requires greater adherence to the international standard than the concept of being "based on". However, the precise boundary between the two is not clear and has not been illustrated by many disputes so far. With regard to the meaning of "based on", the Appellate Body stated that one thing is commonly said to be based on another if the former stands or is founded or built upon or supported by the latter. Further, it stated that a measure based on a standard does not necessarily conform to that standard, such as where only some of the elements of the standard are incorporated into the measure.[70]

In *EC – Hormones* the Appellate Body also explained that for a measure to "conform to" an international standard, it should "embody the international standard completely". It thus appears that the national standard must be identical to the international standard.

The United Stated argued that India's measures did not comply even with the lower of these two standards, in that it was not "based on" the relevant OIE standard. Surprisingly, India responded to this allegation by arguing that its measure "conformed" to the OIE standard—the higher of the two standards.

The Panel found for the United States, mainly because the Indian measure categorically prohibited importation of poultry from entire countries currently or previously affected by LPNAI, and did not permit importation from particular zones of those countries that were free of NAI or HPNAI. This, in the Panel's view, represented a "fundamental departure" from the OIE Terrestrial Code, because the Code precisely envisaged such regional differentiation. The Panel rejected India's contention that an importing country may choose as a "condition of entry" the NAI-free status of the entire exporting country and apply that condition only on a countrywide basis.

13.2.2 Necessity and Scientific Principles: Relationship Between Articles 2.2, 5.1 and 5.2

The *SPS Agreement* aims to ensure that SPS measures are scientifically justified and take relevant scientific factors into account. According to Article 5.1 of the *SPS*

[69] Appellate Body Report, *EC – Hormones,* para. 170.

[70] Appellate Body Report, *EC – Hormones,* para. 163.

Agreement, Members are required to ensure that their SPS measures are based on a risk assessment.

According to well established jurisprudence, this provision should be read together with Article 2.2, which in turn lays down two requirements for SPS measures, namely that: (i) they be applied only to the extent necessary to protect human, animal or plant life or health; and (ii) they have a basis in scientific evidence, except certain cases.

The United States claimed that India's AI measures were inconsistent with Article 2.2 automatically as a result of breaching the risk assessment requirement under Article 5.1. That means that, to find a violation of Article 2.2, the Panel would base its analysis on a mere presumption of inconsistency, without going through a two-tier test of the article.

The Panel ruled on the inconsistency of India's AI measures with Article 2.2, solely basing its reasoning on the presumption of inconsistency, which was previously developed and upheld by the AB in *Australia-Salmon,*[71] *EC-Hormones,*[72] and *Australia-Apples.*[73] While the Panel announced the requirements of the Article 2.2, i.e. that a measure should be based on scientific principles and not maintained without sufficient scientific evidence, it did not conduct the legal analysis further and did not address India's claims, notably the scientific evidence it presented.

Thus, the Panel's finding makes the presumption almost automatic and complainants are likely to argue a violation of the "necessity" requirement of Article 2.2 along with the violation of obligations relating to risk assessment under Article 5 of *SPS Agreement.* Given a rather strict standard of review, the question arises whether would it at all be possible for a respondent to rebut a presumption of Article 2.2 inconsistency.

13.2.3 National Treatment

Member's right to adopt SPS measures is limited in several ways, including the non-discrimination provision, similar to Article I:1 and III:4 of the GATT.

The Panel, relying on the experts' appreciation whether India's surveillance activities would reliably detect LPNAI in poultry, concluded that India's AI measures discriminate between India and other Members. Indeed, while prohibiting imports of certain products listed in S.O. from WTO Members who notify LPNAI to the OIE, India did not have in place a surveillance system capable of detecting that same risk within its territory.

The Panel qualified India's AI measures as "rigid and unbending requirements"[74] because they did not take into account differences that may exist between

---

[71] Appellate Body Report, *Australia – Salmon,* paras. 137 and 138, footnote 166 to para. 213.

[72] Appellate Body Report, *EC – Hormones,* para. 180.

[73] Appellate Body Report, *Australia – Apples,* para. 340.

[74] Panel Report, *India – Agricultural Products,* para. 7.435.

and among WTO Members from which India imports the poultry products at hand. Consequently, the Panel found that India's treatment of foreign poultry amounted to unjustifiable discrimination within the meaning of Article 2.3 of the *SPS Agreement.*

The crux of India's defence under Article 2.3 was that LPNAI is exotic to India. However, after consulting with the OIE experts, the Panel had found that India did not maintain a regime for the surveillance of AI that could reliably detect LPNAI. Indeed, a visual observation "where possible" of "unusual sickness" in birds, qualified by "passive surveillance" by one of the experts, does not seem to be a reliable method of detection of LPNAI. Consequently, India's rationale to rebut the US claim could not be qualified as a "rational connection" between the reasons given for the discriminatory application of the measure and the objective of the measure, the requirement set out by the Appellate Body in *Brazil – Retreated Tyres.*[75] Therefore, the India's AI measures were found to be inconsistent with Article 2.3 of the *SPS Agreement.*

13.2.4 Appropriate Level of Protection Under Article 5.6

The Panel had also made a finding that India's AI measures were more trade-restrictive than required to achieve its appropriate level of protection ("ALOP") under Article 5.6 of the *SPS Agreement.* The Panel reached this finding relying on the arguments put forward by the US.

In order for a complainant to successfully challenge the inconsistency of other Member's measure with Article 5.6 of the *SPS Agreement,* it should establish that there is a reasonably available alternative measure taking into account the technical and economical feasibility. The alternative should also achieve the desired ALOP and should be less trade restrictive than the challenged measure.

The Panel was required to identify India's ALOP in order to adjudicate the claims raised by the US.

In the context of identifying the level of protection achieved by the proposed alternative measures, the Panel found that the OIE Code "provides for an optimal level of security, under which safe trade may be facilitated in order to prevent AI from being introduced into an importing country".[76] Then, the Panel concluded that the measures based on the recommendations of the OIE Code would achieve "a level of protection that is at least as high as India's 'very high' or 'very conservative' level of protection".[77]

The Panel's finding implicitly encourages Members to identify their ALOP as precisely as possible in order for it not to be requalified by the Panel. And since the

[75] Appellate Body Report, *Brazil – Retreated Tyres,* para. 227.

[76] Panel Report, *India – Agricultural Products,* para. 7.581.

[77] Panel Report, *India – Agricultural Products,* para. 7.582.

ALOP is merely an "objective"[78] and not the instrument of implementation of that measure, the clarity and the correct establishment of a Member's appropriate level of protection may play a difference in the analysis of Article 5.6.

13.2.5 Adaptation of SPS Measures to Regional Conditions

When a pest or disease occurs within a country, many countries in the past have banned imports from the entire country, even if the prevalence is limited to certain regions. However, in order for the importing country to comply with its WTO obligations, it is required by Article 6 of the *SPS Agreement* to adapt its SPS measures to the conditions prevailing in the region of origin of the product. This highly improves market access possibilities since imports from the pest-free areas or regions are allowed.

The US had challenged the meaning and the content of the AI measures on their face, because they did not recognize the concept of disease-free areas or areas of low disease prevalence. Consequently, by precluding the recognition of disease-free areas with respect to AI, India's measures precluded it from determining the AI-free areas.

The Panel accepted the US' claim that the measure at issue was not adapted to regional conditions.

Reference

Bohanes J, Salcedo K (2015) WTO Jursiprudence in 2013 at a quick glance. In: Hermann C, Krajewski M, Terhechte JP (eds) European yearbook of international economic law 2015, vol 6. Heidelberg, Springer, pp 337–373

[78] Appellate Body Report, *Australia – Salmon,* para. 200.

Recent Developments in International Investment Law

Catharine Titi

Contents

Abstract International investment law remains a fast evolving and vibrant field of law with ongoing and recently-concluded investment treaty negotiations continually altering the status quo. It is a system at a crossroads of reform, generally focused on safeguarding the right of the host state to regulate and on improving the investor-state dispute settlement (ISDS) mechanism. But reform may also come into play in more far-reaching ways and significant changes are likely to see the day in the near future. One such change concerns the institutional architecture of the resolution of investment disputes, with the possible establishment of a permanent investment court and/or the introduction of an appellate mechanism. Another one relates to the new potential for multilateralism in international investment relations,

C. Titi (✉)
French National Centre for Scientific Research (CNRS), Paris, France

CREDIMI, University of Burgundy, Dijon, France
e-mail: Cathy_titi@hotmail.com

M. Bungenberg et al. (eds.), *European Yearbook of International Economic Law 2016*, European Yearbook of International Economic Law 7,
DOI 10.1007/978-3-319-29215-1_31

with UNCITRAL's Convention on Transparency in Treaty-based Investor-State Arbitration (hereinafter UNCITRAL Transparency Convention) constituting a step in this direction. At the same time, international investment law is a body of jurisprudence. Investor-state tribunals have continued to interpret international investment agreements (IIAs) and grant compensations to aggrieved investors, exercising their authoritative power on how international investment commitments undertaken by contracting parties are to be understood.

1 General Remarks and Trends

International investment law remains a fast evolving and vibrant field of law with ongoing and recently-concluded investment treaty negotiations continually altering the status quo. It is a system at a crossroads of reform, generally focused on safeguarding the right of the host state to regulate and on improving the investor-state dispute settlement (ISDS) mechanism. But reform may also come into play in more far-reaching ways and significant changes are likely to see the day in the near future. One such change concerns the institutional architecture of the resolution of investment disputes, with the possible establishment of a permanent investment court and/or the introduction of an appellate mechanism. Another one relates to the new potential for multilateralism in international investment relations, with UNCITRAL's Convention on Transparency in Treaty-based Investor-State Arbitration (hereinafter UNCITRAL Transparency Convention) constituting a step in this direction. At the same time, international investment law is a body of jurisprudence. Investor-state tribunals have continued to interpret international investment agreements (IIAs) and grant compensations to aggrieved investors, exercising their authoritative power on how international investment commitments undertaken by contracting parties are to be understood.

The chapter is structured in the following manner. The first part explores institutional developments in international investment law, notably in relation to investment treatymaking, the elaboration of new model investment agreements, and the debate on the reform of investor-state dispute settlement. The second part of the chapter focuses on developments in investor-state arbitration and the jurisprudence of investment tribunals. A final section concludes the chapter with an appraisal and outlook on the future.

2 Institutional Developments

2.1 *Negotiations*

In 2014, at least 27 IIAs were concluded, bringing their total number by year end to more than 3250.[1] At least 14 among them were bilateral investment treaties.[2] At the same time, the year 2014 saw the conclusion of negotiations on Mega-Regional agreements including those that involve the European Union, namely the EU-Canada Comprehensive Economic and Trade Agreement (CETA) and (the investment chapter of) the EU-Singapore free trade agreement (FTA).[3] These agreements are the first two EU-wide investment treaties to have been finalised and they reveal the European Union's new investment law policy. They are in harmony with the new generation of North American treaties and incorporate further innovative improvements, such as a code of conduct for arbitrators, leading to a yet newer generation of international investment agreements.[4] In parallel, the European Union has settled on the terms according to which financial responsibility linked to investment dispute settlement on the basis of EU investment agreements is to be apportioned between the Union and its Member States.[5] In general, recently-concluded investment agreements increasingly include pre-establishment commitments, the right of the state to regulate in the public interest, and other sustainable development friendly features.[6]

Other Mega-Regional negotiations are ongoing, including on the Transatlantic Trade and Investment Partnership Agreement (TTIP) between the European Union and the United States,[7] the Trans-Pacific Partnership (TPP),[8] the US-China BIT, and other EU investment negotiations with, inter alia, Japan, Myanmar, Thailand, and Vietnam.[9]

---

[1] UNCTAD, Recent Trends in IIAs and ISDS, IIA Issues Note No. 1, February 2015, p. 2.

[2] UNCTAD, Recent Trends in IIAs and ISDS, IIA Issues Note No. 1, February 2015, p. 2.

[3] The agreements are available through the European Commission's website http://ec.europa.eu/trade/policy/ (last accessed 17 September 2015).

[4] Titi (2015a).

[5] Regulation (EU) No 912/2014 of the European Parliament and of the Council of 23 July 2014 establishing a framework for managing financial responsibility linked to investor-to-state dispute settlement tribunals established by international agreements to which the European Union is party.

[6] UNCTAD, Recent Trends in IIAs and ISDS, IIA Issues Note No. 1, February 2015, p. 3.

[7] On TTIP negotiations, http://ec.europa.eu/trade/policy/in-focus/ttip/ (last accessed 17 September 2015).

[8] On TTP, https://ustr.gov/tpp (last accessed 17 September 2015).

[9] See http://ec.europa.eu/trade/policy/accessing-markets/investment/index_en.htm (last accessed 17 September 2015).

Most recently, in May 2015, the International Energy Charter was formally adopted at a Ministerial Conference in the Netherlands.[10] The International Energy Charter is 'a political declaration aimed at strengthening energy cooperation between the signatory countries',[11] through which the signatories commit to removing investment barriers in the energy sector and to providing a 'stable, transparent legal framework for foreign investments'.[12]

2.2 *Renegotiations, Development of Model Investment Agreements and Terminations*

By early 2015, at least 45 countries and four regional organisations had been reconsidering or reviewing their investment policymaking.[13] This last year has witnessed significant developments in investment treaty revisions, renegotiations and some terminations. In January 2015, Italy gave formal notice to the Depository for the Energy Charter Treaty (ECT) of its intention to withdraw from the ECT.[14] The termination, to become effective in January 2016, does not affect existing investments which will continue to be protected under the ECT's survival clause for a further 20 years. [15] Although Italy's stated reason for withdrawing from the ECT concerns its wish to do away with annual membership fees of around half a million euros, it is also true that the country has started to face claims under the Energy Charter Treaty in relation to investments in renewable energy.[16] The European Union remains a member of the ECT.

At the same time, following in the earlier steps of South Africa, in early 2014, Indonesia gave its notice of termination of the Indonesia-Netherlands bilateral investment agreement and it is in the process of terminating at least 18 of its

[10] See http://www.energycharter.org/fileadmin/DocumentsMedia/Legal/IEC_EN.pdf (last accessed 17 September 2015).

[11] See http://www.energycharter.org/fileadmin/DocumentsMedia/Legal/IEC_EN.pdf (last accessed 17 September 2015).

[12] Point 4 of the International Energy Charter. The text of the Charter is available at: http://www.energycharter.org/fileadmin/DocumentsMedia/Legal/IEC_EN.pdf (last accessed 17 September 2015).

[13] UNCTAD, Recent Trends in IIAs and ISDS, IIA Issues Note No. 1, February 2015, p. 2.

[14] Peterson LE, Italy follows Russia in withdrawing from Energy Charter Treaty, but for surprising reason. IA Reporter, 17 April 2015, http://www.iareporter.com/articles/20150417_1 (last accessed 17 September 2015).

[15] Peterson LE, Italy follows Russia in withdrawing from Energy Charter Treaty, but for surprising reason. IA Reporter, 17 April 2015, http://www.iareporter.com/articles/20150417_1 (last accessed 17 September 2015).

[16] Peterson LE, Italy follows Russia in withdrawing from Energy Charter Treaty, but for surprising reason. IA Reporter, 17 April 2015, http://www.iareporter.com/articles/20150417_1 (last accessed 17 September 2015).

64 BITs.[17] It soon transpired that the purpose of these terminations is the country's intention to renegotiate them on the basis of a new model bilateral investment treaty that is currently being developed.[18] Indonesia's new model may exclude portfolio investment from the treaty's protections and it will likely subject the non-discrimination standards to several exclusions, such as special treatment in favour of domestic small and medium enterprises (SMEs) and preferential treatment granted to least-developed countries. The model may also consider circumscribing fair and equitable treatment, by restricting it to denial of justice and an assurance of police protection from physical harm, and it will probably not cover indirect expropriation. ISDS has been a particular concern and the country may aim to only allow investor claims to proceed where the host state offers its specific consent in a separate letter.[19]

India is another country to have been developing a new model BIT. In contrast with the case of Indonesia, a draft of India's model investment treaty has already become public. This draft model text of 2015 intends to 'create a neutral treaty keeping in mind investor rights while preserving the *right to regulate*'.[20] It is possible that the model goes far in introducing safeguards for the host state leaving little under the treaty umbrella.[21] Some of the model's innovative or unusual features include the following: an enterprise-based definition of investment; exclusion from treaty coverage of some forms of investment, such as portfolio investment; the definition of investor requires 'real and substantial business operations'[22]; the model does not grant investors fair and equitable treatment but protection against extreme situations such as against manifestly abusive treatment or denial of justice[23]; the treaty does not offer most-favoured-nation treatment; it includes

---

[17] See http://unctad-worldinvestmentforum.org/wp-content/uploads/2015/03/Indonesia_side-event-Wednesday_model-agreements.pdf (last accessed 17 September 2015).

[18] See http://unctad-worldinvestmentforum.org/wp-content/uploads/2015/03/Indonesia_side-event-Wednesday_model-agreements.pdf (last accessed 17 September 2015). See further Peterson LE, As Indonesia reconsiders its investment treaties, arbitrators don't want to slow down mining case by separating liability and damages phases. IA Reporter, 28 April 2014, http://www.iareporter.com/articles/20140428 (last accessed 17 September 2015).

[19] The elements discussed here are based on a presentation by Abdulkadir Jailani of Indonesia's Ministry of Foreign Affairs, during UNCTAD's Expert Meeting on the Transformation of the International Investment Agreement Regime on 25 February 2015. The presentation is available at: http://unctad-worldinvestmentforum.org/wp-content/uploads/2015/03/Indonesia_side-event-Wednesday_model-agreements.pdf (last accessed 17 September 2015).

[20] See http://unctad-worldinvestmentforum.org/wp-content/uploads/2015/03/India_side-event-Wednesday_model-agreements.pdf (last accessed 17 September 2015).

[21] The draft text of India's model BIT is available at: https://mygov.in/sites/default/files/master_image/Model%20Text%20for%20the%20Indian%20Bilateral%20Investment%20Treaty.pdf (last accessed 17 September 2015).

[22] Article 1 of the Draft Indian Model BIT (2015).

[23] Article 3 of the Draft Indian Model BIT (2015).

investor obligations[24] and a closely circumscribed access to investor-state dispute settlement.[25]

In early 2015, Brazil adopted a new model 'cooperation and facilitation investment agreement' (CFIA) and concluded two such treaties with Angola and Mozambique.[26] The development is particularly noteworthy given that Brazil, the world's fifth biggest economy for foreign direct investment (FDI),[27] has not ratified any of its old generation bilateral investment treaties signed in the 1990s. Brazil's new agreement departs in several ways from typical bilateral investment treaties.[28] It is structured around three pillars. The first pillar is improved institutional governance, with the setting in place of focal points (ombudsmen) and a joint committee. The second pillar revolves around the development of thematic agendas for investment cooperation and facilitation. And the third pillar concerns the establishment of mechanisms for risk mitigation and dispute prevention. The agreement does not give investors access to investor-state dispute settlement.[29]

Finally, in May 2015, Norway unveiled a new draft model BIT, for which a public consultation is ongoing at the moment of writing.[30] The model takes into account provisions suggested by the EU in the context of the TTIP consultation and in CETA's investment chapter, in view of "many similarities between Norway and a number of EU Member States".[31] Multiple provisions safeguard the host state's right to regulate, including general exceptions modelled after Article XX of the GATT[32] and an essential security interests exception.[33] A remarkable provision, the draft model's expropriation clause, delineates the factors that '[i]n rare circumstances' may lead to a finding of indirect expropriation,[34] while the model's (direct) expropriation provisions 'do not in any circumstances apply to a measure or a series of measures [...] designed and applied to safeguard public interests'. A further

[24] Articles 8 ff. of the Draft Indian Model BIT (2015).

[25] Article 14 of the Draft Indian Model BIT (2015).

[26] Information and the full text of these agreements are available at: http://www.mdic.gov.br//sitio/ (last accessed 17 September 2015).

[27] UNCTAD, World Investment Report 2014, New York and Geneva: UN, p. 4, figure I.3, see also p. 28, figure I.28.

[28] Indeed, on UNCTAD's IIA database, the text of the two agreements is to be found under the section 'other IIAs' and not 'bilateral investment treaties'.

[29] On Brazil's new model, see Titi C, International Investment Law and the Protection of Foreign Investment in Brazil (forthcoming).

[30] See https://www.regjeringen.no/contentassets/e47326b61f424d4c9c3d470896492623/consultation-letter.pdf (last accessed 17 September 2015). Norway's 2007 draft model was abandoned without being adopted.

[31] See explanation relating to the public consultation, available at https://www.regjeringen.no/contentassets/e47326b61f424d4c9c3d470896492623/consultation-letter.pdf (last accessed 17 September 2015), p. 6.

[32] Article [24] of Norway's Draft Model BIT (2015).

[33] Article [26] of Norway's Draft Model BIT (2015).

[34] Article [6] of Norway's Draft Model BIT (2015).

clause modelled after the expropriation provision of the European Convention on Human Rights[35] reserves the right of each party to 'enforce such laws as it deems necessary to control the use of property'.[36] Similarly to the Brazilian model CFIA, Norway's draft model provides for the establishment of a joint committee entrusted with, inter alia, supervising the implementation of the agreement, endeavouring to resolve disputes, deciding to amend the treaty, and determining whether an exception constitutes a valid defence in a given case.

2.3 *Reforming Investor-State Dispute Settlement*

The debate that dominated international investment law and the reform of its architecture has centred on the investor-state dispute settlement mechanism. Sometimes arguments against it have been expressed from unexpected quarters so that doubt was cast on the inclusion of ISDS in some future treaties. Noteworthy in this respect are a European parliamentary committee's opposition to the inclusion of investor-state dispute settlement in TTIP,[37] and the cautioning of the European Committee of the Regions that investor-state dispute settlement provisions that would 'circumvent the ordinary courts entail significant risks, and can therefore be dispensed with'.[38] At the same time, the European Union is a signatory to the International Energy Charter, through parties confirm 'the importance of full access to adequate dispute settlement mechanisms, including national mechanisms and international arbitration'.[39]

Other reactions have focused on reform instead of rejection of ISDS. In a 'Concept Paper' on 'Investment in TTIP and beyond – the path for reform' of May 2015, [40] the European Commission took stock of achievements in negotiations and identified four areas for further improvement. While the first one of these relates to the right to regulate, the remaining three concern the functioning of the

[35] Article 1 of Protocol One of the European Convention on Human Rights.

[36] Article [6] of Norway's Draft Model BIT (2015).

[37] European Parliament, Committee on International Trade, Working document in view of preparing the draft report on Parliament's recommendations to the Commission on the negotiations for the Transatlantic Trade and Investment Partnership (TTIP), 2014–2019, 9 January 2015, http://www.europarl.europa.eu/sides/getDoc.do?type=COMPARL&reference=PE-546.593&format=PDF&language=EN&secondRef=01 (last accessed 17 September 2015), p. 6.

[38] Opinion of the European Committee of the Regions, The Transatlantic Trade and Investment Partnership (TTIP)(2015/C 140/02), available at: http://eur-lex.europa.eu/legal-content/EN/TXT/?qid=1404723846895&uri=OJ:JOC_2015_140_R_0002 (last accessed 17 September 2015), para. 35.

[39] Point 4 of the International Energy Charter.

[40] European Commission, Concept Paper, Investment in TTIP and beyond—the path for reform, May 2015, available at: http://trade.ec.europa.eu/doclib/docs/2015/may/tradoc_153408.PDF (last accessed 17 September 2015).

investor-state dispute settlement mechanism. Notably, they relate to the operating mode of arbitral tribunals (e.g. selection of pre-vetted arbitrators from a roster, so as to 'break the link' between the parties to the dispute and the arbitrators), the establishment of a bilateral appellate mechanism likely modelled on the WTO Appellate Body's institutional set-up and to regulating the relationship between ISDS and domestic *fora* to prevent parallel claims (e.g. through the introduction of a 'no U-turn' clause). Remarkably, the European Commission's 'Concept Paper' envisages further steps beyond TTIP and notably a multilateral system. The very proposals for reform that the paper contains are 'intended as the stepping stones towards the establishment of a multilateral system'.[41]

This discussion on multilateralism is expressed in connection with the wish to include the appellate mechanism not only in TTIP but also in 'all EU trade and investment agreements'.[42] But notably it also comes hand-in-hand with another EU proposal, that of the creation of a permanent investment court.[43] Already, the proposal to create a roster with a fixed list of arbitrators brings ISDS closer to a permanent court.[44] Expressly, the 'Concept Paper' mentions that 'the EU should pursue the creation of one permanent court', which would apply to multiple agreements, including on the basis of an opt-in system.[45] The objective is to multilateralise the court, either as a self-standing institution or by embedding it into an extant 'multilateral' organisation.[46] The European Commission notes that work on how to implement this project, e.g. on the court's architecture, organisation and costs, has already started.[47]

At the same time that the European Commission's 'Concept Paper' became public, other developments in EU Member States concur with the need to create a

[41] European Commission, Concept Paper, Investment in TTIP and beyond—the path for reform, May 2015, available at: http://trade.ec.europa.eu/doclib/docs/2015/may/tradoc_153408.PDF (last accessed 17 September 2015).

[42] European Commission, Concept Paper, Investment in TTIP and beyond—the path for reform, May 2015, available at: http://trade.ec.europa.eu/doclib/docs/2015/may/tradoc_153408.PDF (last accessed 17 September 2015).

[43] European Commission, Concept Paper, Investment in TTIP and beyond—the path for reform, May 2015, available at: http://trade.ec.europa.eu/doclib/docs/2015/may/tradoc_153408.PDF (last accessed 17 September 2015).

[44] European Commission, Concept Paper, Investment in TTIP and beyond—the path for reform, May 2015, available at: http://trade.ec.europa.eu/doclib/docs/2015/may/tradoc_153408.PDF (last accessed 17 September 2015).

[45] European Commission, Concept Paper, Investment in TTIP and beyond—the path for reform, May 2015, available at: http://trade.ec.europa.eu/doclib/docs/2015/may/tradoc_153408.PDF (last accessed 17 September 2015).

[46] European Commission, Concept Paper, Investment in TTIP and beyond—the path for reform, May 2015, available at: http://trade.ec.europa.eu/doclib/docs/2015/may/tradoc_153408.PDF (last accessed 17 September 2015).

[47] European Commission, Concept Paper, Investment in TTIP and beyond—the path for reform, May 2015, available at: http://trade.ec.europa.eu/doclib/docs/2015/may/tradoc_153408.PDF (last accessed 17 September 2015).

permanent court. In May 2015, the German government, which recently had opposed ISDS, made public a draft model agreement for developed countries, prepared by Markus Krajewski.[48] The model agreement advocates, inter alia, the establishment of a permanent international investment tribunal. More particularly, the model suggests the creation of a bilateral tribunal or court created for each specific treaty (an example would be an EU-US Permanent Investment Tribunal for TTIP) with judges—as opposed to arbitrators—selected randomly each individual case, rather than being selected by the parties. This tribunal or court could be complemented by an appellate mechanism. Among the further noteworthy elements of the dispute settlement design of this model is the requirement to exhaust local remedies, unless these remedies are unavailable or manifestly ineffective. Alternatively, initiation of dispute settlement proceedings under the investment agreement could be conditioned on the investor's waiver of any right to start a procedure under domestic courts or tribunals.[49]

Efforts at reforming investor-state dispute settlement may also take place in different quarters. ICSID Secretary-General Meg Kinnear has reportedly expressed ideas about potential changes that can be submitted to member states regarding the establishment of an appellate mechanism, the use of emergency arbitrators, the consolidation of disputes and the introduction of codes of conduct for arbitrators.[50]

Alongside this continuing debate on ISDS, in Latin America some progress has been made with the project on the creation of a regional investment arbitration centre under the auspices of the Union of South American Nations (UNASUR). Negotiations on the centre began following an Ecuadorean proposal in 2008 with the intent to establish a local counterweight to ICSID.[51] The project places emphasis on dispute resolution through consultations or mediation and transparency of proceedings; an appellate mechanism has also been envisaged. [52] In November 2014, UNASUR's Working Group on Responsible Dispute Investment Settlement settled on a constitutive treaty that, if adopted, will create South America's own investment dispute resolution centre.[53]

---

[48] The model is available at: http://www.bmwi.de/BMWi/Redaktion/PDF/M-O/modell-investitionsschutzvertrag-mit-investor-staat-schiedsverfahren-gutachten,property=pdf,bereich=bmwi2012,sprache=de,rwb=true.pdf (last accessed 17 September 2015).

[49] See also http://www.rph1.jura.uni-erlangen.de/material/150429-muster-bit-fr-industriestaaten-krajewski-englische-bersetzung.pdf (last accessed 17 September 2015).

[50] Peterson LE, Ten years after last major reforms, ICSID to float new amendments, including transparency improvements, and possibly appeals process. IA Reporter, 3 July 2014, http://www.iareporter.com/articles/ten-years-after-last-major-reforms-icsid-to-float-new-amendments-including-transparency-improvements-and-possibly-appeals-process/ (last accessed 17 September 2015).

[51] Titi (2014), p. 380.

[52] Titi (2014), p. 380.

[53] See Ecuador, Ministry of Foreign Affairs and Mobility, Expertos de Unasur consolidan texto para la creación del Centro de Solución de Controversias en Materia de Investiones, 7 November 2014, http://www.cancilleria.gob.ec/es/expertos-de-unasur-consolidan-texto-para-la-creacion-del-centro-de-solucion-de-controversias-en-materia-de-inversiones/ (last accessed 17 September 2015).

2.4 Transparency

Investor-state dispute settlement has also been the focus of multilateral transparency initiatives. 2014 saw the entry-into-force of the UNCITRAL Rules on Transparency in Treaty-based Investor-State Arbitration (hereinafter UNCITRAL Transparency Rules), which provide for transparency in investment dispute settlement.[54] The Transparency Rules are applicable to investor-state arbitration pursuant to an agreement concluded on or after 1 April 2014, date of their entry-into-force, unless the parties to the treaty agree otherwise.[55] In some cases, the Transparency Rules may also apply to disputes born on the basis of earlier investment agreements.[56] The Transparency Rules apply to arbitration conducted under the UNCITRAL Rules, but they are also available for use in investor-state dispute settlement initiated under different arbitration rules or in ad hoc proceedings.[57] The CETA incorporates the UNCITRAL Transparency Rules[58] as does the 2014 bilateral investment treaty between Colombia and France.[59] UNCITRAL has also created a 'Transparency Registry' which will perform the role of a 'repository for the publication of information and documents in treaty-based investor-State arbitration'.[60] The Registry will be used not only for disputes decided on the basis of the UNCITRAL Transparency Rules. Documentation relating to the first five cases that has been uploaded on the registry relates to cases brought against Canada under Chapter 11 of the North American Free Trade Agreement (NAFTA), 'with a view to illustrating the educational role played by the Registry as a global reference on transparency in treaty-based investor-State arbitration'.[61]

In view of the fact that the UNCITRAL Transparency Rules do not apply to pre-existing treaties, the UNCITRAL Transparency Convention was elaborated and adopted by UNCITRAL in December 2014.[62] The objective of the Convention is to allow States and regional economic integration organisations the possibility to apply the UNCITRAL Transparency Rules to investor-state dispute settlement under their existing IIAs. Absent reservations by the signatories, the Transparency Rules will apply to disputes where both the home and host economies are parties to

[54] On the adoption of the UNCITRAL Transparency Rules, see Titi (2015b).

[55] Article 1(1) of the UNCITRAL Transparency Rules.

[56] Article 1(2) of the UNCITRAL Transparency Rules.

[57] Article 1(9) of the UNCITRAL Transparency Rules.

[58] See Article X.33 of the draft CETA chapter on investment, version of September 2014. On transparency and the European Union's investment policymaking, see further Titi (2015a).

[59] Article 15 of the Colombia-France BIT (2014).

[60] The Transparency Registry is available at http://www.uncitral.org/transparency-registry/en/introduction.html (last accessed March 2015).

[61] See the Transparency Registry, http://www.uncitral.org/transparency-registry/en/introduction.html (last accessed March 2015).

[62] The Convention is available at http://www.uncitral.org/pdf/english/texts/arbitration/transparency-convention/Transparency-Convention-e.pdf (last accessed 24 September 2015).

the Convention and disputes where only the host state is party to the Convention but the claimant investor agrees to the Rules.[63] The Convention opened for signature on 17 March 2015 in a signing ceremony in Port Louis, Mauritius. At the time of writing, it has been signed by ten states, namely Canada, Finland, France, Germany, Mauritius, Sweden, Switzerland, Syria, United Kingdom, and the United States of America.[64] It is likely that the European Union will also sign up to the Convention.[65]

ICSID is said to be considering emulating the example of UNCITRAL on transparency and putting on the table the question of opening investor-state dispute settlement to greater public scrutiny.[66]

3 Jurisprudence of Arbitral Tribunals

3.1 General Observations

The year 2014 saw the initiation of at least 42 treaty-based investor-state dispute settlement cases, bringing the total to 608 known ISDS disputes.[67] The number of disputes commenced in 2014 was lower than the record highs of 59 and 54 cases in 2013 and 2012 respectively and closer to annual average numbers for the period 2003–2010.[68] Thirty-three disputes were registered with the International Centre for Settlement of Investment Disputes (ICSID), of which three under the ICSID Additional Facility Rules, six cases were filed under the UNCITRAL Arbitration Rules, and the remaining three claims were registered with the Stockholm Chamber of Commerce (SCC) and the International Chamber of Commerce (ICC).[69]

[63] Article 2 of the UNCITRAL Transparency Convention.

[64] For the status of the Convention, see http://www.uncitral.org/uncitral/en/uncitral_texts/arbitration/2014Transparency_Convention_status.html (last accessed 24 September 2015).

[65] See European Commission News Archive, European Commission pushes for full transparency for ISDS in current investment treaties, 29 January 2015, available at: http://trade.ec.europa.eu/doclib/press/index.cfm?id=1247 (last accessed 24 September 2015).

[66] Peterson LE, Ten years after last major reforms, ICSID to float new amendments, including transparency improvements, and possibly appeals process. IA Reporter, 3 July 2014, http://www.iareporter.com/articles/ten-years-after-last-major-reforms-icsid-to-float-new-amendments-including-transparency-improvements-and-possibly-appeals-process/ (last accessed 17 September 2015).

[67] UNCTAD, Investor-State Dispute Settlement: Review of Developments in 2014. IIA Issues Note No. 2, May 2015, p. 2.

[68] UNCTAD, Investor-State Dispute Settlement: Review of Developments in 2014. IIA Issues Note No. 2, May 2015, p. 2.

[69] UNCTAD, Investor-State Dispute Settlement: Review of Developments in 2014. IIA Issues Note No. 2, May 2015, p. 4.

Although 60 % of all new cases were brought against developing countries, the number of claims lodged against developed countries is on the rise.[70] Indeed, Spain in 2014 was the most frequent respondent in investment disputes, following the scaling down of renewable energy subsidies.[71] Other states, such as the Czech Republic and Italy, have faced claims relating to similar measures in the renewable energy sector.[72] New claims concerning the renewable energy sector were initiated in 2015.[73] Of the 42 known investment treaty claims in 2014, 35 were initiated by investors from developed countries and five by investors from developing countries.[74] The majority of cases have been brought by US, Canadian and European investors.[75]

In 2014, at least 43 decisions were rendered in investor-state arbitration, the majority of which are public.[76] This brought the overall number of concluded cases to 356.[77] Eleven decisions upheld tribunal jurisdiction and five decisions rejected such jurisdiction.[78] On the merits, ten cases accepted at least some of the investors' clails and five dismissed all claims.[79] Ten cases are reported to have been settled and five were discontinued.[80] In total, approximately 47 % of cases have been decided in favour of the state and 25 % in favour of the investor; 28 % of cases have been settled.[81]

---

[70] UNCTAD, Investor-State Dispute Settlement: Review of Developments in 2014. IIA Issues Note No. 2, May 2015, p. 2.

[71] UNCTAD, Investor-State Dispute Settlement: Review of Developments in 2014. IIA Issues Note No. 2, May 2015, p. 2.

[72] E.g. see http://www.encharter.org/index.php?id=213. (last accessed 24 September 2015).

[73] See http://www.encharter.org/index.php?id=213. (last accessed 24 September 2015). See also Trevino C, Spain round-up: Even as European Commission throws up red flags, two new claims land at ICSID, and tribunal members are finalized in another. IA Reporter, 27 January 2015 https://www.iareporter.com/articles/spain-round-up-even-as-european-commission-throws-up-red-flags-two-new-claims-land-at-icsid-and-tribunal-members-are-finalized-in-another/ (last accessed 24 September 2015).

[74] In two cases, the investor's home country is not known. UNCTAD, Investor-State Dispute Settlement: Review of Developments in 2014. IIA Issues Note No. 2, May 2015, p. 3.

[75] In two cases, the investor's home country is not known. UNCTAD, Investor-State Dispute Settlement: Review of Developments in 2014. IIA Issues Note No. 2, May 2015, p. 3.

[76] UNCTAD, Investor-State Dispute Settlement: Review of Developments in 2014. IIA Issues Note No. 2, May 2015, p. 4.

[77] UNCTAD, Investor-State Dispute Settlement: Review of Developments in 2014. IIA Issues Note No. 2, May 2015, p. 5.

[78] UNCTAD, Investor-State Dispute Settlement: Review of Developments in 2014. IIA Issues Note No. 2, May 2015, p. 4.

[79] UNCTAD, Investor-State Dispute Settlement: Review of Developments in 2014. IIA Issues Note No. 2, May 2015, p. 4.

[80] UNCTAD, Investor-State Dispute Settlement: Review of Developments in 2014. IIA Issues Note No. 2, May 2015, p. 5.

[81] UNCTAD, Investor-State Dispute Settlement: Review of Developments in 2014. IIA Issues Note No. 2, May 2015, p. 5.

The sections that ensue give a selective overview of some disputes and issues that have been decided by arbitral tribunals since around the beginning of 2014. The analysis will commence with a brief examination of developments in the context of intra-EU disputes. The following section will turn to procedural and jurisdictional aspects of investment dispute settlement. A third section will address the interpretation of substantive investment protections. The remaining sections will deal with compensation awarded in investment arbitration and the review of arbitral decisions by national courts.

3.2 *Intra-EU Disputes*

A quarter of known cases initiated in 2014 are intra-EU disputes, half of which brought under the Energy Charter Treaty.[82] This brings the total of known intra-EU investment disputes to 16 % of all disputes.[83] Among the recently-adjudicated intra-EU cases, the following paragraphs will pay special attention to the Micula v. Romania arbitration.

The facts that gave rise to the Micula v. Romania award[84]: the claim was born from the country's introduction and consequent revocation of economic incentives, including tax incentives and duty exemptions, that were contained in Emergency Government Ordinance 24/1998 (EGO 24) for the development of disfavoured regions in Romania. Romania, which had concluded the 'Europe' Agreement with the European Union in 1995, began its formal accession process in 2000 and eventually joined the EU in 2007.[85] 'As accession talks unfolded, Romania found itself under growing pressure from the EU to align its incentives programs with EU laws designed to promote competition and to limit the granting of so-called state aid to business interests.'[86] The 'competitive fairness of compensating the Swedish investors – at a time when others would not be eligible for such compensation or aid

---

[82] In two cases, the investor's home country is not known. UNCTAD, Investor-State Dispute Settlement: Review of Developments in 2014. IIA Issues Note No. 2, May 2015, p. 3.

[83] In two cases, the investor's home country is not known. UNCTAD, Investor-State Dispute Settlement: Review of Developments in 2014. IIA Issues Note No. 2, May 2015, p. 3.

[84] ICSID Case No. ARB/05/20, *Ioan Micula, Viorel Micula, S.C. European Food S.A., S.C. Starmill S.R.L. and S.C. Multipack S.R.L. v. Romania*, Award, 11 December 2013.

[85] Cite Award. If not citing award: Peterson LE, In Romania case, EU expresses doubts as to legality of ordering EU state to compensate investors for lost incentives. IA Reporter, 6 January 2014 https://www.iareporter.com/articles/in-romania-case-eu-expresses-doubts-as-to-legality-of-ordering-eu-state-to-compensate-investors-for-lost-incentives/ (last accessed 24 September 2015).

[86] Cite Award. If not citing award: Peterson LE, In Romania case, EU expresses doubts as to legality of ordering EU state to compensate investors for lost incentives. IA Reporter, 6 January 2014 https://www.iareporter.com/articles/in-romania-case-eu-expresses-doubts-as-to-legality-of-ordering-eu-state-to-compensate-investors-for-lost-incentives/ (last accessed 24 September 2015).

– was a major concern raised by the European Commission in its amicus curiae intervention in the arbitration'.[87]

The European Commission submitted an amicus curiae brief. According to the European Commission's Written Submission of 20 July 2009, invoked in part in paragraphs 334 to 336 of the *Micula* Award, '[i]f the Tribunal rendered an award that is contrary to obligations binding on Romania as an EU Member State, such award could not be implemented in Romania by virtue of the supremacy of EC law (*sic*), and in particular State aid rules'.[88] Besides, the European Commission invoked the *Eco Swiss* case,[89] where the Court of Justice of the European Union held that the EU competition rules 'are part of the public order which national courts must take into account when they review the legality of arbitral awards under the public policy exception recognized by the 1958 New York Convention on the Recognition and Enforcement of Foreign Arbitral Awards'.[90] And although the European Commission recognised that 'Article 54(1) of the ICSID Convention provides that each Contracting State shall automatically recognize and enforce an ICSID award within its territory as if it were a final judgment of a court in that State', 'it contends that if a national court in the EU were asked to enforce an ICSID award that is contrary to EU law and EU state aid policy rules, the proceedings would have to be stayed under the conditions of Article 234 of the EC Treaty so that the ECJ may decide on the applicability of Article 54 of the ICSID Convention, as transposed into the national law of the referring judge. The Commission notes that "the ICSID Convention is not binding on the EC under Article 300(7) EC, as the terms of the Convention do not allow the EC to become a Contracting Party to it" and concludes that, "[a]ccordingly, the ICSID Convention does not form part of the EC legal order."'[91]

Following delivery of the award which found against Romania, enforcement proceedings were initiated and the European Commission informed Romania in May 2014 of its decision to issue a suspension injunction pursuant to Article 11 (1) of Regulation (CE) No 659/1999 of 22 March 1999, according to which Romania should suspend 'any action which may lead to the execution or implementation of the part of the Award that had not yet been paid, as such execution would constitute unlawful State aid', until the European Commission had taken a

[87] Cite Award. If not citing award: Peterson LE, In Romania case, EU expresses doubts as to legality of ordering EU state to compensate investors for lost incentives. IA Reporter, 6 January 2014 https://www.iareporter.com/articles/in-romania-case-eu-expresses-doubts-as-to-legality-of-ordering-eu-state-to-compensate-investors-for-lost-incentives/ (last accessed 24 September 2015).

[88] ICSID Case No. ARB/05/20, Ioan Micula, Viorel Micula, S.C. European Food S.A., S.C. Starmill S.R.L. and S.C. Multipack S.R.L. v. Romania, Award, 11 December 2013, para. 334.

[89] CJEU, Case C-126/97 *Eco Swiss v. Benetton* ECR [1999] 1-3055, para. 35–41.

[90] ICSID Case No. ARB/05/20, Ioan Micula, Viorel Micula, S.C. European Food S.A., S.C. Starmill S.R.L. and S.C. Multipack S.R.L. v. Romania, Award, 11 December 2013, para. 335.

[91] ICSID Case No. ARB/05/20, Ioan Micula, Viorel Micula, S.C. European Food S.A., S.C. Starmill S.R.L. and S.C. Multipack S.R.L. v. Romania, Award, 11 December 2013, para. 336.

final decision on the compatibility of such aid with EU law.[92] The European Commission's decision fell in October 2014. The Commission considered that 'any execution of the Award of 11 December 2013 would amount to the granting of incompatible "new aid"' and it regretted that Romania had already partially implemented the award by cancelling some of the claimant's outstanding tax debts.[93] In view of these considerations, the Commission has decided to initiate an investigation procedure in accordance with Article 108(2) of the TFEU.[94] Meanwhile, Romania initiated an annulment proceeding against the claimant investor in which the European Commission wished to intervene as amicus curiae, according to a letter dated 15 October 2014.[95] Romania's failure to offer assurances that it would pay the award should the annulment proceeding not be in its favour has resulted in the annulment committee lifting a stay of enforcement.[96] The dispute is at the time of writing still pending.

---

[92] European Commission, State aid SA.38517(2014/C) (ex 2014/NN)—Romania, Implementation of Arbitral award Micula v Romania of 11 December 2013, C(2014) 6848 final, Brussels, 01.10.2014, http://ec.europa.eu/competition/state_aid/cases/254586/254586_1595781_31_11.pdf (last accessed March 2015), para. 6.

[93] European Commission, State aid SA.38517(2014/C) (ex 2014/NN)—Romania, Implementation of Arbitral award Micula v Romania of 11 December 2013, C(2014) 6848 final, Brussels, 01.10.2014, http://ec.europa.eu/competition/state_aid/cases/254586/254586_1595781_31_11.pdf (last accessed March 2015), para. 71.

[94] European Commission, State aid SA.38517(2014/C) (ex 2014/NN)—Romania, Implementation of Arbitral award Micula v Romania of 11 December 2013, C(2014) 6848 final, Brussels, 01.10.2014, http://ec.europa.eu/competition/state_aid/cases/254586/254586_1595781_31_11.pdf (last accessed March 2015), para. 72.

[95] Peterson LE, Tribunal is named for bank's BIT claim vs. Greece as European Commission makes new amicus bid in another ICSID proceeding. IA Reporter, 21 October 2014 https://www.iareporter.com/articles/tribunal-is-named-for-banks-bit-claim-vs-greece-as-european-commission-makes-new-amicus-bid-in-another-icsid-proceeding/ (last accessed 24 September 2015).

[96] Peterson LE, Tribunal is named for bank's BIT claim vs. Greece as European Commission makes new amicus bid in another ICSID proceeding. IA Reporter, 21 October 2014 https://www.iareporter.com/articles/tribunal-is-named-for-banks-bit-claim-vs-greece-as-european-commission-makes-new-amicus-bid-in-another-icsid-proceeding/ (last accessed 24 September 2015).

3.3 *Procedural and Jurisdictional Aspects in Investment Dispute Settlement*

3.3.1 Arbitrator Disqualifications

For the fourth time in the history of investment arbitration under the ICSID Convention, an arbitrator was disqualified in the second *Caratube* dispute.[97] The 'unchallenged' arbitrators conceded that the arbitrator's 'high moral character and recognized competence in the field of law' was not disputed nor was it suggested there was 'proof of actual dependence or bias'; rather was in question 'whether a third party would find that there is an evident or obvious appearance of lack of impartiality or independence based on a reasonable evaluation of the facts' at hand.[98] Concretely, the 'unchallenged' arbitrators found, inter alia, that the challenged arbitrator was 'privy to information that would possibly permit a judgment based on elements not in the record in the present arbitration and hence there is an evident or obvious appearance of lack of impartiality', in light especially of the 'significant overlap in the underlying facts' between an earlier case where their challenged colleague was also arbitrator and the second *Caratube* dispute, 'as well as the relevance of these facts for the determination of legal issues' in the latter.[99] This arbitrator disqualification is particularly important, in light of the numerous unsuccessful arbitrator challenges, notably in light of the fact that arbitrator challenges are determined by the remaining 'unchallenged' arbitrators and colleagues.

3.3.2 ICSID Rule 41(5)

For the first time in a recent ICSID annulment proceeding, the *Elsamex* annulment committee[100] held that ICSID Rule 41(5) may be invoked at annulment in order to dismiss a claim manifestly without legal merit. The committee had to deal with two questions: the first one was whether ICSID Rule 41(5) is applicable in an annulment

[97] ICSID Case No. ARB/13/13, *Caratube International Oil Company LLP & Mr. Devincci Salah Hourani v. Kazakhstan*, Decision on the Proposal for Disqualification of Bruno Boesch, 20 March 2014. The other three known disqualifications under the ICSID Convention took place in ICSID Case No. ARB/98/2, *Victor Pey Casado and President Allende Foundation v. Chile*, decision of 21 February 2006; ICSID Case No. ARB/12/20, *Blue Bank International & Trust (Barbados) Ltd. v. Venezuela*, decision of 12 November 2013; ICSID Case No. ARB/08/5, *Burlington Resources, Inc. v. Ecuador*, decision of 13 December 2013.

[98] ICSID Case No. ARB/13/13, *Caratube International Oil Company LLP & Mr. Devincci Salah Hourani v. Kazakhstan*, Decision on the Proposal for Disqualification of Bruno Boesch, 20 March 2014, para. 64.

[99] ICSID Case No. ARB/13/13, *Caratube International Oil Company LLP & Mr. Devincci Salah Hourani v. Kazakhstan*, Decision on the Proposal for Disqualification of Bruno Boesch, 20 March 2014, para. 89–90.

[100] ICSID Case No. ARB/09/4, *Elsamex, S.A. v. Honduras*, Decision on Elsamex S.A.'s preliminary objection—Annulment proceeding, 7 January 2014, 7 January 2014.

proceeding and the second one which is the scope of ICSID Rule 41(5) in an annulment proceeding.[101] The purpose of the introduction of this provision in 2006 was to avoid unnecessary and costly proceedings, an element that is to the benefit of both parties.[102] If it is manifest to the ad hoc committee that the annulment request cannot be upheld, it must have the competence to terminate the procedure at an early stage.[103] The committee remarked that this interpretation is supported by Rule 53 of the ICSID Arbitration Rules, by virtue of which Rule 41(5) is incorporated *mutatis mutandis* in annulment proceedings.[104]

Having accepted that Rule 41(5) is applicable in annulment proceedings, the committee turned to the second question regarding the 'scope' of its application and notably the question of whether, given the special features of an annulment proceeding, whether the committee must apply a different test.[105] The committee considered that indeed it must apply strict criteria when determining whether a claim manifestly lacks legal merit at the annulment stage. Rule 41(5) would be satisfied and the objection that the claim manifestly lacks legal merit would be accepted if the request for annulment is based on grounds absent from Article 52 of the ICSID Convention, or if the committee acquires the conviction that the grounds invoked for annulment manifestly exceed the scope of those in Article 52, such as when the annulment proceeding is clearly used to introduce an appeal, or if it is manifest that the grounds invoked lack legal basis, even if their factual elements are presumed to exist.[106] In view of this high threshold required for the application of Rule 41(5) in annulment proceedings, the committee could not establish that the respondent's claims lacked manifestly legal merit, which would justify a summary dismissal at this early stage.[107]

[101] ICSID Case No. ARB/09/4, *Elsamex, S.A. v. Honduras*, Decision on Elsamex S.A.'s preliminary objection—Annulment proceeding, 7 January 2014, para. 87.

[102] ICSID Case No. ARB/09/4, *Elsamex, S.A. v. Honduras*, Decision on Elsamex S.A.'s preliminary objection—Annulment proceeding, 7 January 2014, para. 100.

[103] ICSID Case No. ARB/09/4, *Elsamex, S.A. v. Honduras*, Decision on Elsamex S.A.'s preliminary objection—Annulment proceeding, 7 January 2014, para. 100.

[104] ICSID Case No. ARB/09/4, *Elsamex, S.A. v. Honduras*, Decision on Elsamex S.A.'s preliminary objection—Annulment proceeding, 7 January 2014, para. 89, 100. Rule 53 of the ICSID Arbitration Rules provides: 'The provisions of these Rules shall apply *mutatis mutandis* to any procedure relating to the interpretation, revision or annulment of an award and to the decision of the Tribunal or Committee.'

[105] ICSID Case No. ARB/09/4, *Elsamex, S.A. v. Honduras*, Decision on Elsamex S.A.'s preliminary objection—Annulment proceeding, 7 January 2014, para. 101.

[106] ICSID Case No. ARB/09/4, *Elsamex, S.A. v. Honduras*, Decision on Elsamex S.A.'s preliminary objection—Annulment proceeding, 7 January 2014, para. 131.

[107] ICSID Case No. ARB/09/4, *Elsamex, S.A. v. Honduras*, Decision on Elsamex S.A.'s preliminary objection—Annulment proceeding, 7 January 2014, para. 147.

3.3.3 Consent to Investor-State Dispute Settlement

Australia's recently ambivalent relationship to investor-state dispute settlement may have taken a new turn, in light of the *Planet Mining* tribunal's[108] interpretation of a typical Australian arbitration clause to the effect that it does not offer consent to investor-state dispute settlement. The Australia-Indonesia BIT, the treaty under interpretation *in casu*, apart from a nondescript arbitration clause includes in a separate paragraph the provision that if a case is referred to for arbitration, the host state 'shall consent in writing to the submission of the dispute to the Centre within forty-five days of receiving such a request from the investor'.[109] The tribunal noted that '[i]f the host State "shall consent in writing within 45 days" after the investor's request, it follows that consent cannot be located in the Treaty itself and that a separate act is needed'.[110] Although the word 'shall' may imply an obligation for the host state to provide its consent, the tribunal accepted that the sanction for failure to do so would not be to presume that such consent exists.[111]

The *Planet Mining* tribunal's interpretation may have consequences for a dozen other Australian bilateral investment treaties concluded between 1990 and 2002 which contain this clause.[112] In particular, the tribunal remarked that two of these latter treaties, the Australia-Vietnam BIT and the Australia-Sri Lanka BIT, contain language that clearly indicates the possibility for the host state to withhold consent to arbitration.[113] It is noteworthy for instance that Australia-Sri Lanka BIT provides that where a dispute is referred to ICSID by an investor, the host state '*should* consent in writing to the submission of the dispute to the Centre within thirty days of receiving such a request from the investor. *Such consent shall not be unreasonably withheld*'.[114]

Despite finding that the BIT did not contain advance consent to ICSID arbitration, the tribunal was eventually able to find that consent did exist on the basis of a separate document, an approval granted by the host state's investment coordinating board and which covered the claimant investor as shareholder of the company to which it had originally been provided.[115]

---

[108] ICSID Case No. ARB/12/14 and 12/40, *Planet Mining Pty Ltd v. Indonesia*, Decision on Jurisdiction, 24 February 2014.

[109] Article XI(4)(a) of the Australia-Indonesia BIT.

[110] ICSID Case No. ARB/12/14 and 12/40, *Planet Mining Pty Ltd v. Indonesia*, Decision on Jurisdiction, 24 February 2014, para. 161.

[111] ICSID Case No. ARB/12/14 and 12/40, *Planet Mining Pty Ltd v. Indonesia*, Decision on Jurisdiction, 24 February 2014, para. 163.

[112] ICSID Case No. ARB/12/14 and 12/40, *Planet Mining Pty Ltd v. Indonesia*, Decision on Jurisdiction, 24 February 2014, para. 189.

[113] ICSID Case No. ARB/12/14 and 12/40, *Planet Mining Pty Ltd v. Indonesia*, Decision on Jurisdiction, 24 February 2014, para. 191 ff.

[114] Article 13(3)(a) of the Australia-Sri Lanka BIT, emphasis added.

[115] ICSID Case No. ARB/12/14 and 12/40, *Planet Mining Pty Ltd v. Indonesia*, Decision on Jurisdiction, 24 February 2014, para. 200 ff.

3.3.4 Multi-Party Claims

In the *Giovanni Alemanni* case, the respondent claimed that the ICSID Convention does not allow the adjudication of multi-party or mass claims. The tribunal had to deal with the issue of whether the phrase in Article 25(1) of the ICSID Convention 'dispute arising directly out of an investment, between a Contracting State . . . and a national of another Contracting State' denotes a 'dispute between a Contracting State and one, but only one, national of another Contracting State.'[116] It found 'no reasonable basis for implying into the text as it stands of Article 25(1) the additional words 'but only one.'[117] However, the tribunal considered that the question remained open of the respondent's specific consent to the proceedings at hand.[118] The latter had claimed that 'in all cases in which investment tribunals have been prepared in principle to accept multiple claims, that has either been on the basis of express consent by the Respondent *in casu*, or at least tacit consent by the failure to raise express objection on that score' and that 'joinder of multiple claims could only enter into possible consideration if the claims derived from a single legal relationship linking the several claimants.'[119] The tribunal came to the conclusion that in endeavouring to define 'the link that must exist between a group of claimants and between their claims, in the absence of consent by the respondent to the hearing of their claims together', the crucial element lies in the concept 'dispute'.[120] In this respect, the tribunal reiterated that it is possible for a 'dispute' to include more than one party as claimant, although 'the interest represented on each side of the dispute has to be in all essential respects identical for all of those involved on that side of the dispute.' [121] *In casu*, it decided to leave for the merits the decision of whether 'the actual rights of all of the Claimants' and 'the actual effect' of the respondent's conduct on these rights 'were sufficiently the same as to amount to a single 'dispute'',[122] thus postponing an essentially jurisdictional question for the next phase of the dispute.

The earlier *Abaclat* tribunal was the first to accept jurisdiction over a similar multi-party dispute. The *Abaclat* tribunal considered that the multiplicity of

[116] ICSID Case No. ARB/07/8, *Giovanni Alemanni v. Argentina*, Decision on Jurisdiction and Admissibility, 17 November 2014, para. 270.

[117] ICSID Case No. ARB/07/8, *Giovanni Alemanni v. Argentina*, Decision on Jurisdiction and Admissibility, 17 November 2014, para. 271.

[118] ICSID Case No. ARB/07/8, *Giovanni Alemanni v. Argentina*, Decision on Jurisdiction and Admissibility, 17 November 2014, para. 270, 280.

[119] ICSID Case No. ARB/07/8, *Giovanni Alemanni v. Argentina*, Decision on Jurisdiction and Admissibility, 17 November 2014, para. 282.

[120] ICSID Case No. ARB/07/8, *Giovanni Alemanni v. Argentina*, Decision on Jurisdiction and Admissibility, 17 November 2014, para. 292.

[121] ICSID Case No. ARB/07/8, *Giovanni Alemanni v. Argentina*, Decision on Jurisdiction and Admissibility, 17 November 2014, para. 292.

[122] ICSID Case No. ARB/07/8, *Giovanni Alemanni v. Argentina*, Decision on Jurisdiction and Admissibility, 17 November 2014, para. 293.

claimants relates to the question of admissibility rather than jurisdiction.[123] In light of the fact that the ICSID Convention remains silent on the topic, the tribunal noted that it had the power on the basis of Article 44 of the ICSID Convention to 'fill this gap'.[124]

3.3.5 Investor Noncompliance with 'Preconditions to Arbitration'

In the *Giovanni Alemanni* case, the tribunal considered the claimants' noncompliance with the BIT's 'preconditions to arbitration'. These included amicable consultations and an 18-month local remedies requirement. The tribunal remarked that the host state's offer to arbitrate has a legal effect '*only* [...] if the investor accepts the offer on the terms specified by the host State'; neither can the latter 're-write the offer [n]or 'accept' an offer other than that which the host State has made'.[125] It determined thus that the claimants' argument that the 'prior steps' provided for in the BIT are 'not mandatory' should be rejected.[126] In short, the tribunal found 'no warrant for amending or setting aside any of the elements of [the] consent to arbitration which the Contracting Parties have expressed in the BIT, nor indeed [did] it consider itself to have been given any mandate in either the ICSID Convention or the BIT to do so.'[127] It explained that these 'steps' must have some chance of being followed and 'it cannot be supposed that two sophisticated governments could have intended that foreign investors be required to begin an action before the local courts or administrative authorities just for show. The underlying assumption must logically have been that the local courts or administrative authorities would be in a position to pronounce a definitive and binding solution to the dispute [...]. On the other hand, the specification of the time period itself shows unambiguously, to the mind of the Tribunal, that the Contracting States had in view as the intervening step a process that would be potentially effective to settle the issue in dispute.'[128] The tribunal concurred with the *Ambiente Ufficio* decision,[129] which declined to use as criterion the claimant's 'trouble and expense' or the

[123] ICSID Case No. ARB/07/5, *Abaclat and Others v. Argentina*, Decision on Jurisdiction and Admissibility, 4 August 2011, para. 492.

[124] *Abaclat and Others v. Argentina*, Decision on Jurisdiction and Admissibility, 4 August 2011, para. 520.

[125] ICSID Case No. ARB/07/8, *Giovanni Alemanni v. Argentina*, Decision on Jurisdiction and Admissibility, 17 November 2014, para. 305.

[126] ICSID Case No. ARB/07/8, *Giovanni Alemanni v. Argentina*, Decision on Jurisdiction and Admissibility, 17 November 2014, para. 305.

[127] ICSID Case No. ARB/07/8, *Giovanni Alemanni v. Argentina*, Decision on Jurisdiction and Admissibility, 17 November 2014, para. 306.

[128] ICSID Case No. ARB/07/8, *Giovanni Alemanni v. Argentina*, Decision on Jurisdiction and Admissibility, 17 November 2014, para. 311.

[129] ICSID Case No. ARB/08/09, *Ambiente Ufficio S.p.A. and others v. Argentina*, Decision on Jurisdiction and Admissibility, 8 February 2013.

'likelihood that judgment would be reached within the 18 months' and considered instead 'the main issue of substance, i.e. whether recourse to the Argentine courts would have offered the claimants a reasonable prospect of effective redress'.[130] In the circumstances, the tribunal decided that Argentina's judicial system was not shown to be 'reasonably capable of providing effective relief' and so the claimants noncompliance with the BIT's 'preconditions to arbitration' was not a 'jurisdictional bar' to initiating ICSID proceedings.[131]

The *Giovanni Alemanni* decision comes to be added to a significant number of awards deciding in a quasi-individual manner the question of whether failure to comply with 'procedural' or 'jurisdictional' requirements, such as the clauses discussed *in casu*, allow the tribunal to assume jurisdiction over the dispute or not. Although from a different perspective, the same issue was relevant in the *BG* case set-aside proceedings (reported below).

3.3.6 Sovereign Bonds, Definition of Investment (and Adjudication of Economic Crises)

The *Poštová banka* case[132] was in fact an intra-EU dispute, which however appears not to have attracted attention as such, most probably because it related to the sensitive issue of the (intra-EU) management of euro area sovereign debt crises. The dispute was one of the two brought against Greece following that country's 2012 debt restructuring.[133] The rendered *Poštová banka* decision concerned whether the tribunal had in fact jurisdiction to hear the merits of the dispute and revolved inter alia around the question of whether sovereign debt bonds constitute covered investment under the Greece-Slovakia BIT and under the ICSID Convention. In a landmark decision in which the tribunal distanced itself from its Argentine sovereign debt restructuring predecessors, the *Poštová banka* award determined that sovereign debt bonds are not covered by the BIT in question and therefore the claims had to be rejected.

The tribunal did not openly disagree with earlier decisions which, such as in the *Abaclat* case, accepted jurisdiction. In a nuanced approach, it noted that the Greek-Slovakia BIT included a definition of investment that needed to be distinguished from the one interpreted by the Argentine debt restructuring tribunals and which led them to the conclusion that sovereign bonds constituted covered investment under

[130] ICSID Case No. ARB/07/8, *Giovanni Alemanni v. Argentina*, Decision on Jurisdiction and Admissibility, 17 November 2014, para. 315–316.

[131] ICSID Case No. ARB/07/8, *Giovanni Alemanni v. Argentina*, Decision on Jurisdiction and Admissibility, 17 November 2014, para. 316–317.

[132] ICSID Case No. ARB/13/8, Poštová banka, a.s. and ISTROKAPITAL SE v. Greece, Award, 9 April 2015.

[133] The other one is the ICSID Case No. ARB/14/16, *Cyprus Popular Bank Public Co. Ltd. v. Greece,* registered 16 July 2014.

the BIT.[134] Although the treaty under interpretation in *Poštová banka* established that investment 'means any kind of asset', it qualified this by noting 'and in particular, but not exclusively, includes' and adding a list of assets. The broad definition of investment ('any kind of asset') was followed by the specification that 'the term applies especially to a specific group or category'.[135] But the tribunal considered that the latter, even if still broad, is not unlimited.[136] It noted especially that if the chapeau 'investment means every kind of asset and in particular [. . .]' is interpreted in isolation, this would imply that 'any asset of any nature whatsoever would qualify as an investment under the Slovakia-Greece BIT' but in that case the ensuing list of types of assets would appear 'useless or meaningless'.[137]

The tribunal further drew a distinction with the Italy-Argentina BIT applicable in the *Abaclat* case, and remarked that the list of covered investments in the Greece-Slovakia BIT 'does not contain any reference to "obligations" or to "securities," much less to *public* titles or obligations'.[138] No language in this treaty suggests 'that the State parties considered, in the wide category of investments of the list of Article 1(1) of the BIT, public debt or public obligations, much less sovereign debt, as an investment under the treaty'.[139] In the agreement, references to bonds were limited to those issued by companies.[140] The tribunal further rejected the claimants' argument that bonds constituted loans, covered by the Greece-Slovakia BIT[141] and the interpretation they put forward in connection with 'claims to money'.[142] It concluded that there was no investment and the claimants were not investors within the meaning of the BIT; therefore the tribunal lacked jurisdiction *ratione materiae* to hear the merits of the dispute.[143] Having already determined that it did not have

134 ICSID Case No. ARB/13/8, *Poštová banka, a.s. and ISTROKAPITAL SE v. Greece*, Award, 9 April 2015, para. 298 ff., 304 ff.

135 ICSID Case No. ARB/13/8, *Poštová banka, a.s. and ISTROKAPITAL SE v. Greece*, Award, 9 April 2015, para. 314. An apparent contradiction exists between this statement and another statement in paragraph 313, where there the group or category of assets is described as 'not closed, or limited or restrictive'.

136 ICSID Case No. ARB/13/8, *Poštová banka, a.s. and ISTROKAPITAL SE v. Greece*, Award, 9 April 2015, para. 313.

137 ICSID Case No. ARB/13/8, *Poštová banka, a.s. and ISTROKAPITAL SE v. Greece*, Award, 9 April 2015, para. 312.

138 ICSID Case No. ARB/13/8, *Poštová banka, a.s. and ISTROKAPITAL SE v. Greece*, Award, 9 April 2015, para. 331.

139 ICSID Case No. ARB/13/8, *Poštová banka, a.s. and ISTROKAPITAL SE v. Greece*, Award, 9 April 2015, para. 332.

140 ICSID Case No. ARB/13/8, *Poštová banka, a.s. and ISTROKAPITAL SE v. Greece*, Award, 9 April 2015, para. 335.

141 ICSID Case No. ARB/13/8, *Poštová banka, a.s. and ISTROKAPITAL SE v. Greece*, Award, 9 April 2015, para. 336 ff.

142 ICSID Case No. ARB/13/8, *Poštová banka, a.s. and ISTROKAPITAL SE v. Greece*, Award, 9 April 2015, para. 341 ff.

143 ICSID Case No. ARB/13/8, *Poštová banka, a.s. and ISTROKAPITAL SE v. Greece*, Award, 9 April 2015, para. 350.

jurisdiction as the BIT's definition of investment was not satisfied, the tribunal examined in an *obiter dictum* whether sovereign bonds constituted investment under the ICSID Convention. In that case, the majority found that, if the tribunal accept the 'objective' test ('contribution, duration, risk'), the claimants did not have an investment.[144] This latter part of the award is particularly significant, because the tribunal, although narrowing its interpretation to the claims at hand, distanced itself from the Argentine sovereign debt restructuring tribunals and expressly considered that sovereign debt is not investment for the purposes of the ICSID Convention.

The interpretation in *Poštová banka* is noteworthy in that it shows deference to the host state in relation to its economic policymaking and thus allows for the restructuring of sovereign debt without interference and may in the future minimise regulatory chill. This is especially the case, if its reasoning is followed by other tribunals. The decision may also raise some questions regarding the interpretation of non-exhaustive lists in investment treaty provisions.

Ping An v. Belgium is another dispute that arose out of the recent financial and economic crisis in Europe, notably in relation to nationalisations in the banking sector.[145] Although an award was rendered on 30 April 2015,[146] this is not public yet. Reportedly, the decision has dismissed the claims brought against Belgium. It appears that no arguments had been made on the merits prior to the award and that arbitrators had been examining the respondent's jurisdictional objectives.[147]

3.3.7 Disputes Involving the Amount of Compensation for Expropriation

In the *Sanum v. Laos* case, the tribunal considered that Article 8(3) of the Laos-China BIT which allows only 'disputes involving the amount of compensation for expropriation' to be submitted to international arbitration is susceptible to receive many readings. According to the tribunal, '[t]he term "involving" has a wider meaning than other possible terms such as "limited to" which could have been used if the intention of the State Parties had been to limit the jurisdiction of the Tribunal exclusively to disputes on the amount of compensation'. The tribunal

---

[144] ICSID Case No. ARB/13/8, *Poštová banka, a.s. and ISTROKAPITAL SE v. Greece*, Award, 9 April 2015, para. 360 ff.

[145] ICSID Case No. ARB/12/29, *Ping An Life Insurance Company of China, Limited and Ping An Insurance (Group) Company of China, Limited v. Belgium*, registered 19 September 2012.

[146] ICSID Case No. ARB/12/29, *Ping An Life Insurance Company of China, Limited and Ping An Insurance (Group) Company of China, Limited v. Belgium*, Award, 30 April 2015 (not public).

[147] Peterson LE, Belgium prevails in billion dollar ICSID arbitration brought by Chinese investors in failed Fortis bank. IA Reporter, 1 May 2015 http://www.iareporter.com/articles/20150501 (last accessed 24 September 2015).

further observed that this reading is also consistent with the earlier interpretation of the *Tza Yap Shum* tribunal.[148]

3.3.8 Consolidation of Claims

In an unpublished decision of 13 August 2013, reported in the IA Reporter, the Permanent Court of Arbitration (PCA) endorsed the Czech Republic's refusal to allow the consolidation of claims brought by ten foreign investors in connection with measures in the state's photovoltaic sector.[149] The Czech Republic consented to arbitrate jointly some of these claims, with the result that six proceedings will ensue.[150]

3.4 Substantive Matters in Investment Dispute Settlement

The paragraphs that follow address arbitral jurisprudence on investment law's two most important standards: fair and equitable treatment and expropriation.

3.4.1 Fair and Equitable Treatment

The *Micula* tribunal[151] found that Romania had created a legitimate expectation that the incentives would remain in place over a period of 10 years and the early revocation of these incentives in relation to Romania's accession to the EU thwarted the investors' legitimate expectations. The tribunal recognised that the key issue in this respect is to determine 'who bore the risk of regulatory change: the state or the investors who benefited from the existing regulatory regime'.[152]

---

[148] UNCITRAL, PCA Case No. 2013-13, *Sanum v. Laos*, Award on Jurisdiction, 13 December 2013, para. 329.

[149] Peterson LE, Following PCA decision, Czech Republic thwarts move by solar investors to sue in single arbitral proceeding; meanwhile Spain sees new solar claim at ICSID. IA Reporter, 1 January 2014 https://www.iareporter.com/articles/following-pca-decision-czech-republic-thwarts-move-by-solar-investors-to-sue-in-single-arbitral-proceeding-meanwhile-spain-sees-new-solar-claim-at-icsid/ (last accessed 24 September 2015).

[150] Peterson LE, Following PCA decision, Czech Republic thwarts move by solar investors to sue in single arbitral proceeding; meanwhile Spain sees new solar claim at ICSID. IA Reporter, 1 January 2014 https://www.iareporter.com/articles/following-pca-decision-czech-republic-thwarts-move-by-solar-investors-to-sue-in-single-arbitral-proceeding-meanwhile-spain-sees-new-solar-claim-at-icsid/ (last accessed 24 September 2015).

[151] ICSID Case No. ARB/05/20, *Ioan Micula, Viorel Micula, S.C. European Food S.A., S.C. Starmill S.R.L. and S.C. Multipack S.R.L. v. Romania*, Award, 11 December 2013.

[152] ICSID Case No. ARB/05/20, *Ioan Micula, Viorel Micula, S.C. European Food S.A., S.C. Starmill S.R.L. and S.C. Multipack S.R.L. v. Romania*, Award, 11 December 2013, para. 665.

In analysing the investor's legitimate expectations, the tribunal admitted that 'the fair and equitable treatment standard does not give a right to regulatory stability *per se*. The state has a right to regulate, and investors must expect that the legislation will change, absent a stabilization clause or other specific assurance giving rise to a legitimate expectation of stability'.[153] However, the tribunal ended by considering that Romania had breached the claimants legitimate expectations 'with respect to the availability of the EGO 24 incentives' on which the claimants had relied in order to expand their business and which they had reasonably expected to remain in place for 10 years.[154]

More interesting for the interpretation of fair and equitable treatment is the tribunal's findings with reference to some another constitutive element of the standard: the reasonableness of Romania's revocation of the incentives. Concretely, the tribunal addressed 'the question of whether, in pursuit of its objective to join the EU, Romania acted reasonably'.[155] The tribunal took into account the fact that although the EU did not explicitly order the revocation of the incentives, its request to align incompatible state aid regimes with the *acquis communautaire* 'must be interpreted as a request for termination of the incentives as a pre-condition for accession'.[156] In other words, in view of the EU's opinion that the EGO 24 incentives constituted state aid contrary to EU law, their repeal 'related to a rational public policy objective (i.e., EU accession), and there was an appropriate correlation between that objective and the measure adopted to achieve it (i.e., the repeal of the EGO 24 incentives)'.[157] Romania's failure to negotiate with the EU a delay in the revocation date or a transitional period or otherwise mitigate the damages for instance through payment of compensation to the claimants was not unreasonable, given that 'it would have been extremely difficult (perhaps even impossible) to obtain agreement from the EU on any of these alternative solutions'.[158] Otherwise stated, Romania's failure 'to negotiate transitional periods or compensation was not arbitrary, but appears justified under the specific circumstances of the accession negotiations'.[159] However, what the tribunal did consider unreasonable was

[153] ICSID Case No. ARB/05/20, *Ioan Micula, Viorel Micula, S.C. European Food S.A., S.C. Starmill S.R.L. and S.C. Multipack S.R.L. v. Romania*, Award, 11 December 2013, para. 666.

[154] ICSID Case No. ARB/05/20, *Ioan Micula, Viorel Micula, S.C. European Food S.A., S.C. Starmill S.R.L. and S.C. Multipack S.R.L. v. Romania*, Award, 11 December 2013, para. 724–725.

[155] ICSID Case No. ARB/05/20, *Ioan Micula, Viorel Micula, S.C. European Food S.A., S.C. Starmill S.R.L. and S.C. Multipack S.R.L. v. Romania*, Award, 11 December 2013, para. 797.

[156] ICSID Case No. ARB/05/20, *Ioan Micula, Viorel Micula, S.C. European Food S.A., S.C. Starmill S.R.L. and S.C. Multipack S.R.L. v. Romania*, Award, 11 December 2013, para. 802.

[157] ICSID Case No. ARB/05/20, *Ioan Micula, Viorel Micula, S.C. European Food S.A., S.C. Starmill S.R.L. and S.C. Multipack S.R.L. v. Romania*, Award, 11 December 2013, para. 802.

[158] ICSID Case No. ARB/05/20, *Ioan Micula, Viorel Micula, S.C. European Food S.A., S.C. Starmill S.R.L. and S.C. Multipack S.R.L. v. Romania*, Award, 11 December 2013, para. 806.

[159] ICSID Case No. ARB/05/20, *Ioan Micula, Viorel Micula, S.C. European Food S.A., S.C. Starmill S.R.L. and S.C. Multipack S.R.L. v. Romania*, Award, 11 December 2013, para. 825.

Romania's decision to hold the claimants to their obligations while repealing the incentives given to them.[160]

In another case, the *Gold Reserve* tribunal had to interpret the meaning of fair and equitable treatment offered 'in accordance with the principles of international law'.[161] The tribunal remarked that in order to determine these principles, it is necessary to take into account the 'present status of development of public international law in the field of investment protection'.[162] Notably, the tribunal considered that 'public international law principles have evolved since the *Neer* case and that the standard today is broader than that defined in the *Neer* case'.[163] The tribunal concurred with Schwebel that 'the *Neer* award "had nothing to do with the treatment of foreign investors or investments. It did not address what is fair and equitable"' and that "*Neer* is far from what is fair and equitable".[164]

The *Flughafen v. Venezuela* tribunal confirmed doctrinal and jurisprudential interpretations of fair and equitable treatment, as a standard that includes protection against denial of justice.[165] It considered that denial of justice is in any case illicit under customary international law[166] and it is prohibited under the latter.[167] In order to establish that there has been a denial of justice, two conditions need to be present. It is common to consider, first, whether the foreign investor has been treated in a clearly and manifestly anti-juridical manner and, second, whether the foreign investor has exhausted all domestic legal remedies to challenge the anti-juridical decision or has proved that pursuing such remedies would be clearly futile.[168] In the present case, the tribunal found that there had been a denial of justice.[169]

[160] ICSID Case No. ARB/05/20, *Ioan Micula, Viorel Micula, S.C. European Food S.A., S.C. Starmill S.R.L. and S.C. Multipack S.R.L. v. Romania*, Award, 11 December 2013, para. 826.

[161] ICSID Case No. ARB(AF)/09/1, *Gold Reserve Inc. v. Venezuela*, Award, 22 September 2014.

[162] ICSID Case No. ARB(AF)/09/1, *Gold Reserve Inc. v. Venezuela*, Award, 22 September 2014, para. 567.

[163] ICSID Case No. ARB(AF)/09/1, *Gold Reserve Inc. v. Venezuela*, Award, 22 September 2014, para. 567.

[164] ICSID Case No. ARB(AF)/09/1, *Gold Reserve Inc. v. Venezuela*, Award, 22 September 2014, para. 567.

[165] ICSID Case No. ARB/10/19, *Flughafen Zürich A.G. and Gestión e Ingenería IDC S.A. v. Venezuela*, Award, 18 November 2014, para. 376, 630.

[166] ICSID Case No. ARB/10/19, *Flughafen Zürich A.G. and Gestión e Ingenería IDC S.A. v. Venezuela*, Award, 18 November 2014, para. 378, 631.

[167] ICSID Case No. ARB/10/19, *Flughafen Zürich A.G. and Gestión e Ingenería IDC S.A. v. Venezuela*, Award, 18 November 2014, para. 633.

[168] ICSID Case No. ARB/10/19, *Flughafen Zürich A.G. and Gestión e Ingenería IDC S.A. v. Venezuela*, Award, 18 November 2014, para. 635 ff.

[169] ICSID Case No. ARB/10/19, *Flughafen Zürich A.G. and Gestión e Ingenería IDC S.A. v. Venezuela*, Award, 18 November 2014, para. 365.

3.4.2 Expropriation

In *Perenco v. Ecuador*, the tribunal concurred with earlier arbitral jurisprudence on the distinction 'to be drawn between a partial deprivation of value, which is not an expropriation, and a "*complete or near complete deprivation of value*", which can constitute an expropriation'.[170] It remarked that, in accordance with such jurisprudence, concerning 'the amount of deprivation of value required to be shown before an indirect expropriation will be found', in order to have an expropriation a 'very substantial amount of deprivation' is required. Although deprivation need not be total, it has to be very substantial.[171] A 'total loss of the investment's value or a total loss of control by the investor of its investment' were also required by the *Mobil* tribunal, before expropriation could be established.[172] The tribunal considered that both also needed to be of a permanent nature.[173]

3.5 Compensation Awarded: The 'Yukos' Case

At least eight decisions awarded investors compensation in 2014.[174] The most noteworthy development in this respect is a new record high compensation of US $50 billion awarded in the context of the *Yukos* case.[175] The amount initially sought by the claimants was in excess of US$114 billion.[176]

[170] ICSID Case No. ARB/08/6, *Perenco Ecuador Limited v. Ecuador*, Decision on Remaining Issues of Jurisdiction and on Liability, 12 September 2014, para. 672, emphasis in original.

[171] ICSID Case No. ARB/08/6, *Perenco Ecuador Limited v. Ecuador*, Decision on Remaining Issues of Jurisdiction and on Liability, 12 September 2014, para. 673.

[172] ICSID Case No. ARB/07, Mobil Corporation, Venezuela Holdings, B.V., Mobil Cerro Negro Holding, Ltd., Mobil Venezolana de Petróleos Holdings, Inc., Mobil Cerro Negro, Ltd., and Mobil Venezolana de Petróleos, Inc. v. Venezuela, Award, 9 October 2014, para. 286.

[173] ICSID Case No. ARB/07, Mobil Corporation, Venezuela Holdings, B.V., Mobil Cerro Negro Holding, Ltd., Mobil Venezolana de Petróleos Holdings, Inc., Mobil Cerro Negro, Ltd., and Mobil Venezolana de Petróleos, Inc. v. Venezuela, Award, 9 October 2014, para. 286.

[174] UNCTAD, Investor-State Dispute Settlement: Review of Developments in 2014. IIA Issues Note No. 2, May 2015, p. 18.

[175] UNCITRAL, PCA Case No. AA 226, *Hulley Enterprises Limited (Cyprus) v. Russia,* Final Award, 18 July 2014; UNCITRAL, PCA Case No. AA 228, *Veteran Petroleum Limited (Cyprus) v. Russian,* Final Award, 18 July 2014; UNCITRAL, PCA Case No. AA 227, *Yukos Universal Limited (Isle of Man) v. Russian,* Final Award, 18 July 2014.

[176] UNCITRAL, PCA Case No. AA 226, *Hulley Enterprises Limited (Cyprus) v. Russia,* Final Award, 18 July 2014, para. 1694; UNCITRAL, PCA Case No. AA 228, *Veteran Petroleum Limited (Cyprus) v. Russian,* Final Award, 18 July 2014, para. 1694; UNCITRAL, PCA Case No. AA 227, *Yukos Universal Limited (Isle of Man) v. Russian,* Final Award, 18 July 2014, para. 1694.

3.6 *Review of Arbitral Decisions by National Courts: Reversal of BG Award Set-Aside*

The Supreme Court of the United States overturned a 2012 set-aside[177] of the BG award rendered against Argentina in 2007.[178] The award had been set aside in light of the fact that the tribunal had accepted that the state had consented to arbitration, despite the fact that the claimant had not respected an 18-month local remedies clause. In reviewing the decision of the Court of Appeals, the Supreme Court of the United States determined that the provision in question resembled a 'claims-processing requirement' and not one that 'affects the arbitration contract's validity or scope', and for that reason it presumed that the parties intended to leave the authority of decision over that question to the arbitrators.[179] However, two dissenting judges considered that since the treaty's arbitration clause contains a unilateral standing offer by the host state to an investor to 'submit to arbitration under certain conditions, an investor cannot form an arbitration agreement with a Contracting Party under the Treaty until the investor accepts the actual terms of the Contracting Party's offer. Absent a valid excuse, that means litigating its dispute in the Contracting Party's courts to a "final decision" or, barring that, for at least 18 months'.[180]

4 Conclusion and Outlook

While the conclusion of international investment agreements and the filing and adjudication of investor-state disputes continued, some important issues clearly arose in this last year-year and a half. One first such issue concerns the apparent consensus on the need to reform international investment law, an element particularly pronounced in the context of investor-state dispute settlement. In recent years the discussion on reform was concentrated on the need to rebalance investment

[177] United States Court of Appeals, No. 11-7021, *Argentina v. BG Group PLC*, No. 1:08-cv-00485 (2012), http://www.italaw.com/sites/default/files/case-documents/ita0085.pdf (last accessed 9 March 2015).

[178] Supreme Court of the United States, No. 12-138, Opinion in the case *BG Group PLC v. Argentina*, 572 US (2014), http://www.supremecourt.gov/opinions/13pdf/12-138_97be.pdf (last accessed March 2015).

[179] Supreme Court of the United States, No. 12-138, Opinion in the case BG *Group PLC v. Argentina*, 572 US (2014), http://www.supremecourt.gov/opinions/13pdf/12-138_97be.pdf (last accessed March 2015), p. 17.

[180] Supreme Court of the United States, No. 12-138, Opinion in the case *BG Group PLC v. Argentina*, 572 US (2014), Dissenting by Justices Robert and Kennedy, http://www.italaw.com/sites/default/files/case-documents/italaw3117.pdf (last accessed March 2015), p. 9.

agreements—and important achievements have been made in this respect. The latest developments show a shift of focus to improving investment dispute settlement. Noteworthy among others is the proposal to establish a permanent investment court and an appeals mechanism, coming not only from academia but also from policymakers, including the European Union.

The renewed attempt to multilateralise international investment law is another important development with a probably novel chance of succeeding. The adoption of the UNCITRAL Transparency Rules and the Transparency Convention are two first examples, although the latter is yet to enter into force. Multilateralism has also come to be included in seminal policy statements by the European Union.

A final observation concerns the adjudication of economic crises and sovereign debt restructurings. The two recent awards dismissing claims against EU Member States in relation to measures adopted either in relation to a sovereign debt restructuring or nationalisations related to bank bail-outs by the state during an economic crisis, show deference to the host state.[181] The difference with some of the earlier decisions rendered in relation to Argentina's economic crisis and sovereign debt restructuring is striking. The question may be asked whether tribunals are more deferent when the economic policy measures allegedly violating an investment agreement have been taken by developed countries and notably Member States of the European Union. Tribunal deference to host state measures may also be explained by the mounting specticism vis-à-vis investment dispute resolution and particular critiques about the very absence of deference. This development is to be welcomed, especially if it sets a trend to be followed in other arbitral decisions concerning economic crises and sovereign debt restructuring.

References

Titi C (2014) Investment arbitration in Latin America: the uncertain veracity of preconceived ideas. Arbitr Int 30(2):357–386

Titi C (2015a) Investment law and the European Union: towards a new generation of international investment agreements. Eur J Int Law 26(3):639–661

Titi C (2015b) Institutional developments in investor-state dispute settlement and arbitration under the auspices of the International Centre for Settlement of investment disputes. In: Herrmann C, Krajewski M, Terchechte JP (eds) European Yearbook of International Economic Law 2015. Springer, Heidelberg

[181] This is said with the caveat that little is known of the second award at the time of writing.

Recent Developments in IMF Policies and Activities

Ludwig Gramlich

Contents

Abstract During the last 70 years, the Fund has changed its tasks and activities although there were but a few explicit modifications of its Articles of Agreement and the issue of a fair re-allocation of voting rights remained unsolved till now. Thus, the purpose of this overview focusing upon recent developments is to take a closer look at main International Monetary Fund (IMF) fields of activities like surveillance under Art. IV and various forms of financial as well as of technical assistance. Moreover, the role of the Fund as an organization taking actively part in development assistance is dealt with, as well as its relationship with the other 'Bretton Woods' institution, the World Bank, and the World Trade Organization (WTO), since there are many interlinked topics needing intensive cooperation between Fund and the respective partner organization. Finally, the Fund has been

L. Gramlich (✉)
Faculty of Economics and Business Administration, Chemnitz University, 09107 Chemnitz, Germany
e-mail: l.gramlich@wirtschaft.tu-chemnitz.de

M. Bungenberg et al. (eds.), *European Yearbook of International Economic Law 2016*, European Yearbook of International Economic Law 7,
DOI 10.1007/978-3-319-29215-1_32

engaged in strategies and operations how to cope with the deterioration of the financial situation of some Euro zone member States. And of course, there shall be new challenges ahead for the Fund, so a major reform of its legal framework may soon be needed.

1 Introduction

1.1 The IMF at 70

In a speech delivered during the International Monetary Fund (IMF)/World Bank Annual meetings in October 2014,[1] Managing Director Christine Lagarde took a moment to reflect on the 70-year journey the Bretton Woods institutions had made by pointing at "forks in the road". She told the audience:

> "Almost exactly a hundred years ago, the world took a dramatically wrong turn… instead of using technological wonders for the betterment of humanity, they were turned toward massive destruction. The gates of cooperation were bolted shut. Because of this wrong turn, the world went through three decades of carnage, chaos, and calamity. But then something changed. Seventy years ago, in 1944, the world faced another fork in the road. This time, it chose the right path. It was the original "multilateral moment", which gave birth to institutions of cooperation like the Fund and the Bank…
>
> This choice has paid off over the decades—with rising prosperity, greater stability, and lower poverty. The IMF has played an essential role: helping to fight crisis after crisis; helping low-income and transition countries gain a foothold in the global economy; and helping to build capacity, strength, and resilience across our entire membership.

Today, the Fund continues to respond to conditions on the ground, forcefully and flexibly. Since 2008, we have committed almost $700 billion to countries in need, provided training to all of our members, and technical assistance to 90 % of them.[2] Over the last several months alone, we provided fresh financial assistance to Ukraine, the Arab transition countries, and the African nations hit by Ebola.[3]

Seventy years after Bretton Woods, the international community stands at another fork in the road. The tried-and-true modes of cooperation seem to be fraying around the edges. The sustainability of the global economic engine itself is increasingly being questioned. Can it really deliver the jobs, the incomes, the better living standards that people aspire to?

---

[1] The IMF at 70: Making the Right Choices—Yesterday, Today, and Tomorrow, 10 October 2014, http://www.imf.org/external/np/speeches/2014/101014.htm (last accessed 26 June 2015).

[2] Cf. for more details IMF Financial Resources and Liquidity Position 2015, http:www.imf.org/cgi-shl/create_x.pl?liq (last accessed 26 June 2015).

[3] For more information on these topics, cf. references to examples for Fund lending practice below, 2.3.1.2.

There are three key collective choices to be made:

- First, how do we achieve the growth and jobs needed to advance prosperity and ensure social harmony? I would call this the choice between acceleration and stagnation.
- Second, how do we make this interconnected world a more inclusive, safer place for all of us to thrive? This is the choice between stability and fragility.
- Third, how do we strengthen cooperation and multilateralism, instead of isolationism and insularity? This is the choice between solidarity and seclusion".

Lagarde concluded her speech by recommending: "At this key fork in the road, let us choose acceleration over stagnation, stability over fragility, solidarity over seclusion. Let us choose the path of 1944, not 1914".

Since she acted in her role as head of a very prominent intergovernmental organisation, one may ask whether the IMF itself has been endowed with authority broad enough to make the right choices or at least to assist its members adequately when they are discussing appropriate ways and means for improving the overall situation in their respective countries.

1.2 *IMF Policies and Decisions Within the Framework of Legal Responsibilities and Limits*

Earlier contributions on IMF issues in this Yearbook were dealing with "recent legal developments" in the Fund in general,[4] "recent reforms of the finances of the I. M.F.",[5] "recent quota and governance reform at the I.M.F.",[6] the "role of the IMF as a global financial authority"[7] or, in a broader perspective, elaborating upon the "intellectual history of the international regulation of monetary affairs".[8] Thus, it seems appropriate for this essay to move over to some other subjects of importance for IMF activities within the last few years and focus primarily upon surveillance, financial and technical assistance topics. Some other, rather general fields like transparency and governance are also reviewed, as well as cooperation with the other two main universal economic institutions as such a construction consisting of three pillars should already have been put up soon after World War II.

The implementation of reforms by modifying existing provisions of the IMF Articles of Agreement seems rather complex and long-consuming as we can see

[4] Cf. Bergthaler and Bossu (2010), p. 391 ff.

[5] Bergthaler and Steinki (2012), p. 635 ff.

[6] Bergthaler and Giddings (2013), p. 371 ff.

[7] Lastra (2011), p. 121 ff.

[8] Lichtenstein (2014), p. 3 ff.

looking at the still pending IMF quota reform.[9] Thus, changes of Fund policies and practices (as well as their formal consolidation by enacting or altering relevant internal rules and decisions) may primarily result from various events taking place at the international political, financial or economic levels which influence actual decision making in central Fund bodies.

2 Main Issues

2.1 *The IMF's Responsibilities*

According to its own statement, the IMF's primary purpose is "to ensure the stability of the international monetary system - the system of exchange rates and international payments that enables countries (and their citizens) to transact with each other".[10] In fact, Article I of its Articles of Agreement mentions these aspects only at third and fourth place, whereas the aim of promotion of international monetary cooperation by a permanent institutionalized machinery for consultation and collaboration as well as some main objectives of (more general) economic policy are listed at a higher rank. Finally, also the two last main purposes of the Fund do not refer explicitly or even exclusively to monetary matters as they are obliging the organization and its officials to do their utmost to prevent disequilibria in members' balances of payments in general. And finally, a closer look at the wording of the next phrase of Article I shows that the Fund should be guided by these six purposes set forth in this provision "in all its policies and decisions". So, the various bodies of the organization (especially Governing Board and Executive Board) are not only authorized to look at and take into account a broad spectrum of monetary, fiscal, commercial and other economic affairs and activities but that assessment (and to draw consequences when there are relevant disturbances) is their duty, a legal obligation as well as a legitimate behavior. On the other hand, Article X of the Fund agreement makes clear that the Fund must also adequately respect the specific tasks and powers of other corporate actors at the international level by establishing a duty of cooperation for the IMF "within the terms of this Agreement with any general international organization and with public international organizations having specialized responsibilities in related fields".[11]

Within the broad framework of primary IMF law set up by the Articles of Agreement, the Fund's governing bodies may therefore interpret and update the actual mandate which took place in 2012 at the last time when the Executive Board

[9] Cf. Acceptances of the Proposed Amendment of the Articles of Agreement on Reform of the Executive Board and Consents to 2010 Quota Increase, last updated 8 May 2015, http://www.imf.org/external/np/sec/misc/sonsents (last accessed 26 June 2015).

[10] The IMF at a glance, http://www.imf.org/external/about/htm (last accessed 26 June 2015).

[11] Cf. below chapter on the Fund's relationship with World Bank and WTO.

discussed the then current bi-annual working program and followed the proposal of the Managing Director (in her Action Plan[12]) to include all macroeconomic and financial sector issues that bear on global stability into the Fund's fields of activity.[13] Although the IMF does not have any legal authority to enact "hard" secondary law that would be binding upon members or even third persons or institutions, there are indeed various other, "softer" tools to be used to influence member States' behavior rather effectively even if they are not bound (as borrowers) by specific loan conditions. Limits of such rather discretionary powers of intervention are only rarely explicitly laid down in various provisions of the Fund's Articles of Agreement since most interactions between Fund and members are depending on forms of cooperation between both sides which are voluntary at least from a strict legal point of view.[14]

2.2 *Surveillance*

2.2.1 Adjusting to Actual Needs

In today's globalised economy, where the policies of one country typically affect many other countries, close international (monetary, financial and economic) cooperation is essential. The IMF, with its near-universal membership of 188 countries,[15] facilitates this cooperation primarily by using the possibilities which may be derived from Article IV of its Articles of Agreement on "surveillance". There are two main aspects of the Fund's relevant work: on the one hand, bilateral surveillance, which means the appraisal of and advice on the policies of each member country, on the other hand multilateral surveillance, or oversight of the world economy as a whole or at least related to regions or subregions of the globe.

Looking at bilateral surveillance first, 122 consultations were held in 2012, 122 in 2013 and 129 in 2014.[16] Article IV consultations usually take place once a year. IMF economists continually monitor members' economies. In the course of this work, they visit member countries to gather information and exchange views with government and central bank officials considering whether there are risks to domestic and global stability that argue for adjustments in economic or financial

[12] See Press release No. 12/199, 7 June 2012, http://www.imf.org/external/np/sec/pr/2012/pr12199.htm (last accessed 26 June 2015).

[13] Action Plan to the International Monetary and Financial Committee, 18 April 2012, http://www.imf.org/external/pp/longres.aspx?id=4640 (last accessed 26 June 2015).

[14] Of course, there are some exceptions, as provided for, in particular, in Articles V sec. 5, VI sec. and XXVI sec. 2.

[15] Fast Facts, http://www.imf.org/external/about.htm (last accessed 26 June 2015); list of members at: http://wwwimf.org/external/np/sec/memdir/members.aspx (last accessed 26 June 2015).

[16] For relevant documents, cf. http://www.imf.org/external/np/sec/aiv/index/aspx?listby=y (last accessed 26 June 2015).

policies. Discussions mainly focus on exchange rate, monetary, fiscal, and financial policies, as well as macro-critical structural reforms. During their missions in a member country, IMF staff also typically meets with other relevant stakeholders, such as national parliamentarians and representatives of business, labor unions, and civil society, to help better evaluate the country's economic policies and outlook.[17]

Upon its return to the Fund's headquarters, the mission submits a report to the IMF's Executive Board for discussion. The Board's views are subsequently summarized and transmitted to the country's authorities. In 2013 some 96 % of member countries agreed to publication of a Press Release[18] which summarizes the staff's and the Board's views, around 90 % published the Article IV consultation staff report. 95 % of the countries published this report when it was combined with an assessment of a Fund-supported program or other related matters.[19] So, the Fund's surveillance activities and results have become increasingly more transparent.

The IMF also monitors global and regional economic trends, and analyzes spillovers from members' policies onto the global economy. The key instruments of that multilateral surveillance are three regular publications—World Economic Outlook (WEO),[20] Global Financial Stability Report (GFSR),[21] and Fiscal Monitor.[22]

The Fund regularly reviews its surveillance activities. The 2011 Triennial Surveillance Review (TSR)[23] highlighted progress in addressing weaknesses in pre-crisis surveillance but also found gaps still existing. In particular, IMF surveillance was seen as too fragmented, with risk assessments lacking depth and insufficient focus on interconnections and transmission of shocks. The 2011 review report thus recommended improvements in six key areas: interconnectedness, risk assessments, external stability, financial stability, traction, and the legal framework.

Since 2011, the Fund has prepared spillover reports[24] analyzing key global spillovers, with a particular focus on the impact of economic policies in systemic

[17] IMF Surveillance, 13 April 2015, http://www.imf.org/external/np/exr/facts/surv.htm (last accessed 26 June 2015).

[18] Cf., e.g., IMF Executive Board concludes 2015 Article IV consultation with Haiti, Press release No. 15/241, 28 May 2015, http://www.imf/org/external/np/sec/2015/pr15241.htm (last accessed 26 June 2015).

[19] Cf. on possible reasons for remaining intransparency Edwards MS, Coolidge KA, Preston, DA, Who reveals? Transparency and the IMF's Article IV consultations (21 January 2012), http://wp.peio.me/wp-content/uploads/2014/04/Conf5_Edwards-30.09.11.pdf (last accessed 26 June 2015).

[20] For World Economic Outlook Reports, see http://www.imf.org/external/ns/cs.aspx?id=29 (last accessed 26 June 2015).

[21] http://www.imf.org/external/pubs/ft/gfsr/index.htm (last accessed 26 June 2015).

[22] Launched in 2009, http://www.imf.org/external/ns/cs.aspx?id=262 (last accessed 26 June 2015).

[23] Cf. Public Information Notice No. 11/130, 31 October 2011, http://www.imf.org/external/np/sec/pn/2011/pn11130.htm (last accessed 26 June 2015); relevant documents at: http://www.imf.org/external/np/spr/triennial/2011/index.htm (last accessed 26 June 2015).

[24] http://www.imf.org/external/ns/cs.aspx?id=316 (last accessed 26 June 2015).

economies, i.e. the five economies in the world that have the greatest impact on other countries through trade, financial, and other links. Two of these economies are the euro area and the United Kingdom. Since 2012, the IMF has also published Pilot External Sector Reports,[25] which place the external positions of systemically large economies in a globally consistent setting.

Twice a year, the IMF prepares a Global Policy Agenda[26] that pulls together the key findings and policy advice from multilateral reports and defines a future agenda for the Fund and its members.

2.2.1.1 Strengthening Relevant Activities

In recent years, not least caused by the multifold negative effects of the financial crisis which started in 2008, the IMF has undertaken major initiatives to strengthen surveillance to respond to a more globalized and interconnected world. These initiatives include revamping the legal framework for surveillance, deepening analysis of risks and spillovers, strengthening financial surveillance of systemic risk, stepping up assessments of members' external positions, and responding more promptly to concerns of the membership. The Managing Director's Action Plan for Strengthening Surveillance[27] outlined concrete measures to take forward work in these priority areas, which are also discussed in an updated Guidance Note for Surveillance under Article IV.[28] In July 2012, the IMF's Executive Board adopted an Integrated Surveillance Decision[29] that strengthens the legal basis for surveillance in a highly integrated world economy. The Triennial Surveillance Review,[30] furthering initiatives launched in the 2011 Review,[31] proposes steps to improve implementation of reforms in these areas, and also to ensure that surveillance would be well-equipped to address emerging challenges and support sustainable growth in an interconnected post-crisis world.

---

[25] Cf. for more details http://www.imf.org/external/np/spr/2014/esr/ (last accessed 26 June 2015); relevant documents available at: http://www.imforg/external/ns/cs.aspx?id=341 (last accessed 26 June 2015).

[26] See, e.g., the agenda of April 2014 titled 'interconnections, spillovers, and spillbacks', http://www.imf.org/external/np/pp/eng/2014/041214.pdf (last accessed 26 June 2015).

[27] December 2014, http://www.imf.org/external/np/pp/eng/2014/112114.pdf (last accessed 26 June 2015).

[28] 12 October 2012, http://www.imf.org/external/np/pp/eng/2012/101012.pdf (last accessed 26 June 2015).

[29] 17 July 2012, http://www.imf.org/external/np/pp/eng/2012/071712.pdf (last accessed 26 June 2015); cf. also Integrated Surveillance Decision, 30 September 2013, http://www.imf.org/external/np/exr/faxts/isd.htm (last accessed 26 June 2015).

[30] http://www.imf.org/external/np/spr/triennial/2014/index.htm (last accessed 26 June 2015).

[31] Cf. Public Information Notice No. 11/130, 31 October 2011, http://www.imf.org/external/np/sec/pn/2011/pn11130.htm (last accessed 26 June 2015); cf. also Press release No. 14/474, 5 October 2014, http://www.imf.org/external/np/sec/pr/2014/pr14454.htm (last accessed 26 June 2015).

The IMF has started giving more emphasis to financial sector issues in its multilateral and bilateral surveillance, in line with the Financial Surveillance Strategy, approved by the Fund's Executive Board in 2012.[32] Given the potential for financial sector developments to rapidly ignite and propagate crises, effective financial sector surveillance seems more critical than ever. Further on, a review of the Financial Sector Assessment Program (FSAP)[33] was completed in September 2014. FSAP findings provide valuable input to the IMF's broader surveillance of countries' economies, i.e. Article IV consultations. The global financial crisis demonstrated the need for an even more seamless integration of these two strands of the Fund's monitoring work.

The IMF has also been sharpening risk assessments so that potential problems can be spotted, and appropriate policy responses developed, more timely and effectively. In collaboration with the Financial Stability Board (FSB),[34] it has conducted semi-annual Early Warning Exercises to identify and assess low probability but high impact risks to the global economy since November 2008 and moreover also Vulnerabilities Exercises to assess vulnerabilities and emerging risks in individual advanced, emerging market, and low-income countries.[35]

The global crisis underlined the need for more analysis of linkages among economies, which the IMF tries to provide through a number of channels. Spillover reports analyze key global spillovers, focusing in particular on the impact of policies in systemic economies. The 2014 report focused on spillovers from advanced economies' exit from unconventional monetary policies and a broad-based slowdown in emerging market growth.[36] Individual country surveillance, as well as multilateral surveillance reports such as the IMF's main reports (WEO, GFSR) and also various Regional Economic Outlook publications, have deepened their analysis of interconnections and spillovers. Cluster reports are also prepared occasionally on common issues facing groups of countries (e.g., capital flows, macroprudential policies, and unconventional monetary policies).[37] Since 2013, the Fund has undertaken such country analysis emphasizing cross-cutting issues in

---

[32] Cf. Public Information Notice No. 12/111, 21 September 2012, http//www.imf.org/external/np/sec/pn/2012/pn12111.htm (last accessed 26 June 2015); cf. for more details The IMF's Financial Surveillance Strategy, 28 August, 2012, http://www.imf.org/external(np/pp/eng/2012/082812.pdf (last accessed 26 June 2015).

[33] See, in general, Factsheet, 15 April 2015, http://www.imf.org/external/np/exr/facts/fsap.htm (last accessed 26 June 2015); as to the FSAP review focusing upon 'further adaptation to the post-crisis era' see policy paper, 18 August 2014, http://www.imf.org/external/pp/longres.aspx?id=4893 (last accessed 26 June 2015).

[34] http://www.financialstabilityboard.org (last accessed 26 June 2015).

[35] IMF-FSB Early Warning Exercise, 15 April 2015, http://www.imf.org/external/np/exr/facts/ewe.htm (last accessed 26 June 2015); for more details on design and methodological toolkit see http://www.imf.org/external/np/pp/eng/2010/090110.pdf (last accessed 26 June 2015).

[36] 29 July 2014, https://www.imf.org/external/np/pp/eng/2014/062514.pdf (last accessed 26 June 2015).

[37] Cf. background paper on 'Enhanced Surveillance: Interconnectedness and Clusters', 16 March 2012, http://www.imf.org/external/mp/pp/eng/2012/031612.pdf (last accessed 26 June 2015).

a new way of monitoring its member countries. The projects include the Nordic Regional Report, the German-Central European Supply Chain Report, the Baltic Cluster Report, and the Housing Cluster Report.[38] The Fund draws on its analysis of cross-border risks and spillovers in many international fora, such as the Group of 20 (G20) industrialized and emerging market economies[39] and the FSB,[40] to promote policies that support sustainable global growth and financial stability.

Leaders of the G20 pledged at their 2009 Pittsburgh Summit to work together to ensure a lasting recovery and strong and sustainable growth over the medium term.[41] To meet this goal, they launched the Framework for Strong, Sustainable, and Balanced Growth. The backbone of this framework is a multilateral process through which G20 countries identify objectives for the global economy, the policies needed to reach them, and the progress toward meeting these shared objectives—the so-called Mutual Assessment Process (MAP).[42] On the request of the G20, the IMF provides technical analysis to evaluate key imbalances and how members' policies fit together—and whether, collectively, they can achieve the G20's goals. IMF staff was tasked with analyzing—in collaboration with other international institutions—whether policies pursued by individual G20 countries were collectively consistent with the G20's growth objectives. Additionally, in recent years, Fund staff was asked to help the membership develop "indicative guidelines" and to use them in order to identify and evaluate large imbalances among members every 2 years.[43]

2.2.1.2 Post Program Monitoring

Under post-program monitoring (PPM), countries undertake more frequent formal consultations with the Fund than is the case under the IMF's normal surveillance, with a particular focus on macroeconomic and structural policies that have implications for external viability. There are normally two post-program monitoring

---

[38] See, e.g., Baltic Cluster Report, May 2014, http://www.imf.org/external/pubs/ft/scr/2014/cr14117.pdf (last accessed 26 June 2015); German-Central European Supply Chain - Cluster Report, Aug. 2013, http://www.imf.org/external/pubs/ft/scr/2013/cr13263.pdf (last accessed 26 June 2015).

[39] On relevant relations and activities, see http://www.imf.org/external/np/g20/ (last accessed 26 June 2015); IMF Annual Report 2014, p. 54.

[40] On Fund membership in the FSB, cf. Public Information Notice No. 13/33, 22 March 2013, https://www.imf.org/external/np/sec/pn/2013/pn1333.htm (last accessed 26 June 2015); for actual issues of cooperation IMF Annual Report 2014, p. 54 ff.

[41] Cf. Press release No. 09/330, 25 September 2009, https://www.imf.org/external/np/sec/pr/2009/pr09330.htm (last accessed 26 June 2015) on this "historic action" (Strauss-Kahn).

[42] Cf. The G20 Mutual Assessment Process (MAP), 27 March 2015, https://www.imf.org/external/np/exr/facts/g20map.htm (last accessed 26 June 2015).

[43] On results of a review of the Fund's involvement in this process see https://www.imf.org/external/np/pp/eng/2011/051311.pdf (13 May 2011) (last accessed 26 June 2015).

Executive Board consultations during a 12-month period. PPM is intended to help ensure the continued viability of a country's economy after its IMF-supported program has expired.[44] It is presumed that a member country will engage in post-program monitoring with the Fund after its program has expired when its outstanding credit exceeds 200 % of its quota, and when it no longer has a program involvement of any kind with the IMF. The Executive Board can decide on post-program monitoring for a country at any time during the program or after the program expires. Post-program monitoring normally remains in effect until outstanding credit falls below the threshold of 200 % of quota.

2.2.2 Surveillance and Advisory Activities

Multilateral surveillance is closely related to the Fund's "pro-active" advisory activities towards its member countries. Encouraging policies that foster economic stability, reduce vulnerability to economic and financial crises, and raise living standards is implemented by regular assessments of global prospects in the IMF's various reports and other research-based publications like staff discussion notes,[45] working papers[46] as well as journals, e.g. Finance and Development (F&D).[47]

2.3 *Financial Assistance*

2.3.1 Fund "Lending"

Committed amounts under current lending arrangements (as of March 2015) were US$ 163 billion, of which US$ 137 billion have not been drawn.[48] The Fund's biggest borrowers (precautionary loans—amount outstanding as of the same date)

---

[44] Cf. Post-Program Monitoring, 27 March 2015, https://www.imf.org/external/np/exr/facts/ppm.htm; see also, e.g., the case of Iceland, Press release No. 15/114, 13 March 2015, https://www.imf.org/external/np/sec/pr/2015/pr15114.htm (last accessed 26 June 2015).

[45] http://www.imf.org/external/ns/cs.aspx?id=353 (last accessed 26 June 2015).

[46] http://www.imf.org/external/pubs/cat/wp1_sp.aspx (last accessed 26 June 2015).

[47] http://www.imf.org/external/pubs/ft/fandd/2015/06/index.htm (last accessed 26 June 2015).

[48] Fast Facts, http://www.imf.org/external/about.htm (last accessed 26 June 2015).

were four EU countries (Greece,[49] Ireland,[50] Poland[51] and Portugal[52]), Ukraine,[53] Colombia,[54] Mexico[55] and Morocco.[56]

2.3.1.1 General Overview

IMF financing (based upon and in accordance with Art. V of the Fund's Articles of Agreement) is first and foremost intended to provide its members breathing space to correct actual or potential balance of payments problems: national authorities must design adjustment programs in close cooperation with the Fund in order to get support by IMF financing; continued financial assistance is conditional on effective implementation of these programs. The Fund's lending is destined to enable countries to rebuild their international reserves, stabilize their currencies, continue paying for imports, and restore conditions for strong economic growth, while undertaking policies to correct underlying economic and social problems. Unlike development banks (as, e.g., the International Bank for Reconstruction and Development (IBRD)), the IMF does not lend for specific projects.[57]

Over the years, the IMF developed various loan instruments that are tailored to address the specific circumstances of its diverse members. Low-income countries (LICs) may borrow on concessional terms through the Extended Credit Facility (ECF),[58] the Standby Credit Facility (SCF)[59] and the Rapid Credit Facility (RCF).[60] The new concessional facilities became effective in January 2010 under the Poverty Reduction and Growth Trust (PRGT)[61] as part of a broader reform to make the

---

[49] Greece and the IMF, http://www.imf.org/external/country/GRC/ (last accessed 26 June 2015).

[50] Ireland and the IMF, http://www.imf.org/external/country/IRL/ (last accessed 26 June 2015).

[51] Republic of Poland and the IMF, http://www.imf.org/external country/POL/ (last accessed 26 June 2015).

[52] Portugal and the IMF, http://www.imf.org/external/country/PRT/ (last accessed 26 June 2015).

[53] Ukraine and the IMF, https://www.imf.org/external/country/ukr/ (last accessed 26 June 2015).

[54] Colombia and the IMF, https://www.imf.org/external/country/col/ (last accessed 26 June 2015).

[55] Mexico and the IMF, http://www.imf.org/external/country/MEX/ (last accessed 26 June 2015).

[56] Morocco and the IMF, http://www.imf.org/external/country/MAR/ (last accessed 26 June 2015).

[57] See, e.g., http://www.imf.org/external/np/exr/facts/deu/howlendd.htm (last accessed 26 June 2015).

[58] IMF Extended Credit Facility, 13 April 2015, http://www.imf.org/external/np/exr/facts/ecf.htm (last accessed 26 June 2015).

[59] IMF Stand-by Credit Facility (SCF), 13 April 2015, http://www.imf.org/external/np/exr/facts/scf.htm (last accessed 26 June 2015).

[60] IMF Rapid Credit Facility, 5 April 2015, http://www.imf.org/external/np/exr/facts/rcf.htm (last accessed 26 June 2015).

[61] For more details, see Martin M, Watts R, Enhancing the IMF's focus on growth and poverty reduction in low-income countries, April 2012, http://www.eurodad.org/files/pdf/520a34d709fc3.pdf (last accessed 26 June 2015).

Fund's financial support more flexible and better tailored to the diverse needs of LICs. In April 2013, these facilities for LICs were refined to improve the tailoring and flexibility of Fund support.[62] Access limits and norms have been approximately doubled compared to pre-crisis levels.[63] Financing terms have been made more concessional, and the interest rate is reviewed every 2 years (currently zero percent until end-2016).[64] Non-concessional loans are provided mainly through Stand-By Arrangements (SBA),[65] the Flexible Credit Line (FCL),[66] the Precautionary and Liquidity Line (PLL),[67] and the Extended Fund Facility (EFF),[68] which is useful primarily for medium- and longer-term needs. The IMF also may provide emergency assistance via the Rapid Financing Instrument (RFI) to all its members facing urgent balance of payments needs.[69]

When a country intends (or, more precisely, is in need) to borrow from the IMF, it always has to agree to adjust its economic policies to overcome the problems that led it to seek financial assistance (funding) in the first place. The commitments made to realize this policy change, including specific conditionality, are described in the member country's letter of intent, which often includes a memorandum of economic and financial policies.[70] In 2013, 91 % of the member countries that used Fund resources under a program allowed publication of their letters of intent, memoranda on economic and financial policies, or technical memoranda of understanding, and 96 % of stand-alone reports on IMF-supported programs were

[62] See Public Information Notice No. 13/43, 8 April 2013, http://www.imf.org/external/np/sec/pn/2013/pn1343.htm (last accessed 26 June 2015); also review of the Policy on Debt Limits in Fund-Support Programs, 1 March 2013, http://www.imf.org/external/np/pp/eng/2013/030113.pdf (last accessed 26 June 2015).

[63] Cf. also Policy Paper (7 April 2014) presenting an Update on the Financing of the Fund's Concessional Assistance and Proposed Amendments to the PRGT Instrument, http://www.imf.org/external/np/pp/eng/2014/040714a.pdf (last accessed 26 June 2015).

[64] See Press release No. 14/602, 23 December 2014, http://www.imf.org/external/np/sec/pr/2014/pr14602.htm (last accessed 26 June 2015).

[65] IMF Stand-by Arrangement, 10 April 2015, https://www.imf.org/external/np/exr/facts/sba.htm (last accessed 26 June 2015).

[66] The IMF's Flexible Credit Line (FCL), 10 April 2015, https://www.imf.org/external/np/exr/facts/fcl.htm (last accessed 26 June 2015).

[67] The IMF's Precautionary and Liquidity Line (PLL), 13 April 2015, https.//www.imf.org/external/np/exr/facts/pllhtm. (last accessed 26 June 2015).

[68] The IMF's Extended Fund Facility (EFF), 13 April 2015, https://www.imf.org/external/np/exr/facts/eff.htm (last accessed 26 June 2015).

[69] The IMF's Rapid Financing Instrument (RFI), 27 March 2015, https://www.imf.org/external/np/exr/facts/rfi/htm (last accessed 26 June 2015).

[70] For Country's Policy Intentions Instruments, see https://www.imf.org/external/np/loi/mempub_new.asp (last accessed 26 June 2015).

published. All members that requested Fund resources agreed to the publication of a Press Release following the Board discussion.[71]

The loan conditions also serve to ensure that the borrower country will be able to repay the Fund so that IMF resources can be made available to other members in need. Lending reforms approved in 2009[72] streamlined IMF conditionality in order to promote national "ownership" of strong and effective policies. So, under IMF-supported programs, the Fund might help governments to protect and even increase social spending, including social assistance although media and neutral observers news often tell a different story. In particular, the IMF thus promotes measures to increase spending on, and improve the targeting of, social safety net programs that can mitigate the impact of some reform measures on the most vulnerable in society.[73] Whether this aim was reached in Greece which is one of the examples[74] the Fund is presenting to prove that its loan conditions are protecting social spending in a way that is both fiscally-sustainable and cost-effective seems at least doubtful, however.[75]

2.3.1.2 Examples for Fund Lending Practice

The Fund's Articles of Agreement do not contain any explicit provision similar to Art. IV sec. 10 of the IBRD founding treaty which prohibits the Bank and its officers to "interfere in the political affairs of any member" as well as to let their decisions "be influenced . . .by the political character of the member or members concerned". But although the wording of these two agreements are different insofar without any doubt, the IMF and its staff must follow the same guiding principles as its sister organization which are laid down in the second sentence of the provision mention above: "Only economic considerations shall be relevant to their decisions, and these considerations shall be weighed impartially in order to achieve the purposes stated in Article I".[76] Of course, there will hardly ever be any request by a Fund member for financial assistance without some specific (domestic) political background since normally politicians are responsible for bad member States policies causing economic deterioration or financial disturbances in national

[71] http://www.imf.org/external/news/default.aspx?pn (last accessed 26 June 2015) (IMF News – Public Information Notices); for the percentages mentioned above, see Transparency at the IMF, 13 April 2015, http://www.imf.org/external/np/exr/facts/trans.htm (last accessed 26 June 2015).

[72] Cf., e.g., Andersen C, New Rules of Engagement for IMF Loans, 13 April 2009, http://www.imf.org/external/pubs/ft/survey/so/2009/POL041309A.htm (last accessed 26 June 2015).

[73] Protecting the Most Vulnerable under IMF-Supported Programs, 13 April 2015, http://www.imf.org/external/np/exr/facts/protect.htm (last accessed 26 June 2015).

[74] The other countries are Mozambique, Bangladesh, Haiti and Jordan.

[75] More broadly on this topic: Caraway et al (2012), p. 27 ff.

[76] For a 'political economy approach', see Drazen A, Conditionality and Ownership in IMF Lending (July 2002), http://econweb-umd.edu/~drazen/conditionalityIMFStaff.pdf (last accessed 26 June 2015); Dreher et al. (2013) Politics and IMF Conditionality. KOF Working Papers 13-338.

economies. But both Bretton Woods organizations must act and do their best to stop further negative development of member economies and use their financial as well as technical and advisory capacities to promote and enhance necessary reforms. Why things went wrong and whosoever might be held responsible for the current situation should not be a relevant issue at all for IMF decision makers. So it does not matter why but only that the government of a Fund member (whether the old or a new one) seeks assistance, and that its commitments to implement reform policies seem sufficient to enable the use of the IMF resources.

To illustrate the practice of "political neutrality", it might be interesting to look somewhat more closely at the examples Christine Lagarde mentioned in her 2014 speech.[77]

As regards the Ukraine which is a part of the Central, Eastern and Southeastern European region in the Fund's terminology,[78] the case for support economic reforms in that country troubled by "geopolitical tension" was recently summarized by the Fund's First Deputy Managing Director.[79] The Executive Board had a few weeks before it approved $17.5 billion of financing as part of a 4-year program under the IMF's Extended Fund Facility.[80] The goals of that program were, according to Lipton, "simple, yet challenging: to stabilize Ukraine's deeply destabilized finances; to restore growth that has been stagnant for several years; and to support the long-overdue modernization that has lagged behind peers in the region since independence 23 years ago". Following a rapid economic deterioration in 2014, it became increasingly clear that Ukraine's balance of payments and adjustment needs were more than what could be achieved under the original 2 year stand-by agreement with the Fund. But as stabilization alone would hardly be enough to address the crisis. Ukraine also needs to restore growth. A most important measure therefore would be to tackle corruption. And geopolitics of course do count: "If the conflict in the East of the country intensifies—and we all certainly hope it won't—then one has to be concerned about the sustainability of the expected recovery". But nevertheless there is from the Fund's perspective only one answer to the critique that IMF resources would be put at risk in such an uncertain situation: "The Fund's job is to support members in crisis provided they are trying

[77] The IMF at 70: Making the Right Choices—Yesterday, Today, and Tomorrow (10 October 2014), http://www.imf.org/external/np/speeches/2014/10102104.htm (last accessed 26 June 2015).

[78] Central, Eastern and Southeastern Europe, being the object of studies on regional economic issues since 2013; see Press release No. 13/141, 26 April 2014, https://www.imf.org/external/np/sec/pr/2013/pr13141.htm (last accessed 26 June 2015).

[79] Lipton D, The Case for Supporting Ukrainian Economic Reforms, 7 April 2015, http://www.imf.org/external/np/speeches/2015/040715.htm (last accessed 26 June 2015).

[80] See Press release No. 15/105, 11 March 2015, http://www.imf.org/external/np/sec/pr/2015/pr15105.htm (last accessed 26 June 2015); also Country Report No. 15/69, 12 March 2015, http://www.imf.org/external/pubs/cat/longres.aspx?sk=42778.0 (last accessed 26 June 2015).

to put themselves right". And it seems rather remarkable that Lipton adds: "The program has the backing of the Ukrainian people".[81]

The Arab Countries in Transition (Egypt, Jordan, Libya, Morocco, Tunisia and Yemen)[82] have broadly maintained macroeconomic stability, in spite of deepening and spreading conflicts in the region, as well as, in many cases, a challenging internal socio-political environment. At the same time, however, their economies are not delivering the growth rates needed for a meaningful reduction in unemployment, in particular for the youth and women. Notwithstanding diversity of conditions, countries should quickly advance structural reforms to foster higher and more inclusive growth, and continue to strengthen fiscal and external buffers to maintain stability amid heightened uncertainty. Coordinated support from the international community will be crucial in the form of financing, improved trade access, and capacity building assistance. This summary of a policy paper on "economic outlook and key challenges" from fall 2014[83] should be taken in mind when looking more closely on Fund policies towards two of these States: Regarding Tunisia, the Executive Board approved a 4-year Stand-By Arrangement in summer 2013 in the amount of SDR 1.146 billion (about US$ 1.75 billion, or 400 % of Tunisia's quota at the IMF).[84] On May 11, 2015, the Board extended this SBA to December 31, 2015. The extension should provide enough time for the Tunisian authorities to implement the policy measures needed to deliver on forward-looking commitments—notably on the banking and fiscal reforms—which would help reduce vulnerabilities and spur higher and more inclusive growth. Article IV discussions and further reviews under the SBA are also part of the recent decision.[85] The Republic of Yemen received a US$550 million loan under the Extended Credit Facility (ECF)—150 % of its quota—, approved by the Executive Board on September 2, 2014, at the same day Article IV consultations with that country were concluded.[86] In April 2012, Yemen had been the first "Arab spring" country which received a US$ 93 million emergency loan made under the Rapid Credit

[81] For a contrary assessment, cf. Wolff E (author of: Pillaging the World. The History and Politics of the IMF, 2014), 17 February 2015, http://www.globalresearch.ca/imf-loans-to-ukraine-deadly-economic-medicine-aimed-at-total-destabilization/5431677 (last accessed 26 June 2015).

[82] Cf., e.g., Mazarei A, Mirzoev T (2015) Four Years after the Spring, Finance & Development 52, no. 2, http://www.imf.org/external/pubs/ft/fandd/2015/06/marazei.htm (last accessed 26 June 2015); IMF Annual Report 2014, p. 26.

[83] 9 October 2014, htpp://www.imf.org/external/np/pp/eng/2014/100914.htm (last accessed 26 June 2015).

[84] See Press release No. 13/2012, 7 June 2012, http://www.imf.org/external/np/sec/pr/2013/pr13202.htm (last accessed 26 June 2015).

[85] See Press release No. 15/229, 19 May 2015, http://www.imf.org/external/np/sec/pr/2015/pr15229.htm (last accessed 26 June 2015).

[86] See Press release No. 14/408, 2 Sept 2014, http://www.imf.org/external/np/sec/pr/2014/pr14408.htm (last accessed 26 June 2015).

Facility (RCF).[87] Since recently political unrest there did arise again in early 2015, the government's plans to strengthen fiscal and external positions, boost growth, and fight poverty by reducing inefficient fuel subsidies, improving governance, and increasing monthly allowances paid by the Social Welfare Fund might hardly be realized in time, if at all.

The Ebola outbreak put severe pressure on already fragile infrastructure and health care systems in Guinea, Liberia and Sierra Leone. The IMF, recognizing the urgency of the situation, moved quickly to help with an additional $130 million to the three countries so they could fight Ebola.[88] So, e.g., the Executive Board approved a disbursement of an amount equivalent to SDR 32.3 million (25 % of quota) to be drawn from the RCF as well as SDR 25.84 million (20 % of the country's quota) in immediate debt relief under the Catastrophe Containment and Relief (CCR) Trust.[89] The RCF funds are intended to support the authorities' fight against the disease by covering urgent budgetary and balance of payments needs and strengthening international reserves. This additional IMF financing also ought to help catalyze further assistance from the international community, preferably grants. The CCR funds will be applied to immediately repay outstanding debt up to the equivalent of 20 % of Liberia's quota.

2.3.2 Response to the Crisis

In response to the global economic crisis, the IMF strengthened its lending capacity and approved a major overhaul of the mechanisms for providing financial support in April 2009,[90] with further reforms adopted in August 2010[91] and December 2011.[92] Fund lending instruments were improved to provide flexible crisis prevention tools (like PLL and RFI) to members with sound economic fundamentals, policies, and institutional policy frameworks. The IMF doubled loan access limits and boosted its

[87] See Press release No. 12/121, 4 April 2012, http://www.imf.org/external/np/sec/pr/2012/pr12121.htm (last accessed 26 June 2015).

[88] Cf. on measures combating Ebola outbreak: http://www.imf.org/external/pubs/ft/survey/so/2015/NEW020515A.htm (last accessed 26 June 2015).

[89] See Press release No. 15/69, 23 February 2015, http://www.imf.org/external/np/sec/pr/2015/pr1569.htm (last accessed 26 June 2015); see also The Catastrophe Containment and Relief Fund, 13 February 2015, http://www.imf.org/external/np/exr/facts/ccr.htm (last accessed 26 June 2015).

[90] See Public Information Notice No. 09/40, 3 April 2009, http://www.imf.org/external/np/sec/pn/2009/pn0940.htm (last accessed 26 June 2015).

[91] Cf. Goretti M, Joshi B, A Step Closer to a Stronger Global Financial Safety Net, 30 August 2010, http://www.imf.org/external/pubs/ft/survey/so/2010/POL083010A.htm (last accessed 26 June 2015); Press release No. 10/121, 30 August 2010, http://www.imf.org/external/np/sec/pr/2010/pr10321.htm (last accessed 26 June 2015).

[92] Cf. Goretti M, Lanau S, Llaudes R, Porter N, IMF Revamps Lending Options in Response to Global Crisis, 7 December 2011, http://www.imf.org/external/pubs/ft/survey/so/2011/POL120711A.htm (last accessed 26 June 2015).; Press release No. 11/424, 22 November 2011, http://www.imf.org/external/np/sec/pr/2011/pr11424.htm (last accessed 26 June 2015).

lending to the world's poorer countries, supported by the windfall profits from gold sales.[93]

2.4 Technical Assistance

2.4.1 Forms of Non-Financial Assistance

The IMF provides technical assistance and training to help member countries strengthen their capacity to design and implement effective economic and financial policies. The Fund aims to exploit synergies between technical assistance and training—called capacity development—to maximize their effectiveness. Its budget provides for 274 person years in FY 2013 and 285 in FY 2014 for fulfilling that task.[94] Technical assistance is offered in several areas, including tax policy and administration, expenditure management, monetary and exchange rate policies, banking and financial system supervision and regulation, legislative frameworks, and statistics. In FY 2014, low-income countries received over a half (55 %) of all IMF technical assistance while emerging market countries accounted for 57 % of all training delivered through the IMF Institute for Capacity Development[95] program.[96]

Technical assistance should help countries develop more effective institutions, legal frameworks, and policies to promote economic stability and inclusive growth whereas training through practical policy-oriented courses, hands-on workshops, and seminars is intended to strengthen officials' capacity to analyze economic developments and formulate and implement effective policies. Work on technical assistance and training is managed from the IMF's headquarters in Washington, DC, and through a network of nine regional technical assistance centers (RTACs), regional training centers and programs (RTCs and RTPs), topical trust funds, and numerous bilateral donor-supported activities.[97] The IMF works in close coopera-

[93] See Factsheet, Gold in the IMF, 9 April 2015, http://www.imf.org/external/np/exr/facts/gold.htm (last accessed 26 June 2015); more information at PRGT pledges (as of 15 April 2015) at: https://www.imf.org/external/np/fin/prgt/second.htm (last accessed 26 June 2015).

[94] Fast Facts, http://www.imf.org/external/about.htm (last accessed 26 June 2015).

[95] Cf. http://www.imf.org/external/np/ins/English/about.htm (last accessed 26 June 2015) and http://www.imf.org/external/np/INS/English/pdf/brochure,pdf (last accessed 26 June 2015).

[96] See, e.g., on Internal Economics Training, http://www.imf.org/external/mp/ins/courses/internal.aspx (last accessed 26 June 2015).

[97] Cf., e.g., on RTACs, Factsheet, 14 April 2015, http://www.imf.org/external/np/exr/facts/afritac.htm (last accessed 26 June 2015); also policy paper on IMF policies and practices on capacity development, 26 August 2014, http://www.imf.org/external/pp/longres.aspx?id=4891 (last accessed 26 June 2015).

tion with other providers of training and technical assistance and with donor partners.[98]

Technical assistance and training are an important complement to the IMF's other core functions of surveillance and lending. Specialized technical assistance and training from the IMF help build both institutional and human capacity in countries for effective policymaking. Moreover, the IMF's surveillance and lending work often helps identify areas in which technical assistance and training can have the biggest impact. New training courses have been offered, for example, in the areas of inclusive growth, financial inclusion, and external vulnerabilities.[99] In view of these linkages, achieving greater integration between technical assistance, training, surveillance, and lending operations is a key priority for the IMF. The Fund relies on independent external and internal evaluations to assess the effectiveness of its technical assistance and training.[100]

2.4.2 TTFs as Complement to Technical Assistance

Six topical trust funds (TTFs) support IMF technical assistance on specialized thematic areas across all geographic regions. The focus of these TTFs are Anti-Money Laundering/Combating the Financing of Terrorism (AML/CFT), established in 2009,[101] Debt Management Facility II (DMF II), launched in April 2014,[102] as a joint IMF-World Bank trust fund that builds on the success of the DMF's first phase, established in 2008 by the World Bank, Financial Sector Reform Strengthening Initiative (FIRST), a joint IMF-World Bank multi-donor grant facility that funds technical assistance to promote financial sector development in low- and middle-income countries, established in 2002,[103] Managing Natural Resource Wealth (MNRW), launched in 2011 to help recipient countries build capacity to

[98] On Japan—IMF Scholarship Program see http://www.imf.org/external/np/ins/English/scholar.htm (last accessed 26 June 2015); on donors generally http://www.imf.org/external/NP/otm/map/index.htm (last accessed 26 June 2015).

[99] See, e.g., Press release No. 115, 15 March 2015, on IMF co-hosting of a conference on financial inclusion in Central Africa, http://www.imf.org/external/np/sec/pr/2015/pr15115.htm (last accessed 26 June 2015); on inclusive growth see http://imf.smartcatalogiq.com/en/current/Catalog/Courses/HQ/IG/1507/HQIG15-07 (last accessed 26 June 2015).

[100] Cf. for instance task force paper (19 October 2011), http://www.imf.org/external/np/pp/eng/2011/101911.pdf (last accessed 26 June 2015).

[101] See Public Information Notice No. 11/74, 27 June 2011, http://www.imf.org/external/np/sec/pn/2011/pn1174.htm (last accessed 26 June 2015); also The IMF and the Fight against Money Laundering and the Financing of Terrorism, 27 March 2015, http://www.imf.org/external/np/exr/facts/aml.htm (last accessed 26 June 2015).

[102] http://wordlbank.org/en/topic/debt/brief/debt-management-facility (last accessed 26 June 2015); see also Press release, 3 April 2014, http://www.worldbank.org/en/news/press-release/2014/03/31/new-funding-to-help-poor-countries-manage-debt (last accessed 26 June 2015).

[103] https://www.firstinitiative.org/ (last accessed 26 June 2015).

manage their natural resource wealth,[104] Tax Administration Diagnostic Assessment Tool (TADAT), set up in February 2014,[105] and finally Tax Policy and Administration (TPA), a trust fund launched in 2011 to help low- and lower middle-income countries establish well designed and administered tax systems that generate sustainable revenue to pay for essential public services.[106] TTFs complement other delivery modes of IMF technical assistance—including through regional technical assistance centers—and are closely aligned with recipients' development strategies.

The IMF has moreover set up two developed country trust funds to help governmental institutions become more effective, transparent, and accountable, and strengthen their operating and technical capacities. The main areas covered in these funds are revenue mobilization, public financial management, monetary policy, financial sector supervision, and the establishment of statistical systems. The South Sudan Trust Fund was established in 2012,[107] and the Somalia Trust Fund for Capacity Development in Macroeconomic Policies and Statistics started operations in February 2015.[108]

2.4.3 Ensuring "Good" Practices in Member States

Standards and codes are benchmarks of good practices. The term "standards and codes" refers to sets of provisions relating to the institutional environment—the "rules of the game"—within which economic and financial policies are devised and implemented. IMF and IBRD have recognized international standards in 12 policy areas related to their work. In assessing countries' observance of these standards, and helping them to implement reforms where needed, the Fund and the World Bank aim to increase economic and financial stability by strengthening domestic economic and financial institutions.[109]

The IMF developed some standards in a first broader group ("policy transparency") related to data dissemination—Special Data Dissemination Standard

[104] See Press release No. 10/497, 16 December 2010, http://www.imf.org/external/np/sec/pr/2010/pr10497.htm (last accessed 26 June 2015); Program document (November 2010), http://www.imf.org/external/np/otm/2010/110110.pdf (last accessed 26 June 2015).

[105] http://www-tadat.org/ (last accessed 26 June 2015); cf. IMF Annual Report 2014, p. 45.

[106] http://www.imf.org/external/np/otm/2013/tpattf/tpattfininfo.htm (last accessed 26 June 2015); Program document (April 2011) at: https://www.imf.org/external/np/otm/2011/100110.pdf (last accessed 26 June 2015).

[107] See Press release No. 12/323, 19 September 2012, https:/www.imf.org/external/np/sec/pr/2012/pr12323.htm (last accessed 26 June 2015).

[108] See Press release No. 15/102, 9 March 2015, http://www.imf.org/external/np/sec/pr/2015/pr15102.htm (last accessed 26 June 2015).

[109] Cf. Standards and Codes: The Role of the IMF, 27 March 2015, http://www.imf.org/external/np/exr/facts/sc.htm (last accessed 26 June 2015).

(SDDS),[110] General Data Dissemination System (GDDS),[111] and Special Data Dissemination Standard Plus (SDDS Plus).[112] The first three pillars of the Fiscal Transparency Code[113] have already been completed while pillar IV ("resource revenue management") might follow later in 2015.[114] Another topic closely related thereto is monetary and financial policy transparency ("Code of Good Practices on Transparency"[115] concerning these policy fields). Standards in the areas of financial sector regulation and supervision have been set up by specialized standard-setting bodies, like the Basel Committee on Banking Supervision[116] for banking supervision, the International Organization of Securities Commissions[117] for securities regulation and the International Association of Insurance Supervisors[118] in respect of core principles for the insurance sector. In a third broader group of standards ("institutional and market infrastructure"), IMF and World Bank are delivering substantive input, especially concerning issues of insolvency and creditor rights[119] and of market integrity where revised recommendations on anti-money laundering and combatting the financing of terrorism (AML/CFT)[120] were adopted by the Financial Action Task Force (FATF) in February 2012[121] and endorsed by the Fund's Executive Board in March 2014.[122]

---

[110] http://dsbb.imf.org/pages/sdds/home.aspx (established 1996) (last accessed 26 June 2015).

[111] http://dsbb.imf.org/pages/gdds/kome.aspx (established 1997) (last accessed 26 June 2015).

[112] http://dsbb.imf.org/pages/SDDS/Home.aspx?sp=y (established 2012) (last accessed 26 June 2015).

[113] http://blog-pfm.imf.org/files/ft-code.pdf (last accessed 26 June 2015).

[114] Cf. http://www.imf.org/external/np/fad/trans/index.htm (last accessed 26 June 2015); for more details, see policy paper about an update on the Fiscal Transparency Initiative, 18 June 2014, http://www.imf.org/external/pp/longres.aspx?id=4888 (last accessed 26 June 2015); also IMF Annual Report 2014, p. 38.

[115] http://www.imf.org/external/np/mae/mft/code/index.htm (adopted 26 Sept 1999) (last accessed 26 June 2015), and supporting document (adopted 24 July 2000), http://www.imf.org/external/np/mae/mft/sup/index.htm (last accessed 26 June 2015).

[116] Core Principles for Effective Banking Supervision, September 2012, http://www.bis.org/publ/bcbs230.htm (last accessed 26 June 2015).

[117] Objectives and Principles of Securities Legislation, June 2010, http://iosco.org/library/pubdocs/pdf/IOSCOPD323.pdf; referring to an earlier "methodology for assessing implementation" (October 2003), http://www.ebrd.com/downloads/legal/securities/IOSCOPD155.pdf.

[118] Insurance Core Principles, revised version October 2013, http://iaisweb.org/index.cfm?event=getPage&nodeID=25224 (last accessed 26 June 2015).

[119] Creditor Rights and Insolvency Standard (December 2005), http://worldbank.org/ifa/FINAL-ICRStandardMarch2009.pdf (last accessed 26 June 2015).

[120] http://www.fatf-gafi.org/media/fatf/documents/recommendations/pdfs/FATF_Recommendations.pdf (Feb. 2012) (last accessed 26 June 2015).

[121] http://www.fatf-gafi.org/pages/aboutus/ (last accessed 26 June 2015).

[122] Cf. Press release No. 14/167, 11 April 2014, http://www.imf.org/external/np/pp/eng/2014/pr14167.htm (last accessed 26 June 2015); Policy Paper (20 February 2014), http://www.imf.org/external/np/pp/eng/2014/pr022014a.pdf (last accessed 26 June 2015).

In March 2011, a review of the IMF's and the World Bank's work on standards and codes[123] identified scope to adapt standards to a changing environment, better prioritize assessments across countries and policy areas, enhance integration of the Report on the Observance of Standards and Codes (ROSC)[124] findings into the IMF's surveillance and technical assistance, and improve the public availability of ROSCs. The Fund and the World Bank's Executive Boards supported the FSB's decision to combine the accounting and auditing standards under one policy area and introduce a new policy area on crisis resolution and deposit insurance.[125] In August 2014, the Fund's Executive Board approved the first three pillars of a new Fiscal Transparency Code,[126] the groundwork for which was laid in a 2012 IMF policy paper.[127] Fiscal Transparency Evaluations (FTEs), which assess country practices against the new Code, will replace the Fiscal Module of the ROSC as the IMF's principal fiscal transparency diagnostic under the Standards and Codes Initiative.[128]

Another useful tool to help members to establish or improve various national statistics or accounts are manuals, like the Government Statistics Manual,[129] the Manual on Fiscal Transparency,[130] the Quarterly National Accounts Manual[131] or the Balance of Payments Position and International Investment Manual.[132] In May 2015, a Handbook on Securities Statistics[133] was published which has been prepared jointly by the Bank for International Settlements (BIS), the European Central Bank (ECB), and the IMF in response to a request from the Working Group on Securities Databases to develop methodological standards for securities statistics and to improve information on securities markets.[134]

[123] 16 February 2011, http://www.imf.org/external/np/pp/eng/2011/021611.pdf (last accessed 26 June 2015).

[124] http://www-imf.org/external/NP/rocs/rocs.aspx (last accessed 26 June 2015).

[125] For details cf. http://www.financialstabilityboard.org/what-we-do/about-the-compendium-of-standards/key_standards/?page_moved=1 (last accessed 26 June 2015).

[126] http://blog-pfm.imf.org/files/ft-code.pdf (last accessed 26 June 2015).

[127] 7 August 2012, http://www.imf.org/external/np/pp/eng/2012/080712.pdf (last accessed 26 June 2015).

[128] How Does the IMF Encourage Greater Fiscal Transparency?, 27 March 2015, http://www.imf.org/external/np/exr/facts/fiscal.htm (last accessed 26 June 2015).

[129] http://www.imf.org/external/pubs/ft/gfs/nabual/gfs.htm (last accessed 26 June 2015).

[130] https://www.imf.org/external/np/pp/2007/eng/101907m.pdf (2007) (last accessed 26 June 2015).

[131] http://www.imf.org/external/pubs/ft/pna/2000/textbook/index.htm (May 2001) (last accessed 26 June 2015).

[132] http://www.imf.org/external/pubs/ft/bop/2007/bopman6.htm (November 2013) (last accessed 26 June 2015).

[133] http://www.imf.org/external/np/sta/wgsd/pdf/hss.pdf (last accessed 26 June 2015).

[134] See ECB press release, 12 May 2015, https://www.ecb-europa.eu/press/pr/date/2015/html/pr150512.en.html (last accessed 26 June 2015).

2.5 IMF Support for Low-Income Countries

In 2009, the IMF upgraded its support for low-income countries, reflecting the changing nature of economic conditions in these countries and their increased vulnerabilities due to the effects of the global economic crisis. It overhauled its lending instruments, especially to address more directly countries' needs for short-term and emergency support. Concessional lending commitments were about $11 billion in the period 2009–2014. Zero interest applies to all concessional lending through end-2016. The Fund moreover adopted a strategy to support concessional lending of about $2 billion a year over the longer term, financed in part by contributions linked to the distribution of gold sales profits.[135]

To make its financial support more flexible and tailored to the diversity of low-income countries, the IMF established a Poverty Reduction and Growth Trust (PRGT),[136] which has three lending windows, all under highly concessional terms. These windows, which became effective in January 2010 and were further refined in April 2013 to improve the tailoring and flexibility of Fund support,[137] are the Extended Credit Facility (ECF),[138] providing sustained engagement over the medium to long term, in case of protracted balance of payments problems as well as offering more flexibility than before on program extensions, the timing of structural reforms, and formal poverty reduction strategy document requirements, the Standby Credit Facility (SCF),[139] whose task is to provide flexible support to low-income countries with short-term financing and adjustment needs caused by domestic or external shocks, or policy slippages, which targets countries that do not face protracted balance of payments problems but may need help from time to time and can also be used on a precautionary basis to provide insurance, and finally the Rapid Credit Facility (RCF).[140] This third window provides rapid financial support in a single, up-front payout for low-income countries facing urgent financing needs,

[135] Cf. Background note (29 July 2009), https://www.imf.org/external/np/lic/2009/072909.htm (last accessed 26 June 2015); IMF Support for Low-Income Countries, 15 April 2015, https://www.imf.org/external/np/exr/facts/poor.htm (last accessed 26 June 2015).

[136] For details, see 2014 Handbook of IMF Facilities for Low-Income Countries, February 2015, http://www.imf.org/external/np/pp/eng/2014/082714.pdf (last accessed 26 June 2015).

[137] See Public Information Notice No. 13/43, 8 April 2013, http://www.imf.org/external/np/sec/pn/2013/pn1343.htm (last accessed 26 June 2015); also review of the 'Policy on Debt Limits in Fund-Support Programs', 1 March 2013, http://www.imf.org/external/np/pp/eng/2013/030113.pdf (last accessed 26 June 2015). Cf. also Policy Paper (7 April 2014) presenting an "update on the financing of the Fund's concessional assistance and proposed amendments to the PRGT instrument", http://www.imf.org/external/np/pp/eng/2014/040714a.pdf (last accessed 26 June 2015).

[138] IMF Stand-by Credit Facility (SCF), 13 April 2015, http://www.imf.org/external/np/exr/facts/scf.htm (last accessed 26 June 2015).

[139] IMF Rapid Credit Facility, 5 April 2015, http://www.imf.org/external/np/exr/facts/rcf.htm (last accessed 26 June 2015).

[140] For more details, see Martin M, Watts R, Enhancing the IMF's focus on growth and poverty reduction in low-income countries, April 2012, http://www.eurodad.org/files/pdf/520a34d709fc3.pdf (last accessed 26 June 2015).

and offers successive drawings for countries in post-conflict or other fragile situations and also provides flexible assistance without program-based conditionality when use of ECF or SCF is either not necessary (because of the limited nature of needs) or not possible (because of institutional or capacity constraints faced by a borrower). For policy advice and signaling, countries can request non-financial assistance under the Policy Support Instrument (PSI),[141] which supports low-income countries that have macroeconomic stability and thus do not need IMF financial assistance, but may also provide accelerated access to the SCF in case of subsequent financial needs.

In response to the increasing financial needs of low-income countries during the global financial crisis, IMF concessional lending commitments increased significantly from $1.2 billion in 2008 to $3.8 billion in 2009, and an annual average of $1.4 billion during 2010–2014.[142] In addition, more than $18 billion of the $250 billion allocation of IMF Special Drawing Rights (SDRs) went to low-income countries.[143] In 2010, the Fund also established a Post-Catastrophe Debt Relief Trust (PCDR),[144] which allows the IMF to join international debt relief efforts for very poor countries that are hit by the most catastrophic of natural disasters. This allowed the Fund to eliminate Haiti's entire outstanding debt to the IMF following the devastating earthquake in July 2010.[145] In September 2012, the Executive Board approved a partial distribution of the Fund's general reserves attributed to gold sales profits as part of a strategy to make the PRGT sustainable in the longer term.[146] Finally, in February 2015, the IMF transformed the PCDR Trust into the Catastrophe Containment and Relief (CCR) Trust. Three Ebola-afflicted countries (Guinea, Liberia, and Sierra Leone) soon requested assistance from this new trust.[147]

In September 2012, the Executive Board approved a strategy to establish the PRGT as financially self sustaining in the longer term which rests on three pillars: (i) a base annual average lending capacity of about SDR 1¼ billion; (ii) contingent measures activated when average financing needs exceed the base envelope by a

[141] The Policy Support Instrument, 13 April 2015, http://www.imf.org/external/np/exr/facts/psi.htm (last accessed 26 June 2015).

[142] For an early analysis, see Conway P, The IMF and the International Financial Crisis, 28 May 2010, http://www.unc.edu/~pconway/dload/IMF_crisis.pdf (last accessed 26 June 2015).

[143] Special Drawing Right (SDR) Allocations, 5 August 2013, http://www.imf.org/external/np/exr/faq/sdrallocfaqs.htm (last accessed 26 June 2015).

[144] The IMF's Post-Catastrophe Debt Relief Trust Fund, 30 September 2014, http://www.imf.org/external/np/exr/facts/pcdr.htm (last accessed 26 June 2015).

[145] See Press release No. 10/299, 21 July 2010, http://www.imf.org/external/np/sec/pr/2010/pr10299.htm (last accessed 26 June 2015).

[146] See Press release No. 12/368, 28 September 2012, http://www.imf.org/external/np/sec/pr/2012/pr12368.htm; http://www.imf.org/external/np/pp/eng/2012/091712.pdf (last accessed 26 June 2015).

[147] Cf. on measures combating Ebola outbreak: http://www.imf.org/external/pubs/ft/survey/so/2015/2015/NEW20515A.htm (last accessed 26 June 2015).

substantial margin for an extended period; and (iii) the expectation that future modifications to low-income countries (LIC facilities) would also support self-sustainability.[148] In April 2014, amendments to the PRGT instrument necessary to implement the new strategy were approved.[149]

2.6 Europe and the IMF

The IMF is actively engaged in Europe (i.e. the world region) as a provider of policy advice, financing, and technical assistance. The Fund's work in Europe has intensified since the start of the global financial crisis in 2008, and has been further stepped up since mid-2010 as a result of the euro area crisis.[150] In addition to its policy discussions with the 19 individual members of the euro area, IMF staff also holds consultations annually for the euro area as a whole,[151] similar to those held for other currency unions.[152] Here, IMF staff exchange views with counterparts from the ECB, the European Commission and other European institutions in a number of areas, including monetary and exchange rate policies and area-wide fiscal policies, financial sector supervision and stability, trade and cross-border capital flows, as well as other structural policies. An assessment of the economic outlook, external and fiscal position of the euro area as a whole, as well as financial stability assessments are also included in the final staff report as part of the overall assessment. As part of the consultation, staff presents the Fund's views on the economic outlook and policies of the euro area to the Eurogroup, comprising the 19 finance ministers of the "Eurozone".[153]

The IMF pays considerable attention to progress in fostering integration within the euro area to ensure the effective operation of the European Monetary Union. The first-ever EU wide Financial Sector Assessment Program (FSAP), in March

[148] See Public Information Notices No. 108/2012, 13 September 2012, http://www.imf.org/external/np/sec/pn/2012/pn12108.htm (last accessed 26 June 2015), and No. 12/118, 4 October 2012, http://www.imf.org/external/np/sec/pb/2012/pn12118.htm (last accessed 26 June 2015).

[149] See Press release No. 14/84, 5 March 2014, http://www.imf.org/external/np/sec/pr/2014/pr1484.htm (last accessed 26 June 2015).

[150] The IMF and Europe, 10 April 2015, http://www.imf.org/external/np/exr/facts/Europe.htm (last accessed 26 June 2015); see also ECB, The External Representation of the EU and EMU, Monthly Bulletin May 2011, p. 87 ff.

[151] For example, cf. Concluding Statement of the Mission, 19 June 2014, https://www.imf.org/external/np/ms/2014/061914.htm (last accessed 26 June 2015); Press release No. 13/275, 25 July 2013, http://www.imf.org/external/np/sec/pr/2013/pr13275.htm (last accessed 26 June 2015), and Staff report on Euro Area policies, July 2013, http://www.imf.org/external/pubs/ft/scr/2013/cr13231.pdf (last accessed 26 June 2015). For an "early assessment" cf. Pisani J, Sapir A, Wolff GB, EU—IMF Assistance to Euro-Area Countries, 2013; for the view of an ESCB task force see IMF surveillance in Europe, ECB Occasional Paper No. 158, January. 2015.

[152] See, e.g., Press release No. 15/139, 26 March 2015, http://www.imf.org/external/np/sec/pr/2015/pr15139.htm (on West African Economic and Currency Union) (last accessed 26 June 2015).

[153] http://www.consilium.europa.eu/de/council-eu/eurogroup (last accessed 26 June 2015).

2013, outlined important progress in addressing the financial crisis in Europe, but also argued for fast and sustained progress toward a Single Supervisory Mechanism (SSM).[154] In addition, the IMF published papers arguing for a Banking Union to strengthen the EU financial oversight framework and sever bank-sovereign feedback loops; making the case for a Fiscal Union to help address a number of gaps in the euro area's architecture; proposing measures to achieve the dual objectives of restoring external and internal balance; and recommending solutions to address the high youth unemployment problem in the region.[155]

Since the start of the global financial crisis, a number of emerging European countries have requested financial support from the IMF to help them overcome their fiscal and external imbalances. Four members of the euro area—Greece,[156] Portugal,[157] Ireland,[158] and Cyprus[159]—also accessed Fund resources. Access to IMF resources for Europe is being provided through Stand-By Arrangements (SBA), the Flexible Credit Line (FCL), the Precautionary and Liquidity Line (PLL), and the Extended Fund Facility (EFF). Ireland's and Portugal's EFFs concluded in December 2013 and June 2014, respectively, and they then entered into Post-Program Monitoring (PPM).[160] As of March 23, 2015, the IMF had arrangements with 8 countries in Europe with commitments totaling about €71.3 billion or $78.8 billion.[161]

An enhanced cooperation between IMF, the EU, and the ECB in euro area program countries has become known as the "Troika" and, recently, the "institutions"[162] and is aimed at ensuring maximum coherence and efficiency in staff-level

[154] See Press release No. 13/79, 15 March 2013, https://www.imf.org/external/np/sec/pr/2013/pr1379.htm (last accessed 26 June 2015).

[155] Goyal R, Brooks PK, Pradhan M, Tressel T, Dell'Ariccia G, Leckow R, Pazarbasioglu C, A Banking Union for the Euro Area, 13 February 2013, https://www.imf.org/external/pubs/ft/sdn/2013/sdn1301.pdf (last accessed 26 June 2015); Allard C, Brooks PK, Bluedorn JC, Bornhorst F, Christopherson K, Ohnsorge F, Poghosyan T, Toward a Fiscal Union for the Euro Area, September 2013, http://www.imf.org/external/pubs/ft(sdn/2013/sdn1309,pdf (last accessed 26 June 2015); Tressel T, Wang S, Kang JS, Shambaugh J, Adjustment in Euro Area Deficit Countries: Progress, Challenges, and Policies, July 2014, https://www.imf.org/external/pibs/ft/sdn/2014/sdn1407.pdf (last accessed 26 June 2015); Banerji A, Saksonovs S, Lin H, Blavy R, Youth Unemployment in Advanced Economies in Europe: Searching for Solutions, December 2014, http://www.imf.org/external/pubs/ft/sdn/2014/sdn1411.pdf (last accessed 26 June 2015).

[156] Greece and the IMF, http://www.imf.org/external/country/GRC/ (last accessed 26 June 2015).

[157] Portugal and the IMF, http://www.imf.org/external/country/PRT/ (last accessed 26 June 2015).

[158] Ireland and the IMF, http://www.imf.org/external/country/IRL/ (last accessed 26 June 2015).

[159] Cyprus and the IMF, http://www.imf.org/external/country/cyp (last accessed 26 June 2015).

[160] See Press releases No. 13/507, 13 December 2013, https://www.imf.org/external/np/sec/pr/2013/pr13507.htm (last accessed 26 June 2015), and No. 14/380, 1 August 2014, http://www.imf.org/external/np/sec/pr/2014/pr14380.htm (last accessed 26 June 2015).

[161] SBA: Bosnia, Romania, Serbia; EFF: Ukraine; The IMF and Europe, 10 April 2015, http://www.imf.org/external/np/exr/facts/Europe.htm (last accessed 26 June 2015).

[162] On this change in wording, see, e.g., http://www.consilium.europa.eu/en/press/press-releases/2015/02/150220-eurogroup-statement-greece (last accessed 26 June 2015); on the former, see Pisani et al., EU—IMF assistance to euro-area countries, 2013, p. 20 ff.; IMF Annual Report 2014, p. 56.

program discussions with governments on the policies that are needed to put their economies back on the path of sustainable economic growth. While the Fund coordinates closely with the other two partners neither of which is an IMF member, its decisions on financing and policy advice are ultimately taken independently of that process by the Executive Board.[163]

Most of the IMF resources allocated to different activities in Europe are provided by member countries, primarily through their payment of quotas. Starting in early 2009, the IMF signed a number of new bilateral loan and note purchase agreements to bolster its capacity to support member countries during the global economic crisis.[164] In early 2011, the amended and expanded Arrangements to Borrow (NAB)[165] became effective and were activated. At that point, the bilateral agreements of NAB participants were folded into the NAB, and in April 2013, all the 2009 bilateral agreements were terminated.[166] In December 2011, euro area countries committed to providing additional resources to the IMF of up to 150 billion euro. In mid-2012, numerous member countries pledged about $461 billion in additional bilateral commitments to further augment the Fund's resources.

In particular, efforts in recent years to strengthen the international financial system, including in Europe, have triggered additional demands for IMF technical assistance. For instance, the Fund provided assistance to monitor Spain's financial sector, in the context of an ESM-supported program, by providing independent advice, including monitoring the progress on the financial sector reforms to which the government had committed.[167] The IMF also provided assistance on tax policy and revenue administration issues to a number of EU countries.[168] In general, the IMF has increasingly moved to a regional approach to the delivery of technical assistance and training. Thus, the IMF Institute organizes courses for officials from new EU member countries and other economies in transition in Europe and Asia at the Joint Vienna Institute in Austria.[169]

[163] Cf., e.g., Report of the EP's Committee on Economic and Monetary Affairs, Feb. 28, 2014, http://www.europarl.europa.eu/sides/getDoc.do?pubRef=//EP//TEXT+REPORT+A7-2014-0149*0*DOC+XML+V0//EN (last accessed 26 June 2015).

[164] On those instruments, see International Reserves and Foreign Currency Liquidity. Guidelines for a Data Template, 2013, p. 73 ff., http://www.imf.org/external/np/sta/ir/IRPreocessWeb/pdf/guide2013.pdf (last accessed 26 June 2015).

[165] See IMF Standing Borrowing Arrangements, 9 April 2015, http://www.imf.org/external/np/exr/facts/gabnab.htm (last accessed 26 June 2015).

[166] IMF Annual Report 2013, p. 55.

[167] Cf. Spain: Financial Sector Reform—Final Progress Report, February 2014, http://www.imf.org/external/pubs/ft/scr/2014/cr1459.pdf (last accessed 26 June 2015).

[168] See, e.g., IMF Country Report No. 15/112 (technical assistance report on Poland), May 2015, http://www.imf.org/external/pubs/ft/scr/2015/cr15112.pdf (last accessed 26 June 2015).

[169] For more details on that regional training center cf. http://www.jvi.org (last accessed 26 June 2015); also Press release No. 12/242, 28 June 2012, http://www.imf.org/external/np/sec/pr/2012/pr12242 (last accessed 26 June 2015).

2.7 *Governance*

2.7.1 Transparency for Members and at the Fund

Transparency in economic policy and the availability of reliable data on economic and financial developments are critical for sound decision-making and for the smooth functioning of an economy. Transparency helps economies function better and makes them less vulnerable to crises. Greater openness on the part of member countries encourages more widespread public discussion and examination of policies, enhances the accountability of policymakers and the credibility of policies, and facilitates efficient and orderly functioning of financial markets. Greater openness and clarity by the IMF about its own policies and the advice it provides to its member countries contributes to a better understanding of the IMF's own role and operations, building traction for the Fund's policy advice and making it easier to hold the institution accountable. Outside scrutiny should also support the quality of surveillance and IMF-supported programs.[170]

The IMF's approach to transparency is based on the overarching principle that it will strive to disclose documents and information on a timely basis unless strong and specific reasons argue against such disclosure. The principle respects the voluntary nature of publication of documents that pertain to member countries. Publication of country documents prepared for consideration by the IMF Executive Board is typically "voluntary but presumed," meaning that, while voluntary, the publication of these documents is encouraged. A member's consent to publication of a Board document is typically obtained on a non-objection basis. The publication of policy papers is presumed but it is subject to Board approval, while the publication of multi-country documents requires consent either from the Board or the involved members depending on the type of document involved.[171]

The IMF's efforts to improve the understanding of its operations and engage more broadly with the public has been pursued along four broad lines: (i) transparency of surveillance and IMF-supported programs, (ii) transparency of its financial operations; (iii) external and internal review and evaluation; and (iv) external communications.[172] For example, Members' Financial Data—timely information for every member country on its financial position with the IMF—are posted on the IMF's website,[173] as well as news on IMF Financial Activities

[170] Transparency at the IMF, 13 April 2015, http://www.imf.org/external/np/exr/facts/trans.htm (last accessed 26 June 2015); for results of the 2013 review, see http://www.imf.org/external/np/pp/eng/2013/051413.pdf (14 May 2013) (last accessed 26 June 2015).

[171] See Press release No. 13/270, 22 July 2013, http://www.imf.org/external/np/sec/pr/2013/pr13270.htm (last accessed 26 June 2015).

[172] Cf. also Updated Guidance Note on the Fund's Transparency Policy, 8 April 2014, http://www.imf.org/external/pp/longres.aspx?id=4861 (last accessed 26 June 2015).

[173] http://www.imf.org/external/np/fin/tad/exfin1.aspx (last accessed 26 June 2015).

(updated weekly),[174] quarterly data on Financial Transactions,[175] and monthly data on the IMF's Financial Resources and Liquidity Position.[176] Other information posted about the Fund includes the Codes of Conduct for IMF Staff[177] and Executive Directors,[178] recruitment policies,[179] and procurement guidelines.[180]

2.7.2 Better Governance

The IMF places great emphasis on promoting good governance when providing policy advice, financial support, and technical assistance to its member countries. Since poor governance is clearly detrimental to economic activity and welfare, the IMF adopted already in 1997 a policy on how to address economic governance, embodied in the Guidance Note "The Role of the IMF in Governance Issues".[181] In the process of Article IV consultations, the Fund may provide policy advice, when relevant, on governance-related issues. Many of the structural conditions in IMF-supported programs focus on improving governance, including through better fiscal expenditure control, publication of audited accounts of government agencies and state enterprises, streamlined and less discretionary revenue administration, greater transparency in the management of natural resources, the publication of audited central bank accounts, and better enforcement of banking supervision. In all of these areas, the Fund also provides technical assistance that benefits good

[174] http://www.imf.org/cgi-shl/create_x.pl?fa+2015 (last accessed 26 June 2015).

[175] http://www.imf.org/external/pubs/ft/quart/index.htm (last accessed 26 June 2015).

[176] http://www.imf.org/cgi-shl/create_x.pl?liq (last accessed 26 June 2015).

[177] 31 July 1998, http://www.imf.org/external/hrd/code.htm (last accessed 26 June 2015); for more information, cf. IMF, Ethics Office, Annual Reports (e.g., 2013 edition titled "core values: taking action", http://www.imf.org/external/hrd/eo/ar/2013/eoar2013.pdf (last accessed 26 June 2015)).

[178] 14 July 2000, as revised on 1 August 2012, http://www.imf.org/external/hrd/edscode.htm (last accessed 26 June 2015); also The Managing Director's Contract—Applicable Standards of Conduct, 25 October 2008, http://www.imf.org/external/np/omd/2008/eng/pdf/081025a.pdf (last accessed 26 June 2015).

[179] Recruitment Programs, https://www.imf.org/external/np/adm/rec/job/joboppo.htm (last accessed 26 June 2015). Cf. also Momani (2005), p. 167 ff.

[180] IMF Procurement Guide for Suppliers, 1 June 2010, http://www.imf.org/external/np/procure/eng (last accessed 26 June 2015).

[181] Cf. Good Governance. The IMF's Role, http://www.imf.org/external/pubs/ft/exrp/govern/govindex.htm (last accessed 26 June 2015).

governance.[182] In addition, the IMF assists in strengthening countries' capacity to combat corruption by advising on appropriate anti-corruption legal frameworks.[183]

Moreover, the IMF promotes good governance through specific initiatives that tie in with its surveillance, lending, and technical assistance, sometimes in close collaboration with the World Bank and other organizations.[184] Among them are various rules on transparency, like the Code of Good Practices on Fiscal Transparency[185] or the Guide on Resource Revenue Transparency,[186] as well as standards and codes. The Fund also contributes to the international efforts to combat money laundering and the financing of terrorism (AML/CFT), e.g. by establishing a multi-donor Topical Trust Fund for capacity building on AML/CFT,[187] and takes part at the work of the G20 Anti-Corruption Working Group[188] and the OECD Working Group on Bribery in International Business Transactions.[189]

As a means of safeguarding its own resources, the IMF assesses the governance and transparency frameworks within central banks of countries to which it lends money and which are its primary partners according to Article V sec. 1 of the Articles of Agreement. In the process, it promotes sound oversight, internal control,

[182] The IMF and Good Governance (9 April 2015), http://www.imf.org/external/np/exr/facts/gov.htm (last accessed 26 June 2015).

[183] http://www.oecd.org/g20/topics/anticorruption/ (last accessed 26 June 2015); also 1st Monitoring Report, http://www.g20civil.com/documents/Final_G20_Anti-corruption_Working_Group_progress_Report.pdf (last accessed 26 June 2015); 2015–2016 Action Plan, https://g20.org/wp-content/uploads/2014/12/2015-16%20_g20_anti-corruption_action_plan_0 (last accessed 26 June 2015); http://www.oecd.org/corruption/anti-bribery/ (last accessed 26 June 2015).

[184] E.g., the Standards and Codes Initiative, see Standards and Codes: The Role of the IMF, 27 March 2015, http://www.imf.org/external/np/exr/facts/sc.htm (last accessed 26 June 2015); http://www.imf.org/external/np/pp/eng/2011/021611.pdf (last accessed 26 June 2015).

[185] On the actual Code of 2007, see http://blog-pfm.imf.org/files/ft-code.de (last accessed 26 June 2015); on the revision process, cf. http://blog-pfm.imf.org/files/ft-code.pdf (last accessed 26 June 2015); http://www.imf.org/external/np/pp/eng/2012/080712.pdf (last accessed 26 June 2015).

[186] 2007 revised edition, http://www.imf.org/external/np/fad/trans/guide/htm (last accessed 26 June 2015).

[187] See Public Information Notice No. 11/74, 27 June 2011, http://www.imf.org/external/np/sec/pn/2011/pn1174.htm (last accessed 26 June 2015); also The IMF and the Fight against Money Laundering and the Financing of Terrorism, 27 March 2015, http://www.imf.org/external/np/exr/fact s/anl.htm (last accessed 26 June 2015).

[188] http://www.oecd.org/g20/topcs/anti-corruption (last accessed 26 June 2015); also 1st monitoring report, http://www.g20civil.com/documents/Final_G20_Anti-corruption_Working_Group_progress_Report.pdf (last accessed 26 June 2015); 2015–2016 action plan, https://g20.org/wp-content/uploads/2014/12/2015-16%20_g20_anti-corruption_action_plan_0.pdf (last accessed 26 June 2015).

[189] http://www.oecd.org/corruption/antibribery/ (last accessed 26 June 2015).

auditing, and public financial reporting mechanisms in these critical financial institutions.[190]

The Fund also has strong measures in place to ensure integrity, impartiality, and honesty in the discharge of its own professional obligations. To promote good governance within its own organization, the IMF has adopted a number of integrity institutions, including a Code of Conduct for Staff[191]—bolstered by financial certification and disclosure requirements, and sanctions—, a similar Code of Conduct for Members of the Executive Board,[192] and an Integrity Hotline offering protection to "whistleblowers". The IMF Ethics Office advises the institution and its staff on ethics issues, inquires into alleged violations of rules and regulations, and oversees the ethics and integrity training program for all staff members.[193]

An Independent Evaluation Office (IEO) was established in July 2001 to provide objective and independent evaluations on issues related to Fund policies and operations.[194] The Office operates independently of IMF management and at arm's length from the IMF's Executive Board. Both the IEO reports and its work program are publicly available.[195] Further on, the IMF reviews a number of its policies and programs each year. Recent reviews examine the relevance and utilization of the Fund's research,[196] the Fund's performance in the run up to the crisis,[197] and the Fund's interactions with member countries.[198] Typically, reviews

---

[190] Protecting IMF Resources: Safeguards Assessment of Central Banks, 27 March 2015, http://www.imf.org/external/np/exr/facts/safe.htm. See Public Information Notice No. 11/74, 27 June 2011, http://www.imf.org/external/np/sec/pn/2011/pn1174.htm (last accessed 26 June 2015); also The IMF and the Fight against Money Laundering and the Financing of Terrorism, 27 March 2015, http://www.imf.org/external/np/exr/facts/aml.htm (last accessed 26 June 2015); IMF Annual Report 2014, p. 65.

[191] See 31 July 1998, http://www.imf.org/external/hrd/code.htm (last accessed 26 June 2015); for more information, cf. IMF, Ethics Office, Annual Reports (e.g., 2013 edition titled "core values: taking action", http://www.imf.org/external/hrd/eo/ar/2013/eoar2013.pdf (last accessed 26 June 2015)).

[192] See http://www-imf.org/external/hrd/edscode.htm (last accessed 26 June 2015); also The Managing Director's Contract—Applicable Standards of Conduct, 25 October 2008, http://www.imf.org/external/np/omd/2008/endg/pdf/081025a.pdf (last accessed 26 June 2015).

[193] IMF Ethics Advisor—Terms of Reference, 18 May 2011, http://www.imf.org/hrd/eo.htm (last accessed 26 June 2015); also IMF Ombudsperson's Terms of Reference, December 2007, http://www.imf.org/external/hrd/ombuds.htm (last accessed 26 June 2015).

[194] http://www.ieo-imf.org/ieo/pages/ieohome.aspx (last accessed 26 June 2015); IMF Annual Report 2014, p. 67 ff.

[195] See, e.g., Progress Report to the IMFC, 16 April 2015, http://www.ieo-imf.org/ieo/files/whatsnew/IMFC_2015_Progress_Report_to_the_IMFC_on_IEO_Activities.pdf (last accessed 26 June 2015).

[196] IMF Forecasts: Process, Quality, and Country Perspectives, 2014, http://ieo-omf.org/ieo/pages/EvaluationImages181.aspx (last accessed 26 June 2015).

[197] IMF Response to the Financial and Economic Crisis, 2014, http://www.ieo-imf.org/ieo/pages/EvaluationImages227.aspx (last accessed 26 June 2015).

[198] The Role for the IMF as Trusted Advisor, 2013, http://www.ieo-imf.org/ieo/pages/EvaluationImages157.aspx (last accessed 26 June 2015).

are open and inclusive, often drawing on contributions from developing countries, donor agencies, international organizations, and civil society organizations, as well as analyses by IMF and World Bank staff.

2.8 The Fund's Relationship with World Bank and WTO

2.8.1 IMF and IBRD

The International Monetary Fund and the World Bank were both created at an international conference convened in Bretton Woods, New Hampshire, United States in July 1944. The IMF promotes international monetary cooperation and provides policy advise and technical assistance to help countries build and maintain strong economies. It also makes loans and helps countries design policy programs to solve balance of payments problems when sufficient financing on affordable terms cannot be obtained to meet net international payments. IMF loans are short and medium term and funded mainly by the pool of quota contributions that its members provide. The World Bank promotes long-term economic development and poverty reduction by providing technical and financial support to help countries reform particular sectors or implement specific projects—such as, building schools and health centers, providing water and electricity, fighting disease, and protecting the environment. IBRD assistance is generally long term and is funded both by member country contributions and through bond issuance.[199] The IMF and World Bank collaborate regularly and at many levels to assist member countries and work together on several initiatives. In 1989, the terms for their cooperation were set out in a concordat to ensure effective collaboration in areas of shared responsibility.[200]

A Development Committee was established in 1974, whose meetings coincide with the Spring and Annual Meetings of the IMF and the World Bank.[201] In this committee, a group of Fund and World Bank Governors also meets to advise the two institutions on critical development issues and on the financial resources required to promote economic development in low-income countries. The 2007 external review of Bank-Fund collaboration led to a Joint Management Action Plan on World Bank-IMF Collaboration (JMAP) to further enhance the way the two institutions work together.[202] Under the plan, Fund and Bank country teams discuss

[199] For more details, see http://www.worldbank.org/projects/ and http:www.worldbank.org/en/about/what-we-do/brief/ibrd (last accessed 26 June 2015).

[200] The IMF and the World Bank, 27 March 2015, http://www.imf.org/external/np/exr/facts/imfwb.htm (last accessed 26 June 2015); IMF Annual Report 2014, p. 55.

[201] http://web.worldbank.org/WBSITE/EXTERNAL/DEVCOMMEXT/0,,contentMDK:23158487~menuPK:7348076~pagePK:7347738~piPK:7347796~theSitePK:277473,00.html (last accessed 26 June 2015).

[202] 20 September 2007, http://www.imf.org/external/np/pp/2007/eng/092007.pdf (last accessed 26 June 2015).

their country-level work programs, which identify macro-critical sectoral issues, the division of labor, and the work needed in the coming year. A preview of Bank-Fund Collaboration underscored the importance of these joint country team consultations in enhancing collaboration.[203]

The IMF and World Bank also work together to reduce the external debt burdens of the most heavily indebted poor countries under the Heavily Indebted Poor Countries (HIPC) Initiative[204] and the Multilateral Debt Relief Initiative (MDRI)[205] in order to help low-income countries achieve their development goals without creating future debt problems. IMF and Bank staff jointly prepare country debt sustainability analyses under the Debt Sustainability Framework (DSF)[206] developed by the two institutions. In 1999, the IMF and the World Bank launched the Poverty Reduction Strategy Paper (PRSP) approach[207] as a key component in the process leading to debt relief under the HIPC Initiative and an important anchor in concessional lending and the Bank. Whereas the World Bank adopted in July 2014 a new approach to country engagement that no longer requires PRSPs while focusing on the elimination of extreme poverty and promotion of shared prosperity,[208] the Fund continues to rely on the PRSP to provide the link between a Fund-supported program and the poverty reduction and growth objectives of a member country.

Since 2004, the Fund and the Bank have worked together on the Global Monitoring Report (GMR),[209] which assesses progress towards the 2015 UN Millenium Development Goals (MDGs).[210] When New Sustainable Development Goals (SDGs) replace the MDGs in 2015 as the basis for the post-2015 development

[203] Cf. Implementation of the Joint Management Action Plan on Bank-Fund Collaboration, 3 March 2010, http://www.imf.org/np/pp/eng/2010/030310.pdf (last accessed 26 June 2015).

[204] Debt Relief under the Heavily Indebted Poor Countries (HIPC) Initiative, 15 April 2015, http://www.imf.org/external/np/exr/facts/hipc.htm (last accessed 26 June 2015).

[205] The Multilateral Debt Relief Initiative, 15 April 2015, http://www.imf.org/external/np/exr/facts/mdri.htm (last accessed 26 June 2015).

[206] The Joint World Bank-IMF Debt Sustainability Framework for Low-Income Countries, 15 April 2015, http://www.imf.org/external/np/exr/facts/jdsf.htm (last accessed 26 June 2015).

[207] Poverty Reduction Strategy Papers (PRSP), 15 April 2015, http://www.imf.org/external/np/exr/facts/prsp.htm (last accessed 26 June 2015).

[208] World Bank Group: A New Approach to Country Engagement, 29 April 2014, https://consultations.worldbank.org/Data/hub/files/consultation-template/towards-country-partnership-frameworkopenconsultationtemplate/materials/new_approach_to_country_engagement_april_29_1.pdf (last accessed 26 June 2015).

[209] See, e.g., Global Monitoring Report 2014/2015: Ending Poverty and Sharing Prosperity, http://www.worldbank.org/en/publication/global-monitoring-report (last accessed 26 June 2015); also Global Monitoring Reports, http://www.imf.org/external/ns/cs.aspx?id=272 (last accessed 26 June 2015).

[210] The IMF and the Millenium Development Goals, 15 April 2015, http://www.imf.org/external/np/exr/facts/mdg.htm (last accessed 26 June 2015).

agenda,[211] both organizations will continue to support the implementation of the new SDGs and contribute to monitoring progress toward their achievement. The IMF and the World Bank are also working together to make financial sectors in member countries resilient and well regulated. The Financial Sector Assessment Program (FSAP) was introduced in 1999 to identify the strengths and vulnerabilities of a country's financial system and recommend appropriate policy responses.[212]

2.8.2 IMF and World Trade Organization

The IMF and the WTO[213] are international organizations with nearly 150 members in common.[214] While the IMF's central focus is on the international monetary and financial system, and the WTO's is on the international trading system, both work together to ensure a sound system for global trade and payments. With Russia's accession in August 2012,[215] the WTO encompasses all major trading economies.

The Fund and the WTO work together on many levels, with the aim of ensuring greater coherence in global economic policymaking.[216] A cooperation agreement between the two organizations, covering various aspects of their relationship, was signed shortly after the creation of the WTO in 1995.[217] The IMF has observer status in certain WTO bodies,[218] and may participate in meetings of certain WTO committees and working groups. The WTO Secretariat attends meetings of the IMF

---

[211] Cf., for instance, Kenny C (2015) Aiming High, Finance & Development 42, no. 2, http://www.imf.org/external/pubs/ft/fandd/2015/06/kenny.htm (last accessed 26 June 2015).

[212] See Financial System Soundness, 15 April 2015, http://www.imf.org/external/np/exr/facts/pdf.banking.pdf (last accessed 26 June 2015).

[213] The IMF and the World Trade Organization, 9 April 2015, http://www.imf.org/external/np/exr/facts/imfwto.htm (last accessed 26 June 2015).

[214] For the IMF, see Action Plan to the International Monetary and Financial Committee, 18 April 2012, http://www.imf.org/external/pp/longres.aspx?id=4640 (last accessed 26 June 2015); for the WTO: https://www.wto.org/English/thewto_e/whatis_e/tif_e/org6_e.htm (last accessed 26 June 2015).

[215] Russian Federation and the WTO, https://www.wto.org/English/thewto_e/countries_e/Russia_e.htm (last accessed 26 June 2015).

[216] See The IMF and the World Trade Organization, 9 April 2015, http://www.imf.org/external/np/exr/facts/imfwto.htm (last accessed 26 June 2015) and The WTO and the International Monetary Fund, https://www.wto.org/English/thewto_e/coher_e/wto_imf_e.htm (last accessed 26 June 2015).

[217] See WTO and IMF sign cooperation agreement, 9 December 1996, https://www.wto.org/English/news_e/press96_e/pr062_e.htm (last accessed 26 June 2015), and WTO General Council decision WT/L/194, Nov. 18, 1996.

[218] https://www.wto.org/english/thewto_e/igo_obs_e.htm (last accessed 26 June 2015).

Executive Board or the Board Committee on Liaison with the World Bank,[219] and other international organizations on matters of common interest.

WTO agreements require that the Fund must be consulted when the former organization deals with issues concerning monetary reserves, balance of payments, and foreign exchange arrangements. For example, Art. XV GATT or Art. XII GATS allow countries to apply trade restrictions in the event of balance of payments difficulties. The WTO's Balance of Payments Committee bases its assessments of restrictions in considerable part on the IMF's determination of a member's balance of payments situation.[220] In an effort to support progress under the WTO's Doha Round of trade talks, the IMF established the Trade Integration Mechanism (TIM) in April 2004 which is available to all Fund member countries whose balance of payments positions might suffer, albeit temporarily, as a result of multilateral trade liberalization.[221] TIM is not a lending facility, but rather a policy aimed at making Fund resources available under existing IMF facilities more predictably.

3 Conclusion and Outlook

In spring 2015, the total amount of quotas (under Article III of the Fund agreement) was US$ 362 billion, and additional pledged or committed resources were US$ 885 billion.[222] But is the Fund in fact ready to make the right choices within the next few years? Will it be sufficient to streamline some policies and procedures in order to take a more risk based approach and redirect resources to new priorities as the Fund budget seems restrained? Or is there a grave "system malfunction"?

In a recent essay[223] published in a journal issued by the Fund itself, William White describes global imbalances and a "deficient nonsystem" and draws a rather ambiguous picture. "What passes for an international monetary system today is not really a system because it has no rules. It lacks an automatic international

[219] Cf., e.g., Aubon M (2007) Fulfilling the Marrakesh Mandate on Coherence: Ten Years of Cooperation between the WTO, IMF and World Bank, https://www.wto.org/English/res_e/booksp_e/discussion_papers13_e.pdf (last accessed 26 June 2015).

[220] For general information see https://www.wto.org/English/tratop_e/bop_e/bop_e_info_e.htm (last accessed 26 June 2015), for a recent example, WTO news, Members consult with Ukraine on its import surcharge imposed on balance-of-payments grounds, 28 April 2015, https://www.wto.org/English/news_e/news15_e/impl_28apr15_e.htm (last accessed 26 June 2015).

[221] The IMF's Trade Integration Mechanism (TIM), 14 April 2015, https://www.imf.org/external/np/exr/facts/tim.htm (last accessed 26 June 2015).

[222] FY2016—FY 2018 Medium-Term Budget; selected streamlining proposals under the DY2016—FY2018 Medium-Term Budget—implementation issues, May 2015, http://www.imf.org/external/np/pp/eng/2015/032715.pdf (last accessed 26 June 2015).

[223] White WR (2015) System Malfunction, Finance & Development 52, no. 1, http://www.imf.org/external/pubs/ft/fandd/2015/03/white.htm (last accessed 26 June 2015).

adjustment mechanism for current account imbalances. It allows massive spillovers, including gross capital flows, from larger countries (especially the United States) to smaller ones with potentially damaging implications. It is dangerously unanchored with respect to global credit and monetary expansion, and it lacks an international lender of last resort with adequate resources. Voluntary agreement by all large countries to an international monetary system that imposes responsibilities on everyone could play a significant role in reducing the dangers associated with global imbalances. Debtors would effectively import the will to do speedily what needed to be done. Creditors too would be forced to play a role, consistent with the recognition that crises also rebound on them. Getting all actors to recognize the shortcomings of the current nonsystem would be a welcome if difficult first step. However, mobilizing the will of sovereign nations to cooperate to devise a global system that would be in their own longer-term interest will be even more challenging".

And what about the project of an Asian Infrastructure Investment Bank[224] open also to non-regional members when a lot of economic "heavy-weights" are eager to get on board as some IMF members have announced to do?[225] Since the negotiations were successful at last in 2015, what would be the consequence for the Fund's role, at least in Asia? The IMF Managing Director was quite diplomatic when she said in an interview: "The IMF is not in the business of financing infrastructure. This is not what we were set up for 70 years ago. Our mission is financial stability. So we don't compete at all with the activity intended by the AIIB. But, you know, it's an initiative that will fund infrastructure. And if it is done efficiently, projects well-selected, countries' growth lifted, it's good for the global economy".[226] That might not have been the last word in this case. "The times they are a-changing".

References

Bergthaler W, Bossu W (2010) Recent legal developments in the international monetary fund. In: Hermann C, Terhechte JP (eds) European yearbook of international economic law. Springer, Heidelberg, pp 391–404

Bergthaler W, Steinki B (2012) Recent reforms of the finances of the international monetary fund: an overview. In: Hermann C, Terhechte JP (eds) European yearbook of international economic law, vol 3. Springer, Heidelberg, pp 635–666

Bergthaler W, Giddings A (2013) Recent quota and governance reforms at the international monetary fund. In: Hermann C, Krajewski M, Terchechte JP (eds) European yearbook of international economic Law, vol 4. Springer, Heidelberg, pp 371–390

Caraway TL, Rickard SJ, Anner MS (2012) International negotiations and domestic politics: the case of IMF labor market conditionality. Int Organ 66(1):27–61

[224] http://www.aiibank.org/html/aboutus/AIIB/ (last accessed 26 June 2015).

[225] http://www.aiibank.org/html/pagemembers (last accessed 26 June 2015).

[226] Interview with Judy Woodruff, 9 April 2015, http://www.pbs.org/newshour/bb/imf-chief-lagarde-greece-china-uneven-global-recovery (last accessed 26 June 2015).

Dreher A, Sturm JE, Vreeland J (2013) Politics and IMF conditionality. KOF Working Papers 13-338

Lastra RM (2011) The role of the IMF as a global financial authority. In: Hermann C, Terhechte JP (eds) European yearbook of international economic Law, vol 2. Springer, Heidelberg, pp 121–136

Lichtenstein CC (2014) Reflections on the intellectual history of the international regulation of monetary affairs. In: Hermann C, Krajewski M, Terhechte JP (eds) European yearbook of international economic law, vol 5. Springer, Heidelberg, pp 3–16

Momani B (2005) Recruiting and diversifying IMF technocrats. Glob Soc 19(2):167–187

The Road Towards Reform of the International Investment Agreement Regime: A Perspective from UNCTAD

Elisabeth Tuerk and Diana Rosert

Contents

Abstract A shared view is emerging on the need for reform of the International Investment Agreement (IIA) regime to ensure that it is in line with today's sustainable development imperative and that it works for all stakeholders. Over the past years, UNCTAD's Work Programme on IIAs devoted an extensive part of its activities to finding solutions to the challenges the IIA regime is currently facing. The article outlines the reform issues discussed at two recent intergovernmental and multi-stakeholder meetings organized by UNCTAD, the World Investment Forum's IIA Conference in 2014 and the UNCTAD Expert Meeting on the Transformation of the IIA Regime in 2015. It describes recent trends in the IIA regime with a special focus on investment policy developments related to the reform of the

This contribution draws on UNCTAD research and policy analysis, including UNCTAD World Investment Reports and IIA Issues Notes. The views expressed in this article are those of the authors and do not necessarily reflect the views of UNCTAD.

E. Tuerk (✉) • D. Rosert
International Investment Agreements Section, Division on Investment and Enterprise, UNCTAD, Palais des Nations, CH-1211 Geneva, Switzerland
e-mail: Elisabeth.Tuerk@unctad.org; Diana.Rosert@unctad.org

M. Bungenberg et al. (eds.), *European Yearbook of International Economic Law 2016*, European Yearbook of International Economic Law 7,
DOI 10.1007/978-3-319-29215-1_33

IIA regime. These developments are exemplified by new model agreements, treaty terminations, the up-scaling of treaty making through Mega-Regionals and the conclusion of "new generation" investment treaties. All of this indicates that governments have entered into a new phase of investment policymaking. Against this background, the article presents UNCTAD's action menu for reforming the international investment regime as put forward in the World Investment Report 2015. The action menu identifies policy challenges, analyses policy options for key areas of IIA reform and offers guidelines and suggestions for action at different levels of policymaking.

1 Introduction

The International Investment Agreement (IIA) regime is going through a period of reflection, review and revision. In many countries and different settings (in parliaments, at academic conferences and among legal practitioners), concerns about IIAs and investor-State dispute settlement (ISDS) have prompted an at times heated debate about their challenges and opportunities. Today, a broad consensus is emerging that the IIA regime needs to be reformed to ensure that it works for all stakeholders.

Two recent UNCTAD intergovernmental and multi-stakeholder meetings in Geneva addressed pressing reform issues and identified possible solutions. The reform of the IIA regime was at the core of discussions at the IIA Conference taking place during the UNCTAD World Investment Forum 2014. An expert meeting held in 2015 carried forward this work and gave shape to concrete IIA reform options.

Over the past years, UNCTAD's Work Programme on IIAs has devoted extensive research and policy analysis to finding solutions to the challenges the IIA regime is facing. In the World Investment Report 2012, UNCTAD's Investment Policy Framework for Sustainable Development (IPFSD) provided clause-by-clause options for negotiators to strengthen the sustainable development dimension of IIAs.[1] The World Investment Report 2013 summarized five broad options

[1] The IPFSD identified and discussed three major challenges of today's investment policymaking: strengthening the development dimension of IIAs, balancing the rights and obligations of States and investors, and managing the systemic complexity of the IIA regime. It also provided ten core principles for investment policymaking for sustainable development and guidelines for national investment policymaking. See UNCTAD, Investment Policy Framework for Sustainable Development, 2012, http://unctad.org/en/PublicationsLibrary/diaepcb2012d5_en.pdf (last accessed 9 June 2015). On the occasion of the Third International Conference on Financing for Development, UNCTAD launched its updated 2015 version of the Investment Policy Framework, with innovations responding to new insights and feedback on national and international investment policymaking, as well as a plan for investment in sustainable development, aimed to assist countries to mobilize and channel investments into sustainable development related sectors. See UNCTAD, Investment Policy Framework for Sustainable Development, 2015, http://investment-policyhub.unctad.org/ipfsd (last accessed 2 March 2016).

towards reform of investment dispute settlement.[2] In 2014, UNCTAD identified the emerging (and diverging) paths of action in dealing with the existing IIA regime.[3]

Building on this work and on lessons learned from 60 years of IIA rule making, the World Investment Report 2015 offers an action menu for IIA reform.[4] It identifies policy challenges, analyses policy options for key areas of IIA reform (i.e. substantive IIA clauses, investment dispute settlement, and systemic issues) and offers guidelines and suggestions for action at different levels of policymaking (national, bilateral, regional and multilateral). The policy options for reform address the standard elements and typical clauses found in an IIA as well as emerging and innovative issues. As regards the process of IIA reform, the World Investment Report suggests that the best way to make the IIA regime work for sustainable development is to collectively reform the regime to help achieve the objectives of all stakeholders.

This article discusses new investment policy developments related to the reform of the IIA regime. It outlines the reform issues discussed at the IIA Conference 2014 and an UNCTAD Expert Meeting on the Transformation of the IIA Regime in 2015 and describes recent trends in the IIA regime—exemplified by new model agreements, treaty terminations, the up-scaling of treaty making through Mega-Regionals and the conclusion of "new generation" investment treaties. All of this indicates that governments have entered into a new phase of policymaking where they evaluate the costs and benefits of IIAs and reflect on the future objectives and strategies as regards these treaties. Against this background, the article presents UNCTAD's action menu for reforming the international investment regime as put forward in the World Investment Report 2015. In conclusion, it suggests that IIA reform is already underway and that engagement at all levels—national, bilateral, regional and multilateral—is important to deliver an IIA regime in line with today's sustainable development imperative.

---

[2] Promoting alternative dispute resolution, modifying the existing ISDS mechanism through individual IIAs, limiting investors' access to ISDS, introducing an appeals facility, and creating a standing international investment court. See UNCTAD, World Investment Report 2013—Global Value Chains: Investment and Trade for Development, 2013, http://unctad.org/en/pages/DIAE/World%20Investment%20Report/WIR-Series.aspx (last accessed 9 June 2015), p. 113.

[3] UNCTAD, World Investment Report 2014—Investing in the SDGs: An Action Plan, 2014, http://unctad.org/en/pages/DIAE/World%20Investment%20Report/WIR-Series.aspx (last accessed 9 June 2015), p. 126.

[4] UNCTAD, World Investment Report 2015—Reforming International Investment Governance, 2015, http://unctad.org/en/pages/DIAE/World%20Investment%20Report/WIR-Series.aspx (last accessed 9 June 2015).

2 Broad Consensus on the Need for IIA Reform Emerged During the IIA Conference 2014

During the IIA Conference at UNCTAD's Fourth World Investment Forum, held on 16 October 2014 in Geneva, more than 50 high-level representatives from governments, including ministers, as well as senior business representatives, international and civil society organizations convened to address the challenges arising from IIAs and to consider ways to reform the IIA regime.[5] The conference was guided by three main questions: What are the key areas and pressing issues in IIAs and investment dispute settlement that need to be addressed? What are the key ways and means to address these issues? What types of mechanisms and platforms are needed to facilitate the reform?

The conference, attended by an audience of some 300 persons, brought together a broad range of stakeholders and gave a voice to different interests within the investment and development community, helping to bridge divides between supporters and critics of the IIA regime. A broad consensus emerged among government representatives and other stakeholders on the need to improve global investment governance. Many participants also emphasized that IIAs remain an important policy tool to help foster a stable and predictable business climate for the protection and attraction of foreign investment.

The view shared by many speakers was that the IIA regime and the related investment dispute settlement system required systematic and comprehensive reform, but that changes should be introduced gradually and be properly sequenced. Starting from a number of pressing reform issues, the meeting identified concrete and workable solutions to address them. In so doing, the conference participants sketched out the contours of a road map for comprehensive reform of the IIA regime, and called upon UNCTAD, together with governments, regional and intergovernmental organizations and other stakeholders, to further refine the elements of the road map. It was stated that the road map could provide a framework for countries to implement their reform efforts. UNCTAD's Investment Policy Framework for Sustainable Development[6] and the reform paths identified by UNCTAD[7] could serve as valuable starting points.

Many countries considered individual reform efforts to be useful, but also noted that these may not be sufficient in light of the need to address systemic challenges. Some country representatives emphasized that joint, coordinated or multilateral

[5] The list of speakers and their statements are available at: http://unctad-worldinvestmentforum.org/programme/sessions/reforming-the-international-investment-agreements-regime/ (last accessed 9 June 2015).

[6] UNCTAD, Investment Policy Framework for Sustainable Development, 2012, http://unctad.org/en/PublicationsLibrary/diaepcb2012d5_en.pdf (last accessed 9 June 2015). The 2015 version is available at: http://investmentpolicyhub.unctad.org/ipfsd (last accessed 2 March 2016).

[7] UNCTAD, Reform of the IIA Regime: Four Paths of Action and a Way Forward, IIA Issues Note (2015) 3, http://unctad.org/en/PublicationsLibrary/webdiaepcb2014d6_en.pdf (last accessed 9 June 2015).

efforts can be more effective in bringing about needed reforms. It was suggested that UNCTAD, in cooperation with other stakeholders, including international and regional organizations, could provide a multilateral platform for engagement on investment policy issues.

With regard to the most pressing reform issues, the participants identified core treaty provisions and investment arbitration. Many participants emphasized that IIAs must not limit countries' capacity to regulate investment for legitimate national development objectives. Indeed, there was broad consensus on the need for a more coherent and well-designed IIA regime that reflects sustainable development objectives, balances investors' rights and obligations, corresponds to modern economic realities (such as the proliferation of global value chains) and offers a higher degree of predictability. In particular, provisions on definitions of investment and investor, fair and equitable treatment (FET), most-favoured-nation treatment (MFN), indirect expropriation or the umbrella clause were mentioned as needing careful consideration. One country representative, for instance, highlighted the need for reform when discussing the ambiguity of the concept of indirect expropriation.

Stakeholders' suggestions for reform of investment dispute settlement addressed, among others, transparency, frivolous claims, speculative investors, independence of arbitrators, and an appeals mechanism. There were also calls to omit ISDS from investment treaties altogether and consider alternatives to investor-State arbitration. Some participants stressed the importance of alternative dispute resolution, as well as requiring investors to exhaust local remedies as a pre-condition to accessing arbitration. The need to refine substantive legal obligations applied by tribunals was identified as a key, complementary area of reform. Several country delegates called for more technical assistance and capacity-building in this area. The discussions benefitted, among others, from the experience of Argentina, Canada, the Czech Republic, Egypt, Ecuador and Mexico, which are among the most frequent defendants in investor-State arbitrations.

The participants discussed the concrete steps countries can take when reforming their investment treaties, with some countries sharing their experiences in this respect. Among others, the view was put forward that treaties should be subject to rigorous review and careful analysis of core clauses. Several participants stressed the role of domestic laws and contracts for creating a favourable investment climate and attracting investment that promotes sustainable development.

Country representatives and other stakeholders also noted the continued relevance of IIAs—as a tool to attract FDI and to promote sustainable development—and the need to examine and adjust IIAs where necessary. Private sector representatives (e.g. Business and Industry Advisory Committee to the OECD) emphasised the importance of high levels of investor protection in the current IIA regime, while recognizing the need for reform at the same time. Some speakers (e.g. Federation of German Industries) stressed that rather than leading to reduced levels of investor protection, reforms should lead to more balanced treaties that offer legal precision to the benefit of States and investors alike. The countries represented at the conference included those that have been most active in signing IIAs, such as China, Egypt, France, Germany, Switzerland and the United States.

3 IIA Reform Options Explored at the UNCTAD Expert Meeting in 2015

More than 300 experts and delegates from member States, international organizations, NGOs, the private sector and academia attended the UNCTAD Expert Meeting on the Transformation of the IIA Regime from 25 to 27 February 2015 in Geneva.[8] Working in breakout and plenary sessions, the experts explored options for reform of the IIA regime and ISDS, to make them more conducive to sustainable development. The debates centered around four broad themes: the substantive content of IIAs, the sustainable development dimension of IIAs, tools for modernizing the IIA network, and investment dispute settlement. By sharing experiences, identifying best practices and bringing in new ideas, the experts developed a rich menu of options and strategies for governments, IIA policy-makers and negotiators.

There was broad agreement that sustainable development should be the overall objective and guiding principle of IIA reform. Among others, this would help maximize the contribution of IIAs to the implementation of the post-2015 development agenda and the Sustainable Development Goals (SDGs). Some experts emphasized that the reform processes should not undermine the role of IIAs in contributing to transparent, stable and predictable regulatory frameworks in host States. Noting the limitations for individual countries to undertake IIA reform, experts appreciated the possibility of multilateral engagement on this issue. Given the complexity of the regime and the long-term commitments under IIAs, they considered that a step-by-step approach towards reform was preferable.

Many delegates provided insights into their national experiences with regard to concluded or ongoing review processes of their model investment agreements. Brazil presented a new model agreement that focused on investment promotion and facilitation, mitigation of investment risks and dispute prevention. Several delegates, including representatives of Brazil, India, Indonesia, South Africa and the United States, highlighted that the reviews of their model agreements involved a broad range of affected stakeholders.

[8] Information and related documents, including a background note, the chair's summary, presentations, rapporteurs' synopses and the results of the UNCTAD "report-back" project are available at: http://unctad-worldinvestmentforum.org/switzerland2014/followupiia/ (last accessed 2 March 2016).

3.1 *Improving the Substantive Content of IIAs*

With regard to the substantive IIA provisions, the experts stressed the need to promote more clarity in the terms, definitions and concepts used in specific treaty provisions. Discussing the scope and definitions, the experts suggested that the definitions of "investment" and "investor" should be carefully circumscribed in IIAs. Among others, they considered the usefulness of excluding certain types of investment and including additional criteria for covered investors (e.g. requiring substantive business operations in the home State and regulating the dual nationality of natural persons). Several options were proposed to provide more clarifications and guidance on FET in future treaties, such as including an exhaustive list of State obligations or a negative list, linking the FET standard to the international minimum standard of treatment, replacing FET with a different term (e.g. "fair administrative treatment"), and not including a FET provision in the first place, or including it as a political rather than a legally operative standard. The experts considered it useful to add explanatory language on what constituted indirect expropriation, in line with recent treaty practice. However, questions were raised whether the new language would be effective and operative in the context of investment treaty arbitration. A cross-cutting issue that raised concern was the MFN clause, since—in the absence of appropriate action—it can undermine improved formulations of treaty provisions. This makes the MFN clause a crucial provision for IIA reform.

With regard to the recent trend of a greater use of pre-establishment national treatment commitments in IIAs, the negative list approach to undertaking such commitments was discussed. Several challenges were noted, such as the need to undertake an extensive and careful domestic audit of existing non-conforming measures and the inability to foresee which new economic sectors might emerge in the future. Particularly for developing countries conducting such an audit and considering future regulatory needs might be a difficult undertaking in light of limited institutional capacity. The experts also emphasized the need for safeguards and "safety valves" to preserve regulatory space. The positive list approach and best efforts clauses on investment liberalization were also considered.[9]

3.2 *Increasing the Sustainable Development Dimension of IIAs*

The experts highlighted public policy exceptions as an important tool for IIAs. Taking into account concerns that public policy exceptions might give greater

[9] See also Chapter III in UNCTAD, World Investment Report 2015—Reforming International Investment Governance, 2015, http://unctad.org/en/pages/DIAE/World%20Investment%20Report/WIR-Series.aspx (last accessed 9 June 2015).

discretion to States and create uncertainty and the risk of abuse, it was discussed how clauses could be formulated to prevent arbitrariness and discrimination. Procedural mechanisms for applying exceptions clauses could be created (e.g. joint committees of the contracting parties).

The experts expressed different views on the need to include corporate social responsibility (CSR) standards and investor obligations in IIAs, and on their potential nature (binding versus voluntary) and content. One view was that relevant standards for investor conduct should be set in domestic laws and that the inclusion of investor obligations in IIAs could lead to competitive disadvantages for foreign investors. Another view supported the inclusion of investor obligations. It was also noted that more specific rules on the promotion of investment, particularly sustainable development-friendly investments, could be included in IIAs, while the role of domestic law was emphasized as another available tool in achieving a sound business climate. It was also discussed whether IIAs should address incentives or whether this was a matter of domestic law and policy choices only. The experts considered different options to clarify the relationship between IIAs and other areas of international law. Some considered the potential for conflict between the different areas to be limited given the guidance provided by the Vienna Convention on the Law of Treaties. At the same time, it was pointed out that other areas of international law were not always sufficiently taken into consideration in investment arbitration.

3.3 Assessing Tools for Modernizing the IIA Network

The experts discussed the opportunities arising from the increasing trend of regionalism and from multilateral approaches to achieve greater consolidation of the IIA regime and support reform efforts. Some concerns were raised with regard to regional approaches related to the power dynamics between participating States, the impact on non-participating States and overall transparency. It was considered that there were only limited prospects of reaching consensus on reform of the IIA regime at the multilateral level in the near future. One proposal was to foster multilateral engagement through softer instruments, such as model laws, best practices, guidelines, recommendations, toolboxes or checklists for IIA negotiators, and thereby progressively move towards finding common ground.

The experts also addressed the renegotiation of treaties. While it was considered that renegotiation was a viable way forward which would allow contracting parties to coordinate reform, it could pose serious capacity problems to some countries and would depend on mutual consent. With regard to treaty termination, the experts noted that political and economic concerns may deter States from taking such steps. However, termination would not necessarily reduce attractiveness, as investor concerns might be addressed through domestic law and investment facilitation. It was also discussed that contracting parties could make a joint decision to revoke the survival clause before termination.

Treaty interpretation, without amending treaty language, was considered a useful tool. It could focus on the most controversial clauses to which tribunals had attributed contradictory meanings (for example, MFN, FET, umbrella clauses). Among others, contracting parties to a treaty could issue interpretative statements for the specific treaty or non-disputing contracting parties in ISDS proceedings could make submissions to assist in interpretation. The timing of interpretation notes, that is, whether a note was issued before, during or after a dispute, was noted as an issue that could raise fairness concerns.

It was repeatedly suggested that a possible way forward might resemble the opt-in approach of the Convention on Transparency in Treaty-based Investor-State Arbitration developed by the United Nations Commission on International Trade Law (UNCITRAL). This approach could potentially be used to address other key issues, such as FET or indirect expropriation. However, experts considered it a challenge to reach consensus among all States on controversial substantive provisions; the differences in wording found in a myriad of IIAs would further complicate such efforts.

3.4 Reforming Investment Dispute Settlement

The experts discussed the need to reform existing ISDS mechanisms, sharing their national experiences in taking steps in this regard. In light of concerns about a lack of consistency of arbitral awards, erroneous decisions and the limited grounds for annulment under the ICSID Convention, the experts discussed the notion of an appeals mechanism in IIAs and whether having a right to appeal was desirable. They considered that a single, standing appeals mechanism might be preferable to multiple *ad hoc* mechanisms, as it would better address the lack of legal consistency and predictability of arbitral decisions. However, in light of differences in the language of IIAs, an appeals facility would be unlikely to resolve these problems fully, even though it could considerably enhance the regime's legitimacy. The Appellate Body of the World Trade Organization was seen as a possible model, and the International Centre for Settlement of Investment Disputes (ICSID) as a possible forum, albeit with some limitations. Several issues were identified as requiring more detailed analysis (e.g. ways to establish an appeals facility and the potential scope of appellate review).

Some experts considered that an international investment court could resolve concerns related to the overall legitimacy of ISDS and the independence and impartiality of arbitrators, including by providing access to stakeholders other than investors and States (for example, communities affected by investment projects). However, it was noted that the court might raise sovereignty concerns among States, involve costs for a broader range of countries and contribute to the politicization of disputes. It was also pointed out that considerable political will was required for its creation. Several delegates encouraged more research by UNCTAD and other institutions on the prospective court (focusing, for example, on the relationship to ISDS and State–State procedures; jurisdiction; remedies and enforcement mechanism; and best practices of international and regional courts, tribunals and mechanisms).

The experts shared national experiences to circumscribe investors' access to ISDS and to shift focus towards greater reliance on domestic remedies. The difficulties that investors faced when investing abroad and the reasons for retaining investor access to ISDS were part of the discussion as well as the arguments against the provision of ISDS and for the exhaustion of local remedies. Proposals were made to improve ISDS mechanisms, for example, through increased transparency; an arbitrator code of conduct; better use of cooling-off periods; mechanisms for appeals, collective actions by smaller investors, and the early dismissal of frivolous claims; "no-U-turn" or "fork-in-the-road" provisions; clear rules on interest calculation and cost allocation; and enhanced provisions on the right to regulate.

4 Recent Trends in the IIA Regime

4.1 New Approaches to IIAs

Three new approaches to IIAs (by Brazil, India and Indonesia) were revealed at the UNCTAD expert meeting in 2015 and several other innovative models and ideas where launched later that year. At the expert meeting, Brazil presented the key features of its model Cooperation and Facilitation Investment Agreement (CFIA),[10] which was previously announced at the IIA Conference 2014 as an "innovative alternative to traditional IIAs".[11] While the country had signed some BITs in the past but without ratifying any, it signed its first CFIA with Mozambique on 30 March 2015 and ratified it shortly after.[12] Brazil's model CFIA has been developed on the basis of extensive domestic consultations, including with the private sector, and the experience of other countries and international organizations. The model's objectives of promoting cooperation between the parties and

[10] Government of Brazil (Ministério do Desenvolvimento, Indústria e Comércio Exterior), Cooperation and Facilitation Investment Agreement—CFIA (Presentation at the UNCTAD Expert Meeting), 25 February 2015, http://unctad-worldinvestmentforum.org/wp-content/uploads/2015/03/Brazil_side-event-Wednesday_model-agreements.pdf (last accessed 9 June 2015).

[11] Godinho (Secretary of Foreign Trade at Ministry of Development, Industry and Foreign Trade, Brazil), Statement at the UNCTAD IIA Conference 2014, 16 October 2014, http://unctad-worldinvestmentforum.org/wp-content/uploads/2014/10/Godinho.pdf (last accessed 9 June 2015).

[12] Government of Brazil (Ministério do Desenvolvimento, Indústria e Comércio Exterior), Brasil e Moçambique assinam Acordo de Cooperação e Facilitação de Investimentos (ACFI), 30 March 2015, http://www.mdic.gov.br/sitio/interna/noticia.php?area=1&noticia=13678 (last accessed 9 June 2015). CFIAs between Angola and Brazil as well as Brazil and Mexico were also signed in the first half of 2015. See UNCTAD International Investment Agreements Navigator, http://investmentpolicyhub.unctad.org/IIA (last accessed 2 March 2016).

facilitating and encouraging mutual investments are pursued through three main features: (1) the improvement of institutional governance, with the establishment of Focal Points (ombudsmen) and of a Joint Committee made up of government representatives from both parties; (2) the identification of ongoing agendas for investment cooperation and facilitation; and (3) the creation of mechanisms for risk mitigation and dispute prevention. The model includes substantive provisions dealing with expropriation, national treatment (subject to the applicable law) and MFN treatment, compensation for losses, and transparency. The model includes a compulsory mechanism for dispute prevention prior to the establishment of a State–State arbitration procedure (without an ISDS clause). The CFIA also focuses on specific thematic agendas as a way of encouraging and promoting a business-friendly environment. This includes cooperation on business visas, CSR, transfer of funds and transparency of procedures.

India outlined its BIT revision process and key outcomes at the UNCTAD Expert Meeting in February 2015.[13] In April 2015, it made available its new draft model BIT for public comments.[14] The then draft model includes several innovative provisions: an enterprise-based definition of investment (rather than a broad asset-based definition) and a detailed clarification of what is meant by "real and substantial business operations" under the definition of the term "enterprise"; a careful definition of the scope of the treaty; a national treatment provision applicable to investments in "like circumstances"; a new approach replacing the FET clause with a list of State obligations; a test for determining whether indirect expropriation occurred; and a free transfer of funds clause, subject to a detailed list of exceptions. It does not include an MFN clause. The draft model also includes provisions on investor obligations. It further contains a detailed investor-State dispute mechanism that provides for, among other matters, strict time frames for the submission of a dispute to arbitration, the selection of arbitrators and the prevention of conflict of interest. The draft stipulates that investors must first submit their claim before the relevant domestic courts or administrative bodies for the purpose of pursuing domestic remedies, where available. If after exhausting all judicial and administrative remedies no resolution has been satisfactory to the investor within three years, the investor may commence a proceeding under the ISDS article by transmitting a notice of dispute to the respondent party.

Indonesia is currently in the process of developing a new model BIT.[15] According to information available at the time of writing, the new model BIT will consider the exclusion of portfolio investment from the definition of

---

[13] Government of India (Department of Economic Affairs, Ministry of Finance), Transforming the International Investment Agreement Regime: The Indian Experience (Presentation at the UNCTAD Expert Meeting), 25 February 2015, http://unctad-worldinvestmentforum.org/wp-content/uploads/2015/03/India_side-event-Wednesday_model-agreements.pdf (last accessed 9 June 2015).

[14] Draft Indian Model Bilateral Investment Treaty Text, 2015, https://mygov.in/group-issue/draft-indian-model-bilateral-investment-treaty-text/ (last accessed 9 June 2015).

[15] Jailani (Ministry of Foreign Affairs, Indonesia), Indonesia's Experience: IIA Review (Presentation at the UNCTAD Expert Meeting), 25 February 2015, http://unctad-worldinvestmentforum.org/wp-content/uploads/2015/03/Indonesia_side-event-Wednesday_model-agreements.pdf (last accessed 9 June 2015).

investment and will add a contribution to economic development requirement in its definition clauses. National treatment will be subject to exceptions related to special treatment in favour of domestic small and medium-sized enterprises and investments and measures affecting natural resources. The new model will also clarify in greater detail the scope of the FET standard and will provide a list of State obligations including a prohibition against denial of justice in criminal, civil or administrative proceedings and assurance of police protection from any physical harm. Finally, investor-State arbitration will be subject to host country consent. An investor may submit a case to international arbitration if the host country provides a specific consent letter.

Many countries are currently revising or have recently revised their model IIAs. This trend is not limited to a specific group of countries or regions. It involves at least 50 countries and four regional integration organizations, including countries from Africa, Europe, North America, Latin American, Asian countries and economies in transition.

For example, Norway developed a new draft model BIT and opened a public consultation in May 2015.[16] The draft model's definition of investment stipulates that, in order to qualify as an investment, assets must fulfil specific characteristics. The expropriation provision of the draft model stipulates in the last paragraph that "[i]n rare circumstances" the preceding paragraphs apply to indirect expropriation; it provides a list of elements that need to be taken into account in order to determine whether an indirect expropriation has taken place. The daft model contains exceptions relating to essential security interests, cultural policy, prudential regulation and taxation. It also contains a not lowering of standards and a "right to regulate" clause.

Also in May 2015, the European Commission proposed new approaches to key IIA provisions related to the right to regulate and ISDS in its concept paper[17] and the German Federal Ministry for Economic Affairs and Energy made public a memorandum ("Gutachten") on a model BIT for developed countries with a functioning legal system.[18] The Commission's concept paper recognizes the achievements of the concluded negotiations with Canada and Singapore and addresses issues that could be further explored, as a result of the Transatlantic Trade and Investment Partnership (TTIP) public consultations. Four areas are

---

[16] Government of Norway, Consultation—Model investment agreement, 13 May 2015, https://www.regjeringen.no/nb/dokumenter/horing---modell-for-investeringsavtaler/id2411615/ (last accessed 9 June 2015).

[17] European Commission, Investment in TTIP and beyond—the path for reform, Concept Paper, 2015, http://trade.ec.europa.eu/doclib/docs/2015/may/tradoc_153408.PDF (last accessed 9 June 2015).

[18] Federal Ministry for Economic Affairs and Energy, Germany, Modell-Investitionsschutzvertrag mit Investor-Staat Schiedsverfahren für Industriestaaten unter Berücksichtigung der USA, 2015, http://www.bmwi.de/BMWi/Redaktion/PDF/M-O/modell-investitionsschutzvertrag-mit-investor-staat-schiedsverfahren-gutachten,property=pdf,bereich=bmwi2012,sprache=de,rwb=true.pdf (last accessed 9 June 2015).

identified for such further improvement: (1) the protection of the right to regulate, (2) the establishment and functioning of arbitral tribunals, (3) the review of ISDS decisions by an appellate body, and (4) the relationship between domestic judicial systems and ISDS. Some of the suggestions concern the host State's right to regulate in the public interest and the concept paper suggests the inclusion of a clause expressly recognizing the right of States to take measures in pursuance of legitimate public policy objectives according to the level of protection they deem appropriate. With regard to ISDS, it also elaborates on arbitrator selection and qualifications, third-party submissions, and the establishment of a permanent bilateral appeals mechanism. The latter would review awards with respect to errors of law and manifest errors in the assessment of facts. The proposal also envisions the eventual creation of a permanent court and its possible multilateralization.

The suggestion for a model published by the German Federal Ministry for Economic Affairs and Energy addresses reform issues that arose during the TTIP consultation process. It intends to safeguard the State's right to regulate through public policy exceptions and provide options for conferring on foreign investors rights no greater than those enjoyed by domestic investors. For this reason, the model agreement circumscribes and clarifies the content of the FET and of the expropriation standard. Notably, the model suggests the creation of a bilateral tribunal or court for each specific treaty (e.g. EU-US Permanent Investment Tribunal) with judges pre-selected by the parties to the agreement and individual cases being assigned to the judges following rules of distribution that preclude any influence from the disputing parties on the composition of the panel (e.g. distribution by lot, by the order of the filing of disputes or by any other condition). This first instance would have exclusive jurisdiction to hear investment disputes arising under the agreement. The proposed tribunal mechanism is complimented by a standing appellate body. This appellate body would as a second instance "undertake comprehensive scrutiny of the law and restricted scrutiny of the facts" in respect of the awards rendered by the first instance. Submission of a claim by an investor is subject to the exhaustion of domestic remedies, unless such remedies are unavailable or manifestly ineffective. An alternative suggestion conditions initiation of proceedings to the investor's waiver of any rights to start proceedings under national courts or tribunals.

4.2 Other Investment Policy Developments

Countries' search for new model agreements occurs against the background of several other policy developments that UNCTAD has monitored closely in the past few years. A number of countries have put on hold future IIA negotiations, terminated BITs or withdrew from the ICSID Convention. Bolivia withdrew from the ICSID Convention in 2007, Ecuador in 2009 and Venezuela in 2012. The three countries also terminated several IIAs.[19] Following a review of its BITs network, South Africa terminated treaties with several European countries.[20] Between January 2014 and May 2015, Indonesia discontinued 18 of its 64 BITs.[21] South Africa and Indonesia stated their intentions to terminate also other BITs. Botswana and Namibia are currently reconsidering their approaches to BITs.

At the same time, recent years have also seen an up-scaling trend in treaty making, which manifests itself in increasing dynamism (with more countries participating in ever faster sequenced negotiating rounds) and in an increasing depth and breadth of issues addressed.[22] The negotiations of Mega-Regional treaties are a case in point. Taken together, seven Mega-Regional treaties under negotiation at the time of writing (such as TTIP, TPP, and RCEP) or recently concluded (such as the Canada-EU CETA) involve close to 90 countries.[23]

The expansion of the IIA regime continues, with intensified efforts at the regional level. In 2014, countries signed 31 new IIAs (18 BITs and 13 "other IIAs"), bringing the total number of IIAs to 3271 treaties by year-end. A review of new IIAs concluded in 2014 shows that the majority of them include provisions safeguarding the right to regulate for sustainable development objectives, such as those identified in UNCTAD's IPFSD. Of the 18 IIAs reviewed (11 BITs and 7 "other IIAs"), 14 have general exceptions—for example, for the protection of human, animal or plant life or health, or the conservation of exhaustible natural resources. Another 14 treaties contain a clause that explicitly recognizes that the parties should not relax health, safety or environmental standards in order to attract investment. Twelve treaties refer to the protection of health and safety, labour rights, the environment or sustainable development in their preambles.

These sustainable development features are supplemented by treaty elements that aim more broadly at preserving regulatory space for public policies of host countries and/or at minimizing exposure to investment arbitration. These elements include clauses that (1) limit treaty scope (for example, by excluding certain types of assets from the definition of investment); (2) clarify obligations (for example, by including more detailed clauses on FET and/or indirect expropriation); (3) contain

[19] UNCTAD, World Investment Report 2012—Towards a New Generation of Investment Policies, 2012, http://unctad.org/en/pages/DIAE/World%20Investment%20Report/WIR-Series.aspx (last accessed 9 June 2015), p. 87.

[20] Among others, notices of termination were issued to Belgium/Luxembourg in 2012 and to Austria, Denmark and Germany in 2013.

[21] Indonesia sent notices of termination to Bulgaria, Cambodia, China, Egypt, France, Hungary, India, Italy, Kyrgyzstan, the Lao People's Democratic Republic, Malaysia, the Netherlands, Romania, Singapore, Slovakia, Spain, Turkey and Viet Nam.

[22] UNCTAD, World Investment Report 2014—Investing in the SDGs: An Action Plan, 2014, http://unctad.org/en/pages/DIAE/World%20Investment%20Report/WIR-Series.aspx (last accessed 9 June 2015).

[23] UNCTAD, World Investment Report 2014—Investing in the SDGs: An Action Plan, 2014, http://unctad.org/en/pages/DIAE/World%20Investment%20Report/WIR-Series.aspx (last accessed 9 June 2015), p. 118.

exceptions to transfer-of-funds obligations or carveouts for prudential measures; and (4) carefully regulate ISDS (for example, by limiting treaty provisions that are subject to ISDS, excluding certain policy areas from ISDS, setting out a special mechanism for taxation and prudential measures, and/or restricting the allotted time period within which claims can be submitted). Notably, all but one of the treaties concluded in 2014 that were reviewed omit the so-called umbrella clause.

Countries have started to clarify and "tighten" the meaning of individual IIA provisions and to improve ISDS procedures, with the objective of making the process more elaborated, predictable and transparent and of giving contracting parties a stronger role therein. Arguably, the increased efforts for bringing about a "new generation" investment treaties and IIA reform more generally also respond to the developments in investment arbitration and the rapid proliferation of ISDS cases from 326 in 2008 to 608 known cases at the end of 2014. The fact that investment treaty arbitrations increasingly involve both developed and developing countries as defendants contributes to this development.[24] The entry into force of the UNCITRAL Rules on Transparency in Treaty-based Investor-State Arbitration on 1 April 2014[25] and the opening for signature of the Convention on Transparency in Treaty-based Investor-State Arbitration on 17 March 2015[26] also indicate developed and developing countries' interest in addressing concerns about the functioning of the IIA regime and ISDS.

In 2014, the World Investment Report outlined that countries' efforts reveal different paths of action.[27] Some countries aim to maintain the status quo, largely

[24] While the historical average of cases against developed countries is at 28 %, the relative share of the new cases in 2012 (34 %), 2013 (47 %) and 2014 (40 %) was considerably higher. Until the end of 2014, 99 countries—developed and developing ones—were respondents to one or more known treaty-based claims. UNCTAD, Investor-State Dispute Settlement: Review of Developments in 2014, IIA Issues Note (2015) 2, http://investmentpolicyhub.unctad.org/Publications/Details/132 (last accessed 9 June 2015). For updated statistics and lists of cases, see UNCTAD Investment Dispute Settlement Navigator, http://investmentpolicyhub.unctad.org/ISDS (last accessed 2 March 2016).

[25] The UNCITRAL Transparency Rules provide for open oral hearings in ISDS cases as well as the publication of key documents, including notices of arbitration, pleadings, transcripts, and all decisions and awards issued by the tribunal (subject to certain safeguards, including protection of confidential information). By default (in the absence of further action), the Rules apply only to UNCITRAL arbitrations brought under IIAs concluded after 1 April 2014, and thus exclude the pre-existing IIAs from their coverage. See UNCITRAL Rules on Transparency in Treaty-based Investor-State Arbitration, 2014, http://www.uncitral.org/pdf/english/texts/arbitration/rules-on-transparency/Rules-on-Transparency-E.pdf (last accessed 9 June 2015).

[26] The aim of the Convention is to give those States (as well as regional economic integration organizations) that wish to make the UNCITRAL Transparency Rules applicable to their existing IIAs a mechanism to do so. Specifically, and in the absence of reservations by the signatories, the Transparency Rules will apply to disputes where both the respondent State and the home State of the claimant investor are parties to the Convention; and only the respondent State is party to the Convention but the claimant investor agrees to the application of the Rules. See United Nations Convention on Transparency in Treaty-based Investor-State Arbitration, 2015, http://www.uncitral.org/pdf/english/texts/arbitration/transparency-convention/Transparency-Convention-e.pdf (last accessed 9 June 2015).

[27] UNCTAD, World Investment Report 2014—Investing in the SDGs: An Action Plan, 2014, p. 126, http://unctad.org/en/pages/DIAE/World%20Investment%20Report/WIR-Series.aspx (last accessed 9 June 2015).

refraining from changes in the way they enter into new IIA commitments. Others are disengaging from the IIA regime, unilaterally terminating existing treaties or denouncing multilateral arbitration conventions. Many countries are in the process of implementing selective adjustments, modifying models for future treaties but leaving the treaty core and the body of existing treaties largely untouched. Finally, there is the path of systematic reform that aims to comprehensively address the IIA regime's challenges in a holistic manner.

5 Reforming the International Investment Regime: An Action Menu

Today, governments have entered into a phase of evaluating the costs and benefits of IIAs and reflecting on their future objectives and strategies as regards these treaties. Several countries have embarked on a path of IIA reform by revising their model agreements, renegotiating their existing IIAs and concluding "new generation" IIAs with provisions safeguarding the right to regulate for sustainable development objectives. As a result, the IIA regime is going through a period of reflection, review and revision—and there is a noticeable move towards reforming international investment rule making.

Responding to the "pressing need for systematic reform of the global IIA regime", UNCTAD's World Investment Report 2015 offers an action menu that analyses the "what, how and extent" of such reform, i.e. the priority areas, the tools and the depth of IIA reform.[28]

IIA reform can learn from 6 decades of experience with IIA rule making. At least three key lessons learned can be distilled. First, IIAs "bite" (i.e. they may carry risks and involve unanticipated costs) and therefore safeguards are needed. Second, IIAs have limitations as an investment promotion and facilitation tool, since IIAs are only one of many determinants of FDI decision-making, but they also have underused potential. Third, IIAs have wider implications for policy and systemic coherence, as well as for capacity-building due to the broad scope of application of IIAs and the wide range of foreign investment operations which cut across numerous other policy areas at all levels of policymaking within countries (national, subnational, municipal).

These lessons could inform future IIA rule making and help address five main reform objectives identified by UNCTAD (that are challenges at the same time), each accompanied by policy options. IIA reform should aim at:

(1) Safeguarding the right to regulate in the public interest so as to ensure that limits IIAs involve with respect to the sovereignty of States do not unduly

[28] See chapter IV in UNCTAD, World Investment Report 2015—Reforming International Investment Governance, 2015, http://unctad.org/en/pages/DIAE/World%20Investment%20Report/WIR-Series.aspx (last accessed 9 June 2015).

constrain public policymaking. Reform options to achieve this objective include clarifying or circumscribing provisions such as MFN treatment, FET and indirect expropriation, as well as including exceptions (e.g. for public policies or national security).

(2) Reforming investment dispute settlement to address the legitimacy crisis of the current system. Reform options include improving the existing system of investment arbitration (refining the arbitral process, circumscribing access to ISDS), adding new elements to the existing system (e.g. an appeals facility, dispute prevention mechanism) or replacing it (e.g. with a permanent international court, State–State dispute settlement and/or domestic dispute resolution).

(3) Promoting and facilitating investment by effectively expanding this dimension in IIAs. IIA reform options include expanding the investment promotion and facilitation dimension of IIAs together with domestic policy tools, and targeting promotion measures towards sustainable development objectives. These options address home- and host-country measures (inward and outward investment promotion), joint and regional investment promotion initiatives, including an ombudsperson for investment facilitation.

(4) Ensuring responsible investment to maximize the positive impact of foreign investment and minimize its potential negative effects. IIA reform options include adding not lowering of standards clauses and establishing provisions on investor responsibilities, such as clauses on compliance with domestic laws and on corporate social responsibility.

(5) Enhancing the systemic consistency of the IIA regime so as to overcome the gaps, overlaps and inconsistencies of the current system and establish coherence in investment relationships. IIA reform options aim at better managing interactions between IIAs and other areas of law as well as interactions within the IIA regime, with a view to consolidating and streamlining it. They also aim at linking IIA reform to the domestic policy agenda and implementation.

Some of these reform options can be combined and tailored to meet several reform objectives. The compound effect of options also requires careful consideration, since some combinations may result in a treaty that is largely deprived of its traditional investment protection rationale.

Among the most important guidelines for IIA reform is the need to harness IIAs for sustainable development, while also focusing on the key reform areas and following a multilevel, systematic and inclusive approach. Moreover, there are a number of strategic choices to be made at the beginning of a country's reform processes. This includes whether to conclude new IIAs; whether to disengage from existing IIAs; or whether to engage in IIA reform. Other strategic decisions relate to the substance of reform—such as the extent and depth of the reform agenda—and the reform process.

The World Investment Report 2015 suggests that IIA reform calls for processes to be synchronized at the national, bilateral, regional and multilateral levels. Actions at each level require that countries take stock and identify the specific problems, develop a strategic approach and an action plan for reform targeted at these problems, and implement actions. Reform steps at the national level (e.g. new model IIAs) or bilateral level (e.g. renegotiation of IIAs) can play an important role in countries' reform strategies. The World Investment Report 2015 aims to support countries in these efforts by offering policy options and key considerations on important reform issues. At the same time, national and bilateral reform actions risk perpetuating, if not exacerbating, the fragmentation and incoherence of the global IIA regime. A priori, reform initiatives at the multilateral or regional level offer better prospects for consolidating IIA reform efforts and finding common solutions to widely shared concerns. Regional reform processes also have a potential for bringing about change (i.e. through the collective review of the treaty network or through its consolidation).

The World Investment Report draws on a variety of reform proposals and ideas put forward in recent years, by UNCTAD and many others. By presenting reform approaches, guidelines, tools, solutions, and an action menu for the reform process, the Report offers a road map for IIA reform.

6 IIA Reform: New Approaches, Multiple Options and Various Paths

Many countries and regional groupings are in the process of reviewing, reforming and revising their IIAs. During the past few years, new approaches to IIAs have emerged and countries' emerging actions reveal various reform paths. Today, States have a menu of reform options at their disposal—they can pick and choose which reform option to pursue, at what level and intensity of engagement. Countries can and do formulate their own reform packages.

To achieve the common objective of IIA reform, however, engagement at all levels—national, bilateral, regional and multilateral—is important. Given the large number of existing IIAs (3271 treaties by the end of 2014) and the limited potential of reform actions at the national-level to bring about a new and more sustainable development-friendly IIA regime (because by their very nature, these actions are unilateral), it can be argued that only a common approach will deliver an IIA regime in which stability, clarity and predictability help achieve the objectives of all stakeholders: effectively harnessing international investment relations for the pursuit of sustainable development. Through policy analysis, capacity-building and consensus-building activities, UNCTAD can play a role in helping the investment and development community to make the IIA regime work for sustainable development.

Recent Developments in the World Customs Organization

Carsten Weerth

Contents

Abstract This paper investigates recent dynamic developments of the World Customs Organization (WCO) an intergovernmental Organization of 180 contracting parties that rules international customs matters and the co-operation of states in this field of work. During the last 5 years (2011–2015) developments in different legal fields and memberships of legal instruments have resulted in new trends. The major areas of work are explained and recent

---

This paper does not give the position of Germany's Customs Service, the local customs authority Hauptzollamt Bremen, the European Commission or the World Customs Organization; it represents the author's own and privately conducted research.

C. Weerth (✉)
Main Customs Office Bremen, Bremen, Germany

FOM University of Applied Sciences for Economics and Management, Bremen, Germany
e-mail: carsten.weerth@gmx.de

M. Bungenberg et al. (eds.), *European Yearbook of International Economic Law 2016*, European Yearbook of International Economic Law 7,
DOI 10.1007/978-3-319-29215-1_34

developments are highlighted. The WCO as a hub for scientific customs research is presented and new developments with new instruments are introduced.

1 Introduction

This paper investigates recent developments of the World Customs Organization (WCO) an intergovernmental Organization of 180 members that rules international customs matters and the co-operation of states in this field of work. During the last 5 years (2011–2015) developments in different legal fields and memberships of legal instruments have resulted in new trends. This paper builds on a series of three papers of *Wolffgang/Dallimore*[1] which were focusing on special themes and it investigates general trends and new developments in the WCO.

This paper investigates new WCO membership developments, new legal instruments and new areas of work; it analyses these trends in further detail. The WCO membership and the membership to its legal instruments are still growing strongly and at high speed.

2 Membership Development

In June 2015 the WCO had a membership of 180 contracting parties. The last member states that joined were Guinea-Bissau in 2010, South Sudan and Somalia in 2012 and Palestine in 2015.[2] The European Union has a status akin to membership since July 2007—the EU has had rights akin to those of a WCO Member for matters falling within its competency as an interim measure but is listed additionally on the list of members[3]—therefore it is not counted as one of 180 contracting parties. The

[1] See Wolffgang and Dallimore (2012), p. 613; Wolffgang and Dallimore (2013), p. 391 and Dallimore and Wolffgang (2014), p. 379.

[2] See WCO, http://www.wcoomd.org/en/about-us/wco-members/~/media/WCO/Public/Global/PDF/About%20us/WCO%20Members/List%20of%20Members%20with%20membership%20date.ashx (last accessed 28 June 2015).

[3] See WCO, The WCO in brief, Fact file, November 2009, http://www.wcoomd.org/en/about-us/~/media/WCO/Public/Global/PDF/About%20us/WCO%20In%20Brief/DEPL%20OMD%20UK%20A4.ashx (last accessed 28 June 2015), for the WCO history http://www.wcoomd.org/en/about-us/what-is-the-wco/au_history.aspx (last accessed 28 June 2015), and Weerth (2009), p. 267.

Table 1 WCO-membership development in cohorts of 5 years

Years	New members	Rank[a]	Membership (total)
1950–1954	17	4	17
1955–1959	7	11	24
1960–1964	17	4	41
1965–1969	18	3	59
1970–1974	14	6	73
1975–1979	19	2	92
1980–1984	7	11	99
1985–1989	10	10	109
1990–1994	35	1	144
1995–1999	13	7	157
2000–2004	13	7	170
2005–2009	12	9	182
2010–2015	4	14	180[b]

[a]The rank measures the membership rise in 5 year periods and ranks the results

[b]The total number of member countries does not add up because the split up of one former member can result in several new member countries: examples are Czechoslovak Republic into Czech Republic and Slovak Republic. This applies in particular for the USSR and for Yugoslavia but also (most recent) for Sudan and South Sudan

WCO was founded as Customs-Co-Operation Council (CCC) in 1952 and had 17 founding members.[4]

The total membership has risen to 180 contracting parties (the independent State of Palestine as the newest contracting party is not member of the UN but has been granted UN-observer status). Most new member countries acceded after the end of the soviet era (1990–1994) when many new states were founded in former USSR soviet republics and on the Balkan (Table 1).

3 Membership Rise in Established Legal Instruments

3.1 Legal Instruments

The WCO distinguishes between legally binding agreements/conventions, and non-binding legal instruments: recommendations, declarations and resolutions.

[4] See WCO, The WCO in brief, Fact file, November 2009, //www.wcoomd.org/en/about-us/~/media/WCO/Public/Global/PDF/About%20us/WCO%20In%20Brief/DEPL%20OMD%20UK%20A4.ashx (last accessed 28 June 2015), for the WCO history http://www.wcoomd.org/en/about-us/what-is-the-wco/au_history.aspx (last accessed 28 June 2015), and Weerth (2009), p. 268.

The legal instruments of the WCO are listed on its internet page in the rubric "About us → Legal Instruments".[5]

The WCO is also displaying the state of the legal instruments for its member states—that is of importance because not all member states have signed every instrument. These two documents are the so called "summary of position as of 30 June 2014"[6] and "synopsis of position as of 30 June 2014".[7]

This section is about the membership rise in established legally binding instruments.

3.2 International Convention on the Harmonized Commodity Description and Coding System

Its most successful binding legal instrument is the International Convention on the Harmonized Commodity Description and Coding System (HS).[8] In June 2015 the HS has 153 contracting parties (Table 2).[9]

3.3 International Convention on the Simplification and Harmonization of Customs Procedures (Revised Kyoto Convention)

The second most successful binding legal instrument is the International Convention on the simplification and harmonization of Customs procedures (done at Kyoto

[5] See WCO, http://www.wcoomd.org/en/about-us/legal-instruments.aspx (last accessed 28 June 2015).

[6] See WCO, http://www.wcoomd.org/en/about-us/legal-instruments/~/media/A30C5AB2897E4C0484F20A910FB7D6A3.ashx (last accessed 28 June 2015).

[7] See WCO, http://www.wcoomd.org/en/about-us/legal-instruments/~/media/110581D879F447F68B490F2FA8EA662B.ashx (last accessed 28 June 2015).

[8] For the legal text see WCO, http://www.wcoomd.org/en/about-us/legal-instruments/~/link.aspx?_id=002DC5117CE94EE1BC4B6BFFF4319BE9&_z=z (last accessed 28 June 2015), WCO Press releases 2015, see WCO, URL: http://www.wcoomd.org/en/media/newsroom/2015.aspx (last accessed 28 June 2015); Weerth (2015c); and for its significance see Weerth (2008), p. 61 and Wind (2007), p. 80.

[9] See WCO, Position regarding contracting parties (as of 4 November 2014), http://www.wcoomd.org/en/about-us/legal-instruments/~/media/1F153321A5834847B5E4C189E5B5CFAC.ashx (last accessed 28 June 2015).

Table 2 Increase in membership in the legal instrument—Harmonized System (HS)

Year	New members	Membership (total)
2011	3	141
2012	4	145
2013	4	149
2014	2	151
2015	2	153

Table 3 Increase in membership in the legal instrument—Revised Kyoto Convention (RKC)

Year	New members	Membership (total)
2011	7	78
2012	7	85
2013	6	91
2014	6	97
2015	5	102

on 18 May 1973, as amended on 26 June 1999, so called Revised Kyoto Convention, RKC). In June 2015 the RKC has 102 contracting parties.[10]

The WCO is actively lobbying its membership for an accession to the RKC, e.g. by creating media flyers,[11] a research paper on the benefits of the RKC[12] and by help of comprising frequently asked questions.[13]

The RKC has long outnumbered the old Kyoto Convention (KC) which originally had 67 contracting parties.[14]

In May 2015 four countries are still applying the old KC: Burundi, Democratic Republic of Congo, Gambia, and Israel.[15] However, this also applies to the EU-28 since the current Customs Code—Regulation (EEC) No. 2913/92—is based on the old KC. The RKC will be applied within the EU from 1 May 2016 with the so called Union Customs Code—Regulation (EU) No. 952/2013 (Table 3).

[10] See WCO, http://www.wcoomd.org/en/about-us/legal-instruments/~/media/08581EC002E647C690451E3B515584B7.ashx (last accessed 28 June 2015); WCO press releases 2015, see http://www.wcoomd.org/en/media.aspx (last accessed 28 June 2015) and Weerth (2015b).

[11] See WCO (2002), http://www.wcoomd.org/en/topics/facilitation/instrument-and-tools/conventions/~/media/WCO/Public/Global/PDF/Topics/Facilitation/Instruments%20and%20Tools/Conventions/Kyoto%20Convention/Brochures/implement_kyoto_uk.ashx (last accessed 28 June 2015).

[12] See WCO, Benefits of the Revised Kyoto Convention, 2010, http://www.wcoomd.org/en/topics/facilitation/instrument-and-tools/conventions/~/media/WCO/Public/Global/PDF/Topics/Facilitation/Instruments%20and%20Tools/Conventions/Kyoto%20Convention/BenefitsRKC.ashx (last accessed 28 June 2015).

[13] See WCO, http://www.wcoomd.org/en/faq/kyoto_convention_faq.aspx (last accessed 28 June 2015).

[14] See Weerth (2010), p. 80. For the membership of the old KC and the RKC see WCO, http://www.wcoomd.org/en/topics/facilitation/instrument%20and%20tools/conventions/pf_revised_kyoto_conv/instruments.aspx (last accessed 28 June 2015).

[15] See WCO, http://www.wcoomd.org/en/about-us/legal-instruments/~/media/77805587072042468B3B53A00129EF79.ashx (last accessed 28 June 2015).

Table 4 Increase in membership in the legal instrument—Convention on Temporary Admission (Istanbul Convention)

Year	New members	Membership (total)
2011	3	62
2012	2	64
2013	1	65
2014	2	67

3.4 Convention on Temporary Admission (Istanbul Convention)

The third most successful legal binding convention is the Convention on Temporary Admission (Istanbul Convention), concluded on 26 June 1990 (entered into force on 27 November 1993) which had 67 contracting parties in June 2015 (Table 4).[16]

4 New Non-Binding Legal Instruments

Next to the legal binding conventions the non-binding instruments of the WCO are recommendations, declarations and resolutions.

This section is highlighting new non-binding legal instruments of the last 5 years.

In June 2014 the WCO has issued a declaration on the illegal wildlife trade[17] and is reaching out towards a co-operation with other international organizations to address this issue.

In December 2013 the WCO has issued its Dublin Resolution[18] which celebrates the World Trade Organization (WTO) Bali Package and makes a statement about the enhanced co-operation with the WTO.

In June 2013 the WCO council has adopted a recommendation on Customs formalities in connection with the temporary admission of container security devices (CSDs).[19]

[16] See WCO, http://www.wcoomd.org/en/about-us/legal-instruments/~/media/AFF3DFAC1D214A43A5A7CBD9C01CC8D7.ashx (last accessed 28 June 2015).

[17] See WCO, http://www.wcoomd.org/en/about-us/legal-instruments/~/media/BC96FE063BF848AD83E3ADB56B0A79BE.ashx (last accessed 28 June 2015).

[18] See WCO, http://www.wcoomd.org/en/about-us/legal-instruments/~/media/AFC8D1762ACC4689834CB056EB9EAF19.ashx (last accessed 28 June 2015).

[19] See WCO, http://www.wcoomd.org/en/about-us/legal-instruments/recommendations/~/media/C6E5F4DF134C427C923AE8CF99E062C6.ashx (last accessed 28 June 2015).

In June 2012 the WCO council has issued a recommendation concerning the use of advance passenger information (API) and passenger name record (PNR) for efficient and effective customs control.[20]

In December 2011 the WCO policy commission issued a Resolution on Air Cargo Security[21] that stresses the importance of the topic.

In June 2011 the WCO has issued a Resolution on the Role of Customs in Natural Disaster Relief[22] which stresses the importance of customs co-operation after natural disasters in order to help the civic society. A couple of important hints are given how to ensure customs controls without hindering necessary help.

5 WCO's Role in Trade Facilitation

The WCO is taking an active role in trade facilitation which is a topic to the WCO and the WTO alike.

The major legal convention that enhances trade facilitation is the RCK as mentioned above. Furthermore, the Dublin Resolution is stating the importance of the WTO Bali Package and intends a better co-operation with the WTO:

The WCO "will engage immediately with the WTO in respect of the governance and future implementation of the Trade Facilitation Agreement, in particular in the framework of the WTO Trade Facilitation Committee to be established".[23]

One other important aspect is the SAFE Framework of Standards to Secure and Facilitate Global Trade (SAFE Framework) which has been introduced by the WCO as a resolution in June 2005: "Resolution of the Customs Co-operation Council on the Framework of Standards to Secure and Facilitate Global Trade".[24]

168 of the WCO member states have agreed to introduce the SAFE Framework[25] (state of data: March 2014) which makes this non-binding legal instrument the most

[20] See WCO, http://www.wcoomd.org/en/about-us/legal-instruments/recommendations/~/media/58AFD123B1BC41D689BE40D140E81529.ashx (last accessed 28 June 2015).

[21] See WCO, http://www.wcoomd.org/en/about-us/legal-instruments/~/media/745F11ACEF9B45EABC33A31BFD896AB4.ashx (last accessed 28 June 2015).

[22] See WCO, http://www.wcoomd.org/en/about-us/legal-instruments/~/media/A0C1DEE96F944E08BCD48FFDD1A7D4B7.ashx (last accessed 28 June 2015).

[23] See WCO, http://www.wcoomd.org/en/about-us/legal-instruments/~/media/AFC8D1762ACC4689834CB056EB9EAF19.ashx (last accessed 28 June 2015).

[24] See WCO, http://www.wcoomd.org/en/about-us/legal-instruments/~/media/18A4FCBBFBED41688CB72D9A510B4FA8.ashx (last accessed 28 June 2015); for an analysis see Kleine-Holthaus (2007a), p. 57; Kleine-Holthaus (2007b), p. 111; Mikuriya (2007), p. 51 and Dallimore and Wolffgang (2014), p. 379.

[25] See WCO, Compendium of Authorized Economic Operator Programmes, 2014 edition, http://www.wcoomd.org/en/topics/facilitation/instrument-and-tools/tools/~/media/B8FC2D23BE5E44759579D9E780B176AC.ashx (last accessed 28 June 2015).

successful instrument of the WCO. Taiwan is also implementing the SAFE Framework but it is not a WCO member state.[26]

6 The Rise of Capacity Building

The introduction of new tools and legal instruments in more and more WCO member states raises the issue of how this can be accomplished in an easy and successful manner. The capacity building strategy became one of the most important building blocks in the WCO's Strategy for the Twenty-first century.[27]

> The strategy was approved by the WCO Council in 2003[28] and it recognizes the key economic role of customs either as a primary or secondary function to
>
> - Manage the international supply chain,
> - Provide social protection,
> - Generate economic statistical,
> - Maintain revenue streams.[29]

The WCO has defined capacity building as follows:

> All Members of the WCO having the capability to:
>
> - influence, construct and manage policies which meet national requirements, regional and international obligations; and
> - implement and sustain the appropriate operational policy, support systems and procedures to meet these obligations.[30]

A variety of programs and tools is available for different targets.

The SAFE Framework is implemented by help of the COLUMBUS Program and the SAFE Self-Assessment checklist.[31]

The Customs Diagnostic Framework aims to provide a standardized diagnostic tool and project management design and implementation guide to improve the quality of capacity building.[32]

---

[26] See Weerth (2015a), p. 55.

[27] See WCO, The Capacity Building Strategy, http://www.wcoomd.org/en/topics/capacity-building/overview/cb_strategy.aspx (last accessed 28 June 2015); for more on this topic see Weerth (2013).

[28] See WCO, Capacity Building Strategy, http://www.wcoomd.org/en/topics/capacity-building/overview/~/media/WCO/Public/Global/PDF/Topics/Capacity%20Building/Overview/Cap%20buil%20strat.ashx (last accessed 28 June 2015).

[29] See WCO, The Capacity Building Strategy, http://www.wcoomd.org/en/topics/capacity-building/overview/cb_strategy.aspx (last accessed 28 June 2015).

[30] See WCO, The Capacity Building Strategy, http://www.wcoomd.org/en/topics/capacity-building/overview/cb_strategy.aspx (last accessed 28 June 2015).

[31] See WCO, http://www.wcoomd.org/en/topics/capacity-building/instrument-and-tools.aspx (last accessed 28 June 2015).

[32] See WCO, http://www.wcoomd.org/en/topics/capacity-building/instrument-and-tools/cb_diagnostic_framework.aspx (last accessed 28 June 2015).

An Orientation Packet for Decision Makers is designed to help leaders to decide about the needs and directions of their national customs administration.[33]

The Leadership and Management Development Programme that is open to 20 individual leaders per year.[34]

The WCO Fellowship Programme is aiming at senior managers or high-potential middle managers from developing nations that are able to learn customs modernization techniques in the WCO headquarter and other member states.[35] The program has duration of 6 weeks: 4 weeks as an internship with the WCO headquarters in Brussels and 2 weeks as an internship with a modern customs administration.

A WCO Scholarship Programme that is an internal Master Degree programme which is aiming at customs officers from developing nations.[36] This program has been launched in 2000 and is financed by the Japanese Customs Authority.

The Career Development Programme enables individual customs officers from developing nations to make a 10 month internship with the WCO headquarters.[37] This program has been launched in 2009 and is financed by the Japanese Customs Authority.

The general teaching approach for all officers consists out of three elements: capacity building, training and professionalism in customs.[38]

The capacity building approach of the WCO is a regional approach with 26 regional training centres around the world:

---

[33] See WCO, http://www.wcoomd.org/en/topics/capacity-building/instrument-and-tools/orientation-package-for-decision-makers.aspx (last accessed 28 June 2015) and http://www.wcoomd.org/en/topics/capacity-building/instrument-and-tools/~/media/WCO/Public/Global/PDF/Topics/Capacity%20Building/Instruments%20and%20Tools/Orientation%20Package%20Decision%20Makers/Or_package_decision_makers_v2en.ashx (last accessed 28 June 2015).

[34] See WCO, http://www.wcoomd.org/en/topics/capacity-building/activities-and-programmes/cb_leadership_management_development.aspx#Leadership%20and%20Management%20%E2%80%A6the%20basis%20for%20modern%20Customs%20administrations (last accessed 28 June 2015).

[35] See WCO, http://www.wcoomd.org/en/topics/capacity-building/activities-and-programmes/cb_leadership_management_development.aspx#WCO%20Fellowship%20Programme%20%E2%80%A6investing%20in%20the%20future%20Leaders%20of%20the%20Customs%20World (last accessed 28 June 2015).

[36] See WCO, http://www.wcoomd.org/en/topics/capacity-building/activities-and-programmes/cb_leadership_management_development.aspx#WCO%20Fellowship%20Programme%20%E2%80%A6investing%20in%20the%20future%20Leaders%20of%20the%20Customs%20World (last accessed 28 June 2015).

[37] See WCO, http://www.wcoomd.org/en/topics/capacity-building/activities-and-programmes/cb_leadership_management_development.aspx#WCO%20Fellowship%20Programme%20%E2%80%A6investing%20in%20the%20future%20Leaders%20of%20the%20Customs%20World (last accessed 28 June 2015).

[38] See WCO, http://www.wcoomd.org/en/topics/capacity-building/activities-and-programmes/cb_leadership_management_development.aspx#WCO%20Fellowship%20Programme%20%E2%80%A6investing%20in%20the%20future%20Leaders%20of%20the%20Customs%20World (last accessed 28 June 2015).

> Regional Training Centres constitute one of the key components of the regional approach. Forming virtually independent and autonomous entities, the regions are best placed to identify and respond to their Members' training needs. This type of training, which is broader in scope than that offered to individual countries, makes it possible to pool and optimize resources within a single region. Such centres offer a number of advantages: they enable Customs officials from neighbouring countries to forge links with one another and, they facilitate the follow-up of WCO programmes in a region. To date, twenty-six (26) Regional Training Centres (RTCs) have been established: seven in the Asia Pacific Region (China; Fiji; Hong Kong, China; India; Japan, Korea; Malaysia), three in the East and Southern Africa Region (Kenya; South Africa; Zimbabwe), three in the West and Central Africa Region (Burkina Faso; Congo (Rep. of); Nigeria), six in the European Region (Azerbaijan; Hungary; Kazakhstan; The Former Yugoslav Republic of Macedonia; Russian Federation; Ukraine), two in the Americas Region (Brazil; Dominican Republic) and four in North Africa, Near and Middle East (Egypt; Jordan; Lebanon; Saudi Arabia).[39]

7 The WCO: A Hub for Customs Research

One of the major drivers opening the WCO up for the public and inter-disciplinary customs research is Mr. Kunio Mikuriya, the Head of the WCO. Mr. Mikuriya has been Deputy Director of the WCO from 2002 to 2008 and has been elected Secretary General of the WCO in June 2008 and he took office on 1 January 2009.[40] Mr. Mikuriya is an actively publishing and working scientist who received a PhD from the University of Kent, Brussels School of International Studies in International Relations.[41] He serves as an Editorial Board Member to the *Global Trade and Customs Journal* and has published numerous papers and chapters of books and handbooks and of course speeches and journal articles.[42]

New journals and regular periodicals have emerged in the field of international customs research since 2007, of which two are published, co-published or intellectually sponsored by the WCO:

- Global Trade and Customs Journal (Wolters Kluwer)[43]—first volume in 2006,
- World Customs Journal (IUCN and WCO)[44]—first volume in 2007,

[39] See WCO, http://www.wcoomd.org/en/topics/capacity-building/overview/cb_regional_approach/regional_training_centres.aspx?p=1 (last accessed 28 June 2015).

[40] See http://en.wikipedia.org/wiki/Kunio_Mikuriya (last accessed 28 June 2015).

[41] See https://www.kent.ac.uk/brussels/about/past-phd-graduates.html (last accessed 28 June 2015) and WCO, http://www.wcoomd.org/en/about-us/wco-secretariat/the_secretary_general.aspx (last accessed 28 June 2015); the topic of Mikuriya's PhD-thesis was The Evolution of Customs Valuation in the Developing World: From "Deregulation" to Developing "State Capacity".

[42] A selected list of references is available at https://en.wikipedia.org/wiki/Kunio_Mikuriya (last accessed 28 June 2015).

[43] See GTCJ, https://www.kluwerlawonline.com/toc.php?area=Journals&mode=bypub&level=4&values=Journals~~Global+Trade+and+Customs+Journal (last accessed 28 June 2015).

[44] See IUCN and WCO, http://www.worldcustomsjournal.org (last accessed 28 June 2015).

- Customs Scientific Journal (WCO Europe Regional Office for Capacity Building)[45]—first volume in 2011.

A WCO research paper series has been started by the WCO in 2009 and in this series 34 papers have been published until 2015.[46]

Since 2006 the WCO is hosting a yearly research conference the so called PICARD conference.[47] The PICARD Programme stands for "Partnerships in Customs Academic Research and Development" and it was created in 2006 in order to intensify the co-operation of the WCO with academic institutions: The PICARD programme was started "recognizing the importance of knowledge and education in the field of Customs, and that little was known about developments internationally, the WCO initiated a series of meetings with Universities and Academic Institutions during 2005".[48]

The overarching aims of the PICARD programme comprise four pillars:

- Standardization Building: keep PICARD Professional Standards up-to-date with evolving Customs competence;
- Whole-of-career Customs Development Paths: integrate strategic human resource management including the Leadership and Management Development programme;
- Recognition of Customs Education and Training Curricula: build bridges between professional Customs training and national education systems;
- Research: maintain a proactive Customs research agenda and platforms at global and regional levels.[49]

Special conferences are hosted for certain topics such as Information Technology or on Informality.

8 Co-Operation with Other International Agencies

The WCO is strongly co-operation with different international organizations and agencies in order to fulfill its mission, e. g. Secretariat of the Convention on International Trade in Endangered Species of Wild Fauna and Flora (CITES),

[45] See WCO, http://www.rocb-europe.org/leftside/academia/scientific-journal (last accessed 28 June 2015).

[46] See WCO, http://www.wcoomd.org/en/topics/research/activities-and-programmes/research_series.aspx (last accessed 28 June 2015).

[47] See WCO, http://www.wcoomd.org/en/topics/research/picard-conference.aspx (last accessed 28 June 2015).

[48] See WCO, http://www.wcoomd.org/en/topics/capacity-building/activities-and-programmes/cb_picard_overview.aspx (last accessed 28 June 2015).

[49] See WCO, http://www.wcoomd.org/en/topics/capacity-building/activities-and-programmes/cb_picard_overview.aspx (last accessed 28 June 2015).

Frontex, INTERPOL, United Nations Office on Drug and Crimes (UNODC), other United Nations bodies, and the advisory group Global Financial Integrity.[50]

Current co-operation for the law enforcement and development in customs matters has several forms and programs. Co-operations are also in force with the Universal Postal Union (UPU), the WTO, the Organization for Economic Co-operation and Development (OECD), the United Nations Conference for Trade and Development (UNCTAD), the World Bank, the Asian Development Bank, the International Civil Aviation Organization (ICAO), the International Air Transport Association (IATA), the Global Express Association (GEA), etc.

9 Pillars of the WCO (WCO Topics)

The WCO covers ten topics or themes under which headlines its work can be summarized:

- Nomenclature and Classification of Goods,
- Valuation,
- Origin,
- Enforcement and Compliance,
- Procedures and Facilitation,
- Capacity Building*,
- Integrity,
- Research*,
- Key Issues* (Customs Laboratories, Compliance & Enforcement Package, Organizational Development Package, Revenue Package) and
- WCO implementing the WTO TFA*.

The asterisk (*) is showing new and emerging major topics.

For many years the WCO had six major topics but in recent years four new topics have been included (*). Capacity building and research are overarching themes that are covering all topics and key issues and the WCO implementation of the WTO TFA are newly emerging "hot" topics for the WCO.

10 Conclusion

The WCO is still developing and evolving—60 years after its foundation—at a high speed and the evolution has a high dynamic:

[50] See WCO, WCO Enforcement Committee Endorses New Initiatives, http://www.wcoomd.org/en/topics/%C2%ACcapacity-building/activities-and-programmes/learning/~/link.aspx?_id=6CC4E37E783449C392C6193FE7C2F616&_z=z (last accessed 28 June 2015).

WCO membership has risen to 180 contracting parties and its most successful legal instruments, which have 153 contracting states (Harmonized System) and 102 contracting states (Revised Kyoto Convention), are growing continuously.

Binding and non-binding legal instruments in six major topics are the pillars of the WCO work. Four new themes are adding four pillars to make ten fields of WCO action.

The WCO is aiming at harmonizing and raising the customs standards around the globe and thereby to enhance trade facilitation and world trade. Together with the WTO and the WCO member states are trying to create universal customs legislation and to reduce trade barriers.

The WCO is creating a hub of customs research and customs co-operation which enables its member states to learn from each other and for developing member states to receive technical assistance and guidance.

Training, capacity building and development packages together with targeted programs and missions are successfully trying to enhance the customs capabilities of member states around the globe.

References

Dallimore C, Wolffgang HM (2014) The framework of standards and the internationalization of supply chain standards. In: Hermann C, Krajewski M, Terhechte J (eds) European yearbook of international economic law. Springer, New York, pp 379–407

Kleine-Holthaus JD (2007a) Das WCO framework of standards. AW-Prax 13(2):57–62

Kleine-Holthaus JD (2007b) Das WCO framework of standards. AW-Prax 13(3):111–114

Mikuriya K (2007) Supply chain security: the customs community's response. World Customs J 1(2):51–59

Weerth C (2008) Basic principles of customs classifications under the harmonized system nomenclature. Glob Trade Customs J 3(2):61–67

Weerth C (2009) The world customs organization: a short history and its legal milestones. Glob Trade Customs J 4(7/8):267–269

Weerth C (2010) The revised Kyoto convention versus the old one: a capable tool for trade facilitation? Glob Trade Customs J 5(2):79–82

Weerth C (2013) Untersuchung der Ansätze des capacity building der world customs organization und des twinning im Zollbereich der Europäischen Union. Grin, Munich

Weerth C (2015a) AEO-Programm in Taiwan. AW-Prax NewsTicker 21(3):55

Weerth C (2015b) WCO: 102 Vertragsstaaten für die revidierte Kyoto-Konvention. AW-Prax NewsTicker 21(7):154

Weerth C (2015c) Sierra Leone & Djibouti: Beitritt zum Harmonisierten system. AW-Prax NewsTicker 21(7):154

Wind I (2007) Harmonized system – what is it all about? Glob Trade Customs J 2(2):79–86

Wolffgang HM, Dallimore C (2012) The World Customs Organization and its role in the system of world trade. In: Herrmann C, Terhechte J (eds) European Yearbook of International Economic Law. Springer, Berlin/New York, pp 613–633

Wolffgang HM, Dallimore C (2013) The valuation of goods for customs purposes. In: Hermann C, Krajewski M, Terhechte J (eds) European yearbook of international economic law. Springer, Berlin/New York, pp 391–411

Part IV
Book Reviews

Valentina Vadi, Bruno de Witte (Eds.), Culture and International Economic Law

Routledge, 2015, ISBN 9780415723268

Walther Michl

Contents

1 Overview

The book collects the transcripts of the talks delivered at an academic conference on the topic of the volume at Maastricht University in June 2013. It comprises an introduction by the editors and a total of 13 specialised articles which are distributed into four parts. Each of them assesses the interplay between culture and economic interests under the lens of a different branch of international law. Part 1 deals with general international law (especially human rights law), part 2 with international economic law, part 3 with international intellectual property law and part 4 with European law.

W. Michl (✉)
Law Faculty, Ludwig Maximilian University, Prof.-Huber-Platz 2, 80539 Munich, Germany
e-mail: michl@jura.uni-muenchen.de

M. Bungenberg et al. (eds.), *European Yearbook of International Economic Law 2016*, European Yearbook of International Economic Law 7,
DOI 10.1007/978-3-319-29215-1_35

2 Summary of the Contents

2.1 Part 1: Culture and Economic Interests in International Law

Part 1 starts with Francesco Francioni's contribution on "Culture, human rights and international law". It gives the reader a good overview over the inclusion of cultural matters in multilateral international instruments from the 1945 Lemkin genocide convention until the 2007 UN Declaration on the rights of Indigenous peoples as well as over the role of culture particularly in international human rights treaties and UNESCO instruments. Francioni rightly points out that there has been a change in the approach towards the concept of "cultural heritage" under international law in that the focus has shifted from the protection of tangible cultural property to the entrenchment of the traditions and customs of a cultural community. He further elaborates on the human rights protection such cultural heritage enjoys and juxtaposes it with the possibility for individuals to invoke their human rights against collective cultural rights, thus highlighting the oft-forgotten limits to the protection of cultural expressions stemming from the inherent horizontal conflict between different layers of fundamental rights. To wrap it up, Francioni also introduces the reader to the emerging criminalization of offences against cultural goods under international law, above all promoted by the 2003 UNESCO Declaration Concerning the Intentional Destruction of Cultural Heritage—a topic of sad timeliness with regard to the appalling devastation of time-honoured cultural sites in the Middle East by ISIS.

Yvonne Donders' subsequent article is regrettably published under the misleading title "The cultural dimension of economic activities in international human rights jurisprudence". Instead of thoroughly examining the triangle between human rights, cultural diversity and the economy, she focuses exclusively on the example of the use of land by Indigenous peoples—thus leaving aside more obvious issues from the wide area of trade in cultural goods whose protection under international human rights instruments would have been a subject worth dealing with. Instead, Ms Donders provides the reader with a long account of specific cases relating to Article 27 of the International Covenant on Civil and Political Rights (ICCPR) which were decided by the Human Rights Committee and comparable case-law emanating from the Inter-American Commission and Court of Human Rights and the African Commission on Human and Peoples' Rights. In a short conclusion, Ms Donders names the criteria as to when a state interference with the land rights of Indigenous peoples amounts to a violation of human rights and highlights the dialogue between the various international supervisory bodies on this issue.

2.2 *Part 2: Culture and Economic Interests in International Economic Law*

Part 2 starts with Valentina Vadi's article on "Cultural heritage in international economic law". The co-editor of the present volume also concerns herself exclusively with the interplay of economic activities and Indigenous culture heritage. She first analyses the case-law of various international bodies that are predominantly concerned with economic matters with regard to elements of Indigenous cultural heritage—particularly instances in which those elements interacted with rules on free trade or animal protection or in which they interfered with the protection of foreign investments. Peculiar emphasis is laid on the conflict between international economic law and cultural practices relating to subsistence harvest. In the ensuing critical assessment Ms Vadi contends that there is both synergy and collision between economic interests and heritage protection. Her most poignant criticism is aimed at the restricted access of the affected indigenous communities to the relevant economic fora and the limited scope of those fora's jurisdiction. She demands that the relationship between international economic law and other branches of international law be addressed in terms of coordination between the various applicable bodies of norms and that especially the competent fora adopt a holistic approach towards the interpretation and application of international economic agreements so that they become open to the influence of general international law, including international cultural law.

Next are two contributions that focus on the rights of Indigenous peoples with regard to their traditional lands, commonly discussed under the caption "consultation vs consent". The focus of Federico Lenzerini's article titled "Investment projects affecting Indigenous heritage" lies on international investment law and starts by a critical assessment of the two main sources of written law on the material issue, Art. 15(2) of ILO Convention No. 169 and Articles 19 and 32 of the UNDRIP. After that, Lenzerini investigates whether there is a right to free, prior and informed consent for Indigenous peoples under customary international law. He concludes that there is enough practice and evidence to assume an opinio juris in favour of a mandatory consultation process but in most cases no obligation to obtain consent. He goes on to argue, however, that Indigenous Peoples do have a full veto on exploitation projects affecting their lands "when an investment project may seriously prejudice the very cultural identity and integrity of the Indigenous communities concerned" (p. 84)—a standard that is probably too imprecise to have any palpable effect in practice.

In contrast to that, Sarah Sargent's contribution "What's in a name? The contested meaning of free, prior and informed consent in international financial law and Indigenous rights" focuses much more intensely on the aforementioned written rules and juxtaposes them with the standards of the World Bank's International Finance Corporation (IFC) with regard to Indigenous cultural heritage. The latter clearly exclude all sorts of veto rights and are only triggered in certain specific situations that entail potentially adverse impacts to the Indigenous community concerned. Sargent claims that this is incompatible with the standards of the ILO Convention and the UNDRIP although she regards the IFC's current stance as an advancement from the even less charitable positions it had had in the past. Sargent finally suggests that the business model proposed by former UN Special Rapporteur on Indigenous Rights James Anaya be used as a basis for any future business concerning Indigenous land.

Mira Burri's article "The trade versus culture discourse—Tracing its evolution in global law" focuses on the core of the book's topic and investigates into the origins of the perceived opposition between trade and culture. Burri convincingly shows that the issue is a product of Europe's relatively weak position in the audiovisual industry which led to calls for protectionist measures on the old continent. She rightly points out the exceptional nature of Art. IV GATT 1947 and explains the rise of tensions in the Uruguay Round preceding the establishment of the WTO (again between the Europeans and the United States). Burri contends that the irreconcilable differences between the positions of those two main actors are reflected in the design and substance of current WTO law, especially in the highly unusual positive list approach under the GATS. She then describes the UNESCO Convention on Cultural Diversity as the main instrument to counterbalance the economic rules of WTO law but points out that it contains very few obligations, is substantially incomplete and ambiguous in its relation towards other international instruments. Consequently, she rightly gauges it as an instrument of soft rather than hard law with only a minimal impact on the WTO regime as she concludes from the *China—Publications and Audiovisual Products* case. Her final assessment is thus that the lack of interplay between world trade and cultural law leads to legal uncertainty in the realm of international commerce and has so far hindered innovative solutions.

Ana Filipa Vrdoljak's subsequent article on "International exchange and trade in cultural objects" also has a strong historical perspective. A large part of her contribution is concerned with the history of multilateral efforts to regulate the international trade in cultural objects in the inter-war time under the umbrella of the League of Nations and its sub-organisations. She then contrasts the legal instruments of that period with the current UNESCO rules and detects a shift of balance between the aims of preserving national cultural property and facilitating cultural exchange across borders towards a pre-eminence of fighting the illicit trade in cultural objects. Vrdoljak finally points out that the same can be said of most regional and national instruments on the issue and suggests that the two aforementioned aims be regarded as mutually reinforcing rather than mutually exclusive.

2.3 Part 3: Culture and Economic Interests in International Intellectual Property Law

Part 3 is kicked off by Antonietta di Blase's contribution under the caption "Traditional knowledge—Cultural heritage or intellectual property right?". The initial pages are dedicated to the question of how traditional knowledge (TK) can be defined, what its sedes materiae in international treaties is and what the general limits to its protection are, above all the concept of public domain. She then commits a part of the article to the relationship between the instruments protecting TK and the TRIPs agreement. Di Blase rightly points out that ring-fencing TK would probably be inconsistent with TRIPs although there is no explicit case-law on the issue as of yet. However, she contends that Art. 27 paras. 2 and 3 TRIPs would give the Contracting Parties enough leeway for a TK-friendly interpretation. She observes that the States Parties who want to use that possibility tend to resort to instruments outside the scope of TRIPs, e.g. principles applicable to intangible cultural heritage, and thus avoid common titles such as patents or trade-marks. Finally, di Blase gives an overview over the rules on TK stipulated in a number of selected bilateral trade and investment agreements.

Lucas Lixinski's and Louise Buckingham's ensuing contribution has the lengthy title "Propertization, safeguarding and the cultural commons—The turf wars of intangible cultural heritage and traditional cultural expressions". Its core is a juxtaposition of intangible cultural heritage (ICH) and traditional cultural expressions (TCEs) as twin concepts with different institutional anchorings—UNESCO for ICH, WIPO for TCEs. The authors analyse the prerequisites for the protection of traditional culture under both frameworks and, subsequently, their commonalities and differences. They conclude that ICH focuses on social practices while TCEs are concerned with the artefact and contend that that difference has significant impacts on the construction of the two regimes and ultimately on the respective mechanisms of protection. As a consequence, Lixinski and Buckingham characterize the TCEs regime as being harder and more legal which, on the flip side, entails the propertisation of culture at the expense of promoting the circulation of ideas. This a development on which the authors take a critical but balanced stance towards the end of their article.

Finally, Lucky Belder digs into "The digitization of public cultural heritage collections and copyright in public private partnership projects". Her main focus lies on the copyright problems which come along with making library, museum and archive contents accessible via digital media. She also highlights the important role of public private partnerships with global companies such as Google in this context which are used to provide additional funds for the public institutions involved—a phenomenon that leads to an increased emphasis on the economic relevance of cultural heritage. In order to demonstrate the practical difficulties attached to this approach, she undertakes an in-depth analysis of the contracts concluded between Google and the Royal Dutch and British Libraries. Towards the end, she links the topic to the Digital Agenda of the European Union and points out relevant matters emerging from the revision process of the European Copyright law, especially the fairly recent Orphan Works Directive 2012/28/EU and Directive 2013/37/EU amending Directive 2003/98/EC on the Re-use of Public Sector Information.

2.4 Part 4: Culture and Economic Interests in European Law

Part 4 starts with a useful overview over the EU's stakes in the domain of culture by Bruno de Witte under the title "Market integration and cultural diversity in EU law". De Witte contrasts the Union's tough stance on cultural issues in its external trade policy with its relatively low-key role in internal matters due to the restricted nature of the competences under Art. 167 TFEU. He describes the ECJ's approach towards cultural diversity in its decisions on negative integration provisions and takes a particularly critical view of the case-law on free movement which he considers "patchy and unpredictable" as exemplified by the *UTECA* and *Las* cases. As far as positive integration is concerned, de Witte refers to the far-reaching leeway of the EU legislator under the umbrella of the internal market which leads to both a prevalence of economic considerations and a shrinking room to manoeuvre for the Member States.

Rachael Craufurd Smith's contribution "EU media law—Cultural policy or business as usual" complements this overview by examining the nitty-gritty of secondary EU law. She highlights that the initial proposals for European media regulation were driven by political objectives, i.e. creating a European perspective in the lamentably fragmented media coverage on EU issues and safeguarding media pluralism in the Member States. However, all actually important legal acts on the issue have been adopted based on the EU's internal market competence and consequently must seek to abolish rather than to erect trade barriers. Craufurd Smith carefully examines to what extent cultural policies are nevertheless pursued in the Television Without Frontiers Directive, the Audiovisual Media Services Directive and the E-Commerce Directive. Moreover, she describes the role of culture in the EU's industrial and competition policies.

Last but not least, Evangelia Psychogiopoulou examines the role of "Culture in the EU external economic relations", i.e. the place occupied by culture in the EU's trade or trade-related agreements, especially the influence of protocols on cultural cooperation attached to such agreements. The examples chosen are the Economic Partnership Agreement with the Cariforum group of countries, the Free Trade Agreement with Korea and the Association Agreement with the Central American group of countries. Psychogiopoulou describes the various provisions in those agreements which enable horizontal and sectoral cultural cooperation with a clear focus on the coproduction of audiovisual works and their position with regard to specific quotas such as e.g. those stipulated in the Audiovisual Media Services Directive. The author's main argument is that the principles of mutual supportiveness and of simultaneous accommodation of both the UNESCO Convention on the Protection and Promotion of the Diversity of Cultural Expressions and other international obligations require changes to the kinds of agreements the EU chooses to negotiate and conclude.

3 Emerging Lessons

The main lesson to be taken from the contributions seems to be that the international economic fora do not pay enough attention to cultural matters in that they focus too narrowly on the applicable trade rules. There is an urgent need for some kind of harmonious interpretation of the economic agreements at issue in order to accommodate the legitimate cultural concerns of the parties involved. Such a development is also necessary to effectuate the individual rights connected to cultural issues as is evident from the example of the exploitation of Indigenous lands. These issues will need to be addressed in greater detail in future examinations and deserve additional scholarly attention.

4 Particular Strengths of the Book

The particular added value of the book as compared to other academic works is that it provides a comprehensive overview over a broad variety of issues arising at the interface between culture and international trade. The main factor contributing to its high quality is the choice of distinguished authors who had had previous experience in the field they treated. Moreover, the contributions fit well together within the different parts of the volume so that redundancies and duplications are largely avoided. An asset of particular value is the inclusion of generous bibliographies at the end of each article which provide excellent guidance for further readings.

5 Addressees

The volume is of particular interest to all academics that are looking for a reliable starting point for further investigations in the area of trade and culture. Moreover, it can be very helpful for practitioners working on an issue that is treated in one or more of the contributions.

Thomas Cottier, Rosa M. Lastra, Christian Tietje, Lucía Satragno (Eds.), The Rule of Law in Monetary Affairs: World Trade Forum

Cambridge University Press, 2014, ISBN 9781107063631

Alexander Thiele

The global financial crisis as well as the following Eurocrisis were surely a failure of economics. But they were and are also a failure of law: Neither the national nor the European or international legal framework were able to prevent the almost-meltdown of the worldwide financial system or the economic collapse of Greece. The question how to remove these legal deficiencies in order to ensure financial stability for the future has since then become one of the major topics in the public debate. And in quite a few areas we can already find significant changes: New institutions such as the Financial Stability Board or the European Systemic Risk Board (ESRB) have been established in order to acquire a better understanding of systemic risk. Rating agencies are under stricter supervision and banking regulation has at least tightened slightly (though not significantly).

When redesigning the legal framework, however, one faces the difficulty that there is no clear consensus amongst economists what actually needs to be done to achieve financial stability or at least a higher stability than before. Especially with respect to monetary policy and the function of central banks the opinions differ tremendously. There is thus no common and generally accepted economic concept the law would just need to try to incorporate into clear and binding rules for the relevant actors. And then again, it can clearly not be the function of the law to decide these economic disputes with binding force for the future: What if the concept chosen should prove to have been the wrong one? The law so far has reacted to these specialities in two ways: Firstly by relying on soft-law rather than hard-law—foremost when it comes to international arrangements—as this allows more flexibility especially in times of crisis. The states prefer to have the last word since it will usually be them that have to pay the bill if anything should go awry.

A. Thiele (✉)
Georg-August-University of Göttingen, Nikolausberger Weg 17, 37073 Göttingen, Germany
e-mail: alexander.thiele@jura.uni-goettingen.de

M. Bungenberg et al. (eds.), *European Yearbook of International Economic Law 2016*, European Yearbook of International Economic Law 7,
DOI 10.1007/978-3-319-29215-1_36

And secondly, even where we find hard-law the actors are usually equipped with wide discretion. This last aspect was rightly pointed out just recently by the European Court of Justice with respect to the highly disputed OMT-Program the ECB had announced (and only announced!) in 2012.

But is this really the best that law can do in order to contribute to international financial stability? What other normative principles might be able to guide the formulation of policies in this area that affects not only individuals but also the society at large? Decisions taken in this field are far from being mere technical matters and therefore also need sufficient democratic legitimacy. But how can we achieve that? And how can we assure adequate accountability of the relevant actors?

These are just some of the questions asked in the book "The Rule of Law in Monetary Affairs" edited by *Thomas Cottier*, *Rosa M. Lastra*, *Christian Tietje* and (as associate editor) *Lucía Satragno*. Together with 22 other renowned (and mainly European) contributors the editors seek to explore and identify these underlying principles and norms that might contribute to a better (respectively safer) international financial system. They thereby also consider possible common principles with international trade and investment law—monetary affairs have indeed always shown a close interaction with trade and investment (what can be easily confirmed by a brief look at the former Bretton Woods system). The editors make clear, however, that the book does not try to aim at answering all the raised questions once and for all. But as they rightly point out, in order to solve a problem one has to start by asking the right questions. And from this perspective the book appears more than successful as it delivers useful impulses for the ongoing debate by not only giving a competent overview of the current situation but also by proposing first possible solutions for many of the identified problems.

In order to achieve its aim the book is divided into four parts that focus on specific areas. Each part includes between four and seven articles. The following will focus on the first part and will look at the other parts only briefly without discussing all the articles in detail. However, this does obviously not mean that these parts were of any lesser value than the first (introductory) part.

The introductory part with contributions by *Christian Tietje*, *Mario Giovanoli*, *Rosa M. Lastra* and *Jean-Victor Louis* is devoted to the foundations and evolution of the international monetary system. According to the editors this part wants to give an overview of the international monetary system, its present state and likely future development, and describes the current international architecture and institutional aspects. It thereby shows the lack of existing global substantive principles and therefore acts as an (important) introduction for the following parts, making clear why we need a discussion about the role of law in this area in the first place. Special attention is thereby paid to the "unique" role of central banks whose function has indeed changed significantly as they have more and more transformed from mere technical institutions to important actors on the political arena—the ECB is probably the best (but surely not the only) example.

In the first article *Christian Tietje* takes a more historical perspective of the role of law in monetary affairs and tries to develop legal elements of an international financial and monetary order for the future. *Tietje* rightly states that any legal framework in this area has always had to try to find an equilibrium between strengthening regulation and supervision on the one hand and the essential freedoms in financial monetary markets on the other hand. What is new according to *Tietje* is the fact that strengthening regulation and supervision today will only be successful if one takes the need for international regulatory and supervisory cooperation and coordination into account as pure national solutions seem hardly convincing. After giving a brief overview of the development of the international monetary system from 1929 until today *Tietje* concludes that the current international financial and monetary system appears (too) fragmented and incomplete even after the reform efforts since 2008. He thereby identifies two main deficiencies: Firstly the missing regulatory link between trade, finance, sovereign debt and currency issues and secondly the dominance of soft law that stands in the way of a stable international monetary system. The right answer to this can obviously not be the demand for one single "hard" regulation for the whole financial system. This would not only be practically impossible to achieve but also unwise from a legal perspective: Such a regulation would obviously fail to sufficiently consider regional differences and the complexity of the whole matter. And *Tietje* therefore rightly does not propose such a simple answer but rather points to certain principles one will have to consider for an adequate legal solution. These (among others) include (1) the consideration of the necessary domestication of financial markets and products that automatically limits international harmonisation, coordination and cooperation, (2) the necessity of integrating macro- and micro-prudential regulation and supervision but also (3) the adherence to the constitutional values of the UN Charter as well as (4) the integration of the real economy, financial markets, foreign investment and sovereign debt and (5) political (and not administrative!) leadership. One will probably more or less agree to all these principles. What *Tietje's* analysis clearly shows, however, is the fact that we still have quite a long way to go.

Mario Giovanoli takes a closer look at institutional aspects, especially with respect to the actors setting international financial standards (IFS). When it comes to stable financial markets these IFS obviously play a dominant role. Basel II, the international regulatory regime for banks, with its reliance on (complex) bank-internal risk models in actual fact was one of the reasons why banking was able to get so out of control in the first place. Yet the IFS themselves are not set by national parliaments but by International Standard Setting Bodies (ISSB) with the Basle Committee probably being the most prominent. These ISSB appear problematic from a legal perspective for several reasons that *Giovanoli* takes a closer look at (after a brief historical overview): the legitimacy of the standard setting process and the institutions involved, the status of "soft law" rules in international and municipal law, and the implementation of the standards and legal remedies in case of disputes. In his conclusion he finds some reluctance of various financial centres to implement international financial standards. He explains this behaviour by competing national interests and the fear of overregulation and additional costs for the industry. But this reluctance of the states may also relate to the shortcomings as regards legitimacy of the ISSBs and the standard setting process as well as the lack of legal remedies in case of possible violations. However: Even after the financial crisis we have not found a convincing solution regarding the right procedure for the setting of IFS—the Basle Committee is currently working on Basle IV (with the Financial Stability Board taking only marginal influence). And *Giovanoli* does not present one either. Instead he recommends keeping the limits of IFS in mind: They are no substitutes for the prudent behaviour of all the stakeholders, including not only financial institutions and their regulators, but also monetary authorities and politicians. In other words: Neither IFS nor other legal frameworks alone will be able to stabilise the financial markets.

Rosa M. Lastra then turns to the function of central banks in monetary affairs and analyses the evolving role of the US Federal Reserve System and the ECB. Central banking has clearly changed since the financial crisis in 2008. With the help of extraordinary measures the central banks—especially the ECB with its OMT-Program—have helped significantly to prevent a new financial and economic collapse. The financial crisis and even more so the Eurocrisis thus have turned central banks from mere technical institutions that guarantee price stability to important political players responsible also for financial stability. Consequently central banks play a much bigger role also in the public debate—there is probably no regular newspaper reader who would not know the names of *Janet Yellen* or *Mario Draghi*. However, such a mandate change raises difficult legal questions. This is true especially for the ECB whose statute makes it quite clear that the primary objective of the ESCB is price stability—the procedure before the German Constitutional Court (GCC) regarding the OMT-Program made the difficulties more than obvious, even though the ECJ rightly pointed out that the GCC at least in this case was far of the economic and legal track. But even though the statute of the Fed appears to be much more "flexible" in this sense, it remains unclear what such a mandate change might imply for instance for the legal relationship of the central bank to the government. *Lastra* therefore rightly states that the proper understanding of central banking law requires a mix of administrative law, commercial law and international law as well as a constant dialogue with economists. She rightly demands a further development of central banking law and the aspects discussed in her article mark the areas where further research is needed.

The first part is finalised with an article by *Jean-Victor Louis* who comments on the European Economic Monetary Union (EMU) and the law. He thereby concentrates on two aspects: The transformation and evolution of the role of the national central banks (NCBs) within the Eurosystem and the difficulty of insertion of the euro area into the global system. The NCBs play an important role within the Eurosystem and as the ongoing crisis in Greece shows this is true especially in times of crisis: Emergency Liquidity Assistance (ELA) is granted by the NCBs (and not the ECB-Council). However, *Louis* points out that the ECB is not just another central bank within this system next to the NCBs but acts as the "captain" of the team. There are thus provisions within the treaty that establish this (normative) primacy of the ECB. With respect to ELA for instance the ECB-Council may not decide to grant ELA, but can demand the NCB at any time to stop granting ELA immediately. Yet, despite the fact that the NCBs' Governors within the ESCB therefore act as independent experts in the general interest of the Union (and not their national interest) we find no EU rules for the appointment of the Governors (except their term of office). The "Europeanisation" of their task is thus not reflected in the "Europeanisation" of their appointment. And this is true also for the NCBs themselves. They remain national institutions as there are no European provisions that would allow to harmonise for instance the statutes of NCBs. As the behaviour of the German governor *Jens Weidmann* shows this may lead to certain "loyalty-problems". *Weidmann* not only made it quite clear that he disagreed with the official policy of the ECB-Council he was a member of, but even showed up before the GCC to criticise the decisions within a formal court hearing. *Louis* therefore rightly raises the question whether both aspects should not be changed in the future as the loyalty of NCBs and their governors is a necessary condition for maintaining the credibility of the ESCB as a whole. A European appointment procedure might help to make clear that NCBs within the ESCB are European (and not national) in nature and to avoid similar behaviour in the future. As regards the second aspect *Louis* points to the problems that arise due to the fact that the euro area is usually not represented within international institutions as a whole but by the respective national representatives (central bank governors or supervisors). This can amount to problems especially with respect to the IMF which is also why the European Commission recently published a paper including proposals how to achieve a single seat at the IMF for the whole euro area. However, this will obviously only be possible with a change of the IMF-Statute that currently only allows a membership of "countries".

The second part of the book includes articles by *Bernard Hoekman*, *Claus D. Zimmermann*, *Iain Macneil*, *Nadia Rendak*, *Annamaria Viterbo* and *Isabel Feichtner* and focuses on specific policy issues in monetary affairs. The articles cover a wide range of topics: Global governance of international competitiveness spillovers (*Hoekman*); global benchmark interest rates (*Zimmermann*); credit rating agencies and their regulation and financial stability (*Macneil*); monitoring and surveillance of the international monetary system and what might be learnt from the trade field (*Rendak*); the impact of sovereign debt on EU monetary affairs (*Viterbo*) and taxation in times of austerity as a question of political economy (*Feichtner*). All authors show that significant deficiencies within the current legal framework still remain. *Zimmermann* for instance takes a closer look at the Libor-Scandal that has not only led to various banks being fined—beginning with Barclays Bank in 2012—but also initiated a completely revised legal framework for the setting of the Libor rates. *Zimmermann* mainly agrees with these reforms but recommends to at least consider to replace private benchmark rates by alternative benchmarks based on central bank key rates. As regards credit-rating agencies *Macneil* stresses that the regulation following the financial crisis has addressed many of the existing problems such as accountability. Yet, what remains problematic is the issue of over-reliance on ratings by regulators and investors. This was indeed one of the major problems in the run up to the crisis as even the supervisory authorities—for instance the German BaFin—pointed out that the complexity of the financial products made it simply impossible to analyse their risk without the help of credit rating agencies. However, it seems more than doubtful that this reliance-problem will decline due to the reduced leverage of the whole banking system with the implementation of Basel III as *Macneil* suggests: Basel III is no more than a tiny step in the right direction, still mainly relies on internal risk-models without proposing a sufficient clear cut leverage ratio. The reliance problem thus remains to be solved.

The third part looks at the interaction between WTO law and monetary affairs with contributions by *Robert Howse*, *Juan Marchetti*, *Michele Ruta*, *Robert Teh*, *Gabrielle Z. Marceau, John J. Maughan, Mathias Kende. Howse* seeks to find possibilities for an equitable integration of monetary and financial matters, trade and sustainable development. According to *Howse*, the concept of equity thereby can function as a form of "overarching-principle" to support such a coherence as most of the already existing rules depend explicitly or implicitly on some concept of fairness. This approach is surely innovative and with looking at the existing norms first it is surely superior to any concept that wants to create a completely new international order based on such a vague concept as "global justice". But still: This "norm-based equity approach" will only be able to deliver accepted results if one agrees to the form of equity apparently rooted in the existing norms (that is then used for the interpretation of others). Does this appear realistic, especially in times where German legal scholars cannot even agree on the general purpose of the European "No-Bail-Out-Clause"? The other articles of this part look at trade imbalances and multilateral trade cooperation (*Marchetti, Ruta and Teh*); the WTO dispute settlement mechanism in matters involving exchange rates and trade (*Marceau, Maughan*) and monetary affairs in the WTO trade policy review (*Kende*).

The fourth and last part of the book finally analyses the quest for law in monetary policy and includes articles by *Thomas Cottier, Lucía Satragno, Ernst-Ulrich Petersmann, Chistine Kaufmann, Rolf H. Weber, Markus Krajewski, Kern Alexander, François Gianviti* and *Federico Lupo-Pasini. Krajewski* examines the relation between human rights and austerity programmes and thereby shows that the austerity policy of the last 5 years that has been rightly criticised from an economic perspective, also has various legal implications that need to be taken into account within the process of decision-making. Effected are mainly the so-called "second-dimension rights", that is economic, social and cultural rights (ESC rights) which, however, are of no lower value than other human rights. *Krajewski* makes clear that these ESC rights have to play a vital role when it comes to the design of any austerity programme. Austerity programmes thus remain possible but only as long as the measures taken can be justified on the basis of a careful consideration of their effects and of any available alternative. Looking at the current situation in Greece in the summer of 2015 with an unemployment rate above 25 % and an economy more than 25 % below the pre-crisis level one is unsure whether this legal necessity was fully respected when designing these specific economic austerity-programmes—yet without wanting to justify the more than disturbing behaviour of the Greek government during the negotiations (especially in June 2015). In his article that takes a look at international economic law and macro-prudential regulation *Alexander* concludes that the financial crisis triggered intensive regulatory reform efforts to enhance bank risk management and the use of micro-prudential and macro-prudential regulation to achieve financial stability (though one might doubt that these regulatory reforms have actually led to significant changes when it comes to micro-prudential regulation). *Alexander* pleads for a stronger link between micro-prudential supervision of individual banks with broader oversight of the financial system and thus to macro-economic policy. And indeed: It remains extremely difficult for supervisors as well as regulators to mirror detected systemic-risks adequately in micro-prudential rules for the individual institutions. *Alexander* recommends a stronger focus on macroeconomic factors, such as liquidity risks, but also capital adequacy standards that have linkages and reference points in the broader macro economy (for example countercyclical capital rations). Creating this important linkage will definitely remain one of the major tasks of the coming years. The other articles of this last part look at the potential of law and legal methodology in monetary affairs (*Cottier* and *Satragno*), show ways towards a multilayered governance in monetary affairs (*Petersmann*), analyse transparency and monetary affairs (*Kaufmann* and *Weber*), look at the relationship between monetary policy and exchange rate policy (*Gianviti*) and—last but not least—describe the uneasy relationship between monetary stability and investment protection (*Lupo-Pasini*).

To summarise: The book makes clear why it appears to be so difficult to find a functioning legal framework when it comes to international monetary affairs. Yet, it not only asks the right questions but will surely also help to find the right answers. Anything one might miss? Maybe a closer look at a possible insolvency order for states—the situation in Greece has made the necessity for such a legal framework more than obvious. And a concluding article bringing back together the four parts of the book and thereby marking the direction the discussion should go in the future would have been helpful. But otherwise: Goal completed!

Karl Sauvant and Federico Ortino, Improving the International Investment Law and Policy Regime: Options for the Future

Helsinki: Ministry for Foreign Affairs of Finland, 2013; ISBN 978-952-281-217-9

Julien Chaisse

The e-book published in 2013 by Karl Sauvant (Columbia University) and Federico Ortino (King's College London) is an important addition to the literature on international investment law. In a nutshell, this book's contribution is to outline the key features of the international investment regime, identify drivers of change, discuss critical issues, and describe some proposals for reform of the regime. The present review will focus on the suggestions put forward by Sauvant and Ortino and the challenges facing their design and implementation.

The first three Parts of the book set the stage and usefully revisit the structure and changing dynamics of the international investment regime. The three first Parts discuss the key developments which have occurred during the past 2 decades and which are most likely to bear directly on the future evolution of the said regime. The authors rightly point out at the impact of emerging markets and the fact that they play an increasingly prominent role in the world foreign direct investment (FDI) market.[1] At the same time, government expectations about the role and economic

[1] Several developing countries, such as the People's Republic of China (PRC), India, and Korea, represent both the capital-exporting and capital-importing nations. See Ranjan (2014), p. 419, 429–430; Congyan (2009), p. 457, 499; Bath and Nottage (2011).

J. Chaisse (✉)
Faculty of Law, The Chinese University of Hong Kong, Office No 523, Lee Shau Kee Building, 5th Floor, Hong Kong, China

Centre for Financial Regulation and Economic Development (CeFRED), Shatin Campus, Hong Kong, New Territories, China
e-mail: julien.chaisse@cuhk.edu.hk

M. Bungenberg et al. (eds.), *European Yearbook of International Economic Law 2016*, European Yearbook of International Economic Law 7,
DOI 10.1007/978-3-319-29215-1_37

impact of FDI are significantly changing.[2] Importantly for the international community, the number of treaty-based investment disputes is increasing which demonstrates the legalization of investment relationships.[3] As argued by Sauvant and Ortino, such changes are changing the whole landscape of investment rule-making as there is a greater influence of civil society and the current negotiations in the Trans-pacific partnership (TPP) or Transatlantic Partnership (TTIP) can only provide perfect examples.

The changing dynamics of international investment law and policy allows the authors to reassess critical issues affecting the current international investment regime. In this respect, Sauvant and Ortino identify exactly six types of issues which question the legitimacy of international investment law and policy. To start with, there is the purpose of the regime, i.e. the main or ultimate purpose of future treaty-making, which should be clearly identifies by the negotiators. Secondly, the scope of IIAs is an important point because there are several critical issues dealing with the reach of the international investment regime, in particular the scope of IIAs. Although identifying the appropriate scope will depend primarily on the overall goal(s) of an agreement negotiated by the contracting parties, several complex and interconnected options are available to states to make sure that IIAs are indeed effective in achieving economic goals. Thirdly, the substantive content of investment standards is a growing concern as tribunal interpretations often have broaden the scope of many provisions and hence the duties of many governments. Fourthly, Sauvant and Ortino reviews the specific issues raised by investment arbitration. By its very nature and the confidentiality it requires, this type of international dispute settlement mechanism has triggered a number of criticism. Fifthly, the fragmentation of international investment law is also a great concern. Sauvant and Ortino points out at the fact that "States, investors and other stakeholders are now recognizing the need to develop mechanisms that move towards greater coherence. Mechanisms may be needed to achieve a greater alignment of voluntary and binding rules, to address overlapping and "underlapping" jurisdictions and to balance investment protection alongside broader concerns about the impact and effectiveness of international investment as a contributor to development."[4] Finally, a sixth concern relates to the very institutional structure (or lack of) of the regime. While the number of investment claims has sharply increased over the last years, there are still issues as for the enforcement of awards which raised the issues of effectiveness of the international investment law and policy. In this respect, it is essential for the future to improve the regime's institutional framework.

---

[2] See Alvarez (2009), p. 943, 957–959. The purpose of the BIT is to encourage the FDI between the two State-Parties, which hopefully leads to economic growth for both state-parties. On the economic impact of IIAs, see generally Chaisse and Bellak (2015).

[3] See Choi (2007), p. 725, 731. See also Chaisse (2013), p. 332, 334–35.

[4] Sauvant K and Ortino F (2013) Improving the International Investment Law and Policy Regime—Options for the Future. Ministry of Foreign Affairs of Finland, Helsinki, p. 88.

The book last part formulates five solutions to improve the current regime; namely the fact-finding processes, the possibility of consensus-building Working Groups, the formulation of a Model International Investment Agreement, the building of specific mechanisms to improve the investment regime, and commencing the intergovernmental processes. The present review discusses three of these five important proposals. The first important proposal offered by Sauvant and Ortino deals with the fact-finding processes. Such an option is important in the current debate as the investment regime is heavily fragmented and "formalized fact-finding processes could be of assistance to identify and analyze the strengths and weaknesses of the regime and to provide an authoritative account of the current situation."[5] Such processes would require input from a broad range of stakeholders across national and regional boundaries which are detailed by the authors. Sauvant and Ortino also formulate the interesting proposal of a "Model International Investment Agreement." It is true that no international model investment agreement exists which could provide a benchmark for various governments. Sauvant and Ortino are convincing when they say that the "timing for such a Model may be right, given the accumulated stock of agreements and the confluence of a number of important negotiations."[6] Finally, Sauvant and Ortino suggest specific mechanisms to improve the investment regime. Among them, there is the idea that one or two countries could initiate an open stand-alone intergovernmental process to explore the desirability and feasibility of a plurilateral approach (which may eventually turn into a multilateral approach), beginning with the purpose of such an approach. The authors identify the G8 and the G20 as potential candidates for launching such a process. In any event, they agree that any intergovernmental/negotiating process, whether undertaken on a multilateral or plurilateral level, should be supported by an international consensus-building process similar to the one pursued in the preparations of the "Guiding Principles for Business and Human Rights".[7]

Karl Sauvant and Federico Ortino's e-book is both an outstanding work of scholarship and well written. I have no doubt that the book will become an indispensable source for future research in the fields of legal and political science and in other disciplines concerned with international investment law and arbitration; this is mainly because it lays out a number of important proposals which should be seriously taken into account (and if necessary refined) by policy-makers and academics. The international investment regime has reached a stage in its development when we need to reflect on its weaknesses, to ensure that it keeps growing, and, most importantly, to achieve the goals that were assigned to it at the

[5] Sauvant K and Ortino F (2013) Improving the International Investment Law and Policy Regime—Options for the Future. Ministry of Foreign Affairs of Finland, Helsinki, p. 92.

[6] Sauvant K and Ortino F (2013) Improving the International Investment Law and Policy Regime—Options for the Future. Ministry of Foreign Affairs of Finland, Helsinki, p. 112.

[7] See Sauvant K and Ortino F (2013) Improving the International Investment Law and Policy Regime—Options for the Future. Ministry of Foreign Affairs of Finland, Helsinki, p. 136.

beginning: to promote freer capital flows with the aim of ensuring economic development throughout the world.

References

Alvarez JE (2009) Contemporary foreign investment law: an "empire of law" or the "law of empire"? Ala Law Rev 60(4):943–976

Bath V, Nottage L (eds) (2011) Foreign investment and dispute resolution law and practice in Asia. Routledge, London

Chaisse J (2013) Exploring the confines of international investment and domestic health protections—general exceptions clause as a forced perspective. Am J Law Med 39:332–360

Chaisse J, Bellak C (2015) Navigating the expanding universe of investment treaties—creation and use of critical index. J Int Econ Law 18(1):79–115

Choi WM (2007) The present and future of investor state dispute paradigm. J Int Econ Law 10 (3):725–747

Congyan C (2009) China-US BIT negotiations and the future of investment treaty regime. J Int Econ Law 12(2):457–506

Ranjan P (2014) India and bilateral investment treaties—a changing landscape. ICSID Rev 9 (2):419–450

Diane Desierto, Public Policy in International Economic Law: The ICESCR in Trade, Finance, and Investment

Oxford University Press, 2015, ISBN 9780198716938

Kholofelo Kugler

Diane Desierto's book adds to the raging debate on how public policy objectives can and should be incorporated into international economic law (IEL); she focuses on the areas of international trade, finance, and investment. She deems the economic, social, and cultural (ESC) rights enshrined in the International Covenant on Economic, Social, and Cultural Rights, 1966 (ICESCR) such as the rights to self-determination, work, social security, health, education, and to participate in cultural life important international values that should be weaved into the current IEL regime through deliberate, consistent, and systematic means. Of particular concern to her is inherent global inequality, which can be exacerbated when ICESCR rights are disregarded due to the unequal balance of power in the economic relations between developing and developed countries. Desierto's contribution to the current scholarship in this field is a well-researched and balanced monograph that explores ways in which State Parties to the ICESCR (State Parties) and the IEL architecture can operationalise and meaningfully interpret international ESC rights obligations when they cross paths.

In Chapter 1, Desierto introduces her point of departure i.e. inequality is inextricably linked to international law and global economic relations because the economic and political supremacy of some countries over others is firmly and historically entrenched. Although the ideals of 'fairness' and the 'international rule of law' are etched into the international legal psyche, all States are not created

K. Kugler (✉)
Advisory Centre on WTO Law, Avenue Giuseppe-Motta 31-33, 1202 Geneva, Switzerland
e-mail: kholofelo.kugler@acwl.ch

M. Bungenberg et al. (eds.), *European Yearbook of International Economic Law 2016*, European Yearbook of International Economic Law 7,
DOI 10.1007/978-3-319-29215-1_38

equal and thus she engages with the question of inequality and the role of IEL and its institutions in the amelioration and eventual eradication of unjustifiable inequality.[1] She posits that modern international law has embraced the task of addressing inequality through the recognition and implementation of global ESC rights as embodied in the ICESCR, which has been ratified by 164 states to date.[2] Notwithstanding the pervasiveness of these ideals and rights in legal and political discourse, they have not found full incorporation into the design, interpretation, and implementation of the international trade, finance, and investment framework. Desierto concedes that the isolation of international human rights law (IHRL), including the ICESCR, lies equally in its lack of cohesion in enforcement, clarity in scope, and binding effect. Further, the lack of jurisprudence and, hence, the dearth of interpretative guidance has also not helped the ICESCR's plight. Furthermore, the mainstreaming of the 40-year old ICESCR in the development cooperation activities of the United Nations (UN) remains a work in progress, additionally limiting its reach. Nevertheless, she argues that IHRL must no longer be perceived as a burden that IEL is obliged to bear and be "whittled down into a matter of *ex post* treaty interpretation".[3] Desierto supports the coupling of IHRL and IEL in *ex ante* international law making and institution-building, as well as in the *ex post* meaningful interpretation of ESC rights in IEL disputes.

The crux of Desierto's argument is that State Parties' decisions to regulate economic activities under IEL should be designed with the view of preserving the public interest as manifested in their obligation to respect, protect, and fulfil the rights contained in the ICESCR. The Committee for Economic Social and Cultural Rights (CESCR) has stressed the importance of international cooperation for the development and realisation of ESC rights. Desierto recalls that the ICESCR supports the integration of IHRL and IEL by requiring State Parties to integrate ESC rights into, for example, their development activities, fiscal decisions, international commercial contracts, and structural adjustment responsibilities. She maintains that ICESCR obligations can be successfully incorporated into the interpretation of State Parties' economic obligations. Even where treaties do not explicitly reference the ICESCR but allude to IHRL or States' public policy, ESC rights that find expression in the ICESCR can be read into the treaty in the course of its interpretation. She proposes that State Parties redraft their economic treaties in order to build-in ICESCR compliance into the international trade, finance, and investment regime. Her overall proposal rejects generalisations across all IEL institutions and regimes but rather favours a case-by-case and tailored approach to how public policy couched in the ICESR could be vindicated within State Parties' decision-making process within each of these regimes.

[1] Desierto (2015), p. 7.

[2] OHCHR, Status of Ratification Interactive Dashboard, http://indicators.ohchr.org/ (last accessed 21 September 2015).

[3] Desierto (2015), p. 12.

Chapter 2 discusses the role of the State under the ICESCR. At the onset, Desierto highlights the ideological rift that, to a large extent, still prevails over the treatment of civil and political rights vis-à-vis ESC rights. Particularly, the notion propagated by the United States (US) that while the former constitute inalienable, enforceable, and justiciable rights, the latter have an inferior status and are particularly not justiciable. This position is in stark contradistinction to the views of the former Eastern bloc and non-aligned states that demanded the equal treatment of civil and political and ESC rights. It thus not surprising that the US, although a signatory thereof, has not ratified the ICESCR. The disparate ideologies and the CESCR's desire to appease continue to haunt the human rights treaty, resulting in the current challenges with its implementation, particularly its justiciability and legal enforceability, notwithstanding the fact that it contains concrete legal obligations and duties.

Although the ICESCR's faces criticism for being a 'moving target', in this chapter Desierto attempts to rebut the critics by highlighting the evolutive nature of its method of interpretation, identifying the substantive content of State Party duties, emphasising State Parties' minimum core obligations or applicable social protection baseline, and discussing the issue of normative justifiability. She generally indicates that the normative and institutional developments in the ICESCR and its Optional Protocol can and should be considered by State Parties as the bedrock of their public policy imperatives in international economic transactions. She includes case studies on ICESCR-based litigation in South Africa, the Philippines, and India, illuminating the disparate manner in which national courts interpret State Parties' duty to "take all appropriate means" to "achieving progressively the full realization of the rights recognized in the present Covenant" as per Article 2(1) of the ICESCR. While some national courts (notably, South Africa's) have enthusiastically incorporated ESC rights into their local jurisprudence, therefore holding governments accountable to respect, protect, and fulfil ESC rights, some have not yet given full legal effect to these rights.

In Chapter 3, Desierto discusses her problématique in respect of the application of the ICESCR in the rules of the World Trade Organization (WTO). Although she recognises that WTO law does not explicitly refer to IHRL or directly incorporate IHRL instruments such as the ICESCR, human rights form an implicit part of the objectives of the WTO to achieve sustainable development, raise standards of living, and ensure full employment, as expressed in the Preamble of the WTO Agreement. In addition, the now-stalled Doha Development Agenda that was initiated in 2001, placed the issue of development for the world's poorest at the centre of its mandate with regard to (but not limited to) food security, adequate control over natural resources, and the attainment of high standards of health. In this chapter she discusses how State Parties who are also WTO Members (Members) can use the various provisions in WTO law that purposefully grant Members the regulatory flexibility to pursue legitimate public policy objectives for justifying measures that uphold their ICESCR obligations. Desierto posits that the 'necessity test' and the principle of proportionality developed in WTO jurisprudence also gives State Parties the flexibility to justify their ESC rights policies that may be contrary to their international trade obligations. She further suggests that Members may also submit information on their compliance with the ICESCR as part of the information that could be submitted under the WTO's Trade Policy Review Mechanism. Additionally, State Parties could also fulfil their ICESCR obligations through their participation in the WTO political organs, particularly in, for example, agenda-framing and treaty negotiation.

In WTO dispute resolution, short of invoking the ICESCR as applicable law, Desierto suggests that when interpreting WTO treaty obligations, WTO judicial bodies could (as a descriptive or evidentiary tool at minimum) consider the Member's measure pursuant to its ICESCR duties to substantiate the examination of 'public interest' objectives. Such duties can further be interpreted to uphold the principle of good faith, which is pervasive in international law, and also be used to characterise 'reasonableness'. When interpreting exceptions clauses such as GATT Article XX and its GATS counterpart Article XIV, WTO tribunals could give effect to ESC rights in the interpretation of 'public morals' when engaged in the process of 'weighing and balancing' as discussed in WTO case law, including *EC—Seals*.[4] She also cites *Brazil—Retreaded Tyres*[5] as an example of where WTO jurisprudence has given effect to Article 12 of the ICESCR, the right to health, in interpreting GATT Article XX(b)'s "protecting human life or health". Desierto does acknowledge the difficulty in characterising the ICESCR as a relevant rule of international law applicable in the relations between the parties in terms of Article 31(3)(c) of the Vienna Convention on the Law of Treaties[6] (VCLT) as opposed to incorporating it as an evidentiary or informative source. The application of customary rules of interpretation by WTO tribunals is a sensitive issue at the WTO, particularly subsequent to the Appellate Body's decision in *US—Tuna II*[7] where the TBT Committee Decision on international standards was deemed a "subsequent agreement" between the parties to a treaty as contemplated by VCLT Article 31(3)(a).[8]

Chapter 4 analyses how the international financial framework could give effect to ICESCR obligations. Desierto focuses on international development finance and how State Parties, acting as either debtors or creditors, can include their ICESCR obligations in the negotiation and design of intentional project finance agreements. Due to the relatively decentralised nature of the international financial framework, in comparison to WTO law, Desierto proposes an *ex ante* design of international financing agreements that is mindful of ICESCR compliance when parties conduct

[4] Appellate Body Report, *European Communities—Measures Prohibiting the Importation and Marketing of Seal Products*, WT/DS400/AB/R / WT/DS401/AB/R, adopted 18 June 2014.

[5] Appellate Body Report, *Brazil—Measures Affecting Imports of Retreaded Tyres*, WT/DS332/AB/R, adopted 17 December 2007, DSR 2007:IV, p. 1527.

[6] 1155 U.N.T.S. 331, 8 I.L.M. 679, entered into force 27 January 1980.

[7] Appellate Body Report, *United States—Measures Concerning the Importation, Marketing and Sale of Tuna and Tuna Products*, WT/DS381/AB/R, adopted 13 June 2012, DSR 2012:IV, p. 1837.

[8] *US—Tuna II*, para 372.

political and regulatory risk assessments. Such agreements could adopt language, for example in the characterisation of events of default, considering instances where a State Party's debt repayment could be adjusted due to its good faith compliance with its ICESCR obligations and provide renegotiation and risk mitigation options before triggering the repayment consequences. She considers a State-based approach on achieving ICESCR compliance in development finance; affirming the UN-proposed Guiding Principles on Foreign Debt and Human Rights.

According to Desierto, national development initiatives could be enhanced through the global financial system. She therefore proposes reforms for International Financial Institutions (IFIs) to accord high priority to the identification and prevention of financial crises and to strengthen the foundations of international financial stability, as expressed in the Monterrey Consensus on Financing for Development, 2002 and affirmed by the UN's Doha Declaration on Financing for Development, 2008. These instruments allow IFIs to take into account, inter alia, the reduction of poverty and the social cost of loan conditionalities, structural adjustment, and austerity programmes. Desierto acknowledges that IFIs are unmotivated to uphold or engage with ESC rights because, as international organisations, they are not party to the ICESCR. Therefore it is again incumbent on State Parties to implement the political decisions necessary to uphold ICESCR obligations. For as long as the states do not make it an international obligation for IFIs to uphold ESC rights, their disregard of these rights when providing development finance will not constitute an internationally wrongful act and breach of an international obligation of that organisation in terms of Article 4 of the International Law Commission's Draft Articles on the Responsibility of International Organizations.

In Chapter 5, Desierto broaches the subject of the ICESCR in public policymaking in the international investment regime. She stresses that State Parties are obliged to discharge their duties in respect of the ICESCR whether acting as host states or home states; the latter being obliged to regulate the conduct of their nationals who invest abroad. She states that no International Investment Agreement (IIA) to date references the ICESCR as a substantive provision or in its enumeration of applicable law. In addition, due to the diversity and proliferation of IIAs, it would be impossible to pre-identify each individual treaty provision that triggers the issue of a State's regulatory freedom to pursue public interest concerns, which include human rights. She does however opine that host State's defences based on such regulatory freedom have not made much of an impact in investment arbitration jurisprudence. It is hardly disputed that host States who are parties to IIAs and human rights instruments such as the ICESCR are equally subject to each treaty. However, whether the human rights obligations are upheld in investment disputes turns on the arbitral tribunals' interpretation of the affected IIA standard.

She suggests that the IIA anomaly of granting rights and not duties to a third party i.e. the investor can be cured by State Parties concluding treaties that include investor obligations. She provides the Southern African Development Community (SADC) Model Bilateral Investment Treaty and the International Institute for Sustainable Development (IISD) Model IIA for Sustainable Development as notable examples. More tangible measures for human rights compliance by multinational enterprise (MNEs) such as the OECD Guideline for MNEs as well as the UN Global Compact could also serve as inspiration for IIA provisions. She suggest that State Parties can uphold ICESCR rights when determining the 'reasonableness' of their exercise of regulatory freedom as recognised in IIA provisions such as: (i) "in accordance with State law" clauses; (ii) stabilisation clauses; (iii) exceptions or "measures not precluded" clauses; (iv) the definition of investment; and (v) balance of payment provisions. In addition, she proposes that various procedural or structural provisions can be included in IIAs to ensure State Party regulatory freedom. These include ad hoc joint decision mechanisms, inter-State consultative mechanisms, customising the Investor-State Dispute Settlement (ISDS) regime to include an inter-State appellate mechanism, and even the elimination of ISDS altogether. She also suggests the possible inclusion of ICESCR obligations in pre-investment due diligence, specifically in assessing a particular country's political risk profile and including the host State's likelihood to change regulations to comply with its ICESCR in the regulatory risk analysis.

Desierto also posits that the ICESCR can be used as an interpretive aide for IIAs, especially in its incorporation as a "relevant rule of international law" as per VCLT Article 31(3)(c). This is not a completely strange concept to ISDS jurisprudence as in *Micula and ors v. Romania* that particular provision was invoked in the consideration of Article 15 of the Universal Declaration of Human Rights[9] and in *Saluka Investments v. Czech Republic* in order to take account of a customary international law principle that justifies depravation if it resulst from the exercise of a regulation maintaining public order.[10] She also suggests the ICESCR's use as an interpretive tool to accept a host State's good faith compliance with the human rights treaty as an equitable basis to mitigate the amount of compensation.

In her conclusion, Desierto asserts that her proposal to translate ICESCR into trade, finance, and investment decision-making can mitigate the adverse impact on ESC rights in global economic relations. By incorporating ESC rights in economic decision-making State Parties have an opportunity to proactively reject inequality and guarantee minimum social protection for their populations. She hopes that her book gets the conversation going between and among State Parties on how they may best continue to respect, protect, and fulfil the rights enshrined in the ICESCR. She maintains that the use of the ICESCR as a normative foundation to States Parties' various involvements in the global economic sphere will contribute to economic development becoming truly inclusive, sustainable, and equitable.

Desierto's detailed and deliberate arguments makes this book an interesting read, especially for those who grapple with the perennial challenge of the relatively peripheral status of human rights obligations in IEL. Her measured viewpoint gives

[9] *Micula and ors v. Romania* Decision on Jurisdiction and Admissibility, ICSID Case No. ARB/05/20, 24 September 2008, paras. 86–88.

[10] *Saluka Investments v. Czech Republic*, Partial Award, PCA (UNCITRAL), 17 March 2006, paras. 254–255.

one the impression that integrating ICESCR obligations into IEL is not only possible but is indeed an effective manner to manage the intersection of IHRL and IEL obligations, particularly when it appears that the former is a sacrificial lamb. However, there are some immediate red flags that stand out from Desierto's proposal: Firstly, the non-ratification of the ICESCR by the US is the elephant in the room; albeit she briefly mentions it. As an economy, the US boasted the highest amount of total global trade in value and market share in 2014.[11] In the same year it was the number three Foreign Direct Investment recipient and the number one home State.[12] In addition, it yields the most voting power in IFIs such as the International Monetary Fund, World Bank Group (the president being traditionally a US citizen), and the Inter-American Development Bank.[13] The US is also an avid user of international trade and investment dispute resolution mechanisms. It is somewhat utopian to believe that State Parties, even those with the best intentions, will immediately adopt Desierto's proposal when the US is staunchly opposed to giving any force of law to ESC rights. Secondly, as she noted, there is lack of coherence in State Parties' implementation of their ICESCR obligations. Even those countries that have adopted ESC rights as constitutional imperatives implement them in a piecemeal and selective fashion at best; national courts also do not uphold these obligations. Unless a concerted effort is made by State Parties to hold themselves accountable, the success of her proposal is in the balance. In addition, as of March 2016, only 21 countries[14] had ratified the ICESCR's Optional Protocol, which, inter alia, establishes a complaints procedure enabling State Parties to refer violations of ESC rights by another State to the CESCR. The Optional Protocol also provides for a more proactive role for the CESCR to initiate investigations against State Parties based on evidence of treaty non-compliance.[15] This could assist in giving the ICESCR more legal clout and boost its implementation. Thirdly, although the CESCR has done commendable work in its monitoring role and developing the interpretation of the ICESCR in its General Comments and other documents, like other human rights instruments the application of this treaty remains limited. Therefore, incorporating the ICESCR into IEL disputes will relegate the interpretation– and therefore the development of the ICESCR as a

[11] World Integration Trade Solution, http://wits.worldbank.org/CountryProfile/Country/WLD/Year/LTST/Summary (last accessed 22 September 2015).

[12] UNCTAD (2015) World Investment Report 2015, http://www.worldinvestmentreport.org/wir2015/wir2015-ch1-global-investment-trends/#global-fdi-fell-in-2014 (last accessed 22 September 2015).

[13] IMF Members' Quotas and Voting Power, and IMF Board of Governors, https://www.imf.org/external/np/sec/memdir/members.aspx#total (last accessed 22 September 2015); The World Bank, Voting Powers, http://www.worldbank.org/en/about/leadership/VotingPowers (last accessed 22 September 2015), Inter-American Development Bank, Capital Stock and Voting Power. http://www.iadb.org/en/about-us/capital-stock-and-voting-power,3166.html (last accessed 22 September 2015).

[14] http://indicators.ohchr.org/ (last accessed 2 March 2016).

[15] Articles 10 and 11 of the Optional Protocol, http://www.ohchr.org/EN/ProfessionalInterest/Pages/OPCESCR.aspx (last accessed 22 September 2015).

legal text– primarily to IEL tribunals, which could, perhaps, result in the unintended and undesired interpretation of the provisions of the human rights treaty.

In spite of the abovementioned hurdles that challenge Desierto's proposal, her book is a valuable addition to the current IHRL in IEL discourse and a worthwhile acquisition.

Reference

Desierto D (2015) Public policy in international economic law: the ICESCR in trade, finance, and investment. Oxford University Press, New York. doi:10.1093/acprof:oso/9780198716938.001.0001

Juliane Ahner, Investor-Staat-Schiedsverfahren Nach Europäischem Unionsrecht: Zulässigkeit und Ausgestaltung in Investitionsabkommen der Europäischen Union

Mohr Siebeck, 2015, ISBN 9783161537271

Till Patrik Holterhus

After receiving a competence for foreign investments with the Treaty of Lisbon in 2009, the EU unsurprisingly started to negotiate its own bilateral investment treaties (BITs), including typical investor-state dispute settlement (ISDS) mechanisms, in recent years. In this context, especially the EU-Singapore FTA, CETA and TTIP the can be named; all of them basically being trade agreements, but containing distinct investment chapters at the same time. Lately the EU's BIT-negotiations are accompanied by extensive and fierce debates both in public and in academia, not only regarding the legitimacy of ISDS, but also concerning procedural, institutional and even constitutional questions.

Therefore, *Juliane Ahner's* book 'Investor-Staat-Schiedsverfahren nach Europäischen Unionsrecht, Zulässigkeit und Ausgestaltung in Investitionsabkommen der Europäischen Union', examining legitimacy and limitations of ISDS in the context of EU law, focuses on a current and interesting field of legal scholarship. The book, which is written in German and divided into six chapters, exclusively addresses specific aspects of EU-BITs and does not cover EU law issues of BITs between Member States or between Member States and third states.

Ahner starts with a general descriptive overview on the EU policy on foreign investments in chapter one. Besides analyzing the European Commission's approach on existing and future EU-BITs (using this as a benchmark throughout

T.P. Holterhus (✉)
Institute for International Law and European Law, Georg-August-University, Göttingen, Germany
e-mail: tholter@uni-goettingen.de

M. Bungenberg et al. (eds.), *European Yearbook of International Economic Law 2016*, European Yearbook of International Economic Law 7,
DOI 10.1007/978-3-319-29215-1_39

the entire book), she examines the diverse systems and standards of national and international investment protection in general. This includes a precise description of the differing concepts of the term 'investment' in international law (for instance, the definition made by the OECD, the IMF or under the ICSID Convention). Subsequently, *Ahner* broadly outlines the development of the EU's competence of foreign investments over the last decades and the European Commission's policy prior to the treaty of Lisbon.

Chapter two firstly covers the question to what extent the EU's external competences allow the EU to negotiate and conclude BITs, including ISDS, exclusively by itself (hence, without participation of the Member States, as 'EU-only agreements'). By applying coherent legal methodology and interpretation, *Ahner* finds that the EU's explicit competence on common commercial policy in Art. 207 TFEU is limited to foreign direct investments, while not covering the facet of portfolio investments. She does this, *inter alia,* by plausibly referring back to the term of 'investment' that she developed in chapter one. She then considers, but comprehensibly negates that an exclusive EU competence to negotiate and conclude BITs might explicitly derive from Art. 217 TFEU (competence on association agreements), Art. 219 TFEU (competence on agreements concerning monetary or foreign exchange regime matters), Art. 209, 212 TFEU (competence on agreements of development/economic, financial and technical cooperation) or Art. 64 TFEU (competence on measures on the movement of capital). Furthermore, *Ahner* rejects the existence of an implicit exclusive competence pursuant to Art. 216 TFEU. In this regard, she extensively examines possible references in the European Treaties: the freedom of establishment (Art. 50, 53 TFEU), the freedom to provide services (Art. 59, 62, 53 TFEU), the rules of competition (Art. 101 et seqq. TFEU), the common transport policy (Art. 91, 100 TFEU) and the energy policy (Art. 194 TFEU)—to name but a few. Therefore, she reasons that the EU needs to conclude comprehensive BITs, especially if they include ISDS mechanisms, as 'mixed agreements'. Secondly, she examines the binding effects of such mixed BITs, distinguishing between internal (in the multi-level structure of the EU) and external binding effects (on the international level). From an international law perspective, she finds that such mixed BITs are entirely binding on the EU as well as its Member States. This, *Ahner* points out, might only be altered if the EU or a Member State as a party of one BIT explicitly declares on the international level that specific parts of the treaty shall not apply to them.

The third chapter examines the EU's ability to conclude BITs that include an ISDS mechanism, which can render decisions that are binding on the EU institutions, in the context of the so-called autonomy of the EU legal order. Although the ECJ's most recent legal opinion 2/13 on the accession of the EU to the European Convention for the Protection of Human Rights and Fundamental Freedoms could not comprehensively be taken into consideration, *Ahner* still evaluates three main aspects, already developed in earlier legal opinions with references to the autonomy of the EU legal order. Firstly, she denies a violation of Art. 344 TFEU, arguing that ISDS must not be understood as concerning disputes between states and additionally finds that this does not prevent the EU to conclude BITs. Secondly, she stresses the problematic aspect of an extraneous application and interpretation of EU law through arbitral tribunals as a possible violation of the EU institutions' competences, taking into consideration that ISDS arbitral tribunals are generally not only competent to grant compensation but also restitution (and hence, *de facto*, to examine the legality of certain EU measures). Her proposal to make the CJEU's interpretation of EU law binding on arbitral tribunals and to establish a preliminary ruling procedure before the CJEU as a part of every EU-BIT might be a plausible solution for this issue. However, at the same time, it seems rather difficult to combine such an approach with the very idea of an autonomous arbitral jurisdiction in investment law and highly unlikely that a state with whom the EU is negotiating a BIT would agree on such a condition. Thirdly, she points out that an EU-BIT needs to ensure that the determination of the proper defendant (the EU itself or a Member State) in investment arbitration is left to the EU rather than the claimant. Any other provision would violate the EU's internal allocation of competences.

Chapter four then focuses on the question how an EU-BIT could and should be designed, not just to solve potential collisions with the autonomy of the EU legal order (as discussed in chapter three) and the difficulty that the EU, not being a state, is not able to join the ICSID Convention or apply the ICSID Additional Facility Rules, but also to address current criticism regarding the typical composition of international investment arbitration. Among many of the problems currently discussed, *Ahner* confines her examination to forum shopping, jurisdictional divergence through parallel procedures in front of national and international arbitral tribunals and the effect of Most Favoured Nation clauses. She then proposes a comprehensive incorporation of the UNCITRAL's Transparency Rules and discusses the benefits and drawbacks of an appellate mechanism in ISDS, endorsing the chance to establish a coherent substantial investment law (preferably in a multilateral approach).

In the fifth chapter, *Ahner* deals with questions of liabilities in ISDS under EU-BITs, looking at three different aspects. Interpreting the ILC draft articles on state responsibility and the ILC draft articles on the responsibility of international organizations, she, initially, develops a concept of joint liability and (to some extent limited) mutual attribution between the EU and its Member States in ISDS. From there *Ahner*, secondly, concludes that the EU and its Member States could both potentially act as lawful defendants in ISDS under EU-BITs, but again stresses the EU's need to determine the defendant status internally in order to prevent conflicts with the autonomy of the EU legal order. In a third step, she then focuses on the internal allocation of financial responsibilities between the EU and its Member States in case of an ISDS award, devising a right of recourse through Art. 4 Para. 3 TEU. Here, *Ahner* could have considered the latest regulation (EU) No 912/2014, which establishes a framework for managing financial responsibility in investment agreements to which the EU is a party, instead of the former EU-Commission's proposal for that regulation from 2012 (COM (2012) 335).

In summary, one cannot conceal that most of the interesting aspects *Ahner's* book focuses on have been debated in the last months and, thus, several of the arguments and points she puts forward have already been considered or at least touched upon before. Nevertheless, her book has to be acknowledged as a particularly concise and profound examination of these different thoughts and arguments. Especially the broad examination of the (not given) EU competence for portfolio investments needs to be mentioned in this regard. In addition, the chapter on liabilities in ISDS under EU-BIT's is very original. Overall, a valuable contribution, and a book that will find its readers among practitioners and academics.

Aikaterini Titi, The Right to Regulate in International Investment Law

Studies in International Investment Law Series, Nomos/Hart Publishing, 2014, ISBN 9783848710621

Shotaro Hamamoto

States conclude investment treaties to promote and protect foreign investment by accepting international obligations that restrict their rights or powers that they have under international law as well as respective domestic law. But have they not gone too far? If existing investment treaties lay down excessive restrictions on the host State's right to regulate or the 'right to pursue specific public policy goals' (p. 19), how to rectify the situation? These questions attract an increasing number of academics, practicing lawyers, governments, international organizations and, last but not least, civil society, as testified by the rich bibliography of the book. *Titi* tries to answer them in her doctoral thesis submitted to the University of Siegen through an analysis of investment treaties, relevant rules of general international law and investment arbitral jurisprudence.

Investment treaties have not ignored the State's right to regulate. In fact, the 1959 Germany-Pakistan bilateral investment treaty (BIT) already had a provision on it (p. 53). As this very first BIT did, a number of treaties have introduced the host State's right to regulate by explicitly forming exceptions to individual standards of treatment (p. 125). For example, an exception concerning regional economic integration organizations (REIOs) contained in the most-favoured-nation treatment clause allows a State Party to participate in such organizations without extending REIO-specific treatment to investors and/or investments of the other Party to the investment treaty (p. 130). In addition to such specific exceptions, investment treaties frequently provide 'a general regulatory clause applicable to the entire treaty', often modelled after Articles XX and XXI GATT (p. 169). Furthermore, exceptions can be formulated with respect to policy areas (p. 206). For example, a

S. Hamamoto (✉)
Graduate School of Law, Kyoto University, Sakyo, Yoshida Honmachi, Kyoto 606-8501, Japan
e-mail: hamamoto@law.kyoto-u.ac.jp

M. Bungenberg et al. (eds.), *European Yearbook of International Economic Law 2016*, European Yearbook of International Economic Law 7,
DOI 10.1007/978-3-319-29215-1_40

great number of investment treaties 'either contain a general exception leaving taxation matters outside their scope [. . .] or they introduce a specific exception to the national and most-favoured-nation treatment' (p. 211).

Where these exceptions are not applicable, does general international law guarantee the host State's right to regulate? It is quite unlikely, as the rules of general international law available in this context are limited essentially to those relating to circumstances precluding wrongfulness as listed in the International Law Commission's Articles on State Responsibility (p. 236).

What, then, do arbitral tribunals do in the absence of exceptions? Do they recognize 'an *implicit* right to regulate' (p. 275)? In the application of the fair and equitable treatment obligation, which is '[t]he most important standard in investment arbitration' (p. 143), tribunals (for example, *S.D. Myers*, *Saluka*, *BG*, *AWG*, *Parkerings*, *Total* or *Lemire*) have manifested 'some degree of deference' to the State's right to regulate, apparently because fairness and equity require a balancing of interests (p. 277). Difficult problems arise, however, with indirect expropriation, as some tribunals adopt the sole effect doctrine, according to which 'an expropriation is determined exclusively on the basis of the *effect* of the regulatory measure on the investor regardless of state intent relating to the protection of a public interest' (p. 281). Notably, *Roussalis* and *Azurix* tribunals seem to argue that the requirement of compensation in case of expropriation excludes any consideration of purposes of the measure in question (p. 286). It is true that a number of tribunals (for example, *Methanex*, *Feldman*, *Saluka* or *Chemtura*) have adopted the police powers doctrine, according to which 'a measure that falls within the state's police powers does not qualify as indirect expropriation' (p. 281). However, '[o]pting for the police powers doctrine or the sole effect doctrine is a matter of tribunal discretion' (p. 287). It follows that 'in the absence of an express right to regulate, the wide cast of existing interpretations does not permit the deduction that tribunals accommodate host state policy space' (p. 289) and tribunals' '*bon plaisir*' (p. 293) 'may not be safely relied upon by states' (p. 294).

Since neither general international law nor arbitral jurisprudence guarantees the host State's right to regulate, 'it seems preferable that, insofar as a state wishes to reserve its right to regulate, it does so explicitly by means of concrete provisions in its [treaties]' (p. 294). And *Titi* concludes her thesis, looking into a crystal ball: 'we stand at the threshold of a new generation of investment treaties that will be more balanced and will safeguard a modicum of policy space, thus marking a break with the grand old tradition of asymmetric investment protection' (p. 303).

Readers may be surprised at the book's allocation of space. Of its 12 chapters, only one (Chapter XI) is dedicated to an analysis of arbitral jurisprudence and all the others (except for the introduction and the conclusion) are allocated to an extensive and detailed analysis of treaty provisions. Is it because the author underrates the importance of arbitral jurisprudence in the development of international investment law? Unlikely, because *Titi*'s other papers, which include the one entitled "The Arbitrator as a Lawmaker",[1] are filled with an exhaustive analysis of relevant arbitral awards and decisions.[2] It is therefore supposed that the author deliberately dispensed with a detailed analysis of arbitral jurisprudence. Is this a right choice?

At first sight, this is a strange choice, because a more detailed analysis could have led the author to consider that the arbitral jurisprudence is less indifferent to the host State's power to regulate. This is particularly so with respect to indirect expropriation. None of the many tribunals that paid lip service to the sole effect doctrine applied it in reality in cases that they dealt with, while tribunals that found indirect expropriation never forgot to take into account the host State's right to regulate.[3] Having said that, one cannot but agree with *Titi* that such a friendly (or less hostile) attitude of tribunals to the host State's right to regulate depends entirely on their discretion and not on any explicit provision in the applicable treaty. Even the *Chemtura* tribunal, which clearly admitted that a valid exercise of the State's police powers did not constitute an expropriation, failed to explain the legal ground of its finding in light of the clear language of the treaty provision ('a measure tantamount to [. . .] expropriation' (Article 1110(1) NAFTA)) that could have led it to the opposite conclusion. It can safely be said that tribunals are striving for taking into account the host State's right to regulate in applying treaty provisions that do not seem to allow them to do so. However, as *Titi* points out, such efforts may be based solely on '*bon plaisir*' of tribunals and nothing guarantees that they will continue to take into account the host State's right to regulate in future cases.

In fact, it seems that *Titi*'s crystal ball is telling the truth. An increasing number of investment treaties now contain specific and often detailed exceptions. At the very end of her thesis, *Titi* says that 'the new landmark negotiations at the regional level that involve as treaty partners the EU, US and/or Canada, including negotiations on the Trans-Pacific Partnership Agreement (TPP), manifest a sensibility to the right to regulate.' (p. 302). Indeed, both the EU-Canada Comprehensive Economic and Trade Agreement (CETA) and the TPP, the texts of which were disclosed after the publication of *Titi*'s book, contain extremely detailed provisions on fair and equitable treatment and expropriation that provide limitations and/or exceptions intended to preserve the host State's right to regulate.[4]

[1] Catharine Titi, 'The Arbitrator as a Lawmaker: Jurisgenerative Processes in Investment Arbitration', *Journal of World Investment and Trade*, vol. 14, 2013, p. 829.

[2] To quote but a few: Catharine Titi, 'Are Investment Tribunals Adjudicating Political Disputes?', *Journal of International Arbitration*, vol. 32, 2015, p. 261; Catharine Titi, 'Full Protection and Security, Arbitrary or Discriminatory Treatment and the Invisible EU Model BIT', *Journal of World Investment and Trade*, vol. 15, 2014, p. 534.

[3] See the reviewer's paper quoted in *Titi*'s book at p. 287, n. 1561.

[4] For CETA and EU investment law policy, see Catharine Titi, 'Le « droit de réglementer » et les nouveaux accords de l'Union européenne sur l'investissement', *Journal du droit international*, janvier 2015, doctr. 3; Catharine Titi, 'International Investment Law and the European Union', *European Journal of International Law*, vol. 26, 2015, p. 639.

However, the fact remains that there exist some 3500 investment treaties, most of which contain substantive standards without any express limitations or exceptions in favour of the host State's right to regulate. And it is in the application of these treaties that tribunals have bent their efforts to reconcile the host State's right to regulate with the treaty language that seems to grant no particular place for such a right. One day, all of these treaties may perhaps be terminated or replaced with new ones drafted along the lines proposed by *Titi*'s book. Until then, however, what shall we do with these existing treaties? Should we not try to establish a theoretical ground that would require tribunals to take into account the host State's right to regulate even in the absence of explicit limitations or exceptions? These questions are left open.

Printed in the United States
By Bookmasters